CRIMINAL LAW

Cases and Materials

CRIMINAL LAW

Cases and Materials

Fifth Edition

JOHN KAPLAN
Late Jackson Eli Reynolds Professor of Law
Stanford University

ROBERT WEISBERG
Edwin E. Huddleson Jr. Professor of Law
Stanford University

GUYORA BINDER
University of Buffalo Distinguished Professor of Law
State University of New York at Buffalo

ASPEN
PUBLISHERS

1185 Avenue of the Americas, New York, NY 10036
www.aspenpublishers.com

Printed in the United States of America.

1 2 3 4 5 6 7 8 9 0

ISBN 0-7355-4036-5

Library of Congress Cataloging-in-Publication Data

Kaplan, John, 1929–1989.
    Criminal law : cases and materials.—5th ed. / John Kaplan,
Robert Weisberg, Guyora Binder.
        p.   cm.
    Includes bibliographical references and index.
    ISBN 0-7355-4036-5
    1. Criminal law—United States—Cases.   I. Weisberg, Robert,
1946– II. Binder, Guyora. III. Title.

    KF9218.K36   2004
    345.73—dc22

                                                2003063900

About Aspen Publishers

Aspen Publishers, headquartered in New York City, is a leading information provider for attorneys, business professionals, and law students. Written by preeminent authorities, our products consist of analytical and practical information covering both U.S. and international topics. We publish in the full range of formats, including updated manuals, books, periodicals, CDs, and online products.

Our proprietary content is complemented by 2,500 legal databases, containing over 11 million documents, available through our Loislaw division. Aspen Publishers also offers a wide range of topical legal and business databases linked to Loislaw's primary material. Our mission is to provide accurate, timely, and authoritative content in easily accessible formats, supported by unmatched customer care.

To order any Aspen Publishers title, go to *www.aspenpublishers.com* or call 1-800-638-8437.

To reinstate your manual update service, call 1-800-638-8437.

For more information on Loislaw products, go to *www.loislaw.com* or call 1-800-364-2512.

For Customer Care issues, e-mail *CustomerCare@aspenpublishers.com*; call 1-800-234-1660; or fax 1-800-901-9075.

Aspen Publishers
A Wolters Kluwer Company

In memory of John Kaplan, 1929–1989

SUMMARY OF CONTENTS

IV

JUSTIFICATION AND EXCUSE   481

V

ATTRIBUTION OF CRIMINALITY   629

VI

ADDITIONAL OFFENSES   845

TABLE OF CONTENTS

II

THE ELEMENTS OF THE CRIMINAL OFFENSE 93

2

THE CRIMINAL ACT 95

3
_____

THE GUILTY MIND   157

4

CAUSATION   243

III

HOMICIDE OFFENSES   291

13

CRIMINAL LIABILITY OF CORPORATIONS   817

Appendix A

A NOTE ON THE MODEL PENAL CODE

Appendix B

THE MODEL PENAL CODE

PREFACE

The aim of this fifth edition of *Criminal Law* is, of course, to introduce students to the basic purposes, concepts, doctrines, and analytic techniques of the substantive criminal law. The fundamental premise of the book is that the substantive criminal law is a statutory as well as a "common law" subject. While the substantive criminal law, like other basic law courses, exposes students to the arts of common law reasoning, training students in applying statutory standards of liability requires them to understand the basic structure of liability, the fundamental concepts that are as often presupposed as defined in criminal codes, the crucial skills of element analysis, and the considerations of social policy and moral principle that inform the interpretation, application, and evaluation of criminal statutes.

Like most criminal law texts, this book relies first on appellate decisions in actual cases to explicate the doctrines and policy dilemmas of the substantive criminal law. It begins with an introduction that prepares students to read these decisions by explaining how these cases arise, what kinds of substantive issues come up on appeal, what sources of law appellate courts bring to bear on these issues, and what methods of reasoning and argument the courts use to resolve them. While we have continued to include historically significant cases, we have also made a special effort in this edition to include very recent cases illustrating developments in this constantly changing field of law.

Like previous editions, however, this book is not merely a collection of cases. Because criminal law is a statutory subject, this book exposes students to alternative statutory formulations of offenses and defenses, and enables students to become familiar with the influential Model Penal Code. We have continued to interweave cases with journalistic and sociological accounts of crime, historical accounts of the development of the criminal law, and philosophical arguments about criminal justice. We have also continued our commitment to place the substantive criminal law in a realistic social setting in which inequality—whether based on race, gender, or poverty—plays an undeniable role.

Above all, this book is designed not merely to stimulate interest in the fascinating and controversial subject of the criminal law but to explain that subject clearly. We have continued to include throughout the book introductory and transitional material that provides straightforward explanations of the alternative rules applied in each doctrinal area. Notes following principal cases are organized and labeled by legal issue so that students may find quick answers to their most pressing questions. Where appropriate, problems and exercises help students master the analytic skills emphasized throughout the book.

Users of previous editions will find that this one continues to build upon their basic organizational and pedagogical approach.

Chapter 1, on the purposes and limits of punishment, continues to focus on the policy controversy over rising incarceration rates, along with the causes and implications of the recent drop in crime rates, including recent debates over the role of social norms in deterring crime. It adds material on new critiques of retributivism and on the "restorative justice" movement. It updates the Supreme Court's treatment of proportionality with Ewing v. California, the controversial "3-strikes" case, and provides the important holding in Apprendi v. New Jersey, which changes the landscape of sentencing by requiring a jury determination of all facts that can raise the maximum sentence.

Chapter 2, "The Criminal Act," continues its coverage of voluntary acts, omissions, status crimes, prospectivity, legality, and specificity, with two major enhancements. First, it adds a new section on possession crimes, including the case of United States v. Maldonado, on "constructive possession" liability, and also treating the new question of "possession" of Internet files. Second, it revamps the section on legality with the new Supreme Court case of Rogers v. Tennessee on retroactivity and adds the historic case of United States v. Hudson and Goodwin and the Florida decision in State v. Egan on the problem of common law crimes.

In Chapter 3, "The Guilty Mind," we have further streamlined the treatment of mistake of law. We have expanded the treatment of strict liability crimes, adding as principal cases the highly illustrative decisions in People v. Dillard and United States v. Wulff.

Chapter 4, on causation, uses the important nineteenth-century case of Hubbard v. Commonwealth to illustrate the criminal law's traditional focus on violence as a criterion of causal responsibility for resulting harm.

Chapter 5, "Intentional Homicide," offers updated case notes on the factual criteria by which courts determine premeditation, as well as new note material illustrating the broad scope of the MPC's "extreme emotional disturbance" component of voluntary manslaughter. The chapter continues to explore the moral dilemmas posed by the problem of mitigating murder liability based on emotional distress in a society riven by controversies over cultural diversity and gender inequality.

Chapter 6, "Unintentional Homicide," continues to put involuntary manslaughter in contemporary context, with a new note case on "skiing homicide." It also includes fresh historical background on felony murder, debunking familiar claims about its sources and original scope. In addition, we have added the historically important Missouri case of State v. Shock as the chief case on "merger" in felony murder.

Chapter 7, on capital murder, offers the Wyoming case of Olsen v. State as the best new illustration of how state courts interpret and apply the aggravating and mitigating circumstance structure of their death penalty laws. It also includes full treatment of the dramatic Supreme Court decision in Atkins v. Virginia, ruling that execution of the mentally retarded violates the Eighth Amendment.

Chapter 8, on necessary force, lesser evils, and duress, continues to include new material on the battered spouse self-defense doctrine. It also adds a new case from Colorado, People v. Gleghorn, on forfeiture of self-defense by the original aggressor in mutual combat cases.

Chapter 9, on insanity, continues its enhanced focus on the newer cognitive tests, illustrated by the "deific decree" case of People v. Serravo and the notorious recent trial of Andrea Yates, who killed her own children. In addition, the chapter adds a new treatment of the relationship between insanity defenses and competency-to-stand-trial rules, including the case of Sell v. United States on the question of when a defendant can be "medicated into competency," and a look at the New York case of People v. Tortorici.

Chapter 10, "Attempt," expands its treatment of the perennially interesting doctrine of "impossible attempts" with People v. Thousand, a new Michigan case on government Internet stings using fictional children to inculpate pedophiles in attempted sex crimes.

Chapter 11, "Complicity," further streamlines its material on the challenging issue of the mens rea of complicity, and includes the new note case of People v. McCoy, examining "discrepant" liability between principal and accomplice in homicide cases.

Chapter 12, "Conspiracy," expands its consideration of the application of conspiracy doctrine to modern terrorism, with the illustrative text of the indictment in the case of United States v. Zacarias Moussaoui, charged with involvement in the planning of the September 11 attacks. It also includes the new Supreme Court case of United States v. Recio, holding that a conspirator can still be charged even if he "agrees" with confederates who have already been thwarted and arrested.

Chapter 13, on the special rules for criminal liability of corporate entities, adds timely new material on how the scope of enterprise liability was expanded to enable the conviction (and subsequent liquidation) of the Arthur Andersen accounting firm in the wake of the Enron scandal.

Chapter 14, "Theft Offenses," continues to include lively case law on theft-based white collar crimes, including mail fraud and bribery, and expands its treatment of robbery and burglary with two concise new cases, the Arizona decision in Lear v. State, and the Minnesota decision in State v. Colvin.

Finally, Chapter 15, on rape and sexual assault, continues to take account of law reform efforts and scholarly research in this rapidly changing field of law and to offer a comparison and precise element analysis of the broad range of alternative definitions of sexual assault offenses. The new edition builds on the foundation established in the fourth edition and adds new material on the policies underlying statutory rape laws, as well as on the workings of rape shield laws and their interaction with substantive crime definitions.

The point at which government takes a person's life or liberty and justifies it by denouncing that person's actions, purposes, and character is the law's most powerful manifestation. The criminal law therefore poses the most important challenge to our responsibility as citizens to understand, to evaluate, and to improve the law that is enforced in our name. We hope this new book helps our students meet that challenge.

John Kaplan
Robert Weisberg
Guyora Binder

March 2004

ACKNOWLEDGMENTS

Special thanks to colleagues Professors Markus Dubber and Charles Ewing of SUNY Buffalo and Professor Lynne Henderson at University of Nevada-Las Vegas for their wise counsel, and to Michael Ferrara, Mark Noferi, Timothy Riemann, and Mara Silver for their research assistance.

The editors also would like to acknowledge the permission of the authors, publishers, and copyright holders of the following publications for permission to reproduce excerpts herein:

A Death in Mount Hermon, Maine Times, Dec. 16, 1988, sec. 1 at 8. Reprinted by permission.

Alexander, L., & Kessler, K., Mens Rea and Inchoate Crimes, 87 J. Crim. L. & Criminology 1138, 1155, 1169 (1997).

Allen, F., Criminal Justice, Legal Values, and the Rehabilitative Ideal, Justice, Punishment, Treatment: The Correctional Process 193–196 (L. Orland ed. 1973).

American Law Institute, Model Penal Code & Commentaries. Copyright © 1980 by the American Law Institute. Reprinted by permission of the American Law Institute.

Arlen, J., and Kraakman, R., Controlling Corporate Misconduct: An Analysis of Corporate Liability Misconduct Regimes, 72 N.Y.U. L. Rev. 687, 746–49 (1997).

Assault Victim Dies After Feeding Tube Withheld by Court, New York Times, June 15, 1997, sec. 6 at 28. Copyright © 1997 by The New York Times Company. Reprinted by permission.

Ben-Shahar, O. & Harel, A., The Economics of the Law of Criminal Attempts: A Victim-Centered Perspective, 145 U. Pa. L. Rev., 297, 336, 339, 340 (1996). Copyright © 1996 by Omri Ben Shahar and Alon Harel. Reprinted by permission.

Bentham, J., The Theory of Legislation 322–326, 336, 338 (1987). Copyright © 1950, 1987 by Routledge. Used by permission.

Binder, G., & Smith, N., Framed: Utilitarianism and Punishment of the Innocent, 32 Rutgers L. Rev 115, 118, 210–211. Reprinted by permission of Rutgers Law Review.

Braithwaite, J., Crime, Shame, and Reintegration, 62, 101–02 (1989). Copyright © 1989 by Cambridge University Press. Reprinted by permission of John Braithwaite.

Braithwaite, J. & Pettit, P., Not Just Deserts: A Republican Theory of Criminal Justice 2–5 (1990). Copyright © 1990 by Oxford University Press. Reprinted by permission.

Brown, R. M., No Duty to Retreat: Violence and Values in American History and Society 4–30. Copyright © 1991 by Oxford University Press. Used by permission of Oxford University Press, Inc.

Bryden, D., Redefining Rape, 2 Buff. Crim. L. Rev 101, 208–209 (1999). Reprinted with permission of Buffalo Criminal Law Review.

Burke, A., Rational Actors, Self-Defense, and Duress: Making Sense, Not Syndromes, Out of the Battered Woman, 81 North Carolina L. Rev. 211, 245–46, 250–69 (2002). Reprinted by permission of North Carolina Law Review.

Burke, J., Kadish, S., & Kahan, D., Conspiracy, 1 Encyclopedia of Crime and Justice 241–42 (Joshua Dressler, editor in chief, 2d ed., 2002). Copyright © 2002 Macmillan Library Reference USA. Reprinted with permission of the Gale Group.

Byler, W., Removing Children: The Destruction of American Indian Families, 9 Civ. Rts. 19 (Summer 1977). Copyright © 1977 by U.S. Commission on Civil Rights. Reprinted by permission of the author and U.S. Commission on Civil Rights.

Campane, J., Chains, Wheels, and the Single Conspiracy, 50 FBI L. Enforcement Bull. 24, 26–31 (Aug. 1981), 24–30 (Sept 1981). Reprinted by permission of FBI Law Enforcement Bulletin.

Chakravarty, Subrata, Tunnel Vision, Forbes 214, 218, May 21, 1984. Copyright © 1984 by Forbes, Inc. Reprinted by permission.

Coleman, C., 'Guilty but Mentally Ill' Verdict Needed? YES, N.Y.L.J. September 23, 1999, p.2. Reprinted with permission.

Corrado, M., The Abolition of Punishment, 35 Suffolk U. L. Rev. 257 (2001). Reprinted by permission.

Coughlin, A. M., Sex and Guilt, 84 Va. L. Rev., 1, 6–9, 45 (1998). Copyright © 1998 by Virginia Law Review Association. Reprinted by permission.

Dix, G. E., Justification: Self-Defense, 3 Encyclopedia of Crime and Justice 948–949 (Sanford H. Kadish, editor in chief, 1983). Excerpted with permission of Macmillan Library Reference USA, a division of Simon & Schuster, Inc., Copyright © 1983 by the Free Press.

Dripps, D., Criminal Justice Process: 1 Encyclopedia Criminal Justice 362, 364–69 (Joshua Dressler, editor in chief, 2d ed., 2002). Copyright © 2002 Macmillan Library Reference USA. Reprinted with permission of the Gale Group.

Duff, R. A., Trials and Punishments 15, 20–21, 246–47, 254–57, 259–62 (1986). Copyright © 1986 by Cambridge University Press. Reprinted with permission.

Estrich, S., Rape, 95 Yale L.J. 1087, 1099–1101 (1986). Copyright © 1986. Reprinted by permission of the Yale Law Journal and Fred B. Rothman & Company.

Feds Indict Gun Sellers, Aug. 18, 1999. Copyright © 1999 by the Associated Press. Reprinted by permission of the Associated Press.

Feinberg. J., Doing and Deserving: Essays in the Theory of Responsibility, 98, 100–105 (1970). Copyright © 1970. Used with permission.

Fingarette, H., Addiction and Criminal Responsibility, 84 Yale L.J. 413, 428–29, 431–432 (1975). Copyright © 1975. Reprinted by permission of the Yale Law Journal and Fred B. Rothman & Company.

Fletcher, G., Manifest Criminality, Criminal Intent, and the Metamorphosis of Lloyd Weinreb, 90 Yale L.J. 319, 338–40 (1980). Copyright © 1980. Reprinted by permission of the Yale Law Journal and Fred B. Rothman & Company.

Fletcher, G., Rethinking Criminal Law 3–9, 118–119, 132, 134–135, 166–167, 396–401, 524–529, 532–35, 575–578, 613–614, 619–620, 705. Copyright © 1978 by George P. Fletcher. Reprinted by permission of Aspen Law and Business.

Goldstein, A., Excuse: Insanity, 2 Encyclopedia of Crime and Justice 736–740 (Sanford H. Radish, editor in chief, 1983). Excerpted with permission of Macmillan Library Reference USA, a division of Simon & Schuster, Inc. Copyright © 1983 by the Free Press.

Haines, R., Bowman, F., & Woll, J., Federal Sentencing Guidelines Handbook 18–20, 2002. Reprinted with permission of West Group, a division of Thomson West.

Hart, H. L. A. & Honore, A. M., Causation and the Law 64–66 (1959). Copyright © 1959 by Clarendon Press, a division of Oxford University Press. Reprinted by permission.

Hazard, G., Criminal Justice System: Overview, 2 Encyclopedia of Crime and Justice 450, 457–463 (Sanford H. Kadish, editor in chief, 1983). Excerpted with permission of Macmillan Library Reference USA, a division of Simon & Schuster, Inc. Copyright © 1983 by the Free Press. Reprinted by permission.

Ireland, R., Sexual Dishonor and the Unwritten Law in the Nineteenth Century United States, 23 Journal of Social History 27–35 (1992). Reprinted by permission of Journal of Social History.

Jury Acquits Vermont Protestors of Trespass, Boston Globe, Nov. 17, 1984, at 21. Copyright © 1984 by the Associated Press. Reprinted by permission of the Associated Press.

Kahan, D., Social Influence, Social Meaning and Deterrence, 83 Va. L. Rev. 349–50, 354–356, 365, 367–371. Copyright © 1997 by Virginia Law Review. Reprinted by permission.

Katz, L., Bad Acts and Guilty Minds, Conundrums of the Criminal Law 63–64, 80 (1987). Copyright © 1987 by the University of Chicago Press. Reprinted by permission.

Katz, L., Blackmail and Other Forms of Arm-Twisting, 141 U. Pa. L. Rev. 1567, 1597–1598, 1615 (1993). Copyright © by the University of Pennsylvania Law Review. Reprinted by permission.

Kutz, C., Complicity: Ethics and Law for a Collective Age 113, 116–124, 138 (2000). Copyright © 2000 University of California Press. Reprinted by permission.

Lindgren, J., Unraveling the Paradox of Blackmail, 84 Colum. L. Rev. 670–672. Copyright © 1984 by James Lindgren. All rights reserved. Reprinted by permission of Columbia Law Review.

Luna, E., Punishment Theory, Holism, and the Procedural Conception of Restorative Justice, 2003 Utah L. Rev. 207, 230–231. Reprinted with permission of Utah Law Review.

Margolick, D., New Vietnam Debate: Trauma as Legal Defense, New York Times, May 11, 1985, at A1. Copyright © 1985 by The New York Times Company. Reprinted by permission of The New York Times Company.

McCloskey, H, J., A Non-Utilitarian Approach to Punishment, 9 Inquiry 249, 253–254 (1965). Copyright © 1965 by The Norwegian Research Council for Science and the Humanities. Reprinted by permission.

Meares, T. & Kahan, D., When Rights Are Wrong, Boston Review, April/May 1999, sec. 8 at 4. Reprinted by permission.

Midnight Hazing Exercise Proves Fatal at Texas A&M, Peninsula Times Tribune, Sept. 1, 1984, at A6. Copyright © 1984 by the Associated Press. Reprinted by permission of the Associated Press.

Morris, H., A Paternalistic Theory of Punishment, 18 Am. Phil. Q. 263–271 (1981). Copyright © 1981 by The American Philosophical Quarterly. Reprinted with permission.

Morris, H., On Guilt and Innocence, 33–34 (University of California Press, 1976). Reprinted by permission.

Note, Conspiracy: Statutory Reform Since the Model Penal Code, 75 Colum. L. Rev. 1122, 1129–32, 1149–53, 1182–83 (1975). Copyright © 1975 by Columbia Law Review. Reprinted with permission.

Note, Corporate Homicide: The Stark Realities of Artificial Beings and Legal Fictions, 8 Pepperdine L. Rev. 367–70, 372–74, 404–408. Copyright © 1980 by Pepperdine Law Review. Reprinted by permission.

Note, Developments in the Law—Corporate Crime: Regulating Corporate Behavior Through Criminal Sanctions 92 Harv. L. Rev. 1227, 1247–1251. Copyright © 1979 by the Harvard Law Review Association. Reprinted by permission.

Nourse, V., Passion's Progress: Modern Law Reform and the Provocation Defense, 106 Yale L.J. 1331–1334, 1337–38, 1384 (1987). Copyright © 1987 by The Yale Law Journal. Reprinted with permission.

Oberman, M., Turning Girls Into Women: Re-evaluating Modern Statutory Rape Law, 85 Am. J. Crim. L. & Criminology 15, 24–26, 32–33, 37 (1994). Copyright © 1994. Reprinted by permission of the American Journal of Criminal Law.

Packer, H., The Limits of the Criminal Sanction 14, 73–77 (1968). Copyright © 1968 by Stanford University Press and the author. Reprinted by permission of Stanford University Press.

Reason, J., The Psychopathology of Everyday Slips, The Sciences 45, 48–49 (Sept./Oct. 1984). Copyright © 1984 by the New York Academy of Sciences. Reprinted by permission of The Sciences.

Reitz, K., Sentencing: Guidelines, 4 Encyclopedia of Crime and Justice 1429–1440 (Joshua Dressler, editor in chief, 2d ed., 2002). Copyright © 2002 Macmillan Library Reference USA. Reprinted with permission of the Gale Group.

Robinson, P., Causing the Condition of One's Own Defense: A Study in the Limits of Theory in Criminal Law Doctrine, 71 Va. L. Rev. 1, 28–43. Copyright © 1985 by the Virginia Law Review Association. Reprinted by permission.

Robinson, P., Criminal Law Defenses 69–73 (1984). Copyright © 1984 The West Group. Reprinted by permission.

SPECIAL NOTICE

Some citations have been edited from cases for the sake of smoother reading. Footnotes in cases and other quoted materials have generally been eliminated without indication. Those that were not edited, however, have been renumbered to run consecutively with the editors' footnotes. References to the Model Penal Code, unless otherwise indicated, are to American Law Institute, Model Penal Code and Commentaries (1985).

CRIMINAL LAW

Cases and Materials

INTRODUCTION

This book will introduce you to the basic concepts of criminal law, the alternative rules of criminal law considered and adopted by different American jurisdictions, and the processes of reasoning that lawyers and judges engage in when identifying and applying these rules. It is also designed to encourage critical reflection about all three.

Much of the reading in this book consists of reported appellate decisions in criminal cases. In most criminal law courses, such judicial opinions receive the bulk of attention in class discussion. This introductory chapter will assist you in reading these judicial opinions. It will explain how criminal cases come before appellate courts, and what options those courts have in disposing of them. It will alert you to some of the sources of law bearing on the judicial decision in criminal cases, and to the role that considerations of policy and justice may play in those decisions. It will make explicit some widely shared and seldom articulated assumptions about legal reasoning. It will introduce the most influential schemes used to analyze criminal cases into their component issues. Finally, it will discuss the crucial matter of how the burden of proof on these issues is allocated between the prosecution and the defense.

A. THE CAREER OF A CRIMINAL CASE

The bulk of violations of criminal law that come to the attention of law enforcement agencies are reported by victims or other witnesses. Others are discovered by police in the course of routine patrols, or observed in the course of police surveillance or undercover work, or uncovered by government officials in the routine gathering of information on the movements of persons, goods, and money entailed in the workings of a modern administrative state. Most reported crimes are never "solved." The police are most likely to make arrests in crimes against the person because such crimes command the most investigative resources and because reports by the victim (if he or she survives) or other witnesses or physical evidence make it easier to identify the perpetrators. Police investigate homicides most vigorously of all and solve these more than any other crime, in part because they are often able to find the killer among the acquaintances or relatives of the victim.

1. Procedure Before Trial

DONALD DRIPPS, CRIMINAL JUSTICE PROCESS:
1 Encyclopedia Criminal Justice 362, 364-69 (2002)

In the United States the adjudicatory process varies considerably from one jurisdiction to another, although the process throughout the country is highly similar. Most cases originate with an arrest by the police. The Supreme Court has held that the Constitution requires a prompt judicial determination of probable cause to believe that the arrestee has committed an offense. If that judicial probable cause determination was not made prior to arrest by the issuance of a warrant or the return of an indictment by a grand jury, the arrestee must be brought before a judicial officer for a determination of probable cause. Although the time frame prior to this first appearance is not rigidly defined, the Court has recognized a presumption that detention without judicial authorization that lasts longer than forty-eight hours is unconstitutional.

The probable cause hearing need not be more elaborate than the process of issuing an arrest warrant. There does not need to be any formal charge filed at this point, and the Supreme Court has held that the right to counsel does not arise until a charge is filed, whether by indictment, information, or complaint. Nonetheless common practice is to perform several functions at the first appearance in court if the court finds that probable cause indeed exists. Bail or other conditions of pretrial release may be set, counsel for the indigent may be appointed, and a date for further proceedings may be set.

The period between arrest and presentment in court offers the police the opportunity to interrogate the suspect under the *Miranda* rules. Once the suspect is represented by counsel, it is highly unlikely that the suspect will volunteer information, and any questioning by the police after the right to counsel has attached is unconstitutional. The *Miranda* right to counsel is not the Sixth Amendment right to counsel at trial, but a right derived from the Fifth Amendment privilege against self-incrimination. . . . The Supreme Court in *Miranda* accepted the proposition that counsel may be waived without an appearance in Court or consultation with counsel for purposes of interrogation, but has never intimated that such a waiver of the right to counsel at trial would be valid.

After the arrest and a judicial determination of probable cause, the next step in the process is the selection of a charge by the prosecutor. Prosecutors enjoy extremely wide discretion in selecting charges. Consider, for example, a suspect who fired a gun at another man. This might be dismissed as no crime because the suspect was acting in self-defense (or because the prosecutor concludes that although the defendant was not acting in self-defense a jury might conclude otherwise). At the other end of the continuum the case might be charged out as attempted murder or aggravated assault. In between it might be charged out as illegal possession or discharge of a firearm, or a simple assault. If the suspect has prior convictions the prosecutor may but need not add a charge under a recidivism statute such as the *three strikes* laws. Thus prosecutors typically have discretion to expose the suspect to a range of liability extending from zero to a substantial term of years.

Prosecutors decline to proceed in a substantial percentage of cases. In some cases the police themselves never expected a prosecution and made the arrest solely for immediate social control purposes. For example, the police might arrest one or both of the drunks involved in a brawl simply to separate them and prevent further violence, or to prevent one of the inebriates from passing out outdoors on a cold night. In other cases the police might hope for an eventual conviction but the prosecutor may decide the evidence is unlikely to persuade a jury.

Often the prosecutor will agree to drop the criminal charges if the defendant will undertake some alternative program to prevent a recurrence of the offense. The prosecutor may agree with a defendant charged with an offense involving or induced by narcotics to abandon the criminal charge provided the suspect enters a drug treatment program. These so-called *diversion arrangements* are quite common, and there is great variety in the types of programs to which persons might be diverted from the criminal justice system.

Juveniles make up a substantial percentage of the population arrested. All U.S. jurisdictions have by statute created specialized juvenile courts. . . . The applicable statutes typically permit juveniles suspected of serious felonies to be transferred to the general criminal justice system and tried as adults. . . .

In jurisdictions that do not require grand jury indictment the prosecutor may unilaterally file an information accusing the defendant of the crime or crimes the prosecutor has chosen to pursue. About half the states and the federal government require grand jury indictment in felony cases. Whether the charging instrument takes the form of an indictment or an information, the basic purpose of the accusation is to enable the accused to prepare a defense to present at a subsequent trial.

The grand jury usually consists of twenty-three citizens who review cases presented by the prosecutor. Although the grand jurors have the power to refuse to indict, in practice the grand jury very rarely rejects a prosecutor's request for an indictment.

If the case originates with an indictment filed before arrest, the process will differ somewhat. The accused will be either arrested or will surrender to face the charge. At that point the process will continue just as in cases that begin with arrest, with the important qualification that the accused's Sixth Amendment right to counsel has attached even before the arrest. Absent a valid waiver of that right to counsel, so-called critical stages of the process require the presence of defense counsel. Critical stages include interrogation, lineups, and court appearances. They do not include photo identification sessions, the interviewing of witnesses other than the defendant, or the gathering or testing of physical evidence.

Once the charge selected by the prosecutor is filed in court, whether by indictment, information, or complaint, the next step in the process is an arraignment at which the defendant appears in court to hear the charges and enter a plea. If the defendant has not yet retained or been appointed counsel, counsel must be appointed, retained, or waived in open court before entering a plea. Likewise if bail has not been previously set or denied, a pretrial release decision will be made at this point.

If the defendant and the prosecution do not reach a plea agreement and the case goes to trial, there typically will be a *discovery* period, an opportunity for pretrial motions, a preliminary hearing, and a trial. The discovery process has become more extensive but still falls far short of the discovery permitted on the civil side. The principal reasons for the difference are fears that criminal defendants are *more* likely than civil litigants to harass or intimidate witnesses and the belief that the defendant's right not to testify unfairly turns criminal discovery into a one-way street.

The Supreme Court's *Brady* doctrine requires the prosecution to turn over to the defense all material *exculpatory evidence* upon a timely request (*Brady v. Maryland,* 373 U.S. 83 (1963)). Court rules typically require both sides to disclose the names and addresses of the witnesses they intend to call, thus permitting the opposing side to interview the witnesses before trial. In many jurisdictions the defense must give advance notice of the intention to rely on certain defenses, such as insanity, alibi, entrapment, or consent.

The theory of the adversary system is that justice is most likely to emerge from a contest in which the two sides prepare their own cases. In practice the theory is compromised by limited resources. A majority of criminal defendants are represented by publicly provided counsel. There is widespread agreement that the funds provided for indigent defense do not permit anything like an independent investigation by defense counsel in every case. Caseload pressures, often in the range of hundreds of felony files per lawyer per year, require defense counsel to select a few cases for trial while arranging the most favorable plea agreement possible for the rest.

Pretrial motions can be made for a wide variety of purposes, including but not limited to: (1) suppression of otherwise admissible evidence because the evidence was improperly obtained; (2) change of venue; (3) admission or exclusion of evidence; (4) compelling discovery withheld by the other side; (5) determining competence to stand trial; and (6) court appointment of expert witnesses for an indigent defendant. Motions are decided by the court without a jury. If a ruling on a motion turns on disputed facts, the court will hold an evidentiary hearing to determine the facts. Pretrial rulings are ordinarily not appealable by the defense until after a conviction, but are commonly allowed for the prosecution, as otherwise the double jeopardy principle might prevent a retrial even though the government lost the trial because the trial court erroneously ruled on a motion.

Like rulings on motions, the preliminary hearing is conducted by the court without a jury. In theory the preliminary hearing is designed both as a final test of probable cause for a trial and as a discovery tool. Actual practice varies a great deal. In some cases prosecutors introduce their full case, both to encourage a plea from the defense and to preserve the testimony of wavering witnesses. In other cases the prosecutor may put on the minimum needed to go forward to trial out of fear of giving the defense an opportunity for discovery. . . .

Relatively few criminal cases go to trial, fewer still are appealed, and fewer yet become the subject of collateral review. Prosecutors refuse to file charges or dismiss charges in a large number of cases. In the cases prosecutors choose to pursue, the majority end not in trial by jury but by a plea of guilty or a successful motion to dismiss. Statistics vary across jurisdictions, but it would not be uncommon for half of all arrests to result either in no charges or in charges that are later dismissed, for 80 percent of the cases that are not dismissed to end in guilty pleas, and for the remaining cases to be tried. The government typically wins a significant but not overwhelming majority of criminal trials; a 70 percent conviction rate at trial would not be unusual.

These statistics reflect the ubiquity of plea bargaining. Plea bargaining involves the prosecutor trading a reduction in the seriousness of the charges or the length of the recommended sentence for a waiver of the right to trial and a plea of guilty to the reduced charges. Both sides usually have good reasons for settlement. In a case in which the evidence of guilt is overwhelming, the prosecution can avoid the expense and delay of a trial by offering modest concessions to the defendant. When the evidence is less clear-cut the government can avoid the risk of an acquittal by agreeing to a plea to a reduced charge. Because the substantive criminal law authorizes a wide range of charges and sentences for typical criminal conduct, and because the procedural law allows prosecutors wide discretion in selecting charges, the prosecution can almost always give the defense a substantial incentive to plead guilty.

A defendant who is sure to be convicted at trial is likely to take any concessions he can get. The weaker the government's case the more concessions the government will be willing to offer. For the most part the trial process comes into play when the two sides disagree about the likely outcome of a trial. Thus it is not surprising to see that in cases that are not dismissed a very large percentage end in guilty pleas but that the results of trials are far less one-sided. . . .

Plea bargaining is problematic. . . . [B]ecause the substantive criminal law typically authorizes draconian penalties (the three strikes laws, for instance) the prosecution has the power to present defendants with unconscionable pressures. Imagine a defendant with two prior convictions charged with petty theft. The prosecutor offers to drop a three-strikes charge if the defendant pleads guilty. The defendant must now choose between the risk of life in prison if convicted at a trial or a very short term or a suspended sentence following a guilty plea. Although the Supreme Court has accepted such pleas as voluntary, they have every appearance of being practically coerced. [In addition,] the prosecution has the incentive to maximize the benefit of pleading guilty in the weakest cases. The more likely an acquittal at trial the more attractive a guilty plea is to the prosecution. Given caseload pressures prosecutors may simply dismiss the weakest cases. But in a borderline case that does go forward the prosecution may very well threaten the most serious consequences to those defendants who may very well be innocent.

2. Substantive Legal Issues Before Trial

Whether entered in the form of an indictment or an information, the criminal charge identifies the criminal violation, often referring to the statutory provision violated, and alleges facts on the basis of which the grand jury or prosecutor believes the criminal violation occurred. These are the facts that the prosecution is obliged to prove at trial. The charging paper generally describes the facts in vague language that tracks the language of the statutory provision.

The defense will generally have an opportunity to challenge the legal sufficiency of the indictment before trial. The defense may move to have the indictment dismissed on any of three grounds: (1) the crime charged is not, in fact, a violation of the criminal law of the relevant jurisdiction; or (2) the facts alleged, even if true, do not constitute the crime charged; or (3) the evidence proffered at the preliminary hearing does not support the facts alleged.

In almost all American jurisdictions, an act cannot constitute a crime unless it violates a criminal statute, although exactly what this minimal condition means is contestable (see Chapter 2). In addition, conduct cannot constitute a crime if the criminal statute, as applied to the conduct, violates federal or applicable state constitutional law. The clauses of the federal constitution with the greatest bearing on "substantive" criminal law are the prohibitions on the taking of life, liberty, and property without "due process of law" that appear in the Fifth and Fourteenth Amendments; and the Eighth Amendment's prohibition on "cruel and unusual punishments." The application of these constitutional provisions to criminal law will be given some attention in this book, particularly in Chapters 1, 2, 3, and 7.

The facts that must be alleged in order to charge a crime are often referred to as the "elements" of the criminal offense. The prosecution may be required to prove additional facts at trial, depending on the strategies of the defendant. For example, if a homicide defendant claims to have used force justifiably in self-defense, the prosecution may be required to disprove this justification "defense" at trial. But the *absence* of justification is not generally considered an element of the offense and usually need not be alleged in the charge; moreover, as we will shortly see, in some instances it is the defense that must bear the burden of proving certain key facts establishing the *presence* of a defense like justification. Most of the legal questions considered in this book involve the definition of offense elements. Others involve the definition of defenses.

The indictment or information may charge a number of different crimes. The judge may dismiss some or all or none of these charges at a pretrial hearing. Other pretrial motions by the defense may bear on the evidence, objecting, for example, that some of the evidence proffered at the preliminary hearing was unconstitutionally obtained, or is irrelevant, unreliable, or prejudicial. This book does not consider the procedural protections of the Fourth, Fifth, and Sixth Amendments that are often at issue in these evidentiary motions, since these matters are covered in courses or books on criminal procedure. Nor will it consider the rules of evidence, which are covered comprehensively in a distinct set of courses and books. Nevertheless, these matters are relevant to substantive criminal law, since the outcome of evidentiary motions may affect the outcome of a motion to dismiss one or more charges, and since the suppression of certain evidence may make it impossible for the prosecution to prove the facts alleged in a charge.

The dismissal of a charge for failure to allege the elements of a crime or for want of evidence does not preclude the prosecution from charging the same offense again, despite the Fifth Amendment's prohibition on double jeopardy. Moreover, the prosecution may appeal the dismissal of a charge, alleging that the judge made an error of law. A few of the judicial opinions excerpted in this book involve appeals from the dismissal of a charge.

At this early stage, the defense ordinarily may not appeal the denial of a motion to dismiss a charge. If the defendant is found guilty, however, the defense may appeal the conviction on the basis that no actual crime was charged, that the facts alleged did not support the charge, or that the evidence offered at trial was insufficient to justify any jury in finding guilt beyond a reasonable doubt.

3. Procedure at Trial

The accused has a constitutional right to trial by jury for any crime for which the possible sentence is more than six months in jail or prison, unless the accused chooses to waive that right and instead have a "bench" trial before a judge alone. Typically, first the judge and opposing attorneys select a jury, then the judge formally reads the charge and confirms that the accused is pleading not guilty. After pretrial motions on such matters as suppression of challenged evidence, the prosecution makes an opening statement describing the facts it intends to prove and the evidence it expects to offer. The defense may respond with its own opening statement or it may opt to wait until the prosecution has rested. The prosecution then presents witnesses for direct examination, along with physical evidence and documents. The defense can cross-examine each prosecution witness.

When the prosecution has completed its case, the defendant may move for dismissal of the charge on the ground that no reasonable fact finder could find guilt beyond a reasonable doubt. The trial court may accordingly dismiss all or some of the charges. A successful motion to dismiss after the prosecution has presented its case permanently disposes of the charge. The Fifth Amendment prohibition on double jeopardy precludes recharging or retrying the defendant,[1] and so the prosecution cannot appeal if the trial court dismisses on this ground. On the other hand, the defense will not appeal the *denial* of the motion to dismiss at this stage. It will wait, and appeal any resulting conviction.

If any charges remain, the defense has a choice of resting or presenting its own witnesses and exhibits. The prosecution may cross-examine these witnesses, and present rebuttal evidence. Finally, the defense gets one more opportunity to present surrebuttal evidence. The defendant has the right to choose not to testify, and the prosecution may neither call the defendant as a witness nor draw attention to the defendant's failure to testify in any way. Should the defendant choose to testify, however, the prosecution may cross-examine.

After both sides rest and the judge has heard any final motions, each side can make a closing argument, summarizing its case. In a jury trial, the judge then instructs the jury on the elements of the offenses charged, any available defenses, and the nature and allocation of the burden of proof. If the case is tried without a jury, the judge deliberates and decides the case, applying the same legal standards that he or she would instruct a jury to employ.

Jury instructions are generally drawn from three sources: (1) "pattern" jury instructions, which are endorsed and published by appellate courts; (2) instructions requested by the defense or prosecution; and (3) instructions written by the judge based on his or her understanding of the relevant law. If the judge rejects an instruction proposed by the defense and the defendant is convicted, the defendant might later appeal the judge's refusal of the instruction. On the other hand, if the judge rejects a prosecutor's instruction and the defendant is acquitted, the bar against double jeopardy prevents the prosecution from appealing. Much of this book concerns disputes about the proper instruction of juries, since this is the key medium by which judge and jury apply the substantive criminal law doctrines to the facts of the case.

After instruction, the jury deliberates until it reaches a verdict of conviction or acquittal on every charge, or until the judge is convinced that the jury cannot

---

1. Some of the rules of double jeopardy are too complex even to mention here, but note that the prohibition only applies within a particular jurisdiction. Thus, even if a particular state is precluded from recharging or retrying a case, if the same conduct arguably violates a federal criminal statute, then federal prosecutors may still be able to bring a case.

reach a verdict on some charges. Many jurisdictions use 12-person juries and require unanimity in all felony cases, though the federal constitution does not require either practice. If the jury cannot agree on a particular charge, the judge may declare a mistrial, permitting the prosecution to begin another trial, should it so choose. Of course, if the jury acquits, double jeopardy precludes retrial or appeal of an acquittal; on the other hand, if the jury convicts, the defendant may move for a new trial or appeal to a higher court.

After conviction, the judge will normally order a probation report to inform himself or herself on factors in the defendant's background bearing on sentencing. Then, unless the charge carries a completely mandatory sentence, the judge will conduct a sentencing hearing, considering arguments from both sides, and choosing a sentence within the range prescribed by statute, or in conformity with guidelines developed by sentencing commissions in some jurisdictions. In capital cases, the sentencing hearing is quite elaborate, resembling a second trial (see Chapter 7).

4.   Substantive Legal Issues on Appeal

The defendant may appeal a conviction on the *substantive* grounds that:

1. The charge on which he or she was convicted is not a crime, i.e., it is not criminally proscribed, or the criminal proscription is unconstitutional, either in general, or as applied to this defendant. If the court accepts such an argument, it reverses the conviction.
2. The indictment or information did not allege all the necessary elements of the crime. Again, if the court accepts such an argument, it reverses the conviction.
3. The evidence was insufficient to justify any reasonable fact finder in finding all the necessary elements of the crime proved beyond a reasonable doubt. Again, if the court accepts such an argument it reverses the conviction.
4. The jury was improperly instructed on the elements of the offense or on the criteria for a justification or an excuse defense. If such an argument is accepted, the defendant will win a right to a new trial, unless the appellate court also concludes that had the jury been *properly* instructed, it probably *still* would have convicted on the evidence presented (the so-called "harmless error" rule). If the defendant wins a right to a new trial, the prosecution has discretion to retry the defendant or drop the charges.

In this book, you will read judicial dispositions of defense appeals of these four types, as well as the occasional prosecution appeal from the dismissal of a charge. Defendants may also appeal convictions based on procedural or evidentiary errors, but most such appeals are beyond the scope of this book. The one type of evidentiary appeal you may encounter is the claim that (a) evidence supporting a defense was wrongly excluded as irrelevant, because the trial court wrongly disallowed the defense or defined it incorrectly; or (b) prosecution evidence was wrongly admitted as relevant, because the trial court misunderstood the elements of the offense or of the defenses offered. If such an appeal is successful, the defendant normally wins a right to a new trial, subject to the harmless error rule.

B.   SOURCES OF CRIMINAL LAW

How does a judge go about deciding whether the prosecution charged a genuine and constitutionally proscribable criminal offense? How does a judge determine what the prosecution must prove and what evidence a fact finder is justified in accepting as sufficient proof? How can a judge determine the correct instructions to a jury?

Judges can draw on three types of legal sources in resolving these questions: statutes, judicial precedent, and constitutions, though they may invoke considerations of policy and justice in applying any of these sources.

1.   Statutes

All 50 states and the federal government have different criminal statutes; no jurisdiction is bound by another's statute or judicial interpretation of its statute. The federal constitution and some state constitutions have been interpreted to say that criminal defendants can only be charged with violations of a criminal statute (see Chapter 2); though common law rules that have never been put into statutes can often ground a civil cause of action, such as a tort or a breach of conduct, a criminal prohibition usually must have some form of legislative mandate. But because criminal statutes are often vague or ambiguous, courts often have broad discretion in interpreting them. On the other hand, courts may not *overrule* statutes except on constitutional grounds.

GEOFFREY HAZARD, CRIMINAL JUSTICE SYSTEM:
OVERVIEW
2 Encyclopedia of Criminal Justice 450 (1983)

The penal law in virtually all states in the United States is legislative in origin. That is, conduct is not criminally punishable unless it has been proscribed by statute.

The situation was not always thus. In the original common law, which began its development with the Norman domination of England after 1066, crimes and civil wrongs were not clearly distinguished. Moreover, there was no systematic body of criminal prohibitions. Rather, the original common-law offenses consisted of the use of force by the offender in violation of the King's peace and could result in both punitive and compensatory sanctions. It was the use of violence as such, rather than the particular consequences of a violent act, that constituted the wrong. From this foundation, the common law of crimes evolved . . . through judicial decisions interpreting and elaborating the concept of violence into such specific categories as homicide, robbery, arson, and assault. In the later years of the common law's development, particularly from the sixteenth century onward, enactments of Parliament added specific crimes to the array of common-law offenses.

There was, however, no penal code or official systemization of the law of crimes. Commentaries by jurists . . . undertook to group the array of offenses, common-law and statutory, into coherent order according to the nature of the harm inflicted and the intensity and severity of the violation. The law of crimes thus unofficially systematized was nevertheless essentially common law, that is, the pronouncements of courts defining conduct that constituted a crime. In the colonization of British North America, the common law of crimes was received and applied. With the . . . American Revolution, however, a strong movement arose to establish all law, including the criminal law, on the foundation of legislative enactment. Initially, this took the form of legislative enactments that simply declared the common law, including the common law of crimes, to be in effect except as displaced by particular statutory provisions. . . .

The period of social and political upheaval after the American and French revolutions engendered, among many other legal changes, a strong movement toward legislative codification of law, particularly the criminal law. Reform efforts aimed both to order and clarify the law and to ameliorate its severity, for in English law by 1800 more than one hundred different kinds of offenses were punishable by death. A leading reformer was Jeremy Bentham, whose utilitarianism afforded a coherent basis for ordering the law of crimes according to the principle of degrees of social harm. Many reform efforts were launched in the United States, paralleling and to some extent inspired by those of Bentham, as a result of which the law of crimes in many states was recast into more or less coherent penal codes. At least since the late nineteenth century, the criminal law has been expressed in a penal code in all but a few American jurisdictions.

Today the paradigm of penal legislation, both in substance and format, is the Model Penal Code, promulgated by the American Law Institute in 1962. The Code is a comprehensive reformulation of the principles of criminal liability that is drawn from previous codes, decisional law, and scholarly commentary. It has been substantially adopted in many states and is the preeminent source of guidance in revision and reform of substantive criminal law in the United States.

2. Precedent

Understanding the judicial opinions in this book requires awareness of the basic conventions of common law judicial reasoning, conventions that are implicit in most American judicial opinions.

Even though criminal charges now must have a legislative mandate, statutes sometimes unavoidably suffer from ambiguity or vagueness of terms or incompleteness of coverage. Judges therefore often must engage in common law judicial reasoning when they decide how to *interpret* a statute or constitution and when they *supply* rules of law not found in statutes or constitutions. Here are some examples of criminal law questions requiring judges to supply rules:

1. A police officer shoots a fleeing burglar dead. Is the officer guilty of violating a statute prohibiting the intentional or reckless killing of a human being?

2. You find a mail sack full of money in the woods and keep it. Have you violated a statute that simply punishes "theft" without further defining it?

3. Defendant has sexual intercourse with an unwilling person, too drunk to notice that the unwilling person says no. Is the defendant guilty under a statute that simply punishes "rape" without further defining it?

4. Can the state make it a criminal offense to "annoy a police officer" without violating a constitutional clause insuring "due process of law"?

A crucial feature of "common law" systems like those obtaining in American jurisdictions is the practice of stare decisis, or the ascription of legal authority to judicial precedent. An implication of this practice is that in deciding questions like the ones listed above, courts do not only resolve the case in front of them; rather, they provide a rule or standard of decision binding in future cases.

But which future cases? Most students bring to legal study a general impression of legal reasoning as an intuitive process of seeing analogies. According to this conception, if the facts of two cases strike a judge as sufficiently similar, the judge will decide the two cases similarly. This impression is roughly accurate, but it leaves out an important feature of legal reasoning. Judges are concerned only with *relevant* similarity. Many similarities between two cases — the defendants' first names, for an obvious example — are irrelevant. In order to distinguish relevant from irrelevant factual similarities, judges advert to rules, and to justifications for those rules. Usually these justifications (or "rationales," as we will call them) invoke some consideration of fairness or social utility. Chapter 1 will introduce you to a variety of views on the overall purposes of criminal punishment that are often invoked to justify judicially adopted rules in criminal law opinions.

Let us take our first problem, the killing of a fleeing burglar by Officer Duke. Suppose in an earlier case, Officer Wayne had unsuccessfully sought a jury instruction that a police officer could not be guilty under the statute if the officer intended to prevent the escape of a pedestrian observed jaywalking. Until we know more about why the judge refused the requested instruction, we cannot tell if the prior case is *relevantly similar* to Duke's case. Suppose Wayne's judge denied the requested instruction because the statute did not explicitly mention any such defense. Presumably Duke is in the same boat — his requested instruction would also be barred by a rule against nonstatutory defenses. Duke's case is then relevantly similar to Wayne's case. But suppose Wayne's judge denied the requested instruction on the ground that preventing the escape of one suspected of a misdemeanor is not worth killing for. If burglary is a felony, Duke's request is not covered by the *rule* of Wayne's case. Now the question arises whether Duke's killing is covered by the *rationale* of the earlier case — that is, whether preventing the escape of a burglar is a sufficiently valuable purpose to justify killing him or her. If not, burglary is relevantly similar to jaywalking, even though one is a felony and the other a misdemeanor.

When lawyers and judges use an earlier decision as precedent, they do not simply assert that the earlier case was circumstantially similar to the case before the court. They assert that the rule or rationale of the earlier case governs the case before the court.

Lawyers and judges disagree about how much precedent actually constrains judges. For one thing, many judicial opinions do not clearly articulate any rule or rationale. For another, courts often will justify a particular result as compatible with several rival rules — rules that might diverge in other cases, but that coincide in the case before the court. Further, when judges do articulate a rule, they may offer several potentially inconsistent rationales for it. Finally, even a single rule or rationale may not compel any particular choice in the case before the court. As Justice Holmes famously wrote, "abstract propositions do not decide concrete cases." Thus, the rule that preventing the escape of a misdemeanant cannot justify homicide has no clearly necessary implications for one who kills to prevent the escape of a felon. And the rationale that killing is justified only if it serves a sufficiently important purpose does not tell us whether preventing the escape of a burglar is sufficiently important. Thus, judges often have considerable leeway in interpreting and applying precedent. Nevertheless, the conventions of legal reasoning demand that in using a case as precedent, one must ascribe a rule or rationale to it. It is the rule or rationale, rather than the circumstances of the earlier case, that one applies to the current case.

Courts are expected to conform to the past decisions of the highest court of appeal in their jurisdiction. The highest court of appeal in a jurisdiction can change its interpretation of a constitution or statute, and it can reject rules of law it has made. Nevertheless, appellate courts will generally express reluctance to overrule their own precedent, and feel compelled to offer elaborate justifications in the rare cases when they do so. They may assert that social conditions have changed, that scientific knowledge has advanced, or perhaps that the original decision misunderstood the intent of the legislature in drafting the governing statute. Judges will rarely admit to overruling precedent merely because they think it bad policy.

All courts must defer to the United States Supreme Court on federal constitutional law, but state courts need not defer to federal courts on state criminal or state constitutional law. But even where courts are not bound by the statutory or decisional law of other jurisdictions, they may be influenced in their common law reasoning by those other courts, as well as by the writings of legal scholars.

3.   Constitutions

The original Federal Constitution has a number of clauses pertaining to substantive criminal law; for example, the Ex Post Facto clause bars legislatures, state and federal, from punishing acts that occurred before the legislative proscription was passed, and the Bill of Attainder clause bars criminal statutes singling out particular individuals for punishment.

The Due Process Clause of the Fifth Amendment has been interpreted to place a burden of proof beyond a reasonable doubt on federal prosecutors, and the Due Process Clause of the Fourteenth Amendment similarly obligates the states. These due process clauses, along with similarly vague civil rights provisions in state constitutions, also set more substantive boundaries on what a legislature can punish. Thus, the federal and state due process clauses may be invoked in arguments that conduct cannot be punished unless the defendant had notice that it was criminal and that punishment must be pursuant to precisely drafted statutes. Also, in concert with the Eighth Amendment prohibition of "cruel and unusual punishments," these clauses are invoked in arguments that punishment must be for *conduct* rather than for characteristics, conditions, statuses, propensities, desires, or thoughts. These issues are taken up in Chapter 2.

The due process clauses may also play a role in arguments that certain defenses should be available to defendants, or that the prosecution should be required to disprove certain defenses beyond a reasonable doubt. In addition, the Eighth Amendment may set limits on punishments arguably disproportionate to the crime involved (as discussed in Chapter 1) and plays the major role in constraining the scope and nature of death penalty laws (Chapter 7).

To the extent that these constitutional clauses or their state constitutional analogues set limits to criminal liability, courts may not only strike down statutes that transgress those limits, but also, where possible, interpret statutes to avoid such conflicts. Thus constitutional standards of just punishment are potentially relevant to any substantive criminal law issue. Nevertheless, judicial decisions about what elements of a crime must be proved by the prosecution and what defenses must be made available to the defense rarely invoke constitutional standards. For the most part, they apply common law standards of just punishment in interpreting statutes. This means that most judicial precedent concerning just punishment can be overturned by legislative action.

Other civil rights provisions not obviously directed at criminal law set limits on what conduct can be punished. The Equal Protection Clause of the Fourteenth Amendment bars discriminatory legislation by the states, and the Due Process Clause of the Fifth Amendment bars such legislation by the federal government; thus, they may operate to preclude criminal laws that violate constitutional norms against, say, discrimination on the basis of race or national origin. The Thirteenth Amendment bars slavery and involuntary servitude except as punishment for crime. Despite this exception, however, the Thirteenth Amendment is assumed to preclude imprisonment for debt, and to set limits on the use of convict labor, so as to avoid the reinstitution of slavery under the guise of criminal punishment.

The free speech and free exercise of religion clauses of the First Amendment bar some criminal statutes and some decisions to prosecute under otherwise constitutional statutes. The Fourteenth Amendment Due Process Clause applies these limits to the states. And insofar as due process protects abortion, birth control, and consensual sexual intimacy, it precludes criminal prosecution of these practices.

Of course, the Fourth and Fifth Amendments establish procedural rights against unreasonable searches and seizures, double jeopardy, and self-incrimination, and the Sixth Amendment provides rights to trial by jury and to confront witnesses. (All of these rights are now applied against the states by the Fourteenth Amendment's Due Process Clause.) While these rights are inherently procedural, and so beyond the scope of this book, they may nevertheless affect substantive criminal law. Consider one of the problems we posed above. Can a state make it a crime to "annoy a police officer"? One consideration in resolving this question might be the danger that such a statute could be used to punish suspects for refusing to submit to questioning, admit police to their homes, or plead guilty. A court might repel these threats to the procedural rights of defendants by striking down the statute, or by reading restrictive criteria of liability into it — for example, by requiring the prosecution to prove that defendant intentionally impeded the officer in the performance of her duty. Finally, the Sixth Amendment right to a jury trial may figure in arguments that improper jury instructions justify a new trial, particularly if they involved the partial or total exclusion of a valid defense from the jury's consideration.

C.   THE ANALYSIS OF CRIMINAL LIABILITY

1.   The Purpose of Analysis

Judges, lawyers, legislators, and legal scholars often analyze the question of liability for a particular crime by dividing it into discrete issues. The general analytic schemes they deploy, consisting of general principles or criteria for determining the requirements of fair punishment, may be helpful in resolving three important issues:

1. *The scope of legality.* As we noted above, almost all jurisdictions forbid punishment without a pre-established legislative definition of the crime. But the meaning and scope of this principle is unclear and subject to controversy. One purpose of a scheme of analysis is to determine what aspects of criminal liability must be legislatively defined, and what issues can be left to judicial resolution.
2. *Burdens of proof.* Although nowhere mentioned in the federal constitution, the presumption of innocence is assumed to be a requirement of due process. But again, the meaning and scope of this principle is subject to controversy. One purpose of a scheme of analysis is to help identify who bears the burden of proof on various issues. This decision may be confronted at four different levels: (1) The constitutional question of how heavy a burden of proof courts and legislatures *can* place on the defense on different issues. (2) The legislative question of how heavy a burden legislators *should* place on the defense. (3) The interpretive question of what allocation of the burden of proof judges should assume when the legislature is silent. (4) The common law question of how, within constitutional limits, to allocate the burden of proof when judges recognize defenses not provided by statute.
3. *Statutory interpretation.* Statutes defining offenses inevitably leave a great deal unsaid. One purpose served by general schemes of the criteria of criminal liability is to fill in these blanks. These general schemes can be stated explicitly in what is sometimes called "the general part" of a criminal code, or they can be developed judicially and passively accepted by legislatures (who always have the power to change nonconstitutional rules of law developed by judges).

Two of the most influential and widely respected analytic schemes are those reflected in the Model Penal Code, and in the German Penal Code. We offer a brief introduction to each here.

2.   The Model Penal Code Scheme

The basic analytic structure of offenses in the Model Penal Code is summarized in the following excerpt from an important treatise on criminal law defenses.[2]

---

2. Paul Robinson, 1 Criminal Law Defenses §11 (a) (1984).

1. An offense has been committed where an actor has satisfied all elements contained in the definition of the offense. The elements of an offense are of two sorts: objective requirements (actus reus elements) and culpability requirements (including primarily mens rea elements).
2. The objective elements of an offense may include the *conduct* of the actor (or other persons), the *circumstances* under which the conduct takes place, and the *results* stemming from the conduct.
3. Every offense must contain at least one objective element consisting of the conduct of the actor. (This is termed "the act requirement.")
4. The mental or culpability elements of an offense may be purpose (or intention), knowledge, recklessness, negligence, or lack of culpability, with regard to engaging in the conduct, causing the result, or being aware of the circumstances specified as the objective elements. ([Although] . . . negligent and strict liability [should] be avoided. . . .)
5. Every objective element must have a corresponding culpability element and that level of culpability may be different for each of the objective elements of the same offense.

In addition, the Model Penal Code (MPC) defines certain "affirmative defenses," such as necessity, self-defense, duress, and insanity. The MPC treats any circumstance that negates one of these defenses as an objective element of the offense, and so applies the MPC's culpability scheme to these defenses. For example, let us say that self-defense requires an imminent and life-threatening attack. A killer who was negligent in believing such an attack was imminent would thus be guilty of negligent homicide.

3. The German Scheme

The basic structure of the German Penal Code has influenced scholarly analysis of criminal liability around the world for more than a century. It is summarized in the following excerpt from an influential book advocating its increased use by American criminal lawyers. German lawyers divide criminal liability into three issues: the definition of the offense, wrongfulness, and responsibility.[3]

[1] The definition of the offense. This is the set of objective and subjective elements that constitute the incriminating case against the accused. . . . The definition must be read, together with the exceptions represented by claims of justification and excuse, in order to arrive at the conduct that is actually subject to punishment.

The definition consists of objective and subjective elements. If any one of the objective elements is absent, there is no possibility of establishing the offense; and the prosecution fails. . . . [The] subjective element of the definition raises a question of fact about the actor's mental state. It corresponds to the dominant view in the common law about the meaning of mens rea and the Model Penal Code's criteria for "kinds of culpability.". . .

The minimal demand of the *maxim nulla poena sine lege* is that the legislature, and only the legislature, be charged with the authority of enacting definitions of crime. The principle of fair warning requires that the legislature define the prohibitory norms of the society. The demands of legislative specificity are stricter in the category of definition than in the analysis of justification and excuse. . . .

---

3. George Fletcher, Rethinking Criminal Law 575-78 (1978). To avoid confusion, we have substituted "responsibility" for Fletcher's terms, "culpability" and "attribution," which are sometimes used with other meanings in this book.

[2] Wrongdoing and justification. The violation of the prohibitory norm does not entail liability unless it is wrongful. In the typical case, the violation of the definition is wrongful. Yet in extraordinary cases, the conduct might be justified by appeal to a conflicting norm permitting the violation. The paradigmatic instances of justification are lesser evils, self-defense and acting in the name of the law to effect an arrest or prevent an escape from custody. Claims of justification always require a union of objective elements and a subjective intent. The nature of a justification is that the actor has good and sufficient reasons for violating the norm constituting the definition. Justified conduct in violation of the definition is not wrongful, but neither is it perfectly legal, as is conduct that falls outside the scope of the definition. This type of harmful conduct might, for example, support tort liability for the harm done.

[3] [Responsibility] and excuses. The distinction between wrongdoing and . . . [responsibility] corresponds to the distinction between justification and excuse. Claims of justification negate the dimension of wrongdoing; claims of excuse negate the element of . . . [responsibility]. The underlying theory of excusability is that it is unfair to hold the particular suspect accountable for his wrongful act. The diverse grounds of excuse . . . include insanity, duress and various forms of mistake. . . . The functional impact of a justification is to modify the norm by carving out a limited field where the conduct is not wrongful. Valid claims of excuse do not modify the prohibitory norm. Excused conduct is still wrongful: the norm against the conduct remains intact. To recognize an excuse is to judge that the particular suspect cannot be fairly held liable for the violation.

D. BURDENS OF PROOF AND DUE PROCESS

The burden of proof has tactical importance in criminal cases because it determines which side gets the benefit of the doubt in disputed questions. It is also an important "policy" issue because it allocates the risk of error. Thus the normal rule that the prosecution must prove its case beyond a reasonable doubt implies a social or political or moral judgment that we are far more willing to tolerate erroneous acquittals than erroneous convictions. This rule also gives concrete definition to the ideal that the accused are entitled to a "presumption of innocence."

A criminal litigant may face two different kinds of burdens: (1) the burden of production — the duty to introduce at least some *prima facie* evidence in order to compel a fact finder to at least *consider* a claim, and (2) the burden of persuasion — the duty to persuade the fact finder that the totality of evidence presented warrants accepting or rejecting the claim. In addition, criminal litigants may be compelled to meet different *standards* of persuasiveness, ranging from proof "beyond a reasonable doubt" down to proof by mere "preponderance of the evidence."

According to Blackstone, the prosecution was required to prove that the defendant had committed a criminal act, while the defense was required to prove "circumstances of justification, excuse and alleviation," 4 Blackstone's Commentaries 201 (1769). For Blackstone, these included the "excuses" of mistake or accident, circumstances that today would be thought to disprove the mental element of an offense, on which the prosecution now bears the burden of proof. Blackstone's division of the burden of proof was influential in nineteenth-century America. A leading American case was Commonwealth v. York, 50 Mass. (9 Met.) 93 (1845), requiring the defendant to prove the "defense" of provocation.[4]

By the end of the nineteenth century, however, courts had begun to question whether requiring the defense to prove such exculpatory claims was compatible with the principle of the presumption of innocence. A well-known decision expressing this viewpoint was Davis v. United States, 160 U.S. 469 (1895), which placed the burden on the prosecution to disprove claims of insanity in federal cases:

> The plea of not guilty is unlike a special plea in a civil action which, admitting the case averred, seeks to establish substantive grounds of defense by a preponderance of evidence. It is not in confession and avoidance, for it is a plea that controverts the existence of every fact essential to constitute the crime charged. Upon that plea the accused may stand, shielded by the presumption of his innocence, until it appears that he is guilty; and his guilt cannot in the very nature of things be regarded as proved, if the jury entertain a reasonable doubt from all the evidence whether he was legally capable of committing crime.

Davis was not, however, a constitutional ruling. It was merely a common law ruling regarding the burden of proof on a federal charge of murder. In Leland v. Oregon, 343 U.S. 790 (1951), the Supreme Court rejected a due process challenge to Oregon's then-unique practice of requiring defendants to prove insanity beyond a reasonable doubt (at that time about 20 states required defendants to meet a lesser burden). The Court implied, however, that the due process clause might require that the jury be allowed to acquit the defendant of murder if evidence of insanity raised a reasonable doubt that defendant had acted with the requisite mental element of murder. Because the trial court in *Leland* so instructed the jury, the Supreme Court opined that "the burden of proof of guilt, and of all the necessary elements of guilt, was placed squarely upon the state." *Id.* at 795.

In the case of *In re* Winship, 397 U.S. 358 (1970), the Supreme Court made clear that the presumption of innocence was a constitutional principle binding on the states, holding that "the Due Process clause protects the accused against conviction except upon proof beyond a reasonable doubt of every fact necessary to constitute the crime charged." *Id.* at 364. Left unresolved was the question of what facts constituted the crime charged. For example, neither self-defenders nor the insane can be guilty of murder—does this mean that "unlawfulness" and sanity are facts constituting the crime of murder?

The Court addressed this issue in an unfortunately confusing pair of cases in the mid-seventies. In Mullaney v. Wilbur, 421 U.S. 684 (1975), a unanimous court struck down Maine's murder statute, which (1) defined murder as unlawful killing with malice, and (2) defined malice as deliberate and unprovoked cruelty, but (3) presumed intentional killings to be unprovoked unless the defense proved provocation by a preponderance of the evidence. Provoked intentional killings were graded as manslaughters. Justice Powell's opinion for the Court held provocation to be a crucial part of the charge of murder because it determined "the degree of culpability attaching to the criminal homicide."

---

4. On the history of allocations of burden of proof, see George Fletcher, Rethinking Criminal Law 524-35 (1978).

Id. at 696. Yet this formulation was no less ambiguous than *Winship*'s limitation of the presumption of innocence to "the facts constituting the crime charged." Consider these two possible interpretations of "the degree of culpability."

1. The "degree of culpability attaching to the homicide" appears to refer to the grading of the offense. On this interpretation, the prosecution would bear the burden of proof on any issue that could determine what crime, if any, defendant was guilty of. This interpretation would certainly include any defense that could lower homicide liability from murder to manslaughter, but arguably should also include any defense that forecloses liability altogether, such as insanity. On this interpretation of "the degree of culpability," *Mullaney* reversed *Leland* and placed the burden of proof on insanity on the prosecution. Two Justices wrote a separate concurring opinion, in which they reserved the question of the burden of proof on insanity that had been raised in *Leland*.

2. The Model Penal Code equates "culpability" with the mental element of the definition of the offense, listing "purpose, knowledge, recklessness and negligence" as different degrees of "culpability" (as treated in detail in Chapter 3). On this interpretation, the problem with the Maine murder statute was that it shifted the burden onto the defense to disprove part of the statutory definition of murder. If provocation were taken outside of the definition of the offense and treated as an excuse, like insanity, it would no longer affect the "degree of culpability" attaching to the *crime* of homicide, though it would still affect the degree of responsibility attaching to the *defendant*, and so the defendant's liability for the crime.

In the 1977 case of Patterson v. New York, 432 U.S. 197 (1977), by a 5-4 vote the Supreme Court adopted the second interpretation of *Mullaney*. New York's murder statute defined murder simply as intentional killing, without any reference to malice. It offered defendants the opportunity to lower their liability to manslaughter by proving the partial excuse of "extreme emotional disturbance," by a preponderance of the evidence. Since "extreme emotional disturbance" was similar to provocation, the defendant argued that the New York statute was functionally identical to the Maine statute struck down in *Mullaney*. The majority reasoned, however, that New York was still requiring the prosecution to prove every fact defining the crime, including its mental element — or, in the language of the Model Penal Code, its level of culpability. The court held that by reclassifying provocation as an *excuse* rather than a circumstance negating the *mental element* of murder, New York was able to constitutionally shift the burden of proof on the issue. In Sandstrom v. Montana, 442 U.S. 510 (1979), the Supreme Court reaffirmed the prosecution's burden to prove the mental element of the offense, in this case intent to kill. The Supreme Court struck down a jury instruction that "the law presumes that a person intends the ordinary consequences of his voluntary acts."

It was clear in the wake of *Patterson* and *Sandstrom* that while the prosecution is constitutionally required to prove the elements of each offense beyond a reasonable doubt, it is not constitutionally required to bear such a burden on defenses of excuse. Thus, *Patterson* did not resolve the proper allocation of the burden of proof on defenses of justification. Most jurisdictions placed the burden of production on a claim of self-defense on the defendant, but once the defendant has satisfied this burden, almost all jurisdictions required the prosecution to disprove self-defense beyond a reasonable doubt.

In 1982, however, an Ohio Appeals Court ruled that self-defense was "an affirmative defense," one which a defendant charged with an "unlawful" killing was required to prove by a preponderance of the evidence. Just as the *Mullaney* and *Patterson* cases exposed the ambiguity of "culpability" as between the mental element of the offense and the issue of the defendant's responsibility, the Ohio case exposed the ambiguity of "unlawfulness" as between merely satisfying the statutory definition of the offense, and doing so without lawful justification. Indeed, effacing the distinction between justification and excuse, the Ohio court reasoned that if a justified killing could be considered "lawful," then so could a wrongful killing, excusable on grounds of the defendant's insanity. The court concluded that "unlawful" meant simply "defined as an offense by statute," and that prosecutors were only obliged to prove a homicide "unlawful" in that limited sense. They did not need to prove that the homicide was not justified or excused. State v. Morris, 455 N.E.2d 1352 (1982).

Then in 1986, in the case of Martin v. Ohio, 480 U.S. 228, the Supreme Court upheld this position by a 5-4 vote. Citing *Morris,* the majority reasoned that "[i]t is true that unlawfulness is essential for conviction, but the Ohio courts hold that unlawfulness in cases like this is the conduct satisfying the elements of aggravated murder — an interpretation that we are not in a position to dispute." Id. at 235. *Martin* effectively decided that as a matter of federal constitutional law, the presumption of innocence is confined to the definition of the offense, and does not extend to defenses of justification. Nevertheless, many jurisdictions extend the presumption further as a matter of statutory or common law.

New questions were raised about the scope of the prosecution's constitutional burden to prove the mental element of offenses as a result of the Supreme Court's (again, unfortunately) confusing decision in Montana v. Egelhoff, 518 U.S. 37 (1996). Here the Court upheld a Montana statute prescribing that voluntary intoxication "may not be taken into consideration in determining the existence of mental state which is an element of an offense." Four dissenting Justices voted that this statute offended due process by creating an evidentiary presumption that intoxication does not interfere with culpable mental states and thereby reducing the prosecution's burden to prove the mental element of offenses. Four other Justices voted that such an evidentiary presumption would not violate due process. The decisive vote was cast by Justice Ginsburg, who agreed with the dissenters that reducing the prosecution's burden to prove the mental element of the offense would offend due process — but insisted that the Montana statute did not reduce the burden. Instead, she said, the Montana statute permissibly added voluntary intoxication to the culpable mental states constituting the mental element of certain offenses. Justice Ginsburg's interpretation of the Montana statute has been widely criticized, but the fact remains that she joined four other Justices to reaffirm the *Winship-Mullaney-Sandstrom* doctrine that the prosecution must prove the mental element of offenses beyond a reasonable doubt. (Since *Egelhoff* is important for determining a required culpable mental state, it is treated in some detail at the end of Chapter 3.)

The latest question to emerge concerning the constitutional allocation of burden of proof is whether the prosecutorial burden to prove offense elements applies to factual claims considered by judges in sentencing. In McMillan v.

Pennsylvania, 477 U.S. 79 (1986), the Supreme Court held that legislatures have broad discretion to denominate particular circumstances as sentencing factors rather than elements. In this way, legislatures can remove the prosecution's burden to prove these circumstances beyond a reasonable doubt at a jury trial. Shortly thereafter a congressionally established Sentencing Commission issued guidelines for federal judges to use in sentencing all federal offenders. These guidelines were designed to promote uniform and determinate sentencing. One of their most controversial features was that they required judges to enhance sentences on the basis of "relevant" criminal conduct proven by a preponderance of evidence at a sentencing hearing, even if defendant had never been charged with this conduct, or had been acquitted of it at trial.

But two recent Supreme Court decisions raised questions about the constitutionality of sentencing on the basis of unproven "relevant conduct." In Jones v. United States, 526 U.S. 227 (1999), the Court considered a federal carjacking statute that added large sentencing increments if the carjacking resulted in injury or death. The Court decided, 5-4, that such resulting harms were offense elements rather than mere sentencing factors. Justice Souter declared for the Court that "under the due process clause of the Fifth Amendment and the notice and jury trial guarantees of the Sixth Amendment, any fact (other than prior conviction) that increases the maximum penalty for a crime must be charged in an indictment, submitted to a jury, and proven beyond a reasonable doubt." 526 U.S. at 43-44 n.6.

Then, more dramatically, in Apprendi v. New Jersey, 530 U.S. 466 (2000), the Court applied Jones to a hate crime statute that doubled the maximum punishment for a crime committed with a biased motive. Predictably, it required the biased motive to be proved to a jury beyond a reasonable doubt. (Since *Apprendi* is important for the allocation of power to set sentences, it is treated in detail at the end of Chapter 1 on Just Punishment.)

Despite these decisions, every circuit quickly held that "relevant conduct" sentencing remained constitutional as long as it did not raise the maximum penalty for the offense of conviction. In Harris v. United States, 536 U.S. 542 (2002), the Supreme Court agreed, upholding the post-trial finding, on the basis of a preponderance of the evidence, of a fact that increased the *minimum* term of imprisonment for an offense by seven years. However, in Ring v. Arizona, 536 U.S. 584 (2002), the court held that *Apprendi* requires jury determination beyond a reasonable doubt of any circumstances alleged to justify a capital sentence. Some scholars have argued that the *Apprendi* decision's distinction between offense elements and sentencing factors commits the Court to clarify the concept of an offense element,[5] but thus far the Court has not done so.

---

5. *See* Nancy J. King and Susan R. Klein, Essential Elements, 54 Vand. L. Rev. 1467 (2001); Claire Finkelstein, Positivism and the Notion of an Offense, 88 Calif. L. Rev. 335 (2000).

I

JUST PUNISHMENT

The United States has considerably more violent crime and vastly more punishment than any other prosperous democracy. Table 1 provides recent reported offense rates per 100,000 for homicide, robbery, and rape, and incarceration rates for several countries.[1] Disturbing as U.S. crime statistics appear when viewed in comparative perspective, they are actually good news when viewed in historical perspective: In terms of crimes reported to police, homicide rates have dropped 43 percent, and overall violent crime rates have dropped 34 percent since 1991.[2] Yet there has been no corresponding decrease in the incarceration rate, which instead increased by about 21 percent between 1991 and 2001 (although this increase appears to be leveling off). There are now nearly 2 million inmates in the United States,[3] about one-fourth of these imprisoned for drug offenses.[4] About 4 million more Americans are on probation or parole.[5]

There are many possible relationships between the high rates of offending and incarceration in American society. Incarceration may seem like a natural response to crime, but incarceration rates for offenders vary in different countries.

---

1. United States Crime figures (for 2001) are from the Crime in the United States 2001, U.S. Department of Justice, Federal Bureau of Investigation Web site *www.fbi.gov/ucr/cius_01/01crime2.pdf* and incarceration figures (for 2002) are from Bureau of Justice Statistics — Prison and Jail Inmates at Midyear 2002 Web site *www.ojp.usdoj.gov/bjs*. Crime figures for France, Germany, Switzerland, and Japan for 2002, are from International Criminal Police Organization Web site *www.interpol.int/Public/Statistics/ICS/downloadLisp.asp*. Incarceration figures for these countries are from Americans Behind Bars Data Sheet: International Use of Incarceration Web site.

Contrary to common impression, the *overall* crime rate of the United States is matched by that of a few Western European countries, if we include property crimes not involving any harm to the person, such as larceny or burglary of an unoccupied residence. It is in rates of *violent* crime that the United States stands out. See generally Franklin E. Zimring and Gordon Hawkins, Crime Is Not the Problem: Lethal Violence in America (1997).

2. By another measure — anonymous census bureau surveys of individuals reporting whether they have been victimized by crime — the rates of non-fatal violent victimization dropped even more — including decreases of 64 percent for aggravated assault, 63 percent for robbery, and 56 percent for rape/sexual assault.

3. About 1.3 million are in state or federal prisons; the rest are in local jails. *http://www.sentencingproject.org/issues_01.cfm*

4. Timothy Egan, Hard Time: Less Crime, More Criminals, N.Y. Times, March 7, 1999, Late Edition — Final, Sec. 4, p. 1.

5. Overall, as of the end of 2001, more than 5.6 million adult residents of the United States either were serving time or had previously served time in a state or federal prison. www.ojp.usdoj.gov/bjs/pub/press/piusp01pr.htm.

TABLE 1
Violent Crime and Incarceration in Five Wealthy Democracies

	Homicide	Robbery	Rape	Incarceration
United States	5.6	148.5	31.8	702
France	4.07	224.35	17.63	95
Germany	3.23	71.41	10.45	85
Switzerland	2.91	33.40	6.61	80
Japan	1.10	5.48	1.85	37

Japanese offenders, for example, are much more likely to be apprehended than American offenders but less likely to be prosecuted; if prosecuted, they are much more likely to be convicted, but much less likely to be incarcerated.[6]

In America violent crime dropped steadily from the early 1930s to the early 1960s, while incarceration rates remained steady. Yet an increase in violent crime from 1960 to 1980 inspired a sustained increase in incarceration rates that continued even after violent crime rates began to decline. Today's homicide rate is about what it was in the mid-1960s, but the incarceration rate is four times what it was then. Indeed, the unprecedented expansion of incarceration is one of the most dramatic social changes of recent American history. At the same time, the substantial reduction in violent crime during the 1990s, although less dramatic, cries out for explanation.

The most convincing accounts of this drop point to a variety of factors. According to econometrician Steven Levitt of the University of Chicago, about half the decline in violent crime can be ascribed to increases in incarceration rates and in police personnel. Perhaps to the surprise of some, Levitt ascribes almost no causal impact to the strong economy of the 1990s. And surely one of his most surprising — and controversial — findings is that about a fourth of the crime drop can be ascribed to the legalization of abortion in the 1970s. Some of Levitt's conclusions are summarized in the table below:

Percent Decline in Homicide and Violent Crime Attributable to Various Factors[7]

	% decline in homicide	% decline in violent crime
Strong economy	0	0
Changing demographics	0	2
Better policing strategies	1	1
Gun control laws	0	0
Concealed weapons laws	0	0
Increased capital punishment	1.5	0
Increased police	5.5	5.5

6. John Braithwaite, Crime, Shame and Reintegration 62 (1989); A. Didrick Castberg, Japanese Criminal Justice 94-95 (1990).

7. Steven D. Levitt, Understanding Why Crime Fell in the 1990s: Four Factors That Explain the Decline and Seven That Do Not (forthcoming Journal of Economic Perspectives 2004).

Increased incarceration	12	12
Decline of crack use	6	3
Legalized abortion	10	10
All factors considered	36	33.5
Actual decline	42.9	33.6

Punishment is important, then, for two reasons. First, because it has an effect on the important social problem of crime — although how and why are very much contested. Second, because the sheer scale of incarceration today makes the prison an important social institution in its own right. The purpose and proper scope of punishment are therefore questions that may now justly claim every American's attention. As you read, reflect on how and why such high incarceration rates developed, and what goals they advance. As you study criminal law, be mindful that this body of law now affects the lives of many more Americans than ever before.

Beyond its public importance, punishment has special salience for students of criminal law. To the courts that administer it, the criminal law is a system of rules and standards determining the distribution of punishment. For them, and for users of this book, punishment is the criminal law's bottom line. It is the ultimate question presented by every criminal case.

Most of the chapter that follows is devoted to exploring the purposes and limits of punishment. These "theories" of punishment affect legal decision-making in three ways. First, they influence the decisions of legislatures in defining offenses and defenses, prescribing penalties, and allocating resources for police, prisons, prosecutors, parole and probation services, and other social welfare expenditures that may be thought to prevent crime. Second, they influence judges in interpreting and applying criminal statutes. Third, they influence judges in sentencing offenders. The leading theories of punishment have been developed and defended by philosophers and sociologists, but their legal authority is generally established by statute. The following statutory provision is typical.[8]

COLORADO REVISED STATUTES
Title 18. Criminal Code (1999)

§8-1-102. Purpose of code, statutory construction

(1) This code shall be construed in such manner as to promote maximum fulfillment of its general purposes, namely:

(a) To define offenses, to define adequately the act and mental state which constitute each offense, to place limitations upon the condemnation of conduct as criminal when it is without fault, and to give fair warning to all persons concerning the nature of the conduct prohibited and the penalties authorized upon conviction;

(b) To forbid the commission of offenses and to prevent their occurrence through the deterrent influence of the sentences authorized; to provide for

---

8. See also Model Penal Code, §1.02 in Appendix B.

the rehabilitation of those convicted and their punishment when required in the interests of public protection;

(c) To differentiate on reasonable grounds between serious and minor offenses, and prescribe penalties which are proportionate to the seriousness of offenses and which permit recognition of differences in rehabilitation possibilities as between individual offenders;

(d) To prevent arbitrary or oppressive treatment of persons accused or convicted of offenses and to identify certain minimum standards for criminal justice which, within the concept of due process of law, have the stature of substantive rights of persons accused of crime.

1

THE PURPOSES AND LIMITS OF PUNISHMENT

A. AN INTRODUCTORY PROBLEM

Case 1. Edward Jones has been arrested and charged with murder for killing his father.

Jones is a 22-year-old community college graduate working as a computer programmer. He was born into a family of considerable emotional and, occasionally, physical violence. His father was an alcoholic who was prone to abuse his family during drinking bouts. As a young child, Jones was often struck harshly by his father and throughout his life saw his father strike and loudly berate his mother. When Jones was seven years old, his mother sought psychological counseling for him as he alternated between periods of brooding and withdrawal and fits of "acting out" at school.

Jones's father was influenced by fantasies of his wife's sexual infidelity, and on many occasions Jones saw his father denounce her as a whore. Over the years, the mother received several minor bruises at the hands of her husband, though she never suffered broken bones or other serious injuries. Jones's father had once been a successful salesman and had provided well for the family, but his income fluctuated wildly with his drinking, and in recent years he had been frequently unemployed. Jones himself gives part of his salary to his mother, but because of the father's alcoholism and unemployment, his mother, who suffers from arthritis, has had to work full time as a store clerk to help support her younger children. The pressure of work, worry about finances, and the toll of her husband's frequent denunciations have left Jones's mother in a state of constant emotional strain.

Jones came home one evening to see his mother in tears. She recounted that Jones's father had had another alcoholic fit and had screamed at her wildly and shoved her to the couch, though he had inflicted no injuries on her. The father had then stalked off to a bar. Jones had been brooding angrily over his father lately, frustrated and furious over the miserable life his father had imposed on his mother. This incident brought his anger to a fever. Shortly after his father returned that evening and skulked sullenly into the den, Jones took his father's pistol from a drawer and shot his father to death. He immediately turned himself in to the police.

A psychiatrist examining Jones for the court said that Jones was an extremely neurotic and high-strung young man; that he had accumulated anguished hatred for his father; that he could no longer bear his mother's suffering; that he was prone to bouts of depression; but that he was perfectly sane by any legal standard of criminal responsibility.

Jones was charged with second-degree murder, defined by state law as "the intentional killing of another, not in immediate self-defense or in defense of another to save the other from imminent grievous bodily harm." The penalty for second-degree murder is from 10 to 20 years in prison. Because of the sentencing discretion afforded trial judges, the average sentence handed down for this crime is 13 years; because most prisoners are paroled before their sentences expire, the average time actually served for this crime is 8 years plus a period of supervision outside prison.

Case 2. Charles Green has been arrested for breaking into a house and stealing about $100 in jewelry and a small television set. No resident of the house was home at the time.

Green is 23 years old. His father died when he was seven, and his mother supported him and three other children through welfare and unskilled jobs. Because his mother was usually working, Green was unsupervised as a child and from the age of ten was involved with gangs in various forms of petty delinquency. When he was 13, he spent six months in a youth detention center for petty theft. He later completed high school, where he displayed above-average intelligence and got good grades when he tried. Since high school, he has worked off and on in clerical jobs, but has been arrested and convicted three times for breaking and entering and for theft. He has served a total of seven months in the county jail. On one occasion he was arrested for a robbery-mugging, but the charge was dismissed when the complainant refused to testify. Green often uses heroin and cocaine, but his criminal activity began before his use of these drugs. The police suspect that he has committed a large number of larcenies and burglaries and perhaps a few street robberies, but his latest burglary presents them with the clearest case they have been able to make against him. The probation report shows that Green has "antisocial tendencies," but that he suffers from no clinical mental illness and has rejected employment opportunities simply because he does not like to work regularly.

Green has been charged with second-degree burglary, which the state defines as "entering a dwelling without permission with intent to commit therein a larceny." The statutory penalty for this crime is between one and five years in prison or up to a year in the county jail. The average sentence for this crime in the state is 11 months in the county jail.

Notes and Questions

1. Why should Jones be punished? Why should Green?
2. What punishment is appropriate for Jones? For Green?
3. Do you find the criminal statutes under which Jones and Green were charged, and the sentencing ranges they provide, adequate to determine the appropriate punishment?

4. Would it be preferable if the state had only a single criminal law that stated as follows?

> It shall be a crime for any person to commit any act that causes or threatens harm to society, unless the person can present a plausible excuse or justification for the act. The court (or jury) shall determine the proper punishment for the offender upon consideration of all relevant factors.

Return to these questions after you have read the following material.

B. UTILITARIANISM AND RETRIBUTIVISM

... [T]here are two justifications of punishment. What we may call the retributive view is that punishment is justified on the grounds that wrongdoing merits punishment. It is morally fitting that a person who does wrong should suffer in proportion to his wrongdoing. That a criminal should be punished follows from his guilt, and the severity of the appropriate punishment depends on the depravity of his act. The state of affairs where a wrongdoer suffers punishment is morally better than the state of affairs where he does not; and it is better irrespective of any of the consequences of punishing him.

What we may call the utilitarian view holds that on the principle that bygones are bygones and that only future consequences are material to present decisions, punishment is justifiable only by reference to the probable consequences of maintaining it as one of the devices of the social order. Wrongs committed in the past are, as such, not relevant considerations for deciding what to do. If punishment can be shown to promote effectively the interest of society it is justifiable, otherwise it is not.[1]

The criminal justice system we know today is largely the brainchild of utilitarian reformers of the late eighteenth century and the early nineteenth century. Eighteenth-century criminal justice in Europe relied on haphazardly administered capital and corporal punishment, publicly performed with elaborate ceremony, supplemented by informal networks of social control. Punishment even for petty crimes was severe if inflicted, but could often be avoided by those in favor with the rich, wellborn, or influential.[2]

In 1764 the Italian reformer Cesare Beccaria (1738-1794) published the immediately influential *On Crimes and Punishments,* in which he argued for moderate but regular, certain, and swift penalties, proportioned to the threat the offense posed to society. Such penalties — fines and terms of imprisonment — should be just sufficient to deter: excessive punishment was contrary to the interests of society and the rights of its members. The English philosopher and reformer Jeremy Bentham (1748-1832) yoked these ideas to a systematic theory of law: Laws should take the form of legislatively enacted codes, aiming to achieve the greatest happiness and least pain for the greatest number. Bentham's ideas, most fully expressed in his *Introduction to the Principles of Morals and Legislation*

---

1. John Rawls, Two Concepts of Rules, 44 The Philosophical Review 3, 5 (1955).
2. See Douglas Hay, Property Authority, and the Criminal Law, in Hay et al., Albion's Fatal Tree 17-63 (1975).

(1789), achieved influence in England, France, and America. Whether or not due to Beccaria and Bentham, the nineteenth century did witness the proliferation of penitentiaries and criminal codes they had called for, as well as such innovations as regular police forces. Utilitarian thought held that punishment's sole aim was to prevent crime and that it could do so by deterring, reforming, and incapacitating offenders. In America, utilitarian ideas were absorbed into a religiously inspired humanitarian reform movement that identified punishment with penance and spiritual redemption.

Retributivist thought is generally traced to the writings of the eighteenth-century German philosopher Immanuel Kant (1724-1804), especially the Groundwork of the Metaphysic of Morals (1785) and the Metaphysic of Morals (1797):

> Juridical punishment can never be administered merely as a means to promoting another good either with regard to the criminal himself or to civil society, but must in all cases be imposed only because the individual on whom it is inflicted has committed a crime. For one man ought never to be dealt with merely as a means subservient to the purpose of another. . . . He must first be found guilty and punishable, before there can be any thought of drawing from his punishment any benefit for himself or his fellow citizens. The penal law is a categorical imperative; and woe to him who creeps through the serpent-windings of utilitarianism to discover some advantage that may discharge him from the justice of punishment, or even from the due measure of it. . . . What, then is to be said of such a proposal as to keep a criminal alive who has been condemned to death, on his being given to understand that, if he agreed to certain dangerous experiments being performed upon him, he would be allowed to survive. . . . It is argued that physicians might thus obtain new information that would be of value to the commonweal. But . . . justice would cease to be justice, if it were bartered away for any consideration whatsoever.[3]

As this passage indicates, retributivism involves both a limiting principle (there must be no undeserved punishment) and an affirmative justification for punishment (desert justifies punishment). Kant's desert-based philosophy of punishment is said to have influenced the development of German criminal law. But it did not much influence American penal policy until the 1970s, when disappointment with the apparent failure of punishment to prevent crime prompted a search for alternatives to utilitarianism.

JOHN BRAITHWAITE AND PHILIP PETTIT, NOT JUST DESERTS: A REPUBLICAN THEORY OF CRIMINAL JUSTICE
2-5 (1990)

Until the 1970s retributivism — the idea that criminals should be punished because they deserve it — was something of a dead letter in criminology. . . . During and since the Victorian era retributivism had become increasingly

---

3. Immanuel Kant, The Philosophy of Law (Part I of the Metaphysic of Morals) 195 (W. Hastie, trans. 1887).

disreputable, probably unfairly, as an unscientific indulgence of emotions of revenge.

In that period a descendant of utilitarianism dominated criminal justice policy-making. . . . [C]riminologists were motivated by the search for ways of sentencing criminals that would incapacitate them from continuing to offend . . . , that would give the healing and helping professions opportunities to reha-bilitate them, and that would deter both those convicted (specific deterrence) and others who became aware of the punishment (general deterrence).

In that same period, ironically, positive criminology accumulated masses of evidence testifying to the failures of such utilitarian doctrines. All manner of re-habilitation programmes for offenders were tried without any producing con-sistent evidence that they reduce reoffending rates. The deterrence literature also failed to produce the expected evidence that more police, more prisons, and more certain and severe punishment made a significant difference to the crime rate. . . .

The flight to retributivism was not only fuelled by the realization that utili-tarian and preventionist criminology had failed to deliver on its promises. There was also growing documentation of the injustices perpetrated in the name of criminal justice. Indeterminate sentences, on the grounds of rehabilitation or incapacitation, allowed offenders to be locked up until they were "safe" to be re-turned to the community. Many offenders were locked up for extremely long periods for minor crimes; others got very short terms for serious crimes, thanks to their acting skills in feigning rehabilitation. . . . [Rehabilitation and incapac-itation were used to excuse locking up indefinitely some minor offenders who were regarded as subversive or insolent. At the other extreme, bribes were some-times paid to secure the early release of serious offenders, ostensibly on grounds of their remarkable rehabilitation.]

. . . Furthermore, the new retributivists rightly accused . . . [utilitarians] of denying the human dignity of offenders by treating them as determined crea-tures whose behavior could not be accounted for by their own choices to break the law. . . . [I]nstead of holding them responsible for their wrongdoing, [utili-tarians] sought to manipulate [offenders] by curing their sickness (rehabilita-tion), changing the reward-cost calculations that determined their offending (deterrence), and keeping them away from criminal opportunities (incapacita-tion). The retributivists were struck by the injustice, not to mention the futility, of this. So they called for punishment of offenders in proportion to their desert; mostly this meant in proportion to the harmfulness and blameworthiness of their actions.[4]

The new retributivists succeeded in some of their aims — sentencing be-came more determinate, less discretionary, and less focused on rehabilitation. Yet public opinion repudiated rehabilitation largely for different reasons than the philosophers did. The public increasingly saw offenders as incorrigibly dan-gerous and in need of incapacitation. Hence, the new determinate sentencing schemes tended to mandate draconian sentences, especially for repeat offenders,

---

4. [The most influential works invoking retributivism in support of determinate sentencing were Andrew von Hirsch, Doing Justice: The Choice of Punishments (1976); The Twentieth Cen-tury Fund Task Force on Criminal Sentencing, Fair and Certain Punishment (1976); Richard Singer, Just Deserts: Sentencing Based on Equality and Desert (1979). These works converged with nonphilosophical critiques of indeterminate sentencing as arbitrary and unfair in practice.—EDS.]

that were hard to justify in retributivist terms. On the other hand, mandatory sentencing meant that many people would go to prison who were not in fact dangerous, and so whose punishment little served incapacitation.

C.   UTILITARIAN PUNISHMENT

1.   The Utility Principle as a Limit on Punishment

JEREMY BENTHAM, THE THEORY OF LEGISLATION
322-24, 338 (ed. 1931)

The cases in which punishment ought not to be inflicted may be reduced to four heads: when punishment would be — 1st, Misapplied; 2nd, Inefficacious; 3rd, Superfluous; 4th, Too expensive.

I. PUNISHMENTS MISAPPLIED. — Punishments are misapplied wherever there is no real offence, no evil of the first order or of the second order; or where the evil is more than compensated by an attendant good, as in the exercise of political or domestic authority, in the repulsion of a weightier evil, in self-defence, &c. . . .

II. INEFFICACIOUS PUNISHMENTS. — I call those punishments inefficacious which have no power to produce an effect upon the will, and which, in consequence, have no tendency towards the prevention of like acts.

Punishments are inefficacious when directed against individuals who could not know the law, who have acted without intention, who have done the evil innocently, under an erroneous supposition, or by irresistible constraint. Children, imbeciles, idiots, though they may be influenced, to a certain extent, by rewards and threats, have not a sufficient idea of futurity to be restrained by punishments. In their case laws have no efficacy. . . .

III. SUPERFLUOUS PUNISHMENTS. — Punishments are superfluous in cases where the same end may be obtained by means more mild — instruction, example, invitations, delays, rewards. A man spreads abroad pernicious opinions: shall the magistrate therefore seize the sword and punish him? No; if it is the interest of one individual to give currency to bad maxims, it is the interest of a thousand others to refute him.

IV. PUNISHMENTS TOO EXPENSIVE. — If the evil of the punishment exceeds the evil of the offence, the legislator will produce more suffering than he prevents. He will purchase exemption from a lesser evil at the expense of a greater evil. . . .

The following evils are produced by every penal law: — 1st. Evil of coercion. It imposes a privation more or less painful according to the degree of pleasure which the thing forbidden has the power of conferring. 2nd. The sufferings caused by the punishment, whenever it is actually carried into execution. 3rd. Evil of apprehension suffered by those who have violated the law or who fear a prosecution in consequence. 4th. Evil of false prosecutions. This inconvenience appertains to all penal laws, but particularly to laws which are obscure and to imaginary offences. . . . 5th. Derivative evil suffered by the parents or friends of those who are exposed to the rigour of the law. . . .

2. Deterrence

JEREMY BENTHAM, THE THEORY OF LEGISLATION
325-26, 336 (ed. 1931)

FIRST RULE. — The evil of the punishment must be made to exceed the advantage of the offence.

. . . [E]rror is committed whenever a punishment is decreed which can only reach a certain point, while the advantage of the offence may go much beyond.

Some celebrated authors have attempted to establish a contrary maxim. They say that punishment ought to be diminished in proportion to the strength of temptation; that temptation diminishes the fault; and that the more potent seduction is, the less evidence we have of the offender's depravity.

This may be true; but it does not contravene the rule above laid down: for to prevent an offence, it is necessary that the repressive motive should be stronger than the seductive motive. The punishment must be more an object of dread than the offence is an object of desire. An insufficient punishment is a greater evil than an excess of rigour; for an insufficient punishment is an evil wholly thrown away. No good results from it, either to the public, who are left exposed to like offences, nor to the offender, whom it makes no better. What would be said of a surgeon, who, to spare a sick man a degree of pain, should leave the cure unfinished? Would it be a piece of enlightened humanity to add to the pains of the disorder the torment of a useless operation?

SECOND RULE. — The more deficient in certainty a punishment is, the severer it should be.

No man engages in a career of crime, except in the hope of impunity. If punishment consisted merely in taking from the guilty the fruits of his offence, and if that punishment were inevitable, no offence would ever be committed; for what man is so foolish as to run the risk of committing an offence with certainty of nothing but the shame of an unsuccessful attempt? In all cases of offence there is a calculation of the chances for and against; and it is necessary to give a much greater weight to the punishment, in order to counterbalance the chances of impunity.

It is true, then, that the more certain punishment is, the less severe it need be. . . . For the same reason it is desirable that punishment should follow offence as closely as possible; for its impression upon the minds of men is weakened by distance, and, besides, distance adds to the uncertainty of punishment, by affording new chances of escape.

THIRD RULE. — Where two offences are in conjunction, the greater offence ought to be subjected to severer punishment, in order that the delinquent may have a motive to stop at the lesser.

Two offences may be said to be in conjunction when a man has the power and the will to commit both of them. A highwayman may content himself with robbing, or he may begin with murder, and finish with robbery. The murder should be punished more severely than the robbery, in order to deter him from the greater offence. . . .

FOURTH RULE. — The greater an offence is, the greater reason there is to hazard a severe punishment for the chance of preventing it.

We must not forget that the infliction of punishment is a certain expense for the purchase of an uncertain advantage. To apply great punishments to small offences is to pay very dearly for the chance of escaping a slight evil. . . .

In order that a punishment may adapt itself to the rules of proportion above laid down, it should . . . be susceptible of more or less, or divisible, in order to conform itself to variations in the gravity of offences. Chronic punishments, such as imprisonment and banishment, possess this quality in an eminent degree.

JAMES Q. WILSON, THINKING ABOUT CRIME
117-21 (rev. ed. 1983)

The debate over the effect on crime rates of changing the costs and benefits of crime is usually referred to as a debate over deterrence — a debate, that is, over the efficacy (and perhaps even the propriety) of trying to prevent crime by making would-be offenders more fearful of committing crime. But that is something of a misnomer, because the theory of human nature on which is erected the idea of deterrence (the theory that people respond to the penalties associated with crime) is also the theory of human nature that supports the idea that people will take jobs in preference to crime if the jobs are more attractive. In both cases, we are saying that would-be offenders are reasonably rational and respond to their perception of the costs and benefits attached to alternative courses of action. When we use the word "deterrence," we are calling attention only to the cost side of the equation. There is no word in common scientific usage to call attention to the benefit side of the equation; perhaps "inducement" might serve. To a psychologist, deterring persons from committing crimes or inducing persons to engage in non-criminal activities are but special cases of using "reinforcements" (or rewards) to alter behavior.

The reason there is a debate among scholars about deterrence is that the socially imposed consequences of committing a crime, unlike the market consequences of shopping around for the best price, are characterized by delay, uncertainty, and ignorance. In addition, some scholars contend that a large fraction of crime is committed by persons who are so impulsive, irrational, or abnormal that even if there were no delay, uncertainty, or ignorance attached to the consequences of criminality, we would still have a lot of crime.

Imagine a young man walking down the street at night. . . . Suddenly he sees a little old lady standing alone on a dark corner stuffing the proceeds of her recently cashed social security check into her purse. There is nobody else in view. If the boy steals the purse, he gets the money immediately. . . . The costs of taking it are uncertain; the odds are at least fourteen to one that the police will not catch a given robber, and even if he is caught the odds are very good that he will not go to prison, unless he has a long record. On the average, no more than three felonies out of one hundred result in the imprisonment of the offender. In addition to this uncertainty, whatever penalty may come his way will come only after a long delay; in some jurisdictions, it might take a year or more to complete the court disposition of the offender, assuming he is caught in the first place. . . .

Compounding the problems of delay and uncertainty is the fact that society cannot feasibly reduce the uncertainty attached to the chances of being arrested by more than a modest amount, and though it can to some degree increase the probability and severity of a prison sentence for those who are caught, it cannot do so drastically by, for example, summarily executing all convicted robbers or even by sending all robbers to twenty-year prison terms. Some scholars add a further complication: the young man may be incapable of assessing the risks of crime. How, they ask, is he to know his chances of being caught and punished? And even if he does know, is he perhaps "driven" by uncontrollable impulses to snatch purses whatever the risks?

As if all this were not bad enough, the principal method by which scholars have attempted to measure the effect on crime of differences in the probability and severity of punishment has involved using data about aggregates of people . . . rather than about individuals. . . . Isaac Ehrlich, an economist, produced the best known of such analyses using data on crime in the United States in 1940, 1950, and 1960. [H]e found, after controlling for such factors as the income level and age distribution of the population, that the higher the probability of imprisonment for those convicted of robbery, the lower the robbery rate. Thus, differences in the certainty of punishment seem to make a difference in the level of crime. At the same time, Ehrlich did not find that the severity of punishment (the average time served in prison for robbery) had, independently of certainty, an effect on robbery rates in two of the three time periods (1940 and 1960).

But there are some problems associated with studying the effect of sanctions on crime rates using aggregate data of this sort. One is that . . . [t]he observed fact . . . that states in which the probability of going to prison for robbery is low are also states which have high rates of robbery can be interpreted in one of two ways. It can mean *either* that the higher robbery rates are the results of the lower imprisonment rates (and thus evidence that deterrence works) *or* that the lower imprisonment rates are caused by the higher robbery rates. To see how the latter might be true, imagine a state that is experiencing, for some reason, a rapidly rising robbery rate. It arrests, convicts, and imprisons more and more robbers as more and more robberies are committed, but it cannot quite keep up. The robberies are increasing so fast that they "swamp" the criminal justice system; prosecutors and judges respond by letting more robbers off without a prison sentence, or perhaps without even a trial, in order to keep the system from becoming hopelessly clogged. As a result, the proportion of arrested robbers who go to prison goes down while the robbery rate goes up. In this case, we ought to conclude, not that prison deters robbers, but that high robbery rates "deter" prosecutors and judges. . . .

Some commentators believe that these criticisms have proved that "deterrence doesn't work." . . . Such a conclusion is, to put it mildly, a bit premature. . . .

People are governed in their daily lives by rewards and penalties of every sort. We shop for bargain prices, praise our children for good behavior and scold them for bad, expect lower interest rates to stimulate home building and fear that higher ones will depress it, and conduct ourselves in public in ways that lead our friends and neighbors to form good opinions of us. To assert that "deterrence doesn't work" is tantamount to either denying the plainest facts of everyday life or claiming that would-be criminals are utterly different from the rest of us.

DAN M. KAHAN, SOCIAL INFLUENCE, SOCIAL MEANING, AND DETERRENCE
83 Va. L. Rev. 349, 350, 354-56, 365, 367-71 (1997)

Individuals are more likely to commit crimes when they perceive that criminal activity is widespread. In that circumstance, they are likely to infer that the risk of being caught for a crime is low. They might also conclude that relatively little stigma or reputational cost attaches to being a criminal; indeed, if criminal behavior is common among their peers, they may even view such activity as status enhancing. . . .

Empirical studies of why people obey the law . . . reveal a strong correlation between a person's obedience and her perception of others' behavior and attitudes toward the law. Thus, a person's beliefs about whether other persons in her situation are paying their taxes plays a much more significant role in her decision to comply than does the burden of the tax or her perception of the expected punishment for evasion. Likewise, the perception that one's peers will or will not disapprove exerts a much stronger influence than does the threat of a formal sanction on whether a person decides to engage in a range of common offenses — from larceny, to burglary, to drug use.

The role of social influence on law-breaking has even been confirmed experimentally. In one famous . . . study, psychologist Philip Zimbardo . . . placed [a] car, hood up, on the campus of Stanford University, where it remained in pristine condition for over a week. Zimbardo then smashed the windshield with a sledgehammer. At that point, passersby spontaneously joined in the carnage, gleefully visiting further destruction upon the car and (over time) stripping it of valuable parts. The sight of others openly pillaging the car, Zimbardo concluded, had released passersby from their inhibitions against vandalism and theft. . . .

Individuals decide to commit crimes, I've suggested, based in part on their perception of the values, beliefs and behavior of other individuals; the law plays a role in shaping these perceptions. . . . Accordingly, by adopting laws that generate appropriate social meanings, a community should be able to point social influence in a direction that discourages criminality. [This deterrence strategy suggests] the potential utility of policies aimed at suppressing public disorder and visible gang activity, forms of behavior that can generate social influence pressure to engage in crime. . . .

New York City has much less crime today than it did just three years ago. Since 1993, the murder rate there has come down nearly 40 percent, the robbery rate more than 30 percent, and the burglary rate more than 25 percent. These drops are more than double the national average. Overall, crime in New York is at its lowest level in more than a quarter century. What explains this rapid and dramatic turnaround? . . .

What has changed significantly is New York's law-enforcement strategy. Beginning in 1993, the New York City Police Department began to focus intensively on so-called "public order" offenses, including vandalism, aggressive panhandling, public drunkenness, unlicensed vending, public urination, and prostitution. City officials and at least some criminologists credit the larger reduction in crime rates to this recent emphasis on "order maintenance."

But this claim seems to make little sense under the conventional economic conception of deterrence. The legal prices of murder, robbery, and burglary don't depend on how the police respond to vandalism, public drunkenness, prostitution and the like. So why should we think that New York's order-maintenance strategy is in any way responsible for the reduction in the rate of these more serious crimes? The social influence conception of deterrence supplies an answer.

Visible disorder is a self-reinforcing cue about the community's attitude toward crime. James Wilson and George Kelling describe this dynamic as the "broken window" effect. A broken window invites more window-breaking because it is "a signal that no one cares, and so breaking more windows costs nothing." Likewise, prostitution, petty drug dealing, public drunkenness, and the like "lead[ ] to the breakdown of community controls" because they convey that people in the community either don't value or don't expect order.

Disorder is also pregnant with meaning: Public drunkenness, prostitution, aggressive panhandling and similar behavior signal not only that members of the community are inclined to engage in disorderly conduct, but also that the community is unable or unwilling to enforce basic norms. In that circumstance, individuals understandably infer that the odds of being punished for more serious crimes are also low. The very openness of such behavior, moreover, suggests that violating basic norms carries little social sanction. Visible disorder also tells individuals that their own forbearance is unlikely to be reciprocated. In this environment, individuals who are otherwise inclined to engage in crime are much more likely to do so.

The meaning of disorder can also influence the behavior of committed law-abiders in a way that is likely to increase crime. If they can, law-abiding citizens are likely to leave a neighborhood that is pervaded by disorder. Their departure increases the concentration of law breakers, thereby multiplying their interactions with each other and accentuating their mutually reinforcing propensities to engage in crime. Law-abiders who stick it out, moreover, are more likely to avoid the streets, where their simple presence would otherwise be a deterrent to crime. They are also more likely to distrust their neighbors, and thus less likely to join leagues with them in monitoring their community for signs of trouble. The law-abiders' fear of crime thus facilitates even more crime. An order-maintenance strategy should reverse these effects.

Notes and Questions

1. If empirical evidence indicated that life imprisonment for first-offense drunk driving would cut drunk driving rates and associated fatalities in half, would society be justified in imposing such a penalty? What if merely putting such a penalty on the books would completely eliminate drunk driving and, with it, any need to actually impose the penalty?

2. Bentham argues that no deterrent purpose could be served by the punishment of infants and the insane. Is that right? Professor H.L.A. Hart has argued that "it is possible that though . . . the *threat* of punishment could not have operated on them, the actual *infliction* of punishment on those persons, may secure a higher measure of conformity to law on the part of normal persons than is secured by the admission of excusing conditions."[5]

3. Wilson believes that stiff prison sentences probably deter crime, but he doubts that crime is caused by unemployment or that it would be reduced by better job opportunities. See James Q. Wilson and Richard Herrnstein, Crime and Human Nature, 312-13 (1985). Is there any contradiction here?

4. Does the criminal law deter by threatening punishment, or by defining the responsibilities of dutiful citizens? Is either possible without the other?

5. H.L.A. Hart, Punishment and Responsibility 18-20 (1968).

Is Kahan's "social influence" model of crime a modification of deterrence theory, or a rejection of it?

In Germany, which has much lower penalties (and violent crime rates) than the United States, most criminal law scholars conclude that the best rationale for punishment is the goal of "positive general prevention"— that is, punishing offenders in order to reinforce the law-abiding inclinations of most citizens rather than to frighten potential offenders into curbing their criminal impulses. Could such an effect be demonstrated empirically? Is punishment of the guilty the most effective way of inculcating law-abiding inclinations in the general populations?

5. Kahan claims that order-maintenance policing strategies explain the drop in crime in New York City during the 1990s. But recall Steven Levitt's research indicating that changes in policing strategies may have made no causal contribution to the nationwide drop in crime during the 1990s.[6] Another recent study agrees.[7] But two other factors associated with order-maintenance policing may explain part of the drop in crime in New York City. According to Levitt, increases in police account for about one-sixth of the drop in violent crime nationwide, and New York City increased its police force three times more than the national average. Both this increase and the associated drop in violent crime started *before* New York began its order-maintenance policing campaign. That increases in police reduce crime accords with conventional deterrence theory: reducing the incentive to commit crime by increasing the likelihood of apprehension and punishment. Bernard Harcourt has pointed to a second, related link between policing and the drop in crime. He notes that order-maintenance policing involves a large volume of misdemeanor arrests for panhandling, prostitution, subway-fare evasion and the like. These arrests often led to evidence of other crimes or apprehension of suspects wanted for other crimes. According to Harcourt, Kahan's mistake is to assume that arrests for panhandling reduce violent crime by deterring panhandling and so making the streets look more orderly. Harcourt argues that instead, arrests for panhandling reduce violent crime by raising the certainty of punishment for violent crime (a conventional deterrence effect) or by temporarily jailing violent criminals who police claim they suspect of panhandling (an incapacitation effect). In other words, order-maintenance policing may "work" like any vagrancy law, giving police a pretext to "round up the usual suspects."[8]

6. A consistent finding of empirical studies of deterrence is that increases in the certainty of punishment have a greater deterrent effect than increases in the severity of punishment. This is what Beccaria and Bentham suspected, and accounts for many of the reforms they advocated, such as substituting incarceration for capital punishment, and developing a regular police force. But why should certainty have more deterrent effect than severity? Can you think of reasons why the combination of very high penalties and very low apprehension and conviction rates might impede deterrence? Can you think of reasons why very severe penalties might cause a decrease in the certainty of punishment?

6. See pp. 22-23, *supra.*

7. See John Eck and Edward Maguire, "Have Changes in Policing Reduced Violent Crime? An Assessment of the Evidence," The Crime Drop in America 207-265 (Alfred Blumstein and Joel Wallman, eds., 2000).

8. Bernard E. Harcourt, Reflecting on the Subject: A Critique of the Social Influence Conception of Deterrence, the Broken Windows Theory, and Order-Maintenance Policing, New York Style, 97 Mich. L. Rev. 291, 332, 339-42 (1998).

3.   Rehabilitation

While opponents of rehabilitation have often associated it with a psychiatric approach to crime that became prevalent in the 1950s and '60s, rehabilitation was endorsed by early utilitarian reformers like Bentham:

> It is a great merit in a punishment to contribute to the reformation of the offender, not only through fear of being punished again, but by a change in his character and habits. This end may be attained by studying the motive which produced the offence, and by applying a punishment which tends to weaken that motive. A house of correction, to fulfill this object, ought to admit a separation of the delinquents, in order that different means of treatment may be adapted to the diversity of their moral condition.[9]

Today, we tend to think of rehabilitation as an ancillary goal of penal incarceration, involving educational or therapeutic "programs" in prison. But as the following two excerpts reveal, rehabilitation was the original program of prisons.

DAVID ROTHMAN, THE DISCOVERY OF THE ASYLUM
79-88, 105, 107 (1971)

Americans' understanding of the causes of deviant behavior led directly to the invention of the penitentiary as a solution. It was an ambitious program. Its design — external appearance, internal arrangement, and daily routine — attempted to eliminate the specific influences that were breeding crime in the community, and to demonstrate the fundamentals of proper social organization. Rather than stand as places of last resort, hidden and ignored, these institutions became the pride of the nation. A structure designed to join practicality to humanitarianism, reform the criminal, stabilize American society, and demonstrate how to improve the condition of mankind, deserved full publicity and close study. . . . Europeans came to evaluate the experiment and the major powers appointed official investigators. France in 1831 dispatched the most famous pair, Alexis de Tocqueville and Gustave Auguste de Beaumont. [T]he American penitentiary had become world famous.

In the 1820's New York and Pennsylvania began a movement that soon spread through the Northeast, and then over the next decades to many midwestern states. New York devised the Auburn or congregate system of penitentiary organization, establishing it first at the Auburn state prison between 1819 and 1823, and then in 1825 at the Ossining institution, familiarly known as Sing-Sing. Pennsylvania officials worked out the details of a rival plan, the separate system, applying it to the penitentiary at Pittsburgh in 1826 and to the prison at Philadelphia in 1829. . . . Under the Auburn scheme, prisoners were to sleep alone in a cell at night and labor together in a workshop during the day for the course of their fixed sentences in the penitentiary. They were forbidden to converse with fellow inmates or even exchange glances while on the job, at meals, or in their cells. The Pennsylvania system, on the other hand, isolated each prisoner for the entire period of his confinement. According to its blueprint,

9. Jeremy Bentham, The Theory of Legislation, 338 (ed. 1931).

convicts were to eat, work, and sleep in individual cells, seeing and talking with only a handful of responsible guards and selected visitors. They were to leave the institution as ignorant of the identity of other convicts as on the day they entered. As both schemes placed maximum emphasis on preventing the prisoners from communicating with anyone else, the point of dispute was whether convicts should work silently in large groups or individually within solitary cells.

To both the advocates of the congregate and the separate systems, the promise of institutionalization depended upon the isolation of the prisoner and the establishment of a disciplined routine. Convinced that deviancy was primarily the result of the corruptions pervading the community, and that organizations like the family and the church were not counterbalancing them, they believed that a setting which removed the offender from all temptations and substituted a steady and regular regimen would reform him. Since the convict was not inherently depraved, but the victim of an upbringing that had failed to provide protection against the vices at loose in society, a well-ordered institution could successfully reeducate and rehabilitate him. The penitentiary, free of corruptions and dedicated to the proper training of the inmate, would inculcate the discipline that negligent parents, evil companions, taverns, houses of prostitution, theaters, and gambling halls had destroyed. Just as the criminal's environment had led him into crime, the institutional environment would lead him out of it.

The duty of the penitentiary was to separate the offender from all contact with corruption, both within and without its walls. There was obviously no sense to removing a criminal from the depravity of his surroundings only to have him mix freely with other convicts within the prison. . . .

As with any other science, the advocates of moral architecture anticipated that the principles which emerged from the penitentiary experiment would have clear and important applications to the wider society. An arrangement which helped to reform vicious and depraved men would also be effective in regulating the behavior of ordinary citizens in other situations. The penitentiary, by its example, by its discovery and verification of proper principles of social organization, would serve as a model for the entire society. . . .

Tocqueville and Beaumont appreciated how significant both of these purposes were to the first penologists. The institutions, Americans believed, would radically reform the criminal and the society. "Philanthropy has become for them," observed the two visitors, "a kind of profession, and they have caught the *monomanie* of the penitentiary system, which to them seems the remedy for all the evils of society." Proponents described the penitentiary as "a grand theatre, for the trial of all new plans in hygiene and education, in physical and moral reform." The convict "surrendered body and soul, to be experimented upon," and the results, as the Boston Prison Discipline Society insisted, would benefit not only other custodial institutions like alms-houses and houses of refuge, but also "would greatly promote order, seriousness, and purity in large families, male and female boarding schools, and colleges." Perhaps the most dramatic and unabashed statement of these views appeared in a memoir by the Reverend James B. Finley, chaplain at the Ohio penitentiary. "Never, no never shall we see the triumph of peace, of right, of Christianity, until the daily habits of mankind shall undergo a thorough revolution," declared Finley. And in what ways were we to achieve such a reform? "Could we all be put on prison fare, for the space of two or three generations, the world would ultimately be the better for it. Indeed, should society change places with the prisoners, so far as habits are concerned, taking to itself the regularity, and temperance, and sobriety of a good prison," then the grandiose goals of peace, right, and Christianity would be furthered. "As it is," concluded Finley, "taking this world and the next together . . . the prisoner has the advantage."

. . . Once isolated, the prisoner began the process of reform. "Each individual," explained Pennsylvania's supporters, "will necessarily be made the instrument of his own punishment; his conscience will be the avenger of society." Left in total solitude, separated from "evil society . . . the progress of corruption is arrested; no additional contamination can be received or communicated." At the same time the convict "will be compelled to reflect on the error of his ways, to listen to the reproaches of conscience, to the expostulations of religion." Thrown upon his own innate sentiments, with no evil example to lead him astray, and with kindness and proper instruction at hand to bolster his resolutions, the criminal would start his rehabilitation. Then, after a period of total isolation, without companions, books, or tools, officials would allow the inmate to work in his cell. Introduced at this moment, labor would become not an oppressive task for punishment, but a welcome diversion, a delight rather than a burden. The convict would sit in his cell and work with his tools daily, so that over the course of his sentence regularity and discipline would become habitual. He would return to the community cured of vice and idleness, to take his place as a responsible citizen. . . .

The doctrines of separation, obedience, and labor became the trinity around which officials organized the penitentiary. They carefully instructed inmates that their duties could be "comprised in a few words"; they were "to labor diligently, to obey all orders, and preserve an unbroken silence." Yet to achieve these goals, officers had to establish a total routine, to administer every aspect of the institution in accord with the three guidelines, from inmates' dress to their walk, from the cells' furnishings to the guards' deportment. . . .

The functioning of the penitentiary — convicts passing their sentences in physically imposing and highly regimented settings, moving in lockstep from bare and solitary cells to workshops, clothed in common dress, and forced into standard routines — was designed to carry a message to the community. The prison would train the most notable victims of social disorder to discipline, teaching them to resist corruption. And success in this particular task should inspire a general reformation of manners and habits. The institution would become a laboratory for social improvement. By demonstrating how regularity and discipline transformed the most corrupt persons, it would reawaken the public to these virtues. The penitentiary would promote a new respect for order and authority.

EDWARD L. RUBIN,
THE INEVITABILITY OF REHABILITATION
19 Law & Ineq. J. 343, 347, 350-52 (2001)

From its outset, the penitentiary was conceived as a means of rehabilitation. . . . As industrialism spread and public education became the norm, vocational and academic training came to replace remorse and discipline as the principle instrument for rehabilitation. But the basic concept of the penitentiary or prison has remained unchanged since its conception. Convicted felons are separated from their former life, confined in a secure facility, and subjected to some regimen that will change their attitudes and enable them to be productive, law-abiding citizens once they are released. . . .

The concept of rehabilitation decisively determined Western society's preference for incarceration as a mode of punishment. Whatever the aversion to torture, and whatever the impracticality of exile, it was the affirmative desire to reform the criminal that provided the essential argument for developing this expensive, administratively demanding means of punishment. To punishment itself, it adds the desire that a criminal who has completed the term of incarceration will go forth to lead a productive, law-abiding life.

Of the many conceptual bases for this political and social choice, three are particularly notable. The first is a concept of universal citizenship. The developing ideology of the modern nation state . . . led to the belief that every person was a citizen, a member of the state, and needed to understand and fulfill the responsibilities of that position. The criminal, of course, had forfeited his citizenship in some sense, but once his punishment is complete he will necessarily resume that role. Rehabilitation is the attempt to equip him to do so, curing him of the moral blindness that prevented him from perceiving his membership in the secular collectivity of the state.

Second, and closely related, was the idea that every human being has natural rights of a political nature. . . . Pre-Enlightenment society was prepared to regard people as existing for the benefit of others, and equally prepared to treat the criminal as an outcast, as someone who can be exiled or ignored. Modern society sees every person as a rights-bearer, as an equal member of its society. Consequently, it will seek a mode of punishment that will enable the wrongdoer to return to the community and live a productive life.

Finally, the rehabilitative prison was motivated by a new psychology, a belief in personality development as a secular phenomenon. Life was no longer viewed as a prelude to eternal bliss or damnation, nor punishment as a means of obtaining a confession that would save the wrong-doer's soul. Rather, life was a self-contained set of experiences, with its own course of development. Punishment came to be viewed as an event in that development, an event that could alter its course and provide a happier continuation. As John Bender has observed, the contemporaneous development of the novel as the dominant form of fiction was not adventitious. The prison sentence, like the novel, was conceived as a moral progress, a transformation of the individual through a reflective consciousness.

In short, the prison was the product of new attitudes that clustered around the idea of rehabilitation. Rehabilitation was its essential purpose, its goal, and the basis for its design. At present, [imprisonment] is so familiar that it appears inevitable, a fixture in our institutional landscape. But it did not possess this character when it was first devised; at that time, it was a real innovation and an alternative to the familiar punishment of torture or transportation. The reason it seemed like a superior alternative was because it promised to rehabilitate the criminal as well as punish him.

FRANCIS A. ALLEN, CRIMINAL JUSTICE, LEGAL VALUES, AND THE REHABILITATIVE IDEAL
Justice, Punishment, Treatment: The Correctional Process 193-96
(L. Orland ed. 1973)

. . . [U]nder the dominance of the rehabilitative ideal, the language of therapy is frequently employed, wittingly or unwittingly, to disguise the true state of affairs that prevails in our custodial institutions and at other points in the correctional process. Certain measures, like the sexual psychopath laws, have been advanced and supported as therapeutic in nature when, in fact, such a characterization seems highly dubious. Too often the vocabulary of therapy has been exploited to serve a public-relations function. Recently, I visited an institution devoted to the diagnosis and treatment of disturbed children. The institution had been established with high hopes and, for once, with the enthusiastic support of the state legislature. Nevertheless, fifty minutes of an hour's lecture, delivered by a supervising psychiatrist before we toured the building, were devoted to custodial problems. This fixation on problems of custody was reflected in the institutional arrangements which included, under a properly euphemistic label, a cell for solitary confinement. Even more disturbing was the tendency of the staff to justify these custodial measures in therapeutic terms. Perhaps on occasion the requirements of institutional security and treatment coincide. But the inducements to self-deception in such situations are strong and all too apparent. . . .

There is a second sort of unintended consequence that has resulted from the application of the rehabilitative ideal to the practical administration of criminal justice. Surprisingly enough, the rehabilitative ideal has often led to increased severity of penal measures. . . . The tendency of proposals for wholly indeterminate sentences, a clearly identifiable fruit of the rehabilitative ideal, is unmistakably in the direction of lengthened periods of imprisonment. A large variety of statutes authorizing what is called "civil" commitment of persons, but which except for the reduced protections afforded the parties proceeded against, are essentially criminal in nature, provide for absolutely indeterminate periods of confinement. Experience has demonstrated that, in practice, there is a strong tendency for the rehabilitative ideal to serve purposes that are essentially incapacitative rather than therapeutic in character.

. . . The reference to the tendency of the rehabilitative ideal to encourage increasingly long periods of incarceration brings me to my final proposition. It is that the rise of the rehabilitative ideal has often been accompanied by attitudes and measures that conflict, sometimes seriously, with the values of individual liberty and volition.

ELLIOT CURRIE, CONFRONTING CRIME: AN AMERICAN CHALLENGE
236-40 (1985)

The ideological attack on the concept of rehabilitation has usually been accompanied by the argument that nothing more constructive can be done anyway — that we have "tried" rehabilitation and discovered that it "doesn't work." . . .

The conclusion that rehabilitation had failed was based in part on a series of studies reviewing the scattered evaluations of rehabilitation programs up through the mid-sixties, of which the best known was done by Robert Martinson and his colleagues at the City University of New York. Summarizing that research in 1974, Martinson concluded that "with few and isolated exceptions, the rehabilitative efforts that have been reported so far have had no appreciable impact on recidivism." Martinson's conclusion, already gloomy enough, was amplified considerably in the less careful accounts of his work by the media, which quickly began to proclaim that, when it came to rehabilitating criminals, "nothing works."

[T] he critique of rehabilitation, in this sweeping and categorical form, was attractive to both ends of the political spectrum. To the criminological Right, it offered further testimony that the only feasible response to criminal offenders was increased efforts at deterrence and incapacitation, and it served in a deeper sense to confirm the view that crime reflected fundamental flaws in human nature or in the constitution of offenders. . . . For the Left, on the other hand, the apparent failure of rehabilitation frequently supported a very different argument: that given the deep social and economic sources of crime in the United States, little could be gained (and much abuse would be encouraged) by tinkering with offenders in the name of "individual treatment."

EDWARD L. RUBIN,
THE INEVITABILITY OF REHABILITATION
19 Law & Ineq. J. 343 (2001)

The conclusion that rehabilitation is a failure is empirically false. Once the impact of the initial findings had abated, social scientists began to devote more detailed attention to rehabilitative programs and produced more refined, modulated results. Martinson himself withdrew his 1974 declaration that "nothing works" as early as 1979. Meta-analyses and individual program evaluations in the 1980s and 1990s advanced the unsurprising, but previously unrecognized, idea that the effectiveness of rehabilitation programs varies depending on the nature of the intervention and the cooperation of the target group. . . .

Even without these empirical results, however, the declaration that rehabilitation fails to achieve its declared objective is highly suspect. Such a conclusion necessarily depends upon a theory for evaluating social programs, but relatively little thought has been devoted to this topic. . . . When we speak of rehabilitation, we are referring to an effort to remedy a vast array of personal and social problems experienced by some of society's most disadvantaged members. This is not to excuse the criminal — many people experience similar disadvantages and become productive citizens — but to recognize the magnitude of the task. Many prisoners are functionally illiterate or lack a high school degree, many lack training in any legal trade, many are addicted to drugs or alcohol, and many suffer severe psychological and social problems. Each of these problems is difficult to resolve, and all are important to resolve if the criminal is to be rehabilitated. An ex-convict who re-enters society without at least a high school degree, without any vocational skills, still suffering from addiction to illegal drugs or even alcohol, and without some resolution to his psychological or social problems — in short, with any one of the many deficits that he may have had when he was imprisoned — has a poor prognosis. Prison rehabilitation programs attempt to address all these problems, and others. . . . That such efforts do not have one hundred percent success rates is not exactly surprising. . . .

The second argument against rehabilitation is that it authorizes an assault on the prisoner's personality. Critics charge that the rehabilitative model is similar in concept . . . to morally unacceptable reformative techniques such as brainwashing, severe behavior modification, drug therapy and shock treatment. It is also argued that the model, at least in theory, would authorize open-ended sentences that keep offenders incarcerated until prison authorities have judged them to be rehabilitated. . . . Allen goes so far as to suggest that the most complete embodiment of the rehabilitative ideal is to be found in the correctional system of Communist China. . . . The implied metric seems to be that a social program should be condemned if any sort of government, no matter how different than our own, could use it as a rationale for practices that we find unacceptable. However, no program could withstand such a test. Communist China used public education to indoctrinate its children, the Soviet Union used mental health to suppress dissent, and Nazi Germany used recreational programs to foment aggressive attitudes. These lugubrious examples may be useful as a warning against potential abuses, but they cannot, by themselves, be taken as a criticism of an otherwise acceptable program. . . .

In fact, the criticism of rehabilitation as an inducement to abusive practices is almost certainly false when considered in the context of American corrections. Rehabilitation has always been the doctrine espoused by the most progressive elements in the correctional establishment. The rigors of the Auburn and Pennsylvania systems may seem excessive, but they were humane when compared to torture or the death penalty. The rehabilitative approaches that followed were generally more humane, and expressed a sincere concern for the felon as an individual. . . .

The claim that rehabilitation would authorize indeterminately long sentences is equally a product of abstract academic alarmism. . . . Rehabilitation has rarely been used in this country as a principle for determining the convict's sentence. . . . American sentences use the principle of just deserts, or, perhaps more often, rough proportionality — the more serious the crime, in society's judgment, the longer the sentence. In recent years, there has been some effort to consider rehabilitative possibilities when sentencing certain offenders. However, this has not taken the form of indeterminately long prison sentences, but of alternatives to prison such as drug treatment or house arrest. The theoretical possibility that a rehabilitative model might lead to long, open-ended sentences, or of the fact that such sentences were imposed in Communist China, has very little relevance to the actual practice of corrections in the United States.

Even at a more theoretical level, the assertion that rehabilitation ineluctably implies limitless and oppressive treatment is unconvincing. . . . The rehabilitative ideal . . . was based on the ideas of universal citizenship, individual rights, and personal development. Every person, according to these ideas, has value, and even if they have committed crimes, they should not be either discarded or used purely as examples. Rather, an effort should be made to restore them to their place in society and provide them with a fulfilling, productive experience for the remainder of their lives. This view leads directly to the kinds of programs that can be found in most American prisons — to education, vocational training, drug and alcohol treatment, and group therapy. It does not lead to brainwashing, shock therapy, or open-ended sentences; these means are incompatible with ideas of citizenship, individual rights and personal development.

MICHAEL TONRY, MALIGN NEGLECT — RACE, CRIME AND PUNISHMENT IN AMERICA
202-03 (1995)

For drug-abusing offenders, particularly, the case for increased investment in drug-treatment is powerful. From the Justice Department's Drug Use Forecasting (DUF) data from urinalyses of arrested felons, we know that one-half to three-fourths in many cities test positive for recent drug use. From both ethnographic and statistical studies of drug-using offenders, we know that high levels of drug use and high levels of offending are strongly associated. When drug use declines, offending declines. From treatment evaluation studies, we know that participation in well-run methadone maintenance programs and therapeutic communities can demonstrably reduce both later drug use and later criminality of drug-dependent offenders. Finally, also from drug treatment evaluations, we know that the best predictor of successful treatment is time in treatment, even when coerced by legal compulsion.

Together, our knowledge of drug treatment effectiveness argues powerfully for providing treatment on demand for all drug-dependent offenders who want it, and compulsory treatment for many drug-dependent offenders who do not.

Notes and Questions

1. Do offenders have a "right" to opportunities to rehabilitate themselves? Do they have a greater or lesser claim on educational or social services than nonoffenders? If they succeed in rehabilitating themselves, do offenders thereby "deserve" less punishment? If they are given an opportunity to do so and fail, do they deserve more?

2. Was rehabilitation originally conceived as a form of medical therapy? Religious repentance? Something else entirely?

3. Is Rubin's defense of rehabilitation convincing? Or does it amount to a concession that rehabilitation cannot work and that sentencing should not be influenced by the goal of rehabilitation? Is it really true that American sentencing has not been affected by the goal of rehabilitation? Weren't the formerly popular practices of probation and parole expressions of this goal?

4. Some historians, notably Michel Foucault, have seen the new "penitentiaries" of the early nineteenth century as the visible tip of a very large iceberg: a new system of social control that enabled modern industrialized society to function smoothly and relatively peacefully, despite the erosion of traditional sources of authority and networks of community. Foucault portrays this new system of social control — involving organization, regimentation, surveillance, examination, record-keeping, rational incentives, and, perhaps most important, the inculcation of self-awareness — as dispersed across such diverse social institutions as schools, hospitals, factories, military bases, government bureaucracies, and corporations. See Michel Foucault, Discipline and Punish: The Birth of the Prison (Alan Sheridan, trans. 1977).

If most social control is accomplished outside the criminal justice system, should the criminal justice system be blamed for recidivism? On the other hand, if the criminal justice system is not our primary instrument for encouraging law-abiding behavior, should it pursue the goal of rehabilitation at all? Yet if prison administrators should not try to improve the behavior of convicted offenders, what *should* they do with the inmates in their custody?

4.   Incapacitation

Taking away the power of doing Injury. — It is much easier to obtain this end than [to reform the offender]. Mutilations and perpetual imprisonment possess this quality.[10]

a.   *Collective and Selective Incapacitation*

JAMES Q. WILSON, THINKING ABOUT CRIME
145-58 (rev. ed. 1983)

When criminals are deprived of their liberty, as by imprisonment . . . their ability to commit offenses against citizens is ended. We say these persons have been "incapacitated," and we try to estimate the amount by which crime is reduced by this incapacitation.

. . . [T]here is one great advantage to incapacitation as a crime control strategy — namely, it does not require us to make any assumptions about human nature. By contrast, deterrence works only if people take into account the costs and benefits of alternative courses of action and choose that which confers the largest net benefit (or the smallest net cost). . . . Rehabilitation works only if the values, preferences, or time-horizon of criminals can be altered by plan. . . .

Incapacitation, on the other hand, works by definition: Its effects result from the physical restraint of the offender and not from his subjective state. More accurately, it works provided at least three conditions are met: Some offenders must be repeaters; offenders taken off the streets must not be immediately and completely replaced by new recruits; and prison must not sufficiently increase the post-release criminal activity of those who have been incarcerated sufficiently to offset the crimes prevented by their stay in prison.

The first condition is surely true. Every study of prison inmates shows that a large fraction (recently, about two-thirds) of them had prior criminal records before their current incarceration; every study of ex-convicts shows that a significant fraction (estimates vary from a quarter to a half) are rearrested for new offenses within a relatively brief period. In short, the great majority of persons in prison are repeat offenders, and thus prison, whatever else it may do, protects society from the offenses these persons would commit if they were free.

The second condition — that incarcerating one robber does not lead automatically to the recruitment of a new robber to replace him — seems plausible. Although some persons, such as Ernest van den Haag, have argued that new offenders will step forward to take the place vacated by the imprisoned offenders, they have presented no evidence that this is the case, except, perhaps, for certain crimes (such as narcotics trafficking or prostitution), which are organized along business lines. For . . . predatory street crimes . . . — robbery, burglary, auto theft, larceny — there are no barriers to entry and no scarcity of criminal

---

10. Jeremy Bentham, The Theory of Legislation 338 (ed. 1931).

opportunities. . . . In general, the earnings of street criminals are not affected by how many "competitors" they have.

The third condition that must be met if incapacitation is to work is that prisons must not be such successful "schools for crime" that the crimes prevented by incarceration are outnumbered by the increased crimes committed after release attributable to what was learned in prison. It is doubtless the case that for some offenders prison is a school; it is also doubtless that for other offenders prison is a deterrent. The former group will commit more, or more skillful, crimes after release; the latter will commit fewer crimes after release. The question, therefore, is whether the net effect of these two offsetting tendencies is positive or negative. . . . In general, there is no evidence that the prison experience makes offenders as a whole more criminal, and there is some evidence that certain kinds of offenders (especially certain younger ones) may be deterred by a prison experience. . . .

To determine the amount of crime that is prevented by incarcerating a given number of offenders for a given length of time, the key estimate we must make is the number of offenses a criminal commits per year free on the street. If a community experiences one thousand robberies a year, it obviously makes a great deal of difference whether these robberies are the work of ten robbers, each of whom commits one hundred robberies per year, or the work of one thousand robbers, each of whom commits only one robbery per year. In the first case, locking up only five robbers will cut the number of robberies in half; in the second case, locking up one hundred robbers will only reduce the number of robberies by 10 percent.

. . . Working with individual adult criminal records of all those persons arrested in Washington, D.C., during 1973 for any one of six major crimes (over five thousand persons in all), Alfred Blumstein and Jacqueline Cohen suggested that the individual offense rate varied significantly for different kinds of offenders. For example, it was highest for larceny and lowest for aggravated assault. But they also found, as had other scholars before them, that there was not a great deal of specialization among criminals — a person arrested today for robbery might be arrested next time for burglary. The major contribution of their study was the ingenious method they developed for converting the number of times persons were arrested into an estimate of the number of crimes they actually committed, a method that took into account the fact that many crimes are not reported to the police, that most crimes known to the police do not result in an arrest, and that some crimes are likely to be committed by groups of persons rather than by single offenders. Combining all the individual crime rates, the offenders in this study (a group of adults who had been arrested at least twice in Washington, D.C.) committed between nine and seventeen serious offenses per year free.

. . . [C]onfidence in the Blumstein-Cohen estimates was increased when the results of a major study at the Rand Corporation became known. Researchers there had been interviewing prisoners . . . to find out directly from known offenders how much crime they were committing while free. . . . [T]he Rand researchers cross-checked the information against arrest records and looked for evidence of internal consistency in the self-reports. Moreover, the inmates volunteered information about crimes they had committed but for which they had not been arrested. . . .

The Rand group found that the average California prisoner had committed about fourteen serious crimes per year during each of the three years he was free. . . . To state the California findings in slightly different terms, if no one was confined in state prison, the number of armed robberies in California would be about 22 percent higher than it now is. . . .

But the Rand group learned something else which would turn out to be even more important. The "average" individual offense rate was virtually a meaningless term because the inmates they interviewed differed so sharply in how many crimes they committed. A large number of offenders committed a small number of offenses while free and a small number of offenders committed a very large number of offenses. In statistical language, the distribution of offenses was highly skewed. For example, the median number of burglaries committed by the inmates in the three states was about 5 a year, but the 10 percent of the inmates who were the highest-rate offenders committed an average of 232 burglaries a year. The median number of robberies was also about 5 a year, but the top 10 percent of offenders committed an average of 87 a year. As Peter W. Greenwood, one of the members of the Rand group, put it, incarcerating one robber who was among the top 10 percent in offense rates would prevent more robberies than incarcerating eighteen offenders who were at or below the median. . . .

Joan Petersilia and Peter Greenwood, both members of the Rand group, also came to the conclusion that reducing crime by a significant amount through longer prison terms would be very costly. . . .

[A]ll the evidence we have implies that, for crime-reduction purposes, the most rational way to use the incapacitative powers of our prisons would be to do so selectively. Instead of longer sentences for everyone, or for persons who have prior records, or for persons whose present crime is especially grave, longer sentences would be given primarily to those who, when free, commit the most crimes. . . .

But how do we know who these high-rate, repeat criminals are? Knowing the nature of the present offense is not a good clue. The reason for this is quite simple — most street criminals do not specialize. Today's robber can be tomorrow's burglar and the next day's car thief. When the police happen to arrest him, the crime for which he is arrested is determined by a kind of lottery — he happened to be caught red-handed, or as the result of a tip, committing a particular crime that may or may not be the same as either his previous crime or his next one. If judges give sentences based entirely on the gravity of the present offense, then a high-rate offender may get off lightly because on this occasion he happened to be caught snatching a purse. The low-rate offender may get a long sentence because he was unlucky enough to be caught robbing a liquor store with a gun. . . . [W]hile society's legitimate desire for retribution must set the outer bounds of any sentencing policy, there is still room for flexibility within those bounds. We can, for example, act so that all robbers are punished with prison terms, but give, within certain relatively narrow ranges, longer sentences to those robbers who commit the most crimes.

If knowing the nature of the present offense and even knowing the prior record of the offender are not accurate guides to identifying high-rate offenders, what is? . . . In the Rand study, Greenwood and his colleagues discovered . . . that the following seven factors, taken together, were highly predictive of a convicted person being a high-rate offender: he (1) was convicted of a crime while a juvenile (that is, before age sixteen), (2) used illegal drugs as a juvenile, (3) used illegal drugs during the previous two years, (4) was employed less than 50 percent of the time during the previous two years, (5) served time in a juvenile facility, (6) was incarcerated in prison more than 50 percent of the previous two years, and (7) was previously convicted for the present offense.

Using this scale, Greenwood found that 82 percent of those predicted to be low-rate offenders in fact were, and 82 percent of those predicted to be medium- or high-rate offenders also were. To understand how big these differences are, the median California prison inmate who is predicted to be a low-rate offender will in fact commit slightly more than one burglary and slightly less than one robbery per year free. By contrast, the median California inmate who is predicted to be a high-rate offender will commit ninety-three burglaries and thirteen robberies per year free. . . .

ALFRED BLUMSTEIN AND JACQUELINE COHEN, CHARACTERIZING CRIMINAL CAREERS
237 Science 985 (1987)

. . . The probability that an American male would be arrested some time in his life for a nontraffic offense has been estimated at 50 to 60%, a level of participation in crime that is probably an order of magnitude higher than most people would guess. In Great Britain, the lifetime conviction probability for males is estimated to be in the same range — 44%.

These surprisingly high estimates might be dismissed because they include arrests for any kind of offense (other than traffic), and many people may be vulnerable to arrest for minor offenses like disorderly conduct. Subsequent estimates have focused more narrowly on only the FBI "index" offenses (murder, forcible rape, aggravated assault, robbery, burglary, larceny, and auto theft) that comprise the usual reports on "serious" crime published periodically by the FBI. Examining these data for the 55 largest cities . . . the lifetime chance of an index arrest for a male in these cities was estimated to be 25%, with important differences between the races in their participation rates — the chances were 14% for whites and 50% for blacks. . . .

In sharp contrast to the large race difference in participation rates, the recidivism rates for serious crime were about the same for blacks and for whites, about an 85 to 90% chance of rearrest for both groups.

FRANKLIN E. ZIMRING AND GORDON HAWKINS, INCAPACITATION: PENAL CONFINEMENT AND THE RESTRAINT OF CRIME
31-38, 83-84 (1995)

In a . . . review of all the available estimates of the effects of . . . collective incapacitation policies, Jacqueline Cohen concluded that the evidence suggested [at best] "a generalized expectation of potential reduction in serious crimes of about fifteen percent from mandatory five-year prison terms imposed after any felony conviction and about a five percent reduction from the same terms imposed only after repeat felony convictions." . . .

The "[selective] incapacitation theory" that Greenwood and Abrahamse propounded was both similar to the approach of habitual-offender legislation and distinguishable from it: similar in searching for the high-rate offender as a candidate for long prison terms to achieve incapacitation; distinguishable because Greenwood and Abrahamse based the overall allocation of prison space on incapacitation criteria and thus reduced prison sentences for lower-risk offenders. The older habitual-offender approach left prison sentences in non-habitual-offender cases to be decided on other criteria. Thus incapacitative considerations had a pervasive impact on sentencing that had never been claimed for them earlier. . . .

Greenwood and Abrahamse's methods and results were scrutinized and criticized by others who argued that reanalysis of the same data suggested that the original estimates overstated the effects of the proposed selective incapacitation. . . . [R]eanalysis resulted in . . . estimated incapacitation effects that were only about five percent as large as those estimated by Greenwood and Abrahamse.

Finally, Greenwood and Turner undertook a study designed to determine "whether the seven-item scale could be used to predict the individual offense rates of convicted offenders. . . ." . . . It was found that . . . the scale was only about half as accurate in predicting follow-up arrest rates as it was in predicting retrospective self-reported offense rates. . . .

[But] the most important problem in estimating the incapacitation effect of current marginal changes in prison policy from . . . the prisoner surveys is that the historic crime commission rates should not be projected onto the target group of any contemporary change in imprisonment policy. . . .

[M]ost discussions of incapacitation generalize from the average prisoner's crime commission rate to a crime commission rate for criminal offenders just on the margin of prison sanctions. . . . If the relatively small percentage of prisoners who commit offenses at very high rates are more apt to be in prison under any policy option, their criminal proclivities will not be reflected in the crimes prevented by modest upward or downward policy changes. Thus the marginal incapacitation savings from the imprisonment of [an additional offender will be much less than the average prisoner's offense rate]. . . .

MARKUS DIRK DUBBER, RECIDIVIST STATUTES AS A RATIONAL PUNISHMENT
43 Buff. L. Rev. 689, 711 (1996)

Even if one were to assume that Greenwood or others had succeeded in identifying a list of reliable indicators of recidivism, constitutional and moral constraints would cripple the list's predictive potential. For example, Greenwood's list of seven indicators included drug use and unemployment record, both of which are suspect because, insofar as they are relevant to a defendant's culpability, they may exculpate, not inculpate and, at any rate, are conditions which may or may not be attributable to a defendant's earlier culpable choice.

If the intense criminological research on recidivism indicators over the past few decades has taught us anything, it is that the nature of the crime of conviction and prior criminal record are poor indicators of recidivism. This means that habitual offender laws, which without exception predict future criminal behavior based solely on these two unreliable indicators, lead to the unjustified prolonged incarceration of significant numbers of false positives, i.e., persons who, if released, would not commit further crimes. By their very nature, recidivist statutes often do not catch up with an offender until after she is no longer in her crime prime. . . .

Moreover, even by its proponents' standards, incapacitation only "works" (i.e., reduces the crime rate outside of prison) if the places of prison inmates on the street are not taken by an equal or greater number of other offenders. The likelihood of an immediate and complete filling of vacancies is particularly great in organized crime.

Notes and Questions

1. Wilson argues that only selective incapacitation — incarcerating predicted high-rate offenders — was likely to achieve much crime-prevention at an acceptable cost. Zimring and Hawkins and Dubber argue that the recidivist sentencing schemes actually being implemented would not be sufficiently selective to prevent much crime. Yet, according to Steven Levitt, the huge expansion in prison population of the last quarter of the twentieth century was the most significant contributor to the substantial drop in violent crime during the 1990s. Indeed, Levitt concludes that it caused a 12% drop in violent crime, about a third of the total drop. Does the drop in crime prove the critics of incapacitation wrong?

2. According to the recent study by Steven Levitt,[11] another major crime reducer, accounting for a 10% drop in violent crime, was legalized abortion. The rationale is that unwanted children, often born to teenage, impoverished or drug-addicted mothers, are at risk of becoming high-rate offenders. If so, is legalized abortion an incapacitation strategy? Should thinking about abortion in this way change the way one feels about this highly charged issue? Should it change the way one thinks about incapacitation?

b. Prison Violence and the Segregative Function of Incarceration

The conclusion that incarceration automatically incapacitates must be premised on one of two assumptions. Either (1) crime does not occur in prison, or (2) prison crime simply does not count. That violence occurs in prison is widely acknowledged, although the extent is hard to determine; after all, prisoners may face retaliation if they report assaults by either fellow prisoners or guards, and prison officials may have little incentive to ascertain and publicly acknowledge the extent of violence. The most reliable data come from "victimization" studies in which prisoners are interviewed by researchers and asked to report their own experiences of victimization. Yet these studies often do not quantify the number of offenses committed or specify the time interval during which they have been committed. Nor do they indicate how many different offenders may have committed violent offenses. Thus they give us little knowledge on the basis of which to develop comparative in-prison and out-of-prison recidivism rates.

Homicide and suicide. Homicide is the most difficult crime to conceal from authorities, although homicides may be misclassified by prison authorities as

11. See pp. 22-23 *supra.*

suicide, accident, or even natural death. Suicide is another important dimension of prison violence. Research into self-injury and suicide in prison has shown that it is often an effort to escape constant threats of violence from other prisoners.

Officially reported prison homicide rates were quite high in the 1970s, ranging as high as 600 per 100,000 in some states.[12] For 1972 the rate of officially reported homicides for prisons nationwide was 70 per 100,000 compared to 7 for the nation as a whole, and the official suicide rate was approximately 40 compared to 10 for the nation as a whole.[13] It seems fairly clear both from these data and from narrative accounts of prison life during this period that prison was often increasing rather than decreasing homicide, and increasing suicide as well. By 1995, however, the reported homicide rate was down to about 5 and the suicide rate to about 12, although there remained an additional 30 mysterious deaths per 100,000 not attributed to accident or natural causes.[14] One reason for the dramatic decline in homicide rates is the decrease in the average dangerousness of inmates as more and more people are sent to prison, but much of the decline must be ascribed to better — and more restrictive — security measures, better medical care of assault victims, and reduced overcrowding. When one considers the high rates of homicide for the demographic groups from which prisoners are recruited, it is clear that prison is now having an incapacitative effect on homicide.

Assault. Assaults are much less likely to be discovered by prison authorities than homicides. One study noted an officially recorded annual assault rate of 7,000 per 100,000 and generated a victim reported rate of more than 78,000.[15] All indications are that prison assault rates among inmates are much higher than assault rates in the general population and have not declined appreciably over time.[16]

Rape and sexual assault. A difficulty with estimating rates of sexual violence in prison stems from classification problems. Researchers agree that much apparently consensual sexual activity is a response to threats of violence, or to avert the repeat of past violence. On the other hand, not all threats of rape or coercive demands for sexual services reflect an actual willingness to use force — some may be bluffs intended simply to haze or humiliate other prisoners. Nevertheless, studies have found rape rates in prisons and jails varying widely, between 300 and 14,000 per 100,000. Estimated rates of victimization for sexual aggression have ranged from 6,000 to 28,000 per 100,000.[17]

12. David A. Jones, The Health Risks of Imprisonment (1976). Lee Bowker, Prison Victimization 24 (1980).

13. Colin Carriere, The Dilemma of Individual Violence in Prisons, 6 New England Journal on Prison Law 195 (1980).

14. Bureau of Justice Statistics, Sourcebook of Criminal Justice Statistics (1993) Table 6.107.

15. Seventy-eight percent of inmates reported being assaulted within the past year, but did not indicate how often. D. Fuller, T. Orsagh & D. Raber, Violence and Victimization Within the North Carolina Prison System, Paper presented at the 1977 meeting of the Academy of Criminal Justice Sciences.

16. Bureau of Justice Statistics, Sourcebook of Criminal Justice Statistics (1993).

17. Helen Eigenberg, "Rape in Male Prisons," Prison Violence in America, 145-61 (1994); Daniel Lockwood, Issues in Prison Sexual Violence, Prison Violence in America, 97-102 (1994). A recent report by Human Rights Watch surveys the state of the empirical evidence and infers that no fewer than one in ten, but perhaps as many as one in three, jail or prison inmates is victimized by sexual assault during the period of incarceration. Notably, the "line officers"— the guards directly supervising the inmates — offer higher estimates of inmate-on-inmate sexual assault than do higher-ranking officials. Human Rights Watch, No Escape: Male Rape in U.S. Prisons 1-2 (2003).

Because incapacitation theorists have shown almost no curiosity about prison crime rates, "incapacitation" theory appears less concerned with truly incapacitating offenders than with segregating them and thereby redistributing the risk of violent crime from innocents to past offenders. This indifference to violence among inmates seems inconsistent with the utilitarian premise that the welfare of all members of society — offenders included — counts equally. Indeed, the position that only nonoffenders deserve protection from violence would seem to be a principle of retributive desert rather than utility.

One important aspect of retribution is expressive: Inflicting suffering is retributive insofar as it expresses blame, and blaming is a matter of singling out one or more individuals as morally responsible for a harm that may have been caused by the actions and omissions of many people. The blaming of one individual for harm absolves others — both individuals and institutions — from blame, thereby setting an offender apart from the rest of society. The practice of physically segregating offenders, and the policy discourse of "incapacitation" that justifies this practice, both express this segregative implication of blaming. Segregation of offenders not only sets them apart from "society" physically — it also sets them apart from "society" symbolically, by implying that their welfare does not count as social welfare.

The number of people thus excluded from the social welfare calculus — close to 2 million — constitutes a significant portion of America's population. The racial composition of this large inmate population further justifies using the term "segregation" to describe the increasing incarceration demanded in the name of incapacitation. African Americans now face an incarceration rate approximately ten times that faced by whites. About one million African American men are inmates today — as many as were slaves in 1850.

D.   RETRIBUTION

1.   Retribution as a Limit on Punishment

H. J. MCCLOSKEY, A NON-UTILITARIAN APPROACH TO PUNISHMENT
9 Inquiry 249, 253-54 (1965)

. . . [Is] all useful punishment . . . just punishment[?] When the problem of utilitarianism in punishment is put in this way, the appeal of the utilitarian approach somewhat diminishes. It appears to be useful to do lots of things which are unjust and undesirable. Whilst it is no doubt true that harsh punishment isn't necessarily the most useful punishment, and that punishment of the guilty person is usually the most useful punishment, it is nonetheless easy to call to mind cases of punishment of innocent people, of mentally deranged people, of excessive punishment, etc., inflicted because it was believed to be useful. Furthermore, the person imposing such punishment seems not always to be mistaken. . . . We may sometimes best deter others by punishing, by framing, an innocent man who is generally believed to be guilty, or by adopting rough and ready trial procedures, as is done by army courts martial in the heat of battle in respect of deserters, etc.; or we may severely punish a person not responsible for his actions, as so often happens with military punishments for cowardice, and in civil cases involving sex crimes where the legal definition of insanity may fail to cover the relevant cases of insanity. Sometimes we may deter others by imposing ruthless sentences for crimes which are widespread, as with car stealing and shoplifting in food markets. We may make people very thoughtful about their political commitments by having retroactive laws about their political affiliations; and we may, by secret laws, such as make to be major crimes what are believed simply to be anti-social practices and not crimes at all, usefully encourage a watchful, public-spirited behaviour. If the greatest good or the greatest happiness of the greatest number is the foundation of the morality and justice of punishment, there can be no guarantee that some such injustices may not be dictated by it. Indeed, one would expect that it would depend on the details of the situation and on the general features of the society, which punishments and institutions of punishment were most useful. . . .

JOHN RAWLS, TWO CONCEPTS OF RULES
Philosophical Perspectives on Punishment 82, 90-91 (E. Ezorsky ed. 1973)

Try to imagine, then, an institution (which we may call "telishment") which is such that the officials set up by it have authority to arrange a trial for the condemnation of an innocent man whenever they are of the opinion that doing so would be in the best interests of society. The discretion of officials is limited, however, by the rule that they may not condemn an innocent man to undergo such an ordeal unless there is, at the time, a wave of offenses similar to that with which they charge him and telish him for. We may imagine that the officials having the discretionary authority are the judges of the higher courts in consultation with the chief of police, the minister of justice, and a committee of the legislature.

Once one realizes that one is involved in setting up an institution, one sees that the hazards are very great. For example, what check is there on the officials? How is one to tell whether or not their actions are authorized? How is one to limit the risks involved in allowing such systematic deception? How is one to avoid giving anything short of complete discretion to the authorities to telish anyone they like? In addition to these considerations, it is obvious that people will come to have a very different attitude towards their penal system when telishment is adjoined to it. They will be uncertain as to whether a convicted man has been punished or telished. They will wonder whether or not they should feel sorry for him. They will wonder whether the same fate won't at any time fall on them. If one pictures how such an institution would actually work, and the enormous risks involved in it, it seems clear that it would serve no useful purpose. A utilitarian justification for this institution is most unlikely.

GUYORA BINDER & NICHOLAS J. SMITH, FRAMED: UTILITARIANISM AND PUNISHMENT OF THE INNOCENT
32 Rutgers L. Rev. 115, 118, 210-211

. . . [It is] striking . . . that utilitarianism's critics do not cite textual evidence that the originators of utilitarian penology in fact endorsed punishing the innocent or deceiving the public. . . . [T]he charge of framing the innocent rests on a misunderstanding of utilitarian penology as an application of an "act-utilitarian" ethic [requiring individuals to maximize utility]. . . .

Utilitarian penology was not an outgrowth or application of utilitarian ethics. Utilitarians like Beccaria and Bentham were interested in reforming public institutions to better serve the public welfare. Since they thought that individuals were destined to pursue their own welfare they did not see ethical preachments as a particularly useful enterprise. They thought of public utility as a public criterion of judgment for settling political arguments, rather than as a motive for individual action. It was primarily a criterion for use in legislation.

For someone of a skeptical, positivist turn of mind like Bentham, a standard of judgment like utility had no meaning apart from some concrete institutional process of decisionmaking. Bentham endeavored to design institutions that would not so much *maximize* utility as they would *realize* utility by providing a process for identifying it that could be publicly accepted as legitimate. Bentham thought of public confidence that government was guided by the public welfare as the major portion of the public happiness sought.

This larger aim of public confidence or "security" in the utilitarian aims of government necessitated a number of procedural constraints on government action. Thus, all government action should be pursuant to legislation promulgated by democratically elected representatives. Legislation should take the form of clear formal rules, couched in language intelligible to the public, and justified by reasons of public welfare clearly intelligible to the public. It should be faithfully implemented and enforced by executive and judicial officials with little discretion, subject to public monitoring and sanctions for misbehavior. Governmental publicity, education, a free press, and a lucid language of policy analysis and critique were all necessary, to enable the public to assess the performance of government. The entire utilitarian policy process depended upon the circulation of information: the ingathering by government of information about individual interests and social conditions; the outflow of information to the public about the nature, grounds and effects of government decisions; the exchange of information and opinions among members of the public about public needs and the performance of government. This circulation of information was crucial not only to enable government to serve the public interest, but to compel it to do so, and to reassure the public that government was so compelled.

These procedural requisites of utilitarian government combine with other utilitarian constraints to keep utilitarian punishment within narrow channels. Utilitarian penology begins with the idea that punishment is an evil that purposefully destroys welfare. It adds the observation that punishment is nevertheless useful in enforcing public will and deterring malevolence in so far as it can be seen to be precisely directed at wrongdoers. Yet, the weapon of punishment often cannot be aimed with great precision. Errors will be made, and in an interdependent society, the harmful effects of deserved punishment cannot be confined to the guilty. . . . The result is that the use of punishment not only inflicts costly suffering but inevitably threatens the very public security it is designed to serve.

The utilitarian responds in two ways. First, the utilitarian strives to use less destructive methods of social control whenever possible: positive incentives, education, therapeutic treatment, moral persuasion, architecture, surveillance, publicity, and so on. . . . Second, the utilitarian hedges the imposition of punishment with procedural rules designed to assure the public it is as regular and accurate as possible. When conceived as public security, utility turns out to demand much of the familiar civil libertarian agenda in criminal justice. Punishment should be conditioned on offenses that are defined legislatively, prospectively, specifically and publicly. Offenses should be conditioned on voluntariness and culpability so that only deterrable wrongdoing is punished and citizens can be confident they have some control over whether they subject themselves to punishment. Prosecutions should meet exacting standards of proof, and evidentiary reliability. Punishments should be reversible and convictions subject to exhaustive review and appeal. Criminal justice decisionmaking at all levels should be publicly monitored and reviewed. . . .

On this interpretation, utilitarian penology cannot be charged with condoning or demanding punishment of the innocent (except in the limited sense that all efforts to punish the guilty entail risks of inadvertently punishing the innocent and unfairly harming innocent associates of the guilty). Since utilitarian penology does not rest on any ethical theory, it does not entail an ethical obligation on the part of individuals to act so as to maximize utility. Hence, it entails no ethical obligation to bear false witness or frame the innocent or otherwise subvert legal process, even if an individual could know that such an act would maximize utility on a particular occasion. Utilitarian penology could not recommend a government policy of publicly and deliberately punishing innocent people, since this would impose needless suffering, create perverse incentives, and destroy public security. Utilitarian penology could not recommend a government policy of secretly framing the innocent, because a system of criminal justice could only advance its primary aim of public security if it was sufficiently transparent in design to guarantee the public that such acts would be discovered and punished.

HERBERT PACKER, THE LIMITS OF THE CRIMINAL SANCTION
62, 65-66 (1968)

The position I propose to elaborate and defend . . . can be stated summarily as follows:

(1) It is a necessary but not sufficient condition for punishment that it is designed to prevent the commission of offenses.
(2) It is a necessary but not a sufficient condition of punishment that the person on whom it is imposed is found to have committed an offense under circumstances that permit his conduct to be characterized as blameworthy . . .

Law, including the criminal law, must in a free society be judged ultimately on the basis of its success in promoting human autonomy and the capacity for individual growth and development. The prevention of crime is an essential aspect of the environmental protection required if autonomy is to flourish. It is, however, a negative aspect and one which, pursued with single-minded zeal, may end up creating an environment in which all are safe but none is free. The limitations included in the concept of culpability are justified not by an appeal to the Kantian dogma of "just deserts" but by their usefulness in keeping the state's powers of protection at a decent remove from the lives of its citizens.

The case for an essentially preventive view of the function of criminal law is unanswerable; anything else is the merest savagery. But a purely preventive view, reinforced as that view is today by a scientific and deterministic attitude toward the possibilities for controlling human conduct, carries the danger that single-minded pursuit of the goal of crime prevention will slight and in the end defeat the ultimate goal of law in a free society, which is to liberate rather than to restrain. . . . I see an important limiting principle in the criminal law's traditional emphasis on blameworthiness as a prerequisite to the imposition of punishment. But it is a *limiting* principle, not a justification for action. It is wrong to say that we should punish persons simply because they commit offenses under circumstances that we can call blameworthy. It is right to say that we should not punish those who commit offenses unless we can say that their conduct is blameworthy.

ALAN H. GOLDMAN, THE PARADOX OF PUNISHMENT
9 Philosophy & Public Affairs, No. 1, 48-49 (1979)

[T]he mixed theory of punishment . . . endorsed by . . . [several] philosophers in recent years . . . views the social goal of punishment as deterrence, and yet recognizes that we are entitled to pursue this goal only when we restrict deprivation of rights to those forfeited through crime or wrongdoing. . . .

The problem is that while the mixed theory can avoid punishment of the innocent, it is doubtful that it can avoid excessive punishment of the guilty if it is to have sufficient deterrent effect to make the social costs worthwhile. In our society the chances of apprehension and punishment for almost every class of crime are well under fifty percent. Given these odds a person pursuing what he considers his maximum prospective benefit may not be deterred by the threat of an imposition of punishment equivalent to the violation of the rights of the potential victim. If threats of sanctions are not sufficient to deter such people, they would probably fail to reduce crime to a tolerable enough level to make the social costs of the penal institution worthwhile. On the other hand, in order to deter crime at all effectively, given reasonable assumptions about police efficiency at bearable costs, sanctions must be threatened and applied which go far beyond the equivalence relation held to be just. . . .

DAVID DOLINKO, THREE MISTAKES OF RETRIBUTIVISM
39 UCLA L. Rev. 1632-33 (1992)

. . . [S]ince any actual criminal justice system is inherently fallible, any such system will inevitably inflict punishment on some people who are actually innocent and thus do not deserve it. Unless the retributivist rejects all possible systems of legal punishment, therefore, she is endorsing a system that she knows will condemn and punish innocent people. Presumably, she believes that the unjustified punishment of these innocents must be accepted to avoid the far greater injustice that leaving all of the guilty unpunished would produce. But isn't the retributivist then "using" those actually innocent persons who end up wrongly condemned? To be sure, she is ignorant of exactly who these unfortunate persons are. Yet this seems irrelevant: the terrorists who blew up Pan Am Flight 103 over Lockerbie, Scotland, in 1988 were "using" the hapless passengers to score a political point even if (as is likely) they were unaware of the passengers' identities. The retributivist remains "willing to trade the welfare of the innocents who are punished by mistake for the greater good of the punishment of the guilty" and thus, it would seem, committed to sacrificing — "using"— the mistakenly convicted for the benefit of society in general.

MICHAEL L. CORRADO, THE ABOLITION OF PUNISHMENT
35 Suffolk U. L. Rev. 257 (2001)

My point is that the ideas of retribution and desert do not really, when we think about it, limit the authority of the state in any way; that they are consistent with the most serious abuses; and beyond that that they are a kind of mask that makes those abuses easier to live with. . . .

I want to give the name absolute retributivism to the view that desert is not only a limit upon punishment in the strict sense, but also upon all uses of the coercive machinery of the criminal justice system when dealing with rational, morally competent people. The absolute retributivist, if there is any such person, believes that the only thing the state can do to stop sane, rational people from committing crimes is to punish them after the fact. What the state cannot do, again according to the absolute retributivist, is detain people solely for the purpose of deterring other people from committing crimes, or solely to incapacitate the person detained. By contrast, restricted retributivism is the view that retribution or desert is a limitation only on punishment in the strict sense, and not on [other kinds of coercive state actions]. . . .

To explore the question whether we should accept the thesis of absolute retributivism, we should begin by looking at our actual practices. In point of fact, the state does a lot more in the effort to control crime than punish those offenders who are sane and rational. Here is a partial list:

- For those who are adjudged to be dangerous, in the sense of being likely to commit the sorts of crimes with which they have been charged but not yet convicted, the state may detain them without bail until trial — conceivably up to two years.
- For those who are adjudged to have committed a sexual offense (and the judgment need not be the outcome of a criminal trial), the state may first imprison them for a definite term (as punishment for the crime), and then commit them to a mental institution (as preventive detention based upon their dangerousness).
- For those adjudged guilty but mentally ill, the state may first imprison them for a definite term (as punishment for the crime), and then commit them to a mental institution (as preventive detention based upon their dangerousness).
- For those who have committed a third felony, however minor, some states will permit detention so long that it cannot be justified as punishment for a crime, and must be intended to incapacitate on the grounds of dangerousness.

I think . . . the thesis of absolute retributivism is false. One of the primary obligations of the state, with respect to crime, is to protect its citizens, and to insist that protection has no role to play except as an incidental effect of punishment is just foolish. It seems clear that the state has the right to restrain those who might cause harm. The only question is how to limit that right, and in answering that question talk about retribution and desert is of no use at all.

Retribution as a limit . . . is too narrow because there are uses of the state's coercive power, the power to detain, for example, which are not punishment and which seem clearly acceptable. Outside the criminal law, for example, there is quarantine. The state may confine those with a serious contagious illness for the public good, presumably for an indefinite period. . . .

[Within the area of criminal justice] there are cases, I think, in which preventive detention is justified. . . . [S]urely no one would deny that the state has the right to restrain someone clearly bent on serious harm. The real questions are what counts as harm that we cannot bear to let happen and how to identify the person bent on such harm. You can restrict that right of the state as much as you like, but concede it even in one case, and the absolute retributivism thesis is false.

Beyond that, there are much less controversial exercises of state power to control crime that are not limited by retribution. There are injunctions and restraining orders, and there are stalker statutes. All those things are intended to prevent crime, and they envision the detention of people who have not committed any harmful act. The restraining order limits the movement of a person who has not yet committed a crime, on the grounds that he is dangerous. If he violates the order, he will have committed a crime and then may be punished; but what wrong did he do to justify the order in the first place? The restraining order is not issued in retribution for harm done. It is issued to prevent harm in the future — a use of the state's coercive power that is intended to control crime, but which does not involve retribution. . . .

[R]etribution . . . is also too broad because retribution can be stretched to cover any situation you like, to turn dangerousness into retribution, and thereby justify detention. The argument goes like this: the person who is dangerous to society has an obligation, if he is informed of his dangerousness, to have himself restrained so that he does not cause harm — just as he would have an obligation, if he owned a wild beast, to keep it restrained, or if he owned a dangerous automobile, not to take it on the road, or if he had a dangerous weapon to keep it locked up. He has an obligation to take himself out of circulation. Society might provide the means for him to do that, by creating detention centers where those who knew that they were dangerous to society could check in and be detained for the duration of their dangerousness. Society could also create legislation requiring them to do it, and impose a minor sentence, say six months in detention, for those who did not. Is there anything in that scenario that violates the limits of what society may do in the name of punishment? . . .

If absolute retributivism is false, if it is false that the only thing that the state can justifiably do is to punish, then retribution and desert [which only limit punishment] are really no limit on the state's use of power at all.

Notes and Questions

1. The retributivist McCloskey equates "rough and ready" trial procedures with punishment of the innocent; the utilitarian Dolinko argues that all practicable standards of proof entail punishing some innocents. How much

uncertainty about the guilt of offenders can we tolerate without violating retributive limits on punishment? Do we violate these limits by punishing the insane? By punishing those who cause harm accidentally?

2. Rawls and Binder & Smith defend utilitarianism by arguing that it does not require punishment of the innocent. In so doing, they appear to accept retribution or desert as a *limit* on punishment. Packer offers an example of such a *mixed* theory of punishment, which posits prevention as the general justifying aim of punishment, but treats desert as a limitation on the distribution of punishment. Other influential expressions of such a mixed theory include H.L.A. Hart, Punishment and Responsibility 8-13 (1968), and Norval Morris, The Future of Imprisonment (1974). But is such a compromise between prevention and desert possible? Goldman argues that limiting punishment to desert would frustrate deterrence altogether. Corrado, on the other hand, argues that retributive limits are toothless and would not succeed in securing the liberty that Packer is so concerned about. Can both be right?

2. Retribution as an Affirmative Justification for Punishment

a. The Appeal to Intuition

MICHAEL MOORE, LAW AND PSYCHIATRY
233-43 (1984)

Once one grants that there are two sorts of prima facie justifications of punishment — effecting a net social gain (utilitarian) and giving just deserts (retributivist) — one can also see that in addition to the two pure theories of punishment there can also be mixed theories. [T]he popular form of mixed theory asserts that . . . punishment is justified if and only if it achieves a net social gain *and* is given to offenders who deserve it. . . .

It is standard fare in the philosophy of punishment to assert, by way of several thought experiments, counterexamples to the utilitarian thesis that punishment is justified if and only if some net social gain is achieved. . . . [Such] arguments against the pure utilitarian theory of punishment do not by themselves drive one into retributivism. For one can alleviate the injustice of the pure utilitarian theory of punishment by adopting the mixed theory. . . .

[A]nother sort of thought experiment . . . tests whether one truly believes the mixed theory, or is in fact a pure retributivist. . . . Imagine . . . that after [committing a brutal] rape but before sentencing the defendant has gotten into an accident so that his sexual desires are dampened to such an extent that he presents no further danger of rape; if money is also one of his problems, suppose further that he has inherited a great deal of money, so that he no longer needs to rob. Suppose, because of both of these facts, we are reasonably certain that he does not present a danger of either forcible assault, rape, robbery, or related crimes in the future. Since [the rapist] is (by hypothesis) not dangerous, he does not need to be incapacitated, specially deterred, or reformed. Suppose further that we could successfully pretend to punish [him], instead of actually punishing him, and that no one is at all likely to find out. Our pretending to punish him will thus serve the needs of general deterrence and maintain social cohesion, and the cost to the state will be less than if it actually did punish him. Is there anything in the mixed theory of punishment that would urge that [the rapist] nonetheless should really be punished? I think not, so that if one's conclusion is that . . . people like him nonetheless should be punished, one will have to give up the mixed theory of punishment. . . .

Notes and Questions

1. Would you punish Moore's hypothetical defendant?
2. Do you accept his claim that doing so would serve no utilitarian aim? How might Rawls respond to this hypothetical?

b. The Argument from Social Contract

HERBERT MORRIS, ON GUILT AND INNOCENCE
33-34 (1976)

I want to . . . [describe a type of institution] designed to maintain some degree of social control [in which] . . . a central concept is punishment for wrongdoing. . . . The institutions I describe will resemble those we ordinarily think of as institutions of punishment; they will have, however, additional features we associate with a system of just punishment.

Let us suppose that men are constituted roughly as they now are, with a rough equivalence in strength and abilities, a capacity to be injured by each other and to make judgments that such injury is undesirable, a limited strength of will, and a capacity to reason and to conform conduct to rules. Applying to the conduct of these men are a group of rules . . . that prohibit violence and deception and compliance with which provides benefits for all persons. These benefits consist of noninterference by others with what each person values, such matters as continuance of life and bodily security. The rules define a sphere for each person then, which is immune from interference by others. Making possible this mutual benefit is the assumption by individuals of a burden. The burden consists in the exercise of self-restraint by individuals over inclinations that would, if satisfied, directly interfere or create a substantial risk of interference with others in proscribed ways. If a person fails to exercise self-restraint even though he might have and gives in to such inclinations, he renounces a burden which others have voluntarily assumed and thus gains an advantage which others, who have restrained themselves, do not possess. This system, then, is one in which the rules establish a mutuality of benefit and burden and in which the benefits of noninterference are conditional upon the assumption of burdens.

Connecting punishment with the violation of these primary rules, and making public the provision for punishment, is both reasonable and just. First, it is only reasonable that those who voluntarily comply with the rules be provided some assurance that they will not be assuming burdens which others are unprepared to assume. Their disposition to comply voluntarily will diminish as they learn that others are with impunity renouncing burdens they are assuming. Second, fairness dictates that a system in which benefits and burdens are equally distributed have a mechanism designed to prevent a maldistribution in the benefits and burdens. Thus, sanctions are attached to noncompliance with the primary rules so as to induce compliance with the primary rules among those who may be disinclined to obey. In this way the likelihood of an unfair distribution is diminished.

Third, it is just to punish those who have violated the rules and caused the unfair distribution of benefits and burdens. A person who violates the rules has something others have — the benefits of the system — but by renouncing what others have assumed, the burdens of self-restraint, he has acquired an unfair advantage. Matters are not even until this advantage is in some way erased. Another way of putting it is that he owes something to others, for he has something that does not rightfully belong to him. Justice — that is punishing such individuals — restores the equilibrium of benefits and burdens by taking from the individual what he owes, that is, exacting the debt.

JEFFRIE MURPHY, MARXISM AND RETRIBUTION
Punishment, A Philosophy & Pub. Affairs Reader 23-38
(A. John Simmons, et al., eds. 1995)

[C]onsider . . . one sobering fact: of the . . . offenders handled each day by some agency of the United States correctional system, the vast majority (80 percent on some estimates) are members of the lowest 15-percent income level. . . . Unless one wants to embrace the belief that all these people are poor because they are bad, it might be well to . . . [consider the] suggestion that many of them are "bad" because they are poor. . . . At what points will this challenge the credentials of the contractarian retributive theory . . . ?

. . . The retributive theory really presupposes what might be called a "gentlemen's club" picture of the relation between man and society — i.e., men are viewed as being part of a community of shared values and rules. The rules benefit all concerned and, as a kind of debt for the benefits derived, each man owes obedience to the rules. In the absence of such obedience, he deserves punishment in the sense that he owes payment for the benefits. For, as a rational man, he can see that the rules benefit everyone (himself included) and that he would have selected them in the original position of choice. . . .

But to think that [this] applies to the typical criminal, from the poorer classes, is to live in a world of social and political fantasy. [T]hey certainly would be hard-pressed to name the benefits for which they are supposed to owe obedience. . . .

Consider one example: a man has been convicted of armed robbery. On investigation, we learn that he is an impoverished black whose whole life has been one of frustrating alienation from the prevailing socio-economic structure — no job, no transportation if he could get a job, substandard education for his children, terrible housing and inadequate health care for his whole family, condescending-tardy-inadequate welfare payments, harassment by the police but no real protection by them against the dangers in his community, and near total exclusion from the political process. Learning all this, would we still want to talk — as many do — of his suffering punishment under the rubric of "paying a debt to society"? Surely not. Debt for what?

JAMES Q. WILSON AND RICHARD J. HERRNSTEIN,
CRIME AND HUMAN NATURE
330-32 (1985)

Sheldon Danziger and David Wheeler estimated the impact on crime rates in the United States of both absolute differences in income . . . and relative income shares (the ratio of the income of the better off to the income of the less well off). They tested these income variables over time (1949-1970) for the country as a whole and across metropolitan areas in 1960. . . . They found that, over time, either a widening of the absolute income gap or an increase in the ratio of higher to lower incomes was associated with an increase in crime, other things being equal. . . . Across metropolitan areas, absolute differences in income did not affect crime rates, but the shape of income distribution did.

. . . The most recent effort to show the connection between crime and economic inequality was made by Judith and Peter Blau. They found that there was a strong association between inequality in family income and rates of violent crime in 125 U.S. metropolitan areas in 1970, an association that persisted after controlling for race, region, city size, and the level of poverty. . . .

It is not clear that this finding can be interpreted as meaning that people act violently because they believe the distribution of income in their society is unjust. . . . [I]t is a bit puzzling that income inequality is associated with violence but not theft. And even among violent crimes, inequalities are related to homicide and assault but not robbery. If some people feel unjustly treated by a society that gives (in their view) undeservedly high incomes to other people, why wouldn't the aggrieved persons respond by stealing rather than assaulting, especially since most of the victims of such assaults are acquaintances and family members?

Notes and Questions

1. Need society establish just social conditions in order to justly punish? If not, should society take social injustice into account in deciding whom to punish? In deciding how many people to punish, and how severely?

2. Is it just for poor people to bear more of the risk of crime than wealthier people? Would it be fair to redistribute wealth in order to reduce crime?

3. Consider the disastrous life histories of two notorious and much-publicized offenders of the latter twentieth century, Alex Cabarga and Jack Henry Abbott:

When Alex Cabarga was five years old, his parents joined a San Francisco commune that espoused, among other values, open sexuality and marijuana use. At the commune Cabarga fell under the influence of 33-year-old Luis ("Tree Frog") Johnson, a charismatic pedophile. By the age of nine, Cabarga was living with Johnson, who beat and sexually molested him daily. For eight years, Cabarga lived a nomadic life with Johnson. At age 17, Cabarga helped Johnson kidnap an eleven-year-old boy and a two-year-old girl. Cabarga and Johnson held these two children prisoner for ten months, using beatings and starvation to repeatedly coerce the children into performing sex acts with both of them. The children were freed and Cabarga and Johnson were arrested, the day after

Cabarga turned eighteen. Cabarga was charged with about a hundred criminal offenses, and was ultimately sentenced to 25 years in prison.[18]

In Jack Abbott's best-selling 1981 book, *In the Belly of the Beast: Letters from Prison,* he described his life as a "state-raised convict": in foster-care from age nine, in detention from age 12, spending, by his estimate, two or three years of his childhood in solitary confinement, where he experienced claustrophobia and was repeatedly beaten and bound. Shortly after his release from juvenile detention at 18, Abbott was imprisoned again for a petty offense. In prison, he claims, he repelled several sexual assaults, killing one assailant. He earned a 3- to 20-year sentence, serving close to the maximum. As an adult prisoner, Abbott claimed, he spent more than a decade in solitary confinement, and was beaten, starved, shackled, tear-gassed, administered painful and disorienting drugs, kept in total darkness, and held in "strip-cells"—without clothing, bedding, furnishing or plumbing. He wrote that long confinement with other violent offenders trained him to view any dispute as potentially fatal, because his inability to escape potential assailants made homicide seem the only safe solution to conflict. Abbott's eloquent writing won the attention of influential writers who helped win his release on parole at the age of 37. On the morning that Abbott's book was lauded on the front page of the New York Times Book Review, Abbott misunderstood a waiter's efforts to direct him to a bathroom as a violent attack, and stabbed him fatally in the chest.

Both of these offenders committed horrible crimes, yet both were also victims of protracted abuse during their formative years. How does such a background affect an offender's desert? Does an abusive upbringing mitigate an offender's responsibility for his crime? Does society's failure to protect such children forfeit its right to condemn and punish the adult offenders they predictably become? Should the injustice these offenders suffered be deducted from the punishment they owe?[19]

c. *The Expressive Argument*

JOEL FEINBERG, DOING AND DESERVING
98, 100-05 (1970)

. . . [P]unishment is a conventional device for the expression of attitudes of resentment and indignation, and of judgments of disapproval and reprobation, on the part either of the punishing authority himself or of those "in whose name" the punishment is inflicted. Punishment, in short, has a *symbolic significance* largely missing from other kinds of penalties. . . . [W]e can characterize *condemnation* (or denunciation) as a kind of fusing of resentment and reprobation. . . . On the other hand, there are other functions of punishment, . . . that presuppose the expressive function and would be difficult or impossible without it.

18. See Paul H. Robinson, Would You Convict? Seventeen Cases That Challenged the Law 196-216 (1999).

19. Alex Cabarga was charged with multiple crimes and ultimately sentenced to 25 years in prison. Jack Abbott was convicted of manslaughter and returned to prison for a term of 15 years to life.

Authoritative disavowal. Consider the standard international practice of demanding that a nation whose agent has unlawfully violated the complaining nation's rights should punish the offending agent. . . . Punishing the [agent] is an emphatic, dramatic, and well-understood way of *condemning* and thereby *disavowing* his act. . . .

Symbolic nonacquiescence: "Speaking in the name of the people." . . . In the state of Texas, so-called paramour killings were regarded by the law as not merely mitigated, but completely justifiable. Many humanitarians, I believe, will feel quite spontaneously that a great injustice is done when such killings are left unpunished. . . . [They may feel] that paramour killings deserve to be *condemned,* that the law in condoning . . . them . . . expresses the judgment of the "people of Texas," in whose name it speaks, that the vindictive satisfaction in the mind of a cuckolded husband is a thing of greater value than the very life of his wife's lover. The demand that paramour killings be punished may simply be the demand that this lopsided value judgment be withdrawn and that the state *go on record* against paramour killings and the law *testify to the recognition* that such killings are wrongful. . . .

Vindication of the law. Sometimes the state goes on record through its statutes, in a way that might well please a conscientious citizen in whose name it speaks, but then owing to official evasion and unreliable enforcement gives rise to doubts that the law really means what it says. . . . A statute honored mainly in the breach begins to lose its character as law, unless, as we say, it is *vindicated* (emphatically reaffirmed); and clearly the way to do this (indeed the only way) is to punish those who violate it. . . .

Absolution of others. When something scandalous has occurred and it is clear that the wrongdoer must be one of a small number of suspects, then the state, by punishing one of these parties, thereby relieves the others of suspicion and informally absolves them of blame. Moreover, quite often the absolution of an accuser hangs as much in the balance at a criminal trial as the inculpation of the accused. . . .

JEAN HAMPTON, PUNISHMENT AS DEFEAT
Forgiveness And Mercy 124-28, 130 (Jeffrie G. Murphy & Jean Hampton, eds. 1988)

Those who wrong others . . . demean them. They incorrectly believe or else fail to realize that others' value rules out the treatment their actions have accorded the others, and they incorrectly believe or implicitly assume that their own value is high enough to make this treatment permissible. So, implicit in their wrongdoings is a message about their value relative to that of their victims. . . . A retributivist's commitment to punishment is . . . a commitment to asserting moral truth in the face of its denial. If I have value equal to that of my assailant, then that must be made manifest after I have been victimized. By victimizing me, the wrongdoer has declared himself elevated with respect to me, acting as a superior who is permitted to use me for his purposes. A false moral claim has been made. . . . The retributivist demands that the false claim be corrected. The lord must be humbled to show that he isn't the lord of the victim. If I cause the wrongdoer to suffer in proportion to my suffering at his hands, his elevation over me is denied. . . . I master the purported master, showing that he is my peer.

So I am proposing that retributive punishment is the defeat of the wrong-doer at the hands of the victim . . . that symbolizes the correct relative value of wrongdoer and victim. It is a symbol that is conceptually required to reaffirm a victim's equal worth in the face of a challenge to it.

Notes and Questions

1. Notice that the expressive implications of punishment pointed to by Feinberg and Hampton benefit many persons — victims, bystanders, society generally — by vindicating or absolving them. Can punishment be retributive in the sense endorsed by Kant, if it is for the benefit of anyone other than the offender? Does such punishment amount to using the offender as a means?

2. According to Hampton, punishment of the offender serves to express the worth of the victim. Is this punitive aim compatible with the retributive lim-its on punishment? Imagine a young offender who has suffered a deprived and abusive childhood and who is emotionally disturbed, of low intelligence, and ad-dicted to drugs. To feed his habit, the offender snatches a purse. The victim, a skilled brain surgeon, loses her balance, falls into the street, and is hit by a car and suffers permanent paralysis. What punishment would appropriately recog-nize the worth of the victim? What punishment does the offender deserve? Can any sentence do "justice" to both?

E. BEYOND UTILITY AND DESERT: EDUCATIVE AND RESTORATIVE THEORIES OF PUNISHMENT

In the 1980s, after retributivist philosophers had driven rehabilitation from the field, they began to have second thoughts about rehabilitation. They began to wonder whether the religious idea of "repentance" might somehow be central to the idea of punishment.

As we have seen, one of the arguments retributivists developed for punish-ment pointed to its symbolic significance in expressing society's respect for vic-tims and in absolving society of responsibility for crime. But retributivists soon began to wonder whether punishing to make a statement involved an exploita-tive *use* of the offender. They also began to notice that punishment seemed de-signed to communicate something not just to the wider society, but to the of-fender in particular. This led them to the view that punishment entailed efforts to persuade the offender to repent and reform, so that the rehabilitative ideal was inherent in punishment.

This new educative model of punishment provoked efforts to rethink the political values underlying punishment. Perhaps it was less a recognition of the offender's autonomy and moral responsibility for wrongdoing than an expres-sion of society's responsibility to reform and reintegrate the offender. That a society has a responsibility to educate and reintegrate offenders may seem to entail a like responsibility to reaffirm the membership and status of victims by making them whole. Some reformers have advocated efforts to "heal" both offenders and victims under the rubric of "restorative" justice.

HERBERT MORRIS, A PATERNALISTIC THEORY OF PUNISHMENT
18 Amer. Phil. Q. 263, 264-67 (1981)

. . . [A] paternalistic theory of punishment will . . . claim that a principal justification for punishment [is that it] . . . furthers the good of potential and actual wrongdoers. This contrasts with views . . . that it is justice that requires that guilty persons be punished or that it is the utility to society that requires punishment. . . .

. . . The theory I am proposing requires that the practice of punishment promote a particular kind of good for potential and actual wrongdoers. The good is . . . one's identity as a moral person attached to the good.

. . . First, it is a part of this good that one comes to appreciate the nature of the evil involved for others and for oneself in one's doing wrong. This requires empathy. . . ; it also requires the imaginative capacity to take in the implications for one's future self of the evil one has done; it further requires an attachment to being a person of a certain kind.

. . . Second, it is a part of the good that one feel guilt over the wrongdoing, that is, that one be pained at having done wrong, that one be distressed with oneself, that one be disposed to restore what has been damaged, and that one accept the appropriateness of some deprivation, and the making of amends. Not to experience any of this would be to evidence an indifference to separation from others that could only . . . diminish one as a person.

Third, it is also part of the good that one reject the disposition to do what is wrong and commit oneself to forbearance in the future. I assume that this makes possible, indeed that it is inextricably bound up with, one's forgiving oneself, one's relinquishing one's guilt, and one's having the capacity fully to enter into life.

Finally, it is part of the good that one possess . . . a conception of oneself as an individual worthy of respect, a conception of oneself as a responsible person, responsible for having done wrong and responsible [to reflect upon the deed]. . . . This conception of oneself is further nourished by freely accepting the moral conditions placed upon restoring relationships with others and oneself that one has damaged.

It is a moral good, then, that one feel contrite, that one feel the guilt that is appropriate to one's wrongdoing, that one be repentant, that one be self-forgiving and that one have reinforced one's conception of oneself as a responsible being. Ultimately, then, the moral good aimed at by the paternalism I propose is an autonomous individual freely attached to that which is good, those relationships with others that sustain and give meaning to a life. . . .

Now, what more acceptably motivates a parent when it punishes its child than the desire to achieve a goal such as I have described? It would be perverse if the parent were generally to punish primarily from motives of retributive justice or optimal utility for the family. These ends are secondary to . . . the child's acquiring the characteristics of a moral person. . . .

R.A. DUFF, TRIALS AND PUNISHMENTS
15, 20-21, 246-47, 254-57, 259-62 (1986)

. . . As far back as the reign of Henry VIII it was held to be obviously cruel and inhuman to execute a person who had become insane since his commission of a capital offence. . . .

[S]uppose a murderer becomes so disordered that, while she realises *that* she is to be hanged, she cannot understand *why* she is to be hanged; she cannot grasp the connection between what is to be done to her now and what she did in the past which makes her hanging an execution. . . . Her execution might cause her an injury which externally matches the harm caused by, or the wrong involved in, her crime; but it cannot now be a process through which *she* pays for that crime, or restores the balance which her crime disturbed, or expiates or atones for her crime; for she cannot understand, respond to, or participate in her execution as a punishment for what she has done.

The idea that a prisoner should be able to participate in his own execution may at first sound . . . odd. . . . But it suggests that the essential purpose of punishment may be not just to inflict suffering on an offender . . . but to induce suffering which the offender can understand, and to which he can respond, as a punishment for his offence; that what is wrong with hanging someone who is so disordered that he cannot understand his execution in these terms is that it cannot properly count as a *punishment,* since it cannot serve the purpose which is central to the meaning of punishment.

. . . In undertaking a penance I both own and disown my sin: I own it as mine — as a wrong which I have done; but I disown it as an act which I now condemn and repent. . . .

The idea of penance helps us to understand the sense of a voluntary or self-imposed punishment. . . . [But] the *imposition* of punishment on recalcitrant offenders is a central feature of legal systems like our own: so we must ask whether such coercive punishments can be explained and justified as compulsory penances.

. . . A person can find well-being only within a community which is, necessarily, structured by certain shared values and concerns, and within the kinds of relationship which such a community makes possible. A criminal who flouts the just laws of her community thereby injures herself; she separates herself from the values on which the community and her own well-being depend; she damages or destroys her relationships with other members of the community, and separates herself from them. . . . If she would only recognise the moral truth about her criminal attitudes and activities, she would see how they are injurious to her true well-being. . . .

The purpose of punishment, like that of a penance which is imposed on a recalcitrant sinner, is to bring the criminal to understand the nature and implications of her crime; to repent that crime and *thus,* by willing her own punishment as a penance which can expiate her crime, to reconcile herself with the Right and with her community. . . .

We may find elements of such a view in, for instance, the early Quaker view of imprisonment as the appropriate mode of punishment: prison removes the criminal from his corrupting peers, and provides the opportunity for and the stimulus to a reflective self-examination which will induce repentance and self-reform.

JOHN BRAITHWAITE, CRIME, SHAME AND REINTEGRATION
62,101-02 (1989)[20]

[Braithwaite sets out to explain the facts that crime is committed dispro-portionately by males, 15-25 year olds, unmarried people, people living in large cities, people who are highly mobile, young people who do poorly in school, young people who associate with criminals, and people at the bottom of class or race hierarchies; and that the industrialized country with by far the lowest crime rates is Japan.]

. . . A variety of life circumstances increase the chances that individuals will be in situations of greater interdependency, the most important being age (un-der 15 and over 25), being married, female, employed, and having high em-ployment and educational aspirations. Interdependent persons are more sus-ceptible to shaming. More importantly, societies in which individuals are subject to extensive interdependencies are more likely to be communitarian, and sham-ing is much more widespread and potent in communitarian societies. Urbani-zation and high residential mobility are societal characteristics which under-mine communitarianism.

The shaming produced by interdependency and communitarianism can be either of two types — shaming that becomes stigmatization or shaming that is followed by reintegration. The shaming engendered is more likely to become reintegrative in societies that are communitarian. In societies where shaming does become reintegrative, low crime rates are the result because disapproval is dispensed without eliciting a rejection of the disapprovers, so that the poten-tialities for future disapproval are not dismantled. Moreover, reintegrative shaming is superior . . . to stigmatization for conscience-building. . . .

The conclusions of the leading scholars who have studied the social context of Japan's low and declining crime rate can be read as support for the notion of high interdependency in Japanese society (with employers and neighbors as well as families), highly developed communitarianism, and the two characteristics fostering a shaming which is reintegrative. . . .

Shaming that is stigmatizing, in contrast, makes criminal subcultures more attractive because these are in some sense subcultures which reject the rejectors. Thus, when shaming is allowed to become stigmatization for want of reintegra-tive gestures . . . , the deviant is both attracted to criminal subcultures and cut off from other interdependencies (with family, neighbors, church, etc.). Partic-ipation in subcultural groups supplies criminal role models, training in tech-niques of crime and . . . other forms of social support that make choices to engage in crime more attractive. Thus, to the extent that shaming is of the stig-matizing rather than the reintegrative sort, and that criminal subcultures are widespread and accessible in the society, higher crime rates will be the result. While societies characterized by high levels of stigmatization will have higher crime rates than societies characterized by reintegrative shaming, the former will have higher or lower crime rates than societies with little shaming at all de-pending largely on the availability of criminal subcultures.

Yet a high level of stigmatization in the society is one of the very factors that encourages criminal subculture formation by creating populations of outcasts

20. The editors have reordered paragraphs for ease of exposition.

with no stake in conformity, no chance of self-esteem within the terms of conventional society — individuals in search of an alternative culture that allows them self-esteem. A communitarian culture, on the other hand, nurtures deviants within a network of attachments to conventional society, thus inhibiting the widespread outcasting that is the stuff of subculture formation.

ERIK LUNA, PUNISHMENT THEORY, HOLISM, AND THE PROCEDURAL CONCEPTION OF RESTORATIVE JUSTICE
2003 Utah L. Rev. 207, 229-30

[C]ontemporary scholars have begun to question the narrow focus of criminal punishment as state-versus-offender, outside of its social context, and exclusive of other interested parties such as victims, families, and community members. Traditional approaches largely neglect the needs of those directly injured by crime and the resulting damage done to social relationships within an interconnected community. What is needed, some scholars contend, is a punishment theory that takes a broader view of justice in sentencing, mindful of damaged relationships and neglected obligations in civil society. One possibility, commonly described as "restorative justice," has received substantial international interest and has even made inroads in American criminal justice. Although sometimes viewed as a social movement in Western nations rather than a positive or normative theory, restorative justice is nonetheless championed as an alternative to traditional punishment theories, particularly retributivism. . . .

Over the years, restorative justice has been described in similar ways by leading proponents, including the following:

1. Restorative justice is a process of bringing together the individuals who have been affected by an offense and having them agree on how to repair the harm caused by the crime. The purpose is to restore victims, restore offenders, and restore communities in a way that all stakeholders can agree is just.[21]

2. [R]estorative justice is concerned with the broader relationships between offenders, victims, and communities. All parties are involved in the process of settling the offense and reconciliation. Crime is seen as more than simply the violation of the criminal law. Instead, the key focus is on the damage and injury done to victims and communities and each is seen as having a role to play in responding to the criminal act. As a result of meeting with the victims . . . offenders are expected to gain an understanding of the consequences of their behavior and to develop feelings of remorse.[22]

3. Restorative justice is a process that brings victims and offenders together to face each other, to inform each other about their crimes and victimization, to learn about each others' backgrounds, and to collectively reach agreement on a 'penalty' or 'restorative justice sanction.'

21. John Braithwaite, A Future Where Punishment is Marginalized, 46 UCLA L. Rev. 1727, 1743 (1999).
22. Joe Hudson et al., Introduction to Family Group Conferences: Perspectives On Policy And Practice 1, 4 (Joe Hudson et al. eds., 1996).

Restorative justice returns the criminal conflict back to the victims and offenders. It empowers them to address sanctioning concerns together.[23]

4. Crime is a violation of people and relationships. It creates obligations to make things right. [Restorative] justice involves the victim, the offender, and the community in search for solutions which promote repair, reconciliation, and reassurance.[24]

Distilling these and other descriptions, restorative justice would seem to incorporate a number of substantive principles. In particular, crime is not just an act against the state but against particular victims and the community in general, with offending viewed primarily as a breach of social relationships and only secondarily as a violation of the law. The community, family members, and supporters, rather than the state and its justice machinery, are considered the locus of crime control and sanctioning, with the restorative model seeking the active participation of victims, families, and community representatives to address the causes and consequences of offending. Moreover, a primary objective is making amends for the offense, particularly the harm caused to the victim, rather than inflicting pain upon the offender. Accountability is evidenced by recognizing the wrongfulness of one's conduct, expressing remorse for any resulting injury, and taking steps to repair damaged social relationships. Crime creates positive obligations, this approach argues, that require affirmative action on the part of the offender. Various penal practices from around the globe seem to comport with this understanding of restorative justice — family group conferencing in Australia and New Zealand, community reparative boards in Vermont, circle sentencing in Canada, and victim-offender mediation throughout North America and Europe — all aimed at bringing stakeholders together to fashion appropriate resolutions to crime, typically through mediated dialogue.

Notes and Questions

1. Morris and Duff imply that the infliction of suffering is crucial to the morally educative message that punishment conveys. But Japanese "reintegrative shaming," while it no doubt involves anguish for offenders, seems to achieve the goals set forth by these "moral education" theorists without much incarceration. Is that a realistic model for American society?

2. What "moral message" does incarceration communicate to American offenders?

3. Thus far, American use of "restorative" approaches to punishment has been mostly confined to the context of juvenile justice. Could it have broader application to adult offenders?

---

23. Russ Immarigeon, Restorative Justice, Juvenile Offenders and Crime Victims: A Review of the Literature, in Restorative Juvenile Justice: Repairing the Harm of Youth Crime (Gordon Bazemore & Lode Walgrave eds., 1999).

24. Howard Zehr, Changing Lenses: A New Focus for Crime and Justice 181 (1990).

F. PROPORTIONALITY

EWING v. CALIFORNIA
Supreme Court of the United States
123 S. Ct. 1179; 155 L. Ed. 2d 108 (2003)

JUSTICE O'CONNOR announced the judgment of the Court and delivered an opinion in which THE CHIEF JUSTICE and JUSTICE KENNEDY join.

In this case, we decide whether the Eighth Amendment prohibits the State of California from sentencing a repeat felon to a prison term of 25 years to life under the State's "Three Strikes and You're Out" law. . . .

California's three strikes law reflects a shift in the State's sentencing policies toward incapacitating and deterring repeat offenders who threaten the public safety. . . . [Under this law] if the defendant has one prior "serious" or "violent" felony conviction, he must be sentenced to "twice the term otherwise provided as punishment for the current felony conviction." If the defendant has two or more prior "serious" or "violent" felony convictions, he must receive "an indeterminate term of life imprisonment." Defendants sentenced to life under the three strikes law become eligible for parole on a date calculated by reference to a "minimum term," which is the greater of (a) three times the term otherwise provided for the current conviction, (b) 25 years, or (c) the term determined by the court . . . for the underlying conviction, including any enhancements. . . .

On parole from a 9-year prison term, petitioner Gary Ewing walked into the pro shop of the El Segundo Golf Course in Los Angeles County on March 12, 2000. He walked out with three golf clubs, priced at $399 apiece, concealed in his pants leg. . . .

Ewing is no stranger to the criminal justice system. . . . [Ewing has been convicted of numerous misdemeanor and felony offenses, served nine separate terms of incarceration, and committed most of his crimes while on probation or parole. His prior "strikes" were serious felonies including robbery and three residential burglaries, including one in Long Beach. For stealing the golf clubs Ewing] was charged with, and ultimately convicted of, one count of felony grand theft of personal property in excess of $400. . . . As required by the three strikes law, the prosecutor formally alleged, and the trial court later found, that Ewing had been convicted previously of four serious or violent felonies for the three burglaries and the robbery in the Long Beach apartment complex. . . . As a newly convicted felon with two or more "serious" or "violent" felony convictions in his past, Ewing was sentenced under the three strikes law to 25 years to life. . . .

The Eighth Amendment, which forbids cruel and unusual punishments, contains a "narrow proportionality principle" that "applies to noncapital sentences." Harmelin v. Michigan, 501 U.S. 957, 996-997, (KENNEDY, J., concurring in part and concurring in judgment). . . . We have most recently addressed the proportionality principle as applied to terms of years in a series of cases beginning with Rummel v. Estelle, [445 U.S. 263 (1980).]

In *Rummel,* we held that it did not violate the Eighth Amendment for a State to sentence a three-time offender to life in prison with the possibility of parole. Like Ewing, Rummel was sentenced to a lengthy prison term under a recidivism statute. Rummel's two prior offenses were a 1964 felony for "fraudulent use of a credit card to obtain $80 worth of goods or services," and a 1969 felony conviction for "passing a forged check in the amount of $28.36." His triggering offense was a conviction for felony theft — "obtaining $120.75 by false pretenses."

This Court ruled that "having twice imprisoned him for felonies, Texas was entitled to place upon Rummel the onus of one who is simply unable to bring his conduct within the social norms prescribed by the criminal law of the State." . . . We noted that this Court "has on occasion stated that the Eighth Amendment prohibits imposition of a sentence that is grossly disproportionate to the severity of the crime." But "outside the context of capital punishment, successful challenges to the proportionality of particular sentences have been exceedingly rare." Although we stated that the proportionality principle "would . . . come into play in the extreme example . . . if a legislature made overtime parking a felony punishable by life imprisonment," we held that "the mandatory life sentence imposed upon this petitioner does not constitute cruel and unusual punishment under the Eighth and Fourteenth Amendments." . . .

Three years after *Rummel,* in Solem v. Helm, 463 U.S. 277 (1983), we held that the Eighth Amendment prohibited "a life sentence without possibility of parole for a seventh nonviolent felony." The triggering offense in *Solem* was "uttering a 'no account' check for $100." We specifically stated that the Eighth Amendment's ban on cruel and unusual punishments "prohibits . . . sentences that are disproportionate to the crime committed," and that the "constitutional principle of proportionality has been recognized explicitly in this Court for almost a century." The *Solem* Court then explained that three factors may be relevant to a determination of whether a sentence is so disproportionate that it violates the Eighth Amendment: "(i) the gravity of the offense and the harshness of the penalty; (ii) the sentences imposed on other criminals in the same jurisdiction; and (iii) the sentences imposed for commission of the same crime in other jurisdictions."

Applying these factors in *Solem,* we struck down the defendant's sentence of life without parole. We specifically noted the contrast between that sentence and the sentence in *Rummel,* pursuant to which the defendant was eligible for parole. 463 U.S., at 297. . . . Indeed, we explicitly declined to overrule *Rummel.* . . .

Eight years after *Solem,* we grappled with the proportionality issue again in *Harmelin, supra. Harmelin* was not a recidivism case, but rather involved a first-time offender convicted of possessing 672 grams of cocaine. He was sentenced to life in prison without possibility of parole. A majority of the Court rejected Harmelin's claim that his sentence was so grossly disproportionate that it violated the Eighth Amendment. The Court, however, could not agree on why his proportionality argument failed. JUSTICE SCALIA, joined by THE CHIEF JUSTICE, wrote that the proportionality principle was "an aspect of our death penalty jurisprudence" [only]. . . . JUSTICE KENNEDY, joined by two other Members of the Court, concurred in part and concurred in the judgment. JUSTICE KENNEDY specifically recognized that "the Eighth Amendment proportionality principle also applies to noncapital sentences." He then identified four principles of proportionality review — "the primacy of the legislature, the variety of legitimate penological schemes, the nature of our federal system, and the requirement that proportionality review be guided by objective factors" — that "inform the final one: The Eighth Amendment does not require strict proportionality between crime and sentence. Rather, it forbids only extreme sentences that are 'grossly disproportionate' to the crime." JUSTICE KENNEDY's concurrence also stated that *Solem* "did not mandate" comparative analysis "within and between jurisdictions."

The proportionality principles in our cases distilled in JUSTICE KENNEDY's concurrence guide our application of the Eighth Amendment in the new context that we are called upon to consider. . . .

Though three strikes laws may be relatively new, our tradition of deferring to state legislatures in making and implementing such important policy decisions is longstanding. . . . Our traditional deference to legislative policy choices finds a corollary in the principle that the Constitution "does not mandate adoption of any one penological theory." (KENNEDY, J., concurring in part and concurring in judgment). A sentence can have a variety of justifications, such as incapacitation, deterrence, retribution, or rehabilitation. . . . Some or all of these justifications may play a role in a State's sentencing scheme. Selecting the sentencing rationales is generally a policy choice to be made by state legislatures, not federal courts.

When the California Legislature enacted the three strikes law, it made a judgment that protecting the public safety requires incapacitating criminals who have already been convicted of at least one serious or violent crime. Nothing in the Eighth Amendment prohibits California from making that choice. . . .

Against this backdrop, we consider Ewing's claim that his three strikes sentence of 25 years to life is unconstitutionally disproportionate to his offense. . . . The gravity of his offense was not merely "shoplifting three golf clubs." Rather, Ewing was convicted of felony grand theft for stealing nearly $1,200 worth of merchandise after previously having been convicted of at least two "violent" or "serious" felonies. Even standing alone, Ewing's theft should not be taken lightly. His crime was certainly not [like the bad check offense in *Solem*] "one of the most passive felonies a person could commit." . . .

In weighing the gravity of Ewing's offense, we must place on the scales not only his current felony, but also his long history of felony recidivism. Any other approach would fail to accord proper deference to the policy judgments that find expression in the legislature's choice of sanctions. . . .

Ewing's sentence is justified by the State's public-safety interest in incapacitating and deterring recidivist felons, and amply supported by his own long, serious criminal record. . . . To be sure, Ewing's sentence is a long one. But it reflects a rational legislative judgment, entitled to deference, that offenders who have committed serious or violent felonies and who continue to commit felonies must be incapacitated. . . . Ewing's is not "the rare case in which a threshold comparison of the crime committed and the sentence imposed leads to an inference of gross disproportionality." *Harmelin,* 501 U.S., at 1005 (KENNEDY, J., concurring in part and concurring in judgment).

We hold that Ewing's sentence of 25 years to life in prison, imposed for the offense of felony grand theft under the three strikes law, is not grossly disproportionate and therefore does not violate the Eighth Amendment's prohibition on cruel and unusual punishments.

JUSTICE SCALIA, concurring in the judgment.

Proportionality — the notion that the punishment should fit the crime — is inherently a concept tied to the penological goal of retribution. "It becomes difficult even to speak intelligently of 'proportionality,' once deterrence and rehabilitation are given significant weight," *Harmelin, supra,* at 989 — not to mention giving weight to the purpose of California's three strikes law: incapacitation. In the present case, the game is up once the plurality has acknowledged that "the Constitution does not mandate adoption of any one penological theory," and that a "sentence can have a variety of justifications, such as incapacitation, deterrence, retribution, or rehabilitation." That acknowledgment having been made, it no longer suffices merely to assess "the gravity of the offense compared to the harshness of the penalty"; that classic description of the proportionality principle (alone and in itself quite resistant to policy-free, legal analysis) now becomes merely the "first" step of the inquiry. Having completed that step (by a discussion which, in all fairness, does not convincingly establish that 25-years-to-life is a "proportionate" punishment for stealing three golf clubs), the plurality must then *add* an analysis to show that "Ewing's sentence is justified by the State's public-safety interest in incapacitating and deterring recidivist felons."

Which indeed it is — though why that has anything to do with the principle of proportionality is a mystery. Perhaps the plurality should revise its terminology, so that what it reads into the Eighth Amendment is not the unstated proposition that all punishment should be reasonably proportionate to the gravity of the offense, but rather the unstated proposition that all punishment should reasonably pursue the multiple purposes of the criminal law. That formulation would make it clearer than ever, of course, that the plurality is not applying law but evaluating policy.

Notes and Questions

1. *A 5-4 Split.* In Ewing v. California, Justice Thomas concurred on the ground that the Eighth Amendment imposes no proportionality limits. Justices Stevens, Souter, Breyer and Ginsburg dissented, reasoning that the disproportion between Ewing's crime and his sentence was greater than that in *Rummel* and almost as great as that in Solem v. Helm.

2. Consider the sequence of background cases that led to *Ewing:*

Rummell v. Estelle (1980). In Rummel v. Estelle, the Supreme Court affirmed the denial of a writ of habeas corpus for a petitioner serving a life term under a Texas recidivist statute. Rummel was convicted of fraud offenses in 1964, 1969, and 1973. The total amount he acquired by fraud in these three offenses was $230. Because all three offenses were felonies, and because both prior offenses led to imprisonment, Rummel was sentenced to life imprisonment with the possibility of parole after perhaps as "little" as 12 years. The Court emphasized that under the Texas scheme, "a recidivist must twice demonstrate that conviction and actual imprisonment do not deter him from returning to crime once he is released. One in Rummel's position has been both graphically informed of the consequences of lawlessness and given an opportunity to reform, all to no avail." The *Rummel* Court rejected petitioner's contention that only violent crimes could merit life imprisonment. The Court noted the possibility of parole under the Texas statute and suggested that prosecutorial discretion might operate to screen out "truly petty offenders," under the Texas scheme.

Solem v. Helm (1983). In Solem v. Helm, the defendant had previously been convicted of six felonies — none a crime against a person — and in 1979 was charged with writing a bad check for $100. Addressing his Eighth Amendment appeal, the Court adopted the following test:

> [W]e hold as a matter of principle that a criminal sentence must be proportionate to the crime for which the defendant has been convicted. . . . [A] court's proportionality analysis under the Eighth Amendment should be guided by objective criteria, including (i) the gravity of the offense and the harshness of the penalty; (ii) the sentences imposed on other criminals in the same jurisdiction; and (iii) the sentences imposed for commission of the same crime in other jurisdictions. . . . Application of these factors assumes that courts are competent to judge the gravity of an offense, at least on a relative scale. In a broad sense this assumption is justified, and courts traditionally have made these judgments — just as legislatures must make them in the first instance. Comparisons can be made in light of the harm caused or threatened to the victim or society, and the culpability of the offender. . . . There are other accepted principles that courts may apply in measuring the harm caused or threatened to the victim or society. . . . Stealing a million dollars is . . . more serious than stealing a hundred. . . . [A]ssault with intent to murder [is] more serious than simple assault. . . . Turning to the culpability of the offender, there are again clear distinctions that courts may recognize and apply. . . . South Dakota, for example, ranks criminal acts in ascending order of seriousness as follows: negligent acts, reckless acts, knowing acts, intentional acts, and malicious acts. . . .

The *Solem* court went on to argue that the severity of Helm's sentence — life without parole — compared to the relative innocuousness of his crime of issuing a bad check, and the lack of violence in his criminal record, rendered his punishment grossly disproportionate. The court especially emphasized the unavailability of parole in distinguishing Helm's sentence from Rummel's.

Harmelin v. Michigan (1991). Harmelin received a life-without-possibility-of-parole sentence for a single act of cocaine possession — albeit the amount possessed was 672 grams. Like Ewing, his sentence was affirmed by a 5-4 Supreme Court vote. Four justices reaffirmed the proportionality standard of Solem v. Helm, while Justice Scalia and Chief Justice Rehnquist took the view that the Eighth Amendment did not require proportionality in sentences of imprisonment. A three-justice plurality retained a "narrow proportionality principle." Writing for this plurality, Justice Kennedy reasoned as follows:

(1) Legislatures have primary responsibility to determine and apply the purposes of punishment.
(2) "The Eighth Amendment does not mandate any one penological theory." It has long permitted "the penological goals of retribution, deterrence, incapacitation and rehabilitation . . . and competing theories of mandatory and discretionary sentencing. . . ."
(3) Because, in a federal system "state sentencing schemes may embody different penological assumptions," comparisons between prison sentences in different states are unreliable.
(4) Because different sentences might be justified by different penological theories, "we lack clear objective standards to distinguish between sentences for different terms of years."
(5) Therefore, "the Eighth Amendment does not require strict proportionality between crime and sentence. Rather, it forbids only extreme sentences that are grossly disproportionate to the crime."

The three-justice plurality in *Ewing* applied this scheme. But as Justice Scalia's dissent in *Ewing* points out, the second premise raises troubling questions about the coherence of the plurality's "narrow" proportionality principle. Is Justice Scalia correct that any principle of proportionality must be premised on retributivism alone? Was the conception of proportionality the court applied in Solem v. Helm premised on retributivism alone? If so, is that requirement of proportionality still binding after *Harmelin* and *Ewing*? Is any?

But perhaps the concept of proportionality is not necessarily or exclusively retributivist. Recall that other theories of punishment imply limiting principles. The utilitarian rationales for punishment may also be thought to yield principles of proportionality, precluding pointless punishment. Thus deterrence requires that sentences be "proportionate" to the harm and deterrability of the offender's type of crime; considerations of incapacitation and rehabilitation might dictate longer or more determinate sentences for incorrigibly dangerous offenders. Could the plurality be saying that sentences will be deemed constitutionally proportionate so long as they are proportionate in relation to *some* penal purpose? Alternatively, perhaps the plurality is saying that as long as sentences are "grossly" proportionate from a retributive standpoint, legislatures may set punishments on the basis of other policy considerations.

3. *Capital punishment.* The federal constitutional prohibition on cruel and unusual punishment provides an important constraint on the use of the death penalty. Although the Supreme Court has held that the death penalty does not inherently violate the Eighth Amendment, it has prohibited certain practices used by states. (For a more complete discussion of this topic, see *infra* Chapter 7.)

4. *Fines.* The Eighth Amendment prohibits not only cruel and unusual punishment but also the imposition of "excessive fines." In a pair of cases, Austin v. United States, 509 U.S. 602 (1993), and United States v. Bajakajian, 524 U.S. 321 (1998), the Supreme Court applied this principle of proportionality in fines to the controversial practice of civil forfeiture of property used in the commission of crime. In *Austin* the court held that because the purpose of such forfeiture is typically punitive at least in part, such forfeiture qualifies as a fine for purposes of the Eighth Amendment (the ruling does not apply to forfeiture of the proceeds of crime). In *Bajakajian* the court invalidated a statute authorizing forfeiture of currency in amounts larger than $10,000 removed from the country without being duly reported. Bajakajian had failed to report some $350,000 that he had acquired legally and was taking out of the country to pay a lawful debt. An immigrant, Bajakajian apparently feared that government officials would steal the money if they knew of it.

5. *The philosophical debate on recidivist statutes.* Recidivist statutes became increasingly popular in the 1980s and 1990s as part of the new "get-tough" policies that dramatically increased jail and prison populations. These statutes were primarily justified as means to incapacitate the dangerous. Yet surprisingly, recidivist statutes were also defended on retributivist grounds, most notably by Professor Andrew von Hirsch, whose influential 1976 work, Doing Justice, is generally credited with inspiring the movement toward determinate sentencing. An important feature of his argument for desert-based determinate sentencing was his claim that it could also serve the popular legislative goal of incapacitating dangerous offenders. Several retributivist writers questioned von Hirsch's claim. Consider the following argument, by Professor George Fletcher:[25]

---

25. George P. Fletcher, Rethinking Criminal Law 460-66 (1978).

. . . Assuming that prior convictions indicate that a violator is more dangerous, do they also justify a finding of greater desert for the last criminal act?

. . . Von Hirsch's argument is that punishment ought to be inflicted according to desert and that a prior criminal record increases desert. The critical steps in this inference are (1) desert is a function of culpability, [and] (2) a criminal record increases culpability. . . .

We may take as common ground with von Hirsch that punishment ought to be inflicted according to the offender's desert in committing particular criminal offenses. The components of desert are wrongdoing (which von Hirsch calls "harm") and culpability. It is also common ground that a greater degree of wrongdoing justifies greater punishment. The wrongdoing of homicide is greater than a possession offense and therefore a greater punishment is warranted. . . .

Now what is the relationship between wrongdoing and a judgment of culpability based on holding the actor accountable? If the actor is fully accountable, he ought to be fully punished. Yet if his culpability is partial, he ought to be punished less. Lesser culpability justifies a mitigated punishment. . . .

Thus the maximum level of punishment is set by the degree of wrongdoing; punishment is mitigated accordingly as the actor's culpability is reduced. This distinction is critical in understanding our system of criminal law. The wrongdoing of homicide is causing human death; the dimension of wrongdoing is not affected by provocation or diminished capacity. Yet the actor's culpability for the wrongdoing is reduced in these cases and therefore the punishment is properly mitigated. . . .

. . . [L]et us ask how prior convictions affect the offender's desert. It is hard to see how a string of prior burglary convictions could increase the wrongdoing of the current burglary charged in the indictment. Of course two counts of burglary might justify a greater punishment than one. Killing two persons is a greater wrong than killing one. But von Hirsch's proposal is not to relitigate prior criminal acts, presumably already prosecuted and punished, as though they were additional counts in the pending indictment. That would be patently unconstitutional as double jeopardy.

The critical premise in von Hirsch's thesis is not only that diminished culpability serves to reduce punishment, but also that increased culpability may justify increased punishment. . . . [T]he thesis is foreign to our experience of crime and punishment. . . . If an actor . . . [offends] intentionally and voluntarily, his accountability and culpability are complete and there is no need to inquire further into his motives. . . .

If he is arguing against the weight of tradition, von Hirsch should have some good arguments to prove that increased personal culpability merits increased punishment. . . . [His] claim is that

> A repetition of the offense following . . . conviction may be regarded as more culpable, since [the actor] persisted in the behavior after having been forcefully censured for it through his prior punishment.

It is worth noting, initially, the contradictory ways in which repeated offenses may be mustered in arguments for and against the accused. In *Robinson* . . . , repeated acts of addiction tended to excuse the offender, for they hinted at a "condition he was powerless to change." . . . Might we not at least have some doubts about the extent to which repeated offenders are in control of themselves? I am willing to concede that absent a valid excuse, a second offense is voluntary and the actor is accountable and should be punished again. But von Hirsch wants more than that. He claims that the second offense is even more culpable, as though somehow it were more "voluntary" than the first offense.

The key to understanding von Hirsch's argument is the statement: the offender "*persisted* in the behavior." Think of a parent who punishes a teenager who has stayed out too late. The punishment is loss of allowance for a week. If the teenager "persists" in staying out too late, the parent might raise the punishment — after all, the parent seeks compliance with the rules of the house and it might be necessary to raise the punishment in order to achieve it. This example makes von Hirsch's argument at least prima facie plausible.

But let us think more about the case of the teenager. The implication of his "persisting" is not that the offense is more culpable the second time, but that there are signs of an additional wrong of defiance against the parental authority. . . .

Punishment for offenses within the family is different from punishment in a liberal society. . . . If a child persists or threatens to persist in violating the rules of the house, he implicitly undermines parental authority. This is the element of defiance or "rebellion" that constitutes the additional wrong in repeated violations of the rules. . . .

This rebellion against authority is what, to my mind, underlies von Hirsch's argument that a second offense deserves greater punishment than the first. If the family were an appropriate model for civil society, he might be right. But (thank God) the family is not the model for liberal society. Would we have a society in which an offender would risk an additional term in jail if he said, "I will take my punishment, but then I will go back to shoplifting?" Perhaps contrite offenders are punished more leniently, but should proud offenders be punished more severely? Is it a personal wrong to the legislature, to the courts, or to law enforcement personnel for an offender either to threaten or to commit repeat offenses? In raising this issue, we come close, in my mind, to an important difference between a liberal society, based upon the rule of law, and one species of totalitarian society, based upon the cult of personal leadership. . . . [T]his view of authority and defiance clashes with the basic premises of a society based upon formally defined offices. In a society of free and responsible adults, organized to live by the rule of formal authority, the defiant offender is punished according to what he or she does, not according to the implied threat of further disobedience.

Von Hirsch altered his position slightly, in response to these arguments, arguing that first offenders deserved more lenient treatment on the ground that they were only partially culpable.[26] Which side of this debate do you find more convincing: is a second offense more deserving of punishment than a first offense?

Professor Markus Dubber has stressed that neither side in this debate would approve many current recidivist statutes:[27]

> . . . [M]any of the new statutes sweep so broadly that the sentences they mandate often bear no relation to the moral desert of the offender. For example, the newest California recidivist law mandates an indeterminate life sentence for anyone convicted of any third felony if that person had previously been convicted of two serious or violent felonies. For starters, some thirty crimes and their corresponding attempts ranging from any felony with a dangerous weapon to robbery are considered violent or serious felonies under California law. Add to that the recent trend . . . of extending felony status to ever and ever less serious conduct from spraying graffiti to shoplifting, and one ends up with 500 crimes qualifying as a third strike under California's new recidivist law. As a result, the California law has threatened with life imprisonment small time offenders like: the jail inmate who got caught with eight ounces of marijuana; the petty thief who stole $42.52 of hardware; the shoplifter who took sunglasses, a mustache trimmer, a birthday card, and $75 worth of clothes; the "robber" who absconded with pepperoni pizza; the thief who stole a beer from a 7-Eleven, and on and on and on.

26. Andrew von Hirsch, Past or Future Crimes 88-91 (1985).
27. Markus Dirk Dubber, Recidivist Statutes as Arational Punishment, 43 Buff. L. Rev. 689 (1996).

Given the ubiquity of offending, does life imprisonment for such trivial offenses amount to retroactively increasing the punishment for the serious offenses previously committed by these defendants?

G. SENTENCING GUIDELINES

Criticisms of indeterminate sentencing resulted in a wave of sentencing reform legislation in the 1980s beginning with Minnesota's 1980 abolition of parole and establishment of presumptive guidelines for sentencing. In 1984 Congress passed a "Sentencing Reform Act" for the federal criminal justice system, designed to promote determinate sentencing, abolish parole, insure proportionality and uniformity in sentencing, and establish a Sentencing Commission to set up guidelines that would reflect these goals and limit sentencing discretion. The Commission, consisting of judges and academics, devised guidelines that took effect automatically in 1987. While the federal sentencing guidelines have gotten the most attention, guidelines have been adopted in many states and are under study in several more.

As noted in the Introduction, the Supreme Court has recently ruled on the burden of proof for factual allegations used in determining sentences under such guideline schemes, in the case of Apprendi v. New Jersey. We have reproduced portions of this decision in the following material, after a review of the development of sentencing guidelines legislation and explanations of how guidelines work.

KEVIN REITZ, SENTENCING: GUIDELINES,
4 ENCYCLOPEDIA OF CRIME AND JUSTICE
1429-1440 (2002)

The idea of a "commission on sentencing" can be traced to Marvin Frankel's influential writings of the early 1970s, most notably his 1973 book *Criminal Sentences: Law Without Order*. Frankel wanted to replace what he saw as the "lawless" processes of indeterminate sentencing with an alternative model that would promote legal regularity. His chosen vehicles were chiefly *procedural* innovations, and it is possible to identify three fundamental procedural goals in Frankel's plan: (1) The creation of a permanent, expert commission on sentencing in every jurisdiction, with both research and rulemaking capacities; (2) the articulation of broad policies and more specific regulations (later called guidelines) by legislatures and sentencing commissions, to have binding legal authority on case-by-case sentencing decisions made by trial judges; and (3) institution of meaningful appellate review of the appropriateness of individual sentences, so that a jurisprudence of sentencing could develop through the accumulation of case decisions.

Along with these procedural elements, Frankel advocated for two major *substantive* goals: (1) Greater uniformity in punishments imposed upon similarly situated offenders, with a concomitant reduction in inexplicable disparities, including racial disparities in punishment and widely varying sentences based simply on the predilections of individual judges; and (2) a substantial reduction in the overall severity of punishments as imposed by courts throughout the United States, including a general shortening of terms of incarceration, and the expanded use of intermediate punishments. . . .

By midyear 1999, . . . sixteen American jurisdictions were operating with some form of sentencing guidelines (including fifteen states and the federal system). In four additional states, fully developed guideline proposals are under consideration by the state legislatures, and at least three more jurisdictions were in the early stages of deliberations that may eventually lead to commission-based sentencing reform. . . .

Most sentencing guideline systems in America in the late twentieth century used the format of a two-dimensional "grid" or "matrix." . . . Along one axis of the grid, such guidelines rank offense severity on a hierarchical scale. On the other axis, a similar scale reflects the seriousness of the offender's prior criminal history. The guideline sentence in a particular case is derived by moving across the row designated for the offense to be punished, and down the column that corresponds to the offender's past record. . . .

Another central design feature of a sentencing guideline system is the number of severity (or grading) distinctions that the system attempts to capture within the guidelines themselves — as opposed to allowing trial judges discretion to sort among shadings of offense gravity. . . . The grids in state jurisdictions have generally incorporated nine to fifteen levels of offense severity, and four to nine categories for offenders' prior records. . . .

The current federal sentencing guidelines system, inaugurated in 1987, opted for a much more intricate matrix than those used by the states, reflecting a philosophy that the U.S. Sentencing Commission can and should make precise distinctions among cases in advance of adjudication in the courts. The federal grid incorporates forty-three levels of crime seriousness and six categories for prior criminal history, yielding a total of 258 guideline cells. If anything, however, the visual complexity of the federal grid understates the degree to which the federal system attempts to draw fine distinctions among specific cases. Unlike all state guideline systems, offense severity under federal law is not fixed by the crime(s) of conviction. The conviction offense is merely one factor among many fed into a multistep calculation, including "relevant conduct" (other related crimes the defendant probably committed, but for which convictions were not obtained), a point-scale scoring of the "base offense level" (which can go up or down depending on such things as the weight of the drugs involved in a narcotics offense or the amount of money lost in a fraud case), and further point "adjustments" for surrounding circumstances (for example, two points off for "acceptance of responsibility," or two points added for "more than minimal planning"). . . .

Perhaps the most important design feature of existing guideline systems has been the degree of binding legal authority assigned to the sentencing ranges laid out in the guidelines. On one extreme, seven states presently operate with guidelines that are "voluntary," or merely "advisory," to the sentencing judge. In such systems, the court is free to consult or disregard the relevant guideline, and is permitted to impose any penalty authorized by the statute(s) of conviction.

In a bare majority of current guideline structures (nine of sixteen jurisdictions in 1999, including the federal system), the stated guideline range carries a degree of enforceable legal authority. Under the Minnesota scheme, which has been emulated in a number of other states . . . trial courts are instructed that they must use the presumptive sentences in the guideline grid in "ordinary" cases — which in theory include the majority of all sentencing decisions. However, the trial judge retains discretion to "depart" from the guidelines in a case the judge finds to be atypical in some important respect. . . . Ultimately, the appellate courts review whether the trial court has given sufficient reasons for a departure, and whether the degree of departure is consistent with those reasons. . . .

The federal guideline system bears surface similarity to the Minnesota approach, except that the "departure power" retained by trial courts is more strictly limited under federal law than in Minnesota and most other states. . . . A 1997 study found that the chances of a trial court's sentence being reversed on appeal were ten times greater in the federal system than in Minnesota, and fifty times greater than in Pennsylvania. . . .

Among guideline systems as of 2001, nine of sixteen legislatures have chosen to abolish parole release in conjunction with guideline reform — usually under the banner of "truth in sentencing." . . . The remaining seven guideline jurisdictions, however, have retained parole release discretion in some form. . . .

All guideline jurisdictions have found it necessary to create rules that identify the factual issues at sentencing that must be resolved under the guidelines, those that are potentially relevant to a sentencing decision, and those viewed as forbidden considerations that may not be taken into account by sentencing courts. One heated controversy, addressed differently across jurisdictions, is whether the guideline sentence should be based exclusively on crimes for which offenders have been convicted ("conviction offenses"), or whether a guideline sentence should also reflect additional alleged criminal conduct for which formal convictions have not been obtained ("nonconviction offenses"). . . . Sentencing based freely upon both conviction and nonconviction crimes is often called *real-offense sentencing*.

As noted earlier, the federal sentencing guidelines require trial judges to base guideline calculations upon conviction offenses and nonconviction offenses in some circumstances. Under the federal guidelines' "relevant conduct" provision, if a nonconviction crime is related to the offense of conviction (that is, if it is similar in kind or arose from the same episode), and if the defendant's guilt has been established by a preponderance of the evidence during sentencing proceedings, then the trial judge must compute the guideline punishment as though the defendant had been convicted of the nonconviction charge. . . .

State guideline systems have all gone in a different direction than the federal system on this issue. Instead of mandating real-offense sentencing, the consideration of nonconviction crimes is usually restricted to *departure cases* in the states or, in a few jurisdictions, is prohibited outright. All guideline grids set out presumptive sentences based on conviction offenses and prior convictions; no state follows the federal example of adding or substituting nonconviction offenses for purposes of the initial guideline calculation. Thus, presumptive sentences, intended to govern all typical cases, are oriented solely toward conviction crimes. In some guideline states, including all voluntary-guideline jurisdictions, a trial court may deviate from the guidelines in the belief that the defendant's "real" offenses were more numerous or more serious than those reflected in the verdict or guilty plea. . . . In at least three states, even departure sentences based on nonconviction conduct are legally forbidden.

. . . Another difficult issue of fact-finding at sentencing for guideline designers has been the degree to which trial judges should be permitted to consider the personal characteristics of offenders as mitigating factors when imposing sentence. For example: Is the defendant a single parent with young children at home? Is the defendant addicted to drugs but a good candidate for drug treatment? Has the defendant struggled to overcome conditions of economic, social, or educational deprivation prior to the offense? Was the defendant's criminal behavior explicable in part by youth, inexperience, or an unformed ability to resist peer pressure? Most guideline states, once again including all jurisdictions with voluntary guidelines, allow trial courts latitude to sentence outside of the guideline ranges based on the judge's assessment of such offender characteristics. Some states, fearing that race or class disparities might be exacerbated by unguided consideration of such factors, have placed limits on the list of eligible concerns. . . .

Once again, the federal system is an outlier among guideline jurisdictions in its sweeping proscriptions of the consideration of offender characteristics. All of the personal attributes mentioned in the preceding paragraph are treated as forbidden or discouraged grounds for departure in federal law. . . . In contrast to the experience of state judges under state guidelines, U.S. District Court judges complain loudly that the federal guidelines have excised the human component of sentencing decisions. . . .

Marvin Frankel hoped that the rationalizing process of commission-based sentencing reform would ultimately lead to what he viewed as more humane sentencing outcomes overall: a reduced reliance on incarceration. . . . Writing in the early 1970s, Frankel could hardly have predicted that prison and jail confinement rates in America would in fact increase by more than a factor of four in the next twenty-five years. . . . We must ask how much of the incarceration boom has been attributable to the advent of sentncing guidelines.

Some of it clearly has been. In the federal system . . . judges complain regularly that the guidelines . . . force them to impose heavier sentences than they would otherwise have chosen. These claims are consistent with the original legislative and commission intents in promulgating the federal guidelines, as outlined in a 1998 book by Stith and Cabranes: there was widespread political sentiment during the Reagan administration that federal judges had been meting out sentences of undue leniency for many crimes, and the federal guideline reform was directed in large part to preventing that from happening by curtailing the judges' discretion.

Raw statistics suggest that the designers of the federal system got what they wanted. In the first ten years under the new federal guidelines, from 1987 to 1997, the federal imprisonment rate increased by 119 percent. This growth surge was 25 percent greater than the average increase in imprisonment rates for the nation as a whole during the same period. . . .

At the state level, the relationship between guideline reform and sentencing severity has been mixed, but more consistent with Frankel's original vision than the federal experience. A number of state legislatures and commissions have created guideline structures with the express purpose of containing prison growth. . . . In a 1995 study of sentencing commissions operative in the 1980s, Thomas Marvell identified six state commissions that were instructed to consider prison capacity when promulgating guidelines. In all six jurisdictions, Marvell found "comparatively slow prison population growth," prompting him to write that "These findings are a refreshing departure from the usual negative results when evaluating criminal justice reforms."

IV. MINNESOTA SENTENCING GUIDELINES GRID
(August 2003)
Presumptive Sentence Lengths in Months

Italicized numbers within the grid denote the range within which a judge may sentence without the sentence being deemed a departure. Offenders with nonimprisonment felony sentences are subject to jail time according to law.

CRIMINAL HISTORY SCORE

SEVERITY LEVEL OF CONVICTION OFFENSE (Common offenses listed in italics)		0	1	2	3	4	5	6 or more
Murder, 2nd Degree (intentional murder; drive-by shootings)	XI	306 *299-313*	326 *319-333*	346 *339-353*	366 *359-373*	386 *379-393*	406 *399-413*	426 *419-433*
Murder, 3rd Degree Murder, 2nd Degree (unintentional murder)	X	150 *144-156*	165 *159-171*	180 *174-186*	195 *189-201*	210 *204-216*	225 *219-231*	240 *234-246*
Criminal Sexual Conduct, 1st Degree Assault, 1st Degree	IX	86 *81-91*	98 *93-103*	110 *105-115*	122 *117-127*	134 *129-139*	146 *141-151*	158 *153-163*
Aggravated Robbery, 1st Degree Criminal Sexual Conduct, 2nd Degree	VIII	48 *44-52*	58 *54-62*	68 *64-72*	78 *74-82*	88 *84-92*	98 *94-102*	108 *104-112*
Felony DWI	VII	36	42	48	54 *51-57*	60 *57-63*	66 *63-69*	72 *69-75*
Criminal Sexual Conduct, 2nd Degree (a) & (b)	VI	21	27	33	39 *37-41*	45 *43-47*	51 *49-53*	57 *55-59*
Residential Burglary Simple Robbery	V	18	23	28	33 *31-35*	38 *36-40*	43 *41-45*	48 *46-50*
Nonresidential Burglary	IV	12[1]	15	18	21	24 *23-25*	27 *26-28*	30 *29-31*
Theft Crimes (Over $2,500)	III	12[1]	13	15	17	19 *18-20*	21 *20-22*	23 *22-24*
Theft Crimes ($2,500 or less) Check Forgery ($200-$2,500)	II	12[1]	12[1]	13	15	17	19	21 *20-22*
Sale of Simulated Controlled Substance	I	12[1]	12[1]	12[1]	13	15	17	19 *18-20*

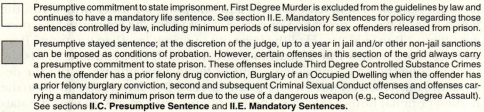

Presumptive commitment to state imprisonment. First Degree Murder is excluded from the guidelines by law and continues to have a mandatory life sentence. See section II.E. Mandatory Sentences for policy regarding those sentences controlled by law, including minimum periods of supervision for sex offenders released from prison.

Presumptive stayed sentence; at the discretion of the judge, up to a year in jail and/or other non-jail sanctions can be imposed as conditions of probation. However, certain offenses in this section of the grid always carry a presumptive commitment to state prison. These offenses include Third Degree Controlled Substance Crimes when the offender has a prior felony drug conviction, Burglary of an Occupied Dwelling when the offender has a prior felony burglary conviction, second and subsequent Criminal Sexual Conduct offenses and offenses carrying a mandatory minimum prison term due to the use of a dangerous weapon (e.g., Second Degree Assault). See sections **II.C. Presumptive Sentence** and **II.E. Mandatory Sentences.**

[1] One year and one day

ROGER W. HAINES JR., FRANK O. BOWMAN III, JENNIFER C. WOLL, FEDERAL SENTENCING GUIDELINES HANDBOOK
18-20 (2002)

The Sentencing Guidelines are like the tax code — mind-numbingly detailed, but carefully constructed, with an overall logic. . . . A defendant's sentence is determined by where the defendant falls on the grid, based on offense level and criminal history category. . . . In simplified form, here are ten steps to use in computing a guidelines sentence.

Step 1. What is the most serious crime of conviction? . . . [Identify the federal criminal statute defining that crime], find the applicable guideline [for that statute] . . . , and find the Base Offense Level for the offense of conviction.

Step 2. What is the Relevant Conduct for this offense of conviction? The concept of relevant conduct is unique to the guidelines. . . . The Base Offense Level includes any other conduct (including *unconvicted conduct*) that involves substantially the same harm. . . . And if the, defendant was involved in a "jointly undertaken criminal activity," relevant conduct . . . includes all "reasonably foreseeable acts" of *others* "in furtherance of" that activity. . . .

Step 3. Are there any Specific Offense Characteristics in the guideline itself? For instance, did the defendant engage in "more than minimal planning?" Was a deadly weapon used? Did bodily injury result? Each, guideline has its own special adjustments. . . .

Step 4. What was the defendant's Role in the Offense? More precisely, what was her Role in the Relevant Conduct? . . . [B]eing an "organizer, leader, manager, or supervisor" earns a defendant a two to four point increase in offense level. On the other side of the coin, being a "minor" participant results in two levels off, and "minimal" participants get four off. . . .

Step 5. Did the defendant Obstruct Justice? If so, add two levels. . . . This includes perjury at trial, but is not limited to post-arrest obstruction. Defendants may obstruct justice by engaging in dangerous high-speed chases to avoid arrest. . . .

Step 6. Was the defendant convicted of Multiple Counts? The second count of equal seriousness adds 2 levels to the overall sentence. . . . But the marginal increase diminishes with the number of counts. . . .

Step 7. Did the defendant show Acceptance of Responsibility? If so, she gets two levels off for remorse and a third level . . . if her offense level is 16 or higher and if she pleads guilty before the government has to prepare for trial. . . .

Step 8. How bad is the defendant's Criminal History? Has she served over a year in prison? If so, . . . add three points for each prior sentence. Add two points for prior sentences of at least 60 days, and one point for lesser priors. Was the defendant on parole, probation or escape status when she committed the present offense? If so, add two. Had she been out of prison less than two years? If so, add two more, unless you added two above, in which case add one. . . . Is the present conviction a felony violent crime or felony drug offense? Is this the defendant's third such offense? If so, she is a Career Offender. . . . She jumps to the highest criminal history category, and her offense level zooms up near the statutory maximum.

Step 9. After all this, is there something the Sentencing Commission forgot to consider? If so, a Departure may be in order. If the defendant cooperates in the investigation of others, the prosecutor may be willing to move for a downward departure. . . . If not, a downward departure may still be possible . . . if the crime was a "single act of aberrant behavior," or . . . where the defendant's criminal history category does not adequately reflect her past criminal history.

Step 10. Is all of this moot because there is a statutory Mandatory Minimum sentence?

A fairly typical federal guideline—this one for robbery—is below.

A SAMPLE FEDERAL GUIDELINE

§2B3.1. Robbery

(a)   Base Offense Level: **20**
(b)   Specific Offense Characteristics
    (1)   If the property of a financial institution or post office was taken, or if the taking of such property was an object of the offense, increase by **2** levels.
    (2)   (A) If a firearm was discharged, increase by **7** levels; (B) if a firearm was otherwise used, increase by **6** levels; (C) if a firearm was brandished or possessed, increase by **5** levels; (D) if a dangerous weapon was otherwise used, increase by **4** levels; (E) if a dangerous weapon was brandished or possessed, increase by **3** levels; or (F) if a threat of death was made, increase by **2** levels.
    (3)   If any victim sustained bodily injury, increase the offense level according to the seriousness of the injury:

Degree of Bodily Injury	Increase in Level
(A) Bodily Injury	add **2**
(B) Serious Bodily Injury	add **4**
(C) Permanent or Life-Threatening Bodily Injury	add **6**

    (D)   If the degree of injury is between that specified in subdivisions (A) and (B), add **3** levels; or
    (E)   If the degree of injury is between that specified in subdivisions (B) and (C), add **5** levels.
    Provided, however, that the cumulative adjustments from (2) and (3) shall not exceed **11** levels.

    (4)   (A) If any person was abducted to facilitate commission of the offense or to facilitate escape, increase by **4** levels; or (B) if any person was physically restrained to facilitate commission of the offense or to facilitate escape, increase by **2** levels.
    (5)   If the offense involved carjacking, increase by **2** levels.
    (6)   If a firearm, destructive device, or controlled substance was taken, or if the taking of such item was an object of the offense, increase by **1** level.
    (7)   If the loss exceeded $10,000, increase the offense level as follows:

Loss (Apply the Greatest)	Increase in Level
(A) $10,000 or less	no increase
(B) More than $10,000	add **1**

(C)	More than $50,000	add **2**
(D)	More than $250,000	add **3**
(E)	More than $800,000	add **4**
(F)	More than $1,500,000	add **5**
(G)	More than $2,500,000	add **6**
(H)	More than $5,000,000	add **7**

MICHAEL TONRY, THE FAILURE OF THE U.S. SENTENCING COMMISSION'S GUIDELINES
39 Crime & Delinquency 131, 135-40 (1993)

Four features of the federal guidelines make them more restrictive than existing state guidelines, and are the source of much of their unpopularity.

First, although the guidelines are in principle "presumptive," and judges have authority to "depart" from them, the grounds for departures are exceedingly limited. Under the governing statute (18 U.S.C. §3553 [b]), judges may depart only on a finding that "there exists an aggravating or mitigating circumstance of a kind, or to a degree, *not adequately taken into consideration by the Sentencing Commission* in formulating the guidelines, that should result in a sentence different from [the guidelines]" (emphasis added). Appellate courts tend to conclude that the Commission must have adequately considered any subject on which it adopted express policy statements.[28]

Second, few approved bases for departures are available and most of the commonsense bases for distinguishing among offenders — for example, a sound employment record, a stable home life, effects of the sentence on dependents — are expressly forbidden. The guidelines provide that age, education, vocational skills, mental and emotional conditions, physical condition including drug dependence and alcohol abuse, employment records, family ties and responsibilities, and community ties are "not ordinarily" relevant in determining whether a sentence should be outside the applicable guideline range. As a result, trial judges have considerable difficulty convincing appellate courts that the Commission did not "adequately consider" offender circumstances.

Third, application of the guidelines is based not on the offense to which the defendant pled guilty or of which he was convicted at trial, but on "actual offense behavior," which the Commission refers to as "relevant conduct." Here is how Judge Heaney summarizes the reach of the relevant conduct rule: "Under the guidelines, however, sentencing judges are routinely required to sentence offenders for 'relevant conduct' which has not been charged in an indictment or information and which was not admitted in a guilty plea or proved at trial.

---

28. A further new restriction on trial judges' power to offer downward departures came in the Prosecutorial Remedies and Other Tools to end the Exploitation of Children Today [PROTECT] Act of 2003. Congress responded to Department of Justice concerns that certain federal trial judges in certain regions had been too generous in granting downward departures, thereby both weakening the deterrent effect of federal sentences and undermining the national uniformity in sentencing that was a premise of the guidelines. While mainly focusing on sentences in child assault cases, Congress also imposed a number of limitations on the power of the federal trial courts to engage in downward departures in federal sentencing generally. Most notably, the new law alters 18 U.S.C. §3742(e), replacing the original provision mandating that appellate courts "shall give due deference to the district court's application of the guidelines to the facts" with a new provision that the Courts of Appeals "shall review de novo the district court's applications of the guidelines to the facts."

Indeed, a court may also increase an offender's sentence for acts of which the offender was acquitted. Uncharged conduct need not be proved beyond a reasonable doubt, but only by a preponderance of the evidence."

An article by the chairman of the Commission argues that the relevant conduct approach is the "cornerstone" of the guidelines. The rationale was that the relevant conduct approach would undermine efforts by prosecutors to manipulate guidelines by dismissing charges to achieve a conviction offense that, under the guidelines, bore the preferred sentence. Every other major American sentencing commission considered and rejected the relevant conduct approach on the basis that prosecutorial manipulation of guidelines, however undesirable, is less undesirable than a sentencing policy that trivializes the significance of convictions based on proof beyond a reasonable doubt. . . .

Fourth, the Commission's guidelines are intended greatly to increase the severity of federal sentencing. [S]entences to probation were greatly reduced; . . . [and] sentences for several categories of offenses — drug crimes, crimes against persons, burglary, and income tax evasion — were increased. . . . The Commission reports that the mean "expected to be served" sentence for all offenders increased from 24 months in July 1984 to 46 months in June 1990.

[Finally], the guidelines have transferred discretion and authority from judges to prosecutors. The Federal Courts Study Committee noted that they "have been told that the rigidity of the guidelines is causing a massive, though unintended, transfer of discretion from the court to the prosecutor."

DANIEL J. FREED, FEDERAL SENTENCING IN THE WAKE OF GUIDELINES
101 Yale L.J. 1681 (1992)

By mid-1988, a number of lawsuits challenged the guidelines as unconstitutional. Some district courts held unprecedented en banc hearings to receive arguments from the Department of Justice and the Commission, both of which supported constitutionality, though on different theories, and from defense attorneys, who argued that the Commission and its guidelines were unconstitutional. Within a year, nearly two hundred judges had written or concurred in decisions holding the new system invalid. In January 1989, the Supreme Court, by an eight-to-one vote, sustained the validity of both the SRA and the Commission. . . . In April 1990, the Federal Courts Study Committee published its final report, containing a chapter sharply critical of the guidelines. It reported that a survey of 270 witnesses found 266 against and four in favor of the guidelines. The detractors all were judges; the four supporters were three Commissioners and Attorney General Richard Thornburgh.

APPRENDI v. NEW JERSEY
Supreme Court of the United States
530 U.S. 466 (2000)

JUSTICE STEVENS delivered the opinion of the Court.

A New Jersey statute classifies the possession of a firearm for an unlawful purpose as a "second-degree" offense . . . punishable by imprisonment for "between five years and 10 years." A separate statute, described by that State's Supreme Court as a "hate crime" law, provides for an "extended term" of imprisonment if the trial judge finds, by a preponderance of the evidence, that "[t]he defendant in committing the crime acted with a purpose to intimidate an individual or group of individuals because of race, color, gender, handicap, religion, sexual orientation or ethnicity." . . . The extended term authorized by the hate crime law for second-degree offenses is imprisonment for "between 10 and 20 years." The question presented is whether the Due Process Clause of the Fourteenth Amendment requires that a factual determination authorizing an increase in the maximum prison sentence for an offense from 10 to 20 years be made by a jury on the basis of proof beyond a reasonable doubt.

At 2:04 A.M. on December 22, 1994, petitioner Charles C. Apprendi, Jr., fired several .22-caliber bullets into the home of an African-American family that had recently moved into a previously all-white neighborhood in Vineland, New Jersey. Apprendi . . . admitted that he was the shooter. After further questioning, . . . he made a statement — which he later retracted — that even though he did not know the occupants of the house personally, "because they are black in color he does not want them in the neighborhood." [Apprendi pleaded to second-degree possession of a firearm for an unlawful purpose, among other offenses.]

. . . The trial judge thereafter held an evidentiary hearing on the issue of Apprendi's "purpose" for the shooting on December 22. Apprendi adduced evidence from a psychologist and from seven character witnesses who testified that he did not have a reputation for racial bias. He also took the stand himself, explaining that the incident was an unintended consequence of overindulgence in alcohol, denying that he was in any way biased against African-Americans, and denying that his statement to the police had been accurately described. The judge, however, found the police officer's testimony credible, and concluded that the evidence supported a finding "that the crime was motivated by racial bias." Having found "by a preponderance of the evidence" that Apprendi's actions were taken "with a purpose to intimidate" as provided by the statute, the trial judge held that the hate crime enhancement applied. . . .

Apprendi appealed, arguing, *inter alia,* that the Due Process Clause of the United States Constitution requires that the finding of bias upon which his hate crime sentence was based must be proved to a jury beyond a reasonable doubt, In re Winship, 397 U.S. 358 (1970). . . . A divided New Jersey Supreme Court affirmed. 731 A. 2d 485 (1999). . . . We granted certiorari and now reverse. . . . [This result] was foreshadowed by our opinion in Jones v. United States, 526 U.S. 227 (1999), construing a federal statute. We there noted that "under the Due Process Clause of the Fifth Amendment and the notice and jury trial guarantees of the Sixth Amendment, any fact (other than prior conviction) that increases the maximum penalty for a crime must be charged in an indictment, submitted to a jury, and proven beyond a reasonable doubt." The Fourteenth Amendment commands the same answer in this case involving a state statute. . . .

[T]he historical foundation for our recognition of these principles extends down centuries into the common law. "[T]o guard against a spirit of oppression and tyranny on the part of rulers," and "as the great bulwark of [our] civil and political liberties," 2 J. Story, Commentaries on the Constitution of the United States 540-541 (4th ed. 1873), trial by jury has been understood to require that "*the truth of every accusation,* whether preferred in the shape of indictment, information, or appeal, should afterwards be confirmed by the unanimous suffrage of twelve of [the defendant's] equals and neighbours. . . ." 4 W. Blackstone, Commentaries on the Laws of England 343 (1769) (hereinafter Blackstone) (emphasis added).

Equally well founded is the companion right to have the jury verdict based on proof beyond a reasonable doubt. "The demand for a higher degree of persuasion in criminal cases was recurrently expressed from ancient times, [though] its crystallization into the formula 'beyond a reasonable doubt' seems to have occurred as late as 1798. It is now accepted in common law jurisdictions as the measure of persuasion by which the prosecution must convince the trier of all the essential elements of guilt." C. McCormick, Evidence §321, pp. 681-682 (1954). . . .

Any possible distinction between an "element" of a felony offense and a "sentencing factor" was unknown to the practice of criminal indictment, trial by jury, and judgment by court as it existed during the years surrounding our Nation's founding. As a general rule, criminal proceedings were submitted to a jury after being initiated by an indictment containing "all the facts and circumstances which constitute the offence, . . . stated with such certainty and precision, that the defendant . . . may be enabled to determine the species of offence they constitute, in order that he may prepare his defence accordingly . . . and *that there may be no doubt as to the judgment which should be given,* if the defendant be convicted." J. Archbold, Pleading and Evidence in Criminal Cases 44 (15th ed. 1862) (emphasis added). The defendant's ability to predict with certainty the judgment from the face of the felony indictment flowed from the invariable linkage of punishment with crime. . . .

Thus, with respect to the criminal law of felonious conduct, "the English trial judge of the later eighteenth century had very little explicit discretion in sentencing. The substantive criminal law tended to be sanction-specific; it prescribed a particular sentence for each offense. The judge was meant simply to impose that sentence (unless he thought in the circumstances that the sentence was so inappropriate that he should invoke the pardon process to commute it)." Langbein, The English Criminal Trial Jury on the Eve of the French Revolution, in The Trial Jury in England, France, Germany 1700-1900, pp. 36-37 (A. Schioppa ed. 1987). . . .

This practice at common law held true when indictments were issued pursuant to statute. Just as the circumstances of the crime and the intent of the defendant at the time of commission were often essential elements to be alleged in the indictment, so too were the circumstances mandating a particular punishment. "Where a statute annexes a higher degree of punishment to a common-law felony, if committed under particular circumstances, an indictment for the offence, in order to bring the defendant within that higher degree of punishment, must expressly charge it to have been committed under those circumstances, and must state the circumstances with certainty and precision. [2 M. Hale, Pleas of the Crown *170]." Archbold, Pleading and Evidence in Criminal Cases, at 51. . . .

We should be clear that nothing in this history suggests that it is impermissible for judges to exercise discretion — taking into consideration various factors relating both to offense and offender — in imposing a judgment *within the range* prescribed by statute. . . . [O]ur periodic recognition of judges' broad discretion in sentencing — since the 19th-century shift in this country from statutes providing fixed-term sentences to those providing judges discretion within a permissible range — has been regularly accompanied by the qualification that that discretion was bound by the range of sentencing options prescribed by the legislature.

The historic link between verdict and judgment and the consistent limitation on judges' discretion to operate within the limits of the legal penalties provided highlight the novelty of a legislative scheme that removes the jury from the determination of a fact that, if found, exposes the criminal defendant to a penalty *exceeding* the maximum he would receive if punished according to the facts reflected in the jury verdict alone. . . .

It was in McMillan v. Pennsylvania, 477 U.S. 79 (1986), that this Court, for the first time, coined the term "sentencing factor" to refer to a fact that was not found by a jury but that could affect the sentence imposed by the judge. That case involved a challenge to the State's Mandatory Minimum Sentencing Act. According to its provisions, anyone convicted of certain felonies would be subject to a mandatory minimum penalty of five years imprisonment if the judge found, by a preponderance of the evidence, that the person "visibly possessed a firearm" in the course of committing one of the specified felonies. . . . [Although] we concluded that the Pennsylvania statute did not run afoul of our previous admonitions against relieving the State of its burden of proving guilt, . . . [w]e did not, . . . budge from the position that (1) constitutional limits exist to States' authority to define away facts necessary to constitute a criminal offense, and (2) that a state scheme that keeps from the jury facts that "expos[e] [defendants] to greater or additional punishment," may raise serious constitutional concern. . . .

In sum, our reexamination of our cases in this area, and of the history upon which they rely, confirms the opinion that we expressed in *Jones*. Other than the fact of a prior conviction, any fact that increases the penalty for a crime beyond the prescribed statutory maximum must be submitted to a jury, and proved beyond a reasonable doubt. . . .[29]

. . . The text of the statute requires the factfinder to determine whether the defendant possessed, at the time he committed the subject act, a "purpose to intimidate" on account of, *inter alia,* race. By its very terms, this statute mandates an examination of the defendant's state of mind — a concept known well to the criminal law as the defendant's *mens rea.* . . . [T]he fact that the language and structure of the "purpose to use" criminal offense is identical in relevant respects to the language and structure of the "purpose to intimidate" provision demonstrates to us that it is precisely a particular criminal *mens rea* that the hate crime enhancement statute seeks to target. The defendant's intent in committing a crime is perhaps as close as one might hope to come to a core criminal offense "element." . . . Despite what appears to us the clear "elemental" nature of

---

29. While a State could, hypothetically, undertake to revise its entire criminal code . . . — extending all statutory maximum sentences to, for example, 50 years and giving judges guided discretion as to a few specially selected factors within that range — this possibility seems remote. Among other reasons, structural democratic constraints exist to discourage legislatures from enacting penal statutes that expose *every* defendant convicted of, for example, weapons possession, to a maximum sentence exceeding that which is, in the legislature's judgment, generally proportional to the crime. . . . In all events, if such an extensive revision of the State's entire criminal code were enacted . . . , or if New Jersey simply reversed the burden of the hate crime finding (effectively assuming a crime was performed with a purpose to intimidate and then requiring a defendant to prove that it was not), we would be required to question whether the revision was constitutional under this Court's prior decisions. . . .

the factor here, the relevant inquiry is one not of form, but of effect — does the required finding expose the defendant to a greater punishment than that authorized by the jury's guilty verdict?

. . . We agree wholeheartedly with the New Jersey Supreme Court that merely because the state legislature placed its hate crime sentence "enhancer" "within the sentencing provisions" of the criminal code "does not mean that the finding of a biased purpose to intimidate is not an essential element of the offense."

The New Jersey procedure challenged in this case is an unacceptable departure from the jury tradition that is an indispensable part of our criminal justice system. Accordingly, the judgment of the Supreme Court of New Jersey is reversed, and the case is remanded for further proceedings not inconsistent with this opinion.

Notes and Questions

1. Recall the question we posed at the end of this chapter's introductory problem: would it be desirable for a jurisdiction to punish only the single crime of causing or threatening social harm, leaving it to the sentencing process to differentiate among offenders? At first glance, nothing seems more at odds with Congress's goals of determinate and proportionate sentencing. But the Commission's guidelines make sentencing "proportionate" to factors other than the actual offense committed. In what ways does the guideline system resemble our hypothetical statute? In what ways is it different? Is it better or worse?

2. Do the problems with the federal sentencing guidelines inhere in the aims of determinate sentencing? Do they inhere in the means of commission-promulgated guidelines?

3. Professor Alan Michaels suggests that the restrictions *Apprendi* imposes on legislative discretion are relatively modest.[30] *Apprendi,* he notes, requires legislatures to state the true maximum penalty for crimes. As for the statute in question, he then argues, the New Jersey legislature could surmount the *Apprendi* obstacle by extending the maximum penalty to twenty years and preventing judges from imposing this maximum for a defendant *lacking* a racially biased motive or "purpose to intimidate." Alternatively, New Jersey could shift the sentencing enhancement to the offense itself, making it an element of the crime. While the sentence imposed on the defendant could have been the same under either of these constructions, the defendant would have been "properly notified" through the statute's provisions as to the penalty he could receive.

4. One criticism of the *Apprendi* decision points out that most convictions result from plea-bargaining rather than trial. Thus prosecutors rarely have to actually bear their burden of proving offense elements beyond a reasonable doubt. But if prosecutors and defendants are precluded from bargaining over sentencing factors, and prosecutors are required to establish sentencing factors by a preponderance of the evidence, real offense sentencing means that the defendant at least gets *some* opportunity to contest *some* of his or her penalty. See Stephanos Bibas, Judicial Fact Finding and Sentencing Enhancements in a World of Guilty Pleas, 110 Yale L.J. 1097 (2001); Jacqueline Ross, Unanticipated

---

30. Truth in Convicting: Understanding and Evaluating *Apprendi,* 12 Fed. Sentencing Rptr. 320 (2000).

Consequences of Turning Sentencing Factors into Offense Elements, 12 Fed. Sent. R. 197 (2000).

5. As noted in the introduction, two subsequent decisions have refined *Apprendi*'s holding. In Harris v. United States, 536 U.S. 545 (2002), the Court refused to require proof to a jury beyond a reasonable doubt of a fact increasing the mandatory minimum (but not extending the sentence beyond the statutory maximum). The court reasoned that when the provision defining the offense prescribes a range of sentences, the jury's verdict has authorized the judge to impose more than the minimum with or without the finding at issue. In Ring v. Arizona, 536 U.S. 584 (2002), the Court extended *Apprendi* in concluding that in the separate penalty hearing in capital punishment cases, the Sixth Amendment grants a capital defendant the right to have a jury determine whether the punishment is life or death. See Chapter 7, *infra*.

6. One of the most controversial aspects of the federal guidelines is "real offense" sentencing based on unproven and uncharged "relevant" conduct. Has *Apprendi*, as modified by *Harris* and *Ring* solved the problem?

II

THE ELEMENTS OF THE CRIMINAL OFFENSE

It is commonly said that a criminal offense consists of two elements: an actus reus (or bad act), and a mens rea (a guilty state of mind). For many crimes, the actus reus involves the causation of some harmful result. Part II examines the general meaning of these requirements of the criminal offense, and the categories of fact that the prosecution must prove to establish each of them.

Though the term "act requirement" may mean the particular actus reus the state must establish beyond a reasonable doubt on a particular criminal charge, Chapter 2 focuses on the more general meaning of the term: the conditioning of just punishment on the proscription of a defined and voluntary instance of conduct. Given the notion of retribution as a "limiting principle of punishment," it follows that moral desert depends on a moral evaluation of actors' choices. Thus, the criminal offense must include some conduct, that is, action or the failure to act where action is called for.

In addition, the limiting principle of retribution may imply that the criminal law should punish proscribed conduct only when it is accompanied by bad thoughts. Chapter 3 examines this principle, and the related assumption that the morally blameworthy person is one who intentionally harms or wrongfully disregards a social interest. Chapter 3 raises the question why we require moral blameworthiness as a requisite of punishment in the first place and then asks how we analyze a particular criminal statute to determine what specific mental states, attached to which specific acts or circumstances, the state must prove to establish "mens rea" or, as it is sometimes called, the "mental element" of the offense. Chapter 3 also explains the distinction between mistakes that negate this mental element, and mistakes that may instead "excuse" defendants from "responsibility" for offenses they nevertheless committed.

The causation of some harmful consequence is part of the act element of many offenses, though not of all. Conversely, the act element of many crimes consists *only* in the causing of some result. Thus the act element of most crimes of homicide is simply the causing of a person's death. Conditioning liability on causing a result raises two large questions: Why punish causation? And what is causation? Chapter 4 examines the philosophical question of why or when actual resulting harm should be an element of a criminal offense. For offenses requiring causation, Chapter 4 examines different approaches to the question of imputing a result to the actions of a particular individual.

2

THE CRIMINAL ACT

It is commonly said that criminal punishment requires that the individual have committed an "act," and that the "actus reus" (criminal or bad act) is a necessary element in the equation establishing criminal liability.

This "act requirement" is really two distinct requirements: (1) the conditioning of just punishment on the proscription, charging, and proof of an "actus reus"; and (2) the particular actus reus the prosecution must charge and prove beyond a reasonable doubt in order to establish liability for a particular crime. This chapter is concerned with the first of these requirements, the "requirement of an act." As for the second, the "actus reus" of many particular offenses (such as the various forms of homicide) includes the causation of harm, which is the subject of Chapter 4; we will examine the "actus reus" of attempt, complicity, conspiracy, theft, and rape in the chapters on those subjects; and we touch on the particular "actus reus" of a number of other crimes as they happen to arise throughout the book.

Considered on its own, the "requirement of an act" is an amorphous idea because of its link to diffuse and contestable ideas about deserved punishment and about the permissible scope of state power. But while Chapter 1 revealed that the purposes of criminal punishment are the subject of lively controversy, it also introduced a proposition about punishment on which there is widespread consensus: Desert is a necessary condition for punishment. This is the concept we called "retribution as a limiting principle of punishment." One approach to interpreting the retributive limits on the criminal law begins with the common sense assumption that moral desert depends on a moral evaluation of actors' choices. This in turn implies a psychological assumption: that human beings are capable of critically evaluating their own desires and resisting them if, on reflection, it appears that pursuing those desires would be wrong. Arguably, people cannot deserve punishment merely for having ignoble desires, but only for failing to resist them. Punishable crime, in other words, should be confined to failures of self-control. That moral precept underlies the many legal issues explored in this chapter.

At the very least, the conditioning of desert on choice implies that deserved punishment must be for some conduct, that is, either action or the failure to act where action is called for. Since we may always be said to be doing or not doing *something* (you will encounter a statute in this chapter that punishes loafing!), punishment must be conditioned on inherently bad conduct, to prevent blame attaching to bad thoughts entertained while one is engaged in some innocuous course of conduct. In addition, if we premise punishment on the assumption that people can exercise choice, punishment must be for *past* conduct; we cannot punish people for falling into some demographic category that is statistically likely to commit crime, or for exhibiting some condition which tends to be a predictor of future crime. Additionally, if the idea of moral choice implies voluntariness, we will want to restrict punishment to voluntary conduct.

But, as the material in this chapter will confirm, judgments of voluntariness are deeply controversial. Moreover, though there is little discernible difference between the claims that, (1) because a particular defendant acted involuntarily, she committed no actus reus, and (2) because she acted involuntarily, she should be excused from responsibility, the law treats these claims differently, and the legal outcome may depend on the way in which the defense is framed. Most notably, the first claim is one that the prosecution may have to disprove beyond a reasonable doubt, while the second may be one the defense must prove by a preponderance of the evidence. (See the Introduction, *supra*.)

Depending on why we think criminal punishment should be restricted to choices manifested in voluntary conduct, we may see further implications to the retributive limit on punishment. We might be concerned that punishing people for thoughts alone, or for involuntary conduct, does not give them a fair chance to avoid liability. In other words, we might view the voluntary conduct requirement as a way to protect autonomy. Alternatively, we might be concerned that criminally punishing thoughts could lead to intrusive government monitoring — that is, the voluntary conduct requirement may be a device for protecting our privacy. Finally, we might be concerned that the intangibility of thoughts makes it temptingly easy to ascribe evil thoughts to persons whom officials wish to punish for some other, illegitimate reason, such as race or ethnicity. Hence, we may view the voluntary conduct requirement as a way of insuring equal status before the law.

All three of these libertarian concerns (autonomy, privacy, and equality) may argue for publicly and prospectively specifying what voluntary conduct will be criminally punishable. Thus, we may not wish to punish everyone who manifests a bad character by making an immoral choice. We may wish to further limit punishment to those who commit acts we define in advance as discrete crimes. (Recall our hypothetical statute from Chapter 1, punishing the single crime of "causing or threatening harm to society.") If we condition punishment on the prior specification of crimes, we enhance the control that individuals have over whether they provoke investigation and punishment, and we set up public standards of deserved punishment against which we can measure the actions of officials charged with investigation and punishment. But note how our expanded conception of the retributive limits on punishment has begun to conflict with retributivism as an affirmative justification for punishment — for now we are suggesting that moral desert is an *insufficient* condition for punishment. In any case, the idea that criminally punishable conduct should be specified in advance is usually referred to as the principle of legality, and traditionally expressed by the maxim, "no crime without a law, no punishment without a law." In this way we may limit the concept of "criminal act" to acts identified as criminal by an appropriate procedure.

While we usually think of a law as the product of a legislature, there is no inherent reason why crimes could not be prospectively defined and proscribed by the judiciary, or an administrative agency, like the United States Sentencing Commission. Yet if the point of the principle of legality is to enhance the autonomy of citizens and control the discretion of officials, it is plausible to think that legality further demands that crimes be defined and proscribed by democratically elected legislators. The retributivist tradition has long associated the idea of autonomy with subjection to a law that is, at least in some attenuated sense, a law of one's own choosing.[1] We may vindicate this conception of autonomy by requiring that criminal law be made with the collective consent of those subject to it. Thus the principle of legality embraces not only the principles of publicity, prospectivity, and specificity, but also that of democracy. This last principle may militate in the direction of legislative definition of crimes.

In sum, "the requirement of an act" may refer to some or all of the following seven conditions for just punishment: that punishment must be for (1) past (2) voluntary (3) wrongful (4) conduct (5) specified (6) in advance (7) by statute. As suggested in the Introduction, *supra,* such ideas about just punishment show up as interpretations of the requirements of constitutional due process, as principles of common law, and as criteria for interpreting statutes.

A. THE NEED FOR AN ACTUS REUS

PROCTOR v. STATE
Criminal Court of Appeals of Oklahoma
176 P. 771 (1918)

GALBRAITH, SPECIAL JUDGE.

The plaintiff in error was convicted of "keeping a place, to wit, a two-story building, with the intent and for the purpose of unlawfully selling, bartering, and giving away spirituous, vinous, fermented and malt liquors," etc.

To the information a demurrer was interposed upon the ground that the information fails to charge a public offense . . . and that section 4 of chapter 26, Session Laws of Oklahoma 1913, on which said information is based, is unconstitutional and void.

The statute under which the charge was laid (section 4 of chapter 26, Session Laws 1913) reads as follows:

Sec. 4. It shall be unlawful for any person to rent to another or keep a place with the intention of, or for the purpose of manufacturing, selling, bartering, giving away, or otherwise furnishing, any spirituous, vinous, fermented or malt liquors. Any person violating any provision of this section shall be punished by a fine of not less than fifty ($50.00) dollars, nor more than two thousand ($2,000.00) dollars, and by imprisonment of not less than thirty (30) days in the county jail, nor more than five (5) years in the state penitentiary.

1. See Guyora Binder, Punishment Theory: Moral or Political? 5 Buff. Crim. L. Rev. 321, 350-366 (2002).

It is alleged upon this appeal that the demurrer to the information was improperly overruled.

It is argued that the above statute is in excess of the power vested in the Legislature, in this, that it makes a mere intention, unexecuted, and not connected with any overt act, a crime, and that this is an impossible thing in organized society under a constitutional government. It is further argued that the ownership of property, namely, "the keeping of a place," is an entirely lawful act and that, when this lawful act is accompanied with an unlawful intent to violate the law at some future and indefinite time, that cannot be declared by statute to be a crime, so long as the unlawful intent is not connected with some overt act, to place the unlawful intent into operation by possession of intoxicating liquors [or] actual "sale or barter"; that this statute runs counter to the first and fundamental principles of law and is absolutely inoperative and void.

It is admitted on behalf of the state that ownership of property, that is, "the keeping of a place," is an innocent and lawful act, but it is contended that this statute was enacted in the exercise of the police power, and that, if the Legislature determined that "the keeping of a place" with the purpose and intent of selling, bartering, and giving away of intoxicating liquors was detrimental to the good morals and public welfare, or was essential in the enforcement of the prohibitory law, it was within the legislative power to declare such use of property to be criminal, and an offense against the law; that the statute itself does not run counter to the fundamental principles of the law; and that it does not condemn the ownership or use of property, a mere "keeping of a place," but, when property is kept or used with the unlawful intent to violate the law, it is within the condemnation of the statute and is properly denominated a crime; that the keeping a place connected with an intent to violate the law constitutes an overt act and may properly be declared to be an offense against the law. The following excerpt from the Attorney General's brief will render his position clear:

> Can it be said that the Legislature intended to make that punishable which is absolutely incapable of proof? An "unexecuted intent" to do a thing amounts merely to a thought, and thoughts without action cannot be punished and were never intended to be punished. But it may be said that, if a person shall establish a building or place without having possession of liquor, and thereafter should say to several of his friends that some time in the future he intended to sell liquors in that particular building or place, what is to prevent his punishment under the laws?
>
> Here we have the keeping of the place and his voluntary statements that he intends to use such place unlawfully in the future. Our answer is that there must exist a present keeping and a present intent, and this keeping and intent, coupled, constitute the overt act. The intent is a question of fact, not of law. No intent, however felonious, unless coupled with some overt act, is criminal.

It will be observed that here is a clear admission on the part of the state that the information in the instant case was insufficient, inasmuch as the unlawful intent was not connected directly with some overt act and therefore that the demurrer thereto was well taken. It cannot be true that "the keeping of a place," coupled with the present intent to violate the law, constitutes an overt act. It is admitted that "the keeping of a place" is an innocent thing, and that an unexecuted criminal intent is not punishable as a crime, and therefore that no crime is charged.

The possession or ownership of liquors is not alleged in the information, nor is it alleged that the liquors were manufactured, bartered, or given away in the place kept. The information does not attempt to charge an overt act or any attempt to place the unlawful intention into execution. As it stands, the information upon its face charges: First, the keeping of a place, an admittedly lawful act; and, second, the possession of an unexecuted unlawful intent to barter, sell, or give away liquor. And it is admitted that this unlawful intent, so long as unexecuted, amounts merely to a thought, and is not subject to punishment. In the language of Mr. Justice Sherwood, of the Supreme Court of Missouri: "With a mere guilty intent unconnected with an overt act, or outward manifestation, the law has no concern." Ex parte Smith, 135 Mo. 223, 36 S.W. 628, 33 L.R.A. 606, 53 Am. St. Rep. 576.

So in the instant case the information merely charges an innocent act, "the keeping of a place," and the possession of an unlawful, unexecuted intent, and attempts to make that a crime. There is no overt act charged in the information in connection with the unlawful intent. It is true the charging part of the information is in the language of the statute, and would be sufficient if the statute defined a crime, but the statute itself fails to define a crime, inasmuch as it attempts to make an innocent act, namely "keeping a place," accompanied with an unlawful and unexecuted intent to violate the law, a crime. This the Legislature had no power to do, whatever may have been its intention in enacting the statute under consideration. To constitute a crime there must be some omission or commission.

intent is not enough alone

An intent to commit a crime is not indictable, and, although the intent is, in general, of the very essence of a crime, some overt act is the only sufficient evidence of the criminal intent. Kelley's Crim. Law & Prac. par. 5; 4 Blackstone Comm. 21, Howell v. Stewart, 54 Mo. 400; State v. Painter, 67 Mo. 84. The essential elements necessary to constitute a crime under the law are enumerated in Blackstone Comm. book 4, p.20, as follows:

> An involuntary act, as it has no claim to merit, so neither can it induce any guilt; the concurrence of the will, when it has its choice either to do or to avoid the fact in question being the only thing that renders human action either praiseworthy or culpable. Indeed, to make a complete crime cognizable by human laws, there must be both a will and an act. For, though, in foro conscientiae, a fixed design or will to do an unlawful act is almost as heinous as the commission of it, yet as no temporal tribunal can search the heart, or fathom the intention of the mind, otherwise than as they are demonstrated by outward actions, it therefore cannot punish for what it cannot know. For which reason, in all temporal jurisdictions, an overt act, or some open evidence of an intended crime, is necessary in order to demonstrate the depravity of the will, before the man is liable to punishment. And, as a vicious will without a vicious act is no civil crime, so, on the other hand, an unwarrantable act without a vicious will is no crime at all. So that to constitute a crime against human laws there must be, first, a vicious will; and, secondly, an unlawful act consequent upon such vicious will.

must also have an act

To the same effect Mr. Bishop, in his work on Criminal Law, vol. 1, announces the rule applicable to the question under consideration as follows, in section 204:

> Now the state that complains in criminal causes, does not suffer from the mere imaginings of men. To entitle her to complain, therefore, some act must have

followed the unlawful thought. This doctrine is fundamental, and, in a general way, universal; but slight differences in its common law applications appear in the books, and now and then a statute is enacted departing from judicial precedent.

In section 206:

Sec. 206. From the foregoing views results the rule established in the legal authorities that an act and evil intent must combine to constitute in law a crime.

And in section 207:

Sec. 207. And generally, perhaps always, the act and intent must, to constitute an offense, concur in point of time.

We quite agree with Justice Sherwood that:

Human laws and human agencies have not yet arrived at such a degree of perfection as to be able without some overt act done, to discern and to determine by what intent or purpose the human heart is actuated.

We conclude that "the keeping of a place" with the unlawful purpose and intent to sell, barter, or give away intoxicating liquors cannot be declared to be a crime, for the reason that such an act, although connected with an unlawful intent, still lacks an essential element necessary to constitute a crime under the law, in this, that the statute fails to connect such unlawful intent with any overt act, as a result or consequence, and further fails to charge the possession of the liquors, the very means essential to the consummation of the unlawful purpose to violate the prohibitory law, and therefore the statute under consideration does not define a crime, and that the information in the instant case did not charge an offense, and the demurrer thereto was well taken, and should have been sustained.

It is therefore ordered that the judgment of conviction be vacated, and the cause remanded, with direction to the trial court to discharge the accused.

Notes and Questions

1. The principle stressed by the court — that the criminal law punishes only a person who has committed an act — needs considerable qualification. According to the court, the prosecutor here failed to charge Proctor with an "overt act" in connection with the alleged culpable intent. What does the court mean by an "overt act"? Did Proctor indeed "do" nothing? How did the prosecutor manage to prove that Proctor had the required evil intent?

2. Is the *Proctor* court concerned that the conduct proscribed by the express terms of the statute caused no one any harm? Should that matter when the legislature has explicitly condemned the conduct?

3. *Purpose of the act requirement.* Courts and scholars often describe the requirement of an act as a fundamental necessity of criminal punishment in a civilized state. Why? Is it that we do not want to punish people merely for their thoughts or for their evil dispositions? If so, why not? Or is it the difficulty of proving evil intent, unless the person has committed some act manifesting it? Or is it

that we feel that the state should allow individuals to know precisely at what point they will be crossing the line beyond which they will incur punishment?

Professor Herbert Packer offers this explanation:[2]

It may hardly seem a startling notion that the criminal law, or law in general for that matter, is concerned with conduct — people's actions (including their verbal and other expressive actions) and their failures to act. Yet there is nothing in the nature of things that compels this focus. The criminal law could be concerned with people's thoughts and emotions, with their personality patterns and character structures. It is true that if this rather than conduct was the focus, it would still be expedient in most cases to ascertain these essentially internal characteristics through inquiry into conduct. But if these internal characteristics were the focus, conduct would simply be evidence of what we are interested in rather than the thing itself; and we would not hesitate to use other evidence to the extent that it became available. If, for example, we could determine through projective tests like the Rorschach or through other and more sophisticated forms of psychological testing that a given individual was likely to inflict serious physical injury on someone, someday, somewhere, and if we viewed conduct as merely evidentiary rather than as a prerequisite, we would presumably not hesitate to inflict punishment on that person for his propensities, or, as the old cliche has it, for thinking evil thoughts. We might rationalize this simply by saying that we were punishing him for the offense of having flunked his Rorschach test, but we would then be acting on a somewhat Pickwickian definition of "conduct."

Why do we not do so? The obvious historical answer is that, aside from a few antiquarian anomalies such as the offense of imagining the King's death, we have not been sufficiently stirred by the danger presented or sufficiently confident of our ability to discern propensities in the absence of conduct to use the instruments of the criminal law in this fashion. For some it may be enough to rejoice that historically this was so and to rest on that historical accident for the present and the future, but I think that a further answer is required. This answer turns, in my view, on the idea of culpability, that necessary but insufficient condition of criminal liability that is an important part of our integrated theory of criminal punishment.

Among the notions associated with the concept of "culpability" are those of free will and human autonomy. I do not mean this in any deep philosophical sense but in a contingent and practical social sense. It is important, especially in a society that likes to describe itself as "free" and "open," that a government should be empowered to coerce people only for what they do and not for what they are.

If this is important for law generally, it is a fortiori important for that most coercive of legal instruments, the criminal law. Now, this self-denying ordinance can be and often is attacked as being inconsistent with the facts of human nature. People may in fact have little if any greater capacity to control their conduct (some say in part, some say in whole) than their emotions or their thoughts. It is therefore either unrealistic or hypocritical, so the argument runs, to deal with conduct as willed or to treat it differently from personality or character.

This attack is, however, misconceived. Neither philosophic concepts nor psychological realities are actually at issue in the criminal law. The idea of free will in relation to conduct is not, in the legal system, a statement of fact, but rather a value preference having very little to do with the metaphysics of determinism and free will. The fallacy that legal values describe physical reality is a very common one. . . . But we need to dispose of it here, because it is such a major impediment to rational thought about the criminal law. Very simply, the law treats man's conduct as

2. The Limits of the Criminal Sanction 73-75, 76 (1968).

autonomous and willed, not because it is, but because it is desirable to proceed as if it were. It is desirable because the capacity of the individual human being to live his life in reasonable freedom from socially imposed external constraints (the only kind with which the law is concerned) would be fatally impaired unless the law provided a locus poenitentiae, a point of no return beyond which external constraints may be imposed but before which the individual is free — not free of whatever compulsions determinists tell us he labors under but free of the very specific social compulsions of the law . . .

It may seem anomalous, particularly to those with some training in the conventional doctrines of the criminal law, that we should fasten here on conduct as limitation on culpability. The orthodox view is that culpability is primarily a matter of the actor's mental state, rather than of the conduct in which he engages . . . And yet, the paradoxical fact is that the limitation of criminal punishment to conduct constitutes the first and most important line of defense against erosion of the idea of culpability, for it keeps the criminal law from becoming purely the servant of the utilitarian ideal of prevention.

Review the reasons Packer offers for confining punishment to acts. Do they also justify confining punishment to acts that manifest an evil or antisocial intent? Or may we punish acts that are equivocal as long as an antisocial intent can be proven with some evidence other than the act itself? This problem is particularly important in defining the requisite conduct element for crimes of attempt. (See Chapter 10.)

4. Note that not all moral systems require an act as a prerequisite to sinning. The Baltimore Catechism teaches that "Actual sin is any willful thought, desire, word, action, or omission forbidden by the law of God."[3]

B.   OMISSIONS

What if it is categorically clear that a defendant committed no act because the charge is that she *omitted* to act? In Jones v. United States, 308 F.2d 307 (D.C. Cir. 1962), Jones was convicted of involuntary manslaughter, a crime involving the causing of death. Shirley Green had a child out of wedlock, and to avoid the embarrassment of having the child in her home, she arranged for Jones, a family friend, to take care of the child in her own home after birth.[4] When the baby was ten months old, officers removed him to the D.C. General Hospital where he was diagnosed as suffering from severe malnutrition and lesions over large portions of his body, apparently caused by severe diaper rash. Following admission, he was fed repeatedly, apparently with no difficulty, and was described as being very hungry. His death, 34 hours after admission, was attributed without dispute to malnutrition. Jones took exception to the failure of the trial court to charge that the jury must find beyond a reasonable doubt, as an element of the crime, that appellant was under a legal duty to supply food and necessities to Anthony Lee. The court held that "under some circumstances the omission of a duty

---

3. This We Believe: By This We Live, Revised Edition of the Baltimore Catechism No. 3, 49-50 (1949).

4. It was uncontested that during the entire period the children were in appellant's home, appellant had ample means to provide food and medical care.

owed by one individual to another, where the omission results in the death of the one to whom the duty is owing, will make the other chargeable with manslaughter, but that . . . [t]his rule of law is always based upon the proposition that the duty neglected must be a legal duty, and not a mere moral obligation."[5] More specifically, it identified four situations in which the failure to act may constitute breach of a legal duty: "One can be held criminally liable: first, where a statute imposes a duty to care for another; second, where one stands in a certain status relationship to another;[6] third, where one has assumed a contractual duty to care for another; and fourth, where one has voluntarily assumed the care of another and so secluded the helpless person as to prevent others from rendering aid."

The *Jones* Court reversed for a new trial, because

> in any of the four situations, there are critical issues of fact which must be passed on by the jury — specifically in this case, whether appellant had entered into a contract with the mother for the care of Anthony Lee or, alternatively, whether she assumed the care of the child and secluded him from the care of his mother, his natural protector. . . . In spite of this conflict, the instructions given in the case failed even to suggest the necessity for finding a legal duty of care. The only reference to duty in the instructions was the reading of the indictment which charged, inter alia, that the defendants "failed to perform their legal duty." A finding of legal duty is the critical element of the crime charged and failure to instruct the jury concerning it was plain error . . .

Though the defendant was successful on appeal in *Jones,* the case makes clear that the state may sometimes punish people for omissions. If a properly instructed jury had found that Jones had undertaken a duty to care for Anthony Lee Green, Jones would be deemed to have caused the death, even though her conduct was entirely passive. Would such a result violate the principle of *Proctor?* Is it not obvious that all citizens face potential criminal liability for such omissions as failure to file income tax returns?

The court in *Jones* sets out four situations in which the failure to act may constitute a breach of a legal duty. What do these situations have in common? Are they broad enough to ensure the punishment for all blameworthy omissions?

Consider Model Penal Code section 2.01(3):

> Liability for the commission of an offense may not be based on an omission unaccompanied by action unless:
> (a) the omission is expressly made sufficient by the law defining the offense; or
> (b) a duty to perform the omitted act is otherwise imposed by law.

Notes and Questions

1. Review again Professor Packer's reasons for conditioning punishment on conduct. Are these purposes achieved when omissions are punished? Does

---

5. Quoting People v. Beardsley, 150 Mich. 205, 206 (1907) (see p. 284, *infra*).
6. 10 A.L.R. Annot. 1137 (1921) (parent to child); Territory v. Manton, 8 Mont. 95, 19 P. 387 (husband to wife); Regina v. Smith, 8 Carr. & P. 153 (Eng. 1837) (master to apprentice); United States v. Knowles, 26 Fed. Cas. 800 (No. 15,540) (ship's master to crew and passengers); cf. State v. Reitze, 86 N.J.L. 407, 92 A. 576 (innkeeper to inebriated customers).

punishing omission amount to anything more than punishing someone for her thoughts alone? Given that we punish omitters for neglecting a duty, we may be punishing some people when they neither act nor think. Does confining punishment to those with customarily recognized duties to act solve these problems? If so, is it important that the duties that can give rise to liability for omissions be specified in a statute?

2. *The scope of duty.* Prof. Michael Moore argues that the rule of limiting criminal liability for omissions to special cases of duty derives from general retributivist principles:[7]

> For we have no duties to prevent many of the world's evils. Our own individual interests in leading lives of beauty, interest, creativity, and enjoyment justify us in not sacrificing those attributes of our lives in the saintly quest to make the world better. Consider the choice faced by the character in Camus's *The Fall:* a woman has fallen (or thrown herself) into the Seine, and he could risk his own life by jumping into the dark waters and trying to save her. Camus's character understandably feels guilty that he did not choose to rescue, but such guilt should not be taken to indicate a failure of duty. Even if the chance of his own drowning was relatively small, and the chances of successful rescue correspondingly high, he had no obligation to put himself at such risk. His felt guilt betokens a negative judgment about himself, namely that he did not live up to the lofty ideals that he professed to admire (as a tireless seeker of social justice). Such negative judgment is a truthful one: he did not behave as virtuously as he might have. But such judgment is about a failure of supererogation, not a failure of obligation. . . .
>
> Notice that the risk and inconvenience justifying not doing certain life-saving actions would hardly justify (active) killings. If a gunman threatens us with a loss of our own life if we do not kill a woman on a bridge over the Seine, yet we could easily escape that threat by jumping into the dark waters and have a good chance of surviving, we cannot justify killing by the risk of drowning were we to jump.[8]

3. Consider the following hypothetical:

A small child is drowning in a public swimming pool as twenty adults look on. The spectators include: various bystanders, the lifeguard, the child's babysitter, a municipal official, the child's cousin, a close friend of the child's parents, and a stranger who had stumbled, accidentally pushing the child into the pool.

Do they all have a duty to save him? Does any one? Does only the adult family member closest to the child have a duty? The one standing closest? The best swimmer? See Wisc. Stat. Ann. (West 1991) §940.34:

Duty to aid victim or report crime:

(1) (a) Whoever violates sub. (2)(a) is guilty of a Class C misdemeanor . . .

(2) (a) Any person who knows that a crime is being committed and that a victim is exposed to bodily harm shall summon law enforcement officers or other assistance or shall provide assistance to the victim . . .

(2)(d) A person need not comply with this subsection if any of the following apply:

1. Compliance would place him or her in danger.

7. Act and Crime 54-56 (1993).
8. But see when the affirmative defense of duress does apply, Chapter 8, *infra*.

2. Compliance would interfere with duties the person owes to others.

3. In the circumstances described under par. (a), assistance is being summoned or provided by others.

Do the restrictions on application of this misdemeanor charge solve the problems of charging for not acting? What about a person who thinks no one else is summoning assistance and still does not summon assistance — would that be a violation of this statute?

Might laws punishing omissions actually disserve law enforcement?[9]

Prof. Eugene Volokh argues against duty-to-help laws, noting that many people who at first hesitate to intervene or report crimes or accidents — out of panic, fear, mistake, hurry, misguided loyalty, or simply reluctance to get involved — later feel remorse and will at least provide useful information, if not help later, unless they are deterred by fear of liability.

4. *Contracts for care.* In Commonwealth v. Pestinikas, 617 A.2d 1339 (Pa. Super. 1992), the court found that the failure to fulfill an oral contract with a sick, elderly person to provide food, medicine, and other necessities can sustain a conviction for murder where it established so clear a breach of promise as to indicate "malice." The defendants in this case had embezzled from the bank account of the victim, who died of starvation and dehydration.

5. *Family status.* New York's highest court has ruled that a stepmother is legally obliged to protect her stepchild even from abuse inflicted by the child's biological parent, who is her husband. People v. Carroll, 93 N.Y.2d 564, 715 N.E.2d 500 (1999) (upholding child endangerment charge in killing of child during ten-day visit of child with defendant and her husband).

6. Does a mother have a "legal duty" to take steps to prevent her husband from raping her daughter where the child had told her of previous assaults? In Degren v. State, 722 A.2d 887 (Md. 1999), the court held that an adult with responsibility for supervising a child may be found guilty of child sexual abuse if the adult fails to prevent abuse by another. The defendant took no action when her husband and another man committed sexual acts on a 12-year-old child; the court construed the statutory term "any act that involves sexual molestation or exploitation of a child" to include "acts of omission" and the word "involves" to cover failure to act. But see Knox v. Commonwealth, 735 S.W.2d 711 (Ky. 1987) (no "legal duty" to prevent rape of child can be inferred from general child abuse and neglect laws).

We will see this question again when we deal, in Chapter 11, with doctrines of complicity, whereby parents who claim to have been "merely present" during the child abuse may be assessed liability. See pp. 695-696, *infra.* We will also revisit the role of duties in attributing harmful results to passive agents in Chapter 4, on the causation of harm.

C. POSSESSION

The *Proctor* court suggested that the outcome might have been different if the defendant had been charged with possessing liquor. But is possession an act?

---

9. Duties to Rescue and the Anticooperative Effects of the Law, 88 Geo. L.J., 105 1999.

More importantly, is it an *actus reus,* a sufficiently bad act to merit criminal liability? According to Model Penal Code Section 2.01 (4), "Possession is an act . . . if the possessor knowingly procured or received the thing possessed or was aware of his control thereof for a sufficient period to have been able to terminate his possession." Does this make possession an *omission?* Is possession merely the *status* of proximity to an object that could be used to cause harm? Does it require the *intention,* or only the *opportunity* to use such an object? Consider the Court's conclusion that the defendant possessed drugs in the following case.

UNITED STATES v. MALDONADO
United States Court of Appeals for the First Circuit
23 F.3d 4 (1994)

BOUDIN, CIRCUIT JUDGE.

On July 2, 1992, a jury convicted Rafael Angel Zavala Maldonado ("Zavala") of possession of cocaine with intent to distribute, in violation of 21 U.S.C. §841(a)(1). On appeal, Zavala argues that the evidence was insufficient to support the conviction. . . . For the reasons set forth, we affirm.

. . . In January 1992, Ruben de los Santos ("Santos"), a seaman serving on board the M/V Euro Colombia, was in the port of Cartagena, Colombia. There, a drug dealer gave Santos sixteen packages of cocaine, amounting to a total of eight kilograms, and asked Santos to deliver them as instructed when the ship docked at the port of Ponce, Puerto Rico.

Santos had earlier been approached by American law enforcement agents attached to the Customs Service, and he accepted the cocaine in Cartagena with the approval of the agents, who intended to track the drugs to their destination. . . . [O]n arriving in Ponce, . . . Santos . . . went to the Hotel Melia in Ponce and asked at the front desk for Mr. Palestino [, as instructed] by the dealer who had given him the cocaine. . . .

When the clerk called from the desk to the room registered to Palestino, the defendant Zavala appeared and gestured to Santos to follow him to room 302. There Santos, who was carrying the cocaine in a bag, told Zavala that he had the drugs to be delivered to Palestino. Zavala said that he was a friend of Palestino and that Palestino would come to the hotel. Using a cellular telephone, Zavala then placed a call, purportedly to Palestino. Then at Santos' urging Zavala called a second time to ask Palestino to come quickly. Zavala asked Santos if they could put the cocaine in another hotel room, saying that he (Zavala) had other friends in the hotel, but Santos refused.

As time passed and Palestino still did not arrive, Santos became increasingly anxious and he proposed to Zavala that they go out of the room for a soda. Zavala agreed, Santos placed the bag with the cocaine in a closet or dressing room in room 302, and the two men left room 302 and entered the corridor. As they went down the stairs, the supervising customs agent detained them. When Santos explained that Palestino had still not arrived, Zavala was taken back to room 302 in custody, accompanied by Santos and one or more agents. There were several more calls to the room purportedly from Palestino, two or three on the cellular telephone and one on the hotel telephone; in each case Santos told the caller that Zavala was out or otherwise occupied.

Shortly after the final call, the operation came to an end. Law enforcement agents [then arrested two men in the hotel whom they believed to be Palestino and his driver, but neither was charged.] . . . Zavala, however, was charged as previously described, and convicted on one count: possession with intent to distribute.

Zavala's primary claim is that an acquittal should have been ordered on grounds of insufficient evidence to prove possession. . . . [T]he conviction for possession can stand only if a reasonable jury could find that Zavala did possess the cocaine within the meaning of 21 U.S.C. §841. If the statute used the term "possess" as a lay juror might understand it prior to instructions from the judge, it might be a stretch to say that Zavala "possessed" the cocaine in the bag. There is no evidence that he even touched the bag or saw the cocaine or that he was ever alone in the room with it or that he had a practical opportunity to remove it from the hotel. These facts explain why Zavala's main argument on appeal is that his relationship to the cocaine cannot be deemed "possession."

The difficulty with the argument is that the concept of possession in the drug statute comes freighted with a history of interpretation. . . . Under settled law, "possession" includes not merely the state of immediate, hands-on physical possession but also "constructive" possession, including possession through another, and joint as well as exclusive possession. Further these concepts can be combined so that, for example, "joint constructive possession" is quite as bad as having the drugs exclusively in one's own pocket. . . .

"Constructive" possession is commonly defined as the power and intention to exercise control, or dominion and control, over an object not in one's "actual" possession. . . . Courts are saying that one can possess an object while it is hidden at home in a bureau drawer, or while held by an agent, or even while it is secured in a safe deposit box at the bank and can be retrieved only when a bank official opens the vault. The problem is not so much with the idea as with deciding how far it should be carried.

Here, we think [it] is at least arguable that Zavala was not shown to possess the drugs while he and Santos were in the room together. Santos apparently had exclusive control of the bag during this period. It contained drugs for which he had not been paid; Zavala was not the named person to whom it was to be delivered; and Santos refused Zavala's suggestion that the bag be entrusted to Zavala's friends in another room. If the agents had broken into the room and arrested Zavala at this point, a directed verdict of acquittal might have been required.

But once both parties departed from the room leaving the drugs inside, the situation altered. It is not that Zavala got closer to the drugs — indeed, he moved further away from them — but rather that two other circumstances changed: first, Santos surrendered his actual possession of them; and second, with the acquiescence of both parties, the drugs were secured in Zavala's room. In the context of this case, we think that a jury could then find both requisites of constructive possession: that Zavala had sufficient power to control the drugs and an intention to exercise that power.

Turning first to the power to exercise control, we begin with the fact that the drugs were left in Zavala's room with his knowledge and consent while Zavala was awaiting the arrival of an accomplice to pay for them. It is fair to describe the location as Zavala's hotel room because he was effectively in occupation and the jury could reasonably infer that he could return there at will.

The evidence showed that the room, although registered in Palestino's name, had been lent to two occupants. It was Zavala who emerged when Santos arrived at the hotel and the room was called; and it was Zavala who took Santos to the room to await "his friend" Palestino.

The location of drugs or firearms in a defendant's home or car is a common basis for attributing possession to the defendant. This is so even if the residence or room is shared by others. . . . The cases do not say that possession is automatic but rather that the location of the object in a domain specially accessible to the defendant can (at least where knowledge is admitted or inferred) be enough to permit the jury to find possession.

location can be enough for jury to infer possession (but it's not mandatory)

Admittedly, Zavala's power to control in this case was diluted because Santos had not yet been paid and might well have resisted any attempt by Zavala to return to the room and carry away the drugs. But by the same token a jury could infer that drugs now stored in Zavala's hotel room, awaiting transfer to Zavala's accomplice, were at least as much within Zavala's power to control as within Santos' power. If each had an effective veto over the other, it would still be joint possession. Two drug dealers with cocaine in the back seat of their car might both possess it even though neither would let the other out of sight.

must also have intent

The issue of intention is quite as important as the issue of power. Someone might have effective power over drugs simply because they were located within reach while their true owner was temporarily absent; but if such a person had power over the drugs (say, as a temporary visitor to the room in which they were located) but had no intention to exercise that power, there might still be no crime. Here, Zavala's connection with the drugs stored in his hotel room was not at all innocent: the drugs were stored there for the purpose (so far as Zavala knew and intended) of facilitating their transfer to his accomplice, Palestino.

In many cases, intention and knowledge are inferred solely from the location of the drugs in an area to which the defendant has a priority of access. Here, Zavala's state of mind is established by independent evidence: his statements that Palestino would be there soon, his suggestion that the drugs be stored temporarily in another room, apparently with his confederates; and by the cellular telephone calls by Zavala and to him seemingly from Palestino. No reasonable jury could have had any doubt that Zavala was there to assist in the transmission of the drugs lodged in his room.

Assuming Zavala's guilty mind, it might still be argued that his precise intention was to aid in the storage and transfer of the drugs but not to "control" the drugs. We think this is too fine a distinction. Defendant's intention to have the drugs stored in his room, incident to their intended transfer to a confederate, seems to us an intention intimately related to his power to control the drugs. If a jury finds this to be constructive possession, we do not think that it has stretched the concept too far or betrayed the intention of Congress. . . .

Affirmed.

Notes and Questions

1. *The elements of possession.* In *Maldonado* the Court identifies two different elements of "constructive" possession: (1) effective power over the thing possessed and (2) the intention to control it. Consider each in turn.

Is mere physical power an adequate test of possession? Presumably a parking attendant has mere custody rather than possession of the cars he parks, because of the limits on his authority to use them. Writing in dissent, Judge Coffin argues that Zavala Maldonado had not yet acquired any authority over the drugs:

> I am persuaded that this reliance on physical power of access understates the law's requirements. . . . [T]he caselaw supports a reading of "power" as the right or authority to exercise control, or dominion and control, over something not in one's actual possession. See . . . United States v. Manzella, 791 F.2d 1263, 1266-67 (7th Cir. 1986) (Posner, J.) (defendant "must have the right (not the legal right, but the recognized authority in his criminal milieu) to possess [the drugs]. . . . Mere association with those who possess the drugs is not good enough."). . . .
>
> For example, in [*United States v.*] *Ocampo-Guarin,* we found sufficient evidence of "power" to establish constructive possession of a suitcase and the cocaine inside it, where the defendant carried baggage claim tickets "which represented her legal right to reclaim the luggage." 986 F.2d at 1410. Similarly, in United States v. Lamare, we upheld a finding of constructive possession of a firearm that had been left as collateral for a towing charge owed by the defendant, because the defendant "could have taken actual possession of the pistol at any time by paying the towing charge . . . and intended to do so." 711 F.2d at 5-6.
>
> The fact that contraband is located in a place specially accessible to a defendant may be sufficient to establish a defendant's power to exercise dominion or control over it, and thus support a finding of constructive possession, if there is a showing that the defendant has the right or authority to exercise control over the object at issue, or if the record is silent as to his right or authority over the contraband. But here the very facts militating against a finding of constructive possession while Santos and Zavala were in the room together — the fact that the drugs had not been paid for, the fact that Zavala was not the intended recipient, and Santos' refusal to follow Zavala's suggestion to transfer them to another room — effectively refute any presumption that Zavala had any claim on the drugs. [23 F.3d at 9-10]

Do Judge Coffin's arguments show that Zavala Maldonado had no possession, or only that he did not have excusive possession? The majority holds that Zavala Maldonado constructively possessed the drugs jointly with Santos. Were these two working together, like members of a relay team, to deliver the drugs, or were they agents of rival commercial interests, each wary of deception and bent on profiting at the expense of the other? Must the prosecution provide evidence that proves the first, or cooperative, characterization — and that excludes the second, or competitive characterization — to prove "joint" possession?

Judge Posner, quoted above in the dissent, would ask whether a broker coordinating a drug transaction has the "recognized authority in his criminal milieu" to possess the drugs. What does this mean? Do some brokers have this authority but not others? How do we identify the rules of a "milieu?"

As to the mental aspect of possession, does Zavala Maldonado's expectation or desire that Palestino receive the drugs when he arrives amount to an intention to control them? If he now intends to deliver the drugs later, does that mean he now intends to control the drugs? What if his intention to deliver the drugs later is contingent on Santos's permission?

Notice an important subtlety here: Zavala Maldonado's offense — possession with intent to distribute — requires two distinct mental states: intent to possess and intent to distribute. Hence his current intention that he will distribute the drugs *later,* when he acquires possession of them, does not entail that he currently intends to exercise control over them now.

2. *Possession jury instructions.* Jury instructions attempt to bridge the gap between the everyday usage definition of possession and that which the court requires of the juror. The Eighth Circuit jury instruction on possession is typical.

8.02 Possession: Actual Constructive, Sole, Joint

The law recognizes several kinds of possession. A person may have actual possession or constructive possession. A person may have sole or joint possession.

A person who knowingly has direct physical control over a thing, at a given time, is then in actual possession of it.

A person who, although not in actual possession, has both the power and the intention at a given time to exercise dominion or control over a thing, either directly or through another person or persons, is then in constructive possession of it.

If one person alone has actual or constructive possession of a thing, possession is sole. If two or more persons share actual or constructive possession of a thing, possession is joint.

Whenever the word "possession" has been used in these instructions it includes actual as well as constructive possession and also sole as well as joint possession. [Manual of Model Criminal Jury Instructions for the District Courts of the Eighth Circuit (2002).]

3. *Proximity and Control.* In United States v. Jenkins, 90 F.3d 814 (3rd Cir. 1996), the defendant challenged the sufficiency of the evidence proving his constructive possession of drugs found on a coffee table in an acquaintance's apartment in close proximity to the defendant. Jenkins was found sitting in the apartment of an acquaintance, sitting in his underwear on a couch near the coffee table on which were placed cocaine and equipment for processing it. Noting that no cocaine residue was found on Jenkins's person, nor were his fingerprints on the equipment, nor was there evidence that the equipment was then being used, the Third Circuit overruled the district court's judgment of conviction for drug possession. The court stated:

The government had no evidence of actual possession of the cocaine powder; consequently, the issue before us is whether there was evidence sufficient to establish constructive possession. Under our precedent, the evidence must show that Jenkins had dominion and control over the drugs. . . . The kind of evidence that can establish dominion and control includes, for example, evidence that the defendant attempted to hide or to destroy the contraband, or that the defendant lied to police about his identity or the source of large amounts of cash on his person. . . . Dominion and control are not established, however, by "mere proximity to the drug, or mere presence on the property where it is located or mere association with the person who does control the drug or the property." Id. at 817-18 (quoting United States v. Brown, 3 F.3d 673, 680 (3rd Cir. 1993)).

Though mere proximity to contraband may not be adequate to convict an otherwise innocent individual of a possession crime, juries are allowed to evaluate the surrounding circumstances and determine whether the defendant was otherwise exercising dominion or control over the item. In People v. Gina, 524 N.Y.S.2d 296 (N.Y. App. 1988), the Court held that a defendant found hiding in the rafters of a burglarized jewelry store was properly convicted of possession of stolen jewels despite the fact that the jewels were in a bag on the floor of the store.

4. *Intercepted possession.* In State v. Clark, 527 S.E.2d 319 (N.C. App. 2001), the police intercepted a package containing 12 pounds of marijuana, removed all but a fraction of a pound of it, and then made a controlled delivery to the defendant-addressee. When that person received the package, did he commit (constructive) possession of the larger amount — and hence face a longer sentence based on the amount? The court held that

> constructive possession has been found when the narcotics were (1) on property in which the defendant had some exclusive possessory interest and there is evidence of his or her presence on the property; (2) on property of which defendant, not an owner, had sole or joint physical custody; or (3) in an area which the defendant frequented, usually near his or her property. Id. at 321.

The court concluded that the doctrine did not extend to this situation: "There is no evidence as to the actual source of the drugs. Although defendant may well have had the requisite intent, there is no evidence he ever had the capability to exercise dominion and control over the original package." Nevertheless, it held that an "appropriate charge under such circumstances would be an attempt" and reduced the conviction to attempted possession.[10]

5. *Duration of possession.* Does the required length of possession depend on what is being possessed? In United States v. Lane, 267 F.3d 715 (7th Cir. 2001), the defendant claimed that his momentary handling of a gun as he purchased it for a friend did not establish possession for purposes of 18 U.S.C. §922(g), which punishes being a felon in possession of a firearm. The court rejected this argument, distinguishing the gun possession law from drug possession under 18 U.S.C. §841. The court held that the drug statute's goal of curbing drug abuse requires that a person be able to control what happens to the drugs, while, in contrast, Congress's goal of keeping guns out of the hands of felons prohibited virtually any contact whatsoever. "Because a defendant can shoot a gun quickly and easily once he holds it in his hands, we conclude that evidence showing that felon held a gun is by itself a factor indicating that he had the ability to exercise control." Id. at 718.

6. *Dominion and control over images.* How does one exercise dominion and control over an electronic image? In United States v. Tucker, 150 F. Supp. 2d 1263 (D. Utah 2001), the court held that Tucker knowingly possessed child pornography, and had this to say regarding Tucker's control of the images:

> . . . Tucker had possession of the child pornography. Tucker had control over the images he viewed on his computer due to the fact that he could detain them on his monitor as long as he liked and control them by, among other things, enlarging and manipulating them. While the images that Tucker received were on his computer screen, he could control them in many ways: he could copy them had he chosen; he could print them had he chosen; he could enlarge them and "zoom-in" on the pictures as he chose; he could show them to other people had he chosen; and he could copy them to other directories — as he attempted to do with the 5-16-98 files found on his c-drive, outside of his cache file. It is true that when Tucker viewed the images, the site and its images were automatically saved on Tucker's cache file, and that Tucker did not play any role in the automatic operation

---

10. On the notion of attempting to commit what is itself a somewhat "inchoate" crime, see pp. 645-648, *infra.*

other than gaining access to the websites and viewing child pornography; yet Tucker also demonstrated ultimate dominion and control over these images because he was able to destroy them by deleting them from his hard drive. That Tucker had possession is not only evidenced by his showing and manipulation of the images, but also by the telling fact that he took the time to delete the image links from his computer cache file. Logically, one cannot destroy what one does not possess and control. Indeed, the ability to destroy is definitive evidence of control. *Id.* at 1267.

How far might this form of possession liability extend? What if Tucker had merely received the images via e-mail "Spam," decided not to delete them, and then examined them later at his leisure? Or what if he had merely neglected to delete them and later discovered that the link to them was still in his inbox and *then* examined them at his leisure?

7. *Possession law enforcement as the new vagrancy.* Increased criminalization of possession and increased penalties for such possession offenses are major contributors to the dramatic recent rise in American incarceration rates, discussed in Part 1, *supra.* According to Professor Markus Dubber, as of 1998, New York law recognized at least 153 possession-based offenses. Also in 1998, over 100,000 individuals were arrested for possession offenses in New York, and one in five jail sentences was for a possession offense. Professor Dubber adds that 1.2 million drug possession arrests were made nationwide in 1998.[11]

Professor Dubber argues that possession offenses have done away with both of the traditional requirements for criminal prosecution, *mens rea* and *actus reus.*

> [P]ossession statutes . . . save prosecutors the trouble of proving that other major ingredient of criminal liability in American criminal law, mens rea, or a guilty mind. This means that many possession statutes, particularly in the drug area — where some of the harshest campaigns in the war on crime have been prosecuted — are so-called strict liability crimes. In other words, you can be convicted of them if you don't know that you are "possessing" a drug of any kind, what drug you are "possessing," how much of it you've got, or — in some states — even that you are possessing anything at all, drug or no drug . . . Possession, however, also does away with the traditional requirement that criminal liability must be predicated on an actus reus, an affirmative act or at least a failure to act (rather than a status, like being in possession of something). So even if some sort of intent (or at least negligence) is required for conviction, there is no need to worry about the actus reus.[12]

Prof. Dubber notes that possession offenses are inchoate offenses, punishing offenders merely for being in a position to use the object "constructively" possessed to cause some harm. He argues that possession offenses have replaced much-criticized and constitutionally suspect vagrancy laws (see the discussion of the principle of Specificity in section G, *infra*) as a tool empowering police to arrest and charge persons they regard as suspicious.

> Blessed with all the definitional flexibility and executory convenience of vagrancy, possession is superior to vagrancy. . . . [U]nlike vagrancy, it can be committed in private as well as in public. This means the state, through a suspicion of

11. Policing Possession: The War on Crime and the End of Criminal Law, 91 J. Crim. L. & Criminology 829, 835 (2001).
    12. Id. at 859-60.

possession, gains entry into the home of suspected [persons] . . . or, while there can detect evidence of possession. . . . Especially if one expansively defines possession to include constructive possession, the criminalization of possession presumptively criminalizes everyone everywhere. . . . [Also,] penalties for vagrancy paled in comparison to those for possession.[13]

D. THE REQUIREMENT OF VOLUNTARINESS

PEOPLE v. NEWTON
Supreme Court, Appellate Division of New York
72 Misc. 2d 646, 340 N.Y.S.2d 77 (1973)

JUSTICE WEINSTEIN.

. . . . On December 7, 1972 petitioner boarded Air International Bahamas' flight #101 bound from the Bahamas to Luxembourg. While on board, the petitioner had concealed on his person a loaded .38 caliber revolver and a quantity of ammunition. At some time during the flight, the captain became aware of the fact that petitioner might possibly be carrying a firearm. There is some indication that the petitioner, severely handicapped and ambulatory only with the aid of prosthetic devices, caused himself to be unruly. The extent to which petitioner was unruly on board the plane, if in fact he was, cannot be ascertained from the evidence before the Court. Suffice it to say that the captain of flight #101, for reasons best known to himself, saw fit to interrupt the course of the plane which was flying over international waters and effected a landing in the County of Queens at the John F. Kennedy International Airport. The landing was made at approximately 12:35 A.M. on December 8, 1972. Officers from the Port Authority Police Department, in response to a radio transmission, went to the runway where the plane, with petitioner on board, was waiting. One of the officers boarded the plane, approached the defendant-petitioner, and inquired of him as to whether or not he had a weapon. The petitioner answered that he did have a weapon which he allowed to be removed from his person. He was then arrested and charged with a violation of section 265.05(2) of the Penal Law of the State of New York after his admission that he had no license to possess or carry the weapon in question. Section 265.05(2) of the Penal Law is as follows:

> Any person who has in his possession any firearm which is loaded with ammunition, or who has in his possession any firearm and, at the same time, has in his possession a quantity of ammunition which may be used to discharge such firearm is guilty of a class D felony.

The Court finds that the petitioner, William Jesse Newton, Jr. did not subject himself to criminal liability by virtue of a voluntary act. Flight #101 was not scheduled to terminate in or pass through the territorial jurisdiction of the United States. The landing at John F. Kennedy International Airport on De-

---

13. Id. at 908-910.

cember 8, 1972 was merely an interruption of flight not attributable to a voluntary action by the petitioner. It is therefore, the opinion of this Court that the Writ of Habeas Corpus be sustained and the petitioner be discharged from custody forthwith.

Notes and Questions

1. Is there any reason for Newton to escape liability under New York criminal law?

2. What act did Newton perform in New York? What could he have done to avoid criminal liability?

3. Does *Newton* raise the same question about criminal liability as did *Proctor*?

4. Should it matter if it is a crime to possess a loaded firearm in either the Bahamas or Luxembourg? Does it matter whether Air International is an American airline? Should it matter whether it is a federal offense to carry a loaded firearm on a United States airline?

MARTIN v. STATE
Court of Appeals of Alabama
17 So. 2d 427 (1944)

SIMPSON, JUDGE.

Appellant was convicted of being drunk on a public highway, and appeals. Officers of the law arrested him at his home and took him onto the highway, where he allegedly committed the proscribed acts, viz., manifested a drunken condition by using loud and profane language.

The pertinent provisions of our statute are: "Any person who, while intoxicated or drunk, appears in any public place where one or more persons are present . . . and manifests a drunken condition by boisterous or indecent conduct, or loud and profane discourse, shall, on conviction, be fined," etc., Code 1940, Title 14, Section 120.

Under the plain terms of this statute, a voluntary appearance is presupposed. The rule has been declared, and we think it sound, that an accusation of drunkenness in a designated public place cannot be established by proof that the accused, while in an intoxicated condition, was involuntarily and forcibly carried to that place by the arresting officer.

Conviction of appellant was contrary to this announced principle and, in our view, erroneous. . . .

Reversed and rendered.

[handwritten marginal note: only reason Def was in a public place is that 2 officer brought him there]

Notes and Questions

1. The statute Martin was accused of violating can be read to require three acts: getting drunk, being in a public place, and engaging in boisterous conduct. Is the point of the court that all three "acts" must be voluntary? Or just the last in the sequence of conduct? If the latter, wasn't Martin boisterous *after* he was carried into a public place?

2. As for the specific components of the crime: Should it matter that it was the police who brought Martin into the street on the way to the police car? Would it matter if instead Martin was thrown out onto the street from a private party for drunken misbehavior? Because of his political beliefs? What if he had gotten drunk in his room but came into the street because his house had caught fire?

3. Should it matter what Martin was originally arrested for? Should it matter whether the arrest was legal? Should it matter if he were innocent of the charges for which he was arrested?

4. What if Martin had been arrested while sober but, while being driven to the police station, discovered a bottle of whiskey in the back of the patrol car and drank it, causing him to be intoxicated on arrival at the police station (assuming the station to be a public place within the meaning of the statute)?

5. *Purpose of the volition requirement.* Why should the law preclude criminal liability in the absence of a voluntary act? Is the point that the criminal law cannot hope to deter involuntary behavior, and thus cannot deter any crime by making an individual liable for actions he or she could not control? Is this true? Or might the requirement of voluntariness be understood as the legal response to the basic intuition that it would be grossly unfair to punish a person who lacked the capacity to conform to the law? Or is it rather, as the drafters of the Model Penal Code asserted, that "the sense of personal security would be undermined in a society where such movement or inactivity could lead to formal social condemnation." The Model Penal Code itself provides:

Section 2.01. Requirement of Voluntary Act . . .

(1) A person is not guilty of an offense unless his liability is based on conduct that includes a voluntary act. . . .

(4) Possession is an act, within the meaning of this Section, if the possessor knowingly procured or received the thing possessed or was aware of his control thereof for a sufficient period to have been able to terminate his possession.

How precisely can we draw the voluntary/involuntary distinction? Are intuitive conceptions of "fairness" helpful? Consider the next case.

PEOPLE v. GRANT
Appellate Court of Illinois, Fourth District
46 Ill. App. 3d 125, 360 N.E.2d 809 (1977)

REARDON, JUSTICE.

The defendant, Seth Grant, was sentenced to 3 to 9 years in the penitentiary after a Logan County jury found him guilty of aggravated battery and obstructing a police officer. The court entered judgment on both verdicts, but only sentenced the defendant for the offense of aggravated battery.

On December 13, 1974, the defendant was a patron at a tavern known as the "Watering Place" in the City of Lincoln where he consumed four drinks consisting of whisky and cola during a 2½-hour period. The defendant then witnessed an altercation between another patron and the tavern owner. The Lincoln police were called to the scene and they forcibly escorted the other patron outside where he continued to resist arrest. A hostile crowd of approximately forty persons accompanied the police and patron as they exited from the tavern and approached the officers' automobile. The crowd was cheering for the patron. Suddenly, the defendant burst through the crowd, and, using a parking meter for leverage, he leaped into the air, striking Officer Raymond Vonderahe twice in the face.

Thereafter, Officer Michael Yarcho placed the defendant under arrest and forcibly led him to the officers' automobile. Yarcho testified that the defendant was very upset and that great force was required to place the defendant in the automobile. Another officer, David Morrow, testified that the defendant was excited, agitated and upset. Morrow also stated that the defendant had not been involved in the altercation prior to his attack on Vonderahe.

The defendant was transported to the Logan County jail and placed in a cell. Approximately one hour after being arrested, one of the jailers discovered the defendant lying on his cot gasping for breath. Defendant's eyes were fixed and his back formed a rigid reversed arch, typical symptoms of a grand mal convulsive seizure. The defendant was immediately transported to a Lincoln hospital by the Lincoln fire department, and then to a Springfield hospital where the defendant remained until December 23, 1974.

The record on appeal reflects that the defendant has a complicated legal and medical history. The defendant suffers from an illness known as psychomotor epilepsy. This history includes a number of violent attacks on other persons which have varied in severity. In some, physical assistance from others was required to subdue the defendant. One, a knife assault in a hospital, was of such violence that a police officer seeking to restrain the defendant was forced to use a weapon. The affray ended only when the defendant was shot in the pelvis and kidney. His past history is replete with emotional outbursts and he has been convicted on separate occasions of involuntary manslaughter and aggravated assault. . . .

Defendant relies on his testimony that his mind went blank at the "Watering Place" and that he remembered nothing until he awoke three days later. He stated that he has had previous blackouts and that he takes medicine for epilepsy. Defendant also relies on Dr. Albert Ludin's testimony that defendant has temporal lobe epilepsy with symptoms described as psychomotor and grand mal seizures. Dr. Ludin expressed his opinion that, at the time the offenses were committed, defendant was suffering from a psychomotor seizure which prevented his conscious mind from controlling his actions.

The jury is not required to accept the conclusions of a psychiatrist . . . and the weight of the psychiatrist's opinion is to be measured by the reasons given for the conclusion and the factual details supporting it. . . .

Here, Dr. Ludin stated that his opinion would be different if the defendant was not telling the truth. Analysis of the record on appeal discloses facts on which the jury could base their opinion that the defendant was being untruthful.

First, defendant alleges that he cannot remember anything that occurred during the three-day period following his arrest. The doctor, however, testified that on December 14, 1974, defendant was alert, awake and in contact with reality. Officer Yarcho also stated that the defendant was alert and not confused when he was arrested. The defendant also responded in an appropriate manner when questioned about his personal history. Next, is Officer Yarcho's troubling testimony that defendant's arrest required a great deal of force. Such testimony coincides with Dr. Ludin's statement that a person having a psychomotor seizure exhibits a great deal of strength. This testimony, however, as the State points out, must be contrasted with Office Yarcho's later testimony that it took four men to place the defendant in an ambulance at the jail, while he initially took the defendant into custody by himself. Furthermore, Officer Yarcho testified that defendant was much stronger during the jail incident than he was during the arrest. Finally, Officer Yarcho stated that in his opinion the defendant was in possession of his "complete faculties" and "normal" at the time of his arrest. The evidence showing that the defendant had a grand mal seizure at the jail does not necessarily reflect that the defendant also had a psychomotor seizure a short time before. While Dr. Ludin did say that sometimes a grand mal seizure is preceded by a psychomotor seizure, he did not say that this always occurs. . . .

The trial court instructed the jury on the question of the defendant's sanity by giving the following instruction which is taken from the Illinois Pattern Jury Instructions, Criminal, No. 24.01 (1968):

> A person is insane and not criminally responsible for his conduct if at the time of the conduct, as a result of mental disease or mental defect, he lacks substantial capacity either to appreciate the criminality of his conduct or to conform his conduct to the requirements of law.

. . . This instruction, however, fails to distinguish behavior by a person lacking ". . . substantial capacity either to appreciate the criminality of his conduct or to conform his conduct to the requirements of law. . . ." from automatic behavior by an individual who possesses the requisite capacity. . . .

The term automatism is defined as the state of a person who, though capable of action, is not conscious of what he is doing. Automatism is not insanity. . . . [I]t is manifested by the performance of involuntary acts that can be of a simple or complex nature. Clinically, automatism has been identified in a wide variety of physical conditions including: epilepsy, organic brain disease, concussional states following head injuries, drug abuse, hypoglycemia and, less commonly, in some types of schizophrenia and acute emotional disturbance. . . . Psychomotor epileptics not only engage in automatic or fugue-like activity, but they may also suffer convulsive seizures.

Section 4-1 of our Criminal Code provides:

> A material element of every offense is a voluntary act, which includes an omission to perform a duty which the law imposes on the offender and which he is physically capable of performing.

While the Illinois Pattern Jury Instructions contain an instruction relating to this statute . . . that instruction was [not] read to the jury in this case. . . .

Ordinarily, a defendant cannot complain on appeal that an instruction was not given if he failed to tender that instruction at trial. . . . [However,] "substantial defects [injury instructions] are not waived by failure to make timely objections thereto if the interests of justice require." Accordingly, we hold that the interests of justice require reversal of the defendant's convictions because the jury instructions are substantially defective in that they do not contain an instruction on the defense of involuntary conduct. We note that courts in other jurisdictions have held that the defendant who introduces evidence of abnormal mental condition, bearing upon the state of mind required for the crime with which he is charged, is entitled to an instruction drawing the jury's attention to that evidence.

We distinguish People v. Espenscheid (1969), 109 Ill. App. 2d 107, 249 N.E.2d 866, which held that the trial court properly refused to give such an instruction because there was no evidence tending to prove that the defendant performed an involuntary act. The entire record on appeal here, especially the testimony of Dr. Ludin, reflects that the defendant suffers from psychomotor epilepsy, which is not insanity. The record reflects that the defendant may have been acting in a state of automatism when he attacked Officer Vonderahe on December 13, 1974. We therefore leave the factual resolution of this question to a jury that is properly instructed.

Although a voluntary act is an absolute requirement for criminal liability under section 4-1 of our Code . . . there is no requirement that every act preceding the actual commission of the offense be voluntary. Thus, the jury may, on remand, determine that the defendant attacked Officer Vonderahe while in a state of automatism, but that he nevertheless committed an offense for which he is criminally responsible if he had prior notice of his susceptibility to engage in violent involuntary conduct brought on by drinking alcoholic beverages or by some other conscious causal behavior. . . .

In Illinois, we have a generally well-reasoned and modern Criminal Code. This Code provides for the affirmative defense of insanity and requires that every offense be the result of a voluntary act. Our legislature has provided that a person found not guilty of an offense by reason of insanity can be committed to a mental health facility for treatment, although no such provision applies to an alleged offender who commits an involuntary act. These provisions are rational and constitute policy responses to a compelling need by a legislature empowered to act.

On remand, the defendant will again run the risk of being convicted for the offenses of aggravated battery or obstructing a police officer if the jury finds that he was not insane when he attacked Officer Vonderahe and that he either consciously committed the offense or recklessly brought about his alleged psychomotor epileptic seizure and its accompanying state of automatism. As some commentators have suggested, the jury plays an important role when the defense is raised:

> [A]utomatism as a result of psychomotor seizures should be [a] valid criminal defense. The dearth of cases employing this defense suggests that the problem is one of proof. If one is sane immediately prior to and after the unlawful act is committed it is difficult to establish that a particular violent act occurred as a result of a psychomotor seizure. (Barrow & Fabing, Epilepsy and the Law 92-93 (1956).)

If the jury finds that the defendant was sane but not responsible for the attack on Officer Vonderahe, then he cannot be committed for the offenses. We find this course to be mandated by our legislature, which only provided for the commitment of persons who are criminally insane . . .

In view of the fact that we are remanding this case for a new trial, we do not address the question of whether the 3 to 9 year sentence of imprisonment imposed by the trial court is excessive. . . .

Reversed and remanded with directions.

Notes and Questions

1. *Involuntary acts.* The Model Penal Code excludes the following from the definition of a voluntary act:

Section 2.01 . . .

(2) The following are not voluntary acts within the meaning of this Section:
    (a) a reflex or convulsion;
    (b) a bodily movement during unconsciousness or sleep;
    (c) conduct during hypnosis or resulting from hypnotic suggestion;
    (d) a bodily movement that otherwise is not a product of the effort or determination of the actor, either conscious or habitual.

Note that the Model Penal Code defines "act" only implicitly (largely by exclusion), and, in so doing, it stresses not so much the notion of a muscular movement or contraction, but rather the element of conscious control. Professor Herbert Packer has explained the reason for this principle as follows: [14]

> [T]he universally recognized doctrine [is] that conduct that occurs while the actor is in an unconscious state — sleepwalking, epileptic seizures, automatism — may not be dealt with criminally. Conduct must be, as the law's confusing term has it, "Voluntary." The term is one that will immediately raise the hackles of the determinist, of whatever persuasion. But, once again, the law's language should not be read as plunging into the deep waters of free will vs. determinism, Cartesian duality, or any of a half-dozen other philosophic controversies that might appear to be invoked by the use of the term "Voluntary" in relation to conduct. The law is not affirming volition; it is excluding, in a crude kind of way, conduct that in any view is not. And it does so primarily in response to the simple intuition that nothing would more surely undermine the individual's sense of autonomy and security than to hold him to account for conduct that he does not think he can control. He may be deluded, if the determinists are right, in his belief that such conduct differs significantly from any other conduct in which he engages. But that is beside the point. He thinks there is a difference, and that is what the law acts upon.

2. *Volition and insanity.* Note an important irony discussed in *Grant*. Had the assault been caused by a diagnosable form of insanity, Grant could have been acquitted on grounds of insanity, but then might have been incarcerated under the civil commitment laws. Yet if the assault were entirely due to an "involuntary action," the state might have been unable to incarcerate Grant at all. Does this make sense? The insanity defense is a large and complex subject we will explore in detail in Chapter 9.

In addition, how does the outcome of this case affect burden of proof?

3. *Hypnosis.* The Model Penal Code Commentary to section 2.01 asserts that acts performed while under hypnotic trance are involuntary: [15]

> The case of hypnotic suggestion also seems to warrant explicit treatment. Hypnosis differs from both sleep and fugue, but as it is characterized by the subject's dependence on the hypnotist, it does not seem politic to treat conduct resulting from hypnotic suggestion as voluntary, despite the state of consciousness involved.

[handwritten margin note: acts in hypnosis are not voluntary]

14. The Limits of the Criminal Sanction 76-77 (1968).
15. Model Penal Code and Commentaries, *supra,* at 221.

The widely held view that the hypnotized subject will not follow suggestions that are repugnant to him was deemed insufficient to warrant treating his conduct while hypnotized as voluntary; his dependency and helplessness are too pronounced.

4. *Sleepwalking.* Acts performed while sleepwalking may also fall outside the definition voluntary behavior necessary to criminal liability. See Model Penal Code §2.01(2)(b).

Sleepwalking killers seem to abound. One Toronto jury acquitted a man of murder for the killing of his mother-in-law, finding that he was sleepwalking when he drove 14 miles to her home, beat her with a tire iron, and stabbed her to death. Witnesses said the defendant, Kenneth Parks, age 24, had a family history of somnabulism, later triggered by stress over his gambling addiction and his embezzlement of $28,000 to cover his gambling losses.[16] On the other hand, a Phoenix jury rejected Scott Falater's sleepwalking defense and found him guilty of first-degree murder in the brutal slaying of his wife, Yarmila. Prosecutors had argued that Falater, 43, who stabbed Yarmila 44 times on January 16, 1997, and held her head under water, had acted after deliberate planning. The defendant, who had a documented history of sleepwalking, had claimed that he was not consciously aware of his actions when he killed Yarmila and had no reason to commit murder. Yarmila, the defense said, was killed when she tried to awaken her sleepwalking husband while he was going through the motions of trying to fix a pool water pump with a hunting knife. Defense attorneys argued that Falater and his wife had a loving marriage for 20 years and that the killing was so inexplicable that the only logical explanation was that Falater was sleepwalking during the incident. But prosecution experts testified that Falater's actions — such as changing his bloody clothes, putting them in Tupperware and placing Tupperware in the trunk of his car — suggested that he was not sleepwalking at all during the attack and that a sleepwalker could not have performed such complicated tasks.[17]

5. *Shock.* In People v. (Huey) Newton, 8 Cal. App. 3d 359, 87 Cal. Rptr. 394 (1970), the court held that the defendant had a right to a jury instruction on the defense of involuntary action due to automatism. Newton, a political activist and leader of the Black Panthers, had been stopped by two police officers and ordered out of his car. Though the evidence was unclear, Newton and one of the officers apparently struggled over a gun, and the gun went off, wounding the officer. The wounded officer then shot Newton in the abdomen from close range and as the fight continued, Newton fired shots, killing the second officer. A medical expert testified for the defense that

> a gunshot wound which penetrates in a body cavity, the abdominal cavity or the thoracic cavity is very likely to produce a profound reflex shock reaction, that is quite different than [*sic*] a gunshot wound which penetrates only skin and muscle and it is not at all uncommon for a person shot in the abdomen to lose consciousness and go into this reflex shock condition for short periods of time up to half an hour or so.

---

16. The jury in Parks's case was instructed that it was not permitted to find him not guilty by reason of insanity. Sleepwalker Innocent in Slaying, Arizona Republic, May 28, 1988, at A29.

17. Falater faced the death penalty, but was ultimately sentenced to life without the possibility of parole. www.courttv.com/trials/falater/062599.

The court rejected the state's argument that such "reflex shock condition" could not constitute involuntary action and remanded the case to let the jury consider Newton's claim that he committed no voluntary act.

Suppose the jury concluded that Newton killed the second officer while in an unconscious state, but that the first officer's shooting of Newton was a justifiable police action. Should it make a difference to Newton's liability if he was responsible for getting himself shot? Would it, according to the court in People v. Grant?

For an argument, relying on Freudian theory, that the notion of conscious intent should be expanded to include "intentions" residing in the unconscious mind, see Daniel I. A. Cohen, The Jurisprudence of Unconscious Intent, 24 J. of Psychiatry & L. 511 (1996).

6. *Anticipating involuntariness.* Consider People v. Decina, 2 N.Y.2d 133, 139-40, 138 N.E.2d 799, 803-04 (1956). Decina had an epileptic seizure while driving and his car struck and killed four people on a sidewalk. The court held that, although the defendant's epileptic seizure was involuntary, he nonetheless was criminally liable.

> Assuming the truth of the indictment, as we must on demurrer, this defendant knew he was subject to epileptic attacks and seizures that might strike at any time.
>
> He also knew that a moving motor vehicle uncontrolled on a public highway is a highly dangerous instrumentality capable of unrestrained destruction. With this knowledge, and without anyone accompanying him, he deliberately took a chance by making a conscious choice of a course of action, in disregard of the consequences which he knew might follow from his conscious act, and which in this case did ensue.
>
> To hold otherwise would be to say that a man may freely indulge himself in liquor in the same hope that it will not affect his driving, and if it later develops that ensuing intoxication causes dangerous and reckless driving resulting in death, his unconsciousness or involuntariness at that time would relieve him from a prosecution under the statute. His awareness of a condition which he knows may produce such consequences as here, and his disregard of the consequences, renders him liable for culpable negligence, as the courts below have properly held. . . . To have a sudden sleeping spell, an unexpected heart or other disabling attack, without any prior knowledge or warning thereof, is an altogether different situation.

Did Decina commit a punishable act? When? Did Grant? When?

E. THE PROHIBITION OF "STATUS" CRIMES

ROBINSON v. CALIFORNIA
Supreme Court of the United States
370 U.S. 660 (1962)

JUSTICE STEWART delivered the opinion of the Court.

A California statute makes it a criminal offense for a person to "be addicted to the use of narcotics." This appeal draws into question the constitutionality of that provision of the state law, as construed by the California courts in the present case.

The appellant was convicted after a jury trial in the Municipal Court of Los Angeles [on evidence that police encountered him in Los Angeles, observed track marks, and heard him admit to occasional use of narcotics.] . . .

This statute . . . is not one which punishes a person for the use of narcotics, for their purchase, sale or possession, or for antisocial or disorderly behavior resulting from their administration. It is not a law which even purports to provide or require medical treatment. Rather, we deal with a statute which makes the "status" of narcotic addiction a criminal offense, for which the offender may be prosecuted "at any time before he reforms." California has said that a person can be continuously guilty of this offense, whether or not he has ever used or possessed any narcotics within the State, and whether or not he has been guilty of any antisocial behavior there.

It is unlikely that any State at this moment in history would attempt to make it a criminal offense for a person to be mentally ill, or a leper, or to be afflicted with a venereal disease. A State might determine that the general health and welfare require that the victims of these and other human afflictions be dealt with by compulsory treatment, involving quarantine, confinement, or sequestration. But, in the light of contemporary human knowledge, a law which made a criminal offense of such a disease would doubtless be universally thought to be an infliction of cruel and unusual punishment in violation of the Eighth and Fourteenth Amendments.

We cannot but consider the statute before us as of the same category. . . . [N]arcotic addiction is an illness . . . which may be contracted innocently or involuntarily. We hold that a state law which imprisons a person thus afflicted as a criminal, even though he has never touched any narcotic drug within the State or been guilty of any irregular behavior there, inflicts a cruel and unusual punishment in violation of the Fourteenth Amendment. To be sure, imprisonment for ninety days is not, in the abstract, a punishment which is either cruel or unusual. But the question cannot be considered in the abstract. Even one day in prison would be a cruel and unusual punishment for the "crime" of having a common cold. . . . Reversed.

JUSTICE HARLAN, concurring.

I am not prepared to hold that on the present state of medical knowledge it is completely irrational and hence unconstitutional for a State to conclude that narcotics addiction is something other than an illness nor that it amounts to cruel and unusual punishment for the State to subject narcotics addicts to its criminal law. Insofar as addiction may be identified with the use or possession of narcotics within the State (or, I would suppose, without the State), in violation of local statutes prohibiting such acts, it may surely be reached by the State's criminal law. But in this case the trial court's instructions permitted the jury to find the appellant guilty on no more proof than that he was present in California while he was addicted to narcotics. Since addiction alone cannot reasonably be thought to amount to more than a compelling propensity to use narcotics, the effect of this instruction was to authorize criminal punishment for a bare desire to commit a criminal act.

JUSTICE WHITE, dissenting.

I am not at all ready to place the use of narcotics beyond the reach of the States' criminal laws. I do not consider appellant's conviction to be a punishment for having an illness or for simply being in some status or condition, but rather a conviction for the regular, repeated or habitual use of narcotics immediately prior to his arrest and in violation of the California law. . . .

The Court clearly does not rest its decision upon the narrow ground that the jury was not expressly instructed not to convict if it believed appellant's use of narcotics was beyond his control. The Court recognizes no degrees of addiction. The Fourteenth Amendment is today held to bar any prosecution for addiction regardless of the degree or frequency of use, and the Court's opinion bristles with indications of further consequences. If it is "cruel and unusual punishment" to convict appellant for addiction, it is difficult to understand why it would be any less offensive to the Fourteenth Amendment to convict him for use on the same evidence of use which proved he was an addict.

Notes and Questions

1. Was Robinson truly punished for who he was, not for what he did? If so, how did the state gather the evidence against him? What might the prosecution's evidence have been? Could it have been used to prove Robinson guilty under some other, constitutionally sound charge?

2. *Addiction and volition.* For a provocative argument denying the "automatic" or "involuntary" consequences of drug use, consider the following by philosopher Herbert Fingarette: [18]

Narcotics constitute the most effective analgesics (pain relievers) known to medicine, and their use is a widespread and conventional procedure for medical relief of substantial pain. Yet only a small fraction of the many millions of patients who receive morphine ever attempt to take the drug again, and only an exceedingly small proportion of addicts owe their dependence to medically initiated narcotic use. These data alone prove that repeated use of narcotics does not automatically hook users to continued use of the drug. . . .

Among the minority of drug users who do develop addiction, many give it up. Contrary to widespread skepticism about drug rehabilitation, there has been substantial success in measures to control and eliminate addiction in the United States. Skeptics probably assume that anything less than 100 percent success in achieving total, permanent abstention from narcotics as the result of exposure to any one program is a failure and proof of the hopelessness of the task. This conclusion is unreasonable and misleading. More important than such total successes are the days spent free of drug use and the direction of the trend for a population even though specific individuals may relapse on occasion. Impressive achievement in these latter aspects is often overlooked because attention is focused on the relapse incidents. . . .

On the other hand, the social inducements to adopt addictive patterns of behavior are often maximal. A very large proportion of new addicts in the United States today are young, psychologically immature, occupationally unskilled, socially uprooted, poor and disadvantaged. Many engaged in crime before they were addicted. The myth of the addict as a helpless slave to his habit only lends further strength to the inducements for addicts to continue addictive patterns. It provides

18. Addiction and Criminal Responsibility, 84 Yale L.J. 413, 428-29, 431-32 (1975).

such persons with a rationale for ignoring alternatives to crime and the drug culture. Young people who are disadvantaged, and alienated, may find the foundation of a socially authenticated identity in addiction. For such persons, drug use provides at last a "constructive" focal activity in life, generating its own occupational responsibilities, opportunities for success and achievement, social status, and ideological, philosophical, or religious meaning. The "hustling" required by drug addiction is not always a burden or a separation from a socially productive life; for certain groups it may be one natural outgrowth of the values of an alienated subculture, values that are by definition inconsistent with those of the dominant society. When some writers characterize the addict as one who will seek the drug at "great risk" or "at the cost of unbelievable sacrifices," the sacrifice in question may be one of values important only to the writer and not to the addict. A person who has developed roots in conventional society and skills for leading a productive life is substantially less likely to find a meaningful social identity in the drug culture, and such a person can more readily abandon addiction once it develops.

Because addiction in this country has far deeper social roots than physiological ones, judicious use of sanctions and threats of sanctions, especially if coupled with suitable constructive aid, can be an effective tool in deterring addicts from continuing drug use.

On the other hand, recent medical research on the neurobiology of endorphins suggests that some chemical imbalances that promote substance abuse result from either genetic "hard-wiring"[19] or the experience of traumatic victimization in early life.[20] Should judges or juries try to assess these differing views of addiction? Can they?

3. Justice Harlan's concurrence concludes that "since addiction alone cannot reasonably be thought to amount to more than a compelling propensity to use narcotics, the effect of this instruction was to authorize criminal punishment for a bare desire to commit a criminal act." Does due process forbid punishment for future dangerousness? If so, how is that compatible with punishing possession of burglary tools, counterfeiting equipment, and the like? How is it compatible with punishing attempts? How is it compatible with sentencing on the basis of "selective incapacitation" — that is, incarcerating those offenders deemed most likely to commit future crimes, for longer terms than other offenders? (See pp. 45-52, *supra*.)

4. *Powell v. Texas.* Six years after *Robinson,* the Court appeared to retreat in Powell v. Texas, 392 U.S. 514 (1968). The facts of *Powell* were as follows:

[The defendant] was arrested and charged with being found in a state of intoxication in a public place, in violation of Texas Penal Code, Art. 477 (1952) which reads as follows: "Whoever shall get drunk or be found in a state of intoxication in any public place, or at any private house except his own, shall be fined not exceeding one hundred dollars."

Appellant was tried . . . found guilty, and fined $20. . . . His counsel urged that appellant was "afflicted with the disease of chronic alcoholism," that "his

19. Amanda J. Roberts & George Koob, The Neurobiology of Addiction, 21 Alcohol Health & Research World 101 (1997).

20. Joseph Volpicelli, et al., The Role of Uncontrollable Trauma in the Development of PTSD and Alcohol Addiction, 23 Alcohol Research & Health 256 (1999).

appearance in public while drunk was . . . not of his own volition," and therefore that to punish him criminally for such conduct would be cruel and unusual, in violation of the . . . U.S. Constitution. [Id. at 517.]

Only four Justices agreed with this claim. A second block of four Justices voted to affirm the conviction reasoning:

Appellant . . . seeks to come within the application of the Cruel and Unusual Punishment Clause announced in Robinson v. California, 370 U.S. 660 (1962), which involved a state statute making it a crime to "be addicted to the use of narcotics." This Court held there that a "state statute which imprisons a person thus afflicted (with narcotic addiction) as a criminal, even though he has never touched any narcotic drug within the State or been guilty of any irregular behavior there, inflicts a cruel and unusual punishment. . . .

On its face the present case does not fall within that holding, since appellant was convicted, not for being a chronic alcoholic, but for being in public while drunk on a particular occasion. The State of Texas thus has not sought to punish a mere status, as California did in *Robinson;* nor has it attempted to regulate appellant's behavior in the privacy of his own home. Rather, it has imposed upon appellant a criminal sanction for public behavior which may create substantial health and safety hazards, both for appellant and for members of the general public, and which offends the moral and esthetic sensibilities of a large segment of the community. This seems a far cry from convicting one for being an addict, being a chronic alcoholic, being "mentally ill or a leper. . . ."

. . . If Leroy Powell cannot be convicted of public intoxication, it is difficult to see how a State can convict an individual for murder, if that individual, while exhibiting normal behavior in all other respects, suffers from a "compulsion" to kill. [Id. at 532-34.]

Justice White, who had dissented in *Robinson,* provided the fifth vote to uphold Powell's conviction. But he wrote a separate opinion, asserting:

If it cannot be a crime to have an irresistible compulsion to use narcotics, Robinson v. California . . . , I do not see how it can constitutionally be a crime to yield to such a compulsion. Punishing an addict for using drugs convicts for addiction under a different name. Distinguishing between the two crimes is like forbidding criminal conviction for being sick with flu or epilepsy but permitting punishment for running a fever or having a convulsion. Unless *Robinson* is to be abandoned, the use of narcotics by an addict must be beyond the reach of the criminal law. Similarly, the chronic alcoholic with an irresistable urge to consume alcohol should not be punishable for drinking or for being drunk.

Powell's conviction was for the different crime of being drunk in a public place. Thus even if Powell was compelled to drink, and so could not be constitutionally convicted for drinking, his conviction in this case can be invalidated only if there is a constitutional basis for saying that he may not be punished for being in public while drunk. . . . I cannot say that the chronic [alcoholic] who proves his disease and a compulsion to drink is shielded from conviction when he has knowingly failed to take feasible precautions against committing a criminal act, here the act of going to or remaining in a public place. On such facts, the alcoholic is like a person with smallpox, who could be convicted for being on the street, but not for being ill, or like the epileptic, punishable for driving a car but not for his disease.

Does *Powell* overrule *Robinson?* Consider two possible rationales for the *Robinson* decision:

Gloss #1: Involuntary conduct cannot be punished. Robinson cannot stop being an addict without medical assistance. Hence he is an addict involuntarily.

Gloss #2: Punishment must be for past, not future, conduct. Being an addict implies the desire or propensity to commit punishable acts in the future.

Now reread Justice White's "swing" opinion in *Powell*. Although he dissented in *Robinson,* does he actually reject either of the two glosses above? The *Powell* decision has often been read as confining *Robinson* to the requirement that punishment be for past conduct rather than future propensities (Gloss # 2). But is this reading compelled by the language of the opinions? Not according to the judge in Pottinger v. City of Miami, 810 F. Supp. 1551 (S.D.Fla. 1992):

> . . . Plaintiffs . . . filed this action in December of 1988 on behalf of themselves and approximately 6,000 other homeless people living in the City of Miami. Plaintiffs' complaint alleges that the City of Miami . . . has a custom, practice and policy of arresting, harassing and otherwise interfering with homeless people for engaging in basic activities of daily life — including sleeping and eating — in the public places where they are forced to live. Plaintiffs further claim that the City has arrested thousands of homeless people for such life-sustaining conduct under various City of Miami ordinances and Florida Statutes. . . .
>
> Plaintiffs contend that the City's arrests of class members under various ordinances prohibit them from lying down, sleeping, standing, sitting or performing other essential, life-sustaining activities in any public place at any time. Plaintiffs argue that their status of being homeless is involuntary and beyond their immediate ability to alter and that the conduct for which they are arrested is inseparable from their involuntary homeless status. Consequently, plaintiffs argue, application of these ordinances to them is cruel and unusual in violation of the eighth amendment.
>
> [The court summarized *Robinson* and *Powell.*]
>
> As a number of expert witnesses testified, people rarely choose to be homeless. Rather, homelessness is due to various economic, physical or psychological factors that are beyond the homeless individual's control.
>
> Professor Wright testified that one common characteristic of homeless individuals is that they are socially isolated; they are part of no community and have no family or friends who can take them in. Professor Wright also testified that homelessness is both a consequence and a cause of physical or mental illness. Many people become homeless after losing their jobs, and ultimately their homes, as a result of an illness. Many have no home of their own in the first place, but end up on the street after their families or friends are unable to care for or shelter them. . . .
>
> . . . Because of the unavailability of low-income housing or alternative shelter, plaintiffs have no choice but to conduct involuntary, life-sustaining activities in public places. The harmless conduct for which they are arrested is inseparable from their involuntary condition of being homeless. . . .
>
> Accordingly, the court finds that [the city's] conduct violates the eighth amendment ban against cruel and unusual punishment and therefore that the defendant is liable on this count.

However homelessness otherwise differs from alcoholism, does *Pottinger* convincingly distinguish *Powell?* Compare Joyce v. San Francisco, 846 F. Supp. 843 (N.D. Cal. 1994), refusing to enjoin San Francisco from enforcing a New York style order-maintenance policing program including arrests of the homeless for sleeping in public. The court called *Pottinger* a "dubious extension of *Robinson* and *Powell.*"

JOHNSON v. STATE
Supreme Court of Florida
602 So. 2d 1288 (Fla. 1992)

HARDING, JUSTICE.

. . . The issue before the court is whether section 893.12(l)(c) l., Florida Statutes (1989), permits the criminal prosecution of a mother, who ingested a controlled substance prior to giving birth for delivery of a controlled substance to the infant during the thirty to ninety seconds following the infant's birth, but before the umbilical cord is severed.

[The court announced that it was adopting as its own opinion the analysis in Judge Sharp's dissent in the lower court.]

Johnson appeals from two convictions for delivering a controlled substance to her two minor children in violation of section 893.13(1)(c)1., Florida Statutes (1989). The state's theory of the case was that Johnson "delivered" cocaine or a derivative of the drug to her two children via blood flowing through the children's umbilical cords in the sixty-to-ninety second period after they were expelled from her birth canal but before their cords were severed . . .

. . . On October 3, 1987, Johnson delivered a son. The birth was normal with no complications. There was no evidence of fetal distress either within the womb or during the delivery. About one and one-half minutes elapsed from the time the son's head emerged from his mother's birth canal to the time he was placed on her stomach and the cord was clamped.

The obstetrician who delivered Johnson's son testified he presumed that the umbilical cord was functioning normally and that it was delivering blood to the baby after he emerged from the birth canal and before the cord was clamped. Johnson admitted to the baby's pediatrician that she used cocaine the night before she delivered. A basic toxicology test performed on Johnson and her son was positive for . . . a . . . "breakdown" product of cocaine.

In December 1988, Johnson, while pregnant with a daughter, suffered a crack overdose. Johnson told paramedics that she had taken $200 of crack cocaine earlier that evening and that she was concerned about the effects of the drug on her unborn child. Johnson was then taken to the hospital for observation.

Johnson was hospitalized again on January 23, 1989, when she was in labor. Johnson told Dr. Tompkins, an obstetrician, that she had used rock cocaine that morning when she was in labor. With the exception of finding meconium stain fluid in the amniotic sack, there were no other complications with the birth of Johnson's baby daughter. Approximately sixty-to-ninety seconds elapsed from the time the child's head emerged from her mother's birth canal until her umbilical cord was clamped.

The following day, the Department of Health and Rehabilitative Services investigated an abuse report of a cocaine baby concerning Johnson's daughter. Johnson told the investigator that she had smoked pot and crack cocaine three to four times every other day throughout the duration of her pregnancy with her daughter. Johnson's mother acknowledged that Johnson had been using cocaine for at least three years during the time her daughter and son were born. . . .

I submit there was no medical testimony adequate to support the trial court's finding that a "delivery" occurred here during the birthing process, even if the criminal statute is applicable. The expert witnesses all testified about blood flow from the umbilical cord to the child. But that blood flow is the child's and the placenta through which it flows, is not part of the mother's body. No witness testified in this case that any cocaine derivatives passed from the mother's womb to the placenta during the sixty-to-ninety seconds after the child was expelled from the birth canal. That is when any "delivery" would have to have taken place under this statute, from one "person" to another "person."

Further, there was no evidence that Johnson timed her dosage of cocaine so as to be able to transmit some small amount after her child's birth. Predicting the day or hour of a child's birth is difficult to impossible even for experts. Had Johnson given birth one or two days later, the cocaine would have been completely eliminated, and no "crime" would have occurred. But since she went into labor which progressed to birth after taking cocaine when she did, the only way Johnson could have prevented the "delivery" would have been to have severed the cord before the child was born which, of course, would probably have killed both herself and her child. This illustrates the absurdity of applying the delivery-of-a-drug statute to this scenario.

However, in my view, the primary question in this case is whether section 893.13(l)(c)1. was intended by the Legislature for it to apply to the delivery of cocaine derivatives to a newborn during a sixty-to-ninety second interval, before severance of the umbilical cord . . .

In 1982, sections 415.501-514 were enacted to deal with the problem of child abuse and neglect. . . . To further this end, the Legislature required that a comprehensive approach for the prevention of abuse and neglect of children be developed for the state. The statute defined an "abused or neglected child" as a child whose physical or mental health or welfare was harmed, or threatened with harm, by the acts of omissions of the parent or other person responsible for the child's welfare. As originally defined, "harm" included physical or mental injury, sexual abuse, exploitation, abandonment, and neglect. 415.503(7), Fla. Stat. (1983).

In 1987, a bill was proposed to broaden the definition of "harm" to include physical dependency of a newborn infant upon certain controlled drugs. However, there was a concern among legislators that this language might authorize criminal prosecutions of mothers who give birth to drug-dependent children. . . . The bill was then amended to provide that no parent of a drug-dependent newborn shall be subject to criminal investigation solely on the basis of the infant's drug dependency. In the words of the sponsor of the House bill:

> This clearly states that the individual would not be subject to any investigation solely upon the basis of the infant's drug dependency. The prime purpose of this bill is to keep the families intact. It's not for the purpose of investigation. . . .
>
> Again, there is a well-founded anxiety that we are looking to arrest Moms. We're not looking to do that. What we are looking to do is we're looking to intervene on behalf of many different state policies.

From this legislative history, it is clear that the Legislature considered and rejected a specific statutory provision authorizing criminal penalties against mothers for delivering drug-affected children who received transfer of an illegal drug derivative metabolized by the mother's body, in utero. In light of this express legislative statement, I conclude that the Legislature never intended for the general drug delivery statute to authorize prosecutions of those mothers who take illegal drugs close enough in time to childbirth that a doctor could testify that a tiny amount passed from mother to child in the few seconds before the umbilical cord was cut. Criminal prosecution of mothers like Johnson will undermine Florida's express policy of "keeping families intact" and could destroy the family by incarcerating the child's mother when alternative measures could protect the child and stabilize the family. . . .

this crime would defeat the purpose of keeping families intact

Some experts estimate that as many as eleven percent of pregnant women have used an illegal drug during pregnancy, and of those women, seventy-five percent have used cocaine. . . . Others estimate that 375,000 newborns per year are born to women who are users of illicit drugs. . . .

It is well-established that the effects of cocaine use by a pregnant woman on her fetus and later on her newborn can be severe. On average, cocaine-exposed babies have lower birth weights, shorter body lengths at birth, and smaller head circumferences than normal infants. . . . Cocaine use may also result in sudden infant death syndrome, neural-behavioral deficiencies as well as other medical problems and long-term developmental abnormalities. . . . The basic problem of damaging the fetus by drug use during pregnancy should not be addressed piecemeal, however, by prosecuting users who deliver their babies close in time to use of drugs and ignoring those who simply use drugs during their pregnancy. . . .

[P]rosecuting women for using drugs and "delivering" them to their newborns appears to be the least effective response to this crisis. Rather than face the possibility of prosecution, pregnant women who are substance abusers may simply avoid prenatal or medical care for fear of being detected. Yet the newborns of these women are, as a group, the most fragile and sick, and most in need of hospital neo-natal care. . . .

In summary, I would hold that section 893.13(l)(c) 1. does not encompass "delivery" of an illegal drug derivative from womb to placenta to umbilical cord to newborn after a child's birth. Johnson, 578 So. 2d at 421-27 (Sharp, J., dissenting).

. . . [For the reasons indicated in Judge Sharp's dissent,] we quash the decision below . . . and remand with directions that Johnson's two convictions be reversed.

Notes and Questions

1. Did Johnson commit an "act" as that term has been defined through the cases? Was she prosecuted for the twin statuses of being an addict and being pregnant? Is being under the influence of a drug an act or a status? What about being in labor (also describable as "giving birth")?

2. Would Powell v. Texas, *supra,* allow punishment here?

3. Did the court determine whether the defendant had committed an "act" sufficient as a premise for punishment, or did it determine that punishing her was poor social policy?

4. *Social and legal context.* Most women who have appealed convictions for "delivering" cocaine to their unborn infants have won reversal by arguing for a

narrow interpretation of statutory terms like "delivery" — as in *Johnson;* and most who have appealed convictions under child abuse or child endangerment statutes have won reversal by arguing that the statutory term "child" excludes the unborn. But see Whitner v. State, 492 S.E.2d 777 (S.C. 1997) (court must include viable fetus under definition of "child" in the endangerment statute to ensure consistency with earlier holding that feticide is covered by homicide law). Nevertheless, Prof. Dorothy Roberts argues, the hidden political and constitutional issues underlying these cases require airing:

> [T]he prosecution of crack-addicted mothers diverts public attention from social ills such as poverty, racism, and a misguided national health policy and implies instead that shamefully high Black infant death rates are caused by the bad acts of individual mothers. Poor Black mothers become the scapegoats for the causes of the Black community's ill health. Punishing them assuages any guilt the nation might feel at the plight of an underclass with infant mortality at rates higher than those in some less developed countries. Making criminals of Black mothers apparently helps to relieve the nation of the burden of creating a health care system that ensures healthy babies for all its citizens.[21]

Prof. Roberts, noting that despite the many appellate reversals many defendants are forced into plea bargains, and that between 60 and 75 percent of defendants in these cases have been black, argues that such prosecutions violate equal protection and privacy rights. She also argues that prosecuting cocaine-taking mothers perversely disserves infant health by deterring mothers from seeking health services out of fear of detection or of intrusive and discriminatory investigation, and also that links between prosecutors, hospital bureaucracies, and clinicians inspired by these laws have led to deprivation of parental rights even where they have not led to criminal convictions.[22]

F. LEGALITY

UNITED STATES v. HUDSON AND GOODWIN
Supreme Court of the United States
11 U.S. (7 Cranch) 32 (1812)

This was a case certified from the Circuit Court for the District of *Connecticut,* in which, upon argument of a general demurrer to an *indictment* for a libel on the President and Congress of the United States, contained in the *Connecticut Currant,* of the 7th of May, 1806, charging them with having in secret voted two millions of dollars as a present to Bonaparte for leave to make a treaty with Spain, the judges of that Court were divided in opinion upon the question, whether the Circuit Court of the United States had a common law jurisdiction in cases of libel.

21. Punishing Drug Addicts Who Have Babies: Women of Color, Equality, and the Right of Privacy, 104 Harv. L. Rev. 1419, 1436 (1991).
22. Unshackling Black Motherhood, 95 Mich. L. Rev. 938 (1997).

JOHNSON, J.

The only question which this case presents is, whether the Circuit Courts of the United States can exercise a common law jurisdiction in criminal cases. . . . In no other case for many years has this jurisdiction been asserted; and the general acquiescence of legal men shews the prevalence of opinion in favor of the negative of the proposition.

The course of reasoning which leads to this conclusion is simple, obvious, and admits of but little illustration. The powers of the general Government are made up of concessions from the several states — whatever is not expressly given to the former, the latter expressly reserve. The judicial power of the United States is a constituent part of those concessions, — that power is to be exercised by Courts organized for the purpose, and brought into existence by an effort of the legislative power of the Union. Of all the Courts which the United States may, under their general powers, constitute, one only, the Supreme Court, possesses jurisdiction derived immediately from the constitution, and of which the legislative power cannot deprive it. All other Courts created by the general Government possess no jurisdiction but what is given them by the power that creates them, and can be vested with none but what the power ceded to the general Government will authorize them to confer.

It is not necessary to inquire whether the general Government, in any and what extent, possesses the power of conferring on its Courts a jurisdiction in cases similar to the present; it is enough that such jurisdiction has not been conferred by any legislative act, if it does not result to those Courts as a consequence of their creation. . . .

The only ground on which it has ever been contended that this jurisdiction could be maintained is, that, upon the formation of any political body, an implied power to preserve its own existence and promote the end and object of its creation, necessarily results to it. . . .

But if [this principle is] admitted as applicable to the state of things in this country, the consequence would not result from it which is here contended for. If it may communicate certain implied powers to the general Government, it would not follow that the Courts of that Government are vested with jurisdiction over any particular act done by an individual in supposed violation of the peace and dignity of the sovereign power. The legislative authority of the Union must first make an act a crime, affix a punishment to it, and declare the Court that shall have jurisdiction of the offence.

Certain implied powers must necessarily result to our Courts of justice from the nature of their institution. But jurisdiction of crimes against the state is not among those powers. To fine for contempt — imprison for contumacy — inforce the observance of order, &c. are powers which cannot be dispensed with in a Court, because they are necessary to the exercise of all others: and so far our Courts no doubt possess powers not immediately derived from statute; but all exercise of criminal jurisdiction in common law cases we are of opinion is not within their implied powers.

Notes and Questions

1. *Hudson and Goodwin* was decided against the background of political struggles between the Federalists and the Jeffersonian Republicans. The

Federalist-controlled Congress had authorized prosecutions of criminal libels under the hated Sedition Act of 1798. These prosecutions, along with other abuses, prompted the Kentucky and Virginia resolutions, authored by Jefferson and Madison respectively, propounding a theory of federal powers as revocable delegations from the sovereign states. The Sedition Act was allowed to lapse after the Republican electoral victory of 1800. Some Federalists, notably Justice Story, continued to feel that the effective conduct of diplomacy and war required the use of criminal law to punish both officials who refused to carry out the policies of the executive branch and private citizens who interfered with or subverted these policies. Yet the memory of Federalist misuse of such powers to suppress political opposition effectively discredited this argument.

Hudson and Goodwin established that the federal courts could impose liability only for crimes defined by statute. Does Justice Johnson's reasoning depend only on the nature of the federal constitution as establishing a government of limited powers? Or would the same arguments apply to state courts? Consider, in this regard, the following case.

STATE v. EGAN
Supreme Court of Florida
287 So. 2d 1 (1973)[23]

BOYD, JUSTICE.

On November 29, 1971, the grand jury, in and for Broward County, Florida, returned an indictment charging appellee . . . with . . . the common-law offense of nonfeasance. [Nonfeasance is a form of official misconduct, involving an omission or failure to perform a legal duty. Common law criminal liability is authorized by Section 775.01, Florida Statutes, which provides that the English common law of crimes will apply on any subject not regulated by statute.]

A motion to dismiss was filed challenging the constitutionality of Section 775.01. . . . [T]he lower court entered its order striking down Section 775.01 on the ground that it was '. . . in violation of [the Florida Constitutions, Article I, Section 9 (due process) and Article I, Section 16 (right to be informed of the nature of accusations)]. . . .' The controlling issue, as stated by the lower court, was whether Section 775.01 is too vague and indefinite to sufficiently inform a defendant of the charge placed against him. . . .

The legislative antecedents of Section 2.01, Florida Statutes expressly made the common law of England a part of the law of this jurisdiction. And for more than 100 years, this common law has been in effect in this jurisdiction, except insofar as it has been modified or superseded by statute. . . .

Section 775.01 provides:

'The common law of England in relation to crimes, except so far as the same relates to the modes and degrees of punishment, shall be of full force in this state where there is no existing provision by statute on the subject.'

What is there, then, about the above quoted statute that is vague? The statute simply makes the common law of England in relation to crimes, with certain

---

23. The editors have reordered some paragraphs for ease of exposition.

exceptions, the law of this state. . . . Where the legislative intent as evidenced by a statute is plain and unambiguous, then there is no necessity for any construction or interpretation of the statute, and the courts need only give effect to the plain meaning of its terms. . . .

As to the validity of the indictment in the case *sub judice* which charged appellee with . . . a common law offense, appellant relies on LaTour v. Stone, 139 Fla. 681 (1939). . . . [*LaTour* was a habeas corpus petition, attacking an information charging several city officials with official misconduct because the only applicable statute provided punishment only for state officers guilty of malpractice in office.] . . . However, this Court pointed out that the common law of England in relation to crimes was in full force in this jurisdiction, absent a statutory provision on the subject. The Court then reasoned:

> It, therefore, follows that if the Information charges any offense it must be found to be an offense under the common law. . . . "In general, it may be said that any . . . person occupying an official or quasi official position, may be guilty of [the common law offense of malfeasance in office]." . . . "All such crimes as especially affect public society are indictable at common law. The test is not whether precedents can be found in books, but whether they injuriously affect the public police and economy." . . . "The common law is sufficiently broad to punish as a misdemeanor, although there may be no exact precedent, any act which directly injures or tends to injure the public to such an extent as to require the state to interfere and punish the wrongdoer, as in the case of acts which injuriously affect public morality, or obstruct, or pervert public justice, or the administration of government." 190 So. at 707-708.

[In the instant case], the lower court indicated that a search was made of the common law of England in an effort to find where the offense of nonfeasance was discussed. We emphasize, however, that American courts, particularly Florida appellate courts, do not look solely to English cases to determine what the common law is. The words used in our statute, 'common law of England' refer to such common law, not only as declared by the English courts but also as declared by the courts of the American states. . . . Appellee was given specific direction in the indictment as to where the common law could be found which described the offense with which he was charged. The pertinent part of each count of the indictment reads:

> '. . . in violation of the common law of England, as enunciated in La Tour v. Stone, 190 So. 704 . . . as adopted by F.S. 775.01 and punishable as provided in F.S. 775.02. . . .'[24]

[The *LaTour* decision defined common law nonfeasance as follows:]

> At common law a failure or neglect of an officer to perform a ministerial duty imposed upon him by law renders him guilty of a misdemeanor. . . . Where however, the duty which has not been performed, is one involving discretion, the failure to perform it is not per se an indictable offense in the absence of willful and corrupt motives. . . . 190 So. at 709.

---

24. Section 775.02, F.S.A.: 'When there exists no such provision by statute, the court shall proceed to punish such offense by fine or imprisonment, but the fine shall not exceed five hundred dollars, nor the imprisonment twelve months.'

We think, however, that the lower court's main objection to Section 775.01 is that the statute does not set forth in express verbiage the common law which is made a part of the law of this jurisdiction. To put it another way, the statute imposes the duty upon the reader thereof to ascertain for himself what the common law is. The opinion of the lower court notwithstanding, there are some things so well known that the legislature may justly assume that the courts will take judicial notice thereof. . . .

Surely, no legislative adoption is necessary to affirm the existence of the common law. Just as surely, however, it is urged that a statutory enactment is essential to repeal, abrogate, or change the rules or doctrine of the common law. . . . While, admittedly, a court can and should strike down any common law crime that fails to pass constitutional muster, it is emphasized that it is the province of the legislature and not of the court to modify the rules of the common law. The court has no more right to abrogate the common law than it has to repeal the statutory law. In other words, courts may properly extend old principles to new conditions, determine new or novel questions by analogy, and even develop and announce new principles made necessary by changes wrought by time and circumstance. Under our constitutional system of government, however, courts cannot legislate. They cannot abrogate, modify, repeal, or amend rules long established and recognized as parts of the law of the land. . . .

Another basic argument in support of the lower court's action in striking down Section 775.01 is that there is no longer any necessity for the statute and that it should be discarded. This argument seems strange . . . because the instant case affords an excellent example of the necessity of resorting to the common law for the proper crime with which to charge a defendant. . . .

In Ducksworth v. Boyer, 125 So. 2d 844 (Fla. 1960) this Court had occasion to resort to the common law in holding that a person lawfully confined for civil contempt, who escaped from confinement, could be punished for the common law offense of prison break, even though he was not confined for a misdemeanor or a felony. Clearly, if this Court had not had the right to rely on the common law, then the offender would have been able to violate the law with impunity.

. . . Whenever a principle of the common law has been once clearly established, the courts of this country must enforce it until repealed by the legislature, as long as there is a subject matter for the principle to operate on, and although the reason, in the opinion of the court, which induced its original establishment may have ceased to exist. . . .

Accordingly, the order of the trial court is quashed, and the cause remanded for further proceedings consistent herewith.

Notes and Questions

1. *Nonfeasance.* According to Professors Perkins and Boyce:

> Illustrations of nonfeasance in office include the refusal of the officer upon whom the duty rests to apprehend or prosecute a known offender, to execute criminal process entrusted to him, or to deliver a copy of certain proceedings to one entitled thereto. It would also be nonfeasance in office if an officer should refuse to take reasonable steps to prevent the lynching of a prisoner in his custody.[25]

25. Rollin M. Perkins and Ronald N. Boyce, Criminal Law 546 (1982).

Surely a legal system cannot effectively impose duties on public officials without some means of enforcement. But is criminal punishment the only available enforcement sanction? Whose responsibility is it to determine the enforcement sanction, the legislature or the courts? If the legislature chose to confine the official misconduct offense to state officers, should the court extend it to others? Or should we ascribe to the legislature the intention of leaving the regulation of other officials to the common law?

2. *Notice.* Does F.S. 775.01 give Florida officials adequate notice that they face criminal liability for nonfeasance? Does the case of LaTour v. Stone? Are potential defendants any better informed by the publication of legal rules in statutes rather than in case reports? If there had been no prior case of common law prosecution of official misconduct in Florida, could the indictment still have been upheld? Could the Florida courts have relied on ancient English cases? Could they have exercised common law powers to define a new offense, based on considerations of social utility or moral desert? And if they can exercise their common law powers to create new crimes, why can't they exercise these same powers to abolish old crimes? Is it because the legislature mandated such old crimes by passing F.S. 775.01? Could the defendant have been charged with nonfeasance even without this statute?

Does the importance of notice depend on the purpose of punishment? Is notice of criminal prohibitions necessary in order to rehabilitate or incapacitate violators? Is it important to deserved punishment? Can the criminal law deter effectively without publicizing criminal prohibitions and penalties? Could uncertainty about the scope of criminal prohibitions enhance deterrence? Would it deter only undesirable behavior or acceptable behavior as well?

3. *Common law crimes.* According to Professor Wayne LaFave:

> In the United States, the following conduct has been held criminal although no statute made it so: conspiracy; attempt to commit a crime; solicitation to commit a crime; uttering grossly obscene language in public; burning a body in the cellar furnace; keeping a house of prostitution; maliciously killing a horse; blasphemy; negligently permitting a prisoner to escape; discharging a gun near a sick person; public drunkenness; offenses against the purity of elections; libel; being a common scold; indecent assault; false imprisonment; misprison of felony; creating a public nuisance; eavesdropping; and violations of international law. . . .[26]

Nevertheless, almost all of these examples date from before World War II. Most American jurisdictions have dispensed with common law crimes. As Model Penal Code Article 1.05(1) provides, "No conduct constitutes an offense unless it is a crime or violation under this Code or another statute of this State." Many states have adopted similar provisions, including California, Texas, New York, Pennsylvania, Ohio, Illinois, New Jersey, Georgia, Tennessee, Missouri, Wisconsin and Arizona. Others, such as Indiana, have abolished common law crimes judicially. *See* Ledgerwood v. State, 134 Ind. 81, 33 N.E. 631 (1893). While Florida authorizes punishment of common law crimes by statute, some states punish common law crimes without such a statute. *See* Street v. State, 307 Md. 262, 513 A.2d 870 (1986) (cabdriver who kept passenger locked in cab during dispute about changing a large bill convicted of common law crime of unlawful

---

26. Wayne R. LaFave, Criminal Law (2003) 78-79 (citations omitted).

imprisonment); In re Antoine H., 319 Md. 101, 570 A.2d 1239 (1990) (hindering police officer); Commonwealth v. Triplett, 426 Mass. 26, 584 S.E.2d 271 (1979) (common law obstruction of justice includes witness tampering, but not interference with investigation); In re May, 584 S.E.2d 271 (N.C. 2003) (affray).

The following case applies a statutory provision abolishing the common law of crimes, and also brings to bear federal constitutional prohibitions on retroactive punishment.

ROGERS v. TENNESSEE
Supreme Court of the United States
532 U.S. 451 (2001)

JUSTICE O'CONNOR delivered the opinion of the Court.

. . . At common law, the year and a day rule provided that no defendant could be convicted of murder unless his victim had died by the defendant's act within a year and a day of the act. The Supreme Court of Tennessee abolished the rule as it had existed at common law in Tennessee and applied its decision to petitioner to uphold his conviction. The question before us is whether, in doing so, the court denied petitioner due process of law in violation of the Fourteenth Amendment.

I

Petitioner Wilbert K. Rogers was convicted in Tennessee state court of second degree murder. [Defendant stabbed James Bowdery in the heart, causing cardiac arrest, leading to brain damage and a coma. Bowdery died of a kidney infection, a common complication of comas, after 15 months.] Based on this evidence, the jury found petitioner guilty under Tennessee's criminal homicide statute. The statute, which makes no mention of the year and a day rule, defines criminal homicide simply as "the unlawful killing of another person which may be first degree murder, second degree murder, voluntary manslaughter, criminally negligent homicide or vehicular homicide." Tenn. Code Ann. §39-13-201 (1997). Petitioner appealed his conviction . . . arguing that, despite its absence from the statute, the year and a day rule persisted as part of the common law of Tennessee and, as such, precluded his conviction. . . .

The Supreme Court of Tennessee affirmed. . . . The court observed that it had recognized the viability of the year and a day rule in Tennessee in *Percer* v. *State*, 118 Tenn. 765, 103 S. W. 780 (1907), and that, "[d]espite the paucity of case law" on the rule in Tennessee, "both parties . . . agree that the . . . rule was a part of the common law of this State." . . . After reviewing the justifications for the rule at common law, however, the court found that the original reasons for recognizing the rule no longer exist. Accordingly, the court abolished the rule as it had existed at common law in Tennessee.

The court disagreed with petitioner's contention that application of its decision abolishing the rule to his case would violate the *Ex Post Facto* Clauses of the State and Federal Constitutions. Those constitutional provisions, the court observed, refer only to legislative Acts. The court then noted that in *Bouie* v. *City of Columbia* . . . this Court held that due process prohibits retroactive application of any "'judicial construction of a criminal statute [that] is unexpected and indefensible by reference to the law which has been expressed prior to the conduct in issue.'" . . . The court concluded, however, that application of its decision to petitioner would not offend this principle. We . . . now affirm.

II

Although petitioner's claim is one of due process, the Constitution's *Ex Post Facto* Clause figures prominently in his argument. The Clause provides simply that "[n]o State shall . . . pass any . . . ex post facto Law." Art. I, §10, cl. 1. The most well-known and oft-repeated explanation of the scope of the Clause's protection was given by Justice Chase, who long ago identified, in dictum, four types of laws to which the Clause extends:

> "1st. Every law that makes an action done before the passing of the law, and which was innocent when done, criminal; and punishes such action. 2d. Every law that aggravates a crime, or makes it greater than it was, when committed. 3d. Every law that changes the punishment, and inflicts a greater punishment, than the law annexed to the crime, when committed. 4th. Every law that alters the legal rules of evidence, and receives less, or different, testimony, than the law required at the time of the commission of the offense, in order to convict the offender." *Calder* v. *Bull*, 3 Dall. 386, 390 (1798) (*seriatim* opinion of Chase, J.). As the text of the Clause makes clear, it "is a limitation upon the powers of the Legislature, and does not of its own force apply to the Judicial Branch of government." *Marks* v. *United States*, 430 U.S. 188, 191 (1977).

We have observed, however, that limitations on *ex post facto* judicial decisionmaking are inherent in the notion of due process. In *Bouie* v. *City of Columbia*, [378 U.S. 347 (1964)] . . . , we considered the South Carolina Supreme Court's retroactive application of its construction of the State's criminal trespass statute to the petitioners in that case. The statute prohibited "entry upon the lands of another . . . after notice from the owner or tenant prohibiting such entry. . . ." The South Carolina court construed the statute to extend to [black] patrons of a drug store who had received no notice prohibiting their entry into the store, but had refused to leave the store when asked. Prior to the court's decision, South Carolina cases construing the statute had uniformly held that conviction under the statute required proof of notice before entry. None of those cases, moreover, had given the "slightest indication that that requirement could be satisfied by proof of the different act of remaining on the land after being told to leave."

We held that the South Carolina court's retroactive application of its construction to the store patrons violated due process. Reviewing decisions in which we had held criminal statutes "void for vagueness" under the Due Process Clause, we noted that this Court has often recognized the "basic principle that a criminal statute must give fair warning of the conduct that it makes a crime." Deprivation of the right to fair warning, we continued, can result both from vague statutory language and from an unforeseeable and retroactive judicial expansion of statutory language that appears narrow and precise on its face. . . . We found that the South Carolina court's construction of the statute violated this principle because it was so clearly at odds with the statute's plain language and had no support in prior South Carolina decisions.

. . . Petitioner contends that the *Ex Post Facto* Clause would prohibit the retroactive application of a decision abolishing the year and a day rule if accomplished by the Tennessee Legislature. He claims that the purposes behind the Clause are so fundamental that due process should prevent the Supreme Court of Tennessee from accomplishing the same result by judicial decree. . . .

To the extent petitioner argues that the Due Process Clause incorporates the specific prohibitions of the *Ex Post Facto* Clause as identified in *Calder,* petitioner misreads *Bouie.* To be sure, our opinion in *Bouie* does contain some expansive language that is suggestive of the broad interpretation for which petitioner argues. Most prominent is our statement that "[i]f a state legislature is barred by the *Ex Post Facto* Clause from passing . . . a law, it must follow that a State Supreme Court is barred by the Due Process Clause from achieving precisely the same result by judicial construction." This language, however, was dicta. Our decision in *Bouie* was rooted firmly in well established notions of *due process.* Its rationale rested on core due process concepts of notice, foreseeability, and, in particular, the right to fair warning as those concepts bear on the constitutionality of attaching criminal penalties to what previously had been innocent conduct. And we couched its holding squarely in terms of that established due process right, and not in terms of the *ex post facto*–related dicta to which petitioner points. Contrary to petitioner's suggestion, nowhere in the opinion did we go so far as to incorporate jot-for-jot the specific categories of *Calder* into due process limitations on the retroactive application of judicial decisions. . . .

In the context of common law doctrines (such as the year and a day rule), there often arises a need to clarify or even to reevaluate prior opinions as new circumstances and fact patterns present themselves. Such judicial acts, whether they be characterized as "making" or "finding" the law, are a necessary part of the judicial business in States in which the criminal law retains some of its common law elements. Strict application of *ex post facto* principles in that context would unduly impair the incremental and reasoned development of precedent that is the foundation of the common law system. The common law, in short, presupposes a measure of evolution that is incompatible with stringent application of *ex post facto* principles. . . . Accordingly, we conclude that a judicial alteration of a common law doctrine of criminal law violates the principle of fair warning, and hence must not be given retroactive effect, only where it is "unexpected and indefensible by reference to the law which had been expressed prior to the conduct in issue."

III

Turning to the particular facts of the instant case, the Tennessee court's abolition of the year and a day rule was not unexpected and indefensible. The year and a day rule is widely viewed as an outdated relic of the common law. Petitioner does not even so much as hint that good reasons exist for retaining the rule, and so we need not delve too deeply into the rule and its history here. Suffice it to say that the rule is generally believed to date back to the 13th century . . . ; that the primary and most frequently cited justification for the rule is that 13th century medical science was incapable of establishing causation beyond a reasonable doubt when a great deal of time had elapsed between the injury to the victim and his death; and that, as practically every court recently to have considered the rule has noted, advances in medical and related science have so undermined the usefulness of the rule as to render it without question obsolete. . . .

For this reason, the year and a day rule has been legislatively or judicially abolished in the vast majority of jurisdictions recently to have addressed the issue. . . . Common law courts frequently look to the decisions of other jurisdictions in determining whether to alter or modify a common law rule in light of changed circumstances, increased knowledge, and general logic and experience. Due process, of course, does not require a person to apprise himself of the common law of all 50 States in order to guarantee that his actions will not subject him to punishment in light of a developing trend in the law that has not yet made its way to his State. At the same time, however, the fact that a vast number of jurisdictions have abolished a rule that has so clearly outlived its purpose is surely relevant to whether the abolition of the rule in a particular case can be said to be unexpected and indefensible by reference to the law as it then existed.

Finally, and perhaps most importantly, at the time of petitioner's crime the year and a day rule had only the most tenuous foothold as part of the criminal law of the State of Tennessee. The rule did not exist as part of Tennessee's statutory criminal code. And while the Supreme Court of Tennessee concluded that the rule persisted at common law, it also pointedly observed that the rule had never once served as a ground of decision in any prosecution for murder in the State. . . .

The judgment of the Supreme Court of Tennessee is accordingly affirmed.

this rule was tenuous anyway

JUSTICE SCALIA, with whom JUSTICE STEVENS and JUSTICE THOMAS join, and with whom JUSTICE BREYER joins as to Part II, dissenting.

The Court today approves the conviction of a man for a murder that was not murder (but only manslaughter) when the offense was committed. It thus violates a principle — encapsulated in the maxim *nulla poena sine lege*— which "dates from the ancient Greeks" and has been described as one of the most "widely held value-judgment[s] in the entire history of human thought." J. Hall, General Principles of Criminal Law 59 (2d ed. 1960). Today's opinion produces, moreover, a curious constitution that only a judge could love. One in which (by virtue of the *Ex Post Facto* Clause) the elected representatives of all the people cannot retroactively make murder what was not murder when the act was committed; but in which unelected judges can do precisely that. . . .

not fair that judges can change even though leg can't

I

. . . At the time of the framing, common-law jurists believed (in the words of Sir Francis Bacon) that the judge's "office is *jus dicere,* and not *jus dare;* to interpret law, and not to make law, or give law." Bacon, Essays, Civil and Moral, in 3 Harvard Classics 130 (C. Eliot ed. 1909) (1625). Or as described by Blackstone, . . . "judicial decisions are the principal and most authoritative *evidence,* that can be given, of the existence of such a custom as shall form a part of the common law." 1 W. Blackstone, Commentaries on the Laws of England *69 (1765) (emphasis added).

Blackstone acknowledged that the courts' exposition of what the law was could change. *Stare decisis,* he said, "admits of exception, where the former determination is most evidently contrary to reason . . ." *Ibid.* But "in such cases the subsequent judges do not pretend to make a new law, but to vindicate the old one from misrepresentation." To fit within this category of bad law, a law must be "manifestly absurd or unjust." It would not suffice, he said, that "the particular reason [for the law] can at this distance of time [not be] precisely assigned." "For though [its] reason be not obvious at first view, yet we owe such a deference to former times as not to suppose they acted wholly without consideration." . . . "A custom once reasonable and tolerable, if after it become grievous, and not answerable to the reason, whereupon it was grounded, yet is to be . . . taken away by act of parliament." 2 E. Coke, Institutes of the Laws of England 664 (1642). . . .

It is true that framing-era judges in this country considered themselves authorized to reject English common-law precedent they found "barbarous" and "ignorant," see 1 Z. Swift, A System of the Laws of the State of Connecticut 46 (1795) (hereinafter Swift). That, however, was not an assertion of *judges'* power to *change* the common law. For, as Blackstone wrote, the common law was a law for England, and did not automatically transfer to the American Colonies; rather, it had to be adopted. In short, the colonial courts felt themselves perfectly free to pick and choose which parts of the English common law they would adopt. . . . This discretion not to adopt would not presuppose, or even support, the power of colonial courts subsequently to change the accumulated colonial common law. . . .

Nor is the framing era's acceptance of common-law crimes support for the proposition that the Framers accepted an evolving common law. The acknowledgment of a new crime, not thitherto rejected by judicial decision, was not a *changing* of the common law, but an *application* of it. At the time of the framing, common-law crimes were considered unobjectionable, for "a law founded on the law of nature may be retrospective, because it always existed," *Blackwell* v. *Wilkinson*, Jefferson's Rep. 73, 77 (Va. 1768) (argument of then-Attorney General John Randolph). . . .

What occurred in the present case, then, is precisely what Blackstone said — and the Framers believed — would not suffice. The Tennessee Supreme Court made no pretense that the year-and-a-day rule was "bad" law from the outset; rather, it asserted, the need for the rule, as a means of assuring causality of the death, had disappeared with time. Blackstone — and the Framers who were formed by Blackstone — would clearly have regarded that *change* in law as a matter for the legislature, beyond the *power* of the court. It may well be that some common-law decisions of the era in fact changed the law while purporting not to. But that is beside the point. What is important here is that it was an undoubted point of principle, at the time the Due Process Clause was adopted, that courts could not "change" the law. That explains why the Constitution restricted only the legislature from enacting *ex post facto* laws. Under accepted norms of judicial process, an *ex post facto* law (in the sense of a judicial holding, not that a prior decision was erroneous, but that the prior valid law is hereby retroactively *changed*) was simply not an option for the courts. This attitude subsisted, I may note, well beyond the founding era, and beyond the time when due process guarantees were extended against the States by the Fourteenth Amendment. . . .

II

Even if I agreed with the Court that the Due Process Clause is violated only when there is lack of "fair warning" of the impending retroactive change,

I would not find such fair warning here. It is not clear to me, in fact, what the Court believes the fair warning consisted of. Was it the mere fact that "[t]he year and a day rule is widely viewed as an outdated relic of the common law"? So are many of the elements of common-law crimes, such as "breaking the close" as an element of burglary, or "asportation" as an element of larceny. Are all of these "outdated relics" subject to retroactive judicial rescission? Or perhaps the fair warning consisted of the fact that "the year and a day rule has been legislatively or judicially abolished in the vast majority of jurisdictions recently to have addressed the issue." But why not count in petitioner's favor (as giving him no reason to expect a change in law) those even more numerous jurisdictions that have chosen *not* "recently to have addressed the issue"? And why not also count in petitioner's favor (rather than *against* him) those jurisdictions that have abolished the rule *legislatively,* and those jurisdictions that have abolished it through *prospective* rather than *retroactive* judicial rulings (together, a large majority of the abolitions, see 922 S. W. 2d, at 397, n. 4, 402 (listing statutes and cases))? That is to say, even if it was predictable that the rule would be changed, it was *not* predictable that it would be changed *retroactively,* rather than in the *prospective* manner to which legislatures are restricted by the *Ex Post Facto* Clause, or in the *prospective* manner that most other courts have employed. . . .

Finally, the Court seeks to establish fair warning by discussing at great length, how unclear it was that the year-and-a-day rule was ever the law in Tennessee. [However,] the Supreme Court of Tennessee is the authoritative expositor of Tennessee law, and has said categorically that the year-and-a-day rule was the law. . . . As far as I can tell, petitioner had nothing that could fairly be called a "warning" that the Supreme Court of Tennessee would retroactively eliminate one of the elements of the crime of murder. . . .

Notes and Questions

1. Let us assume that the principle of prospectivity has two functions: ensuring fair notice to defendants so they can conform their conduct to the law, and preventing ad hominem or discriminatory criminalization (that is, punishing conduct on the basis of who committed it, rather than its wrongfulness or harmfulness). As to the fair notice function, didn't Rogers have adequate notice that he might end up convicted of murder when he attempted to murder his victim? Is it plausible that he relied on the year-and-a-day rule to exculpate him when he planned his victim's murder? If the defendant had fair notice that he could be convicted of murder, the only remaining issue is whether, as in *Bouie,* allowing the court to alter its construction of the elements of the offense poses the risk of discriminatory treatment.

In *Bouie,* the court criminalized conduct (remaining after notice to leave) not defined as criminal by the trespass statute. In *Rogers,* the Tennessee court eliminated its own judicially created *exception* to the statutory offense definition punishing causation of death. Is it important that the law being altered to the defendant's detriment in *Rogers* was judge-made? If, as Justice Scalia argues, courts cannot alter criteria of causation by eliminating the year-and-a-day rule, can they ever change their minds about how to instruct juries on the meaning of any statutory offense element? Only when doing so benefits the defense in the case at bar?

2. Justice Scalia claims that the Framers believed that (1) the common law rested on truths of nature, and (2) therefore judges could not alter it, but

(3) judges could correct their own mistaken opinions about it. Is causation a question of science, a fact of nature about which judges can be wrong? If so, can't judges correct their definition of causation, consistently with Justice Scalia's conception of the original understanding of due process?

How might Justice Scalia have decided *Egan*?

3. *The Keeler case.* In its famous decision in Keeler v. Superior Court, 2 Cal. 3d 619, 87 Cal. Rptr. 481 (1970), the California Supreme Court quashed a murder charge for a defendant who intentionally killed a fetus by viciously beating his ex-wife, who was then eight months pregnant by another man. The doctor who removed the fetus testified that it was mature enough to be viable — that even if prematurely born at that age it would have had a 75 to 96 percent chance of survival. The court reasoned:

> Penal Code section 187 provides: "Murder is the unlawful killing of a human being, with malice aforethought." The dispositive question is whether the fetus which petitioner is accused of killing was, on February 23, 1969, a "human being" within the meaning of the statute. If it was not, petitioner cannot be charged with its "murder" and prohibition will lie.
>
> Section 187 was . . . taken verbatim from the first California statute defining murder, part of the Crimes and Punishments Act of 1850. . . . We conclude that in declaring murder to be the unlawful and malicious killing of a "human being" the Legislature of 1850 intended that term to have the settled common law meaning of a person who had been born alive, and did not intend the act of feticide — as distinguished from abortion — to be an offense under the laws of California. . . .
>
> The People urge, however, that the sciences of obstetrics and pediatrics have greatly progressed since [that time], to the point where with proper medical care a normally developed fetus prematurely born at 28 weeks or more has an excellent chance of survival, i.e., is "viable"; that the common law requirement of live birth to prove the fetus had become a "human being" who may be the victim of murder is no longer in accord with scientific fact, since an unborn but viable fetus is now fully capable of independent life; and that one who unlawfully and maliciously terminates such a life should therefore be liable to prosecution for murder under section 187. We may grant the premises of this argument. . . . But we cannot join in the conclusion sought to be deduced: we cannot hold this petitioner to answer for murder by reason of his alleged act of killing an unborn — even though viable — fetus. To such a charge there are two insuperable obstacles, one "jurisdictional" and the other constitutional.
>
> Penal Code section 6 declares in relevant part that "No act or omission" accomplished after the code has taken effect "is criminal or punishable, except as prescribed or authorized by this code, or by some of the statutes which it specifies as continuing in force and as not affected by its provisions, or by some ordinance, municipal, county, or township regulation. . . ." This section embodies a fundamental principle of our tripartite form of government, i.e., that subject to the constitutional prohibition against cruel and unusual punishment, the power to define crimes and fix penalties is vested exclusively in the legislative branch. Stated differently, there are no common law crimes in California. . . .
>
> Applying these rules to the case at bar, we would undoubtedly act in excess of the judicial power if we were to adopt the People's proposed construction of section 187. As we have shown, the Legislature has defined the crime of murder in California to apply only to the unlawful and malicious killing of one who has been born alive. . . . Whether to . . . extend liability for murder in California is a determination solely within the province of the Legislature. For a court to simply declare, by judicial fiat, that the time has now come to prosecute under section 187

one who kills an unborn but viable fetus would indeed be to rewrite the statute under the guise of construing it. . . .

The second obstacle to the proposed judicial enlargement of section 187 is the guarantee of due process of law. Assuming arguendo that we have the power to adopt the new construction of this statute as the law of California, such a ruling, by constitutional command, could operate only prospectively. . . .

The first essential of due process is fair warning of the act which is made punishable as a crime. . . . This requirement of fair warning is reflected in the constitutional prohibition against the enactment of ex post facto laws. When a new penal statute is applied retrospectively to make punishable an act which was not criminal at the time it was performed, the defendant has been given no advance notice consistent with due process. And precisely the same effect occurs when such an act is made punishable under a preexisting statute but by means of an unforeseeable judicial enlargement thereof. (Bouie v. City of Columbia (1964) 378 U.S. 347.) . . .

We conclude that the judicial enlargement of section 187 now urged upon us by the People would not have been foreseeable to this petitioner, and hence that its adoption at this time would deny him due process of law. . . .

Keeler is decided on two grounds: (1) the "legislativity" of criminal lawmaking required by the California Penal Code, and (2) the prospectivity of criminal lawmaking required by the Due Process Clause of the Fourteenth Amendment. Does *Rogers* narrow the holding of *Bouie* enough to overrule *Keeler,* on the issue of prospectivity? If a court can expand murder liability by altering the meaning of causing death, can it *expand* murder by altering the meaning of human being? Does it depend on whether these terms appear in the statute? Note that it is an accepted canon of statutory construction that "contemporary or practical interpretation" should play a role in statutory interpretation. While "[t]he common law meanings of words used may always be important in determining the exact meaning which was intended," criminal laws should be "given their common and ordinary meaning so that they may be understood by all."[27] Does Rogers's act fit the "ordinary meaning" of killing a human being? Does Keeler's?

Would Keeler have had any reasonable claim that he had been denied fair warning that his act was illegal? If he knew he was at least committing a crime, does it make a difference whether he was aware which crime he was committing?

4. *Legality and defenses.* The legality principle clearly places limits on the courts' ability to define and proscribe common law crimes. But what about the power of courts to recognize common law defenses not provided by statute? Can courts fashion a self-defense exception to a statute that defines murder simply as "the intentional killing of a human being?" Should they be able to do so only if the statute appears to delegate authority to the courts to define justifications, say by defining murder as "the *unlawful* killing of a human being with malice aforethought?" Assuming that the principle of legality permits courts to provide defendants with extrastatutory defenses, does it also allow courts to take them away or narrow them? Take our second statute, defining murder as "the unlawful killing of a human being." Let us imagine that courts in the relevant jurisdiction have, in the past, instructed jurors that a killing is "lawful" if necessary to repel a violent attacker from one's home. May a court now instruct a jury that such a killing is "lawful" only if the defendant could not safely retreat?

27. Arthur Sutherland, Statutory Construction Section 59.08 (1986).

G. SPECIFICITY

CHICAGO v. MORALES
Supreme Court of the United States
527 U.S. 41 (1999)

JUSTICE STEVENS announced the judgment of the Court and delivered the opinion of the Court with respect to Parts I, II, and V, and an opinion with respect to Parts III, IV, and VI, in which JUSTICE SOUTER and JUSTICE GINSBURG join.

In 1992, the Chicago City Council enacted the Gang Congregation Ordinance, which prohibits "criminal street gang members" from "loitering" with one another or with other persons in any public place. The question presented is whether the Supreme Court of Illinois correctly held that the ordinance violates the Due Process Clause of the Fourteenth Amendment to the Federal Constitution.

I

Before the ordinance was adopted, the city council's Committee on Police and Fire conducted hearings to explore the problems created by the city's street gangs, and more particularly, the consequences of public loitering by gang members. . . .

The council found that a continuing increase in criminal street gang activity was largely responsible for the city's rising murder rate, as well as an escalation of violent and drug related crimes. It noted that in many neighborhoods throughout the city, "the burgeoning presence of street gang members in public places has intimidated many law abiding citizens." 177 111. 2d 440, 445, 687 N.E.2d 53, 58 (1997). Furthermore, the council stated that gang members "establish control over identifiable areas . . . by loitering in those areas and intimidating others from entering those areas; and . . . [m]embers of criminal street gangs avoid arrest by committing no offense punishable under existing laws when they know the police are present. . . ." Ibid. It further found that "loitering in public places by criminal street gang members creates a justifiable fear for the safety of persons and property in the area" and that "[a]ggressive action is necessary to preserve the city's streets and other public places so that the public may use such places without fear." Moreover, the council concluded that the city "has an interest in discouraging all persons from loitering in public places with criminal gang members."

The ordinance creates a criminal offense punishable by a fine of up to $500, imprisonment for not more than six months, and a requirement to perform up to 120 hours of community service. Commission of the offense involves four predicates. First, the police officer must reasonably believe that at least one of the two or more persons present in a "public place" is a "criminal street gang membe[r]." Second, the persons must be "loitering," which the ordinance defines as "remain[ing] in any one place with no apparent purpose." Third, the officer must then order "all" of the persons to disperse and remove themselves "from the area." Fourth, a person must disobey the officer's order. If any person, whether a gang member or not, disobeys the officer's order, that person is guilty of violating the ordinance.

Two months after the ordinance was adopted, the Chicago Police Department promulgated General Order 92-4 to provide guidelines to govern its enforcement. That order purported to establish limitations on the enforcement discretion of police officers "to ensure that the anti-gang loitering ordinance is not enforced in an arbitrary or discriminatory way." . . . The limitations confine the authority to arrest gang members who violate the ordinance to sworn "members of the Gang Crime Section" and certain other designated officers, and establish detailed criteria for defining street gangs and membership in such gangs. . . . In addition, the order directs district commanders to "designate areas in which the presence of gang members has a demonstrable effect on the activities of law abiding persons in the surrounding community," and provides that the ordinance "will be enforced only within the designated areas." . . . The city, however, does not release the locations of these "designated areas" to the public.

II

During the three years of its enforcement, the police issued over 89,000 dispersal orders and arrested over 42,000 people for violating the ordinance. . . .

The Illinois Supreme Court . . . held "that the gang loitering ordinance violates due process of law in that it is impermissibly vague on its face and an arbitrary restriction on personal liberties." . . . Like the Illinois Supreme Court, we conclude that the ordinance enacted by the city of Chicago is unconstitutionally vague.

III

Vagueness may invalidate a criminal law for either of two independent reasons. First, it may fail to provide the kind of notice that will enable ordinary people to understand what conduct it prohibits; second, it may authorize and even encourage arbitrary and discriminatory enforcement. . . . Accordingly, we first consider whether the ordinance provides fair notice to the citizen and then discuss its potential for arbitrary enforcement.

IV

"It is established that a law fails to meet the requirements of the Due Process Clause if it is so vague and standardless that it leaves the public uncertain as to the conduct it prohibits. . . ." Giaccio v. Pennsylvania, 382 U.S. 399, 402-03 (1966). The Illinois Supreme Court recognized that the term "loiter" may have a common and accepted meaning, . . . but the definition of that term in this ordinance — "to remain in any one place with no apparent purpose" — does not. It is difficult to imagine how any citizen of the city of Chicago standing in a public place with a group of people would know if he or she had an "apparent purpose." If she were talking to another person, would she have an apparent purpose? If she were frequently checking her watch and looking expectantly down the street, would she have an apparent purpose?

Since the city cannot conceivably have meant to criminalize each instance a citizen stands in public with a gang member, the vagueness that dooms this ordinance is not the product of uncertainty about the normal meaning of "loitering," but rather about what loitering is covered by the ordinance and what is not. The Illinois Supreme Court emphasized the law's failure to distinguish between innocent conduct and conduct threatening harm.[28] [S]tate courts have uniformly invalidated laws that do not join the term "loitering" with a second specific element of the crime.

The city's principal response to this concern about adequate notice is that loiterers are not subject to sanction until after they have failed to comply with an officer's order to disperse. "[W]hatever problem is created by a law that criminalizes conduct people normally believe to be innocent is solved when persons receive actual notice from a police order of what they are expected to do." We find this response unpersuasive for at least two reasons.

First, the purpose of the fair notice requirement is to enable the ordinary citizen to conform his or her conduct to the law. "No one may be required at peril of life, liberty or property to speculate as to the meaning of penal statutes." Lanzetta v. New Jersey, 306 U.S. 451, 453 (1939). Although it is true that a loiterer is not subject to criminal sanctions unless he or she disobeys a dispersal order, the loitering is the conduct that the ordinance is designed to prohibit. If the loitering is in fact harmless and innocent, the dispersal order itself is an unjustified impairment of liberty. If the police are able to decide arbitrarily which members of the public they will order to disperse, then the Chicago ordinance becomes indistinguishable from the law we held invalid in Shuttlesworth v. Birmingham, 382 U.S. 87, 90 (1965). Because an officer may issue an order only after prohibited conduct has already occurred, it cannot provide the kind of advance notice that will protect the putative loiterer from being ordered to disperse. . . .

Second, the terms of the dispersal order compound the inadequacy of the notice afforded by the ordinance. It provides that the officer "shall order all such persons to disperse and remove themselves from the area." This vague phrasing raises a host of questions. After such an order issues, how long must the loiterers remain apart? How far must they move? If each loiterer walks around the block and they meet again at the same location, are they subject to arrest or merely to being ordered to disperse again? As we do here, we have found vagueness in a criminal statute exacerbated by the use of the standards of "neighborhood" and "locality." . . .

The Constitution does not permit a legislature to "set a net large enough to catch all possible offenders, and leave it to the courts to step inside and say who could be rightfully detained, and who should be set at large." United States v. Reese, 92 U.S. 214, 221 (1876). This ordinance is therefore vague "not in the sense that it requires a person to conform his conduct to an imprecise but

---

28. 177 Ill. 2d, at 452, 687 N.E.2d, at 61. One of the trial courts that invalidated the ordinance gave the following illustration: "Suppose a group of gang members were playing basketball in the park, while waiting for a drug delivery. Their apparent purpose is that they are in the park to play ball. The actual purpose is that they are waiting for drugs. Under this definition of loitering, a group of people innocently sitting in a park discussing their futures would be arrested, while the 'basketball players' awaiting a drug delivery would be left alone." Chicago v. Youkhana, Nos. 93 MCI 293363 et al. (111. Cir. Ct., Cook Cty., Sept. 29, 1993).

comprehensible normative standard, but rather in the sense that no standard of conduct is specified at all." Coates v. Cincinnati, 402 U.S. 611, 614 (1971).

V

The broad sweep of the ordinance also violates "the requirement that a legislature establish minimal guidelines to govern law enforcement." Kolender v. Lawson, [461 U.S., 352, 358 (1983)]. There are no such guidelines in the ordinance . . . As we discussed in the context of fair notice, . . . the principal source of the vast discretion conferred on the police in this case is the definition of loitering as "to remain in any one place with no apparent purpose."

As the Illinois Supreme Court interprets that definition, it "provides absolute discretion to police officers to determine what activities constitute loitering." . . . We have no authority to construe the language of a state statute more narrowly than the construction given by that State's highest court. . . .

Nevertheless, the city disputes the Illinois Supreme Court's interpretation, arguing that the text of the ordinance limits the officer's discretion in three ways. First, it does not permit the officer to issue a dispersal order to anyone who is moving along or who has an apparent purpose. Second, it does not permit an arrest if individuals obey a dispersal order. Third, no order can issue unless the officer reasonably believes that one of the loiterers is a member of a criminal street gang.

Even putting to one side our duty to defer to a state court's construction of the scope of a local enactment, we find each of these limitations insufficient. That the ordinance does not apply to people who are moving — that is, to activity that would not constitute loitering under any possible definition of the term — does not even address the question of how much discretion the police enjoy in deciding which stationary persons to disperse under the ordinance. Similarly, that the ordinance does not permit an arrest until after a dispersal order has been disobeyed does not provide any guidance to the officer deciding whether such an order should issue. The "no apparent purpose" standard for making that decision is inherently subjective because its application depends on whether some purpose is "apparent" to the officer on the scene.

Presumably an officer would have discretion to treat some purposes — perhaps a purpose to engage in idle conversation or simply to enjoy a cool breeze on a warm evening — as too frivolous to be apparent if he suspected a different ulterior motive. Moreover, an officer conscious of the city council's reasons for enacting the ordinance might well ignore its text and issue a dispersal order, even though an illicit purpose is actually apparent.

It is true, as the city argues, that the requirement that the officer reasonably believe that a group of loiterers contains a gang member does place a limit on the authority to order dispersal. . . . But this ordinance, for reasons that are not explained in the findings of the city council, requires no harmful purpose and applies to non-gang members as well as suspected gang members. It applies to everyone in the city who may remain in one place with one suspected gang member as long as their purpose is not apparent to an officer observing them. Friends, relatives, teachers, counselors, or even total strangers might unwittingly engage in forbidden loitering if they happen to engage in idle conversation with a gang member.

Ironically, the definition of loitering in the Chicago ordinance not only extends its scope to encompass harmless conduct, but also has the perverse consequence of excluding from its coverage much of the intimidating conduct that motivated its enactment. As the city council's findings demonstrate, the most harmful gang loitering is motivated either by an apparent purpose to publicize the gang's dominance of certain territory, thereby intimidating nonmembers, or by an equally apparent purpose to conceal ongoing commerce in illegal drugs. As the Illinois Supreme Court has not placed any limiting construction on the language in the ordinance, we must assume that the ordinance means what it says and that it has no application to loiterers whose purpose is apparent. The relative importance of its application to harmless loitering is magnified by its inapplicability to loitering that has an obviously threatening or illicit purpose.

Finally, in its opinion striking down the ordinance, the Illinois Supreme Court refused to accept the general order issued by the police department as a sufficient limitation on the "vast amount of discretion" granted to the police in its enforcement. We agree. . . . That the police have adopted internal rules limiting their enforcement to certain designated areas in the city would not provide a defense to a loiterer who might be arrested elsewhere. Nor could a person who knowingly loitered with a well-known gang member anywhere in the city safely assume that they would not be ordered to disperse no matter how innocent and harmless their loitering might be.

VI

In our judgment, the Illinois Supreme Court correctly concluded that the ordinance does not provide sufficiently specific limits on the enforcement discretion of the police "to meet constitutional standards for definiteness and clarity." We recognize the serious and difficult problems testified to by the citizens of Chicago that led to the enactment of this ordinance. . . . However, in this instance the city has enacted an ordinance that affords too much discretion to the police and too little notice to citizens who wish to use the public streets.

Accordingly, the judgment of the Supreme Court of Illinois is
Affirmed.

Notes and Questions

1. What exactly is the actus reus of the crime covered by this ordinance? To "loiter"? To "not promptly obey" an order to disperse? To "remain in any one place with no apparent purpose"? To give the appearance of being a street gang member?

2. *Notice and the average citizen.* Is the problem that it is not clear enough to the average citizen who might risk arrest? Surely the average citizen knows precisely when she is being given an order to disperse. Can it be seriously argued that the term "disperse" is too vague? So is the problem that the citizen clearly told to disperse does not know how to avoid being given that order? Or that she does not have any way of knowing whether the order had a legal basis?

On the other hand, is the problem with the ordinance that it is not clear enough to the average police officer who might seek to make an arrest? But is the relevant standard — that the officer, based on his or her experience, observe some indications that people on the site are members of a street gang, and that the individual in question stands in a single place for some measurable period of time with no apparent activity underway — so different from what we legitimately ask the police to do all the time in order to protect the peace, to stop disorderly conduct, to disperse people from accident or potential crime scenes?

3. *Loitering and gangs.* Does the Court say that loitering, as defined in the statute, is a constitutionally protected act? Or does it suggest that the law is unconstitutional solely because it did not define the act precisely enough? Consider this suggestion in Justice O'Connor's concurring opinion:

> Nevertheless, there remain open to Chicago reasonable alternatives to combat the very real threat posed by gang intimidation and violence. For example, the Court properly and expressly distinguishes the ordinance from laws that require loiterers to have a "harmful purpose," from laws that target only gang members, and from laws that incorporate limits on the area *and* manner in which the laws may be enforced. In addition, the ordinance here is unlike a law that "directly prohibits" the "presence of a large collection of obviously brazen, insistent, and lawless gang members and hangers-on on the public ways," that "intimidates residents." Indeed, as the plurality notes, the city of Chicago has several laws that do exactly this. Chicago has even enacted a provision that "enables police officers to fulfill . . . their traditional functions," including "preserving the public peace." (Thomas, J., dissenting.) Specifically, Chicago's general disorderly conduct provision allows the police to arrest those who knowingly "provoke, make or aid in making a breach of peace." See Chicago Municipal Code §8-4-010 (1992).
>
> In my view, the gang loitering ordinance could have been construed more narrowly. The term "loiter" might possibly be construed in a more limited fashion to mean "to remain in any one place with no apparent purpose other than to establish control over identifiable areas, to intimidate others from entering those areas, or to conceal illegal activities." Such a definition would be consistent with the Chicago City Council's findings and would avoid the vagueness problems of the ordinance as construed by the Illinois Supreme Court. As noted above, so would limitations that restricted the ordinance's criminal penalties to gang members or that more carefully delineated the circumstances in which those penalties would apply to nongang members.

Are these suggestions consistent with Justice Stevens's opinion?

4. In Papachristou v. Jacksonville, 405 U.S. 156, 162-71 (1972), the Supreme Court struck down a vagrancy law that punished many classes of persons, including "Rogues and vagabonds, . . . common gamblers . . . common drunkards, common night walkers, thieves, pilferers or pick pockets, traders in stolen property, lewd wanton and lascivious persons, . . . common railers and brawlers, . . . habitual loafers, and disorderly persons." Are these acts or statuses? In other words, is the problem that they define conduct vaguely, or that they do not punish conduct at all, but mere propensities?

Justice Douglas's famous opinion in *Papachristou* offered an essay on vagrancy and the void-for-vagueness principle:

> Living under a rule of law entails various suppositions, one of which is that "[all persons] are entitled to be informed as to what the State commands or forbids." Lanzetta v. New Jersey, 306 U.S. 451, 453.

Lanzetta is one of a well-recognized group of cases insisting that the law give fair notice of the offending conduct. In the field of regulatory statutes governing business activities, where the acts limited are in a narrow category, greater leeway is allowed.

The poor among us, the minorities, the average householder are not in business and not alerted to the regulatory schemes of vagrancy laws; and we assume they would have no understanding of their meaning and impact if they read them. Nor are they protected from being caught in the vagrancy net by the necessity of having a specific intent to commit an unlawful act.

The Jacksonville ordinance makes criminal activities which by modern standards are normally innocent. "Nightwalking" is one. Florida construes the ordinance not to make criminal one night's wandering, Johnson v. State, 202 So. 2d, at 855, only the "habitual" wanderer or, as the ordinance describes it, "common night walkers." We know, however, from experience that sleepless people often walk at night, perhaps hopeful that sleep-inducing relaxation will result.

Luis Munoz-Marin, former Governor of Puerto Rico, commented once that "loafing" was a national virtue in his Commonwealth and that it should be encouraged. It is, however, a crime in Jacksonville.

"[P]ersons able to work but habitually living upon the earnings of their wives or minor children"— like habitually living "without visible means of support"— might implicate unemployed pillars of the community who have married rich wives.

"[P]ersons able to work but habitually living upon the earnings of their wives or minor children" may also embrace unemployed people out of the labor market, by reason of a recession or disemployed by reason of technological or so-called structural displacements.

Persons "wandering or strolling" from place to place have been extolled by Walt Whitman and Vachel Lindsay. The qualification "without any lawful purpose or object" may be a trap for innocent acts. Persons "neglecting all lawful business and habitually spending their time by frequenting . . . places where alcoholic beverages are sold or served" would literally embrace many members of golf clubs and city clubs.

Walkers and strollers and wanderers may be going to or coming from a burglary. Loafers or loiterers may be "casing" a place for a holdup. Letting one's wife support him is an intra-family matter, and normally of no concern to the police. Yet it may, of course, be the setting for numerous crimes.

The difficulty is that these activities are historically part of the amenities of life as we have known them. They are not mentioned in the Constitution or in the Bills of Rights. These unwritten amenities have been in part responsible for giving our people the feeling of independence and self-confidence, the feeling of creativity. These amenities have dignified the right of dissent and have honored the right to be nonconformists and the right to defy submissiveness. They have encouraged lives of high spirits rather than hushed, suffocating silence. . . .

A direction by a legislature to the police to arrest all "suspicious" persons would not pass constitutional muster. A vagrancy prosecution may be merely the cloak for a conviction which could not be obtained on the real but undisclosed grounds for the arrest. . . .

Those generally implicated by the imprecise terms of the ordinance — poor people, nonconformists, dissenters, idlers — may be required to comport themselves according to the life style deemed appropriate by the Jacksonville police and the courts. Where, as here, there are no standards governing the exercise of the discretion granted by the ordinance, the scheme permits and encourages an arbitrary and discriminatory enforcement of the law. It furnishes a convenient tool for "harsh and discriminatory enforcement by local prosecuting officials, against particular groups deemed to merit their displeasure." Thornhill v. Alabama, 310 U.S. 88, 97-98. . . .

. . . Of course, vagrancy statutes are useful to the police. Of course, they are nets making easy the roundup of so-called undesirables. But the rule of law implies equality and justice in its application. Vagrancy laws of the Jacksonville type teach that the scales of justice are so tipped that even-handed administration of the law is not possible. The rule of law, evenly applied to minorities as well as majorities, to the poor as well as the rich, is the great mucilage that holds society together.

The Jacksonville ordinance cannot be squared with our constitutional standards and is plainly unconstitutional.

5. *Majoritarianism and due process.* Consider this commentary by Profs. Tracey Meares and Dan Kahan,[29] attacking the Illinois Supreme Court decision in *Morales* that was soon thereafter affirmed by the United States Supreme Court:

. . . The ACLU attacked the ordinance as a throwback to the pre-Papachristou era, when police officers used vague loitering ordinances to intimidate and harass racial minorities. A state court (in a case now on appeal to the Illinois Supreme Court) agreed, describing the ordinance as an exercise of power reminiscent of a police state.

The picture of Chicago's gang-loitering ordinance that the ACLU and the court painted is simply false. The law was enacted not to oppress the City's minority residents; rather, it sprang from the grievances of these very citizens, who demanded effective action to rid their neighborhoods of drive-by shootings, fighting, and open-air drug dealing. The ordinance was passed by an overwhelming margin in the Chicago City Council, with key support from Aldermen representing the city's most impoverished, crime-ridden districts, whose residents are predominantly racial and ethnic minorities.

The claim that the ordinance invited arbitrary or discriminatory enforcement was also unfounded. In fact, the ordinance was accompanied by a carefully considered set of guidelines. For example, only a small number of officers in each police district were permitted to enforce the ordinance. They could do so, moreover, only in specified areas of a district with demonstrated gang activity. Before specifying enforcement "hot spots" district commanders were to consult with community residents.

What's more, it appears that the ordinance succeeded in decreasing crime before the courts intervened. Police data indicate that aggressive enforcement of the ordinance had led to substantial decreases in gang- and narcotics-related homicides and aggravated batteries in the districts with the most serious problems.

Blocking the policies makes law-enforcement protection less effective while adding no new political checks against law-enforcement abuses.

. . . The 1960s conception of rights insists on hyper-specific rules because it assumes that white political establishments can't be relied upon to punish law enforcers who abuse discretion to harass minorities. That anxiety is no longer so well founded: law enforcers in America's big cities are accountable to political establishments that more fairly represent African-Americans. Uncompromising hostility to discretion is therefore inappropriate.

That doesn't mean that the law should regard discretion as an unvarnished good. Even assuming political accountability, unbounded discretion creates a risk that individual law enforcers will be able to disregard the will of the community without detection. It also creates the risk that officials will concentrate burdens on a powerless or despised segment of the community, thereby undermining the

29. 24 Boston Rev., Apr.-May, 1999, at 4, 8.

principle of community burden-sharing. Hyper-specific rules are unnecessary under the principle of "guided discretion," but this principle does require communities to allocate authority in a manner that minimizes these risks.

Chicago's anti-gang loitering ordinance is a good example of a law-enforcement policy that satisfies the guided-discretion principle. That law was implemented through regulations that clearly specified who counted as a "gang member," what kinds of behavior counted, which officers could enforce the law, and in what neighborhood areas it could be enforced. When evaluated against these regulations, misuse of the ordinance would have been easy to spot. Given these safeguards, courts should have upheld the gang-loitering ordinance, whether or not it satisfied the demand for hyper-precision associated with the 1960s conception of rights.

. . . Douglas criticized vagrancy laws on the ground that the legal abstractions used to defend them were out of keeping with contemporary circumstances — namely, the discriminatory enforcement of vagrancy laws against effectively disenfranchised minorities. But circumstances have changed since 1960. Today African-Americans exercise considerable political clout in our nation's inner-cities; and far from being terrorized by anti-loitering laws, curfews and building searches, many inner-city residents support these measures as potent weapons against the crime that drastically diminishes their economic and social prospects.

What assumptions do Meares and Kahan make about the relationship between effective law enforcement, majority rule, historical circumstance, and due process rights?

For a comprehensive treatment of new, so-called "quality-of-life" policing schemes, and an argument that political and administrative measures to manage police discretion are more effective than constitutional review of "vagueness," see Debra Livingston, Police Discretion and the Quality of Life in Public Places: Courts, Communities, and the New Policing, 97 Colum. L. Rev. 551 (1997).

6. *Specificity today.* Is it still possible to draft a constitutionally valid vagrancy law? Consider the following effort by the drafters of the Model Penal Code:

Section 250.6. Loitering or Prowling. A person commits a violation if he loiters or prowls in a place, at a time, or in a manner not usual for lawabiding individuals under circumstances that warrant alarm for the safety of persons or property in the vicinity. Among the circumstances which may be considered in determining whether such alarm is warranted is the fact that the actor takes flight upon appearance of a peace officer, refuses to identify himself, or manifestly endeavors to conceal himself or any object. Unless flight by the actor or other circumstance makes it impracticable, a peace officer shall prior to any arrest for an offense under this section afford the actor an opportunity to dispel any alarm which would otherwise be warranted, by requesting him to identify himself and explain his presence and conduct. No person shall be convicted of an offense under this Section if the peace officer did not comply with the preceding sentence, or if it appears at trial that the explanation given by the actor was true and, if believed by the peace officer at the time, would have dispelled the alarm.

Does the Code's emphasis on "alarming" loitering solve the void-for-vagueness problem?

7. *Scope of the specificity principle.* Even relatively uncontroversial criminal laws, such as the homicide laws, give juries broad moral and political discretion to define criminal conduct under vague categories such as "reasonableness." If the involuntary manslaughter law requires the jury to determine whether the victim's death was "reasonably foreseeable," or if the voluntary manslaughter law

requires it to find that a "reasonable" person in the defendant's position would have been provoked into the heat of passion, are these laws void for vagueness? In a famous antitrust opinion in Nash v. United States, 229 U.S. 373, 376-78, (1913), Justice Holmes said

> [T]he law is full of instances where a man's fate depends on his estimating rightly, that is, as the jury subsequently estimates it, some matter of degree. If his judgment is wrong, not only may he incur a fine or a short imprisonment, as here; he may incur the penalty of death. "An act causing death may be murder, manslaughter, or misadventure according to the degree of danger attending it" by common experience in the circumstances known to the actor. "The very meaning of the fiction of implied malice in such cases at common law was, that a man might have to answer with his life for consequences which he neither intended nor foresaw." Commonwealth v. Pierce, 138 Mass. 165, 178. Commonwealth v. Chance, 174 Mass. 245, 252. "The criterion in such cases is to examine whether common social duty would, under the circumstances, have suggested a more circumspect conduct." 1 East P.C. 262. If a man should kill another by driving an automobile furiously into a crowd he might be convicted of murder however little he expected the result. If he did no more than drive negligently through a street he might get off with manslaughter or less. And in the last case he might be held although he himself thought that he was acting as a prudent man should . . . We are of opinion that there is no constitutional difficulty in the way of enforcing the criminal part of the act.

In State v. Musser, 118 Utah 537, 223 P.2d 193 (1950), the defendants, charged with counseling and practicing polygamy, were convicted under a statute making it a crime "to commit any act injurious . . . to public morals. . . ." In striking the act as void for vagueness, the concurring judge explained the ruling as follows:

> I might pose the question: How all-inclusive is the phrase "contrary to public morals"? It must be conceded it has wide coverage unless limited by other judicial or legislative pronouncements. It has been suggested that the phrase can be interpreted so as to indicate a legislative intent to limit its effect to those acts which are specified by the legislature in other sections of the statutes as being injurious to public morals. . . .
>
> In interpreting a statute, the legislature will be presumed to have inserted every part for a purpose and to have intended that every part be given effect. Significance and meaning should, if possible, be accorded every phrase, and a construction is favored which will render every word operative rather than one which makes some phrases or subsections nugatory. If we adopt the foregoing rule of construction we must hold dial subsection (5) is a catch-all provision without guides, standards or limits.
>
> There are situations when conspiracies to teach certain dogmas, tenets, or beliefs might be deemed inimical to public morals by some jurists and by some jurors, and yet not be defined by the legislature as crimes. The teaching of card-playing might be considered by some as being in that category, although the legislature may not have made such teaching a crime. It is in this aspect that subsection (5) becomes vagrant and wandering and has no limits. Courts and juries might determine that certain teachings offend against public morals and yet the parties doing the teaching might not be advised by statute or otherwise that they were committing a crime. The standards for an offense would thus be fixed by those who heard the evidence and not by the legislature, whose duty it is to define the crime with some degree of particularity.
>
> In the final analysis, each individual has his own moral codes, private and public, and what acts might be considered as injurious to public morals are as

numerous as the opinions of man. The law requires that crimes be defined with more certainty than that.

8. *Specificity and intent.* Many courts — including the Supreme Court — have held that the presence of a sufficiently exacting intent requirement can save an otherwise unconstitutionally vague statute; i.e., that a statute is constitutionally acceptable even where the prohibited conduct is very vaguely defined if some "evil" intent is required for the conduct to become criminal. See People v. Superior Court (Caswell), 46 Cal. 3d 381, 250 Cal. Rptr. 515, 518-19, 524 (1988) (statute punishing anyone "who loiters in or about any toilet open to the public for *the purpose* of engaging in or soliciting any lewd or lascivious or any unlawful activity") (emphasis added). Does this notion suggest a way that Chicago might successfully redraft its loitering ordinance?

Just why does an intent requirement immunize a statute from a vagueness challenge? Wasn't this the problem with the very first case in this chapter, Proctor v. State, *see* pp. 97-100, *supra*?

Just as courts are more willing to uphold vague statutes if they contain an intent requirement, courts are more willing to uphold vague statutes that proscribe conduct only within a limited area, such as in public lavatories or on public buses, as in People v. Superior Court (Caswell). Does this rationale simply afford the legislature the opportunity to enact what would otherwise be unconstitutionally vague statutes if the statutes are limited to places that poor persons or members of minorities are likely to frequent? Aren't these the areas where protection against police discrimination is most needed?

9. *Rejected challenges.* Although void-for-vagueness challenges are still made, they are rarely successful. Courts have rejected challenges to allegedly vague terms in obscenity statutes, 511 Detroit Street, Inc. v. Kelley, 807 F.2d 1293, 1295-97 (6th Cir. 1986) (unlawful to disseminate obscene material as a "predominant and regular part of [one's] business" if materials are a "principal part or substantial part of the stock in trade at that [business]"); child pornography statutes, United States v. Smith, 795 F.2d 841, 847 n.4 (9th Cir. 1986) (prohibition on mailing "visual depiction" of child pornography); larceny statutes, United States v. Jones, 677 F. Supp. 238, 240-41 (S.D.N.Y. 1988) (in prosecution for sale of information about government's plans for prosecution overheard from government agents, lawfully obtained, nonpublic information is a "thing of value"; sale "without authority" is sufficiently clear); assault statutes, United States v. Fitzgerald, 676 F. Supp. 949, 950-54 (N.D.Cal. 1987) (prohibition on assault resulting in "serious bodily injury"); and mining statutes, United States v. Doremus, 658 F. Supp. 752, 756-59 (D. Idaho 1987) (prohibition on "violating any term . . . of a[n] . . . approved operating plan" and "damaging any natural feature or other property of the United States"); State v. Crowdell, 234 Neb. 469, 451 N.W.2d 695 (1990) (upholding a Nebraska law defining child abuse as placing a child "in a situation that endangers his or her life or health" or depriving the child of "necessary food, shelter, clothing, or care"); Posters 'n' Things, Ltd. v. United States, 511 U.S. 513 (1994) (upholding statute punishing the sale of "drug paraphernalia" and specifying several ways of identifying such merchandise).

10. *Jane L. v. Bangerter.* Courts do, however, continue to rely on the void-for-vagueness doctrine to invalidate statutes. For example, in Jane L. v. Bangerter, 61 F.3d 1493 (10th Cir. 1995), a Utah statute stated that "[l]ive unborn children may not be used for experimentation, but when advisable, in the best medical

judgment of the physician, may be tested for genetic defects," and made violation of that statute a felony. In a civil action, plaintiffs asked the court to declare the statute unconstitutionally vague and hence unenforceable. The court noted:

"Experimentation" is an ambiguous term that lacks a precise definition. What tests and procedures constitute experimentation? There are at least three possible answers: 1) those procedures that a particular doctor or hospital have not routinely conducted; 2) those procedures performed on one subject that are designed to benefit another subject; and 3) those procedures that facilitate pure research and do not necessarily benefit the subject of experimentation. . . . Testimony in the record highlights the ambiguities in the term "experimentation." For example, one doctor testified that "experimentation" can have two distinct meanings: 1) "[W]hen you do things to see — just wonder 'What would happen if I did this? What would happen if I gave a fetus this drug; what would be the outcome[?]'"; and 2) doing a procedure without a "data base of many cases to rely upon." Because there are several competing and equally viable definitions, the term "experimentation" does not place health care providers on adequate notice of the legality of their conduct. . . .

Defendants argue that the district court cured the statute's ambiguity and vagueness by interpreting "used for experimentation" as prohibiting only those experiments that do not benefit either mother or fetus. . . .

In an effort to cure the fatal ambiguity in the statute, the district court grafted its own meaning onto the statute's language. We do not understand how "used for experimentation" translates to "tests or medical techniques which are designed solely to increase a researcher's knowledge and are not intended to provide any therapeutic benefit to the mother or child." Jane L. II, 794 F. Supp. at 1550. The district court blatantly rewrote the statute, choosing among a host of competing definitions for "experimentation." This is an improper use of judicial power . . .

Finally, the district court interpreted "used for experimentation" to prohibit only those procedures that provide no benefit to mother or fetus. Although curing some of the imprecision in the term "experimentation," this construction is not free from ambiguity. What does "benefit" mean? If the mother gains knowledge from a procedure that would facilitate future pregnancies but inevitably terminate the current pregnancy, would the procedure be deemed beneficial to the mother? Does the procedure have to be beneficial to the particular mother and fetus that are its subject? In vitro fertilization exposes and fertilizes several ova to assure that one can be implanted in the mother. The other ova are destroyed. Would this common procedure be proscribed under the statute because some ova are subjected to non-therapeutic experimentation, i.e., of no benefit to the ovum or the mother? Accordingly, we conclude that the district court's interpretation is itself unconstitutionally vague.

The criminal law must clearly demarcate criminal conduct from permitted action. Section 310 does not do that here. During the course of the proceedings, one doctor testified that he had developed a procedure to cure a fatal abnormality in a fetus. Not only was he unsure whether this treatment constituted experimentation for the purposes of the statute, but he was also reluctant to testify for fear that his actions "could theoretically be considered illegal under the Utah statute that was in effect" when he began the treatment. Because of the vagaries of the statute, individuals like this doctor may avoid conduct that would not be proscribed in order to avert criminal liability to the detriment of beneficial research. By failing to draw a clear line between proscribed and permitted conduct, section 310 violates established legal principles that provide a crucial backdrop to our criminal legal system.

3

THE GUILTY MIND

In Chapter 2, we examined the view that the criminal law should punish proscribed conduct rather than mere evil thoughts or desires unaccompanied by any action. In this chapter, we examine the legal implications of the complementary view, that the criminal law should punish proscribed conduct only when that conduct is accompanied by bad thoughts.

The fundamental intuitions behind this view are first, that the retributive limits on the criminal law discussed in Chapter 1 restrict punishment to those who are morally blameworthy, and second, that our core image of the morally blameworthy person is one who intentionally harms a person. The difficulty is that intent to harm is only an imperfect proxy for moral blameworthiness: We blame some people for being so self-absorbed or "thoughtless" that they fail to inform themselves about the potentially harmful consequences of their actions to others. Conversely, we might excuse people who deliberately inflict harm under duress or in the grip of psychosis. No matter how detailed the rules we write to capture these moral intuitions, we will of course encounter immoral actors who violated no rule, and rule violators who seem blameless. If, instead, we allocate punishment on the basis of flexible standards of moral blameworthiness, we provoke the concerns about legality, notice, retroactivity, arbitrariness, and discrimination explored in Chapter 2. Moreover, in a bureaucratically regulated modern society, riven by political and moral disagreements, we may find it easier to agree that conduct is immoral because it is clearly illegal than to agree that conduct should be punished because it is clearly immoral.

This chapter concerns itself primarily with efforts to link punishment to moral blame by conditioning liability on bad thoughts; the related issue of excusing the blameless of responsibility is considered in greater detail in Chapters 8 and 9. But as this chapter will demonstrate, these two issues cannot always be separated. Any characterization of a thought as bad risks being understood as a more global conclusion that the actor was morally blameworthy and deserved punishment.

The criminal law generally conceives bad thoughts as (1) the desire to harm others or violate some other social duty; or (2) disregard for the welfare of others or for some other social duty. Violations of social duties not directly imposing harm on others might include such "victimless crimes" as possessing or ingesting drugs, or such "regulatory" offenses as driving an unregistered vehicle.

One can manifest a "guilty mind," or mens rea, by implementing an ignoble desire, or by acting uninfluenced by a noble desire, such as a concern for the safety of others.

In the last chapter, we saw that the phrase "act requirement" may refer to the general precept that just punishment depends upon proof of proscribed conduct, or to the conduct proscribed by a particular statutory provision. The phrase "mens rea requirement" is similarly ambiguous. It may refer to a general precept that punishment depend on proof that defendant acted with a guilty mind, or to the particular "mental state" the prosecution must prove to establish the defendant's guilt for a particular crime.

The first part of this chapter will explore the view that just punishment depends upon proof of a guilty mind, and will address the question of when, if ever, a person who acts with no culpable "mental state" may nonetheless suffer criminal punishment. Like all conceptions of just punishment, ideas about whether and when the state must prove mens rea may be seen as requirements of constitutional due process, or simply as principles of justice that should guide legislation, statutory interpretation and common law adjudication.

But even if courts view the dependence of punishment on proof of a guilty mind as a constitutional principle, they may apply it in more than one way. Courts (a) may strike down statutes for failing to require proof of a guilty mind, or they (b) may interpret statutes to require proof of a guilty mind. When they do the latter, they may leave ambiguity as to whether they regard their interpretation of a statute as constitutionally required, or as reflecting implicit legislative intent, or simply as a judicially developed notion of justice. Thus the general question of whether the prosecution must prove a "guilty mind" cannot be neatly separated from the problem of deciding, on the basis of some legal authority, what mental state the prosecution must prove to sustain a particular criminal charge.

Criminal statutes may specify what the prosecution must prove the defendant desired or knew or should have known. Statutes that are based on the Model Penal Code provide interpreters with a fair amount of guidance on this issue, although, as we shall see, sometimes such statutes provide interpreters with conflicting instructions.

The second part of this chapter introduces the different culpable mental states the Model Penal Code deploys in defining crimes, and the default rules it provides when statutory provisions do not sufficiently define the "mental element" of an offense. This scheme looms large in this chapter and throughout the rest of this book. Yet in reading this material, it is important to remember that many jurisdictions, including the increasingly important federal criminal justice system, have not adopted the Model Penal Code. Especially in these jurisdictions, statutory definitions of offenses often say little or nothing about the culpable mental state the prosecution must prove. In interpreting these spare statutory provisions, judges may be influenced by the conceptions of just punishment explored in the first part of this chapter and by the Model Penal Code scheme explored in the second part of this chapter. They will also draw upon the common law tradition that identifies the purpose of mental criteria of liability as insuring that punishment will only be imposed for immoral conduct.

As interpreted by courts, statutory offenses generally require the defendant's awareness of some circumstance or the likelihood of some harmful result. Thus the problem of defining the mens rea requirement, or, as it is sometimes called, the "mental element" of an offense, generally arises when a defense attorney argues that defendant should be acquitted because she may have been unaware of some fact. The third and fourth parts of this chapter will immerse you in the analysis of such "mistakes." You will find this analysis complicated by two distinctions: (1) the distinction between mistakes negating the mental element of the offense and mistakes negating responsibility, and (2) the distinction between mistakes of fact and mistakes of law.

The first distinction involves concepts explored above in this book's Introduction. Recall that a defendant may concede that she satisfied the definition of an offense but argue that she did so with justification (hence the act was not wrongful), or that she was not responsible for her offense. Claims about what the defendant knew or felt at the time that she fulfilled the act element of an offense may exonerate her by negating the mental element of the offense. But even if the defendant fulfilled the mental element of an offense, she may still be able to argue that what she knew or felt excused her of responsibility; that is, even where the state can establish the elements of the offense beyond a reasonable doubt, her mental or emotional condition may provide an affirmative defense. We saw, for example, that the emotional disturbance that would negate the mental element of murder in one state might partially excuse a killing in another. The result in either state is a reduction of the defendant's liability from murder to manslaughter; but if a state classifies the absence of emotional disturbance as part of the mental element of murder, it is constitutionally required to prove that absence beyond a reasonable doubt. So, too, with mistakes. If they negate the mental element of the charged offense, the state must disprove them beyond a reasonable doubt. If they do not, mistakes may still be thought to excuse the charged offense. But the legislative or judicial decision whether to excuse a mistake may turn on different considerations from those involved in defining the mental element of an offense. And if a mistake negates responsibility rather than the definition of the offense, the defendant may be required to bear the burden of proof.

The second distinction is suggested by the ancient maxim that "ignorance of the law is no excuse." The intuition behind this maxim is that if the criminal law genuinely punishes morally blameworthy behavior, the mere fact that a particular offender expected to escape punishment for her conduct provides no moral reason not to punish her. As Holmes put it, "the fact that crimes are generally sins is one of the practical justifications for requiring a man to know the law."[1] But what about regulatory offenses that are immoral primarily in the sense that one who commits them shirks one of the common burdens of modern citizenship — in other words offenses that are immoral merely because they are illegal? And how can we reconcile the legality concerns explored in Chapter 2 with the precept that ignorance of the law is no excuse?

This maxim has sometimes been invoked as a consideration in interpreting the mental element of offenses. Other legal decision makers have understood the maxim to apply only when defendants seek to excuse themselves of responsibility on the basis of a mistake. In their view, a mistake about a legal circumstance or result may negate the mental element of the offense if the circumstance or result is part of the act element of the offense. This chapter's third part focuses on the analysis of mistake generally; the fourth part focuses on "mistakes of law."

---

1. Oliver Wendell Holmes, The Common Law 125 (1881).

This chapter's fifth part explores another issue at the boundary between the mental element of an offense and the defendant's responsibility for the offense. As we have noted, the mental element of an offense may involve knowing certain facts or desiring certain ends. Yet efforts to excuse defendants sometimes involve claims, backed by expert testimony, that their cognitive or volitional capacities were impaired at the time they committed the offense. May the jury also consider this evidence in deciding whether the prosecution has met its burden of proving that the defendant fulfilled the mental element of the offense? Or should juries simply presume that defendants have a capacity to act with mens rea?

A.   THE REQUIREMENT OF A GUILTY MIND

PEOPLE v. DILLARD
California Court of Appeal
154 Cal. App.3d 261, 201 Cal. Rptr. 136 (1984)

PANELLI, J.

A jury found Moses Dillard, Jr., guilty of the misdemeanor offense of carrying a loaded firearm on his person in a public place, in violation of Penal Code section 12031. . . . The question presented is whether knowledge that the firearm is loaded is an element of the offense of carrying a loaded firearm in a public place. We hold that such knowledge is not an element of the offense and affirm the judgment.

In the early morning hours of June 1, 1981, Oakland Police Officer Luis Torres observed appellant riding a bicycle on the 1300 block of 100th Avenue in Oakland. Appellant was carrying what appeared to be a rifle case. Torres activated the lights on his patrol car and asked appellant to stop. Appellant complied. In response to the officer's request, he placed the rifle case on the ground, stepped away from it, and stood by the patrol car.

Officer Torres unzipped the rifle case and lifted out the rifle. The rifle, a 30.30 Winchester, had one round of ammunition inside the chamber and six additional rounds inside the cylinder. Seven more rounds were loose in the case.

Appellant testified that the rifle belonged to him and that he had picked it up from his stepfather's house about three hours before he was stopped. He did not open the carrying case between the time he picked up the weapon and his stop by Torres.

Relying on *People v. Harrison (1969)* 1 Cal.App.3d 115, 120, the court ruled inadmissible as irrelevant evidence tending to show that appellant was unaware that the rifle was loaded. The court rejected defense counsel's offer of proof, outside the presence of the jury, that appellant's stepfather had taken the rifle hunting, that appellant had loaned it to him for this purpose on several prior occasions, that his stepfather had never before returned the rifle to appellant loaded, and that on the day of the offense appellant had acted in reliance on his stepfather's past conduct. Over defense objection, the court instructed the jury that knowledge that the weapon is loaded is not an element of the offense. . . .

Penal Code section 12031 provides in pertinent part: "[Aside from special enumerated circumstances,] every person who carries a loaded firearm on his or her person or in a vehicle while in any public place or on any public street . . . is guilty of a misdemeanor." In People v. Harrison, the court in dictum stated that the section "does not require knowledge that the gun was loaded, as the statute prohibits the carrying of a loaded firearm and does not specify knowledge it is loaded as an element of the crime." Appellant argues that to construe section 12031 as not requiring knowledge that the weapon is loaded violates his due process right to present a defense (see *Chambers v. Mississippi*, 410 U.S. 284 (1973), and violates the basic principle of common law . . . that to constitute a crime there must be a union of act and wrongful intent (see *People v. Vogel (1956) 46 Cal.2d 798, 801*).

In *United States v. Balint*, 258 U.S. 250 (1922), the Supreme Court stated: "While the general rule at common law was that the scienter was a necessary element in the indictment and proof of every crime, and this was followed in regard to statutory crimes even where the statutory definition did not in terms include it [citation], there has been a modification of this view in respect to prosecutions under statutes the purpose of which would be obstructed by such a requirement. It is a question of legislative intent to be construed by the court."

In California the common law concept of scienter, or mens rea is codified in section 20. [Section 20 provides: "In every crime or public offense there must exist a union, or joint operation of act and intent, or criminal negligence."] Nevertheless, notwithstanding the admonition of *section 20* and the common law tradition upon which it is based, the courts, albeit with some reluctance, have recognized that certain kinds of regulatory offenses enacted for the protection of the public health and safety are punishable despite the absence of culpability or criminal intent in the accepted sense. "Although criminal sanctions are relied upon, the primary purpose of the statutes is regulation rather than punishment or correction. The offenses are not crimes in the orthodox sense, and wrongful intent is not required in the interest of enforcement." [*People v. Vogel, supra,* 46 Cal.2d at 801.] As the Supreme Court stated in Morissette v. United States:

> Many of these offenses are not in the nature of positive aggressions or invasions, with which the common law so often dealt, but are in the nature of neglect where the law requires care, or inaction where it imposes a duty. Many violations of such regulations result in no direct or immediate injury to person or property but merely create the danger or probability of it which the law seeks to minimize. . . . In this respect, whatever the intent of the violator, the injury is the same, and the consequences are injurious or not according to fortuity. Hence, legislation applicable to such offenses, as a matter of policy, does not specify intent as a necessary element. The accused, if he does not will the violation, usually is in a position to prevent it with no more care than society might reasonably expect and no more exertion than it might reasonably exact from one who assumed his responsibilities. . . . Under such considerations, courts have turned to construing statutes and regulations which make no mention of intent as dispensing with it and holding that the guilty act alone makes out the crime.' [342 U.S. 246, 255-56 (1952)].

With these principles in mind, we consider whether it was the legislative intent to exclude knowledge that the weapon is loaded as an element of the offense of carrying a loaded weapon in a public place. *Section 12031* was enacted in 1967 as one of a series of statutes directed to prohibiting the carrying of

[handwritten margin note: sometimes, can have a crime w/out knowledge/ intent]

loaded weapons in specified public places. Other provisions of the 1967 act prohibited the carrying of a loaded weapon into the State Capitol, the office of any
legislator or constitutional officers, or on the grounds of any public school
(§171c), and prohibited carrying a loaded weapon within the Governor's Man-
sion or on its grounds (§171d). The act was declared an urgency statute "necessary for the immediate preservation of the public peace, health or safety." As
facts constituting such necessity, the Legislature cited the danger to the peace
and safety of the people of this state from the increased incidence of organized
groups or individuals publicly arming themselves, and the inadequacy of existing laws to protect the people from "either the use of such weapons or from violent incidents arising from the mere presence of such armed individuals in
public places."

   . . . The carrying of a loaded weapon in a public place, we believe, falls
within the class of cases involving "acts that are so destructive of the social order,
or where the ability of the state to establish the element of criminal intent would
be so extremely difficult if not impossible of proof, that in the interest of justice
the legislature has provided that the doing of the act constitutes a crime, regardless of knowledge or criminal intent on the part of the defendant." . . . (*In
re Marley (1946) 29 Cal.2d 525, 529.) Section 12031* is, in our view, a quintessential
public welfare statute which embraces a legislative judgment that in the interest
of the larger good, the burden of acting at hazard is placed upon a person who,
albeit innocent of criminal intent, is in a position to avert the public danger.

   The potential danger to the public safety from the prohibited conduct is
dramatically illustrated by the facts of the instant case. Officer Torres, an expert
in the operation and use of rifles, testified that the 30.30 Winchester is a 'very
high-powered rifle' that is primarily used for bear and deer hunting. As examples of the rifle's extraordinary force, he stated that one round fired would
penetrate not only a police vest, '[i]t would go through the window, through the
vest, through [the officer] and through the car.' 'If you were to line up six jurors and fire at the first one, the last one would be fatally wounded.' The weapon
had no safety latch and the chances of its going off if it were dropped from appellant's bicycle were about 75 percent. Without question, society has a legitimate interest in placing on the possessor of such a weapon the burden of ascer-
taining at his peril that it is unloaded before he ventures forth with it in public.
Moreover, one who carries such a weapon in ignorance of the fact that it is
loaded could in some circumstances pose a greater threat to the public safety
than one who willfully violates the law by carrying the weapon with knowledge
that it is loaded. The latter, at least, presumably would handle the weapon with
the greater care its potential danger dictates, whereas the former would be unaware of the need for caution. Thus, if appellant, as he contends, were truly unaware that the rifle was loaded, the public safety was endangered by that very fact
as he rode with it on his bicycle and when he placed it on the ground at Officer
Torres' direction.

   Appellant was presumed to know that it is unlawful to carry a loaded
firearm in a public place. . . .

   Appellant's contention that to dispense with the requirement of knowledge
violates his due process right to present a defense is meritless. Since knowledge
that the weapon is loaded is not an element of the offense of violation of *section
12031,* lack of such knowledge is not a defense. Hence, no right of appellant's
was infringed.

Notes and Questions

1. The court says it is inferring the intent of the California legislature not to require mental culpability as an element of the offense. How does the court know this? From direct evidence of what the legislators intended? Or indirectly, by virtue of the category of crime into which this statute falls? Is the key criterion that the forbidden act is very "destructive of the social order," or that the nature of the conduct is such that a culpable mental state would be "extremely difficult if not impossible of proof?" How well do those criteria apply to this law? How much do they distinguish this law from others where the court would not infer strict liability? What do you suppose was the social context that led to passage of the law?

2. What if Dillard had not even known there was a gun in his backpack in the first place, because his stepfather had put it in there entirely without his knowledge? Would the court have had to read the statute the same way? Would the doctrine of constructive possession, see pp. 106-10, *supra,* have helped the defendant in that case? Would a jury then have any (legitimate) choice to acquit? Conversely, since Dillard did really know he was carrying a gun, was he really morally blameless for the risk that it was loaded?

3. Note that the *Dillard* court abruptly dismisses the defendant's due process argument as meritless because knowledge was not an element of the offense. Does that mean that strict liability statutes can never violate due process? In *Balint,* the famous United States Supreme Court case cited in *Dillard,* the trial court had quashed Balint's indictment for selling a narcotic substance without obtaining without written permission from the IRS as required by federal law, holding that it had wrongly failed to charge that Balint had known the nature of the drugs he was selling. Reversing and reinstating the indictment, Chief Justice Taft noted:

> It has been objected that punishment of a person for an act in violation of law when ignorant of the facts making it so, is an absence of due process of law. But that objection is considered and overruled in Shevlin-Carpenter Co. v. Minnesota, 218 U.S. 57, 69, 70, in which it was held that in the prohibition or punishment of particular acts, the State may in the maintenance of a public policy provide "that he who shall do them shall do them at his peril and will not be heard to plead in defense good faith or ignorance." Many instances of this are to be found in regulatory measures in the exercise of what is called the police power where the emphasis of the statute is evidently upon achievement of some social betterment rather than the punishment of the crimes as in cases of mala in se. So, too, in the collection of taxes, the importance to the public of their collection leads the legislature to impose on the taxpayer the burden of finding out the facts upon which his liability to pay depends and meeting it at the peril of punishment. Again where one deals with others and his mere negligence may be dangerous to them, as in selling diseased food or poison, the policy of the law may, in order to stimulate proper care, require the punishment of the negligent person though he be ignorant of the noxious character of what he sells.
>
> The question before us, therefore, is one of the construction of the statute and of inference of the intent of Congress. . . .
>
> . . . [T]he emphasis . . . of the [Narcotic] Act is in securing a close supervision of the business of dealing in these dangerous drugs by the taxing officers of the Government[;] . . . it merely uses a criminal penalty to secure recorded evidence of the disposition of such drugs as a means of taxing and restraining the traffic. Its

manifest purpose is to require every person dealing in drugs to ascertain at his peril whether that which he sells comes within the inhibition of the statute, and if he sells the inhibited drug in ignorance of its character, to penalize him. Congress weighed the possible injustice of subjecting an innocent seller to penalty against the evil of exposing innocent purchasers to danger from the drug, and concluded that the latter was the result preferably to be avoided. Doubtless considerations as to the opportunity of the seller to find out the fact and the difficulty of proof of knowledge contributed to this conclusion. [258 U.S. at 252-54]

Does Chief Justice Taft imply that due process never requires that a criminal offense include such a mental element? Or is he saying that some kinds of offenses may be strict liability and others may not?

4. *What is strict liability?* Before we return to the question of constitutional limits on strict liability, we need to understand the nature and purpose of strict liability in more detail.

In tort law, liability without fault is quite common. "Strict" or "absolute" liability is a consequence of the courts' view that under some conditions, as between an "innocent" plaintiff and an "innocent" defendant, the defendant should have to bear the loss. The argument often runs in economic terms as follows: If a defendant bears all the costs of his activity, she will engage in the "optimal" level of the activity. If the activity is a business, she can purchase insurance against liability and spread the cost among all her customers. If the activity cannot remain economically viable once its costs are "internalized" in this way, it is not socially valuable.

Do these principles apply in criminal cases? Recall the materials in Chapter 1 about the limitations on criminal punishment. Do they suggest that the tort arguments should not apply, and that the criminal law should punish someone only for conduct that may be regarded as his or her fault?

What exactly does "strict liability" mean? We can distinguish at least three uses of the term: liability without moral fault (*substantive strict liability*); liability without any culpable mental state with respect to any objective element (*pure strict liability*); and liability without any culpable mental state with respect to at least one such element (*impure strict liability*).

Consider an offense with three objective elements: (a) possessing (b) inhibited drugs (c) with hallucinogenic properties. If liability does not depend on awareness of any of these three elements, it is a pure strict liability offense. If it depends on awareness of one or two of these three elements it is an impure strict liability offense. And if, perhaps as a result of pure or impure strict liability, morally blameless persons are punished, it is a substantive strict liability offense.[2]

Let us say that Smith makes some pills combining an amphetamine with a hallucinogen. Smith sells some to Brown, describing them as "uppers" but neglecting to tell Brown they contain hallucinogens. One pill falls to the ground, where Jones later picks it up, not knowing its contents. Brown puts some of the pills in a wallet, later stolen by Williams, who is unaware that the pills are inside.

What form of strict liability, if any, is involved if only Smith is guilty? If only Smith and Brown are guilty? If Smith, Brown, and Jones are guilty, but Williams is not? If Brown, Smith, and Williams are guilty, but Jones is not? If all four are guilty?

2. These terms are taken from Kenneth W. Simons, When Is Strict Liability Just? 87 J. Crim. L. & Criminology 1075 (1997).

Pure strict liability offenses are unusual, because with the exceptions of possession, omission, and causation, most conduct terminology implies some awareness of what one is doing. The controversial cases usually involve impure strict liability under circumstances that also seem to involve substantive strict liability.

5. *The Model Penal Code and strict liability.* According to the Model Penal Code, section 2.05, when the state imposes even partial strict liability, the criminal offense may be punished only as a violation. Section 1.04(5) distinguishes a violation from a crime, by defining the former as an offense punishable only by "a fine, or fine and forfeiture, or other civil penalty [that] shall not give rise to any disability or legal disadvantage based on conviction of a criminal offense." Consider the Model Penal Code's explanation of this decision:

> This [section] makes a frontal attack on absolute or strict liability in the penal law, whenever the offense carries the possibility of criminal conviction, for which a sentence of probation or imprisonment may be imposed. The method used is not to abrogate strict liability completely, but to provide that when conviction rests upon that basis the grade of the offense is reduced to a violation. . . .
>
> This position is affirmed not only with respect to offenses defined by the penal code; it is superimposed on the entire corpus of the law so far as penal sanctions are involved. Since most strict liability offenses involve special regulatory legislation, . . . this superimposition is essential if the principle of no criminality . . . for strict liability offenses is to be made effective.
>
> . . . The liabilities involved are indefensible, unless reduced to terms that insulate conviction from the type of moral condemnation that is and ought to be implicit when a sentence of probation or imprisonment may be imposed. It has been argued, and the argument undoubtedly will be repeated, that strict liability is necessary for enforcement in a number of areas where it obtains. But if practical enforcement precludes litigation of the culpability of alleged deviation from legal requirements, the enforcers cannot rightly demand the use of penal sanctions for the purpose. Crime does and should mean condemnation and no court should have to pass that judgment unless it can declare that the defendant's act was culpable. This is too fundamental to be compromised. The law goes far enough if it permits the imposition of a monetary penalty in cases where strict liability has been imposed.[3]

6. *Formal and substantive strict liability.* The Model Penal Code attempts to tie liability to fault by conditioning liability on some level of awareness of every act, circumstance, and result that defines the actus reus of the offense. Professor Kenneth Simons argues that the attempt to avoid substantive strict liability by formally defining fault cannot succeed:

> Imagine that a legislature considers adopting a strict liability statute that punished any person who causes a forest fire, with or without fault. Instead, the legislature actually enacts a law prohibiting any person from knowingly carrying a match in or near a forest, with a penalty of five years imprisonment if that conduct causes a forest fire. Does such a law cure the retributive defects of strict liability, by adding a mens rea requirement? In a formal sense it does. But the cure hardly suffices. In substance, the law is similar to a law simply prohibiting a person from causing a forest fire. One might handle a match carefully, without any fault, and still, unfortunately, thereby contribute to a forest fire. . . .

3. American Law Institute, Model Penal Code and Commentaries, Part I, §2.05, at 282-83 (1985).

Conventional analysis expresses a formal conception of strict liability and fault. This conception accepts offense elements as given, requires an analysis of culpability as to each of these elements considered separately, and assumes that if some minimally acceptable form of culpability as to each of those elements is shown, then criminal liability expresses some genuine form of fault . . .

By contrast, a substantive conception of strict liability and fault examines the offense elements themselves, considers the interrelationship between offense elements, culpability terms, and the relevant ultimate harm, and requires a substantive criterion of fault that might not correspond simply and directly to formal culpability requirements. Knowing possession of firearms, or of burglar's tools, or of matches . . . are instances of formal fault, but not necessarily substantive fault, since the legislature might only be interested in these forms of "knowing" . . . conduct insofar as they create a significant risk of other harms. And they might not. Or, even if they do, the level of punishment for these nonconsummate offenses might be excessive in light of the modest degree to which the conduct poses the risk.[4]

7. *Inferring or imputing strict liability.* American courts frequently confront statutes that contain no express mental state element at all. What resources do they have to determine when the legislature truly intended to impose some form of strict liability? What constitutional power do they have to constrain this legislative choice when they see it?

One of the most famous judicial pronouncements on this subject comes from Justice Jackson's opinion in Morissette v. United States, 342 U.S. 246 (1952), also quoted in *Dillard.* The defendant, a junk dealer, openly entered an air force practice bombing range and appropriated spent bomb casings that had been lying about for years, exposed to the weather and rusting away. He flattened them out and sold them at a city junk market at a profit of $84. He was indicted and convicted of violating 19 U.S.C. §641, which made it a crime "knowingly to convert" government property. There was no question that the defendant knew that what he took and sold were air force bomb casings. His defense was that he honestly believed that they had been abandoned by the air force and that he was therefore violating no one's rights by taking them. The Court reversed, and Justice Jackson said:

The contention that an injury can amount to a crime only when inflicted by intention is no provincial or transient notion. It is as universal and persistent in mature systems of law as belief in freedom of the human will and a consequent ability and duty of the normal individual to choose between good and evil. A relation between some mental element and punishment for a harmful act is almost as instinctive as the child's familiar exculpatory "But I didn't mean to," and has afforded the rational basis for a tardy and unfinished substitution of deterrence and reformation in place of retaliation and vengeance as the motivation for public prosecution. . . .

Crime, as a compound concept, generally constituted only from concurrence of an evil-meaning mind with an evil-doing hand, was congenial to an intense individualism and took deep and early root in American soil. As the states codified the common law of crimes, even if their enactments were silent on the subject, their courts assumed that the omission did not signify disapproval of the principle but merely recognized that intent was so inherent in the idea of the offense that it required no statutory affirmation.

4. When is Strict Liability Just?, 87 J. Crim. L. & Criminology 1075, 1085-88, 1121-24 (1997).

However, the [*Balint* offense belongs] to a category of another character, with very different antecedents and origins. The crimes there involved depend on no mental element but consist only of forbidden acts or omissions. This, while not expressed by the Court, is made clear from examination of a century-old but accelerating tendency, discernible both here and in England, to call into existence new duties and crimes which disregard any ingredient of intent. The industrial revolution multiplied the number of workmen exposed to injury from increasingly powerful and complex mechanisms, driven by freshly discovered sources of energy, requiring higher precautions by employers. Traffic of velocities, volumes and varieties unheard of came to subject the wayfarer to intolerable casualty risks if owners and drivers were not to observe new cares and uniformities of conduct. Congestion of cities and crowding of quarters called for health and welfare regulations undreamed of in simpler times. Wide distribution of goods became an instrument of wide distribution of harm when those who dispersed food, drink, drugs, and even securities, did not comply with reasonable standards of quality, integrity, disclosure and care. Such dangers have engendered increasingly numerous and detailed regulations which heighten the duties of those in control of particular industries, trades, properties or activities that affect public health, safety or welfare.

While many of these duties are sanctioned by a more strict civil liability, lawmakers, whether wisely or not, have sought to make such regulations more effective by invoking criminal sanctions to be applied by the familiar technique of criminal prosecutions and convictions. This has confronted the courts with a multitude of prosecutions, based on statutes or administrative regulations, for what have been aptly called "public welfare offenses." These cases do not fit neatly into any of such accepted classifications of common-law offenses, such as those against the state, the person, property, or public morals. Many of these offenses are not in the nature of positive aggressions or invasions, with which the common law so often dealt, but are in the nature of neglect where the law requires care, or inaction where it imposes a duty. Many violations of such regulations result in no direct or immediate injury to person or property but merely create the danger or probability of injury which the law seeks to minimize. . . .

Neither this court nor, so far as we are aware, any other has undertaken to delineate a precise line or set forth comprehensive criteria for distinguishing between crimes that require a mental element and crimes that do not. We attempt no closed definition, for the law on the subject is neither settled nor static. The conclusion reached in [*Balint*] has our approval and adherence for the circumstances to which it was there applied. A quite different question here is whether we will expand the doctrine of crimes without intent to include those charged here.

Stealing, larceny, and its variants and equivalents, were among the earliest offenses known to the law that existed before legislation; they are invasions of rights of property which stir a sense of insecurity in the whole community and arouse public demand for retribution, the penalty is high and, when a sufficient amount is involved, the infamy is that of a felony. . . . State courts of last resort, on whom fall the heaviest burden of interpreting criminal law in this country, have consistently retained the requirement of intent in larceny-type offenses. . . .

Congress, therefore, omitted any express prescription of criminal intent from the enactment before us in the light of an unbroken course of judicial decision in all constituent states of the Union holding intent inherent in this class of offense, even when not expressed in statutes. Congressional silence as to mental elements in an Act merely adopting into federal statutory law a concept of crime already so well defined in common law and statutory interpretation by the states may warrant quite contrary inferences than the same silence in creating an offense new to general law, for whose definition the courts have no guidance except the Act. Because the offenses before this Court in [*Balint*] were of this latter class, we cannot accept them as authority for eliminating intent from offenses incorporated from the common law. . . .

The Government asks us by a feat of construction radically to change the weights and balances in the scales of justice. The purpose and obvious effect of doing away with the requirement of a guilty intent is to ease the prosecution's path to conviction, to strip the defendant of such benefit as he derived at common law from innocence of evil purpose, and to circumscribe the freedom heretofore allowed juries. Such a manifest impairment of the immunities of the individual should not be extended to common-law crimes on judicial initiative. . . . [342 U.S. at 250-63]

What distinctions can be drawn between *Morissette* on the one hand, and *Dillard* and *Balint* on the other? Is the difference simply that narcotics and loaded guns are more dangerous than spent bomb casings? Was the defendant in *Balint* more blameworthy than the defendant in *Morissette?*

Is *Morissette* premised on a substantive rule of constitutional law, that due process forbids strict liability for certain kinds of crime? Or is it premised on a rule of interpretation, that certain kinds of criminal statutes should be read to require "mens rea" unless Congress is very explicit to the contrary? Is there a difference? How far can interpretation go before it amounts to overturning the statute? How well does *Morissette* help a court to discern whether a statute is one of strict liability or not — or help a legislature determine if it *should* be? Is the key criterion the venerability of the criminal prohibition? The severity of the punishment? Consider the following case:

UNITED STATES v. WULFF
United States Court of Appeals for the Sixth Circuit
758 F.2d 1121 (6th Cir. 1985)

MILBURN, CIRCUIT JUDGE.

The United States appeals the judgment of the district court dismissing an indictment that charged the defendant, Robert Wulff, with offering to sell migratory bird parts in violation of the Migratory Bird Treaty Act ("MBTA"), *16 U.S.C. §703.* This case raises the question of whether a felony conviction for the sale of a migratory bird part in violation of the MBTA is violative of the due process clause of the Fifth Amendment of the United States Constitution. Because a felony conviction under the Act does not require proof of scienter, because the crime is not one known to the common law, and because the felony penalty provision is severe and would result in irreparable damage to one's reputation, we affirm the decision of the district court and declare the felony provision of the Act, §707(b)(2), unconstitutional.

On September 15, 1983, a federal grand jury returned a one-count indictment charging the defendant with selling migratory bird parts in violation of 16 U.S.C. §§703 and 707(b)(2). Section 707(b)(2) provides as follows:

(b) Whoever, in violation of *sections 703* to *711* of this title, shall — . . .
(2) sell, offer for sale, barter or offer to barter, any migratory bird shall be guilty of a felony and shall be fined not more than $2,000 or imprisoned not more than two years, or both.

The indictment was based on a sale made by the defendant to a special agent of the United States Fish and Wildlife Service of a necklace made of red-tailed hawk and great-horned owl talons. Both birds are protected species under the Migratory Bird Treaty Act. . . .

The defendant . . . filed a "Motion to Dismiss Indictment or Enter Order Directing Charge of Misdemeanor," arguing that because section 707(b)(2) does not require guilty knowledge, imposition of a felony conviction would be a violation of due process. The district court agreed and directed that if the defendant was convicted of a violation, he would be sentenced under the misdemeanor provision of the Act, rather than the felony provision. . . .

[The court summarized the *Morissette* holding.]

The district court [also relied on] the case of *Holdridge v. United States*, 282 F.2d 302 (8th Cir.1960):

> [W]here a federal criminal statute omits mention of intent and where it seems to involve what is basically a matter of policy, where the standard imposed is, under the circumstances, reasonable and adherence thereto properly expected of a person, where the penalty is relatively small, where conviction does not gravely besmirch, where the statutory crime is not taken over from the common law, and where congressional purpose is supporting, the statute can be construed as one not requiring criminal intent. The elimination of this element is then not violative of the due process clause. *Id. at 310.* . . .

Applying these legal precedents to the facts before it, the district court noted that the felony statutory penalty involved in this case included a maximum sentence of two (2) years' imprisonment or a fine of Two Thousand ($2,000.00) Dollars, or both. The district court felt that these were not "relatively small penalties." The district court further noted that a convicted felon loses his right to vote, his right to sit on a jury and his right to possess a gun, among other civil rights, for the rest of his life. The district court was of the opinion that a felony conviction irreparably damages one's reputation. . . .

Dilemmas similar to the one presented in this case have been resolved in the past by reading a requirement of scienter into an otherwise silent statute. However, this court has previously held that Congress did not intend for scienter to be an element of the offense under the MBTA. [citing cases.]

These cases are distinguishable in that the convictions therein were under the misdemeanor penalty provisions of the MBTA or the regulations promulgated thereunder. . . . [W]e are concerned with the construction of the felony provision of the MBTA. In our opinion, we cannot read a requirement of scienter into *section 707(b)(2)* because the crime is not one known to the common law. An element of scienter can be read into an otherwise silent statute only where the crime is one borrowed from the common law. . . .

. . . The question before us today is not whether scienter is an element of the offense or whether Congress made a rational choice in legislating a felony conviction for the commercialization of protected birds. Rather, we must decide whether the absence of a requirement that the government prove some degree of scienter violates the defendant's right to due process.

. . . Extrapolating from *Holdridge*, the proper test would appear to be as follows: The elimination of the element of criminal intent does not violate the due process clause where (1) the penalty is relatively small, and (2) where conviction does not gravely besmirch. . . . [S]ection 707(b)(2) does not meet these criteria. The felony penalty carries a maximum sentence of two (2) years' imprisonment or Two Thousand ($2,000.00) Dollars fine, or both. "This is not, in this Court's mind, a relatively small penalty." [United States v. Pierre, 578 F.Supp. 1424, 1429

(D.S.D. 1983)] In addition, as the district judge noted, a felony conviction irreparably damages one's reputation,[5] and in Michigan a convicted felon loses, among other civil rights, his right to sit on a jury and his right to possess a gun.

We are of the opinion that in order for one to be convicted of a felony under the MBTA, a crime unknown to the common law which carries a substantial penalty, Congress must require the prosecution to prove the defendant acted with some degree of scienter. Otherwise, a person acting with a completely innocent state of mind could be subjected to a severe penalty and grave damage to his reputation. This, in our opinion, the Constitution does not allow.

to have felony conviction for a crime unknown to common law, must have scienter

Notes and Questions

1. When a statute does not include any express mental culpability requirement, how does a court decide whether strict liability applies — and who has the authority to decide that? *Wulff* holds that due process forbids strict liability for a felony statute and also that the Court may not read a mens rea requirement into a statute where the legislature has not explicitly done so. But if it is so unthinkable to impose felony liability without mental culpability, should we not infer that the legislature intended to require mental culpability, unless it was absolutely explicit to the contrary? If the notion is so unthinkable, is it likely that that was what the legislature thought? In that light, note two alternative views to the *Wulff* approach, as the following two notes illustrate.

2. *Reading in a culpability requirement.* In Baender v. Barnett, 255 U.S. 224 (1921), the defendant, charged with possessing tools to make counterfeit coin, complained that though the indictment charged "willful" or "knowing" possession, those mental elements had no basis in the statute, which, he contended, therefore violated due process. The Court agreed that due process required a mental culpability component in the law, but concluded it was authorized to construe the statute as containing one:

> . . . The statute is not intended to include and make criminal a possession which is not conscious and willing. While its words are general, they are to be taken in a reasonable sense, and not in one which works manifest injustice or infringes constitutional safeguards.
>
> In so holding we but give effect to a cardinal rule of construction recognized in repeated decisions of this and other courts. A citation of three will illustrate our view. In Margate Pier Co. v. Hannam, 3 B. & Ald. 266, 270, Abbott, C. J., quoting from Lord Coke, said: 'Acts of Parliament are to be so construed, as no man that is innocent, or free from injury or wrong, be by a literal construction punished or endamaged.' In United States v. Kirby, 7 Wall. 482, 486 (19 L. Ed. 278), this court said: 'All laws should receive a sensible construction. General terms should be so limited in their application as not to lead to injustice, oppression, or an absurd consequence. It will always, therefore, be presumed that the Legislature intended exceptions to its language, which would avoid results of this character. The reason of the law in such cases should prevail over its letter. The common sense of man approves the judgment mentioned by Puffendorf, that the Bolognian law, which enacted 'that whoever drew blood in the streets should be punished with the utmost severity,' did not extend to the surgeon who opened the vein of a person that

---

5. "[T]he infamy is that of a felony, which, says Maitland, is '. . . as bad a word as you can give to a man or thing.'" *Morissette, supra,* 342 U.S. at 260, 72 S.Ct. at 248 (footnote omitted).

fell down in the street in a fit. The same common sense accepts the ruling, cited by Plowden, that the statute of 1 Edward II, which enacts that a prisoner who breaks prison shall be guilty of felony, does not extend to a prisoner who breaks out when the prison is on fire — "for he is not to be hanged because he would not stay to be burnt." And in United States v. Jin Fuey Moy, 241 U.S. 394, 401, we said: 'A statute must be construed, if fairly possible, so as to avoid, not only the conclusion that it is unconstitutional, but also grave doubts upon that score.'

3. *Finding strict liability constitutional.* In United States v. Engler, 806 F.2d 425 (3d Cir. 1986), involving the very same migrant bird statute and the very same legal posture as *Wulff*, the government argued that its trial proof had established that the defendant had in fact exhibited knowledge with respect to the conduct elements of the crime and therefore that the court could simply follow *Baender* in supplying the missing scienter element and reinstating the indictments. The court found this solution unnecessary and *Wulff* wrong:

> . . . *Wulff* . . . made a judgment call that does not withstand reasonable analysis. [It holds] that the differences between a felony fine of $2,000 and a misdemeanor fine of $500, between a two-year felony sentence and a six-month misdemeanor sentence, between the stigma of a felony conviction and that of a misdemeanor conviction turn the trick on constitutionality. Mechanical jurisprudence has no place here. The constitutionality of acts of Congress should not be determined by such nice distinctions, with tight mathematical formulas derived from a pocket calculator or a computer spread sheet. The differences between the objective penalties of the misdemeanor and felony provisions of the Act [are], for due process purposes, *de minimis*. Moreover, we are unwilling to accept that it is axiomatic, or proved by experience or empirical data, that there is, in the *Morissette* formulation, a "grave danger to an offender's reputation" when he is sentenced to two years imprisonment (eight months actual incarceration) under the felony provision, but no such danger when he is sentenced to six months imprisonment (six months actual incarceration) under the misdemeanor provision. Nor should the differences in the fines compel the conclusion that one's reputation is not besmirched by a $500 fine, but is unconstitutionally tarnished by an additional levy of $1500. . . . [806 F.2d at 434.]

Note that at early common law, felonies were defined as crimes that had the potential of being punishable by death. These included homicide, mayhem, arson, rape, robbery, burglary, larceny, prison breach, and rescue of a felon. In England, though this list was expanded by statute, Parliament continued to emphasize capital punishment as the chief characteristic of a felony, and "misdemeanor" was the label ultimately applied to all other, non-capital offenses. In light of modern regulatory laws like the MBTA, is the line between felony and misdemeanor now an anachronism?

Could judges consult social science to determine how severely a criminal charge tarnishes one's reputation?

4. *A constitutional test for strict liability.* Professor Alan Michaels has suggested the following principle to explain the Supreme Court's cases on the constitutionality of strict liability:

> [S]trict liability is constitutional when, but only when, the intentional conduct covered by the statute could be made criminal by the legislature. . . . [This] principle . . . flows naturally from two relatively uncontroversial propositions. The first is that the legislature normally may not punish the exercise of a fundamental

can't punish for exercising a right or for involuntary conduct

right. For example, a law that made voicing an opinion in public a crime would be unconstitutional. The second is that punishment must be predicated on some voluntary act or omission covered by a statute. For example, a law that made stuttering a crime would be unconstitutional. . . .

A sketch of the application of [this] test to the crime of bigamy clarifies the concept. Bigamy has two elements: (i) marrying another while (ii) being married. Historically, most jurisdictions applied strict liability to the second element — being married — and many states continue to do so. Thus, even if a woman reasonably believed that her first husband was deceased, or that she was divorced from her first husband, she could nevertheless be punished for bigamy if she remarried and that belief turned out to be mistaken. Is this use of strict liability constitutional? . . . [T]he decisive issue is whether the Constitution would permit the state to punish the woman under an otherwise identical statute without the strict liability element, that is, could the state constitutionally punish her simply for knowingly getting married? . . . Because the fundamental right to marry prohibits the state from making a crime of all marriages [strict liability would not appropriate].[6]

Because the Michaels test relies on some independent test of the constitutional protection for particular conduct, the area of First Amendment free expression provides a test ground for his approach. Consistent with his view is the early obscenity decision in Smith v. California, 361 U.S. 147 (1959). There the Court held that the First Amendment required that any law condemning possession of obscene material must contain some scienter component.

We have held that obscene speech and writings are not protected by the constitutional guarantees of freedom of speech and the press. [But we do not] recognize any state power to restrict the dissemination of books which are not obscene; and we think this ordinance's strict liability feature would tend seriously to have that effect, by penalizing booksellers, even though they had not the slightest notice of the character of the books they sold. The appellee and the court below analogize this strict liability penal ordinance to familiar forms of penal statutes which dispense with any element of knowledge on the part of the person charged, food and drug legislation being a principal example. . . . There is no specific constitutional inhibition against making the distributors of food the strictest censors of their merchandise, but the constitutional guarantees of the freedom of speech and of the press stand in the way of imposing a similar requirement on the bookseller. . . . If the contents of bookshops and periodical stands were restricted to material of which their proprietors had made an inspection, they might be depleted indeed. The bookseller's limitation in the amount of reading material with which he could familiarize himself, and his timidity in the face of his absolute criminal liability, thus would tend to restrict the public's access to forms of the printed word which the State could not constitutionally suppress directly.

It is argued that unless the scienter requirement is dispensed with, regulation of the distribution of obscene material will be ineffective, as booksellers will falsely disclaim knowledge of their books' contents or falsely deny reason to suspect their obscenity. We might observe that it has been some time now since the law viewed itself as impotent to explore the actual state of a man's mind. Eyewitness testimony of a bookseller's perusal of a book hardly need be a necessary element in proving his awareness of its contents. The circumstances may warrant the inference that he was aware of what a book contained, despite his denial.

How does the Court's approach differ from that of Prof. Michaels?

6. Alan Michaels, Constitutional Innocence, 112 Harv. L. Rev. 828, 834-35, 877-78 (1999) (paragraphs reordered).

By contrast, in United States v. X-Citement Video, 513 U.S. 64 (1994), the Protection of Children Against Sexual Exploitation Act, 18 U.S.C. §2252, did contain an explicit mental state term, creating criminal liability for any person who "knowingly transports or ships in interstate or foreign commerce . . . any visual depiction, if (A) the producing of such depiction involves the use of a minor engaging in sexually explicit conduct and (B) such depiction is of such conduct. . . ." The lower court had struck down the law for its lack of a mental state element for the section dealing with minors. On appeal, Chief Justice Rehnquist noted that "the presumption in favor of a *scienter* element should apply to each of the statutory elements which criminalize otherwise innocent conduct" and so inferred that "knowingly" applied to the fact that a minor was used in the film, even if this was not the most natural grammatical reading of Congress's prose. The Chief Justice noted that the offense in question was punishable by up to ten years in jail, and concluded that it "is not a public welfare offense. Persons do not harbor settled expectations that the contents of magazines and films are generally subject to stringent public regulation. . . . Rather, the statute is more akin to the common law offenses against the 'state, person, property, or public morals,' *Morissette, supra,* at 255." Is that a logical statement? Is it a fair reading of *Morissette?* Is this approach different from that of Prof. Michaels? What if the statute had not used the word "knowingly" or any other culpability term?

5. Even where a statute is construed to legitimately impose strict liability as a matter of law, the legal system sometimes covertly requires some level of blameworthiness. This is especially true in the commercial or corporate context where a defendant might in effect be charged with vicarious liability for the actions of someone in her enterprise. In United States v. Dotterweich, 320 U.S. 277 (1943), the CEO of a pharmaceutical firm was charged with the misdemeanor of selling misbranded and adulterated drugs, in violation of the Federal Food, Drug, and Cosmetic Act. Relying on *Balint,* Justice Frankfurter concluded that the misdemeanor provision fell safely within the category of malum prohibitum or regulatory crime. But notably, he stressed that the statute only effectively applied to those who stood "in responsible relation" to the illegal shipment. Moreover, he stated:

> It would be too treacherous to define . . . the class of employees which stands in such responsible relation. To attempt a formula embracing the variety of conduct whereby persons may responsibly contribute in furthering a transaction forbidden by an Act of Congress, to wit, to send illicit goods across state lines, would be mischievous futility. In such matters the good sense of prosecutors, the wise guidance of trial judges, and the ultimate judgment of juries must be trusted. Our system of criminal justice necessarily depends on "conscience and circumspection in prosecuting officers," Nash v. United States, 229 U.S. 373, 378, even when the consequences are far more drastic than they are under the provision of law before us. [Id. at 285]

Is Justice Frankfurter reassuring us that strict liability is permissible because it is not really strict liability? Was Dotterweich punished for being generally careless in the way he ran the company, even if he did not have the foggiest idea that an employee was misbranding a shipment? Alarmed by the Frankfurter approach, Justice Murphy, in dissent, said:

> To erect standards of responsibility is a difficult legislative task and the opinion of this Court admits that it is "too treacherous" and a "mischievous futility" for us to

engage in such pursuits. But the only alternative is a blind resort to "the good sense of prosecutors, the wise guidance of trial judges, and the ultimate judgment of juries." Yet that situation is precisely what our constitutional system sought to avoid. Reliance on the legislature to define crimes and criminals distinguishes our form of jurisprudence from certain less desirable ones. [Id. at 293-94]

In a similar case under the same statute, United States v. Park, 421 U.S. 658 (1975), the defendant, the president of Acme Markets, was charged with shipping contaminated food. Upholding the conviction, the Court stated:

The requirements of foresight and vigilance imposed on responsible corporate agents are beyond question demanding, and perhaps onerous, but they are no more stringent than the public has a right to expect of those who voluntarily assume positions of authority in business enterprises whose services and products affect the health and well-being of the public that supports them. . . .
. . . The duty imposed by Congress on responsible corporate agents is, we emphasize, one that requires the highest standard of foresight and vigilance, but the Act, in its criminal aspect, does not require that which is objectively impossible. The theory upon which responsible corporate agents are held criminally accountable for "causing" violations of the Act permits a claim that a defendant was "powerless" to prevent or correct the violation. . . . [Id. at 672-73]

Is this standard the same as that in *Dotterweich?* What if some of Acme's food had suffered contamination that could not be prevented by any technology currently available to Acme or any other company, but which could have been prevented if Acme had invested in research and development of more advanced technology? How well can we distinguish the state of the industry art or custom from the scientifically feasible?

6. In light of *Dotterweich* and *Park*, consider Professor Henry M. Hart's opposition to the use of strict liability to impose criminal sanction on morally blameless individuals:[7]

Moral, rather than crassly utilitarian, considerations re-enter the picture when the claim is made, as it sometimes is, that strict liability operates, in fact, only against people who are really blameworthy, because prosecutors only pick out the really guilty ones for criminal prosecution. This argument reasserts the traditional position that a criminal conviction imports moral condemnation. To this, it adds the arrogant assertion that it is proper to visit the moral condemnation of the community upon one of its members on the basis solely of the private judgment of his prosecutors. Such a circumvention of the safeguards with which the law surrounds other determinations of criminality seems not only irrational, but immoral as well.
     But moral considerations in a still larger dimension are the ultimately controlling ones. In its conventional and traditional applications, a criminal conviction carries with it an ineradicable connotation of moral condemnation and personal guilt. Society makes an essentially parasitic, and hence illegitimate, use of this instrument when it uses it as a means of deterrence (or compulsion) of conduct which is morally neutral. This would be true even if a statute were to be enacted proclaiming that no criminal conviction hereafter should ever be understood as casting any reflection on anybody. For statutes cannot change the meaning of

7. The Aims of the Criminal Law, 23 Law & Contemp. Probs. 401, 424 (1958).

words and make people stop thinking what they do think when they hear the words spoken. But it is doubly true — it is ten-fold, a hundred-fold, a thousand-fold true — when society continues to insist that some crimes *are* morally blameworthy and then tries to use the same epithet to describe conduct which is not.

LAMBERT v. CALIFORNIA
Supreme Court of the United States
355 U.S. 225 (1957)

JUSTICE DOUGLAS delivered the opinion of the Court.

Section 52.38 (a) of the Los Angeles Municipal Code defines "convicted person" as follows:

> "Any person who, subsequent to January 1, 1921, has been or hereafter is convicted of an offense punishable as a felony in the State of California, or who has been or who is hereafter convicted of any offense in any place other than the State of California, which offense, if committed in the State of California, would have been punishable as a felony."

Section 52.39 provides that it shall be unlawful for "any convicted person" to be or remain in Los Angeles for a period of more than five days without registering; it requires any person having a place of abode outside the city to register if he comes into the city on five occasions or more during a 30-day period; and it prescribes the information to be furnished the Chief of Police on registering.

Section 52.43 (b) makes the failure to register a continuing offense, each day's failure constituting a separate offense.

Appellant, arrested on suspicion of another offense, was charged with a violation of this registration law. The evidence showed that she had been at the time of her arrest a resident of Los Angeles for over seven years. Within that period she had been convicted in Los Angeles of the crime of forgery, an offense which California punishes as a felony. Though convicted of a crime punishable as a felony, she had not at the time of her arrest registered under the Municipal Code. At the trial, appellant asserted that 52.39 of the Code denies her due process of law. . . . The trial court denied this objection. The case was tried to a jury which found appellant guilty. . . . The case is here on appeal. . . . [W]e now hold that the registration provisions of the Code as sought to be applied here violate the Due Process requirement of the Fourteenth Amendment.

The registration provision, carrying criminal penalties, applies if a person has been convicted "of an offense punishable as a felony in the State of California" or, in case he has been convicted in another State, if the offense "would have been punishable as a felony" had it been committed in California. No element of willfulness is by terms included in the ordinance nor read into it by the California court as a condition necessary for a conviction.

We must assume that appellant had no actual knowledge of the requirement that she register under this ordinance, as she offered proof of this defense which was refused. The question is whether a registration act of this character violates due process where it is applied to a person who has no actual knowledge of his duty to register, and where no showing is made of the probability of such knowledge.

We do not go with Blackstone in saying that "a vicious will" is necessary to constitute a crime, 4 Bl. Comm. *21, for conduct alone without regard to the intent of the doer is often sufficient. There is wide latitude in the lawmakers to declare an offense and to exclude elements of knowledge and diligence from its definition. But we deal here with conduct that is wholly passive — mere failure to register. It is unlike the commission of acts, or the failure to act under circumstances that should alert the doer to the consequences of his deed. Cf.; United States v. Balint, 258 U.S. 250; United States v. Dotterweich, 320 U.S. 277, 284. The rule that "ignorance of the law will not excuse" (Shevlin-Carpenter Co. v. Minnesota, *supra,* p. 68) is deep in our law, as is the principle that of all the powers of local government, the police power is "one of the least limitable." District of Columbia v. Brooke, 214 U.S. 138, 149. On the other hand, due process places some limits on its exercise. Engrained in our concept of due process is the requirement of notice. Notice is sometimes essential so that the citizen has the chance to defend charges. Notice is required before property interests are disturbed, before assessments are made, before penalties are assessed. Notice is required in a myriad of situations where a penalty or forfeiture might be suffered for mere failure to act. . . .

Registration laws are common and their range is wide. Many such laws are akin to licensing statutes in that they pertain to the regulation of business activities. But the present ordinance is entirely different. Violation of its provisions is unaccompanied by any activity whatever, mere presence in the city being the test. Moreover, circumstances which might move one to inquire as to the necessity of registration are completely lacking. At most the ordinance is but a law enforcement technique designed for the convenience of law enforcement agencies through which a list of the names and addresses of felons then residing in a given community is compiled. The disclosure is merely a compilation of former convictions already publicly recorded in the jurisdiction where obtained. Nevertheless, this appellant on first becoming aware of her duty to register was given no opportunity to comply with the law and avoid its penalty, even though her default was entirely innocent. She could but suffer the consequences of the ordinance, namely, conviction with the imposition of heavy criminal penalties thereunder. We believe that actual knowledge of the duty to register or proof of the probability of such knowledge and subsequent failure to comply are necessary before a conviction under the ordinance can stand. As Holmes wrote in The Common Law, "A law which punished conduct which would not be blameworthy in the average member of the community would be too severe for that community to bear." Id., at 50. Its severity lies in the absence of an opportunity either to avoid the consequences of the law or to defend any prosecution brought under it. Where a person did not know of the duty to register and where there was no proof of the probability of such knowledge, he may not be convicted consistently with due process. Were it otherwise, the evil would be as great as it is when the law is written in print too fine to read or in a language foreign to the community.

JUSTICE FRANKFURTER, whom JUSTICE HARLAN and JUSTICE WHITTAKER join, dissenting.

The present laws of the United States and of the forty-eight States are thick with provisions that command that some things not be done and others be done, although persons convicted under such provisions may have had no awareness of what the law required or that what they did was wrongdoing. The body of decisions sustaining such legislation, including innumerable registration laws, is almost as voluminous as the legislation itself. The matter is summarized in United States v. Balint, 258 U.S. 250, 252: "Many instances of this are to be found in regulatory measures in the exercise of what is called the police power where the emphasis of the statute is evidently upon achievement of some social betterment rather than the punishment of the crimes as in cases of mala in se."

Surely there can hardly be a difference as a matter of fairness, of hardship, or of justice, if one may invoke it, between the case of a person wholly innocent of wrongdoing, in the sense that he was not remotely conscious of violating any law, who is imprisoned for five years for conduct relating to narcotics, and the case of another person who is placed on probation for three years on condition that she pay $250, for failure, as a local resident, convicted under local law of a felony, to register under a law passed as an exercise of the State's "police power." Considerations of hardship often lead courts, naturally enough, to attribute to a statute the requirement of a certain mental element — some consciousness of wrongdoing and knowledge of the law's command — as a matter of statutory construction. Then, too, a cruelly disproportionate relation between what the law requires and the sanction for its disobedience may constitute a violation of the Eighth Amendment as a cruel and unusual punishment, and, in respect to the States, even offend the Due Process Clause of the Fourteenth Amendment.

But what the Court here does is to draw a constitutional line between a State's requirement of doing and not doing. . . . One can be confident that Mr. Justice Holmes would have been the last to draw such a line. . . .

If the generalization that underlies, and alone can justify, this decision were to be given its relevant scope, a whole volume of the United States Reports would be required to document in detail the legislation in this country that would fall or be impaired. I abstain from entering upon a consideration of such legislation, and adjudications upon it, because I feel confident that the present decision will turn out to be an isolated deviation from the strong current of precedents — a derelict on the waters of the law. Accordingly, I content myself with dissenting.

Notes and Questions

1. The Court in *Lambert* acknowledges that *Balint* and other cases allow legislatures to enact regulatory offenses that "exclude elements of knowledge and diligence" from their definition. What then, is the salient aspect of the California registration law that moves the Court to make an exception here? What, after *Lambert*, is the minimal constitutional requirement of a mental element for criminal liability?

As the court notes, the offense defined by the Los Angeles ordinance was a crime of omission. Its actus reus therefore consisted of passive conduct by one with a legal duty to act under the circumstances. Is the court saying that due process always requires the prosecution to prove that omitters were aware of the legal duty they are charged with violating? Is that "the generalization" that the majority fears would affect so much legislation?

Perhaps the court is imposing a requirement of culpability only for some crimes of omission: where there are no "circumstances which might move one to inquire as to the necessity of registration" or "circumstances that should alert the doer to the consequences of his deed." Is the court saying that a reasonable person should be aware that certain kinds of activities are commonly regulated, and so conditioned on the fulfillment of legal duties? But what kind of activities? Commerce in dangerous commodities like drugs or explosives? What of a law requiring felons to register before they undertake paid baby-sitting?

The state, of course, could argue that ex-felons inherently pose a danger and should realize they might be subject to regulation. But is being an ex-felon, or a dangerous person, an *activity* or a *status*? Is the problem with the Lambert ordinance that it makes being an ex-felon in Los Angeles a status offense? Recall Robinson v. California, pp. 121-23, *supra*. Is the test simply whether certain kinds of regulations are customary? If felon registration ordinances were sufficiently widespread, would that relieve the prosecution of having to prove knowledge of a duty to register?

Professor Michaels's "constitutional innocence" test, p. 171, *supra,* implies that a strict liability failure-to-register-offense would be unconstitutional no matter how prevalent it was. Michaels asks whether the state could constitutionally punish Lambert's conduct absent the strict liability element. Take away the failure to register and Lambert is being punished for (1) the status of being an ex-felon and (2) exercising her constitutional right to travel by entering and remaining within Los Angeles.

> The principle that made Lambert "innocent" as a constitutional matter, but did not make Balint or Dotterweich so, is that the only intentional conduct covered by the statute that she engaged in was conduct that the legislature could not punish. Lambert was rightly decided because the intentional conduct covered by the ordinance that Lambert engaged in — being in Los Angeles — was not punishable by the legislature because of her constitutional right to travel. Balint and Dotterweich, in contrast, engaged in intentional conduct covered by the statutes they were charged with — selling drugs — that the legislature did have the power to punish. [112 Harv. L. Rev. at 862]

2. *The scope of* Lambert: *gun possession.* In United States v. Hutzell, 217 F.3d 966 (8th Cir. 2001), the court addressed 18 U.S.C. §922(g)(9), which makes it unlawful for anyone "who has been convicted in any court of a misdemeanor crime of domestic violence, to . . . possess . . . any firearm." Cody Hutzell pleaded guilty to a state charge of "domestic abuse assault," a misdemeanor. More than two years later, during an argument with his girlfriend, Hutzell fired a gun and was subsequently charged with violating §922(g)(9), which was enacted *after* his assault conviction.

Hutzell maintained that his conviction was improper, first, because he personally was unaware of §922(g)(9) at the time of the argument with his girlfriend and, further, because no one could be presumed to have had notice that the conduct described in the statute was in fact unlawful. The court nevertheless agreed with the government that 18 U.S.C. §924(a)(2), which provides the penalties for those who "knowingly" violate §922(g), required it to prove only that Hutzell knew of *the facts* constituting the offense (his domestic violence conviction and his gun possession), not that he also knew that it was illegal for him to possess a gun. Hutzell argued that, as in *Lambert,* nothing about the conduct that §922(g)(9) proscribes should have alerted him that it might be illegal. Writing for the Court, Judge Arnold responded:

Lambert carves out a very limited exception to the general rule that ignorance of the law is no excuse. The *Lambert* principle applies, for instance, only to prohibitions on activities that are not per se blameworthy. Even assuming that this requirement is met here, *Lambert* is nevertheless unavailing to Mr. Hutzell if his lack of awareness of the prohibition is objectively unreasonable. . . . [A]n individual's domestic violence conviction should itself put that person on notice that subsequent possession of a gun might well be subject to regulation. . . . Although an individual's right to bear arms is constitutionally protected, the possession of a gun, especially by anyone who has been convicted of a violent crime, is nevertheless a highly regulated activity, and everyone knows it. [Id. at 968-69]

Dissenting, Judge Bennett noted that "mere possession" (rather than active use) of a firearm after conviction of a domestic violence offense is "unaccompanied by any activity whatever," and is therefore just as passive as "mere presence in the city" after a felony conviction. Furthermore, Judge Bennett argued, given the wide prevalence of legal gun possession and the existence of legitimate uses for guns in American society, possession of a firearm is not "per se blameworthy." Finally, Judge Bennett argued:

[H]utzell's continued possession of a firearm from a time when such possession was legal to a time when it was suddenly forbidden, without notice that his status as a person able to possess firearms had changed, did not constitute "circumstances which might move one to inquire as to the necessity of" conforming to new regulations. In contrast, . . . acquisition of a firearm after a domestic violence conviction is [such a circumstance] because acquisition of a firearm would bring one into renewed contact with registration and permit requirements for firearms. Similarly, transportation of a firearm across state lines may give rise to such a duty to inquire, at least if one has been convicted of . . . a serious offense.

. . . [T]he law in question here is so obscure that not only are most of the people to whom it might be applicable unaware of its existence, most state-court judges, those most involved in administration of domestic abuse statutes, appear to be unaware of it, and routinely fail to advise persons convicted of domestic abuse or subject to domestic abuse restraining orders of their potential liability for firearm possession under federal law. [Id. at 976-77]

Assuming for the moment a Second Amendment right to gun possession, does Professor Michaels's "constitutional innocence" test permit the result in *Hutzell*? Does Section 922(g)(9) in essence combine a constitutionally impermissible status offense with the constitutionally protected "conduct" of possessing a firearm? The dissent apparently assumes that the constitution allows punishing gun possession by ex-offenders, as long as there is adequate notice. The majority responds that the dangers of firearms put the defendant on notice. But suppose that at the time of his domestic violence conviction he had duly inquired whether it affected his continued right to possess a firearm, and learned that it did not? Is it reasonable to expect him to renew his inquiry every year? Every day?

3. Lambert *and sex offender registration laws.* The registration law in *Lambert* finds echoes in the advent of new sexual offender registration laws, which have proved unusually fertile grounds for constitutional attacks on strict liability. For example, in Giorgetti v. State, 821 So.2d 417 (Fla. Ct. App. 2002), the defendant was convicted of violating a state law requiring sexual offenders to file an official report of any change in personal address within 48 hours of the move, and punishable as a felony subject to up to 5 years' imprisonment. The court reversed

his conviction because, in its view, the trial court had wrongly instructed the jury that "[t]he State does not have to prove the elements of intent [or] malicious or wrongful mental attitude." The court relied on Chicone v. State, 684 So. 2d 736 (Fla. 1996), which adopted as a rule of statutory interpretation that felonies should be presumed to require culpability absent explicit imposition of strict liability in the statute defining the offense. *Chicone* relied in turn on *Morissette*'s disfavoring of severe penalties for strict liability offenses. Could the *Giorgetti* court have relied on *Lambert* to rule strict liability unconstitutional for a sex-offender registration statute? Would *Lambert* apply if sex offenders are a particularly dangerous class of ex-convicts? Would it apply to statutes providing some procedure to notify ex-offenders of their obligation to register?

B.   CATEGORIES OF CULPABILITY

REGINA v. FAULKNER

Court of Crown Cases Reserved Ireland

13 Cox C.C. 550 (1877)

. . . The indictment was as follows: "That Robert Faulkner, on the 26th day of June, 1876, on board a certain ship called the Zemindar, the property of Sandback, Tenne, and Co., on a certain voyage on the high seas, then being on the high seas, feloniously, unlawfully, and maliciously, did set fire to the said ship. . . ."

It was proved that the Zemindar was on her voyage home with a cargo of rum, sugar, and cotton, worth 50,000 [pounds]. That the prisoner was a seaman on board, that he went into the forecastle hold, opened the sliding door in the bulk head, and so got into the hold where the rum was stored; he had no business there, and no authority to go there, and went for the purpose of stealing some rum, that he bored a hole in the cask with a gimlet, that the rum ran out, that when trying to put a spile in the hole out of which the rum was running, he had a lighted match in his hand; that the rum caught fire; that the prisoner himself was burned on the arms and neck; and that the ship caught fire and was completely destroyed. At the close of the case for the Crown, counsel for the prisoner asked for a direction of an acquittal on the ground that on the facts proved the indictment was not sustained, nor the allegation that the prisoner had unlawfully and maliciously set fire to the ship proved. The Crown contended that inasmuch as the prisoner was at the time engaged in the commission of a felony, the indictment was sustained, and the allegation of the intent was immaterial.

At the second hearing of the case before the Court for Crown Cases Reserved, the learned judge made the addition of the following paragraph to the case stated by him for the court.

> It was conceded that the prisoner had no actual intention of burning the vessel, and I was not asked to leave any question to the jury as to the prisoner's knowing the probable consequences of his act, or as to his reckless conduct.

The learned judge told the jury that although the prisoner had no actual intention of burning the vessel, still if they found he was engaged in stealing the rum, and that the fire took place in the manner above stated, they ought to find him guilty. The jury found the prisoner guilty on both counts, and he was sentenced to seven years penal servitude. The question for the court was whether the direction of the learned judge was right, if not, the conviction should be quashed. . . .

DOWSE, B. gave judgment to the effect that the conviction should be quashed.

BARRY, J. A very broad proposition has been contended for by the Crown, namely, that if, while a person is engaged in committing a felony, or, having committed it, is endeavouring to conceal his act, or prevent or spoil waste consequent on that act, he accidently does some collateral act, which if done wilfully would be another felony either at common law or by statute, he is guilty of the latter felony. I am by no means anxious to throw any doubt upon, or limit in any way, the legal responsibility of those who engage in the commission of felony, or acts mala in se; but I am not prepared without more consideration to give my assent to so wide a proposition. No express authority either by way of decision or dictum from judge or text writer has been cited in support of it. . . .

FITZGERALD, J. I concur in opinion with my brother Barry, that the direction of the learned judge cannot be sustained in law, and that therefore the conviction should be quashed. I am further of opinion that in order to establish the charge . . . the intention of the accused forms an element in the crime to the extent that it should appear that the defendant intended to do the very act with which he is charged, or that it was the necessary consequence of some other felonious or criminal act in which he was engaged, or that having a probable result which the defendant foresaw, or ought to have foreseen, he, nevertheless, persevered in such other felonious or criminal act. The prisoner did not intend to set fire to the ship — the fire was not the necessary result of the felony he was attempting; and if it was a probable result, which he ought to have foreseen, of the felonious transaction on which he was engaged, and from which a malicious design to commit the injurious act with which he is charged might have been fairly imputed to him, that view of the case was not submitted to the jury. . . . Counsel for the prosecution in effect insisted that the defendant, being engaged in the commission of, or in an attempt to commit a felony, was criminally responsible for every result that was occasioned thereby, even though it was not a probable consequence of his act or such as he could have reasonably foreseen or intended. No authority has been cited for a proposition so extensive and I am of opinion that it is not warranted by law. . . .

O'BRIEN, J. I am also of opinion that the conviction should be quashed, and I was of that opinion before the case for our consideration was amended by my brother Lawson. I had inferred from the original case that his direction to the jury was to the effect now expressly stated by amendment, and that, at the trial, the Crown's counsel conceded that the prisoner had no intention of burning the vessel, or of igniting the rum; and raised no questions as to prisoner's imagining or having any ground for supposing that the fire would be the result or consequence of his act in stealing the rum. With respect to Reg. v. Pembliton

(12 Cox C.C. 607), it appears to me there were much stronger grounds in that case for upholding the conviction than exist in the case before us. In that case the breaking of the window was the act of the prisoner. He threw the stone that broke it; he threw it with the unlawful intent of striking some one of the crowd about, and the breaking of the window, was the direct and immediate result of his act. And yet the Court unanimously quashed the conviction upon the ground that, although the prisoner threw the stone intending to strike some one or more persons, he did not intend to break the window. The courts above have intimated their opinion that if the jury (upon a question to that effect being left to them) had found that the prisoner, knowing the window was there, might have reasonably expected that the result of his act would be the breaking of the window, that then the conviction should be upheld. During the argument of this case the Crown counsel required us to assume that the jury found their verdict upon the ground that in their opinion the prisoner may have expected that the fire would be the consequence of his act in stealing the rum, but nevertheless did the act recklessly, not caring whether the fire took place or not. But at the trial there was not even a suggestion of any such ground, and we cannot assume that the jury formed an opinion which there was no evidence to sustain, and which would be altogether inconsistent with the circumstances under which the fire took place. The reasonable inference from the evidence is that the prisoner lighted the match for the purpose of putting the spile in the hole to stop the further running of the rum, and that while he was attempting to do so the rum came in contact with the lighted match and took fire. . . .

KEOGH, J. I have the misfortune to differ from the other members of the Court. I think it very fortunate for the prisoner that this case has lasted so long, and has received such elaborate consideration, for I cannot be considered as violating judicial confidence when I state that if the case were decided when the arguments closed the conviction would stand. . . . I am . . . of opinion, that the conviction should stand, as I consider all questions of intention and malice are closed by the finding of the jury, that the prisoner committed the act with which he was charged whilst engaged in the commission of a substantive felony. On this broad ground, irrespective of all refinements as to "recklessness" and "wilfulness," I think the conviction is sustained. . . .

Notes and Questions

1. Faulkner obviously did not intend to burn the ship. But was he nevertheless properly culpable for the ship's loss? Did he foresee the possibility of a fire? Should he have? Is Faulkner's responsibility for burning the ship increased by the fact that it happened while he was stealing rum? Would he be less culpable if he had been sent by the captain to fetch some rum and had, equally carelessly, lit a match that set the rum afire? According to the judges, must Faulkner have intended to burn the ship in order to be liable, or will some lesser form of culpability do?

2. The Malicious Damage Act, the statute under which Faulkner was prosecuted, made it a crime "feloniously, unlawfully, and maliciously" to set fire to the ship. Does the legislature's choice of adverbs help us determine what state of mind should be necessary for punishment under the statute? Are the judges

in the majority contending that Faulkner set fire to the ship "feloniously," but not "maliciously?" Or do "feloniously," "unlawfully," and "maliciously" all mean the same thing: that defendant acted with whatever mental state justifies punishment under the statute?

3. *Mens rea in the common law.* The notion that crime required an act of will entered the common law from canon law in the Middle Ages. As Professor Anthony Dillof recounts,

> [t]he jurist most associated with the introduction of mens rea into the criminal law is [the thirteenth century author] Henry Bracton. A cleric as well as a judge, Bracton wrote, "a crime is not committed unless the intention to injure exists." The requisite intention to injure, however, was not defined with any great care. It appears that any fault on the part of the actor would be sufficient. Accordingly, Bracton has been understood as adopting the canonist doctrine [that] . . . one acting unlawfully is held responsible for all the consequences of his conduct.[8]

Would Bracton have classified Faulkner's mental state as an "intent to injure"? Would he have held Faulkner criminally responsible for burning the ship?

Bracton's idea had little immediate influence. Edward Coke coined the maxim that an evil act required a "mens rea" in 1641, but made no effort to define this requirement for each crime.[9] Common law judges sometimes treated accident or mistake as relevant to liability — but they ordinarily viewed such claims as excuses. Blackstone's Commentaries — the most widely used lawbook in early America — classified mistake and accident with insanity and duress as "excuses from punishment for disobedience to the laws."[10] Did Faulkner have an "excuse" for damaging the ship? Would the fact that he was only trying to steal, not to burn, excuse him?

The idea of a mental element probably makes its first appearance in Francis Bacon's 1596 Elements of the Common Law. Bacon divided crimes into a malicious intent and a harmful result, but did not see each crime as having a distinctive mental element. Instead, he decreed that a "general" malicious intent could be transferred among crimes of like gravity: "*In criminalibus sufficit generalis malitia intentionis cum facto paris gradus.*"[11] Bacon reasoned: "All crimes have their conception in a corrupt intent, and have their consummation and issuing in some particular fact; which though it might not be the fact at which the intention of the malefactor levelled, yet the law giveth him no advantage of the error, if another particular ensue of as high a nature."[12] In the early eighteenth century William Hawkins offered a similar "general rule, that where ever a man intending to commit one felony, happens to commit another, he is as much guilty as if he had intended the felony he actually commits."[13]

---

8. Anthony Dillof, Transferred Intent: An Inquiry into the Nature of Criminal Culpability, 1 Buff. Crim. L. Rev. 501, 509 (1998); see Henry De Bracton, On the Laws and Customs of England, 289, 341, 384, 424 (George E. Woodbine ed. & Samuel E. Thorne transl. 1968); Francis Sayre, Mens Rea, 45 Harv. L. Rev. 974, 984-985 (1932); Guyora Binder, The Rhetoric of Motive and Intent, 6 Buff. Crim. L. Rev. 1, 7-27 (2003).

9. Sir Edward Coke, The Third Part of the Institutes of the Common Law of England 107 (1986) (Reprint of 1797 ed.).

10. William Blackstone, 4 Commentaries on the Laws of England *20-21 (1769).

11. Francis Bacon, 4 Works of Francis Bacon 55 (1826).

12. Id.

13. William Hawkins, Pleas of the Crown (1716-1721) at 74.

Soon thereafter, Justice Sir Peter King held that some crimes required a specific, and hence non-transferable intent, in the case of Rex v. Woodbourne and Coke, 16 St. Tr. 53 (1722). Charged with the statutory felony of maiming with intent to disfigure, Woodbourne and Coke argued that they had intended to kill rather than disfigure their victim, and so were guilty only of the misdemeanor of attempted murder! King agreed, arguing that

> There are some cases where an unlawful or felonious intent, to do one act, may be carried over to another act, done in prosecution thereof; and such other act will be felony, because done in prosecution of an unlawful intent. . . . But now the indictment on this statute is for a particular intent; for purposely . . . slitting Mr. Crispe's nose, with an intention in so doing to maim or disfigure.[14]

Lord Mansfield offered a slightly different distinction in the libel prosecution Rex v. Woodfall, 5 Burrows 2667 (1770). Mansfield held that the prosecution need only persuade the jury that the defendant intentionally published a libel "malicious" in its effect, not that he did so with malicious intent. Mansfield wrote: "When an act, in itself indifferent, becomes criminal if done with a particular intent, then the intent must be proved and found; but when the act is in itself unlawful, the proof of justification or excuse lies on the defendant, and in failure thereof, the law implies a criminal intent." With this notion of "implied criminal intent," Mansfield reinterpreted all offenses as requiring proof of intent. Is Mansfield's dictum helpful in the *Faulkner* case? Was Faulkner's act unlawful in itself? What was Faulkner's act? Stealing? Damaging property? Lighting a match? Spilling rum?

4. *General and specific intent.* King's distinction between transferable and non-transferable intentions, and Mansfield's distinction between inherently unlawful acts and innocent acts rendered criminal by a particular intent, inspired early efforts to develop a systematic classification of mental states for crimes. In his influential nineteenth century treatise, the American Joel Prentiss Bishop offered the theory that crimes ordinarily required both an intention to "do a forbidden thing" and a harmful result. Yet the harm produced need not be the specific harm intended: A "general" intent to commit some crime sufficed to make the offender criminally responsible for any harm caused. As long as the intended result was roughly as bad as the result produced, the unlawful intent would "transfer" to the actual, but unintended, result. Yet Bishop excepted certain crimes from this doctrine of a transferable or "general" intent to do wrong. These crimes required a "specific" intent that could only transfer to a result of the same kind intended:

> The doctrine of the transfer of the intent to the unintended act . . . is limited in its application; because of the peculiar character of many of the specific offenses. Thus . . . to constitute some crimes . . . there must exist a precise and specific intent, for which no other, however heinous in itself, will be a substitute. So there are certain acts, which are not in their nature wrong, but only wrong when done with some particular intent. . . . There are some crimes requiring . . . the concurrence of two or more separate intents; as, an intent to do wrong in general, or to do a particular wrong, with an ulterior purpose beyond. Thus, in larceny there must be, first, an intent to trespass on another's personal property; secondly . . . the

14. 16 St. Tr. 79.

further intent to deprive the owner of his ownership therein. So burglary consists in the intent, which must be executed, to break in the night-time into a dwelling house; and the further concurrent intent, which may be executed or not, to commit therein some crime which is a felony. In these and other like cases, the particular or ulterior intent must be proved, in addition to the more general one, in order to make out the offence. . . . But aside from these and other special doctrines, the rule is, that, if a man intends to do what he is conscious the law, which everyone is presumed to know, forbids, there need not be any other evil intent.[15]

Under Bishop's formulation, then, which crimes required proof of "specific" intent? The answer: (1) all offenses explicitly so defined by statute, (2) all attempts (see Chapter 10, *infra*) and other "inchoate" crimes, and (3) any other crimes, like burglary and larceny, for which common law courts had defined an intent element. Readers of Bishop's treatise would have described *Faulkner* as a decision that England's Malicious Damage Act defined a crime of "specific" rather than "general" intent. Do you agree, or do you think the judges in Faulkner were rejecting Bishop's idea of transferable or "general" intent?

American judges and jurists tried to use Bishop's terminology to solve a wide array of problems. As a result, the phrases "general intent" and "specific intent" took on a variety of different meanings:

(a) According to one version of the distinction, "specific intent" refers to the mental element of any crime, while "general intent" refers to the broader question of defendant's blameworthiness or guilt, including both the defendant's mens rea and responsibility. According to this version, a fact that negates "specific intent" negates the mental element of the offense. A fact that negates general intent is an excuse or affirmative defense.

(b) According to a second version of the distinction, a "general intent" is simply an intention to do the act proscribed: to enter another's property in the case of trespass. A "specific intent" is an *unexecuted* intention to do some further act or accomplish some further result. Thus, an unexecuted intention to kill turns the general intent crime of trespass into the specific intent crime of burglary (requiring entry of another's property with intent to commit a felony therein). Under this formulation, specific intent crimes often contain a "lesser included offense" (e.g., trespass is the lesser included offense of burglary); general intent crimes do not. A defendant without the secondary or "specific" intent, could still be convicted of the lesser included, general intent crime.

(c) A third version of the distinction associates "general intent" with the traditional presumptions that an actor intends the "natural and probable results" and the "legal consequences" of his conduct. Offenses to which these presumptions apply are "general intent" offenses. If, however, the prosecutor must prove the defendant intended a *particular* result, or intended that his action have a *particular* legal consequence, the offense is a "specific intent" offense. Thus, bigamy is a "general intent crime," if the prosecution must prove only an intent to remarry; it is a "specific intent crime" if the prosecution must also prove the offender's knowledge that he or she remains legally married to a living spouse. Today, the Supreme Court's due process decisions require proving rather than presuming of the mental element of an offense, but it remains permissible to punish unintended consequences (see the Introduction, *supra* at p. 19-20).

15. Joel Prentiss Bishop, 1 Commentaries on the Criminal Law 229, 220-222 (1st ed., 1856).

Hence, the terminology of presumptions is disappearing, but the terminology of general and specific intent survives.

(d) A fourth version of the distinction equates "specific intent" with "purpose" and "general intent" with knowledge or recklessness or negligence. Thus a general intent offense punishes for consequences she expected, or knowingly risked or should have expected. A specific intent offense punishes her only for consequences she desired. An example is Louisiana's statutory definition of criminal intent:

Criminal Intent

Criminal intent may be specific or general:

(1) Specific criminal intent is that state of mind which exists when the circumstances indicate that the offender actively desired the prescribed criminal consequences to follow his act or failure to act.

(2) General criminal intent is present . . . when the circumstances indicate that the offender, in the ordinary course of human experience, must have adverted to the prescribed criminal consequences as reasonably certain to result from his act or failure to act."[16]

We have suggested that the *Faulkner* court treated malicious damage as a "specific intent" crime. But is that accurate if we use version (b) of the distinction? What if we use version (d)?

5. *Criticisms of general and specific intent.* Modern scholars criticize the terminology of general and specific intent on five grounds.

First, as noted above, it is ambiguous: An offender who acted with "general intent" may have acted with (a) no excuse, (b) a proven intent to achieve the actual results of her conduct only, (c) a presumed (rather than proven) intent to achieve the actual results of her conduct, or (d) recklessness or negligence. An offender who acted with "specific intent" may have acted with (a) the culpable mental state required by the definition of an offense, (b) a proven intent to achieve some result beyond that actually achieved, (c) a proven (rather than presumed) intent to achieve the actual results of her conduct, or (d) intent (rather than recklessness or negligence).

Second, a distinction between general and specific intent is not very useful for an offense with more than two elements. Consider burglary, which might be defined as (1) entering the (2) dwelling (3) of another (4) without permission (5) with the intent to commit a felony therein. Which of these five elements must the offender intend? It does no good to say burglary is a specific intent offense, because that implies only that the intent to enter is not enough. There are four other elements. Which of these must the offender specifically intend?

Third, the terminology of general and specific intent wrongly implies that intent is the only kind of mental culpability possible. A lawmaker might wish to condition burglary on intending to enter a building and commit a felony, while being reckless or negligent as to whether the building is a dwelling and whether the actor has permission to enter.

Fourth, "general intent" is often a misleading euphemism: An offense that conditions liability on having reasons to expect a result or know of a

16. L.S.A. 14-10 (1997).

circumstance is a crime of negligence, not intent. If the term "general intent" means culpability for undesired results, it is too imprecise: it does not distinguish between results the actor actually expected and those the actor merely had reason to expect. It also does not distinguish among results that seem certain, probable, or possible.

Fifth, even though the phrase "general intent" need not mean "presumed intent," it is best avoided because of its historic association with unconstitutional presumptions.

6. *Normative and descriptive terminology.* Could the drafters of the malicious damage act have avoided ambiguity by using more precise terminology? Consider the following argument by Prof. George Fletcher, that any terminology used to specify subjective criteria of liability will inevitably suffer from the same ambiguity.[17]

One of the persistent tensions in legal terminology runs between the descriptive and normative uses of the same terms. Witness the struggle over the concept of malice. The term has a high moral content, and when it came into the law as the benchmark of murder, it was presumably used normatively and judgmentally. Yet . . . English jurists have sought to reduce the concepts of malice to the specific mental states of intending and knowing. California judges, in contrast, have stressed the normative content of malice in a highly judgmental definition, employing terms like "base, anti-social purpose" and "wanton disregard for human life." For the English, malice is a question of fact; did the actor have a particular state of consciousness (intention or knowledge)? In California, malice is a value judgment about the actor's motives, attitudes and personal capacity. . . .

The confusion between normative and descriptive language is so pervasive in Anglo-American criminal law that it affects the entire language of discourse. There appear to be very few terms that are exempt from the ambiguity. The term "intent" may refer either to a state of intending (regardless of blame) or it may refer to an intent to act under circumstances . . . that render an act properly subject to blame. The term "criminal intent" does not resolve the ambiguity, for a criminal intent may simply be the intent to do the act, which, according to the statutory definition, renders the act "criminal," i.e., punishable under the law. . . .

It is obvious that the very word "criminal" is affected by the same tension between descriptive and normative illocutionary force. When used normatively, "criminal" refers to the type of person who by virtue of his deeds deserves to be branded and punished as a criminal. When used descriptively, as in the phrase, "criminal act" it may refer to any act the legislature has declared to be "criminal." Thus the term "criminal intent" may mean the intent to act under circumstances that make it just to treat the criminal as an actor in the pejorative sense. . . . But it is equally plausible to use the term "criminal intent" to refer to the intent or knowledge sufficient to commit the crime as defined by the legislature. . . .

It would seem that the term "culpability" ordinarily has normative force, for in non-legal English, a person is culpable only if he is justly to blame for his conduct. It would follow that if conduct were excused by virtue of duress or insanity, the actor would not be culpable. Yet the Model Penal Code defines acting purposely and knowingly as "kinds of culpability." . . . [I]t would . . . follow that if a person committed larceny while subject to duress, he would be acquitted . . . [despite having] acted culpably. . . .

Descriptive theorists . . . are apt to see problems of insanity, duress and mistake as extrinsic to the analysis of *mens rea* and criminal intent. Normative theorists,

17. Rethinking Criminal Law 396-401 (1978).

in contrast, . . . integrate these "defensive" issues into their formulation of the minimum conditions for liability [by arguing that] there is no mens rea or "criminal
intent" when the intentional commission of the offense is excused by reason of
duress, insanity, or reasonable mistake. . . . [T]he normative theory of culpability
provides an important . . . premise in the argument requiring the prosecution to
disprove claims of duress, insanity and mistake beyond a reasonable doubt. . . .

One might be inclined to think that this tension between normative and descriptive usage could be eliminated simply by coining new terms that are patently
either normative or descriptive. Yet we have seen that "intent" may be employed
normatively, and "culpability" descriptively. The faith that new terminology would
eliminate the problem of ambiguity ignores the underlying problem. . . . Descriptive theorists seek to minimize the normative content of the criminal law in order
to render it, in their view, precise and free from the passions of subjective moral
judgment. . . . ; the reality of judgment, blame and punishment in the criminal process generates the contrary pressure and insures that the quest for a value-free science of law cannot succeed. . . .

Professor Fletcher clearly identifies himself with the normative theorists of criminal law. Is his objection to the reform proposals of descriptive theorists that they
remain ambiguous, or that they achieve precision at the cost of rendering the
criminal justice process blind to moral considerations?

As Fletcher notes, modern movements to reform the substantive criminal
law have focused on attempts to obviate problems of the sort raised by the
Faulkner case, and to avoid ambiguous formulas like "general and specific intent." Such efforts have aimed at creating a systematic scheme of mental states
that distinguishes them along a hierarchy of culpability and clarifies which mental state should be assigned to each element of a criminal statute. The most important of these efforts at codification is the Model Penal Code, and the heart
of the Code lies in the following sections.

MODEL PENAL CODE
American Law Institute, Model Penal Code and Commentaries (1985)

Section 1.13. General Definitions

(9) "element of an offense" means (i) such conduct or (ii) such attendant circumstances or (iii) such a result of conduct as
    (a) is included in the description of the forbidden conduct in the definition
of the offense; or
    (b) establishes the required kind of culpability; or
    (c) negatives an excuse or justification for such conduct; or
    (d) negatives a defense under the statute of limitations; or
    (e) establishes jurisdiction or venue;
(10) "material element of an offense" means an element that does not relate
exclusively to the statute of limitations, jurisdiction, venue or to any other matter
similarly unconnected with (i) the harm or evil, incident to conduct, sought to be
prevented by the law defining the offense, or (ii) the existence of a justification or
excuse for such conduct. . . .

Section 2.02. General Requirements of Culpability

(1) *Minimum Requirements of Culpability.* Except as provided in Section 2.05,
a person is not guilty of an offense unless he acted purposely, knowingly, recklessly

or negligently, as the law may require, with respect to each material element[18] of the offense.

(2) *Kinds of Culpability Defined.*

(a) *Purposely.* A person acts purposely with respect to a material element of an offense when:

(i) if the element involves the nature of his conduct or a result thereof, it is his conscious object to engage in conduct of that nature or to cause such a result; and

(ii) if the element involves the attendant circumstances, he is aware of the existence of such circumstances or he believes or hopes that they exist.

(b) *Knowingly.* A person acts knowingly with respect to a material element of an offense when:

(i) if the element involves the nature of his conduct or the attendant circumstances, he is aware that his conduct is of that nature or that such circumstances exist; and

(ii) if the element involves a result of his conduct, he is aware that it is practically certain that his conduct will cause such a result.

(c) *Recklessly.* A person acts recklessly with respect to a material element of an offense when he consciously disregards a substantial and unjustifiable risk that the material elements exist or will result from his conduct. The risk must be of such a nature and degree that, considering the nature and purpose of the actor's conduct and the circumstances known to him, its disregard involves a gross deviation from the standard of conduct that a law-abiding person would observe in the actor's situation.

(d) *Negligently.* A person acts negligently with respect to a material element of an offense when he should be aware of a substantial and unjustifiable risk that the material element exists or will result from his conduct. The risk must be of such a nature and degree that the actor's failure to perceive it, considering the nature and purpose of his conduct and the circumstances known to him, involves a gross deviation from the standard of care that a reasonable person would observe in the actor's situation.

Notes and Questions

1. Note that the language of the Model Penal Code is quite complicated. Can you describe any of these blameworthy states of mind in more readily understandable terms, without sacrificing the Code's precision of meaning?

2. *Understanding the MPC terminology.* Even if all can agree that, in general, some culpable state of mind must attach to a voluntary act in order to justify the

---

18. [The Model Penal Code provides in section 1.13:

(9) "element of an offense" means (i) such conduct or (ii) such attendant circumstances or (iii) such a result of conduct as

(a) is included in the description of the forbidden conduct in the definition of the offense; or

(b) establishes the required kind of culpability; or

(c) negatives an excuse or justification for such conduct; or

(d) negatives a defense under the statute of limitations; or

(e) establishes jurisdiction or venue;

(10) "material element of an offense" means an element that does not relate exclusively to the statute of limitations, jurisdiction, venue or to any other matter similarly unconnected with (i) the harm or evil, incident to conduct, sought to be prevented by the law defining the offense, or (ii) the existence of a justification or excuse for such conduct. . . .

For more on the history and significance of the Model Penal Code, see Appendix A, *infra.* — EDS.]

condemnation of the law, the issue does not end here. We can, in various ways, specify different kinds of culpable states of mind. As we will see, the modern trend in American jurisdictions is to use the categories of culpability adopted and refined by the Model Penal Code. Though these are not the only ways one could slice the concept of a culpable state of mind, they do accord with certain of our basic intuitions.

Imagine for instance a parent who has come into a room and found that her child has just smashed a valuable vase:

Parent: You smashed that vase deliberately! (This is her most serious charge — that the child's conscious object was to break the valuable vase; in other words, that the child had "purpose.")

Child: No, that is not what I wanted to do at all. I didn't want to break the vase.

Parent (presumably trained as a lawyer): Even if that is true, you knew that when you let the vase hit the ground it would break, even though you might only have wanted to make a loud noise.

Child: No, I did not know that it would break at all, especially since my friend dropped a vase at his house and it didn't break, but I realize now that his is made of unbreakable plastic.

Parent: Even so, you knew that the vase *might* break. You recognized the risk when you dropped it or threw it to the ground, and despite this recognition you acted anyway. You took the chance. In other words, you were reckless.

Child: No, I didn't. It never occurred to me that the vase might break. I was sure it wouldn't.

Parent: In that case, *you should have known* that the vase would break. You are six years old and we expect a six-year-old to have knowledge that such a result would occur. In other words, you were negligent.

Child: From now on you can expect me to have this knowledge, but it is too much to ask of a six-year-old, who has had no previous experience dropping vases, to realize that they might break.

Parent (adopting a kind of mental state that the quoted passage from the Model Penal Code did not mention, but that the trial judge instructed the jury to apply in Regina v. Faulkner): You should not have been playing with the vase to begin with. You should have been in your room resting at the time.

Child: In that case, I should be punished only for not resting in my room or for playing with the vase, but not for the more serious offense of breaking it.

Parent (impressed with his child's argument for his lack of a culpable state of mind with respect to the vase, but nonetheless eager to punish): It does not matter; I will punish you for breaking the vase because you are *strictly liable.*

Child: That is fundamentally unjust.

3. *The MPC commentary.* The comments to the Model Penal Code give a more detailed exposition of the culpable states of mind it has classified in section 2.02, General Requirements of Culpability:[19]

> This section expresses the Code's basic requirement that unless some element of mental culpability is proved with respect to each material element of the offense, no valid criminal conviction may be obtained [except as provided in Section 2.05]. . . .

19. American Institute, Model Penal Code and Commentaries, Part I, at 229-44 (1985).

. . . The Code provision on rape will afford an illustration [of the Model Code's approach]. Under Section 213.1 (1), a purpose to effect the sexual relation is clearly required. But other circumstances are also made relevant by the definition of the offense. The victim must not have been married to the defendant and her consent to sexual relations would, of course, preclude the crime. Must the defendant's purpose have encompassed the facts that he was not the husband of the victim and that she opposed his will? These are certainly entirely different questions. Recklessness may be sufficient for these circumstances of the offense, although purpose is required with respect to the sexual result that is an element of the offense. . . . [The Code] delineates four levels of culpability: purpose, knowledge, recklessness and negligence. It requires that one of these levels of culpability must be proved with respect to each "material element" of the offense, which may involve (1) the nature of the forbidden conduct or (2) the attendant circumstances, or (3) the result of conduct. The question of which level of culpability suffices to establish liability must be addressed separately with respect to each material element, and will be resolved either by the particular definition of the offense or the general provisions of this section.

The purpose of articulating these distinctions in detail is to advance the clarity of draftsmanship in the delineation of the definitions of specific crimes . . . and to dispel the obscurity with which the culpability requirement is often treated when such concepts as "general criminal intent," "mens rea," "presumed intent," "malice," "wilfulness," "scienter" and the like have been employed. What Justice Jackson called "the variety, disparity and confusion" of judicial definitions of "the requisite but elusive mental element" in crime [Morissette v. United States, 342 U.S. 246, 252 (1952)] should, insofar as possible, be rationalized by a criminal code." . . .

. . . In defining the kinds of culpability, the Code draws a narrow distinction between acting purposely and knowingly, one of the elements of ambiguity in legal usage of the term "intent." Knowledge that the requisite external circumstances exist is a common element in both conceptions. But action is not purposive with respect to the nature or the result of the actor's conduct unless it was his conscious object to perform an action of that nature or to cause such a result. . . .

. . . [T]here are areas where the discrimination is required and is made under traditional law, which uses the awkward concept of "specific intent." This is true in treason, for example, insofar as purpose to aid the enemy is an ingredient of the offense, and in attempts, complicity and conspiracy, where a true purpose to effect the criminal result is requisite for liability. . . .

. . . An important discrimination is drawn between acting either purposely or knowingly and acting recklessly. As the Code uses the term, recklessness involves conscious risk creation. It resembles acting knowingly in that a state of awareness is involved, but the awareness is of risk, that is of a probability less than substantial certainty; the matter is contingent from the actor's point of view. Whether the risk relates to the nature of the actor's conduct or to the existence of the requisite attendant circumstances, or to the result that may ensue, is immaterial; the concept is the same. . . .

. . . [The Code requires, however, that the risk thus consciously disregarded by the actor be "substantial" and "unjustifiable" to be considered reckless.] Even substantial risks . . . may be created without recklessness when the actor is seeking to serve a proper purpose, as when a surgeon performs an operation that he knows is very likely to be fatal but reasonably thinks to be necessary because the patient has no other, safer chance. Some principle must, therefore, be articulated to indicate the nature of the final judgment to be made after everything has been weighed. . . . There is no way to state this value judgment that does not beg the question in the last analysis; the point is that the jury must evaluate the actor's conduct and determine whether it should be condemned. The Code proposes . . . that this difficulty be accepted frankly, and that the jury be asked to measure the substantiality and justifiability of the risk by asking whether its disregard, given the actor's perceptions, involved a gross deviation from the standard of conduct that a law-abiding person in the actor's situation would observe. . . .

. . . The fourth kind of culpability is negligence. It is distinguished from [acting purposely, knowingly or recklessly] in that it does not involve a state of awareness. A person acts negligently . . . when he inadvertently creates a substantial and unjustifiable risk of which he ought to be aware . . . [considering its nature and degree, the nature and the purpose of his conduct and the care that would be exercised by a reasonable person in his situation]. [A]gain it is quite impossible to avoid tautological articulation of the final question. The tribunal must evaluate the actor's failure of perception and determine whether, under all the circumstances, it was serious enough to be condemned. The jury must find fault, and must find that it was substantial and unjustified; that is the heart of what can be said in legislative terms. . . .

. . . [S]ome critics have opposed any penal consequences for negligent behavior. Since the actor is inadvertent by hypothesis, it has been argued that the "threat of punishment for negligence must pass him by, because he does not realise that it is addressed to him." So too, it has been urged that education or corrective treatment, not punishment, is the proper social method for dealing with persons with inadequate awareness, since what is implied is not a moral defect. This analysis, however, oversimplifies the issue. . . . [K]nowledge that conviction and sentence, not to speak of punishment, may follow conduct that inadvertently creates improper risk does supply [people] with an additional motive to take care before acting, to use their faculties and draw on their experience in gauging the potentialities of contemplated conduct. To some extent, at least, this motive may promote awareness and thus be effective as a measure of control. . . . [L]egislators act on these assumptions in a host of situations, and it would be dogmatic to assert that they are wholly wrong. Accordingly, negligence, as here defined, should not be wholly rejected as a ground of culpability that may suffice for purposes of penal law, though it should not generally be deemed sufficient in the definition of specific crimes and it should often be differentiated from conduct involving higher culpability.

4. *Applying culpable mental states to act elements.* Professors Paul Robinson and Jane Grall have constructed the following Chart 1 to clarify application of the Model Penal Code's culpable mental states to different kinds of objective elements.[20]

5. *Culpability terms for wrongdoing and responsibility.* A distinctive aspect of the Model Penal Code's culpability scheme is its extension of the concept of mens rea to knowledge of circumstances bearing on wrongdoing and responsibility. Traditional conceptions of the mental element of the offense limit the mental element of the offense to awareness of, or attitudes toward, circumstances included in the definition of the offense. While the distinction between the definition of the offense and the defenses of justification and excuse currently delineates the constitutionally requisite allocation of the burden of proof beyond a reasonable doubt, see pp. 14-20 in the Introduction, *supra,* the Model Penal Code ignores that distinction for purposes of determining the mental element of the offense. Section 1.12 of the Model Penal Code defines as a "material element of an offense" all conduct, attendant circumstances, and results included

---

20. Element Analysis in Defining Criminal Liability: The Model Penal Code and Beyond, 35 Stan. L. Rev. 681, 695 (1983).

CHART 1
Model Penal Code §2.02(2) Culpability Definitions

A person acts [culpability level] with respect to
[type of objective element] when:

Type of objective element

	Circumstance	*Result*	*Conduct*
Purposely	he is aware of such circumstances or hopes they exist	it is his conscious object . . . to cause such a result	it is his conscious object to engage in conduct of that nature
Knowingly	he is aware. . . that such circumstances exist	he is aware that it is practically certain that his conduct will cause such a result	he is aware that his conduct is of that nature
Recklessly	he consciously disregards a substantial and unjustifiable risk that the material element exists	he consciously disregards a substantial and unjustifiable risk that the material element . . . will result from his conduct	
Negligently	he should be aware of a substantial and unjustifiable risk that the material element exists	he should be aware of a substantial and unjustifiable risk that the material ele- ment . . . will result from his conduct	

in the definition of the offense, establishing the required kind of culpability, *or negating a justification or excuse.* Recall that section 2.02 requires a culpable mental state with respect to each "material element." Could the inclusion of justifying and excusing circumstances among the material elements of an offense provide one reason why drafters of the Model Penal Code might want different mental states for different material elements?

6. *Knowledge, willful ignorance, and acceptance.* In United States v. Jewell, 532 F.2d 697 (9th Cir. 1976), the defendant claimed that, though he knew of a secret compartment in the automobile that he drove into the United States and knew of facts indicating that marijuana had been placed there, "he deliberately avoided positive knowledge . . . to avoid responsibility in the event of discovery."

The court held that this "willful blindness" was equivalent to knowledge, and hence that the defendant "knowingly brought marijuana into the United States" in violation of the law.

Consider the Model Penal Code approach to this issue, in section 2.02(7):

Requirement of Knowledge Satisfied by Knowledge of High Probability. When knowledge of the existence of a particular fact is an element of an offense, such knowledge is established if a person is aware of a high probability of its existence, unless he actually believes that it does not exist.

Is this a satisfying solution to cases like *Jewell*? Does "knowledge" accurately describe the mental state being punished here? If a juror knows that 90 percent of criminal defendants are guilty, and does not actually believe a particular defendant to be innocent, does she know that defendant is guilty? May she convict?

One commentator concludes that cases like *Jewell* show that the Model Penal Code is wrong to define culpability by reference to cognitive states like knowledge, rather than desire states. Professor Alan Michaels argues that we should condemn the likes of Jewell for *accepting* harm, not *expecting* it. To accept harm, he argues, is not necessarily to wish it, or even expect it, but to be willing that it occur if necessary to achieve some other purpose. For Michaels, it is this volitional attitude of acceptance that renders even the knowing wrongdoer culpable.

Is the accepting actor "as bad" as the knowing actor? Well, what is it that makes the knowing actor morally culpable in the first place? It is not of course, the knowledge that a particular action will be harmful. There is nothing wrong with the knowledge if the person chooses not to act. . . . What makes the knowing actor morally culpable is . . . the fact that . . . knowledge she would cause harm was not sufficient to stop her from acting. . . . This is the core definition of acceptance. Acceptance and knowledge thus represent the same level of culpability.[21]

Do you agree? Aristotle thought that those who cause harm unwittingly but later fail to regret it are nevertheless culpable because their lack of regret implies that they would not have acted differently had they known the harm they would cause.[22] In a similar spirit, Michaels proposes that juries decide not whether a defendant anticipated harm, but whether such knowledge would have dissuaded the defendant from acting. But is it fair or prudent to condition liability on the answer to a hypothetical question? Is Michaels right that the Model Penal Code focuses too much on cognition rather than desire?

7. *Recklessness.* Professor Kenneth Simons offers a similar criticism of the Model Penal Code's definition of recklessness as the conscious awareness of a substantial risk of harm. Simons writes:

Many modern legal standards devalue desire states relative to belief or cognitive states. For example, the influential Model Penal Code differentiates criminal recklessness from negligence in only one respect: recklessness requires conscious

---

21. Alan C. Michaels, Acceptance: The Missing Mental State, 71 So. Ca. L. Rev. 953, 967 (1998).
22. Aristotle, Nichomachean Ethics III.1.1110b (Martin Ostwald transl., 1962).

awareness of a substantial and unjustifiable risk, while negligence requires that the actor *should* have been aware of such a risk. Yet a traditional and defensible view sees recklessness as culpable *indifference* to risk. The terms "indifference," "not caring," and "callousness" all describe a culpable *desire* state — not a desire to harm, but an insufficiently strong *aversion* to harm, or a desire or willingness to create a *risk* of harm. The modern account of recklessness, emphasizing cognitive awareness of a risk, ignores or conceals the moral quality that "culpable indifference" expresses.[23]

8. *Negligence.* One of the most controversial issues in the drafting of the Model Penal Code was whether to permit the criminalization of negligence. The Code permits only the legislature — not courts — to condition crimes on negligence, and only if they do so explicitly. Herbert Wechsler, the Code's principal drafter, advised that "liability for negligence should be deemed the exceptional and not the ordinary case."[24] But if culpability is ordinarily conditioned on awareness of wrongdoing, is it ever fair to punish negligent wrongdoers? Jerome Hall thought not:

> . . . [N]egligent behavior implies inadvertence and must therefore be sharply distinguished from voluntary harmdoing, i.e., conduct that includes at least an awareness of possible harm. If, for example, one who is about to drive an automobile knows that he is ill or very tired or if he drinks alcoholic beverages knowing this will incapacitate him, subsequent damage may justifiably be attributed to his immediately prior conduct. . . . [But] this would seem to fall within the Model Penal Code's definition of recklessness as conscious disregard for "a substantial and unjustifiable risk.". . . With respect to negligent damage, neither at the time of damage, nor shortly prior to it . . . does the defendant have knowledge, belief or suspicion that he is endangering anything socially valued. . . .
>
> [Some argue] that negligent harm-doers exhibit such an indifference to social values, such a calloused character, that they deserve punishment. But this extends the meaning of "fault" to include ignorance and insensitivity. Although these characteristics are to be deplored, they do not amount to voluntary harm-doing. Such an insensitive person is by definition *not aware of* his dangerous behavior.[25]

Hall argues here that when we criminalize truly negligent or inadvertent harm, we wrongly punish character rather than any voluntary conduct. But consider Aristotle's argument that the negligent actor is criminally responsible for his character: "[A] man is himself responsible for becoming careless, because he lives in a loose and carefree manner; he is likewise responsible for being unjust or self-indulgent, if he keeps on doing mischief or spending his time in drinking and the like. For a given kind of activity produces a corresponding character."[26]

Hall responded by questioning whether prosecutors could actually prove in any given case that current carelessness had been caused by the offender's past

---

23. Kenneth W. Simons, Rethinking Mental States, 72 B.U.L. Rev. 463, 466 (1992). For a thoughtful critique of the Simoins approach, arguing that desire states are often too vague or conflicting to serve usefully as culpability criteria, and that the MPC survives Simons's challenge, see Kimberly Kessler Ferzan, Don't Abandon the Model Penal Code Yet! Thinking Through Simons's Rethinking, 5 Buff. Crim. L. Rev. 185 (2002).

24. Herbert Wechsler, On Culpability and Crime: The Treatment of Mens Rea in the Model Penal Code, 339 Annals 24, 31 (1962).

25. Jerome Hall, Negligent Behavior Should Be Excluded From Penal Liability, 63 Colum. L. Rev. 632, 634-37 (1963).

26. Aristotle, n.17 *supra,* at III.5.1114a.

wrongdoing, and suggested that faulty character was often shaped by upbringing and environment. Professor Kyron Huigens, counters that responsibility for a negligent character need not depend on causing one's self to develop it. Huigens compares criminalizing negligence to imposing criminal liability

> in the face of seemingly good excuses premised on social disadvantage . . . or other factors which are beyond the control of the accused, but which strongly determine her wrongdoing by depriving her of any operative conception of the good or right. . . . Regardless of the causal connections between choices in the past and present mistakes, there is a clear connection between present mistakes and one's character. What is blameworthy is not a particular state of consciousness, but the person whose life plan and past choices have brought him to heedless disaster.[27]

Should the criminal law punish people for having a careless character rather than for knowing wrongdoing?

9. Michaels, Simons, and Huigens all claim that the cognitive emphasis of the Model Penal Code misses such other dimensions of culpability as desire, motivation, and character. Do they, like Fletcher, think it is misguided to try to describe culpable mental states? Or are they trying to describe these mental states more accurately than the Model Penal Code?

10. *Faulkner under the MPC.* Review the facts of Regina v. Faulkner, and assume that Faulkner was prosecuted under the Model Penal Code. Section 220.1(1) (a) of the Code provides that a person is guilty of arson "if he starts a fire or causes an explosion with the purpose of . . . destroying" an occupied building or vehicle. Is Faulkner guilty of arson? If not, is he guilty of one of the following Model Penal Code offenses?

Section 220.2. Causing or Risking Catastrophe

(1) *Causing Catastrophe.* A person who causes a catastrophe by explosion, fire, flood . . . or other harmful or destructive force or substance . . . commits a felony of the second degree if he does so purposely or knowingly, or a felony of the third degree if he does so recklessly.

Section 220.3. Criminal Mischief

(1) *Offense Defined.* A person is guilty of criminal mischief if he:
    (a) damages tangible property of another purposely, recklessly, or by negligence in the employment of fire, explosives, or other dangerous means. . . .
    (b) purposely or recklessly tampers with tangible property of another so as to endanger person or property. . . .
(2) *Grading.* Criminal mischief is a felony of the third degree if the actor purposely causes pecuniary loss in excess of $5,000, or a substantial interruption or impairment of public communication, transportation . . . or other public service. It is a misdemeanor if the actor purposely causes pecuniary loss in excess of $100, or a petty misdemeanor if he purposely or recklessly causes pecuniary loss in excess of $25. Otherwise criminal mischief is a violation.

11. *The persistence of general and specific intent.* The Model Penal Code eschews the terminology of general and specific intent for the reasons indicated earlier.

---

27. Kyron Huigens, Virtue and Criminal Negligence 1 Buff. Crim. L. Rev. 431, 453-54 (1998).

Notwithstanding that most states have adopted the culpability terminology of the Model Penal Code, some states and the federal system have not. Many modern courts still use the dichotomy between general and specific intent. For example:

In United States v. Doe (R.S.W.), 136 F.3d 631 (3d Cir. 1998), the court construed a federal arson statute punishing "maliciously burning" a building on a federal reservation. Defendant lit a paper towel dispenser in a school bathroom and blew the flame out, but then unwittingly reignited it by opening the door to leave. In contrast to the *Faulkner* court, the *Doe* court ruled that arson was a "general intent" crime and reasoned that because the defendant committed a blameworthy act and was conscious of a risk of serious damage, she could be liable, notwithstanding her lack of intent to burn the school.

In State v. Neuzil, 589 N.W.2d 708 (Iowa 1999), the court construed a stalking offense that punishes "purposely engaging in a course of conduct directed at a specific person that would cause a reasonable person to fear bodily injury to, or the death of, that specific person or a family member." The court held that this language did not require a "specific intent" to provoke fear, but only a "general intent" to engage in the conduct that in fact causes such fear.

C. MISTAKE AND MENS REA DEFAULT RULES

REGINA v. PRINCE
Court for Crown Cases Reserved
L.R. 2 Crim. Cas. Res. 154 (1875)

Case stated by DENMAN, J.

At the assizes for Surrey, held at Kingston-upon-Thames, on the 24th of March last, Henry Prince was tried upon the charge of having unlawfully taken one Annie Phillips, an unmarried girl, being under the age of sixteen years, out of the possession and against the will of her father. The indictment was framed under s.55 of 24 & 25 Vict. c.100.[28]

He was found guilty.

All the facts necessary to support a conviction existed, unless the following facts constituted a defence. The girl Annie Phillips, though proved by her father to be fourteen years old on the 6th of April following, looked very much older than sixteen, and the jury found upon reasonable evidence that before the defendant took her away she had told him that she was eighteen, and that the defendant bona fide believed that statement, and that such belief was reasonable.

If the Court should be of the opinion that under these circumstances a conviction was right, the defendant was to appear for judgment at the next assizes for Surrey; otherwise the conviction was to be quashed. . . .

---

28. By 24 & 25 Vict. c. 100, s.55, "Whosoever shall unlawfully take or cause to be taken any unmarried girl, being under the age of sixteen years, out of the possession and against the will of her father or mother, or of any other person having the lawful care or charge of her, shall be guilty of a misdemeanor, and being convicted thereof shall be liable, at the discretion of the Court, to be imprisoned for any term not exceeding two years, with or without hard labour."

June 26. The following judgments were delivered:

The following judgment (in which COCKBURN, C.J., MELLOR, LUSH, QUAIN, DENMAN, ARCHIBALD, FIELD, and LINDLEY, J.J., and POLLOCK, B., concurred) was delivered by BLACKBURN, J. . . .

The question, therefore, is reduced to this, whether the words in 24 & 25 Vict. c.100, s.55, that whosoever shall take "any unmarried girl, being under the age of sixteen, out of the possession of her father," are to be read as if they were "being under the age of sixteen, and he knowing she was under that age." No such words are contained in the statute, nor is there the word "maliciously," "knowingly" or any other word used that can be said to involve a similar meaning.

The argument in favour of the prisoner must therefore entirely proceed on the ground that, in general, a guilty mind is an essential ingredient in a crime, and that where a statute creates a crime, the intention of the legislature should be presumed to be to include "knowingly" in the definition of the crime, and the statute should be read as if that word were inserted, unless the contrary intention appears. We need not inquire at present whether the canon of construction goes quite so far as above stated, for we are of opinion that the intention of the legislature sufficiently appears to have been to punish the abduction, unless the girl, in fact, was of such an age as to make her consent an excuse, irrespective of whether he knew her to be too young to give an effectual consent and to fix that age at sixteen. The section in question is one of a series of enactments beginning with s.48, and ending with s.55, forming a code for the protection of women, and the guardians of young women. These enactments are taken with scarcely any alteration from the repealed statute, 9 Geo. 4, c.31, which had collected them into a code from a variety of old statutes all repealed by it.

Section 50 enacts, that whosoever shall "unlawfully and carnally know and abuse any girl under the age of ten years," shall be guilty of felony. Section 51, whoever shall "unlawfully and carnally know and abuse any girl being above the age of ten years, and under the age of twelve years," shall be guilty of a misdemeanor.

It seems impossible to suppose that the intention of the legislature in those two sections could have been to make the crime depend upon the knowledge of the prisoner of the girl's actual age. It would produce the monstrous result that a man who had carnal connection with a girl, in reality not quite ten years old, but whom he on reasonable grounds believed to be a little more than ten, was to escape altogether. He could not, in that view of the statute, be convicted of the felony, for he did not know her to be under ten. He could not be convicted of the misdemeanor, because she was in fact not above the age of ten. It seems to us that the intention of the legislature was to punish those who had connection with young girls, though with their consent, unless the girl was in fact old enough to give valid consent. The man who has connection with a child, relying on her consent, does it at his peril, if she is below the statutable age. . . .

The following judgment (in which KELLY, C. B., CLEASBY, POLLOCK, and AMPHLETT, B. B., and GROVE, QUAIN, and DENMAN, J. J., concurred) was delivered by BRAMWELL, B.

. . . [T]he question is whether he is guilty where he knows, as he thinks, that she is over sixteen. This introduces the necessity for reading the statute with some strange words introduced; as thus: "Whosoever shall take any unmarried girl, being under the age of sixteen, and not believing her to be over the age of sixteen, out of the possession," etc. Those words are not there, and the question is, whether we are bound to construe the statute as though they were, on account of the rule that the mens rea is necessary to make an act a crime. I am of opinion that we are not, nor as though the word "knowingly" was there, and for the following reasons: The act forbidden is wrong in itself, if without lawful cause; I do not say illegal, but wrong. I have not lost sight of this, that though the statute probably principally aims at seduction for carnal purposes, the taking may be by a female with a good motive. Nevertheless, although there may be such cases, which are not immoral in one sense, I say that the act forbidden is wrong.

Let us remember what is the case supposed by the statute. It supposes that there is a *girl*— it does not say a woman, but a girl — something between a child and a woman; it supposes she is in the *possession* of her father or mother, or other person having lawful *care or charge* of her; and it supposes there is a *taking*, and that that taking is *against the will* of the person in whose possession she is. It is, then, a *taking of a girl*, in the *possession* of someone, *against his will*. I say that done without lawful cause is wrong, and that the legislature meant it should be at the risk of the taker whether or not she was under sixteen. I do not say that taking a woman of fifty from her brother's or even father's house is wrong. She is at an age when she has a right to choose for herself; she is not a *girl*, nor of such tender age that she can be said to be in the *possession* of or under the *care or charge* of anyone. I am asked where I draw the line; I answer at when the female is no longer a girl in anyone's possession.

But what the statute contemplates, and what I say is wrong, is the taking of a female of such tender years that she is properly called a *girl*, can be said to be in another's *possession*, and in that other's *care or charge*. No argument is necessary to prove this; it is enough to state the case. The legislature has enacted that if anyone does this wrong act, he does it at the risk of her turning out to be under sixteen. This opinion gives full scope to the doctrine of mens rea. If the taker believed he had the father's consent, though wrongly, he would have no mens rea; so if he did not know she was in anyone's possession, nor in the care or charge of anyone. In those cases he would not know he was doing the *act* forbidden by the statute — an act which, if he knew she was in possession and in care or charge of anyone, he would know was a crime or not, according as she was under sixteen or not. He would not know he was doing an act wrong in itself, whatever was his intention, if done without lawful cause. . . .

DENMAN, J. . . .

. . . Bearing in mind the previous enactments relating to the abduction of girls under sixteen, and the general course of the decisions upon those enactments, and upon the present statute, and looking at the mischief intended to be guarded against, it appears to me reasonably clear that the word "unlawfully," in the true sense in which it was used, is fully satisfied by holding that it is equivalent to the words "without lawful excuse," using those words as equivalent to "without such an excuse as being proved would be a complete legal justification for the act, even where all the facts constituting the offence exist."

Cases may easily be suggested where such a defence might be made out, as, for instance, if it were proved that he had the authority of a Court of competent jurisdiction, or of some legal warrant, or that he acted to prevent some illegal violence not justified by the relation of parent and child, or school-mistress, or other custodian, and requiring forcible interference by way of protection.

In the present case the jury find that the defendant believed the girl to be eighteen years of age; even if she had been of that age, she would have been in the lawful care and charge of her father, as her guardian by nature. Her father had a right to her personal custody up to the age of twenty-one, and to appoint a guardian by deed or will, whose right to her personal custody would have extended up to the same age. The belief that she was eighteen would be no justification to the defendant for taking her out of his possession, and against his will. By taking her, even with her own consent, he must at least have been guilty of aiding and abetting her in doing an unlawful act, viz. in escaping against the will of her natural guardian from his lawful care and charge. This, in my opinion, leaves him wholly without lawful excuse or justification for the act he did, even though he believed that the girl was eighteen, and therefore unable to allege that what he has done was not unlawfully done, within the meaning of the clause. In other words, having knowingly done a wrongful act, viz. in taking the girl away from the lawful possession of her father against his will, and in violation of his rights as guardian by nature, he cannot be heard to say that he thought the girl was of an age beyond that limited by the statute for the offence charge against him. He had wrongfully done the very thing contemplated by the legislature: He had wrongfully and knowingly violated the father's rights against the father's will. And he cannot set up a legal defence by merely proving that he thought he was committing a different kind of wrong from that which in fact he was committing.

BRETT, J. . . .

. . . [I]f the facts had been as the prisoner, according to the findings of the jury, believed them to be, and had reasonable ground for believing them to be, he would have done no act which has ever been a criminal offence in England; he would have done no act in respect of which any civil action could have ever been maintained against him; he would have done no act for which, if done in the absence of the father, and done with the continuing consent of the girl, the father could have had any legal remedy. . . .

Upon all the cases I think it is proved that there can be no conviction for crime in England in the absence of a criminal mind or mens rea.

Then comes the question, what is the true meaning of the phrase? I do not doubt that it exists where the prisoner knowingly does acts which would constitute a crime if the result were as he anticipated, but in which the result may not improbably end by bringing the offence within a more serious class of crime. As if a man strikes with a dangerous weapon, with intent to do grievous bodily harm, and kills, the result makes the crime murder. The prisoner has run the risk. So, if a prisoner [does] the prohibited acts, without caring to consider what the truth is as to facts — as if a prisoner were to abduct a girl under sixteen without caring to consider whether she was in truth under sixteen — he runs the risk. So if he without abduction defiles a girl who is in fact under ten years old, with a belief that she is between ten and twelve. If the facts were as he believed he would be committing the lesser crime. Then he runs the risk of his crime resulting in the greater crime. It is clear that ignorance of the law does not excuse.

It seems to me to follow that the maxim as to mens rea applies whenever the facts which are present to the prisoner's mind, and which he has reasonable ground to believe, and does believe to be the facts, would, if true, make his acts no criminal offence at all. . . .

Notes and Questions

1. Does the statute say that Prince has to know anything to be convicted of the crime? Suppose the statute read: "It shall be a misdemeanor to knowingly take an unmarried girl, being below the age of 16, out of the possession and against the will of her father." Would this clarify whether Prince could be convicted if he mistakenly believed Annie Phillips was over 16?

2. Note that *Prince* was decided only a few years before *Faulkner*. Do the two decisions seem consistent? What accounts for the different outcomes of the two cases? Do the two courts view malicious damage and abduction of a minor as different kinds of offenses? Do they view accident and mistake as different kinds of defenses? Do they employ different conceptions of mens rea?

3. Do the four opinions in *Prince* have differing views as to what is necessary for Prince's conviction? Which, if any, of the judges would hold Prince guilty regardless of his moral blameworthiness? As for those who would not, how would they determine whether Prince was blameworthy? Does blameworthiness mean any more or less than exhibiting the culpable state of mind implicitly required by the statute? Which opinion is most persuasive?

4. Judge Blackburn offers an interesting argument that the legislature could not have intended knowledge of the victim's age to be an element of section 55 of the statute, because section 51 of the same statute punishes sexual abuse of a child between the ages of ten and twelve. Why does the wording of section 51 have this implication for section 55? What if section 51 had punished sexual abuse of a child "under the age of twelve" rather than "above the age of ten and under the age of twelve"?

5. Consider Judge Brett's opinion, arguing that Prince was unpunishable because the act he believed he was committing was no crime. Brett approves of punishing for a "greater crime" one who, if the facts were as he believed, would be guilty only of a "lesser crime." If Prince deserves to be judged on the basis of the act he *thought* he was committing, why not the felon who reasonably believes he is committing only a misdemeanor? Is it because, unlike Prince, the latter knows his action is "unlawful"?

On the logic of Brett's argument, one who transports an adult, mistakenly believing the adult consents, should be acquitted of kidnapping. Suppose that Prince believed both that Phillips was over the age of 16 and that she consented to go with him — but believed each to be true with a probability of 60 percent. On this assumption, Prince believes it only 36 percent probable that Phillips competently consented, 40 percent probable that he unlawfully abducted a minor, and 24 percent probable that he unlawfully abducted a nonconsenting adult. He believes it probable he committed some crime, but does not know which. What result, on Brett's view?

6. *Bramwell's "doctrine of mens rea."* Consider Judge Bramwell's opinion, arguing that even if Phillips were as old as she allegedly claimed to be, Prince acted immorally. Judge Bramwell claims that his rationale for convicting Prince gives

[handwritten margin note: if facts prisoner believes would not constitute a crime, then → no crime]

"full scope to the doctrine of mens rea." What does he mean by this? What is his conception of that doctrine?

Recall that while the Model Penal Code insists that the defendant must have a "culpable mental state" with respect to every "material element," including the absence of justifying circumstances, traditional doctrine limits the mental element of the offense to knowledge or attitudes about circumstances defining the offense. What conduct and circumstances define the statutory offense here? Can we assume that any circumstance mentioned in the statute is part of the definition of the offense? Suppose the statute read as follows: "It shall be a misdemeanor to take an unmarried girl out of the possession and against the will of her father. Such taking shall be lawfully justified if in execution of a warrant; if necessary to prevent the imminent injury or unlawful abuse of the girl; or upon the consent of the girl, she being at least sixteen years of age." Would the age of the girl be part of the "act element" of this statute? If not, would "the doctrine of mens rea" afford Prince a defense?

Now reconsider the actual statute under which Prince was charged. Is it clear that the age of the girl is part of the definition of the offense rather than a circumstance precluding the assertion of consent as a justification?

Finally, if we assume that the age of the girl was not part of the definition of the offense, would it be necessary to argue, as Judge Bramwell does, that Prince's conduct, though mistaken, was *immoral*? Compare these three glosses on Judge Bramwell's argument:

Gloss #1:   The "doctrine of mens rea" does *not* require that offenders know all the circumstances defining their offenses. It requires *only* that offenders deserve punishment. If all the circumstances were as Prince believed them to be, he would have displayed mens rea because his act would have been immoral, though not proscribed by law. Though not punishable, his act would have been deserving of punishment. Hence, his punishment gives full scope to the doctrine of mens rea.

Gloss #2:   The "doctrine of mens rea" *does* require that offenders know all the circumstances defining their offenses. But it *also* requires that offenders deserve punishment. These two requirements can be reconciled if we treat the *definition of the offense* as including *only* those circumstances about which a mistake absolves the defendant of moral blame. Prince's mistake about Annie Phillips's age does not absolve him of moral blame; hence, her age is not part of the act element of the offense. Hence, his conviction gives full scope to the doctrine of mens rea.

Gloss #3:   The "doctrine of mens rea" *does* require that offenders know all the circumstances defining their offense. But it *also* requires that offenders deserve punishment. These two requirements can be reconciled by acquitting all defendants who are unaware of a circumstance defining the charged offense; *and also by excusing* all defendants whose mistakes absolve them of moral responsibility. Prince's mistake did not negate the mental element of the offense, because Annie Phillips's age was not a circumstance defining Prince's conduct as an offense; and Prince's mistake did not excuse him of responsibility because what he thought he was doing was immoral. Hence his conviction gives full scope to the doctrine of mens rea.

7. Several American courts adopted reasoning similar to that of the *Prince* court in determining the mental element of adultery, statutory rape, and abduction of a minor for purposes of prostitution. One turn-of-the-century

American treatise cited several such cases for the general proposition that, "If a man is engaged in the commission of an immoral act, even though it may not be indictable, and unintentionally commits a crime, it is generally no defense for him to show that he was ignorant of the existence of the circumstances rendering his act criminal."[29]

PEOPLE v. RYAN
Court of Appeals of New York
82 N.Y.2d 497, 626 N.E.2d 51, 605 N.Y.S.2d 235 (1993)

KAYE, CHIEF JUDGE: Penal Law §220.18(5) makes it a felony to "knowingly and unlawfully possess . . . six hundred twenty-five milligrams of a hallucinogen." The question of statutory interpretation before us is whether "knowingly" applies to the weight of the controlled substance. We conclude that it does and that the trial evidence was insufficient to satisfy that mental culpability element. . . .

I.

Viewed in a light most favorable to the People, the evidence revealed that on October 2, 1990, defendant asked his friend David Hopkins to order and receive a shipment of hallucinogenic mushrooms on his behalf. Hopkins agreed, and adhering to defendant's instructions placed a call to their mutual friend Scott . . . and requested the "usual shipment." Tipped off to the transaction, . . . [an] investigator . . . located the package . . . then borrowed a Federal Express uniform and van and delivered the package to Hopkins, the addressee, who was arrested upon signing for it.

Hopkins explained that the package was for defendant and agreed to participate in a supervised delivery to him. In a telephone call recorded by the police, Hopkins notified defendant that he got the package, reporting a "shit load of mushrooms in there." Defendant responded, "I know, don't say nothing." At another point Hopkins referred to the shipment containing two pounds. The men agreed to meet. . . .

At the meeting, after a brief conversation, Hopkins handed defendant a substitute package. . . . Moments after taking possession, defendant was arrested. He was later indicted for attempted criminal possession of a controlled substance in the second degree. . . .

The case proceeded to trial, where the evidence summarized above was adduced. Additionally, the police chemist testified that the total weight of the mushrooms in Hopkins' package was 932.8 grams (about two pounds), and that a 140 gram sample of the package contents contained 796 milligrams of psilocybin, a hallucinogen. . . . [No] evidence [was offered] as to how much psilocybin would typically appear in two pounds of mushrooms.

At the close of the People's case, defendant moved to dismiss for insufficient proof that he knew the level of psilocybin in the mushrooms. . . . [The motion] denied, defendant was convicted as charged. . . .

29. William L. Clark & William L. Marshall, A Treatise on the Law of Crimes (1900).

The Appellate Division affirmed. The court held that a defendant must know the nature of the substance possessed, and acknowledged that the weight of the controlled substance is an element of the crime. . . . [H]owever, . . . the court held that "the term 'knowingly' should be construed to refer only to the element of possession and not the weight requirement." . . .

We now reverse.

II.

Although the present case involves an attempt, analysis begins with the elements of the completed crime, second degree criminal possession of a controlled substance. Penal Law §220.18(5) provides:

> A person is guilty of criminal possession of a controlled substance in the second degree when he knowingly and unlawfully possesses: . . .
> 5. six hundred twenty-five milligrams of a hallucinogen.

. . . At issue is whether defendant must . . . know the weight of the material possessed. That is a question of statutory interpretation, as to which the Court's role is clear: our purpose is not to pass on the wisdom of the statute or any of its requirements, but rather to implement the will of the Legislature. . . .

In effectuating legislative intent, we look first of course to the statutory language. Read in context, it seems evident that "knowingly" does apply to the weight element. Indeed, given that a defendant's awareness must extend not only to the fact of possessing something ("knowingly . . . possesses") but also to the nature of the material possessed ("knowingly . . . possesses . . . a hallucinogen"), any other reading would be strained. Inasmuch as the knowledge requirement carries through to the end of the sentence . . . , eliminating it from the intervening element — weight — would rob the statute of its obvious meaning. We conclude, therefore, that there is a mens rea element associated with the weight of the drug.

That reading is fortified by two rules of construction ordained by the Legislature itself. First, a "statute defining a crime, unless clearly indicating a legislative intent to impose strict liability, should be construed as defining a crime of mental culpability" (Penal Law §15.15[2]). If any material element of an offense lacks a mens rea requirement, it is a strict liability crime (Penal Law §15.10). Conversely, a crime is one of "mental culpability" only when a mental state "is required with respect to every material element of an offense" (id.).

By ruling that a defendant need not have knowledge of the weight, the Appellate Division in effect held, to that extent, that second degree criminal possession is a strict liability crime (see Penal Law §15.10). That is an erroneous statutory construction unless a legislative intent to achieve that result is "clearly indicated" (Penal Law §15.15[2]).

In a similar vein, the Legislature has provided in Penal Law §15.15(1):

> Construction of statutes with respect to culpability requirements.
> 1. When the commission of an offense defined in this chapter, or some element of an offense, requires a particular culpable mental state, such mental state is ordinarily designated in the statute defining the offense by use of the terms

"intentionally," "knowingly," "recklessly" or "criminal negligence," or by use of terms, such as "with intent to defraud" and "knowing it to be false," describing a specific kind of intent or knowledge. When one and only one of such terms appears in a statute defining an offense, it is presumed to apply to every element of the offense unless an intent to limit its application clearly appears." . . .

Accordingly, if a single mens rea is set forth, as here, it presumptively applies to all elements of the offense unless a contrary legislative intent is plain.

We discern no "clear" legislative intent to make the weight of a drug a strict liability element, as is required before we can construe the statute in that manner (Penal Law §§15.15[1], [2]). Moreover, the overall structure of the drug possession laws supports the view that a defendant must have some knowledge of the weight.

There are six degrees of criminal possession of a controlled substance, graded in severity from a class A misdemeanor up to an A-I felony. The definition of each begins identically: "A person is guilty of criminal possession of a controlled substance in the . . . degree when he knowingly and unlawfully possesses . . ." The primary distinctions between one grade or another relate to the type and weight of the controlled substance. . . . To ascribe to the Legislature an intent to mete out drastic differences in punishment without a basis in culpability would be inconsistent with notions of individual responsibility and proportionality prevailing in the Penal Law. . . .

III.

The People's contrary argument is based in part on a concern that it would be "prohibitively difficult," if not impossible, to secure convictions if they were required to prove that a defendant had knowledge of the weight. We disagree.

Often there will be evidence from which the requisite knowledge may be deduced, such as negotiations concerning weight, potency or price. Similarly, for controlled substances measured on an "aggregate weight" basis (see, e.g, Penal Law §220.06[2]), knowledge of the weight may be inferred from defendant's handling of the material, because the weight of the entire mixture, including cutting agents, is counted. . . .

By contrast, that same inference may be unavailable for controlled substances measured by "pure" weight, like psilocybin . . . [that] are customarily combined [or found] with other substances. . . . Although we cannot simply read the knowledge requirement out of the statute, these "compelling practical considerations" may inform our interpretation of that element. . . .

. . . A purpose of the knowledge requirement, . . . is to avoid over-penalizing someone who unwittingly possesses a larger amount of a controlled substance than anticipated. That legislative purpose can be satisfied, among other ways, with evidence that the pure weight of the controlled substance possessed by defendant is typical for the particular form in which the drug appears. This correlation between the pure weight typically found, and the pure weight actually possessed, substantially reduces the possibility that a person will unjustly be convicted for a more serious crime. . . .

IV.

With the foregoing principles in mind, we consider whether there was sufficient evidence to convict defendant of attempted second degree possession, an A-II felony.

Certainly there was sufficient evidence from which the jury could conclude, beyond a reasonable doubt, that defendant attempted and intended to possess a two-pound box of hallucinogenic mushrooms. It is also undisputed that, upon testing, the mushrooms in the particular box defendant attempted to possess . . . contained more than 650 milligrams of psilocybin. . . . Although in these circumstances defendant could properly be convicted of attempting to possess the amount of psilocybin that would typically appear in two pounds of hallucinogenic mushrooms, there was no evidence linking psilocybin weight to mushroom weight. . . . We thus conclude on this record that there was insufficient evidence to satisfy the knowledge requirement within the meaning of the statute. . . .

Notes and Questions

1. The court says, "By ruling that a defendant need not have knowledge of the weight, the Appellate Division in effect held, to that extent, that second degree criminal possession is a strict liability crime." Does that seem true? Was Ryan held as "strictly" liable as Dillard or Balint or Dotterweich?

The court bases its conclusion on New York Penal Law §15.10, which provides that "if an offense or some material element thereof does not require a culpable mental state on the part of the actor, such offense is one of 'strict liability.'" By this definition, was Prince held "strictly liable"?

2. *Default culpability.* The New York statutory provision defining the drug offense was ambiguous as to whether the culpability term "knowingly" applied to possession only, or also to the amount possessed. The court resolved this ambiguity by invoking two statutory default rules: New York Penal Law §15.15(2), which disfavors strict liability with respect to any element absent clear legislative intent, and §15.15(1), which distributes any culpability term specified in the offense definition to every element, absent clear legislative intent to the contrary.

These default rules parallel Model Penal Code §2.02(1) and §2.02(4). Section 2.02(1) provides that "a person is not guilty of an offense unless he acted purposely, knowingly, recklessly or negligently with respect to each material element of the offense" unless one of two exceptions occurs, which are specified in §2.05: either the offense is a mere "violation," not punishable by incarceration, or "a legislative purpose to impose absolute liability for such offenses or with respect to any material element thereof plainly appears."[30] Section 2.02(4) provides

> *Prescribed culpability requirement applies to all material elements.* When the law defining an offense prescribes the kind of culpability that is sufficient for the commission of an offense, without distinguishing among the material elements thereof, such provision shall apply to all the material elements of the offense, unless a contrary purpose plainly appears.

---

30. Unlike NYPL §15.15(2), Section 2.05 limits the exception for provisions manifesting a purpose to impose strict liablity to offenses defined outside the code and limits such offenses to violations.

Suppose the New York Penal Law had a provision like §2.02(1), barring strict liability, but did not have a "distributive default rule" paralleling §2.02(4). What level of culpability would then be required with respect to the weight of the drug? What result would be reached in *Ryan*?

3. *The legislative response to* Ryan. In an effort to overrule the *Ryan* decision, the New York legislature rewrote NYPL §220.18 to read:

> A person is guilty of criminal possession of a controlled substance in the second degree when he knowingly and unlawfully possesses . . .
> (5) a hallucinogen and said hallucinogen weighs six hundred and twenty five milligrams or more.

Does this change, substituting "and said hallucinogen weighs" for "weighing," change the mental element of the offense? Does it change the application of §15.15(1) and §15.15(2) to §220.18? If so, does that make §220.18 a crime of strict liability with respect to the weight of the drug, or one of negligence?

4. *The recklessness default rule.* The Rhode Island Supreme Court invoked yet another Model Penal Code default rule in determining the mental element of a child abuse offense in State v. Lima, 546 A.2d 770 (R.I. 1988):

> The defendant, a native of Portugal who had resided in the United States some seventeen years at the time the incident in question occurred, was convicted of first-degree child abuse for allegedly lowering the victim, a two-and-a-half-year-old boy, into a tub of scalding water. Lima completed five years of schooling in her native Portugal. She served as a babysitter for nine children, including the victim. . . .
>
> . . . The trial justice committed reversible error in refusing to instruct the jury that an intentional act is required to convict under §11-9-5.3, the child-abuse statute. Counsel for defendant requested an instruction that "in order to find the Defendant guilty of child abuse you must find beyond a reasonable doubt that the Defendant intentionally burned the child in hot water." As noted above, the trial justice refused to so instruct the jury.
>
> As a general proposition, where the requisite intent is not defined in a statute establishing a criminal offense such intent should be explicated in an instruction. Nowhere in his charge to the jury did the trial justice instruct it that in order to find defendant guilty, the jury was required to find beyond a reasonable doubt that defendant intentionally inflicted upon the victim a physical injury that caused said child to become permanently disfigured or disabled.
>
> Our review of the record, and most specifically the charge as given, indicates that the jury may have convicted defendant because she injured the child by placing him in the water, without finding that she inflicted the injury intentionally. As a result, there must be a new trial.
>
> We note that a number of states apply a standard similar to that set forth in the Model Penal Code, §2.02(3) at 226 (A.L.I. 1985) (the code), in situations in which the requisite level of intent is not set forth within the statutory scheme in question. The code provides that "[w]hen the culpability sufficient to establish a material element of an offense is not prescribed by law, such element is established if a person acts purposely, knowingly or recklessly with respect thereto." Id. We deem such standard to be appropriate in the instant matter. Thus, upon retrial we direct the trial justice to instruct the jury in accordance with the standard set forth above. See State v. Adams, 404 N.E.2d 144, 146 (Oh. 1980) (requiring only a showing of recklessness in an "endangering children" statute). We view such an instruction as protecting a defendant from a conviction predicated upon an act devoid of mens rea while at the same time protecting a class of defenseless victims from physical abuse.

Note that *Lima* relies on Model Penal Code §2.02(3), which establishes reck-lessness as the default level of culpability. The New York Penal Law applied in *Ryan* lacks this recklessness default rule. The court found that knowledge of the weight possessed was required only because "knowledge" governed the weight element, and so had to be "distributed" to the weight element. But what culpa-bility would the *Ryan* court have required with respect to possession and the weight possessed if no culpability term had appeared in the statute? Was this level of culpability established by the evidence?

What result would be reached in the *Ryan* case if no culpability term ap-peared in the drug statute, but New York had a "recklessness default rule," like the MPC's §2.02(3)?

5. Without the "recklessness default rule" of §2.02(3), the Model Penal Code would still have a default culpability standard: negligence, the minimal level of culpability required for criminal liability by §2.02(1). Why, then, is §2.02(3) necessary? Should negligence suffice for default culpability under the Code? The Commentary to §2.02(3) explains the policy behind the default cul-pability provision:

> Subsection (3) provides that unless the kind of culpability sufficient to estab-lish a material element of an offense has been prescribed by law, it is established if a person acted purposely, knowingly or recklessly with respect thereto. This accepts as the basic norm what usually is regarded as the common law position. More im-portantly, it represents the most convenient norm for drafting purposes. When purpose or knowledge is to be required it is conventional to be explicit. And since negligence is an exceptional basis of liability, it should be excluded . . . unless ex-plicitly prescribed.[31]

6. *State v. Guest.* Compare the Model Penal Code default rules to the ap-proach taken by the Alaska Supreme Court in State v. Guest, 583 P.2d 836 (Alaska Sup. Ct. 1978), construing a statutory rape statute that did not specify what level of culpability attached to the element of the victim's age:

> The question presented in the State's petition for review is whether an honest and reasonable mistake of fact regarding a victim's age may serve as a defense to a charge of statutory rape.
> On April 7, 1977, the respondents, Moses Guest and Jacob Evan, were charged with the statutory rape of T.D.G., age fifteen. . . .[32]
> . . . The parties entered into a stipulation that "the evidence expected to be presented at trial will support a reasonable belief on the part of each defendant that the alleged victim, age 15, was sixteen years of age or older at the time of the alleged act of sexual intercourse." In light of that stipulation, the court ordered that it would instruct the jurors as follows:

>> It is a defense to a charge of statutory rape that the defendant reasonably and in good faith believed that the female person was of the age of sixteen years or older even though, in fact, she was under the age of sixteen years. If from all the evidence you have a reasonable doubt as to the question whether defendant reasonably and in good faith believed that she was sixteen years of age or older, you must give the defendant the benefit of that doubt and find him not guilty.

31. Model Penal Code and Commentaries, *supra*, at 244.
32. AS 11.15.120 provides in relevant part:

Rape. (a) a person who . . . being 16 years of age or older, carnally knows and abuses a person under 16 years of age, is guilty of rape.

The state brings a petition for review from that order.

Respondents concede that in most jurisdictions a reasonable mistake of age is not a defense to a charge of statutory rape. Although the validity of this defense to a statutory rape charge has not been decided in Alaska, we were presented with a similar issue in Anderson v. State, 384 P.2d 669 (Alaska 1963), where the charge was contributing to the delinquency of a minor by a consensual act of sexual intercourse. We said that "[a]ppellant's belief that prosecutrix was over the age of eighteen, even though it may have some support, is no excuse" and "[p]ersons having illegal relations with children do so at their [own] peril." Id. at 671.

We recognized in Speidel v. State, 460 P.2d 77 (Alaska 1969), that consciousness of wrongdoing is an essential element of penal liability. "It is said to be a universal rule that an injury can amount to a crime only when inflicted by intention — that conduct cannot be criminal unless it is shown that one charged with criminal conduct had an awareness or consciousness of some wrongdoing." . . .

Our opinion in *Speidel* stated that there are exceptions to the general requirement of criminal intent which are categorized as "public welfare" offenses. These exceptions are a rather narrow class of regulation, "caused primarily by the industrial revolution, out of which grew the necessity of imposing more stringent duties on those connected with particular industries, trades, properties, or activities that affect public health, safety or welfare." The penalties for the infraction of these strict liability offenses are usually relatively small and conviction of them carries no great opprobrium.

Statutory rape may not appropriately be categorized as a public welfare offense. It is a serious felony. If the offender is less than nineteen years of age, he may be imprisoned for up to twenty years. If he is nineteen years of age or older, he may be punished by imprisonment for any term of years.

We believe that the charge of statutory rape is legally unsupportable under the principles of *Speidel,* unless a defense of reasonable mistake of age is allowed. To refuse such a defense would be to impose criminal liability without any criminal mental element. The defense of reasonable mistake of fact is generally allowed in criminal cases to permit the defendant to show that he lacked criminal intent.[33] When [the opportunity to offer such a defense] is foreclosed the result is strict criminal liability.

Although AS 11.15.120 is silent as to any requirement of intent, this is true of many felony statutes. The requirement of criminal intent is then commonly inferred. In fact, in such cases, where the particular statute is not a public welfare type of offense, either a requirement of criminal intent must be read into the statute or it must be found unconstitutional.

Since statutes should be construed where possible to avoid unconstitutionality, it is necessary here to infer a requirement of criminal intent.

It has been urged in other jurisdictions that where an offender is aware he is committing an act of fornication he therefore has sufficient criminal intent to justify a conviction for statutory rape because what was done would have been

---

33. The defense of mistake has been generally explained as follows:

Instead of speaking of ignorance or mistake of fact or law as a defense, it would be just as easy to note simply that the defendant cannot be convicted when it is shown that he does not have the mental state required by law for commission of that particular offense. For example, to take the classic case of the man who takes another's umbrella out of a restaurant because he mistakenly believes that the umbrella is his, it is not really necessary to say that the man, if charged with larceny, has a valid defense of mistake of fact; it would be more direct and to the point to assert that the man is not guilty because he does not have the mental state (intent to steal the property of another) required for the crime of larceny. Yet, the practice has developed of dealing with such mistakes as a matter of defense, perhaps because the facts showing their existence are usually brought out by the defendant. . . . LaFave & Scott, Criminal Law, §47 at 356-57 (1972).

unlawful under the facts as he thought them to be. We reject this view. While it is true that under such circumstances a mistake of fact does not serve as a complete defense, we believe that it should serve to reduce the offense to that which the offender would have been guilty of had he not been mistaken. See Model Penal Code §2.04(2) (Proposed Official Draft 1962).[34] Thus, if an accused had a reasonable belief that the person with whom he had sexual intercourse was sixteen years of age or older, he may not be convicted of statutory rape. If, however, he did not have a reasonable belief that the victim was eighteen years of age or older, he may still be criminally liable for contribution to the delinquency of a minor. . . .

For the foregoing reasons, we hold that a charge of statutory rape is defensible where an honest and reasonable mistake of fact as to the victim's age is shown. Anderson v. State, *supra,* is overruled to the extent that its holding is inconsistent with the views expressed herein. The order of the superior court is affirmed.

The *Guest* court states that "if an accused had a reasonable belief that the person with whom he had sexual intercourse was sixteen years of age or older, he may not be convicted of statutory rape." What level of culpability does the court thereby attach to the element of the age of the victim? What, then, does the court mean when it states that it must "infer a requirement of criminal intent"? What level of culpability would the Model Penal Code default rules provide?

7. *Inferring culpability in federal statutes.* Federal criminal law is not governed by any statutory mens rea default rules. Yet as we saw in *Balint, Dotterweich,* and *Morissette,* federal courts must determine the relevance of mistakes to criminal liability when the statute defining the offense is silent. Rather than following definite rules, federal courts often resort to flexible standards in deciding how much culpability to require for each offense. In *Morissette,* the Supreme Court conditioned higher requirements of culpability on such factors as severe punishment, actual harm rather than mere risk, action rather than omission, and common law as opposed to modern regulatory origins. How might these factors apply to the offenses at issue in *Ryan, Lima,* and *Guest?* Note that the Model Penal Code default rules specify a culpability level for each material element of an offense. The *Morissette* factors do not.

8. *A default rule exercise.* Consider §2.02(4) of the Model Penal Code, which distributes any culpability term appearing in the definition of an offense to all material elements. In this regard, note that the Code defines burglary as follows in §221.1:

> (1) *Burglary Defined.* A person is guilty of burglary if he enters a building or occupied structure . . . with purpose to commit a crime therein . . . unless the actor is . . . privileged to enter.
>
> (2) *Grading.* Burglary is a felony of the second degree if it is perpetrated in the dwelling of another at night. . . . Otherwise, burglary is a felony of the third degree.

Of what offenses, if any, are the following people guilty under this section, and under §§2.02(3), 2.02(4) and 2.04?

(a) Susan agreed to feed the cat in her friend Betty's townhouse while Betty was away. Susan misremembered the number of Betty's house

---

34. . . . Although ignorance or mistake would otherwise afford a defense to the offense charged, the defense is not available if the defendant would be guilty of another offense had the situation been as he supposed. In such a case, however, the ignorance or mistake of the defendant shall reduce the grade and degree of the offense of which he may be convicted to those of the offense of which he would be guilty had the situation been as he supposed.

and went to the house next door. She found the door unlocked, entered, and then realized she was in the wrong house. But she spotted some expensive pieces of jewelry and left with them.

(b) Brad saw a small brick building and decided to break in and look for something valuable he could fence for narcotics money. It was night time, and the building appeared to be a small warehouse with no one in it. He broke in and was surprised to find Fred, who was actually renting it for sleeping quarters.

(c) Hugh was driving down the alley of a residential neighborhood at night when he noticed an unlatched window in the back of a small, well-maintained bungalow. It did not look like anyone was home, so he broke into the house hoping to steal a VCR and a television set, or other household goods. In fact, the building was used only as a yarn shop. No one lived there and there were no household goods. Hugh left empty-handed.

Notice that the burglary statute mentions "purpose." Does "purpose" apply to all elements of the crime? Does §2.02(2) help? Does §2.02(3)?

Refer briefly again to hypothetical (a), above. In addition to applying §2.02 in the conventional way, notice that the hypothetical also presents an issue of "concurrence" of Susan's act and Susan's mental state. Put simply, criminal liability requires this concurrence. It is not larceny for a person to carry off the property of another with an innocent mind and then decide later to keep it forever without permission. It is not intentional battery to accidentally strike one's enemy and then, on realizing that has happened, to rejoice at the latter's pain.[35] Note, however, that §2.02, if applied at the correct moment in the sequence of action, should produce the same result.

Section 2.04(2) of the Code deals specifically with the problem of mistake and grading:

> Although ignorance or mistake would otherwise afford a defense to the offense charged, the defense is not available if the defendant would be guilty of another offense had the situation been as he supposed. In such case, however, the ignorance or mistake of the defendant shall reduce the grade and degree of the offense of which he may be convicted to those of the offense of which he would be guilty had the situation been as he supposed.

Does this help the analysis of the above hypotheticals?

9. *More default rule exercises.* How would the Model Penal Code default rules apply to the following statutory offenses? How would the *Morissette* factors apply? For each offense, try to identify the material elements and assign a culpability term — or strict liability — to each.

(a) Any person who transports any toxic material, without a permit to do so, shall be guilty of a misdemeanor.

(b) Any person who knowingly transports any toxic material, thereby placing another person in imminent physical danger, shall be guilty of a felony.

(c) Any person who, within 100 yards of a stream or wetlands, while knowingly transporting any toxic material, drives negligently, shall be guilty of a misdemeanor.

---

35. See Wayne LaFave & Austin Scott, Criminal Law §3.11(a) (2d ed. 1986).

(d) Any person who causes environmental damage to a body of fresh water as a result of negligently discharging material that person knows to be toxic, shall be guilty of a felony.

10. *Affirmative defenses and burdens of production.* The *Guest* opinion characterizes an honest and reasonable mistake of age as a "defense" to a charge of statutory rape. However, as the excerpt from LaFave and Scott makes clear, the court conceives of a "defense" as merely a restatement of the rule that the prosecution must prove that the defendant possessed the requisite culpable mental state when he committed the crime. If the defendant proves that, because of a mistake of fact, he did not possess the mens rea, then he is not guilty. This is the classical "mistake of fact defense." Thus, in *Guest,* the prosecutor must prove beyond a reasonable doubt that Guest was negligent, but Guest could refute this by offering evidence that he made a reasonable mistake of fact. Such a defense is an "affirmative defense" only in the sense that it allocates the burden of production, not the burden of proof, to the defendant. This is also how Model Penal Code §1.12 defines the term "affirmative defense":

Proof Beyond a Reasonable Doubt; Affirmative Defenses; Burden of Proving Fact When Not an Element of an Offense; Presumptions

(1) No person may be convicted of an offense unless each element of such offense is proved beyond a reasonable doubt. In the absence of such proof, the innocence of the defendant is assumed.

(2) Subsection (1) of this Section does not:

(a) require the disproof of an affirmative defense unless and until there is evidence supporting such defense; or

(b) apply to any defense which the Code or another statute plainly requires the defendant to prove by a preponderance of evidence.

(3) A ground of defense is affirmative, within the meaning of Subsection (2)(a) of this Section, when:

(a) it arises under a section of the Code which so provides; or

(b) it relates to an offense defined by a statute other than the Code and such statute so provides; or

(c) it involves a matter of excuse or justification peculiarly within the knowledge of the defendant on which he can fairly be required to adduce supporting evidence.

D.   "MISTAKE OF LAW"

1.   Introduction to Mistake of Law

St. German's 1518 "Dialogues Between a Doctor and a Student" asserted that "Ignorance of the law . . . doth not excuse . . . but in few cases; for every man is bound at his peril to take knowledge what the law of the realm is . . . ; but ignorance of the deed . . . may excuse in many cases."[36] Blackstone concurred:

Ignorance or mistake is another defect of will; when a man, intending to do a lawful act, does that which is unlawful. For here the deed and the will acting separately,

36. Dialogue II, c. 46.

there is not that conjunction between them, which is necessary to form a criminal act. But this must be an ignorance or mistake of fact, and not an error in point of law. As if a man, intending to kill a thief or housebreaker in his own house kills one of his own family, this is no criminal action: but if a man thinks he has a right to kill a person excommunicated or outlawed wherever he meets him, and does so; this is wilful murder. For a mistake in point of law, which every person of discretion is bound and presumed to know, is in criminal cases no sort of defence.[37]

Given what you have already learned about contemporary criminal law, the maxims "knowledge of law is presumed" and "ignorance of the law is no excuse" should trouble you for two reasons.

First, *notice* is an important value in constitutional law, reflected in prohibitions on retroactive punishment and excessively vague statutes. We have seen that the *Lambert* decision requires the prosecution to prove *actual knowledge* of the legal duty violated for some crimes of omission. Where there is nothing alerting persons that the law might impose a duty, knowledge of such a duty is *not* presumed, but must be treated as part of the mental element of the offense.

Second, because due process requires the prosecution to bear the burden of proof on all elements of offenses, the law disapproves of presumptions generally (see the discussion of Sandstrom v. Montana in the Introduction, *supra*). If knowledge of a law is part of the mental element of a particular offense, the prosecution must prove that defendant actually had that knowledge. The Model Penal Code reflects this view by including mistakes of law in its general treatment of mistake in §2.04(1)(a): "Ignorance or mistake as to a matter of fact or law is a defense if the ignorance or mistake negatives the purpose, knowledge, belief, recklessness, or negligence required to establish a material element of the offense."

This provision acknowledges that many conduct, circumstance, and result elements involve legal concepts. For example, Model Penal Code §224.13 punishes one disposing of "property . . . entrusted to him as a fiduciary . . . in a manner which he knows is unlawful and involves substantial risk of loss or detriment to . . . a person for whose benefit the property was entrusted." An offender cannot culpably commit such a crime without considerable legal knowledge.

Because the mental element of every offense must be proven, not presumed, contemporary lawmakers are unlikely to proclaim that everyone is presumed to know the law. Instead, they may assert that knowledge that one's act is a criminal offense is not ordinarily an element of that offense. Thus, Model Penal Code §2.02(9) provides:

Culpability as to illegality of conduct. Neither knowledge nor recklessness or negligence as to whether conduct constitutes an offense or as to the existence, meaning or application of the law determining the elements of an offense is an element of such offense, unless the definition of the offense or the Code so provides.

This provision really just restates the principle that the mental element of the offense consists of culpable mental states with respect to the acts (or omissions), circumstances, and results that define the actus reus. Once the prosecution proves the defendant had the required culpable mental state for each conduct, circumstance and result element in the offense definition, it has established the mental element of the offense. *This means that the prosecution need not also prove*

37. William Blackstone, 4 Commentaries on the Laws of England *27 (1769).

that the defendant knew the offense definition itself, unless the statute actually defines the offense to require such knowledge.

Some modern statutes *do* require that offenders be aware of the offense definition, or part of it. For example, federal regulatory offenses often attach penalties to the violation of a regulation governing some business activity. The regulation might be found in one statutory provision and the criminal penalty for its violation in another. So we might say that part of the offense definition is in the regulatory provision, and another part is in the penal provision. If the penal provision explicitly conditions punishment on knowledge of the regulatory provision, we might say that the offense requires knowledge of part of the offense definition. But unless a statute clearly requires knowledge of the offense definition, Model Penal Code §2.02(9) denies that knowledge of the offense definition is part of the mental element of the offense.

This position may seem unfair if it results in people being convicted of crimes who had no idea they were doing anything illegal. A possible response to this concern is to excuse from responsibility those offenders who had no fair notice that their conduct was illegal. One version of such an excuse is provided by Model Penal Code §2.04(3):

> A belief that conduct does not legally constitute an offense is a defense to a prosecution for that offense based upon such conduct when:
>
> (a) the statute or other enactment defining the offense is not known to the actor and has not been published or otherwise reasonably made available prior to the conduct alleged; or
> (b) he acts in reasonable reliance upon an official statement of the law, afterward determined to be invalid or erroneous, contained in (i) a statute or other enactment; (ii) a judicial decision, opinion or judgment; (iii) an administrative order or grant of permission; or (iv) an official interpretation of the public officer or body charged by law with responsibility for the interpretation, administration or enforcement of the law defining the offense.

Section 2.04(4) places the burden of proof for this excuse on the defendant. Moreover, relatively few states have as yet adopted it. Why might this be so?

While the Model Penal Code provides one version of a mistake of law excuse, other definitions are possible. We might excuse all those offenders who reasonably believed their conduct legal, or who relied on advice of counsel. The point of a mistake of law excuse is to avoid punishing those offenders who cannot fairly be held responsible for their offenses. By contrast, a mistake of law that negates the mental element of the offense implies that the defendant committed no offense to begin with.

In Blackstone's day, all culpability arguments were seen as excuses to be proven by the defendant. If ignorance of law was no excuse, it could have no exculpatory significance at all. Today, however, the prosecution is required to prove the mental element of the offense, and this element may include some legal knowledge. So mistakes of law can *acquit* the defendant, without *excusing* her. Today, "ignorance of the law is no excuse," means only that once the prosecution has proven the mental element of the offense, the defense may not offer a mistake of law as a reason to excuse the defendant from responsibility for her offense. In that limited sense, ignorance of the law *is* no excuse in some jurisdictions, but not in all.

We will begin with two principal cases illustrating the modern approach to mistake of law as a negation of mens rea, including the disparate treatment of mistakes about the offense definition (United States v. Baker) and mistakes about particular actus reus elements (People v. Bray). A third case, Cheek v. United States, provides an example of a federal regulatory offense requiring proof of knowledge of a regulatory provision. After considering these cases on mens rea, we will proceed to consider a principal case viewing mistake of law as an excuse, Commonwealth v. Twitchell.

2.   Mistake of Law and Mens Rea

PEOPLE v. BRAY
California Court of Appeal
52 Cal. App. 3d 494, 124 Cal. Rptr. 913 (1975)

GERALD BROWN, PRESIDING JUSTICE.

James Eugene Bray appeals the judgment following his jury conviction on two counts of being a felon in possession of a concealable firearm.

Bray's meritorious contention is the trial court should have instructed the jury that ignorance or mistake of fact is a defense to the crime.[38]

In 1969 Bray pled guilty in Kansas to being an accessory after the fact. At sentencing, the Kansas prosecutor recommended Bray be granted probation because he had no previous criminal record, he had been unwilling to participate in the crime but had gotten involved by driving a friend away from the scene and he had cooperated fully with the district attorney's office. Bray was placed on two years summary probation which he successfully completed before moving to California in 1971. While in California Bray first worked at Convair Aircraft and later was employed by the County of San Diego in the Department of Public Health. Near the end of 1973 he transferred to the district attorney's office.

In January 1972, Bray filled out an application to vote in the State of California. He discussed the problems he had had in Kansas with the Deputy of the Registrar of Voters and asked if he would be allowed to vote. The Deputy could not answer the question and suggested he say on the registration form he had been convicted of a felony and fill out a supplementary explanatory form to find out if he, in fact, had committed a felony. This Bray did; he was allowed to vote.

In early July of 1973, Bray applied for a part-time job as a guard with ADT Sterling Security Company. On the application he answered that he had been arrested or charged with a crime but had not been convicted of a felony. At the bottom of the page Bray explained the circumstances surrounding his arrest and period of probation. In September he received a notice from the Bureau of

38. Bray requested jury instructions from CALJIC [The book of California Jury Instructions] reading:

CALJIC 4.35 — Ignorance or Mistake of Fact

An act committed or an omission made under an ignorance or mistake of fact which disproves any criminal intent is not a crime.

Thus a person is not guilty of a crime if he commits an act or omits to act under an honest and reasonable belief in the existence of certain facts and circumstances which, if true, would make such an act or omission lawful.

Collection and Investigative Services that he had been registered as a guard or patrolman.

Later in July of 1973 Bray bought a .38 caliber revolver from a pawn shop, Western Jewelry and Loan Company, to use in guard assignments requiring an armed patrolman. On one of the required forms he said he had not been convicted of a felony; on another he said he had not been convicted of a crime with a punishment of more "than one year." After the statutory five-day waiting period, the gun was delivered to him.

On September 14, 1973, Bray filled out an application for a job as a contract compliance investigator. In response to the question asking whether he had been convicted of a felony or misdemeanor, Bray answered with a "?". He again explained the circumstances surrounding his arrest and the sentence he received.

On November 16, 1973, and April 12, 1974, Bray filled out job applications for positions as an audio-visual technician and as an eligibility worker I. In each instance he answered that he had been convicted of a "felony or misdemeanor"; in each instance he explained his Kansas arrest and sentence.

In July of 1974, two investigators from the district attorney's office conducted a search with a warrant of Bray's house and car. Bray voluntarily led the investigators to a closet where he kept the .38 and a .22 pistol.

In order to gain a conviction under the relevant statute, the prosecutor must prove (1) conviction of a felony and (2) ownership, possession, custody or control of a firearm capable of being concealed on the person. There was no question here that Bray had been in possession of a concealable firearm; there was no question he had been convicted of the crime of being an "accessory after the fact" in Kansas. Bray says there must be proof he knew he was a felon. Or, in the alternative, he says mistake of fact is a defense and the court erred in denying this requested instruction.

It appears to be a question of first impression whether Penal Code §12021 [the statute in question] requires proof of the defendant's knowledge of his felony status, and whether such a prosecution may be defended by showing the defendant lacked knowledge he was a felon. The prevailing trend of decisions is to avoid constructions of penal statutes which would impose strict liability. The Attorney General agrees the statute should not be one of strict liability but then says it is not necessary for the People to prove the defendant had knowledge.

In considering the role of knowledge, whether the defendant knew he had committed an offense is irrelevant. The question here is whether the defendant must know of the existence of those facts which bring him within the statute's proscription. Even though §12021 does not explicitly require knowledge, the defendant must know he has possession of a concealable weapon. In addition, as to whether a defendant must know he is an alien under §12021, this court, in dictum, has said:

> Knowledge that one is in the State of California might conceivably be relevant in the case of a person who unwittingly had overstepped the boundary of a neighboring state, who might have been carried into the state against his will, or as the result of mistake in taking some vehicle of public transportation. In the present case, defendant knew he was no longer in Mexico. (People v. Mendoza, 251 Cal. App. 2d 835,843.)

Likewise, knowledge that one is a felon becomes relevant where there is doubt the defendant knew he had committed a felony. Here, even the prosecution had substantial difficulty in determining whether the offense was considered a felony in Kansas. In arguing to the court the necessity of a Kansas attorney's expert testimony, the district attorney said, " . . . in even our own jurisdiction, let alone a foreign jurisdiction such as the State of Kansas, it's extremely difficult to determine whether a sentence was a felony or a misdemeanor." Although the district attorney had great difficulty in determining whether the Kansas offense was a felony or a misdemeanor, he expects the layman Bray to know its status easily. There was no doubt Bray knew he had committed an offense: there was, however, evidence to the effect he did not know the offense was a felony. Without this knowledge Bray would be ignorant of the facts necessary for him to come within the proscription of §12021. Under these circumstances the requested instructions on mistakes or ignorance of fact and knowledge of the facts which make the act unlawful should have been given.

Notes and Questions

1. In the California statute under which Bray is here charged, what is the mens rea attached to the fact that the possessor of the gun had formerly been convicted of a felony? What was the defendant's mens rea? What result would MPC §2.04(1)(a) dictate here?

2. In *Bray,* note that the court implicitly and necessarily concludes that the crime of which Bray was convicted in Kansas was indeed a felony. How must it have determined this? And why did Bray himself misunderstand this? But did Bray understand the California law on gun possession?

3. The mistake made by the defendant was about a law rather than the usual mistake of fact. If a defendant makes a mistake of law that deprives him of the mens rea necessary for being found guilty of a crime, should we nonetheless treat him as if he had that mens rea? Why would we do that?

In most cases where a defendant's objective conduct falls within the terms of a criminal statute but he or she is nonetheless not blameworthy, the reason is that because of a mistake of fact the defendant lacks the mens rea required for the crime. This, however, is not always the case. Let us assume that a statute provides that it is a crime for someone with a living wife to go through a marriage ceremony with someone else, attaching the mens rea of recklessness, let us say, to the issue of whether one has a living wife. In such a case it should not matter whether the defendant was wrongly convinced that his wife had perished in an airplane crash or was equally convinced that his divorce from her was valid. It is true that the former error could be categorized as a mistake of fact and the latter a mistake of law, but since either would deprive the accused of the mens rea attached to his having a living wife, which the statute makes necessary for guilt, the distinction is not significant.

This is just as well because, although we may be convinced that we know the difference between a question of fact and of law, some questions might be open to characterization either way. Thus, while we usually think of the question of whether a person is dead as being one of fact (Did she perish in the airplane accident? We have not heard from her for a long time and she would be very old now, so she is probably dead.), the question of whether a person is dead could also be one of law and might arise where we are completely familiar with all the facts (He is lying in a hospital, having fluids pumped in and out of him with his heart beating only because of electrical stimulation, and having a flat electroencephalograph, which has shown no sign of brain activity for two months.). In this case, whether or not he was dead would be a question of law.

4. Consider the British case of Regina v. Smith (David), 2 Q.B. 354, 58 Cr. App. 320 (1974). Smith was a tenant in a flat and installed some electric wiring for use with stereo equipment and also, with the landlord's permission, installed ceiling and wall panels and floorboards. Under the hoary, if hypertechnical, law of "fixtures," the ceilings, walls, and floors became the property of the landlord once installed or "affixed" to the real estate. After a dispute with the landlord, Smith gave notice of terminating the lease and then, in removing the stereo wires, damaged the ceilings, walls, and floor. Understandably unversed in the law of fixtures, Smith told police he honestly believed the property he destroyed was his own. The court dismissed the charge of "damaging property of another" on the ground that the prosecution had not proven that Smith did so intentionally. Accepting the court's construction of the mental element of "damaging property of another," how would the Model Penal Code resolve this case?

Smith, like divorce cases, might tempt one to assume that it is errors of *civil* law that can be exculpating, while errors of *criminal* law are not. But note that, as in *Bray,* even an error of criminal law can exculpate if it negates the mens rea required by the criminal statute. So under the approach suggested by the Model Penal Code and employed by the court in *Bray,* mistakes negating mens rea are limited neither to mistakes of fact, nor to mistakes of civil law. An alternative is to say that Bray did not misunderstand the *governing* criminal law under which he was currently being prosecuted in California, but rather a *non-governing* law that became incorporated into the governing law as an element. We could then say that though a legislature can choose to make any mental factor an element of the crime, in the great majority of statutes, awareness of the governing law is not made such an element. See MPC §2.02(9), *supra.*

UNITED STATES v. BAKER
United States Court of Appeals for the Fifth Circuit
807 F.2d 427 (1986)[39]

Paul Baker appeals his conviction for trafficking in counterfeit goods, claiming that an element of the offense is knowledge of the criminality of the conduct and that the jury should have been so charged. We reject his contention and affirm his conviction.

Prior to 1984 trademark counterfeiting was addressed by the civil penalties found in the Lanham Act, 15 U.S.C. §§1051-1127. In 1984, however, Congress determined that "penalties under [the Lanham] Act have been too small, and too infrequently imposed, to deter counterfeiting significantly." S. Rep. No. 526, 98 Cong., 2d Sess. 5 (1984). Accordingly, Congress enacted the Trademark Counterfeiting Act of 1984, criminalizing much of the conduct that formerly had been subject only to civil penalties. The statute subjects to criminal penalties anyone who

> intentionally traffics or attempts to traffic in goods or services and knowingly uses a counterfeit mark on or in connection with such goods or services.

39. [Some footnote material has been placed in the text for ease of exposition.—Eds.]

Id. §1502(a) (codified at 18 U.S.C. §2320).

Paul Baker was convicted under this new statute for dealing in counterfeit watches. He does not dispute that he intentionally dealt in the watches. He also admits that he knew the "Rolex" watches he sold were counterfeit. His contention is that the statute requires that he act with knowledge that his conduct is criminal. He asserts that he did not know trafficking in counterfeit goods is criminal and that he would not have done so had he known he was committing a crime. The district court denied a motion to dismiss on this ground and refused to instruct the jury that Baker could not be convicted if he did not have the purpose to "disobey or disregard the law." Baker's sole contention on appeal is that the statute requires knowledge that the conduct is criminal and that the district court's rulings were thus erroneous. . . .

The statute clearly sets out the elements of the crime and the mental state required for each element. The defendant must intentionally deal in goods and he must knowingly use a counterfeit mark in connection with those goods. There is no ambiguity in this language and nothing in the statute suggests that any other mental state is required for conviction. . . .

It is not surprising that Congress would allow conviction of one who knows that he is selling bogus "Rolex" watches even though he does not know his conduct is punishable as a crime. While it is true that "the general principle that ignorance or mistake of law is no excuse is usually greatly overstated" (American Law Institute, Model Penal Code §2.02 comment 131 (Tent. Draft no. 4 1955)), the principle continues to be valid to the extent that ordinarily "the criminal law does not require knowledge that an act is illegal, wrong, or blameworthy." United States v. Freed, 401 U.S. 601, 612 (1971) (Brennan J., concurring). A noted treatise in the area summarizes this principle as follows:

> It bears repeating here that the cause of much of the confusion concerning the significance of the defendant's ignorance or mistake of law is the failure to distinguish two quite different situations: (1) that in which the defendant consequently lacks the mental state required for commission of the crime and thus . . . has a valid defense; and (2) that in which the defendant still had whatever mental state is required for commission of the crime and only claims that he was unaware that such conduct was proscribed by the criminal law, which . . . is ordinarily not a recognized defense.[40]

Baker's contention clearly falls within the second of the situations described.

Baker's claim is merely that, even though he had the mental states required by the face of the statute, he should not be convicted because he did not know that Congress had passed a statute criminalizing his conduct. This clearly is not the law. A defendant cannot "avoid prosecution by simply claiming that he had not brushed up on the law." Hamling v. United States, 418 U.S. 87, 123 (1974).

Notes and Questions

1. What is the mental element of the counterfeiting offense defined by 18 U.S.C. §2320? Does it include knowledge that counterfeiting is illegal? What

40. W. LaFave & A. Scott, Criminal Law §47, at 362-63 (1972).

result would MPC §2.04(1)(a) dictate in this case? What result would MPC §2.02(9) dictate? Are these provisions really saying the same thing?

2. The excerpt from LaFave and Scott enunciates the principle that ignorance of the offense definition is no defense. On this principle, defendant may be acquitted for ignorance that conditions specified in the definition were present; but may not be acquitted merely because she did not know that such conditions constituted defining elements of a proscribed offense.

3. Consider Hopkins v. State, 69 A.2d 456 (Md. 1950):

DELAPLAINE, JUDGE: This appeal was taken by the Rev. William F. Hopkins, of Elkton, from the judgment of conviction entered upon the verdict of a jury in the Circuit Court for Cecil County for violation of the statute making it unlawful to erect or maintain any sign intended to aid in the solicitation or performance of marriages.

The State charged that on September 1, 1947, defendant maintained a sign at the entrance to his home . . . in Elkton and also a sign along a highway leading into the town, to aid in the solicitation and performance of marriages. Four photographs were admitted in evidence. . . . [T]he sign in Elkton [containing the name "Rev. W. F. Hopkins," was illuminated at night, as was] . . . the other sign along the highway containing the words, "W. F. Hopkins, Notary Public, Information." . . .

The State showed that during the month of August, 1947, thirty ministers performed 1,267 marriages in Cecil County, and of this number defendant performed 286, only three of which were ceremonies in which the parties were residents of Cecil County.

The Act of 1943, now under consideration, was passed by the Legislature of Maryland to curb the thriving business which unethical ministers had built up as a result of the tremendous increase in the numbers of couples coming into the State to be married following the passage of stringent marriage laws in nearby States. . . .

Defendant contended that the judge erred in excluding testimony offered to show that the State's Attorney advised him in 1944 before he erected the signs, that they would not violate the law. It is generally held that the advice of counsel, even though followed in good faith, furnishes no excuse to a person for violating the law and cannot be relied upon as a defense in a criminal action. Moreover, advice given by a public official, even a State's Attorney, that a contemplated act is not criminal will not excuse an offender if, as a matter of law, the act performed did amount to a violation of the law. These rules are founded upon the maxim that ignorance of the law will not excuse its violation. If an accused could be exempted from punishment for crime by reason of the advice of counsel, such advice would become paramount to the law.

While ignorance of fact may sometimes be admitted as evidence of lack of criminal intent, ignorance of the law ordinarily does not give immunity from punishment for crime, for every man is presumed to intend the necessary and legitimate consequences of what he knowingly does. In the case at bar defendant did not claim that the State's Attorney misled him regarding any facts of the case, but only that the State's Attorney advised him as to the law based upon the facts. Defendant was aware of the penal statute enacted by the Legislature. He knew what he wanted to do, and he did the thing he intended to do. . . . For these reasons the exclusion of the testimony offered to show *that* defendant had sought and received advice from the State's Attorney was not prejudicial error. . . . [69 A.2d at 458-60]

What were the elements of Hopkins's crime? What may we infer were, in the court's view, the actus reus elements of the crime? What mens rea attached to each element? Did Hopkins have the required mens rea? Precisely what mistake did Hopkins make? Even if Hopkins had the required mens rea, *should he nevertheless be excused from responsibility for his offense?* Would MPC §2.04(3) have helped him if Maryland had adopted it?

4. *Willful violations of a regulatory statute.* The principle that mistakes about the offense definition do not negate mens rea requires two caveats. First, it is not always clear whether a legal provision is part of the definition of the charged offense. Second, the principle does not apply where a court concludes that knowledge of some part of the offense definition is an element of the offense. Suppose that Consumer Law Code section 101 provides that "no product may be sold at a higher price than advertised," and section 102 provides that "willful violation of section 101 is a misdemeanor." Is section 101 part of the offense definition? Many federal regulatory offenses are defined in this way, and federal courts have sometimes viewed "willful" violation of a regulation to require knowledge of the regulation. Consider the following case.

CHEEK v. UNITED STATES
Supreme Court of the United States
498 U.S. 192 (1991)

JUSTICE WHITE delivered the opinion of the court.

Title 26, §7201 of the United States Code provides that any person "who willfully attempts in any manner to evade or defeat any tax imposed by this title or the payment thereof" shall be guilty of a felony. Under 26 U.S.C. §7203, "[a]ny person required under this tide . . . or by regulations made under authority thereof to make a return . . . who willfully fails to . . . make such return" shall be guilty of a misdemeanor. This case turns on the meaning of the word "willfully" as used in §§7201 and 7203.

Petitioner John L. Cheek has been a pilot for American Airlines since 1973. He filed federal income tax returns through 1979 but thereafter ceased to file returns. He also claimed an increasing number of withholding allowances — eventually claiming 60 allowances by mid-1980 — and for the years 1981 to 1984 indicated on his W-4 forms that he was exempt from federal income taxes. . . .

As a result of his activities, petitioner was indicted for 10 violations of federal law. He was charged with six counts of willfully failing to file a federal income tax return for the years 1980, 1981, and 1983 through 1986, in violation of 26 U.S.C. §7203. He was further charged with three counts of willfully attempting to evade his income tax for the years 1980, 1981, and 1983 in violation of 26 U.S.C. §7201. In those years, American Airlines withheld substantially less than the amount of tax petitioner owed because of the numerous allowances and exempt status he claimed on his W-4 forms. The tax offenses with which petitioner was charged are specific intent crimes that require the defendant to have acted willfully.

At trial, the evidence established that between 1982 and 1986, petitioner was involved in at least four civil cases that challenged various aspects of the federal income tax system. In all four of those cases, the plaintiffs were informed by the courts that many of their arguments, including that they were not taxpayers within the meaning of the tax laws, that wages are not income, that the Sixteenth Amendment does not authorize the imposition of an income tax on individuals, and that the Sixteenth Amendment is unenforceable, were frivolous or had been repeatedly rejected by the courts. During this time, petitioner also attended at least two criminal trials of persons charged with tax offenses. In addition, there was evidence that in 1980 or 1981 an attorney had advised Cheek that the courts had rejected as frivolous the claim that wages are not income.

Cheek represented himself at trial and testified in his defense. He admitted that he had not filed personal income tax returns during the years in question. He testified that as early as 1978, he had begun attending seminars sponsored by, and following the advice of a group that believes, among other things, that the federal income tax is unconstitutional. Some of the speakers at these meetings were lawyers who purported to give professional opinions about the invalidity of the federal income tax laws. Cheek produced a letter from an attorney stating that the Sixteenth Amendment did not authorize a tax on wages and salaries but only a gain on profit. Petitioner's defense is that, based on the indoctrination he received from this group and from his own study, he sincerely believed that the tax laws were unconstitutionally enforced and that his actions during the 1980-86 period were lawful. He therefore argued that he had acted without the willfulness required for conviction of the various offenses with which he was charged.

In the course of the instructions, the trial court advised the jury that to prove "willfulness" the Government must prove the voluntary and intentional violation of a known legal duty, a burden that could not be proved by showing mistake, ignorance or negligence. The court further advised the jury that an objectively reasonable good-faith misunderstanding of the law would negate willfulness but mere disagreement with the law would not. The court described Cheek's beliefs about the income tax system and instructed the jury that if it found that Cheek "honestly and reasonably believed that he was not required to pay income taxes or to file tax returns," a not guilty verdict should be returned.

After several hours of deliberation, the jury sent a note to the judge that stated in part: "We have a basic disagreement between some of us as to if Mr. Cheek honestly and reasonably believed that he was not required to pay income taxes. . . . Page 32 [the relevant jury instruction] discusses good-faith misunderstanding and disagreement. Is there any additional clarification you can give us on this point?"

The District Judge responded with a supplemental instruction containing the following statements:

> [A] person's opinion that the tax laws violate his constitutional rights does not constitute a good faith misunderstanding of the law. Furthermore, a person's disagreement with the government's tax collection systems and policies does not constitute a good faith misunderstanding of the law.

At the end of the first day of deliberation, the jury sent out another note saying it still could not reach a verdict because "[w]e are divided on this issue as to if Mr. Cheek honestly & reasonably believed that he was not required to pay income tax." When the jury resumed its deliberations, the District Judge gave the jury an additional instruction. This instruction stated in part that "[a]n honest but unreasonable belief is not a defense and does not negate willfulness," and that "[a]dvice or research resulting in the conclusion that wages of a privately employed person are not income or that the tax laws are unconstitutional is not objectively reasonable and cannot serve as the basis for a good-faith misunderstanding of the law defense." The court also instructed the jury that "[p]ersistent refusal to acknowledge the law does not constitute a good faith misunderstanding of the law." Approximately two hours later, the jury returned a verdict finding petitioner guilty on all counts.

Petitioner appealed his conviction, arguing that the District Court erred by instructing the jury that only an objectively reasonable misunderstanding of the law negates the statutory willfulness requirement. The United States Court of Appeals for the Seventh Circuit rejected that contention and affirmed the convictions. . . .

The general rule that ignorance of the law or mistake of law is no defense to a criminal prosecution is deeply rooted in the legal system. . . . Based on the notion that the law is definite and knowable, the common law presumed that every person knew the law. . . .

The proliferation of statutes and regulations has sometimes made it difficult for the average citizen to know and comprehend the extent of the duties and obligations imposed by the tax laws. Congress has accordingly softened the impact of the common-law presumption by making specific intent to violate the law an element of certain federal criminal tax offenses. Thus, the Court almost 60 years ago interpreted the statutory term "willfully" as used in the federal criminal tax statutes as carving out an exception to the traditional rule. This special treatment is largely due to the complexity of the tax laws. In United States v. Murdock, 290 U.S. 389 (1933), the Court recognized that:

> Congress did not intend that a person by reason of a bona fide misunderstanding as to his liability for the tax, as to his duty to make a return, or as to the adequacy of the records he maintained, should become a criminal by his mere failure to measure up to the prescribed standard of conduct.

The Court held that the defendant was entitled to an instruction with respect to whether he acted in good faith based on his actual belief. In *Murdock,* the Court interpreted the term "willfully" as used in the criminal tax statutes generally to mean "an act done with a bad purpose" or with an "evil motive."

Willfulness, as construed by our prior decisions in criminal tax cases, requires the Government to prove that the law imposed a duty on the defendant, that the defendant knew of this duty, and that he voluntarily and intentionally violated that duty. We deal first with the case when the issue is whether the defendant knew of the duty purportedly imposed by the provision of the statute or regulation he is accused of violating, a case in which there is no claim that the provision at issue is invalid. In such a case, . . . the issue is whether, based on all the evidence, the Government has proved that the defendant was aware of the duty at issue, which cannot be true if the jury credits a good-faith misunderstanding and belief submission, whether or not the claimed belief or misunderstanding is objectively reasonable.

In this case, if Cheek asserted that he truly believed that the Internal Revenue Code did not purport to treat wages as income, and the jury believed him, the Government would not have carried its burden to prove willfulness, however unreasonable a court might seem such a belief. . . . We thus disagree with the Court of Appeals' requirement that a claimed good-faith belief must be objectively reasonable if it is to be considered as possibly negating the Government's evidence purporting to show a defendant's awareness of the legal duty at issue. . . .

Cheek asserted in the trial court that he should be acquitted because he believed in good faith that the income tax law is unconstitutional as applied to him and thus could not impose any legal duty upon him of which he should have been aware . . . [Some cases have] construed the willfulness requirement in the criminal provisions of the Internal Revenue Code to require proof of knowledge of the law. This was because in "our complex tax system, uncertainty often arises even among taxpayers who earnestly wish to follow the law" and "[i]t is not the purpose of the law to penalize frank difference of opinion or innocent errors made despite the exercise of reasonable care," United States v. Bishop, 412 U.S. 346.

Claims that some of the provisions of the tax code are unconstitutional are of a different order. They do not arise from innocent mistakes caused by the complexity of the Internal Revenue Code. Rather, they reveal full knowledge of the provisions at issue and a studied conclusion, however wrong, that those provisions are invalid and unenforceable. . . .

We do not believe that Congress contemplated that such a taxpayer, without risking criminal prosecution, could ignore the duties imposed on him by the Internal Revenue Code and refuse to utilize the mechanisms provided by Congress to present his claims of invalidity to the courts and to abide by their decisions. There is no doubt that Cheek, from year to year, was free to pay the tax that the law purported to require, file for a refund, and if denied, present his claims of invalidity, constitutional or otherwise, to the courts. Also, without paying the tax, he could have challenged claims of tax deficiencies to the Tax Court, with the right to appeal to a higher court if unsuccessful. Cheek took neither course in some years, and when he did he was unwilling to accept the outcome. As we see it, he is in no position to claim that his good-faith belief about the validity of the Internal Revenue Code negates willfulness or provides a defense to criminal prosecution under §§7201 and 7203. . . .

We thus hold that in a case like this, a defendant's views about the validity of the tax statutes are irrelevant to to the issue of willfulness, need not be heard by the jury, and if they are, an instruction to disregard them would be proper. For this purpose, it makes no difference whether the claims of invalidity are frivolous or have substance. It was therefore not error in this case for the District Judge to instruct the jury not to consider Cheek's claims that the tax laws were unconstitutional. However, it was error for the court to instruct the jury that petitioner's asserted beliefs that wages are not income and that he was not a taxpayer within the meaning of the Internal Revenue Code should not be considered by the jury in determining whether Cheek had acted willfully. [Case remanded.]

Notes and Questions

1. If the statute punished "knowingly" evading the tax imposed by statute, would the result be the same? Is the court splitting hairs in ascribing a different meaning to the term "willfully?" Note that the primary definition of "willful" in the Oxford English Dictionary is "asserting or disposed to assert one's will against persuasion, instruction or command." (Compact Edition 1971, p. 3778) Can one violate a regulation "willfully" (in this sense) without being aware of the regulation one is violating?

2. *Mistake of constitutional law.* What level of culpability must the jury ascribe to Cheek with respect to his violation of a statute or regulation to find him liable for "willful" tax evasion? What level of culpability, if any, must the jury ascribe to

Cheek with respect to the constitutionality of the statute or regulation he violates to find him liable for "willful" tax evasion? Does the court adequately justify this disparate treatment of the two different sources of legal rules? The court suggests that it is particularly unfair to expect citizens to know the tax law, but that citizens may be presumed to know constitutional law. Does this distinction make sense? Note that philosophers of law will often point to technical statutes like the tax code for examples of precise rules, and to the Constitution for examples of vague legal standards like "due process."

Consider the "Jim Crow" era Alabama case of Green v. State, 58 Ala. 190 (1877). In 1866, the Alabama legislature passed an antimiscegenation statute. In 1872, at the height of Reconstruction, the statute was held unconstitutional by the Alabama Supreme Court. Burns v. State, 48 Ala. 195 (1872). The defendant in Green, a white woman, married a black man in reliance on the latter decision, and was then charged and convicted under the statute. The Alabama Supreme Court, newly composed of supporters of "Jim Crow," not only overturned the earlier decision, thereby upholding the constitutionality of the antimiscegenation law — the Court also upheld Green's conviction!

3. *Cheek* is no longer an isolated case. According to Prof. Sharon Davies:

> "Knowledge of illegality" has now been construed to be an element in a wide variety of [federal] statutory and regulatory criminal provisions, including the federal tax provisions, the federal false statement provisions, the federal anti-structuring provisions, the federal firearms provisions, the Medicare and Medicaid anti-kickback provisions, the Occupational Safety and Health Act, the Child Support Recovery Act, and the Trading with the Enemy Act. Proof of knowledge of illegality has also been required to support a conviction for willfully misapplying student loan funds, willfully exporting an aircraft, willfully attempting to export weapons or ammunition, willfully [importing] monetary instruments in excess of $5,000 . . . , willfully neglecting to submit for induction into the army, intentionally using the contents of [illegally recorded] telephone conversations . . . , and knowingly acquiring or possessing food stamps in a manner not authorized by law. . . . These constructions establish that . . . ignorance or mistake of law has already become an acceptable [defense] in a number of regulatory and nonregulatory settings, particularly in prosecutions brought under statutes requiring proof of "willful" conduct on the part of the accused. Under the reasoning employed in these cases, at least 160 additional federal statutes . . . are at risk of similar treatment.[41]

In 1998, however, the Supreme Court held that "'willfully' dealing in firearms without a federal license . . . requires proof that the defendant knew that his conduct was unlawful . . . [but] not that he also knew of the federal licensing requirement." Bryan v. United States, 524 U.S. 184, 193-95 (1998). Bryan bought guns in secretive "straw man" deals, but he arguably did not know that he needed a license when he sold them. In holding that proof of knowledge of the regulation violated was not required, the Court distinguished *Cheek* and other cases as involving "highly technical statutes that presented the danger of ensnaring individuals engaged in apparently innocent conduct." Is this a valid distinction here? But the Court also noted that even if Bryan was not specifically aware of the licensing requirement, his conduct hardly evinced any good-faith

---

41. Sharon L. Davies, The Jurisprudence of Ignorance: An Evolving Theory of Excusable Ignorance, 48 Duke L. J. 341, 344-47 (1998).

belief in the legality of the deals, since he used the "straw purchasers" to acquire pistols he could not have purchased himself; that the purchasers made false statements to the sellers; that he assured the straw purchasers that he would file the serial numbers off the guns; and that he resold the guns on street corners known for drug dealing. Is there any way then that Bryan could still have had a good claim under *Cheek?*

3. Mistake of Law as an Excuse

COMMONWEALTH v. TWITCHELL
Supreme Judicial Court of Massachusetts
416 Mass. 114, 617 N.E.2d (1993)

WILKINS, JUSTICE: David and Ginger Twitchell appeal from their convictions of involuntary manslaughter in connection with the April 8, 1986, death of their two and one-half year old son Robyn. Robyn died of the consequences of peritonitis caused by the perforation of his bowel which had been obstructed as a result of an anomaly known as Meckel's diverticulum. There was evidence that the condition could be corrected by surgery with a high success rate.

The defendants are practicing Christian Scientists who grew up in Christian Science families. They believe in healing by spiritual treatment. During Robyn's five-day illness from Friday, April 4, through Tuesday, April 8, they retained a Christian Science practitioner, a Christian Science nurse, and at one time consulted with Nathan Talbot, who held a position in the church known as the "Committee on Publication." As a result of that consultation, David Twitchell read a church publication concerning the legal rights and obligations of Christian Scientists in Massachusetts. That publication quoted a portion of G.L. c.273, §1, as then amended, which . . . read . . . : "A child shall not be deemed to be neglected or lack proper physical care for the sole reason that he is being provided remedial treatment by spiritual means alone in accordance with the tenets and practice of a recognized church or religious denomination by a duly accredited practitioner thereof." G.L. c. 273, §1 (1992 ed.). . . .

[T]he jury would have been warranted in finding that the Twitchells were wanton or reckless in failing to provide medical care for Robyn, if parents have a legal duty to provide a child with medical care in such circumstances and if the spiritual treatment provision of G.L. c. 273, §1, did not protect them from manslaughter liability. . . .

The Commonwealth presented its case on the theory that each defendant was guilty of involuntary manslaughter because the intentional failure of each to seek medical attention for their son involved such "a high degree of likelihood that substantial harm will result to" him as to be wanton or reckless conduct. Commonwealth v. Welansky, 316 Mass. 383 (1944) [see p. 361, *infra*]. . . . A charge of involuntary manslaughter based on an omission to act can be proved only if the defendant had a duty to act and did not do so. Commonwealth v. Welansky, *supra*. . . . [A] parental duty of care has been recognized in the common law of homicide in this Commonwealth. . . . There is, . . . quite apart from G.L. c.273, §1, a common law duty to provide medical services for a child, the breach of which can be the basis, in the appropriate circumstances, for the conviction of a parent for involuntary manslaughter.

The defendants argue that the spiritual treatment provision in G.L. c.273, §1, bars any involuntary manslaughter charge against a parent who relies, as they did, on spiritual treatment and who does not seek medical attention for his or her child, even if the parent's failure to seek such care would otherwise be wanton or reckless conduct. We disagree. . . .

Section 1 of G.L. c.273 provides no complete protection to a parent against a charge of involuntary manslaughter that is based on the parent's wanton or reckless failure to provide medical services to a child. . . . The spiritual treatment provision refers to neglect and lack of proper physical care, which are concepts set forth earlier in §1, as then amended, as bases for punishment: (1) neglect to provide support and (2) wilful failure to provide necessary and proper physical care. These concepts do not underlie involuntary manslaughter. Wanton or reckless conduct is not a form of negligence. . . . Wanton or reckless conduct does not involve a wilful intention to cause the resulting harm. See Commonwealth v. Welansky. . . . An involuntary manslaughter verdict does not require proof of wilfulness. . . . Commonwealth v. Welansky. . . . Thus, by its terms, the spiritual treatment provision in §1 does not apply to involuntary manslaughter. . . .

The defendants argue that the failure to extend the protection of the spiritual treatment provision to them in this case would be a denial of due process of law because they lacked "fair warning" that their use of spiritual treatment could form the basis for a prosecution for manslaughter. Fair warning is part of the due process doctrine of vagueness. . . . Even if a statute is clear on its face, there may not be fair warning in the circumstances of particular defendants. The defendants here argue that they have been denied fair warning in three different ways. They contend that fair warning . . . is denied because they were officially misled by an opinion of the Attorney General of the Commonwealth. . . .

In May 1975, the Attorney General gave an opinion on a number of topics to the deputy director of the Office for Children. Rep. A.G., Pub. Doc. No. 12, at 139 (1975). The relevant portion of that opinion . . . answers a general question "whether parents who fail to provide medical services to children on the basis of religious beliefs will be subject to prosecution for such failure." Id. at 140. A reasonable person not trained in the law might fairly read the Attorney General's comments as being a negative answer to the general question whether in any circumstances such parents may be prosecuted. It is true that the answer comes to focus on negligent failures of parents, and we know that wanton or reckless failures are different. But an answer that says that children may receive needed services "notwithstanding the inability to prosecute parents in such cases" (id.), and issues no caveat concerning homicide charges, invites a conclusion that parents who fail to provide medical services to children on the basis of religious beliefs are not subject to criminal prosecution in any circumstances. . . .

Although the Twitchells were not aware of the Attorney General's opinion, they knew of a Christian Science publication called "Legal Rights and Obligations of Christian Scientists in Massachusetts." . . . It is obvious that the Christian Science Church's publication on the legal rights and obligations of Christian Scientists in Massachusetts relied on the Attorney General's 1975 opinion. That opinion was arguably misleading because of what it did not say concerning criminal liability for manslaughter. If the Attorney General had issued a caveat concerning manslaughter liability, the publication (which, based on such portions of it as appear in the record, is balanced and fair) would have referred to it in all reasonable likelihood. Nathan Talbot, who served as the Committee on Publication for the church and with whom the Twitchells spoke on the Sunday or Monday before Robyn's death, might well have given the Twitchells different advice.

Although it has long been held that "ignorance of the law is no defence," . . . there is substantial justification for treating as a defense the belief that conduct is not a violation of law when a defendant has reasonably relied on an official statement of the law, later determined to be wrong, contained in an official interpretation of the public official who is charged by law with the responsibility for the interpretation or enforcement of the law defining the offense. See Model Penal Code §2.04(3)(b) (Proposed Official Draft 1962). . . . There is special merit to such a rule if religious beliefs are involved and if the defendant was attempting to comply with the law while adhering, as far as possible, to his religious beliefs and practices. . . . Federal courts have characterized an affirmative defense of this nature as "entrapment by estoppel." . . . The defense rests on principles of fairness grounded in Federal criminal cases in the due process clause of the Fifth Amendment to the United States Constitution. . . . The defense generally involves factual determinations . . . based on the totality of the circumstances attending the prosecution, although the authority of the government official making the announcement is obviously a question of law.

The Twitchells were entitled to present such an affirmative defense to the jury. The Attorney General was acting in an area of his official responsibilities. He is the chief law officer of the Commonwealth, with the power to set a unified and consistent legal policy for the Commonwealth. . . . He is statutorily empowered to "give his opinion upon questions of law submitted to him" by the executive branch or the Legislature. G.L. c.12, §9 (1992 ed.). Whether a person would reasonably conclude that the Attorney General had ruled that §1 provided protection against a manslaughter charge is a question of fact. Whether the defendants in turn reasonably relied on the church's publication and on the advice of the Committee on Publication, assuming that the construction of the Attorney General's opinion was reasonable, also presents questions of fact. . . . In the resolution of these factual questions, the relevant portion of the Attorney General's opinion and the relevant portion of the church's publication will be admissible. The jury should also be advised of the terms of the spiritual treatment provision of §1. . . . For these reasons, the judgments must be reversed, the verdicts must be set aside, and the cases remanded for a new trial, if the district attorney concludes that such a prosecution is necessary in the interests of justice.

Notes and Questions

1. The *Twitchell* court cites Model Penal Code §2.04(3), creating an excuse based on an official statement of law. Why excuse mistakes made in reliance on an official statement of law rather than simply excuse all reasonable mistakes? Is such an excuse aimed at absolving blameless offenses, or restraining official arbitrariness?[42]

42. For a comprehensive treatment of excuse based on official misstatement of law, and a call for a flexible due process defense for reasonable reliance, see John T. Parry, Culpability, Mistake, and Official Interpretations of Law, 25 Am. J. Crim. L. 1 (1997).

2. Is the court raising any question about whether the Twitchells had a duty to provide medical care and whether they acted in "wanton and reckless" disregard of that duty? If the Twitchells concededly caused their child's death wantonly and recklessly, what issue is left for the jury to resolve?

3. The court implies that if the Twitchells made a reasonable mistake of law, convicting them for manslaughter would be a violation of the constitutional due process principle of specificity, which is one aspect of the larger principle of legality we studied in Chapter 2. Does this imply that the denial of such a defense in a case like *Baker* was a constitutional violation? What about in *Hopkins*?

4. Is one more likely to think the Massachusetts legislature wished to avoid punishing those who seek to cure their sick children through prayer alone, if one believes this course of conduct is morally right? In satisfying the jury that their interpretation of the child welfare and homicide law was "reasonable," should the Twitchells have to prove it was reasonable for the average citizen, or may they ask the jury to take into account the Twitchells' religious beliefs?

5. *Reliance on Private Legal Advice.* In *Twitchell* the court allowed the excuse defined by Model Penal Code §2.04 (3)(b), reasonable reliance upon an official statement of law. But should this excuse be broadened to include reasonable reliance on consultation of a privately retained attorney? Is such reliance inherently unreasonable? Does a rule excusing mistake of law in reliance on a private attorney risk creating bad incentives for lawyers and clients?

The MPC, of course, does not offer such an excuse, and very few jurisdictions have done so, at least as a matter of stated doctrine. But in the famous case of Long v. State, 44 Del. 262, 65 A.2d 489 (1949), the Delaware Supreme Court awarded defendant a new trial for bigamy to allow him to present such an excuse. Defendant had remarried following an out of state divorce that an attorney had erroneously assured him was valid in Delaware. The trial court refused to allow testimony concerning the lawyer's advice, on two grounds: that a mistake concerning the legality of a divorce did not negate the mental element of the offense, and that "ignorance of the law is no excuse." The Delaware Supreme Court agreed with the trial court that, as defined by the Delaware criminal code, the mental element of bigamy required only knowing remarriage with knowledge that one's first spouse was probably still alive. The mental element did not include belief in the continuing legal validity of the earlier marriage. Yet, while holding defendant's alleged mistake irrelevant to the *mental element of the offense,* the court rejected the maxim that ignorance of the law is no *excuse.* If proven reasonable, defendant's alleged mistake was relevant to his guilt because it excused him from responsibility. The court reasoned that mistake of law is ordinarily

disallowed as a defense in spite of the fact that it may show an absence of the criminal mind. The reasons for disallowing it are practical considerations dictated by deterrent effects upon the administration and enforcement of the criminal law, which are deemed likely to result if it were allowed as a general defense. As stated in . . . [Perkins, Ignorance and Mistake in Criminal Law 88 U. Pa. L. Rev. 35,] 41: " . . . But if such ignorance were available as a defense in every criminal case, this would be a constant source of confusion to juries, and it would tend to encourage ignorance at a point where it is peculiarly important to the state that knowledge should be as widespread as is reasonably possible. In the language of one of the giants of the profession, this is a point at which 'justice to the individual is rightly outweighed by the larger interests on the other side of the scales'" [quoting Holmes].

Similar considerations are involved when we disallow ignorance or mistake of law as a defense to a defendant who engages in criminal conduct (even though not obviously immoral or anti-social) where his ignorance or mistake consists merely in (1) unawareness that such conduct is or might be within the ambit of any crime; or (2) although aware of the existence of criminal law relating to the subject of such conduct, or to some of its aspects, the defendant erroneously concludes (in good faith) that his particular conduct is for some reason not subject to the operation of any criminal law. But it seems to us significantly different to disallow mistake of law where (3) together with the circumstances of the second classification, it appears that before engaging in the conduct, the defendant made a bona fide, diligent effort, adopting a course and resorting to sources and means at least as appropriate as any afforded under our legal system, to ascertain and abide by the law, and where he acted in good faith reliance upon the results of such effort. It is inherent in the way our legal system functions that the criminal law consequences of particular contemplated conduct cannot be determined in advance with certainty. . . . Hence, in the sense in which we are concerned with the expression, a "mistake of law" of the second or third classification refers to the failure of predictions of legal consequences to come to pass. No matter how logical, plausible and persuasive may be the bases for a prediction (assumptions, abstract legal rules, reasoning, etc.) a mistake of law arises if the prediction does not eventuate; and there is no mistake of law if the prediction eventuates.

With these thoughts in mind, let us examine how the considerations which justify the rejection of a mistake of the first and second classifications operate with respect to a mistake of the third classification. The objection of tending to "encourage ignorance" of the law would hardly seem applicable. The very conditions of the third classification include a diligent effort, in good faith, by means as appropriate as any available under our legal system, to acquire knowledge of the relevant law. The objection of difficulties of proof, including facilitation of subterfuge, is applicable, if at all, in a far less degree than in the case of mistakes of the first and second classifications. For them, the facts are essentially confined to the defendant's subjective state of mind. The conditions of the third classification are not so limited. They include an affirmative showing of effort to abide by the law, tested by objective standards rather than the defendant's subjective state of mind.

Any deterrent effects upon the administration of the criminal law which might result from allowing a mistake of the third classification as a defense seem greatly outweighed by considerations which favor allowing it. To hold a person punishable as a criminal transgressor where the conditions of the third classification are present would be palpably unjust and arbitrary. Most of the important reasons which support the prohibition of ex post facto legislation are opposed to such a holding. It is difficult to conceive what more could be reasonably expected of a "model citizen" than that he guide his conduct by "the law" ascertained in good faith, not merely by efforts which might seem adequate to a person in his situation, but by efforts as well designed to accomplish ascertainment as any available under our system.

The court placed the burden of proof on the defendant to show reasonable reliance on his attorney's advice at his new trial. But why should defendant bear the burden on this issue? Are you persuaded by the court's reasons? By the way, how might Reverend Hopkins have fared under the approach taken by the court in *Long*? What about *Baker*?

On the other hand, note that where a statute, unlike the one in *Twitchell*, punishes "willful" conduct and so otherwise is construed as making knowledge of the law an element of the offense, *see Cheek, supra,* a defendant's claim that she was misled by a private attorney may at least support her argument that she lacks that knowledge. But see United States v. Petrie, 302 F.3d 1280 (11th Cir. 2002) (claim that defendant did not willfully violate money-laundering law because misled by attorney fails where defendant had not disclosed all relevant facts to attorney and so lacked good faith).

6. *Mistakes of law and social norms.* Recently, a number of defendants have argued that their homicide liability should be reduced from murder to manslaughter because of the role of foreign cultural, moral, or legal norms in motivating their homicidal acts. See Chapter 5, *infra,* for discussion of these "cultural defenses."

If socialization in a foreign culture can arguably have an exculpating effect, what about socialization in a deviant American subculture? Recall the Jack Abbott case discussed in Chapter 1. Does acclimation to the brutal norms prevailing in maximum security prisons excuse wrongdoing? See the discussion of Abbott's trial for homicide in Chapter 8.

Finally, what if the defendant's mistake results from acclimation to social norms prevailing in the wider community? Consider the following argument:

> The theory suggested by Holmes as underlying the general rule is that "to admit the excuse at all would be to encourage ignorance where the lawmaker has determined to make men know and obey, and justice to the individual is rightly outweighed by the larger interests on the other side of the scales." If ignorance of the law were a defense, it would be difficult for the state to bring home to its citizens knowledge of new regulations affecting their rights and duties, or of new crimes, and thus to establish the new rules in social mores of the community.[43]

Is it fair to inculcate new mores by making examples of particular offenders? Consider the relative blameworthiness of defendants who claim unfamiliarity with new laws: (1) punishing failure to wear a seat belt, or (2) expanding the scope of rape liability to encompass any coerced sex in dating situations.[44]

E. CAPACITY FOR MENS REA

HENDERSHOTT v. PEOPLE
Supreme Court of Colorado
653 P.2d 385 (1982)

JUSTICE QUINN: In April 1979 the defendant [Lee Roy Hendershott] was living in the rooming house of Patricia Styskal, whom he had dated intermittently for approximately three years. Problems developed in their relationship due to the defendant's excessive drinking, and on April 28, 1979, Ms. Styskal told the defendant he would have to move out. . . . At approximately 11:00 P.M. Ms. Styskal returned home and found the defendant waiting in her bedroom.

43. Livingston Hall & Selig J. Seligman, Mistake of law and Mens Rea, 8 U. Chi. L. Rev. 641, 648 (1941)
44. This issue is treated in Ch. 15, *infra.*

The defendant accused her of having been out with another man. He then struck, kicked, and began to choke her. She was able to escape and fled to a neighbor's home. The police, who were immediately summoned, found the defendant unconscious in an upstairs bedroom of Ms. Styskal's home, and he was immediately arrested and charged with third degree assault.

In the course of pretrial discovery the district attorney learned that defense counsel intended to offer at trial expert opinion evidence in order to establish that the defendant, due to adult minimal brain dysfunction [a condition similar to hyperactivity in children, characterized by heightened anxiety and a lack of impulse control approaching an automatic response to stimuli], lacked the requisite culpability of "knowingly" or "recklessly" [causing bodily injury] essential to the crime of assault in the third degree. The district attorney filed a pretrial motion to exclude this evidence, arguing that section 18-1-803, C.R.S., restricts evidence of impaired mental condition to specific intent crimes and that third degree assault was not a specific intent offense. Section 18-1-501, C.R.S., states that all crimes "in which the mental culpability requirement is expressed as 'intentionally' or 'with intent' are declared to be specific intent offenses [and] . . . all crimes in which the mental culpability requirement is expressed as 'knowingly' or 'willfully' are general intent crimes." Because the mental element of "recklessly" represents a less serious form of culpability than the element of "knowingly," a crime with the culpability requirement of "recklessly" is obviously not one of specific intent. The county court ruled the evidence inadmissible as a matter of law in prosecutions for crimes not requiring specific intent. . . . The jury found the defendant guilty. . . . The district court affirmed his conviction. . . . We granted certiorari to consider the issue whether opinion evidence of a mental impairment due to a mental disease or defect may be admitted to negate the mens rea for a nonspecific intent crime such as assault in the third degree. . . .

It is not open to question that the power to define criminal conduct and to establish the legal components of criminal liability is vested with the General Assembly. . . . Once a person is charged with violating the criminal law, [however,] basic principles of constitutional law come into play and apply throughout the prosecution of the case. It is axiomatic that an accused is presumed innocent of the charge, and this presumption extends to every element of the crime including the requisite mens rea. Additionally, due process of law requires the prosecution to prove beyond a reasonable doubt every fact necessary to constitute the crime charged before the accused may be convicted and subjected to punishment. In Re Winship, 397 U.S. 358 (1970), Sandstrom v. Montana, 442 U.S. 510 (1979), Patterson v. New York 432 U.S. 197 (1977), Mullaney v. Wilbur, 421 U.S. 684 (1975). . . .

In addition to establishing the essential elements of criminal conduct, it is within the legislature's prerogative to formulate principles of justification or excuse, usually denominated affirmative defenses, and to limit these defenses to a particular category of crimes, so long as the basic rights of the criminally accused are not thereby impaired. The formulation and the limitation of affirmative defenses, however, must be distinguished from the accused's right to present reliable and relevant evidence to controvert the prosecution's case against him. . . .

[I]t would be a violation of due process to require the prosecution to establish the culpable mental state beyond a reasonable doubt while, at the same time, to prohibit a defendant from presenting evidence to contest this issue. Such a prohibition assumes all the features of an impermissible presumption of culpability. . . . A rule precluding the defendant from contesting the culpability element of the charge would render the prosecution's evidence on that issue uncontestable as a matter of law, in derogation of the presumption of innocence and the constitutional requirement of prosecutorial proof of guilt beyond a reasonable doubt. . . .

The trial court's refusal to permit the defendant to offer mental impairment evidence establishing that he lacked the requisite [knowledge or recklessness] for third degree assault due to adult minimal brain dysfunction was based on section 18-1-803, C.R.S., which provides: "Evidence of an impaired mental condition though not legal insanity may be offered in a proper case as bearing upon the capacity of the accused to form the specific intent if such an intent is an element of the offense charged." The trial court construed this section to prohibit the admission of all mental impairment evidence in prosecutions for nonspecific intent crimes and the district court adopted the same construction. This construction, in our view, cannot be justified as a legitimate constitutional option. . . .

An accused is not only entitled to the presumption of innocence on all elements of a charge but also is protected against a conviction unless the prosecution establishes the requisite mens rea by proof beyond a reasonable doubt. . . . The trial court's exclusion of the mental impairment evidence rendered the prosecution's evidence uncontestable as a matter of law on the issue of mens rea, thus adversely implicating the constitutional presumption of innocence. . . .

A reasonable doubt as to guilt may arise not only from the prosecution's case, but also from defense evidence casting doubt upon what previously may have appeared certain. Denying the defendant any opportunity to controvert the prosecution's case by reliable and relevant evidence of mental impairment, . . . downgrades the prosecution's burden to something less than that mandated by due process of law.

We therefore disapprove the trial court's ruling as violative of due process of law and hold that reliable and relevant mental impairment evidence is admissible, upon proper foundation, to negate the culpability element of the criminal charge. Our holding conforms to the Model Penal Code which provides: "Evidence that the defendant suffered from a mental disease or defect shall be admissible whenever it is relevant to prove that the defendant did or did not have a state of mind which is an element of the offense." Model Penal Code §4.02(1). . . .

The People have urged a contrary holding and have raised several policy arguments to that end. . . . The People initially argue that the admission of mental impairment evidence to negate the mens rea for crimes not involving a specific intent would render the insanity defense an unnecessary option in prosecutions for such offenses. . . . A person who is criminally insane is excused from criminal responsibility for his actions because, due to a mental disease or defect, he lacks the capacity to distinguish right from wrong with respect to the act or to adhere to the right or refrain from the wrong. This is not to say, however, that legal sanity is a proxy for mens rea. The prosecution's burden of proof on the requisite mens rea for a crime is no less where the defendant has previously been adjudicated legally sane in a sanity trial. . . . To prohibit the defendant in this case from contesting the mens rea of "knowingly" or "recklessly" except by raising the insanity defense would be nothing short of a conclusive presumption of culpability and, as previously noted, would be constitutionally intolerable. . . .

The People next point to the problems of proof which arise when psychiatric testimony is admissible. In the People's view these problems are due primarily to the inexact and tentative nature of psychiatry. . . . This argument, however, overlooks the essentially subjective character of the issues relating to criminal culpability. These issues involve moral, legal and medical components and rarely, if ever, will they be resolved on the basis of objective scientific evidence. . . . Nonetheless, there is no reason to believe that psychiatric testimony is any less helpful to the fact finder in resolving whether a defendant acted "knowingly" or "recklessly" than in determining whether he had the capacity to form the "specific intent." . . .

The People's last policy argument is that the protection of the community justifies the exclusion of mental impairment evidence in nonspecific intent crimes. The logic of the People's argument is that, notwithstanding the lack of mens rea for the commission of a criminal offense, mentally disturbed persons should not be completely set at liberty upon their acquittal. As we see it, the solution of the problem posed by the People does not lie in barring the admission of mental impairment evidence to negate the requisite culpability for the crime charged, but rather in providing for the confinement and treatment of persons who are mentally ill and pose a danger to themselves or others. . . .

In approving the admissibility of mental impairment evidence by psychiatric or psychological experts in order to negate the culpability element of a crime, we recognize a significant distinction between this type of evidence and evidence of self-induced intoxication. . . . In People v. Del Guidice, 199 Colo. 41, 606 P.2d 840 (1979), we held that self-induced intoxication was not an affirmative defense to second degree murder and, therefore, evidence of voluntary intoxication was not admissible to negate the culpability element of "knowingly" for that offense. . . . It is a matter of common knowledge that the excessive use of liquor or drugs impairs the perceptual, judgmental and volitional faculties of the user. Also, because the intoxication must be "self-induced," the defendant necessarily must have had the conscious ability to prevent this temporary incapacity from coming into being at all. Self-induced intoxication, therefore, by its very nature involves a degree of moral culpability. . . . Thus, when a defendant chooses to knowingly introduce intoxicants into his body to the point of becoming temporarily impaired in his powers of perception, judgment and control, the policy enunciated in *Del Guidice* prohibits him from utilizing his intoxication as a defense to crimes requiring the mens rea of "knowingly," "willfully," "recklessly" or "with criminal negligence." There is nothing in *Del Guidice*, however, that is inconsistent with permitting a defendant to contest these culpability elements by evidence of a mental impairment caused by a known mental disease or defect. . . . Unlike voluntary drunkenness, a mental impairment such as minimal brain dysfunction is not a condition that may be induced or avoided by conscious choice. . . .

The judgment is reversed and the cause is remanded to the district court with directions to return the case to the county court for a new trial in accordance with the views herein expressed.

Notes and Questions

1. As the Court notes in *Hendershott,* it follows the Model Penal Code approach of allowing evidence of psychological impairment to negate the mental element of all crimes. Only about ten states do so. A much larger number allow in such evidence to negate "specific intent" only. And some do not permit it to negate mens rea at all.

2. Recall the four meanings of general and specific intent discussed in note 4 after *Faulkner,* pp. 184-86, *supra.* Which meaning is this distinction given in *Hendershott?*

The traditional rule that voluntary intoxication could only negate specific intent often presumed that every specific intent crime contained a lesser included general intent crime. Thus, the category of "specific intent crimes" was often limited to compound crimes, involving the commission of one crime with the intent of committing another. "General intent crimes" did not require an intention to cause a secondary harm. On this view, any mental impairment — whether based on voluntary intoxication or insanity — negates only "specific intent," then intoxication can only mitigate liability, not eliminate it.

3. How rigorous a standard of "mental disease or defect" must a court apply in admitting psychological evidence offered to negate an element of the offense? In United States v. Bright, 517 F.2d 584 (2d Cir. 1975), the defendant was charged with unlawful possession of stolen checks "knowing the same to have been stolen." 18 U.S.C. §1708. Bright admitted that she had possessed welfare checks stolen from the mail. She said that she had cashed them for a man named Scott, who was an acquaintance of her "boyfriend," after Scott told her he had received the checks in payment of debts owed him but that he had no bank account of his own. She claimed that out of naivete she believed everything Scott told her was true. The defense sought to introduce the testimony of a psychiatrist that though Bright suffered no clinically defined mental illness, she had a "dependent, childlike character" and that she "unconsciously 'needed' to believe" that she could trust the word of men. In effect, her "passive dependent personality" required her to deny the possibility that her male friends would deceive her, and thus she did not truly believe or "know" that the checks were stolen. The appellate court upheld the trial judge's refusal to admit this evidence.

Did the court unfairly exclude logically relevant evidence? Was the problem with the evidence that Bright's personality was irrelevant to judging the credibility of her claim that she believed Scott, or was it that it invades the jury's function to have a psychiatrist offer a conclusion on the credibility of a witness?

4. That a defendant is delusional seems relevant to the judgment whether a defendant knew of a fact or a risk. Thus it seems plausible to claim that insanity can diminish one's capacity to act knowingly or recklessly. But can insanity similarly diminish one's capacity to act *negligently?* Rather than describing a mental state, negligence calls for a moral judgment as to what a person in defendant's situation should have known, or taken the trouble to learn. If we conclude that a particular defendant should not have been expected to act reasonably because of a mental impairment, are we just saying that her mental condition diminishes her responsibility?

5. *Voluntary intoxication.* Are you persuaded by the Colorado court's distinction between voluntary intoxication and mental disease as causes of inca-

pacity to harbor mens rea? Is it necessarily negligent or reckless to become intoxicated? Even if it is, can we also equate voluntary intoxication with *knowledge* that one will cause harm, as this court seems to? Compare *Hendershott* to the following case.

STATE v. CAMERON
Supreme Court of New Jersey
104 N.J. 42, 514 A.2d 1302 (1986)

CLIFFORD, J.

This appeal presents a narrow, but important, issue concerning the role that a defendant's voluntary intoxication plays in a criminal prosecution. The specific question is whether the evidence was sufficient to require the trial court to charge the jury on defendant's intoxication, as defendant requested. The Appellate Division reversed defendant's convictions, holding that it was error not to have given an intoxication charge. We . . . now reverse.

Defendant, Michele Cameron, age 22 at the time of trial, was indicted for second degree aggravated assault, in violation of N.J.S.A. 2C:12-1(b)(1); possession of a weapon, a broken bottle, with a purpose to use it unlawfully, contrary to N.J.S.A. 2C:39-4(d); and fourth degree resisting arrest, a violation of N.J.S.A. 2C:29-2. A jury convicted defendant of all charges. . . . The charges arose out of an incident of June 6, 1981, on a vacant lot in Trenton. The unreported opinion of the Appellate Division depicts the following tableau of significant events:

The victim, Joseph McKinney, was playing cards with four other men. Defendant approached and disrupted the game with her conduct. The participants moved their card table to a new location within the lot. Defendant followed them, however, and overturned the table. The table was righted and the game resumed. Shortly thereafter, defendant attacked McKinney with a broken bottle. As a result of that attack he sustained an injury to his hand, which necessitated 36 stitches and caused permanent injury.

Defendant reacted with violence to the arrival of the police. She threw a bottle at their vehicle, shouted obscenities, and tried to fight them off. She had to be restrained and handcuffed in the police wagon.

The heart of the Appellate Division's reversal of defendant's conviction is found in its determination that voluntary intoxication is a defense when it negates an essential element of the offense — here, purposeful conduct. We agree with that proposition. Likewise are we in accord with the determinations of the court below that all three of the charges of which this defendant was convicted — aggravated assault, the possession offense, and resisting arrest — have purposeful conduct as an element of the offense; and that a person acts purposely "with respect to the nature of his conduct or a result thereof if it is his conscious object to engage in conduct of that nature or to cause such a result" (quoting N.J.S.A. 2C:2-2(b)(1)). We part company with the Appellate Division, however, in its conclusion that the circumstances disclosed by the evidence in this case required that the issue of defendant's intoxication be submitted to the jury. . . .

Under the common law intoxication was not a defense to a criminal charge. . . . Notwithstanding the general proposition that voluntary intoxication is no defense, the early cases nevertheless held that in some circumstances intoxication could be resorted to for defensive purposes — specifically, to show the absence of a specific intent.

The exceptional immunity extended to the drunkard is limited to those instances where the crime involves a specific, actual intent. When the degree of intoxication is such as to render the person incapable of entertaining such intent, it is an effective defence. If it falls short of this it is worthless. [Warner v. State, *supra*, 56 N.J. L. at 686, 690, 29 A. 505 (1894).]

The principle that developed from the foregoing approach — that intoxication formed the basis for a defense to a "specific intent" crime but not to one involving only "general" intent — persisted for about three-quarters of a century. See, e.g., State v. Mack, 90 A. 1120 (E.&A. 1914) ("if defendant was so intoxicated or in such a condition of mind because he was getting over a debauch that his faculties were prostrated and rendered him incapable of forming a specific intent to kill with . . . willful, deliberate and premeditated character, then although it is no defence or justification, his offence would be murder in the second degree"). . . .

Eventually the problems inherent in the application of the specific-general intent dichotomy surfaced. In State v. Maik [60 N.J. 203, 287 A.2d 715 (1972)], this Court dwelt on the elusiveness of the distinction between "specific" and "general" intent crimes, particularly as that distinction determined what role voluntary intoxication played in a criminal prosecution. . . .

Which brings us to the Code. N.J.S.A. 2C:2-8 provided:

a. Except as provided in subsection d. of this section, intoxication of the actor is not a defense unless it negatives an element of the offense.
b. When recklessness establishes an element of the offense, if the actor, due to self-induced intoxication, is unaware of a risk of which he would have been aware had he been sober, such unawareness is immaterial.
c. Intoxication does not, in itself, constitute mental disease within the meaning of chapter 4.
d. Intoxication which (1) is not self-induced . . . is an affiirmative defense if by reason of such intoxication the actor at the time of his conduct lacks substantial and adequate capacity either to appreciate its wrongfulness or to conform his conduct to the requirement of the law. . . .

As is readily apparent, self-induced intoxication is not a defense unless it negatives an element of the offense. Code Commentary at 67-68. Under the common-law intoxication defense, as construed by the Commission, intoxication could either exculpate or mitigate guilt "if the defendant's intoxication, in fact, prevents his having formed a mental state which is an element of the offense and if the law will recognize the proof of the lack of that mental state." Thus, the Commission recognized that under pre-Code law, intoxication was admissible as a defense to a "specific" intent, but not a "general" intent, crime.

The original proposed Code rejected the specific/general intent distinction, choosing to rely instead on the reference to the four states of culpability for offenses under the Code: negligent, reckless, knowing, and purposeful conduct, N.J.S.A. 2C:2-2(b). Although the Code employs terminology that differs from that used to articulate the common-law principles referable to intoxication, the Commission concluded that the ultimately enacted statutory intoxication defense would achieve the same result as that reached under the common law. In essence, "[t]hat which the cases now describe as a 'specific intent' can be equated, for this purpose, with that which the Code defines as 'purpose' and 'knowledge.' See §2C:2-2b. A 'general intent' can be equated with that which the Code defines as 'recklessness,' or criminal 'negligence.'" Code Commentary at 68. Therefore, according to the Commissioners, N.J.S.A. 2C:2-8(a) and (b) would serve much the same end as was achieved by the common-law approach. Specifically, N.J.S.A. 2C:2-8(a) permits evidence of intoxication as a defense to crimes requiring either "purposeful" or "knowing" mental states but it excludes evidence of intoxication as a defense to crimes requiring mental states of only recklessness or negligence. N.J.S.A. 2C:2-8 was modeled after the Model Penal Code (MPC) §2.08. The drafters of the MPC, as did the New Jersey Commission, criticized the specific-general intent distinction.

The policy reasons for requiring purpose or knowledge as a requisite element of some crimes are that in the absence of those states of mind, the criminal conduct would not present a comparable danger, or the actor would not pose as significant a threat. Moreover, the ends of legal policy are better served by subjecting to graver sanctions those who consciously defy legal norms. It was those policy reasons that dictated the result that the intoxication defense should be available when it negatives purpose or knowledge. The drafters [of the Model Penal Code] concluded: "If the mental state which is the basis of the law's concern does not exist, the reason for its non-existence is quite plainly immaterial." Id. at 358.

Thus, when the requisite culpability for a crime is that the person act "purposely" or "knowingly," evidence of voluntary intoxication is admissible to disprove that requisite mental state. . . .

The foregoing discussion establishes that proof of voluntary intoxication would negate the culpability elements in the offenses of which this defendant was convicted. The charges — aggravated assault, possession of a weapon with a purpose to use it unlawfully, and resisting arrest — all require purposeful conduct (aggravated assault uses "purposely" or "knowingly" in the alternative). The question is what level of intoxication must be demonstrated before a trial court is required to submit the issue to a jury. What quantum of proof is required?

The guiding principle is simple enough of articulation. . . . See State v. Stasio [396 A.2d 1143 (1979)]:

> [I]t is not the case that every defendant who has had a few drinks may successfully urge the defense. . . . What is required is a showing of such a great prostration of the faculties that the requisite mental state was totally lacking. That is, to successfully invoke the defense, an accused must show that he was so intoxicated that he did not have the intent to commit an offense. Such a state of affairs will likely exist in very few cases. [396 A.2d 1129 (Pashman, J., concurring and dissenting).] . . .

Measured by the foregoing standard, it is apparent that the record in this case is insufficient to have required the trial court to grant defendant's request to charge intoxication. . . .

True, the victim testified that defendant was drunk, and defendant herself said she felt "pretty intoxicated," "pretty bad," and "very intoxicated." But these are no more than conclusory labels, of little assistance in determining whether any drinking produced a prostration of faculties.

More to the point is the fact that defendant carried a quart of wine, that she was drinking (we are not told over what period of time) with other people on the vacant lot, that about a pint of the wine was consumed, and that defendant did not drink this alone but rather "gave most of it out, gave some of it out." Defendant's conduct was violent, abusive, and threatening. But with it all there is not the slightest suggestion that she did not know what she was doing or that her faculties were so beclouded by the wine that she was incapable of engaging in purposeful conduct. That the purpose of the conduct may have been bizarre, even violent, is not the test. The critical question is whether defendant was capable of forming that bizarre or violent purpose, and we do not find sufficient evidence to permit a jury to say she was not.

Defendant's own testimony, if believed, would furnish a basis for her actions. She said she acted in self-defense, to ward off a sexual attack by McKinney and others. She recited the details of that attack and of her reaction to it with full recall and in explicit detail, explaining that her abuse of the police officers was sparked by her being upset by their unfairness in locking her up rather than apprehending McKinney.

Ordinarily, of course, the question of whether a defendant's asserted intoxication satisfies the standards enunciated in this opinion should be resolved by the jury. But here, viewing the evidence and the legitimate inferences to be drawn therefrom in the light most favorable to defendant, . . . there is no suggestion . . . that defendant's faculties were so prostrated by her consumption of something less than a pint of wine as to render her incapable of purposeful or knowing conduct. The trial court correctly refused defendant's request. . . .

Notes and Questions

1. *The Model Penal Code.* As the court mentions in *Cameron,* the Model Penal Code rejects the specific/general intent distinction. Instead, the Code, like the New Jersey statute, allows consideration of evidence of intoxication only to negate certain levels of culpability:

Section 2.08. Intoxication

(1) [Voluntary] intoxication of the actor is not a defense unless it negatives an element of the offense.
(2) When recklessness establishes an element of the offense, if the actor, due to self-induced intoxication, is unaware of a risk of which he would have been aware had he been sober, such unawareness is immaterial.

In State v. Warren, 518 A.2d 218 (N.J. 1986), the court stated that, "[a]s a matter of logic, intoxication that negates purpose or knowledge should also negate recklessness. . . . As a matter of policy, however, the drafters of the Code concluded that intoxication should not exonerate a defendant from crimes involving recklessness." What is this policy? The *Cameron* court notes that allowing an intoxication defense to apply only to purpose or knowledge crimes will yield substantially the same result as allowing the defense to apply only to specific intent crimes. Is the policy behind subsection (2) of the Code the same as the policy behind the specific/general intent distinction? Does subsection (2) say that anyone who voluntarily becomes intoxicated is reckless as to the consequences, or is it an exception to subsection (1)?

MONTANA v. EGELHOFF
Supreme Court of the United States
518 U.S. 37 (1996)

[Defendant's conviction for "purposely or knowingly" causing death was overturned by the Montana Supreme Court on the ground that the jury had been instructed, pursuant to Mont. Code Ann. §45-2-203, that respondent's "intoxicated condition" could not be considered "in determining the existence of a mental state which is an element of the offense." The Montana Supreme Court held intoxication relevant to the mental element of the charged offense and struck down §45-2-203 as violating defendant's due process right to present evidence relevant to an essential element of the offense. The United States Supreme Court reversed. Justice O'Connor, in a 4-justice plurality, took the view that excluding evidence relevant to the mental element of an offense violated due process by presuming culpability rather than innocence. Justice Scalia, with three others, took the view that a state could indeed exclude exculpatory evidence relevant to mens rea. Here is Justice Ginsburg's controlling "swing" opinion:]

JUSTICE GINSBURG, concurring in the judgment: The Court divides in this case on a question of characterization. The State's law, Mont. Code Ann. §45-2-203 (1995), prescribes that voluntary intoxication "may not be taken into consideration in determining the existence of a mental state which is an element of [a criminal] offense." For measurement against federal restraints on state action, how should we type that prescription? If §45-2-203 is simply a rule designed to keep out "relevant, exculpatory evidence," Justice O'Connor maintains, Montana's law offends due process. If it is, instead, a redefinition of the mental state element of the offense, on the other hand, Justice O'Connor's due process concern "would not be at issue," for "[a] state legislature certainly has the authority to identify the elements of the offenses it wishes to punish," and to exclude evidence irrelevant to the crime it has defined.

Beneath the labels (rule excluding evidence or redefinition of the offense) lies the essential question: Can a State, without offense to the Federal Constitution, make the judgment that two people are equally culpable where one commits an act stone sober, and the other engages in the same conduct after his voluntary intoxication has reduced his capacity for self-control? For the reasons that follow, I resist categorizing §45-2-203 as merely an evidentiary prescription, but join the Court's judgment refusing to condemn the Montana statute as an unconstitutional enactment.

Section 45-2-203 does not appear in the portion of Montana's Code containing evidentiary rules (Title 26), the expected placement of a provision regulating solely the admissibility of evidence at trial. Instead, Montana's intoxication statute appears in Title 45 ("Crimes"), as part of a chapter entitled "General Principles of Liability." No less than adjacent provisions governing duress and entrapment, §45-2-203 embodies a legislative judgment regarding the circumstances under which individuals may be held criminally responsible for their actions.

As urged by Montana and its amici, §45-2-203 "extract[s] the entire subject of voluntary intoxication from the mens rea inquiry," thereby rendering evidence of voluntary intoxication logically irrelevant to proof of the requisite mental state. Thus, in a prosecution for deliberate homicide, the State need not prove that the defendant "purposely or knowingly caused the death of another," in a purely subjective sense. To obtain a conviction, the prosecution must prove only that (1) the defendant caused the death of another with actual knowledge or purpose, or (2) that the defendant killed "under circumstances that would otherwise establish knowledge or purpose 'but for' [the defendant's] voluntary intoxication." Accordingly, §45-2-203 does not "lighten the prosecution's burden to prove [the] mental state element beyond a reasonable doubt," as Justice O'Connor suggests, for "the applicability of the reasonable-doubt standard . . . has always been dependent on how a State defines the offense that is charged," Patterson v. New York, 432 U.S. 197 (1977).

Comprehended as a measure redefining mens rea, §45-2-203 encounters no constitutional shoal. States enjoy wide latitude in defining the elements of criminal offenses, see, e.g., Martin v. Ohio, 480 U.S. 228 (1987), Patterson, 432 U.S. at 201-02. . . . When a State's power to define criminal conduct is challenged under the Due Process Clause, we inquire only whether the law "offends some principle of justice so rooted in the traditions and conscience of our people as to be ranked as fundamental." Patterson, 432 U.S. at 202. Defining mens rea to eliminate the exculpatory value of voluntary intoxication does not offend a "fundamental principle of justice," given the lengthy common-law tradition, and the adherence of a significant minority of the States to that position today. . . . Other state courts have upheld statutes similar to §45-2-203, not simply as evidentiary rules, but as legislative redefinitions of the mental-state element. Legislation of this order, if constitutional in Arizona, Hawaii, and Pennsylvania, ought not be declared unconstitutional by this Court when enacted in Montana.

If, as . . . Justice O'Connor . . . agree[s], it is within the legislature's province to instruct courts to treat a sober person and a voluntarily intoxicated person as equally responsible for conduct — to place a voluntarily intoxicated person on a level with a sober person — then the Montana law is no less tenable under the Federal Constitution than are the laws, with no significant difference in wording, upheld in sister States. The Montana Supreme Court did not disagree with the courts of other States; it simply did not undertake an analysis in line with the principle that legislative enactments plainly capable of a constitutional construction ordinarily should be given that construction. The Montana Supreme Court's judgment, in sum, strikes down a statute whose text displays no constitutional infirmity. . . .

Notes and Questions

1. Justice Ginsburg writes, "Beneath the labels . . . lies the essential question: Can a State, without offense to the Federal Constitution, make the judgment that two people are equally culpable where one commits an act stone sober, and the other engages in the same conduct after his voluntary intoxication has reduced his capacity for self-control?" Is this the "essential" question, or do the labels matter? Is the essential question whether Montana *did* define intoxication as a mental element of murder, not whether they could have? Should the U.S. Supreme Court accept the Montana Supreme Court's answer to this question?

2. What exactly is the mental element of murder in Montana, according to Justice Ginsburg? Is it: (1) Causing death *knowingly, purposely or in a state of voluntary intoxication?* (2) Causing death *knowingly, purposely or because voluntary intoxication has reduced [defendant's] capacity for self-control?* (3) Causing death

knowingly or purposely, including when voluntary intoxication has reduced defendant's capacity for self-control? (4) Causing death *with actual knowledge or purpose, or under circumstances that would otherwise establish knowledge or purpose but for [the defendant's] voluntary intoxication?* Can you tell what this latter standard means?

Try applying these standards to the following three hypotheticals, suggested by Professor Ronald Allen in a critique of Justice Ginsburg's opinion:[45] (1) A drunk person is driving a car, blacks out, and runs over somebody. (2) A drunk person is in a bar with a gun in his waistband. He trips and falls; the gun goes off killing somebody. (3) A drunk person in a bar pulls out a gun and jokingly points it at someone else. The gun goes off, killing the other person. The perpetrator did not intend to shoot and does not know whether he pulled the trigger.

Try drafting mental element language, to go in a statute or jury instruction, that excludes evidence of voluntary intoxication but that acquits in these three cases.

45. Ronald J. Allen, Foreword: Montana v. Egelhoff — Reflections on the Limits of Legislative Imagination and Judicial Authority, 87 J. Crim. L. & Criminology 633, 638 (1997).

4

CAUSATION

We saw in Chapter 2 that a criminal act is a basic constituent of liability. Together with its corresponding mental element (see Chapter 3), the criminal act defines the offense that the prosecution is constitutionally required to prove. The principle that the conduct element of an offense must involve a criminal act may connote a number of different ideas: that the act be legislatively proscribed, or that it manifest a bad purpose, or that it cause harm.

The causation of some harmful consequence is part of the act element of many offenses, though not of all. Conversely, the act element of many crimes consists *only* in the causing of some result. Thus, the act element of most crimes of homicide is simply the causing of a person's death.

Conditioning liability on causing a result raises two large questions: *Why* punish causation? And *what is* causation?

It is not self-evident why we should ever condition punishment on the causing of harm. As we saw in Chapter 3, since the late eighteenth century, criminal liability has increasingly been conditioned on the proof of culpable mental states. Should not a culpable mental state, manifested by some act, be enough for liability? If Marcia tried to cause harm, why should her liability depend on whether she was lucky enough to succeed? If we know that George recklessly ran over a bicyclist, what moral difference does it make that the bicyclist miraculously escaped injury?

One common sense answer is that harm seems tangible, a matter of indisputable fact. But while harm itself may be a brute fact, causal responsibility for harm certainly is not. Consider this scenario: Joe, a liquor store clerk, is killed by Lewis in a robbery. Lewis was conceived at 11:06 P.M., Nov. 18, 1974. If anything had been different — if Lewis's parents had conceived a child earlier or later or not at all, or under slightly different circumstances — Lewis probably would not have existed to kill Joe. So the antecedent conditions for any result are infinite, stretching back in time through endless chains of circumstance. Large and tragic consequences turn on countless natural occurrences and human decisions that seem unimportant at the time. Yet common sense tells us that we cannot count all of these as causes. Perhaps Lewis's parents bear some responsibility for raising an armed robber — but we would not describe the conception of Lewis as the killing of Joe, any more than we would describe the conception of

Joe as the killing of Joe. Yet both were necessary conditions to Joe's death, but for which the death would not have occurred.

Probably the time and circumstances of most deaths are affected by human decisions. But the law singles out a small number of deaths as homicides, deaths that are "caused" by human action. This attribution of causal responsibility is a normative judgment. The chief question of this chapter is by what normative criteria that judgment should be made.

This chapter reviews five strategies for limiting causation.

1. *But-for causation.* Criminal law generally confines causes to the class of necessary conditions or acts "but for" which the harmful result would not have occurred. An exception is often made for simultaneous sufficient conditions, as when two assailants simultaneously shoot a victim. These rules are sometimes said to define "factual" causation, as opposed to the additional limitations that are said to define the artificial concept of "legal" causation.

2. *Violent acts.* The common law of crimes was originally concerned primarily with suppressing conspicuous violence. As a result, necessary conditions for a harmful result were only perceived as criminal if they appeared violent — most often, blows aimed at hurting or injuring. Gradually, this category was expanded to include other acts judged to be dangerous, and so this limitation tended to be replaced by the following one.

3. *Foreseeability.* A relatively contemporary limitation on legal causation, borrowed from tort law, requires a connection between the actor's culpable mental state and the result. For example, if defendant is charged with recklessly causing injury, the injury resulting from defendant's reckless action must be one she "foresaw," in order for us to conclude that her recklessness "caused" it, and negligent action "causes" harm only if it leads to harm that is reasonably "foreseeable." This *psychological* conception of causation as a function of culpable mental states is often referred to as "proximate causation," although this term sometimes refers to other standards.

4. *Intervening events.* The common law traditionally absolved defendants of causal responsibility for creating a necessary condition for harm if it could identify an "intervening" event that "broke the chain" of direct causation. Generally an event might be said to "break the chain of causation" if it was a necessary condition for the harmful result, subsequent to defendant's act, and not caused by defendant's act. The notion that such an "intervening" event breaks the chain of causation is inconsistent with a foreseeability standard, which would dictate that if the actor could have foreseen the "intervening" event she is responsible for creating a condition necessary for the intervening event to cause harm. Rather than distinguish between foreseeable and unforeseeable intervening events, the common law developed categorical rules that the link between necessary conditions and results would be severed by "intervening actions" and long intervals of time.

(a) *Intervening voluntary actions.* Premised on free will, the common law generally assumed that individuals were the exclusive cause of their own actions. Hence, providing the necessary means for another person to do harm was not to cause the harm oneself (although it might make one complicit in the other person's act of causing harm).

(b) *Temporal intervals.* A lengthy interval between cause and result raises a number of problems. First, the longer the interval, the more plausible it becomes that but for defendant's action the victim might have suffered some other misfortune. Second, the longer the interval, the more plausible it becomes that some other undetected factor has caused the result. For these and other reasons, the common law traditionally limited the time period within which necessary conditions could legally cause a result. But as the *Rogers* case in Chapter 2 revealed, advancing medical knowledge has caused most jurisdictions to abandon such limits.

A necessary condition to a resulting harm, particularly a violent blow, if not superseded by an intervening event, is often referred to as a "direct cause."

5. *Duties.* As we saw in Chapter 2, passive conduct can "cause" harm. Theoretically we could all be liable for any harm we might have prevented with more diligent investigation and more energetic action. Any such omission is a necessary condition to the harmful result. But it is not a sufficient one, because criminal law generally limits the causal responsibility of omitters to those who have some duty to act, resulting from statute, status, contract, or undertaking. Thus, where passive conduct is a necessary condition for a result, it must be combined with a duty to act to constitute a cause.

As we shall see, proximate cause standards, direct cause standards, and the ascription of causal responsibility on the basis of duty to act may yield quite different outcomes in a given case. The criminal law's criteria of causation all turn on such normative issues as what states of affairs should be regretted as unfortunate, when an actor should have foreseen a result, to which of two contributing actors a misfortune should be attributed, or who has a duty to prevent harm. Thus, at the most basic level, our two original questions (What is causation? Why punish it?) are answered the same way: Causation of harm is actually a normative conclusion that, absent justifying conditions, defendant has wronged someone.

A. "BUT FOR" CAUSATION

REGINA v. MARTIN DYOS
Central Criminal Court
Crim. L. Rev. 660-62 (1979)

CANTLEY, J.

A Friday night dance at a Community Center was attended by a group of seven youths. The deceased, RM, was one of these as was also SK who at one stage danced near two girls — "he was cocky and showing off."

The boyfriend, BT, of one of the girls was incensed by this; when the seven left shortly before the end of the dance he encouraged the four friends with him to follow to "give us a hand."

At the exit to the dance hall there was some general abuse and threats directed at SK.

The seven went towards the railway station to find a taxi; the five followed at a distance continuing their abuse and threats. When the seven crossed the road the five followed, and were by now closing up.

One of the five, MD, and possibly others, were seen to pick up stones/bricks and throw them. One stone thrown by MD hit PS, one of the seven, on the back of the head. Momentarily stunned, he turned, took off his jacket, challenged the five, advanced, and hit BT.

This immediately turned into a scuffle or fight involving for certain PS, SK, MB, and RM from the seven and BT, IS, and KW of the five. The fight lasted no more than a minute or so as RM was spotted lying in the road by his twin brother GM, bleeding from severe head injuries — whereupon the five fled and emergency services was called.

One of RM's injuries, that to his right forehead, was caused by a brick held by MD. What had happened, in MD's own words to the police was this:

> Matey threw a punch at me and I ran away . . . I was hit in back by brick as I was going to jump on wall . . . I picked up a brick and started towards one I thought had chucked brick at me . . . [H]e started to run and I went to throw it but I was running and I hit him before I could let it go. I misjudged the distance.

RM survived nine days before succumbing to his injuries; in the meantime all involved were questioned. No evidence was offered against any of the seven; all of the five were indicted with unlawful assembly to which they pleaded guilty, affray which they all denied, MD alone being charged with murder and grievous bodily harm . . . to RM.

At the post mortem it was found that apart from a very few slight marks on the right hand side of the body, legs, and arms, all the injuries were confined to the head, of which the two principal were the one caused by MD to the right forehead and one behind the right ear for which there was no evidence as to the cause.

As to the cause of death the following is a summary of the pathologist's conclusions:

1. The cause of death was cerebral contusion due to a fractured skull.
2. RM received two or more separate blows. There was no evidence as to whether they were caused by the same or different objects, be it metal, wood, masonry, and/or a shod foot.
3. Both principal wounds were potentially fatal.
4. No distinction was made as to the seriousness of either wound.
5. Either wound would "very probably" cause death.
6. There was no certain way of telling which injury came first.
7. There was a "reasonable and sensible" possibility that the deceased might have recovered from the first injury, whichever that was.

In addition to the medical evidence, there was no evidence as to how the second injury was caused, apart from speculation at the time of RM hitting one of the many passing vehicles or of his being swung around and thrown into the traffic. Likewise apart from traces of blood on at least one of the five's shoes (which probably came from kicking SK in the mouth) there was no evidence of blood being found on any blunt object, shoe, brick or kerb. Nor were there any traces of material such as the brick dust in the wounds.

The only evidence against MD was that he struck the one blow to the right forehead; and there was no evidence of joint enterprise as to either wound.

On the count of murder the trial judge upheld the defence submission at the close of the prosecution that it would be unsafe to leave the count to the jury.

These submissions were as follows:

The Crown had failed to prove that MD was responsible for the cause of death because,

(a) the pathologist's evidence was that it was a reasonable and sensible possibility that the injury behind the ear caused the death, and . . . there was no evidence that MD was responsible for it,

(b) and conversely there was no evidence that the injury which MD (admitted) having caused, was in fact beyond a reasonable doubt the cause of death. MD could only be guilty if death was a natural and probable consequence of his act.

Even if the forehead injury caused by MD was the first injury there was a reasonable and sensible possibility of recovery.

MD's act cannot be held to be the cause of death if that even would or could have occurred without it.

Before the count of murder could go to the jury the Crown had to exclude the possibility . . . that death was not caused by another injury.

It was conceded by the defence that if as a result of what MD did the Crown could show, e.g., that RM was struck by a passing car, then MD's act would have been a substantial cause of death. There was no evidence of this (and in fact the Crown sought to exclude this possibility).

If the ear injury was caused by a brick and that was the cause of death (and the pathologist said both were reasonable possibilities) there was no evidence that MD (or anyone else) did it.

Therefore, in sum:

(1) there was another injury

(2) that injury may reasonably have been the cause of death

(3) that injury cannot be shewn not to have been the cause of death. . . .

After the judge's ruling MD changed his plea to guilty on Count 1 (affray) and Count 4 (grievous bodily harm). . . .

Notes and Questions

1. Certainly MD's action *could have* caused the death. Why should it make a difference whether or not it actually did? That issue has nothing to do with the moral guilt of the defendant, does it? The comments to Model Penal Code section 2.03 defend the causation requirement as follows:[1]

How far the penal law ought to attribute importance in the grading of offenses to the actual result of conduct, as opposed to results attempted or threatened, presents a significant and difficult issue. Distinctions of this sort are essential, at least when severe sanctions are involved, for it cannot be expected that jurors will lightly return verdicts leading to severe sentences in the absence of the resentments aroused by the infliction of serious injuries. Whatever abstract logic may suggest, a prudent legislator cannot disregard these facts in the enactment of a penal code.

Is this the best defense of the requirement of causation that one can make?

1. American Law Institute, Model Penal Code and Commentaries, Part I, at 257 (1985).

2. *Necessary conditions and simultaneous sufficient conditions.* Philosophers have debated for centuries about what we mean by "cause." One way of looking at the matter is to regard the question of whether one event caused another as involving a "thought experiment." To do this, we attempt to envision the world as it would have been if everything had been the same but the allegedly causal event had not occurred. If, in that hypothetical situation, the alleged result would have occurred anyway, we can say that the first event did not cause the second. On the other hand, if, in our hypothetical world, the second event, which is alleged to be the result, would not have occurred, then we can say that the first event was a cause of the second.

A crucial point here is that under this kind of broad definition of cause, every event has many, many causes — the vast majority of which are uninteresting from our point of view. As a result, it simply is not an argument to say that event *A* did not cause a result because event *B* did. Since an event may have many causes, the specification of one does not in any way eliminate others.

Professor Glanville Williams has explained the requirement of but-for causation in the following dialogue:[2]

> *Surely the notion of but-for causation is ridiculously wide, because it takes us back to Adam and Eve. The criminal's mother is a but-for cause of his crimes, and so is his grandmother, and all his ancestors to infinity.*

That is perfectly true, but two factors limit the judicial inquiry. First, one starts with the defendant who is charged; his mother does not come into it, much less Adam and Eve. Secondly, but-for causation is only half the story; the defendant who was the but-for cause of the harm is not responsible unless his conduct was also the imputable cause. We still have to deal with imputable causation. . . .

> *What about two but-for causes contributed by different defendants? Doesn't your definition imply the paradox that if two persons independently cause an event, neither causes it?*

To provide for this, an exception for cases of multiple causation has to be inserted into the definition. It is possible for two sufficient causes, C1 and C2, to be present together, so that E follows both, when usually it follows only one or the other. Both C1 and C2 are causes, even though in the particular situation one or other (as the case may be) was not necessary to be present. An example is where two fatal wounds are given independently at the same time. . . .

> *Suppose that D1's shot entered the lung and would have caused the victim's death in an hour, but D2's entered the heart and killed him instantaneously?*

Then, of course, only D2 has killed him. D1 is guilty of an attempt.

The but-for cause is sometimes referred to as the factual cause, or the de facto cause, or the scientific cause. The important thing is to distinguish it from cause in another sense, "imputable" (or "legal" or "effective" or "direct" or "proximate") cause. . . .

Does the Martin Dyos case provide an example of two independent but simultaneous sufficient conditions for death? Why is not MD guilty?

---

2. Textbook of Criminal Law 379-81 (1983).

3. *Problems with "but-for" causes.* If the cause of death includes any act, "but for" which death would have occurred later, we can get some strange results. For example, in 1993, prosecutors in Los Angeles decided to charge a rapist with murder in the death, from heart disease and pneumonia, of his 79-year-old victim, one month after the attack. Prosecutors conceded that Mary Lee Ward did not die as a result of physical injuries suffered during the attack, but they claimed that the brutal rape robbed the sickly victim, who also suffered from lung cancer, of her "will-to-live." The district attorney was quoted as saying that "but for the rape, she would have lived more than one month."[3] In 1994 in Buffalo, New York, 71-year-old Eleanor Szablicki suffered a fatal heart attack after discovering that burglars had ransacked her home of 48 years while she was away. The medical examiner ruled the death a homicide.[4] In Oklahoma City in 1984, 67-year-old Mildred Pruner, who suffered a fatal heart attack in court as she described how she was robbed at gunpoint, was ruled a homicide victim by Oklahoma's chief medical examiner.[5] Did the rapist "kill" Ward? Did the burglar "kill" Szablicki? Did the robber "kill" Pruner? If not, why not?

Or, consider the following hypothetical posed by Professor Leo Katz:[6]

> Henri plans a trek through the desert. Alphonse, intending to kill Henri, puts poison into his canteen. Gaston also intends to kill Henri but has no idea what Alphonse has been up to. He punctures Henri's canteen and Henri dies of thirst. Who has caused Henri's death? Was it Alphonse? How could it be, since Henri never swallowed the poison. Was it Gaston? How could it be, since he only deprived Henri of some poisoned water that would have killed him more swiftly even than thirst. Was it neither then? But if neither had done anything, Henri would still be alive. So who killed Henri?

Notice that neither Alphonse's nor Gaston's act appears to be a but-for cause of Henri's death, and that Gaston, whose act leads more directly to Henri's death, actually prolongs his life. How would Williams resolve this case?

Katz points to another difficulty with but-for causation:[7]

> Suppose we know that A caused B and B caused C. Then we can conclude that A caused C. Causation, logicians would say, is transitive. Now suppose we know that if A had not happened, B would not have happened, and if B had not happened C would not have happened. Still, we cannot infer that if A had not happened C would not have happened. The "but for" relationship is not transitive and hence is not the same thing as causation. . . . It may be true that "If Kennedy had not been president, he would not have been killed." It may also be true that "If Kennedy had not been killed, he would have been reelected." But that does not imply that "If Kennedy had not been President he would have been reelected." . . .
>
> You may remember that [in Frank Capra's movie *It's a Wonderful Life*] . . . , some money disappears and drives the Jimmy Stewart character, George Bailey, close to suicide. It drives him to suicide because he doesn't appreciate the intransitivity of the "but for" relationship. He reasons thus: If he had never been born, that money

3. Los Angeles Times, Mar. 21, 1993, at B1.
4. Woman's Fatal Heart Attack Ends Story Filled With Irony, Buffalo News, Nov. 29, 1994, City Edition, at 1.
5. Witness's Fatal Heart Attack in Court Is Ruled Homicide, San Jose Mercury News, May 25, 1984, at 6A.
6. Leo Katz, Bad Acts and Guilty Minds: Conundrums of the Criminal Law 210 (1987).
7. Id. at 234.

would never have disappeared. (That's probably true.) If the money had not disappeared, a lot of people would be a lot happier, namely his wife, his brother, his uncle, his friends, and his customers. (That, too, is probably true.) From this, he incorrectly concludes that if he had never been born, a lot of people would be a lot happier. It takes Clarence, the Angel Second Class, to convince him of the fallacy of his reasoning by showing him what the world would look like if he had never been born: his wife would have [been lonely and loveless] . . . , his brother would have drowned, his uncle would have gone mad, his former employer would have gone to jail, his customers would not have gotten loans, and so on. What Clarence shows George Bailey is that the "but for" relationship is not transitive.

Many contemporary philosophers refer to "but-for" causes as mere "causal conditions" rather than "causes." While there may be infinitely many "causal conditions" for a result, there can be only one cause. Richard Taylor explains:[8]

According to the . . . widely held conception, a causal condition of an event is any sine qua non condition under which that event occurred or any condition which was such that, had the condition not obtained, that event (its effect) would not have occurred, and the cause of that event is the totality of those conditions. If this is so . . . then it at once follows that the cause — that is, the totality of those necessary conditions — is also sufficient for the occurrence of the event in question. Once one has enumerated all the conditions necessary for the occurrence of a given event, that totality of conditions will at once be sufficient for its occurrence [because] . . . no further conditions will be necessary.

Notice that Taylor's conception of causation as the entire set of conditions necessary to bring about a result solves the transitivity problem pointed out by Katz. But if "the cause" of a result is the set of all its necessary conditions, can any human action ever be "the cause" of harm? Is this an adequate or useful conception of causation for the criminal law?

4. *Legal causation.* Probably the most influential work on legal causation is that of H.L.A. Hart & A.M. Honoré, who argue that but-for causation does not accord with common sense or ordinary use of the term "cause." They argue that ordinary use places further limits on causation. Thus they object to the characterization of but-for causation as "factual" or "scientific" causation, and the characterization of all further limitations as the expression of a specialized "legal" conception of causation.[9]

. . . [T]he view that whenever a man is murdered with a gun his death was the consequence of . . . the manufacturer of the bullet . . . introduces an unfamiliar, though, of course, a possible way of speaking about familiar events. It is not that this unrestricted use of "consequence" is unintelligible or never found; it is indeed used to refer to bizarre or fortuitous connections or coincidences: but the point is that the various causal notions employed for the purposes of explanation, attribution of responsibility or the assessment of contributions to the course of history carry with them implicit limits. . . .

[T]he . . . proposition, defining consequence in terms of "necessary condition," . . . is the corollary of the view that, if we look into the past of any given event, there is an infinite number of events, each of which is a necessary condition of the given event and so, as much as any other, is its cause. This is the "cone" of

8. Richard Taylor, Causation, 2 Encyclopedia of Philosophy 63 (1967).
9. Causation and the Law 341 (1950).

causation, so called because, since any event has a number of simultaneous conditions, the series fans out as we go back in time. . . .

Legal theorists have developed this account of cause and consequence to show what is "factual," "objective," or "scientific" in these notions: this they call "cause in fact" and it is usually stressed as a preliminary to the doctrine that any more restricted application of these terms in the law represents nothing in the facts or in the meaning of causation, but expresses fluctuating legal policy or sentiments of what is just or convenient. Moral philosophers have insisted in somewhat similar terms that the consequences of human action are "infinite": this they have urged as an objection against the utilitarian doctrine that the rightness of a morally right action depends on whether its consequences are better than those of any alternative action in the circumstances. "We should have to trace as far as possible the consequences not only for the persons affected directly but also for those indirectly affected and to these no limit can be set." . . . Yet, . . . this objection seems to rest on a mistake as to the sense of "consequence." The utilitarian assertion that the rightness of an action depends on its consequences is not the same as the assertion that it depends on all those later occurrences which would not have happened had the action not been done, to which indeed "no limit can be set." . . .

[T]hough we could, we do not think in this way in tracing connections between human actions and events. Instead, whenever we are concerned with such connections, whether for the purpose of explaining a puzzling occurrence, assessing responsibility, or giving an intelligible historical narrative, we employ a set of concepts restricting in various ways what counts as a consequence. These restrictions colour all our thinking in causal terms; when we find them in the law we are not finding something invented by or peculiar to the law. . . .

No short account can be given of the limits thus placed on "consequences" because these limits vary, intelligibly, with the variety of causal connection asserted.

Thus we may be tempted by the generalization that consequences must always be something intended or foreseen or at least foreseeable with ordinary care: but counter-examples spring up from many . . . context[s] where causal statements are made. If smoking is shown to cause lung cancer, this discovery will permit us to describe past as well as future cases of cancer as the effect or consequence of smoking even though no one foresaw or had reasonable grounds to suspect this in the past. What is . . . foreseeable certainly controls the scope of consequences in certain varieties of causal statement but not in all. . . .

[T]he voluntary intervention of a second person very often constitutes the limit. If a guest sits down with a table laid with knife and fork and plunges the knife into his hostess's breast, her death is not in any context thought of as caused by, or the effect or result of, the waiter's action in laying the table; nor would it be linked with this action as its consequence for any of the purposes, explanatory or attributive, for which we employ causal notions. Yet . . . there are many other . . . case[s] where a voluntary action or the harm it does are naturally attributed to some prior neglect of precaution. . . .

Finally, we may think that a simple answer is already supplied by Hume and Mill's doctrine that causal connection rests on general laws asserting regular connection; yet, even in the type of case to which this important doctrine applies, reference to it alone will not solve our problem. For we often trace a causal connection between an antecedent and a consequent which themselves very rarely go together: we do this when the case can be broken down into intermediate stages, which themselves exemplify different generalizations, as when we find that the fall of a tile was the cause of someone's death, rare though this be. Here our problem reappears in the form of the question: When can generalizations be combined in this way?

Notice that Hart and Honoré mention three different ways of further limiting but-for causation: limiting causes to necessary conditions for a result (1) foreseeable by the actor, (2) achieved without the voluntary action of another, or (3) regularly following such a condition.

R. v. BENGE

Maidstone Crown Court

44 F. & F. 504 (1865)

The prosecution arose out of a fatal railway accident, which occurred on the South Eastern Railway at a place called Staplehurst, where there was a bridge, about two miles in the direction towards London from a station called Headcorn. The tidal trains of that day would be due at Staplehurst at 3:15 P.M., on Friday, the 9th of June. The prisoner Benge was foreman of a gang of plate-layers, who had been employed to repair the rails within a certain distance, including the portion of the line at Staplehurst, and for that purpose it would be necessary to take up and replace the rails. . . . The time at which the work was done at any part of the line was left to the direction of the prisoner Benge, as the foreman of the gang. And he was furnished with a time book, in which the precise time of the arrival of the various trains on each day was marked; for each week in columns headed by the name of the day of the week. . . . The hour of arrival of the tidal train varied of course with the tide, and was different on each day. And on the day in question the prisoner Benge had looked at the column for Saturday — the next day — instead of Friday, the 9th. The time of arrival on the Saturday would be 5:20 P.M.; whereas the time for Friday, the day in question, would be 3:15. Thinking that the time would be 5:20, the prisoner Benge, when the last of the trains before the tidal train had passed, which was at 2:50 P.M., directed his gang to take up the rails at Staplehurst bridge, and they were accordingly taken up. There was, it will be seen, barely half an hour between the time at which the 2:50 train passed, and the time — 3:15 — at which the tidal train would arrive; [while] . . . the job would . . . [require] about an hour. . . .

It was usual . . . to send on one of the gang as a signal man with a flag in his hand, who was to go on at least 1000 yards in the direction in which the expected train was to come, and when he had got that distance he was to stand and raise a flag when it appeared, which would be seen at a distance of above 500 yards, and thus would give a distance of 1500 yards, or nearly a mile, between the train and the spot at which the rails were up, so as to allow of ample time to stop the train. Books of printed rules were in the hands of the foreman of plate-layers, and among others, of the prisoner; and these rules expressly provided that rails should not be taken up without these precautions. On the occasion in question one of the men of the prisoner's gang, named Wills, was sent forward as signal man, . . . and instead of going 1000 yards he went, as he said, only 540 yards; and there he stood till he saw the advancing train, and moved his flag. He was observed, but not until the train was too near to be stopped. The engine-driver was not paying a very sharp look-out, and though so soon as he saw the signal man he gave the signal to stop, and the steam was shut off, and the brakes put on, it was too late to stop the train, which was going at the rate of 50 miles an hour, and it came on to the bridge, and then running off the line at the spot where the rails were up, it dashed on to the bridge, and the catastrophe ensued in which many lives were lost. . . .

Ribton, for the prisoner, submitted that there was no evidence of any criminal act or default on his part which had caused the death. It appeared that the accident could not have happened, notwithstanding the mistake which the prisoner had undoubtedly committed, if other servants of the company had done their duty; if for instance, the flagman had gone far enough with the signal, or if the engine-driver had kept a sufficient look-out, and had seen the signal, as then he must have seen it earlier than he did, and in time enough to stop the train.

Pigott, B., said, that assuming culpable negligence on the part of the prisoner which materially contributed to the accident, it would not be material that others also by their negligence contributed to cause it. Therefore he must leave it to the jury whether there was negligence of the prisoner which had been the substantial cause of the accident. In summing up the case to the jury, he said their verdict must depend on whether the death was mainly caused by the culpable negligence of the prisoner. Was the accident mainly caused by the taking up of the rails at a time when an express train was about to arrive, was that the act of the prisoner, and was it owing to culpable negligence on his part? His counsel had urged that it was not so, because the flagman and engine-driver had been guilty of negligence, which had [also] contributed to cause the catastrophe; but they, in their turn, might make the same excuse, and so, if it was valid, no one could be criminally responsible at all. This would be an absurd and unreasonable conclusion, and showed that the contention of the prisoner's counsel could not be sound. Such was not the right view of the law — that if the negligence of several persons at different times and places contributed to cause an accident, any one of them could set up that his was not the sole cause of it. It was enough against any one of them that his negligence was the substantial cause of it. Now, here the primary cause was certainly the taking up of the rails at a time when the train was about to arrive, and when it would be impossible to replace them in time to avoid the accident. And this the prisoner admitted was owing to his own mistake. . . . [I]t was true that the company had provided other precautions to avoid any impending catastrophe, and that these were not observed upon this occasion; but was it not owing to the prisoner's culpable negligence that the accident was impending, and if so, did his negligence the less cause it, because if other persons had not been negligent it might possibly have been avoided?

Verdict — Guilty.

Notes and Questions

1. Was Benge's carelessness in misreading the schedule a *necessary* condition to the resulting deaths? Was it a *sufficient* condition? What about the failure of Wills, the signalman, to position himself a full 1000 yards ahead of the bridge (despite written instructions that this was a necessary precaution)? Was that a necessary condition to the resulting death, given the failure of the engineer to keep watch for a signal? Was it a sufficient condition? Was the engineer's inattention a necessary condition to the resulting deaths, given the signalman's failure to give warning early enough? Was it a sufficient condition? If Benge's negligent mistake was necessary but insufficient to cause death, and if the negligent mistakes of the signalman and engineer were each sufficient (once the tracks

were pulled up) but each unnecessary (because of the negligence of the other), who caused the deaths? Do the tests provided by the court help resolve this question? Who "materially contributed to the accident"? Whose negligence was "the substantial cause"? Is it necessary to choose one "main" or "primary" cause, or could all three be causally responsible?

2. *The Baby José case.* For a modern illustration of this problem, consider the death of the infant José Martinez, from an overdose of medication administered in a Houston hospital. According to a newspaper account,[10] José suffered from a septal defect, a small hole between the chambers in his heart which interfered with the efficiency of its pumping action. The attending physician prescribed Digoxin, a drug which swells the heart tissue. The attending physician and a resident worked out the proper dosage together: 0.09 milligrams. But the resident misrecorded the dosage on the treatment order form as 0.9 milligrams. The attending physician checked over the treatment order form but did not spot the error. A copy of the order form was sent to the hospital pharmacy where the pharmacist set it aside because he recognized that the dosage was wrong, and paged the resident. But the resident had gone home and never answered the page. A second copy of the order form arrived at the pharmacy, where an assistant filled the prescription. The pharmacist simply checked that the dosage matched the order form, forgetting that he had set aside an earlier copy. The order and the medicine were sent to the pediatric ward, where a nurse, suspecting the dosage was excessive, asked a resident to check the order. The resident recalculated the dosage, and got 0.09 milligrams, but failed to notice the difference between his result and the and 0.9 milligrams on the order. He told the nurse the order was right. Still concerned, the nurse nevertheless administered the medication, which almost immediately swelled the heart tissue to the point of immobility, causing the baby's death. Who killed José Martinez? The attending physician? The first resident? The pharmacist? The second resident? The nurse? All of them? None? Was a crime committed?

B. VIOLENT ACTS

HUBBARD v. COMMONWEALTH
Court of Appeals of Kentucky
304 Ky. 818, 202 S.W.2d 634 (1947)

Opinion of the Court by STANLEY, COMMISSIONER:

R. W. Dyche died of a heart attack. Robert Hubbard has been adjudged guilty of killing him and sentenced to two years' imprisonment on a charge of voluntary manslaughter. . . .

Hubbard was at home on furlough from the army in August, 1945. He was arrested for being drunk in a public place and taken before the County Judge of Laurel County. Being too drunk to be tried, he was ordered to jail, but refused to go peaceably. Dyche, the jailer, and Newman, a deputy, took hold of him.

10. Lisa Belkin, "Getting Past Blame"; How Can We Save the Next Victim? New York Times, June 15, 1997, sec. 6, at 28.

The prisoner resisted and struck Newman. In the scuffle both fell to the floor and Hubbard lay on his back "kicking at" anybody or anything within reach. Dyche had hold of him. He said, "I have done all I can; you will have to help me," or "Somebody is going to have to take my place; I am done." Judge Boggs took hold of the prisoner and persuaded him to get up; but he continued to resist as he was being taken to jail by Newman and another person. Dyche followed them out of the courthouse. He put his hand over his heart and sat down. In a few minutes he got down on the ground where he "rolled and tumbled" until he died within a half hour. Hubbard never struck Dyche at all, and he received no physical injury. He had been suffering for some time with a serious condition of the heart, and had remarked to a friend several hours before that he was feeling bad. Three doctors testified that his death was due to acute dilatation of the heart, but that the physical exercise and excitement was calculated to accelerate his death. . . .

The only inquiry we need make is whether the facts constitute involuntary manslaughter. . . . The death of Dyche was charged to have resulted from the commission by Hubbard of a misdemeanor not of a character likely to endanger life. The Attorney General frankly concedes that the defendant was at least entitled to an instruction on involuntary manslaughter, and expresses grave doubt whether he is guilty of any culpable homicide. The only theory of guilt is that his unlawful act in resisting arrest contributed to Dyche's death or accelerated it.

There is a close line of distinction between criminal responsibility and innocence where the facts approach or are similar to those presented here. One cannot escape culpability because factors other than his act contributed to the death of another or hastened it, such as where he was suffering from some fatal malady or had a predisposed physical condition, as being in feeble health, without which a blow or other wound would not have been fatal. Under most modern decisions death caused or accomplished through fright, fear or nervous shock may form a basis for criminal responsibility. On the other hand, it is held that to warrant a conviction of homicide the act of the accused must be the proximate cause of death; that if there was an intervening cause for which the accused was not responsible and but for which death would not have occurred, he is blameless.

We have a case in our jurisprudence like the present one in principle. A woman became frightened because of the unlawful discharge of a pistol on a public highway by the defendant, and because of the fright she gave premature birth to a child, after which she became sick and died. We held that while the woman had been badly frightened by the unlawful act of the defendant and her miscarriage was caused by it, her death was not the natural or probable consequence of the defendant's unlawful act. Commonwealth v. Couch, 106 S.W. 830.

Somewhat like this case is People v. Rockwell, 39 Mich. 503, where the defendant knocked a man down with his fist and a horse jumped on him or kicked him, inflicting injuries from which he died. The defendant was held not responsible. In Ex parte Heigho, 18 Idaho 566, Heigho had gone to the home of Barton where they engaged in a violent fight. Barton's mother-in-law became badly frightened and died within thirty minutes. An autopsy revealed she had died of a species of heart attack. The case was before the court on a writ of habeas corpus sought by Heigho. . . . The sole question was whether there was a sufficient disclosure of a public offense for which the prisoner should be held on a preliminary examination. The court believed it would be unsafe and unreasonable and often unjust to hold as a matter of law that under no state of facts should a prosecution for manslaughter be sustained where death was caused by fright, fear or terror alone, even though no hostile demonstration or overt act was directed at the person of the deceased; hence the writ of habeas corpus was denied.

In Letner v. State, 156 Tenn. 68, 299 S.W. 1049, the defendant had fired into a river near a boat for the purpose of merely frightening the occupants. One of them leaped overboard in order to avoid the apparent danger of being shot, and in so doing overturned the boat, with the result that one of the other occupants was drowned. The court held that the defendant having set in motion a series of forces which resulted in the death of the man, his act was the proximate cause of his death and the accused could not avoid the consequences of his wrongful act by relying on a supervening cause which resulted naturally and proximately from that act.

It seems to us that where the cause of death was not due to a corporal blow or injury (essential under the early common law) or to some hostile demonstration or overt act directed toward the person of the decedent, there is no criminal liability unless death or serious bodily harm was the probable and natural consequence of an indirect, unlawful act of the accused. If there is reasonable doubt of this it would be unjust to punish the accused.

In the present case the misdemeanor of the defendant must be regarded as too remote — not in time, to be sure, but as the cause. The failure of the man's diseased heart was the cause. The deceased knowing he had a serious condition of the heart undertook a task which he knew would excite him or create an emotional state of mind, which he also well knew he should have avoided. The evidence is that he had theretofore exercised such wise discretion. His intervening act in rolling and tumbling in pain on the courthouse yard, instead of lying quiet and still, was probably as much responsible for his ensuing death as was the initial excitement caused by the conduct of the accused. . . . It is, at least, speculative to say that the act of the defendant in this case was sufficiently proximate to impose criminal responsibility upon him for the unfortunate death. We are of opinion, therefore, that the court should have directed an acquittal.

Notes and Questions

1. *Direct and proximate cause.* Note that the court offered two reasons why the defendant's act of resisting arrest could not be treated as the cause of death. First, death was "not due to a corporal blow or injury (essential under the early common law)." Second, "death or serious bodily harm" was not a "probable and natural consequence" of defendant's "indirect, unlawful act." In other words, Hubbard's resisting arrest was neither a direct cause nor a proximate cause of Dyche's death.

2. *The requirement of a direct blow at common law.* The actus reus of homicide at common law was never merely conduct that was a necessary condition to a subsequent death. The common law of crimes was royal law, concerned with enforcing the king's peace. Accordingly it was particularly directed against conspicuous acts of violence. The actus reus of all forms of homicide at common law was *killing,* which according to Hale's Pleas of the Crown typically involved

"giving a mortal stroke."[11] Thus to "kill" usually meant to cause death by means of a battery — a blow intended to wound or hurt. While killing also included such deliberate cruelties as "exposing a sick or weak person or infant unto the cold to the intent to destroy him," "imprisoning a man so strictly that he dies," "starving," "poisoning," and "strangling or suffocation,"[12] the common law's focus on violence set limits to the concept of killing. Thus

> If a man either by working upon the fancy of another or possibly by harsh or unkind usage puts another into such passion of grief or fear, that the party either dies suddenly, or contracts some disease, whereof he dies, tho . . . this may be murder or manslaughter in the sight of God, yet *in foro humano* it cannot come under the judgment of felony, because no external act of violence was offered, whereof the common law can take notice, and secret things belong to God.[13]

Is Hale's definition of killing adequate for a modern society? How would it apply to the *Benge* case? What result would it dictate in the *Hubbard* case? What about the *Rockwell* and *Heigho* cases, where a blow was given, but not to the person who died? What about the *Couch* and *Letner* cases, where a shot was fired, but did not hit anyone?

The *Rockwell* and *Heigho* cases appear to have reached opposite results. Are they reconcilable? Similarly the *Couch* and *Letner* cases appear to have reached opposite results. Are they reconcilable? How does the *Hubbard* court distinguish *Heigho* and *Letner* from the result in Hubbard?

3. *"Probable and natural consequences."* Why does the *Hubbard* court think Dyche's death was not a "probable and natural consequence" of Hubbard's resisting arrest? Is it because resisting arrest does not usually provoke heart attacks in arresting officers? Is it because Dyche brought his death upon himself by stressing himself imprudently?

Hale appears to limit homicide to two categories: causing death by means of a blow and causing death intentionally by some other means. Yet some of his examples suggest that he might include very reckless violations of a duty of care, such as abandoning an infant or subjecting a prisoner to life-threatening conditions of confinement. The *Hubbard* court expands this idea into a separate category of homicide by an "indirect, unlawful act" that "probably" and "naturally" causes death. The next section examines this and related standards of proximate causation.

4. *Direct causation and intervening events.* Apart from the examples in the previous note, Hale limited unintended killing to fatal blows. The causation question that concerned him was the effect on causal responsibility of events subsequent or prior to such a blow. Hale reasoned that

> If a man give another a stroke, which, it may be, is not in itself so mortal, but that with good care he might be cured, yet if he die within a year and a day, it is homicide or murder. . . . But if the wound or hurt be not mortal, but with ill applications . . . of unwholesome salves or medicines the party dies . . . it seems it is not homicide. . . .
>
> But if a man receives a wound, which is not itself mortal, but either for want of helpful applications, or neglect thereof, it turns to gangrene, or a fever, and that

11. Sir Matthew Hale, I The History of the Pleas of the Crown (1680) 425.
12. Id. 431-432.
13. Id. 429.

gangrene or fever be the immediate cause of death, yet this is murder or manslaughter in him that gave the stroke or wound. . . .

If a man be sick of some such disease, which possibly by course of nature would end his life in half a year, and another gives him a wound or hurt, which hastens his end by irritating or provoking the disease to operate more violently or speedily, this . . . is homicide. . . .[14]

Is the result in *Hubbard* consistent with these principles? Did Hubbard hasten the course of Dyche's heart disease? Did he do so by administering a "wound or hurt"? A later section of this chapter will consider what kinds of intervening events "break the chain" of defendant's causal responsibility. But bear in mind that originally, the chain of causal responsibility had to begin with a battery.

C.   PROXIMATE CAUSE: FORESEEABILITY AND RELATED LIMITATIONS

COMMONWEALTH v. RHOADES
Supreme Judicial Court of Massachusetts
401 N.E.2d 342 (1980)

[Defendant Rhoades was charged with deliberately setting a fire in an apartment he was visiting in Chelsea.]

The first alarm for the three alarm blaze was sounded at 11:03 P.M. Among the firefighters responding to the second alarm was Captain James Trainor. When Trainor entered the burning building in an attempt to rescue persons thought to be trapped inside, he was outfitted in standard fire-fighting gear: rubber coat, helmet, boots and a self-contained breathing apparatus. The temperature outside was in the 20s. Attempting to assist those fighting the fire, Trainor encountered intense heat and thick smoke, and experienced difficulty in getting air through his face mask. While on the roof of the building, Trainor collapsed; taken to a hospital in Everett, he was pronounced dead on arrival. The Commonwealth's medical expert concluded that the combination of cold weather, stress, and smoke inhalation precipitated the coronary thrombosis which caused Trainer's death. . . .

Experts concluded that the fire was set. [The defendant was charged with arson and second-degree murder for the death of Captain Trainor. He appealed the conviction for second-degree murder on the grounds that the charge to the jury did not adequately describe the causal connection that must exist between a defendant's act and a person's death.]

. . . The trial judge charged the jury that if Captain Trainor died "as a result" of Rhoades' act, or if Rhoades' act "in any way contributed to hasten, or was part of the proximate cause" of Trainor's death, then Rhoades could be liable for second degree murder. The judge charged that if the jury found beyond a reasonable doubt, that Rhoades' act was a "contributing cause" of Trainor's death, then Rhoades would be criminally liable. The overall effect of this charge was to

14. Id. at 428.

leave the jury with the impression that if Rhoades' act in setting the fire in any way constituted a link, no matter how remote, in the chain of events leading to Trainor's death, Rhoades should be convicted. We conclude that this formulation exposed Rhoades to potential liability for events not proximately caused by his felonious act in setting the fire.[15] See State v. Newman, 162 Mont. 450, 461-62, 513 P.2d 258, 265 (1973) (charge that the jury must find that defendant's act "contributed to or was the proximate cause of" the victim's death held to misstate the law because disjunctively phrased). . . .

This misimpression is not corrected by the impact of the instructions evaluated as a whole. Nothing said to the jury by the judge indicated that proximate cause in Captain Trainer's death "is a cause, which, in the natural and continuous sequence, produces the death, and without which the death would not have occurred." California Jury Instructions, Criminal 8.55 (4th rev. ed. 1979).

The judge, apparently responding to the defendant's theory that he was criminally responsible only if he were the sole cause, merely attempted to instruct the jury that if Rhoades' conduct contributed to Trainer's death, Rhoades could be convicted. . . . He emphasized that the fire need not be the sole cause, but failed to instruct the jury clearly that the defendant's conduct must be the efficient cause, the cause that necessarily sets in operation the factors which caused the death. The judgment on the indictment charging Rhoades with the death of Captain Trainor is therefore reversed, the verdict set aside, and the case remanded to the Superior Court for further proceedings consistent with this opinion.

Notes and Questions

1. What was wrong with the trial judge's instruction in this case? Was it a failure to make clear that defendant's action must be a necessary condition? Or a failure to make clear that a cause is something more than a necessary condition? Or both?

2. The decision points out that California Jury Instruction 8.55 defines "proximate cause" as one that produces the result by a "natural and continuous sequence."

Recall the three limitations on but-for causation considered by Hart and Honoré. Which (if any) of these three limitations is implied by the phrase "natural and continuous sequence"?

Does it mean "without interruption by human action"? Does it mean "without interruption by some unusual event or circumstance"? Does it mean a "familiar sequence of events"? A "predictable" or "foreseeable sequence"? A "sequence foreseeable by the defendant"?

3. *Proximate cause hypotheticals.* Consider whether the following cases produce death in a "natural and continuous sequence" (and if not, why not):

    a. Defendant clubs Lee on the head in a bank parking lot as Lee returns to her car from an automatic teller machine. Defendant grabs Lee's wallet

---

15. A finding that Rhoades' conduct was the proximate cause of Trainor's death is an inference that a jury could well have drawn from the evidence in this case. . . . The Commonwealth's medical expert found that Trainor's efforts in fighting the fire "precipitated" the thrombosis that caused his death. The defendant's expert testified that the stress of fighting the fire "contributed to" Trainor's "final thrombosis." Nevertheless, a defendant is entitled to have the law correctly explained to the jury.

and leaves her lying unconscious in the parking lot. Later, Lee is run over and killed by a driver who does not see her.

b. Same facts, but Lee is not run over. She awakes unharmed several hours later. Lee's baby, however, left in a locked car on a hot day, has died of dehydration.

c. Driving drunk, defendant hits a fire hydrant on a cold night, causing a flood that freezes on the road. Later, another driver, Pat, skids on the icy road and is killed in a crash.

d. Same hypothetical, but Pat is driving 20 miles an hour over the speed limit.

e. A variation on Commonwealth v. Rhoades: Fighting a fire deliberately set by defendant, a firefighter dies of a heart attack brought on in part by exertion and smoke inhalation. The firefighter suffered from a serious heart condition, and his supervisor had violated department rules by failing to put him on medical leave.

f. The facts in *Rhoades,* but the firefighter had violated department guidelines by unnecessarily entering a smoke-filled room.

4. *Proximate cause and culpability.* Consider the Model Penal Code's conception of causation:

Section 2.03. Causal Relationship Between Conduct and Result; Divergence Between Result Designed or Contemplated and Actual Result or Between Probable and Actual Result

(1) Conduct is the cause of a result when:

(a) it is an antecedent but for which the result in question would not have occurred; and

(b) the relationship between the conduct and result satisfies any additional causal requirements plainly imposed by law.

(2) When purposely or knowingly causing a particular result is a material element of an offense, the element is not established if the actual result is not within the purpose or the contemplation of the actor unless:

(a) the actual result differs from that designed or contemplated, as the case may be, only in the respect that a different person or different property is injured or affected or that the injury or harm designed or contemplated would have been more serious or more extensive than that caused; or

(b) the actual result involves the same kind of injury or harm as that designed or contemplated and is not too accidental in its occurrence to have a just bearing on the actor's liability or on the gravity of his offense.
[Alternative: and it occurs in a manner that the actor knows or should know is rendered substantially more probable by his conduct.]

(3) When recklessly or negligently causing a particular result is a material element of an offense, the element is not established if the actual result is not within the risk of which the actor is aware, or in the case of negligence, of which he should be aware unless:

(a) the actual result differs from the probable result only in the respect that a different person or different property is injured or affected or that the probable injury or harm would have been more serious or more extensive than that caused; or

(b) the actual result involves the same kind of injury or harm as the probable result and is not too accidental in its occurrence to have a just bearing on the actor's liability or on the gravity of his offense.

[Alternative: and it occurs in a manner that the actor knows or should know is rendered substantially more probable by his conduct.]

Notice how the meaning of causing a result changes depending on the culpable mental state required with respect to that result. As a consequence, whether or not defendant caused a result may depend on the offense she is charged with. Does this make sense? The Model Penal Code's fluid standard of causation may be explained as an effort to condition liability on a determination that the defendant's culpable mental state caused the proscribed result. But can mental states cause results? While this is an odd way of speaking, there is one consideration in its favor:

It has often been observed that our ideas of mechanistic causation . . . stem from our own first person experience as actors, making events in the world happen via our bodies. This has led some to conclude that human actions are our paradigm of the causal relation. . . . On this view, human actions are the only clear cases of causation, all causal relations between natural events being such only by analogy to these strong paradigms.[16]

MPC §2.03(2) poses the question whether the harm resulting from defendant's action was of a kind the defendant intended. On the other hand, MPC §2.03(3) asks whether the harm was one the defendant expected or should have expected. To what extent do we anticipate *kinds of* results, rather than particular results? If Leslie shoots at Bill and instead fatally hits Mike, has she killed intentionally (because she intended to kill someone) or merely killed recklessly (because shooting at one person poses a risk to bystanders)? MPC §2.03(2) characterizes Leslie's killing of Mike as intentional, though she did not intend to kill him. Does this make sense? Perhaps, on the view that Leslie's intent to kill resulted in Mike's death. But what if Leslie's shot at Bill merely startles Mike, causing him to swerve his car into oncoming traffic, with the result that he is killed in a crash? Would MPC §2.03(2) permit a finding of intentionally causing death on this scenario?

If, on the other hand, we treat bystander killings as merely reckless, we face this problem: Suppose Leslie shoots at Bill's head and accidentally hits his heart. She missed her intended target, but knew there was a chance she would miss Bill's head but wound or even kill Bill anyway. Should we conclude that Leslie killed Bill recklessly while failing in an attempt to kill him intentionally?

Perhaps we should conclude that our expectations of harm are general rather than specific. But do the categories of harm we expect have determinate boundaries? If not, does it make sense to tie causation to these expectations, as the Model Penal Code does?

5. *Applying MPC §2.03(3)*. Recall the Huey Newton case from Chapter 2, see p. 120, *supra*. Suppose in a similar case the evidence indicated that officer Trigger wrongfully shot suspect Desperado, who, in an unconscious state of shock, proceeded to shoot and kill officer Duck. Would Trigger's shooting of Desperado be a "proximate cause" of Duck's death under the instruction favored by the Supreme Judicial Court in *Rhoades*? If wrongful death was a predictable outcome

16. Michael Moore, Act and Crime: The Philosophy of Actions and Its Implications for the Criminal Law 274 (1993).

of shooting the suspect, should it matter that the wrongful death ensued in a fluky way?

Suppose Officer Trigger is charged with reckless homicide under the Model Penal Code. Would Trigger have recklessly caused Duck's death under MPC §2.03(3)?

Reconsider the deaths of Ward, Szablicki, and Pruner, p. 249, *supra,* in light of MPC §2.03(3). In all three cases, crime victims later die of heart attacks that officials ascribe to the emotional impact of the crime. Did the offenders in any of these cases cause the deaths of their victims according to the standards in MPC §2.03(3)?

6. *Strict liability and proximate cause.* Many state legislatures have passed DWI-manslaughter statutes that authorize manslaughter convictions for defendants involved in fatal accidents while driving drunk. One such statute was challenged by a defendant on the ground that the statute did not require any causal connection between the defendant's intoxication and the resulting death. Baker v. State, 377 So. 2d 17 (Fla. 1979). Rather, the statute required only that the defendant was intoxicated at the time he operated the vehicle, and that a death resulted from the operation of the vehicle by the defendant. (Baker was making a legal left turn at a relatively safe speed, but had a Blood Alcohol Content of 0.17, when he saw a bicyclist and tried in vain to avoid a collision.) The statute did not require that the defendant's intoxication cause the resulting death, but the Supreme Court of Florida upheld it on the ground that driving while intoxicated is reckless and that deterrence of such reckless conduct would be reduced by requiring a causal connection between the reckless conduct and the death. Does this make sense? Does deterrence also justify convicting drunk drivers of vehicular homicide when nobody dies? Should we instead simply raise penalties for acts of culpable risk-taking, and eliminate the causation of harm as an element of crime?

Model Penal Code §2.03(4) requires a causal connection for strict liability offenses: "When causing a particular result is a material element of an offense for which absolute liability is imposed by law, the element is not established unless the actual result is a probable consequence of the actor's conduct." What result would you reach in *Baker* under this standard?

7. *Negligence and proximate cause.* Can we ever actually tell what harm negligence or recklessness causes? A choice is negligent if it is likely to lead to "more" harm — say, "more" deaths — than an alternative. It is reckless if this likelihood is known to the actor. But when a particular death occurs, can we ever tell if it is an "extra" death, caused by negligence or recklessness? Professor Leo Katz points out that "typically what negligent conduct does is to see to it that instead of one group of people being killed or injured, another larger group is."[17] This raises a problem illustrated by the following hypothetical, based on one developed by Katz:[18]

> The manager of a power company has decided that it will be profitable to build a power plant to serve two neighboring cities, Bigburg and Smalltown.
> If she builds the plant in Smalltown, it is foreseeable that an average of 10 additional people per year will die of cancer there, but because the plant will result

17. Leo Katz, p. 249, *supra.*
18. Id., 249-50.

in improved street lighting there will be 5 fewer traffic deaths in Smalltown, and 10 fewer traffic deaths in Bigburg.

If she builds the plant in Bigburg, it is foreseeable that an average of 20 additional people per year will die of cancer there; but again, 5 fewer will die in Smalltown and 10 fewer in Bigburg due to improved lighting.

The average age of the additional people expected to die of cancer if the plant is built is 60, while the average age of those expected to be saved from traffic deaths is 40.

The manager decides to build the plant and sites it in Bigburg because the expected profits will be higher. In the first year of operation, cancer deaths and traffic deaths in the two towns change as predicted.

Assume that you are a prosecutor in a jurisdiction that criminally punishes the offense of negligent homicide. You are deciding whether to charge the manager with this offense. Has the manager negligently caused any deaths? How many? Which ones? Would she have negligently caused any deaths if she situated the plant in Smalltown? If she decided not to build the plant at all?

8. *The many meanings of "proximate cause."* "Proximate cause" usually denotes a standard of causation that, like MPC §2.03, limits causation to results expected by the actor. But the term can have other meanings.

For one thing, "proximate cause" standards do not always link a probability standard to the defendant's requisite culpable mental state. A condition necessary to a result may proximately cause that result if it does so regularly, or predictably, or commonly, regardless of what culpable mental state is required to make that proximate cause a crime. "Proximate cause" is of course a spatial metaphor, suggesting that some causes are too distant or remote from their results to count as legal causes; or, that at the time of acting, the danger of an unfortunate consequence may be "remote" from the view of an actor, or a reasonable person in the actor's place; or, perhaps that the chances of misfortune resulting from an act are "remote," in the sense of attenuated by a series of low probability necessary conditions. All of these senses of causal "remoteness" and "proximity" have an affinity to the related metaphor of "chains of causation." The chain of causation linking a condition to a result can have a "weak link" if it depends on an improbable event. It can be too long temporally. It can be "broken" by intervening causes, whether natural or human. Sometimes these extensions of the metaphor of the causal chain are also referred to as "proximate cause" limitations. These traditional limitations on causation are taken up in the next section.

D. INTERVENING CAUSES

COMMONWEALTH v. ROOT
Supreme Court of Pennsylvania
403 Pa. 571, 170 A.2d 310 (1961)

CHARLES ALVIN JONES, CHIEF JUSTICE.

The appellant was found guilty of involuntary manslaughter for the death of his competitor in the course of an automobile race between them on a highway. . . . On appeal from the judgment of sentence entered on the jury's verdict, the Superior Court affirmed. We granted allocatur because of the important question present as to whether the defendant's unlawful and reckless conduct was a sufficiently direct cause of the death to warrant his being charged with criminal homicide.

The testimony . . . discloses that, on the night of the fatal accident, the defendant accepted the deceased's challenge to engage in an automobile race; that the racing took place on a rural 3-lane highway; that the night was clear and dry, and traffic light; that the speed limit on the highway was 50 miles per hour; that, immediately prior to the accident, the two automobiles were being operated at varying speeds of from 70 to 90 miles per hour; that the accident occurred in a no-passing zone on the approach to a bridge where the highway narrowed to two directionally-opposite lanes; that, at the time of the accident, the defendant was in the lead and was proceeding in his right hand lane of travel; that the deceased, in an attempt to pass the defendant's automobile, when a truck was closely approaching from the opposite direction, swerved his car to the left, crossed the highway's white dividing line and drove his automobile on the wrong side of the highway head-on into the oncoming truck with resultant fatal effect to himself.

This evidence would of course amply support a conviction of the defendant for speeding, reckless driving and, perhaps, other violations of The Vehicle Code. . . . In any event, unlawful or reckless conduct is only one ingredient of the crime of involuntary manslaughter. Another essential and distinctly separate element of the crime is that the unlawful or reckless conduct charged to the defendant was the direct cause of the death in issue. The first ingredient is obviously in this case but, just as plainly, the second is not.

While precedent is to be found for application of the tort law concept of "proximate cause" in fixing responsibility for criminal homicide, the want of any rational basis for its use in determining criminal liability can no longer be properly disregarded. When proximate cause was first borrowed from the field of tort law and applied to homicide prosecutions in Pennsylvania, the concept connoted a much more direct causal relation in producing the alleged culpable result than it does today. Proximate cause, as an essential element of a tort founded in negligence, has undergone in recent times, and is still undergoing, a marked extension. More specifically, this area of civil law has been progressively liberalized in favor of claims for damages for personal injuries to which careless conduct of others can in some way be associated. To persist in applying the tort liability concept of proximate cause to prosecutions for criminal homicide after the marked expansion of civil liability of defendants in tort actions for negligence would be to extend possible criminal liability to persons chargeable with unlawful or reckless conduct in circumstances not generally considered to present the likelihood of a resultant death.

The instant case is one of first impression in this State; and our research has not disclosed a single instance where a district attorney has ever before attempted to prosecute for involuntary manslaughter on facts similar to those established by the record now before us. The closest case, factually, would seem to be Commonwealth v. Levin, 135 A.2d 764 (1957), which affirmed the defendant's conviction of involuntary manslaughter. In the *Levin* case two cars were racing on the streets of Philadelphia at speeds estimated at from 85 to 95 miles per hour. The defendant's car, in the left hand lane, was racing alongside of the car in which the deceased was a passenger when the defendant turned his automobile sharply to the right in front of the other car thereby causing the driver of the latter car to lose control and smash into a tree, the passenger being thrown to the road and killed as a result of the impact. It is readily apparent that the elements of causation in the *Levin* case were fundamentally different from those in the present case. Levin's act of cutting his automobile sharply in front of the car in which the deceased was riding directly forced that car off of the road and into the tree. The defendant's reckless and unlawful maneuver was the direct cause of the crucial fatality. In the instant case, the defendant's conduct was not even remotely comparable. Here, the action of the deceased driver in recklessly and suicidally swerving his car to the left lane of a 2-lane highway into the path of an oncoming truck was not forced upon him by an act of the defendant; it was done by the deceased and by him alone, who thus directly brought about his own demise. The *Levin* case was properly decided but it cannot, by any ratiocination, be utilized to justify a conviction in the present case.

Legal theory which makes guilt or innocence of criminal homicide depend upon such accidental and fortuitous circumstances as are now embraced by modern tort law's encompassing concept of proximate cause is too harsh to be just. A few illustrations should suffice to so demonstrate.

In Mautino v. Piercedale Supply Co., 12 A.2d 51 (1940) — a civil action for damages — we held that where a man sold a cartridge to a person under 16 years of age in violation of a State statute and the recipient subsequently procured a gun from which he fired the cartridge injuring someone, the injury was proximately caused by the act of the man who sold the cartridge to the underage person. If proximate cause were the test for criminal liability and the injury to the plaintiff in the Mautino case had been fatal, the man who sold the bullet to the underage person (even though the boy had the appearance of an adult) would have been guilty of involuntary manslaughter, for his unlawful act would, according to the tort law standard, have been the proximate cause of the death.

In Schelin v. Goldberg, 146 A.2d 648 (1958), it was held that the plaintiff, who was injured in a fight, could recover in tort against the defendants, the owners of a taproom who prior to the fight had unlawfully served the plaintiff drinks while he was in a visibly intoxicated condition, the unlawful action of the defendants being held to be the proximate cause of the plaintiff's injuries. Here, again, if proximate cause were the test for criminal liability and the plaintiff had been fatally injured in the fight, the taproom owners would have been guilty of involuntary manslaughter, for their unlawful act would have been no less the proximate cause of death.

In Marchl v. Dowling & Company, 41 A.2d 427 (1945), it was held that where a truck driver had double parked his truck and the minor plaintiff was struck by a passing car when she walked around the double parked truck, the truck driver's employer was held liable in tort for the plaintiff's injuries on the ground that the truck driver's act of double parking, which violated both a State statute and a city ordinance, was the proximate cause of the plaintiff's injuries. Here, also, if proximate cause were the test for criminal liability and the plaintiff's injuries had been fatal, the truck driver would have been guilty of involuntary manslaughter since his unlawful act would have been the proximate cause of the death for which his employer was held liable in damages under respondeat superior. To be guilty of involuntary manslaughter for double parking would, of course, be unthinkable, yet if proximate cause were to determine criminal liability, such a result would indeed be a possibility.

Even if the tort liability concept of proximate cause were to be deemed applicable, the defendant's conviction of involuntary manslaughter in the instant case could not be sustained under the evidence. The operative effect of a supervening cause would have to be taken into consideration. . . . But, the trial judge refused the defendant's point for charge to such effect and erroneously instructed the jury that "negligence or want of care on the part of [the deceased] is no defense to the criminal responsibility of the defendant. . . ."

Under the uncontradicted evidence in this case, the conduct of the defendant was not the proximate cause of the decedent's death as a matter of law.

In [Johnson v. Angretti, 361 Pa. 602, 73 A.2d 666 (1950),] while Angretti was driving his truck eastward along a highway, a bus, traveling in the same direction in front of him, stopped to take on a passenger. Angretti swerved his truck to the left into the lane of oncoming traffic in an attempt to pass the bus but collided with a tractor-trailer driven by the plaintiff's decedent, who was killed as a result of the collision. In affirming the entry of judgment n.o.v. in favor of the defendant bus company, we held that any negligence on the part of the bus driver, in suddenly bringing his bus to a halt in order to pick up a passenger, was not a proximate cause of the death of the plaintiff's decedent since the accident "was due entirely to the intervening and superseding negligence of Angretti in allowing his truck to pass over into the pathway of the westbound tractor-trailer. . . ."

In the case now before us, the deceased was aware of the dangerous condition created by the defendant's reckless conduct in driving his automobile at an excessive rate of speed along the highway but, despite such knowledge, he recklessly chose to swerve his car to the left and into the path of an oncoming truck, thereby bringing about the head-on collision which caused his own death.

To summarize, the tort liability concept of proximate cause has no proper place in prosecutions for criminal homicide and more direct causal connection is required for conviction. . . . In the instant case, the defendant's reckless conduct was not a sufficiently direct cause of the competing driver's death to make him criminally liable therefor. . . .

EAGEN, JUSTICE, dissenting.

The opinion of the learned Chief Justice admits, under the uncontradicted facts, that the defendant, at the time of the fatal accident involved, was engaged in an unlawful and reckless course of conduct. Racing an automobile at 90 miles per hour, trying to prevent another automobile going in the same direction from passing him, in a no-passing zone on a two-lane public highway, is certainly all of that. Admittedly also, there can be more than one direct cause of an unlawful death. To me, this is self-evident. But, says the majority opinion, the defendant's recklessness was not a direct cause of the death. With this, I cannot agree.

If the defendant did not engage in the unlawful race and so operate his automobile in such a reckless manner, this accident would never have occurred. He helped create the dangerous event. He was a vital part of it. The victim's acts were a natural reaction to the stimulus of the situation. The race, the attempt to pass the other car and forge ahead, the reckless speed, all of these factors the defendant himself helped create. He was part and parcel of them. That the victim's response was normal under the circumstances, that his reaction should have been expected and was clearly foreseeable, is to me beyond argument. That the defendant's recklessness was a substantial factor is obvious. All of this, in my opinion, makes his unlawful conduct a direct cause of the resulting collision. . . .

The majority opinion states, "Legal theory which makes guilt or innocence of criminal homicide depend upon such accidental and fortuitous circumstances as are now embraced by modern tort law's encompassing concept . . . is too harsh to be just." If the resulting death had been dependent upon "accidental and fortuitous circumstances" or, as the majority also say, "in circumstances not generally considered to present the likelihood of a resultant death," we would agree that the defendant is not criminally responsible. However, acts should be judged by their tendency under the known circumstances, not by the actual intent which accompanies their performance. Every day of the year, we read that some teenagers, or young adults, somewhere in this country, have been killed or have killed others, while racing their automobiles. Hair-raising, death-defying, law-breaking rides, which encompass "racing" are the rule rather than the exception, and endanger not only the participants, but also every motorist and passenger on the road. To call such resulting accidents "accidental and fortuitous," or unlikely to result in death, is to ignore the cold and harsh reality of everyday occurrences. . . .

While the victim's foolhardiness in this case contributed to his own death, he was not the only one responsible and it is not he alone with whom we are concerned. It is the people of the Commonwealth who are harmed by the kind of conduct the defendant pursued. Their interests must be kept in mind.

I, therefore, dissent and would accordingly affirm the judgment of conviction.

Notes and Questions

1. The court distinguishes another drag-racing case, *Levin*, where the defendant swerved dangerously in front of his opponent, causing the opponent to smash into a tree. Should there be any difference between the liability attaching to Levin's conduct and Root's? Didn't Root act dangerously and recklessly by drag racing at up to 90 miles an hour? Could he not foresee that his driving — or even that issuing the challenge to race — might cause his opponent's death?

Does the court concede that Root might have foreseen, and hence proximately caused, his opponent's death, and yet demand something more for homicide liability? How would you define the extra element?

Does the court's use of the term "direct cause" illuminate the issue? The court says that Root's opponent "directly brought about his own demise," and that his action in swerving into the wrong lane "was not forced upon him by any act of the defendant." Is this reasoning convincing?

2. The court summarizes three civil tort cases, *Mautino, Schelin,* and *Marchl,* and says that if Root is guilty of homicide, it would follow that the civil defendants in those cases would themselves be criminally liable. Carefully review the facts of those cases. Is the court correct that the criminal liability of the tort defendants would logically follow from Root's? If so, would punishing them criminally be unjust?

3. What if Root's opponent had killed the truck driver with whom he collided, as well as himself? Would that alter the court's view of Root's liability? For a case suggesting just that result, see Jacob v. State, 184 So. 2d 711 (Fla. 1966).

What if the person killed were a passenger in the car of Root's opponent? For a case finding liability under such circumstances see State v. Shimon, 182 N.W.2d 113 (Iowa 1970). Why might one hold drag racer #1 liable for the death of a third party killed by the reckless driving of drag racer #2? Because #1 caused #2's reckless action, or merely because #1 acquiesced in it? If #1's liability is based on consent to #2's reckless act causing death, #1 is liable as an accomplice to #2. See Chapter 11, *infra,* for the elements of complicity.

4. The dissent in *Root* vigorously argues for Root's liability. What would the dissenting judge have said about the homicide liability of friends of the drag racers who had helped plan the race and had stood by and cheered, instead of calling the police or otherwise stopping the dangerous activity? Recall the discussion of omission liability in Chapter 2. Did bystanders have a duty to try to stop the race? Based on what? Is there any basis for ascribing a higher duty to Root? See the discussion of duties as a limitation on causation by omission, below.

5. Suppose that Root and deceased had been playing Russian Roulette instead of drag racing, and that deceased had shot himself in the head. For a case upholding a manslaughter conviction on similar facts, see Commonwealth v. Atencio, 189 N.E.2d 223 (Mass. 1963). Can you distinguish these two results?

6. The drafters for the California Joint Legislative Committee for Revision of the Penal Code (Tent. Draft No. 2, 1968) suggested one interesting change in the causation rule when they focused on the intervening actions of a person other than the defendant. Note the emphasized clauses below:

Section 408. Causation: Responsibility for Causing a Result

(1) An element of an offense which requires that the defendant have caused a particular result is established when his conduct is an antecedent but for which the result would not have occurred, and,

(a) if the offense requires that the defendant intentionally or knowingly cause the result, that the actual result, as it occurred,

(i) is within the purpose or contemplation of the defendant, *whether the purpose or contemplation extends to natural events or to the conduct of another.* . . .

(b) if the offense requires that the defendant recklessly or negligently cause the result, that the actual result, as it occurred,

(i) is within the risk of which the defendant was or should have been aware, *whether that risk extends to natural events or to the conduct of another.* . . .

7. *Intervening actor problems.* To what extent can it be said that one person causes the act of another human being? If the doctor in charge of a mental institution carelessly leaves the door unlocked when he leaves the padded cell of a homicidal maniac and the maniac escapes and kills someone, should the doctor be criminally liable for having caused the death? Does the fact that the maniac himself would be irresponsible under the insanity defense make it easier to attach liability to the doctor? If so, what about the prison guard who negligently leaves the cell door of a violent (though criminally responsible) murderer open, permitting the criminal to kill his enemy in a nearby cell?

In State v. Wassil, 233 Conn. 174, 658 A.2d 548 (1995), the defendant bought heroin for himself and another man, Groleau. Groleau injected the heroin into his own arm and soon lost consciousness. The defendant and a friend, Kiley, attempted unsuccessfully to awaken the unconscious man. Wassil then prevented Kiley from calling 911 and told him to leave. Wassil finally called 911 one hour after Groleau had lost consciousness, but the paramedic team was unable to revive

Groleau. The Supreme Court of Connecticut affirmed the conviction of manslaughter in the first degree, holding that Wassil's delivery of the heroin to Groleau was the proximate cause of the death, and that Groleau's conduct in injecting the drugs himself was not an efficient intervening cause of death.

Was there enough causal connection in this case, or is it more like prosecuting a bullet manufacturer for murder, or a waiter for setting the table with a knife later used for murder?

Assume that the Model Penal Code standard applied to Henry II of England (which it most certainly did not). Should he be guilty of the reckless or negligent homicide of Thomas à Becket? Angry with the Archbishop for having frustrated his plans, Henry II expostulated (apparently with no thought of having the churchman killed), "Will not someone rid me of this meddlesome priest?" Several of his knights, seeking to curry favor with the king and believing that he wished this event to occur, went and murdered Becket in the Canterbury Cathedral.

8. *The defendant as an intervening actor.* Can the defendant's own non-culpable action constitute an intervening cause of death, absolving her of responsibility for an earlier culpable action, but for which death would not have occurred? In the British case of Thabo Meli v. R., on appeal from the High Court of Basutoland, the appellants, acting under a preconceived plan first to kill the victim and then to fake an "accident," had deliberately given him liquor and when he was in a semi-intoxicated state they hit him on the head. The Privy Council assumed for its opinion that the appellants then believed that their victim was dead. They then rolled the body over a low cliff and faked the scene to resemble an accident. The medical evidence showed that the victim's subsequent death was due not to the blow inflicted by the appellants but to exposure. The defense argued that the first act, though exhibiting mens rea, was not the cause, and the second, which was the cause, exhibited no culpable mens rea. The court found this argument too nuanced and affirmed the conviction. [1954] 1 W.L.R. 228, 230, sub nom. Meli v. The Queen; the report at [1954] 1 All E.R. 373, 374.

In R. v. Church, [1966] 1 Q.B. 59, the accused claimed that he had struck the deceased during a fight. Believing that she was dead, he threw her in a river. The medical evidence showed that although the injuries she had suffered were likely to have caused unconsciousness and eventually death, the deceased was alive when thrown into the water and death was caused by drowning. The jury acquitted the accused of murder, but the Court of Criminal Appeal held that the jury should have been told that it could still convict of murder, if it regarded the appellant's conduct, from the moment he first struck her to the moment when he threw her into the river, as a series of acts designed to cause death or grievous bodily harm.

Is it fairer to treat these cases as single chains of causation, or as sets of legally discrete acts?

UNITED STATES v. HAMILTON
United States District Court, District of Columbia
182 F. Supp. 548 (1960)

HOLTZOFF, DISTRICT JUDGE. The evidence in this case establishes the following salient facts. On the afternoon and evening of December 2, 1959, a number of men had gathered in a poolroom on Georgia Avenue near Lamont Street for the purpose of recreation. The defendant and the deceased were in that group. They played several games of pool. They imbibed intoxicating beverages in the rear of the establishment, and they also carried on desultory conversations. There was an exchange of banter between the deceased and the defendant, which developed into an argument, and finally into an acrimonious quarrel. . . . Both the deceased and the defendant were asked by the person in charge of the poolroom to leave. . . . Accordingly, both of them went outside and a fight started on Lamont Street. In the course of the fight, the deceased was knocked down by the defendant. While he was lying on the ground, the defendant apparently exploded in a fit of ungovernable rage and jumped on the face of the deceased and kicked him in the head as well.

The deceased was taken to the District of Columbia General Hospital, arriving there at 11:30 P.M. [He] was in a semi-comatose condition. He was violent and in shock. Blood was coming from his face.

Promptly upon arrival at the hospital, the deceased came into the competent hands of the Chief Resident of the Neurological Service, who . . . did everything possible that could be done for his patient. A blood transfusion was given to the deceased, his airways were cleansed, and tubes inserted into his nasal passages and trachea in order to maintain the breathing process. In view of the fact that he was violent, it was necessary to restrain the patient by fastening leather handcuffs on him. The doctor saw the patient several times during the night. In addition, the registered nurse in charge of the ward in which the deceased was placed, saw him at least every half hour or every thirty-five minutes. The deceased was in a room with only one other patient. A licensed practical nurse was constantly in attendance in that room. It is obvious that the patient received incessant and continuous care and treatment at the hands of both the medical and nursing staff of the hospital.

During the night it became desirable to change the bed clothes of the deceased, because they had become bloody. To accomplish this result, it was necessary to remove the restraints from the patient. They were not put back, because by that time, the patient was no longer violent and was resting better than when he arrived. About 6:30 in the morning, the patient had a convulsion, and immediately thereafter, he himself, with his own hands, pulled out the tubes. At 7:30 A.M., the patient died.

The Deputy Coroner, who performed the autopsy and who himself is an experienced physician, found the cause of death to be asphyxiation due to aspiration or inhalation of blood caused by severe injuries to the face, including multiple fractures of the nasal bones. The attending physician testified that the cause of death was asphyxia. In other words, the two physicians agree as to the cause of death. It should be said at this point that the purpose of the tubes was to assist in keeping the airways clear in order that the patient might breathe normally. It is claimed by able counsel for the defendant that the immediate cause of death was the fact that the patient pulled out the tubes, and that, therefore, he brought about his own death. This contention requires a consideration of the applicable principles of law.

It is well established that if a person strikes another and inflicts a blow that may not be mortal in and of itself but thereby starts a chain of causation that leads to death, he is guilty of homicide. This is true even if the deceased contributes to his own death or hastens it by failing to take proper treatment.

The principles of the common law on this subject are summarized in Hale's Pleas of the Crown, vol. 1, p. 427, in a passage that has been frequently quoted. He says:

> If a man give another a stroke, which it may be, is not in itself so mortal, but that with good care he might be cured, yet if he die of this wound within a year and a day, it is homicide or murder, as the case is, and so it hath been always ruled.

And, again, Hale says:

> But if a man receives a wound, which is not in itself mortal, but either for want of helpful applications, or neglect thereof, it turns to a gangrene, or a fever, and that gangrene or fever be the immediate cause of his death, yet, this is murder or manslaughter in him that gave the stroke or wound, for that wound, tho it were not the immediate cause of his death, yet, if it were the mediate cause thereof, and the fever or gangrene was the immediate cause of his death, yet the wound was the cause of the gangrene or fever, and so consequently is causa causati.

Judicial decisions applying this doctrine are too numerous to require a review. Suffice it to say that these principles have been adopted and applied in the District of Columbia, in Hopkins v. United States, 4 App. B.C. 430, 439. In that case, the defendant had struck the deceased. Several weeks later the deceased died, and the autopsy showed that the death was caused by the blow that had been inflicted by the defendant. It was argued that the defendant was not guilty of homicide, because the deceased had neglected to take medical treatment after he was struck and that his failure to do so either caused or contributed to bringing about his death. This contention was overruled, and it was held that the mere fact that the deceased had neglected to procure proper treatment for the effects of the blow or wound did not relieve the defendant of his responsibility for the homicide.

Hawkins' Pleas of the Crown, Volume 1, Chapter 31, Section 10, summarizes this principle very succinctly. He says:

> But if a person hurt by another, die thereof within a year and a day, it is no excuse for the other that he might have recovered, if he had not neglected to take care of himself.

It is urged by defense counsel, however, that this case should not be governed by the principles just discussed, because, in this instance, the deceased was not guilty merely of neglect, but took affirmative action which contributed to his death, namely, pulling out the tubes. The evidence is far from clear whether the action of the deceased in pulling out the tubes was a reflex action, or whether he was then only semi-conscious, or whether it was a conscious, deliberate act on his part. It is not necessary, however, to resolve this question of fact, because even if the act of the deceased in pulling out the tubes was conscious and deliberate, it would not help the defendant. First, there is not sufficient evidence to justify a finding that if the tubes had remained in the trachea and nasal passages of the deceased, he would have continued to live. Second, and quite irrespective of that consideration, even if it were to be assumed, arguendo, that the deceased might have lived if he had not pulled out the tubes, this circumstance would not have any effect on the liability and responsibility of the defendant for the death of the deceased.

In People v. Lewis, 124 Cal. 551, 559, the facts were as follows. The defendant inflicted a gunshot wound on the deceased. This wound was mortal. The deceased, however, procured a knife and cut his throat, and thereby brought about his death sooner than would have been the case if it had resulted from the original wound. The defendant was convicted of manslaughter, and the conviction was affirmed by the highest court of California.

An even more extreme case is Stephenson v. State, 179 N.E. 633 (Ind.). There the defendant attempted to rape the deceased, and seriously, but not mortally, wounded her. She took poison and died as a result of the poisoning. The defendant was convicted of murder in the second degree, and the Supreme Court of Indiana affirmed the conviction. As against the argument in behalf of the defendant that there was no homicide, since the deceased took her own life by committing suicide, the Court held that the jury was justified in finding that the defendant by his acts or conduct rendered the deceased distracted and mentally irresponsible and that her taking poison was a natural and probable consequence of the unlawful and criminal treatment that the defendant had inflicted on the deceased.

Here the question before the Court is whether the defendant should be deemed guilty of homicide or guilty merely of assault with a dangerous weapon. The Court is of the opinion that the injuries inflicted on the deceased by the defendant were the cause of death in the light of the principles of law heretofore discussed, and that, therefore, the defendant should be adjudged guilty of homicide.

Accordingly, the Court finds the defendant guilty of manslaughter.

Notes and Questions

1. If we believe that Hamilton caused his victim's death, can we at the same time believe that the victim intentionally or voluntarily pulled out his lifesaving tubes? Or must we believe that the victim did not exercise any volition?

2. *Temporal intervals.* The *Hamilton* opinion quotes the common law rule that a defendant may be liable for the death of his victim if the victim dies within a year and a day of the injury. As we saw in Rogers v. Tennesee, p. 136, *supra,* many jurisdictions have abolished the year-and-day rule as outmoded by improvements in medical science.

3. *Languishing victims.* Should the defendant be liable for the death of the victim in the following news article?[19] What about liability for those individuals who made the decision to disconnect the victim's life support system? After all, they probably acted with a clearer intent to end the life of the victim than did the defendant when he stabbed the victim four years earlier.

Assault Victim Dies after Feeding Tube Withheld by Court

Portland, Me.— Mark Weaver, whose life-support system was disconnected eight days ago over the objections of the man who stabbed him, died Friday, nearly four years after the stabbing left him in a coma.

19. New York Times, Apr. 9, 1989, at 24.

Mr. Weaver, 28 years old, "died peacefully," said his mother, Sylvia Lane. "He never had a moment's pain," she said.

Noel Pagan, who served three years in prison for stabbing Mr. Weaver in a street fight in 1985, sought unsuccessfully in court to force Mr. Weaver's family to keep him alive on a feeding tube. Prosecutors have said Mr. Pagan, who is on probation, could face a murder charge after Mr. Weaver's death. They now say they need a technical determination of the cause of death before deciding whether to press charges.

"The medical examiner will conduct an autopsy and make a report to us, and then we will make a decision," Attorney General James E. Tierney said. . . .

Mr. Pagan's lawyer, Robert Mullen, said that if new charges were filed, he would move to have them thrown out. He cited two possible grounds: double jeopardy and a Maine legal provision under which a person must die no more than a year and a day after an assault for the assailant to be charged with murder or manslaughter.

While Mark Weaver languished in a coma for years before his death he did not suffer (although surely his family did). But if the victim of an assault suffers during a long convalescence, we face the question whether the interval between the attack and the death should decrease the assailant's liability or increase it. What punishment is appropriate in the following case?

Woman Dies Seven Years after Husband Shot Her[20]

Chicago — Penny Dunn never walked again and rarely left her hospital bed after her husband shot her in the face during an argument over a telephone bill seven years ago. Her suffering ended quietly with her death last week.

Over the last year, Mrs. Dunn, 42, had several bouts with pneumonia and grew increasingly depressed, family members said. On Thursday, the Cook County medical examiner ruled she died of complications from the gunshot wound.

"I guess maybe she knew that her time was coming," said her mother, Alice Cygan. "She just didn't care anymore."

Dunn shot his wife in the face as she sat on the edge of her bed in November 1986. . . . The gunshot left her unable to walk and barely able to speak. . . .

Criminal Court Judge Donald Joyce acquitted Dunn of attempted murder, convicting him instead of aggravated battery and unlawful use of a weapon. He served two years of a five-year prison term.

Police said Friday they were looking at records of the case to see if additional charges would be filed.

4. *Mistreatment and failure to treat.* Glanville Williams[21] discusses these "victim aggravated" cases:

What if the victim having received an injury foolishly refuses treatment, so that his condition becomes worse?

The rule excluding from consideration the contributory negligence of the victim leading to his first injury does not necessarily entail the conclusion that the attacker is liable for an aggravation of the injury brought about by the victim. This is a separate question. As a matter of justice, it might be thought that the attacker

---

20. Sarah Nordgren, Buffalo News, A.P., Jan. 30, 1994, at A10.
21. Textbook of Criminal Law 397-99 (1983).

ought not generally to be liable for the result of the aggravation; but the cases go the other way.

First, it is clear law that if D inflicts a serious injury on V, and V refuses, however unreasonably, to receive medical treatment and so dies from the injury, D is responsible for the death. The latest decision is *Blaue*. Blaue stabbed V, penetrating her lung. She was taken to hospital, but, being a Jehovah's Witness, refused to have a blood transfusion, and died. The transfusion would probably have saved her. The judge directed the jury that they would get some help from the cases to which counsel had referred in their speeches, and said that they might think they had little option but to reach the conclusion that the stab wound was the operative cause of death — or a substantial cause of death. The jury convicted of manslaughter by reason of diminished responsibility (the diminished responsibility, of course, having nothing to do with the question of causation), and the conviction was affirmed on appeal.

Although the case follows certain ancient authorities, preferring them to opinions expressed in "textbooks intended for students or as studies in jurisprudence," it fails to notice that all the cases dated from a time when medical science was in its infancy, and when operations performed without hygiene carried great danger to life. It was therefore open to the court for the benefit of the defendant to consider the question afresh, and there were several reasons for doing so. . . .

The best reason for the decision, though not one given in the judgment, is that Blaue would have been guilty of unlawful homicide if the victim had had no chance of obtaining medical assistance, and therefore (it may be said) should be equally guilty if the victim chose not to avail herself of such assistance. Still, there is a difference. The decision means that if the death penalty for murder were restored, the attacker might be hanged purely as a result of the unreasonable decision of the victim not to accept preferred medical help. . . .

Assuming that *Blaue* settles the law, there is doubtless one limitation upon the rule, namely, that it does not apply where the injury inflicted by the defendant was trifling.

What if the victim is guilty of a positive act of foolishness aggravating his injury?

In general the aggravation will again be placed at the door of the defendant, at any rate if the victim's act was within the range of reasonable foresight. . . .

[W]here the victim took understandable measures to relieve his suffering, or went on with his ordinary life without fully realising the danger caused by the wound, his conduct does not necessarily sever the causal connection that the law sees between the wound and the death. But the cases do not decide that no supervening act of rashness by the deceased affects the responsibility of the defendant. If the victim's acts were not reasonably foreseeable, and particularly if the wound given were not in itself likely to cause death, and the victim by egregious folly introduced infection into it, a jury might well find, and be in effect required to find, that the defendant's act did not substantially contribute to the death.

5. *Cases on negligent treatment.* Professor Williams's summary of the legal principles that apply where a person injured by the defendant dies after improper treatment by doctors is consistent with the majority approach in American law. In Baylor v. United States, 407 A.2d 664 (D.C. App. 1979), the defendant struck his wife during an argument, causing a two-inch laceration in her spleen. She lay in pain while the ambulance was delayed in arriving, and then waited two hours for doctors to diagnose the problem and decide to operate on her spleen. After the operation, she suffered lung problems that led to pneumonia, and she died of cardiac arrest two weeks after her injury. The court

of appeals affirmed the husband's conviction of involuntary manslaughter. It held that the hospital's negligence did not negate his liability for homicide, since he could reasonably have foreseen the possibility that the victim would receive negligent treatment.

In *Baylor,* the court noted that the victim had suffered a dangerous wound from which she would have died without treatment. At least one court has held that the defendant might nevertheless be innocent of homicide when the wound inflicted by the defendant would not have caused the victim's death even if left untreated, but the victim received improper or negligent treatment that led to death. Wright v. State, 374 A.2d 824 (Del. Supr. 1977). Does this distinction make sense? Is the idea that the negligent treatment was not a necessary condition to the death because the victim would have died without treatment? But is that the right comparison? Should we ask what would have happened if doctors had not treated the victim at all? Or should we ask what would have happened if doctors had not treated the victim negligently?

Many courts relieve the defendant of liability where the doctors treating the victim provide "grossly negligent" treatment. In People v. Stewart, 40 N.Y.2d 692, 389 N.E.2d 487 (1976), the defendant stabbed the victim in the stomach. The surgeons succeeded in closing the stomach wound, but while the victim was on the operating table, the surgeons noticed he had an incarcerated hernia, wholly unrelated to the stab wound, which they also proceeded to treat. While the surgeons worked, the anesthesiologist apparently exhibited "gross negligence" in monitoring the victim's intake supply. The victim suffered massive brain and coronary damage and died a month later without ever regaining consciousness. An expert witness testified that it was probably sound medical practice for the surgeons to treat the hernia while they had already opened the victim's abdomen to treat the stab wound, but that the patient would probably have survived the operation to correct the stab wound if the surgeons had left the hernia untreated. On these facts, the court reduced the conviction from manslaughter to assault. The court concluded that the defendant could not be guilty of homicide if the victim's death was "solely attributable to grossly negligent treatment."

Even if the quoted principle is correct, did the court correctly apply the principle to the facts?

Can you distill a rule from the decisions in *Wright* and *Stewart?* Apply this rule to the facts in *Hamilton.* Would the victim's resistance to treatment constitute an intervening cause of death? If not, is the result in *Hamilton* inconsistent with the intervening actor rule? What about the court's argument for this result? Note that *Hamilton* approvingly cites cases in which victims inflicted aggravating injuries on themselves. One of these is reproduced below.

STEPHENSON v. STATE[22]
Supreme Court of Indiana
179 N.E. 633 (Ind. 1932)

[With the help of several accomplices, Stephenson abducted Madge Oberholtzer, whom he had known socially for several months. Over the next

22. [The *Stephenson* case took place in a politically charged atmosphere. David Curtis Stephenson, the defendant in the case, was the leader of the Ku Klux Klan of Indiana when the

days, Stephenson repeatedly assaulted, bit, and attempted to rape her. Oberholtzer secretly obtained and ingested bichloride of mercury. She became violently ill and Stephenson discovered she had taken the poison. Oberholtzer refused Stephenson's offer to take her to a hospital. Stephenson then decided to return Oberholtzer to her home in Indianapolis, a long trip during which she became violently sick, vomited repeatedly, and screamed for a doctor. Stephenson did nothing to alleviate her suffering during the trip. Stephenson brought her to his home in Indianapolis, from whence she was carried home. After arriving home, Oberholtzer received medical treatment for bite-wounds and poisoning. Although her wounds healed, she died ten days after being returned to her home. The doctor ascribed death to a combination of shock, loss of food, loss of rest, the effect of the poison, lack of early treatment and the general impact of what had happened to her. Stephenson was found guilty of second-degree murder and the Supreme Court affirmed.]

PER CURIAM: . . . Appellant very earnestly argues that the evidence does not show appellant guilty of murder. He points out in his brief that after they reached the hotel, Madge Oberholtzer left the hotel and purchased a hat and the poison, and voluntarily returned to his room, and at the time she took the poison she was in an adjoining room to him, and that she swallowed the poison without his knowledge, and at a time when he was not present. From these facts he contends she took her life by committing suicide; that her own act in taking poison was an intervening responsible agent which broke the causal connection between his acts and the death, that his acts were not the proximate cause of her death, but the taking of poison was the proximate cause of her death. . . .

      . . . In the case of Rex v. Beech [23 Cox Crim. Cas. 181 (1912)], the prosecutrix was the village nurse and lived alone. At 11:45 P.M. on an evening in November the appellant came to her house when she was in bed. He entered the house by breaking a window and went upstairs to the bedroom occupied by the prosecutrix. The door was locked and the appellant threatened to break it open if the prosecutrix would not let him in. She refused and the appellant then tried to burst open the door. The prosecutrix called out, that if he got in he would not find her in the room, and as the appellant continued his attack upon the door the prosecutrix jumped out of the window sustaining injuries. The prosecutrix also testified that the appellant had attempted to interfere with her on a previous occasion when she had threatened to take poison if he touched her. The court approved the proposition as stated by the lower court as follows: "Whether the conduct of the prisoner amounted to a threat of causing injury to the young woman; was the act of jumping the natural consequence of the conduct of the prisoner and was the grievous bodily harm the result of the conduct of the prisoner." The court held that if these questions were answered in the

organization was at the height of its power, with 200,000 members in 1920 in Indiana alone, and millions nationwide. He was credited with reviving the Klan and widening its base, and considered the most powerful man in Indiana. After his conviction, and angered that Gov. Ed Jackson of Indiana would not pardon him, Stephenson released his "little black box," which implicated a number of highly placed state officials in Klan activities. The case and its fall-out effectively destroyed the Klan in Indiana, and may have reversed its ascendancy as a national political force. The story of Stephenson and the trial is told in a 1989 NEC movie, "Cross of Fire." See Kogan, The Heart of Evil: Well Crafted "Cross of Fire" Depicts the Klan in Its Heyday, Chicago Tribune, November 3, 1989, at Tempo sec., p.l.; Hill, The Rise and Fall of the KKK: "Cross of Fire"'s Story of the Man Under the Sheet, Washington Post, Nov. 5, 1989, at TV Tab sec., p.8. —EDS.]

affirmative he would be guilty. In Rex v. Valade (Que.), 22 Rev. De. Jur. 524, 26 Can. Cr. Cas. 233, where the accused induced a young girl to go along with him to a secluded apartment, and there had criminal sexual intercourse with her, following which she jumped from a window to the street to get away from him and was killed by the fall. The accused was held guilty of murder. Bishop in his work on Criminal Law, Vol. 2, 9th Edition, page 484, says, "When suicide follows a wound inflicted by the defendant his act is homicidal, if deceased was rendered irresponsible by the wound and as a natural result of it." . . . We do not understand that the rule laid down by Bishop, *supra*, that the wound which renders the deceased mentally irresponsible is necessarily limited to a physical wound. We should think that the same rule would apply if a defendant engaged in the commission of a felony such as rape . . . inflicts upon his victim both physical and mental injuries, the natural and probable result of which would render the deceased mentally irresponsible and suicide followed, we think he would be guilty of murder.

In the case at bar appellant is charged with having caused the death of Madge Oberholtzer while engaged in the crime of attempted rape. The evidence shows that appellant together with Earl Gentry and the deceased left their compartment on the train and went to a hotel about a block from the depot, and there appellant registered as husband and wife, and immediately went to the room assigned to them. This change from their room on the train to a room in the hotel is of no consequence, for appellant's control and domination over the deceased was absolute and complete in both cases. The evidence further shows that the deceased asked for money with which to purchase a hat, and it was supplied her by "Shorty," at the direction of appellant, and that she did leave the room and was taken by "Shorty" to a shop and purchased a hat and then, at her request, to a drug store where she purchased the bichloride of mercury tablets, and then she was taken back to the room in the hotel, where about 10:00 o'clock A.M. she swallowed the poison. Appellant argues that the deceased was a free agent on this trip to purchase a hat, etc., and that she voluntarily returned to the room in the hotel. This was a question for the jury and the evidence would justify them in reaching a contrary conclusion. Appellant's chauffeur accompanied her on this trip, and the deceased had, before she left appellant's home in Indianapolis, attempted to get away and also made two unsuccessful attempts to use the telephone to call help. She was justified in concluding that any attempt she might make, while purchasing a hat or while in the drug store, to escape or secure assistance would be no more successful in Hammond than it was in Indianapolis. We think the evidence shows that the deceased was at all times from the time she was entrapped by the appellant at his home on the evening of March 15th till she was returned to her home two days later, in the custody and absolute control of appellant. Neither do we think the fact that the deceased took the poison some four hours after they left the drawing-room on the train or after the crime of attempted rape had been committed necessarily prevents it from being part of the attempted rape. Suppose they had not left the drawing-room on the train, and instead of the deceased taking poison she had secured possession of the appellant's revolver and shot herself or thrown herself out of the window of the car and died from the fall. We can see no vital difference. At the very moment Madge Oberholtzer swallowed the poison she was subjected to the passion, desire and will of the appellant. She knew not what moment she would be subjected to the same demands that she was while in the drawing-room on the train. What would have prevented appellant from compelling her to submit to him at any moment? The same forces, the same impulses, that would impel her to shoot herself during the actual attack or throw herself out of the car window after the attack had ceased, was pressing and overwhelming her at the time she swallowed the poison. The evidence shows that she was so weak that she staggered as she left the elevator to go to the room in the hotel, and was assisted, by appellant and Gentry. That she was very ill so much so that she could not eat, all of which was the direct and proximate result of the treatment accorded her by the appellant. We think the situation no different here than we find in the *Beech* case or the *Valade* case, *supra.* To say that there is no causal connection between the acts of appellant and the death of Madge Oberholtzer would be a travesty of justice. The whole criminal program was so closely connected that we think it should be treated as one transaction, and should be governed by the same principles of law as was applied in the case of Rex v. Beech and Rex v. Valade, *supra.* We therefore conclude that the evidence was sufficient and justified the jury in finding that appellant by his acts and conduct rendered the deceased distracted and mentally irresponsible, and that such was the natural and probable consequence of such unlawful and criminal treatment, and that the appellant was guilty of murder in the second degree as charged in the first count of the indictment.

Notes and Questions

1. The *Stephenson* court characterizes Oberholtzer's despondency and resulting suicide as "natural and probable," i.e., the foreseeable consequence of the abduction and assault. Was it the intended consequence? Stephenson was convicted of second degree murder, which required the jury to find that Stephenson "purposely" killed Oberholtzer.

Under the Indiana murder statute then in force, the jurors could have convicted Stephenson of first degree murder without finding any purpose to kill, if they had agreed merely that he had "caused poison to be administered to her," or that he had caused death "in the . . . attempt to perpetrate a rape." But, oddly, the jury convicted on the lesser charge of second degree murder, which did require purpose.

2. Is it crucial for the result in this case that the victim's suicidal act was "mentally irresponsible"? Consider the following two scenarios:

Scenario #1: Stephenson offers a ride to Oberholtzer, an acquaintance. She accepts. While driving at a high speed, Stephenson suddenly brandishes a knife at Oberholtzer and threatens her. She leaps from the car and dies as a result of her injuries.

Scenario #2: Stephenson offers a ride to Oberholtzer, an acquaintance. She accepts. While driving at a high speed, Stephenson suddenly waves a best-selling paperback in her face, and says "this is the best new translation of Proust ever — you *must* read it!" Oberholtzer, startled, leaps from the car and dies as a result of her injuries.

In which scenario is Oberholtzer's response more rational? In which scenario is Stephenson more causally responsible for Oberholtzer's death?

Perhaps the crucial question is not whether Oberholtzer is mentally responsible for her suicidal act but whether Stephenson is responsible for her suicidal act, by depriving her of either the mental capacity or the practical opportunity to make a better choice.

3. The *Stephenson* court emphasizes that Oberholtzer remained in Stephenson's custody and control throughout the abduction, including when she purchased and took the poison. Is this important to Stephenson's liability? Does he have an obligation to prevent the suicide? If Oberholtzer, though still distraught, had already been freed by the time she poisoned herself, would Stephenson be off the hook for the homicide?

Suppose that instead of taking poison during the abduction, Oberholtzer had languished in a depression for a year afterwards, and then fatally poisoned herself. Would Stephenson still be guilty of murder? Suppose, still traumatized by the crime a year later, Oberholtzer had instead shot and killed someone she wrongly believed was about to assault her? Would Stephenson be liable for that, too? If Stephenson is not causally responsible for these later deaths, why not? Because they are unforeseeable? Because the temporal interval is too long? Because Stephenson is no longer in a position to prevent the death?

4. *Causing suicide.* When is one person causally responsible for the self-destructive act of another? In Persampieri v. Commonwealth, 175 N.E. 2d 387 (1961), the Massachusetts Supreme Judicial Court upheld a manslaughter conviction on these facts:

> The petitioner's wife was emotionally disturbed, she had been drinking, and she had threatened to kill herself. The petitioner, instead of trying to bring her to her senses, taunted her, told her where the gun was, loaded it for her, saw that the safety was off, and told her the means by which she could pull the trigger. He thus showed a complete disregard of his wife's safety and the possible consequences of his conduct.

In State v. Bier, 591 P.2d 1115 (1979), the Montana Supreme Court affirmed a negligent homicide conviction, despite evidence that the victim, defendant's then very intoxicated wife, shot herself during a marital argument:

> Defendant stated that . . . intent on leaving and avoiding further quarrel, [he] went into the bedroom to ready his departure. Mrs. Bier stood in the bedroom doorway, apparently to block his exit. Defendant reached into the closet, pulled a gun from its holster, cocked it and cast it on the bed stating words to the effect that to stop him she'd have to shoot him. Defendant turned away and his wife picked up the gun, held it with both thumbs on the trigger and pointed it at her head. Defendant shouted "that damn thing's loaded" and either grabbed or slapped at the gun to avert its aim. It discharged and Mrs. Bier collapsed on the floor. . . . Mrs. Bier never regained consciousness and died six days after the shooting. . . .
>
> Defendant . . . contends he should not be held responsible to have foreseen his wife's alleged suicide attempt. Generally, where a crime is based on some form of negligence the state must show not only that defendant's negligent conduct was the "cause in fact" of the victim's death, but also that the victim was foreseeably endangered, in a manner which was foreseeable and to a degree of harm which was foreseeable. . . . Clearly the risk created by defendant's conduct under the circumstances (that in a highly intoxicated state his wife would shoot either the defendant or herself) was a foreseeable risk. Indeed, he challenged her to use the gun.

Does supplying or loading a gun under such circumstances "cause" the victim to pull the trigger? Or is this like holding a waiter liable for setting the table with a steak knife later used in a homicide?

Is it even crucial to the reasoning of the court in these cases that the defendant supplied or loaded the gun? The Massachusetts court implies that defendant had an obligation to try to dissuade the victim from committing suicide. Was his failure to do so by itself sufficient to constitute a cause of death? Is it important in these cases that defendant and victim were married?

Are the results in *Persampieri* and *Bier* compatible with the position reached by the court in the following famous case?

PEOPLE v. KEVORKIAN
Supreme Court of Michigan
527 N.W.2d 714 (1994)

[Defendant filed a motion to quash the information and dismiss murder charges concerning assisted suicides. The Circuit Court, Oakland County, granted defendant's motion to dismiss, and the state appealed. The Court of Appeals reversed and remanded, and defendant appealed to the Michigan Supreme Court.]

MICHAEL F. CAVANAGH, CHIEF JUSTICE, and BRICKLEY and ROBERT P. GRIFFIN, JUSTICES. . . .

Before . . . [Michigan's Assisted Suicide] statute was enacted, defendant [Dr. Jack] Kevorkian allegedly assisted in the deaths of Sherry Miller and Marjorie Wantz on October 23, 1991. . . . Each woman was said to be suffering from a condition that caused her great pain or was severely disabling. Each separately had sought defendant Kevorkian's assistance in ending her life. The women and several friends and relatives met the defendant at a cabin in Oakland County on October 23, 1991.

According to the testimony presented at the defendant's preliminary examination, the plan was to use his "suicide machine." The device consisted of a board to which one's arm is strapped to prevent movement, a needle to be inserted into a blood vessel and attached to IV tubing, and containers of various chemicals that are to be released through the needle into the bloodstream. Strings are tied to two of the fingers of the person who intends to die. The strings are attached to clips on the IV tubing that control the flow of the chemicals. As explained by one witness, the person raises that hand, releasing a . . . fast-acting barbiturate. . . . "When the person falls asleep, the hand drops, pulling the other string, which releases another clip and allows potassium chloride to flow into the body in concentrations sufficient to cause death."

The defendant tried several times, without success, to insert the suicide-machine needle into Ms. Miller's arm and hand. He then left the cabin, returning several hours later with a cylinder of carbon monoxide gas and a mask apparatus. He attached a screw driver to the cylinder, and showed Ms. Miller how to use the tool as a lever to open the gas valve.

The defendant then turned his attention to Ms. Wantz. He was successful in inserting the suicide-machine needle into her arm. The defendant explained to Ms. Wantz how to activate the device so as to allow the drugs to enter her bloodstream. The device was activated, and Ms. Wantz died.

The defendant then placed the mask apparatus on Ms. Miller. The only witness at the preliminary examination who was present at the time said that Ms. Miller opened the gas valve by pulling on the screw driver. The cause of her death was determined to be carbon-monoxide poisoning.

The defendant was indicted on two counts of open murder. He was bound over for trial following a preliminary examination. However, in circuit court, the defendant moved to quash the information and dismiss the charges, and the court granted the motion.

A divided Court of Appeals reversed. . . . The Court of Appeals majority relied principally on People v. Roberts, 178 N.W. 690 (1920).

In *Roberts*, the defendant's wife was suffering from advanced multiple sclerosis and in great pain. She previously had attempted suicide and, according to the defendant's statements at the plea proceeding, requested that he provide her with poison. He agreed, and placed a glass of poison within her reach. She drank the mixture and died. The defendant was charged with murder. He pleaded guilty, and the trial court determined the crime to be murder in the first degree.

The defendant appealed [unsuccessfully]. . . . [T]he *Roberts* Court concluded: We are of the opinion that when defendant mixed the paris green with water and placed it within reach of his wife to enable her to put an end to her suffering by putting an end to her life, he was guilty of murder by means of poison within the meaning of the statute, even though she requested him to do so. By this act he deliberately placed within her reach the means of taking her own life, which she could have obtained in no other way by reason of her helpless condition. [178 N.W. 690.] . . .

We must determine . . . whether *Roberts* remains viable. . . . Under the common-law definition, "[m]urder is where a person of sound memory and discretion unlawfully kills any reasonable creature in being, in peace of the state, with malice prepense or aforethought, either express or implied." Implicit in this definition is a finding that the defendant performed an act that caused the death of another. To convict a defendant of criminal homicide, it must be proven that death occurred as a direct and natural result of the defendant's act. . . .

Early decisions indicate that a murder conviction may be based on merely providing the means by which another commits suicide. However, few jurisdictions, if any, have retained the early common-law view that assisting in a suicide is murder. The modern statutory scheme in the majority of states treats assisted suicide as a separate crime, with penalties less onerous than those for murder.

Recent decisions draw a distinction between active participation in a suicide and involvement in the events leading up to the suicide, such as providing the means. Frequently, these cases arise in the context of a claim by the defendant that the prosecution should have been brought under an assisted suicide statute. The courts generally have held that a person may be prosecuted for murder if the person's acts went beyond the conduct that the assisted suicide statute was intended to cover.

For example, in People v. Cleaves, 229 Cal. App. 3d 367, 280 Cal. Rptr. 146 (1991), the defendant was charged with first-degree murder in the strangulation death of another man. [The decedent in *Cleaves* was suffering from AIDS and wanted the defendant's assistance in strangling himself.] The trial court had refused a defense request to instruct the jury on the statutory offense of aiding and abetting a suicide, and the jury convicted him of second-degree murder.

. . . In holding that the trial judge properly refused to instruct the jury under the assisted suicide statute, the appeals court said:

[The statute] provides: "Every person who deliberately aids, or advises, or encourages another to commit suicide, is guilty of a felony." As explained by our Supreme Court, the "key to distinguishing between the crimes of murder and of assisting suicide is the active or passive role of the defendant in the suicide. If the defendant merely furnishes the means, he is guilty of aiding a suicide; if he actively participates in the death of the suicide victim, he is guilty of murder." [In re Joseph G, 34 Cal. 3d 429, 436; 194 Cal. Rptr. 163 (1983).] The statute providing for a crime less than murder "'does not contemplate active participation by one in the overt act directly causing death. It contemplates some participation in the events leading up to the commission of the final overt act, such as furnishing the means for bringing about death, the gun, the knife, the poison, or providing the water, for the use of the person who himself commits the act of self-murder. But where a person actually performs, or actively assists in performing, the overt act resulting in death, such as shooting or stabbing the victim, administering the poison, or holding one under water until death takes place by drowning, his act constitutes murder, and it is wholly immaterial whether this act is committed pursuant to an agreement with the victim. . . .'" [quoting People v. Matlock, 51 Cal.2d 682, 694 (1959)]

In the years since 1920, when *Roberts* was decided, interpretation of causation in criminal cases has evolved in Michigan to require a closer nexus between an act and a death than was required in *Roberts*. . . .

In the context of participation in a suicide, the distinction recognized in In re Joseph G, *supra* at 436, constitutes the view most consistent with the overwhelming trend of modern authority. There, the California Supreme Court explained that a conviction of murder is proper if a defendant participates in the final overt act that causes death, such as firing a gun or pushing the plunger on a hypodermic needle. However, where a defendant is involved merely "in the events leading up to the commission of the final overt act, such as furnishing the means . . . ," a conviction of assisted suicide is proper. Id.

. . . [T]his Court has modified the common law when it perceives a need to tailor culpability to fit the crime more precisely than is achieved through application of existing interpretations of the common law. . . . For the reasons given, we perceive such a need here. Accordingly, we would overrule *Roberts* to the extent that it can be read to support the view that the common-law definition of murder encompasses the act of intentionally providing the means by which a person commits suicide. Only where there is probable cause to believe that death was the direct and natural result of a defendant's act can the defendant be properly bound over on a charge of murder.[23] Where a defendant merely is involved in the events leading up to the death, such as providing the means, the proper charge is assisting in a suicide.

23. However, there may be circumstances where one who recklessly or negligently provides the means by which another commits suicide could be found guilty of a lesser offense, such as involuntary manslaughter. There are a number of cases in which providing a gun to a person known to the defendant to be intoxicated and despondent or agitated has constituted sufficient recklessness to support such a conviction. For example, in People v. Duffy, 79 N.Y.2d 611, 613, 595 N.E.2d 814 (1992), the defendant provided a gun to the intoxicated and despondent decedent, who had said he wanted to kill himself, and urged him to "blow his head off." The decedent proceeded to shoot himself. Duffy was . . . [convicted of] recklessly caus[ing] the death (N.Y. Penal Law, §125.15[1]). The New York Court of Appeals concluded:

[T]he conduct with which defendant was charged clearly fell within the scope of section 125.15[1]'s proscription against recklessly causing the death of another person. As the People aptly observe, a person who, knowing that another is contemplating immediate suicide, deliberately prods that person to go forward and furnishes the means of bringing about death may certainly be said to have "consciously disregard[ed] a substantial and unjustifiable risk" that his actions would result in the death of that person. . . .

... [W]e remand this matter to the circuit court for reconsideration of the defendant's motion to quash in light of the principles discussed in this opinion.

BOYLE, JUSTICE, dissenting in part.

I do not agree with the lead opinion's redefinition of the statutory offense of murder to exclude participation in the events leading up to the death, including, without limitation, providing the means and all other acts save that of the final act precipitating death. A person who participates in the death of another may be charged with murder, irrespective of the consent of the deceased. . . . The acts shown in the Oakland County case establish causation as a matter of law for purposes of bindover. Thus, the trial court erred in quashing the information, and the decision of the Court of Appeals should be affirmed.

Criminal homicide has been a statutory offense in Michigan since 1846. The crime is not defined by reference to its elements but by reference to the common law. . . . There is no dispute that at the time these offenses were committed, the Legislature had shown no disposition to depart from the common-law definition of murder as including assisted suicide. The lead opinion today would alter the definition of murder by changing the causation requirement in the context of suicide to exclude from liability for criminal homicide those who intentionally participate in the events that directly cause death with the intention that death occur.

However, the intended results of the plaintiff's acts were the results actually obtained, and the acts were both the cause in fact and the proximate or foreseeable cause of the decedents' deaths. The lead opinion would thus redefine murder as it is defined in our statutes and has created a special causation standard, unknown in any other jurisdiction. . . .

The fact that an active participant in the death of another risks jury determination that the circumstances are not so compelling as to benefit from their mercy-dispensing power tests the situation and the actions by the only repository of authority within the judicial reach. Whether death has been caused for good, bad, or mixed reasons, or whether the person is in fact presently incurable or suffering intolerable and unmanageable pain, and has a fixed and rational desire to die, are issues that should be addressed by a jury or the Legislature, not by this Court as a matter of law. . . .

In a society that draws a line that dictates that it is better that many go free than that one innocent person should be convicted, something approaching the principles protecting against error that are extended to the criminally accused should be extended to the victims of those who are willing to participate in suicide and to cause death, as long as they do not pull the final trigger. . . . To the extent that this Court reduces culpability for those who actively participate in acts that produce death, we do so at the risk of the most vulnerable members of our society — the elderly, the ill, the chronically depressed, those suffering from a panoply of stressful situations: adolescence, loss of employment, the death of a child or spouse, divorce, alcoholism, the abuse of other mind-altering substances, and the burden of social stigmatization.

Notes and Questions

1. The dissenting judge claims that the majority has adopted a novel standard of causation unknown in other jurisdictions. Is that right? Has the majority simply followed the intervening actor rule?

2. The majority attempts to distinguish People v. Duffy, a case finding causation on facts similar to the facts in *Persampieri*. Is this attempt successful? Perhaps Kevorkian's "victims" had better reasons to kill themselves than Duffy's or Persampieri's, but how was his causal role any smaller? How would the *Kevorkian* court decide *Bier*?

3. The dissent charges that the majority's holding provides little protection for vulnerable and psychologically instable people from being bullied or manipulated into suicide. Is that charge fair? Suppose Kevorkian had provided aid and encouragement for the suicide of a 17-year-old athlete, despondent after becoming paralyzed in a car accident. Would the *Kevorkian* court permit a murder charge to stand on those facts?

If the lack of meaningful consent on the part of suicide victim is an element of homicide-by-assisted suicide, who should bear the burden of proof on this issue? The dissent argues that permitting prosecutors to charge murder in cases of assisted suicide would force those who aid or encourage suicide to face a jury and persuade it that the suicide was fully consensual. Is it consistent with the presumption of innocence to force defendants to prove this?

Finally, if assisting a mentally irresponsible person to commit suicide is a form of homicide, what mens rea must defendant have with respect to defendant's capacity to consent?

4. Following the state Supreme Court's invitation, the state of Michigan continued to prosecute Dr. Kevorkian under the common law of crimes. Twice the jury acquitted him, but on March 26, 1999, after a trial in which he served as his own lawyer, Kevorkian was convicted of second degree murder after he directly administered a lethal dose of drugs at the request of a 52-year-old man suffering from Lou Gehrig's disease, and he now is in prison, still pursing appeals, and eligible for parole in 2007.

Meanwhile, the Supreme Court of the United States has upheld the constitutionality of state statutes making it a crime to assist a suicide. The court found the punishment of suicide assistance sufficiently rooted in tradition and common law and sufficiently reflected in contemporary law so as not to violate due process. Washington v. Glucksberg, 521 U.S. 702 (1997). It also found no violation of equal protection in a law that made aiding or attempting suicide illegal, even though that law permitted a patient to refuse even lifesaving treatment. Vacco v. Quill, 521 U.S. 793 (1997).

E.   CAUSATION BY OMISSION: DUTIES

PEOPLE v. BEARDSLEY
Supreme Court of Michigan
150 Mich. 205, 113 N.W. 1128 (1907)

McALVAY, C.J.

Respondent was convicted of manslaughter before the circuit court for Oakland county, and was sentenced to the state prison at Jackson for a minimum term of one year and a maximum term not to exceed five years.

He was a married man living at Pontiac, and at the time the facts herein narrated occurred he was working as a bartender and clerk at the Columbia Hotel. He lived with his wife in Pontiac, occupying two rooms on the ground floor of a house. Other rooms were rented to tenants, as was also one living room in the basement. His wife being temporarily absent from the city, respondent arranged with a woman named Blanche Burns, who at the time was working at another hotel, to go to his apartments with him. He had been acquainted with her for some time. They knew each other's habits and character. They had drunk liquor together, and had on two occasions been in Detroit and spent the night together in houses of assignation. On the evening of Saturday, March 18, 1905, he met her at the place where she worked, and they went together to his place of residence. They at once began to drink, and continued to drink steadily, and remained together, day and night, from that time until the afternoon of the Monday following, except when respondent went to his work on Sunday afternoon. There was liquor at these rooms, and when it was all used they were served with bottles of whisky and beer by a young man who worked at the Columbia Hotel, and who also attended respondent's fires at the house. . . . On Monday afternoon, about 1 o'clock, the young man went to the house to see if anything was wanted. At this time he heard respondent say they must fix up the rooms, and the woman must not be found there by his wife, who was likely to return at any time. During this visit to the house the woman sent the young man to a drug store to purchase, with money she gave him, . . . morphine tablets. . . . She concealed the morphine from respondent's notice, and was discovered putting something into her mouth by him and the young man as they were returning from the other room after taking a drink of beer. She in fact was taking morphine. Respondent struck the box from her hand. Some of the tablets fell on the floor, and of these respondent crushed several with his foot. . . . All together it is probable she took from three to four grains of morphine. The young man went away soon after this. Respondent called him by telephone about an hour later, and after he came to the house requested him to take the woman into the room in the basement which was occupied by a Mr. Skoba. She was in a stupor, and did not rouse when spoken to. The young man proceeded to take her downstairs. While doing this, Skoba arrived, and together they put her in his room on the bed. Respondent requested Skoba to look after her, and let her out the back way when she waked up. Between 9 and 10 o'clock in the evening, Skoba became alarmed at her condition. He at once called the city marshal and a doctor. An examination by them disclosed that she was dead.

. . . In the brief of the prosecutor, his position is stated as follows:

> It is the theory of the prosecution that the facts and circumstances attending the death of Blanche Burns in the house of respondent were such as to lay upon him a duty to care for her, and the duty to take steps for her protection, the failure to take which was sufficient to constitute such an omission as would render him legally responsible for her death. . . . There is no claim on the part of the people that the respondent was in anyway an active agent in bringing about the death of Blanche Burns, but simply that he owed her a duty which he failed to perform, and that in consequence of such failure of his part she came to her death.

Upon this theory a conviction was asked and secured.

The law recognizes that under some circumstances the omission of a duty owed by one individual to another, where such omission results in the death of the one to whom the duty is owing, will make the other chargeable with manslaughter. . . . This rule of law is always based upon the proposition that the duty neglected must be a legal duty, and not a mere moral obligation. It must be a duty imposed by law or by contract, and the omission to perform the duty must be the immediate and direct cause of death. . . . One authority has briefly and correctly stated the rule, which the prosecution claims should be applied to the case at bar, as follows:

> If a person who sustains to another the legal relation of protector, as husband to wife, parent to child, master to seaman, etc., knowing such person to be in peril, willfully and negligently fails to make such reasonable and proper efforts to rescue him as he might have done, without jeopardizing his own life, or the lives of others, he is guilty of manslaughter at least, if by reason of his omission of duty the dependent person dies. . . . So one who from domestic relationship, public duty, voluntary choice, or otherwise, has the custody and care of a human being, helpless either from imprisonment, infancy, sickness, age, imbecility, or other incapacity of mind or body is bound to execute the charge with proper diligence, and will be held guilty of manslaughter, if by culpable negligence he lets the helpless creature die.

. . . Seeking for a proper determination of the case at bar by the application of the legal principles involved, we must eliminate from the case all consideration of mere moral obligation, and discover whether respondent was under a legal duty towards Blanche Burns at the time of her death, knowing her to be in peril of her life, which required him to make all reasonable and proper effort to save her, the omission to perform which duty would make him responsible for her death. This is the important and determining question in this case. . . . The record in this case discloses that the deceased was a woman past 30 years of age. She had been twice married. She was accustomed to visiting saloons and to the use of intoxicants. She previously had made assignations with this man in Detroit at least twice. There is no evidence or claim from this record that any duress, fraud, or deceit had been practiced upon her. On the contrary, it appears that she went upon this carouse with respondent voluntarily, and so continued to remain with him. Her entire conduct indicates that she had ample experience in such affairs.

It is urged by the prosecutor that the respondent "stood towards this woman for the time being in the place of her natural guardian and protector, and as such owed her a clear legal duty which he completely failed to perform." The cases establish that no such legal duty is created based upon a mere moral obligation. The fact that this woman was in his house created no such legal duty as exists in law and is due from a husband towards his wife, as seems to be intimated by the prosecutor's brief. Such an inference would be very repugnant to our moral sense. Respondent had assumed either in fact or by implication no care or control over his companion. Had this been a case where two men under like circumstances had voluntarily gone on a debauch together, and one had attempted suicide, no one would claim that this doctrine of legal duty could be invoked to hold the other criminally responsible for omitting to make effort to rescue his companion. How can the fact that in this case one of the parties was a woman change the principle of law applicable to it? Deriving and applying the law in this case from the principle of decided cases, we do not find that such legal duty as is contended for existed in fact or by implication on the part of respondent towards the deceased, the omission of which involved criminal

liability. We find no more apt words to apply to this case than those used by
Mr. Justice Field, . . . "In the absence of such obligations, it is undoubtedly the
moral duty of every person to extend to others assistance when in danger . . .
and, if such efforts should be omitted by any one when they could be made without imperiling his own life, he would by his conduct draw upon himself the just
censure and reproach of good men; but this is the only punishment to which he
would be subjected by society." . . .

had only a moral obligation, if any

The conviction is set aside, and respondent is ordered discharged.

Notes and Questions

1. Was it foreseeable that Burns might die if Beardsley did not seek medical attention for her? If so, then what difference should it make what sort of
relationship they had?

You may recall from Chapter 2, *supra,* that there are only four traditionally
recognized sources of duties to aid: status-relations (like marriage); statutory
obligations; contract; and undertaking (where the offer of aid may preclude
others from aiding a victim). Are any of these present in the facts of the *Beardsley*
case?

sources of duties

Professor Graham Hughes calls for a generalized duty to prevent foreseeable harm:

> [I]n the immense complexity and interdependency of modern life, those who
> elect to pursue certain activities or calling must, for the welfare of their fellow cit-
> izens, submit to a host of regulations, some of which will naturally and properly im-
> pose positive duties to act. . . .
>
> . . . In a civilized society, a man who finds himself with a helplessly ill person
> who has no other source of aid should be under a duty to summon help, whether
> the person is his wife, his mistress, a prostitute, or a Chief Justice. The *Beardsley* de-
> cision deserves emphatic repudiation by the jurisdiction which was responsible.[24]

Can you see any problems with Hughes's theory?

2. Professor George Fletcher defends the *Beardsley* decision and draws the
duty to aid more narrowly:

> It would be a mistake to read this case as holding that duties to aid should be
> limited in the common law to marital or legitimate relationships. The point that
> the court stressed in justifying the reversal was that there was an element of risk in
> the weekend assignation and that the victim . . . undertook those risks with her eyes
> open. The affair had not gone far enough to establish the degree of interdepen-
> dence that would support a legal duty to do more than defendant did. . . . The de-
> fendant himself was intoxicated and hardly in a position to think clearly about
> what should be done to help a friend in distress.
>
> . . . [W]ith the exception of drinking sprees, the binding together of people
> to confront common risks entails reciprocal duties of aid. The common cases
> would be seamen going to sea, mountaineers joined in a single party, astronauts in
> a single spaceship — these would be fairly clear cases of joint enterprises entailing
> reciprocal duties.[25]

24. Hughes, Criminal Omissions, 67 Yale L.J. 590, 600, 624 (1958).
25. George Fletcher, Rethinking Criminal Law 613-14 (1978).

3. *Duties and victim self-harm.* One possible ground for decision in *Beardsley* is the fact that the deceased had brought her need for help upon herself by abusing a drug. In other words, we might think that Beardsley's causal responsibility for Burns's death was precluded by Burns's own voluntary action. Can a passive actor be held causally responsible for a result produced by the voluntary action of another person?

In general, where one person has a duty to seek medical attention for another person's illness or injury, this duty is unaffected by the source of the other person's malady. Because a voluntarily inflicted injury precedes neglect to treat an injury, it is not an intervening cause. Hence, violating a duty to seek treatment for a voluntarily inflicted injury may be a cause of death. The more difficult question is whether failure to prevent a voluntary action can ever be a cause of death.

4. *Creating risk and duty to aid.* Professor George Fletcher comments:

In the typical case of derivative liability for failing to avert harm, the defendant comes on the scene after the potential victim has fallen into jeopardy. . . . Yet in other cases that seem more difficult, the defendant himself is the one who creates the danger to the potential victim. This can happen in a variety of ways. The suspect assaults the victim and leaves him lying, disabled, in the street. Or he, without fault on his part, runs down a pedestrian and leaves him there, bleeding. In another variation, he rapes a girl and she, distraught, falls into a stream and drowns while he looks on with satisfaction.

The preliminary distinction required in the analysis of these cases is whether the defendant is criminally culpable for causing the original state of distress. If he is, there is considerable support for a duty to prevent complications of the original crime. . . .

At the other end of the spectrum are those cases in which the defendant justifiably inflicts injury in self-defense and then leaves the victim to die. The consensus . . . is that there is no liability for death resulting from a justified blow. . . .

The difficult, middle range of cases are those in which the defendant causes the distress to the person in need of aid [without fault on the part of either.] . . . This is a contested field . . . particularly in the area of road accidents.[26]

Fletcher suggests that creating risk should impose a duty to avert harm only if the actor is at fault for creating the risk. If we accept this suggestion, can we justify the result in Commonwealth v. Cali, 141 N.E. 510 (Sup. Jud. Ct., Mass. 1923):

The defendant having been indicted, tried and convicted under G.L. c. 266, §10, of burning a building in Leominster belonging to Maria Cali, which at the time was insured against loss or damage by fire, with intent to injure the insurer, the case is here on his exceptions to the denial of his motion for a directed verdict, and to rulings at the trial. . . .

The only evidence as to the origin, extent and progress of the fire were the statements of the defendant to the police inspector, *and* as a witness. The jury who were to determine his credibility and the weight to be given his testimony could find notwithstanding his explanations of its origin as being purely accidental, that when all the circumstances were reviewed he either set it, or after the fire *was* under way purposely refrained from any attempt to extinguish it in order to obtain

26. Id. at 619-20.

the benefit of the proceeds of the policy, which when recovered, would be applied by the mortgagee on his indebtedness. If they so found, a specific intent to injure the insurer had been proved. The motion and the defendant's requests insofar as not given were denied rightly. . . .

The instructions to the jury that: "If a man does start an accidental fire what is his conduct in regard to it? A question — as if after the fire has started accidentally, and he then has it within his power and ability to extinguish the fire and he realizes and knows that he can, and then he forms and entertains an intent to injure an insurance company, he can be guilty of this offense. It is not necessary that the intent be formed before the fire is started," — also show no error of law.

If the defendant was not proven to have been at fault in starting the fire, why did he have a duty to put it out? If he had none, how did he cause the building to burn or cause injury to the insurer?

5. *Duties to protect from crime.* Can we ever cause death by failing to prevent the voluntary criminal conduct of another? In Palmer v. State, 223 Md. 341 (1960), defendant was convicted of manslaughter after her infant died from the effects of beatings by her lover, a Mr. McCue (who was likewise convicted of manslaughter). The Maryland Supreme Court affirmed Ms. Palmer's conviction, writing:

> . . . [T]he appellant's conduct and actions in permitting and, in fact, compelling this poor little defenseless urchin to remain in an environment where she was subjected to merciless, inhumane, and inordinate brutality of a protracted nature, manifested a recklessness of justice and the rights and feelings of the tiny infant in such a manner so as to support the finding that the appellant's conduct and actions displayed "a wanton or reckless disregard of human life." The actions of McCue were so outrageous as to put any reasonable person on guard that the child's life was in real and imminent peril. . . .
>
> The question of proximate cause here turns largely upon the foreseeability of the consequence of the defendant's permitting McCue to "discipline" the child by repeated and violent beatings. The trial judge, as the trier of facts in this case, found that there was a causal connection between the mother's negligence and the death. We think the evidence sufficient to sustain his conclusion.
>
> There seems to be no doubt that the direct and immediate cause of . . . [the victim's] death was the violent blow or blows inflicted upon her by McCue on September 3rd. But we do not deem this action upon his part to amount to an "intervening efficient cause" (as distinguished from one that is concurrent or contributing), as that term is used in the statement of the doctrine of proximate cause. McCue's brutal striking of the child so as to cause her death would constitute a ground of defense for the appellant's gross negligence only if it were the sole cause of the injury. . . .
>
> . . . McCue's violent and unrestrained actions were of such a nature as to put any ordinary, reasonable person on notice that the child's life was truly and realistically in immediate peril. The appellant easily could, and should, have removed . . . [the child] from this danger. Her failure to do so . . . is sufficient . . . to support a finding . . . that her gross and criminal negligence was a contributing cause [of death].

Why does the court treat McCue's abuse of the victim as a "concurrent or contributing" rather than an "intervening efficient" cause? Is it because the death was foreseeable?

III

HOMICIDE OFFENSES

The common law recognized two broad categories of homicide: murder and manslaughter. It generally deemed murder as the killing of one human being by another with "malice aforethought." By itself, the latter phrase offers little help in analyzing homicide cases, since it has no very precise meaning. In particular, be forewarned that "malice aforethought" does *not* necessarily involve "premeditation." (As we will see below, premeditation is one of the factors that may aggravate a murder from second-degree to first-degree murder, once we otherwise establish that the homicide was murder and not manslaughter.)

Perhaps the best that can be said for the term "malice aforethought" is that it describes a cluster of criteria that distinguish murder, in its various forms, from manslaughter (thus deemed as an unlawful killing without malice). "Malice" can then best be described as an intention to cause, or a willingness to undertake, a serious risk of causing the death of another, when that intent or willingness is based on an immoral or unworthy aim. The gradations of homicide then turn on refinements of the extent of the risk undertaken, the degree of consciousness of the risk, and the degree of unworthiness of the motivating aim.

Murder is then generally defined as an unjustified killing manifesting (1) purpose to cause death; or (2) intent to inflict serious bodily harm; or (3) extreme recklessness with respect to a serious risk of harm to another's life, where the risky action manifests so unworthy or immoral a purpose as to suggest callous indifference to human life; or (4) under the so-called felony-murder rule, a willingness to undertake even a very small risk of death where the risky conduct is so unworthy as to establish guilt of a serious felony. Thus, it is best not to invoke the terms "malice" or "malice aforethought" for any of their common-sense connotations; rather, "malice" is a code word encompassing the states of mind outlined above.

Early in the nineteenth century, American legislatures began classifying murders according to degree. Though the states have exhibited and continue to exhibit some variety, the typical structure is as follows: A murder becomes first-degree if it is both intentional and premeditated, or if it involves a killing during the course of one of several major felonies specified by statute — such as robbery, burglary, rape, arson, or mayhem. Otherwise, a murder is second-degree. The traditional and continuing significance of the degree distinction lies in gradations of punishment: The penalty for first-degree murder is generally a prison term of at least 15 years and up to a life sentence, with or without the possibility of parole. Punishment for second-degree murder is a term of years in prison, usually in the range of 5 to 15 years. But the most dramatic difference in gradation concerns the death penalty. Generally, the only crime for which the death penalty is even theoretically possible is first-degree murder, and where a first-degree murder is prosecuted as a "capital murder" (i.e., where the prosecutor seeks the death penalty), a defendant who avoids a death sentence will almost always face a life sentence, often without the possibility of parole. In the roughly 37 states that have capital punishment, a separate statute specifies the substantive criteria and special trial procedures for determining whether a defendant convicted of first-degree murder should receive a life sentence or a death sentence. See Chapter 7, *infra*.

Manslaughter, as noted, is homicide without malice. Roughly speaking, it consists of (1) voluntary manslaughter, which means an intentional killing that lacks malice because the killer either acted in the heat of passion after "adequate provocation" or acted in the honest but unreasonable belief that the killing was necessary for self-defense;[1] (2) involuntary manslaughter, which normally means a killing committed recklessly or highly negligently. Some states break involuntary manslaughter into two crimes — reckless manslaughter and the slightly less serious crime of negligent homicide, and some create a special rule for vehicular manslaughter. Some retain an analogy to the felony murder rule called the misdemeanor-manslaughter rule, making it involuntary manslaughter to cause death by risking fatal harm where the underlying act establishes guilt of some misdemeanor.

Note then that some murders are intentional and some are unintentional, and the same is true of acts of manslaughter.

In the following chapters, we develop these classifying criteria in great detail, treating both the distinction between murder and manslaughter and the different degrees of murder. Nevertheless, we organize the material according to the intuitively simpler criteria of intentional killings (whether murder or manslaughter) in Chapter 5 and then unintentional killings (whether murder or manslaughter) in Chapter 6. Finally, in Chapter 7, we treat the special constitutional and statutory doctrines governing the death penalty for first-degree murder.

Here are some sample state homicide statutes. They are worth examining as a general introduction to the grades of homicide as well as a reference source as you study the cases that follow.

Typical state homicide statutes. The Kansas and Alabama statutes typify the classical structure of manslaughter and murder and the difference in degrees of murder.

Kan. Stat. Ann. (1995 & Supp. 2002)

§21-3401. Murder in the First Degree

Murder in the first degree is the killing of a human being committed:
   (a) Intentionally and with premeditation; or
   (b) in the commission of, attempt to commit, or flight from an inherently dangerous felony [including kidnapping, robbery, rape, burglary, or arson].

---

1. Though note that a few states, like Illinois, see p. 298, *infra*, treat these factors only as reducing first-degree murder to second-degree murder.

Murder in the first degree is a class A felony [punishable by death or by life imprisonment].

§21-3402. Murder in the Second Degree

Murder in the second degree is the killing of a human being committed
    (a) Intentionally; or
    (b) unintentionally but recklessly manifesting extreme indifference to the value of human life.
Murder in the second degree is [punishable by 12-14 years in prison][2]

§21-3403. Voluntary Manslaughter

Voluntary manslaughter is the intentional killing of a human being committed:
    (a) Upon a sudden quarrel or in the heat of passion; or
    (b) upon an unreasonable but honest belief that circumstances existed that justify deadly force. . . . Voluntary manslaughter is [punishable by 6-7 years in prison].

§21-3404. Involuntary Manslaughter

Involuntary manslaughter is the unintentional killing of a human being committed:
    (a) Recklessly;
    (b) in the commission of, or an attempt to commit, or flight from any felony, other than an inherently dangerous felony [as included in §21-3401, above] that is enacted for the protection of human life or safety or a misdemeanor that is enacted for the protection of human life and safety. . . .
    (c) during the commission of a lawful act in an unlawful manner. Involuntary manslaughter is [punishable by 4-5 years in prison].

§21-3405. Vehicular Homicide

Vehicular homicide is the unintentional killing of a human being committed by the operation of an automobile, airplane, motor boat or other motor vehicle in a manner which creates an unreasonable risk of injury to the person or property of another and which constitutes a material deviation from the standard of care which a reasonable person would observe under the same circumstances.

Vehicular homicide is a . . . misdemeanor [punishable by a term not to exceed 1 year in jail].

---

2. Kansas has adopted so-called determinate sentencing, which uses complex formulas for weighing various factors and imposes on the sentencing judge a much narrower range of possible sentence than more traditional indeterminate sentencing.

Ala. Code (1994 & Supp. 2002)

§13A-6-2. Murder

(a) A person commits the crime of murder if:

(1) With intent to cause the death of another person, he causes the death of that person or of another person; or

(2) under circumstances manifesting extreme indifference to human life, he recklessly engages in conduct which creates a grave risk of death to a person other than himself, and thereby causes the death of another person; or

(3) he commits or attempts to commit arson in the first degree, burglary in the first or second degree, escape in the first degree, kidnapping in the first degree, robbery in any degree, sodomy in the first degree or any other felony clearly dangerous to human life, and, in the course of and in furtherance of the crime that he is committing or attempting to commit, or in immediate flight therefrom, he, or another participant if there be any, causes the death of any person.

(b) A person does not commit murder under subdivision (a) (1) or (a) (2) of this section if he was moved to act by a sudden heat of passion caused by provocation recognized by law, and before there had been a reasonable time for the passion to cool and for reason to reassert itself. The burden of injecting the issue of killing under legal provocation is on the defendant, but this does not shift the burden of proof. This subsection does not apply to a prosecution for, or preclude a conviction of, manslaughter or other crime.

(c) Murder is [punishable by death or by life imprisonment].

§13A-6-3. Manslaughter

(a) A person commits the crime of manslaughter if:

(1) He recklessly causes the death of another person, or

(2) He causes the death of another person under circumstances that would constitute murder under Section 13A-6-2; except, that he causes the death due to a sudden heat of passion caused by provocation recognized by law, and before a reasonable time for the passion to cool and for reason to reassert itself,

(b) Manslaughter is [punishable by 2-20 years in prison. If a firearm or other deadly weapon (not including a vehicle) is used, then the minimum sentence is 10 years].

§13A-6-4. Criminally Negligent Homicide

(a) A person commits the crime of criminally negligent homicide if he causes the death of another person by criminal negligence.

(b) The jury may consider statutes and ordinances regulating the actor's conduct in determining whether he is culpably negligent under subsection (a) of this section.

(c) Criminally negligent homicide is a . . . misdemeanor [punishable by not more than 1 year in jail or at hard labor], except in cases in which said criminally negligent homicide is caused by the driver of a motor vehicle who is driving in violation of the [drunk-driving law]; in such cases criminally negligent homicide is [punishable by a term of 1-10 years in prison].

The California structure. The California homicide law generally follows the classical structure, with some unusual vocabulary ("express malice" and "implied malice") and a few unusual provisions that will be examined in case law in the chapters upcoming.

Cal. Penal Code (West 1999 & Supp. 2003)

§187. Murder Defined . . .

(a) Murder is the unlawful killing of a human being . . . with malice aforethought.

§188. Malice, Express Malice, and Implied Malice Defined

Such malice may be express or implied. It is express when there is manifested a deliberate intention unlawfully to take away the life of a fellow creature. It is implied, when no considerable provocation appears, or when the circumstances attending the killing show an abandoned and malignant heart.[3]

When it is shown that the killing resulted from the intentional doing of an act with express or implied malice as defined above, no other mental state need be shown to establish the mental state of malice aforethought. Neither an awareness of the obligation to act within the general body of laws regulating society nor acting despite such awareness is included within the definition of malice. [The minimum punishment for first-degree murder is 25 years to life in prison; for second-degree murder, it is 15 years.]

§189. Murder; Degrees

All murder which is perpetrated by means of a destructive device or explosive, knowing use of ammunition designed primarily to penetrate metal or armor, poison, lying in wait, torture, or by any other kind of willful, deliberate, and premeditated killing, or which is committed in the perpetration of, or attempt to perpetrate, arson, rape, carjacking, robbery, burglary, mayhem, or any act punishable under [Sections 286-89, covering sexual assaults against minors], or any murder which is perpetrated by means of discharging a firearm from a motor vehicle, intentionally at another person outside of the vehicle with the intent to inflict death, is murder of the first degree. All other kinds of murders are of the second degree. . . .

---

3. This hoary and colorful phrase is a traditional term for extreme recklessness. See *Mayes v. The People*, in Chapter 6, pp. 382, *infra*.

§191.5. Gross Vehicular Manslaughter While Intoxicated

(a) Gross vehicular manslaughter while intoxicated is the unlawful killing of a human being without malice aforethought, in the driving of a vehicle, where the driving was in violation of [the drunk-driving laws], and the killing was the proximate result of the commission of a lawful act which might produce death, in an unlawful manner, and with gross negligence . . .

(c) Gross vehicular manslaughter while intoxicated is punishable by imprisonment in the state prison for 4, 6, or 10 years.

(d) This section shall not be construed as prohibiting or precluding a charge of murder under Section 188 upon facts exhibiting wantonness and a conscious disregard for life to support a finding of implied malice, or upon facts showing malice consistent with the holding of the California Supreme Court in People v. Watson, 30 Cal. 3d 290.[4]. . .

§192. Manslaughter; Voluntary, Involuntary, and Vehicular . . .

Manslaughter is the unlawful killing of a human being without malice. It is of three kinds:

(a) Voluntary — upon a sudden quarrel or heat of passion.

(b) Involuntary — in the commission of an unlawful act, not amounting to felony; or in the commission of a lawful act which might produce death, in an unlawful manner, or without due caution or circumspection. . . .

(c) Vehicular —

(1) Except as provided in Section 191.5 [gross vehicular manslaughter while intoxicated], driving a vehicle in the commission of an unlawful act, not amounting to felony, and with gross negligence; or driving a vehicle in the commission of a lawful act which might produce death, in an unlawful manner, and with gross negligence. [Punishable by a jail sentence of not more than 1 year, or by imprisonment for 2, 4, or 6 years.]

(2) [The conduct described in paragraph (1), but without gross negligence, is punishable by not more than 1 year in jail.]

"Gross negligence," as used in this section, shall not be construed as prohibiting or precluding a charge of murder . . . upon facts exhibiting wantonness and a conscious disregard for life to support a finding of implied malice, or upon facts showing malice, consistent with the holding of the California Supreme Court in People v. Watson, 30 Cal. 3d 290.

The Pennsylvania degree structure. Pennsylvania, the first state to divide murder into degrees, now adds a third degree version of murder and includes under that rubric certain killings resulting from the use of illegal drugs.

Pa. Cons. Stat. Ann. (Purdon 1998 & Supp. 2003)

Tit 18, §2502. Murder

(a) *Murder of the first degree.* A criminal homicide constitutes murder of the first degree when it is committed by an intentional killing.

---

4. See this case in Chapter 6, pp. 390, *infra.*

(b) *Murder of the second degree.* A criminal homicide constitutes murder of the second degree when it is committed while defendant was engaged as a principal or an accomplice in the perpetration of a felony [punishable by life in prison].

(c) *Murder of the third degree.* All other kinds of murder shall be murder of the third degree. Murder of the third degree is a felony of the first degree [punishable by up to 20 years in prison].

(d) *Definitions.* As used in this section the following words and phrases shall have the meanings given to them in this subsection. . . .

"Intentional killing." Killing by means of poison, or by lying in wait, or by any other kind of willful, deliberate and premeditated killing.

"Perpetration of a felony." The act of the defendant in engaging in or being an accomplice in the commission of, or an attempt to commit, or flight after committing, or attempting to commit robbery, rape, or deviate sexual intercourse by force or threat of force, arson, burglary or kidnapping.

§2503. Voluntary Manslaughter

(a) *General rule.* A person who kills an individual without lawful justification commits voluntary manslaughter if at the time of the killing he is acting under a sudden and intense passion resulting from serious provocation by:

(1) the individual killed; or

(2) another whom the actor endeavors to kill, but he negligently or accidentally causes the death of the individual killed. . . .

(c) Grading — Voluntary manslaughter is [punishable by up to 10 years in prison].

§2504. Involuntary Manslaughter

(a) *General rule.* A person is guilty of involuntary manslaughter when as a direct result of the doing of an unlawful act in a reckless or grossly negligent manner, or the doing of a lawful act in a reckless or grossly negligent manner, he causes the death of another person.

(b) Grading — Involuntary manslaughter is [punishable by a maximum of five years in prison].

§2506. Drug Delivery Resulting in Death

(a) *General rule.* A person commits murder of the third degree who administers, dispenses, delivers, gives, prescribes, sells, or distributes any controlled substance or counterfeit controlled substance in violation of [the Controlled Substance Act], and another person dies as a result of using the substance.

(b) *Mandatary minimum sentence.* A person convicted under subsection (a) shall be sentenced to a mandatory minimum term of imprisonment of 5 years. . . .

The Illinois Alternative. Illinois does not permit mitigation of murder to voluntary manslaughter like other states, but does allow the typical mitigation criteria to lower first-degree to second-degree murder. In another interesting variation, Illinois provides a special voluntary manslaughter law for killing of a fetus (outside the context of an otherwise legal abortion) — the only voluntary manslaughter provision in Illinois.

Illinois Compiled Statutes Ann. (2002)

720 ILCS 5/9-1

Sec. 9-1. First Degree Murder . . .

(a) A person who kills an individual without lawful justification commits first degree murder if, in performing the acts which cause the death:

(1) he either intends to kill or do great bodily harm to that individual or another, or knows that such acts will cause death to that individual or another; or

(2) he knows that such acts create a strong probability of death or great bodily harm to that individual or another; or

(3) he is attempting or committing a forcible felony other than second degree murder. [Punishable by a term of 20 years to 60 years where not part of a capital charge.]

720 ILCS 5/9-2

Sec. 9-2. Second Degree Murder.

(a) A person commits the offense of second degree murder when he commits the offense of first degree murder as defined in paragraphs (1) or (2) of subsection (a) of Section 9-1 of this Code and either of the following mitigating factors are present:

(1) At the time of the killing he is acting under a sudden and intense passion resulting from serious provocation by the individual killed or another whom the offender endeavors to kill, but he negligently or accidentally causes the death of the individual killed; or

(2) At the time of the killing he believes the circumstances to be such that, if they existed, would justify or exonerate the killing under the principles stated in Article 7 [on affirmative defenses] of this Code, but his belief is unreasonable.

(b) Serious provocation is conduct sufficient to excite an intense passion in a reasonable person. . . .

(d) Sentence. Second Degree Murder is a Class 1 felony [punishable by a term of 4 to 20 years.]

720 ILCS 5/9-2.1

Sec. 9-2.1. Voluntary Manslaughter of an Unborn Child.

(a) A person who kills an unborn child without lawful justification commits voluntary manslaughter of an unborn child if at the time of the killing he is acting under a sudden and intense passion resulting from serious provocation by another whom the offender endeavors to kill, but he negligently or accidentally causes the death of the unborn child.

Serious provocation is conduct sufficient to excite an intense passion in a reasonable person.

(b) A person who intentionally or knowingly kills an unborn child commits voluntary manslaughter of an unborn child if at the time of the killing he believes the circumstances to be such that, if they existed, would justify or exonerate the killing under the principles stated in Article 7 of this Code, but his belief is unreasonable.

(c) Sentence. Voluntary Manslaughter of an unborn child is a Class 1 felony [punishable by 4 to 15 years].

(d) For purposes of this Section, (1) "unborn child" shall mean any individual of the human species from fertilization until birth, and (2) "person" shall not include the pregnant woman whose unborn child is killed.

(e) This Section shall not apply to acts which cause the death of an unborn child if those acts were committed during any abortion, as defined in Section 2 of the Illinois Abortion Law of 1975, as amended, to which the pregnant woman has consented. This Section shall not apply to acts which were committed pursuant to usual and customary standards of medical practice during diagnostic testing or therapeutic treatment.

Minnesota special first-degree factors. Minnesota, along with traditional premeditation formula and the felony-murder rule for the generic serious felonies, adds some unusual factors determining first-degree murder, including the following:

Minnesota Statutes Ann. (2002)

609.185 Murder in the First Degree

(a) Whoever does any of the following is guilty of murder in the first degree and shall be sentenced to imprisonment for life: . . .

(5) causes the death of a minor while committing child abuse, when the perpetrator has engaged in a past pattern of child abuse upon the child and the death occurs under circumstances manifesting an extreme indifference to human life;

(6) causes the death of a human being while committing domestic abuse, when the perpetrator has engaged in a past pattern of domestic abuse upon the victim or upon another family or household member and the death occurs under circumstances manifesting an extreme indifference to human life. . . . ["Family or household member" includes (1) spouses and former spouses; (2) parents and children; (3) persons related by blood; (4) persons who are presently residing together or who have resided together in the past; (5) persons who have a child in common regardless of whether they have been married or have lived together at any time; (6) a man and woman if the woman is pregnant and the man is alleged to be the father, regardless of whether they have been married or have lived together at any time; and (7) persons involved in a significant romantic or sexual relationship.]. . . .

(7) causes the death of a human being while committing, conspiring to commit, or attempting to commit a felony crime to further terrorism and the death occurs under circumstances manifesting an extreme indifference to human life. [A crime is committed to "further terrorism" if it is a felony and

is "a premeditated act involving violence to persons or property that is intended to: (1) terrorize, intimidate, or coerce a considerable number of members of the public in addition to the direct victims of the act; and (2) significantly disrupt or interfere with the lawful exercise, operation, or conduct of government, lawful commerce, or the right of lawful assembly."]

Model Penal Code. The special homicide provision of the MPC somewhat modifies the classical structure of manslaughter. It avoids the terms "voluntary" and "involuntary" in defining manslaughter and unites these in a single section, and then distinguishes the form of manslaughter based on recklessness from criminally negligent homicide. More strikingly, the MPC provides for only one degree of murder and retains only the most minimal form of the felony murder rule found in most states.

Model Penal Code (1962 Official Draft, 1985 Edition)

§210.2. Murder

(1) Except as provided in Section 210.3(1) (b), criminal homicide constitutes murder when:

(a) it is committed purposely or knowingly; or

(b) it is committed recklessly under circumstances manifesting extreme indifference to the value of human life. Such recklessness and indifference are presumed if the actor is engaged or is an accomplice in the commission of, or an attempt to commit, or flight after committing or attempting to commit robbery, rape or deviate sexual intercourse by force or threat of force, arson, burglary, kidnapping or felonious escape.

(2) Murder is a felony of the first degree [punishable by imprisonment or capital punishment].

§210.3. Manslaughter

(1) Criminal homicide constitutes manslaughter when:

(a) it is committed recklessly; or

(b) a homicide which would otherwise be murder is committed under the influence of extreme mental or emotional disturbance for which there is reasonable explanation or excuse. The reasonableness of such explanation or excuse shall be determined from the viewpoint of a person in the actor's situation under the circumstances as he believes them to be.

(2) Manslaughter is a felony of the second degree [having a minimum punishment of 1-3 years in prison and a maximum sentence of 10 years].

§210.4. Negligent Homicide

(1) Criminal homicide constitutes negligent homicide when it is committed negligently.

(2) Negligent homicide is a felony of the third degree [with a 1- to 2-year minimum sentence and a maximum of 5 years in prison].

New York and its extensive first-degree criteria. The New York homicide law is unusual in its highly specific delineations of criteria for some forms of murder. These were adopted as part of New York's reinstitution of the death penalty in 1995, and these delineations, though designed to make certain killings eligible for capital punishment, also serve to distinguish first from second-degree murder in non-capital cases. If the state proves one of these criteria, it establishes first-degree murder, and then may use any proven criterion as an aggravating circumstance in a death penalty hearing. In addition, New York is notable for using the Model Penal Code's formulation of "extreme emotional disturbance" in defining voluntary manslaughter.

New York Penal Code (1999 & Supp. 2003)

§125.10. *Criminally Negligent Homicide*

A person is guilty of criminally negligent homicide when, with criminal negligence, he causes the death of another person.

Criminally negligent homicide is [punishable by a term of up to 4 years in prison].

§125.12. *Vehicular Manslaughter in the Second Degree*

A person is guilty of vehicular manslaughter in the second degree when he:

(1) commits the crime of criminally negligent homicide as defined in section 125.10, and. . . .

(2) causes the death of such other person by operation of a vehicle in violation of . . . [the drunk-driving provision] of the vehicle and traffic law . . .

Vehicular manslaughter in the second degree is [punishable by up to 7 years in prison].

§125.15. *Manslaughter in the Second Degree*

A person is guilty of manslaughter in the second degree when:

(1) He recklessly causes the death of another person. . . .

(2) Manslaughter in the second degree is [punishable by a term of up to 15 years in prison].

§125.20. *Manslaughter in the First Degree*

A person is guilty of manslaughter in the first degree when:

(1) With intent to cause serious physical injury to another person, he causes the death of such person or of a third person; or

(2) With intent to cause the death of another person, he causes the death of such person or of a third person under circumstances which do not constitute murder because he acts under the influence of extreme emotional disturbance, as defined in paragraph (a) of subdivision one of section 125.25.

The fact that homicide was committed under the influence of extreme emotional disturbance constitutes a mitigating circumstance reducing murder to manslaughter in the first degree and need not be proven in any prosecution initiated under this subdivision; or . . .

(4) Being eighteen years old or more and with intent to cause physical injury to a person less than eleven years old, the defendant recklessly engages in conduct which creates a grave risk of serious physical injury to such person and thereby causes the death of such person.

Manslaughter in the first degree is [punishable by up to 25 years in prison].

§125.25. Murder in the Second Degree

A person is guilty of murder in the second degree [punishable by minimum of 15-25 years in prison] when:

(1) With intent to cause the death of another person, he causes the death of such person or of a third person; except that in any prosecution under this subdivision, it is an affirmative defense that:

(a) The defendant acted under the influence of extreme emotional disturbance for which there was a reasonable explanation or excuse, the reasonableness of which is to be determined from the viewpoint of a person in the defendant's situation under the circumstances as the defendant believed them to be. Nothing contained in this paragraph shall constitute a defense to a prosecution for, or preclude a conviction of, manslaughter in the first degree or any other crime; or . . .

(2) Under circumstances evincing a depraved indifference to human life, he recklessly engages in conduct which creates a grave risk of death to another person, and thereby causes the death of another person; or

(3) Acting either alone or with one or more other persons, he commits or attempts to commit robbery, burglary, kidnapping, arson, rape in the first degree, sodomy in the first degree, sexual abuse in the first degree, aggravated sexual abuse, escape in the first degree, or escape in the second degree, and, in the course of and in furtherance of such crime or of immediate flight therefrom, he, or another participant, if there be any, causes the death of a person other than one of the participants; except that in any prosecution under this subdivision, in which the defendant was not the only participant in the underlying crime, it is an affirmative defense that the defendant:

(a) Did not commit the homicidal act or in any way solicit, request, command, importune, cause or aid the commission thereof; and

(b) Was not armed with a deadly weapon, or any instrument, article or substance readily capable of causing death or serious physical injury and of a sort not ordinarily carried in public places by law-abiding persons; and

(c) Had no reasonable ground to believe that any other participant was armed with such a weapon, instrument, article or substance; and

(d) Had no reasonable ground to believe that any other participant intended to engage in conduct likely to result in death or serious physical injury.

(4) Under circumstances evincing a depraved indifference to human life, and being eighteen years old or more the defendant recklessly engages in conduct which creates a grave risk of serious physical injury or death to another person less than eleven years old and thereby causes the death of such person.

Murder in the second degree is [punishable by up to a term of life in prison].

§125.27. Murder in the First Degree

A person is guilty of murder in the first degree when:

(1) With intent to cause the death of another person, he causes the death of such person or of a third person; and

(a) either:

(i) the intended victim was a police officer . . . who was at the time of the killing engaged in the course of performing his official duties, and the defendant knew or reasonably should have known that the intended victim was a police officer; or

(ii) the intended victim was a peace officer . . . who was at the time of the killing engaged in the course of performing his official duties, and the defendant knew or reasonably should have known that the intended victim was such a uniformed court officer, parole officer, probation officer, or employee of the division for youth; or

(iii) the intended victim was an employee of a state correctional institution or was an employee of a local correctional facility . . . who was at the time of the killing engaged in the course of performing his official duties, and the defendant knew or reasonably should have known that the intended victim was an employee of a state correctional institution or a local correctional facility; or

(iv) at the time of the commission of the killing, the defendant was confined in a state correctional institution [under a life sentence], or at the time of the commission of the killing, the defendant had escaped from such confinement or custody while serving such a sentence and had not yet been returned to such confinement or custody; or

(v) the intended victim [or his/her immediate family member] was a witness to a crime committed on a prior occasion and the death was caused for the purpose of preventing the intended victim's testimony in any criminal action or proceeding . . . , or the intended victim [or his/her immediate family member] had previously testified in a criminal action or proceeding and the killing was committed for the purpose of exacting retribution for such prior testimony; . . . or

(vi) the defendant committed the killing or procured commission of the killing pursuant to an agreement with a person other than the intended victim to commit the same for the receipt, or in expectation of the receipt, of anything of pecuniary value from a party to the agreement or from a person other than the intended victim acting at the direction of a party to such agreement; or

(vii) the victim was killed while the defendant was in the course of committing or attempting to commit and in furtherance of robbery, burglary in the first degree or second degree, kidnapping in the first degree, arson in the first degree or second degree, rape in the first degree, sodomy in the first degree, sexual abuse in the first degree, aggravated sexual abuse in the first degree or escape in the first degree, or in the course of and furtherance of immediate flight after committing or attempting to commit any such crime or in the course of and furtherance of immediate flight after attempting to commit the crime of murder in the second degree; provided however, the victim is not a participant in one of the aforementioned crimes . . . ; or

(viii) as part of the same criminal transaction, the defendant, with intent to cause serious physical injury to or the death of an additional person or persons, causes the death of an additional person or persons; provided, however, the victim is not a participant in the criminal transaction; or

(ix) prior to committing the killing, the defendant had been convicted of murder as defined in this section or section 125.25 of this article, or had been convicted in another jurisdiction of an offense which, if committed in this state, would constitute a violation of either of such sections; or

(x) the defendant acted in an especially cruel and wanton manner pursuant to a course of conduct intended to inflict and inflicting torture upon the victim prior to the victim's death. As used in this subparagraph, "torture" means the intentional and depraved infliction of extreme physical pain; "depraved" means the defendant relished the infliction of extreme physical pain upon the victim evidencing debasement or perversion or that the defendant evidenced a sense of pleasure in the infliction of extreme physical pain; or

(xi) the defendant intentionally caused the death of two or more additional persons within the state in separate criminal transactions within a period of twenty-four months when committed in a similar fashion or pursuant to a common scheme or plan; or

(xii) the intended victim was a judge . . . and the defendant killed such victim because such victim was, at the time of the killing, a judge; and

(b) The defendant was more than eighteen years old at the time of the commission of the crime.

(2) In any prosecution under subdivision one, it is an affirmative defense that:

(a) The defendant acted under the influence of extreme emotional disturbance for which there was a reasonable explanation or excuse, the reasonableness of which is to be determined from the viewpoint of a person in the defendant's situation under the circumstances as the defendant believed them to be. Nothing contained in this paragraph shall constitute a defense to a prosecution for, or preclude a conviction of, manslaughter in the first degree or any other crime except murder in the second degree. . . . [Murder in the first degree is punishable by life imprisonment or death.]

Some facts about homicide in the United States. Who are the perpetrators and victims of homicide in the United States? How and when do they kill?

Any empirical inquiry requires a working definition of the crimes for which one is seeking statistics. The most reliable source of homicide statistics is the FBI's Uniform Crime Reports for the United States (UCR), which collects statistics from state and local police and prosecutors. These figures are based on the charging decisions or classifications of local authorities — not on actual convictions. The definition of homicide used by the FBI covers most but not all of the gradations of homicide outlined in this introduction and examined in this Part. It includes all killings meeting the definition of murder (whether first-degree or lower, whether intentional or unintentional) and all "nonnegligent" man-slaughter. The definition excludes any cases of negligent homicide or acts of justifiable or excusable homicide.

With those caveats in mind, we can infer the following from the UCR for 2002:

- The American murder rate peaked in 1980 and again in 1990 at about 10 murders per 100,000 people. A slow decline then occurred, and in the mid-1990s, there were about 22,000 homicides per year, or a rate of about 7.5 (still by far the highest rate among large industrialized democracies). The rate began dropping somewhat faster after the mid-1990s, and 2002 saw about 16,000 murders, for a rate of 5.6 per 100,000 people (hence over a 40 percent drop from 1990).
- The most homicidal month in 2002 was July, and the least homicidal was February.
- In terms of region, the South has by a slight margin the highest rate, and the Northeast the lowest, with the West and Midwest in between.
- In terms of victims, 77 percent were males, and 10 percent were under 18 years of age, and 25 percent were under 22 years of age; approximately half were Black, and almost half were White, with other racial categories making up the small remainder.
- In terms of offenders, 90 percent were male, 5 percent were under 18, and 22 percent were under 22; among those offenders identified by race, approximately 50 percent were Black, and 48 percent were White, but 29 percent of the offenders were not identified by race.
- Homicide is typically intraracial: 85 percent of White victims were killed by White offenders; 91 percent of Black victims were killed by Black offenders.
- Approximately 90 percent of male victims and 90 percent of female victims are killed by male offenders.
- Firearms (most often handguns) were used in 67 percent of the homicides.
- It has always been true that a great fraction of killers know their victims personally, but the exact figures are unclear. In 2002, about 13 percent of killers were related to their victims, and another 35 percent in some way were acquainted. While 14 percent were clearly strangers, as many as 40 percent of the pairings were undetermined. Among female victims, about 28 percent were killed by husbands or boyfriends, while 3 percent of male victims were killed by wives or girlfriends.
- About 34 percent of the murders appeared to result from arguments, 17 percent were caused by or associated with some independent felonious activity, and 7 percent (and increasing markedly) were juvenile gang killings.

5

INTENTIONAL HOMICIDE

A. INTENTIONAL MURDER (SECOND-DEGREE)

As noted in the Introduction to this Part, see p. 291, *supra,* the starting point of the law of homicide is that intent to kill establishes the "malice" or "malice aforethought" necessary for murder. Intent to kill would seem to be an easy concept to understand in the abstract. But as with mens rea generally in a criminal case, intent to kill is often difficult to prove, especially where the prosecution has no eyewitnesses and where the defendant, on ambiguous circumstantial evidence, claims he caused the victim's death only accidentally. Consider this case:

FRANCIS v. FRANKLIN
Supreme Court of the United States
471 U.S. 307 (1985)

JUSTICE BRENNAN delivered the opinion of the Court. . . .

Respondent Raymond Lee Franklin, then 21 years old and imprisoned for offenses unrelated to this case, sought to escape custody on January 17, 1979, while he and three other prisoners were receiving dental care at a local dentist's office. The four prisoners were secured by handcuffs to the same 8-foot length of chain as they sat in the dentist's waiting room. At some point Franklin was released from the chain, taken into the dentist's office and given preliminary treatment, and then escorted back to the waiting room. As another prisoner was being released, Franklin, who had not been reshackled, seized a pistol from one of the two officers and managed to escape. He forced the dentist's assistant to accompany him as a hostage.

In the parking lot Franklin found the dentist's automobile, the keys to which he had taken before escaping, but was unable to unlock the door. He then fled with the dental assistant after refusing her request to be set free. The two set out across an open clearing and came upon a local resident. Franklin demanded this resident's car. When the resident responded that he did not own one, Franklin made no effort to harm him but continued with the dental assistant until they came to the home of the victim, one Collie. Franklin pounded on the heavy wooden front door of the home and Collie, a retired 72-year-old carpenter, answered. Franklin was pointing the stolen pistol at the door when Collie arrived. As Franklin demanded his car keys, Collie slammed the door. At this moment Franklin's gun went off. The bullet traveled through the wooden door and into Collie's chest killing him. Seconds later the gun fired again. The second bullet traveled upward through the door and into the ceiling of the residence.

Hearing the shots, the victim's wife entered the front room. In the confusion accompanying the shooting, the dental assistant fled and Franklin did not attempt to stop her. Franklin entered the house, demanded the car keys from the victim's wife, and added the threat "I might as well kill you." When she did not provide the keys, however, he made no effort to thwart her escape. Franklin then stepped outside and encountered the victim's adult daughter. He repeated his demand for car keys but made no effort to stop the daughter when she refused the demand and fled. Failing to obtain a car, Franklin left and remained at large until nightfall.

Shortly after being captured, Franklin made a formal statement to the authorities in which he admitted that he had shot the victim but emphatically denied that he did so voluntarily or intentionally. He claimed that the shots were fired in accidental response to the slamming of the door. He was tried in the Superior Court of Bibb County, Georgia, on charges of malice murder . . . and kidnaping. His sole defense to the malice murder charge was a lack of the requisite intent to kill. To support his version of the events Franklin offered substantial circumstantial evidence tending to show a lack of intent. He claimed that the circumstances surrounding the firing of the gun, particularly the slamming of the door and the trajectory of the second bullet, supported the hypothesis of accident, and that his immediate confession to that effect buttressed the assertion. He also argued that his treatment of every other person encountered during the escape indicated a lack of disposition to use force.

On the dispositive issue of intent, the trial judge instructed the jury as follows:

> A crime is a violation of a statute of this State in which there shall be a union of joint operation of act or omission to act, and intention or criminal negligence. A person shall not be found guilty of any crime committed by misfortune or accident where it satisfactorily appears there was no criminal scheme or undertaking or intention or criminal negligence. The acts of a person of sound mind and discretion are presumed to be the product of the person's will, but the presumption may be rebutted. A person of sound mind and discretion is presumed to intend the natural and probable consequences of his acts, but the presumption may be rebutted. A person will not be presumed to act with criminal intention but the trier of facts, that is, the Jury, may find criminal intention upon a consideration of the words, conduct, demeanor, motive and all other circumstances connected with the act for which the accused is prosecuted.

Approximately one hour after the jury had received the charge and retired for deliberation, it returned to the courtroom and requested reinstruction on the element of intent and the definition of accident. Upon receiving the requested reinstruction, the jury deliberated 10 more minutes and returned a verdict of guilty. . . .

Franklin levels his constitutional attack at the following two sentences in the jury charge: "The acts of a person of sound mind and discretion are presumed to be the product of a person's will, but the presumption may be rebutted. A person of sound mind and discretion is presumed to intend the natural and probable consequences of his acts, but the presumption may be rebutted." . . . The federal constitutional question is whether a reasonable juror could have understood the two sentences as a mandatory presumption that shifted to the defendant the burden of persuasion on the element of intent once the State had proved the predicate acts.

The challenged sentences are cast in the language of command. They instruct the jury that "acts of a person of sound mind and discretion *are presumed* to be the product of the person's will," and that a person *"is presumed* to intend the natural and probable consequences of his acts" (emphasis added). These words carry precisely the message of the language condemned in [Sandstrom v. Montana, 442 U.S. 510 (1979)] ("[t]he law presumes that a person intends the ordinary consequences of his voluntary acts"). The jurors "were not told that they had a choice, or that they *might* infer that conclusion; they were told only that the law presumed it. It is clear that a reasonable juror could easily have viewed such an instruction as mandatory." 442 U.S., at 515 (emphasis added). The portion of the jury charge challenged in this case directs the jury to presume an essential element of the offense — intent to kill — upon proof of other elements of the offense — the act of slaying another. In this way the instructions "undermine the factfinder's responsibility at trial, based on evidence adduced by the State, *to find* the ultimate facts beyond a reasonable doubt."

The language challenged here differs from *Sandstrom* of course, in that the jury in this case was explicitly informed that the presumptions "may be rebutted." The State makes much of this additional aspect of the instruction in seeking to differentiate the present case from *Sandstrom*. This distinction does not suffice, however, to cure the infirmity in the charge. Though the Court in *Sandstrom* acknowledged that the instructions there challenged could have been reasonably understood as creating an irrebuttable presumption, it was not on this basis alone that the instructions were invalidated. Had the jury reasonably understood the instructions as creating a *mandatory rebuttable* presumption the instructions would have been no less constitutionally infirm.

An irrebuttable or conclusive presumption relieves the State of its burden of persuasion by removing the presumed element from the case entirely if the State proves the predicate facts. A mandatory rebuttable presumption does not remove the presumed element from the case if the State proves the predicate facts, but it nonetheless relieves the State of the affirmative burden of persuasion on the presumed element by instructing the jury that it must find the presumed element unless the defendant persuades the jury not to make such a finding. A mandatory rebuttable presumption is perhaps less onerous from the defendant's perspective, but it is no less unconstitutional. Our cases make clear that "[s]uch shifting of the burden of persuasion with respect to a fact which the State deems so important that it must be either proved or presumed is impermissible under the Due Process Clause." . . .

When combined with the immediately preceding mandatory language, the instruction that the presumptions "may be rebutted" could reasonably be read as telling the jury that it was required to infer intent to kill as the natural and probable consequence of the act of firing the gun unless the defendant persuaded the jury that such an inference was unwarranted. The very statement that the presumption "may be rebutted" could have indicated to a reasonable juror that the defendant bore an affirmative burden of persuasion once the State proved the underlying act giving rise to the presumption. Standing alone, the challenged language undeniably created an unconstitutional burden-shifting presumption with respect to the element of intent. . . .

The jury, of course, did not hear only the two challenged sentences. The jury charge taken as a whole might have explained the proper allocation of burdens with sufficient clarity that any ambiguity in the particular language challenged could not have been understood by a reasonable juror as shifting the burden of persuasion. The State argues that sufficient clarifying language exists in this case. In particular, the State relies on an earlier portion of the charge instructing the jurors that the defendant was presumed innocent and that the State was required to prove every element of the offense beyond a reasonable doubt. The State also points to the sentence immediately following the challenged portion of the charge, which reads: "[a] person will not be presumed to act with criminal intention. . . ."

As we explained in *Sandstrom,* general instructions on the State's burden of persuasion and the defendant's presumption of innocence are not "rhetorically inconsistent with a conclusive or burden-shifting presumption," because "[t]he jury could have interpreted the two sets of instructions as indicating that the presumption was a means by which proof beyond a reasonable doubt as to intent could be satisfied." In light of the instructions on intent given in this case, a reasonable juror could thus have thought that, although intent must be proved beyond a reasonable doubt, proof of the firing of the gun and its ordinary consequences constituted proof of intent beyond a reasonable doubt unless the defendant persuaded the jury otherwise. These general instructions as to the prosecution's burden and the defendant's presumption of innocence do not dissipate the error in challenged portion of the instructions. . . ."

Sandstrom v. Montana made clear that the Due Process Clause of the Fourteenth Amendment prohibits the State from making use of jury instructions that have the effect of relieving the State of the burden of proof on the critical question of intent in a criminal prosecution. Today we reaffirm the rule of *Sandstrom* and the wellspring due process principle from which it was drawn. . . .

Notes and Questions

1. How should the court have instructed the jury on the issue of intent to kill?

Would the jury instructions rejected by Justice Brennan have significantly benefited the prosecution in the *Franklin* case?

2. *The meaning of intent.* Professor Lloyd Weinreb has commented:[1]

> . . . Intent to kill has nothing to do with motive as such. While the circumstances that give rise to the intent may mitigate culpability, the law makes no differentiation between a killing with a benevolent motive, like euthanasia, and any other intentional killing.

1. Lloyd Weinreb, Homicide: Legal Aspects, 2 Encyclopedia of Crime and Justice 858, 859 (1983).

Also consider the commentary to Model Penal Code, §210.2:[2]

> *Purposeful or Knowing Homicide.* Under Section 210.2(1) (a), both purposeful and knowing homicides are classified as murder, assuming the absence of justification or excuse under Articles 2 and 3 of the Code and the absence of mitigation based on mental or emotional disturbance under Section 210.3(1) (b). This result reflects the judgments that purpose and knowledge should be assimilated for grading purposes, as was generally the case with prevailing law, and that no further grading distinctions, save for the possibility of provocation or similar mitigating circumstances, can usefully be made with respect to sentences to imprisonment. . . .
>
> As defined in Section 2.02, "purposely" and "knowingly" refer to the actor's subjective state of mind. It is, therefore, misleading to speak, as some courts are prone to do, of a "presumption" that a person intends the natural or probable consequences of his acts. Liability under Section 210.2(1) (a) may not rest merely on a finding that the defendant purposely or knowingly did something which had death of another as its natural and probable consequence. Rather, the prosecution must establish that the defendant engaged in conduct with the conscious objective of causing death of another or at least with awareness the death of another was practically certain to result from his act. Of course, the required state of mind may be proved circumstantially, and a finding of purpose or knowledge may be a permissible inference from the character of the defendant's conduct and the circumstances under which it took place.

3. *"Malice" and intent.* Does the term "malice" add any meaning to modern murder statutes? In a surprising and controversial decision, State v. Myers, 244 Neb. 905, 510 N.W.2d 58 (1994), the Nebraska Supreme Court ruled that to establish second-degree murder the jury had to find both intent to kill and "malice." The fallout from *Myers* was powerful: 62 prison inmates convicted of murder sought and won retrials, ending in reduced charges for a number of them; public outcry was great, and one justice who had voted in the majority lost his seat on the court. Four years later, after a change in court personnel, the court reversed itself and held that the term "malice" was essentially surplusage, presumably leaving it to the defendant to bring affirmative defenses to establish "absence of malice." See State v. Burlison, 583 N.W.2d 31 (Neb. 1998).

4. *The presumption of intent.* Is it true that a person usually intends the probable consequences of her actions? Consider the following passage from sociologist Jack Katz.[3]

> The practical objective of those who kill is not necessarily to kill. In the non-predatory assault or homicide, "much of the violence is of an impulsive nature. An argument gets out of hand or two old enemies meet on the street, and a fight ensues. It is often difficult to tell who is the victim and who is the offender."[4]
>
> Recognizing these findings, contemporary writers on homicide and assault routinely note that whether an event ends in a criminal homicide or an aggravated assault depends on such chance factors as the distance to the hospital; the quality of medical services available; whether a gun was used and, if so, its caliber; whether "a head reeling from a punch strikes a rail or concrete floor"; or whether the knife chanced to hit a vital organ.

2. American Law Institute, Model Penal Code and Commentaries, Pt. II, at 20-21.
3. Seductions of Crime 32 (1989).
4. Richard Block, Violent Crime 88 (1977).

5. *"Transferred" intent.* What if Gray purposely shoots to kill Smith but misses Smith and kills Johnson? Is Gray guilty of the intentional killing of Johnson? The virtually universal rule is that he is guilty, thanks to the hoary legal fiction that his intent to kill Smith is "transferred" to his unintended killing of Johnson. Can we reach this result without the notion of "transferred intent"? See People v. Scott, 14 Cal. 4th 544, 59 Cal. Rptr. 178 (1996) (reaffirming transferred intent rule under which defendant is guilty of both intentional killing of dead victim and attempt on target; the intent is "transferred" to but not "used up" by killing); but see Anthony Dillof, Transferred Intent: An Inquiry into the Nature of Criminal Culpability, 1 Buff. Crim. L. Rev. 501 (1998) ("transferred intent" doctrine is inconsistent with tort principle that duty runs to individuals, not world at large; better to rest liability on recklessness).

B. PREMEDITATED MURDER (FIRST-DEGREE)

UNITED STATES v. WATSON
District of Columbia Court of Appeals
501 A.2d 791 (1985)

ROGERS, ASSOCIATE JUDGE.

Appellant appeals his conviction for first degree murder, D.C. Code §22-2401 (1981), of Metropolitan Police Officer Donald Lunning on the ground that there was insufficient evidence of premeditation and deliberation. Consistent with our standard of review, we hold that a reasonable jury could reasonably find, from the evidence in the government's case-in-chief, that appellant had formed the decision to kill upon reaching for the loose gun, and that he gave further thought about this decision when the officer pleaded for his life. Accordingly, we affirm.

In reviewing the denial of a motion for a judgment of acquittal notwithstanding the verdict, this court must determine "'whether there was sufficient evidence from which a reasonable juror could fairly conclude guilt beyond a reasonable doubt.'" Jones v. United States, 477 A.2d 231, 246 (D.C. 1984) (quoting Head v. United States, 451 A.2d 615, 622 (D.C. 1982)). We view the evidence in the "light most favorable to the government, giving full play to the right of the jury to determine credibility, weighing the evidence, and draw justifiable inferences of fact," Hall v. United States, 454 A.2d 314, 317 (D.C. 1982), and do not distinguish between direct and circumstantial evidence. We may reverse only where the government has produced no evidence from which a reasonable mind might infer guilt beyond a reasonable doubt.

First degree murder is a calculated and planned killing while second degree murder is unplanned or impulsive. The government must therefore prove beyond a reasonable doubt that the accused acted with premeditation and deliberation, the thought processes necessary to distinguish first degree murder from second degree. See *Hall, supra,* 454 A.2d at 317. As set forth in [State v. Frendak, 408 A.2d 364, 371 (NJ. 1979)]:

To prove premeditation, the government must show that a defendant gave "thought before acting to the idea of taking a human life and [reached] a definite decision to kill." Deliberation is proved by demonstrating that the accused acted with "consideration and reflection upon the preconceived design to kill; turning it over in the mind, giving it second thought." Although no specific amount of time is necessary to demonstrate premeditation and deliberation, the evidence must demonstrate that the accused did not kill impulsively, in the heat of passion, or in an orgy of frenzied activity.

"[S]ome appreciable time must elapse" between the formation of design to kill and actual execution of the design to establish that reflection and consideration amounted to deliberation. Bostic v. United States, 94 F.2d 636, 639 (D.C. App. 1937). The time need not be long. Thus, the government is not required to show that there was a "lapse of days or hours, or even minutes," Bostic, 94 F.2d at 639, and the time involved may be as brief as a few seconds. Although reflection and consideration, and not lapse of time, are determinative of deliberation, Bostic, 94 F.2d at 639, "[l]apse of time is important because of the opportunity which it affords for deliberation." Bostic, 94 F.2d at 639. The evidence of premeditation and deliberation must be sufficient to persuade, not compel, a reasonable juror to a finding of guilty.

Viewing the evidence most favorably to the government, the government's case-in-chief showed that during the investigation of a stolen car, two police officers saw the stolen car pull into the parking lot of 3729 Jay Street, N.E. They ordered the driver to stop by shouting, "Police. Hold it." The driver of the car, appellant, jumped out, looked at the officers, and ran toward an apartment complex; Officer Lunning, with his gun drawn, pursued. Appellant ran through the archway of 3749 Jay Street, N.E. and then through the open door of the Davis' apartment at 3712-A Hayes Street, N.E. Three young girls, ages approximately 14, 13 and 9, were sitting at a table doing their homework. Appellant asked to use the telephone, and after dialing, he asked the responding party "[Are] they still out there?" He sat down at the table, where the girls were sitting, and held his head in his hands.

Officer Lunning entered the open door of the apartment holding his gun in front of him and told appellant "Police, you are under arrest." Appellant asked, "For what?" When appellant refused to cooperate with being handcuffed, the officer said, "Do you want me to blow your m —— f —— head off?" Appellant stood up. As the officer reached for his hand to put on the handcuffs, appellant said, "You are not going to put those things on me." Appellant grabbed the officer in a bear hug around the waist. Eventually the two men fell over a table. The officer's gun, which had been pointed downwards as he had tried to handcuff appellant, dropped onto the floor.

The two men scuffled, rolling over each other, until appellant had the officer in a position where he could not move: appellant had his knee in the officer's chest and, with his hands, held down the officer's hands. At this point, according to two of the girls, the officer told appellant, "It wasn't worth it." Then, with the officer still flat on his back, appellant reached out and grabbed the loose gun. He proceeded to hold the gun to the officer's chest. The officer now repeated, "It wasn't worth it." One of the girls then ran back to the back of the apartment, a distance of approximately twenty feet. She was inside the bathroom when, within seconds, she heard a shot. Another girl ran from the apartment, approximately sixteen feet, and heard a shot while outside. She next saw appellant coming down the steps as he was leaving the apartment complex holding the gun in his hand. The officer followed shortly, holding his chest and eventually fell to the ground.

The gun was fired approximately thirty to thirty-six inches from Officer Lunning's body while he was lying on the floor. The bullet entered at the midline of the top of the officer's abdomen on the right side. Appellant was uninjured when he was arrested at the scene, suffering only scrapes on his kneecap. Appellant was six feet four inches tall and weighed 218 pounds. Officer Lunning was five feet nine inches tall and weighed approximately 220 pounds.

A neighbor testified that when appellant ran into 3694 Hayes Street, N.E. and asked to use her sister's telephone, she heard him say into the telephone, "I just shot the police; could you come and get me?" He also said he "had something on him and the police were chasing him so he hit [the officer] with the gun." The sister who lived in the apartment corroborated this testimony, and also testified that appellant told her he was carrying drugs and offered her money if she would hide him.

"Premeditation and deliberation may be inferred from sufficiently probative facts and circumstances." *Hall, supra*, 454 A.2d at 317.[5] In the instant case the jury could reasonably find that when appellant sat at the table, after making the telephone call, he was anticipating the officer's arrival and planning how to escape. He knew the officer had drawn his gun, and a juror could infer that appellant realized he would have to disarm the officer in order to escape. Appellant, who was five inches taller, and described by one of the girls as much larger than the officer, initiated the struggle while the officer was pointing his gun at him. He struggled with the officer and caused him to drop his gun. He then continued to struggle with the officer until he gained complete physical control of the officer. One of the girls testified that the officer did not have a chance to get the loose gun. A juror could reasonably find that when the officer said, "It wasn't worth it," and appellant grabbed the gun, the officer was pleading for his life or at least suggesting to appellant that avoiding arrest for stealing a car was not worth assaulting an officer. Since there was nothing blocking appellant's escape from the apartment, a juror could further infer that by grabbing the loose gun and holding it to the officer's chest instead of fleeing, appellant had made the decision to kill the officer.

Before a shot was fired, however, the officer had time to repeat, "It wasn't worth it." Two of the girls also had time to run from the room into another part of the apartment or outside of the apartment building. In addition, appellant rose up and stood over the officer. At no time was anything or anyone impeding appellant's escape from the apartment. Considering the lapse of time before

5. This court has sustained a trial court's finding of sufficient evidence to submit the issue of premeditation and deliberation to the jury where a planned and calculated intent to kill could be inferred from: evidence of prior threats of hostility between the accused and the victim, [Harris v. United States, 375 A.2d 505, 508 (D.C. 1977)]; evidence of a motive, which suggested a purposeful or reasoned killing, *Jones, supra*, 477 A.2d at 246-47 (fight about money); *Hall, supra*, 454 A.2d at 317-18 (jilted lover); the manner and circumstances of the killing, for example, an interruption and subsequent continuation of the killing, *Hall, supra*, 454 A.2d at 317-18 (having to adjust gun during murder); evidence of the accused's behavior before the killing, *Frendak, supra*, 408 A.2d at 371 (keeping apprised of the victim's schedule and stalking him); O'Connor v. United States, 399 A.2d 21, 26 (D.C. 1979) (anticipating and preparing for a confrontation). Also, in the absence of evidence "truly probative of premeditation and deliberation," the origin of the murder weapon is of "undeniable significance" [Hemphill v. United States, 402 F.2d 187, 190 (D.C. Cir. 1968)] ("prosecutor's failure to bring out whether defendant brought murder weapon with him" important factor in finding no premeditation and deliberation); compare [Belton v. United States, 382 F.2d 150, 152 (D.C. Cir. 1967)] (bringing loaded gun to scene permits inference of premeditation and deliberation); *Frendak, supra*, 408 A.2d at 364 (same).

appellant fired the gun, a juror could reasonably infer from all the circumstances that the officer's second plea was asking appellant to reconsider the decision to kill him, and that appellant had sufficient time to, and did reaffirm his decision to kill the officer. Although these events occurred within a short period of time, there was evidence before the jury from which it could find that there were two significant pauses in the action — when appellant had immobilized the officer and when the officer repeated his plea — which afforded appellant time to premeditate and deliberate.

Appellant argues that the absence of eyewitness testimony about the events which occurred from the time appellant had the gun pointed in the officer's chest and the firing of the gun demonstrates the jury was left to speculate on whether the officer's remarks had any impact on defendant's thought process. He notes that no evidence was presented of his facial gestures or hand movements which would indicate the officer's remarks affected him. Of course, eyewitness testimony is not required for the government to meet its burden of proof; circumstantial evidence will suffice. This jurisdiction has long recognized that the jury is entitled to consider all of the circumstances preceding and surrounding the shooting to determine "whether reflection and consideration amounting to deliberation actually occurred." *Bostic, supra,* 94 F.2d at 638-39.

Appellant also urges us to hold that like the appellant in *Bostic, supra,* he acted in fear, panic and self-defense arising from the officer's threat, when he entered the apartment, to shoot appellant's "head off," and the officer's attempt later to grab his gun as appellant pointed it at him. He relies also on the testimony of one of the girls that the officer was acting kind of crazy and appellant looked frightened. Evidence that the officer had tried to grab his gun was not in evidence during the government's case-in-chief. But, in any event, we are satisfied that a juror could reasonably infer from the government's evidence that the totality of the circumstances cast substantial doubt on appellant's claim that he fired out of fear, in a panic, or in self-defense when the officer allegedly reached for the gun.

The government's evidence showed that although he was facing an officer with a drawn gun, appellant, having waited for the officer to arrive, initiated the physical struggle with him. Even after he had immobilized the officer and had grabbed the gun, appellant did not shoot immediately, but held the gun in the officer's chest. When he fired the gun he did not fire a series of shots, as though in a panic, but a single shot, which went directly into the right side of the officer's chest. Combined with the evidence of appellant's motive to escape, these circumstances could cause a reasonable juror to conclude that appellant did not shoot in a panic but acted with deliberation, having decided to kill the officer in order to assure his escape, and that he reflected upon his decision before pulling the trigger, and did not shoot in a frenzy or in the heat-of-passion.[6]

Accordingly, we find no reason to disturb the trial court's implicit finding that the evidence viewed most favorably to the government is not such that a reasonable juror must have a reasonable doubt, and the issue was properly left to the jury.

Affirmed.

6. Appellant's appearance shortly after he shot the officer is also consistent with such a conclusion. The woman who was in her sister's apartment in the neighborhood, testified that when he admitted he had shot an officer, appellant did not appear to be frightened, only confused, and that he was still clearly focusing on how to escape.

Notes and Questions

1. Under the court's approach, would Watson be guilty of first-degree murder if he had grabbed Officer Lunning's gun and shot him the moment they first encountered each other on the street? After Watson had run into the apartment, but the moment Lunning entered it? Under what theory of punishment might Watson be less culpable under those circumstances? The court takes pains to note that Watson had time to, and did in fact, reconsider and reaffirm his decision to kill. Would he be a less culpable killer if he were the sort never to take this extra mental step at all?

Of what relevance might it be that Watson initially fled from Lunning? That he was not himself armed?

2. *Retribution and premeditation.* According to Sir James Stephen:[7]

> As much cruelty, *as* much indifference to the life of others, a disposition at least as dangerous to society, probably even more dangerous, is shown by sudden as by premeditated murders. The following cases appear to me to set this in a clear light. A man passing along the road, sees a boy sitting on a bridge over a deep river and, out of mere wanton barbarity, pushes him into it and so drowns him. A man makes advances to a girl who repels him. He deliberately but instantly cuts her throat. A man civilly asked to pay a just debt pretends to get the money, loads a rifle and blows out his creditor's brains. In none of these cases is there premeditation unless the word is used in a sense as unnatural as "aforethought" in "malice aforethought," but each represents even more diabolical cruelty and ferocity than that which is involved in murders premeditated in the natural sense of the word.

Does Stephen reflect a retributivist view of the criminal law? Does his criticism of the premeditation formula take account of the deterrent or incapacitative functions of the criminal law?

3. *Duration.* According to the court in *Watson,* "no specific amount of time is necessary to demonstrate premeditation and deliberation," and the government need not show a "lapse of days or hours, or even minutes," but "some appreciable time must elapse." How do you reconcile these statements? Is it that seconds must elapse? Would it be sufficient, even if not necessary, that minutes elapsed? What might be happening during those minutes?

4. *Criteria of premeditation.* However vague the definitions of premeditation given in jury instructions by the trial court, appellate courts often cite various evidentiary factors in determining whether the evidence was sufficient to support a jury verdict of first-degree murder. These include: earlier hostility between the accused and the victim, *e.g.,* State v. Cross, 577 N.W.2d 721 (Minn. 1998) (killer's demonstrated pattern of abusing spouse helps establish that he killed her with premeditation); self-interested motive, *e.g.,* Jones v. United States, 477 A.2d 231 (D.C. 1984) (fight about money); the manner and circumstances of the killing, *e.g.,* Hall v. United States, 454 A.2d 314 (D.C. 1982) (interruption and subsequent continuation of the killing, where defendant adjusted gun during murder); Beasley v. State, 774 So. 2d 649 (Fla. 2000) (murder weapon, a hammer, had been wrapped in cloth); the accused's behavior before the killing, *e.g.,* State v. Frendak, 408 A.2d 364 (N.J. 1979) (keeping apprised of victim's schedule and

---

7. 3 A History of the Criminal Law in England 94 (1883).

stalking him); the origin of the murder weapon, *e.g.*, Belton v. United States, 382 F.2d 150 (D.C. Cir. 1967) (bringing loaded gun); Busey v. United States, 747 A.2d 1153 (D.C. App. 2000) (no evidence that defendant somehow might have happened to find gun inside apartment — no testimony, for example, of gun already in bedroom where murder occurred the decedent was murdered; of physical signs suggesting a struggle in the bedroom between defendant and decedent over the weapon).

In People v. Garcia, 78 Cal. App. 4th 1422, 1428, 93 Cal. Rptr. 2d 796, 798-800 (2000), the court found these facts sufficient to support a premeditation verdict:

> Garcia owed Chiquete money relating to a marijuana deal, and Chiquete had spoken to him twice about it, but Garcia had not paid. When Chiquete spoke to him about the debt a third time, Garcia killed him. . . . There was no history of threats or violence by Chiquete, nor was he armed on any of the previous occasions he had spoken to Garcia about repaying the money owed. When Chiquete went to speak with Garcia on the day he was killed, he again was unarmed and wearing only a pair of pants — making it impossible to carry or conceal a weapon in his waistband, under his shirt, in a jacket, etc. Chiquete and Garcia did not argue or raise their voices. Yet, while Chiquete was standing with his hands down at his sides, Garcia pulled out a loaded, .9-millimeter handgun, held it straight out in front of his body and shot Chiquete through the heart from close range.

On the other hand, in State v. Long, 45 S.W.3d 611, 621 (Tenn. Crim. App. 2000), the court found the following factors consistent with intent to kill but *insufficient* to support a verdict of premeditation:

> (a) the "victim had engaged in sexual relations with other men"; (b) Defendant "admitted that Ramona 'slept around' and that he was 'angry with her' for that"; (c) Defendant "admitted that he had 'beat the hell out of her before' in the past due to her indiscretions"; (d) the "victim had expressed her fear" of Defendant; (e) when "the victim's mother and sister went to the defendant's in search of Ramona that the defendant told them that she had left with another individual" (sic); (f) Defendant told the same story in (e) to Jackson County Sheriff's Deputy Kenneth Bean; (g) Defendant "acted normally when a group of friends came to his house to shoot pool after Ramona's death"; (h) when officers came to Defendant's home on August 6, 1996, Defendant asked Deputy Doug Burgess "What if I killed her?"; (i) Defendant recovered Ramona's body for law enforcement after hiding it; (j) Ramona died from a close range gunshot wound to the right temple; (k) Ramona had a knife wound on her neck; (l) Defendant admitted that he caused the knife wound; (m) Ramona's hands did not test positive for particles of gunshot primer residue.

Did the appellate court in *Long* intrude too far on the jury's decision?

5. *Quality of reflection.* One of the major background cases to *Watson*, Austin v. United States, 382 F.2d 129 (D.C. Cir. 1967), reviewed the history of the premeditation rule:

> The reports reflect the effort of some courts to carry out the legislative conception, by interpreting "deliberation" to call for elements which the word normally signifies — that the determination to kill was reached calmly and in cold blood rather than under impulse or the heat of passion and was reached some appreciable time prior to the homicide. The more widespread judicial tendency was marked by a restrictive reading of the statutory terms. "The statutory scheme was

apparently intended to limit administrative discretion in the selection of capital cases. As so frequently occurs, the discretion which the legislature threw out the door was let in the window by the courts."

Judge, later Justice, Cardozo, in a memorable 1928 address,[8] voiced his concern over the judicial attenuation of premeditation and deliberation. He spoke against the background of the New York experience, where, although the courts had abandoned their early statement that it sufficed if intention preceded the act though the act followed instantly, they held that the time for deliberation need not be long, and seconds might suffice, provided there was time for a choice to kill or not to kill. Judge Cardozo said:

> There can be no intent unless there is a choice, yet . . . the choice without more is enough to justify the inference that the intent was deliberate and premeditated. The presence of a sudden impulse is said to mark the dividing line, but how can an impulse be anything but sudden when the time for its formation is measured by the lapse of seconds? Yet the decisions are to the effect that seconds may be enough. . . . The present distinction is so obscure that no jury hearing it for the first time can fairly be expected to assimilate and understand it. I am not at all sure that I understand it myself after trying to apply it for many years and after diligent study of what has been written in the books. Upon the basis of this fine distinction with its obscure and mystifying phraseology, scores of men have gone to their death. [Id. at 134-35.]

Criticizing a jury instruction that focused on the duration of thought, not the "degree of meditation," the court stated,

> In homespun terminology, intentional murder is in the first degree if committed in cold blood, and is murder in the second degree if committed on impulse or in the sudden heat of passion. These are the archetypes, that clarify by contrast. The real facts may be hard to classify and may lie between the poles. A sudden passion, like lust, rage, or jealousy, may spawn an impulsive intent yet persist long enough and in such a way as to permit that intent to become the subject of a further reflection and weighing of consequences and hence to take on *the* character of a murder executed without compunction and "in cold blood." The term "in cold blood" does not necessarily mean the assassin lying in wait, or the kind of murder brilliantly depicted by Truman Capote in *In Cold Blood* (1965). Thus the common understanding might find both passion and cold blood in the husband who surprises his wife in adultery, leaves the house to buy a gun at a sporting goods store, and returns for a deadly sequel. The analysis of the jury would be illuminated, however, if it is first advised that a typical case of first degree is the murder in cold blood; that murder committed on impulse or in sudden passion is murder in the second degree; and then instructed that a homicide conceived in passion constitutes murder in the first degree only if the jury is convinced beyond a reasonable doubt while there was an appreciable time after the design was conceived and that in this interval there was a further thought, and a turning over in the mind — and not a mere persistence of the initial impulse of passion. [Id. at 137.]

Would the *Austin* court's distinction between hot-blooded and coldblooded killings help a jury more than the standard used in the *Watson* case?

Is *deliberation* the same thing as *premeditation*? In Kazalyn v. State, 825 P.2d 578, 583 (Nev. 1992), the Nevada Supreme Court had defined premeditation

---

8. What Medicine Can Do for Law, reprinted in Law and Literature 70, 96-101 (1931).

as, "a design, a determination to kill, distinctly formed in the mind at any moment before or at the time of the killing," and then stated, "[I]f the jury believes from the evidence that the act constituting the killing has been preceded by and has been the result of premeditation . . . it is willful, deliberate and premeditated murder." In Byford v. State, 994 P.2d. 700 (Nev. 2000), the court changed course, concluding that *Kazalyn* improperly collapsed willfulness and deliberation into the definition of premeditation, raising the risk that a jury's finding of premeditation would automatically create a finding of the other necessary elements and blurring the distinction between first and second-degree murder. It established a new jury instruction, including this language:

> Deliberation is the process of determining upon a course of action to kill as a result of thought, including weighing the reasons for and against the action and considering the consequences of the action.
>
> A deliberate determination may be arrived at in a short period of time. But in all cases the determination must not be formed in passion, or if formed in passion, it must be carried out after there has been time for the passion to subside and deliberation to occur. A mere unconsidered and rash impulse is not deliberate, even though it includes the intent to kill. [Id. at 714]

How significant is this change? Would Justice Cardozo have found it helpful?

6. *Righteous rage.* Many premeditation cases involve violent butchery far beyond what is necessary to kill the victim. Courts and juries then struggle over whether this gratuitous violence supports or weakens a finding of premeditation. Sociologist Jack Katz has proffered an analysis of what he calls "righteous slaughter" killings that may technically be premeditated but which evince psychological subtleties that the premeditation formula is too crude to capture. Katz describes a category of filing where the killer is motivated by powerful rage at humiliation he blames on the victim and sets out to kill as if engaged in an obligatory ritual of sacrifice:[9]

1. The would-be-killer must interpret the scene and the behavior of the victim in a particular way. He must understand not only that the victim is attacking what he, the killer, regards as an eternal human value, but that the situation requires a last stand in defense of his basic worth.
2. The would-be killer must undergo a particular emotional process. He must transform what he initially senses as an eternally humiliating situation into a rage. In rage, the killer can blind himself to his future, forging a momentary sense of eternal unity with the Good.
3. The would-be-killer must successfully organize his behavior to maintain the required perspective and emotional posture while implementing a particular project. The project is the honoring of the offense that he suffered through a marking violently drawn into the body of the victim. Death may or may not result, but when it does, it comes as a sacrificial slaughter.

Then, when the killer attacks, he curses and denounces the victim as if to proclaim the moral significance of his act and may utter a threat of obliteration ("I'll blow you away" or "wipe you out"), not just of the victim's future existence, but of any trace of his or her prior existence on earth.[10]

9. Seductions of Crime, at 18-19.
10. Id. at 37.

In a case like this, should the jury focus on the defendant's rage and deluded but sincere sense of justification, or on his "organization" of the killing as a "project"?

7. *Mercy killing.* Consider the following:

Mercy Killer Gets Probation, $10,000 Fine [11]

San Diego — A 71-year-old woman who admitted strangling her bedridden husband with a nylon stocking was placed on probation yesterday by a judge who said, "She wanted to release him and free him of his pain." Dorothy Healy of La Jolla had pleaded guilty earlier to voluntary manslaughter in the slaying of her 92-year-old husband, Walter, and could have been jailed for up to 11 years. But Municipal Judge Frederic Link said he saw moral and ethical reasons why Mrs. Healy committed the homicide. He ordered her to serve five years' probation, pay a $10,000 fine and perform 1,000 hours of community-service work.

"Mr. Healy was in severely declining health," the judge said. He suffered loss of hearing. He had had a series of strokes since 1973 and was in constant pain and almost totally bedridden.

"But for the valiant efforts of Dorothy Healy, Mr. Healy probably would not have lived as long as he did. Walter Healy had often said he didn't want to go to a hospital or a rest home. Mrs. Healy believed in what she was doing. She had said: 'Walter would thank me. Walter would appreciate what I did.'" Healy suffered from emphysema, arteriosclerosis and other illnesses. Mrs. Healy first told authorities that her husband of 48 years had died in his sleep on March 20. She was arrested when an autopsy revealed he had been strangled. She told police she used a nylon stocking to kill him.

"I didn't want to believe that this sweet little old thing could possibly have anything to do with killing her husband," San Diego County Deputy Coroner Chuck Bolton said after her arrest.

How would you defend Mrs. Healy against a charge of first-degree murder under *Watson?*

8. *The MPC position.* The drafters of the Model Penal Code solved the problem of distinguishing between premeditated and "merely intentional" murder by abandoning the distinction altogether, providing for only a single degree of murder. The drafters argued that the originating purpose behind the distinction was to isolate those cases for which capital punishment would be automatic. Now that there can be no "automatic" death penalty, see p. 433, *infra,* the distinction serves no purpose. The drafters also took the view that the factors that might normally separate first-degree from second-degree murder will, in any event, play a role in the judge's discretionary sentencing or will take the form of arguments for mitigation of the murder charge to manslaughter. They commented:[12]

. . . [W]e think it plain that the case for a mitigated sentence does not depend on a distinction between impulse and deliberation; the very fact of long internal struggle may be evidence that the actor's homicidal impulse was deeply

---

11. San Francisco Chronicle, June 20, 1984, at 4.

12. American Law Institute, Model Penal Code and Commentaries, §210.6, comment at 70 (Tent. Draft No. 9, 1959).

aberrational, far more the product of extraordinary circumstances than a true reflection of the actor's normal character, as, for example, in the case of mercy killings, suicide pacts, many infanticides and cases where a provocation gains in its explosive power as the actor broods about his injury.

9. *Mental disorder.* What sort of evidence might a defendant introduce to negate a charge of premeditating a particular killing by showing that he was somehow incapable of premeditation in general?

In Commonwealth v. Gould, 405 N.E.2d 927 (Mass. 1980), the defendant was convicted of first-degree premeditated murder for stabbing his former girlfriend to death. Gould suffered from a "long-standing, constant delusional belief system" that he had a Messianic role, and he felt obligated to kill her because she was "impure." He was diagnosed as paranoid schizophrenic. However, he was unable to win a verdict of not guilty by reason of insanity because he could not establish, as required by Massachusetts law, that at the time of the killing he was unable to appreciate the wrongfulness of his act or to exercise self-restraint. The court held that Gould was entitled to offer evidence of his mental condition in an effort to persuade the jury that even if he was guilty of an intentional killing, he was unable to premeditate one. The court noted that evidence of voluntary drug or alcohol intoxication was admissible to negate premeditation and found Gould's mental disorder at least as probative.

Does it make sense to find someone sane enough to intend to kill and yet not sane enough to premeditate? What does this distinction imply about the meaning of premeditation?

C. VOLUNTARY MANSLAUGHTER

1. The Theory of Mitigation

Manslaughter encompasses two very different kinds of killings. Voluntary manslaughter differs from involuntary manslaughter in that it is intentional; the defendant has with knowledge or purpose killed another human being rather than having done so with gross negligence or recklessness or merely with the intent to commit some other crime.

While an intentional killing is generally murder, the criminal law reduces the murder to voluntary manslaughter where there has been "provocation" that has caused the defendant to act in "the heat of passion." In one quaint formulation:

"Malice aforethought" implies a mind under the sway of reason, whereas "passion" whilst it does not imply a dethronement of reason, yet it is the *furor brevis*, which renders a man deaf to the voice of reason so that, although the act was intentional of death, it was not the result of malignity of heart, but imputable to human infirmity. Passion and malice are, therefore, inconsistent motive powers, and hence an act which proceeds from the one, cannot also proceed from the other. [Hannah v. Commonwealth, 149 S.E.2d 419, 421 (Va. 1929)].

PEOPLE v. WALKER
Illinois Court of Appeals
204 N.E.2d 594 (1965)

MR. JUSTICE DRUCKER delivered the opinion of the court.

Defendant appeals from a conviction of murder and the sentence of four-teen years, after a bench trial. He urges that he was not proved guilty beyond a reasonable doubt but that in any event he was guilty of manslaughter and not murder.

The testimony of Albert McClinton, the State's main witness, reveals that on the night of June 2, 1961, he, Claude Jenkins, a Mrs. Brown and the defendant were drinking and talking on a porch at 3310 South Indiana Avenue in Chicago; that a man he did not know, John Stenneth (hereinafter referred to as the deceased), approached and demanded that they gamble; that when he was refused he drew a knife and started toward them; that McClinton grabbed two bottles and told deceased he would hit him if "you comes up on me with that knife"; that defendant and Jenkins told McClinton to come back but that every time he turned deceased ran up and tried to cut him; that defendant and Jenkins came up and backed deceased down the street; that deceased was cutting at both of them but that he did not see either defendant or Jenkins get cut. McClinton further testified that defendant threw a brick which hit deceased and knocked him down; that all three ran up and stood around the deceased; that defendant picked up deceased's hand with the knife in it and said "he would cut his throat with his own knife"; that he cut the deceased and walked away. McClinton then said "You shouldn't have cut the man. I told you not to cut the man, I told you not to cut the man" and defendant answered: "You told me not to cut the man. He cut me." . . . Defendant's main contention is that, under the law, if a killing occurs during the course of a fight and before the blood of the killer has had time to cool, the offense is not murder but voluntary manslaughter. In support of his view, defendant cites People v. Bissett, 92 N.E. 949:

> . . . It is indispensible, before one can be convicted of the crime of murder, that the act be done with malice aforethought, either express or implied. Here the element of malice, under the case as made by the People, was wholly wanting. Under our statute the crime committed could not have been more than manslaughter, which to use the language of the statute, "is the unlawful killing of a human being with-out malice, express or implied, and without any mixture of deliberation whatever. It must be voluntary, upon a sudden heat of passion, caused by a provocation ap-parently sufficient to make the passion irresistible. . . . In cases of voluntary manslaughter, there must be a serious and highly provoking injury inflicted upon the person killing, sufficient to excite an irresistible passion in a reasonable per-son, or an attempt by the person killed to commit a serious personal injury on the person killing. The killing must be the result of that sudden, violent impulse of pas-sion supposed to be irresistible; for if there should appear to have been an interval between the assault or provocation given, and the killing, sufficient for the voice of reason and humanity to be heard, the killing shall be attributed to deliberate re-venge, and punished as murder." That Russell was inflicting upon plaintiff in error a highly provoking injury at the time he voluntarily seized him and demanded he turn over to him the contents of his pocket is clearly shown by the testimony of every witness to the assault. *That from the time the affray began until Russell was shot and killed there was not the slightest pause in the activities of the two men engaged, and not the slightest opportunity offered plaintiff in error to deliberate or reason in regard to the matter, is*

clearly shown. Under this state of facts the plaintiff in error, if guilty at all, is guilty of no graver offense than that of manslaughter, and upon motion for a new trial the verdict of the jury should have been set aside. (92 N.E.2d at 522.) (Emphasis supplied. . . .)

In the instant case, the deceased was an aggressive, intoxicated belligerent who menaced strangers because they would not gamble with him. According to every witness he kept swinging his knife at one and all. Defendant went to McClinton's aid; defendant had no words with deceased whom he had never seen before; when he was cut by the deceased, he knocked him down by striking him with a brick. It is undisputed that defendant never had a knife. He grabbed deceased's hand with the knife in it and stabbed deceased with the knife in deceased's hand. The affray was a continuous one. It lasted six minutes according to defendant. McClinton testified that:

I don't know exactly how much time elapsed between the time I first saw this man and when Leroy cut him with his own knife. Everything happened pretty fast. I guess it wasn't as long as 15 minutes. It all happened pretty fast.

In his summation in the trial court, the Assistant State's Attorney said:

. . . I think the defendant used too much force in attempting to restrain the attack of the deceased. And I think that after he was attacked and was cut by the deceased, that he became impatient and that is when he performed the stabbing on the deceased. . . .

We find that under the evidence defendant was guilty of voluntary manslaughter and remand the cause to the Circuit Court with directions to enter a finding of guilty of voluntary manslaughter and to impose a sentence for that crime appropriate to the facts and circumstances of this cause and to whatever other matters in aggravation or mitigation may be made available to the trial court. . . .

Notes and Questions

1. What was Walker's mens rea at the time of the killing? Are the conventional mental state categories, as delineated in Model Penal Code §2.02, sufficient to address this question?

2. Did Stenneth's actions *justify* the killing? Did he deserve to die? If so, why does Walker face any criminal charge at all? If not, why does Walker win a reversal?

Assuming that an intentional, unjustified killing would be punishable by a very long prison sentence (let us say 15 years to life), why does Walker merit a much shorter sentence? Was he responsible for his actions? How does the doctrine of "provocative temptation" square with the various principles or purposes of criminal punishment discussed in Chapter 1? With general deterrence? Specific deterrence? Any others?

3. In many jurisdictions, provocation is not the only reason to reduce an unlawful intentional killing from murder to voluntary manslaughter. In particular, where a person kills in the unreasonable and mistaken belief that he must do so in self-defense, or kills in the face of an actual threat of death or serious injury where he himself was the initiator or provoker of the threat from the victim, the

charge of intentional murder might be compromised to one of voluntary manslaughter. We address these situations later in Chapter 8, treating claims of justified or excused defensive force. By the way, could Walker have raised a self-defense claim?

4. *The Meaning of provocation.* The Model Penal Code Commentaries to section 210.3 discuss the provocation doctrine as it existed at common law.[13]

> At most, therefore, provocation affects the quality of the actor's state of mind as an indicator of moral blameworthiness. Provocation is thus properly regarded as a recognition by the law that inquiry into the reasons for the actor's formulation of an intent to kill will sometimes reveal factors that should have significance in grading. It is a concession to human weakness and perhaps to non-deterrability, a recognition of the fact that one who kills in response to certain provoking events should be regarded as demonstrating a significantly different character deficiency than one who kills in their absence.
>
> Although statements of the rule vary slightly, common law provocation has two essential requirements. The first is objective in character. The provocation must be "adequate," and adequacy is measured by reference to the objective standard of the reasonable man. . . . The second requirement is subjective in nature. The defendant must in fact have been provoked; he must have acted in response to the provocation. . . .[14] He also must not have acted from any previously settled intention to kill. These requirements necessitate a subjective assessment of the particular individual's state of mind at the time of the killing. These elements of the rule of provocation will each be examined in turn.
>
> Provocation is said to be "adequate" if it would cause a reasonable person to lose his self-control. Of course, a reasonable person does not kill even when provoked, but events may so move a person to violence that a homicidal reaction, albeit unreasonable in some sense, merits neither the extreme condemnation nor the extreme sanctions of a conviction of murder. The underlying judgment is thus that some instances of intentional homicide may be as much attributable to the extraordinary nature of the situation as to the moral depravity of the actor. This observation supplies the essential rationale for the law of provocation: "The more strongly most persons would be moved to kill by circumstances of the sort that provoked the actor to the homicidal act, and the more difficulty they would experience in resisting the impulse to which he yielded, the less does his succumbing serve to differentiate his character from theirs." This rationale explains the rule's secure grounding in an objective view of what constitutes sufficient provocation. The lighter the provocation, when understood in terms of the way ordinary people would react, "the more basis there is for ascribing the actor's act to an extraordinary susceptibility to intense passion, to an unusual deficiency in those other desires which counteract in most men the desires which impel them to homicidal acts, or to an extraordinary weakness of reason and consequent inability to bring such desires into play." Yet it is also clear that some characteristics of the individual actor must be considered. A taunting attack that would seem trivial to the ordinary citizen may be extremely threatening to the blind man. And a person experiencing an adverse reaction to chemotherapy cannot be expected to maintain the same judgment and restraint that he would otherwise possess. The common

13. Model Penal Code and Commentaries, *supra*, at 54-60.

14. [But this requirement that the defendant have been impassioned in fact rarely arises as an independent factor where the objective criterion is established, see State v. Perdue, 792 N.E.2d 747 (Ohio App. 2003) (voluntary manslaughter not established where though decedent had acted in a provocative rage, no witnesses described the defendant himself as manifesting any anger at all). — EDS.]

law viewed such concessions grudgingly, however, and the courts took a firm stance against individualization of the standard for determining adequacy of provocation.

Traditionally, the courts have also limited the circumstances of adequate provocation by casting generalizations about reasonable human behavior into rules of law that structured and confined the operation of the doctrine. Thus, the decisions usually required that the provocation arise from some action of the deceased or at least that the defendant reasonably so believe. Further, there emerged a series of categories defining conduct that a jury might deem adequate provocation. First and foremost, physical attack might constitute provocation, though not every technical battery could suffice. Of course, even a violent blow would be inadequate if the deceased were entitled to use force, as for example in self-defense. Mutual combat became another established category of provocation. Less clearly, a threat of physical attack might constitute provocation, at least in extreme cases. Unlawful arrest would sometimes suffice, and the law frequently recognized witnessing adultery as provocation for intentional homicide of either the unfaithful spouse or the paramour. Certain other acts — chiefly violent or sexual assault on a close relative — might also constitute adequate provocation. Most importantly, the courts excluded some situations from the jury's consideration altogether. Thus, it became an established rule at common law that words alone, no matter how insulting, could not amount to adequate provocation. The only apparent exception concerned informational words disclosing a fact that would have been adequate provocation had the actor observed it himself.

The second branch of the common-law rule of provocation is subjective rather than objective in character. Circumstances sufficient to rob a reasonable man of self control will not mitigate a resulting homicide unless the defendant in fact acted in a sudden heat of passion. Passion usually means rage, but it also includes fear or any violent and intense emotion sufficient to dethrone reason. Thus, a person of exceptional restraint or maturity of judgment is held to a higher standard than is his more susceptible counterpart. The same rule applies to cooling time. One who kills after adequate provocation and before a reasonable man would regain self-control is nonetheless guilty of murder if he recovered from the affront with unusual quickness. The underlying rationale is that the individual whose passions are not aroused by provocation merits the same condemnation and punishment as one who kills without provocation of any sort.

5. *Rationale for mitigation.* Why does the criminal law mitigate the grading and punishment for a "provoked" killing? Consider two categories of explanation:

Partial Justification: Every provoked killer thinks he has a good reason to kill. If he truly had a good reason that would cause a rational person to kill, he should merit complete exoneration — as we will see in Chapter 8 on justification defenses. If he somewhat exaggerates the premise for killing or if killing is an excessive reaction to an otherwise plausible reason for force, the law splits the difference and reduces the crime from murder to manslaughter. As a retributive matter, he deserves some punishment, but not as much as an unprovoked killer. As a utilitarian matter, the law would seem to be trying to find the optimal level of deterrence. It seeks not to deter all action in the face of provocation — only excessively violent action.

If partial justification is the basis for the mitigation claim, might we not generate several criteria for the claim?

(a) The provocation would have to come from the victim.
(b) Words themselves would never be "adequate" provocation.

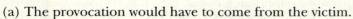

(c) The victim's defensive force against the killer's initiating force could never be a provocation.

(d) The killer must have some strong evidence that the wrong he avenges really occurred.

Partial Excuse: Now assume that there is no social value whatsoever in Walker's killing Stenneth. We give Walker no "partial moral credit" for the killing, but we do recognize that he was so enraged that his actions were slightly less voluntary, and hence slightly less culpable, than if he had not been provoked. As a retributive matter, the killing is less ascribable to malevolent character; as a utilitarian matter, Walker is less deferrable because of his rage, but also less dangerous in general, because it was partly an external force that "motivated" the killing.

If partial excuse is the basis for the mitigation claim, might we not generate several criteria for the claim?

(a) The killer must act immediately after the provocation.

(b) The victim need not have been the cause of the provocation.

(c) The victim's defensive force against the killer's initiating force could be a provocation.

(d) The killer may have been wholly, though understandably, mistaken in ascribing bad conduct to the victim.

6. *Burden of proof.* Approaching provocation as either a justification or an excuse raises the question of burden of proof. As discussed in the Introduction, *supra,* were provocation an affirmative defense, the defendant would have the burden of establishing it, probably by a preponderance. But if provocation is an element of the crime of voluntary manslaughter, or if the malice necessary to murder includes the absence of provocation, would it be the burden of the prosecution to disprove provocation beyond a reasonable doubt? In states still using old common law rules of provocation, a version of the latter is used: Once the defendant bears the burden of *production,* i.e., coming forth with some plausible evidence of provocation, the prosecution must disprove provocation or heat of passion beyond a reasonable doubt. See, *e.g.,* Commonwealth v. Acevedo, 695 N.E.2d 1065 (Mass. 1998). The Model Penal Code itself adopts the same rule, Model Penal Code §1.12(2). Nevertheless most of the states that have adopted the MPC's substantive "extreme emotional disturbance" rule require the defendant to prove EED as an affirmative defense, by a preponderance of the evidence.[15]

---

15. Uncertainty about burden of proof can lead to ironic legal outcomes. Recognizing that the heat-of-passion doctrine is a "concession to human frailty," juries often rely on voluntary manslaughter as a compromise between murder and acquittal. If the defendant is acquitted of murder but convicted of voluntary manslaughter, can he then appeal on the grounds that the components of the heat-of-passion doctrine were not established — i.e., that the facts were insufficient to establish "adequate provocation"? If so, and if an appellate court accepted his argument on appeal, double jeopardy would bar the court from declaring the defendant guilty of murder but also from retrying him on either charge. Would the defendant then go free, even though the jury probably wanted him to be punished for something? At least two courts facing this problem have declared that they indeed had no choice but to free to defendant. State v. Perdue, 792 N.E.2d 747 (Ohio App. 2003); State v. Cooley, 536 S.E.2d 666 (S.C. 2000). What must these courts have assumed was the proper burden of proof on heat-of-passion? How could the trial court or the prosecutor have avoided this problem?

7. *Scope of mitigation.* Should there also be intermediate crimes like "mitigated theft" or "mitigated assault" to mitigate the punishment of other criminals who may have been moved by the heat of passion? The historical reason for limiting the mitigation to homicide cases is simple: The doctrine traditionally served to change murder to manslaughter at a time in English history when the automatic punishment for murder was the death penalty, and judges and juries had no legal discretion to spare the life of a convicted murder. Since that premise has disappeared from American criminal law, do we still need the provocation-manslaughter doctrine at all?

Return to these categories of explanation as we examine the ground rules for "adequate provocation" in more detail.

2. "Cooling Time"

EX PARTE FRALEY
Oklahoma Criminal Court of Appeals
109 P. 295 (1910)

RICHARDSON, J.

This is an original application in this court by M. F. Fraley for a writ of habeas corpus, by which he seeks to be let to bail pending the final hearing and determination of a charge of murder filed against him in Osage county. . . .

Petitioner contends that he should be let to bail . . . because the proof of his guilt of a capital offense is not evident or the presumption thereof great. . . .

Petitioner did not testify in the examining trial, nor were any witnesses introduced in his behalf. The testimony taken, which is uncontradicted in this court, shows: That the deceased, Dan Parker, on April 11, 1910, was sitting upon or leaning against a railing in front of a drug store in the city of Pawhuska. That he had been in that position for some 10 or 15 minutes engaged in conversation with some gentlemen beside him in regard to the sale of certain walnut timber. That the petitioner came around the corner, walked up in front of the deceased, said, "Hello, Dan," and without further warning immediately fired two shots into the deceased in quick succession. That the deceased jumped up, threw up his hands, staggered, and fell off the sidewalk. The petitioner thereupon walked around an obstruction and fired four more shots into the deceased. That the petitioner then walked off, and, after going some distance, turned and came back, and putting his pistol close to the head of the deceased, snapped it a time or two, and said: "You damned son of a bitch! I told you I'd kill you. You killed my boy." The substance of the foregoing facts are testified to positively by seven eyewitnesses, and they stand in the record undisputed. It is further shown that after the deceased fell off the sidewalk his pistol fell out of his pocket; but the evidence nowhere tends to show that the deceased ever at any time had his pistol in his hand, or that he ever made any effort or demonstration to draw it. No previous conversation or difficulty of any kind or character between the petitioner and the deceased was shown or intimated.

The testimony does not show it, but it was stated by counsel for the petitioner in presenting this case, that the deceased, some 9 or 10 months previously, had shot and killed the son of the petitioner, and that the deceased had been acquitted; and it is urged here that, when the petitioner saw the deceased

on this occasion, the recollection of that event must have engendered in him a
passion which overcame him, that the killing was committed in the heat of such
passion, was without premeditation, and therefore not murder. To this we cannot assent. . . . In Ragland v. State, 125 Ala. 19, 27 So. 983, four hours intervening
between the provocation and the killing was held as a matter of law to be sufficient
cooling time to preclude the reduction of a homicide to manslaughter. Perry v.
State, 102 Ga. 365, 30 S.E. 903, arid Rockmore v. State, 93 Ga. 123, 19 S.E. 32, each
hold three days as a matter of law sufficient. Commonwealth v. Aiello, 180 Pa. 597,
36 A. 1079, holds from 1 to 2 hours sufficient, and State v. Williams, 141 N.C. 827,
53 S.E. 823, holds 15 minutes sufficient. And the authorities are all agreed that
the question is not alone whether the defendant's passion in fact cooled, but also
was there sufficient time in which the passion of a reasonable man would cool? If
in fact the defendant's passion did cool, which may be shown by circumstances,
such as the transaction of other business in the meantime, rational conversations
upon other subjects, evidence of preparation for the killing, etc., then the length
of time intervening is immaterial. But if in fact it did not cool, yet if such time intervened between the provocation and the killing that the passion of the average
man would have cooled, and his reason have resumed its sway, then still there
is no reduction of the homicide to manslaughter. If the fatal wound be inflicted
immediately following a sufficient provocation given, then the question as to
whether the defendant's passion thereby aroused had in fact cooled, or as to
whether or not such time had elapsed that the passion of a reasonable man would
have cooled, is a question of fact to be determined upon a consideration of all the
facts and circumstances in evidence; but, when an unreasonable period of time
has elapsed between the provocation and the killing, then the court is authorized
to say as a matter of law that the cooling time was sufficient.

Ordinarily one day, or even half a day, is in law much more than a sufficient
time for one's passion to cool; and a killing committed upon a provocation given
some 9 or 10 months before, is not, on account of that provocation or any passion engendered thereby, reduced to manslaughter. A deliberate killing committed in revenge for an injury inflicted in the past, however near or remote, is
"murder."

The uncontradicted testimony in this case convinces us that the proof of
the petitioner's guilt of a capital offense is evident, and that he is not therefore
entitled to bail as a matter of right. . . .

Notes and Questions

1. *Rationale for "cooling time" rules.* According to the Model Penal Code
Commentaries to section 210.3:[16]

> The courts supplemented their rules about adequate provocation by requiring that
> there not elapse between provocation and resulting homicide sufficient time for a
> reasonable man to cool off. For the reasonable man, at least, passion subsides and
> reason reasserts its sway as the provoking event grows stale. The courts refused to
> allow mitigation of intentional homicide where the actor had enjoyed a reasonable
> opportunity for his passion to cool. Generally, this rule obtained even where the

16. Model Penal Code and Commentaries, *supra,* at 59-60.

defendant in fact did not cool off but was still enraged at the time he killed. This view is consistent with the application of an objective, reasonable-person test to the cooling period as well as to the existence of provocation. If a reasonable person would have cooled off before the killing occurred, the passion was held to have subsided, and the provocation was no longer effective to reduce the homicide from murder to manslaughter. Although some courts allowed a subsequent event to revive prior provocation, others applied the cooling-time limitation with surprising strictness. In the famous case of State v. Gounagias [153 P. 9 (Wash. 1915)], the deceased committed sodomy on the unconscious defendant and subsequently spread the news of his accomplishment. Those who learned of the event taunted and ridiculed the defendant until he finally lost control and killed his assailant some two weeks after the sodomy. The court rejected the defendant's theory that the cumulative effect of reminders of former wrongs could support a sudden passion and allow mitigation and held that the passage of time precluded the original act of sodomy from being a basis for mitigation. In other instances of cumulative provocation, however, courts have held that the cooling time began with the occurrence of the last provocative event preceding the homicide.

2. If the killing of Fraley's son was legally adequate provocation, why does Fraley lose?

3. *When does the provocative event occur?* The court seems to assume that by killing Fraley's son, Parker "provoked" Fraley within the meaning of the law. Is that necessarily true? How do we square this assumption with Parker's acquittal? Can you imagine facts supporting Parker's acquittal that would either support or undermine the court's assumption?

In People v. Nesler, 16 Cal. 4th 561, 66 Cal. Rptr. 2d 454 (1997), Elie Nesler, whose seven-year-old son was allegedly sexually assaulted by one Daniel Driver, attended the preliminary hearing in Driver's criminal prosecution. Both she and her son had to testify. Nesler was overwrought by the trauma her son had suffered since the attack; she also had consumed a high dose of methamphetamine that morning. Further aroused after Driver supposedly smirked at her and her son during their testimony, Nesler pulled out a gun from her sister's purse and shot Driver to death. She was later convicted of voluntary manslaughter.

> . . . [I]n a tape-recorded statement, defendant said that she had not intended to kill Driver at the hearing and did not know whether she had done the right thing, but was tired of all the pain Driver had caused, and that he deserved to die. Defendant thought that [her son's] pain had destroyed her sense of right and wrong. She said that when Driver smirked at her son outside the courthouse, she would have killed him right there had she already taken possession of the gun. [Id. at 567, 66 Cal. Rptr. at 458] [17]

Did Nesler have a better provocation claim than Fraley?

4. *Indirect provocation.* Note that learning indirectly of harm done to a relative of the killer, as opposed to harm to the killer himself, may constitute adequate provocation. Note also that some courts give some defendants some leeway in terms of cooling time in these situations. In People v. Brooks, 185 Cal. App. 3d 687, 230 Cal. Rptr. 86 (1986), the defendant killed the murderer of his brother two hours after he learned of the murder. At some point during the two-hour

---

17. [The case was remanded to the trial court, but solely on the issue of juror misconduct during discussion of Nesler's insanity plea. Eds.]

gap, Brooks was told that the decedent, Todd, was the likely killer. During the rest of the time before killing Todd, Brooks ran around the neighborhood in an excited state, gathering confirming information. The court held that he was entitled to a voluntary manslaughter instruction.

5. *Gradual provocation.* Why should the law mitigate a killing if it is done rashly on the spur of the moment but not where the killing is the result of a long process of anguished brooding? In State v. Gounagias, 153 P. 9 (Wash. 1915), discussed in the Model Penal Code excerpt above, the Washington Supreme Court discussed the criteria of adequate provocation and reasonable cooling time, where the deceased had humiliated the accused by sodomizing him and then, over a course of two weeks, had bragged about his sexual triumph over the accused to other men in their town. The court concluded:

> The offered evidence makes it clear that the appellant knew and appreciated for days before the killing the full meaning of the words, signs, and vulgar gestures of his countrymen, which, as the offer shows, he had encountered from day to day for about three weeks following the original outrage, wherever he went. The final demonstration in the coffeehouse was nothing new. It was exactly what the appellant, from his experience for the prior three weeks, must have anticipated. To say that it alone tended to create the sudden passion and heat of blood essential to mitigation is to ignore the admitted fact that the same thing had created no such condition on its repeated occurrence during the prior three weeks. To say that these repeated demonstrations, coupled with the original outrage, *culminated* in a sudden passion and heat of blood when he encountered the same character of demonstration in the coffeehouse on the night of the killing, is to say that sudden passion and heat of blood in the mitigative sense may be a cumulative result of repeated reminders of a single act of provocation occurring weeks before, and this, whether that provocation be regarded as the original outrage or the spreading of the story among appellant's associates, both of which he knew and fully realized for three weeks before the fatal night. This theory of the cumulative effect of reminders of former wrongs, not of new acts of provocation by the deceased, is contrary to the idea of sudden anger as understood in the doctrine of mitigation. In the nature of the thing *sudden* anger cannot be cumulative. A provocation which does not cause instant resentment, but which is only resented after being thought upon and brooded over, is not a provocation sufficient in law to reduce intentional killing from murder to manslaughter, or under our statute to second degree murder, which includes every inexcusable, unjustifiable, unpremeditated, intentional killing. . . .
>
> The evidence offered had no tendency to prove sudden anger and resentment. On the contrary, it did tend to prove brooding thought, resulting in the design to kill. It was therefore properly excluded.

6. *Other provoked emotions.* Should the "cooling off" period apply to "provoked fear" as opposed to "provoked anger" cases? In People v. Tapia, 204 Cal. App. 3d 1055, 251 Cal. Rptr. 823 (1988), the court mandated a manslaughter instruction for two addicts accused of killing their supplier out of fear:

> Thus, the concept of a "cooling off period" fits nicely into the typical heat-of-passion case in which some event or series of events provokes the defendant to anger. Anger, at least once provoked to a boiling point, generally diminishes with time so that over time, one expects "passion to subside and reason to return." Where passion is the result of fear rather than anger, however, the typical pattern of explosive provocation followed by abating emotional intensity is not necessarily

applicable. While anger is essentially a retrospective emotion, focussing back on the source of the provocation, fear has a significant prospective component, looking forward to what might happen. [204 Cal. App. 3d at 1062.]

3.   The Common Law and Its Categories and Rules

a.   Adultery and Other "Adequate Provocations"

ROWLAND v. STATE
Supreme Court of Mississippi
35 So. 826 (1904)

TRULY, J.

Appellant was indicted for the murder of his wife, Becky Rowland, sentenced to imprisonment for life, and appeals. His story is as follows: His wife had been for about two months prior to the homicide living with Lou Pate, at whose house the killing occurred. Appellant and his wife were on good terms, and he was in the habit of visiting her and staying one night with her each week, or every two weeks. Lou Pate's house consisted of two rooms. In the front room were two beds — one occupied by Lou and her husband, and the other usually occupied by Becky Rowland. In the back room there was one bed. On the night of the killing, appellant reached Pate's house about 10 o'clock, hitched his horse, and noticed John Thorn's also hitched to the fence. Coming up to the house, he heard a man and a woman talking in the back room, in which there was no light. Listening, he discovered that John Thorn and Becky Rowland (appellant's wife) were in the room, and heard Thorn say, "Make haste." This aroused his suspicions, and he attempted to open the back door to the room; but it being latched, he went to the front door, pushed it open, and went into the front room, where, by the dim light of a lamp burning at the foot of their bed, he saw Lou Pate and her husband in bed asleep. He spoke to them, and also called his wife's name. Getting no answer, he stepped through the partition door into the back room, and discovered his wife and Thorn in the very act of adultery. They sprang up as they caught sight of him, and both rushed by him through the doorway into the front room; his wife blowing out the lamp as she passed the foot of the bed. Appellant fired at Thorn, and killed his wife. Lou Pate, the only eyewitness introduced by the state, corroborated the story of appellant in its main features. She testified that Thorn came to the house about first dark, and, when she and her husband went to bed, Thorn and Becky were seated in the same room, talking; that she was awakened by hearing appellant speak, and saw him standing in her room; that he went to the door between the rooms, and then Becky ran out of the back room into the front room, and blew out the lamp just as appellant shot; that she did not see Thorn run out of the back room, and did not know how or when he got out of the house, but that after the shooting his horse was still hitched to the fence. Becky was in her nightclothes when killed.

On this state of case, the court instructed the jury on behalf of the state as follows: "The court instructs the jury that murder is the killing of a human being without authority of law, by any means or in any manner, when done with the deliberate design to effect the death of the person killed; and if the jury believe from the evidence in this case, beyond a reasonable doubt, that the defendant so killed the deceased, Becky Rowland, then the jury will find the defendant guilty as charged in the bill of indictment."

In Reed v. State, 62 Miss. 410, it is said: "If he had caught the offender in the act of adultery with his wife, and had slain him on the spot, the crime would have been extenuated to manslaughter; such provocation, in legal contemplation, being sufficient to produce that brevis furor which for the moment unsettles reason." And this was recognized as the rule at common law. 4 Bla. Com. 191. In Mays v. State, 88 Ga. 403, 14 S.E. 560 — a case strikingly in point — quoting and approving the statement of the law by Gilpin, C.J., in State v. Pratt, 1 Houst. (Del.) 265, it is said:

> In order to reduce the crime from murder to manslaughter, it is necessary that it should be shown that the prisoner found the deceased in the very act of adultery with his wife. I do not mean to say that the prisoner must stand by and witness the actual copulative conjunction between the guilty parties. If the prisoner saw the deceased in bed with his wife, or saw him leaving the bed of the wife, or if he found them together in such position as to indicate with reasonable certainty to a rational mind that they had just then committed the adulterous act, . . . it will be sufficient to satisfy the requirements of the law in this regard; and if, under such circumstances, he then and there struck the mortal blow, his offense would amount to manslaughter only.

And in principle there can be no difference in the degree of the crime, whether the betrayed husband slays the faithless wife or her guilty paramour. In either event the crime proven has uniformly been held to be, not murder, but manslaughter. . . .

. . . Making an application of the foregoing principle of law to the case at bar, we find that the conviction for murder was not warranted by the facts, and cannot be sustained. In some jurisdictions, homicide under the circumstances disclosed by this record is held to be justifiable; and we have been unable to find any decision of a court of last resort, which, in the absence of express statute, upheld a conviction for murder under similar facts. Accepting the story of the state's witness as absolutely true, deceased and Thorn were surprised by appellant under such conditions and amid such surroundings as to demonstrate with absolute certainty that they were then actually committing adultery. This fact alone, in legal contemplation, is adequate provocation to reduce the grade of the homicide, if then instantly committed, from murder to manslaughter.

From an extended examination of the authorities bearing on this question, we conclude that there was no testimony upon which to base the second instruction granted for the state, as hereinbefore quoted. There are no facts disclosed by this record to warrant the jury in finding that appellant acted from a "deliberate design to effect the death of the person killed." The law, from the earliest ages, recognizing and considering the passions and frailties of man, in its mercy, has said that deliberation cannot be predicated of the deeds of a man situated as was the appellant at the moment of the homicide. . . .

Notes and Questions

1. Is the "reasonable man" the same figure as the "reasonable person"?

2. *Male honor.* "The earliest manslaughter law developed to mitigate punishment when a killing resulted from a 'chance medley,' common during the

sixteenth and seventeenth centuries. Thus, manslaughter began as a reaction to male violence."[18] Indeed, this description applies to homicide law more generally. In the United States today, over 90 percent of people arrested for homicide in the United States and 78 percent of homicide victims are male. Women are much more likely to be the victim of homicide than the perpetrator. See the Introduction to this Part, p. 305, *supra*.

"What is invariably overlooked [by criminologists] is that the factor that is most highly related to violent crimes is not race, nor social class, but sex."[19] "Homicide is overwhelmingly a male act."[20] The overwhelming "maleness" of violent crime has led one scholar to declare that

> [t]he primary cause of violence in this country is related to notions that connect masculinity and violence, plus the power imbalance between the sexes that allows men to act out this dangerous connection. . . . Until the dangerous consequences of this culture's idea of masculine behavior are recognized and changed, male violence toward women, as well as toward other males, will not be halted.[21]

Given its origins in male combat, its focus on anger as the paradigm emotion invoked under proving circumstances, and the way in which courts have dealt with cases involving adultery, is it fair to say that manslaughter/provocation doctrine is quite "male"?

3. *The rules and their boundaries.* The strictest version of this category of provocation required proof that the defendant actually witnessed the physical act of intercourse between his wife and the paramour. By mid-nineteenth century, however, many American courts had taken what purported to be a more psychologically realistic view of this form of provocation. Consider Price v. State, 18 Tex. Ct. App. (1885):

> Our statute uses the expression "taken in the act of adultery with the wife." The question is as to the proper meaning or construction of these terms. Do the words, when properly construed, mean that the husband must discover, find, or see the wife and adulterer in the very act of illicit intercourse or copulation in order to constitute the offense denominated "taken in the act of adultery"?
> Such positive proofs of the commission of the crime of adultery are not required, and are rarely attainable. As a crime, adultery itself may be established and proven by circumstantial testimony. (Richardson v. The State, 34 Texas, 142.) Should the law hold the husband to a greater or higher degree of proof than itself requires to establish a given fact? It is a late hour of the night — the parties are found in a corn crib some distance from the house, lying down in the dark. They refuse, at first, to answer when called; then, when the wife answers, she denies that any one is with her, — when deceased gets up he clutches the gun, — defendant finds that the one whose previous conduct and "carrying on" with his wife has excited his suspicions is the one he has thus found in company with his wife. What would any reasonable, sensible man have concluded from these circumstances? In other words, how did the matter reasonably appear to defendant? To him are not these facts "confirmations strong as proofs of holy writ"? Could it have been otherwise than that he had caught the parties in the act of adultery, either just as they were about to commit, or just after they had in fact committed it? His voice when

---

18. Laurie J. Taylor, Provoked Reason in Men and Women: Heat-of-Passion Manslaughter and Imperfect Self-Defense, 33 UCLA L. Rev. 1679, 1684 (1986).
19. Diana Russell, Rape in Marriage 108 (1982).
20. Taylor, *supra*, at 1679.
21. Russell, *supra*, at 108.

he called, perhaps, had arrested them in the very act of carnal coition, and if that were so, then were not the parties caught or taken by him in adultery? . . .

As to a proper construction of the expression "taken in the act," we cannot believe that the law requires or restricts the right of the husband to the fact that he must be an eye-witness to physical coition of his wife with the other party. As we have seen, adultery can be proven by circumstances, and the circumstances in this case were not hearsay so far as this defendant was concerned; they transpired in his own presence, sight and hearing. . . .

Mr. Bishop's rule, as above quoted, also commends itself to us as both just and proper: "If a husband is not actually witnessing his wife's adultery, but knows it is transpiring, and in an overpowering passion, no time for cooling having elapsed, he kills the wrong-doer, the offense is reduced to manslaughter."

Similarly, Walker had a plausible claim of provocation because the facts fell into the categories of physical battery or mutual combat. According to the common law, had Stenneth merely insulted Walker with contumacious or even threatening words, however abusive, then Walker would not have been able to press his provocation claim before the jury. But as *Price* demonstrates for adultery cases, the historical trend has been toward relaxing these categorical rules. In Elsmore v. State, 104 S.W.2d 493 (Tex. Crim. 1937), Elsmore had become distressed when a man named Shaw began publicly cursing him with remarks like "There is nothing to that little s.o.b. except wind. I will finish him if he starts anything. I will stomp his guts out." Shaw was even reported as saying "that the town was too small for both of them." These threats and denunciations were regularly reported to Elsmore. Finally, hearing that Shaw was getting drunk and violent (though he was easily disarmed by other townspeople), Elsmore grabbed his own gun, approached Shaw, and shot him to death. The court stated,

> Under the former law of manslaughter, as it existed prior to the adoption of the present law relating to murder, insulting words or gestures, or an assault and battery so slight as to show no intention to inflict pain, or injury to property unaccompanied by violence was not adequate cause. The statute as it existed at that time limited the grounds constituting adequate cause; first, to an assault and battery by the deceased causing pain or bloodshed; second, a serious personal conflict, in which great injury is inflicted by the person killed, etc., but said statutes have been repealed and no statute exists now which specifies the acts of the deceased constituting adequate cause. Hence the question of whether or not adequate cause existed is a matter left entirely to the jury to be determined from all the relevant facts and circumstances proven and if they fairly raise the issue, it should be submitted. It seems that the legislature by repealing the statute intended that insulting words or gestures might be sufficient to constitute adequate cause. Therefore, the reasonable conclusion to be drawn from the repeal of said statute, is that the legislature intended that any cause which would commonly produce a degree of anger, rage, resentment, or terror in a person of ordinary temper sufficient to render the mind incapable of cool reflection is [manslaughter]. [Id. at 494-95.]

4. *Gender and property.* The "sight of adultery" category of provocation was the first exception to the older rule requiring physical attack or mutual combat. An early English case, Regina v. Mawgridge, [1707] Kel. 1, 117, reprinted in 84 Eng. Rep. 1107, illustrates the courts' sympathy for the man who kills (in this case the paramour) in a jealous rage over his wife's adultery:

> [J]ealousy is the rage of a man, and adultery is the highest invasion of property. . . .
> If a thief comes to rob another, it is lawful to kill him. And if a man comes to rob a

man's posterity and his family, yet to kill him is manslaughter. So is the law though it may seem hard, the killing in the one case should not be as justifiable as the other. . . . So that a man cannot receive a higher provocation. [Id. at 1115.]

The court added,

Although this is the highest possible invasion of property, a man is not justifiable in killing another, whom he taketh in adultery with his wife; for it savours more of sudden revenge than of self-preservation; but this law hath been executed with great benignity. [Id.]

Earlier concepts of male property provide antecedents for this principle. Under Roman law, husbands were justified in killing their adulterous wives.[22] The husband's authority had to remain inviolate to ensure certainty about the pedigree of the male children who would inherit the father's possessions and reputation. Thus, some commentators argue that the provocation doctrine "endorses men's ownership of women's sexuality by expressing violent reactions to their wives' infidelity."[23] Though both men and women kill their sexual partners, they do so under very different circumstances. Women rarely react with violence to their husbands' infidelity. Rather, women's chief motive for killing their mates is self-defense.[24] Indeed, it is hard to find cases where a woman has her charge or punishment mitigated on provocation grounds when she has killed her husband or her husband's lover. In 1946, the British courts at least formally announced that the adultery-provocation doctrine could aid female defendants as well as male. Holmes v. D.P.P., [1946] 2 All E.R. 124, 128. And one American court has held that a woman who is maddened to kill by the sight of her husband's adultery may be guilty of manslaughter, and indeed that a woman may merit acquittal if she kills to prevent the act of adultery. Scroggs v. State, 93 S.E.2d 583 (Ga. App. 1956).

5. *The "honor" defense.* Though most jurisdictions have followed the manslaughter doctrine of the common law, until the 1960s and 1970s a few states made it *justifiable,* and thus wholly innocent, for a husband to kill his wife's lover.[25] Georgia actually limited this justification doctrine to killings aimed at preventing rather than punishing adultery. Scroggs v. State, *supra* (manslaughter where the killing occurred after the adultery; a rare case involving the aggrieved wife as defendant). Delaware, though not offering the total defense of justification, until recently limited punishment for a man provoked to killing by his wife's adultery to a $1,000 fine and one year in prison. Del. Code. Ann. tit. 11, §575(a), (b) (1953). Texas applied the total justification defense to cases where

22. R. Emerson Dobash & Russell B. Dobash, Wives: The "Appropriate" Victims of Marital Violence, 2 Victimology 426, 428 (1978). In addition, during the Middle Ages, women in Spain, Italy, France, and Britain could be flogged in the public streets, exiled for years, or executed if they were caught in any adulterous offenses. Cato the Censor said in the fifth century B.C.: "If you catch your wife in adultery, you could put her to death with impunity, she, on her part, would not dare to touch you with her finger; and it is not right that she should." Id. at 428.

23. E.g., Taylor, *supra*, at 1670.

24. Researchers have found that the most common motivation for men killing their partners is a perception that the woman was rejecting the man or his dominance. Barnard, Vera, Vera and Newman, Till Death Do Us Part: A Study of Spouse Murder, 10 Bull. Am. Acad. Psychiatry & L. 271, 274 (1982). The men experienced this rejection as potential or actual desertion. Over half the male defendants in one study were separated from their spouses/victims at the time of the killing. Female defendants charged with killing their mates were separated from the mates only 9.1 percent of the time.

25. Taylor, *supra*, at 1694.

the husband killed the paramour, not the wife. Reed v. State, 59 S.W.2d 122 (Tex. Crim. 1933).

In some other states that followed the common law principle that adultery-provocation could merely mitigate the crime down to manslaughter, the so-called honor defense nevertheless gave the juries an opportunity to nullify the manslaughter rule and acquit those husband-killers who claimed to have killed to protect their honor. See Roberts, The Unwritten Law, 10 Ky. L.J. 456, 49 (1922). The acquittal was often under the somewhat contrived rubric of an insanity claim. Comment, Recognition of the Honor Defense under the Insanity Plea, 43 Yale L. J. 809, 812 (1934). In Commonwealth v. Whitler, 2 Brewster 388 (Pa. Ct. of Oyer & Terminer 1868), where the defendant killed the paramour with an ax on discovering his wife in bed with him, the defense lawyer

> admitted that the Court had held [since 1793] that where a person had found an-other in the act of adultery with his wife and killed him in the first transport of pas-sion, the offence was manslaughter, and that Courts had so held from that time down — but he argued that no jury had ever convicted a husband of any offence, under such a state of facts, either in England or in this country, from that time to this, although more than two hundred years had passed since that decision, and as many as twenty-five persons had been tried for the murder of the seducers of their wives. [Id. at 388.]
>
> Notwithstanding this defense argument, the judge refused to instruct the jury that adultery provided a complete defense. Nevertheless, the jury then acquitted Whitler of all charges. Id. at 390.[26]

At least one state Supreme Court actually *endorsed* the use of the honor defense in the case of a wife's adultery, Biggs v. Georgia, 29 Ga. 723, 728-29 (1860):

> Has an American jury ever convicted a husband or father of murder or manslaugh-ter, for killing the seducer of his wife or daughter? . . . Is it not [the jury']s . . . right to determine whether in reason or justice, it is not justifiable in the sight of Heaven and earth, to slay the murderer of the peace and respectability of a family, as one forcibly attacks habitation and property? . . . What is the annihilation of houses or chattels by fire and faggot, compared with the destruction of female innocence; robbing woman of that priceless jewel, which leaves her a blasted ruin? . . . Our sacked habitations may be rebuilt, but who shall repair this desolation?

Do you think the *Biggs* court would have viewed the case differently had there been firm proof that the wife had fully consented to the adultery, or even had seduced the paramour?

On a contemporary note, see Outrage over 18 Months for Man Who Killed His Wife in "Heat of Passion," New York Times, Oct. 21, 1995, at 9 (public out-cry when defendant who found wife in adulterous act killed her after 4 hours of arguing pleads guilty to voluntary manslaughter and sentenced to 18 months, and when judge expresses regret that he had to imprison defendant at all, wondering "how many men could walk away without inflicting some corporal punishment?").

6. *Provocation and old moral norms.* The underlying reasons for mitigating the killing of the adulterous wife or paramour may have been still more complex.

---

26. [Do you regret that double jeopardy would bar a prosecution appeal here? — Eds.]

Robert M. Ireland suggests that the doctrine reflects a nineteenth-century cultural and moral conflict over sexual morality. The rise of an urban middle class loosened traditional restraints on sexuality and gave women more independence. Yet this change may have had paradoxical effects for women:[27]

> Marriage replaced parenthood as the fundamental familial relationship and the republican wife assumed the theoretical role of as the model of republican virtue. This concept, together with the evangelical Protestant re-thinking that deemphasized the significance of woman in the creation of original sin and republican middle-class hostility against loose European and American aristocratic sexual mores, combined to help formulate the conception of the pure, highly moral, sexually passionless female. Until the latter part of the eighteenth century women were commonly regarded as sexually more passionate than men. Because middle-class Americans regarded the family as the bulwark of an American society threatened by the new freedoms unleashed by the growth of industry and cities and because they considered wives the guardians of republican morality within the family and society itself, they found it convenient and logical to transform women from sexually the most passionate to sexually the least to the point of non-existence. Pure, sexually dispassionate women could more readily serve as guardians of republican middle-class morality than potentially lustful women.

At the same time, new social models for men emerged; men were to avoid sexual overindulgence as a threat to health as well as social stability, but since men nevertheless had "naturally" greater sexual appetites than women, a minority of men inevitably escaped these restraints and created the specter of demonic libertinism.

> Part of the ideology of republican virtue that created the republican wife also conceived the anti-republican libertine whose seductions of once virtuous women were described as the works of Satan. . . .
>
> Those conflicts, in turn, caused middle-class Victorian Americans to fear for the survival of the very foundations of American society, the family, marriage, and republican virtue.
>
> In short, although Americans had always placed a premium on sexual virtue, they value it more highly in the nineteenth century than at any time in their history. [Thus,] Americans occasionally adopted extreme measures in order to protect their notions of sexual propriety. . . . It is no wonder that they invented and perfected the higher law that excused the assassination of the libertine whom they regarded as the satanic embodiment of that conduct which most threatened the sexual ideals they in turn considered vital to the preservation of republicanism. . . .
>
> Often in these cases the "fallen" woman actually had been more aggressive in the pursuit of forbidden sexual pleasure than the alleged libertine, yet efforts of prosecutors and defenders of "libertines" to prove such aggressiveness inevitably failed to undermine public wrath over perceived male libertinism or to convince the jury to convict the heralded avenger of sexual dishonor.
>
> The tendency of the unwritten law to tolerate or ignore husbandly abuse complemented its fantasy about the preservation of successful marriages. Traditional defenders of paramouricide argued that libertines had destroyed once happy marriages by preying upon defenseless wives. In reality these marriages had soured long before the libertines made their appearance.

27. Sexual Dishonor and the Unwritten Law in the Nineteenth Century United States, 23 Journal of Social History 27, 28-35 (1992).

7. *Provocation and mistake.* What if a defendant sincerely believed that his wife had committed adultery under conditions that would constitute adequate provocation but was mistaken about the facts? In State v. Yanz, 50 A. 37 (Conn. 1901), the defendant discovered his wife in the isolated company of another man, under compromising circumstances; assuming — perhaps wrongly — that they had just engaged in adultery, the defendant killed the other man. The court ruled that Yanz was entitled to an instruction invoking the provocation doctrine on the facts as he reasonably perceived them to be:

> The law justifies a jury in calling it manslaughter when, on finding his wife in the act of adultery, a man, in the first transport of passion, kills her paramour. This is because from a sudden act of this kind, committed under the natural excitement of feeling induced by so gross an outrage, malice, which is a necessary ingredient of the crime of murder, cannot fairly be implied. The excitement is the effect of a belief, from ocular evidence, of the actual commission of adultery. It is the belief, so reasonably formed, that excites the uncontrollable passion. Such a belief, though a mistaken one, is calculated to induce the same emotions as would be felt were the wrongful act in fact committed. [Id. at 39.]

The dissent disagreed as follows:

> To make the offense manslaughter, the injury must have been done. Intentional unlawful killing in a rage is murder, and not manslaughter. Anger thirsting for the blood of an enemy is in itself an earmark of murder, no less than revenge or brutal ferocity; but when it is provoked by the wrongful act of the person slain, who thus brings upon himself the fatal blow, given in the first outbreak of rage, caused by himself, the offense is manslaughter; not only because the voluntary act is, in a way, compelled by an ungovernable rage but also because the victim is the aggressor; and his wrong, although it cannot justify, may modify, the nature of the homicide thus induced. [Id. at 40.]

Does the dissent have a different theory of the purpose of the manslaughter/ provocation doctrine?

What happens if a "reasonably provoked" person kills the provoker but, in the course of the fatal encounter, also kills another? In Carter v. State, 843 So.2d 812 (Ala. 2002), the jury convicted the defendant of voluntary manslaughter on the first killing and intentional murder on the second, under the so-called "transferred intent" theory. The appellate court affirmed the murder conviction, finding no unjust inconsistency. It cited the common law "transferred intent" principle, in which, when a killer who intends to kill one person misses but then accidentally kills another, the mens rea from the attempt is applied to the second. It then noted that in this case when the intent to kill was proved as part of the voluntary manslaughter count, and that while the heat-of-passion doctrine "overlooks or forgives the 'malice'" in that situation, the relevant intent is still there to be "transferred." Id. at 815. Does this outcome make sense, if the provoked killer has engaged in a single course of outraged conduct? Does it detach heat-of-passion too far from the notion of mens rea?

8. *Adultery in a modern context.* If you were a judge in a common law jurisdiction and were cautious about extending the concept of adequate provocation too far beyond the sight-of-adultery category, would you permit the provocation issue to go to the jury in the following cases?

(a) Smith brags to Brown that Smith has just committed adultery with Brown's wife.
(b) Smith brags to Brown that Smith long ago had an intense affair with Brown's wife:
   • after the Browns were married.
   • before the Browns were married.
(c) Green tells Brown that Smith has just committed adultery with Brown's wife.
(d) Smith approaches Brown and calls Brown's wife an adulteress.

9. *New provocation categories.* If you were a judge in a jurisdiction that was wary of creating new categories of adequate provocation beyond those established by the common law, would you permit a manslaughter instruction in the following cases, where Lee kills Sandy because

(a) Sandy defrauded Lee in a scheme that ruined Lee's business and left Lee bankrupt?
(b) Sandy, a new plant manager who is racially bigoted, refuses to give well-earned promotions to several black employees, including Lee?
(c) Sandy, an insensitive slum owner, evicts Lee and Lee's family for alleged delinquency in rent or for complaining about conditions in their apartment?

b. Provocation Under Reform Rules

PEOPLE v. BERRY
Supreme Court of California
18 Cal. 3d 509, 134 Cal. Rptr. 415 (1976)

SULLIVAN, JUSTICE.

Defendant Albert Joseph Berry was charged by indictment with one count of murder (Pen. Code §187). . . . A jury found defendant guilty as charged. . . . Defendant was sentenced to state prison for the term prescribed by law. He appeals from the judgment of conviction.

Defendant contends that there is sufficient evidence in the record to show that he committed the homicide while in a state of uncontrollable rage caused by provocation and . . . therefore that it was error for the trial court to fail to instruct the jury on voluntary manslaughter as indeed he had requested. He claims . . . that he was entitled to an instruction on voluntary manslaughter as defined by statute (§192) since the killing was done upon a sudden quarrel or heat of passion. . . .

Defendant, a cook, 46 years old, and Rachel Pessah, a 20-year-old girl from Israel, were married on May 27, 1974. Three days later Rachel went to Israel by herself, returning on July 13, 1974. On July 23, 1974, defendant choked Rachel into unconsciousness. She was treated at a hospital where she reported her strangulation by defendant to an officer of the San Francisco Police Department. On July 25, Inspector Sammon, who had been assigned to the case, met with Rachel and as a result of the interview a warrant was issued for defendant's arrest.

While Rachel was at the hospital, defendant removed his clothes from their apartment and stored them in a Greyhound bus depot locker. He stayed overnight at the home of a friend, Mrs. Jean Berk, admitting to her that he had choked his wife. On July 26, he telephoned Mrs. Berk and informed her that he had killed Rachel with a telephone cord on that morning at their apartment. The next day Mrs. Berk and two others telephoned the police to report a possible homicide and met Officer Kelleher at defendant's apartment. They gained entry and found Rachel on the bathroom floor. A pathologist from the coroner's office concluded that the cause of Rachel's death was strangulation. Defendant was arrested on August 1, 1974, and confessed to the killing.

At trial defendant did not deny strangling his wife, but claimed through his own testimony and the testimony of a psychiatrist, Dr. Martin Blinder, that he was provoked into killing her because of a sudden and uncontrollable rage so as to reduce the offense to one of voluntary manslaughter. He testified that upon her return from Israel, Rachel announced to him that while there she had fallen in love with another man, one Yako, and had enjoyed his sexual favors, that he was coming to this country to claim her and that she wished a divorce. Thus commenced a tormenting two weeks in which Rachel alternately taunted defendant with her involvement with Yako and at the same time sexually excited defendant, indicating her desire to remain with him. Defendant's detailed testimony, summarized below, chronicles this strange course of events.

After their marriage, Rachel lived with defendant for only three days and then left for Israel. Immediately upon her return to San Francisco she told defendant about her relationship with and love for Yako. This brought about further argument and a brawl that evening in which defendant choked Rachel and she responded by scratching him deeply many times. Nonetheless they continued to live together. Rachel kept taunting defendant with Yako and demanding a divorce. She claimed she thought she might be pregnant by Yako. She showed defendant pictures of herself with Yako. Nevertheless, during a return trip from Santa Rosa, Rachel demanded immediate sexual intercourse with defendant in the car, which was achieved; however upon reaching their apartment, she again stated that she loved Yako and that she would not have intercourse with the defendant in the future.

On the evening of July 22d defendant and Rachel went to a movie where they engaged in heavy petting. When they returned home and got into bed, Rachel announced that she had intended to make love with defendant, "But I am saving myself for this man Yako, so I don't think I will." Defendant got out of bed and prepared to leave the apartment whereupon Rachel screamed and yelled at him. Defendant choked her into unconsciousness.

Two hours later defendant called a taxi for his wife to take her to the hospital. He put his clothes in the Greyhound bus station and went to the home of his friend Mrs. Berk for the night. The next day he went to Reno and returned the day after. Rachel informed him by telephone that there was a warrant for his arrest as a result of her report to the police about the choking incident. On July 25th defendant returned to the apartment to talk to Rachel, but she was out. He slept there overnight. Rachel returned around 11 A.M. the next day. Upon seeing defendant there, she said, "I suppose you have come here to kill me." Defendant responded, "yes," changed his response to "no," and then again to "yes," and finally stated, "I have really come to talk to you." Rachel began screaming. Defendant grabbed her by the shoulder and tried to stop her screaming. She continued. They struggled and finally defendant strangled her with a telephone cord.

Dr. Martin Blinder, a physician and psychiatrist, called by the defense, testified that Rachel was a depressed, suicidally inclined girl and that this suicidal impulse led her to involve herself ever more deeply in a dangerous situation with defendant. She did this by sexually arousing him and taunting him into jealous rages in an unconscious desire to provoke him into killing her and thus consummating her desire for suicide. Throughout the period commencing with her return from Israel until her death, that is from July 13 to July 26, Rachel continually provoked defendant with sexual taunts and incitements, alternating acceptance and rejection of him. This conduct was accompanied by repeated references to her involvement with another man; it led defendant to choke her on two occasions, until finally she achieved her unconscious desire and was strangled. Dr. Blinder testified that as a result of this cumulative series of provocations, defendant at the time he fatally strangled Rachel, was in a state of uncontrollable rage, completely under the sway of passion.

We first take up defendant's claim that on the basis of the foregoing evidence he was entitled to an instruction on voluntary manslaughter as defined by statute which is "the unlawful killing of a human being, without malice . . . upon a sudden quarrel or heat of passion." (§192.) In People v. Valentine (1946) 28 Cal. 2d 121 this court, in an extensive review of the law of manslaughter, specifically approved the following quotation from People v. Logan (1917) 175 Cal. 45 as a correct statement of the law:

> In the present condition of our law *it is left to the jurors* to say whether or not the facts and circumstances in evidence are sufficient to lead them to believe that the defendant did, or to create a reasonable doubt in their minds as to whether or not he did, commit his offense under a heat of passion. The jury is further to be admonished and advised by the court that this heat of passion must be such a passion as would naturally be aroused in the mind of an ordinarily reasonable person under the given facts and circumstances, and that, consequently, no defendant may set up his own standard of conduct and justify or excuse himself because in fact his passions were aroused, unless further the jury believes that the facts and circumstances were sufficient to arouse the passions of the ordinarily reasonable man. . . . For the fundamental of the inquiry is whether or not the defendant's reason was, at the time of his act, so disturbed or obscured by some passion — not necessarily fear and never, of course, the passion for revenge — to such an extent as would render ordinary men of average disposition liable to act rashly or without due deliberation and reflection, and from this passion rather than from judgment. [emphasis in original]

We further held in *Valentine* that there is no specific type of provocation required by section 192 and that verbal provocation may be sufficient. In People v. Borchers (1958) 50 Cal. 2d 321, 329, in the course of explaining the phrase "heat and passion" used in the statute defining manslaughter we pointed out that "passion" need not mean "rage" or "anger" but may be any "[v]iolent, intense, high-wrought or enthusiastic emotion" and concluded there "that defendant was aroused to a heat of 'passion' by a series of events over a considerable period of time. . . ." Accordingly we there declared that evidence of admissions of infidelity by the defendant's paramour, taunts directed to him and other conduct, "supports a finding that defendant killed in wild desperation induced by long continued provocatory conduct." We find this reasoning persuasive in the case now before us. Defendant's testimony chronicles a two-week period of provocatory conduct by his wife Rachel that could arouse a passion of jealousy, pain and sexual rage in an ordinary man of average disposition such as to cause him to act rashly from this passion. It is significant that both defendant and Dr. Blinder testified that the former was in the heat of passion under an uncontrollable rage when he killed Rachel.

The Attorney General contends that the killing could not have been done in the heat of passion because there was a cooling period, defendant having waited in the apartment for 20 hours. However, the long course of provocatory conduct, which had resulted in intermittent outbreaks of rage under specific provocation in the past, reached its final culmination in the apartment when Rachel began screaming. Both defendant and Dr. Blinder testified that defendant killed in a state of uncontrollable rage, of passion, and there is ample evidence in the record to support the conclusion that this passion was the result of the long course of provocatory conduct by Rachel, just as the killing emerged from such conduct in *Borchers*. The Attorney General relies principally on People v. Bufarale (1961) 193 Cal. App. 2d 551, 559-63, 14 Cal. Rptr. 381, but the reliance is misplaced. *Bufarale* merely held that the defendant's killing of a married woman with whom he had been living was not, as a matter of law, upon the heat of passion since the defendant's act was one of vengeance, preceded by neither a quarrel with, nor by adequate provocatory conduct on the part of, the victim, who had decided to return to her husband.

As to Count One, charging a violation of Section 187, the judgment is reversed.

Notes and Questions

1. Did Pessah "provoke" Berry within the conventional meaning of the concept of legally adequate provocation?

2. By what "reasonable man" standard is Berry being measured?

3. *The scope of the California standard.* In Commonwealth v. Vatcher, 781 N.E.2d 1277 (Mass. 2003), a father shot to death his eleven-year-old son. The boy had a number of physical and developmental disabilities, and, on the day of the killing, had had an "extended temper tantrum" in which he vandalized the house and cursed at, struck, and kicked his father. The father, convicted of murder, argued that he was entitled to a voluntary manslaughter instruction, partly because the "broader context" of the family situation and his "persistent difficulties" with the child permitted a finding of provocation. The court disagreed, holding that this family history if anything showed that the child's actions that day "would have come as no surprise to the defendant." Id. at 1282. Would Vatcher have won under *Berry*? Might expert testimony have helped him?

4. *The expert witness and reasonableness.* How exactly was Dr. Blinder's testimony relevant in this case? Did the jury need the expert testimony of a psychiatrist to determine whether Berry had acted in the heat of passion? Did his testimony bear in any way on the question of whether a reasonable person would have been provoked into the heat of passion in these circumstances? How was testimony of Pessah's suicidal tendency relevant to the question of provocation? If Pessah had indeed been goading Berry to help her complete her suicidal wish, why did she seek legal protection from him? When the psychiatrist's only

information about Pessah came from Berry, why was he allowed to testify as to Pessah's mental state? What are the implications of Dr. Blinder's testimony for our assumptions about volition and determinism?

The Supreme Court of Oregon has strictly limited psychiatric testimony on provocation claims. Relying on the principle that experts should not testify even implicitly as to "ultimate" conclusions that belong within the jury's province, the court has forbidden psychiatric experts to testify as to "defendant's personality traits," whether "the murder was or was not an intentional act," and whether "the defendant acted under 'extreme emotional disturbance.'" State v. Wille, 858 P.2d 128 (Or. 1993). Had these rules applied in California, what would Dr. Blinder have been able to say to the jury in *Berry*?[28]

5. *The "reformed" provocation standard.* After *Berry*, how would you state California's definition of legally adequate provocation? The California standard, though it draws on old "heat of passion" verbiage, represents the "reform" of provocation doctrine exemplified by the Model Penal Code, and reflected in the laws of at least a third of the states. The MPC substantive provision on provocation reads:

Section 210.3. Manslaughter

(1) Criminal homicide constitutes manslaughter when . . .

(a) a homicide which would otherwise be murder is committed under the influence of extreme mental or emotional disturbance for which there is reasonable explanation or excuse. The reasonableness of such explanation or excuse shall be determined from the viewpoint of a person in the actor's situation under the circumstances as he believes them to be.

In many states, this expanded notion of provocation is known as "extreme emotional disturbance" or "EED."

Do such new versions of the provocation formula evince moral or legal progress? Prof. Victoria Nourse provides a comprehensive review of contemporary cases, focusing on some of the surprising consequences of the "reform" version of what she calls the "passion defense."[29] Nourse canvasses almost 300 state court opinions to identify those cases in which a defendant was at least allowed to get to a jury on the provocation claim; she sorts those cases into three types of jurisdiction: the so-called common law states that retain the fairly rigid original categories; the MPC-type states; and a mixed category. Her data reveal that, as the more traditional cases suggest, most provocation claims arise in "intimate" or domestic situations, but that a remarkable number of the cases — almost all

28. Haunting ironies can be found in journalistic accounts of the personal life of Dr. Martin Blinder, the expert psychiatric witness in the *Berry* case. Blinder is well-known in the San Francisco Bay Area for his important testimony in a number of high-profile homicide cases, and is the author of such books as *Choosing Lovers* and *Lovers, Killers, Husbands and Wives*. Journalist Mike Weiss reports that Blinder himself has been married twice and that both his wives committed suicide, and also describes a complex personal and legal dispute with another woman, who was his patient. "Mayhem Shadowed Therapist's Life; Expert On Relationships Examines Why Many of His Have Ended Badly," San Francisco Chronicle, May 22, 2001, at A1. Blinder's second wife, Dorothy Braco, from whom he had been estranged, apparently fell into a dispute with him that might have involved her fear that he would disown their son in favor of his new woman partner. Braco entered Blinder's house and stabbed him in the arm, shortly before she went to the Golden Gate Bridge and leapt to her death. In an interview he granted Weiss, Blinder speculated on a possible psychological defense Braco might have used had she lived and been prosecuted for her assault on him.

29. Victoria Nourse, Passion's Progress: Modern Law Reform and the Provocation Defense, 106 Yale L.J. 1331, 1332-33 (1997).

arising in the MPC jurisdictions — turn not on reaction to *infidelity* so much as reaction to *separation*.

> A significant number of the reform cases I studied involve no sexual infidelity whatsoever, but only the desire of the killer's victim to leave a miserable relationship. Reform has permitted juries to return a manslaughter verdict in cases where the defendant claims passion because the victim left, moved the furniture out, planned a divorce, or sought a protective order. Even infidelity has been transformed under reform's gaze into something quite different from the sexual betrayal we might expect — it is the infidelity of a fiancée who danced with another, of a girlfriend who decided to date someone else, of the divorcee found pursuing a new relationship months after the final decree. In the end, reform has transformed passion from the classical adultery to the modern dating and moving and leaving.

Nourse critically reviews the history of the provocation doctrine from the old rigid category rules to the new doctrines, like that of California and the MPC, which purport to focus on the emotional condition of the defendant rather than the objective provocatory circumstances:

> The history of the passion defense, from the common law to the Model Penal Code, is the history of a "passion" that is increasingly private and personal. Once an honor code, then heated blood, now a state of mind, the idea of passion has moved steadily inward. . . . The Model Penal Code was the logical culmination of this shift. It took the "reasonable person" model a step further by asking juries not only to look into persons' minds but also to identify their personal characteristics. What had moved from norm to body to mind was now a question of *identity*.
>
> By embracing this shift, MPC reformers never intended to endorse outdated norms about relationships. By eliminating the category of adultery and extending coverage to nontraditional relationships, reformers no doubt saw themselves as taking the progressive position on gender issues. What reformers did not envision, however, was that their intellectual method might betray their purpose. Internalizing the defense within the minds of reasonable defendants simply ignored the normative questions about relations that remained.[30]

As a result, Nourse argues:

> The law in practice does something more than protect self-control. Courts and lawyers have not measured claims of passion by "quickened heartbeats" or "shallow breathing," but by judgments about the equities of relationships. Judgments disguised — and therefore rendered more powerful and resistant to change — by a jurisprudence pretending to make no judgments at all.
>
> . . . Reform of the passion defense . . . [has bound] women to the emotional claims of husbands and boyfriends long ago divorced or rejected. Reform in other areas of the law has encouraged battered women to leave their victimizers. Reform of the passion defense, however, discourages such departures, allowing defendants to argue that a battered wife who leaves has, by that very departure, supplied a reason to treat the killing with some compassion. . . .
>
> . . . The intellectual move here is one I call the "personification" of the defense, a move that places all of the normative questions into the form of questions about the qualities and attributes of persons and thus disguises both the essential

---

30. Id. at 1384.

normativity of the inequity and the fact that the Model Penal Code's concealed normative commitments are to relationships rather than persons.[31]

Nourse acknowledges the call of the re-reformers, especially feminists, to abolish the defense, but she would salvage it under very limited circumstances, where

> the defendant and the victims stand on an equal emotional and normative plane. When a man kills his wife's rapist, his emotional judgments are inspired by a belief in a "wrong" that is no different from the law's own . . . When a man kills his departing wife, claiming that her departure outraged him, this normative equality disappears. There is no reason to suspect that the victim would have agreed to a regime in which "leaving" was a wrong that the law would punish. To embrace the defendant's emotional judgments in these latter circumstances not only allows the defendant to serve as judge and executioner, but also as a legislator.[32]

In short, she would allow provocation as a "warranted excuse" where the defendant can win not only our sympathy, but also our legally sanctioned concurrence to the moral view that precipitated his or her action.

Does Nourse establish that modern reform of provocation doctrine reinforces certain social judgments that cause heightened emotion, rather than accommodate spontaneous emotion itself?

6. *The significance of the MPC reform.* In Dandova v. State, 72 P.2d 325 (Alaska App. 2003), the defendant and Schumacher, the father of her child, had separated shortly after Dandova came to believe that Schumacher had sexually abused the child. A bitter custody and financial dispute ensued, in which, in Dandova's view, Schumacher had vengefully reduced her to poverty. Two years later, news of a new lawsuit Schumacher was filing against her and the unexpected sighting of him driving a new vehicle reinflamed Dandova's anger over earlier wrongs and led her to shoot him. Affirming the trial court's refusal to allow a heat-of-passion claim, the court construed Alaska law as rejecting the more flexible Model Penal Code rule in favor of the more objective common law standard. Would Dandova have won under the MPC?

7. *Prior acts as evidence.* Under normal rules of evidence, earlier misconduct is not admissible to prove that a defendant committed the illegal act under issue in the case. Yet in State v. McCarthy, 536 N.E.2d 917 (Ill. 1989), the court admitted evidence that McCarthy had committed batteries on the victim — his girlfriend — and her mother six weeks before the killing. This evidence purportedly showed that McCarthy did not kill in the heat of passion. Did it? How would the *McCarthy* holding apply to *Berry*?

8. How "extreme" must "extreme emotional disturbance" be? See State v. Ott, 686 P.2d 1001, 1009 (Or. 1984) (rejecting trial instruction that "extreme" means "the outermost or furtherest, most remote in any direction, final" on ground that it would confound provocation claim with mental illness claim).

9. *Provocation and fear.* The provocation doctrine has been criticized for focusing too narrowly on anger as the predictable emotional response to provocative acts, thus excluding those who kill because of fear or other disorienting

---

31. Id. at 1333-34.
32. Id. at 1337-38.

emotions.[33] In People v. Tapia, p. 330, *supra,* the court ruled that the trial judge should have given a manslaughter instruction in a case involving two heroin addicts who were former tenants and customers of a violent heroin supplier. After the dealer made several threats to kill the two addicts, they killed him in a surprise attack. Holding that prolonged fear might provide sufficient provocation to support a manslaughter verdict, the court stated:

> Traditionally and stereotypically, the heat-of-passion theory applies where the victim provokes the defendant to intense anger and the defendant kills as a result. . . . It is well-established in California that intense emotions other than anger may support a heat-of-passion theory. . . . In particular, fear has been recognized as a motivation for an intentional killing which may mitigate the defendant's culpability. . . . There is no question in this case that the series of beatings, assaults and threats to which Tapia and Diaz were subjected, coupled with their knowledge of Garcia's reputation for violence, was such as to make any rational person fear for his life. Moreover, the facts are certainly susceptible of the interpretation that defendant's decision to kill Garcia was a product of such a fear. [204 Cal. App. 3d at 1061.]

Of course, if Tapia had killed Garcia to fend off an immediate threat of serious harm, he might have had a self-defense claim, and, had the claim been successful, he would have been wholly exculpated. Moreover, as we will see in Chapter 8, *infra,* if Tapia had a reasonable and sincere, if mistaken, belief that Garcia was about to strike him a serious blow, he might have at least mitigated his charge to voluntary manslaughter under the rubric of "imperfect self-defense." What, then, is the point of permitting him a provocation claim on these facts? Does "provoked fear" fit in any coherent way with the traditional notion of heat-of-passion?

10. *Youth and other factors.* Recall that the MPC speaks of "the viewpoint of a person in the actor's situation under the circumstances as he believes them to be." Just what goes into the definition of the actor's "situation" as opposed to the identity of the actor? In Director of Public Prosecutions v. Camplin, House of Lords, [1978] 2 All E.R. 168, the court held that the defendant, a 15-year-old boy who had been sexually assaulted by the deceased, should be held to the standard of a reasonable person of his young age, rather than the more abstracted standard of the "reasonable man." The trial court had instructed the jury to consider whether

> the provocation was sufficient to make a reasonable man in like circumstances act as the defendant did. Not a reasonable boy, as [defense counsel] would have it, or a reasonable lad; it is an objective test — a reasonable man. [Id. at 170.]

In overturning the murder conviction, Lord Diplock noted that the traditional character called "the reasonable man"

> has established his (or her) role in the law of provocation under a variety of different sobriquets in which the noun "man" is frequently replaced by "person" and the adjective "reasonable" by "ordinary," "average" or "normal." At least from as early as 1914 the test of whether the defence of provocation is entitled to succeed has been a dual one: the conduct of the deceased to the accused must be such as (1) might cause in any reasonable or ordinary person and (2) actually causes in the accused a sudden and temporary loss of self-control as the result of which he

---

33. E.g., Dolores Donovan & Stephanie Wildman, Is the Reasonable Man Obsolete? A Critical Perspective on Self-Defense and Provocation, 14 Loyola Los Angeles L. Rev. 435 (1981).

commits the unlawful act that kills the deceased. But until the 1957 Act was passed there was a condition precedent which had to be satisfied before any question of applying this dual test could arise. The conduct of the deceased had to be of such a kind as was capable in law of constituting provocation; and whether it was or was not was a question for the judge, not for the jury. [Id. at 171.]

Lord Diplock then applied the terms of the new law, section 3 of the 1957 act, noting that the purpose of the law was to "mitigate in some degree the harshness of the common law of provocation":

> Section 3 of the 1957 Act is in the following terms:
>
>> Where on a charge of murder there is evidence on which the jury can find that the person charged was provoked (whether by things done or by things said or by both together) to lose his self-control, the question whether the provocation was enough to make a reasonable man do as he did shall be left to be determined by the jury; and in determining that question the jury shall take into account everything both done and said according to the effect which, in their opinion, it would have on a reasonable man. [Id. at 173.]

Lord Diplock then concluded,

> In my opinion a proper direction to a jury on the question left to their exclusive determination by §3 of the 1957 Act would be on the following lines. The judge should state what the question is, using the very terms of the section. He should then explain to them that the reasonable man referred to in the question is a person having the power of self-control to be expected of an ordinary person of the sex and age of the accused, but in other respects sharing such of the accused's characteristics as they think would affect the gravity of the provocation to him, and that the question is not merely whether such a person would in like circumstances be provoked to lose his self-control but also would react to the provocation as the accused did. . . . [Id. at 175.]

Lord Morris of Borth-y-Guest concurred:

> In my view it would now be unreal to tell the jury that the notional "reasonable man" is someone without the characteristics of the accused: it would be to intrude into their province. A few examples may be given. If the accused is of particular colour or particular ethnic origin and things are said which to him are grossly insulting it would be utterly unreal if the jury had to consider whether the words would have provoked a man of different colour or ethnic origin, or to consider how such a man would have acted or reacted. The question would be whether the accused if he was provoked only reacted as even any reasonable man in his situation would or might have reacted. If the accused was ordinarily and usually a very unreasonable person, the view that on a particular occasion he acted just as a reasonable person would or might have acted would not be impossible of acceptance. . . . The jury had to consider whether a young man of about the same age as the accused but placed in the same situation as that which befell the accused could, had he been a reasonable young man, have reacted as did the accused and could have done what the accused did. For the reasons which I have outlined the question so to be considered by the jury would be whether they considered that the accused, placed as he was, and having regard to all the things that they find were said, and all the things that they find were done, only acted as a reasonable young man might have acted, so that, in compassion, and having regard to human frailty, he could to some extent be excused even though he had caused death. [Id. at 177.]

Should a defendant with a physical disability be judged according to the degree of insult likely to be felt by a reasonable person with the same disability? See Rex v. Raney, [1942] 29 C.A. 14 (murder conviction reduced to manslaughter where man with one leg provoked by deceased's act of knocking away one of his crutches). What if the defendant claims to be inherently bad-tempered? Habitually drunk?

11. *The MPC and the reasonable person.* How does the Model Penal Code identify those cases where the "reasonable person" standard will be modified by facts peculiar to the defendant's situation or character? See Model Penal Code §210.3, *supra.* The drafters of the Code have defended their approach as follows in the Commentaries:[34]

The critical element in the Model Code formulation is the clause requiring that reasonableness be assessed "from the viewpoint of a person in the actor's situation." The word "situation" is designedly ambiguous. On the one hand, it is clear that personal handicaps and some external circumstances must be taken into account. Thus, blindness, shock from traumatic injury, and extreme grief are all easily read into the term "situation." This result is sound, for it would be morally obtuse to appraise a crime for mitigation of punishment without reference to these factors. On the other hand, it is equally plain that idiosyncratic moral values are not part of the actor's situation. An assassin who kills a political leader because he believes it is right to do so cannot ask that he be judged by the standard of a reasonable extremist. Any other result would undermine the normative message of the criminal law. In between these two extremes, however, there are matters neither as clearly distinct from individual blameworthiness as blindness or handicap nor as integral a part of moral depravity as a belief in the lightness of killing. Perhaps the classic illustration is the unusual sensitivity to the epithet "bastard" of a person born illegitimate. An exceptionally punctilious sense of personal honor or an abnormally fearful temperament may also serve to differentiate an individual actor from the hypothetical reasonable man, yet none of these factors is wholly irrelevant to the ultimate issue of culpability. The proper role of such factors cannot be resolved satisfactorily by abstract definition of what may constitute adequate provocation. The Model Code endorses a formulation that affords sufficient flexibility to differentiate in particular cases between those special aspects of the actor's situation that should be deemed material for purpose of grading and those that should be ignored. There thus will be room for interpretation of the word "situation," and that is precisely the flexibility desired. There will be opportunity for argument about the reasonableness of explanation or excuse, and that too is a ground on which argument is required. In the end, the question is whether the actor's loss of self-control can be understood in terms that arouse sympathy in the ordinary citizen. Section 210.3 faces this issue squarely and leaves the ultimate judgment to the ordinary citizen in the function of a juror assigned to resolve the specific case.

12. *Situation and character.* Consider this perspective from Professor Mark Kelman:[35]

Courts include or exclude certain traits of the defendant in the profile of the typical individual to whom the defendant's conduct is to be compared. . . . Presumably, everyone tries to exclude from his vision of the typical man to whom the

---

34. Model Penal Code and Commentaries, *supra,* at 62-63.
35. Interpretive Construction in the Substantive Criminal Law, 33 Stan. L. Rev. 591, 636-37, 646 (1981).

defendant is to be compared all the narrow-focused traits the defendant has that the criminal law is designed to alter — hot-headedness, hypersensitivity, proclivity to violence — but this line ultimately collapses. . . . As we take a broader, more categorical view of the typical provoked defendant, fewer and fewer defendants appear to have acted reasonably.

If we hypothesize that people have "true" characters outside the fortuitous circumstances in which they live, we should at least search for a full determinist account. The behavior of the former battered child tells us nothing of the defendant's "true character," just as the behavior of the coerced, threatened thief tells us nothing of his "real nature." And, if character is nothing but a summary of *actual* behavior given *actual* life circumstances, then it is part of a defendant's "character" that he "is" a killer if he has, given the pressures he has faced, killed.

What would be the effect of taking the subjective approach to voluntary manslaughter to its logical extreme? What if the law mitigated an intentional killing to manslaughter whenever the killer at the time of the crime was in an irrational passion or frenzy similar to what we observe in "legally provoked" killers, but where no legal provocation occurred? This situation would arise when a person, though not legally insane, suffers from an unstable personality that makes him or her overreact to stressful experiences.

In a new book freshly reappraising the heat-of-passion doctrine, Prof. Cynthia Lee suggests an approach to the "reasonable person" issue called "switching":

> For example, in a case in which a male defendant asserts that he was provoked by his female partner's actual or perceived infidelity, jurors would assess the reasonableness of the defendant's emotions from the perspective of a woman in the defendant's situation. If the case involved a female defendant who killed her male partner after catching him in bed with another woman, jurors would think about whether they would grant the provocation mitigation if the female defendant was a man. In cases in which a heterosexual male defendant employs a gay panic argument, the jury could assess the reasonableness of the defendant's emotions and actions from the perspective of a gay man faced with an unwanted nonviolent heterosexual advance from a woman.[36]

Would this approach make the MPC standard more practical for jurors? Fairer for defendants? Will it always be clear which factors need to be "switched"?

4. Cultural Norms and the Reasonable Person

Just how flexible is the concept of the "reasonable person" in terms of the cultural values and origins of particular defendants? At least twice in recent years, American courts have accepted guilty pleas to manslaughter from Japanese women who intentionally killed their children because their husbands, having committed adultery, had "shamed" their families.[37] In both cases, the defendants asserted that the killings followed the principle of *oyako-shinju,* which many women follow in Japan. Obviously, these are not "provocation" cases in any conventional sense, but if the killings are intentional, must we not try to fit them

---

36. Murder and the Reasonable Man 253 (2003).
37. Cultural Defense — A Legal Tactic, Los Angeles Times, July 15, 1988, at 1, 28, 29, 31.

into the category of voluntary manslaughter? Is the point that a "reasonable woman" raised in the tradition of *oyako-shinju* would be tempted to kill her children and merits only partial punishment? How does this mitigation claim compare with the sort of claim of mistake of law made by a new arrival from a very different culture? See p. 231, *supra.* Consider the following case:

PEOPLE v. WU
Court of Appeal of California, Fourth Appellate District
235 Cal. App. 3d 614, 286 Cal. Rptr. 868 (1991)

TIMLIN, ACTING P. J.

I

Helen Wu, also known as Helen Hamg Ieng Chau (defendant), was convicted of the second degree murder of her son, Sidney Wu (Sidney), following trial by jury. . . .

The prosecution's theory seems to have been that defendant killed Sidney because of anger at Sidney's father, and to get revenge. The defense's theory was that defendant believed that Sidney, who lived with his father in the United States, was looked down upon and was ill-treated by everyone except his paternal grandmother because he had been born out of wedlock, and that when she learned that the grandmother was dying of cancer, she felt trapped and, in an intense emotional upheaval, strangled Sidney and then attempted to kill herself so that she could take care of Sidney in the afterlife.

The only issues on appeal are whether the trial court committed prejudicial error by refusing to give two instructions requested by defendant, one related to the defense of unconsciousness, and one related to the effect her cultural background might have had on her state of mind when she killed Sidney. . . .

II

Defendant was born in 1943 in Saigon, China. At the age of 19, in about 1962 or 1963, she moved to Macau. She married and had a daughter, who was 25 years old at the time of the trial of this matter in February 1990. In 1963, she met Gary Wu (Wu), the son of one of her friends. That same year Wu went to the United States, and married Susanna Ku. He opened several restaurants in the Palm Springs area.

After eight years of marriage, defendant was divorced, and became employed, writing statistics for greyhound races. She was apparently betrothed to remarry in the mid-1970s, but her fiancé developed lung cancer and died. His sister, Nancy Chung (Chung), became defendant's close friend and confidante. According to Chung, Chung's brother made her promise to help defendant because defendant was a kind, moral person, not greedy, but too trusting.

In 1978 or 1979, defendant was contacted by Wu, who had heard that she was divorced and had a daughter. Wu told her his marriage was unsatisfactory because his wife could not have children. According to defendant, Wu told her he planned to divorce his wife. They discussed the possibility that defendant could come to the United States and conceive a child for Wu. Defendant believed Wu would marry her after he divorced his wife. Defendant was in love with Wu, and Wu gave defendant money to deposit in a joint bank account and sent her $20,000 so she could apply for a visa to the United States.

In November 1979, defendant came to the United States. When defendant arrived, he hugged and kissed her, told her his divorce proceedings would be completed soon and he definitely would marry her. Defendant lived with Wu's mother. Wu's wife believed she was a family friend. At Wu's request defendant had brought $15,000 of the money he had sent her and they opened a joint account together.

In December 1979 or January 1980, Wu and his wife Susanna were divorced; however, Wu did not tell defendant that he had obtained a divorce. Defendant conceived a child by Wu in the early part of 1980 and then moved into an apartment, where she was visited by Wu. After the child, Sidney, was born in November 1980, Wu apparently made no overtures regarding marriage. Depressed, defendant, who could not speak English, could not drive, and who had no support system in the United States, told Wu she intended to return to Macau, apparently expecting that this information would cause him to try to persuade her to stay.

Wu did not try to persuade defendant to stay, so in February 1981, she returned home but left Sidney with Wu. She could not take the baby because no one knew she had a baby and she and Sidney would have been humiliated in China. She told only her closest friend, Chung, who had already learned of defendant's pregnancy from Chung's daughters who were going to college in the United States, that she had borne a child out of wedlock; such a thing was apparently considered to be particularly shameful among people of defendant's culture.

From 1981 to 1988 defendant regularly asked Wu to bring Sidney to visit her, but to no avail. In 1981, Wu said he could only come for the summer and defendant told him she wanted Sidney to stay and if he could not, then she did not want to see him because it would be harder after he left. In 1984, Wu asked defendant to visit him but she did not want to come until she was married, then she and her son would have dignity and status.

In September 1987, Wu told defendant he needed money for his restaurant business. She finally told him that if he would bring Sidney to visit her, she would loan him money for his restaurants.

In January 1988, Wu brought Sidney, who was then seven years old, to visit defendant in Hong Kong. Defendant showed him $100,000 cash and a receipt for a certificate of deposit of a million Hong Kong dollars. Both the cash and the deposited funds had been loaned to defendant by Chung, after defendant admitted to Chung that she had lured Wu into bringing Sidney to see her with the promise of a loan. On that visit, Wu proposed marriage, but defendant declined, depressed over the fact that the marriage proposal seemed to be because of "her" money, and because she did not know if Wu was still married or not. Defendant was so discouraged by these beliefs that she attempted to throw herself out of the window of Chung's apartment, but was restrained by Chung, Chung's daughter, and a servant.

According to Chung, Wu, while in Hong Kong, suggested that if Chung invested money in his restaurant business, he could be her sponsor for American citizenship, because the communists would be taking over control of Hong Kong in a few years. Chung declined, saying she did not know anything about the restaurant business. Wu then said there was another way to help her, and when she asked how, he said he could marry her. Chung asked, "What about Helen?" Wu replied by indicating that there was enough time for him to first marry Chung and to later marry defendant. Wu later wrote Chung a letter suggesting the marriage, which he followed up with a telephone call asking if Chung had received his letter. Chung politely cooled these advances by denying she had received the letter, which, however, she saved, and which was produced at trial. Chung did not tell defendant of Wu's advances.

During the next year defendant worked and traveled with Chung. She wanted to see Sidney but she did not know if Wu was still married and did not want to upset her son's life. In August 1989, defendant, who was on a vacation trip to Las Vegas and San Francisco with Chung, as Chung's guest, apparently heard that Wu's mother, Sidney's paternal grandmother, was terminally ill, so she came to Palm Springs to visit. While there, she was told by the grandmother that when the grandmother died, she, defendant, should take Sidney because Wu would not take good care of him. She was given similar advice by Sandy, Wu's cousin.

Toward the end of August, Wu told defendant that they were going to Las Vegas. Defendant stated she did not want to go. Wu told her it was important that she go, as "she was the main character" because they were going to be married. Defendant and Wu were married on September 1. On September 5, they went to Los Angeles to consult an attorney about immigration law. Defendant, following the marriage and consultation, was still of the opinion that Wu had married her because of his belief that she had a lot of money. During the drive home from Los Angeles, this belief was reinforced by Wu's comments. When she asked if he had married her for her money, he responded that until she produced the money, she had no right to speak. Defendant asked Wu whether the marriage was not worthwhile simply for the purpose of legitimizing Sidney, and Wu replied that many people could give him children. Defendant told Wu he would be sorry. She later explained that remark meant that she was thinking about returning to Macau and killing herself.

After the trip to the lawyer, defendant told Wu to get her a plane ticket for September 16 so that she could return to Macau. She asked him not to let Sidney know that she was leaving, because she wished to have 10 days of happiness with her son. Wu wanted, to know if defendant was going to get the money, which made her very angry. Defendant gave Wu $6,300, her own money, and told him he liked money too much.

On September 9, the evening of the killing, defendant was playing with Sidney. Earlier that day defendant had interceded on Sidney's behalf when Wu hit Sidney when Sidney would not get out of the family car. Wu had gone to the restaurant to put on two birthday parties, apparently for his friend Rosemary. Defendant and Sidney played and talked, and defendant told Sidney that she knew what he liked because of the mother-child bond between them.

Sidney told defendant that Wu said she was "psychotic" and "very troublesome." He then told defendant that Rosemary was Wu's girlfriend, and that the house they lived in belonged to Rosemary. He also told her that Wu made him get up early so Wu could take Rosemary's daughters to school in the morning and if he did not get up, Wu would scold and beat him. He said Wu loved Rosemary more than him. Defendant began to think about what she had been told by Sidney's grandmother and Sandy concerning her taking care of Sidney. She began to experience heart palpitations and to have trouble breathing. She told

Sidney she wanted to die, and asked him if he would go too. He clung to her neck and cried. She then left the bedroom, and obtained a rope by cutting the cord off a window blind. She returned to the bedroom and strangled Sidney. According to defendant, she did not remember the strangling itself. She stopped breathing, and when she started breathing again, she was surprised at how quickly Sidney had died. She then wrote a note to Wu to the effect that he had bullied her too much and "now this air is vented. I can die with no regret," but did not mention Sidney's killing in the note. She then attempted to strangle herself, failed, went to the kitchen and slashed her left wrist with a knife, and then returned to the bedroom and lay down next to Sidney on the bed, having first placed a waste-paper basket under her bleeding wrist to catch the blood so that the floor would not be dirtied.

Wu returned home several hours later, and discovered defendant and Sidney. He called the police, and the paramedics were also summoned. The police determined that Sidney was dead. The paramedics tested defendant's vital signs, and determined that although her pulse and blood pressure were normal, she exhibited a decreased level of consciousness. . . .

Defendant was charged with murder (Pen. Code, §187) and, following a trial by jury, was convicted of second degree murder.

III

A. THE TRIAL COURT COMMITTED REVERSIBLE ERROR BY REFUSING TO INSTRUCT THE JURY ON THE DEFENSE OF UNCONSCIOUSNESS

[The court held here that the defendant had presented sufficient evidence to warrant the following instruction:

> A person who commits what would otherwise be a criminal act, while unconscious, is not guilty of a crime.
> This rule of law applies to persons who are not conscious of acting but who perform acts while asleep or while suffering from a delirium of fever, or because of an attack of [psychomotor] epilepsy, a blow on the head, the involuntary taking of drugs or the involuntary consumption of intoxicating liquor, or any similar cause. . . .

The court held that a reasonable jury could have found that although defendant might have consciously contemplated killing Sidney before she actually strangled him, the actual act of strangulation was committed while she was in a fugue state, i.e., in a state in which she acted without conscious thought and was unconscious of her act of strangulation at the time she committed it. A reasonable jury could have further concluded that defendant "knew" she had strangled Sidney not because she had been consciously aware of her acts as she strangled the child, but because she later inferred that she must have strangled him.]

B. UPON RETRIAL, THE TRIAL COURT SHOULD, IF SO REQUESTED, INSTRUCT THE JURY ON HOW EVIDENCE OF DEFENDANT'S CULTURAL BACKGROUND RELATES TO DEFENDANT'S THEORY OF THE CASE

Defendant contends that the trial court erred by refusing to give an instruction which pinpointed a significant aspect of her theory of the case, i.e., an instruction which told the jury it could choose to consider the evidence of defendant's cultural background in determining the presence or absence of the various mental states which were elements of the crimes with which she was charged. Because we have already determined that the judgment must be reversed because of the failure to give an instruction on unconsciousness, we will address the issue of the propriety of an instruction pinpointing the cultural background theory of defendant's case for purposes of guiding the trial court on retrial.

Defendant requested the following instruction:

> You have received evidence of defendant's cultural background and the relationship of her culture to her mental state. You may, but are not required to, consider that the [*sic*] evidence in determining the presence or absence of the essential mental states of the crimes defined in these instructions, or in determining any other issue in this case.

At trial, the prosecutor objected to this instruction on the ground that

> it's real touchy, in a major case, to be messing around with non-pattern jury instructions . . . People smarter than myself have put together all the pattern jury instructions. I think they have covered every conceivable type of crime, certainly in this case they have, and I don't think that we need to be giving the jury extra instructions.

In addition, the People stated the concern that there was no appellate law on the subject of instructions on "cultural defenses," and that

> the problem, apparently, to me, is that the jury has heard evidence about that, and whether we called it cultural defense, I don't know, but they certainly have heard the word "culture" probably a thousand times in this trial; maybe not a thousand, but hundreds. . . .

The trial court expressed the concern that the instruction would be "telling [the jury] that is the law." Although defendant's attorney specifically pointed out that the instruction merely told the jury that it could either consider or not consider the evidence of cultural background in determining defendant's mental state at the time of the crime, the trial court disagreed that that was the instruction's effect.

Ultimately, the court refused to give the instruction, commenting that it did not want to put the "stamp of approval on [defendant's] actions in the United States, which would have been acceptable in China."

On appeal, the People do not contend that the instruction should not have been given because there was no established appellate law on such an instruction, but instead contend that failure to give the requested instruction was not error, because . . . defendant's defense as to mental states was sufficiently covered by the other instructions . . . given . . .

Here, the instruction, assuming it is legally correct, is clearly applicable to the facts of this case, as there was ample evidence of both the defendant's cultural background, and how it could have affected her mental state at the time of the charged offense.

The issue then is whether it was a correct statement of the law that the jury may consider evidence of defendant's cultural background in determining the presence or absence of the "essential mental states of the crimes defined in these instructions, or in determining any other issue in this case."

The essential mental states at issue here were (1) premeditation and deliberation, (2) malice aforethought, and (3) specific intent to kill. Generally speaking, all relevant evidence is admissible (Evid. Code, §351), and the trier of fact may consider any admitted evidence. Here, the admission of evidence of defendant's cultural background was never objected to by the People; there is no argument that the evidence was relevant. The question then is, on what issues was such evidence relevant? As discussed below, this evidence clearly related to certain mental states, which are elements of the charged offense.

First, the evidence of defendant's cultural background was clearly relevant on the issue of premeditation and deliberation. The prosecution's theory was that defendant's statements on days before the killing to Wu and other family members indicated that she had planned to take revenge on Wu by killing Sidney in a Medea-like gesture. The evidence of defendant's cultural background offered an alternative explanation for the statements (that defendant intended to kill herself) and also for motive behind the killing, that explanation being that the killing of Sidney (as opposed to defendant's own planned suicide) was not deliberate and premeditated, but instead occurred immediately after defendant learned from Sidney himself facts conclusively confirming, in defendant's mind, the statements by Gramma and Sandy, and her own observations, that Sidney was not loved by Wu and was badly treated.

Second, the evidence of defendant's cultural background was also relevant on the issue of malice aforethought and the existence of heat of passion at the time of the killing, which eliminates malice and reduces an intentional killing to voluntary manslaughter. (Pen. Code, §192.) The court recognized that "heat of passion" was an issue in this case because it instructed the jury regarding heat of passion negating malice and further instructed the jury regarding the lesser included offense of manslaughter.

. . . However, as this court stated in *Berry*, "there is no specific type of provocation required by [Penal Code] section 192 [defining manslaughter] and . . . verbal provocation may be sufficient." (18 Cal. 3d at 515.)

. . . In People v. Borchers (1958) 50 Cal. 2d 321, 329, . . . in the course of explaining the phrase "heat of passion" used in the statute defining manslaughter[,] we pointed out that "passion" need not mean "rage" or "anger" but may be any "[v]iolent, intense, high-wrought or enthusiastic emotion" and concluded there "that defendant was aroused to a heat of 'passion' by a series of events over a considerable period of time. . . ." (50 Cal. 2d at p.328, 329.) . . .

Here, there was evidence that defendant had experienced a series of events for a 10-year period before and during her stay in late August and early September 1989 with Wu in California, from which the jury could have concluded that defendant was suffering from "pre-existing stress" at the time that Sidney told her things which confirmed her fear that Sidney, because he was not legitimate and because he had no mother to care for him, was not well-treated, and that things were going to get worse for him upon the death of his Gramma. The testimony related to defendant's cultural background was relevant to explain the source of such stress, as well to explain how Sidney's statements could have constituted "sufficient provocation" to cause defendant to kill Sidney in a "heat of passion."

The experts on transcultural psychology specifically testified that, in their opinion, defendant was acting while in an emotional crisis during the time that she obtained the knife and cord, strangled Sidney and then slashed her own wrist, and that her emotional state was intertwined with, and explainable by reference to, her cultural background. Specifically, the following testimony was given:

Dr. Chien testified:

A.   So when all of this thought came up to her mind, all of a sudden she said she couldn't breathe. She almost got into some kind of state that she did not know what she was doing other than thinking that, "There's no way out other than bringing the son together with her to the other life."

After then describing the Chinese belief in an afterlife, he testified that:

A.   She told me wondering that is a heaven, paradise. She thought the only way to find out a way out is to bring this Sidney to go together so the mother and son can finally live together in the other heaven, other world if that cannot be done in this realistic earth.

Dr. Chien further testified:

And at that time, she said during the strangulation or that kind of emotional heat — obviously, she was under the heat of passion when she realized that her son was unwanted son, uncared by Gary, passed around from one woman to the other woman, and now the grandmother is dying and she was planning to leave, "What will happen to Sidney?"

And all this information came up to her mind to stimulate all her guilt feeling which was probably more than ordinary guilt feeling that some depressive person would feel.

I must say that guilt feeling is quite a common symptom in depressive patients, and for that many depressed person would commit suicide.

But in this case, Helen had some realistic reason to be 200 percent or 300 percent more guilty in addition to her normal guilt feeling that came from depression. She would feel that she couldn't really do the duty to the son, so the only way to fulfill her duty when she realized her son was neglected and not to be cared by anybody in the future, she thought the way to go is to the heaven.

So obviously, obviously she strangulated her son and she kind of start being after to breathe again after the strangulation and realize how quickly a boy who is not a small boy could be killed by her small stature.

Dr. Chien was asked about the significance of the "depression in [defendant's] thought processes" on her decision to strangle Sidney and he testified:

A.   It was very — in my expertise as a transcultural psychiatry, in my familiarity, with my familiarity with the Chinese culture translate and from the information interview I obtain from Helen, she thought she was doing that out from the mother's love, mother's responsibility to bring a child together with her when she realized that then; was no hope for her or a way for her to survive in this country or in this earth.

Q.   Well, are you telling us that the death of Sidney was her act of love?

A.   Yes. It's a mother's altruism. This may be very difficult for the Westerner to understand because I have dealt with many other so-called children who are sent to me from the children bureau. Children can be easily taken away from the mother in our agencies' mind. Social worker, when they discovered child abuse case or whatever else, children can be easily taken away from the parents.

But in the Asian culture when the mother commits suicide and leave the children alone, usually they'll be considered to be a totally irresponsible behavior, and the mother will usually worry what would happen if she died, "Who is going to take care of the children? Anybody [*sic*— "Nobody"?] can supply the real love that mother could provide," so and so. . . .

Q. Well, based upon what you heard from Helen and reviewed from the materials, was Helen in a fugue state when she strangled Sidney?

A. Obviously.

Q. Why is it obvious?

A. Because that kind of emotion, mixed emotional of the despair, anger, disappointment, depression, sadness, hopelessness, everything all sudden come up to her mind that she thought the only way out is to go to the heaven together with the son. And that is not kind of comfortable thing for people to think long time ahead or to plan. So obviously, she was under a kind of heat of emotion or I call it heat of passion that went out like a dreamy state."

Dr. Terry Gock, a clinical psychologist who interviewed defendant for a total of nine and a half hours in three interview sessions and a witness for the defense, testified on direct examination that on the day Sidney was killed, defendant was experiencing a very high level of emotional turmoil, i.e., an emotional crisis, which he described as "when our, when our feelings are so conflicting, so confused and so, so distressful that we, that we don't perhaps know exactly how to plan a course of action, plan a solution in the most rational way." He testified that in his opinion, defendant's cultural background was very intertwined with her emotional state on the evening of the killing. Specifically, Dr. Gock testified:

It is very difficult to divorce ourselves from our culture and act in a totally culturally different way. And so, you know, she in many ways is a product of her past experiences, including her culture. And also when she experience certain things, like some of the information that she, that she got from her son that evening, it was, it was very distressful for her. And in some sense the kind of alternatives that she, if you would perhaps, you know, it's not as rational as an alternative that the only way she saw out was perhaps — you know, maybe that's the best word is the way she saw how to get out of that situation was quite culturally determined. . . .

And then in terms of what are some of the alternatives then for her. In — perhaps in this country, even with a traditional woman may, may see other options. But in her culture, in her own mind, there are no other options but to, or her at that time, but to kill herself and take the son along with her so that they could sort of step over to the next world where she could devote herself, all of herself to the caring of the son, caring of Sidney.

Q. Was that the motive for killing him?

A. Motive, if you will, yes.

Q. What was her purpose?

A. Her purpose is to, is that she, is, in many ways is, is a benevolent one. It's a positive one where she believed — and this, this sounds sort of implausible to some, some of us whose, who are raised in another culture. That what she believed was that she was not exactly killing but, through death, both of them would be reunited in the next world where she could provide the kind of caring that Sidney did not get in this world.

On cross-examination, Dr. Gock agreed that defendant must have made a decision to kill Sidney, and then decided what instrumentality to use, where to get it, and when to use it, but noted that the way the questions were being presented by the prosecuting attorney suggested "a lot of thought processes," "[a]nd what I'm saying is that when one is emotionally distressed or one's feelings are all worked up, a lot of times we don't think in that kind of ways and we do things at, that afterwards we may be able to sort it out in that kind of a way, but at that time they were not separate elements like that."

There was also testimony from Professor Juris G. Draguns, a clinical psychologist and an expert in the area of cross-cultural psychology. He discussed, among other things, a "classical sociological study of suicide," which contained information about suicide and filicide, noting that the author:

> [D]escribed the situation of these combined, of killing oneself and one's child as follows. She's talking then about American mothers for the most part in Chicago in the 1920s. These mothers apparently did not yet regard their infant children as separate personalities with an independent right to live but, rather, as part of themselves, sharing their troubles, and to be taken on with them into death.
>
> Except in extreme ends to which it leads, this attitude of interpreting the interests and attitudes of another, in terms of one's own interest, is not abnormal nor even unusual. In cases in which this attitude leads to murder before a suicide, the person committing the murder does not regard himself as doing anything criminal or even wrong. He is moved by love, pity, sympathy. He is removing someone from the wicked world before the wickedness has touched him. He's doing kindness by removing the other from suffering, which he has endured and which, therefore, the other also endures or will in time encounter. . . .

Because the requested instruction was, for the most part, a correct statement of the law, and because it was applicable to the evidence and one of defendant's two basic defenses in this case, upon retrial defendant is entitled to have the jury instructed that it may consider evidence of defendant's cultural background in determining the existence or nonexistence of the relevant mental states. . . .

Notes and Questions

1. Was it inconsistent for Wu to plead both that she was unconscious and that she acted in a manner consistent with her cultural values?

2. What is the operative definition of "culture" in this case? What is "transcultural psychiatry," and what is its relevance to homicide law?

3. *Laws and cultural norms.* At what point must the criminal law be willing to undermine culture? Lawyers report increasing use of so-called cultural defenses, usually with the expectation of mitigating punishment rather than winning acquittal. In one California case, an Ethiopian immigrant shot a woman who he feared was using witchcraft against him and presented expert testimony by a professor of anthropology that Ethiopians from the Eritrea area do indeed believe that an evil spirit inflicts pain through use of a woman agent. How would you compare this expert testimony with that of Dr. Blinder in the *Berry* case, above? What responsibility did this man have to "unlearn" his old beliefs?

In Washington state, Dong Lu Chen was convicted of second-degree manslaughter for smashing his wife's head eight times with a hammer when he suspected her of carrying on an affair.[38] Washington State Supreme Court Justice Edward Pincus explained that Chen "is not a loose cannon. He never displayed psychopathic tendencies. This guy's not going to do it again and he has suffered." Stan Mark, program director at the Asian American Legal Defense and Education Fund complained, "It has nothing to do with his being Chinese or having a Chinese background. In modern China, under Socialist law, it is not acceptable conduct."

Do Mark and Pincus agree about the general reason for criminal punishment? See Chapter 1, *supra*. Monona Yin of the Committee Against Anti-Asian Violence said that although she too opposes the sentence given Chen, she believes that cultural considerations should play a part in the courtroom. "Culture informs everything each person does," Yin said, "We are acutely aware of the pressures on an immigrant. But is adultery justification for extreme violence? I would say no." Is Yin contradicting herself? Or is she suggesting that certain emotions are so strong and certain crimes so heinous that they overwhelm cultural considerations? To which emotions and crimes would she allow the application of cultural considerations?

Prof. Cynthia Lee notes the irony that provocation claims by defendants from foreign cultures may succeed in American courts most when they happen to converge with the cultural stereotypes that dominate American law generally. Thus, she argues, Dong Lu Chen received a light sentence (probation and time served) because his provocation claim, though allegedly rooted in Chinese culture, happened to map on to the traditional American favor shown "male honor" claims.[39]

4. Note that the court does not hesitate to allow the "heat of passion claim" even though the victim of the killing could hardly be described as the provoker. The logic of the reform or MPC approach, turning objective provocation into the condition of extreme emotional disturbance, would argue in favor of allowing reduction to manslaughter even where the victim of the killing is wholly innocent. Thus, see Model Penal Code Commentaries sec. 210.3 (Revised Commentaries, 1980), at 60-61 ("[T]he Code does not require that the actor's emotional distress arise from some injury, affront, or other provocative acts perpetrated upon him by the deceased.").

5. In State v. Raguseo, 622 A.2d 519 (Conn. 1993), the jury considering a provocation claim in a murder case sent the following poignant request for further instruction to the judge: "definition 'norm.' Whose 'norm' are we comparing the action/thought process to —, the 'norm' for the defendant or the 'norm' for society?" Id. at 535 n.3 (Berdon, J., dissenting).

Is there any coherence to the idea of a culture-specific motivation? One commentator argues against a key foundation of the concept of a cultural defense — the notion that "acting in a culturally motivated manner" establishes lesser blameworthiness — on the ground that all human volition is influenced by forces that by some manipulation of definition can be called "cultural."[40]

---

38. Washington Post (April 10, 1989, at A3).
39. Murder and the Reasonable Man 113-114 (2003).
40. Neal Gordon, The Implications of Memetics for the Cultural Defense, 50 Duke L.J. 1809 (2001).

6

UNINTENTIONAL HOMICIDE

A. INVOLUNTARY MANSLAUGHTER

1. Negligent and Reckless Homicide

Francis Wharton, in his Treatise on Criminal Law, says:

> There are many cases in which death is the result of an occurrence, in itself unexpected, but which arose from negligence or inattention. How far in such cases the agent of such misfortune is to be held responsible, depends upon the inquiry, whether he was guilty of gross negligence at the time. Inferences of guilt are not to be drawn from remote causes, and the degree of caution requisite to bring the case within the limits of misadventure, must be proportioned to the probability of danger of attending the act immediately conducive to the death.[1]

COMMONWEALTH v. WELANSKY
Supreme Judicial Court of Massachusetts
55 N.E.2d 902 (1944)

LUMMUS, JUSTICE.

On November 28, 1942, and for about nine years before that day, [Barnett Welansky] maintained and operated a "night club" in Boston, having an entrance at 17 Piedmont Street, for the furnishing to the public for compensation of food, drink and entertainment, consisting of orchestra and band music, singing and dancing. . . . Barnett Welansky . . . is called in this opinion simply the defendant, since his codefendants were acquitted by the jury. . . .

The defendant was accustomed to spend his evenings at the night club, inspecting the premises and superintending the business. On November 16, 1942, he became suddenly ill, and was carried to a hospital, where he remained . . . [on the night in question]. During his stay at the hospital, although employees

---

1. Treatise on Criminal Law 382 (1880).

visited him there, he did not concern himself with the night club, because as he testified, he "knew it would be all right" and that "the same system . . . [he] had would continue" during his absence. There is no evidence of any act, omission or condition at the night club on November 28, 1942 (apart from the lighting of a match hereinafter described), that was not within [defendant's] usual and regular practice. . . . Under these circumstances the defendant was not entitled to a verdict of not guilty on the ground that any acts or omissions on the evening of November 28, 1942, were the transitory and unauthorized acts or omissions of servants or other persons, for which the defendant could not be held criminally responsible.

The physical arrangement of the night club on November 28, 1942, as well as on November 16, 1942, when the defendant last had personal knowledge of it, was as follows. [The main entrance was on Piedmont Street. A revolving door led to the foyer, off of which were the Caricature Bar, the Main Dining Room, the office, and a stairway down to the Melody Lounge and kitchen. A new Cocktail Lounge was accessible through the dining room and Caricature Bar. Apart from the front entrance, there was a customer exit in a corridor at the far side of the Cocktail Lounge. There were also five "emergency" exits: one hidden in the corridor with the office, locked shut; one inward-swinging door in the same hallway, blocked by checked coats; two inward-swinging doors that only employees would know about; and the principal exit in the Main Dining Room. This emergency exit led to Shawmut Street and consisted of two doors with panic bars, obscured by hooked wooden doors and blocked by tables in the dining room.]

We come now to the story of the fire. A little after ten o'clock on the evening of Saturday, November 28, 1942, the night club was well filled with a crowd of patrons. It was during the busiest season of the year. An important football game had attracted many visitors to Boston. . . . Witnesses were rightly permitted to give their estimates, derived from their observations, of the number of patrons in various parts of the night club. . . . [Those estimates ranged from 980 to 1,250 people in the entire establishment.] Yet it could have been found that the crowd was no larger than it had been on other Saturday evenings before the defendant was taken ill, and that there had been larger crowds at earlier times. . . . The defendant testified that the reasonable capacity of the night club, exclusive of the new Cocktail Lounge, was six hundred fifty patrons. He never saw the new Cocktail Lounge with the furniture installed, but it was planned to accommodate from one hundred to one hundred twenty-five patrons.

A bartender in the Melody Lounge noticed that an electric light bulb which was in or near the coconut husks of an artificial palm tree in the corner had been turned off and that the corner was dark. He directed a sixteen-year-old bar boy . . . to cause the bulb to be lighted. A soldier sitting with other persons near the light told the bar boy to leave it unlighted. But the bar boy got a stool, lighted a match in order to see the bulb, turned the bulb in its socket, and thus lighted it. The bar boy blew the match out, and started to walk away. Apparently the flame of the match had ignited the palm tree and that had speedily ignited the low cloth ceiling near it, for both flamed up almost instantly. The fire spread with great rapidity across the upper part of the room, causing much heat. The crowd in the Melody Lounge rushed up the stairs, but the fire preceded them. People got on fire while on the stairway. The fire spread with great speed across the foyer and into the Caricature Bar and the main dining room, and thence into the Cocktail Lounge. Soon after the fire started the lights in the night club went out. . . . The crowd was panic stricken, and rushed and pushed in every direction through the night club, screaming, and overturning tables and chairs in their attempts to escape.

The door at the head of the Melody Lounge stairway was not opened until firemen broke it down from outside with an axe and found it locked by a key lock, so that the panic bar could not operate. Two dead bodies were found close to it, and a pile of bodies about seven feet from it. The door in the vestibule of the office did not become open, and was barred by the clothing rack. The revolving door soon jammed, but was burst out by the pressure of the crowd. The head waiter and another waiter tried to get open the panic doors from the main dining room to Shawmut Street, and succeeded after some difficulty [i.e., hammering one of the doors with a table]. The other two doors to Shawmut Street were locked, and were opened by force from outside by firemen and others. Some patrons escaped through them, but many dead bodies were piled up inside them. . . . Some employees, and [492] patrons, died in the fire. . . .

The defendant, his brother James Welansky, and [employee] Jacob Goldfine, were indicted for manslaughter. . . .

[Counts 7 to 12 alleged that the defendants] did for a period of time prior to and including November 28, 1942, maintain and operate a night club, to which [they] invited members of the general public; that [they were] under a legal duty to [their] invitees to use reasonable care to keep [the] premises safe for their use; . . . that in reckless disregard of such duty to one [naming a victim] who was lawfully upon said premises pursuant to such invitation to the general public, and of the probable harmful consequences to him of their failure to perform said duty, they and each of them did "wilfully, wantonly and recklessly neglect and fail to fulfill their said legal duty and obligation to the said" victim, by reason whereof he . . . died.

The defendant was found guilty. . . . He was sentenced to imprisonment in the State prison upon each count for a term of not less than twelve years and not more than fifteen years, the first day of said term to be in solitary confinement and the residue at hard labor, the sentences to run concurrently. . . .

The Commonwealth disclaimed any contention that the defendant intentionally killed or injured the persons named in the indictments as victims. It based its case on involuntary manslaughter through wanton or reckless conduct.

To convict the defendant of manslaughter, the Commonwealth was not required to prove that he caused the fire by some wanton or reckless conduct. Fire in a place of public resort is an ever present danger. It was enough to prove that death resulted from his wanton or reckless disregard of the safety of patrons in the event of fire from any cause. . . .

Usually wanton or reckless conduct consists of an affirmative act, like driving an automobile or discharging a firearm, in disregard of probable harmful consequences to another. But whereas in the present case there is a duty of care for the safety of business visitors invited to premises which the defendant controls, wanton or reckless conduct may consist of intentional failure to take such care in disregard of the probable harmful consequences to them or of their right to care.

To define wanton or reckless conduct so as to distinguish it clearly from negligence and gross negligence is not easy. Sometimes the word "wilful" is prefaced to the words "wanton" and "reckless" in expressing the concept. That only blurs it. Wilful means intentional. In the phrase "wilful, wanton or reckless conduct," if "wilful" modifies "conduct" it introduces something different from wanton or reckless conduct, even though the legal result is the same. Wilfully causing harm is a wrong, but a different wrong from wantonly or recklessly causing harm. If "wilful" modifies "wanton or reckless conduct" its use is accurate. What must be intended is the conduct, not the resulting harm. . . .

The standard of wanton or reckless conduct is at once subjective and objective. . . . Knowing facts that would cause a reasonable man to know the danger is equivalent to knowing the danger. The judge charged the jury correctly when he said,

> To constitute wanton or reckless conduct, as distinguished from mere negligence, grave danger to others must have been apparent and the defendant must have chosen to run the risk rather than alter his conduct so as to avoid the act or omission which caused the harm. If the grave danger was in fact realized by the defendant, his subsequent voluntary act or omission which caused the harm amounts to wanton or reckless conduct, no matter whether the ordinary man would have realized the gravity of the danger or not. But even if a particular defendant is so stupid [or] so heedless . . . that in fact he did not realize the grave danger, he cannot escape the imputation of wanton or reckless conduct in his dangerous act or omission, if an ordinary normal man under the same circumstances would have realized the gravity or the danger. A man may be reckless within the meaning of the law although he himself thought he was careful.

The essence of wanton or reckless conduct is intentional conduct, by way of either commission or of omission where there is a duty to act, which conduct involves a high degree of likelihood that substantial harm will result to another. Wanton or reckless conduct amounts to what has been variously described as indifference to or disregard of probable consequences to that other. . . .

The words "wanton" and "reckless" are thus not merely rhetorical or vituperative expressions used instead of negligent or grossly negligent. They express a difference in the degree of risk and in the voluntary taking of risk so marked as compared with negligence, as to amount substantially and in the eyes of the law to a difference in kind. . . . [T]he rule is that "negligence and willful and wanton conduct are so different in kind that words properly descriptive of the one commonly exclude the other."

. . . [I]t is now clear in the Commonwealth that at common law conduct does not become criminal until it passes the borders of negligence and gross negligence and enters into the domain of wanton or reckless conduct. There is in Massachusetts at common law no such thing as "criminal negligence."

The Commonwealth was properly allowed to show that an exit . . . and fire doors . . . called for by the plans that were approved by the building department of the city of Boston under St. 1907, c.550, §12, as amended, had not been provided when the defendant last had knowledge of the premises on November 16, 1942, although he planned to open the Cocktail Lounge the next day; that the mode of construction of the Cocktail Lounge indicated that he did not intend to provide either; and that they had not been provided at the time of the fire. As planned, the fire doors were to be held open by fusible plugs that would melt and allow the door to close automatically in case of fire. They and the exits might have afforded some protection to persons in the Cocktail Lounge. The violation of such statute is not negligence per se but sometimes is evidence of

negligence. Standing by itself, it would not warrant a finding of wanton or reckless conduct. But it might be considered with other evidence. There was no error
in its admission. . . .

Judgments affirmed.

Notes and Questions

1. What "wanton and reckless" acts did Welansky perform? When? What
risks did he advert to? When? The court says that "the Commonwealth was not
required to prove that he caused the fire by some wanton or reckless conduct."
What did the prosecutor have to prove *was* wanton and reckless?

What relevant "wilful" or "intentional conduct" acts did Welansky perform?

2. Ultimately, what is the Massachusetts standard for involuntary manslaughter? Reread the trial court's charge to the jury. Does the instruction really require recklessness? Or can the prosecutor rely on proof of either recklessness or
some especially egregiously gross negligence? Does this case suggest that the two
can be morally equivalent? On which ground is Welansky guilty?

3. *Reckless and negligent homicide.* Though many jurisdictions treat recklessness and gross negligence as equal or alternative bases for involuntary
manslaughter, the Model Penal Code takes some pains to distinguish the two —
it requires recklessness for manslaughter but provides a lesser homicide crime
for which negligence will suffice. The Code Comments explain the purpose of
the drafters:[2]

> It is a fair summary of common-law homicide that three levels of risk-creation were
> recognized: that which was sufficient for a conviction of murder, that which was
> sufficient for a conviction of manslaughter, and that which was sufficient only for
> civil liability. The lines between these three categories were at best unclear. . . .
>
> Sections 210.3(1)(a) and 2.02(2)(c) resolve these issues under the Model
> Code with respect to the offense of manslaughter. Section 210.3(1)(a) treats reck-
> less homicide as manslaughter. Under Section 2.02(2)(c), a person acts recklessly
> with respect to the death of another when he consciously disregards a substantial
> and unjustifiable risk that his conduct will cause that result. Additionally, the na-
> ture and degree of risk must be such that, considering all the circumstances, its dis-
> regard "involves a gross deviation from the standard of conduct that a law-abiding
> person would observe in the actor's situation." . . .
>
> Under the Model Code, liability for manslaughter cannot be premised on
> negligence. Statutes derived from the common law classify unintentional homi-
> cide as involuntary manslaughter without any attempt to distinguish conscious dis-
> regard of homicidal risk from inadvertent risk creation. This failure to differenti-
> ate across a broad spectrum of culpability raises serious grading difficulties. On the
> one hand, involuntary manslaughter may be graded as is its voluntary counterpart,
> in which case disproportionately severe sanctions are assigned to conduct that is
> merely negligent. On the other hand, reduced penalties may be authorized for
> involuntary manslaughter, in which case persons guilty of serious wrongdoing
> benefit from formal categorization with less culpable homicides. Section 210.3(1)
> (a) refines the traditional definition of manslaughter by demanding proof of con-
> scious disregard of perceived homicidal risk. In such instances, punishment as a

2. American Law Institute, Model Penal Code and Commentaries, Part II, at 52-87 (1980).

felony of the second degree is warranted. Negligent homicide is relegated to a separate provision carrying lesser sanctions. . . .

. . . The essence of the difference between recklessness and negligence as those terms are defined in Section 2.02 of the Model Code is that the reckless actor must "consciously disregard" a substantial and unjustifiable homicidal risk created by his conduct, whereas the negligent actor need only disregard a risk of which he "should be aware." Inadvertence to risk is thus the basis upon which condemnation for negligence proceeds, coupled with the judgment that the actor's failure to perceive the risk involves a "gross deviation from the standard of care that a reasonable person would observe in the actor's situation." . . .

In summary, therefore, the Model Penal Code was drafted against a background of inconsistency and imprecision in determining the content of negligence for purposes of criminal homicide. There was also a general failure to focus upon the need for a grading differential between conduct involving conscious risk creation and conduct involving inadvertence. The most common situation was that negligent homicide was treated as a species of involuntary manslaughter, with judicial formulation of the appropriate standard expressed in a jumble of language that obscured the essential character of the inquiry.

. . . Conscious risk creation is adequately covered by the Model Code in the crime of manslaughter and, in some instances of especially grievous conduct, in the crime of murder. Whether there is need to include the inadvertent risk creator within the penal prohibition presents an issue of principle that deserves explicit consideration.

It has been urged that inadvertent negligence is not a sufficient basis for criminal conviction, both on the utilitarian ground that threatened sanctions cannot influence the inadvertent actor and on the moral ground that criminal punishment should be reserved for cases involving conscious fault. The utilitarian argument is that the inadvertent actor by definition does not perceive the risks of his conduct, and thus cannot be deterred from risk creation. The moral argument is that the legitimacy of criminal condemnation is premised upon personal accountability of the sort that is usually and properly measured by an estimate of the actor's willingness consciously to violate clearly established societal norms. Those who hold this view argue that the actor who does not perceive the risks associated with his conduct presents a moral situation different in kind from that of the actor who knows exactly what he is doing and what risks he is running and who nevertheless makes a conscious choice condemned by the penal law.

These arguments are canvassed in more detail in the commentary to Section 2.02, as is the basis of the Model Code response to them. Suffice it to say here that neither contention was regarded by the Institute as persuasive. Criminal punishment of negligent homicide is not impotent to stimulate care that might otherwise not be taken, nor is a person's failure to use his faculties for the protection of others an improper basis for condemnation. The Model Code definition of negligence insists on proof of substantial fault and limits penal sanctions to cases where "the significance of the circumstances of fact would be apparent to one who shares the community's general sense of right and wrong." Justice is safeguarded by insisting upon that gross deviation from ordinary standards of conduct which is contemplated by the Model Code definition of negligence. Liability for inadvertent risk creation is thus properly limited to cases where the actor is grossly insensitive to the interests and claims of other persons in society.

On the other hand, the distinction between conscious and inadvertent risk creation is important both for assessing the dangerousness of the actor's conduct and for evaluating the gravity of his moral fault. For that reason, the Model Code punishes negligent homicide as an offense of lesser grade than manslaughter. The range of sanctions authorized for negligent homicide under Section 210.4 falls considerably short of that prevailing at the time the Code was drafted in states where manslaughter was a single category. The penalties provided, however, are somewhat higher than the norm for involuntary manslaughter in states where voluntary and involuntary manslaughter were distinguished for purposes of sentence. Given the ameliorative powers vested in the courts by the Model Code, these sanctions do not seem excessive.

4. *A reprise on the "wanton or reckless" standard.* The *Welansky* standard came back for review nearly 60 years later in Commonwealth v. Levesque, 766 N.E.2d 50 (Mass. 2002), another notorious fatal fire case. *Levesque,* like *Welansky,* raises not only the question of defendants' level of culpability, but also the question of to what act that culpability attached. The facts were as follows:

For several months prior to December 3, 1999, the defendants lived in a room on the second floor of the vacant five-story warehouse. The warehouse was a cold storage building and, as such, had brick walls, wood framing, and a compartmentalized floor plan with many small windowless rooms insulated with cork and styrofoam. The second floor where the defendants stayed had some windows, but those windows were boarded up. The room occupied by the defendants contained a bed, closet, and personal effects, including clothing, blankets, a radio, a wooden end table, and a kerosene heater. The defendants had an operable cellular telephone, food, and pets. Because there was no electricity, a flashlight, candles, and a heater were used for light. On more than one occasion, the defendants had an overnight guest in these quarters. . . .

On the afternoon of December 3, 1999, between 4:15 P.M. and 4:30 P.M., the defendants had a physical altercation in their bedroom at the warehouse that resulted in the knocking over of a lit candle. A fire started and the defendants tried unsuccessfully to put the fire out with their feet and a pillow. The fire spread rapidly until everything in the room began to burn. The defendants searched for the cat and dog that lived in the warehouse with them but the search was futile. The defendants left the warehouse and did not report the fire to the authorities.

After leaving the warehouse, the defendants passed several open businesses and shopping mall stores where public telephones were available. Between 4 and 5 P.M., the general manager of Media Play store saw the defendants in his store and heard Julie Barnes say, "I can't believe I lost all my stuff. . . . I lost everything. I don't have anything. I lost all my stuff. I can't believe I lost everything." Thomas Levesque replied, "Don't worry about it. Let's go." After leaving Media Play, the defendants walked around the mall until they left to get dinner. They returned to the mall where they first went back to Media Play to listen to more music, and then went to a Sports Authority store to get a job application. The defendants subsequently went to Regina Guthro's house where Levesque remained until the next morning. Barnes spent the night with Bruce Canty at a hotel where both Barnes and Canty viewed the ongoing warehouse fire from their hotel room window. . . .

The fire was not reported until 6:13 P.M. that evening when an emergency caller reported the fire. Sergeant O'Keefe, an expert in arson and fire investigations, stated that "the significance of the delay in reporting [the fire] ha[d] a great deal to do with what kind of fire the Worcester Fire Department got to that day." After arriving on the scene, fire fighters were informed that there might be homeless persons inside the warehouse. The fire fighters entered the warehouse in an effort to locate any persons that might have been inside, and to evaluate their tactics to combat the fire. It was during these efforts that six fire fighters went into the building and never returned. Rescuers recovered their remains during the eight days that followed. . . .

[An] investigation . . . revealed that the warehouse fire, which originated in the defendants' second-floor "makeshift" bedroom, was most likely accidental and the result of an open candle flame in contact with combustible material. [Id. at 54-55.]

The defendants managed to persuade the trial judge to quash the manslaughter indictment against them on two grounds: that they owed no duty to report the fire, and that the evidence was insufficient to demonstrate wanton and reckless conduct. Reversing, and restoring the charges, the Supreme Judicial Court quickly dismissed the claim that because the defendants started the fire accidentally, they had not undertaken any duty to remedy it by an affirmative act.

> . . . The civil law creates a specific duty that we may apply to the situation in this case. The Restatement (Second) of Torts §321 (1) (1965) reads: "If the actor does an act, and subsequently realizes or should realize that it has created an unreasonable risk of causing physical harm to another, he is under a duty to exercise reasonable care to prevent the risk from taking effect."
> . . . We agree with this principle and apply it to this case; where one's actions create a life-threatening risk to another, there is a duty to take reasonable steps to alleviate the risk. The reckless failure to fulfill this duty can result in a charge of manslaughter. [Id. at 56-57.]

Then, on the question of sufficiency of the evidence, the court ruled:

> . . . Although, in this case, the defendants apparently could not have successfully put out the fire, they could have given reasonable notice of the danger they created. It was for the grand jury (and later, the petit jury) to decide whether the defendants' failure to take additional steps was reasonable, and if not, whether the defendants' omission constituted wanton or reckless conduct.
> . . . The words "wanton" and "reckless" constitute conduct that is "different in kind" than negligence or gross negligence. [*Welansky*] at 400. It has been defined as "intentional conduct . . . involv[ing] a high degree of likelihood that substantial harm will result to another." Id. at 399. . . .
> . . . The following testimony was sufficient in this regard: the defendants attempted to put out the fire and were unsuccessful, thus demonstrating they were cognizant of the fire's rapid spread; they observed the fire consume their possessions over a short period of time; they were forced to abandon their attempts to rescue their pets, again evidencing their awareness of the peril posed by the fire's rapid spread; they possessed a cellular telephone and passed several open stores after their exit from the warehouse, thus allowing the grand jury to infer that the defendants had multiple opportunities and the means to call for help if they chose to do so. Further, the testimony that the defendants went shopping and calmly ate a meal after leaving the building refutes any suggestion that panic might explain a failure to report the fire. Finally, the fact that the defendants may have faced criminal liability for trespass had they informed authorities that they had been living in the warehouse provided a motive for their failure to report the fire.
> The defendants also assert that their conduct could not have been reckless because it was unforeseeable that such grievous harm would result to the fire fighters who responded. The Superior Court judge agreed, noting that fire fighters ordinarily do not lose their lives in the course of fighting a fire, and that even the fire fighters themselves failed to appreciate the gravity of the danger. However, an uncontrolled fire is inherently deadly to all who may come into contact with it, whether fire fighters or ordinary citizens. The defendants are charged with this knowledge. [Id. at 58-59]

Recall the discussion of omissions as the legal equivalents of acts in Chapter 2, pp. 102-105, *supra*. Is it fair to extend the categories of legal duty to act to the situation in *Levesque*? If the defendants' negligent setting of the fire was the predicate for their ultimate liability, does that mean they are essentially being punished for negligence, not "wanton and reckless" conduct? In any event, has the court made out a good case of reckless failure to report? To what risk did the defendants consciously advert? Did the court apply the same standard it had in *Welansky*?

5. *Psychology of negligence.* Often criminal negligence consists in making a catastrophic blunder. In many cases we associate this negligence — as opposed to recklessness — with colossal stupidity. One psychologist[3] who has studied the issue argues that this is not the case:

> Two years ago, during NATO training exercises over West Germany, the pilot of a Royal Air Force Phantom jet accidentally fired a live Sidewinder missile at a Royal Air Force Jaguar. The Jaguar pilot parachuted safely to earth, but his twelve-million-dollar aircraft was destroyed. Earlier that same year, the top deck of a double-decker bus traveling on a country road in south Wales was sheared off when the driver tried to pass under a low bridge. Six passengers died in the accident. And in 1977, the pilot of a Boeing 747 jumbo jet, about to make the short hop from Santa Cruz, on the island of Tenerife, to Las Palmas, on the island of Gran Canaria, off the coast of northwest Africa, failed to wait for takeoff clearance from the control tower. Roaring down the tarmac at a speed of 150 miles an hour, the plane crashed into another 747 still taxiing on the runway. Of the 637 passengers and crew aboard the two craft, 577 were killed.
>
> There is a natural tendency to suppose that disasters such as these are the product of some rare species of monumental blunder, but the evidence suggests otherwise. In fact, the mental errors that lead to horrendous accidents are indistinguishable in nature from the trivial, absentminded slips and lapses of everyday life. The true hallmark of absentminded errors, whatever their consequences, is not inexperience or ineptitude but misapplied competence — habit gone wrong, in a sense. . . .
>
> It seems clear from our close examination of slips and lapses that whenever thoughts, words, or actions depart from their planned course, they tend to go in the direction of something familiar, expected, and in keeping with existing knowledge structures. Or, more briefly: errors tend to be more conservative than intentions — and the more frequently a particular routine is set in motion and achieves the desired outcome, the more likely it is to recur unbidden at the wrong time, as a slip of habit. William James likened habits to flywheels: once set in motion, they require little additional effort to keep them going. But habits are hard to control.
>
> These findings underscore a crucial point about absentminded errors: they are characteristic of highly skilled activities — a problem of the expert, not the beginner. That seems to run contrary to common sense, since people expend a great deal of effort to acquire skills so that they will not make mistakes. Yet, paradoxically, the probability of making an absentminded error increases with proficiency at a particular task. The more skilled we become at an activity, the fewer demands it makes upon consciousness. . . .

Should the pilots and driver described above be treated as criminals? How do their "professional" disastrous errors compare to the following one? Is the father's obviously sincere reaction to the child's death relevant to his liability?

---

3. James Reason, The Psychopathology of Everyday Slips, The Sciences 45, 48, 49 (Sept./Oct. 1984).

No Charges for Prof in Baby's Hot Death[4]

Prosecutors have decided not to file criminal charges against a Wayne State University assistant professor whose 5-month-old son died in a hot minivan while he taught a class.

Assistant Prosecutor Nancy Diehl said today 47-year-old Thomas Fungwe may have been negligent for forgetting the baby in the back seat of his parked van for nearly five hours but did not commit "gross negligence" and cannot be charged with involuntary manslaughter.

Before leaving the baby in the van and locking it, the father had dropped off two older sons at a day camp. The baby was supposed to be dropped off at a daycare center but instead Fungwe forgot about him and went to class at the university's Detroit campus.

Later in the day passersby tried to reach the baby. By the time Fungwe arrived, it was too late.

Police said Thorence Fungwe's body temperature exceeded 108 degrees when he arrived at a hospital and was pronounced dead on arrival.

A university spokesman says the professor was "absent-minded" and grief-stricken.

2. Involuntary Manslaughter in Contemporary Settings

STATE v. WILLIAMS
Court of Appeals of Washington
484 P.2d 1167 (1971)

HOROWITZ, CHIEF JUDGE.

Defendants, husband and wife, were charged by information filed October 3, 1968, with the crime of manslaughter for negligently failing to supply their 17-month-old child with necessary medical attention, as a result of which he died on September 12, 1968. Upon entry of findings, conclusions and judgment of guilty, sentences were imposed on April 22, 1969. Defendants appeal.

The defendant husband, Walter Williams, is a 24-year-old full-blooded Sheshont Indian with a sixth-grade education. His sole occupation is that of laborer. The defendant wife, Bernice Williams, is a 20-year-old part Indian with an eleventh-grade education. At the time of the marriage, the wife had two children, the younger of whom was a 14-month-old son. Both parents worked and the children were cared for by the 85-year-old mother of the defendant husband. The defendant husband assumed parental responsibility with the defendant wife to provide clothing, care and medical attention for the child. Both defendants possessed a great deal of love and affection for the defendant wife's young son.

The court expressly found:

> That both defendants were aware that William Joseph Tabafunda was ill during the period September 1, 1968, to September 12, 1968. The defendants were ignorant. They did not realize how sick the baby was. They thought that the baby had a toothache and no layman regards a toothache as dangerous to life. They loved the baby and gave him aspirin in hopes of improving its condition. They did not take the baby to a doctor because of fear that the Welfare Department would take the baby away from them. They knew that medical help was available because of

4. UPI, July 27, 1999.

previous experience. They had no excuse for not taking the baby to a doctor. The defendants Walter L. Williams and Bernice J. Williams were negligent in not seeking medical attention for William Joseph Tabafunda.

That as a proximate result of this negligence, William Joseph Tabafunda died. . . .

Defendants take no exception to findings but contend that the findings do not support the conclusions that the defendants are guilty of manslaughter as charged. . . .

. . . On the question of the quality or seriousness of breach of the duty, at common law, in the case of involuntary manslaughter, the breach had to amount to more than mere ordinary or simple negligence — gross negligence was essential. In Washington, however, RCW 9.48.060 . . . and RCW 9.48.150 supersede both voluntary and involuntary manslaughter as those crimes were defined at common law. Under these statutes the crime is deemed committed even though the death of the victim is the proximate result of only simple or ordinary negligence.

The concept of simple or ordinary negligence describes a failure to exercise the "ordinary caution" necessary to make out the defense of excusable homicide. Ordinary caution is the kind of caution that a man of reasonable prudence would exercise under the same or similar conditions. If, therefore, the conduct of a defendant, regardless of his ignorance, good intentions and good faith, fails to measure up to the conduct required of a man of reasonable prudence, he is guilty of ordinary negligence because of his failure to use "ordinary caution." If such negligence proximately causes the death of the victim, the defendant, as pointed out above, is guilty of statutory manslaughter. . . .

. . . The law does not mandatorily require that a doctor be called for a child at the first sign of any indisposition or illness. The indisposition or illness may appear to be of a minor or very temporary kind, such as a toothache or cold. If one in the exercise of ordinary caution fails to recognize that his child's symptoms require medical attention, it cannot be said that the failure to obtain such medical attention is a breach of the duty owed. In our opinion, the duty as formulated in People v. Pierson, 176 N.Y. 201, 68 N.E. 243 (1903) . . . properly defines the duty contemplated by our manslaughter statutes. The court there said:

> We quite agree that the Code does not contemplate the necessity of calling a physician for every trifling complaint with which the child may be afflicted, which in most instances may be overcome by the ordinary household nursing by members of the family; that a reasonable amount of discretion is vested in parents, charged with the duty of maintaining and bringing up infant children; and that the standard is at what time would an ordinarily prudent person, solicitous for the welfare of his child and anxious to promote its recovery, deem it necessary to call in the services of a physician.

It remains to apply the law discussed to the facts of the instant case. . . . Because of the serious nature of the charge against the parent and stepparent of a well-loved child, and out of our concern for the protection of the constitutional rights of the defendants, we have made an independent examination of the evidence to determine whether it substantially supports the court's express finding on proximate cause and its implied finding that the duty to furnish medical care became activated in time to prevent death of the child.

Dr. Gale Wilson, the autopsy surgeon and chief pathologist for the King County Coroner, testified that the child died because an abscessed tooth had been allowed to develop into an infection of the mouth and cheeks, eventually becoming gangrenous. This condition, accompanied by the child's inability to eat, brought about malnutrition, lowering the child's resistance and eventually producing pneumonia, causing the death. Dr. Wilson testified that in his opinion the infection had lasted for approximately 2 weeks, and that the odor generally associated with gangrene would have been present for approximately 10 days before death. He also expressed the opinion that had medical care been first obtained in the last week before the baby's death, such care would have been obtained too late to have saved the baby's life. Accordingly, the baby's apparent condition between September 1 and September 5, 1968, became the critical period for the purpose of determining whether in the exercise of ordinary caution defendants should have provided medical care for the minor child.

The testimony concerning the child's apparent condition during the critical period is not crystal clear, but is sufficient to warrant the following statement of the matter. The defendant husband testified that he noticed the baby was sick about 2 weeks before the baby died. The defendant wife testified that she noticed the baby was ill about a week and a half or 2 weeks before the baby died. The evidence showed that in the critical period the baby was fussy; that he could not keep his food down; and that a cheek started swelling up. The swelling went up and down, but did not disappear. In that same period, the cheek turned "a bluish color like." The defendants, not realizing that the baby was as ill as it was or that the baby was in danger of dying, attempted to provide some relief to the baby by giving the baby aspirin during the critical period and continued to do so until the night before the baby died. The defendants thought the swelling would go down and were waiting for it to do so; and defendant husband testified, that from what he had heard, neither doctors nor dentists pull out a tooth "when it's all swollen up like that." There was an additional explanation for not calling a doctor given by each defendant. Defendant husband testified that "the way the cheek looked . . . and that stuff on his hair, they would think we were neglecting him and take him away from us and not give him back." Defendant wife testified that the defendants were "waiting for the swelling to go down," and also that they were afraid to take the child to a doctor for fear that the doctor would report them to the welfare department, who, in turn, would take the child away. "It's just that I was so scared of losing him." They testified that they had heard that the defendant husband's cousin lost a child that way. The evidence showed that the defendants did not understand the significance or seriousness of the baby's symptoms. However, there is no evidence that the defendants were physically or financially unable to obtain a doctor, or that they did not know an available doctor, or that the symptoms did not continue to be a matter of concern during the critical period. Indeed, the evidence shows that in April 1968, defendant husband had taken the child to a doctor for medical attention.

In our opinion, there is sufficient evidence from which the court could find, as it necessarily did, that applying the standard of ordinary caution, i.e., the caution exercisable by a man of reasonable prudence under the same or similar conditions, defendants were sufficiently put on notice concerning the symptoms of the baby's illness and lack of improvement in the baby's apparent condition in the period from September 1 to September 5, 1968, to have required them to have obtained medical care for the child. The failure so to do in this case is ordinary or simple negligence, and such negligence is sufficient to support a conviction of statutory manslaughter.

The judgment is affirmed.

Notes and Questions

1. What is the legal standard the court applies here? Would the defendants be guilty of manslaughter under the Model Penal Code? Would they be guilty of anything else?

Consider the question of timing and causation in *Williams,* examining the sequence of the baby's symptoms and the pathologist's report. Could the defendants have argued that by the time they could have reasonably been expected to bring the baby to the doctor, it would have been too late for medical science to save the baby anyway?

2. *The reasonable person in social context.* Is it relevant that the defendants were members of an insular minority that has suffered discrimination in the United States? Should the same standard of care be applied to them as to members of the country's dominant mainstream? Does the stated standard of care need changing, or does some other aspect of the court's approach? What would be the consequences if the standard of care were to vary with the characteristics of the defendant?

Can the *Williams* case be decided without the following information? William Byler, executive director of the Association on American Indian Affairs, Inc., writes,[5]

> Surveys of States with large Indian populations conducted by the Association on American Indian Affairs (AAIA) in 1969 and again in 1974 indicate that approximately 25-35 percent of all Indian children are separated from their families and placed in foster homes, adoptive homes, or institutions. . . .
>
> The disparity in placement rates for Indian[s] and non-Indians is shocking. . . . In the State of Washington, the Indian adoption rate is 19 times greater and the foster care rate 10 times greater [than for non-Indians, i.e., Indian children are much more likely to be taken from their families than other children, while Indians are usually placed with non-Indian foster care or adoptive families]. . . .
>
> How are we to account for this disastrous situation? The reasons . . . include a lack of rational Federal and State standards governing child welfare matters, a breakdown in due process, economic incentives, and the harsh social conditions in so many Indian communities. . . .
>
> . . . Very few Indian children are removed from their families on the grounds of physical abuse. . . .
>
> In judging the fitness of a particular family, many social workers, ignorant of Indian cultural values and social norms, . . . frequently discover neglect or abandonment where none exists.
>
> For example, the dynamics of the Indian extended families are largely misunderstood. An Indian child may have scores of, perhaps more than a hundred, relatives who are counted as close, responsible members of the family. Many social workers . . . consider leaving the child with persons outside the nuclear family as neglect and thus as grounds for terminating parental rights. . . .

5. Removing Children: The Destruction of American Indian Families, 9 Civil Rights 19 (Summer 1977).

. . . [In one case,] social workers asserted that, although they had no evidence that the mother was unfit, it was their belief that an Indian reservation is an unsuitable environment for a child and that the pre-adoptive parents were financially able to provide a home and a way of life superior to the one furnished by the natural mother. . . .

The abusive actions of social workers would largely be nullified if more judges were themselves knowledgeable about Indian life and required a sharper definition of the standards of child abuse and neglect. . . .

. . . It is an unfortunate fact of life for many Indian parents that the primary service agency to which they must turn for financial help also exercises police powers over their family life and is, most frequently, the agency that initiates custody proceedings. . . .[6]

The parents in Byler's article seem to be blameless. Are the system's abuses relevant to the parents in *Williams*?

3. Recall the case of Commonwealth v. Twitchell, discussed in Chapter 3, *supra*, p. 226. Do religious beliefs have special immunity from manslaughter prosecution, where ignorance does not?

4. The *Williams* court notes the somewhat unusual standard of "simple" or "ordinary" negligence for involuntary manslaughter under Washington law, as opposed to the more common "gross negligence" or recklessness. For a survey and analysis of how states array themselves around this distinction, see Leslie Yalof Garfield, A More Principled Approach to Criminalizing Negligence: A Prescription for the Legislature, 65 Tenn. L. Rev. 875 (1998).

5. *Medical manslaughter.* Diagnosed in 1951 as having tuberculosis, Roger Mozian died of the illness in 1963. With treatment by a medical doctor, the disease had remained dormant for ten years but then re-arose. When his doctor recommended hospitalization and drug treatment, Mozian instead sought treatment from Dr. Gian-Cursio, a New York–licensed chiropractic physician who practiced "natural hygiene." Having been advised that Mozian had tuberculosis, Dr. Gian-Cursio treated the patient with a vegetarian diet and fasting. In the winter of 1962, he sent Mozian to a licensed chiropractor in Florida for similar treatment. In May 1963, Mozian was hospitalized and treated with "drugs and other approved treatment" but died within days. There was testimony that if Mozian had received approved medical care instead of the treatment provided by the chiropractic physicians, his disease could have been controlled. Upholding the conviction, the court stated that

criminal negligence exists where the physician or surgeon, or person assuming to act as such, exhibits gross lack of competency, or gross inattention, or criminal indifference to the patient's safety. . . . [T]his may arise from his gross ignorance of the science of medicine or surgery and of the effect of the remedies employed, through his gross negligence in the application and selection of remedies and his lack of proper skill in the use of instruments, or through his failure to give proper instructions to the patient as to the use of medicines. . . . [Gian-Cursio v. State,

6. [Congress responded to these problems by enacting the Indian Child Welfare Act of 1978, 25 U.S.C. §§1901-63. Congress found "that an alarmingly high percentage of Indian families are broken up by the removal, often unwarranted, of their children from them by nontribal public and private agencies and that an alarmingly high percentage of such children are placed in non-Indian foster and adoptive homes and institutions. . . ." §1901(4). The law was meant to establish minimum federal standards for the removal of Indian children and to assure that any necessary placements of the children would "reflect the unique values of Indian culture." §1902. — Eds.]

180 So. 2d 396, 399 (Fla. Dist. Ct. App. 1965, quoting Hampton v. State, 39 So. 2d 421, 424 (Fla. 1905))]

Were the chiropractic physicians criminally negligent? Is it significant that they were state-licensed in their field? Does it matter that Mozian chose of his own free will the treatment he wanted?

6. *Hazing.* Journalists regularly provide reports like the following, which can be pressed into the reckless/negligent homicide mold.

Midnight Hazing Exercise Proves Fatal at Texas A&M[7]

College Station, Texas (AP) — Despite a memo ordering a halt to such hazing, a cadet member of a Texas A&M University military corps group was rousted from his bed and forced to perform "motivational exercise" until he suffered fatal heat stroke, it was announced Friday.

. . . [Bruce] Goodrich and his roommate, John McIntosh, were awakened at 2:30 A.M. Thursday by three juniors in their unit of the corps who took them out for . . . nearly an hour of running, push-ups and sit-ups in 77 degree temperatures and 79 percent humidity, officials said. . . .

The three students overseeing the exercises could be suspended or expelled if they are found guilty of violating university policy. . . .

Goodrich's heart had stopped and his body temperature was 104 degrees when he was taken by police to St. Joseph Hospital . . . after McIntosh, who was not injured, could not revive him. Goodrich died at the hospital later Thursday.

"This was a most unfortunate accident — a tragedy — and I know that no one regrets it more than those involved. Their grief is, of course, shared by all of us," A&M President Frank E. Vandiver said in a prepared statement. . . .

Col. Donald Burton, commandant of the Corps of Cadets, said he specifically outlawed such exercises in orders issued in January 1983.

"The majority of this stuff was indeed knocked off," he said. "But periodically, you'll always have some cadet who tries to get it started again. If something positive doesn't come of this [death], we're damned fools."

Bob Wiatt, director of security and traffic for Texas A&M, said he expected to offer evidence to a grand jury for investigation. The panel likely would be asked to consider charges of involuntary manslaughter or negligent homicide, he said. . . .

Should the reasonable person expect less than an hour of exercise to kill a military cadet?

The majority of states now have laws against hazing. Texas's law, enacted in 1987, defines hazing as "including but not limited to . . . any type of physical activity, such as sleep deprivation, exposure to the elements, confinement in a small space, calisthenics, or other activity that subjects the student to an unreasonable risk of harm or that adversely affects the mental or physical health or safety of the student." Tex. Educ. Code Ann. §§37.151 (Vernon 1996). Recognizing the influence of peer pressure, the legislature provided that consent by the victim is not a defense. Violation resulting in death is a misdemeanor, punishable by a fine of $5,000 to $10,000, one to two years in jail, or both. The law specifically "does not affect or repeal any penal law of this state." §37.156. Does this law fill a gap in the criminal law? Does it just give the prosecutor a "sure" conviction, as an alternative to the harsher manslaughter charge?

7. *Hunting.* Consider this story.

7. Peninsula Times Tribune, Sept. 1, 1984, at A-6.

A Death in Mount Hermon[8]

It's not hard to believe that Donald Rogerson thought he might find deer . . . when he and a companion decided to go hunting. . . . Then again, it's not hard to believe he might have found a house in the forest before he found a deer. . . .

As it turns out, Rogerson, 45, did find a house in the woods, and a bullet from his rifle found the owner of that house [37-year-old Karen Ann Wood] as she walked in her backyard. . . . [A] grand jury's subsequent failure to indict Rogerson for manslaughter [has triggered vigorous] . . . public debate. . . .

[The fact that the victim was wearing white mittens became a key piece of evidence in that debate.] . . . [A] Maine warden at the scene told a reporter that, along with the absence of any blaze orange on the victim, the mittens could have been mistaken for the white tail of a deer. . . .

[A] friend of the Wood family . . . [said], "The most abhorrent aspect of the reporting has been the insinuation that somehow Karen shares the blame for her death. . . . One could get the impression from reports that she was wearing antlers and a target as she walked deep in the woods."

Frederick Badger, the Wood family attorney, . . . cites factors other than "blame the victim" for the refusal of the grand jury to indict Rogerson. One is an attitude by natives toward people from out-of-state (the Wood family had moved to the Bangor area from Iowa and upstate New York) that makes them second-class citizens. . . .

Another factor, Badger believes, was the news coverage on the day after the shooting that portrayed the remorseful Rogerson, a grocery store produce manager, as a loving father, scoutmaster, and conscientious worker. "If Mr. Rogerson had been an unemployed carpenter, I think he would have been indicted," Badger says. "His remorse is no comparison to the loss suffered by the family. Nice people and fine people can be neglectful."

Lewis Vafiades, Rogerson's attorney, [says], . . . "We had evidence that he was in a lawful area, he was not aware of the house, and that he actually shot at a deer. . . . He says he did see a deer and there had been a couple of deer in the area."

Warden Sgt. Sargent says he is not permitted to discuss evidence in the case, including whether investigators found evidence of deer . . . in the vicinity where Karen Wood was shot. Sources close to the attorney general's case, however, . . . [note that if deer tracks or droppings had been found nearby, it] might have resulted in a lesser charge than manslaughter being filed. . . .

One attorney who was skeptical about the handling of the case says it is rare for a grand jury in Maine not to return an indictment. "There's an old saying that a grand jury will indict a ham sandwich if a prosecutor asks them to," he said. "A hunter who shoots at a target he can't positively identify seems like a prima facie case of criminal negligence."

. . . [S]everal private attorneys noted that prosecutors could return with a lesser charge of assault with a deadly weapon . . . [or] come back to a different grand jury and try again for a manslaughter indictment.[9]

Of course, even apart from the hunting context, guns are frequently involved in involuntary manslaughter cases. Is there definitionally some level of

8. Wilson, A Death in Mount Hermon, Maine Times, Dec. 16, 1988, §1, at 8.
9. Update: On December 8, 1989, one year after the first grand jury refused to indict Rogerson, a second grand jury did in fact indict him for manslaughter. Deer Hunter Is Indicted in Accidental Killing of Woman in Maine, New York Times, Dec. 9, 1989, at 11. The local media reported that the first grand jury's action may have been due to the presence on it of the nephew of Rogerson's lawyer. Prosecutors said that they found no evidence of bias but that they refiled the case merely to negate any public inference of bias. The indictment left Rogerson facing a maximum sentence of 20 years if convicted. He went to trial and was acquitted on October 17, 1990.

culpability when someone points a gun at a person and pulls the trigger? Is it always reckless, always negligent, or sometimes neither? Of what significance is a defendant's belief that the gun is not loaded? Does a defendant have to examine the gun immediately before shooting to verify that it is unloaded? What if the person shooting does not know how to tell if a gun is loaded — does that augment or excuse negligence? For what, if anything, should parents/guardians be criminally liable when young children kill with the accessible family gun? Consider the following tragedy:[10]

> [Nine-year-old Derrick "Kye" Smith] was passing the afternoon at his grandparents' while his mother worked as a nurse's aide. He and a cousin were sitting on a sofa studying baseball cards when his two-year-old brother toddled into the room with a revolver picked up from a dresser elsewhere in the house. Sensing danger, another cousin, also 9, grabbed the gun. It fired, and the bullet struck Kye. He was dead on arrival at a local hospital.

Recall from Chapter 2 the discussion of liability for omission of a duty, pp. 102-105, *supra*. Is there a duty to keep guns and children apart? What could be the charge in such a case? Would the purpose of charging grieving family members be deterrence, or something else?

8. *Skiing*. Skiing accidents began to emerge in the 1990s as another new context for involuntary manslaughter prosecutions. In State v. Hall, 999 P.2d 207 (Colo. 2000), the Colorado Supreme Court held that Nathan Hall had to stand trial for the death of Alan Cobb, with whom Hall, then 18 years old, collided at a Vail resort in 1997.

> Several witnesses stated that Hall was skiing very fast. Allen and the other eyewitnesses all said that Hall was travelling too fast for the conditions, at an excessive rate of speed, and that he was out of control. Allen said that Hall passed him on the slope travelling three times faster than Allen, himself an expert skier. Sandberg presented testimony that Hall was a ski racer, indicating that Hall was trained to attain and ski at much faster speeds than even skilled and experienced recreational skiers. The witnesses said that Hall was travelling straight down the slope at such high speeds that, because of his lack of control, he would not have been able to stop or avoid another person.
>   . . . The coroner said that although he could not estimate Hall's speed from Cobb's injuries, Hall must have been travelling with "a significant amount of speed" to generate sufficient force to cause a basal skull fracture and brain injuries like Cobb's. Additionally, Hall crashed through [another skier's] skis and poles after he struck Cobb — breaking one of the poles in half — indicating a very high speed and great deal of force. Hall came to rest over eighty feet past Cobb's body, further suggesting that Hall was skiing at exceptionally high speeds. . . .
>   In addition to Hall's excessive speed, Hall was out of control and unable to avoid a collision with another person. All the witnesses said Hall was not traversing the slope and that he was skiing straight down the fall line. Hall was back on his skis, with his ski tips in the air and his arms out to his sides to maintain balance. Allen said that Hall was bounced around by the moguls on the slope rather than skiing in control and managing the bumps. Hall admitted to Deputy Mossness that he first saw Cobb when he was airborne and that he was unable to stop when he saw people below him just before the collision. Hence, in addition to finding that Hall was skiing at a very high rate of speed, a reasonably prudent person could have

10. Death by Gun, Time 30, 46 (July 17, 1988).

concluded that Hall was unable to anticipate or avoid a potential collision with a skier on the trail below him.

While skiing ordinarily carries a very low risk of death to other skiers, a reasonable person could have concluded that Hall's excessive speed, lack of control, and improper technique for skiing bumps significantly increased both the likelihood that a collision would occur and the extent of the injuries that might result from such a collision, including the possibility of death, in the event that a person like Cobb unwittingly crossed Hall's downhill path. [A detective] testified that he was aware of only two other deaths from skier collisions on Vail mountain in the past eleven years, but a reasonable person could have determined that Hall's conduct was precisely the type of skiing that risked this rare result.

We next ask whether a reasonable person could have concluded that Hall's creation of a substantial risk of death was unjustified. To the extent that Hall's extremely fast and unsafe skiing created a risk of death, Hall was serving no direct interest other than his own enjoyment. Although the sport often involves high speeds and even moments where a skier is temporarily out of control, a reasonable person could determine that the enjoyment of skiing does not justify skiing at the speeds and with the lack of control Hall exhibited. Thus, a reasonable person could have found that Hall's creation of a substantial risk was unjustifiable. . . .

. . . A violation of a skier's duty in an extreme fashion, such as here, may be evidence of conduct that constitutes a "gross deviation" from the standard of care imposed by statute for civil negligence. Hall admitted to Deputy Mossness that as he flew off a knoll, he saw people below him but was unable to stop; Hall was travelling so fast and with so little control that he could not possibly have respected his obligation to avoid skiers below him on the slope. Additionally, Hall skied in this manner for some time over a considerable distance, demonstrating that his high speeds and lack of control were not the type of momentary lapse of control or inherent danger associated with skiing. Based on the evidence, a reasonable person could conclude that Hall's conduct was a gross deviation from the standard of care that a reasonable, experienced ski racer would have exercised knowing that other people were on the slope in front of him and that he could not see the area below the knolls and bumps over which he was jumping. . . .

[W]e next ask whether a reasonably prudent person could have entertained the belief that Hall consciously disregarded that risk. Hall is a trained ski racer who had been coached about skiing in control and skiing safely. Further, he was an employee of a ski area and had a great deal of skiing experience. Hall's knowledge and training could give rise to the reasonable inference that he was aware of the possibility that by skiing so fast and out of control he might collide with and kill another skier unless he regained control and slowed down. . . .

Although the risk that he would cause the death of another was probably slight, Hall's conduct created a risk of death. Hall's collision with Cobb involved enough force to kill Cobb and to simulate the type of head injury associated with victims in car accidents. Even though it is a rare occurrence, the court heard testimony that two skiers in the past eleven years died on Vail mountain alone from skier-to-skier collisions. . . . [Id. at 222-224]

By the court's reasoning, would a person of lesser training and expertise but otherwise skiing the same way have been guilty of manslaughter? At trial, Hall was acquitted on the manslaughter charge but convicted of the lesser crime of negligent homicide. Was it fair for the jury to infer that Hall had not adverted to the risk of death?[11]

11. Hall, who had faced up to six years in prison, was sentenced to 90 days in jail, ordered to perform 240 hours of public service and barred from drinking alcohol and engaging in any recreational skiing as part of a probationary term. Jean Hellwege, Trial, Feb. 2001, at 1. Does this sentence seem commensurate with the conviction? With Hall's actual conduct?

What effect might prosecutions like that of Hall have on the ski industry? On other recreational sports and industries?

9. *Vehicular homicide.* The automobile is now so common in our society — as are car-related fatalities — that many states have defined a category of criminal homicide less severe than involuntary manslaughter, or even less severe than negligent homicide, for those who accidentally kill while operating an automobile. In support of such laws, some argue that invoking the general manslaughter principle would expose too large a percentage of the population to the risk of prosecution for a very serious crime. No doubt legislators realize that they would be among the people exposed to criminal liability. Reckless or negligent killings by car may be the form of homicide most likely to cross class lines — stiff laws would not be for "them," but for all of us.

Of course, a hugely overwhelming majority of negligent homicide cases involve automobiles. But because driving is a routine part of most of our lives, and because people naturally tend to identify with the occasionally careless driver, juries are often loath to convict even a grossly negligent driver of manslaughter, a crime whose very name suggests violent criminality. Therefore, many states have enacted statutes with lesser penalties and less stigmatic names to increase the likelihood that *some* punishment will be meted out in cases of vehicular homicide.

Another justification for such a statute is that, unlike many other kinds of negligent conduct that do not result in death, negligent driving is punishable even if no one is killed or injured. Thus, the entire burden of deterring grossly negligent conduct does not have to fall on those whose negligence in fact causes a death. On the other hand, does the likelihood of only a misdemeanor penalty for drunk driving (when no injuries occur) teach that such behavior is not really considered dangerous, rather than deterring a broad class of potentially dangerous drivers?

Vehicular homicide falls under the negligent homicide section of the Model Penal Code. Comment 4 to §210.4 defends the decision not to have a separate vehicular homicide section:[12]

> . . . [T]he structure of the Model Code homicide offenses obviates any necessity for special treatment of vehicular homicide. The case for such legislation arose in the first instance from the indiscriminate punishment of both reckless and negligent homicide as the serious crime of manslaughter. Under Section 210.4, this problem is solved by punishing all forms of negligent homicide as an offense of lesser grade. Furthermore, as is explained in the commentary to Section 2.02, the Model Code is opposed in principle to the imposition of criminal sanctions for ordinary negligence. If the evidence does not make out a case of negligent homicide, as defined in the Model Code, liability for the homicide, as distinct from the traffic offense, is unwarranted.

Consider Porter v. State, 88 So. 2d 924 (Fla. 1956):

> The accident resulting in the death of the decedent occurred at 9:30 A.M. on a Saturday morning at a street intersection on the outskirts of the city of Bradenton, but apparently outside the city limits. The appellant was proceeding north on a street which was well marked with "stop" signs prior to its intersection with the street upon which the decedent was travelling in a westerly direction, and which

12. Model Penal Code and Commentaries, *supra,* at 90.

was marked only with a "slow" sign. The right front of appellant's car collided with the left front and side of decedent's car. There was ample evidence from which the jury could find that the appellant was driving at the rate of 60 or 65 miles per hour and did not stop before entering the intersection. [Id. at 974]

The state Supreme Court reversed the conviction, finding insufficient evidence of gross negligence to support the verdict. One judge stated:

> The accident occurred outside the city limits on a country road in the daylight. There is no evidence in the record establishing the speed limit in this area so we must presume that it was sixty miles per hour. The evidence in the light most favorable to the State establishes the speed of the car at about sixty miles per hour. The driver was perfectly sober and there is no suggestion to the contrary. The sole evidence of reckless driving is that he failed to stop or slow down at a stop street which crossed the highway on which he was travelling. The record shows there was a stop sign on the right side of the road 112 feet from the intersection but there is no evidence in the record that the defendant had ever traversed this road before or was familiar with the locality.
>
> To sustain the conviction of the defendant in this case is tantamount to holding that if a person is killed because of the failure of a driver of an automobile to stop at a stop sign, such conduct constitutes in itself negligence of such gross and flagrant character that it evinces a reckless disregard of human life.
>
> There are few, if any, of us who have not through momentary lapse of attention — particularly on strange roads — been guilty of traversing stop streets without slowing down. Such, no doubt, constitutes such negligence as to support a damage action, but I do not think it was ever intended that negligence of that kind was sufficient to support a verdict of manslaughter. [Id. at 926]

Should a driver who ignores a stop sign at over 60 miles per hour escape criminal liability for a death caused by his driving? Would a manslaughter charge have been more appropriate if Porter had been drunk? If the accident had happened at night? If Porter had been in his own neighborhood? Why?

Alcohol-related car accidents quickly followed the development of the automobile. Courts considered resultant manslaughter convictions without the help of specific vehicular homicide statutes, e.g., Williams v. State, 161 Miss. 406 (1931) ("To drive an automobile on a public street or highway while intoxicated is prohibited . . . , and is therefore negligence in any case; is culpable if the intoxication of the driver is such as to render him incapable of driving the automobile with the care essential to the safety of persons then in the automobile and of others on or near the street or highway; and at common law . . . a homicide of which it is the direct and proximate cause is manslaughter.") Of course, most states now have statutes dealing directly with drunk-driving homicide, *e.g.,* Model Penal Code §191.5 (1999): "[G]ross vehicular manslaughter [is] the unlawful killing of a human being without malice aforethought, in the driving of a vehicle, where the driving was in violation of Section 23152 [driving under the influence] . . . and the killing was . . . the proximate result of the commission of an unlawful act, not amounting to a felony, and with gross negligence." If a drunk driver, staying in her lane, drives 50 miles per hour in a 45 mile-per-hour zone and strikes a pedestrian who surprisingly and foolishly darted out from between parked cars, should the statute apply?

Mothers Against Drunk Driving and similar lobbyists have argued that intoxicated drivers who kill should be charged with murder, not manslaughter.

This new category of murder prosecution is discussed later in this chapter, *infra,* pp. 390-392.

8. *Seat belts and homicide.* A new twist has been added in recent years to the vehicular manslaughter arena with the adoption of seat belt laws in many states. Consider the following story:[13]

> In a rare prosecution, the father of a 6-year-old boy killed in a car crash was charged with manslaughter because the youngster wasn't wearing a seat belt.
>
> The case was proceeding because an example needs to be made — parents are responsible for the safety of their children, the prosecutor said.
>
> Walter G. Sylvia Jr. of Acton was driving his son, Michael, to school when he lost control of his auto on a winding road near Santa Clarita. The vehicle flipped twice and Michael was killed.
>
> Authorities say Sylvia, 49, was going too fast and that the boy would have lived had he worn a seat belt.
>
> "I don't understand why they are doing this to me," Sylvia said last week. "I don't know what they hope to accomplish." . . . .
>
> "The point is to be made to all parents that it is your responsibility that your child is buckled in — no matter how much they fight, kick, scream," Davis-Springer said.
>
> Sylvia later told California Highway Patrol officers that about 25 minutes into the trip, Michael unbuckled his seat belt to push back his seat and cover himself with a blanket. At that moment, Sylvia lost control of his Honda Civic. Michael was thrown from the car and died about an hour later.
>
> Sylvia insists that he lost control while trying to avoid a passing car that had cut him off. The CHP said there is no evidence another car was involved.
>
> Sylvia said he has been devastated by the loss of his youngest son and cannot comprehend why charges have been filed against him. . . .

What was Sylvia's crime? Was it placing Michael in the car? What if Sylvia had not buckled Michael in correctly? Did the prosecutor really think that a one-year jail sentence would act as a greater deterrent to others than the loss of a 6-year-old son? Why else would she attempt to prosecute this case? (Eventually, the charges against Sylvia were dropped.)

In Commonwealth v. Mitchell, 41 S.W.3d 434 (Ky. 2001), the defendant was convicted of reckless homicide and sentenced to a year in prison after his daughter was thrown from the family car during an accident. Mitchell had placed the infant in a car seat that was neither secured to the automobile nor buckled, and the accident occurred when he did not yield the right of way to an oncoming pickup truck. To establish the "gross deviation" component of the homicide charge, the prosecution thought it sufficient to rely on the Kentucky Seatbelt Statute, which required children to be strapped in. The court reversed the conviction, noting that under the statute a violation cannot establish civil liability or contributory negligence in tort cases, and is punishable only by a $50 fine. Could the prosecutor have proved reckless homicide despite the limitations in the statute? Would it actually have been easier for the prosecutor to win such a case if the legislature had never enacted a statute requiring seat belts for children?

13. San Jose Mercury News (AP) (Oct. 15, 1990, at 6B).

B.   RECKLESS MURDER

MAYES v. THE PEOPLE
Supreme Court of Illinois
106 Ill. 306, 46 Am. Rep. 698 (1883)

MR. JUSTICE SCHOLFIELD delivered the opinion of the Court: Plaintiff in error, by the judgment of the court below, was convicted of the crime of murder, and sentenced to the penitentiary for the term of his natural life. . . .

It is contended the facts proved do not constitute murder. They are, briefly, these: The deceased was the wife of plaintiff in error, and came to her death by burning, resulting from plaintiff in error throwing a beer glass against a lighted oil lamp which she was carrying, and thereby breaking the lamp and scattering the burning oil over her person. Plaintiff in error came into the room where his wife, his mother-in-law and his young daughter were seated around a table engaged in domestic labors, about nine o'clock at night. He had been at a saloon nearby, and was, to some extent, intoxicated, — not, however, to the degree of unconsciousness, for he testifies to a consciousness and recollection of all that occurred. When he sat down, the deceased, noticing that one side of his face was dirty, asked him if he had fallen down. He replied that it was none of her business. She then directed the daughter to procure water for him with which to wash his face, which being done, he washed his face, and he then directed the daughter to procure him a clean beer glass, which she did. He had brought some beer with him from the saloon, and he then proceeded to fill the glass with the beer and handed it to the deceased. She took a sup of it, and then offered it to her mother, who declined tasting it. The deceased then brought plaintiff in error his supper, but he declined eating it, and was about to throw a loaf of bread at the deceased when she took it from his hands and returned it to the cupboard. After this, having sat quietly for a few minutes, he asked for arsenic. No reply was made to this request, and thereupon he commenced cursing, and concluded by saying that he would either kill deceased or she should kill him. He wanted a fire made, but deceased told him it was bed time and they did not need any fire. He then picked up a tin quart measure and threw it at the daughter. Thereupon deceased started, with an oil lamp in her hand, toward a bed-room door, directing the daughter to go to bed, and as the deceased and daughter were advancing toward the bed-room door, he picked up the beer glass, which is described as being a large beer glass, with a handle on one side, and threw it with violence at the deceased. It struck the lamp in her hand and broke it, scattering the burning oil over her person and igniting her clothes. Plaintiff in error made no effort to extinguish the flames, but seems to have caught hold of the deceased, temporarily, by her arms. This occurred on Monday night, and on Saturday of that week she died of the wounds caused by this burning.

The plaintiff in error claims that he was only intending to pitch the beer glass out of doors — that he did not design hitting the deceased, and that the striking of the lamp was therefore purely an accident. In this he is positively contradicted by his daughter and mother-in-law, the only witnesses of the tragedy besides himself. He says, to give plausibility to his story, that the door leading into the yard was open, and that deceased and daughter had to pass between him and that door in going to the bedroom, and that deceased was near the edge of the door and moving across the door when he pitched the glass. They both say this door was closed, and that he *threw* the glass. The language of his mother-in-law, in regard to the throwing, is: "He threw at her with vengeance a heavy tumbler"; and his daughter's language is: "He picked up a tumbler and threw it with such force that it struck the lamp." We can not say the jury erred in believing the mother-in-law and daughter, and disbelieving plaintiff in error.

. . . The plaintiff in error asked the court to instruct the jury, "that to constitute a murder there is required an union of act and intent, and the jury must believe, beyond a reasonable doubt, both that the weapon used was thrown with the intent to inflict bodily injury upon the person of Kate Mayes, and if they have a reasonable doubt as to whether his intent was to strike his wife or not, the jury should give the prisoner the benefit of such doubt, and acquit him." The court refused to give this as asked, but modified it by adding: "Unless the jury further believe, from the evidence, beyond a reasonable doubt, that all the circumstances of the killing of Kate Mayes, (if the evidence shows that she was killed by defendant,) shows an abandoned and malignant heart on the part of the defendant," and then gave it. Plaintiff in error then also asked the court to instruct the jury as follows:

"The court instructs the jury, for the defendant, that intention to commit a crime is one of the especial ingredients of an offence, and the People are bound to show, beyond a reasonable doubt, that the defendant threw the glass in question at the deceased with the intention to do her bodily injury, and if you believe, from the evidence, that there is a reasonable doubt as to the defendant having thrown said glass with intent to do her bodily injury, the jury will give the defendant the benefit of said doubt, and acquit the defendant."

This, also, the court refused to give as asked, but modified it by adding: "Unless all the circumstances of the killing of Mrs. Mayes (if she is shown, beyond a reasonable doubt, to have been killed by defendant) show an abandoned and malignant heart on the part of the defendant," and then gave it. Exceptions were taken to the rulings in these modifications, so the question whether they were erroneous is properly before us.

We perceive no objection to these rulings. Malice is an indispensable element to the crime of murder. But our statute, repeating the common law rule, says: "Malice shall be implied when no considerable provocation appears, or when all the circumstances of the killing show an abandoned and malignant heart." (Rev. Stat. 1874, p.374, sec. 140). And hence it is said: "When an action, unlawful in itself, is done with deliberation, and with intention of mischief or great bodily harm to particulars, or of mischief indiscriminately, fall where it may, and death ensue, against or beside the original intention of the party, it will be murder." (Wharton on Homicide, 45.) And as illustrative of the principle, the author says: "Thus, if a person, breaking in an unruly horse, willfully ride him among a crowd of persons, the probable danger being great and apparent, and death ensue from the viciousness of the animal, it is murder. . . . So, if a man mischievously throw from a roof into a crowded street, where passengers are constantly passing and repassing, a heavy piece of timber, calculated to produce death on such as it might fall, and death ensue, the offence is murder at common law. And upon the same principle, if a man, knowing that people are passing along the street, throw a stone likely to do injury, or shoot over a house or wall with intent to do hurt to people, and one is thereby slain, it is murder on account of previous malice, though not directed against any particular individual.

It is no excuse that the party was bent upon mischief generally." To like effect is, also, 1 Russell on Crimes, (7th Am. ed.) 540, *541; 1 Wharton on Crim. Law, (7th ed.) sec. 712b. So, here, it was utterly immaterial whether plaintiff in error intended the glass should strike his wife, his mother-in-law, or his child, or whether he had any specific intent, but acted solely from general malicious reck-lessness, disregarding any and all consequences. It is sufficient that he mani-fested a reckless, murderous disposition, — in the language of the old books, "A heart void of social duty, and fatally bent on mischief." A strong man who will violently throw a tin quart measure at his daughter — a tender child — or a heavy beer glass in a direction that he must know will probably cause it to hit his wife, sufficiently manifests malice in general to render his act murderous when death is the consequence of it. He may have intended some other result, but he is re-sponsible for the actual result. Where the act is, in itself, lawful, or, even if un-lawful, not dangerous in its character, the rule is different. In cases like the pres-ent, the presumption is the mind assented to what the hand did, with all the consequences resulting therefrom, because it is apparent he was willing that any result might be produced, at whatever of harm to others. In the other case, the result is accidental, and, therefore, not presumed to have been within the con-templation of the party, and so not to have received the assent of his mind.

Notes and Questions

1. Precisely what was Mayes's mens rea with respect to the fatal result of his act? How would the rejected jury instructions have made a difference?

2. *"Abandoned and malignant heart" murder.* We find in *Mayes* one of the commonest verbal formulations of the state of mind necessary to establish non-intentional murder — "an abandoned and malignant heart." The court cites at least one other common law formulation — "a heart void of social duty, and fa-tally bent on mischief." As we will see, versions of these and other colorful for-mulations persist quite vigorously in contemporary homicide law. What function does such a formulation serve before a jury? Does it succeed in describing a particular mental state? Does it (mistakenly?) cause the jury to think in vaguely normative terms about "malice"? Does it cause the jury to assess issues of the defendant's character beyond his mens rea for the immediate crime?

3. *Extreme indifference and gross recklessness.* The Model Penal Code Commen-tary to section 210.2 explains:[14]

> *Reckless Homicide Manifesting Extreme Indifference.* Section 210.2(1)(b) also pro-vides that criminal homicide constitutes murder when it is "committed recklessly under circumstances manifesting extreme indifference to the value of human life." This provision reflects the judgment that there is a kind of reckless homicide that cannot fairly be distinguished in grading terms from homicides committed pur-posely or knowingly.
>
> Recklessness, as defined in Section 2.02(2)(c), presupposes an awareness of the creation of substantial homicidal risk, a risk too great to be deemed justifiable by any valid purpose that the actor's conduct serves. Since risk, however, is a matter of degree and the motives for risk creation may be infinite in variation, some

14. Model Penal Code and Commentaries, *supra*, at 21-26 (1980).

formula is needed to identify the case where recklessness may be found and where it should be assimilated to purpose or knowledge for purposes of grading. Under the Model Code, this judgment must be made in terms of whether the actor's conscious disregard of the risk, given the circumstances of the case, so far departs from acceptable behavior that it constitutes a "gross deviation from the standard of conduct that a law-abiding person would observe in the actor's situation." Ordinary recklessness in this sense is made sufficient for a conviction of manslaughter under Section 210.3(1) (a). In a prosecution for murder, however, the Code calls for the further judgment whether the actor's conscious disregard of the risk, under the circumstances, manifests extreme indifference to the value of human life. The significance of purpose or knowledge as a standard of culpability is that, cases of provocation or other mitigation apart, purposeful or knowing homicide demonstrates precisely such indifference to the value of human life. Whether recklessness is so extreme that it demonstrates similar indifference is not a question, it is submitted, that can be further clarified. It must be left directly to the trier of fact under instructions which make it clear that recklessness that can fairly be assimilated to purpose or knowledge should be treated as murder and that less extreme recklessness should be punished as manslaughter.

Insofar as Subsection (1)(b) includes within the murder category cases of homicide caused by extreme recklessness, though without purpose to kill, it reflects both the common law and much pre-existing statutory treatment usually cast in terms of conduct evidencing a "depraved heart regardless of human life" or some similar words. Examples usually given include shooting into a crowd or into an occupied house or automobile, though they are not, of course, exhaustive.

Some indication of the content of this concept as a means of differentiating murder and manslaughter may be afforded by prior decisional law. One case involved a game of Russian roulette, where the defendant pointed a revolver loaded with a single cartridge at his friend. The weapon fired on the third try, and the fatal wound resulted. The court affirmed the conviction for murder, despite ample evidence that the defendant had not desired to kill his friend, with the statement that "malice in the sense of a wicked disposition is evidenced by the intentional doing of an uncalled-for act in callous disregard of its likely harmful effects on others." In another case, the defendant's claimed intention was to shoot over his victim's head in order to scare him. The court held that, even crediting this assertion, the jury could find the defendant guilty of murder on the ground that his act showed "such a reckless disregard for human life as was the equivalent of a specific intent to kill." A third illustration involved a defendant who fired several shots into a house which he knew to be occupied by several persons. The court affirmed his conviction of murder because the defendant's conduct was "imminently dangerous" and "evinced a wicked and depraved mind regardless of human life." Other acts held to show sufficient recklessness to justify a conviction of murder include shooting into a moving automobile and throwing a heavy beer glass at a woman carrying a lighted oil lamp. The Model Code formulation would permit a jury to reach the same conclusion in each of these cases. . . .

Given the Model Code definition of recklessness, the point involved is put adequately and succinctly by asking whether the recklessness rises to the level of "extreme indifference to the value of human life." As has been observed, it seems undesirable to suggest a more specific formulation. The variations referred to above retain in some instances greater fidelity to the common-law phrasing but they do so at great cost in clarity. Equally obscure are the several attempts to depart from the common law to which reference has been made. The result of these formulations is that the method of defining reckless murder is impaired in its primary purpose of communicating to jurors in ordinary language the task expected of them. The virtue of the Model Penal Code language is that it is a simpler and more direct method by which this function can be performed.

4. *Fatal games*. In the famous case of Commonwealth v. Malone, 47 A.2d 445 (Pa. 1946), the defendant appealed from a second-degree murder conviction for the killing of 13-year-old William Long. Defendant and Long were friends at the time of the shooting. The court set out the facts as follows:

> On the evening of February 26th, 1945, when the defendant went to a moving picture theater, he carried in the pocket of his raincoat a revolver which he had obtained at the home of his uncle on the preceding day. In the afternoon preceding the shooting, the decedent procured a cartridge from his father's room and he and the defendant placed it in the revolver.
>
> After leaving the theater, the defendant went to a dairy store and there met the decedent. Both youths sat in the rear of the store ten minutes, during which period the defendant took the gun out of his pocket and loaded the chamber to the right of the firing pin and then closed the gun. A few minutes later, both youths sat on stools in front of the lunch counter and ate some food. The defendant suggested to the decedent that they play "Russian Poker." Long replied: "I don't care; go ahead." The defendant then placed the revolver against the right side of Long and pulled the trigger three times. The third pull resulted in a fatal wound to Long. The latter jumped off the stool and cried: "Oh! Oh! Oh!" and Malone said: "Did I hit you, Billy? Gee, Bad, I'm sorry." Long died from the wounds two days later.
>
> The defendant testified that the gun chamber he loaded was the first one to the right of the firing chamber and that when he pulled the trigger he did not "expect to have the gun go off." He declared he had no intention of harming Long, who was his friend and companion.

The court then held that the facts justified a conviction of second-degree murder:

> A specific intent to take life is, under our law, an essential ingredient of murder in the first degree. At common law, the "grand criterion" which "distinguished murder from other killing" was malice on the part of the killer and this malice was not necessarily "malevolent to the deceased particularly" but "any evil design in general; the dictate of a wicked, depraved and malignant heart"; 4 Blackstone 199. . . .
>
> When an individual commits an act of gross recklessness for which he must reasonably anticipate that death to another is likely to result, he exhibits that "wickedness of disposition, hardness of heart, cruelty, recklessness of consequences, and a mind regardless of social duty" which proved that there was at that time in him "the state or frame of mind termed malice." . . .
>
> The killing of William H. Long by this defendant resulted from an act intentionally done by the latter, in reckless and wanton disregard of the consequences which were at least sixty percent certain from his thrice attempted discharge of a gun known to contain one bullet and aimed at a vital part of Long's body. This killing was, therefore, murder, for malice in the sense of a wicked disposition is evidenced by the intentional doing of an uncalled-for act in callous disregard of its likely harmful effects on others.

The court reasoned that the gun had a 60-percent chance of going off because it had five chambers and one bullet, and Malone pulled the trigger three times. If the gun had gone off on the first pull (20-percent chance), would the risk that Malone took have manifested an extreme indifference to human life? The defendant testified that the bullet was in the chamber to the right of the firing pin. Assuming that was true, what crime did Malone commit? If the defendant was correct, how could the gun have gone off?

5. Why do people play Russian Roulette (as opposed to Malone's "Russian Poker")? Consider the following comment by sociologist Jack Katz:[15]

> We have left [the] arena of physical challenge to begin specifying what it is about illicit action that some males . . . find fascinating. It is something about the possibility of losing everything that develops when the stakes suddenly rise, and it is something about pretensions, whether in the form of a pimp's social pretentiousness, a poker player's bluff, or the strutting braggadocio of a badass. The essential challenge is moral rather than physical.

Is the killer's motivation relevant to assessing his culpability? Compare Malone's motivation to Mayes's. Who better fits Katz's description of this existential risk-taker?

6. Consider the following cases:

a. Medical murder. In People v. Protopappas, 201 Cal. App. 3d 152, 246 Cal. Rptr. 915 (1988), the defendant, a dentist and oral surgeon, was convicted of three counts of second-degree murder for killing patients. In all three cases: the patient had some medical problem, of which Protopappas was aware, which made her overly sensitive to anesthesia; Protopappas gave her a massive overdose of anesthesia, often using improper chemicals; he failed to monitor her condition during and after the surgery even when warned that the patient was in grave danger, often delegating the medical care to inexperienced partners who knew little or nothing about anesthesia; and he failed to pursue proper means of resuscitation. On all three counts, there was voluminous expert testimony that the defendant's deviation from safe medical practice was overwhelmingly dangerous. The judge instructed the jury that it was murder if the state proved

> an intentional act or acts involving a high degree of probability that they will result in death, which act or acts are done for a base, anti-social purpose and with a wanton disregard for human life.

Does this language make murder out of negligence? The court thought so but held the error harmless because defendant's awareness of the risk had been clearly established. What meaning might the jury give to "base, anti-social purpose" in a case where it was obviously in the defendant's economic self-interest to protect the lives of his patients? Is this, as the court said, "the health care equivalent of shooting into a crowd or setting a lethal mantrap in a dark alley"?

b. Murderous animals. In Berry v. Superior Court, 208 Cal. App. 3d 783 (1989), the defendant was charged with second-degree murder when his pet pit bull dog mauled a neighbor's two-year-old boy to death. The defendant sought dismissal of the charges on the ground that the evidence could in no way support a murder charge. The evidence was roughly as follows:

Berry kept his dog, Willy, tethered near his house. He knew that his immediate neighbors had several small children, and he had told them that the dog was dangerous but had reassured them that his fence kept the dog secured. In fact, the fence was partly open, giving children access to the area where the dog was tethered. There was no evidence that the dog had ever attacked a human being, but there was considerable evidence that the dog had been specifically bred and trained to be a fighting dog. In fact, in purchasing the dog, Berry had

15. Seductions of Crime 244 (1988).

apparently relied on the seller's word that "a dog won't go an hour with Willy and live." Berry furthered the dog's training and prepared him for paid competition. An expert testified that pit bulls are trained to attack swiftly and silently, without warning, and that the likelihood of a trained pit bull making an unprovoked attack on a human being was, with respect to a dog like Willy, "unpredictable." In assessing California's line between murder and manslaughter, the Court of Appeal observed,

> Our high court has drawn this line placing in the more culpable category not only those deliberate life-endangering acts which are done with a subjective awareness of the risk involved, but also life-endangering conduct which is "only" done with the awareness the conduct is contrary to the laws of society. Although behavior in the latter category may not be as morally heinous as the former, the difference in culpability does not require the latter crime to be legally shifted into manslaughter slots.

In a Kansas case, State v. Davidson, 987 P.2d 335 (Kan. 1999), the defendant owned several violent Rottweiler dogs who had frequently broken through her flimsy fence, chased and nipped at young children, attacked neighbors' dogs, and threatened and frightened adult neighbors, baring their teeth and growling menacingly. One morning three of her dogs chased a young boy at his school bus stop and eventually mauled him to death. Davidson had received some instruction in a dog sport called Schutzhund, whereby one trained dogs to do tracking and protection work, but, according to Schutzhund experts, she violated Schutzhund principles by failing to teach her dogs obedience and by kenneling them in a group and thereby risking "pack behavior." In affirming the conviction for "extreme indifference" murder, the court said: "The State is not required to prove that the defendant knew her dogs would attack and kill someone. It was sufficient to prove that her dogs killed [the boy] and that she could have reasonably foreseen that the dogs could attack or injure someone as a result of what she did or failed to do."

Under these rulings, what is the mens rea for murder when the defendant knowingly engages in highly anti-social acts?

7. *Intoxication.* Recall the discussion in Chapter 3 about the admissibility of evidence of voluntary intoxication to negate the defendant's mens rea for the crime. See pp. 236-242, *supra.* Recall that even though intoxication is sometimes admissible to negate a required "specific intent," the Model Penal Code, at least, virtually forbids the use of intoxication testimony to negate a mens rea of recklessness where the defendant, if sober, would have been aware of the risk perceived. Model Penal Code §2.08. Should the Code rule also apply in charges of "grossly reckless" murder? The answer was affirmative in State v. Dufield, 549 A.2d 1205 (N.H. 1988), where the defendant was convicted of murder for brutally maiming and killing his sister. The defendant had argued that since "extreme indifference" murder required a higher mental state than reckless manslaughter, that higher mental state, like knowledge or purpose, could be negated by intoxication. The court disagreed, viewing the second-degree murder charge here as requiring not so much a higher mental state than reckless manslaughter as a more extreme degree of divergence from law-abiding conduct:

> [T]he function of proving the existence of "circumstances manifesting extreme indifference" is to establish, not a subjective state of mind, but a degree of divergence from the norm of acceptable behavior even greater than the "gross deviation" from

the "law-abiding" norm, by which reckless conduct is defined. On this view, the words in question would describe a way of objectively measuring such a deviation, in which case any voluntary intoxication that might have blinded a defendant to the risks of such extremely deviant behavior would be as irrelevant as it would be to proof of the less culpable deviation required to establish mere recklessness. [Id. at 1206-07.]

Assuming you agree with the result, do you think this is the best rationale for the result?

In one study, more than half the people who shot to death friends or relatives were intoxicated and fired the gun within a few seconds of brandishing it, and many killed unintentionally.[16] What legal implications follow?

What if the defendant commits a grossly reckless act in disregard of human life, not intending to kill, but also feeling provoked? Is he then guilty of *voluntary* manslaughter, or is that an oxymoron, given the lack of intent? Does provocation make his purpose less "anti-social" or "malignant"? In People v. Lasko, 23 Cal. 4th 101, 999 P.2d 666 (2000), the defendant fell into a bitter dispute with the victim over a debt, and, in the course of a struggle, hit him with a bat. The court noted that despite the statutory designation of "voluntary manslaughter," the actual statutory definition — "upon a sudden quarrel or heat of passion" — nowhere requires intent. Thus, the court held that, assuming the highest mental state the prosecution could prove was "implied malice" — i.e., gross recklessness—the defendant was entitled to a voluntary manslaughter instruction. The court stressed that otherwise, a defendant who intended to kill, and was thus even more culpable, would have an unfair advantage in avoiding a murder conviction. Note that under this ruling, a defendant can insist that he receive a voluntary manslaughter instruction to avoid a murder charge, but he is not entitled to reduce the charge to involuntary manslaughter.

8. *Intent to do serious bodily injury.* The common law definition of murder allowed intent to do serious bodily injury to substitute for intent to kill. For example, in Commonwealth v. Dorazio, 365 Pa. 291, 74 A.2d 125 (1950), the defendant, Dorazio, was a former professional heavyweight boxer who had once fought (and lost to) Joe Louis for the heavyweight championship. At the time in question, Dorazio worked at a brewery where two rival unions were engaged in a bitter jurisdictional dispute. He was securing signatures to a petition for his union when he encountered the victim along with two other members of the rival union. He struck the victim, chased him, and beat him on his head and body. When the victim's companions arrived and tried to pull Dorazio off, Dorazio struck them and knocked them down. He then returned to beating the now unconscious victim. The victim was taken to the hospital, treated and released, but died later that day from a hemorrhage from a fracture of the skull, apparently caused by Dorazio's fists. Dorazio was convicted of second-degree murder.

The Supreme Court of Pennsylvania upheld the conviction. It noted that intent to inflict "serious bodily harm" murder does not require an intent to do permanent or fatal injury. However, to prevent every fatal assault from being classed as murder, this doctrine is generally limited to cases where the assailant used a deadly weapon. Normally, fists would not qualify as a deadly weapon, but here the court held otherwise, reasoning that the "size of the assailant, the

16. San Francisco Chronicle, June 19, 1989, at B4 (from the Washington Post).

manner in which the fists are used, the ferocity of the attack and its duration and the provocation are all relevant to the question of malice." [Id. at 130.]

How useful is the "intent to do bodily harm" formula? Could Dorazio have been convicted of abandoned and malignant heart murder? Consider this:[17]

The Model Penal Code eliminates intent to injure as a separate basis of liability for murder. The drafters concluded that proper cases for liability of this type will be included without it. The only clear case of murder under the common law that is excluded under the Code is one in which the actor inflicts serious injury while taking express precautions not to kill his victim, and the victim dies anyway. Such a case would in any event fall within some category of criminal homicide — manslaughter, if not murder. On the other hand, retention of the common-law classification leaves the possibility that unless the degree of seriousness of the intended injury is emphasized, an unintentional killing not accompanied by the same culpability as an intentional killing will be treated in the same way. Some jurisdictions follow the lead of the Model Penal Code; many others retain this category of murder.

9. *Vehicular murder.* In 1981, the Supreme Court of California held that a drunk driver who causes a fatal car accident can be charged with second-degree murder. People v. Watson, 30 Cal. 3d 290, 179 Cal. Rptr. 43 (1981). The facts of the case were as follows:

In the late night and early morning hours of January 2 and 3, 1979, defendant Robert Watson consumed large quantities of beer in a Redding bar. Approximately an hour and a half after leaving the bar, defendant drove through a red light on a Redding street and avoided a collision with another car only by skidding to a halt in the middle of the intersection. After this near collision, defendant drove away at high speed, approached another intersection and, although he again applied his brakes, struck a Toyota sedan. Three passengers in the Toyota were ejected from the vehicle and the driver and her six-year-old daughter were killed. Defendant left 112 feet of skid marks prior to impact, and another 180 feet of skid marks to the vehicle's point of rest.

The applicable speed limit at the accident scene was 35 miles per hour. Expert testimony based on the skid marks and other physical evidence estimated defendant's speed immediately prior to applying his brakes at 84 miles per hour. At point of impact, the experts concluded that defendant's speed was approximately 70 miles per hour. Eyewitness Henke testified that defendant's car passed him "real fast" (estimated by Henke at 50 to 60 miles per hour) shortly before the collision. According to Henke, defendant swerved from the slow lane into the fast lane, suddenly braked and skidded into the intersection, and thereupon struck the other vehicle. Henke believed that the traffic light was green when defendant entered the intersection.

Defendant's blood alcohol content one-half hour after the collision was .23 percent, more than twice the percentage necessary to support a finding that he was legally intoxicated. [Id. at 293-94.]

The court rejected defendant's claim that the state's vehicular manslaughter statute precluded a murder charge and held that the evidence would support a finding of "implied malice." Chief Justice Bird, dissenting, asserted:

. . . The act of speeding through a green light at 55 or 60 miles per hour in a 35-mile-per-hour zone was dangerous, but was not an act likely to result in the

17. Lloyd Weinreb, Homicide: Legal Aspects, 2 Encyclopedia of Crime and Justice.

death of another. It was 1 o'clock in the morning. The person whose car respondent nearly collided with testified that he saw no other cars around. . . .

The fact that respondent was under the influence of alcohol made his driving more dangerous. A high percentage of accidents is caused by such drivers. No one holds a brief for this type of activity. However, a rule should not be promulgated by this court that driving while under the influence of alcohol is sufficient to establish an act "likely to kill." Death or injury is not the probable result of driving while under the influence of alcohol. Thousands, perhaps hundreds of thousands, of Californians each week reach home without accident despite their driving intoxicated.

The majority also fail to demonstrate that it is reasonable to infer that respondent had a conscious disregard for life. Can a conscious disregard for life be established by the fact that several hours *before* the accident respondent drove his car to a bar? The majority hold as a matter of law that he "must have known" he would have to drive his car later and that he wilfully drank alcohol until he was under its influence.

How does respondent's state of mind at the time he drove to the bar and began drinking justify an inference that he had a reckless state of mind at the time of the accident? This meager evidence does not justify the inference that by drinking alcohol he harbored a conscious disregard for life when he later drove his car! I submit that the majority's reasoning that such an inference may be drawn to support a finding of implied malice will be used to establish second degree murder in every case in which a person drives a car to a bar, a friend's home, or a party, drinks alcohol so that he is under its influence, drives away and is involved in a fatal accident. . . .

The majority's reasoning also perpetuates the fiction that when a person drinks socially, he wilfully drinks to come under the influence of alcohol and with this knowledge drives home at a later time. This unfounded conclusion ignores social reality. "[T]ypically [a person] sets out to drink without becoming intoxicated, and because alcohol distorts judgment, he overrates his capacity, and misjudges his driving ability after drinking too much." [Taylor v. Superior Ct. 24 Cal. 3d 890, 890, 908 (1979).]

Clearly, evidence regarding respondent's drinking earlier in the evening bears little relevance to his state of mind at the time of the accident. The majority's reliance on evidence of respondent's presumed state of mind before he began driving violates the basic principle that a crime cannot be committed unless there is unity of act and intent. (Pen. Code, §20.)

The majority's errors are compounded by the fact that they improperly *presume* that respondent harbored a conscious disregard for life. Thus, they state that respondent "must have known" he would drive after drinking and that it "may be presumed that [he] was aware of the hazards of driving while intoxicated." These presumptions improperly dilute the requirement that the prosecution must *prove* the accused's intent to commit an act likely to kill with conscious disregard for life. [Id. at 306 (emphasis added).]

Is the Chief Justice correct when she says the majority opinion will support a finding of implied malice to establish second-degree murder whenever a drunk driver is involved in a fatal accident?

Is the Chief Justice correct when she says driving under the influence may "show lack of a conscious appreciation of the risk presented to others"? Why does the majority seem to say the more drunk you are the more reckless? Can this conflict be resolved? Is it significant that Watson hit his brakes?

In 1983, California amended its vehicular manslaughter statute to read,

Gross negligence, as used in this section, shall not be construed as prohibiting or precluding a charge of murder under Section 188 upon facts exhibiting wantonness and a conscious disregard for life to support a finding of implied malice, or upon facts showing malice, consistent with the holding of the California Supreme Court in People v. Watson (1981) 30 Cal. 3d 290.

10. *The meaning of fatal recklessness: attitude or cognition?* Recent work in criminal jurisprudence has raised the question whether the actual cognition of great risk of death is — or should be — the basis for reckless manslaughter or grossly reckless murder. Prof. Samuel Pillsbury argues[18] that grossly reckless and negligent homicide should be reconfigured to focus not on awareness of risk, but *indifference* to risk; he draws on modern neurological theories of consciousness that reject the simple dualism of conscious and unconscious mental processes, and posits that people should often be held responsible for choosing the scope and limitations of their range of awareness and perception. Thus, where a defendant claims he lacked awareness of risk, the key question should be whether the defendant had a nonculpable reason for *not* perceiving or responding to that risk.

Do people choose what they perceive and do not perceive? Do they choose to become unperceptive? Do pathologically indifferent people *choose* at some point to lack empathy?

C.   HOMICIDE IN THE COURSE OF ANOTHER CRIME

1.   Felony Murder: An Introduction

STATE v. MARTIN

Supreme Court of New Jersey

573 A.2d 1359 (1990)

POLLOCK, J.

On June 29, 1983, defendant and four others from Keyport attended a party in the apartment of Lois Baker on the third floor of a three-story wood-framed building in Keansburg. Defendant, who claimed he was intoxicated, stated that he had smoked marijuana and consumed four beers before the party, and four more beers and four shots of Southern Comfort at the party. Paul Wade, one member of the Keyport group, became involved in two altercations with other guests, including Mike Kilpatrick. After the second altercation, Baker told everyone from Keyport to leave. On leaving, defendant and Wade vandalized a motorcycle that they thought belonged to Kilpatrick. . . .

Within fifteen minutes after defendant left Baker's apartment, another guest noticed that the building was on fire. Everyone escaped, except Barbara Quartz, who had fallen asleep after drinking alcoholic beverages at the party. She died of asphyxiation due to smoke inhalation and carbon monoxide intoxication.

According to defendant, he set the fire by lighting a paper bag containing trash that he found in the hallway by Lois Baker's door. Defendant testified:

> I picked up the bag and walked down the steps with it. I was just, you know, throwing it around making a mess, you know, and I set it down and I lit up a cigarette.

___

18. Crimes of Indifference, 49 Rutgers L. Rev. 105 (1996).

And the match — I lit the paper bag on fire, you know, 'cause I thought maybe it would burn up the garbage, you know, not to spread or anything, just make, like make a mess of the bottom of the landing. And then, then I left. . . . I put the match on the bag and lit the bag, the top of the bag on fire. I thought it would make a mess of things. I didn't understand. I mean I didn't figure that it would, you know, cause a fire and spread or catch on anything. I thought it would just, you know, burn the garbage and go right out. I didn't mean to hurt nobody.

The State's version of the setting of the fire differed materially from that of defendant. According to the State's experts, Frederick Dispensiere of the Monmouth County Prosecutor's Office, and Daniel Slowick, a fire insurance investigator, the fire was set by spreading kerosene between the ground floor and the second floor. . . .

Defendant, Daniel Martin, was found guilty of . . . felony murder, arson, and aggravated arson arising out of the death of a woman in a building that he set on fire. . . . The Appellate Division affirmed. . . . Because the charge incorrectly instructed the jury on the standard for finding that defendant's act caused the death of the victim, we reverse defendant's murder conviction.

Under the New Jersey Penal Code, causation . . . is a term of art, the meaning of which varies with the mental state of the actor. It means one thing when an offense is committed knowingly or purposely, and something else for a crime of strict or absolute liability such as felony murder. . . . [T]he New Jersey Code is based substantially on the Model Penal Code. The underlying premise of both codes is that problems regarding variations between the actual and designed or contemplated results are problems of culpability rather than metaphysical problems of causation. Consequently, in assessing whether a defendant's conduct is the cause of a remote result, both codes focus on whether the actual result justly bears on the defendant's culpability for the offense. . . .

The felony-murder verdict arose under *N.J.S.A.* 2C:11-3a(3), which imposes liability when

the actor, acting either alone or with one or more other persons, is engaged in the commission of arson [or robbery, sexual assault, burglary, kidnapping, carjacking or criminal escape] and in the course of such crime . . . , any person causes the death of a person other than one of the participants; except that in any prosecution under this subsection, in which the defendant was not the only participant in the underlying crime, it is an affirmative defense that the defendant:

(a) Did not commit the homicidal act or in any way solicit, request, command, importune, cause or aid the commission thereof; and

(b) Was not armed with a deadly weapon, or any instrument, article or substance readily capable of causing death or serious physical injury and of a sort not ordinarily carried in public places by law-abiding persons; and

(c) Had no reasonable ground to believe that any other participant was armed with such a weapon, instrument, article or substance; and

(d) Had no reasonable ground to believe that any other participant intended to engage in conduct likely to result in death or serious physical injury.

At common law, if the victim died during the course of the commission of the felony, the perpetrator was guilty of murder. Theoretically, the intent to commit the felony, even in the absence of an intent to kill, was transferred to the death of the victim. . . . More recently, felony murder has been viewed not as a crime of transferred intent, but as one of absolute or strict liability. . . . The historical justification for the rule is that it serves as a general deterrent against the commission of violent crimes. The rationale is that if potential felons realize that they will be culpable as murderers for a death that occurs during the commission of a felony, they will be less likely to commit the felony. . . .

To the extent that the felony-murder rule holds an actor liable for a death irrespective of the actor's mental state, the rule cuts across the grain of criminal law. Generally, people are not criminally culpable for the consequences of their acts unless those consequences were intended, contemplated, or foreseeable. Because the felony-murder rule runs counter to normal rules of criminal culpability, it received careful consideration from the drafters of the Model Penal Code and from the New Jersey Commission. The drafters of the Model Penal Code objected to the rule as "a form of strict liability to which we are opposed." *Model Penal Code* §2.01.1 (Tent. Draft No. 9 (1959)). Although it ultimately recommended retention of the rule, the New Jersey Commission stated that "principled justification in its defense is hard to find." II *N.J. Code* §2C:11-3 commentary at 157. Ultimately, the Commission incorporated the advice of Oliver Wendell Holmes, Jr., who wrote:

> [I]f experience shows, or is deemed by the lawmaker to show, that somehow or other deaths which the evidence makes accidental happen disproportionately often in connection with other felonies, or with resistance to officers, or if on any other ground of policy it is deemed desirable to make special efforts for the prevention of such deaths, the law-maker may consistently treat acts which, under the known circumstances, are felonious, or constitute resistance to officers, as having a sufficiently dangerous tendency to put under a special ban. The law may, therefore, throw on the actor the peril, not only of the consequences foreseen by him, but also of consequences which, although not predicted by common experience, the legislator apprehends. [*The Common Law* 49 (1963).]

To comprehend the New Jersey Code's approach to felony murder, one must consider the pre-existing law, the Model Penal Code, and the New Jersey Commission's modifications of that Code. Before the enactment of the New Jersey Code, this State recognized a broad felony-murder rule. The predecessor statute provided:

> any person, [who] in committing or attempting to commit arson, burglary, kidnapping, rape, robbery, sodomy or any unlawful act . . . of which the probable consequences may be bloodshed, kills another, or if the death of anyone ensues from the committing or attempting to commit any such crime or act [was guilty of murder].

Even under that statute, the State was required to prove not only that the felony was the cause-in-fact or "but-for" cause, but also that it was the proximate cause of the victim's death. Thus, the proximate-cause test limited the harsh effect of the common-law felony-murder rule. Because of its vagueness, however, the test created problems of its own.

The Model Penal Code took a different approach. Instead of treating felony murder as an absolute-liability offense, the Model Penal Code created a presumption of recklessness when a homicide occurred in the course of the commission of certain felonies, including arson. . . . If not rebutted, that presumption would support a conviction for murder.

Initially, the New Jersey Commission agreed with that approach. In a tentative draft of the New Jersey Code, the Commission recommended adoption of the Model Penal Code's treatment of felony murder, concluding that "[b]eyond this, we submit that the felony-murder doctrine, as a basis for establishing the criminality of homicide, should be abandoned." *New Jersey Law Commission* (Tentative Draft at 310 (Jan. 1971)). As an alternative, the Commission mentioned the New York Code, *id.* at 313-14, which "allows a limited affirmative defense as to the non-perpetrator participant in the felony where that person is able to demonstrate that he did not assume a homicidal risk." II *N.J. Code* §2C:11-3 commentary at 157.

In its final report, the New Jersey Commission rejected the Model Penal Code's approach . . . [but] provided an affirmative defense, similar to that provided in New York, for perpetrators who did not assume a homicidal risk. . . . Consequently, an accomplice, as distinguished from the primary actor, may establish the defense by proving that he or she did not commit the homicidal act, was not armed with a deadly weapon, and had no reason to believe that any other participant was so armed or "intended to engage in conduct likely to result in death or serious physical injury." *N.J.S.A.* 2C:11-3a(3)(a) to -3a(3)(d). Those four factors focus on whether the accomplice undertook a homicidal risk or could have foreseen that the commission of the felony might result in death. . . .

. . . [A]mendments, enacted in 1979 and 1981 in response to this Court's decision in *State v. Canola,* 374 A.2d 20 (1977), extend the reach of the statute. In *Canola,* four perpetrators attempted to rob a jewelry store. During the course of the robbery, the owner killed one of the perpetrators and then was himself killed. The defendant was convicted of felony murder of both the owner and the other perpetrator. [This court reversed] the conviction [for the death] of the other perpetrator. . . . According to the Court, a felon could not be liable for any death, even of a non-felon, when the death was caused by someone other than a participant in the commission of the felony [because the statute punished only deaths caused by a "participant" and "in the course of and in furtherance of" the felony]. . . . The Legislature responded by [eliminating] the requirement[s] that the death be caused by one of the participants . . . [and] that the death occur "in furtherance of" the commission of the felony. . . .

Concerning absolute-liability offenses, the New Jersey Code states:

> When causing a particular result is a material element of an offense for which absolute liability is imposed by law, the element is not established unless the actual result is a probable consequence of the actor's conduct. [*N.J.S.A.* 2C:2-3e.]

In effect, subsection e provides that the actual result — death, in the case of felony murder — "is not established unless" it is the "probable consequence of the [commission of the felony]." However, a question remains about the meaning of "probable consequences."

The term "probable consequence" is undefined in the Model Penal Code or Commentary, the New Jersey Commission Report, the New Jersey Code, or anywhere else in the legislative history. Our review of that history leads us to conclude that the Legislature . . . did not intend a drastic change in the law of felony murder. . . .

Pre-Code cases originally employed the term "probable consequence" or the equivalent when referring to the risk of death created by the felon's acts. In *State v. Cooper,* the former Supreme Court stated that an unintentional killing occurring during the commission or attempt to commit a felony constitutes a felony murder, "especially if death were a probable consequence of the act." 13 *N.J.L.* 360, 370 (1833). . . .

In an attempt to focus more closely on the meaning of "probable consequence," we listed this case for reargument. . . . At oral argument, defendant urged that probable consequence in the felony-murder context means variously that the victim's death must not be too remote or depend on the act of another, and that the death cannot be accidental, unanticipated, or remote. By comparison, the State contended that "probable consequence" means that the victim's death need be only foreseeable, and not the result of an independent or intervening cause. Significantly, both counsel urge that probable consequences means something more than "but for" causation. The point to be derived from prior law, the language and history of the Code, and the argument of counsel is that some deaths are too remotely related to the commission of the felony to justify holding the actor responsible not only for the commission of the felony, but for murder. . . .

. . . The Model Penal Code Commentary supports the proposition that the meaning of "probable consequence" is closely related to the concept of foreseeability. In the commentary to the accomplice-liability section of the Model Penal Code, 2.06, the commentators recognize that the "probable consequence" test is substantially similar to a test of foreseeability. As they observe: "To say that the accomplice is liable if the offense committed is 'reasonably foreseeable' or the 'probable consequence' of another crime is to make him liable for negligence." *Model Penal Code and Commentaries* §2.06 at 312 n. 42 (1985). Although not directly related to felony-murder analysis, the commentary lends support to the interchangeability of the terms "probable consequence" and "reasonable foreseeability."

Keeping in mind that the New Jersey Commission predicated its version of the felony-murder rule on New York law, the causation test developed by the New York courts is illuminating. Those courts have rejected the notion that "but-for" causation is sufficient to sustain a felony-murder conviction. To find a defendant guilty of felony murder, New York courts require that the "death [be] a reasonably foreseeable and non-accidental consequence" of the felony. *People v. Flores,* 124 Misc. 2d 478, 481, (Sup. Ct. 1984) . . .

In sum, pre-Code case law and the Model Penal Code draw on notions of foreseeability. To the extent that the Legislature looked to those sources, "probable consequence" may be interpreted in their light. . . . We can [define] . . . "probable consequence" by recourse to the terms used to define causation in 2C:2-3 for crimes committed knowingly, purposely, or recklessly, or with criminal negligence. For those offenses, in addition to other prescribed requirements, the result must "not be too remote, accidental in its occurrence, or dependent on another's volitional act to have a just bearing on the actor's liability or the gravity of his offense." As previously noted, however, the Legislature amended *N.J.S.A.* 2C:11-3 to provide that culpability for felony murder may attach when the killing is committed by one other than the felon, such as the victim or a police officer. As that amendment intimates, such killings are not "[too] dependent on another's volition to have a just bearing on the actor's liability." In brief, deaths occurring as a result of self-defense or retaliation are not "too dependent on another's volition," but are the foreseeable result of the risk created by the felon. Although the legislative intent is not entirely clear, we conclude that the Legislature recognized that some deaths will occur in the course of a felony that are too remotely related or accidental to warrant holding the actor liable.

. . . The court should instruct the jury that the defendant, whether a sole perpetrator or an accomplice, is liable for felony murder only if the death is not too remote, accidental in its occurrence, or too dependent on another's volitional act to have a just bearing on the defendant's culpability.

Two examples define the outer limits of the problem. On the one hand, a bank robber would not be liable for felony murder if at "the moment a bank robber stepped into the bank, an employee pushing the button for a burglar alarm was electrocuted." *Model Penal Code and Commentaries* §2.03(4) comment at 264 (1985). On the other hand, in a robbery of a store in which "the shopkeeper fires at the robber but instead kills an innocent bystander," the death would not be too remote for the defendant to be guilty of felony murder. Senate Judiciary Committee, *Statement to Senate Committee Substitute,* No. 1537, §14 (1981). . . .

As the foregoing examples illustrate, in a multiple-perpetrator felony, the focus should be on the relationship between the victim's death and the felony, not the individual roles of the various perpetrators. Hence, in such a felony, an otherwise culpable accomplice may be liable for the death of the victim even if he or she was not the gunman who killed the victim, but was merely a lookout for the driver of a getaway car. The point is that a defendant should be exculpated only when a death occurs in a manner that is so unexpected or unusual that he or she could not justly be found culpable for the result. . . .

. . . In the instant case, the trial court failed to instruct the jury that defendant would not be liable for the felony murder of the victim if her death was "too remote, accidental in its occurrence, or too dependent on another's volitional act to have a just bearing on the defendant's culpability." Instead, the trial court instructed the jury:

> Now, under this law [felony murder] it does not matter whether the act which caused death is committed recklessly or unintentionally or accidentally. The perpetrator is as guilty of murder as he would be if he had purposely or knowingly committed the act which caused the death. . . .

. . . Because the trial court did not adequately charge the jury on causation under *N.J.S.A.* 2C:2-3, we reverse the judgment of conviction for murder, and remand the cause to the Law Division.

Notes and Questions

1. In the absence of the felony murder rule (that is, applying the homicide doctrines already studied), does Martin merit murder liability on his account of the facts? On the prosecution's account?

2. According to the court, how did the trial court's instructions on felony murder lead to an unjust result? Under the correct felony murder instruction, is it clear that Martin would be guilty of murder? On his account of the facts? On the prosecution's?

3. Notice that the New Jersey felony murder provision contains no culpability term. As the court points out, many modern commentators characterize — and criticize — felony murder as a crime of strict liability. The court in *Martin* also characterizes felony murder in New Jersey as a "strict liability" or "absolute liability" offense. Nevertheless, it insists that causation of death necessarily

requires culpability with respect to the risk of death. Accordingly, it requires that the resulting death must be "probable," "reasonably foreseeable," "negligent," and "not too accidental to have a just bearing on defendant's culpability." In short, while paying fealty to the common description of felony murder as a strict liability crime, the court effectively conditions it on the culpable mental state of negligence. How does this standard compare with the approach to this issue taken by MPC §210.2(1) (b)?

While the court emphasizes that causing death requires culpability, does the statute even require that the *felons* cause death? Note that the legislature eliminated language requiring that death be caused by "a participant" and "in furtherance of" the felony. Did the legislature thereby eliminate any requirement that the felon culpably cause the death of the victim? Or did the legislature determine that felons can sometimes be causally responsible and culpable for deaths caused during a felony by non-felons? An example might be the death of a bystander caused by a stray shot from the gun of a resisting robbery victim.

4. Notice, on the other hand, that the legislature excludes liability for the deaths of co-felons. Why? Isn't it foreseeable that a fellow robber might be shot by a resisting victim, or that a fellow arsonist might be trapped in a burning building? Is imposing a risk on a co-felon less wrongful than imposing a risk on a victim or bystander? Does a felon "impose" risk on an accomplice at all, or does the accomplice "assume the risk"? (We examine this question at pp. 410-411, *infra*.)

5. The New Jersey statute also includes a defense for felons who (1) did not commit the act causing death, (2) were not armed, (3) had no reason to think a co-felon would commit an act likely to cause death, and (4) had no reason to think a co-felon was armed. What purpose is served by this defense? Is it necessary in light of the New Jersey Supreme Court's interpretation of the causation standard?

6. The New Jersey statute conditions felony murder only on particular enumerated felonies that lead to death, including arson. New Jersey's original felony murder statute, dating back to 1828, applied to arson, burglary, robbery, and rape and any other crime "of which the probable consequences may be bloodshed." Is it possible to commit arson *without* reasonably foreseeing a risk of death? Does the commission of some felonies necessarily entail culpability with respect to death? Is this true of all the felonies enumerated in the New Jersey statute? (Below, at pp. 415-418, we examine the question of which felonies are sufficiently dangerous to serve as "predicate felonies" for the felony murder rule.)

7. *Felony murder in historical perspective.* American courts and scholars have long believed that American law received a sweeping felony murder rule from England. William Clark and William Marshall summed up this prevailing view on the origin of American felony murder rules in their early twentieth century treatise on crimes:

> At common law, malice was implied as a matter of law in every case of homicide while engaged in the commission of some other felony, and such a killing was murder whether death was intended or not. . . . On this principle, it was murder at common law to unintentionally kill another in committing, or attempting to commit, burglary, arson, rape, robbery, or larceny. The doctrine has repeatedly been recognized and applied in this country, and is to be regarded as still in force, except where it has been expressly abrogated by statute. The decisions at common law do not require that the act done shall have been of such a nature as to endanger life

or threaten great bodily harm. . . . If it had been otherwise, the doctrine would have been altogether unnecessary, because the killing would be murder because of the *tendency* of the act, without regard to its being done in the commission of a felony.[19]

But this view of the origins of our felony murder rules appears mistaken on a number of points. First, England had not yet developed a felony murder rule of its own by the time of the American Revolution. While a broad felony murder rule, imposing liability for accidental killing in the course of any felony, was proposed by eighteenth-century English scholars Hawkins and Foster, and was discussed favorably in some eighteenth century English cases, such a rule was not applied. By the time of the American revolution, English courts had gone no farther than to impose murder liability on persons who: (1) mistakenly killed one person in an attempt to kill or wound another; (2) killed in defending themselves against resistance to a crime (the crime precluding a claim of self-defense or provocation); or (3) agreed with others to kill or wound for a criminal purpose, one of them killing for that purpose. The distinction between felonies and other offenses was of no particular significance in these cases.

Even if England had developed a felony murder rule by the time of the American Revolution, it could not have been received into the law of any particular American jurisdiction without an explicit legislative or judicial endorsement. English constitutional law held that the common law did not apply to the colonies. Colonial charters authorized governing authorities to enact law as "compatible" with the common law as might be "convenient" for local conditions. During the Revolutionary period, Americans were ambivalent about English law and generally regarded the common law as authoritative only as it had been locally applied in a particular colony. They were particularly suspicious of English criminal law, which leading reformers criticized as overly harsh. Some Americans also saw judicial definition of crimes as potentially tyrannical. So rules of English criminal law were only authoritative where a legislature enacted them or a court decided to receive them.

English courts did not apply any felony murder rule until the last half of the nineteenth century, sparking an immediate controversy. This belated felony murder rule was much narrower than the one proposed a century and a half before. It conditioned felony murder liability on causing death by an act of violence or an act manifestly dangerous to human life, in the perpetration or attempt of a felony.

The first legally binding felony murder rules were enacted, not in England, but in America. Pennsylvania, in 1794, enacted a statute aggravating murder to murder in the first degree if committed in the attempt of the felonies of arson, burglary, robbery or rape. Illinois, in 1826, passed the first statute explicitly mandating that killing in the course of any felony was murder — if the circumstances of the killing manifested an "abandoned and malignant heart." New Jersey and New York passed felony murder statutes soon after. Over the course of the nineteenth century, most American states passed either felony murder statutes like the Illinois or New York statutes, or graded murder statutes like Pennsylvania's, or both. Most of these statutes were applied to impose murder liability for some unintended killings in the course of felonies. The first reported felony murder convictions were obtained under the Pennsylvania and New York statutes in the 1840s, well before any reported felony murder cases in England.

19. William Clark & William Marshall, A Treatise on Crimes (1900) 515-16.

Because the original American felony murder rules derived from diverse statutes rather than a unitary common law, it is difficult to generalize about their scope. But most of these rules were considerably narrower than the sweeping rule described by Clark and Marshall, at least as put into practice. In states with enumerated felony grading statutes, felony murder liability was almost always first degree murder liability, predicated on these enumerated felonies. Many states applied their felony murder statutes only to predicate felonies involving violence or danger to life.

Felony murder liability was also limited by nineteenth century ideas about the causation element of murder. In the great majority of nineteenth century American felony murder cases that we have found, the act causing death was an intentional battery: usually shooting, sometimes stabbing, strangling, clubbing, or beating. A few nineteenth century felony murder cases explored the problem of accomplice liability for killings in the course of felonies. These cases divided fairly evenly over whether felons had to intend the act causing death, or only the underlying felony. We have found no cases imposing liability for the death of a co-felon.[20]

8. *Types of modern felony-murder laws:* Almost all states retain some form of the felony murder rule, despite the Model Penal Code's disapproval. Their statutes can be classified in many ways, but the most salient factors are the particular categories of felonies that trigger the rule, the degree to which these felonies can augment homicide liability, the extent to which these felonies can reduce the culpability otherwise required for a particular grade of homicide liability, and the scope of accomplice liability.

a. *Predicate felonies:* The most important factor in classifying felony murder rules is the range of felonies that can serve as "predicates" for murder liability under a particular rule. To include a felony under the rule is to declare that the felony is sufficiently dangerous per se that a person committing it can be viewed as accepting the risk of murder liability. Most states rely on statutes that explicitly enumerate a few distinct felonies (traditionally arson, robbery, burglary, and rape, and sometimes others) as bases for felony murder. Some states predicate felony murder on any dangerous or "forcible" felony, or any felony involving use of a deadly weapon. Some statutes enumerate predicate felonies for first degree murder, and leave open to judicial construction which felonies, if any, might serve as predicates for second degree murder. (See pp. 415-417, *infra.*) A few states rely on general legislation that applies the felony-murder rule for any felony that leads to death; but where statutes do not limit predicate felonies, courts may nevertheless limit them to those to dangerous to life.

b. *Aggravating liability:* Another issue in analyzing felony murder statutes is determining how the attempt of a predicate felony augments homicide liability beyond what would otherwise be imposed for causing death with a given level of culpability. The predicate felony may, as Clark and Marshall suggested, make otherwise accidental or nonculpable homicides into murders, of first or second degree. It may raise only involuntary manslaughters, involving negligent or reckless causation of death, to either first or second-degree murder. It may raise intentional or grossly reckless killings from second degree to first-degree murder. Finally, the felony may serve as an aggravating circumstance, triggering consideration of a capital sentence for what would otherwise be noncapital murder

20. This history is explained in detail in Guyora Binder, The Origins of American Felony Murder Rules, forthcoming 2004).

(see the constitutional limits on the death penalty for felony murder in Chapter 7, pp. 459-64, *infra.*) Note that a felony murder rule may or may not hold a defendant *strictly* liable for causing death in the course of a felony. A felony murder rule is *any rule reducing the culpability with respect to death required for a particular grade of murder when committed in the course of certain felonies.*

Note that a few states, including Kentucky, Michigan, and Hawaii, have no felony murder rule at all. Hawaii, for example, requires purpose to cause death for all murder. Haw. Rev. Stat. §707.701 (2003).

c. *Culpability:* While most statutes do not explicitly condition felony murder liability on any culpable mental state, some do. And some courts have construed otherwise ambiguous statutes to require culpability. Thus:

- A few states expressly condition felony murder on a mens rea of gross recklessness with respect to death, hence elevating what might otherwise be second-degree murder (or possibly involuntary manslaughter) to first-degree murder when done in the course of a dangerous felony. *E.g.,* Ark. Stat. Ann., §45-10-102 (1997); see Labastida v. State, 931 P.2d 1334 (Nev. 1996) (parent's felony child neglect in face of beatings of child by another establishes "implied malice" necessary to establish felony murder).

- Some states condition felony murder on recklessness, hence making first-degree murder out of a homicide that would otherwise be involuntary manslaughter, if done in the course of a dangerous felony. *E.g.,* State v. Ortega, 112 N.M. 554, 817 P.2d 1196 (1991) (felony murder may rest on a greatly dangerous act done with "knowledge that the act creates a strong probability of death or great bodily harm").

- Some states expressly require proof of negligence, thus removing the strict liability component from felony murder. The Delaware first-degree murder statute mandates that the accused at least have acted with criminal negligence in the course of committing certain enumerated felonies or recklessly in the course of committing nonenumerated felonies. Del. Code, tit. 11, §636(a)(2),(6) (2001).

d. *Accomplice liability:* In many states, the felony-murder rule can also make the defendant liable for the homicidal behavior of an accomplice to the independent felony. Suppose a driver waits in a getaway car, while his co-felon robs a store. The storekeeper resists, and the robber shoots him. Is the co-felon liable? Some jurisdictions take the position that as a felon, he is liable for any death caused by the felony (or during its commission, or by any act in furtherance of it). Others require that he have some degree of culpability for the act causing death. A compromise position between these two is the affirmative defense contained in the New Jersey statute.

9. *Purposes of the felony murder rule.* Given New Jersey's limitation of felony murder to (1) enumerated dangerous felonies (2) of which the "probable consequence" is death (3) that kill nonparticipants (4) where the felons expect one of their number to impose a risk of death or carry a lethal weapon, it seems fair to conclude that New Jersey's felony murder rule requires a form of negligence. But why does such negligence justify murder liability? The New Jersey Supreme Court invokes Justice Holmes's argument that felony murder liability deters dangerous crimes. Do you find this rationale convincing? Is it also possible to justify felony murder liability on retributivist grounds, as deserved? Or are the drafters of the New Jersey Penal Code right, that "principled justification" of felony murder liability "is hard to find"?

a. *A taxonomy of rationales.* Different jurisdictions and commentators have posited some of the following penological justifications for the felony rule, some chiefly retributive and some utilitarian:

(1) The independent felony establishes, as a fact, that the defendant acted with the sort of mens rea that would otherwise establish murder liability — gross recklessness or "wanton indifference."

(2) The intention to commit a felony is as "malicious" a mental state as the intention to kill.

(3) A felony murder rule, by raising the stakes to murder where a death occurs in the course of a felony, will deter prospective criminals from committing the felony.

(4) A felony murder rule will induce those who will commit felonies to take the greatest pains to commit those felonies safely, since they know they will be responsible for any fatal outcomes.

What do you think of these rationales? Is #1 logically correct? Is #2 persuasive? Does #3 make sense, when presumably we already impose serious punishment for the underlying felony itself? Does #4 seem realistic, when in the case of a felon who commits the felony in a dangerous way, there is no bar to punishing him separately for both the felony and, say, reckless homicide?

b. *Felony murder and deterrence:* Deterrence-based rationales for felony murder assume that the mere act of committing the predicate felony raises a substantial risk of death. Most state statutes have enumerated at least some major felonies as automatically involving the rule, and probably the commonest examples of enumerated felonies are robbery, burglary, and rape. So are these crimes clear instances of felonies raising a substantial risk of death?

When they considered the felony murder rule, the drafters of the Model Penal Code noted the following statistics measuring the relation of total felonies to those resulting in homicides for robbery, rape, and burglary:[21]

> In fact, the number of all homicides which occur in the commission of such crimes as robbery, burglary, or rape is lower than might be expected. For example, comparison of the figures for solved and unsolved homicides from M. Wolfgang, Criminal Homicide (1958), with statistics on basic felonies taken from the FBI Uniform Crime Reports, reveals the following for Philadelphia from 1948-1952 (see table below).

Relation of Total Felonies to Homicides Occurring During the Felony, Philadelphia, 1948-1952

Offense	No. of crimes reported	No. accompanied by homicide	%	No. per 1,000
Robbery	6,432	38	0.59	5.9
Rape	1,133	4	0.35	3.5
Burglary	27,669	1	0.0036	0.036
Auto Theft	10,315	2	0.019	0.1

21. Model Penal Code and Commentaries, *supra,* at 38 n.6.

With probabilities so low, would the felony-murder rule deter anybody from committing a felony? If it did, would the small reduction in risk justify the increased penalty? Assuming that the vast majority of fatal robberies are those involving use of a firearm, would the deterrent effect of the rule be much greater if the rule were limited to robbery with a firearm? Or especially lethal firearms?

c. *Felony murder and desert:* Retributivists often challenge the felony murder rule as a species of strict liability, arguing that without some culpable mens rea toward the risk of death, the defendant does not merit murder, much less first-degree murder liability. Thus, defenders of the rule are often put in the difficult position of trying to justify extreme punishments for a strict liability rule. But could defenders of the rule refuse to concede the premise of the strict liability attack? Recall that State v. Martin described New Jersey's felony murder rule as requiring "foreseeability" and "culpability." Felony murder statutes usually set as a premise for murder liability the commission of a "predicate felony," which by itself poses a heightened risk of death. In light of that requirement, consider this perspective from Prof. Kenneth Simons:[22]

> On first impression, any grading differential for which no formal culpability is required seems inconsistent with retributivism. . . .
>
> But this analysis is incorrect. Often, culpably doing X, which happens to cause Y, amounts to negligence (or to a higher culpability, such as recklessness) as to Y. Consider a more specific felony murder example. If armed robbery is the predicate felony, then it is not difficult to conclude that an armed robber should foresee, and often does foresee, a significant risk that the robbery will result in a death. Thus, the robber is ordinarily negligent and often reckless as to the risk of death.
>
> This analysis suggests that formal strict liability as to death (i.e., the lack of any explicit culpability requirement) can nevertheless be consistent with substantive culpability. But the question remains: how much of a differential in punishment does such culpability justify? An armed robber who causes death had engaged in a serious felony, and has, let us assume, recklessly caused death. So his punishment for felony-murder can at least be as severe as the combined punishment that retributive principles permit for the felony and for the reckless homicide. But can the punishment be more?
>
> I believe that it can, insofar as knowingly creating a risk of death in the context of another criminal act is more culpable than knowingly creating a risk of death in the context of an innocent or less culpable act. A reckless homicide growing out of a seriously wrongful activity is a much more culpable homicide on that account. . . .
>
> Now consider a more complex case than the armed robber (who ordinarily is aware of a substantial risk that he might cause death, or who at least should reasonably be aware of such a risk). Suppose instead that the foreseeability of death resulting from a particular felony is just below the threshold that we require for negligent homicide. For example, consider an unarmed bank robbery in which the risk of death (from a guard or police officer) is real but not sufficient to surpass that threshold. Should we conclude that the bank robber has displayed no culpability as to the risk of death, so that liability for that death is genuinely strict?
>
> We should not reach that conclusion, because the conclusion rests on too narrow a conception of negligence, one that applies the concept of negligence only to an isolated element of the offense, not to the offender's conduct more generally. . . . As John Gardner has put the matter, his commission of a felony "changes his normative position."

22. When Is Strict Liability Just? 87 J. Crim. L. & Criminology, 1075, 1121-24 (1997).

Even if retributivists concede that felony murder operates as a negligence rule, they may attack its punishment upgrades as unfairly severe. But perhaps even this attack can be answered. The mens rea for any homicide properly involves the weighing of two factors: the extent of the defendant's willingness to impose a risk of death on others, and the moral worth of the purpose for which the defendant imposes the risk. For example, the gross recklessness that gives rise to murder liability requires recklessness in the course of an unworthy or immoral purpose — otherwise it would be punishable only as manslaughter. Even intentional homicide may be punishable only as manslaughter if committed under "adequate provocation" or under an honest but unreasonably mistaken belief that defensive force was necessary. Perhaps, then, negligently causing death in the furtherance of a felonious purpose is as bad as recklessly causing death in furtherance of an immoral purpose, which in turn is as bad as intentionally causing death without provocation. On this view, the moral wrong captured by the concept of felony murder is a kind of exploitation — a willingness to impose a risk of death on others in pursuit of a malign goal. The risk may be small, but the evil purpose renders even that small risk thoroughly reprehensible.[23]

10. *Reprise on foreseeability and causation.* In People v. Stamp, 2 Cal. App. 3d 203, 82 Cal. Rptr. 598 (1969), defendants Koory and Stamp,

> armed with a gun and a blackjack, entered the rear of the building housing the offices of General Amusement Company, [and] ordered the employees they found there to go to the front of the premises, where the two secretaries were working. [Lehman, the third co-felon, waited, and was later apprehended, in the getaway car.] Stamp, the one with the gun, then went into the office of Carl Honeyman, the owner and manager. Thereupon Honeyman, looking very frightened and pale, emerged from the office in a "kind of hurry." He was apparently propelled by Stamp who had hold of him by an elbow.
>
> The robbery victims were required to lie down on the floor while the robbers took the money and fled out the back door. As the robbers, who had been on the premises 10 to 15 minutes, were leaving, they told the victims to remain on the floor for five minutes so that no one would "get hurt."
>
> Honeyman, who had been lying next to the counter, had to use it to steady himself in getting up off the floor. Still pale, he was short of breath, sucking air, and pounding and rubbing his chest. As he walked down the hall, in an unsteady manner, still breathing hard and rubbing his chest, he said he was having trouble "keeping the pounding down inside" and that his heart was "pumping too fast for him." A few minutes later, although still looking very upset, shaking, wiping his forehead and rubbing his chest, he was able to walk in a steady manner into an employee's office. When the police arrived, almost immediately thereafter, he told them he was not feeling very well and that he had a pain in his chest. About two minutes later, which was 15 to 20 minutes after the robbery had occurred, he collapsed on the floor. At 11:25 he was pronounced dead on arrival at the hospital. The coroner's report listed the immediate cause of death as heart attack.
>
> The employees noted that during the hours before the robbery Honeyman had appeared to be in normal health and good spirits. The victim was an obese, sixty-year-old man, with a history of heart disease, who was under a great deal of pressure due to the intensely competitive nature of his business. Additionally, he did not take good care of his heart.

23. See Guyora Binder, Meaning and Motive in the Law of Homicide, 3 Buff. Crim. L. Rev. 755, 770-774 (2000); Guyora Binder, The Rhetoric of Motive and Intent, 6 Buff. Crim. L. Rev. 1, 84-86 (2002).

Three doctors . . . testified that although Honeyman had an advanced case of atherosclerosis, a progressive and ultimately fatal disease, . . . but for the robbery there would have been no fatal seizure at that time. The fright induced by the robbery was too much of a shock to Honeyman's system. . . . [2 Cal. App. 3d at 207-208.]

The court affirmed the defendants' first-degree convictions and life sentences, under Cal. Penal Code, §189 (see p. 295, *supra*), stating:

There is no requirement that the killing occur, "while committing" or "while engaged in" the felony, or that the killing be "a part of" the felony, other than that the few acts be a part of one continuous transaction. Thus the homicide need not have been committed "to perpetrate" the felony. There need be no technical inquiry as to whether there has been a completion or abandonment of or desistance from the robbery before the homicide itself was completed. . . .

The doctrine is not limited to those deaths which are foreseeable. Rather a felon is held strictly liable for *all* killings committed by him or his accomplices in the course of the felony. . . . [2 Cal. App. 3d at 210.]

The defendants argued that the trial court erred by refusing this proffered instruction: "Where the defendant's criminal act is not the proximate cause of the death and the sole proximate cause was the negligent or reckless conduct of the victim, a conviction is unwarranted." . . . The court held that the following instruction, which the jury received, was sufficient:

The proximate cause of death is that cause which, in natural and continuous sequence, unbroken by any efficient intervening cause, produces the death, and without which the result would not have occurred. It is the efficient cause — the one that necessarily sets in operation the factors that accomplish the death.

If a person unlawfully does an act or unlawfully sets in operation factors which are a proximate cause of another person's death, such conduct of the former constitutes an unlawful homicide even though the unlawful act or the factors set in operation were not the only cause of the death, and although the person killed had been already enfeebled by disease, injury, physical condition or other cause and although it is probable that a person in sound physical condition would not have died as a result of the act or the factors set in operation, and although it is probable that the act or the factors set in operation only hastened the death of the deceased person and that he would have died soon thereafter anyhow from another cause or other causes. [Id. at 211-212 n.4.]

What type of homicide, if any, would the defendants in *Stamp* be guilty of if there were no felony-murder rule? Did the defendants "kill" the victim? Did their robbery cause the victim's death? Does the court require that the death be instrumental to the robbery? Does it require that the act causing the death be instrumental to the robbery? Would the convictions stand under the *Martin* test in New Jersey? How different is the California test?

One court reached a result similar to that in the *Stamp* case while nevertheless applying a foreseeability standard. In People v. Brackett, 510 N.E.2d 877 Ill. (1987), an 85-year-old woman who had suffered a rape and aggravated battery fell into a deep depression that caused her to refuse to eat. Doctors inserted a tube to feed her, but breathing difficulties resulting from the attack led to her choking to death on the tube. The court upheld the felony murder charge because the fact of death from the attack, if not the specific means of death, was foreseeable. Note that the court in *Stamp* conditions felony murder liability on killing in the course of a "felony inherently dangerous to life." If a felony is inherently dangerous to life, can a resulting death be unforeseeable, according to the reasoning of *Brackett*? Was Honeyman's death within the scope of the danger ordinarily posed by robbery? Was the death of Brackett's victim within the scope of the danger ordinarily posed by rape?

2. Causal Limitations

One means of limiting felony murder liability, illustrated in the *Martin* case, is to require a close causal connection between the felony and the resulting death. This connection may be established by requiring that death be the "foreseeable" or "probable" result of the felony (as in *Martin*); or that the act causing death be committed by a participant in the felony (as required in New Jersey before 1979); or that a felon directly "kill" rather than merely somehow cause death; or that death be caused "in the commission" of the felony, or "in furtherance" of the felony (as was required in New Jersey before 1981); or that the person killed be a non-participant in the felony. This section will explore several of these criteria of causal linkage between felony and death.

PEOPLE v. HICKMAN
Appellate Court of Illinois
12 Ill. App. 3d 412, 297 N.E.2d 582 (1973)

SCOTT, JUSTICE.

[Defendants Rock and Hickman along with several others were surprised by the police as they emerged from a burglary; they attempted to escape and] ran through the bushes while in the meantime Sergeant Cronk ran to the rear of the warehouse where he noticed two people running in a northwesterly direction. Sergeant Cronk yelled "halt — police" several times but his commands were ignored. He lost sight of the two fleeing individuals but within seconds thereafter saw a man carrying a handgun running towards the bushes at the northwest corner of the parking lot. Sergeant Cronk, believing that this approaching individual was one of the burglars . . . and referring to the handgun, ordered the person to "drop it." When there was no compliance to this warning Sergeant Cronk fired his shotgun at the individual, who was later discovered to be Detective William Loscheider of the Joliet police force. Loscheider was killed by this shot from his fellow officer's gun.

Approximately one-half hour later the defendants Rock and Hickman were arrested as they were walking on a street approximately two and a half blocks from the warehouse. Neither of the defendants had a weapon on his person. . . .

. . . [W]e must determine whether the actual shooting which caused the death of an innocent victim must have been performed by the defendants or someone acting in concert with them in order to comply with the requirements of the felony-murder doctrine.

Our criminal code contains statutory provisions relating to the felony-murder doctrine, being Ch. 38, Sec. 9-1 (a) (3), Ill. Rev. Stat., which provides:

(a) A person who kills an individual without lawful justification commits murder if, in performing the acts which cause the death: . . . (3) He is attempting or committing a forcible felony other than voluntary manslaughter.

The defendants urge an interpretation of this statute to the effect that the person who kills or performs the acts which cause death must be the same person as the one who is attempting or committing a forcible felony before liability for murder can be imposed.

While the syntax of the words involved in our felony-murder statute could be interpreted on the restrictive and narrow lines urged by the defendants, we do not believe that in statutory construction we are bound to consider only the wording used in the statute. The court in construing a statute may consider the notes and reports of the commission pursuant to which the statutory provision was adopted. Turning our attention to the committee comments in regard to the statute in question we find on page 9 of Smith Hurd Ill. Ann. Stat., Ch. 38, the following comments in regard to the application of Sec. 9-1 (a) (3), the felony-murder provision:

It is immaterial whether the killing in such a case is intentional or accidental, or is committed by a confederate without the connivance of the defendant . . . or even by a third person trying to prevent the commission of the felony.

In support of the committee comment that one can be guilty of murder where the killing resulted from the act of third person trying to prevent the commission of a felony, there is cited the case of People v. Payne, 359 Ill. 246, 194 N.E. 539[,] where armed robbers entered the home of two brothers. One of the brothers discharged a weapon to prevent the robbery as did one of the robbers. The other brother was killed and it could not be determined whether he was killed by his brother or the robber. Our Supreme Court in affirming the defendant's conviction of murder stated:

Where several persons conspire to do an unlawful act, and another crime is committed in the pursuit of the common object, all are alike guilty of the crime committed, if it is a natural and probable consequence of the execution of the conspiracy. . . . It reasonably might be anticipated that an attempted robbery would meet with resistance, during which the victim might be shot either by himself or someone else in attempting to prevent the robbery, and those attempting to perpetrate the robbery would be guilty of murder.

. . . [I]n *Payne* the court clearly adopted the theory that a defendant and co-conspirators acting in concert with him can be held responsible for a killing of an innocent third party during the commission of a forcible felony even though the killing was not actually done by a person acting in concert with the defendant or his co-conspirators. . . .

The defendants both in the trial court and in this appeal urge that the applicable law is set forth in the case of People v. Morris, 1 Ill. App. 3d 566, 274 N.E.2d 898. In *Morris* the defendant and two cohorts entered a restaurant armed for the purpose of committing a robbery. A struggle ensued between a patron and one of the cohorts during which gunfire erupted and the cohort was killed. The defendant Morris, one of the would-be robbers, was charged with murder of his co-conspirator under the theory of the felony-murder doctrine and was convicted of the crime of murder by the trial court. The reviewing court reversed the trial court holding that the felony-murder doctrine is not applicable against a surviving felon when a co-felon is justifiably killed during commission of a forcible felony.

We do not believe that the rationale of the *Morris* case is controlling in the instant case since *Morris* presented a factual situation which differed in one very significant detail. In *Morris,* unlike the case before us, the victim was not an innocent third party. In *Morris* the victim was not free from culpability but was in fact an individual who was attempting to commit a felony. We do not . . . indulge in the fanciful theory that the victim being a felon assumed the risk and thereby constructively consented to his death, but we do hold that he assisted in setting in motion a chain of events which was the proximate cause of his death and therefore in the criminal law as in the civil law there is no redress for the victim.

Clearly the case of People v. Payne, 359 Ill. 246, 194 N.E. 539, and the case now before us are distinguishable from *Morris* in that unlike *Morris,* innocent parties were killed. We interpret *Payne* as setting forth the rule that he whose act causes in any way, directly, or indirectly, the death of an innocent victim is guilty of murder by virtue of the felony-murder doctrine.

. . . There should be no doubt about the "justice" of holding a felon guilty of murder who engages in a robbery followed by an attempted escape and thereby inevitably calls into action defensive forces against him, the activity of which results in the death of an innocent human being.

[*conviction reversed*]

Notes and Questions

1. What would the defendants be guilty of in this case without the felony murder rule?

2. Does it accord more with your sense of justice to convict Hickman of just burglary or of murder as well?

3. Recall the description of New Jersey felony murder law in *Martin,* above. How would New Jersey's affirmative defense apply to Hickman? This defense is also available in New York and several other states. How would Hickman have fared under the test applied in New Jersey's earlier *Canola* case? How would Hickman fare under New Jersey's requirement that the death be the "probable consequence" of defendant's conduct and "not too remote or accidental to bear justly" on his culpability?

4. *California's limits.* California law takes a categorically more restrictive view of the *Hickman* situation, as laid out in People v. Washington, 62 Cal. 2d 777, 44 Cal. Rptr. 442 (1965). The facts were these:

> Shortly before 10 P.M., October 2, 1962, Johnnie Carpenter prepared to close his gasoline station. He was in his office computing the receipts and disbursements of the day while an attendant in an adjacent storage room deposited money in a vault. Upon hearing someone yell "robbery," Carpenter opened his desk and took out a revolver. A few moments later, James Ball entered the office and pointed a

revolver directly at Carpenter, who fired immediately, mortally wounding Ball. Carpenter then hurried to the door and saw an unarmed man he later identified as defendant running from the vault with a moneybag in his right hand. He shouted "Stop." When his warning was not heeded, he fired and hit defendant who fell wounded in front of the station. [62 Cal. 2d at 779.]

In a famous opinion by Chief Justice Traynor, the court said:

> . . . The felony-murder doctrine ascribes malice aforethought to the felon who kills in the perpetration of an inherently dangerous felony. That doctrine is incorporated in section 189 of the Penal Code, which provides in part: "All murder . . . committed in the perpetration or attempt to perpetrate . . . robbery . . . is murder of the first degree." . . .
>
> When a killing is not committed by a robber or by his accomplice but by his victim, malice aforethought is not attributable to the robber, for the killing is not committed by him in the perpetration or attempt to perpetrate robbery. It is not enough that the killing was a risk reasonably to be foreseen and that the robbery might therefore be regarded as a proximate cause of the killing. Section 189 requires that the felon or his accomplice commit the killing, for if he does not, the killing is not committed to perpetrate the felony. . . . To include such killings within §189 would expand the meaning of the words "murder . . . which is committed in the perpetration . . . [of] robbery . . ." beyond common understanding.
>
> The purpose of the felony-murder rule is to deter felons from killing negligently or accidentally by holding them strictly responsible for killings they commit. This purpose is not served by punishing them for killings committed by their victims.
>
> It is contended, however, that another purpose of the felony-murder rule is to prevent the commission of robberies. Neither the common-law rationale of the rule nor the Penal Code supports this contention. In every robbery there is a possibility that the victim will resist and kill. The robber has little control over such a killing once the robbery is undertaken as this case demonstrates. To impose an additional penalty for the killing would discriminate between robbers, not on the basis of any difference in their own conduct, but solely on the basis of the response by others that the robber's conduct happened to induce. An additional penalty for a homicide committed by the victim would deter robbery haphazardly at best. To "prevent stealing, [the law] would do better to hang one thief in every thousand by lot." (Holmes, The Common Law, p. 58.) . . .
>
> To invoke the felony-murder doctrine when the killing is not committed by the defendant or by his accomplice could lead to absurd results. Thus, two men rob a grocery store and flee in opposite directions. The owner of the store follows one of the robbers and kills him. Neither robber may have fired a shot. Neither robber may have been armed with a deadly weapon. If the felony-murder doctrine applied, however, the surviving robber could be convicted of first degree murder, even though he was captured by a policeman and placed under arrest at the time his accomplice was killed. [Id. at 780-783.]

Did the majority in *Washington* remove a meaningful deterrent to the commission of armed robberies? Can it be argued that any shooting or gun battle can be attributed to the armed robbers, because of their presence, even if a victim or police officer shoots first? In *Stamp,* the accomplices did not have to directly perform the killing to be guilty of felony murder. Is the fact that there was in *Washington* an intervening action (the victim shooting the co-felon) sufficient to distinguish *Stamp*?

Two recent cases follow the *Hickman* "proximate cause" theory of felony murder. See People v. Dekens, 695 N.E.2d 474 (Ill. 1998) (robbery victim shoots co-felon); Palmer v. State, 704 N.E.2d 124 (Ind. 1999) (in kidnapping case, felony murder upheld when defendant held a gun to one officer's head, and in the struggle, one officer accidentally shot the other).

5. *Felon as victim.* Does it matter if the victim is a co-felon? Should the court be less concerned with giving prosecutors a tool to convict when the victim is a felon, rather than an innocent person? Under *Washington* what would have been the result if Carpenter had missed Ball and killed a passerby? What about under the New Jersey statute?

In an old case testing the limits of the felony-murder rule, People v. Cabaltero, 31 Cal. App. 2d 52, 87 P.2d 364 (1939), the appellant combined with Dasalla, Ancheta, and Flores to commit a robbery at a farm run by Nishida. During the robbery, Ancheta unnecessarily fired a shot at two workers who came upon the scene; in anger for this foolish act, Dasalla shot Ancheta to death. The court held that section 189 "was designed to include and that its provisions apply to any killing by one engaged in the commission of any of the specified felonies, irrespective of the status of the person killed and regardless of whether the killing is accidental or intentional. . . ." On the other hand, the *Cabaltero* court confidently distinguished People v. Ferlin, 203 Cal. 587, 265 P. 230, where one Skala, who was Ferlin's accomplice to an act of arson (for insurance fraud), accidentally burned himself to death outside Ferlin's presence. The court disapproved of any murder charge against Ferlin on the ground that Skala had killed himself. Was the court in *Cabaltero* justified in distinguishing *Ferlin*? Can *Washington* be squared with *Cabaltero*?

On what rationale is the felony murder rule designed to protect felons?

6. *The Pennsylvania cases.* Pennsylvania developed its felony murder doctrine in a series of cases similar to those in this chapter. In Commonwealth v. Almeida, 362 Pa. 596, 68 A.2d 595 (1949), a police officer was killed by other officers attempting to apprehend robbers. The court explicitly expanded the felony murder doctrine by espousing a doctrine of proximate cause, attaching liability for any death proximately resulting from commission of the felony. If the risk of death was foreseeable and death occurred, the felon was guilty of felony murder.

In Commonwealth v. Thomas, 382 Pa. 639, 117 A.2d 204 (1955), the defendant was charged with the killing of his accomplice by the victim of their robbery. The court, reasoning from *Almeida*, held the defendant liable. *Thomas* was overruled three years later by Commonwealth v. Redline, 391 Pa. 486, 137 A.2d 472 (1958). In *Redline* the defendant initiated a gun battle and his accomplice was killed by a police bullet. Reversing Redline's felony murder conviction, the court distinguished *Almeida* by distinguishing "excusable" and "justifiable" homicides. The killing of an innocent person, as in *Almeida*, was merely an excusable killing while the killing of a co-felon was a justifiable one. The court stated that

> the victim of the homicide was one of the robbers who, while resisting apprehension in his effort to escape was shot and killed by a policeman in the performance of his duty. Thus, the homicide was justifiable and, obviously, could not be availed of, on any rational legal theory, to support a charge of murder. How can anyone, no matter how much of an outlaw he may be, have a criminal charge lodged against him for the consequence of the lawful conduct of another person? [137 A.2d at 483.]

The court then held that, "in order to convict for felony murder, the killing must have been done by the defendant or by an accomplice or confederate or by one acting in furtherance of the felonious undertaking." *Almeida* and its proximate cause approach were explicitly overruled in Commonwealth ex rel. Smith v. Meyers, 438 Pa. 218, 261 A.2d 550 (1970), 12 years after *Redline.* The court in *Meyers,* though, rejected *Redline*'s distinction between excusable and justifiable killings. Why do you think that distinction was rejected?

7. *The "regular" murder "back-up."* *Washington* forbade the use of the felony murder rule in California when any person other than one of the felons committed the killing. Nevertheless, the court did not bar other means of imposing murder liability on felons who may indirectly cause death, especially by initiating gun battles, noting that such felons may be guilty of "abandoned and malignant heart" murder. This approach was applied in Taylor v. Superior Court, 3 Cal. 3d 578, 91 Cal. Rptr. 275 (1970), where one robber threatened a liquor store owner with a gun, provoking the shopkeeper's wife to open fire, killing another robber. Taylor, who waited in a getaway car, was charged with the murder of his co-felon. He moved to have the murder charge set aside on the grounds that *Washington* forbade a felony murder count, and there was no evidence of murder on any other theory. The state Supreme Court affirmed the trial court's denial of his motion on the ground that the actions of Daniels and Smith were "provocative of lethal resistance" and that the two men had initiated the gun battle "with conscious disregard for human life and with natural consequences dangerous to life." Id. at 584-85. Hence, Taylor could be an accomplice to second-degree "abandoned and malignant heart" murder.

8. *A felony murder exercise:* A and his accomplice, B, had committed a residential burglary and made their escape in a Cadillac. Shortly thereafter, police approached the parked car when B was driving it alone. Before the police could frisk B, he fired at one officer and began running. Another officer fired and killed B. Apply the different rules and rationales above to determine whether the felony murder rule might apply to A.

9. Notice that the defendants in *Hickman* were trying to escape when the fatality occurred. Should that matter? Consider the next case.

PEOPLE v. GLADMAN
Court of Appeals of New York
41 N.Y.2d 124, 359 N.E.2d 420 (1976)

JASEN, JUDGE.

At trial, the People submitted overwhelming evidence . . . that on the night of December 29, 1971, the defendant shot and killed Nassau County Police Officer Richard Rose in a bowling alley parking lot. The events of that evening can be briefly recited. At approximately 8:00 P.M., defendant obtained a ride to the County Line Shopping Center in Amityville, New York. Ten minutes later, he entered a delicatessen, produced a gun, and demanded money from the clerk. The clerk turned over about $145 in cash and checks. After the robbery, Gladman left the shopping center and walked through the surrounding neighborhood, eventually arriving at the County Line Bowling Alley. In the meantime, the robbery had been reported to the Nassau County Police Department and an alert was transmitted over the police radio. Two officers arrived at the delicatessen at

8:16 P.M., just minutes after the defendant had left. A description of the robber was obtained and broadcast over the police radio. Normal police procedure required that unassigned patrol cars proceed to the vicinity of the crime area and any nearby major intersections in an effort to seal off potential avenues of escape. As Gladman walked onto the parking lot of the bowling alley, he saw a police car turn and enter the lot. He hid under a parked car. Patrolman Rose, the lone officer in the car, emerged from his vehicle and walked over to defendant's hiding place. The defendant got up from underneath the car with his gun concealed between his legs. The officer ordered the defendant to put his weapon on the car hood; instead, the defendant turned and fired. Patrolman Rose, mortally wounded, struggled to his police car and attempted to use the radio to summon the assistance of brother officers. He collapsed on the seat. The defendant commandeered the automobile of a bowling alley patron and made good his escape. An off-duty New York City police officer used Rose's radio to broadcast a signal for help. The report of the shooting went over the police radio at 8:24 P.M. Eyewitnesses fixed the time of the altercation at approximately 8:25 P.M. The bowling alley was located less than one-half mile from the robbed delicatessen.

Defendant was subsequently captured, identified by eyewitnesses, . . . indicted [and convicted]. . . .

. . . The principal issue on this appeal is whether the jury was properly permitted to conclude that the shooting of Officer Rose occurred in the immediate flight from the delicatessen robbery. . . .

Under old statutes which did not specifically address the issue it was early held that a killing committed during an escape could . . . constitute a felony murder . . . where the defendants got away with some loot. A different result was reached in People v. Huter, 184 N.Y. 237, 77 N.E. 6, where . . . hot pursuit . . . "did not operate to continue the burglary after the defendant had abandoned the property that he undertook to carry away and had escaped from the premises burglarized." . . . These kinds of analyses soon led to the development of some rather arbitrary rules. . . .

The later New York cases indicate some dissatisfaction with the strict legal rules that had developed and tended to leave the question of escape killings to the jury as a question of fact, under appropriate instructions. The charge was to point out "generally that the killing to be felony murder must occur while the actor or one or more of his confederates is engaged in securing the plunder or in doing something immediately connected with the underlying crime, that escape may . . . be a matter so immediately connected with the crime as to be part of its commission but that, where there is . . . a complete intervening desistence from the crime, as by the abandonment of the loot and running away, the subsequent homicide is not murder in the first degree without proof of deliberation and intent." The question of termination of the underlying felony was then left to the jury as a fact question.

The New York approach was more rigid than that developed in other jurisdictions. The majority of the States tended to follow the "res gestae" theory — i.e., whether the killing was committed in, about and as a part of the underlying transaction. California had adopted the res gestae theory, at least insofar as robbery is concerned, holding that a robbery is not complete if the "conspirators have not won their way even momentarily to a place of temporary safety and the possession of the plunder is nothing more than a scrambling possession." . . .

The 1967 Penal Law limited the application of the felony murder concept to nine serious and violent predicate felonies. At the same time, it was provided that the doctrine would apply to a killing committed in "immediate flight." This change was intended to do away with many of the old technical distinctions relating to "abandonment" or "completion."

Under the new formulation, the issue of whether the homicide occurred in "immediate flight" from a felony is only rarely to be considered as a question of law for resolution by the court. Only where the record compels the inference that the actor was not in "immediate flight" may a felony murder conviction be set aside on the law. Rather, the question is to be submitted to the jury, under an appropriate charge. The jury should be instructed to give consideration to whether the homicide and the felony occurred at the same location or, if not, to the distance separating the two locations. Weight may also be placed on whether there is an interval of time between the commission of the felony and the commission of the homicide. The jury may properly consider such additional factors as whether the culprits had possession of the fruits of criminal activity, whether the police, watchmen or concerned citizens were in close pursuit, and whether the criminals had reached a place of temporary safety. These factors are not exclusive; others may be appropriate in differing factual settings. If anything, past history demonstrates the fruitlessness of attempting to apply rigid rules to virtually limitless factual variations. No single factor is necessarily controlling; it is the combination of several factors that leads to a justifiable inference.

In this case, the jury could properly find, as a question of fact, that the killing of Officer Rose occurred in immediate flight from the delicatessen robbery. The shooting occurred less than 15 minutes after the robbery and less than a half mile away. The defendant had made off with cash proceeds and was attempting to secure his possession of the loot. The police had reason to believe that the robber was still in the immediate vicinity and had taken steps to seal off avenues of escape. In this regard, the absence of proof as to why Officer Rose turned into the bowling alley parking lot is no deficiency. The standard is not whether the police officer subjectively believed that the defendant was the robber. Indeed, the defendant's own apprehension may be more valuable. The defendant's response to the observation of the police car was to seek an immediate hiding place. This indicates that the defendant perceived that the police were on his trail. The record does not indicate that the officer knew or supposed that defendant committed a crime; it does indicate that the defendant feared that the officer possessed such knowledge. Additionally, the defendant had not reached any place of temporary safety. In short, there is evidence from which the jury could conclude, as it did, that the defendant was in immediate flight from the robbery and that he shot the officer in order to make good his escape with the loot. The jury was properly charged as to the relevant considerations and we see no basis for disturbing its findings. . . .

Notes and Questions

1. Does the court lay down any standards with which to measure the duration of a felony? If not, why not? Is flexibility in this instance good or bad? Why?

2. *Immediate flight.* If a felon is chased by police officers for two hours after committing a crime, is he still in immediate flight? What if the chase is ten

hours? Two days? Does it make sense for purposes of the felony murder rule to say that the felony has ceased if the pursuers lose the felon's trail, allowing the felon to reach a place of temporary safety, even though they regain the trail quickly? In order to answer this kind of question do we have to know which answer comports best with the policies underlying the felony murder rule? What are those policies? Why should a felony ever end — at least before the felons have all been brought to justice?

In Franks v. State, 636 P.2d 361 (Okla. Cr. 1981), the defendant robbed a supermarket and drove off the scene unpursued; several minutes later he was stopped for speeding and running a stop sign by an officer unaware of the robbery; the defendant assaulted the officer, took his gun, fired at him, and then drove off; the officer, who had run from the gunshots, was unable to pursue by car; a few minutes later, Franks ran another stop sign and struck another car, killing a child passenger. The court reversed the felony murder conviction for want of a causal "nexus" between either the robbery of the grocery store or the attack against the officer and the child's death. Is this too generous under *Gladman*? Should it matter that Franks took the officer's gun?

But in State v. Colenburg, 773 S.W.2d 184 (Mo. App. 1989), the felony murder conviction was upheld where the defendant had received a stolen car and committed the felony of "tampering" with its VIN number, and then, almost seven months later, fatally struck a child with the car. The court held that at the time of the accident, the defendant was still driving the car without the owner's consent. Would *Gladman* permit this result? Is the result in *Colenburg* consistent with the reasoning in the earlier auto-theft case of State v. Chambers, 524 S.W.2d 826 (Mo. 1975) (see p. 417, *infra*)?

3. *The "purposive scope" of the felony.* Consider Stouffer v. State, 703 A.2d 861 (Md. App. 1997). Stouffer, along with two accomplices, decided to attack one Fiddler because they suspected Fiddler was an informant to narcotics detectives. Fiddler was found dead by the side of a road, the victim of a stabbing and beating. Forensic evidence, including the absence of blood at the scene, led state experts to testify that the attack had begun elsewhere, that Fiddler was forcibly moved while still alive, and that after he died his body was dumped at the roadside. Stouffer was convicted of kidnapping and felony murder. The appellate court affirmed the kidnapping conviction but reversed the felony-murder verdict, declaring that the homicide was not "committed in the perpetration of a felony."

> In our determination of whether the homicide was committed in the perpetration of the underlying felony, we are not concerned with the point in time at which the intent to commit the underlying felony was formed. Rather, we consider dispositive whether the overarching intent — which we shall refer to with a capital "I" — driving the criminal enterprise is the intent essential to the underlying felony or the intent which is the mens rea of the resulting homicide, regardless of whether the intent is formed before or after the homicide. Conceptually, when this Intent coincides with the requisite intent of the underlying felony, the resulting homicide is felony murder. The corollary, of course, is that where that intent coincides with the mens rea of homicide, the homicide is not felony murder.
>
> There was no direct or inferential evidence before the trier of fact that the announced purpose of Stouffer's mission — to scare Fiddler — was to be accomplished by forcibly confining and transporting him. All of the evidence indicates that the means to be employed in intimidating Fiddler or placing him in fear as a consequence of him being a "narc" or "sticking his nose where it didn't belong" was

the infliction of serious bodily harm in a reckless and dangerous manner with indifference to the consequences, i.e., as Stouffer reportedly said, "I do not give a damn if the guy lived or died."

The felony-murder rule was conceived at common law to relieve the State of its obligation to prove an intent to kill when a felon embarked on a dangerous course of conduct which, because of that conduct, resulted in death. . . . The rationale was to dissuade one from engaging in a dangerous course of conduct whereby a greater harm might logically result; it was not the object to dissuade a course of conduct, the aim of which was to inflict great bodily injury from resulting in a far lesser harm.

The felony must be a sine qua non, i.e., but for the felony, the deceased would not have been killed. [Id. at 875-76.]

Is *Stouffer*'s purposive test preferable to *Gladman*'s focus on the temporal scope of the felony?

3. Dangerous Felony Limitations

As we have seen, both utilitarian and retributivist arguments for felony murder liability presume that the rule will be predicated on especially dangerous felonies. In many states, legislatures have enumerated specific felonies (most often robbery, burglary, rape, and perhaps arson and kidnapping) as predicates for the felony murder rule. In a few states, the statutes speak of "dangerous" or "serious" felonies and leave it to the courts to determine which felonies fill that category. In some states this is the sole felony-murder rule and can produce a first-degree murder. In others, enumerated felonies can establish first-degree murder but nonenumerated felonies, if sufficiently dangerous, can establish second-degree murder. Under these statutes, courts may employ notions of foreseeability in a categorical way. That is, they can hold as a matter of law that certain felonies are so inherently dangerous that death is a legally foreseeable result, but others are not.

In a truistic sense, any felony that results in death is dangerous. But the illogical implications of that truism should seem obvious: Any time a commission of a particular felony led to death, we would have to declare that type of felony categorically "dangerous" in the legal sense. Absurd examples come to mind quickly: Lee, a gasoline executive, calls Sandy, a rival, to announce that he is planning a price-fixing arrangement with another seller, Pat, so that Lee and Pat can dominate the market. Price-fixing is illegal and can sometimes be a felony under the antitrust laws. Pat is horrified upon hearing the deal arranged by Lee and Sandy and drops dead on the spot from a heart attack. Felony-murder? Hardly, but as the controversial California second-degree felony murder doctrine demonstrates (see *infra*), resolving this illogic while retaining the notion of nonenumerated felonies for second-degree murder is not easy:

i. *Danger in the abstract:* Consider the following facts, taken from a California Supreme Court decision, People v. Patterson, 262 Cal. Rptr. 195, 49 Cal. 3d 615 (1989):

[T]he victim Jennie Licerio and her friend Carmen Lopez had been using cocaine on a daily basis in the months preceding Licerio's death. On the night of November 25, 1985, the two women were with defendant [Patterson] in his motel room.

There, all three drank "wine coolers," inhaled "lines" of cocaine, and smoked "coco puffs" (hand-rolled cigarettes containing a mixture of tobacco and cocaine). Defendant furnished the cocaine. When Licerio became ill, Lopez called an ambulance. Defendant stayed with the two women until the paramedics and the police arrived. The paramedics were unable to revive Licerio, who died of acute cocaine intoxication.

Recall the "abandoned and malignant heart" standard discussed earlier in this chapter, pp. 382-395, *supra*. Given the above facts, would a prosecutor be able to prove that Patterson had exhibited the requisite "gross recklessness" or "wanton indifference" for murder? Does one necessarily manifest such a mental state by supplying cocaine? Did Patterson himself manifest it by the particular way he supplied Licerio cocaine? The court said:

> While Health and Safety Code section 11352 includes drug offenses other than the crime of furnishing cocaine, which formed the basis for the prosecution's theory of second degree felony murder here, we conclude that the inquiry into inherent dangerousness must focus on the felony of furnishing cocaine, and not on section 11352 as a whole. We further hold that — consistent with the established definition of the term "inherently dangerous to life" in the context of implied malice as an element of second degree murder — a felony is inherently dangerous to life when there is a high probability that its commission will result in death. . . .
>
> [I]n determining whether defendant committed an inherently dangerous felony, we must consider the elements of the felony "in the abstract." . . . Because Health and Safety Code section 11352 also proscribes conduct other than that involved here (furnishing cocaine), the issue still to be resolved is whether we must consider only the specific offense of furnishing cocaine or the entire scope of conduct prohibited by the statute.
>
> The determination whether a defendant who furnishes cocaine commits an inherently dangerous felony should not turn on the dangerousness of other drugs included in the same statute, such as heroin and peyote; nor should it turn on the danger to life, if any, inherent in the transportation or administering of cocaine. Rather, each offence set forth in the statute should be examined separately to determine its inherent dangerousness. . . . [49 Cal. 3d at 619-625.]

The court in *Patterson* then reaffirmed the second-degree felony murder doctrine, provided that the predicate felony has a high probability of causing death. The court, however, did not reach the question of whether Patterson's particular offense — furnishing cocaine — is inherently dangerous to human life. Instead, the Court of Appeal was directed to remand the case to the trial court for it to decide the question of inherent dangerousness of furnishing cocaine "in the abstract," rather than as committed by Patterson. In another case, the California Supreme Court explained the reason for this limitation:

> [T]here is a killing in every case where the rule might potentially be applied. If in such circumstances a court were to examine the particular facts of the case prior to establishing whether the underlying felony is inherently dangerous, the court might well be led to conclude the rule applicable despite any unfairness which might redound to so broad an application: the existence of the dead victim might appear to lead inexorably to the conclusion that the underlying felony is exceptionally hazardous. [People v. Burroughs, 35 Cal. 3d 824, 210 Cal. Rptr. 319 (1984).]

Thus, under California law, when a court decides whether a particular felony can serve as the predicate for the felony murder rule, it must consider that felony without any reference to the facts of their particular killing. Otherwise, the very rule-like quality of the rule will dissolve, and the rule will not serve any purpose independent of the usual "grossly reckless" murder doctrine. The difficult question is which felonies belong on either side of the "inherently dangerous" line.[24]

The following is a sample of offenses the California courts have found to be suitable proxies for "malice": People v. Taylor, 112 Cal. App. 3d 348, 169 Cal. Rptr. 290 (1980) (furnishing heroin); People v. Kelso, 64 Cal. App. 3d 538, 134 Cal. Rptr. 364 (1976) (kidnaping); People v. Mattison, 4 Cal. 3d 177, 93 Cal. Rptr. 185 (1971) (supplying methyl alcohol to drink); People v. Nichols, 3 Cal. 3d 150, 89 Cal. Rptr. 721 (1970) (burning a car). And here are some ruled to lack "inherent danger in the abstract," in cases where, by definition, the particular felonious act led to death: People v. Phillips, 64 Cal. 2d 574, 51 Cal. Rptr. 225 (1966) (grand theft medical fraud, where defendant chiropractor encouraged the parents of child with eye cancer to forgo surgery and seek alternative (and quickly futile) treatment from him instead); People v. Satchell, 6 Cal. 3d 28, 98 Cal. Rptr. 33 (1971) (possession of a firearm by an ex-felon and possession of a sawed-off shotgun); People v. Lovato, 258 Cal. App. 290, 65 Cal. Rptr. 638 (1968) (possession of a concealable weapon by an alien).

Are you persuaded by the court's effort at distinguishing inherently dangerous from noninherently dangerous felonies? Is the *Patterson* standard so close a proxy for malice that it seriously weakens the felony murder doctrine? What evidence would be useful to a trial judge in determining whether the drug offense is inherently dangerous to human life in the abstract?

Should a court look at all possible violations of an entire criminal statute to determine whether it was possible to commit the crime without danger, as opposed to some specific subsection the defendant violated? In People v. Lopez, 6 Cal. 3d 45, 98 Cal. Rptr. 44 (1971), the defendant's accomplice killed someone during the course of an escape from jail. The statute barring escape specified different penalties for violent and nonviolent escapes. The court held, however, that the statute essentially identified only one central offense, i.e., escape, and that it could be committed with or without violence; thus, the offense as a whole — including violent escapes — could not be deemed inherently dangerous.

What is the point of looking at the statute that way? Is that the way prospective felons look at it?

ii. *Danger in the commission.* While many courts look to the least dangerous means of committing a statutory offense in the abstract, other states have been willing to examine the facts in their felony murder cases. The circumstances of the commission of the offense, as well as its abstract definition, are used to determine dangerousness. In this way, the felony as committed gives evidence about the defendant's mens rea.

In State v. Chambers, 524 S.W.2d 826 (Mo. 1975), defendant and his accomplice stole a pickup truck from Hi Dollar Joe Burtrum's, towing it away at night, with no lights, after drinking. They swerved into the opposing lane and crashed into a car, killing four passengers. The predicate felony for the second-degree murder conviction was theft of a motor vehicle. The Missouri Supreme

---

24. Cf. State v. Jones, 516 S.E.2d 405 (N.C. App. 1999) (under N.C. Gen. Stat. Section 14-17, drunk driving can be assault with a deadly weapon qualifying under an enumerated category called "other felony committed or attempted with the use of a deadly weapon").

Court affirmed, noting, "The collision and resulting deaths attest to the violence and danger in such actions." Following the "common law felony murder rule," the court held that any felony can be the basis for second-degree felony murder if done in a sufficiently dangerous way.

Consistent in theory, if different in result, is Ford v. State, 262 Ga. 602, 423 S.E.2d 255 (1992). Ford, a convicted felon, accidentally discharged his gun while cleaning it; the bullet penetrated an adjoining wall and killed a resident in the next apartment. The court forbade use of the rule in cases like Ford's, where the defendant was unaware that another person was present just on the other side of the wall.

4. The Independent Felonious Purpose Limitation

STATE v. SHOCK
Supreme Court of Missouri
68 Mo. 552 (1878)

HOUGH, J. — [Defendant was convicted of first degree murder.] . . . The evidence on the part of the State tended to show that on the 6th day of March, 1878, the defendant beat the deceased, who was a boy between five and six years of age, with a piece of sycamore fishing-pole, about three feet long and one and a half inches in diameter, for some minutes, accompanying his beating with oaths; that he left the room in which he was beating the boy, went into the yard, procured a piece of grapevine about one and one-fourth inches in diameter, returned to the house and resumed the beating, which lasted in all about fifteen minutes. During the beating the child did not scream or cry, but groaned and moaned, and after several days, died of the injuries so received at the hands of the defendant. An inquest was held, at which the body was examined. The child's head was found to be covered with bruises, its back beaten to a jelly and its skull fractured. On the part of the defendant evidence was introduced tending to show that the deceased was very weakly and sickly; that the defendant did not beat it on the day named, and that the wounds on its head were caused by its falling down stairs. The deceased was a son of a cousin of the wife of the defendant, and it appears that it had been at the house of the defendant for about two months. . . .

The only question of importance presented for our determination, arises upon the action of the court in giving, at the instance of the prosecuting attorney, the following instructions:

4. "To constitute murder in the first degree, it is not necessary that the fatal beating, wounding or striking be given with the specific intent to kill; it is sufficient if it be given willfully and maliciously, and with the intent to inflict great bodily harm, and death ensue."

13. "If the jury believes, from the evidence, that it was not the intention of the defendant to kill the child Scott, by whipping him, but that he did intend to do him great bodily harm, and in so whipping him, death ensued, he is guilty of murder in the first degree."

It is contended on behalf of the State that the foregoing instructions were fully warranted by the decision of this court in the case of the *State v. Jennings* (18 Mo. 435). . . . In [that] case . . . , which was a most atrocious case of lynching, the infliction of which was continued for several hours, under circumstances of the greatest cruelty and brutality, there was no occasion for any effort on the part of the State to make a case of constructive murder in the first degree, as the facts of the case justified the jury in finding the defendant guilty of a willful, deliberate and premeditated killing. The following instruction, however, was given in that case: 6. "If the jury believe from the evidence that it was not the intention of those concerned in lynching Willard, to kill him, but that they did intend to do him great bodily harm, and that in so doing death ensued, such killing is murder in the first degree by the statutes of this State." Judge Ryland, who delivered the opinion of this court, approved this instruction in the following language: "The sixth instruction is correct under the statutes of this State (see Crimes and Punishments, R. C., 1845, §1, 38). Homicide, committed in the attempt to perpetrate any arson, rape, robbery, burglary or other felony, shall be deemed murder in the first degree. The 38th section makes the person by whose act or procurement, great bodily harm has been received by another, guilty of what is by our law called a felony; that is, guilty of such an offense as may be punished by imprisonment in the penitentiary."

There [is an error] in the foregoing extract. . . . Section 1 is as follows: "Every murder which shall be committed by means of poison, or by lying in wait, or by any other kind of willful, deliberate and premeditated killing, or which shall be committed in the perpetration or attempt to perpetrate any arson, rape, robbery, burglary or other felony, shall be deemed murder in the first degree." . . . It will be observed that the statute does not say that every homicide committed in the manner therein pointed out, shall be murder in the first degree, but that every murder so committed, shall be murder in the first degree. The object of the first and second sections of the statute, is to divide the crime of murder into two degrees, and they deal with that crime as it existed at common law. This is made manifest by the language of the second section, which is as follows: "All other kinds of murder at common law, not herein declared to be manslaughter, or justifiable or excusable homicide, shall be deemed murder in the second degree." So that in every case under the first section, the first, though not the sole, inquiry to be made is, whether the homicide was murder at common law; if not, it cannot be murder in the first degree under the statute. At common law a homicide committed in the willful and malicious infliction of great bodily harm was murder, though death was not intended; but this was not so because such infliction of great bodily harm was in itself a felony, in the perpetration of which the homicide was committed, but because such infliction of great bodily harm was an act *malum in se,* and the party was, therefore, held answerable for all the harm that ensued. But as such a homicide, death not being intended, is not a willful, deliberate and premeditated killing, and is not a murder committed in the perpetration or attempt to perpetrate any of the felonies specially designated in the first section, but a simple unintentional killing only, it has been universally classed as murder in the second degree, in [other] States. . . . But as murder in the second degree with us comprehends only such homicides as are intentional but without deliberation, it cannot be so classed in this State. How it shall be classed under our statute must depend upon the construction to be given to the words "other felony," in the first section. . . .

We are of the opinion that the words "other felony" used in the first section refer to some collateral felony, and not to those acts of personal violence to the deceased which are necessary and constituent elements of the homicide itself, and are, therefore, merged in it, and which do not, when consummated, constitute an offense distinct from the homicide. . . . As this section, as before shown, includes only such murders as were murders at common law, it may well be doubted whether the words "other felony" can be held to include offenses which were not felonies at common law. This point, however, we do not now decide, it being unnecessary in the present case. But the statute evidently contemplates such "other felony" as could be consummated, although the murder should also be committed. . . . The arson, rape, robbery, burglary may each be perpetrated and the murder also be committed. But when great bodily harm has been inflicted, and death immediately or speedily ensues therefrom, what felony has been committed, either at common law or under our statutes, in addition to the murder? . . .

On the facts of this case, we think the jury might properly have been instructed as to the law of murder in the first degree, on the theory of a willful, deliberate and premeditated killing, and also as to the law of manslaughter in the fourth degree. It was to be expected, of course, that the circuit court would, in passing upon the instructions presented at the trial of this case, be governed by the decision of this court in the case of the *State v. Jennings;* but the doctrine of that case . . . is overruled. . . . The judgment will be reversed and the cause remanded.

HENRY, J., concurring. The obvious meaning of section 1, art. 2, of the act in relation to crimes and punishments, is that every homicide committed in the perpetration or attempt to perpetrate any arson, rape, robbery, burglary, or other felony, which was murder at common law, should be deemed murder under that section, and classed with those murders committed by means of poison, lying in wait, etc. It was not intended to enlarge the class of constructive murders, but only to recognize those designated, and assign them their places in the classification made by that section. If the construction contended for by the State prevail, it will nullify many provisions of the criminal code. For instance: "Every person who shall administer to any woman, pregnant with a quick child, any medicine, drug or substance whatsoever, or shall use, or employ any instrument, or other means, with intent thereby to destroy such child, unless the same shall have been necessary to preserve the life of such mother, or shall have been advised by a physician to be necessary for that purpose, shall, if the death of such child, or the mother thereof, ensue from the means so employed, be deemed guilty of manslaughter in the second degree." Wag. Stat., §10, p. 447. If one administer medicine or employ other means, with the intent to destroy the child and the death of the mother ensue from the means so employed, the offense, by the express terms of the statute, is manslaughter in the second degree: yet, under the construction placed upon the first section in the *Jennings case,* as the homicide was committed in the perpetration of a felony, it would be murder of the first degree, notwithstanding the statute expressly declares that it shall be manslaughter in the second degree.

If one assault another with intent to kill, he is guilty of a felony under Wag. Stat., sec. 32 p. 449. If the assault be premeditated, but not deliberate, and death ensue, the offense would be murder of the second degree. If made in a heat of passion, it would be manslaughter, unless the doctrine of the *Jennings* case be correct, under which it would, in either case, be murder in the first degree, because the commission of the homicide was in the perpetration of a felony, thus making what was manslaughter at common law, and murder in the second degree under our statute, murder of the first degree, a result not to be thought of but with abhorrence. . . .

It is clear from the whole scope and spirit of the act that it was intended to mitigate the severity of the common law in regard to murder, but this construction of the first section would make our code more severe. . . .

NORTON, J., dissenting. . . . The felony committed by B in inflicting great bodily harm on A, under unjustifiable or inexcusable circumstances, is no more merged in the killing of A if death is occasioned thereby, than would the felony of B in committing a rape on A, resulting in A's death. If B starts out with a fixed felonious purpose to "inflict great bodily harm" on A, under circumstances neither excusable nor justifiable, without intending to kill but to stop with the infliction of great bodily harm and death ensues, the felony committed in inflicting the great bodily harm is no more merged in the killing than would a rape perpetrated by B upon A, which resulted in the death of A, be merged or lost sight of in the death of A. The crime in either case would be murder in the first degree, notwithstanding the violence used in committing the rape and in inflicting the injuries occasioning the death would necessarily be directed against the person killed and would be the sole cause of the death, though not inflicted with a murderous intent and purpose. It is said in the statute that murder "committed in the perpetration or attempt to perpetrate any arson, rape, robbery, burglary or other felony, shall be murder in the first degree." In all these enumerated cases the General Assembly has declared the law that the perpetrator shall be held guilty of murder in the first degree, without further proof that the death was the ultimate result which the will, deliberation and premeditation of the party accused sought. Neither of the two specified crimes of rape or robbery could be committed without an assault directed against the person of the one raped or robbed. So there are included in the words, "other felony," a large number of crimes classified as felonies, which could not be committed except by violence directed against the person. It is made a felony by our statute for one person, on purpose and of malice, to cut or disable the tongue, or to cut off or disable any limb or member of another with intent to kill, maim or disfigure him. Now, if A, in feloniously cutting off the tongue of B, or in feloniously castrating him with no other intent than to maim or disfigure him, occasions his death, can it be said that it was not the intention of the Legislature that he should be held answerable for murder in the first degree, although his specific intent was only to maim and not to kill, and that the felony thus committed, being directed against the person whose death was occasioned by its commission was not, for that reason, such a felony as was contemplated by the General Assembly in the use of the words, "other felony," in defining the crime of murder in the first degree? . . .

I cannot subscribe to the doctrine announced, that the words "other felony," used in the first section, defining murder in the first degree, refer to some collateral felony, and not to those acts of personal violence to the deceased which are necessary and constituent elements of the homicide itself, and are, therefore, merged in it. . . .

Notes and Questions

1. Is the result in *Shock* just? Judge Hough writes that the evidence would support an instruction on premeditated and intentional murder, but is it clear that Shock intended to kill his victim? As Judge Hough concedes, Shock's

conduct would probably have given rise to second degree murder liability on a gross recklessness theory in other states, but Missouri lacked gross recklessness murder liability at the time. Should the felony murder doctrine have been made broader to cover this kind of case?

Shortly after the *Shock* decision, the Missouri legislature replaced the term "or other felony" in the definition of first degree murder with the term "or mayhem," restricting felony murder to the enumerated felonies of arson, burglary, rape, robbery and mayhem, and thereby rendering the merger doctrine enunciated in *Shock* superfluous. Notably, the merger doctrine was first developed in New York, which also formerly did not restrict felony murder to enumerated felonies. See People v. Rector, 19 Wend. 569 (1838) (assault merges with murder). The doctrine also can play a role in states like California, which permit second degree felony murder on the basis of non-enumerated felonies. See People v. Ireland, 70 Cal. 2d 522, 450 P.2d 580 (Cal. 1969) (assault merges with murder).

2. *Rationale of the merger rule.* Assume that Smith is convicted of voluntary manslaughter for killing Brown intentionally but with "adequate provocation." Can the prosecution then charge Smith with felony murder, making the obvious point that manslaughter is very inherently dangerous, in both the abstract and the particular? As Judge Henry's concurrence points out, without some kind of "independent felony" or "merger" limitation, every manslaughter would be murder. But does that mean that the merger limitation must extend to felony assault, as in *Shock?* As Judge Norton points out in dissent, the enumerated predicate felonies of robbery and rape include assaults. Is there any principled way to explain why these can be predicate felonies but assault cannot?

Recall that one possible rationale for the felony murder rule would characterize felony murder as a form of exploitation — a selfish willingness to impose a foreseeable risk of death on others in furtherance of some particularly unworthy purpose of one's own. See *supra,* p. 404. Does that not account of felony murder require a merger doctrine? Could one argue that imposing a risk of death on someone for the purpose of hurting him is hostile, but not exploitative?

3. *Child abuse.* If assault is so integrally related to homicide as to "merge" with the homicide, does it follow that the same is true of felony child abuse? Does it matter from the standpoint of the merger doctrine that beating a child is more dangerous than beating an adult? Does it matter that it is crueler? Consider State v. Lucas, 759 P.2d 90 (Kan. 1988):

> At the times of the crimes of which defendant was convicted, he was living in Olathe with Jean Woodside and her two daughters, Shaina (age 18 months at the time of her death) and Shannon (age 3 years). Mrs. Woodside worked . . . and attended school . . . evenings. Defendant had the children in his care every evening and frequently in the daytime. At approximately 10:30 P.M. on July 6, 1986, defendant called 911 . . . to request medical assistance for Shaina. . . . Officer James Stover. . . . found the defendant . . . standing over the unconscious body of Shaina. . . . Officer Stover asked defendant what had happened and defendant gave a lengthy detailed account of how he had placed the two little girls in the tub for their evening bath, shut the glass shower doors, and gone downstairs to watch television. Sometime later he had returned upstairs to check on the children and had found Shaina floating face down in the tub. . . .
>
> . . . The child was pronounced dead at the hospital. A number of suspicious injuries were observed on her body at the hospital . . . and numerous bruised areas on many different parts of her body. . . .

. . . [A]n autopsy was performed which showed Shaina had suffered severe multiple blows to the head. . . . The coroner . . . found it probable Shaina had met her death by losing consciousness in a body of water and drowning. . . .

. . . A few days before Shaina's death, Mrs. Woodside had observed Shaina in a dazed condition. . . . Defendant told her that he had "ranked" the child. He explained this consisted of holding his hand over the child's face until she passed out from lack of oxygen. . . . He generally explained Shaina's injuries, when observed by others, as arising from accidents or efforts at discipline.

. . . [D]efendant contends the district court erred in failing to dismiss the charge of felony murder as the child abuse charge merged into the felony murder and could not constitute the requisite collateral felony to support the felony-murder charge. . . .

In Kansas, as in many other states, the application of felony murder has been limited by judicial decision to situations where: (1) the underlying felony is inherently dangerous to human life; and (2) the elements of the underlying felony are so distinct from the homicide as not to be an ingredient of the homicide. . . .

K.S.A. 1987 Supp. 21-3609 provides: "Abuse of a child is willfully torturing, cruelly beating or inflicting cruel and inhuman corporal punishment upon any child under the age of 18 years."

Clearly, abuse of a child as defined [above] is a felony inherently dangerous to human life and no contrary assertion is made herein. Rather, the issue herein is whether the underlying or collateral felony is so distinct from the homicide as not to be an ingredient of the homicide. If the underlying felony does not meet this test it is said to merge with the homicide and preclude the application of felony murder. . . . Otherwise, all degrees of homicide would constitute murder in the first degree, regardless of the defendant's intention or premeditation. . . .

It was the State's theory that Shaina died as a result of a severe beating to her head administered by the defendant from which she lost consciousness and drowned in the bathtub. There was no claim that any of the other acts of abuse caused or contributed to her death. The defendant could have been found guilty of abuse of a child based solely on the fatal beating and convicted of felony murder solely on the fatal beating. . . .

Had an adult been beaten on the head, lost consciousness as a result thereof, and drowned . . . we would have no hesitancy in holding that the aggravated battery . . . was an integral part of the homicide and that it merged therewith and could not serve as the underlying felony. Can a different result logically be reached by designating the beating as abuse of a child rather than aggravated battery? We believe not. . . .

If additional protection for children is desired, the Kansas Legislature might well consider legislation which would make the death of a child occurring during the commission of the crime of abuse of a child, or aggravated battery against a child, first- or second-degree felony murder.

Judge Herd dissented:

. . . The majority repeatedly compares the beating and death of children with that of adults to prove its logic that our limitations to the statute should apply to a continuing course of child abuse. The majority states that if the legislature feels the death of children by felonious abuse from their caretakers is a more serious concern in our society than other assaults, the legislature should enact a statute making it so. The legislature has already spoken on that issue and made all homicides resulting from commission of a felony . . . felony murder. . . .

. . . [A]cts of torture do not deserve the protection from the severity of the felony-murder rule given defendants charged with assault. The age of the victim and the continuing nature of the torture are the elements which distinguish child abuse from assault. These elements create a circumstance in which the danger to the victim is so great that the felony-murder doctrine is justifiably imposed.

4. *The narrow Illinois approach.* In Illinois, *only* voluntary manslaughter is excluded as nonindependent. "A person who kills an individual without lawful justification commits murder if, in performing the acts which cause the death: . . . . He is attempting or committing a forcible felony other than voluntary manslaughter." (Ill. Rev. Stat.1985, ch. 38, par. 9-1(a)(3).) Thus, an aggravated battery upon a police officer, causing gunfire in which another officer was fatally shot, can be felony murder. People v. Jenkins, 545 N.E.2d 986 (Ill. App. 1 Dist. 1989). Can that be squared with *Moran*? Why would the prosecutor need felony murder in such a case? How might the legislature have solved this problem?

5. *Merger in first-degree cases.* What about merger in first-degree felony murder? Assume that an armed robber goes into a store and kills the store owners while in the process of robbing them. What if, as a defense to a felony murder charge, defendant argues that armed robbery is just assault with a deadly weapon coupled with larceny, and that any charge of murder for a killing arising out of armed robbery necessarily includes assault with a deadly weapon and cannot support a felony murder instruction? Is this argument to extend the merger rule sound? The court in People v. Burton, 6 Cal. 3d 375, 491 P.2d 793 (1971), said no: "In the case of armed robbery, as well as the other felonies enumerated in section 189 of the Penal Code, there is an *independent felonious purpose,* namely in the case of robbery to acquire money or property belonging to another." Is the court correct?

How much room is there for felony murder between the merger doctrine and the rule requiring an inherently dangerous felony with a high probability of causing death?

5.   Two Variants of Felony Murder

a.   *Misdemeanor Manslaughter*

A common law doctrine known as the misdemeanor manslaughter or "unlawful act" doctrine creates a form of manslaughter liability parallel to felony murder. Although the Model Penal Code and a majority of states have abolished this misdemeanor manslaughter rule, it has been retained by a number of states that have not revised their criminal codes and by a dozen more that kept the common law rule in their reformed laws.

For example, in United States v. Walker, 380 A.2d 1388 (D.C. Sup. Ct. 1977), the defendant was charged with involuntary manslaughter and carrying a pistol without a license (D.C. Code 1973, §22-3204). While carrying a pistol without a license, Walker dropped it in the stairwell of an apartment building, and the gun went off, fatally wounding a bystander. The defense offered expert firearms testimony that when the hammer of the pistol was not cocked, it would fire on impact only if dropped at a particular angle. These proffers constitute the only explanation in the record of the incident underlying the indictment. The court defined involuntary manslaughter as: "(1) an unlawful killing of a human being (2) with either (a) the intent to commit a misdemeanor dangerous in itself *or* (b) an unreasonable failure to perceive the risk of harm to others." *Walker* had violated D.C. Code 1973, §22-3204:

> No person shall within the District of Columbia carry either openly or concealed on or about his person, except in his dwelling house or place of business or on other land possessed by him, a pistol, without a license therefor issued as hereinafter provided. . . .

Walker argued that the plain intent of section 3204 was to stop the prohibited conduct *before* danger of injury arises, and that such danger is not a necessary concomitant of the offense. He offered the following hypothetical:

> [T]wo persons [are] walking peaceably on a public street carrying holstered pistols. One . . . has a license to carry a pistol, but the other has no license. The second person is violating section 3204, and the first is not. Yet there is no difference between them in terms of the danger presented to others. . . .

The court nevertheless concluded that carrying a pistol without a license necessarily exposes the public to so serious risk of harm that when any death results the defendant merits a manslaughter charge. It added:

> Congress has expressly required one who seeks the license to be "a suitable person to be so licensed." Issuance of these licenses is the responsibility of the Chief of the Metropolitan Police Department, and is subject to restrictive regulations which, among other things, require the applicant to be of sound mind, to be without prior criminal record, not be an alcoholic or user of narcotics, to "be trained and experienced in the use, functioning and safe operation of the pistol," and finally, "to be free from physical defects which would impair his safe use of the weapon."
>
> Thus, taking up appellee's hypothetical of the two persons carrying pistols on a public street, one of whom is licensed and the other of whom is not, we conclude that Congress intended to preclude the non-licensee from being on the street with his weapon because of the danger he posed to the community as a result (1) of the inherent dangerousness of the weapon he carried, and (2) of the absence of any evidence of his capability to carry safely such a dangerous instrumentality. . . . Id. at 1391.

Was Walker guilty of negligence in his handling of the pistol? In the court's view, need a conviction be based on such a finding? Note that the court does not seem interested in the mens rea of the defendant with respect to the death. Rather, the court merely asks whether the death resulted from the commission of a misdemeanor. What moral theory allows this kind of increase in criminal liability where the result of committing a relatively minor crime is the death of a human being? Is this the view that the court rejected in Regina v. Faulkner, discussed in Chapter 3, *supra*, p. 180? Is the element analysis of the Model Penal Code designed to prevent just this?

As noted, the Model Penal Code rejected the misdemeanor-manslaughter rule. The commentary to section 210.3 of the recent edition of the Code explains why:[25]

> . . . Recently, courts and legislatures have acted to limit the misdemeanor-manslaughter rule in a variety of ways that in general parallel limitations developed

---

25. Model Penal Code and Commentaries, *supra*, at 75-77.

on the felony-murder rule. It has been held to apply generally to misdemeanors mala in se rather than mala prohibita. The authorities are divided on the question whether the misdemeanor-manslaughter rule can be based on an underlying crime that is itself one of strict liability, and there is substantial unanimity in limiting the rule's scope by confining notions of causation. At a minimum, death of another must result from the course of conduct constituting an unlawful act. Mere coincidence of time and place of the unlawful act and a homicide is insufficient; there must be a direct causal connection between the unlawful act and the homicide. . . . E.g., Commonwealth v. Williams, 133 Pa. Super. 104, 1 A.2d 812 (1938), where the defendant, a good driver who had failed to renew his driver's license, was forced off the road into a telephone pole by another vehicle, resulting in the death of his passenger. The court reversed a conviction of manslaughter because the unlawful act of driving without a license did not cause the death. . . . Some courts go farther and require that the homicide must be caused by that aspect of the defendant's conduct that renders it unlawful. Thus, for example, a death caused while speeding would not fall within the rule if driving at the posted speed would not have avoided the occurrence.

However explained and confined, the misdemeanor-manslaughter rule is objectionable. . . .

. . . It dispenses with proof of culpability and imposes liability for a serious crime without reference to the actor's state of mind. This result is not only morally unjustified, but it also operates quite inequitably among individuals. Application of the rule in the context of traffic offenses illustrates the point. Speed limits are in part set to prevent accidents dangerous to life. Occasionally, speeding causes the death of another in circumstances in which the actor was unaware of the risk of death and indeed cannot even be judged negligent with respect thereto. Subjecting such a driver, who is engaged in behavior so like many others, to a severe prison term introduces an unfair haphazardness to criminal punishment. For reasons explained more fully in connection with the felony-murder rule, the Model Code rejects any form of strict liability in the law of homicide.

In Todd v. State, 594 So. 2d 802 (Fla. Ct. App. 1992) the misdemeanor-manslaughter doctrine was found inapplicable where a theft from a church caused the heart attack of a congregant. Would this suggest that the critical element in misdemeanor manslaughter is the foreseeability of the harm? Judge Griffin, writing for the majority, explained, "Although the petty theft did trigger a series of events that concluded in the death of Mr. Voeglitin and was, in that sense, a 'cause' of the death, the petty theft did not encompass the kind of direct, foreseeable risk of physical harm that would support a conviction of manslaughter." [Id. at 806.] Which mental state is Judge Griffin demanding for conviction?

b. Felony Murder as Sentencing Enhancement

In some jurisdictions, proof that an enumerated nonhomicidal felony in fact caused death in a particular case may significantly upgrade punishment, but the technical device is a "sentencing enhancement" rather than a higher grade of offense. The prime example is federal criminal law.

Federal statutes criminalizing certain enumerated acts affecting interstate commerce enhance criminal liability "if death results." See United States v. Nelson, 920 F. Supp. 825 (M.D. Tenn. 1996) (bank robbery); United States v. Hayes,

589 F.2d 811 (5th Cir. 1979) (civil rights violations). Thus, in the Oklahoma City bombing case, the defendant was charged, among other things, with using a weapon of mass destruction against people and property, in violation of 18 U.S.C. §2332(a). Under that statute, if the prosecutor proves the act and mental state requirements of that charge, and if the jury also finds that death resulted, the defendant is sentenced under the rules for first-degree murder, including a possible death sentence. Timothy McVeigh claimed that by this means, the government unfairly avoided any need to prove a culpable mental state with respect to death, or to have the homicide allegation screened by the grand jury, because the "death results" component was not treated as an element of the statutory crime. The trial court held that Congress had intended just this arrangement. See United States v. McVeigh, 940 F. Supp. 1571 (D. Colo. 1996).

Second, the Federal sentencing guidelines, in section 5K2.1,[26] provide for an upward departure from the guidelines for any offense for which death results. This section effectively functions as a kind of second-degree felony murder rule, allowing enhancement for deaths caused in the perpetration of felonies not inherently dangerous to life, but where death was intentionally or knowingly risked. Courts have tended, despite the language, to treat this as a negligence standard. See United States v. White, 979 F.2d 539 (7th Cir. 1992); cf. United States v. Iheqworo, 959 F.2d 26 (5th Cir. 1992) (death results from sale of unusually pure heroin; jury acquits of responsibility for death but judge departs upward because of knowing risk).

Note that these holdings may be reconsidered in light of United States v. Jones and Apprendi v. New Jersey (see Introduction, *supra*, pp. 20, 87-92), holding that punishment cannot exceed the maximum provided by the statute defining the offense unless proven to a jury beyond a reasonable doubt.

---

26. For a discussion of the guidelines, see pp. 79-92, *supra* in Chapter 1.

7

CAPITAL MURDER AND THE
DEATH PENALTY

As the previous chapters have shown, the criminal law draws important distinctions among types of homicides in order to determine the appropriate punishment, or range of punishment, for a particular killing. Though the difference in punishment between voluntary manslaughter and second-degree murder, or between second- and first-degree murder, might be a decade of the defendant's life, no distinction drawn by the criminal law is so important and stark as the one between life imprisonment and the death penalty. Generally, a defendant is not even "eligible" for the death penalty unless he or she is convicted of the state's equivalent of first-degree murder. But under modern American law, the prosecutor who seeks the execution of a defendant convicted of first-degree murder must seek to prove yet a higher degree of murder in a special proceeding, usually called the "penalty trial." The doctrines of criminal law applied in the penalty trial are the focus of this chapter.

A. AN HISTORICAL AND CONSTITUTIONAL SUMMARY

The American law of the death penalty has passed through three broad phases. In brief: (1) At the time of Independence, most homicide, and certainly all murder, was automatically punishable by death. (In fact other felonies, including robbery, burglary, and grand larceny, often carried a mandatory death penalty.) The automatic death penalty, inherited by the colonies from English law, continued in almost all the states well into the nineteenth century, although the states gradually created a two-degree scheme of murder and restricted the death penalty to first-degree murders. (2) Then, from roughly the middle of the nineteenth century to the 1970s, the states used their first-degree murder definitions to decide which defendants were eligible for the death penalty; but they left the choice between life and death to the unguided discretion of the judge or jury that had decided the guilt issue.

(3) After decades of constitutional wrangling, death penalty law has now settled into a fairly stable third phase. Typically, after a jury finds the defendant

guilty of "capital" or first-degree murder, it retests the defendant's liability against a still narrower "super-first-degree" murder law by deciding whether the offender or the offense exhibited certain "aggravating" factors. The jury, in the penalty trial, then comparatively evaluates those aggravating factors against any mitigating factors about the crime or the criminal and decides whether the defendant should live or die.

These developments in American capital punishment raise broad constitutional, philosophical, and empirical questions. But, in a course in criminal law — as opposed to one in criminology, philosophy, or constitutional law — these broader questions should serve as background to the more concrete question of how the death penalty law actually operates under state and federal death penalty statutes today. Thus, after a summary of the constitutional developments, we will examine capital punishment law as the last step in the continuum of homicide law.

The Fifth Amendment to the Constitution says that no person "shall be deprived of life . . . without due process of law." The language obviously suggests that the authors of the Bill of Rights had no categorical objection to the death penalty. And indeed the law in the colonies and in the states after Independence used the mandatory death penalty as the major instrument for punishing murders.

The only potential constitutional restraint on the death penalty lay in the Eighth Amendment prohibition of cruel and unusual punishments. But the Supreme Court has held, in Gregg v. Georgia, 428 U.S. 153, 169-70 (1976), that the authors of the Eighth Amendment, obviously aware of the prevalence of capital punishment, did not believe that the death penalty per se was unconstitutional. Rather, the "cruel and unusual punishments" clause, drawn from the English Bill of Rights of 1689, was concerned with more particular matters. First, it prohibited any punishments not officially authorized by statute or not lying within the sentencing court's jurisdiction. Second, it proscribed brutal, gratuitously painful methods of torture or execution. Although the authors of the Eighth Amendment may have intended to prohibit a severe punishment such as death for a minor crime, they certainly did not view the death penalty as unconstitutionally excessive or disproportionate for the crime of murder.[1]

For more than a century and a half after Independence, capital punishment proceeded in the United States with virtually no constitutional scrutiny. The state law of capital punishment, however, changed significantly. The state legislatures gradually rejected the automatic death penalty scheme for two related reasons. First, many legislators may have simply felt that not all murderers — even first-degree murderers — were equally culpable or that all deserved death. In short, the law of murder did not sufficiently distinguish killers according to the blameworthiness of their crimes or the moral aspects of their characters. Second, the automatic death penalty law had a paradoxically lenient effect. Jurors who believed a defendant was guilty of capital murder but did not believe he or she deserved to die would simply "nullify" the law of homicide by acquitting the defendant of the murder charge.

Slowly but steadily during the nineteenth century, the states changed their death penalty laws to a system that openly and expressly gave juries the discretion they had previously exercised in a subversive fashion. The model was very simple. The judge first instructed the jury in the law of first-degree murder so the jury

<hr/>

1. See generally Anthony Granucci, "Nor Cruel and Unusual Punishments Inflicted": The Original Meaning, 57 Calif. L. Rev. 839 (1969).

could determine whether the defendant was "eligible" for the death penalty. If the jury so found, it was then to decide, as part of the same deliberation, whether the defendant should be executed or, instead, sentenced to life imprisonment. The trial court gave the jury little, if any, legal guidance on how to make the choice. Nor did the jury have the benefit of extensive information about the defendant's background, character, or previous criminal record, beyond whatever narrow information the law of evidence allowed the parties to offer on the question of the defendant's guilt on the murder charge. The system had changed from one of no jury discretion to one of total — and virtually unguided — jury discretion. This new system constituted the American law of the death penalty until 1972. Though a few states had wholly abolished capital punishment late in the nineteenth century or during the twentieth century, the great majority retained the system of jury-discretionary capital punishment until that year.

By the 1950s, the jury-discretion scheme of capital punishment had come under great political and philosophical scrutiny. Many opponents of the death penalty attacked it in absolute terms, arguing that there was no empirical proof that it was superior to life imprisonment in deterring serious crime, and that a morally mature society should not use death as an instrument for revenge or retribution. But the legal attacks on the death penalty during the 1960s also focused on the way the death penalty operated in practice. Though giving discretion to the jury softened the severity of the old automatic death penalty, it also permitted arbitrary and discriminatory administration. Many complained that a comparison of the crimes and criminal records of those executed and with crimes and records of those who received life sentences yielded no rational pattern in the results. And unfortunately, many noted, the one potential pattern that did emerge was one of racial discrimination: Death sentences appeared to issue disproportionately against black defendants or, more subtly, against defendants accused of killing whites, or — most disproportionately of all — against black men convicted of raping white women.

In McGautha v. California, 402 U.S. 183 (1971), the Court held that the standardless jury discretion schemes of the states did not violate the Due Process clause of the Fourteenth Amendment. Somewhat hypertechnically, the Court restricted its decision to the application of the Due Process clause, avoiding any decision on the application of the Eighth Amendment. But Justice Harlan's opinion for the court contained a prescient warning that whatever the constitutional rubric, any effort to impose legal regulation on the morally complex question of capital punishment would be futile:

> To identify before the fact those characteristics of criminal homicides and their perpetrators which call for the death penalty, and to express these characteristics in language which can be fairly understood and applied by the sentencing authority, appear to be tasks which are beyond present human ability. [Id. at 204.]

Justice Harlan believed the Court should not force the state legislatures to devise guiding rules for the death penalty, because the visceral decision of whether to kill a defendant could not be reduced to legal rules.

Just one year later, a majority of the Court rejected Justice Harlan's warning. In the landmark case of Furman v. Georgia, 408 U.S. 238 (1972), the Court, by a vote of five to four, struck down all the death penalty schemes in the United States as they then operated. Unfortunately, there was not a majority opinion in *Furman*. Indeed, each of the five judges in the majority wrote his own opinion. Thus, at best one can glean from the *Furman* opinions some general themes, rather than a single guiding principle. Two of the Justices, Brennan and Marshall, took the view that the death penalty under all circumstances violated the Eighth Amendment because it served no legitimate deterrent or retributive purpose, and because it violated "evolving standards of decency." The swing votes, cast by Justices Douglas, Stewart, and White, were more guarded. The consensus of their views was that the wanton, unpredictable infliction of the death penalty under the unguided discretion schemes, as well as the discriminatory infliction of the death penalty on the basis of race, violated the Eighth Amendment. The result of *Furman,* then, was that the states could restore the death penalty only if they designed new capital punishment laws that so restricted or guided jury discretion as to remove the arbitrary and discriminatory effects decried by the *Furman* plurality.

Immediately after *Furman,* roughly three-quarters of the states did enact new laws aimed at satisfying the somewhat elusive demands of *Furman.* The new capital punishment statutes took two forms, each designed to solve the problem of unguided jury discretion. (1) A handful of states, in an act of historical irony, returned to the mandatory or automatic death penalty. They created special categories of egregious first-degree murder, such as the premeditated murder of a police officer, or premeditated murder in the course of an enumerated felony, and declared the death penalty automatic for anyone convicted of such murders. Thus, these states "solved" the problem of unguided or excessive jury discretion by eliminating jury discretion altogether. (2) The other type of statute, adopted by the majority of the reenacting states, can be termed "guided discretion" statutes. Under these statutes, the court conducts a separate sentencing hearing (usually before the jury, but, under a few original post-*Furman* statutes, the judge alone) after the defendant is convicted of first-degree or "capital" murder. The sentencer then chooses either the death penalty or life imprisonment (sometimes with the possibility of parole, sometimes not) but is guided in that choice by a process of balancing aggravating and mitigating factors. The sentencer must find the presence of certain aggravating factors and also take into account any relevant mitigating factors. This model of the guided discretion statute has now become the established norm for the death penalty in America, and we will examine it in some detail below.

In 1976, in Gregg v. Georgia, *supra,* and companion cases from Florida, Texas, North Carolina, and Louisiana, the Supreme Court returned to the death penalty to determine whether the new statutes had resolved the problems identified four years earlier in *Furman.* Once again, the Court produced no majority decision, but the holding of *Gregg* was clear. First, over the dissents of Justice Brennan and Marshall, the Court, in a plurality opinion by Justice Stewart, flatly rejected the argument that the death penalty was in all circumstances unconstitutional under the Eighth Amendment. Summarizing the jurisprudence of the Eighth Amendment, Justice Stewart stated that a punishment was constitutional so long as it comported with "evolving standards of human decency," as reflected in "contemporary public attitudes," and with the Eighth Amendment concept of the "dignity of man." The death penalty met the first test because public attitudes, reflected in such objective evidence as the reenactment of death penalty laws by a majority of state legislatures after *Furman* and numerous jury verdicts of death under these new laws, demonstrated that the death penalty did not violate contemporary standards of decency. And the death penalty did not violate the "dignity of man" because it could serve legitimate deterrent and retributive purposes. The Court acknowledged that the empirical evidence of the deterrent value of the death penalty was inconclusive at best, but, in the absence of a clear answer, the Justices gave the benefit of the doubt on this issue of penological policy to the legislatures. Moreover, said Justice Stewart, retribution was a legitimate, time-honored justification for the criminal law, especially since retributive action by the state could channel aggressive energies in society that might otherwise lead to lawless, vengeful action by private citizens. Finally, Justice Stewart concluded that whatever the fairness of inflicting death for less serious crimes, the death penalty was not invariably excessive for the crime of murder.

Having concluded that the death penalty did not necessarily violate the Eighth Amendment, the Court proceeded to examine the new post-*Furman* statutes. In Woodson v. North Carolina, 428 U.S. 280 (1976), and Roberts v. Louisiana, 428 U.S. 325 (1976), the Court struck down the revived automatic death penalty statutes. The plurality in *Woodson* and *Roberts* viewed the automatic-death statutes as misguided efforts to solve the problem of jury discretion. The Justices believed that the Eighth Amendment implied a principle of respect for the individuality of all criminal defendants, and were therefore unwilling to tolerate a death penalty law that forbade individualized distinctions of culpability among murderers guilty of a given category of crime. Moreover, the plurality returned to the classic problem of jury nullification that had helped undermine the old automatic statutes more than a century before. It declared that the inevitable tendency of jurors to render "false acquittals" to spare a guilty but sympathetic defendant from death would lead to further arbitrary or capricious administration of the death penalty.

In its key holding in Gregg v. Georgia, however, the Court upheld the guided discretion statutes as constitutionally satisfactory solutions to the problems of unfettered jury discretion diagnosed in *Furman*. Citing the Model Penal Code's death penalty provisions in section 210.6 as a particularly satisfactory model, Justice Stewart approved the new Georgia statute and noted several features that supported its constitutionality, though he avoided saying that any of these particular features was constitutionally required: The statute created a separate sentencing proceeding at which the state and the defendant could offer evidence not presented at the guilt phase; the statute offered the jury express guidance in identifying aggravating circumstances and requiring the jury to find at least one of the aggravating circumstances enumerated in the statute before it voted for death; the jury was instructed to consider any individualized mitigating circumstances that might outweigh the aggravating circumstances; the defendant had a right of automatic appeal to the state supreme court for review of the death sentence; and the state supreme court was required to conduct a "proportionality review" of every sentence, ensuring that the sentence was not arbitrary or prejudicial, or disproportionate in comparison to sentences handed down in similar Georgia cases.[2] In companion cases, the Court upheld the constitutionality of similar statutes in Proffitt v. Florida, 428 U.S. 242 (1976), and Jurek v. Texas, 428 U.S. 262 (1976). Though the Florida and Texas statutes differed from the Georgia law in their schemes for establishment of aggravating and mitigating circumstances, the Court found that they provided similarly adequate safeguards against arbitrary and discriminatory application of capital punishment.

2. In 1984, the Court held that the proportionality review was not constitutionally mandated. Pulley v. Harris, 465 U.S. 37 (1984).

The 1976 cases thus restored the death penalty in America under the model of the guided discretion statutes. (States like North Carolina and Louisiana, whose automatic-death laws were struck down in 1976, quickly enacted new death penalty laws to meet the model approved in *Gregg*.) The year after *Gregg*, Gary Gilmore was executed in Utah, becoming the first person to suffer the death penalty in America since the pre-*Furman* litigation had effectively suspended the death penalty in 1967.

The Supreme Court has indicated that the death penalty is unconstitutional for any crime other than murder. See, e.g., Coker v. Georgia, 433 U.S. 584 (1977), where the court held that the death penalty was unconstitutionally excessive for the crime of rape of an adult woman.[3] But almost 4,000 murderers have entered death row under the new statutes. Protracted federal and state appeals have prevented or delayed the execution of the vast majority of these prisoners, but through 1999, more than 575 people have been executed under the new laws, and the rate of execution has been steadily increasing.

The Death Penalty Information Center compiles nationwide statistics on death row inmates. As of November 2003 it provided the following key facts and figures:

Race of Death Row Inmates

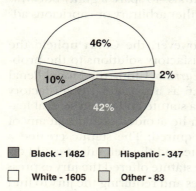

- Black - 1482
- White - 1605
- Hispanic - 347
- Other - 83

Size of Death Row: 1968-2000

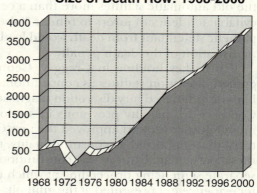

Death Row Inmates by State *

California	625	Tennessee	105	Virginia	29	Kansas	7
Texas	453	Louisiana	92	U.S. Govt.	26	U.S. Military	7
Florida	380	Nevada	88	Idaho	21	Nebraska	7
Penn.	241	S. Carolina	77	Delaware	19	Colorado	6
N. Carolina	214	Missouri	69	Maryland	15	Montana	6
Ohio	207	Mississippi	69	New Jersey	15	New York	6
Alabama	194	Arkansas	41	Washington	12	S. Dakota	4
Arizona	127	Indiana	39	Utah	11	New Mexico	2
Georgia	116	Kentucky	38	Connecticut	7	Wyoming	2
Oklahoma	110	Oregon	31	Illinois	7		

TOTAL: 3,525 *

*When added, state totals are slightly higher because some inmates are sentenced in more than one state.
Source: NAACP LDF *Death Row, U.S.A.* (7/1/03) (includes cases with temporary reversals)

---

3. One lower court has read *Coker* to permit the death penalty for the nonfatal aggravated rape of a child, though the case reviewed a pretrial order, not a conviction and sentence. State v. Wilson, 685 So. 2d 1063 (La. 1996).

Total 879

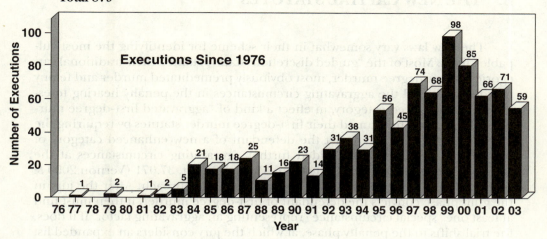

Race of Defendants Executed

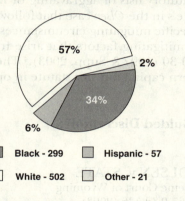

57%

2%

34%

6%

■ Black - 299   ■ Hispanic - 57

□ White - 502   ■ Other - 21

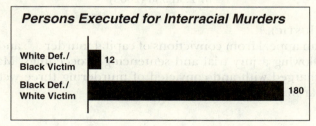

Persons Executed for Interracial Murders

White Def./ Black Victim   12

Black Def./ White Victim   180

Race of Victims in Death Penalty Cases

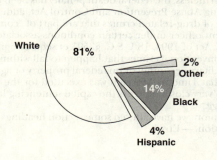

White

81%

2% Other

14% Black

4% Hispanic

B. THE NEW CAPITAL STATUTES

The new laws vary somewhat in their scheme for identifying the most culpable killers. Most of the "guided discretion" states retained their traditional categories of first-degree murder, most obviously premeditated murder and felony murder, and used the aggravating circumstances in the penalty hearing to establish an enhanced category, in effect a kind of "aggravated first-degree murder." Other states fine-tuned their first-degree murder statutes by requiring the jury *at the guilt stage* to convict the defendant of a new enhanced category of "capital murder," and then added further aggravating circumstances at the penalty stage. See, e.g., Tex. Code Crim. Proc. Ann. art. 37.071 (Vernon 2000 & Supp. 2004). California has taken an intermediate approach: After the jury in the guilt phase convicts the defendant of first-degree murder, it then must find at least one "special circumstance" representing an aggravating factor. If it does, the trial shifts to the penalty phase, at which the jury considers an expanded list of aggravating circumstances. Cal. Penal Code §190.2 (West 1999 & Supp. 2003). Most states created detailed statutory lists of aggravating or mitigating circumstances like the Wyoming statute's in the *Olsen* case that follows below, but a few states do not enumerate any specific mitigating circumstances, simply requiring the sentencer to consider any mitigating factors that arise from the evidence. See, e.g., Ga. Code Ann. §17-10-30 (1997 & Supp. 2003).[4] The following recent case exemplifies a typical modern capital murder statute in operation.

1. The Structure of "Guided Discretion": An Exemplary Case

OLSEN v. STATE
Supreme Court of Wyoming
67 P.3d 536 (2003)

GOLDEN, JUSTICE.[5]

[T]his is an appeal from convictions of capital murder . . . and sentences of death, . . . following a jury trial and sentencing proceedings. Martin J. Olsen (Olsen) was charged with and convicted of murdering three victims during a robbery at a bar in Worland, Wyoming. . . .

---

4. Though federal criminal law once played a greater role in capital punishment, especially for such crimes as treason or interstate kidnapping, almost all executions in the post-*Gregg* era have been under state law. Nevertheless, the federal death penalty has been revived recently: Section 848 of the Comprehensive Drug Abuse Prevention and Control Act, added in 1988, makes it a capital crime to kill in the course of drug-related crimes that are part of "continuing criminal enterprise" or to kill a law enforcement officer under certain conditions associated with drug crimes. And in the Federal Death Penalty Act of 1994, 18 U.S.C. §3591 et seq., Congress added new death penalties for a wide variety of conventional crimes that happen to fall within federal jurisdiction, such as those occurring among military personnel or on federal property or against federal officials (hence it was under federal law that Timothy McVeigh was executed for the 1995 Oklahoma City bombing). The 1994 federal law very closely mirrors the capital sentencing law of the Model Penal Code, cited with approval in *Gregg*.

5. [In editing this opinion, we have altered some section headings and the order of some paragraphs, for ease of exposition. — EDS.]

We find . . . no errors in the guilt phase of Olsen's trial. Therefore, we affirm Olsen's convictions of capital/first degree murder and robbery. We do find error, however, in the sentencing phase of Olsen's trial in the following matters: (1) insufficient evidence to support the jury's finding of the aggravating circumstance that the murders were especially atrocious or cruel, being unnecessarily torturous to the victims; (2) insufficient evidence to support the jury's finding of the aggravating circumstance that Olsen knowingly created a great risk of death to two or more persons; [and] (3) improper jury instructions on the law of mitigating circumstances [and] the decision-making process. . . . Consequently, we set aside Olsen's sentence of death and remand for a new sentencing hearing to be conducted with a new jury impaneled for that purpose.

[I. FEDERAL PRECEDENT]

In 1994, . . . in *Tuilaepa v. California,* 512 U.S. 967 (1994), [the Supreme Court] explained that its decisions require that a jury's discretion in sentencing defendants to death must be genuinely narrowed; however, once that is accomplished, the jury must be allowed the widest possible discretion to not choose death. To accomplish these constitutional requirements, there are two different aspects of the capital decision-making process: the eligibility decision and the selection decision. A defendant is eligible for the death penalty in a homicide case when the trier of fact finds one aggravating circumstance or its equivalent at either the guilt or sentencing phase. Aggravating circumstances must meet two requirements: the circumstance may not apply to every defendant convicted of murder; it must apply only to a subclass of defendants convicted of murder (genuine narrowing); and the circumstance must not be unconstitutionally vague.

The selection decision determines whether an eligible defendant should receive the death penalty and requires an individualized determination on the basis of the character of the individual and the circumstances of the crime. The individualized determination requirement is met when the jury can consider relevant mitigating evidence of the character and record of the defendant and the circumstances of the crime. The eligibility decision requires an answer to the factual question of "what was the rationale for imposing a sentence of death" while the selection decision does not necessarily have to answer a factual question, but can be open-ended in assessing the defendant's culpability. . . .

[II. FACTS]

. . . On the night of January 20, 1997, sometime between 11:00 P.M. and midnight, Olsen entered the Little Chief Bar in Worland. He instructed two patrons to lie down on the floor and robbed the bar. After having the bartender also lay face down on the floor, he shot all three in the back of the head, firing a fourth shot seconds later when it appeared that one victim was not dead. He left the bar, went to a convenience store and pumped gas into his pickup. He chatted with the store clerk until asked if he knew why the police were active in the area. At this question, he became agitated, left, and went home and packed. Before he left his home, he confessed the murders to his mother and then fled in his vehicle. After he left, his mother called the police, told them Olsen was involved, and within a few hours, Olsen was apprehended. He was advised of his rights, and spent much of the rest of the day confessing the murders to police. Several of these confessions were recorded on audiotape and videotape.

. . . During a recorded interview conducted at 7:05 A.M. at the Buffalo judicial center, Olsen claimed that he did not remember confessing to his mother, . . . continued to admit that he had shot three people in the back of the head, but . . . explained that his motive for killing them was fright and intoxication. . . .

[The court offered further details on the background of the killings, including evidence that Olsen was intoxicated at the time, that he had suffered organic brain damage since birth, resulting in an aneurism that caused severe learning and behavioral problems, and that on the night of the murders he had taken a relatively new drug to control related seizures.]

. . . The . . . jurors . . . ultimately return[ed] a verdict finding Olsen guilty of three counts of premeditated, first degree murder, three counts of first degree felony murder, and one count of aggravated robbery.

[III. SENTENCING PHASE]

1. [Wyoming Death Penalty Statute]
   [Wyo. Stat. Ann. §6-2-102] provides that:
   a) . . . Upon conviction of a person for murder in the first degree the judge shall conduct a separate sentencing hearing to determine whether the defendant should be sentenced to death or life imprisonment. . . .
   b) The . . . jury shall hear evidence as to any matter that the court deems relevant to a determination of the sentence, and shall include matters relating to any of the aggravating or mitigating circumstances enumerated in subsections (h) and (j) of this section. . . .
   c) Upon conclusion of the evidence and arguments the judge shall give the jury appropriate instructions, including instructions as to any aggravating or mitigating circumstances, as defined in subsections (h) and (j) of this section, . . .
   (i) After hearing all the evidence, the jury shall deliberate and render a sentence based upon the following:
   (A) Whether one (1) or more aggravating circumstances exist beyond a reasonable doubt as set forth in subsection (h) of this section;
   (B) Whether, by a preponderance of the evidence, mitigating circumstances exist as set forth in subsection (j) of this section; and
   (C) The mere number of aggravating or mitigating circumstances found shall have no independent significance.
   (ii) Based upon the considerations in paragraph (i) of this subsection, the jury shall unanimously determine whether the defendant should be sentenced to death or life imprisonment. The jury shall consider aggravating and mitigating circumstances unanimously found to exist, and each individual juror may also consider any mitigating circumstances found by that juror to exist; . . .
   e) The death penalty shall not be imposed unless at least one of the aggravating circumstances set forth in subsection (h) of this section is found. . . . If the jury cannot, within a reasonable time, agree on the punishment to be

imposed, the judge shall impose a life sentence. The jury, if its verdict is a sentence of death, shall designate in writing signed by the foreman of the jury:

(i) The aggravating circumstance or circumstances which it unanimously found beyond a reasonable doubt;

(ii) The mitigating circumstance or circumstances which it unanimously found by a preponderance of the evidence; and

(iii) The mitigating circumstance or circumstances which any individual juror found by a preponderance of the evidence. . . .

h) Aggravating circumstances are limited to the following:

(i) The murder was committed by a person:

(A) Confined in a jail or correctional facility;

(B) On parole or on probation for a felony;

(C) After escaping detention or incarceration; or

(D) Released on bail pending appeal of his conviction.

(ii) The defendant was previously convicted of another murder in the first degree or a felony involving the use or threat of violence to the person;

(iii) The defendant knowingly created a great risk of death to two (2) or more persons;

(iv) The murder was committed while the defendant was engaged, or was an accomplice, in the commission of, or an attempt to commit, or flight after committing or attempting to commit, any aircraft piracy or the unlawful throwing, placing or discharging of a destructive device or bomb;

(v) The murder was committed for the purpose of avoiding or preventing a lawful arrest or effecting an escape from custody;

(vi) The murder was committed for compensation, the collection of insurance benefits or other similar pecuniary gain;

(vii) The murder was especially atrocious or cruel, being unnecessarily torturous to the victim;

(viii) The murder of a judicial officer, former judicial officer, district attorney, former district attorney, defending attorney, peace officer, juror or witness, during or because of the exercise of his official duty;

(ix) The defendant knew or reasonably should have known the victim was less than seventeen (17) years of age or older than sixty-five (65) years of age;

(x) The defendant knew or reasonably should have known the victim was especially vulnerable due to significant mental or physical disability;

(xi) The defendant poses a substantial and continuing threat of future dangerousness or is likely to commit continued acts of criminal violence;

(xii) The defendant killed another human being purposely and with premeditated malice and while engaged in, or as an accomplice in the commission of, or an attempt to commit, or flight after committing or attempting to commit, any robbery, sexual assault, arson, burglary or kidnapping. . . .

j) Mitigating circumstances shall include the following:

(i) The defendant has no significant history of prior criminal activity;

(ii) The murder was committed while the defendant was under the influence of extreme mental or emotional disturbance;

(iii) The victim was a participant in the defendant's conduct or consented to the act;

(iv) The defendant was an accomplice in a murder committed by another person and his participation in the homicidal act was relatively minor;

(v) The defendant acted under extreme duress or under the substantial domination of another person;

(vi) The capacity of the defendant to appreciate the criminality of his conduct or to conform his conduct to the requirements of law was substantially impaired;

(vii) The age of the defendant at the time of the crime;

(viii) Any other fact or circumstance of the defendant's character or prior record or matter surrounding his offense which serves to mitigate his culpability.

[IV.   APPLICATION]

Olsen contends that three of the four aggravating factors of which he was convicted were, as a matter of law, improperly applied to the facts of his case. The aggravating factors submitted to the jury were: (1) Olsen created a great risk of death to two or more persons; (2) the murders were committed for the purpose of avoiding or preventing a lawful arrest; (3) the murders were especially atrocious or cruel, being unnecessarily torturous to the victims; (4) Olsen posed a substantial and continuing threat of future dangerousness or was likely to commit continued acts of criminal violence; (5) Olsen killed another human being purposely and with premeditated malice and while engaged in the commission of a robbery.

1. Atrocious or Cruel Aggravating Circumstance

. . . The first aggravating circumstance which Olsen complains was improperly applied states the "murder was especially atrocious or cruel, being unnecessarily torturous to the victim." . . . The trial court instructed the jury that atrocious means

> outrageously wicked and vile; cruel means designed to inflict a high degree of pain with utter indifference to, or even enjoyment of, the suffering of others. What is intended to be included in this circumstance are those murders where the actual commission of the crime was accompanied by such additional acts of serious physical or mental abuse of the victims as to set it apart from the normal first degree murder; that is, a particularly consciousless or pitiless crime which is unnecessarily torturous to the victims. . . .

. . . Part of extensive 1989 amendments to the statute, this aggravating circumstance previously read, "especially heinous, atrocious or cruel," and survived a vagueness challenge in [*Hopkinson v. State I*]; 632 P.2d 79 (Wyo. 1981), when we held that the statutory language provided the jury adequate guidance when imposing the death penalty. That decision focused on the "especially heinous" portion of the statute's wording and found that the murder to be so classified must demonstrate that the consciencelessness of the defendant is not only an outrage but also a dangerous and unrestrainable threat to society. It found Florida's interpretation instructive:

> That court has recognized that while it is arguable "that all killings are atrocious, still, we believe that the Legislature intended something 'especially' heinous, atrocious or cruel when it authorized the death penalty for first degree murder."

As a consequence the court has indicated that the eighth statutory provision is directed only at "the conscienceless or pitiless crime which is unnecessarily torturous to the victim." We cannot say that the provision, as so construed, provides inadequate guidance to those charged with the duty of recommending or imposing sentences in capital cases." [Hopkinson, 632 P.2d at 154 (quoting Proffitt v. Florida, 428 U.S. at 255-56.]

. . . In this case, there was no evidence of physical torture, and Olsen's jury was presented with argument that conviction was appropriate under this aggravating circumstance because "uncertainty as to his or her ultimate fate" constituted mental torture. . . .

Relying upon Olsen's statements, the State describes the murders as establishing that mental anguish was caused by Olsen's having the victims lay down on the floor and wait to be shot, and that the mental anguish must have increased for at least two of the victims after the first victim was shot. This set of facts does not establish any intentional infliction of mental torture that proves beyond a reasonable doubt the murders were "especially atrocious or cruel, being unnecessarily torturous to the victim." The facts of *Hopkinson v. State II,* 664 P.2d 43 (Wyo. 1983), establish the extreme degree of physical torture contemplated by the statutory language. In that case, the evidence was that, before death, the murder victim, while tied down, received over 140 burns on his body, including his eyes; five knife cuts on his neck and breasts; a bullet wound; bludgeoning; and extreme physical torture that could only have been intentionally inflicted over several hours. . . . In comparison, the evidence of this case establishes a degree of mental anguish that, while significant, is not sufficient to be atrocious by proof beyond a reasonable doubt. Were we to decide otherwise, we would not be upholding the clear legislative intent to limit Wyoming's death penalty to the most culpable of murderers.

2. Great Risk of Death Aggravating Circumstance

We next consider Olsen's challenge to the aggravating circumstance that he "knowingly created a great risk of death to two or more persons." We have upheld application of this factor in *Engberg v. State,* 686 P.2d 541 (Wyo. 1984), finding:

. . . Engberg seriously endangered the lives of Kay Otto and other persons present in the parking lot at the time of the robbery and murder, as well as that of his victim, Vernon Rogers. In shooting errantly at persons in parked vehicles in the lot, Engberg manifested an utter disregard for lives of innocent persons . . .

The State did not present any evidence or suggest that there were other bystanders involved who were threatened with grave harm as Olsen shot his intended victims. In applying this aggravating circumstance to Olsen, the State argued its basis was the harm inflicted upon the victims of his crime in a multiple homicide. The State defends its application by referring us to decisions in the jurisdictions of Oklahoma, Louisiana, and Mississippi, providing an interpretation that "where there is more than one victim, where they are in the same building, room, or place, and within the same time frame, their killing may be said to have created a great risk of death to two or more persons." In contrast, Arizona has limited similar language to "those factual situations where a grave risk of death has been created which threatens persons other than the intended victims." Arizona v. Tison, 633 P.2d 335 (Ariz. 1981).

The State's contention that the legislature intended the death penalty to apply to multiple homicide comports neither with the plain language of the statutory circumstance because the legislature could easily have included "multiple homicide" language, nor with an intent to restrict use of the death penalty to the most culpable of murderers. States that have included multiple homicide as an aggravating circumstance do so in addition to the inclusion of the aggravating circumstance of creating a great risk of death to others, and they use explicit, plain language.

. . . The State concedes that bystanders' lives other than the intended victims were not directly endangered during Olsen's crimes. It was reversible error to submit an instruction on this aggravating factor to the jury.

3. Purpose of Avoiding or Preventing a Lawful Arrest Aggravating Circumstance

Olsen was charged with committing the murders "for the purpose of avoiding or preventing a lawful arrest or effecting an escape from custody." In applying this aggravating circumstance to Olsen, the State contended the evidence showed that after the bartender told him that he would not get away with his crime, Olsen realized the witnesses in the bar could identify him and he then executed them. Olsen contends that application of the aggravator under these circumstances permits it to be valid in any homicide case, because in virtually every homicide there is a witness silenced, and an arrest thus potentially prevented. He points out that such application would call into question the constitutional validity of the aggravator because "there [would be] no principled way to distinguish this case, in which the death penalty is imposed, from the many cases in which it was not." He urges that no evidence establishes and this court cannot find that the dominant motive for the murder was the elimination of witnesses. He contends that the aggravating circumstance is properly limited to those cases where it is the dominant motive, as illustrated by those situations involving an imminent arrest or those cases where the victim of the murder is a witness to an earlier independent crime.

[*Hopkinson v. State II,* 664 P.2d at 58-59] considered the application of this factor. This court found the evidence established that the victim was an accomplice murdered because he was to testify before a grand jury about Hopkinson's role in an earlier multiple murder. The State contends that limiting this factor to witnesses in an ongoing investigation as in *Hopkinson* would make this aggravating circumstance practically indistinguishable from the aggravating circumstance in §6-2-102(h)(viii) [(involving the murder of judicial officers, lawyers, jurors, or witnesses in a case)].

. . . We have already determined that it is the legislative intent to limit application of the death penalty to the most culpable of crimes. Plainly, the legislature intended that the death penalty apply to those murders motivated to avoid or prevent a lawful arrest or effect an escape from custody although the murders also occurred during commission of a robbery, the aggravating circumstance articulated in §6-2-102(h)(xii).

The evidence supports finding that the only motive for the execution-type killings after the victims had cooperated and the robbery was accomplished was as Olsen admitted, namely, to eliminate identification witnesses. . . . Olsen's concern that in virtually every homicide there is a witness silenced, and an arrest thus potentially prevented, does not arise when the State is required to prove beyond a reasonable doubt that the dominant motive is to eliminate witnesses to a crime.

In this case, sufficient evidence supports finding that this aggravating circumstance existed. Olsen stated that none of the victims resisted him during the robbery and the robbery was accomplished before he shot them. Olsen stated that he shot the victims because they could identify him. This evidence established that Olsen's dominant motive for the murders was to eliminate the witnesses to his crime of robbery and established for the jury beyond a reasonable doubt the aggravating circumstance of murder to avoid or prevent a lawful arrest.

4. Premeditated Felony Murder Aggravating Circumstance

Olsen contends that after he was convicted of premeditated first degree murder and felony murder, the premeditation and robbery elements of those crimes were used to establish the "premeditated felony murder" aggravating circumstance in violation of *Engberg*. . . .

. . . In [*Engberg v. Meyer,* 820 P.2d 70, 89-91 (Wyo. 1991)] the robbery established an essential element of the crime of felony murder and of two aggravating circumstances: the murder was committed while the defendant was engaged in the commission of a felony, and the murder was committed for pecuniary gain.[6] *Engberg's* holding was very specific: We now hold that where an underlying felony is used to convict a defendant of felony murder only, elements of the underlying felony may not again be used as an aggravating factor in the sentencing phase.

. . . Olsen was convicted of both felony murder and premeditated first degree murder, and *Engberg* does not apply. We disagree with Olsen's claim that permitting this aggravating factor does not narrow the class of persons to be sentenced to death. Once Olsen was convicted of premeditated first degree murder, this aggravating circumstance constitutionally submitted the question of whether he was eligible for the death penalty on the basis that he was engaged in the commission of a robbery. . . .

[V. LAW OF MITIGATING CIRCUMSTANCES]

. . . Olsen's sentencing jury was instructed to consider whether twenty-one specifically listed mitigating circumstances existed by a preponderance of the evidence.

. . . Defense counsel listed the mitigating circumstances that were unrefutedly established by the evidence:

1. Unrefuted that he is loved by his family.
2. Unrefuted that he is a loving father.
3. Unrefuted about AVM.[7]
4. Unrefuted that his intelligence has declined to low average.
5. Unrefuted that he is a model prisoner, unrefuted that he is not future dangerous.
6. Unrefuted that he is loyal to his friends.

---

6. [Note that this was possible because at the time of *Engberg*, an earlier version of the Wyoming death penalty law made it an aggravating circumstance that the defendant "was engaged . . . in the commission . . . of any robbery," Engberg v. Meyer, 820 P.2d at 89, whereas the current version of aggravating circumstance (xii) requires that the killer both premeditate and act in the course of a robbery.—Eds.]

7. [This refers to "arteriovenous malformation," a congenital, organic condition that deprives the brain of normal blood flow.—Eds.]

7. Unrefuted that he had a high level of alcohol in his system at the time of the offense.
8. Unrefuted that he is young.
9. Unrefuted that he saved his sister's life.
10. Unrefuted that his capacity to conform his conduct to the requirements of the law was substantially impaired.
11. Unrefuted that he was under the influence of extreme or emotional disturbance.
12. Unrefuted that he cooperated and confessed and has the ability to be constructive in prison.
13. Unrefuted that he was self-destructive and suffering from marital problems and depressed.
14. Unrefuted that this was only a robbery, not other crimes.
15. Debatable whether he had a significant criminal history, but nothing as a youth and no felony convictions.

Although the existence of a number of these mitigating circumstances was unrefuted, and would reasonably be expected to have been considered in the jury's weighing process, . . . no mitigating circumstances were unanimously found to exist by a preponderance of the evidence. Individual jurors did find that two of the listed mitigating circumstances existed, and individual jurors wrote in six other mitigating circumstances found to exist that were not listed on the verdict form. . . . Olsen contends that improper instructions precluded the jury from considering relevant mitigating evidence in its consideration of an appropriate penalty.

. . . The specific instructions that Olsen challenges are Instruction No. 12, which instructed the jury that it "may consider whether a defendant has established the existence of any mitigating factors," and Instruction No. 13, which instructed that the jury "may consider any fact or circumstance of Martin Olsen's character or prior record or matter surrounding his offense which serves to mitigate his culpability." Olsen challenges the discretionary language presented by the term "may," contending that the statutory language and constitutional principles require mandatory language such as "shall." . . . Olsen contends that the jury's failure to find any of the mitigating factors specifically listed on the verdict form despite the fact that each was established upon reasonable testimony, and many were unrefuted, or did not involve credibility, establishes the inadequacies of Instruction Nos. 12 and 13. The State replies that the completed verdict form where the jury determined that no specifically listed mitigating factor was unanimously agreed upon, but individual jurors found some of the specifically listed factors and wrote in others, proves the jury understood the instructions and did consider the mitigating evidence and the mitigating circumstances proposed by Olsen.

. . . A jury's unanimous decision that mitigating circumstances do not exist does not make the evidence irrelevant. The mitigating circumstances not unanimously found to be present by the jury did not become "irrelevant" to mitigation merely because one or more jurors either did not believe that the circumstance had been proved as a factual matter, or did not think that the circumstance, though proved, mitigated the offense. . . . "It is not enough simply to allow the defendant to present mitigating evidence to the sentencer. The sentencer must also be able to consider and give effect to that evidence in imposing sentence." Penry, 492 U.S. at 319.

. . . The statutory phrase "the jury shall consider aggravating and mitigating circumstances" is significant under Wyoming's death penalty statutory scheme. This phrase describes the process intended to distinguish between a penalty of life imprisonment and death. . . . That the statute intends this consideration to be a "mental balancing process," "a reasoned judgment," and a consideration of the "substantiality and persuasiveness" of all of the circumstances is clear from its prohibition that the mere numbers of each are not to be considered.

. . . After reviewing instructions from other states as well as Olsen's proposed instruction, we believe a more accurate instruction would be:

> The weighing of aggravating and mitigating circumstances does not mean a mere mechanical counting of factors on each side of an imaginary scale, or the arbitrary assignment of weights to any of them. You are free to assign whatever moral or sympathetic value you deem appropriate to each and all of the various factors you are permitted to consider. In weighing the various circumstances you determine under the relevant evidence which penalty is justified and appropriate by considering the totality of the aggravating circumstances with the totality of the mitigating circumstances. In reaching a reasoned, moral judgment about which penalty is justified and appropriate, you must decide how compelling or persuasive the totality of the mitigating factors are when compared against the totality of the aggravating factors. You cannot be governed or influenced by sentiment, passion or prejudice, however, you may consider mercy, and decline to impose the death penalty after a thoughtful consideration of the evidence. To return a judgment of death, each of you must be persuaded that the aggravating circumstances are so substantial in comparison with the mitigating circumstances that it warrants death instead of a life sentence.

In examining all of the other submitted jury instructions, we see that Olsen's jury received inconsistent instruction in the steps of the statutory process it is to engage in and no useful instruction in how it is to engage in this statutory process. We recommend that the trial court instruct on the principles just set forth. . . .

We hold that the jury instructions about mitigating circumstances do not correctly state the law mandated by §6-2-102(d), and this failure is reversible error. Upon remand for resentencing, jury instructions should reflect the intended statutory process and clarify the jury's decision process in comparing the totality of aggravating and mitigating circumstances.

[VI. INSTRUCTION IN RESPONSE TO JURY QUESTIONS ABOUT PAROLE]

After a short time deliberating during the sentencing phase, the jury sent a note to the court asking:

> If sentenced to three life terms would the Defendant ever have a chance for parole for any possible reason. . . .

Despite defense counsel's objections, the district court answered this question with this supplemental instruction:

> Under the laws of the State of Wyoming, the governor has the power to grant reprieves, commutations and pardons after conviction for all offenses. . . . This means that the governor has the power to commute each life sentence to a term of years. If the governor were to commute each life sentence to a term of years then and only then could the parole board consider the possibility of parole. . . .

The United States Supreme Court has held that it is not unconstitutional for a court to tell the jury about the possibility of executive clemency. California v. Ramos, 463 U.S. 992 (1983). Despite the State's assurance that this instruction does inform the jury that Olsen would be eligible for parole, it does not. . . . [W]e agree with Olsen that the instruction is insufficient under Simmons v. South Carolina, 512 U.S. 153 (1994), because it did not inform the jury of Olsen's immediate statutory ineligibility for parole.

Just as in Olsen's case, future dangerousness was an issue in *Simmons;* however, the trial court refused to instruct the jury that defendant was statutorily ineligible for parole should it elect to impose a life term in prison rather than the death penalty. The plurality . . . observed that "[t]he Due Process Clause does not allow the execution of a person 'on the basis of information which he had no opportunity to deny or explain.'"

Accordingly, Olsen's jury should have been instructed that, under the statute, a sentence of life imprisonment means that he would not be eligible for parole.

[VII. Summary]

We have invalidated two of the four aggravating circumstances for which Olsen was convicted. Although he was properly convicted of two aggravating circumstances, his sentence cannot be affirmed. "An automatic rule of affirmance in a weighing state [is] invalid . . . for it would not give defendants the individualized treatment that would result from actual reweighing of the mix of mitigating factors and aggravating circumstances." [Clemons v. Mississippi, 494 U.S. 738 (1990).]

. . . We [also] conclude that Olsen's jury was not properly instructed on the law of mitigating circumstances as intended by Wyoming's death penalty statute. We vacate the sentence of death and remand for a new sentencing hearing.[8]

Notes and Questions

1. *Who is the sentencer?* In the new death penalty statutes enacted after *Furman* and approved in *Gregg,* most of the states delegated to juries the power to impose death, but in a handful the power lay solely with the trial judge, and in a few states, most notably Florida, the jury could make recommendation on life

---

8. [The court also determined that prejudicial error occurred when (1) the jury was not properly instructed on the statutorily required decision-making process, the law of mitigating circumstances and the mitigating circumstance of duress; (2) the jury was not provided an adequate verdict form; and (3) victim impact evidence was improperly admitted.]

or death but the final power lay with the judge. Now in light of its recent decision, the Supreme Court has steered the states substantially toward a requirement that capital defendants have the right to a jury at the penalty phase. The
post-*Furman* Arizona statute had wholly entrusted the death penalty decision to
the trial judge. This law had been upheld in Walton v. Arizona, 497 U.S. 639
(1990), where the Court stated that aggravating factors were not "elements of
the offense," but rather "sentencing considerations." But recall that in Apprendi
v. New Jersey, 530 U.S. 466 (2000), see the Introduction, p. 20, *supra,* the Court
held that if a State makes an increase in a defendant's maximum authorized
punishment contingent on the finding of a fact, that fact — no matter how the
State labels it — must be found by a jury beyond a reasonable doubt. In short, a
defendant may not be exposed to a penalty exceeding the maximum he would
receive if punished according to the facts reflected in the jury verdict alone. In
Ring v. Arizona, 536 U.S. 584 (2002), the Court returned to the Arizona law and
noted that once a jury found the defendant guilty of all the elements of an offense that carries death as its maximum penalty, it was left to the judge to decide
whether that maximum penalty, rather than a lesser one, ought to be imposed.
Hence, in *Ring,* the Court read *Apprendi* as forbidding the Arizona scheme.

Read narrowly, the *Ring* decision mandates that factors — namely aggravating circumstances — making a criminal defendant death-eligible must be
determined by a jury rather than by a judge. Under such a reading, the death
sentence itself need not necessarily be determined by a jury. But states whose
laws were affected by *Ring* have differed dramatically in how they interpret the
holding. For example, the Delaware Supreme Court has held that while the jury
must determine the existence of any statutory aggravating factor, "[t]he final
sentencing decision . . . remains with the judge." Brice v. State, 815 A.2d 314
(Del. 2003). Other state courts have held that *Ring* requires that a jury weigh aggravating and mitigating factors and then make the final determination as to
whether mitigating circumstances are sufficient to warrant life rather than
death; Arizona v. Ring, 65 P.3d 915 (Ariz. 2003); Johnson v. State, 59 P.3d 450
(Nev. 2002). Of course, read more broadly, *Ring* may mandate that all states now
adopt full jury decision-making at the penalty phase.[9]

2. *Aggravating Circumstances.* Review the list of aggravating circumstances
enumerated in the Wyoming statute, at p. 439, *supra.* It is extremely typical of
those of other capital punishment jurisdictions, and closely maps the list prescribed by the Model Penal Code, a list which was favorably cited in Gregg v.
Georgia opinion. The rules and principles of aggravating circumstances, as well
as the countervailing rules and principles of mitigating circumstances, merit
some detailed attention, as provided in the following subsections.

a. *The concept of aggravation.* These typical aggravating circumstances bear an
interesting relationship to the traditional homicide categories. For example, section (h)(xii) partly duplicates the first-degree felony-murder rule. Subsections
(v) and (vi) seem to overlap slightly with the concerns of the felony murder rule

---

9. Perhaps surprisingly, in the first round of post-*Ring* cases in Arizona, juries imposed death
10 out of 12 times, a far greater rate than had been true under pure judge-sentencing in recent
years. One possible reason is that judges who had previously given lawyers months to compile mitigating evidence have been imposing strict time constraints on the defense to avoid keeping juries
impaneled for extensive periods, though many believe judges and lawyers will adapt to the new system in the long run. Robert S. Greenberger, A Death Penalty Turnabout, Wall St. J., Aug. 6, 2003,
p. A4.

but distinguish murders on the basis of "motive," an issue normally irrelevant to the criminal law once the required technical mens rea is established. Subsection (iii) is curious: It aggravates a first-degree murder where the defendant, in effect, exhibited an "abandoned and malignant heart" with respect to the possible deaths of other people, even if those others were not killed. The most controversial of these factors, the "atrocious or cruel" provision in subsection (vii), which we will examine below, seems like a vague exhortation to the sentencer to identify whatever aggravating aspects of the particular crime have evaded the other categories.

Finally, note that it is an aggravating circumstance under subsection (i) that the murderer was already under a sentence of imprisonment. Does that factor make the murder more culpable? Or is it that a prisoner cannot be deterred from killing by any punishment less than death?[10]

We now examine in more detail some of the legal issues surrounding several typical aggravating factors, noting when and how they arise in *Olsen:*

b. *Previous felonies.* Why is it an aggravating circumstance that the defendant previously committed another felony involving violence? Subsection (ii) enhances punishment on the basis of the defendant's previous criminal record. Under normal rules of evidence, a defendant's earlier crimes cannot be introduced at a criminal trial to help prove the defendant's predisposition to commit a new offense. Yet in traditional discretionary sentencing by the judge in noncapital cases, the trial judge always looks at the defendant's criminal record. The states have transposed this element of discretionary noncapital sentencing into the new criminal "trial" of the penalty phase. If Olsen had committed previous aggravated assaults or kidnappings, how would that have affected the question whether he deserved death for this murder? Does the presence of this factor suggest that in the penalty phase the defendant is being "tried" not just for her crime but for the "culpability" of her entire life and character?

Note that when the legislature tries to create a new aggravating factor it produces the same sort of problems of statutory interpretation and doctrinal coherence that we encountered in the traditional homicide grading laws. With respect to the "prior violent felony" circumstance, is subsection (ii) careless in the phrase "a felony involving the use or threat of violence to the person"? What if the previous conviction was for burglary of an empty house? Does burglary generally involve violence or the threat of violence? If so, should it matter that this particular defendant committed a burglary in a careful, nonviolent way? Compare the issue of the "inherently dangerous felony" in the discussion of felony murder, pp. 415-417, *supra.*

What if a defendant robs and kills a person, and then, as part of the same criminal transaction, robs another person, say, a companion of the murder victim? Would the second robbery be an aggravating factor with respect to the murder? Many courts say yes.[11]

10. In Sumner v. Shuman, 483 U.S. 66 (1987), the Supreme Court held that a Nevada statute categorically imposing the death penalty on a prison inmate convicted of murder while serving a life sentence without possibility of parole violated the Eighth Amendment, because it failed to require individualized sentencing.

11. Some states permit evidence showing the defendant committed the previous crime even if he or she was never formally convicted. See, e.g., Ark. Crim. Code 5-4-604 (1997); Parker v. Norris, 64; F.3d 1178 (8th Cir. 1995). The ironic result is that the defendant will contest the evidence, so that the penalty phase of the murder trial includes a mini-criminal trial where he contests his guilt of the previous felony, *e.g.,* People v. Haskett, 30 Cal. 3d 841, 640 P.2d 776 (1982), Elledge v. State, 346 So. 2d 998, 1001 (Fla. 1977).

Though prior convictions almost always serve as aggravating circumstances, one commentator has argued that prior imprisonment should serve as a mitigating circumstance, because of the psychic and physical abuse most prison inmates suffer.[12]

c. *Felony murder as aggravation.* At his guilt phase, Olsen was convicted of both robbery and of felony murder, in addition to premeditated murder. Is it fair for the state to then count the felony again as an aggravating circumstance at the penalty phase, so that the defendant automatically enters the penalty phase with one strike against him? Many state courts, like Wyoming's here, limit this bonus to cases where, as in *Olsen,* the premeditation count would have sufficed to establish first-degree murder anyway. *E.g.,* State v. Cherry, 298 N.C. 86, 257 S.E.2d 551 (1979). On the other hand, as a matter of federal constitutional law, the Supreme Court would permit the prosecutorial "bonus" even in the case where the underlying murder charge was solely based on a felony murder ground, as in the *Engberg* case cited in *Olsen.* In Lowenfeld v. Phelps, 484 U.S. 231 (1988), the defendant had been convicted of three counts of first-degree murder, an essential statutory element of which was a finding of his intent "to kill or inflict great bodily harm upon more than one person." Only this finding at the guilt phase made the murder first-degree, rather than second-degree. In the sentencing phase, the jury then found the aggravating circumstance that the defendant has "knowingly created a risk of death or great bodily harm to more than one person." The Court upheld the death sentence, noting that the statutory scheme narrowed the group of those eligible for the death penalty at the guilt phase, rather than the sentencing phase, and it was constitutional so long as this narrowing occurred somewhere along the way.

Now under *Lowenfeld,* can a state create a regime whereby all statutory aggravating factors are found at the guilt phase, thereby ensuring that the defendant enters the penalty phase with one or more strikes against him? See United States v. McVeigh, 944 F. Supp. 1478 (D. Colo. 1996) (aggravating factors include destruction of motor vehicle, transport of explosives, destruction of government property by explosives; "double-counting" permissible where extra crimes that form part of aggravating circumstance contain some of same elements as crimes charged in indictment, but not where a whole crime charged in the indictment is separately charged as an aggravator).

d. *"Atrocious or cruel."* One aggravator used against Olsen was that the killing was done in "an atrocious or cruel" manner (the verbal formulas for this type of aggravator vary among the statutes, but usually use the word "heinous"). If treated as a distinct crime, would this factor pass the vagueness test of City of Chicago v. Morales, *supra,* p. 144? Does it satisfy the *Gregg* mandate of carefully guided discretion? The positive answer in *Olsen* finds qualified support in Godfrey v. Georgia, 446 U.S. 420 (1980). There, the defendant argued that the aggravating circumstance that the killing was "outrageously or wantonly vile, horrible, or inhuman in that it involved torture, depravity of mind, or an aggravated battery to the victim" was unconstitutionally vague.

A plurality of the Court (a) declared that on their face, the words of this provision were unconstitutionally vague; (2) conceded that in recent cases, the Georgia Supreme Court had attempted to establish certain guiding criteria for

---

12. James Robertson, Closing the Circle: When Prior Imprisonment Ought to Mitigate Capital Murder, 11 Kan. J. L. & Pub. Pol. 415 (2001).

this provision, such as that the killing involved torture or aggravated battery on the conscious victim before death occurred, but (3) concluded that these criteria had not worked to sufficiently justify the aggravator in this particular case:

> The petitioner's crimes cannot be said to have reflected a consciousness materially more "depraved" than that of any person guilty of murder. His victims were killed instantaneously. They were members of his family who were causing him extreme emotional trauma. Shortly after the killings, he acknowledged his responsibility and the heinous nature of his crimes. [Id. at 433.]

Other state courts have struggled to avoid the *Godfrey* problem by giving some coherent meaning to the "heinous, atrocious, or cruel" aggravating circumstance through case-by-case comparison and distinction of facts. In Florida, for example, the circumstance cannot rest solely on proof that the killing was "premeditated, cold, and calculated," Lewis v. State, 398 So. 2d 432 (Fla. 1981), or because the defendant killed the victim in the presence of the victim's family, Riley v. State, 366 So. 2d 19 (Fla. 1978). In State v. Johnson, 751 A.2d 298 (Conn. 2000), the defendant fatally shot a policeman with one or two shots. The court noted that the victim had remained conscious long enough after the last shot to shout "Oh, my God" and to turn on the car's strobe light, and that he had suffered pain from shrapnel in his arm. Nevertheless, the court invalidated the "heinousness" circumstance:

> Given the manner in which Bagshaw was murdered and the speed with which he died, as reprehensible as the attack was, there is no principled way to distinguish this case from the "ordinary" gunshot death or to differentiate it from the norm of capital felonies. . . .
>
> Although there are cases in which a near instantaneous death by gunfire could satisfy the "heinous" factor, typically such cases have involved extreme fear, emotional strain and terror during the events leading up to the murder. See, e.g., Henyard v. State, 689 So.2d 239, 254 (Fla. 1996), (defendant's abduction of mother and her three and seven year old daughters, rape and shooting of mother, followed by execution of girls, sufficiently terrifying to children to constitute cruel, heinous and atrocious aggravating factor). Fortunately, this case was not accompanied by such cruelty. Six seconds of being the target of the defendant's fusillade and up to ninety seconds of consciousness following being struck by one bullet do not suffice to meet the heinous, atrocious or cruel aggravating factor. Short of an instantaneous death, which . . . is quite rare, occurring only when there is a direct injury to the brain stem or sufficient trauma to the brain cavity, virtually any gunshot wound will involve some pain. . . .
>
> Moreover, with regard to Bagshaw's victim's shrapnel arm wound, the evidence does not demonstrate whether that wound preceded or followed the fatal chest wound, and thus it is uncertain whether Bagshaw was even conscious when that wound was inflicted. . . .
>
> Although Bagshaw's last words certainly evoke great sympathy, such words do not demonstrate extreme psychological pain above and beyond that necessarily accompanying any killing that is not absolutely instantaneous. Moreover, the ability to activate the lights merely demonstrates that the trooper was conscious. [Id. at 340-43].

This quoted section is a small fraction of the court's discussion of the nuances of the killing, a discussion that takes up 12 dense pages in the West Reporter. Does this incredibly fine parsing of the psychological and physical phenomena of homicidal trauma sensibly fall within the competence of the judicial system?

e. *Pecuniary gain.* In numerous cases, the apparently discrete categories created by the statutory aggravating circumstances seem to duplicate each other and apply to the exact same evidentiary facts. Some courts have therefore strained to construe the circumstances narrowly and avoid the overlap. A good example is the common circumstance that the murder was committed for the purpose of "pecuniary gain." Can this circumstance arise any time a murder occurs in the course of a robbery or larceny-based burglary? Should it have applied in *Olsen*? Seeking to avoid this overlap, a few courts have construed the circumstance to apply only in cases of murder for hire or murder to obtain insurance proceeds or inheritances of bequests. See, e.g., State v. Simants, 197 Neb. 549, 250 N.W.2d 881 (Neb. 1977).

f. *Avoiding or preventing arrest.* Why was it an aggravating factor that Olsen committed the murder for the purpose of avoiding or preventing arrest? If he acted with intent or purpose in killing the victim, how does his motive increase his culpability? Would this circumstance apply in virtually every case of an intentional killing of a robbery or burglary or rape victim? Similarly, why is it an aggravating circumstance that the victim was a judicial officer, attorney peace officer, or witness (subsection viii)? How does the *Olsen* court resolve the potential overlap problem here?

In light of these "motive" factors, should it mitigate an intentional killing that the defendant acted with the purpose or motive of removing from society a person known to be a criminal but not then in the act of committing a serious crime?

Do the courts' difficulties in applying these overlapping criteria support Justice Harlan's warning in McGautha v. California, p. 431, *supra*?

g. *Some miscellaneous aggravators.* In Leslie v. Warden, 59 P.3d 440 (Nev. 2002), the Nevada Supreme Court ruled that the circumstance that the murder was committed "at random and without any apparent motive" was meant to apply to situations where the killer selected his victim without a specific or discernable purpose, and could not be used in the generic case of a murder during the course of a robbery where the defendant kills the robbery victim or a witness-bystander.

The Florida statute contains an aggravating circumstance that the murder was committed "in a cold, calculated, and premeditated manner without any pretense of moral or legal justification." Fla. Stat. Ann. §921.141 (5) (i) (Supp. 1997). By what definition of premeditation can a premeditated killing be distinguished from a "cold, calculated" killing?

h. *Nonstatutory aggravating factors.* In some states the prosecutor is allowed to prove to the jury certain "nonstatutory" aggravating factors, such as the victim's youth and vulnerability. Though the guided discretion statutes approved in Gregg v. Georgia expressly define certain aggravating circumstances, prosecutors may be inclined to argue the presence of other aggravating circumstances that have a basis in the evidence, but that fall outside the circumstances expressly enumerated in the statute. Is it consistent with *Furman* and *Gregg* that the sentencer rely on such "nonstatutory" aggravating circumstances in reaching a death verdict? In Zant v. Stephens, 462 U.S. 862 (1983), and Barclay v. Florida, 463 U.S. 939 (1983), the Supreme Court found no constitutional flaw in such reliance, so long as the sentencer found at least one statutory aggravator.

For example, in *Barclay,* the trial judge who ordered the defendant's execution over a jury's recommendation of life found an aggravating circumstance that Barclay had been convicted of breaking and entering with intent to commit grand larceny, even though the only prior crimes that constituted statutory aggravating circumstances in Florida were those inherently involving violence.

i. *Victim impact statements.* In Payne v. Tennessee, 501 U.S. 808 (1991), the Court ruled that the Eighth Amendment erects no categorical barrier to "victim impact" evidence describing the victim's personal characteristics and the emotional and other effects of the murder on the victim's family. The trial court had permitted testimony and prosecutorial argument on the emotional effect on a young boy of the murder of his mother and young sister. The Court rejected the argument that evidence relating to the character of the victim or the peculiar circumstances or sufferings of the victim's family does not reflect on the defendant's blameworthiness or moral desert. Rather, it said, degree of harm is often a measure in determining both the elements of an offense and the degree of punishment. Thus, the "specific harm" caused by the defendant is an important factor in determining his appropriate punishment, both for the legislature in drawing general guidelines and the jury in exercising its sentencing discretion. Although capital sentencing jurisprudence aims for procedures that ensure that the jury focus on the defendant as a unique individual, the Court held that a state may constitutionally decide that it is relevant as well for the sentencer to consider the victim as a unique individual.

Does victim impact testimony improperly shift the trial's focus to the victim's worth, making it tactically impossible for the defense to rebut this evidence? Does victim impact testimony encourage juries to discriminate among victims on the basis of their worth to society? In Mosley v. State, 983 S.W.2d 249 (Texas Ct. Crim. App. 1999), the court said that trial judges should exclude testimony about the character of the victim that encourages the jury to compare the victim with other members of society in terms of worth or morality. Can that distinction hold?

After *Payne,* is the defendant entitled to present evidence proffered by the victim's family that they oppose the death penalty for him? The answer was negative in Lynn v. Reinstein, 68 P.3d 412 (Ariz. 2003) (victim's husband not allowed to recommend a life sentence over prosecutor's objection).

2. Mitigating Circumstances

a. *The concept of mitigation.* Review the numerous mitigating factors enumerated in the Wyoming statute, see pp. 439-440, *supra.* The Model Penal Code prescribes a similar list of mitigating circumstances, although, as we will see below, the actual enumeration is less significant than might appear, since the defendant has a constitutional right to present any mitigating evidence or circumstances, whether listed by statute or not.

Some of the enumerated mitigating factors in the typical statute, such as subsection (i) on the absence of a serious criminal record, are simply the obverse of the aggravating circumstances. Others closely resemble various conventional homicide doctrines that would normally serve as defenses to, or reduce the grade of, the defendant's liability. Thus subsection (ii) is like "heat of passion" in voluntary manslaughter; subsection (v) resembles the duress defenses we will examine later in Part V; subsection (vi) obviously resembles the insanity defense; and subsection (iv) seems designed to reflect the criminal law's ambivalence about the felony murder rule. (As we will see below in the case of *Tison v. Arizona*, p. 459, *infra,* the Supreme Court itself was beset by this ambivalence.) Note for now that these factors often call for the same sort of evidence that might be offered at the guilt phase to reduce the grade of homicide or to serve as a complete defense. If the evidence, by hypothesis, has proved insufficient to save the defendant from a first-degree murder conviction, does it make sense for it to be reconsidered at sentencing?

b. *The scope of mitigation.* Like aggravating factors, mitigating factors are often expressly enumerated in the state's capital murder statute. See Model Penal Code §210.6. Three issues then arise. First, can the state limit mitigating factors to those enumerated in the statute? Second, if the state cannot so limit mitigating factors by statute, are there any conceptual or topical boundaries as to what mitigating factors the defense can proffer? Third, in ruling on the admissibility of mitigating factors proffered by the defense, how much leeway does the trial judge have in admitting or excluding evidence on the basis of its probative value?

The clear negative answer to the first question came in Lockett v. Ohio, 438 U.S. 586 (1978). Sandra Lockett was the getaway driver in an armed robbery of a pawnshop. While she sat in the car, one of her accomplices accidentally killed the robbery victim. At her sentencing hearing, however, Lockett tried to offer as a mitigating circumstance the fact that she had not herself caused or intended the victim's death. At the time, the Ohio death penalty statute enumerated three mitigating circumstances: That the victim of the killing had helped cause his own death; that the defendant had acted under duress, coercion, or strong provocation; or that the offense primarily resulted from the defendant's mental impairment. Even though the sentencing judge heard her evidence about her minor participation in the killing, the judge was not allowed to count that evidence as a mitigating factor because it did not fall within any of the enumerated statutory mitigating categories. The Supreme Court vacated her death sentence.

> . . . [W]e . . . conclude that the Eighth and Fourteenth Amendments require that the sentencer, in all but the rarest kind of capital case, not be precluded from considering, as a mitigating factor, any aspect of a defendant's character or record and any of the circumstances of the offense that the defendant proffers as a basis for a sentence less than death. . . . The need for treating each defendant in a capital case with that degree of respect due the uniqueness of the individual is far more important than in noncapital cases. A variety of flexible techniques — probation, parole, work furloughs, to name a few — and various post-conviction remedies may be available to modify an initial sentence of confinement in noncapital cases. The nonavailability of corrective or modifying mechanisms with respect to an executed capital sentence underscores the need for individualized consideration as a constitutional requirement in imposing the death sentence.
>
> . . . [A] statute that prevents the sentencer in all capital cases from giving independent mitigating weight to aspects of the defendant's character and record and to circumstances of the offense proffered in mitigation creates the risk that the death penalty will be imposed in spite of factors which may call for a less severe penalty. [Id. at 604-05.]

Note that the mitigating factor at issue in *Lockett* related to the specific circumstances of the murder for which she was on trial rather than to broader matters concerning her character and background. After *Lockett* the Supreme Court made clear that the entire character and background of the defendant was indeed relevant to the sentencing decision. In Eddings v. Oklahoma, 455 U.S. 104 (1982), Eddings, who was 16 years old at the time of his crime and arrest, was convicted of murdering a highway patrol officer who had stopped him for reckless driving. At the penalty phase, the defense had tried to establish that Eddings's parents had divorced when he was five, that he had then lived with his alcoholic mother entirely without any supervision, and that he was then sent to his father and was seriously abused. The trial court had blocked admission of this evidence on the ground that it did not bear on the immediate circumstances of the killing or, under the normal rules of homicide, go to establish any legal defense to murder:

> . . . [It] is clear that the trial judge did not evaluate the evidence in mitigation and find it wanting as a matter of fact; rather he found that as a matter of law he was unable even to consider the evidence.
>
> The Court of Criminal Appeals took the same approach. It found that the evidence in mitigation was not relevant because it did not tend to provide a legal excuse from criminal responsibility. Thus the court conceded that Eddings had a "personality disorder," but cast this evidence aside on the basis that "he knew the difference between right and wrong . . . and that is the test of criminal responsibility." Similarly, the evidence of Eddings' family history was "useful in explaining" his behavior, but it did not "excuse" the behavior. From these statements it appears that the Court of Criminal Appeals also considered only that evidence to be mitigating which would tend to support a legal excuse from criminal liability. [Id. at 112-13.]

The Supreme Court rejected this line of reasoning under *Lockett:*

> Just as the state may not by statute preclude the sentencer from considering any mitigating factor, neither may the sentencer refuse to consider, as a matter of law, any relevant mitigating evidence. In this instance, it was as if the trial judge had instructed a jury to disregard the mitigating evidence Eddings proffered on his behalf. The sentencer, and the Court of Criminal Appeals on review, may determine the weight to be given relevant mitigating evidence. But they may not give it no weight. . . . [W]hen the defendant was 16 years old at the time of the offense there can be no doubt that evidence of a turbulent family history, of beatings by a harsh father, and of severe emotional disturbance is particularly relevant. . . . [Id. at 113-115.]

By far the most common mitigating circumstances proffered by capital defendants are that they were abused or neglected as children, or suffer from some mental illness short of legal insanity, or were beclouded by drugs or alcohol when they killed their victims.[13] Prof. Phyllis Crocker argues that the constitutional mandate of individualized sentencing has foundered on the courts' failure to ensure that juries differentiate guilt from punishment issues, and that the word and concept "culpability" dangerously blurs the distinction, especially in confusing guilt-phase insanity defense concepts and penalty phase mitigation.[14]

---

13. See Gary Goodpaster, The Trial for Life: Effective Assistance of Counsel in Death Penalty Cases, 58 N.Y.U. L. Rev. 299 (1983).

14. Concepts of Culpability and Deathworthiness: Differentiating Between Guilt and Punishment in Capital Cases, 66 Fordham L. Rev. 21 (1997).

In *Lockett* and *Eddings,* has the Court come full circle from *McGautha*? That is, in requiring highly flexible death sentencing procedures with individualized consideration of the offender and the offense, unrestrained by statutory categories, has the Court in effect restored to the sentencer the unguided, subjective discretion that was held illegitimate in *Furman*? Especially after the Court's holding in *Zant* and *Barclay, supra,* that the sentencer can consider nonstatutory aggravating factors as well? Also, by permitting factors like the "troubled childhood" claim at the penalty phase, has the Court opened up the whole vexing range of determinist explanations of criminal behavior, which the criminal law has essentially suppressed at the guilt stage? See the discussion in Chapter 1.

c. *Limits on mitigation.* In an important footnote in *Lockett,* the Court admonished:

> Nothing in this opinion limits the traditional authority of a court to exclude, as irrelevant, evidence not bearing on the defendant's character, prior record, or the circumstances of his offense. [438 U.S. at 604 n.12.]

How much does that exclude? And why?

One possible exclusion was rejected in Skipper v. South Carolina, 476 U.S. 1 (1986). At his penalty trial, Skipper tried to present the testimony of two jailers and a visitor as to his good behavior in jail during the seven months between his arrest and the trial. The Supreme Court held that *Lockett* permitted him to offer this testimony, reasoning that since juries are allowed to consider evidence that a defendant has a record of disruptive or dangerous behavior in prison as aggravating, "evidence that the defendant would not pose a danger if spared (but incarcerated) must be considered potentially mitigating." Id. at 5.

But despite *Skipper,* the limiting footnote in *Lockett* has had some bite, since the mitigating evidence has to be about the defendant personally, and not some more general factor or issue that could sway a jury to mercy. Examples of factors usually held outside the scope of *Lockett* include evidence about the likely general conditions the defendant would face as a life prisoner — including the certainty of confinement and lower-than-expected cost, Cherrix v. Commonwealth, 257 Va. 292, 513 S.E.2d 642 (1999); testimony from social scientists on the dubious deterrent value of the death penalty, or from journalists on the physical agonies a person suffers in the electric chair or the gas chamber, Gall v. Commonwealth, 607 S.W.2d 97, 112 (Ky. 1980); or testimony from theologians about the questionable religious basis for retribution, Johnson v. State, 416 So. 2d 383, 392 (Miss. 1982). Thus, courts often say that the sentencer cannot reexamine general questions of criminal law policy decided by the legislature (though they occasionally permit this type of testimony as a matter of trial court discretion). Finally, in Franklin v. Lynaugh, 487 U.S. 164 (1988), the Court held that a defendant did not have an Eighth Amendment right to a jury instruction that the jury could consider as a mitigating factor at the penalty phase any residual or "lingering" doubt about the defendant's guilt that it carried over from the guilt phase, though, again, some states still permit this. Can such "lingering doubt" be viewed as a mitigation circumstance?

d. *"Reverse mitigating circumstances."* Can the prosecution fashion an *aggravating* circumstance by manipulating the meaning of a particular enumerated *mitigating* circumstance? In People v. Kuntu, 196 Ill.2d 105, 752 N.E.2d 380 (2001), at the penalty phase the defendant established the circumstance of

"No significant history of prior criminal activity." During her closing argument, the prosecutor addressed the defendant's clean record: "I suggest to you that in this particular case, you can consider that as aggravation because . . . It tells you that up until age 26 this guy . . . knew the difference between right and wrong." The Court held this argument illegal:

> The legislature has chosen a specific scheme to ensure that the death penalty is not applied in an arbitrary and capricious manner. As part of this legislative scheme, the legislature has defined certain facts as inherently mitigating. . . . Neither this court nor a trial prosecutor has the authority to change the legislative scheme and convert a fact that the legislature has determined to weigh in favor of not sentencing a defendant to death into a fact that weighs in favor of sentencing a defendant to death. [752 N.E.2d at 402].

The court also dismissed state's contention that the remark was appropriate as a rebuttal to the defendant's introduction of "diminished intellectual capacity" as a reason he should not receive the death penalty, but it indicated that the prosecutor's creative use of a normally extenuating factor would have been proper had the legislature not already earmarked absence of criminal history as mitigating. Is there any legal way the prosecutor could have made this point?

3.   Weighing the Circumstances

a. *Formulas for the jury.* In *Olsen*, the defendant's long list of proffered mitigating items was "unrefuted," and yet on its verdict form the jury did not unanimously find any mitigating circumstances, and individual jurors only found a few. According to the court, by what principle could the jury have fairly rejected "unrefuted" mitigating evidence.

On the other hand, the court held that the instruction on mitigating circumstances was not consistent with the Wyoming statute. What was the error in the instruction? What misinterpretation of the death penalty law did the court fear the jury may have made? Review the instruction the court required for retrial, on p. 445. How does that solve the problem the court perceived?

State legislatures have authorized a variety of formulas for taking comparative account of aggravating and mitigating circumstances. Compare the formula required by the *Olsen* court to the one mandated by the Model Penal Code statute, §210.2:

> The [sentencing jury] shall take into account the aggravating and mitigating circumstances enumerated in Subsections (3) and (4) and any other facts that it deems relevant, but it shall not impose or recommend sentence of death unless it finds one of the aggravating circumstances enumerated in Subsection (3) and further finds that there are no mitigating circumstances sufficiently substantial to call for leniency.

In another variation, the Idaho Supreme Court has held that the sum of all mitigating circumstances should be weighed against each individual aggravating circumstance in order to give the defendant a stronger "presumption of life." State v. Charboneau, 774 P.2d 299 (1989).

Do you find a practical difference among these schemes? Do these types of instructions provide a psychologically realistic alternative to merely counting up the circumstances? Are they comprehensible to the average juror? Do they provide an objective intellectual process for comparing aggravating and mitigating circumstances so as to satisfy *Furman*?

Recall that in 1976 the Supreme Court invalidated mandatory death penalties imposed by statute regardless of aggravating and mitigating circumstances. But is there anything wrong with a "weighing formula" that tells jurors that a death sentence is mandatory after they conclude that the aggravators clearly dominate the mitigators? The Pennsylvania law provides that "[t]he verdict must be a sentence of death if the jury unanimously finds at least one or more aggravating circumstances which outweigh any mitigating circumstances." 42 Pa. Cons. Stat. §9711. In Blystone v. Pennsylvania, 494 U.S. 299 (1990), the Court held:

> At sentencing, petitioner's jury found one aggravating circumstance present in this case — that petitioner committed a killing while in the perpetration of a robbery. No mitigating circumstances were found. Petitioner contends that the mandatory imposition of death in this situation violates the Eighth Amendment requirement of individualized sentencing since the jury was precluded from considering whether the severity of his aggravating circumstance warranted the death sentence. We reject this argument. The presence of aggravating circumstances serves the purpose of limiting the class of death-eligible defendants, and the Eighth Amendment does not require that these aggravating circumstances be further refined or weighed by a jury. The requirement of individualized sentencing in capital cases is satisfied by allowing the jury to consider all relevant mitigating evidence.

Blystone essentially holds that a judge is not required to tell the jury, "You are free to choose life over death, even if you think that the balance of aggravators over mitigators legally calls for death." Of course, in fact, if not in law, a jury normally does have unbridled discretion to exercise mercy in behalf of a defendant, since just as a verdict of acquittal, under double jeopardy principles, cannot be appealed by the prosecution, in almost all states a verdict of life rather than death by a sentencing jury is irreversible. Is it sound to instruct a jury not to exercise discretion that it in fact possesses? Does the *Gregg* decision support such an instruction? Under what conditions might a jury find itself in this dilemma?

Note that a few state death penalty statutes do not use the language of comparative weighing at all. In Georgia, for example, the jury is told that it should "consider, any mitigating circumstances or aggravating circumstances otherwise authorized by law and any of the . . . statutory aggravating circumstances which may be supported by the evidence." It is then told that "a sentence of death shall not be imposed [unless the jury finds] at least one statutory aggravating circumstance and [makes] a recommendation that such sentence be imposed." See, e.g., Ga. Code Ann. §17-10-31 (1997 & Supp. 2003).[15]

b. *Ensuring jury responsibility.* All statutes governing jury death sentencing require that a death verdict be unanimous.[16] Though burden of proof and

_____

15. A key consequence of the weighing/nonweighing distinction is that in a nonweighing state, the aggravating circumstance serves more as a predicate to make the defendant eligible for death, rather than as a factor to be balanced against mitigating evidence. Thus, when an appellate court finds that one of several aggravating circumstances was invalid, it can more readily conclude that the invalid finding did not taint the death verdict. Clemons v. Mississippi, 484 U.S. 738, 744-45 (1990).

16. Many also require that a life verdict be unanimous, though in some of those where the jury deadlocks on either the presence of aggravating circumstances or on the ultimate life vs. death verdict, the court must hand down a default term of life with the possibility of parole, rather than de-

standard of proof rules vary somewhat, note the fairly typical rule in Wyoming — that aggravating factors must be proved beyond a reasonable doubt and that mitigating factors must be found by a preponderance of the evidence. Given the potential breadth and even vagueness of mitigating circumstances, does a standard of proof derived from conventional trials make sense to juries?

But even beyond the unanimity rule, courts and legislatures treat the jury's death vs. life decision as an especially delicate one, with legal fine-tunings of the type of information the jury may or may not or must be given. In *Olsen*, recall the issue of the instruction on parole. What risk did the court think that the trial judge's instruction on parole had posed, and how would the instruction on retrial prevent that risk? In California v. Ramos, 463 U.S. 992 (1983), the Court declined to require the states to inform capital juries about possible executive clemency. But in Simmons v. South Carolina, 512 U.S. 154 (1994), the Court held that due process required informing the penalty-phase jury that the defendant was categorically ineligible for parole if spared the death penalty, at least where the prosecution expressly rested its case for the death penalty on his future dangerousness. See also Kelly v. South Carolina, 534 U.S. 246 (2002) (prosecutor cannot skirt *Simmons* rule by characterizing evidence of defendant's violent tendencies as evidence of bad character meriting retribution, rather than of future dangerousness). At the same time, to ensure that the jury fully appreciate its responsibility, the Court has forbidden prosecutors to reassure jurors that any death penalty they impose will be reviewed by an appellate court. Caldwell v. Mississippi, 472 U.S. 320 (1985). In a further refinement, in Kelly v. South Carolina, the Supreme Court held that the court is required to inform the jury that the defendant would be ineligible for parole if given a life sentence, even where the jury was provided a third sentencing alternative along with life and death.

For a provocative argument that the broad standards by which capital juries are guided ensure moral responsibility far better than more mechanical rules would, see Steven Semararo, Responsibility in Capital Sentencing, 39 San Diego L. Rev. 79 (2202) (also recommending moiré narrative jury instructions and greater appellate scrutiny to ensure reasoned verdicts).

C. CATEGORICAL LIMITS ON THE DEATH PENALTY

Recall that although the Supreme Court has established that the death penalty is not absolutely forbidden by the Eighth Amendment, it has essentially limited its use to cases of murder, Coker v. Georgia, p. 434, *supra*. Moreover, in recent years, that Court has invoked Eighth Amendment principles of proportionality to determine whether there are particular types of murders — or murderers — outside the legal bounds of capital punishment. The following cases show where and how the Court has drawn those lines.

---

clare a mistrial and a retrial. See, e.g., S. C. Code Ann. 16-3-20(b)(c) (2003 Cum. Supp.). Note also that Wyoming's statute is explicit that there is no requirement of unanimity as to the presence of particular mitigating circumstances. See Mills v. Maryland, 486 U.S. 367 (1988) (death sentence vacated where likely that jurors falsely believed they all had to agree on existence of particular mitigating circumstance for any one juror to give circumstance weight in vote on sentence).

1.   The Mens Rea Limit: A Reprise on Felony Murder

TISON v. ARIZONA
Supreme Court of the United States
481 U.S. 137 (1987)

JUSTICE O'CONNOR delivered the opinion of the Court.

The question presented is whether the petitioners' participation in the events leading up to and following the murder of four members of a family makes the sentences of death imposed by the Arizona courts constitutionally permissible although neither petitioner specifically intended to kill the victims and neither inflicted the fatal gunshot wounds. . . .

Gary Tison was sentenced to life imprisonment as the result of a prison escape during the course of which he had killed a guard. After he had been in prison a number of years, Gary Tison's wife, their three sons Donald, Ricky, and Raymond, Gary's brother Joseph, and other relatives made plans to help Gary Tison escape again. The Tison family assembled a large arsenal of weapons for this purpose. Plans for escape were discussed with Gary Tison, who insisted that his cellmate, Randy Greenawalt, also a convicted murderer, be included in the prison break. . . .

On July 30, 1978, the three Tison brothers entered the Arizona State Prison at Florence carrying a large ice chest filled with guns. The Tisons armed Greenawalt and their father, and the group, brandishing their weapons, locked the prison guards and visitors present in a storage closet. The five men fled the prison grounds in the Tisons' Ford Galaxy automobile. No shots were fired at the prison.

After leaving the prison, the men abandoned the Ford automobile and proceeded on to an isolated house in a white Lincoln automobile that the brothers had parked at a hospital near the prison. At the house, the Lincoln automobile had a flat tire; the only spare tire was pressed into service. After two nights at the house, the group drove towards Flagstaff. As the group traveled on back roads and secondary highways through the desert, another tire blew out. The group decided to flag down a passing motorist and steal a car. Raymond stood out in front of the Lincoln; the other four armed themselves and laid in wait by the side of the road. One car passed by without stopping, but a second car, a Mazda occupied by John Lyons, his wife Donnelda, his 2-year-old son Christopher and his 15-year-old niece, Theresa Tyson, pulled over to render aid.

As Raymond showed John Lyons the flat tire on the Lincoln, the other Tisons and Greenawalt emerged. The Lyons family was forced into the backseat of the Lincoln. Raymond and Donald drove the Lincoln down a dirt road off the highway and then down a gas line service road farther into the desert; Gary Tison, Ricky Tison and Randy Greenawalt followed in the Lyons' Mazda. The two cars were parked trunk to trunk and the Lyons family was ordered to stand in front of the Lincoln's headlights. The Tisons transferred their belongings from the Lincoln into the Mazda. They discovered guns and money in the Mazda which they kept and they put the rest of the Lyons' possessions in the Lincoln.

Gary Tison then told Raymond to drive the Lincoln still farther into the desert. Raymond did so, and, while the others guarded the Lyons and Theresa Tyson, Gary fired his shotgun into the radiator, presumably to completely disable the vehicle. The Lyons and Theresa Tyson were then escorted to the

Lincoln and again ordered to stand in its headlights. Ricky Tison reported that John Lyons begged, in comments "more or less directed at everybody," "Jesus, don't kill me." Gary Tison said he was "thinking about it." . . . John Lyons asked the Tisons and Greenawalt to "[g]ive us some water . . . just leave us out here, and you all go home." Gary Tison then told his sons to go back to the Mazda and get some water. Raymond later explained that his father "was like in conflict with himself . . . [w]hat it was, I think it was the baby being there and all this, and he wasn't sure about what to do." . . .

The petitioners' statements diverge to some extent, but it appears that both of them went back towards the Mazda, along with Donald, while Randy Greenawalt and Gary Tison stayed at the Lincoln guarding the victims. Raymond recalled being at the Mazda filling the water jug "when we started hearing the shots." . . . Ricky said that the brothers gave the water jug to Gary Tison who then, with Randy Greenawalt went behind the Lincoln, where they spoke briefly, then raised the shotguns and started firing. . . . In any event, petitioners agree they saw Greenawalt and their father brutally murder their four captives with repeated blasts from their shotguns. Neither made an effort to help the victims, though both later stated they were surprised by the shooting. The Tisons got into the Mazda and drove away, continuing their flight. Physical evidence suggested that Theresa Tyson managed to crawl away from the bloodbath, severely injured. She died in the desert after the Tisons left.

Several days later the Tisons and Greenawalt were apprehended after a shootout at a police roadblock. Donald Tison was killed. Gary Tison escaped into the desert where he subsequently died of exposure. Raymond and Ricky Tison and Randy Greenawalt were captured and tried jointly for the crimes associated with the prison break itself and the shootout at the roadblock; each was convicted and sentenced.

The State then individually tried each of the petitioners for capital murder of the four victims as well as for the associated crimes of armed robbery, kidnaping, and car theft. The capital murder charges were based on Arizona felony-murder law providing that a killing occurring during the perpetration of robbery or kidnapping is capital murder, . . . and that each participant in the kidnapping or robbery is legally responsible for the acts of his accomplices. . . . Each of the petitioners was convicted of the four murders under these accomplice liability and felony-murder statutes. . . .

In Enmund v. Florida, 458 U.S. 782 (1982), this Court reversed the death sentence of a defendant convicted under Florida's felony-murder rule. Enmund was the driver of the "get-away" car in an armed robbery of a dwelling. The occupants of the house, an elderly couple, resisted and Enmund's accomplices killed them. The Florida Supreme Court found the inference that Enmund was the person in the car by the side of the road waiting to help his accomplices escape sufficient to support his sentence of death. . . .

This Court, citing the weight of legislative and community opinion, found a broad societal consensus, with which it agreed, that the death penalty was disproportional to the crime of robbery-felony murder "in these circumstances." Id., at 788. The Court noted that although 32 American jurisdictions permitted the imposition of the death penalty for felony murders under a variety of circumstances, Florida was one of only eight jurisdictions that authorized the death penalty "solely for participation in a robbery in which another robber takes life." Id., at 789. Enmund was, therefore, sentenced under a distinct minority regime, a regime that permitted the imposition of the death penalty for felony-murder *simpliciter*. At the other end of the spectrum, eight States required a finding of intent to kill before death could be imposed in a felony-murder case and one State required actual participation in the killing. The remaining States authorizing capital punishment for felony murders fell into two somewhat overlapping middle categories: three authorized the death penalty when the defendant acted with recklessness or extreme indifference to human life, and nine others, including Arizona, required a finding of some aggravating factor beyond the fact that the killing had occurred during the course of a felony before a capital sentence might be imposed. Arizona fell into a subcategory of six States which made "minimal participation in a capital felony committed by another person a [statutory] mitigating circumstance." Id., at 792. Two more jurisdictions required a finding that the defendant's participation in the felony was not "relatively minor" before authorizing a capital sentence. Id., at 791.

After surveying the States' felony-murder statutes, the *Enmund* Court next examined the behavior of juries in cases like Enmund's in its attempt to assess American attitudes towards capital punishment in felony-murder cases. Of 739 death row inmates, only 41 did not participate in the fatal assault. All but 16 of these were physically present at the scene of the murder and of these only 3, including Enmund, were sentenced to death in the absence of a finding that they had collaborated in a scheme designed to kill. The Court found the fact that only 3 of 739 death row inmates had been sentenced to death absent an intent to kill, physical presence or direct participation in the fatal assault persuasive evidence that American juries considered the death sentence disproportional to felony-murder *simpliciter*.

Against this background, the Court undertook its own proportionality analysis. . . . [T]he Court found that Enmund's degree of participation in the murders was so tangential that it could not be said to justify a sentence of death. It found that neither the deterrent nor the retributive purposes of the death penalty were advanced by imposing the death penalty upon Enmund. The *Enmund* Court was unconvinced "that the threat that the death penalty will be imposed for murder will measurably deter one who does not kill and has no intention or purpose that life will be taken." 458 U.S., at 798-99. In reaching this conclusion, the Court relied upon the fact that killing only rarely occurred during the course of robberies and such killing as did occur even more rarely resulted in death sentences if the evidence did not support an inference that the defendant intended to kill. The Court acknowledged, however, that "[i]t would be very different if the likelihood of a killing in the course of a robbery were so substantial that one should share the blame for the killing if he somehow participated in the felony." Id., at 799.

That difference was also related to the second purpose of capital punishment, retribution. The heart of the retribution rationale is that a criminal sentence must be directly related to the personal culpability of the criminal offender. . . . Since Enmund's own participation in the felony murder was so attenuated and since there was no proof that Enmund had any culpable mental state, Enmund v. Florida, *supra*, 458 U.S., at 790-91, the death penalty was excessive retribution for his crimes.

Enmund explicitly dealt with two distinct subsets of all felony murders in assessing whether Enmund's sentence was disproportional under the Eighth Amendment. At one pole was Enmund himself: the minor actor in an armed robbery, not on the scene, who neither intended to kill nor was found to have had any culpable mental state. . . . *Enmund* also clearly dealt with the other polar case: the felony murderer who actually killed, attempted to kill, or intended to kill. . . . The Tison brothers' cases fall into neither of these neat categories.

. . . As petitioners point out, there is no evidence that either Ricky or Raymond Tison took any act which he desired to, or was substantially certain would, cause death.

The Arizona Supreme Court did not attempt to argue that the facts of this case supported an inference of "intent" in the traditional sense. Instead, the Arizona Supreme Court attempted to reformulate "intent to kill" as a species of foreseeability. The Arizona Supreme Court wrote:

> Intend [*sic*] to kill includes the situation in which the defendant intended, contemplated, or anticipated that lethal force would or might *be* used or that life would or might be taken in accomplishing the underlying felony. State v. (Raymond Curtis) Tison, 142 Ariz., at 456, 690 P.2d, at 757.

. . . Indeed, the possibility of bloodshed is inherent in the commission of any violent felony and this possibility is generally foreseeable and foreseen; it is one principal reason that felons arm themselves. The Arizona Supreme Court's attempted reformulation of intent to kill amounts to little more than a restatement of the felony-murder rule itself. Petitioners do not fall within the "intent to kill" category of felony murderers for which *Enmund* explicitly finds the death penalty permissible under the Eighth Amendment.

On the other hand, it is equally clear that petitioners also fall outside the category of felony murderers for whom *Enmund* explicitly held the death penalty disproportional: their degree of participation in the crimes was major rather than minor, and the record would support a finding of the culpable mental state of reckless indifference to human life. . . .

Raymond Tison brought an arsenal of lethal weapons into the Arizona State Prison which he then handed over to two convicted murderers, one of whom he knew had killed a prison guard in the course of a previous escape attempt. By his own admission he was prepared to kill in furtherance of the prison break. He performed the crucial role of flagging down a passing car occupied by an innocent family whose fate was then entrusted to the known killers he had previously armed. He robbed these people at their direction and then guarded the victims at gunpoint while they considered what next to do. He stood by and watched the killing, making no effort to assist the victims before, during, or after the shooting. Instead, he chose to assist the killers in their continuing criminal endeavors, ending in a gun battle with the police in the final showdown.

Ricky Tison's behavior differs in slight details only. Like Raymond, he intentionally brought the guns into the prison to arm the murderers. He could have foreseen that lethal force might be used, particularly since he knew that his father's previous escape attempt had resulted in murder. He, too, participated fully in the kidnapping and robbery and watched the killing after which he chose to aid those whom he had placed in the position to kill rather than their victims.

These facts not only indicate that the Tison brothers' participation in the crime was anything but minor, they also would clearly support a finding that they both subjectively appreciated that their acts were likely to result in the taking of innocent life. The issue raised by this case is whether the Eighth Amendment prohibits the death penalty in the intermediate case of the defendant whose participation is major and whose mental state is one of reckless indifference to the value of human life. . . .

. . . Four States authorize the death penalty in felony-murder cases upon a showing of culpable mental state such as recklessness or extreme indifference to human life. Two jurisdictions require that the defendant's participation be substantial and the statutes of at least six more, including Arizona, take minor participation in the felony expressly into account in mitigation of the murder. These requirements significantly overlap both in this case and in general, for the greater the defendant's participation in the felony murder, the more likely that he acted with reckless indifference to human life. At a minimum, however, it can be said that all these jurisdictions, as well as six States which *Enmund* classified along with Florida as permitting capital punishment for felony-murder *simpliciter,* and the three States which simply require some additional aggravation before imposing the death penalty upon a felony murderer, specifically authorize the death penalty in a felony-murder case where, though the defendant's mental state fell short of intent to kill, the defendant was a major actor in a felony in which he knew death was highly likely to occur. On the other hand, even after *Enmund,* only 11 States authorizing capital punishment forbid imposition of the death penalty even though the defendant's participation in the felony murder is major and the likelihood of killing is so substantial as to raise an inference of extreme recklessness. This substantial and recent legislative authorization of the death penalty for the crime of felony murder regardless of the absence of a finding of an intent to kill powerfully suggests that our society does *not* reject the death penalty as grossly excessive under these circumstances.

. . . A narrow focus on the question of whether or not a given defendant "intended to kill," however, is a highly unsatisfactory means of definitively distinguishing the most culpable and dangerous of murderers. Many who intend to, and do, kill are not criminally liable at all — those who act in self-defense or with other justification or excuse. Other intentional homicides, though criminal, are often felt undeserving of the death penalty — those that are the result of provocation. On the other hand, some nonintentional murderers may be among the most dangerous and inhumane of all — the person who tortures another not caring whether the victim lives or dies, or the robber who shoots someone in the course of the robbery, utterly indifferent to the fact that the desire to rob may have the unintended consequence of killing the victim as well as taking the victim's property. This reckless indifference to the value of human life may be every bit as shocking to the moral sense as an "intent to kill." Indeed it is for this very reason that the common law and modern criminal codes alike have classified behavior such as occurred in this case along with intentional murders. . . . [W]e hold that the reckless disregard for human life implicit in knowingly engaging in criminal activities known to carry a grave risk of death represents a highly culpable mental state, a mental state that may be taken into account in making a capital sentencing judgment when that conduct causes its natural, though also not inevitable, lethal result. . . .

. . . We will not attempt to precisely delineate the particular types of conduct and states of mind warranting imposition of the death penalty here. Rather, we simply hold that major participation in the felony committed, combined with reckless indifference to human life, is sufficient to satisfy the *Enmund* culpability requirement. . . . The Arizona courts have clearly found that the former exists; we now vacate the judgments below and remand for determination of the latter. . . .

Notes and Questions

1. Does the Court mean that the behavior of voters, legislators, judges, and juries is a guide to setting constitutional limits on the decisions of voters, legislators, judges, and juries? Does the notion of "evolving standards of decency" help us avoid circularity here?

2. *Reckless indifference. Tison* establishes as a sufficient (and perhaps necessary) mens rea for the death penalty "reckless indifference for human life" with "substantial participation in the felony." Recall the "abandoned and malignant heart" formula of state murder statutes, pp. 382-389, *supra.* Has the Court actually adopted this formulation of mens rea as its minimal requirement for death? What would the Tison brothers have been convicted of in a state that did not have a felony murder statute? First-degree murder? Second-degree? Manslaughter?

3. *Defining the fatal act.* The majority in *Tison* reasoned that since some of the most heinous murders do not require a specific intent to kill, this specific intent was not required for the imposition of the death penalty. Justice Brennan took sharp issue with the line of reasoning, stating that

> this case, like *Enmund,* involves accomplices who *did not kill.* Thus, although some of the "most culpable and dangerous of murderers" may be those who killed without specifically intending to kill, it is considerably more difficult to apply that rubric convincingly to those who not only did not intend to kill, but who also have not killed. [Id. at 169-70.]

As we will see in Chapter 11 on Complicity and Chapter 12 on Conspiracy, Justice Brennan's distinction may appear questionable in light of traditional doctrines of vicarious liability. Could any participant in a violent felony not be considered to have caused death?

The *Tison* Court distinguished the felony murderer who actually killed from one who does not. In the case of the actual killer, the court reaffirmed that states could "continue to exact [the death penalty] in accordance with local law when the circumstances warranted." Is this consistent with the rest of their holding in *Tison*? If accomplices in a felony murder must have a minimum level of mens rea to be executed, why not the principal? Recall People v. Stamp, p. 404, *supra.* If Stamp was held to have actually killed, would it make sense to allow him to be executed strictly for his actus reus without first determining his mens rea? If there is a constitutional requirement of extreme recklessness for death eligibility in some cases, why should it not apply to all cases?

ATKINS v. VIRGINIA
Supreme Court of the United States
536 U.S. 304 (2002)

JUSTICE STEVENS delivered the opinion of the Court.

Those mentally retarded persons who meet the law's requirements for criminal responsibility should be tried and punished when they commit crimes.

Because of their disabilities in areas of reasoning, judgment, and control of their impulses, however, they do not act with the level of moral culpability that characterizes the most serious adult criminal conduct. Moreover, their impairments can jeopardize the reliability and fairness of capital proceedings against mentally retarded defendants. Presumably for these reasons, in the 13 years since we decided Penry v. Lynaugh, 492 U.S. 302 (1989), the American public, legislators, scholars, and judges have deliberated over the question whether the death penalty should ever be imposed on a mentally retarded criminal. The consensus reflected in those deliberations informs our answer to the question presented by this case: whether such executions are "cruel and unusual punishments" prohibited by the Eighth Amendment to the Federal Constitution.

I

Petitioner, Daryl Renard Atkins, was convicted of abduction, armed robbery, and capital murder, and sentenced to death. At approximately midnight on August 16, 1996, Atkins and William Jones, armed with a semiautomatic handgun, abducted Eric Nesbitt, robbed him of the money on his person, drove him to an automated teller machine in his pickup truck where cameras recorded their withdrawal of additional cash, then took him to an isolated location where he was shot eight times and killed.

Jones and Atkins both testified in the guilt phase of Atkins' trial.[17] Each confirmed most of the details in the other's account of the incident, with the important exception that each stated that the other had actually shot and killed Nesbitt. Jones' testimony, which was both more coherent and credible than Atkins', was obviously credited by the jury and was sufficient to establish Atkins' guilt.[18] At the penalty phase of the trial, the State introduced victim impact evidence and proved two aggravating circumstances: future dangerousness and "vileness of the offense." To prove future dangerousness, the State relied on Atkins' prior felony convictions as well as the testimony of four victims of earlier robberies and assaults. To prove the second aggravator, the prosecution relied upon the trial record, including pictures of the deceased's body and the autopsy report.

In the penalty phase, the defense relied on one witness, Dr. Evan Nelson, a forensic psychologist who had evaluated Atkins before trial and concluded that he was "mildly mentally retarded." His conclusion was based on interviews with people who knew Atkins, a review of school and court records, and the administration of a standard intelligence test which indicated that Atkins had a full scale IQ of 59.[19]

---

17. Initially, both Jones and Atkins were indicted for capital murder. The prosecution ultimately permitted Jones to plead guilty to first-degree murder in exchange for his testimony against Atkins. As a result of the plea, Jones became ineligible to receive the death penalty.

18. Highly damaging to the credibility of Atkins' testimony was its substantial inconsistency with the statement he gave to the police upon his arrest. Jones, in contrast, had declined to make an initial statement to the authorities.

19. . . . At the sentencing phase, Dr. Nelson testified: "[Atkins'] full scale IQ is 59. Compared to the population at large, that means less than one percentile. . . . Mental retardation is a relatively rare thing. It's about one percent of the population." According to Dr. Nelson, Atkins' IQ score "would automatically qualify for Social Security disability income." Dr. Nelson also indicated that of the over 40 capital defendants that he had evaluated, Atkins was only the second individual who met the criteria for mental retardation. He testified that, in his opinion, Atkins' limited intellect had been a consistent feature throughout his life, and that his IQ score of 59 is not an "aberration, malingered result, or invalid test score."

The jury sentenced Atkins to death, but the Virginia Supreme Court ordered a second sentencing hearing because the trial court had used a misleading verdict form. At the resentencing, Dr. Nelson again testified. The State presented an expert rebuttal witness, Dr. Stanton Samenow, who expressed the opinion that Atkins was not mentally retarded, but rather was of "average intelligence, at least," and diagnosable as having antisocial personality disorder. The jury again sentenced Atkins to death.

The Supreme Court of Virginia affirmed the imposition of the death penalty. Atkins [contended] "that he is mentally retarded and thus cannot be sentenced to death." The majority of the state court rejected this contention, relying on our holding in *Penry*. The Court was "not willing to commute Atkins' sentence of death to life imprisonment merely because of his IQ score."

Justice Hassell and Justice Koontz dissented. They rejected Dr. Samenow's opinion that Atkins possesses average intelligence as "incredulous as a matter of law," and concluded that "the imposition of the sentence of death upon a criminal defendant who has the mental age of a child between the ages of 9 and 12 is excessive." In their opinion, "it is indefensible to conclude that individuals who are mentally retarded are not to some degree less culpable for their criminal acts. By definition, such individuals have substantial limitations not shared by the general population. A moral and civilized society diminishes itself if its system of justice does not afford recognition and consideration of those limitations in a meaningful way."

Because of the gravity of the concerns expressed by the dissenters, and in light of the dramatic shift in the state legislative landscape that has occurred in the past 13 years, we granted certiorari to revisit the issue that we first addressed in the *Penry* case. 533 U.S. 976 (2001).

II

. . . A claim that punishment is excessive is judged not by the standards that prevailed in 1685 when Lord Jeffreys presided over the "Bloody Assizes" or when the Bill of Rights was adopted, but rather by those that currently prevail. As Chief Justice Warren explained in his opinion in *Trop v. Dulles,* 356 U.S. 86 (1958): "The basic concept underlying the Eighth Amendment is nothing less than the dignity of man. . . . The Amendment must draw its meaning from the evolving standards of decency that mark the progress of a maturing society." Id., at 100-101.

Proportionality review under those evolving standards should be informed by "objective factors to the maximum possible extent," see [Harmelin v. Michigan, 501 U.S. at 957, 1000 (1991)]. We have pinpointed that the "clearest and most reliable objective evidence of contemporary values is the legislation enacted by the country's legislatures." Penry, 492 U.S. at 331. . . .

We also acknowledged in [Coker v. Georgia, 438 U.S. 584 (1977)] that the objective evidence, though of great importance, did not "wholly determine" the controversy, "for the Constitution contemplates that in the end our own judgment will be brought to bear on the question of the acceptability of the death penalty under the Eighth Amendment." 433 U.S. at 597. . . .

Thus, in cases involving a consensus, our own judgment is "brought to bear," by asking whether there is reason to disagree with the judgment reached by the citizenry and its legislators.

Guided by our approach in these cases, we shall first review the judgment of legislatures that have addressed the suitability of imposing the death penalty on the mentally retarded and then consider reasons for agreeing or disagreeing with their judgment.

III

The parties have not called our attention to any state legislative consideration of the suitability of imposing the death penalty on mentally retarded offenders prior to 1986. In that year, the public reaction to the execution of a mentally retarded murderer in Georgia apparently led to the enactment of the first state statute prohibiting such executions. In 1988, when Congress enacted legislation reinstating the federal death penalty, it expressly provided that a "sentence of death shall not be carried out upon a person who is mentally retarded." In 1989, Maryland enacted a similar prohibition. It was in that year that we decided *Penry,* and concluded that those two state enactments, "even when added to the 14 States that have rejected capital punishment completely, do not provide sufficient evidence at present of a national consensus." 492 U.S. at 334.

Much has changed since then. Responding to the national attention received by the [Georgia] execution and our decision in *Penry,* state legislatures across the country began to address the issue. . . . In 1990 Kentucky and Tennessee enacted statutes similar to those in Georgia and Maryland, as did New Mexico in 1991, and Arkansas, Colorado, Washington, Indiana, and Kansas in 1993 and 1994. In 1995, when New York reinstated its death penalty, it emulated the Federal Government by expressly exempting the mentally retarded. Nebraska followed suit in 1998. There appear to have been no similar enactments during the next two years, but in 2000 and 2001 six more States — South Dakota, Arizona, Connecticut, Florida, Missouri, and North Carolina — joined the procession. The Texas Legislature unanimously adopted a similar bill, and bills have passed at least one house in other States, including Virginia and Nevada.

It is not so much the number of these States that is significant, but the consistency of the direction of change. Given the well-known fact that anticrime legislation is far more popular than legislation providing protections for persons guilty of violent crime, the large number of States prohibiting the execution of mentally retarded persons (and the complete absence of States passing legislation reinstating the power to conduct such executions) provides powerful evidence that today our society views mentally retarded offenders as categorically less culpable than the average criminal. The evidence carries even greater force when it is noted that the legislatures that have addressed the issue have voted overwhelmingly in favor of the prohibition. Moreover, even in those States that allow the execution of mentally retarded offenders, the practice is uncommon. . . . The practice, therefore, has become truly unusual, and it is fair to say that a national consensus has developed against it.[20]

20. Additional evidence makes it clear that this legislative judgment reflects a much broader social and professional consensus. For example, several organizations with germane expertise have adopted official positions opposing the imposition of the death penalty upon a mentally retarded offender. In addition, representatives of widely diverse religious communities in the United States,

To the extent there is serious disagreement about the execution of mentally retarded offenders, it is in determining which offenders are in fact retarded. In this case, for instance, the Commonwealth of Virginia disputes that Atkins suffers from mental retardation. Not all people who claim to be mentally retarded will be so impaired as to fall within the range of mentally retarded offenders about whom there is a national consensus. As was our approach in Ford v. Wainwright, with regard to insanity, "we leave to the States the task of developing appropriate ways to enforce the constitutional restriction upon its execution of sentences." 477 U.S. 399 (1986).

IV

This consensus unquestionably reflects widespread judgment about the relative culpability of mentally retarded offenders, and the relationship between mental retardation and the penological purposes served by the death penalty. Additionally, it suggests that some characteristics of mental retardation undermine the strength of the procedural protections that our capital jurisprudence steadfastly guards.

. . . [C]linical definitions of mental retardation require not only subaverage intellectual functioning, but also significant limitations in adaptive skills such as communication, self-care, and self-direction that became manifest before age 18. Mentally retarded persons frequently know the difference between right and wrong and are competent to stand trial. Because of their impairments, however, by definition they have diminished capacities to understand and process information, to communicate, to abstract from mistakes and learn from experience, to engage in logical reasoning, to control impulses, and to understand the reactions of others. There is no evidence that they are more likely to engage in criminal conduct than others, but there is abundant evidence that they often act on impulse rather than pursuant to a premeditated plan, and that in group settings they are followers rather than leaders. Their deficiencies do not warrant an exemption from criminal sanctions, but they do diminish their personal culpability.

In light of these deficiencies, our death penalty jurisprudence provides two reasons consistent with the legislative consensus that the mentally retarded should be categorically excluded from execution. First, there is a serious question as to whether either justification that we have recognized as a basis for the death penalty applies to mentally retarded offenders. Gregg v. Georgia, 428 U.S. 153 (1976), identified "retribution and deterrence of capital crimes by prospective offenders" as the social purposes served by the death penalty. Unless the imposition of the death penalty on a mentally retarded person "measurably contributes to one or both of these goals, it 'is nothing more than the purposeless

---

reflecting Christian, Jewish, Muslim, and Buddhist traditions, have filed an *amicus curiae* brief explaining that even though their views about the death penalty differ, they all "share a conviction that the execution of persons with mental retardation cannot be morally justified." Moreover, within the world community, the imposition of the death penalty for crimes committed by mentally retarded offenders is overwhelmingly disapproved. Finally, polling data shows a widespread consensus among Americans, even those who support the death penalty, that executing the mentally retarded is wrong. Although these factors are by no means dispositive, their consistency with the legislative evidence lends further support to our conclusion that there is a consensus among those who have addressed the issue.

and needless imposition of pain and suffering,' and hence an unconstitutional punishment." Enmund, 458 U.S. at 798.

With respect to retribution — the interest in seeing that the offender gets his "just deserts"— the severity of the appropriate punishment necessarily depends on the culpability of the offender. Since *Gregg,* our jurisprudence has consistently confined the imposition of the death penalty to a narrow category of the most serious crimes. For example, in Godfrey v. Georgia, 446 U.S. 420, 64 (1980), we set aside a death sentence because the petitioner's crimes did not reflect "a consciousness materially more 'depraved' than that of any person guilty of murder." Id., at 433. If the culpability of the average murderer is insufficient to justify the most extreme sanction available to the State, the lesser culpability of the mentally retarded offender surely does not merit that form of retribution. Thus, pursuant to our narrowing jurisprudence, which seeks to ensure that only the most deserving of execution are put to death, an exclusion for the mentally retarded is appropriate.

With respect to deterrence — the interest in preventing capital crimes by prospective offenders — "it seems likely that 'capital punishment can serve as a deterrent only when murder is the result of premeditation and deliberation,'" *Enmund,* 458 U.S. at 799. Exempting the mentally retarded from that punishment will not affect the "cold calculus that precedes the decision" of other potential murderers. Gregg, 428 U.S. at 186. Indeed, that sort of calculus is at the opposite end of the spectrum from behavior of mentally retarded offenders. The theory of deterrence in capital sentencing is predicated upon the notion that the increased severity of the punishment will inhibit criminal actors from carrying out murderous conduct. Yet it is the same cognitive and behavioral impairments that make these defendants less morally culpable — for example, the diminished ability to understand and process information, to learn from experience, to engage in logical reasoning, or to control impulses — that also make it less likely that they can process the information of the possibility of execution as a penalty and, as a result, control their conduct based upon that information. Nor will exempting the mentally retarded from execution lessen the deterrent effect of the death penalty with respect to offenders who are not mentally retarded. Such individuals are unprotected by the exemption and will continue to face the threat of execution. Thus, executing the mentally retarded will not measurably further the goal of deterrence.

The reduced capacity of mentally retarded offenders provides a second justification for a categorical rule making such offenders ineligible for the death penalty. The risk "that the death penalty will be imposed in spite of factors which may call for a less severe penalty," Lockett v. Ohio, 438 U.S. 586 (1978), is enhanced, not only by the possibility of false confessions,[21] but also by the lesser ability of mentally retarded defendants to make a persuasive showing of mitigation in the face of prosecutorial evidence of one or more aggravating factors. Mentally retarded defendants may be less able to give meaningful assistance to their counsel and are typically poor witnesses, and their demeanor may create an unwarranted impression of lack of remorse for their crimes. As *Penry* demonstrated, moreover,

---

21. Despite the heavy burden that the prosecution must shoulder in capital cases, we cannot ignore the fact that in recent years a disturbing number of inmates on death row have been exonerated. As two recent high-profile cases demonstrate, these exonerations include mentally retarded persons who unwittingly confessed to crimes that they did not commit.

reliance on mental retardation as a mitigating factor can be a two-edged sword that may enhance the likelihood that the aggravating factor of future dangerousness will be found by the jury. 492 U.S. at 323-325. Mentally retarded defendants in the aggregate face a special risk of wrongful execution.

Our independent evaluation of the issue reveals no reason to disagree with the judgment of "the legislatures that have recently addressed the matter" and concluded that death is not a suitable punishment for a mentally retarded criminal. We are not persuaded that the execution of mentally retarded criminals will measurably advance the deterrent or the retributive purpose of the death penalty. Construing and applying the Eighth Amendment in the light of our "evolving standards of decency," we therefore conclude that such punishment is excessive and that the Constitution "places a substantive restriction on the State's power to take the life" of a mentally retarded offender. Ford, 477 U.S. at 405.

The judgment of the Virginia Supreme Court is reversed and the case is remanded for further proceedings not inconsistent with this opinion.

Notes and Questions

1. The *Atkins* Court articulated that the basic test for cruel and unusual punishment is the "progress of a maturing society" and whether a punishment offends "evolving standards of decency." Current Eighth Amendment jurisprudence dictates that the most reliable indicator of "decency" is state law. The Supreme Court reasons that since state legislators represent the will of the people, "standards of decency" can be determined by the actions of state legislators. Consequently, the opinions in both *Atkins* and *Tison* contain elaborate catalogs of current state laws.

Once again, does this mean that the behavior of voters, legislators, judges, and juries is a guide to setting constitutional limits on the decisions of voters, legislators, judges, and juries? Does the notion of "evolving standards of decency" help us avoid circularity here?

2. *National consensus?* In *Atkins*, the Court relies on legislation in 18 states that exempts the mentally retarded from the death penalty. It further points to the "consistency of the direction of change."

In his dissent, Justice Scalia writes that "[s]eldom has an opinion of this Court rested so obviously upon nothing but the personal views of its members." 536 U.S. at 338. He asks how an agreement among 47 percent of the states that permit capital punishment could possibly amount to a consensus, especially when that number does not include some of the states with the largest populations. Regarding the "direction of change," Justice Scalia also notes that because states only recently began to except the mentally retarded, there is no other direction for the "consensus" to go, and that the legislation the majority relies upon is still "in its infancy" and has not been assessed in the long term. Though the Court claims to use an objective standard, does it have an objective definition of "consensus?"

3. *Indicators of decency.* In determining whether or not a consensus exists the *Atkins* Court looked further than just state legislation, pointing to (1) the positions of civic and religious organizations; (2) international opinion; (3) empirical data from public opinion polls; and (4) the justices' "own judgment."

Nevertheless, that expanded methodology is not without question. In a scathing dissent, Chief Justice Rehnquist writes that only "the work product of legislatures and sentencing jury determinations" should be indicators of American conceptions of decency. He states that "the viewpoints of other countries simply are not relevant" and that the views of professional organizations and religious groups should not be "accorded any weight." Do you agree?

4. *A note on the age limit.* The method of constitutional analysis used in *Atkins* and *Tison* has been applied to other questions, but often produces uncertain results. The Supreme Court has held that the execution of a defendant 15 years or younger violates evolving standards but that the execution of a 16-year-old does not. In Thompson v. Oklahoma, 487 U.S. 815 (1988), Thompson was sentenced to death for a murder that he committed when he was 15; he had been previously convicted for assault and battery three times as a juvenile and was tried for murder as an adult. All four participants in the crime were sentenced to death. The Supreme Court overturned Thompson's death sentence. The four justices in the plurality found a clear social consensus that execution of an individual who killed before the age of 16 violated evolving standards of decency. The dissent, however, noting that a death sentence for a 15-year-old killer was theoretically possible in 19 states, did not find any such consensus.

The argument of the dissenters in *Thompson* later prevailed for killers 16 years old or older. In Stanford v. Kentucky (decided with Wilkins v. Missouri), 492 U.S. 361 (1989), a majority of the court found no constitutional infirmity where 16- and 17-year-old killers were sentenced to death. The test was whether the death penalty in these cases overstepped traditional or evolving societal norms. In this case, the sentences clearly did not breach common law standards since "the common law set the rebuttable presumption of incapacity to commit any felony at the age of 14, and theoretically permitted capital punishment to be imposed on anyone over the age of 7." Id. at 368. Neither, found the Court, did the sentences offend evolving standards of decency. Placing the burden of proof on the defendants, the Court held that because only 15 states decline to impose the death penalty on 16-year-olds, and only 12 on 17-year-olds, the defendants failed to establish the degree of national agreement required to label a punishment cruel and unusual.

5. *Culpability and the death penalty.* The Court stated that "the severity of the appropriate punishment necessarily depends on the culpability of the offender." In *Tison*, the Court examined the level of involvement in a crime necessary to satisfy the culpability requirement. It held that "major participation" and "reckless indifference to human life" was enough. In *Atkins,* the Court examined the level of intelligence necessary. It held that "[i]f the culpability of the average murderer is insufficient to justify the most extreme sanction available to the State, the lesser culpability of the mentally retarded offender surely does not merit that form of retribution." However, the Court itself states that "[m]entally retarded persons frequently know the difference between right and wrong. . . ." What, then, is the correlation between intelligence and moral culpability? Is the death penalty never appropriate retribution for a defendant like Atkins regardless of the severity of the crime?

6. *States' application of* Atkins. *Atkins* represents a categorical exemption — that mentally retarded offenders are ineligible for the death penalty. However, as the Supreme Court stated, "we leave to the States the task of developing appropriate ways to enforce the constitutional restriction upon its execution of

sentences." The impact of *Atkins* depends primarily upon which definition of "mentally retarded" is employed. That said, the definitions used by the states have been varied. Some states use IQ as the primary indicator of mental retardation. Arizona and Arkansas, for example, have established a rebuttable presumption that a defendant with an IQ below 65 is mentally retarded. See Ariz. Rev. Stat. §13-703.02(G) (2001); Ark. Code Ann. §5-4-618 (Michie 1993). Other states do not have an IQ requirement but instead have employed their own statutory definitions of mentally retarded. For example, Missouri requires deficits in two or more "adaptive behaviors" which include self-care, social skills, functional academics and community use. Mo. Rev. Stat. §565.030 (2001). Kansas specifies that a defendant does not fall under *Atkins* unless his or her impairments make it difficult to "appreciate the criminality of one's conduct or to conform one's conduct to the requirements of law." Kan. Stat. Ann. §21-4623 (2002). Do you view this diversity of definitions as inevitable and reasonable or do you believe that a more uniform standard should be established? Should that standard be developed by legislatures or by the Court?

The varied application of *Atkins* raises a host of questions for future decisions. Should there be a threshold IQ for *Atkins* defendants? Should the defendant be required to prove the onset of retardation before a certain age? Should a judge or jury determine whether a capital defendant falls under *Atkins*? Should that decision be made during trial or later during the sentencing phase? Who should carry the burden of proof?

2. Victim/Race Discrimination and the Eighth Amendment

McCLESKEY v. KEMP
Supreme Court of the United States
481 U.S. 279 (1987)

JUSTICE POWELL delivered the opinion of the Court.

[McCleskey, a black man, was convicted and sentenced to death for the murder of a white police officer.]

... McCleskey next filed a petition for a writ of habeas corpus in the federal District Court for the Northern District of Georgia. His petition raised 18 claims, one of which was that the Georgia capital sentencing process is administered in a racially discriminatory manner in violation of the Eighth and Fourteenth Amendments to the United States Constitution. In support of his claim, McCleskey proffered a statistical study performed by Professors David C. Baldus, George Woodworth, and Charles Pulaski (the Baldus study) that purports to show a disparity in the imposition of the death sentence in Georgia based on the race of the murder victim and, to a lesser extent, the race of the defendant. The Baldus study is actually two sophisticated statistical studies that examine over 2,000 murder cases that occurred in Georgia during the 1970s. The raw numbers collected by Professor Baldus indicate that defendants charged with killing white persons received the death penalty in 11% of the cases, but defendants charged with killing blacks received the death penalty in only 1% of the cases. The raw numbers also indicate a reverse racial disparity according to the race of the defendant: 4% of the black defendants received the death penalty, as opposed to 7% of the white defendants.

Baldus also divided the cases according to the combination of the race of the defendant and the race of the victim. He found that the death penalty was assessed in 22% of the cases involving black defendants and white victims; 8% of the cases involving white defendants and white victims; 1% of the cases involving black defendants and black victims; and 3% of the cases involving white defendants and black victims. Similarly, Baldus found that prosecutors sought the death penalty in 70% of the cases involving black defendants and white victims; 32% of the cases involving white defendants and white victims; 15% of the cases involving black defendants and black victims; and 19% of the cases involving white defendants and black victims.

Baldus subjected his data to an extensive analysis, taking account of 230 variables that could have explained the disparities on nonracial grounds. One of his models concludes that, even after taking account of 39 nonracial variables, defendants charged with killing white victims were 4.3 times as likely to receive a death sentence as defendants charged with killing blacks. According to this model, black defendants were 1.1 times as likely to receive a death sentence as other defendants. Thus, the Baldus study indicates that black defendants, such as McCleskey, who kill white victims have the greatest likelihood of receiving the death penalty.[22]

The District Court held an extensive evidentiary hearing on McCleskey's petition. . . . It concluded that McCleskey's "statistics do not demonstrate a prima facie case in support of the contention that the death penalty was imposed upon him because of his race, because of the race of the victim, or because of any Eighth Amendment concern." McCleskey v. Zant, 580 F. Supp. 338, 379 (N.D. Ga. 1984). As to McCleskey's Fourteenth Amendment claim, the court found that the methodology of the Baldus study was flawed in several respects. Because of these defects, the Court held that the Baldus study "fail[ed] to contribute anything of value" to McCleskey's claim. Id., at 372 (emphasis omitted). . . .

The Court of Appeals for the Eleventh Circuit . . . carefully reviewed the District Court's decision on McCleskey's claim. 753 F.2d 877 (1985). It assumed the validity of the study itself and addressed the merits of McCleskey's Eighth and Fourteenth Amendment claims. That is, the court assumed that the study "showed that systematic and substantial disparities existed in the penalties imposed upon homicide defendants in Georgia based on the race of the homicide victim, that the disparities existed at a less substantial rate in death sentencing based on race of defendants, and that the factors of race of the victim and defendant were at work in Fulton County." Id., at 895. Even assuming the study's validity, the Court of Appeals found the statistics "insufficient to demonstrate discriminatory intent or unconstitutional discrimination in the Fourteenth Amendment context, [and] insufficient to show irrationality, arbitrariness and

---

22. Baldus's 230-variable model divided cases into eight different ranges, according to the estimated aggravation level of the offense. Baldus argued in his testimony to the District Court that the effects of racial bias were most striking in the mid-range cases. "[W]hen the cases become tremendously aggravated so that everybody would agree that if we're going to have a death sentence, these are the cases that should get it, the race effects go away. It's only in the mid-range of cases where the decisionmakers have a real choice as to what to do. If there's room for the exercise of discretion, then the [racial] factors begin to play a role." App. 36. Under this model, Baldus found that 14.4% of the black-victim mid-range cases received the death penalty, and 34.4% of the white-victim cases received the death penalty. See Exhibit DB 90, reprinted in Supplemental Exhibits 54. According to Baldus, the facts of McCleskey's case placed it within the mid-range.

capriciousness under any kind of Eighth Amendment analysis." Id., at 891. . . .
The court concluded:

> Viewed broadly, it would seem that the statistical evidence presented here, assum-
> ing its validity, confirms rather than condemns the system. . . . The marginal dis-
> parity based on the race of the victim tends to support the state's contention that
> the system is working far differently from the one which Furman v. Georgia con-
> demned. In pre-*Furman* days, there was no rhyme or reason as to who got the death
> penalty and who did not. But now, in the vast majority of cases, the reasons for a
> difference are well documented. That they are not so clear in a small percentage
> of the cases is no reason to declare the entire system unconstitutional. Id., at 899.

The Court of Appeals affirmed the dismissal by the District Court of McCleskey's
petition for a writ of habeas corpus, with three judges dissenting as to McCleskey's
claims based on the Baldus study. We granted certiorari, and now affirm.

McCleskey's first claim is that the Georgia capital punishment statute violates the Equal Protection Clause of the Fourteenth Amendment.[23] He argues
that race has infected the administration of Georgia's statute in two ways: persons who murder whites are more likely to be sentenced to death than persons
who murder blacks, and black murderers are more likely to be sentenced to
death than white murderers. As a black defendant who killed a white victim, Mc-
Cleskey claims that the Baldus study demonstrates that he was discriminated
against because of his race and because of the race of his victim. In its broadest
form, McCleskey's claim of discrimination extends to every actor in the Georgia
capital sentencing process, from the prosecutor who sought the death penalty
and the jury that imposed the sentence, to the State itself that enacted the capital punishment statute and allows it to remain in effect despite its allegedly discriminatory application. We agree with the Court of Appeals, and every other
court that has considered such a challenge, that this claim must fail.

[The court first rejected the argument the Baldus study proved that the
death penalty violated equal protection, because McCleskey could not show that
either the state or the prosecutor acted with discriminatory intent. It then reviewed the history of Eighth Amendment claims against the death penalty, and
essentially reaffirmed the guided discretion of modern death penalty statutes.]

[A]bsent a showing that the Georgia capital punishment system operates in
an arbitrary and capricious manner, McCleskey cannot prove a constitutional violation by demonstrating that other defendants who may be similarly situated
did *not* receive the death penalty. In *Gregg*, the Court confronted the argument
that "the opportunities for discretionary action that are inherent in the processing of any murder case under Georgia law," Gregg v. Georgia [428 U.S. 153,
199 (1976)], specifically the opportunities for discretionary leniency, rendered

---

23. Although the District Court rejected the findings of the Baldus study as flawed, the Court
of Appeals assumed that the study is valid and reached the constitutional issues. Accordingly, those
issues are before us. As did the Court of Appeals, we assume the study is valid statistically without
reviewing the factual findings of the District Court. Our assumption that the Baldus study is statistically valid does not include the assumption that the study shows that racial considerations actually enter into any sentencing decisions in Georgia. Even a sophisticated multiple regression analysis such as the Baldus study can only demonstrate a *risk* that the factor of race entered into some
capital sentencing decisions and a necessarily lesser risk that race entered into any particular sentencing decision.

the capital sentences imposed arbitrary and capricious. We rejected this contention:

> The existence of these discretionary stages is not determinative of the issues before us. At each of these stages an actor in the criminal justice system makes a decision which may remove a defendant from consideration as a candidate for the death penalty. *Furman,* in contrast, dealt with the decision to impose the death sentence on a specific individual who had been convicted of a capital offense. Nothing in any of our cases suggests that the decision to afford an individual defendant mercy violates the Constitution. *Furman* held only that, in order to minimize the risk that the death penalty would be imposed on a capriciously selected group of offenders, the decision to impose it had to be guided by standards so that the sentencing authority would focus on the particularized circumstances of the crime and the defendant. Ibid.[24]

Because McCleskey's sentence was imposed under Georgia sentencing procedures that focus discretion "on the particularized nature of the crime and the particularized characteristics of the individual defendant," id., at 206, we lawfully may presume that McCleskey's death sentence was not "wantonly and freakishly" imposed, id., at 207, and thus that the sentence is not disproportionate within any recognized meaning under the Eighth Amendment.

Although our decision in *Gregg* as to the facial validity of the Georgia capital punishment statute appears to foreclose McCleskey's disproportionality argument, he further contends that the Georgia capital punishment system is arbitrary and capricious in *application,* and therefore his sentence is excessive, because racial considerations may influence capital sentencing decisions in Georgia. We now address this claim.

To evaluate McCleskey's challenge, we must examine exactly what the Baldus study may show. Even Professor Baldus does not contend that his statistics *prove* that race enters into any capital sentencing decisions or that race was a factor in McCleskey's particular case.[25] Statistics at most may show only a likelihood that a particular factor entered into some decisions. There is, of course, some risk of racial prejudice influencing a jury's decision in a criminal case. There are similar risks that other kinds of prejudice will influence other criminal trials. The question is at what point that risk becomes constitutionally unacceptable. . . . McCleskey asks us to accept the likelihood allegedly shown by the Baldus study as the constitutional measure of an unacceptable risk of racial prejudice influencing capital sentencing decisions. This we decline to do. . . .

---

24. The Constitution is not offended by inconsistency in results based on the objective circumstances of the crime. Numerous legitimate factors may influence the outcome of a trial and a defendant's ultimate sentence, even though they may be irrelevant to his actual guilt. If sufficient evidence to link a suspect to a crime cannot be found, he will not be charged. The capability of the responsible law enforcement agency can vary widely. Also, the strength of the available evidence remains a variable throughout the criminal justice process and may influence a prosecutor's decision to offer a plea bargain or to go to trial. Witness availability, credibility, and memory also influence the results of prosecutions. Finally, sentencing in state courts is generally discretionary, so a defendant's ultimate sentence necessarily will vary according to the judgment of the sentencing authority. The foregoing factors necessarily exist in varying degrees throughout our criminal justice system.

25. According to Professor Baldus:

> "McCleskey's case falls in [a] grey area where . . . you would find the greatest likelihood that some inappropriate consideration may have come to bear on the decision. In an analysis of this type, obviously one cannot say that we can say to a moral certainty what it was that influenced the decision. We can't do that."

McCleskey's argument that the Constitution condemns the discretion allowed decisionmakers in the Georgia capital sentencing system is antithetical to the fundamental role of discretion in our criminal justice system. Discretion in the criminal justice system offers substantial benefits to the criminal defendant. Not only can a jury decline to impose the death sentence, it can decline to convict, or choose to convict of a lesser offense. Whereas decisions against a defendant's interest may be reversed by the trial judge or on appeal, these discretionary exercises of leniency are final and unreviewable. . . . [A] prosecutor can decline to charge, offer a plea bargain, or decline to seek a death sentence in any particular case. Of course, "the power to be lenient [also] is the power to discriminate," K. Davis, Discretionary Justice 170 (1973), but a capital punishment system that did not allow for discretionary acts of leniency "would be totally alien to our notions of criminal justice." Gregg v. Georgia, 428 U.S., at 200, n.50.

At most, the Baldus study indicates a discrepancy that appears to correlate with race. Apparent disparities in sentencing are an inevitable part of our criminal justice system. . . . As this Court has recognized, any mode for determining guilt or punishment "has its weaknesses and the potential for misuse." Singer v. United States, 380 U.S. 24, 35 (1965). Despite these imperfections, our consistent rule has been that constitutional guarantees are met when "the mode [for determining guilt or punishment] itself has been surrounded with safeguards to make it as fair as possible." [Id., at 35.] Where the discretion that is fundamental to our criminal process is involved, we decline to assume that what is unexplained is invidious. In light of the safeguards designed to minimize racial bias in the process, the fundamental value of jury trial in our criminal justice system, and the benefits that discretion provides to criminal defendants, we hold that the Baldus study does not demonstrate a constitutionally significant risk of racial bias affecting the Georgia capital-sentencing process.

Two additional concerns inform our decision in this case. First, McCleskey's claim, taken to its logical conclusion, throws into serious question the principles that underlie our entire criminal justice system. The Eighth Amendment is not limited in application to capital punishment, but applies to all penalties. Thus, if we accepted McCleskey's claim that racial bias has impermissibly tainted the capital sentencing decision, we could soon be faced with similar claims as to other types of penalty. Moreover, the claim that his sentence rests on the irrelevant factor of race easily could be extended to apply to claims based on unexplained discrepancies that correlate to membership in other minority groups, and even to gender. Similarly, since McCleskey's claim relates to the race of his victim, other claims could apply with equally logical force to statistical disparities that correlate with the race or sex of other actors in the criminal justice system, such as defense attorneys, or judges. Also, there is no logical reason that such a claim need be limited to racial or sexual bias. If arbitrary and capricious punishment is the touchstone under the Eighth Amendment, such a claim could — at least in theory — be based upon any arbitrary variable, such as the defendant's facial characteristics, or the physical attractiveness of the defendant or the victim, that some statistical study indicates may be influential in jury decision making. As these examples illustrate, there is no limiting principle to the type of challenge brought by McCleskey. The Constitution does not require that a State eliminate any demonstrable disparity that correlates with a potentially irrelevant factor in order to operate a criminal justice system that includes capital punishment. As we have stated specifically in the context of capital punishment, the Constitution does not "plac[e] totally unrealistic conditions on its use." Gregg v. Georgia, 428 U.S., at 199, n.50.

Second, McCleskey's arguments are best presented to the legislative bodies. It is not the responsibility — or indeed even the right — of this Court to determine the appropriate punishment for particular crimes. . . . Legislatures also are better qualified to weigh and "evaluate the results of statistical studies in terms of their own local conditions and with a flexibility of approach that is not available to the courts," Gregg v. Georgia, *supra*, 428 U.S., at 186. Capital punishment is now the law in more than two-thirds of our States. It is the ultimate duty of courts to determine on a case-by-case basis whether these laws are applied consistently with the Constitution. Despite McCleskey's wide ranging arguments that basically challenge the validity of capital punishment in our multi-racial society, the only question before us is whether in his case the law of Georgia was properly applied. We agree with the District Court and the Court of Appeals for the Eleventh Circuit that this was carefully and correctly done in this case. . . .

Notes and Questions

1. In a study similar to Baldus's, Samuel Gross and Robert Mauro[26] examined the patterns of capital sentencing since *Furman* in eight states.[27] They found substantially the same results:

> There has been racial discrimination in the imposition of the death penalty under post-*Furman* statutes in the eight states that we examined. The discrimination that we found is based on the race of the victim, and it is a remarkably stable and consistent phenomenon. Capital sentencing disparities by race of victim were found in each of the eight states, despite their diversity. The legitimate sentencing variables that we considered could not explain these disparities, whether we controlled for these variables one at a time, organized them into a scale of aggravation, or used multiple regression analysis. . . . The data show "a clear pattern, unexplainable on grounds other than race," (Washington v. Davis, 426 U.S. 229, 266 (1976)), or at least unexplainable short of some improbable inanimate conspiracy of numbers.[28]

2. Justice Stevens, in a separate dissent, accepted the Baldus study as sound, and agreed with the other dissenters that "[i]f society were indeed forced to choose between a racially discriminatory death penalty (one that provides heightened protection against murder 'for whites only') and no death penalty at all, the choice mandated by the Constitution would be plain." But he did not agree with two of the other dissenting justices that Georgia's death penalty statute could not be further refined:

> One of the lessons of the Baldus study is that there exist certain categories of extremely serious crimes for which prosecutors consistently seek, and juries

---

26. Patterns of Death, 37 Stan. L. Rev. 27 (1984). The Baldus study examined more variables, whereas Gross and Mauro controlled for sample selection bias.

27. Arkansas, Florida, Georgia, Illinois, Mississippi, North Carolina, Oklahoma, Virginia.

28. More recently, a study in Maryland found that while roughly in 1,311 death-penalty eligible cases from 1978 to 1999 the victims were evenly split between blacks and whites, in 80 percent of the 76 cases where the death sentence was imposed the victim was white. Adam Liptak, Death Penalty Found More Likely When Victim is White, New York Times, Jan. 8, 2003, at A12.

consistently impose, the death penalty without regard to the race of the victim or the race of the offender. If Georgia were to narrow the class of death-eligible defendants to those categories, the danger of arbitrary and discriminatory imposition of the death penalty would be significantly decreased, if not eradicated. [481 U.S. at 367.]

Current death penalty statutes, however, have the built-in procedural protection of bifurcated penalty and guilty-phase trials, as well as "due process" protections in the penalty phase. The statutes also require a finding that aggravating circumstances outweigh mitigating circumstances before a death penalty is legal. How is it possible to narrow the category of murderers who are "death-eligible" further? If the statutes were to narrow death-eligibility to those who consistently get the death penalty, would that be so different from the mandatory death sentences condemned in *Woodson*? Is guided-discretion inevitably a self-destructive concept? See David Baldus, George Woodworth, & Charles Pulaski, Jr., Reflections on the "Inevitability" of Racial Discrimination in Capital Sentencing and the "Impossibility" of Its Prevention, Detection, and Correction, 51 Wash. & Lee. L. Rev. 359 (1994) (inevitability of racial discrimination, as implied by *McCleskey*, is overstated; new efforts in Florida and New Jersey to monitor death sentences for equity have shown promise).

In the wake of *McCleskey*, one factor in explaining racial disproportion in use of the death penalty may be the salience of rape-murder. As noted earlier, in *Coker v. Georgia* the Court forbade the death penalty for non-homicidal rape (at least in the case of an adult victim) in part because the death penalty for rape had been used so disproportionately to punish black defendants who allegedly raped white victims. But as Prof. Phyllis Crocker has detailed, rape contends to be the most dramatic aggravating circumstance in influencing juries in capital murder cases and may continue to reinforce prejudicial racial and gender stereotypes.[29]

3. The *McCleskey* majority rejected Justice Stevens's argument and reaffirmed the *Gregg* holding that the Georgia death penalty statute is constitutional. Does this mean they must choose between a racially discriminatory death penalty or no death penalty at all? What does that say about the death penalty? About the criminal justice system?

4. Recall that Gregg v. Georgia encouraged, though did not require,[30] states to address equity and caprice issues through comparative "proportionality review" of their capital cases. Some states have taken up the message enthusiastically, others not at all.

How should comparative proportionality review be conducted? Should the case in question be compared only to cases where the death was upheld? Originally imposed? Sought by the prosecutor? Was theoretically chargeable? Note that the narrower and more egregious the set of cases, the more skewed the sample will be since there will, by definition, be fewer cases where an arguably more culpable killer received life. On the other hand, the wider the pool, the more difficult it will be to tell whether some procedural or extraneous factor

---

29. Phyllis L. Crocker, Crossing the Line: Rape-Murder and the Death Penalty, 26 Ohio Northern University Law Rev. 689 (2000); Is the Death Penalty Good for Women, 4 Buff. Crim. L. Rev. 917 (2001).

30. See n.2, *supra*.

prevented ultimate imposition of the death penalty, and the more difficult it may be to determine the criteria of culpability of moral desert necessary for the comparison. See In re Proportionality Review 735 A.2d 528 (N.J. 1999). The New Jersey Supreme Court postponed decision on the state constitutionality of the statute that required proportionality review only in cases where the death penalty was imposed. Instead, it ordered a study requiring comparison to all cases where capital charges were filed. For a massive study of the premises and practices of "proportionality review" and an evaluation of the performance of state courts in reviewing death sentences for equity, see Leigh Bienen, The Proportionality Review of Capital Cases by State High Courts after *Gregg:* Only "The Appearance of Justice"? 87 J. Crim. L. & Criminology 130 (1996) (noting success of New Jersey courts' efforts).

5. Consider the following final perspective:[31]

> There may never be a social consensus on the role of capital punishment, but a social engineer might try to identify a sort of culturally optimal number of executions that would best compromise among the competing demands made by the different constituencies of the criminal justice system.
>
> The most obvious approach is to have some executions, but not very many. A small number of executions offers a logical, if crude, compromise between the extreme groups who want either no executions or as many as possible. It would also satisfy those who believe that execution is appropriate only for a small number of especially blameworthy killers, at least if the right ones are selected. It might further satisfy those who do not believe there is a discernible and small category of most blameworthy killers, but who believe that a small number of executions might adequately serve general deterrence and make a necessary political statement about society's attitude toward crime. But our hypothetical social engineer would want to consider other points of view or factors as well in designing his culturally optimal number. Too many executions would inure the populace to the fact of state killing and thereby deprive the death penalty of its value as a social symbol. Or too many executions might have the opposite effect of morally offending people with the spectacle of a bloodbath. On the other hand, if the number were too low in comparison with the number of murders, capital punishment might not serve general deterrence. Or if we execute too few people, we may not produce a big enough statistical sample to prove that the death penalty meets any tests of rationality or nondiscrimination.
>
> We might therefore imagine a socially stabilizing design for the death penalty which leads to just the right number of executions to keep the art form alive, but not so many as to cause excessive social cost. It is, of course, fanciful to imagine any political institution having the skill or authority to take a systemic approach to executions. Under the current capital punishment laws, judges have some opportunity to manipulate the rate of execution. Legislators theoretically can affect the execution rate by changing the substantive laws of murder and punishment. But between the constitutional restrictions on death sentencing and the voters' general demand for capital punishment, legislators in most states probably do not have a great deal of room to maneuver. A prosecutor can ensure that any given murder defendant will not face execution, but because he cannot control the jury or judges he can never guarantee that a defendant is executed. A juror can at best control the rate of execution in one case. But judges, especially appellate judges,

---

31. Robert Weisberg, Deregulating Death, 1983 Sup. Ct. Rev. 303, 386-87.

have a good deal of freedom to control the number of executions within the pool of capital claimants who come before them.

Viewing the statistics of the last decade, one might imagine that in a rough, systemic way, judges have indeed manipulated death penalty doctrine to achieve a culturally optimal number of executions. That number is very close to zero, but it must be viewed in light of a very different number — the number of death sentences.

If we somewhat fancifully treat the judiciary as a single and calculating mind, we could say that it has conceived a fiendishly clever way of satisfying the competing demands on the death penalty: We will sentence vast numbers of murderers to death, but execute virtually none of them. Simply having many death sentences can satisfy many proponents of the death penalty who demand capital punishment, because in a vague way they want the law to make a statement of social authority and control. It will also satisfy jurors who want to make that statement in specific cases with the reassurance that the death sentence will never really be carried out. And we can at the same time avoid arousing great numbers of people who would vent their moral and political opposition to capital punishment only on the occasion of actual executions. Once a murderer enters the apparently endless appellate process, much of the public ceases to pay attention.

Twenty years after this excerpt was written, there are about 3,500 people on death row, and an average of about 63 executions per year have occurred in the last decade. At what rate would the argument cease to hold true?

IV

JUSTIFICATION AND EXCUSE

The defenses of justification and excuse cut across the entire criminal law. In both defenses, the actor concedes that she has committed a criminal act, with the mens rea required by the definition of the crime. The actor has, in short, committed an offense. Nevertheless, the actor offers a plausible argument of desert or utility why she should not suffer punishment. This introduction will review frequently noted differences between the two types of defense (justification and excuse) and the two types of argument for each (desert and utility). Then it will review arguments against efforts to distinguish justification and excuse.

A. DISTINGUISHING JUSTIFICATION AND EXCUSE

What are the differences between defenses of justification and defenses of excuse? The most important concern (1) the wrongness of defendant's conduct, (2) the relative importance of legality in the definition of each type of defense, (3) the allocation of burden of proof, and (4) the treatment of third parties (persons other than the principal perpetrator or the victim).

(1) *Wrongdoing.* An actor can claim justification when, in committing an offense, she has advanced a social interest or vindicated a right of sufficient weight that the criminal law should neither disapprove nor discourage her conduct. A defense of justification is a claim that, though the actor fulfilled the definition of a criminal offense, she *did no wrong.* A justification denies the wrongfulness of particular conduct that concededly constitutes an offense.

An actor can excuse the *wrongful* commission of a criminal offense when circumstances so limited the voluntariness of her conduct that she is not morally blameworthy for it or could not have been deterred from it. An excuse denies a particular actor's responsibility for conduct that is concededly wrong.

(2) *Legality.* Defenses of justification supplement statutory offenses to complete the criminal law's definition of our legal duties. If legal actors know of the availability of defenses of justification, they can make responsible choices, exercise their rights, and conform their behavior to the law. In other words, the

481

criteria of justification are "conduct rules" for actors subject to the criminal law, as well as "decision rules" for persons charged with administering the law.[1]

Excuses, by contrast, are premised on the actor's incapacity to make a responsible choice under the circumstances. Thus, the availability of excuses need not and should not enter into the decision making of actors. Criteria of excuse are only decision rules for courts or juries, not conduct rules for actors. This distinction between the audiences for criteria of justification and criteria of excuse implies that there is less need to insure the specificity, publicity, and prospectivity of criteria of excuse.

Must criteria of justification be as precise as definitions of offenses? Often they are not. Criteria of justification are sometimes judicially developed rather than legislatively enacted; where embodied in statutes, they may take the form of vague, flexible standards rather than precise, inflexible rules. Courts, legislators, and scholars all assume that applying criteria of justification requires more discretion than applying definitions of offenses. A defense of justification identifies a situational exception to an overbroad prescriptive rule.

Thus, defenses of justification embody a tension between (1) the *discretion* required for judging the defendant's conduct and (2) the *obligation to inform the public* of what conduct is illegal. A common resolution of this tension between discretion and publicity is to require that criteria of justification be prospective and public, but not specific. Thus, criteria of justification are not so much "decision *rules*" for courts and "conduct *rules*" for individuals as they are decision *standards* and conduct *standards*.

Because claims of excuse, like claims of justification, invite situation-specific moral judgment, they also seem to require discretionary *standards* of decision rather than inflexible *rules*. Because defenses of excuse do not set standards for conduct, they do not embody the same tension between moral discretion and publicity that defenses of justification do.

There is one more reason for the defenses of justification and excuse to be specified by statute: the importance of democratic participation in criminal lawmaking. But precise statutory rules would impede the situation-specific moral discretion these defenses seem to require. An alternative that achieves some democratic participation while preserving situation-specific moral discretion is delegating the discretionary application of vague standards to juries. Juries arguably perform their most useful role where we wish to combine discretionary decision making with democratic participation.

(3) *Burden of proof.* You will recall from the Introduction that due process as currently understood by the Supreme Court requires the prosecution to bear the burden of proof beyond a reasonable doubt on all of the defining elements of an offense, but not on defenses of justification and excuse. You may also recall that most jurisdictions nevertheless place such a burden on the prosecution on the issue of wrongdoing, or justification. Why is this? Simply because the criteria of justification are part of the criminal law's prescriptive norms of conduct. Until the prosecution has proven that defendant committed an offense without justification, it has not established that defendant did anything wrong.

(4) *Third parties.* Justifications exonerate conduct as right, and excuses exonerate persons as blameless for wrongful conduct. It follows that third parties

---

1. See Meir Dan-Cohen, Decision Rules and Conduct Rules: On Acoustic Separation in Criminal Law, 97 Harv. L. Rev. 625 (1984).

may justifiably assist, and may not interfere with, justified conduct. By contrast, third parties may not assist, and may interfere with, conduct that is excused but wrongful. One who assists the excused but wrongful commission of an offense could be liable for the offense as an accomplice, unless she also has an excuse.

B. JUSTIFICATION, EXCUSE, AND THE PURPOSES OF PUNISHMENT

The distinction between justification and excuse is often difficult to apply in practice. To see why, we need to pose a more fundamental question. Why do we justify or excuse offenses?

You will recall from Chapter 1 that punishment is generally justified on the grounds that it controls crime and achieves retribution. These are very different goals, associated with the different philosophical theories of utilitarianism and retributivism respectively. Each of these theories implies a different approach to defining justifiable and excusable conduct. Yet few jurisdictions — indeed few people — consistently embrace either theory of punishment: Most people draw ideas from both. The result is that defenses that seem like justifications from a "moral" or retributive point of view may seem like excuses from a "policy" or utilitarian point of view, and vice versa. In any case, many of the controversies and hard cases in the law of justification and excuse can be seen as debates between these two points of view.

(1) *The utilitarian perspective.* If punishment is meant to achieve the optimal level of crime control, it should deter harmful conduct, without imposing more harm than it prevents. To a utilitarian, all conduct is harmful that does not "maximize utility" — that is, achieve the greatest social benefit for the least possible cost. Utilitarians recognize that sometimes it is hard to tell what course of action is most socially beneficial and that gathering enough information to decide the best course of action can be prohibitively costly. Moreover, utilitarians do not think all harmful or socially costly behavior should be punished, because punishment involves social cost. Thus, punishment is beneficial only to the extent the conduct involved is quite harmful and punishment can significantly reduce it. On the other hand, since utilitarians are not very concerned about desert, they may be willing to enact draconian punishments for petty offenses, if those punishments will so deter the offenses that they will rarely have to be applied.

(2) *Utilitarian justifications.* To the extent that we are utility minded we will justify offenses *necessary to prevent a greater evil.* A pure utilitarian expects each actor to selflessly aim at maximizing the general good, rather than her own. Thus utilitarians will be skeptical of claims that self-defense is always justified. Certainly, the self-defender will have a *duty to retreat,* if possible, rather than kill her assailant. Similarly, she may not justifiably kill in defense of any interest less weighty than life itself — her use of force must be *proportionate* to the interest defended. While the utilitarian self-defender can clearly take one life to save several, she may not take several lives in defense of one. Nor is it obvious that utilitarianism justifies taking one life to save another.

(3) *Utilitarian excuses.* These doubts that defensive force *is justified* do not preclude *excusing* defensive force. Utilitarian thought generally approves

excusing wrongful conduct that is hard to deter because of (1) the high cost to the actor of abstaining from the conduct; or (2) the actor's incapacity to discern or act in her own best interest. The first category might include *defense of self* or loved ones, as well as *duress* (committing a crime under threat of violence) or *necessity* (stealing to feed a starving child). The second category might include *insanity* or *addiction*.

On the other hand, there are utilitarian arguments against excusing "undeterrable" offenders. One can argue that the public is not very discriminating about the particular circumstances or characteristics the law considers exculpatory; that is, the public is likely to be deterred as much by the punishment of an undeterrable as by that of a deterrable offender. One can point out that since all offenders were undeterred by the threat of punishment, the argument for excusing the undeterrable leads to the implausible conclusion that no one need ever be punished.

(4) *The retributivist perspective.* To the extent that we emphasize the retributive function of punishment, we may define both justification and excuse differently. To a retributivist, the only legitimate reason to punish is that punishment is deserved because of responsibility for wrongdoing. Retributivists usually identify conduct as wrongful if it violates someone else's rights. Similarly, retributivists generally see conduct as justified if the actor has a right to engage in it. Where utilitarians see only one choice as "right" or "justified"—the one that maximizes utility—retributivists tend to see any choice as justified that falls within the actor's rights.

(5) *Retributivist justifications.* It follows from the preceding discussion that retributivists are likely to see many offenses as justified that a utilitarian would not.

This is particularly apparent in the area of necessary force. To the pure retributivist, force, even deadly force, may be justified in defense of any right, no matter how insignificant, against a wrongdoer. It is permissible to kill many aggressors to save one innocent. In addition, the defender has no duty to retreat and thereby spare her attacker's life. On the other hand, the retributivist may be more committed to the requirement that defense *be*—rather than merely *appear*—necessary. Suppose Jean defends herself based on a reasonable but false belief that she is about to be attacked. Since the belief is false, the resulting use of force violates the rights of an innocent. To a retributivist, such a rights violation cannot be justified. But because it was based on a reasonable mistake, it may be excused.

While retributivists are more likely than utilitarians to justify necessary defense, they are less likely than utilitarians to justify offenses as the lesser of two evils. We cannot justifiably violate the rights of others to spare ourselves or society a greater cost.

(6) *Retributivist excuses.* The retributivist reason for excusing offenders is very different from the utilitarian. Rather than excusing those who are difficult to deter, retributivists would excuse those who cannot fairly be blamed for the wrong acts they perpetrate. In practice, these may turn out to be many of the same people the utilitarian would excuse as undeterrable — those who are under duress, or who commit offenses to assuage hunger, or who suffer from mental disease. It includes offenders who commit offenses because of fear of an imminent threat to the safety of the offender or a loved one. On the other hand, the retributivist will neither justify nor excuse an offense necessary to prevent a

"greater" evil that does not imminently threaten the offender or a loved one. Here the offender commits what the retributivist considers to be an act of wrongdoing, and does it out of sober calculation rather than desperate fear.

(7) *The reasonable person.* We have encountered "reasonable person" standards before in this book. In weighing charges involving the mens rea of negligence, jurors are often asked whether a reasonable person in the defendant's situation would have been aware of some risk. When considering whether a mistake of governing law should excuse a defendant, jurors in some special cases are asked to decide whether the mistake was reasonable. In deciding whether a defendant who killed was provoked, jurors are often asked to compare defendant's reactions to that of the average or the reasonable person.

Reasonable person standards are quite prevalent in the areas of justification and excuse. But their function is very different depending on whether one sees criminal punishment as primarily utilitarian or retributive in purpose.

(8) *The reasonable utilitarian.* When a utilitarian asks whether an offense was justified she is not interested in whether the offense actually was the best available action; nor is she interested in whether it appeared to be, given the information defendant had. She wants to know whether it would have appeared best, at the time committed, to a person who had made the socially optimal investment in information. To the utilitarian considering whether an offense was justified, *the optimally informed person* is the "reasonable person."

When a utilitarian considers whether an offense should be excused, she is no longer asking whether it was the best choice. Now she wants to know whether it was a deferrable choice. In determining this she may compare the defendant to a quite different hypothetical person: *the average person.* This average person is the "reasonable person" for purposes of excusing.

Here the utilitarian will encounter a problem: It may not be possible to distinguish the person who *was not* deterred from the person who *could not* be deterred. The utilitarian is tempted to solve this problem by asking whether similar people in similar circumstances would likely have been deterred by the threat of punishment. Now the reasonable person has become the *average person with defendant's characteristics in defendant's circumstances.* But if similar and similarly circumstanced persons would have been deterred, how does that prove that this particular defendant could have been deterred? The defendant may always argue that a person with identical characteristics in identical circumstances would not have been deterred. The inquiry into how the "reasonable person" would have acted may appear to answer the question whether defendant was deterrable, but it really just restates it.

(9) *The reasonable retributivist.* From a retributivist standpoint, the "reasonable person" is irrelevant to justification. Justification means acting within one's rights, not doing what a reasonable person would have mistakenly thought was within her rights.

The standard of the reasonable person, however, *is* relevant to retributivist excuses. Retributivism holds that punishment is deserved for acts that manifest bad character. Ordinarily, the commission of an act of wrongdoing — an unjustified offense — manifests bad character. An excuse, however, precludes the inference from a bad act to a bad character. Hence, the excuse should be based on circumstances external to the character of the defendant. To the retributivist, the defendant should not be able to plead her own propensity to commit crimes as a reason to avoid punishment.

In deciding whether the defendant's bad act manifests bad character, the retributivist wants to know whether a "reasonable person" could have acted as defendant did, facing the same circumstances. The "reasonable person" here means *the person of good character*. But how does comparison to this hypothetical person help the jury judge the character of a particular defendant confronted with a difficult situation? The jurors may ask themselves what they would do in the same circumstances, but what if the "circumstances" the defendant points to are an abused childhood, or socialization in a foreign culture, or a mental disorder? Can the "reasonable person" really help us distinguish exculpatory misfortunes from inculpatory character flaws? Once again, the reasonable person standard does not answer the crucial question (here, of responsibility rather than deterrability); it merely restates it.

(10) *Retributivism and the insanity defense.* The insanity defense is one excuse that clearly does not require any test of the reasonableness of defendant's conduct and is therefore anomalous from the retributivist perspective. The retributivist preference for excusing on the basis of circumstances external to the defendant's character raises a particularly troubling problem with the insanity defense: The defendant who pleads insanity appears to excuse herself on the basis of her flawed character. A retributivist account of the insanity defense therefore requires some criterion for distinguishing insanity from bad character. The legal system generally delegates this problem to medical experts, but this does not really answer the retributivist's concern. The term "mental disease" is often merely a metaphor: Psychiatric symptoms are not really caused by germs. A psychiatrist may sometimes be able to point to some other kind of external cause for the defendant's mental disorder, but often she may not. Sometimes a psychiatrist can show congenital physiological causes of behavior, but whether these should excuse is a deep moral question. A psychiatrist may be able to show how an offense fit in to a defendant's characteristic pattern of thought and behavior but cannot answer the moral question whether those psychological characteristics should exculpate or inculpate the defendant.

C. COMBINING JUSTIFICATION AND EXCUSE

Having summarized the divergent conceptions of justification and excuse implied by our society's leading rationales for punishment, we return to the problem of distinguishing justification and excuse. Justification and excuse are difficult to distinguish in practice because:

(a) Retributivism considers some offenses justified that utilitarianism considers wrong, but possibly excusable in whole or in part (e.g., disproportionate defensive force).

(b) Utilitarianism considers some offenses justifiable that retributivism considers wrong (e.g., offenses aimed at avoiding a greater evil) but possibly excusable (e.g., if the greater evil imminently and personally threatens the offender).

(c) Within utilitarianism, the boundary separating justified from wrong actions is fuzzy, because it depends on contestable judgments about

      (i) the information to be ascribed to "reasonable person" and (ii) the best course of action in light of that information.

(d) While the use of a "reasonable person" standard connotes a defense of excuse for retributivists, it may indicate either a justification or an excuse for utilitarians.

(e) Lawmakers who disagree or are uncertain whether some conduct is justifiable may "compromise" by excusing it.

(f) Jurors or legislators may readily agree that a particular defendant or class of defendants should be acquitted without being able to agree on the reasons.

The introduction to Article 3 of the Model Penal Code, in fact, defends the drafters' decision not to draw a bright line between justification and excuse:[2]

The plan of the Code makes a rough analytical distinction between excuse and justification as defenses to a criminal prosecution, even when their procedural significance is the same. . . .

The Model Code does not, however, attempt to draw a fine line between all those situations in which a defense might more precisely be labeled a justification and all those situations in which a defense might more precisely be labeled an excuse. Thus, it treats in justification sections those cases in which an actor mistakenly perceives the circumstances or the necessity for force; in some of the cases, at least, it might be said that the actor is really offering an excuse for his conduct rather than a full-fledged justification. The Code's approach is based on a skepticism that any fine line between excuse and justification can sensibly be drawn, and on the belief that any possible value of attempting such a line would be outweighed by the cost of complicating the content of relevant provisions.

To say that someone's conduct is "justified" ordinarily connotes that the conduct is thought to be right, or at least not undesirable; to say that someone's conduct is "excused" ordinarily connotes that the conduct is thought to be undesirable but that for some reason the actor is not to be blamed for it. Usually one can say whether a defense that is offered is justificatory or excusatory, but there are some troublesome borderline cases. Suppose an actor makes a mistake of fact that is not only reasonable but also consistent with the highest standards of perception and apprehension. For example, relying on the consistently prevailing wind, a person sets a fire that will destroy private property but will also stop the advance of a large forest fire that looks as if it will destroy much more property. A sudden unexpected shift in the wind renders the forest fire harmless, while the set fire does the expected amount of property damage. In retrospect it is regrettable that the second fire was set, and one might consider a defense of setting it an "excuse" for an unfortunate occurrence. But based on all available information, the act of setting the fire was appropriate, and society would hope that similar fires would be set by persons with similar available information; thus the conduct of setting the fire was justified. Whether in this circumstance, one speaks of "justification" or "excuse" is a question of vague linguistic boundary lines rather than of substantive judgment.

In other circumstances there may be genuine doubt as to how behavior should be judged. Self-defense serves as an acceptable reason for the use of deadly force both because it is often desirable that people defend their lives and because it is thought that people will "naturally" defend themselves if they believe their lives are

---

2. American Law Institute, Model Penal Code and Commentaries, Part I, at 2-4 (1985).

in danger. For many cases of self-defense it would probably be generally agreed that the use of deadly force was actually desirable, but for others, e.g., resistance by one family member to attack by another, there would be disagreement whether the use of deadly force was actually desirable or should merely be accepted as a natural response to a grave threat.

There is little point in trying to "purify" justification provisions of all situations in which it might be said that the defense offered is really an excuse. The main aim of a criminal code is to differentiate conduct that warrants criminal sanctions from conduct that does not. If it is clear that conduct will not be subject to criminal sanctions, the effort to establish precisely in each case whether that conduct is actually justified or only excused does not seem worthwhile, especially since, in regard to the difficult cases, members of society may disagree over the appropriate characterization. Moreover, insofar as determinations of justification and excuse are made by juries and both sorts of defenses are offered in difficult cases, a general verdict of acquittal would conceal the precise defense accepted even if the criminal code drew a fine line between justification and excuse.

8

DEFENSIVE FORCE, NECESSITY, AND DURESS

This chapter will examine three defenses with a common characteristic: All three assert that an offense should not be punished if it was committed to avert some other harm.

We will begin with the issue of necessary force: the use of force in self-defense, defense of another, defense of property, and law enforcement. As we have noted, self-defense has traditionally been offered by retributivists as the paradigmatic example of a justification defense, and is often analyzed as a justification claim by utilitarians as well.

The next section will take up two related defenses: "choice of evils" and "necessity." "Choice of evils" reflects a utilitarian conception of justification. Although often asserted in similar fact-situations, the defense of "necessity" involves a claim of excuse, based on the idea that an imminent danger to the defendant or a loved one gave the defendant no choice but to commit the offense. Accordingly, she should not be held responsible for her offense. The two defenses are so similar that the term "necessity" is often used to encompass both, and courts that recognize a defense of "necessity" do not always specify which of these two defenses they have in mind.

Finally, we will conclude with the related defense of duress, a claim that the defendant's capacity to choose was impaired by a serious, imminent threat of harm from another person.

In the next chapter we will consider a pure excuse defense — insanity — whose many complexities require a separate treatment.

A. DEFENSIVE FORCE

1. Elements and Rationales

PEOPLE v. LA VOIE
Supreme Court of Colorado
395 P.2d 1001 (1964)

MOORE, JUSTICE. The defendant . . . was accused of the crime of murder. . . . At the conclusion of the evidence, the trial court, on motion of counsel for defendant, directed the jury to return a verdict of not guilty. It was the opinion of the trial court that the evidence was insufficient to warrant submission of any issue to the jury in that the sum total thereof established a clear case of justifiable homicide. The district attorney objected, and the case is here on writ of error requesting this court to render an opinion expressing its disapproval of the action of the trial court in directing the verdict of not guilty. . . .[1]

. . . The defendant was employed as a pharmacist at the Kincaid Pharmacy, 7024 West Colfax Avenue, Lakewood, Colorado. His day's work ended at about 12:30 A.M. After leaving his place of employment, he obtained something to eat at a nearby restaurant and started on his way home. He was driving east on West Colfax Avenue, toward the city of Denver, at about 1:30 A.M. An automobile approached his car from the rear. The driver of this auto made contact with the rear bumper of defendant's car and thereupon forcibly, unlawfully, and deliberately accelerated his motor, precipitating the defendant forward for a substantial distance and through a red traffic light. There were four men in the automobile who were under the influence of intoxicating liquor in varying degrees. Prior to ramming the car of the defendant they had agreed to shove him along just for "kicks." The defendant applied his brakes to the full; but the continuing force from behind precipitated him forward, causing all four wheels to leave a trail of skid marks. When defendant's car ultimately came to a stop the auto containing the four men backed away a few feet. The defendant got out of his car and as he did so he placed a revolver beneath his belt. He had a permit to carry the gun. The four men got out of their auto and advanced toward the defendant threatening to "make you eat that damn gun," to "mop up the street with you," and also directed vile, profane and obscene language at him. The man who was in advance of his three companions kept moving toward defendant in a menacing manner. At this point the defendant shot him. As a result, he died at the scene of the affray. . . .

The law of justifiable homicide is well set forth by this court in the case of Young v. People, 47 Colo. 352, 107 P. 274:

> . . . When a person has reasonable grounds for believing, and does in fact actually believe, that danger of his being killed, or of receiving great bodily harm, is imminent, he may act on such appearances and defend himself, even to the extent of taking human life when necessary, although it may turn out that the appearances were false, or although he may have been mistaken as to the extent of the real or actual danger.

The defendant was a stranger to all four occupants of the auto. He was peaceably on his way home from work, which terminated after midnight. Under the law and the circumstances disclosed by the record, defendant had the right to defend himself against the threatened assault of those whose lawlessness and utter disregard of his rights resulted in the justifiable killing of one of their number.

The judgment is affirmed.

---

1. [Under federal double jeopardy principles, the prosecution is barred from appealing a judge's directed verdict of acquittal, and so La Voie himself was no longer at risk of conviction here. But some states nevertheless permit the prosecutor to request a higher court opinion disapproving the trial court verdict, as a guide to future cases. — EDS.]

Notes and Questions

1. *Justifying defensive force.* Assuming that the men in the car were in fact intending to kill La Voie, why does he deserve acquittal? Is it because his life is worth more than any of their lives, once they initiate an illegal attack on him? Did his attacker "forfeit" what would normally be his own legally protected right to life? Or is it that La Voie had a right to defend a sphere of autonomy from outside interference? Consider the following discussion by Professor Paul Robinson:

Defensive force justifications differ from general justifications in that they always concern threats of harm from a human aggressor to the particular interest that is the subject of the defense—to the actor himself in self-defense, to other persons in the defense of others, and to property in the defense of property. Defensive force justifications rely on the same balancing of evils that is the basis of the lesser evils defense. Where a gang of thugs, rather than a natural forest fire, threatens the lives of the inhabitants of a town, the defense of others will permit defensive force against the attackers, just as the lesser evils justification permits the setting of a fire to create a firebreak. In the former case, however, an innocent person, such as the owner of the firebreak field, need not bear the harm of the justified conduct; rather, it is borne by the culpable attackers. Consequently, there is not as strong a need for the strict balancing of physical harms commonly done in lesser evils; that is, the actor may be permitted to kill three attacking thugs in order to save three innocent townspeople even though the physical harm caused (three lives) is not less than the physical harm threatened (three lives). One may even permit the killing of three attacking thugs to save one innocent person, though the harm caused is clearly greater, because society highly values the protection of innocents and deplores unjustified aggression.

Permitting the actor to cause greater physical harm than he avoids does not mean that the balancing of harms of the general justification defense has been rejected. The aggressors' culpability may be seen as discounting the value of their lives in the balance. Or, what is perhaps a better characterization of the process, one may properly add to the evil of physical harm to an innocent, a variety of intangible evils that arise from such aggression, evils that may well be more significant to society than the physical harm threatened. In the case of the thugs, for example, the lives of the three thugs are balanced against the lives of the three townspeople *plus* the compelling societal interest in preserving the right of bodily autonomy and condemning unjustified aggression.

The same process occurs in the protection of property. The harm of physical injury to a thief is balanced against the owner's interest in retaining the threatened property plus the societal interest in preserving a right to property ownership and condemning unjustified aggression. Again, the more intangible societal interests may be more significant than the particular owner's interest in retaining the particular item threatened. But even the weight of these societal interests has a limit—the limit is generally surpassed when human life is taken in defense of property. A human life, even a culpable aggressor's, is still likely to be assigned a more significant value than property.

The same balancing principles apply when the actor kills another to save his own life. But self-defense is unique among defensive force justifications, and is sometimes theoretically troublesome. First, by definition only one human life can be at stake on the side of the actor; if there are more, a defense of others is available. This forces difficult choices because the frequent situation of one life for one life demands complete reliance on intangible societal interests to break the deadlock. There is no reason, however, that the analysis should vary. The community is generally willing to give sufficient weight to the intangible interests to permit the killing of the aggressor.

Self-defense is also unique among defensive force situations because the actor makes the justification decision at a moment when he is in a difficult position. Taking this into account, it seems appropriate that many jurisdictions provide liberal excuse provisions for an actor who makes a mistake as to a self-defense justification, as well as liberal rules governing the admission of evidence relevant to those mistakes, such as evidence concerning the battered-wife syndrome. Some jurisdictions have gone further to say that an attack on a person may produce a state of coercion in him that should be recognized as duress. If the actor is in fact justified, however, there is no need for such excuses. Just because the self-defense situation may give rise to an excuse does not, as some commentators suggest, change the fact that it may also provide a justification. If *A* is permitted to intervene to save the life of *another* by killing an unjustified attacker, one can hardly deny *A* a justification when *A* is the intended victim, simply because *A* would *also* be excused for having acted in a state of confusion or coercion.[2]

2. *Mistaken self-defense.* Why do we care what the men in the car actually intended? Does that issue bear on justification or excuse?

On the other hand, the court notes that La Voie was allowed to act on the appearance of a threat of deadly force. Why should La Voie enjoy an acquittal if he mistakenly failed to realize that the other men were only harassing him but were never intending him any grievous harm? Could we still say the attacker "forfeited" his right to life by virtue of culpably creating the appearance of a fatal threat? What mental state would the attacker have had to possess? Can it still then be a matter of La Voie's life being worthier? Or would there be another rationale here — that we are willing to excuse La Voie from the crime of intentional homicide because his mind was disrupted by fear of his own death? Under the rules of most jurisdictions, La Voie would be entitled to full acquittal by means of "perfect self-defense" if the other men were in fact threatening deadly or grievous harm, or if La Voie had reasonably perceived them to be doing so. On the other hand if this belief was unreasonable he might have only an imperfect self-defense claim. In many jurisdictions this would afford him no defense. But, as we shall see below, pp. 508-09, *infra*, in many jurisdictions imperfect self-defense would reduce a killer's liability from murder to manslaughter. See In re Christian S., 7 Cal. 4th 768, 30 Cal. Rptr. 33, (1994) (16-year-old who shot and killed "skinhead" gang member who had repeatedly threatened him could claim "honest but unreasonable fear of immediate harm").

3. *Defense of others.* Though we usually speak of *self*-defense, there is an exactly parallel doctrine of defense of others. If *A* aims deadly force at *B* and if *B* would have a self-defense justification to kill *A* in response, then if *C* comes along and observes *A* attacking *B*, *C* would have a virtually identical justification response in killing *A* in order to save *B*. A minority of states say that in the case of defense of others, the killer must be factually accurate in perceiving that the deadly force is necessary — an honest and reasonable mistake will not work. Also in most states, this doctrine does not require *C* to have any special relationship with *B*.

4. *The Model Penal Code.* The MPC contains an elaborate formula for determining when the use of force in self-defense is noncriminal. Note that under

---

2. Paul Robinson, Criminal Law Defenses 69-73 (1984).

the MPC the right to use *deadly* force is subject to more stringent rules than is the right to use force in general.

Section 3.04. Use of Force in Self-Protection

(1) *Use of Force Justifiable for Protection of the Person.* Subject to the provisions of this Section and of Section 3.09, the use of force upon or toward another person is justifiable when the actor believes that such force is immediately necessary for the purpose . . . of protecting himself against the use of unlawful force by such other person on the present occasion.

(2) *Limitations on Justifying Necessity for Use of Force.*

(A) The use of force is not justifiable under this Section:

(i) to resist an arrest that the actor knows is being made by a peace officer, although the arrest is unlawful; or

(ii) to resist force used by the occupier or possessor of property or by another person on his behalf, where the actor knows that the person using the force is doing so under a claim of right to protect the property, except that this limitation shall not apply if:

(a) the actor is a public officer acting in the performance of his duties or a person lawfully assisting him therein or a person making or assisting in a lawful arrest; or

(b) the actor has been unlawfully dispossessed of the property and is making a re-entry or recaption justified by Section 3.06; or

(c) the actor believes that such force is necessary to protect himself against death or serious bodily injury.

(B) The use of deadly force is not justifiable under this Section unless the actor believes that such force is necessary to protect himself against death, serious bodily injury, kidnapping or sexual intercourse compelled by force or threat; nor is it justifiable if:

(i) the actor, with the purpose of causing death or serious bodily injury, provoked the use of force against himself in the same encounter; or

(ii) the actor knows that he can avoid the necessity of using such force with complete safety by retreating or by surrendering possession of a thing to a person asserting a claim of right thereto or by complying with a demand that he abstain from any action that he has no duty to take, except that:

(a) the actor is not obliged to retreat from his dwelling or place of work, unless he was the initial aggressor or is assailed in his place of work by another person whose place of work the actor knows it to be; and

(b) a public officer justified in using force in the performance of his duties or a person justified in using force in his assistance or a person justified in using force in making an arrest or preventing an escape is not obliged to desist from efforts to perform such duty, effect such arrest or prevent such escape because of resistance or threatened resistance by or on behalf of the person against whom such action is directed.

(C) Except as required by paragraphs (A) and (B) of this Subsection, a person employing protective force may estimate the necessity thereof under the circumstances as he believes them to be when the force is used, without retreating, surrendering possession, doing any other act that he has no legal duty to do or abstaining from any lawful action.

(3) *Use of Confinement as Protective Force.* The justification afforded by this Section extends to the use of confinement as protective force only if the actor takes all reasonable measures to terminate the confinement as soon as he knows that he safely can, unless the person confined has been arrested on a charge of crime.

PEOPLE v. GLEGHORN
California Court of Appeal
193 Cal. App. 3d 199, 238 Cal. Rptr. 82 (1987)

STONE, PRESIDING JUSTICE.

May a person who enters the habitat of another at 3 o'clock in the morning for the announced purpose of killing him, and who commences to beat the startled sleeper's bed with a stick and set fires under him, be entitled to use deadly force in self defense after the intended victim shoots him in the back with an arrow? Upon the basis of these bizarre facts, we hold that he may not, and instead, must suffer the slings and arrows of outrageous fortune (with apologies to William Shakespeare and Hamlet, Act III, sc. 1).

Kelsey Dru Gleghorn appeals his conviction by jury of one count of simple assault, and one count of battery with the infliction of serious bodily injury. He contends the trial court erred in denying his motion for mistrial based on his allegation of inconsistent verdicts and insufficient evidence to support the conviction on count II and erred in instructing the jury pursuant to CALJIC 5.42. We find no error and affirm the judgment.

This case is a parable of the dangers of weaponry in the hands of unreasonable powers who become unduly provoked over minor irritations. Melody Downes shared her house with several persons, including appellant. She rented her garage to Michael Fairall for $150 per month. She believed he was to give her a stereo as part of the rent. He believed her intent was only to borrow it. He asked for the return of the stereo; she said she sold it.

Fairall, a man of obvious sensitivity, smashed all the windows of her automobile, slashed the tires, and dented the body. Not quite mollified, he kicked in her locked door, scattered her belongings in the bedroom, and broke an aquarium, freeing her snake. . . . Ms. Downes advised appellant of Fairall's behavior; he apparently took umbrage. On the fateful night in question, Fairall, having quaffed a few, went to the garage he called home and then to bed, a mattress laid upon a lofty perch in the rafters. He was rudely awakened by a pounding on the garage door accompanied by appellant's request that he come out so that appellant might kill him. Fairall wisely advised him that they could exchange pleasantries in the morning.

Undeterred, appellant opened the garage door, entered with stick in hand and began beating on the rafters, yelling for Fairall to come down. In the darkness, Fairall claimed he could see sparks where the board hit the rafters. Appellant said that if Fairall did not come down, he would burn him out. No sooner said than done, appellant set a small fire to some of Fairall's clothes.

Fairall, who happened to have secreted a bow and quiver of arrows in the rafters to prevent its theft, loosed one but did not see where it landed. Fairall, abandoning his weapons, swung down from the rafters and was immediately hit from behind. He yelled for someone to bring a hose and attempted to extinguish the fire with his hands. Meanwhile, appellant, in an ill humor from the gash in his back caused by the arrow, continued to beat him, causing a two-inch-wide vertical break in Fairall's lower jaw, tearing his lips, knocking out 6 to 10 teeth, mangling two fingers, and lacerating his arm, stomach and back. Fairall also suffered burns on the palms of his hands.

Fairall testified under a grant of immunity given concerning the vandalism of the car. . . .

The jury returned verdicts of guilty of simple assault as a lesser included offense of assault by means of force likely to incur great bodily injury on count I and of battery with the infliction of serious bodily injury on count II. Appellant moved for a new trial on grounds that the verdicts were contrary to the law or evidence. He contends that since the jury found his acts prior to being shot constituted only simple assault, Fairall was not justified in replying with deadly force. Since the victim responded with deadly force, he continues, he was entitled to defend himself with deadly force. Ergo, he could not be convicted of battery with the infliction of serious bodily injury.

Not every assault gives rise to the right to kill in self-defense. Penal Code section 197 explains when homicide is justifiable, i.e., "2. When committed in defense of habitation, property, or person, against one who manifestly intends or endeavors, by violence or surprise, to commit a felony, or against one who manifestly intends and endeavors, in a violent, riotous or tumultuous manner, to enter the habitation of another for the purpose of offering violence to any person therein; or, [¶] 3. . . . when there is reasonable ground to apprehend a design to commit a felony or to do some great bodily injury, and imminent danger of such design being accomplished. . . ." However, to repel a slight assault, the person assaulted is not authorized to resort to unduly violent measures.

Generally, if one makes a felonious assault upon another, or has created appearances justifying the other to launch a deadly counterattack in self-defense, the original assailant cannot slay his adversary in self-defense unless he has first, in good faith, declined further combat, and has fairly notified him that he has abandoned the affray. However, when the victim of simple assault responds in a sudden and deadly counterassault the original aggressor need not attempt to withdraw and may use reasonably necessary force in self-defense.

Appellant contends that, since he initially committed only a simple assault, he was legally justified as a matter of law in standing his ground, even though he was the initial attacker, and in utilizing lethal force against Fairall. He asserts that the jury did not follow special instruction number 5 which stated: "Where the original aggressor is not guilty of a deadly attack, but of a simple assault or trespass, the person assaulted has no right to use deadly or other excessive force. [¶] And, where the counter assault is so sudden and perilous that no opportunity be given to decline further to fight and he cannot retreat with safety he is justified in slaying in self-defense." . . .

The right of self-defense is based upon the appearance of imminent peril to the person attacked. The right to defend one's person or home with deadly force depends upon the circumstances as they reasonably appeared to that person. That right cannot depend upon the appellant's supposedly non-felonious secret intent. Similarly, justification does not depend upon the existence of actual danger but rather upon appearances, i.e., if a reasonable person would be placed in fear for his or her safety, and defendant acted out of that fear.

Moreover, even though a person is mistaken in judgment as to the actual necessity for the use of extreme measures, if he was misled through no fault or carelessness on his part and defends himself correctly according to what he supposed the facts to be, his act is justifiable. These are usually questions of fact for the jury to resolve. It is beyond the province of this court to reweigh the evidence. . . .

Here, the jury could reasonably infer from the evidence that: (1) Fairall acted reasonably upon the appearances that his life was in danger or (2) even if Fairall acted unreasonably in shooting appellant with the arrow and appellant was justified in responding with deadly force, appellant continued to beat his attacker long after the attacker was disabled. If a person attacked defends himself so successfully that his attacker is rendered incapable of inflicting injury, or for any other reason the danger no longer exists, there is no justification for further retaliation. This principle is embodied in CALJIC 5.52 and 5.53 (1983 rev.), both of which were given to the jury.

The evidence supports a finding that Fairall did not threaten or take any action against appellant after Fairall descended from the loft. On the other hand, if the jury found, as it could have, that Fairall was justified in reasonably fearing for his life on the appearances of appellant's actions, appellant never obtained the right of self-defense in the first place. We find no error.

Notes and Questions

1. Why should Gleghorn forfeit what would otherwise have been his right to self-defense? According to the court, under what circumstances does someone initiating a fight retain a right of self-defense? When can he regain a right otherwise forfeited?

2. If Gleghorn, as the original aggressor, loses his self-defense claim, then he seems liable for the intentional assault on Fairall. But his real culpability lies in his original aggressive act that caused the situation that led to Fairall attacking him with deadly force and then Gleghorn responding with deadly force. Following this reasoning, if Gleghorn had killed Fairall, what homicide crime would he have committed?

3. Note that Gleghorn and Fairall were co-occupants of their residence. Should this affect the outcome? We consider this question in the context of examining duty to retreat, see pp. 515-518, *infra*.

4. *Creating the conditions of one's own defense.* According to one commentator,[3] the issue presented by *Gleghorn* is but one facet of a much broader problem, that of defendants who create the conditions of their own defense:

> Assume that an actor sets a fire that threatens a nearby town to create the conditions that will justify his using his enemy's farm as a firebreak. Denying a justification defense might dissuade him from undertaking such a scheme, but if it fails to dissuade him, the unavailability of the defense may reduce his incentive to set the firebreak and save the town. Once the justifying conditions exist, regardless of the cause, society benefits if the actor undertakes the justified conduct. Moreover, if the defense is denied, the owner of the field, who values his crop more than he does the lives of the townspeople, may lawfully interfere with the actor's attempt to set fire to the field.
>
> Denying the defense to the actor who has created the justifying circumstances also creates an anomalous situation in which the actor and another person may work side by side engaging in the same conduct — here, setting fire to the same field — yet one will be justified and the other will not. It is the nature of justified conduct that it either is or is not justified — depending on whether it causes a net societal benefit — regardless of the particular state of mind, past or present, of the actor.

3. Paul Robinson, Causing the Condition of One's Own Defense: A Study in the Limits of Theory in Criminal Law Doctrine, 71 Va. L. Rev. 1, 28-43 (1985) (emphasis in original).

These problems may be avoided, however, and such a grand schemer may be properly punished, if his liability is based on his initial conduct in causing the justifying circumstances and on his culpable state of mind, at that time, as to causing the justified harm. In the culpably-caused-need-for-a-firebreak case, the actor might be liable for setting the forest fire in the first place and for the damage it caused. His subsequent conduct in saving the town by setting the firebreak would remain justified, and thus would be encouraged and protected. Indeed, the actor retains a special incentive to set the firebreak, for if the town burns down and kills or injures someone, he may be liable for this additional harm. . . .

Where the actor is not only culpable as to causing the defense conditions, but also has a culpable state of mind *as to causing himself to engage in the conduct constituting the offense,* the state should punish him for causing the ultimate justified or excused conduct. His punishment, however, is properly based on his initial conduct of causing the defense conditions with his accompanying scheming intention, not on the justified or excused conduct that he subsequently performs.

This . . . analysis accounts for different degrees of culpability as to the ultimate offense. If at the time of starting the forest fire the actor is only aware of a risk that his conduct will cause him (or others) to burn the firebreak, he is properly held liable only for recklessly causing the destruction of the firebreak.

2.   The Reasonable Self-Defender: The Case of the Battered Spouse

STATE v. LEIDHOLM
Supreme Court of North Dakota
334 N.W.2d 811 (1983)

VANDE WALLE, JUSTICE.

Janice Leidholm was charged with murder for the stabbing death of her husband, Chester Leidholm, in the early morning hours of August 7, 1981, at their farm home near Washburn. She was found guilty by a McLean County jury of manslaughter and was sentenced to five years' imprisonment in the State Penitentiary with three years of the sentence suspended. Leidholm appealed from the judgment of conviction. We reverse and remand the case for a new trial.

I

According to the testimony, the Leidholm marriage relationship in the end was an unhappy one, filled with a mixture of alcohol abuse, moments of kindness toward one another, and moments of violence. The alcohol abuse and violence was exhibited by both parties on the night of Chester's death.

Early in the evening of August 6, 1981, Chester and Janice attended a gun club party in the city of Washburn where they both consumed a large amount of alcohol.[4] On the return trip to the farm, an argument developed between Janice and Chester which continued after their arrival home just after midnight.

---

4. A Breathalyzer test administered to Janice shortly after the stabbing, at approximately 3:30 A.M., showed her blood-alcohol content was .17 of 1 percent. The analysis of a blood sample from Chester showed his blood-alcohol content was .23 of 1 percent.

Once inside the home, the arguing did not stop; Chester was shouting, and Janice was crying.

At one point in the fighting, Janice tried to telephone Dave Vollan, a deputy sheriff of McLean County, but Chester prevented her from using the phone by shoving her away and pushing her down. At another point, the argument moved outside the house, and Chester once again was pushing Janice to the ground. Each time Janice attempted to get up, Chester would push her back again.

A short time later, Janice and Chester re-entered their home and went to bed. When Chester fell asleep, Janice got out of bed, went to the kitchen, and got a butcher knife. She then went back into the bedroom and stabbed Chester. In a matter of minutes Chester died from shock and loss of blood.

II

. . . The first, and controlling, issue we consider is whether or not the trial court correctly instructed the jury on self-defense. Our resolution of the issue must of necessity begin with an explanation of the basic operation of the law of self-defense as set forth in Chapter 12.1-05 of the North Dakota Century Code. . . .

[12.1-05-03. *Self-Defense.* A Person is justified in using force upon another person to defend himself against danger of imminent unlawful bodily injury. . . .

12.1-05-07. *Limits on the use of force — Excessive Force — Deadly Force*

1. A person is not justified in using more force than is necessary and appropriate under the circumstances.

2. Deadly force is justified. . . .

b. When it is used in lawful self-defense, or in lawful defense of others, if such force is necessary to protect the actor or anyone else against death, serious bodily injury, or the commission of a felony involving violence. The use of deadly force is not justified if it can be avoided, with safety to the actor and others, by retreat or other conduct involving minimal interference with the freedom of the person menaced. . . . But . . . (2) no person is required to retreat from his dwelling or place of work unless he was the original aggressor or is assailed by a person who he knows also dwells or works there.]

Conduct which constitutes self-defense may be either justified [Section 12.1-05-03, N.D.C.C.] or excused [Section 12.1-05-08, N.D.C.C.]. Although the distinction between justification and excuse may appear to be theoretical and without significant practical consequence, because the distinction has been made in our criminal statutes we believe a general explanation of the difference between the two concepts — even though it requires us to venture briefly into the pathway of academicism — is warranted.

A defense of justification is the product of society's determination that the *actual existence* of certain circumstances will operate to make proper and legal what otherwise would be criminal conduct. A defense of excuse, contrarily, does not make legal and proper conduct which ordinarily would result in criminal liability; instead, it openly recognizes the criminality of the conduct but excuses it because the actor believed that circumstances actually existed which would justify his conduct when in fact they did not. In short, had the facts been as he supposed them to be, the actor's conduct would have been justified rather than excused. . . .

In the context of self-defense, this means that a person who believes that the force he uses is necessary to prevent imminent unlawful harm is *justified* in using such force if his belief is a correct belief; that is to say, if his belief corresponds with what actually is the case. If, on the other hand, a person *reasonably* but incorrectly believes that the force he uses is necessary to protect himself against imminent harm, his use of force is *excused*.

The distinction is arguably superfluous because whether a person's belief is correct and his conduct justified, or whether it is merely reasonable and his conduct excused, the end result is the same, namely, the person avoids punishment for his conduct. Furthermore, because a correct belief corresponds with an actual state of affairs, it will always be a reasonable belief; but a reasonable belief will not always be a correct belief, viz., a person may reasonably believe what is not actually the case.[5] Therefore, the decisive issue under our law of self-defense is not whether a person's beliefs are correct, but rather whether they are reasonable and thereby excused or justified. . . .

Section 12.1-05-08, N.D.C.C., which sets forth the general conditions that excuse a person's conduct, states:

> A person's conduct is excused if he believes that the facts are such that his conduct is necessary and appropriate for any of the purposes which would establish a justification or excuse under this chapter, even though his belief is mistaken. However, if his belief is negligently or recklessly held [i.e., unreasonably], it is not an excuse in a prosecution of an offense for which negligence or recklessness, as the case may be, suffices to establish culpability. Excuse under this section is a defense or affirmative defense according to which type of defense would be established had the facts been as the person believed them to be.

The first sentence of Section 12.1-05-08, N.D.C.C., in combination with Section 12.1-05-03, N.D.C.C., which contains the kernel statement of self-defense, yields the following expanded proposition: A person's conduct is excused if he *believes* that the use of force upon another person is necessary and appropriate to defend himself against danger of imminent unlawful harm, even though his belief is mistaken.[6] Thus we have a statement of the first element of self-defense, i.e., a person must actually and sincerely believe that the conditions exist which give rise to a claim of self-defense. . . .

From the next sentence of Section 12.1-05-08 we may infer that, besides being actual and sincere, a person's belief that the use of force is necessary to protect himself against imminent unlawful harm must be reasonable. Here, we have the second element of self-defense, namely, a person must reasonably believe that circumstances exist which permit him to use defensive force. . . .

If, therefore, a person has an actual and reasonable belief that force is necessary to protect himself against danger of imminent unlawful harm, his conduct is justified or excused. If, on the other hand, a person's actual belief in the necessity of using force to prevent imminent unlawful harm is unreasonable, his

5. For example, a person may reasonably, but mistakenly, believe that a gun held by an assailant is loaded.

6. If the danger against which a person uses force to defend himself is "death, serious bodily injury, or the commission of a felony involving violence," the person may use deadly force [Section 12.1-05-07, N.D.C.C.], which is deemed as that force which a person uses with the intent of causing, or which he knows creates a substantial risk of causing, death or serious bodily injury." Sec. 12.1-05-12(2), N.D.C.C.

conduct will not be justified or excused. Instead, he will be guilty of an offense for which negligence or recklessness suffices to establish culpability. For example, if a person recklessly believes that the use of force upon another person is necessary to protect himself against unlawful imminent serious bodily injury *and* the force he uses causes the death of the other person, he is guilty of manslaughter. And if a person's belief is negligent in the same regard, he is guilty of negligent homicide. . . .

Under both approaches, if a person reasonably believes self-defense is necessary, his conduct is excused or justified. And even though under our view an unreasonable belief may result in a conviction for either manslaughter or negligent homicide, and under theirs an unreasonable belief may result only in a conviction for manslaughter, they are the same to the extent that an honest but unreasonable belief will never result in a conviction for murder.

It must remain clear that once the factfinder determines under a claim of self-defense that the actor honestly and sincerely held the belief that the use of defensive force was required to protect himself against imminent unlawful injury, the actor may not be convicted of more than a crime of recklessness or negligence; but, if the factfinder determines, to the contrary, that the actor did not honestly and sincerely hold the requisite belief under a claim of self-defense, the actor may not appeal to the doctrine of self-defense to avoid punishment, but will be subject to conviction for the commission of an intentional and knowing crime.

As stated earlier, the critical issue which a jury must decide in a case involving a claim of self-defense is whether or not the accused's belief that force is necessary to protect himself against imminent unlawful harm was reasonable. However, before the jury can make this determination, it must have a standard of reasonableness against which it can measure the accused's belief.

Courts have traditionally distinguished between standards of reasonableness by characterizing them as either "objective" or "subjective." An objective standard of reasonableness requires the factfinder to view the circumstances surrounding the accused at the time he used force from the standpoint of a hypothetical reasonable and prudent person. Ordinarily, under such a view, the unique physical and psychological characteristics of the accused are not taken into consideration in judging the reasonableness of the accused's belief.

This is not the case, however, where a subjective standard of reasonableness is employed. See State v. Wanrow, 88 Wash. 2d 221, 559 P.2d 548 (1977). Under the subjective standard the issue is not whether the circumstances attending the accused's use of force would be sufficient to create in the mind of a reasonable and prudent person the belief that the use of force is necessary to protect himself against immediate unlawful harm, but rather whether the circumstances are sufficient to induce in *the accused* an honest and reasonable belief that he must use force to defend himself against imminent harm.

Neither Section 12.1-05-03, nor Section 12.1-05-08, explicitly states the viewpoint which the factfinder should assume in assessing the reasonableness of an accused's belief. Moreover, this court has not yet decided the issue of whether Sections 12.1-05-03 and 12.1-05-08 should be construed as requiring an objective or subjective standard to measure the reasonableness of an accused's belief under a claim of self-defense. Finally, the legislative history of our self-defense statutes, as well as the commentaries to the codified criminal statutes which form the basis of the North Dakota Criminal Code, give no indication of a preference for an objective standard of reasonableness over a subjective standard, or vice versa.[7] . . .

Because (1) the law of self-defense as developed in past decisions of this court has been interpreted to require the use of a subjective standard of reasonableness [State v. Hazlett, 113 N.W. 371, 380-81 (1907); State v. Jacobs, 222 N.W.2d 586, 588-89 (N.D. 1974)], and (2) we agree with the court in *Hazlett* that a subjective standard is the more just, and (3) our current law of self-defense as codified in Sections 12.1-05-03, 12.1-05-7, and 12.1-05-08 does not require a contrary conclusion, that is to say, our current law of self-defense is consistent with either a subjective or objective standard, we now decide that the finder of fact must view the circumstances attending an accused's use of force from the standpoint of the accused to determine if they are sufficient to create in the accused's mind an honest and reasonable belief that the use of force is necessary to protect himself from imminent harm. . . .

The practical and logical consequence of this interpretation is that an accused's actions are to be viewed from the standpoint of a person whose mental and physical characteristics are like the accused's and who sees what the accused sees and knows what the accused knows. For example, if the accused is a timid, diminutive male, the factfinder must consider these characteristics in assessing the reasonableness of his belief. If, on the other hand, the accused is a strong, courageous, and capable female, the factfinder must consider these characteristics in judging the reasonableness of her belief.

In its statement of the law of self-defense, the trial court instructed the jury:

> The circumstances under which she acted must have been such as to produce in the mind of reasonably prudent persons, regardless of their sex, similarly situated, the reasonable belief that the other person was then about to kill her or do serious bodily harm to her.

In view of our decision today, the court's instruction was a misstatement of the law of self-defense. A correct statement of the law to be applied in a case of self-defense is:

> [A] defendant's conduct is not to be judged by what a reasonably cautious person might or might not do or consider necessary to do under the like circumstances, but what he himself in good faith honestly believed and had reasonable ground to believe was necessary for him to do to protect himself from apprehended death or great bodily injury.

The significance of the difference in viewing circumstances from the standpoint of the "defendant alone" rather than from the standpoint of a "reasonably cautious person" is that the jury's consideration of the unique physical and psychological characteristics of an accused allows the jury to judge the reasonableness of the accused's actions against the accused's subjective impressions of the need to use force rather than against those impressions which a jury determines that a hypothetical reasonably cautious person would have under similar circumstances. . . .

---

7. One defense in Chapter 12.1-05, N.D.C.C., which involves an objective standard, is entrapment. In Section 12.1-05-11(2), N.D.C.C., the Legislature, by the specific words "likely to cause *normally law-abiding persons* to commit the offense," eliminated the subjective test for that defense.

Hence, a correct statement of the law of self-defense is one in which the court directs the jury to assume the physical and psychological properties peculiar to the accused, viz., to place itself as best it can in the shoes of the accused, and then decide whether or not the particular circumstances surrounding the accused at the time he used force were sufficient to create in his mind a sincere and reasonable belief that the use of force was necessary to protect himself from imminent and unlawful harm. . . .

Leidholm argued strongly at trial that her stabbing of Chester was done in self-defense and in reaction to the severe mistreatment she received from him over the years. Because the court's instruction in question is an improper statement of the law concerning a vital issue in Leidholm's defense, we conclude it amounts to reversible error requiring a new trial.

III

Although we decide that this case must be sent back to the district court for a new trial, there still remain several other issues raised by Leidholm on appeal which must be addressed to ensure a proper disposition of the case on remand.

Expert testimony was presented at trial on what has come to be commonly referred to as the "battered woman syndrome." Such testimony generally explains the "phenomenon" as one in which a regular pattern of spouse abuse[8] creates in the battered spouse low self-esteem and a "learned helplessness," i.e., a sense that she cannot escape from the abusive relationship she has become a part of. See Comment, The Admissibility of Expert Testimony on the Battered Woman Syndrome in Support of a Claim of Self-Defense, 15 Conn. L. Rev. 121 (1982).

The expert witness in this case testified that Janice Leidholm was the victim in a battering relationship which caused her to suffer battered woman syndrome manifested by (1) a psychological condition of low self-esteem and (2) a psychological state of "learned helplessness." On the basis of the expert testimony, Leidholm offered the following proposed instruction on battered woman syndrome:

> A condition known or described by certain witnesses as the "battered wife syndrome" if shown by the evidence to have existed in the accused at the time she allegedly committed the crime charged, is not of itself a defense. However, as a general rule, whether an accused was assaulted by the victim of the homicide prior to the commission of a fatal act by the accused may have relevance in determining the issue of self-defense.
>
> Whenever the actual existence of any particular purpose, motive or intent is a necessary element to the commission of any particular species or degree of crime, you may take into consideration evidence that the accused was or had been assaulted by the victim in determining the purpose, motive or intent with which the act was committed.
>
> Thus, in the crime of murder of which the accused is charged in this case, specific intent is a necessary element of the crime. So, evidence the accused acted or failed to act while suffering the condition known as the "battered wife syndrome" may be considered by the jury in determining whether or not the accused

---

8. Typically, the pattern begins with a tension-building phase, followed by an intermediate phase where one spouse physically, with undoubted psychological effects, abuses the other, and a final phase where the battering spouse feels remorse for his actions and then attempts to "make up" with the battered spouse.

acted in self-defense. The weight to be given the evidence on that question, and the significance to attach to it in relation to all the other evidence in the case, are for you the jury to determine.

The court's refusal to include the proposed instruction in its charge to the jury, Leidholm contends, was error.

The instruction on battered woman syndrome was designed to support Leidholm's claim of self-defense by focusing the jury's attention on the psychological characteristics common to women who are victims in abusive relationships, and by directing the jury that it may consider evidence that the accused suffered from battered woman syndrome in determining whether or not she acted in self-defense. The instruction correctly points out that battered woman syndrome is *not of itself* a defense. In other words, "The existence of the syndrome in a marriage does not of itself establish the legal right of the wife to kill the husband, the evidence must still be considered in the context of self-defense." . . .

There is nothing in the proposed instruction at issue which would add to or significantly alter a correct instruction on the law of self-defense. The jury's use of a subjective standard of reasonableness in applying the principles of self-defense to the facts of a particular case requires it to consider expert testimony, once received in evidence, describing battered woman syndrome and the psychological effects it produces in the battered spouse when deciding the issue of *the existence* and *reasonableness* of the accused's belief that force was necessary to protect herself from imminent harm. If an instruction given is modeled after the law of self-defense which we adopt today, the court need not include a specific instruction on battered woman syndrome in its charge to the jury.

IV

An inseparable and essential part of our law of self-defense limits the use of deadly force to situations in which its use is necessary to protect the actor against death or serious bodily injury. However, the use of deadly force by an actor in self-defense is not justified if a retreat from the assailant can be accomplished with safety to the actor and others. Thus, before, it can be said that the use of deadly force is "necessary" to protect the actor against death or serious injury, it must first be the case that the actor cannot retreat from the assailant with safety to himself and others. In short, the use of deadly force is not necessary (and therefore not justified) within the meaning of our law of self-defense unless the actor has no safe avenue of retreat.

The practical effect of this statement is that the jury must first satisfy itself that an actor could not safely retreat before it can find that the actor's use of deadly force was necessary to protect himself against death or serious injury. And the way in which the jury determines whether or not the actor could not retreat safely is by considering whether or not the actor honestly and reasonably believed that he could not retreat from his attacker with safety. . . .

The duty to retreat, however, is not a rule without exceptions. Section 12.1-05-07(2)(b), N.D.C.C., provides, in part:

> (2) *no person is required to retreat from his dwelling*, or place of work, *unless* he was the original aggressor or *is assailed by a person who he knows also dwells* or works *there*. (Emphasis added.)

Included within the trial court's instruction to the jury on the law of self-defense was a statement roughly equivalent to the underscored language above. Leidholm maintains that the principle stated by this language violates the Equal Protection Clause, the Due Process Clause, and the Privileges and Immunities Clause of Article 14, Section 1, of the Amendments to the United States Constitution. Her argument seems to be that making an individual's duty to retreat from his dwelling dependent upon the status of the assailant unduly discriminates against the accused if the attacker is a cohabitant. We find no merit in this argument.

If the facts and circumstances attending a person's use of deadly force against an assailant who is a cohabitant are sufficient to create in his own mind an honest and reasonable belief that he cannot retreat from the assailant with safety to himself and others, his use of deadly force is justified or excused, and his failure to retreat is of no consequence.

This is a certain corollary to the guiding principle in our law of self-defense that the reasonableness of an accused's belief is to be measured against the accused's subjective impressions and not against the impressions which a jury might determine to be objectively reasonable.

Leidholm also argues it was error for the trial court to instruct the jury that manslaughter is a lesser included offense of murder.

Whether or not a lesser included offense instruction on manslaughter is appropriate in a murder trial depends upon the particular facts and circumstances of the case. We have no question that the court's instruction on manslaughter was warranted in this case.

Moreover, any time the court instructs a jury on self-defense, it must of necessity include a special instruction on manslaughter as well as an instruction on negligent homicide. The difference between self-defense and manslaughter is the reasonableness of the accused's belief that the use of force is necessary to prevent imminent unlawful harm. If the accused's belief is reasonable, he will be found to have acted in self-defense. If unreasonable, he is guilty of either manslaughter or negligent homicide, depending upon whether his belief was held recklessly or negligently, respectively. . . .

The judgment of conviction is reversed and the case is remanded to the district court of McLean County for a new trial.[9]

Notes and Questions

1. Did Janice Leidholm have any choice, other than to choose between her life and her husband's? Can she plausibly argue that she reasonably believed her life was in imminent danger if her husband was asleep when she killed him? Were there any avenues of retreat, literally or figuratively, that she could have yet explored? Did she face *imminent* death or grievous harm? By what standard of

---

9. [After the case was reversed, Ms. Leidholm worked out a plea agreement under which she would plead guilty to manslaughter but could not be sentenced to more than one year imprisonment with three months suspended. She would also get credit for the time she had already spent in jail, some 76 days. A sentencing hearing was then held at which she presented evidence to the judge that her sentence should be less than specified in the agreement. The judge agreed and gave her a suspended sentence. — Ed.]

behavior is she to be judged? What led the jurors to convict Janice of manslaughter, rather than either convicting her of manslaughter or wholly acquitting her?

2. To put these issues in more technical terms, consider the component questions that Leidholm's self-defense claim posed for the jury:

- Did Janice actually face a threat of death or grievous bodily harm? An imminent threat?
- Did she reasonably perceive that she faced such a threat? That it was imminent?
- Did she correctly infer that killing Chester was necessary to save her from death or grievous harm? That it was necessary on this very evening?
- Did she at least reasonably infer that killing Chester was necessary to save her from death or grievous harm? That it was necessary on this very evening?

Now review the instructions the jury received in the case. How did the instructions affect their answers to these questions? According to the appellate court, how did it wrongly affect those answers? How would the correct instructions properly influence the jury's answers? How would the admission or exclusion of the expert testimony in this case affect the answers to these questions?

By the way, how is it relevant that both Janice and Chester were intoxicated the night of the killing?

3. Now, what does the court mean by a "subjective" standard? Does the word "subjective" actually describe the standard the court adopts? Must the defendant still act "reasonably" in some sense? What other legal standards does this so-called "subjective" standard resemble? For example, which of the standards for heat-of-passion manslaughter in Chapter 5, pp. 339-349, *supra*.

4. *Justification or excuse?* Does Leidholm's self-defense argument amount to a justification or an excuse? What consequences follow from answering this question one way or the other?

Recall the discussion in this chapter's introduction of the reasons for and against distinguishing justification from excuse. One commentator offers a further reason for upholding the justification/excuse distinction, in the context of a battered spouse case:[10]

> [T]he feminist theory starts with the premise that battered women's acts of self-defense are justifiable rather than merely excusable. Although both excusable and justifiable self-defense fully pardon the defendant from criminal liability, an important ideological distinction separates the two. Society holds an excusable act to be wrong, but tolerates it because of the actor's state of mind. The actor claims "I couldn't help myself," or "I didn't mean to do it." Society perceives a justified act of self-defense as correct and even laudable behavior. Unlike excuse, justification posits the act as right, and therefore not condemnable; the substance of the deed rather than the person's state of mind is at issue.
>
> Whether society justifies a woman for taking a man's life while defending herself or excuses her for thinking she was worth defending is crucial for battered women. By focusing on the actor as wrong but pardonable, excusable self-defense would imply that her response was typically and idiosyncratically emotional. The doctrine would perpetuate the views that the woman could not have been rational

---

10. Phyllis Crocker, The Meaning of Equality for Battered Women Who Kill Men in Self-Defense, 8 Harv. Women's L.J. 121, 130-31 (1985).

in assessing the danger and that the legal system must compensate for her mental and physical weaknesses.

Justification, on the other hand, would assume that society values a woman's and a man's lives equally, and thus considers women's lives worthy of self-defense. It would recognize that a woman has the capacity to correctly and reasonably perceive that the act is warranted, legitimate, and justified. Justification would encourage, indeed would compel, a legal recognition that a woman's capacity for reasonable judgment — comparable to that of a man's — can be the basis for engaging in the "correct behavior" of self-defense.

5. *Gender and the self-defense instruction.* A leading case on the battered woman defense claim is State v. Wanrow, 88 Wash. 2d 221, 559 P.2d 548 (1977), cited by the court in *Leidholm.* In *Wanrow* the jury received the following instruction:

> However, when there is no reasonable ground for the person attacked to believe that his person is in imminent danger of death or great bodily harm, and it appears to him that only an ordinary battery is all that is intended, and all that he has reasonable grounds to fear from his assailant, he has a right to stand his ground and repel such threatened assault, yet he has no right to repel a threatened assault with naked hands, by the use of a deadly weapon in a deadly manner, unless he believes, and has reasonable grounds to believe, that he is in imminent danger of death or great bodily harm.

The court rejected the instruction as erroneous and prejudicial:

> The second paragraph of instruction No. 10 not only establishes an objective standard, but through the persistent use of the masculine gender leaves the jury with the impression the objective standard to be applied is that applicable to an altercation between two men. The impression created — that a 5 ft. 4 in. woman with a cast on her leg and using a crutch must, under the law, somehow repel an assault by a 6 ft. 2 in. intoxicated man without employing weapons in her defense, unless the jury finds her determination of the degree of danger to be objectively reasonable — constitutes a separate and distinct misstatement of the law and, in the context of this case, violates the respondent's right to equal protection of the law. The respondent was entitled to have the jury consider her actions in the light of her own perceptions of the situation, including those perceptions which were the product of our nation's "long and unfortunate history of sex discrimination." Frontiero v. Richardson, 411 U.S. 677, 684 (1973). Until such time as the effects of that history are eradicated, care must be taken to assure that our self-defense instructions afford women the right to have their conduct judged in light of the individual physical handicaps which are the product of sex discrimination. To fail to do so is to deny the right of the individual woman involved to trial by the same rules which are applicable to male defendants. . . . The portion of the instruction above quoted misstates our law in creating an objective standard of "reasonableness." It then compounds that error by utilizing language suggesting that the respondent's conduct must be measured against that of a reasonable male individual finding himself in the same circumstances.

In determining whether the jury would be influenced by the sexism the court found in this instruction, would it make a difference what portion of the jury consisted of women?

6. *The sleeping batterer.* Though many courts have followed *Leidholm* in permitting a broad reading of the self-defense concept for battered wives, others

have drawn one clear, hard line: They reject the defense when the husband is sleeping at the time the wife slays him. In State v. Norman, 378 S.E.2d 8 (N.C. 1988), the defendant shot her sleeping husband to death after 25 years of abuse (during which he beat her and forced her to work as a prostitute). Nevertheless, the North Carolina Supreme Court rejected the defendant's claim of self-defense:

> The evidence tended to show that no harm was "imminent" or about to happen to the defendant when she shot her husband. The uncontroverted evidence was that her husband had been asleep for some time when she walked to her mother's house, returned with the pistol, fixed the pistol after it jammed and then shot her husband three times in the back of the head. The defendant was not faced with an instantaneous choice between killing her husband or being killed or seriously injured. Instead, all of the evidence tended to show that the defendant had ample time and opportunity to resort to other means of preventing further abuse by her husband. There was no action underway by the decedent from which the jury could have found that the defendant had reasonable grounds to believe either that a felonious assault was imminent or that it might result in her death or great bodily injury. Additionally, no such action by the decedent had been underway immediately prior to his falling asleep.
>
> . . . The relaxed requirements for perfect self-defense proposed by our Court of Appeals would tend to categorically legalize the opportune killing of abusive husbands by their wives solely on the basis of the wives' testimony concerning their subjective speculation as to the probability of future felonious assaults by their husbands. Homicidal self-help would then become a lawful solution, and perhaps the easiest and most effective solution, to this problem. [Id. at 13-14.]

How does the North Carolina court's notion of "imminence" differ from that of the court in *Leidholm*?

In State v. Stewart, 763 P.2d 572 (Kan. 1988), the defendant had suffered severe physical and sexual abuse by her husband. The court noted, however, that she had exhibited great indecision as to whether to kill her husband, to flee him, to seek psychiatric help for herself, or to stay in the marriage. One evening, after her husband threatened her with violence and forced sex on her, he fell asleep, and she took his gun and killed him. The Kansas Supreme Court held that she was not entitled to a self-defense instruction.

> Here, however, there is an absence of imminent danger to defendant: Peggy told a nurse at the Oklahoma hospital of her desire to kill Mike. She later voluntarily agreed to return home with Mike when he telephoned her. She stated that after leaving the hospital Mike threatened to kill her if she left him again. Peggy showed no inclination to leave. In fact, immediately after the shooting, Peggy told the police that she was upset because she thought Mike would leave her. Prior to the shooting, Peggy hid the loaded gun. The cars were in the driveway and Peggy had access to the car keys. After being abused, Peggy went to bed with Mike at 8 P.M. Peggy lay there for two hours, then retrieved the gun from where she had hidden it and shot Mike while he slept.
>
> Under these facts, the giving of the self-defense instruction was erroneous. Under such circumstances, a battered woman cannot reasonably fear imminent life-threatening danger from her sleeping spouse. [Id. at 578.]

Is the court confounding different weaknesses in Mrs. Stewart's self-defense claim? If she did have reasonable grounds to believe that killing her husband was necessary to save her life, should it matter that he was sleeping? If she lacked such grounds, would it matter that he was awake?

7. *Does imminence really mean imminence?* Prof. Victoria Nourse argues that though the courts invoke "imminence" as a criterion because duration of time is an objective measure of necessity, "imminence" is in fact something of a red herring.[11] Surveying hundreds of court decisions from many jurisdictions over a 20-year period, Nourse identified those decisions purporting to resolve "imminence" issues and discovered that in a surprising majority, there was no meaningful issue of imminence at all, because the killing occurred during a direct confrontation. Rather, she concludes, courts use "imminence" as a code word for the possibility of retreat before confrontation occurred.

> It turns out that the battered women cases in my survey, like their male counterparts, raise imminence most often in confrontational situations, where the defendant kills when she sees a gun, where the victim is advancing, or during an actual brawl. If that is right, then the problem of the battered woman case may not be one of fact, but of law. We do not ask of the man in the barroom brawl that he leave the bar before the occurrence of an anticipated fight, but we do ask the battered woman threatened with a gun why she did not leave the relationship. If, when courts are saying "imminence," they import meanings that demand retreat *before* the confrontation, they are applying a rule that the law itself disavows (for any defendant). And, if that is right, we need not subjectify the law for the disfavored; instead, we must deal with the potential for objective rules to contradict themselves, to perpetuate meanings that they disavow.[12]

8. *Psychological harm.* Professor Charles Ewing offers a way of modifying the battered wife self-defense claim that sidesteps empirical questions about the battered wife's ability to measure her risk of death. He suggests a doctrine of "psychological self-defense [that] would justify the use of deadly force where such force appeared reasonably necessary to prevent the infliction of extremely serious psychological injury."[13] The latter is deemed as "gross and enduring impairment of one's psychological functioning that significantly limits the meaning and value of one's physical existence." Meeting the objection that a person's interest in physical existence must outweigh all other interests, Ewing responds that many of the conventional rules of self-defense — that a justified killing may be in response to a threat of serious injury and not death, or that under certain conditions the self-defender has no duty to retreat — already allow personal autonomy to outweigh physical existence in certain conflicts. Does Ewing meet the objection? Can you make other objections?

Ewing's proposal is anomalous in that it offers the battered spouse's psychological condition as the basis of a justification rather than an excuse. Would it be better to characterize the defense he proposes as an excuse?

9. *The manslaughter alternative.* What should the defendant in *Leidholm* be guilty of on retrial if the jury determines that she honestly, but unreasonably, believed her life was in imminent danger? Doesn't the Model Penal Code flatly provide in the first few lines of section 3.04(1) and again in the first few lines of

11. Victoria Nourse, Self-Defense and Subjectivity, 68 U. Chi. L. Rev. 1235 (2001).
12. Id. at 1237-38 (emphasis in original).
13. Psychological Self-Defense: A Proposed Justification for Battered Women Who Kill, 14 Law & Human Behavior 579, 587-89 (1990).

section 3.04(2)(b) that the defense is proper when the "actor believes" the force is necessary? In this regard, one must consider another relevant provision of the Code, section 3.09:

Section 3.09 . . . Reckless or Negligent Use of Otherwise Justifiable Force; . . .

(2) When the actor believes that the use of force upon or toward the person of another is necessary for any of the purposes for which such belief would establish a justification under Sections 3.03 to 3.08 but the actor is reckless or negligent in having such belief or in acquiring or failing to acquire any knowledge or belief which is material to the justifiability of his use of force, the justification afforded by those Sections is unavailable in a prosecution for an offense for which recklessness or negligence, as the case may be, suffices to establish culpability.

(3) When the actor is justified under Sections 3.03 to 3.08 in using force upon or toward the person of another but he recklessly or negligently injures or creates a risk of injury to innocent persons, the justification afforded by those Sections is unavailable in a prosecution for such recklessness or negligence towards innocent persons.

In addition, the Comments to section 3.04 explain this apparent discrepancy.[14]

Prevailing rules respecting self-defense, both common law and statutory, similarly demanded belief in the necessity of the defensive action. They usually added, however, a requirement of a reasonable ground for the belief, the precise statement of which varied somewhat with the jurisdiction. Two consequences followed for this requirement: (1) a mistaken belief in the necessity of force or the degree of force employed might suffice to exculpate; but (2) the actor's negligence in making the mistake might strip him of any defensive claim, thus permitting his conviction of a purposeful offense, even of murder.

The Model Code sections are grounded on the belief that the second consequence is wrong. Compare, for example, the actor who purposely kills in order to reap financial reward and the actor who purposely kills while believing in the existence of circumstances that would, if they actually existed, exonerate on self-defense grounds. If the second actor was mistaken — if the circumstances were not in fact as he believed them to be — it is unjust to view him as having the same level of culpability as the first actor. It is unjust to put him at that level even if he was negligent or reckless in forming his belief, though to be sure in that case it would be appropriate to view him as culpable. This lesser degree of culpability should not be left merely to influence prosecutorial decisions to seek lesser charges or judicial decisions to mitigate sentences, but should be reflected in the criminal code. If the actor was reckless or negligent as to the existence of circumstances that would justify his conduct, he should then be subject to conviction of a crime for which recklessness or negligence, as the case may be, is otherwise sufficient to establish culpability. Negligence in this context would permit a conviction of negligent homicide rather than purposeful murder, while recklessness would permit a conviction of manslaughter. The defendant should thus be classified according to the culpability he actually manifested toward the material elements[15] of his offense. This solution is worked out for Article 3 by Sections 3.09(2) and 3.02(2), and is also embodied as a general principle of liability in Section 2.02(10).

---

14. American Law Institute, Model Penal Code and Commentaries, Part I, §3.04, at 35-37.

15. The term "material element," as established by Section 1.13(9) and (10), includes such conduct, circumstances or results as negative an excuse or justification.

10. *The expert witness.* In Ibn-Tamas v. United States, 407 A.2d 626 (D.C. Ct. App. 1979), the defendant attempted to introduce expert testimony of Dr. Lenore Walker. Dr. Walker

> had studied 110 women who had been beaten by their husbands. Her studies revealed three consecutive phases in the relationships: "tension building," when there are small incidents of battering; "acute battering incident," when beatings are severe; and "loving-contrite," when the husband becomes very sorry and caring. Dr. Walker then testified that women in this situation typically are low in self-esteem, feel powerless, and have few close friends, since their husbands commonly "accuse[] them of all kinds of things with friends, and they are embarrassed. They don't want to cause their friends problems, too." Because there are periods of harmony, battered women tend to believe their husbands are basically loving, caring men; the women assume that they, themselves, are somehow responsible for their husbands' violent behavior. They also believe, however, that their husbands are capable of killing them, and they feel there is no escape. Unless a shelter is available, these women stay with their husbands, not only because they typically lack a means of self-support but also because they fear that if they leave they will be found and hurt even more. Dr. Walker stressed that wife batterers come from all racial, social and economic groups (including professionals), and that batterers commonly "escalate their abusiveness" when their wives are pregnant. She added that battered women are very reluctant to tell anyone that their husbands beat them. Of those studied, 60 percent had never done so before (Dr. Walker typically found them in hospitals), 40 percent had told a friend, and only 10 percent had called the police.
>
> When asked about appellant, whom she had interviewed, Dr. Walker replied that Mrs. Ibn-Tamas was a "classic case" of the battered wife. Dr. Walker added her belief that on the day of the killing, when Dr. Ibn-Tamas had been beating his wife despite protests that she was pregnant, Mrs. Ibn-Tamas' pregnancy had had a "major impact on the situation. . . . [T]hat is a particularly crucial time."
>
> Dr. Walker's testimony, therefore, arguably would have served at least two basic functions: (1) it would have enhanced Mrs. Ibn-Tamas' general credibility in responding to cross-examination designed to show that her testimony about the relationship with her husband was implausible; and (2) it would have supported her testimony that on the day of the shooting her husband's actions had provoked a state of fear which led her to believe she was in imminent danger ("I just knew he was going to kill me"), and thus responded in self-defense. Dr. Walker's contribution, accordingly, would have been akin to the psychiatric testimony admitted in the case of Patricia Hearst "to explain the effects kidnapping, prolonged incarceration, and psychological and physical abuse may have had on the defendant's mental state at the time of the robbery, insofar as such mental state is relevant to the asserted defense of coercion or duress." Dr. Walker's testimony would have supplied an interpretation of the facts which differed from the ordinary lay perception ("she could have gotten out, you know") advocated by the government.

The court reversed the trial judge's exclusion of Dr. Walker's testimony as a matter of law and sent the matter back for further hearings on the admissibility of her study.

A clear majority of states now permit the defendant to introduce expert testimony on the "battered woman syndrome" of the sort admitted in *Leidholm.* See State v. Hickson, 630 So. 2d 172 (Fla. 1993). But several courts impose the following limitation, described in State v. Hennum, 441 N.W.2d 793, 799 (Minn. 1989):

> In allowing the admission of battered woman syndrome evidence, we set some limits on the use of expert testimony on this subject. We hold that in future cases

expert testimony regarding battered woman syndrome will be limited to a description of the general syndrome and the characteristics which are present in an individual suffering from the syndrome. The expert should not be allowed to testify as to the ultimate fact that the particular defendant actually suffers from battered woman syndrome. This determination must be left to the trier of fact. Each side may present witnesses who may testify to characteristics possessed by the defendant which are consistent with those found in someone suffering from battered woman syndrome. This restriction will remove the need for a compelled adverse medical examination of the defendant. Since the expert will only be allowed to testify as to the general nature of battered woman syndrome, neither side need conduct an examination of the defendant.

Does the distinction between "general" and "particular" evidence offered here make a practical difference? Will a jury overly defer to an expert who testifies as to the defendant's actual state of mind?

Critique of expert testimony. Despite courts' widespread acceptance of BWS testimony, Dr. Walker's research has not escaped criticism for methodological flaws that may reduce its viability under the usual evidentiary criteria for admission of expert testimony. Among the criticisms are that Walker's selection of subjects contained no control group of women who were not battered, while on the other hand none of her subjects was ever charged with criminal violence; that Walker lumped together scores for such variables as fear, anxiety, depression, and hostility, rather than test their separate effects; that subjects were asked leading questions; and that the study lacked objective measures of the time frame for the emotional cycle that Walker describes.[16] And reviewing these empirical critiques, Prof. Alafair Burke has argued that Walker's findings do not logically support her theory of "learned helplessness."[17]

... Walker's battered woman syndrome ultimately fails to provide a satisfactory explanation for why the battered woman kills during a non-confrontational moment. If one believes the cycle theory of violence, then one believes that the victim of domestic violence endures a constant and heightened fear of abuse, even if her batterer is peaceful or even sleeping. If one also believes the theory of learned helplessness, then one believes that the domestic violence victim is not only living in a constant reign of terror, but also suffering from a cognitive incapacity to recognize any method of escape. One would expect, therefore, the domestic violence victim to remain passive even when her batterer is seemingly calm or even sleeping, because she nonetheless is fearful of an imminent attack and because of her incapacity to recognize the ability to do anything other than remain passive. . . .

... Walker has difficulty explaining why the woman's cognitive priority suddenly shifts from survival skills within the abusive relationship to escape skills that require use of force to survive outside the relationship.

Walker's likely explanation for the discrepancy between the passivity connoted by the learned helplessness theory and the action necessary to act in self-defense is that the battered woman who kills does so not because of her learned helplessness, but because she has overcome it. Walker, for example, concludes that women leave abusive relationships when they become more angered, disgusted,

16. David Faigman, Note, The Battered Woman Syndrome and Self-Defense: A Legal and Empirical Dissent, 72 Va. L. Rev. 619, 636-43 (1986); see also David Faigman and Amy Wright, The Battered Woman Syndrome in the Age of Science, 39 Ariz. L. Rev. 67, 109-110 (1997).

17. Alafair Burke, Rational Actors, Self-Defense, and Duress: Making Sense, Not Syndromes, Out of the Battered Woman, 81 North Carolina L. Rev. 211, 245-46 (2002).

and hostile, and less fearful, anxious, and depressed. Walker acknowledges, however, that her findings "do not indicate why some women become disgusted and angry enough to leave a relationship and others do not." [Lenore E. Walker, The Battered Woman Syndrome 89 (1984)]. Similarly, Walker's findings fail to explain why some women kill their abusers and others remain in a battering relationship to their peril.

More importantly, though, Walker's conclusion that a woman's passivity ends when she overcomes learned helplessness does little to assist women like Norman and Hennum. If the battered woman has overcome her learned helplessness and can appreciate exit options, then the syndrome fails to explain why she exercises the option of deadly force. Additionally, if Walker's explanation for the shift from passivity to action is that the woman's emotions have shifted to anger, disgust, and hostility, then the use of force would appear to be out of revenge rather than the need for self-protection.[18]

But Prof. Burke by no means rejects the battered wife defense. Rather, she argues that if we recognize the actual impediments to safe escape for battered wives (such as the lack of sufficient shelters or police protection), and if we relax the requirement of "imminence" in favor of a broadened view of "necessity," then conventional self-defense doctrine can quite well accommodate the battered wife:

> . . . A woman's participation in an abusive relationship can be understood without depicting domestic violence victims as homogenous, irrational, and cognitively impaired. In light of individual factual circumstances that vary from woman to woman, a domestic violence victim's decision to remain in a battering relationship may not evidence cognitive incapacity. It may, in fact, demonstrate that the woman is a rational actor making a reasoned decision based upon an evaluation of her viable escape options and the value she assigns to competing priorities.
>
> Viewing battered women as rational actors choosing among options that are limited by their factual circumstances has ramifications for their self-defense and duress claims. The doctrinal impediment for battered women who used defensive force during non-confrontational moments has been the requirement of a reasonable fear of imminent harm. The prevailing approach uses the fiction of battered woman syndrome as a means to argue that domestic violence victims meet this requirement. An alternative approach, however, is to question directly the requirement of "imminency" and change the scope of self-defense to encompass justified uses of force.[19]

If Burke's reconstruction of the data on battered women is correct, is she right that the "rational" battered wife defense will be as legally effective as the approach she criticizes?

11. *Duty to retreat.* The defendant in *Leidholm* argued that the trial judge's instruction on retreat was defective. Why have a retreat rule? If we are going to have one, why create a dwelling exception? If we do not ordinarily require self-defenders to retreat from their homes, why do so where the attacker lives there, too?

---

18. Burke concludes, that, ironically, the "learned helplessness" theory espoused by Walker would far more logically support a defense theory of duress in cases where the battered spouse is coerced by the batterer into committing crimes against third persons. Id. at 250-66; we consider the battered wife and the duress defense, see pp. 576-78, *infra.*

19. Burke, *supra,* note 17, at 266-69.

According to Professor George Dix:[20]

> The rationale for the retreat rule is not difficult to ascertain, at least in part. It rests upon the view that human life, even the life of an aggressor, is sufficiently important that it should be preserved when to do so requires only the sacrifice of the much less important interest in standing one's ground (Model Penal Code, 1958, §3.04).
>
> Opponents of a retreat requirement urge that, at least on some occasions, compelling a threatened person to retreat or punishing such a person for not retreating involves an exceptionally grievous insult to the person's dignity that should be avoided. Further, while human life is unquestionably of major value, one who assaults another under circumstances justifying deadly force in response can reasonably be regarded as having forfeited as least some of the respect to which most persons and their lives are entitled.
>
> *When retreat is required.* The traditional retreat rule contains a clear exception for attack in one's own residential premises — one's "castle." A person assaulted in his dwelling need not retreat before using deadly force, even if a safe opportunity exists. Modern developments have raised significant question as to the meaning of this exception and its scope. Perhaps the most frequent question is whether one is required to retreat when assaulted in one's business premises. A majority of courts have expanded the "castle" exception to cover business premises, apparently on the assumption that the indignity of being compelled to flee one's place of business is little different from being forced to flee from one's home. When one is attacked on the porch of one's home, must one, under the rule, retreat at least into the structure? . . . Modern apartment living presents further difficulties. For example, must one who is accosted in an apartment-house hallway at least retreat into his or her own apartment? . . .
>
> *Requirement of safe retreat.* Those jurisdictions requiring retreat apply the requirement only when the defendant has an opportunity to retreat in safety. The case of Commonwealth v. Eberle, 474 Pa. 548, 379 A.2d 90 (1977), illustrates the tendency to hold the prosecution to a substantial showing of a safe opportunity. Eberle's assailant, while intoxicated, lunged at her, and she stabbed him with the knife she had in her hand. Evidence introduced at trial showed that to reach the door of the apartment in which the assault occurred, she would have had to go around a corner. The apartment was cluttered, and diagrams introduced into evidence showed that there were some objects between the defendant and the doorway. There was no indication that the door was unlocked and could be easily opened in a hurry, and no evidence demonstrated that once Eberle got into the hallway outside the apartment she would be in a place of safety. In light of these considerations, and assuming a duty to retreat existed, the court concluded that the prosecution had failed to show that an opportunity to retreat in safety had been presented.
>
> *The Model Penal Code and the retreat rule.* Although the retreat rule remains a minority one among American jurisdictions, it received significant impetus when it was incorporated into the Model Penal Code (1962) as Section 3.04(2)(b)(ii). Modern American statutory formulations of self-defense vary. A number embody the retreat requirement; others do not. . . .
>
> Despite the Model Penal Code's effort to breathe new vigor into the traditionally minority position, the retreat rule seems likely to wither. While society is undoubtedly developing greater sensitivity for human life and less sympathy for extrajudicial battles to resolve disputes, there is also an increasing willingness to trust juries and to avoid complex and arguably inflexible rules designed to reduce

20. Justification: Self-Defense, Encyclopedia of Crime and Justice 948-49 (1983).

jury discretion. It is likely that [in the future] no absolute duty to retreat will be formally imposed. Juries, however, will be told to consider any failure to make use of retreat opportunities in evaluating the reasonableness of responding to attacks with deadly force.

12. *Some historical background.* In Erwin v. State, 29 Ohio St. 186, 199 (1876), the Supreme Court of Ohio rejected the duty to retreat in famous language:

The law, out of tenderness for human life and the frailty of human nature, will not permit the taking of it to repel mere trespass, or even to save a life where the assault is provoked; but a true man who is without fault is not obliged to fly from an assailant, who by violence or surprise maliciously seeks to take his life or do him enormous bodily harm.

And in Runyan v. State, 57 Ind. 80 (1877), the court rejected any duty to retreat as well, saying that a broad right of self-defense is "founded on the law of nature; and is not, nor can be, superseded by any law of society." And more specifically, the court said that "the tendency of the American mind seems to be very strongly against" any duty to retreat — perhaps suggesting that retreat is un-American cowardice. These and other authorities were approvingly summarized in the first Justice Harlan's opinion in Beard v. United States, 158 U.S. 550 (1895), relieving assaulted killers of any obligation to retreat. The historical significance of this distinctly American doctrine is discussed by Richard Maxwell Brown:[21]

The English common-law "duty to retreat" was a powerful means to produce a society of civility, for obedience to the duty to retreat — really a duty to flee from the scene altogether or, failing that, to retreat to the wall at one's back — meant that in the vast majority of disputes no fatal outcome would occur. . . .

In a minority of American states the English common-law doctrine of duty to retreat did survive, but one of the most important transformations in American legal and social history occurred in the nineteenth century when the nation as a whole repudiated the English common-law tradition in favor of the American theme of no duty to retreat: that one was legally justified in standing one's ground to kill in self-defense. . . . The centuries-long English legal severity against homicide was replaced in our country by a proud new tolerance for killing in situations where it might have been avoided by obeying a legal duty to retreat. This undoubtedly had an impact on our homicide rate, helping to make it the highest on earth among our peer group of the modern, industrialized nations of the world. It is impossible to say how many lives have been lost in this country as a result of the change in the law from the duty to retreat to the legal right to stand one's ground, but the toll of victims during the nineteenth and twentieth centuries may well be, indirectly but significantly, in the tens of thousands. . . .

In his 1762 essay on homicide, Foster declared . . . that "the injured party may repel force by force in defence of his person" against one attempting to commit a felony — such as a robbery or murder — upon him. In such a case, wrote Foster, the self-defender was not "obliged to retreat" but might "pursue his adversary till he findeth himself out of danger, and if in a conflict between them he happeneth to kill, such killing is justifiable." In 1803, another English commentator, Edward Hyde East, echoed Foster's view. . . .

. . . [T]he Foster-East doctrine had no practical impact in England, whose Criminal Law Act of 1967 retained the age-old duty to retreat, but such an impact

21. No Duty to Retreat: Violence and Values in American History and Society 4-30 (1991).

soon occurred in America. In a Massachusetts case of 1806, Commonwealth v. Selfridge, the Foster-East mitigation of duty to retreat was cited and upheld. . . .

Bishop followed Foster and East in the turn away from the duty to retreat. Indeed, Bishop was such an ardent exponent of the Americanized doctrine of no duty to retreat that he wrote that "if a man murderously attacked by another flies instead of resisting, he commits substantially [the] offense of misprision of felony." Bishop [implied] that the law did not give one the option of flight or resistance but, rather, commanded resistance. . . .

. . . Two of the most influential state supreme court stipulations of no duty to retreat came in 1876 and 1877, respectively, in the "true man" and "American mind" decisions from Ohio and Indiana. . . .

The language of the supreme court in Ohio with its emphasis on the action of a "true man" and of the Indiana court with its repudiation of what it saw as legalized cowardice illustrates a running theme in the language of the American state supreme court judges who grappled with the issue of the duty to retreat versus standing one's ground: a concern for the values of masculine bravery in a frontier nation.

For example, in an earlier case focusing on the retreat requirement, a Tennessee judge had scathingly referred to the defendant, a hunter named Grainger, as a "timid, cowardly man," and this case, Grainger v. State (1830) — which significantly increased the right of violent self-defense — was ever after referred to as the "timid hunter" case.

In State v. Bartlett (1902), the Missouri court viewed standing one's ground as a sacred right of human liberty "as dear in the eye of the law" as human life and magisterially declared that the "idea of the nonnecessity of retreating from any locality where one has the right to be is growing in favor, as all doctrines based upon sound reason inevitably will." . . . Taking the highest ground of all was the Wisconsin supreme court, which in 1909 announced that self-defense was a "divine right" by which a man might "stand his ground" in preference to the obsolete "flight rule" embodying the "ancient doctrine" of Blackstone and "early common-law writers." "Retreat to the wall," said the court, "may well have been all right in the days of chivalry, so called" but "has been pretty generally" and "in this state very definitely, abandoned."

The line of cases viewing the duty to retreat as "un-American" seems to have culminated in Justice Holmes's opinion in Brown v. United States, 256 U.S. 335 (1921), where, perhaps motivated by his own brutal experiences as a Union soldier in several devastating Civil War battles,[22] Holmes famously said: "Detached reflection cannot be demanded in the presence of an uplifted knife." Id. at 343.

13. *Focus on the dwelling context.* The dwelling exception to the retreat rule has its own venerable history in those states that otherwise do require retreat. In New York v. Tomlins, 107 N.E. 496, 497-98 (N.Y. 1914), the defendant claimed self-defense when attacked in his home by his son. In reversing the defendant's conviction because the duty to retreat instruction was given, Justice Cardozo explained the historical basis of the privilege of nonretreat from the home:

It is not now and never has been the law that a man assailed in his own dwelling is bound to retreat. If assailed there, he may stand his ground and resist the attack. He is under no duty to take to the fields and the highways, a fugitive from his own home. More than 200 years ago it was said by Lord Chief Justice Hale: In case a man "is assailed in his own house, he need not flee as far as he can, as in other cases

22. See id. at 34-36.

of se defendendo, for he hath the protection of his house to excuse him from flying, as that would be to give up the protection of his house to his adversary by flight." Flight is for sanctuary and shelter, and shelter, if not sanctuary, is in the home. . . . The rule is the same whether the attack proceeds from some other occupant or from an intruder. [Id. at 497-98.]

See Stuart Green, Castles and Carjackers: Proportionality and the Use of Deadly Force in Defense of Dwellings and Vehicles, 1999 Ill. L. Rev. 1 (enumerating the foundations of the right to use deadly force in defense of premises: a person's special vulnerability in his or her home; a distinct privileged property interest; the threat to privacy and dignity as in rape and kidnapping, and the need for maximum deterrence of unjustified aggression; and arguing that it is some aggregation of these that legitimates the right).

Co-occupants and retreat. But must a person threatened with death or grievous harm retreat from her own residence when the attacker shares the residence? In Cooper v. United States, 512 A. 2d 1002 (D.C. App. 1986), the defendant killed his brother in the apartment they shared with their mother. The court held that Cooper was not entitled to a "castle" instruction:

> Indeed, all co-occupants, even those unrelated by blood or marriage, have a heightened obligation to treat each other with a degree of tolerance and respect. That obligation does not evaporate when one co-occupant disregards it and attacks another. [Id. at 1006.]

But in recent years the phenomenon of the battered wife has come to undo that exception to the residence exception to the retreat rule. In Weiand v. State, 732 So. 2d 1044 (Fla. 1999), where a wife shot her abusive husband to death in their home, the trial court only gave the instruction applicable in all self-defense cases regarding the duty to retreat:

> The fact that the defendant was wrongfully attacked cannot justify her use of force likely to cause death or great bodily harm if by retreating she could have avoided the need to use that force. [Id. at 1048.]

Moreover, the prosecutor's closing argument stressed:

> She had to exhaust every reasonable means of escape prior to killing him. Did she do that? No. Did she use the phone that was two feet away? No. Did she go out the door that her baby was sitting next to? No. Did she get in the car that she had driven all over town drinking and boozing it up all day? No. [Id. at 1048-1049.]

Reversing the conviction, the court held that Weiand indeed had a privilege not to retreat here, noting that otherwise it would be allowing the anomaly, for example, that a mother facing attack from her 19-year-old son would have to retreat from her home if he lived in the home, but not if he happened to live elsewhere.

> However, the privilege of nonretreat from the home stems not from the sanctity of property rights, but from the time-honored principle that the home is the ultimate sanctuary. As has been asked rhetorically, if the duty to retreat from the home is applied to a defendant attacked by a co-occupant in the home, "whither shall he

flee, and how far, and when may he be permitted to return?" Jones v. Alabama, 76 Ala. 8, 16 (Ala. 1884).

The omission of the jury instruction on the privilege of nonretreat from the home is not cured by the jury instruction given in all self-defense cases that there is no legal duty to retreat if retreating would increase the danger of death or great bodily harm. [This instruction was] incomplete because, without the privilege of nonretreat instruction, the jury may have believed that the defendant had a duty to retreat from her home. . . .

Studies show that women who retreat from the residence when attacked by their co-occupant spouse or boyfriend may, in fact, increase the danger of harm to themselves due to the possibility of attack after separation. According to Dr. Lenore Walker, "[t]he batterer would often rather kill, or die himself, than separate from the battered woman." Lenore E. Walker, Terrifying Love: Why Battered Women Kill and How Society Responds 65 (1989). . . . A leading expert in the field cites one study which revealed that forty-five percent of the murders of women "were generated by the man's 'rage over the actual or impending estrangement from his partner.'" Donald G. Dutton, The Batterer: A Psychological Profile 15 (1995). . . . [Id. at 1052-1053.]

The court then went on to consider "the views of jurists in the minority position, who have expressed a concern that eliminating a duty to retreat from the residence will actually increase violence." The court added:

> While there may be more opportunities for violence in the domestic setting, no empirical data has been presented, either through expert testimony or studies, demonstrating any correlation between eliminating a duty to retreat from the home and an increase in incidents of domestic violence. In contrast, a duty to retreat from the home adversely affects victims of domestic violence by placing them at greater risk of death or great bodily harm. [Id. at 1056.]

The court finally resolved the key instructional issue as follows:

> Nonetheless, we conclude that [a] "middle ground" instruction . . . satisfies any concern that eliminating a duty to retreat might invite violence. This instruction imposes a limited duty to retreat within the residence to the extent reasonably possible, but no duty to flee the residence. Accordingly, we adopt the following instruction:
>
> > If the defendant was attacked in [his/her] own home, or on [his/her] own premises, by a co-occupant [or any other person lawfully on the premises] [he/she] had a duty to retreat to the extent reasonably possible without increasing [his/her] own danger of death or great bodily harm. However, the defendant was not required to flee [his/her] home and had the lawful right to stand [his/her] ground and meet force with force even to the extent of using force likely to cause death or great bodily harm if it was necessary to prevent death or great bodily harm to [himself/herself]. [Id. at 1056-1057.]

Weiand now represents the view of the majority of states that otherwise would specifically require retreat from one's dwelling when attacked by a legal co-occupant.[23] The Minnesota Supreme Court has noted a pragmatic reason for

---

23. Only a few states now impose a duty to retreat when attacked in the home by a co-occupant or invited guest. See, e.g., State v. Shaw, 441 A.2d 561 (Conn. 1981); Oney v. Commonwealth, 9 S.W.2d 723 (Ky. 1928); State v. Grierson, 69 A.2d 851 (N.H. 1949); State v. Crawford, 66 S.E. 110 (W. Va. 1909); State v. Ordway, 619 A.2d 819 (R.I. 1992).

joining this majority, approving this as a "bright-line rule" which "eliminates the need to define and differentiate between residents, non-residents, invited guests, unwanted guests, etc., because the status of the aggressor is irrelevant." State v. Glowacki, 630 N.W.2d 392, 400 (Minn. 2001). Similarly, the Model Penal Code, which recognizes a duty to retreat under most circumstances, does not impose a duty to retreat when necessary to defend against death or great bodily harm from a co-occupant of the dwelling. Model Penal Code §3.04(2)(b) (ii)(A), commentary at 56 (1985). Conversely, Massachusetts, New Jersey, and North Dakota have statutes imposing a duty to retreat when attacked in the home by someone with a legal right to be on the premises.[24]

14. *The sociology of battering.* For striking insights on domestic violence, see Neil Jacobson and John Gottman, When Men Batter Women (1998). This study of abusive males finds two distinct types: "Pit Bulls" and "Cobras." "Pit Bulls" confine their violent behavior to those they love; they feel deep jealousy, fear abandonment, and try to deprive partners of independence; are prone to rage, stalking, and public attacks; become physiologically aroused in argument; have some potential for rehabilitation, are more likely to have had abusive fathers, and less likely to have criminal records. By contrast, "cobras" are aggressive toward all people — and even pets; they are not emotionally dependent, but do want their partners to cater to all desires; they threaten with knives or guns; calm down internally as they become more aggressive; are difficult to treat with therapy; and are more likely to have criminal records and to abuse drugs or alcohol. "Pit bulls" are easier to leave in the short run but in the long run are more dangerous; they are the ones who shoot their spouses on the courthouse steps. By contrast, once a woman escapes a "cobra," he likely will go on to a new conquest.

A recent study by the Bureau of Justice Statistics shows significant declines in two key areas of domestic violence. The rate at which women suffered criminal violence declined between 1993 and 2001; and the number of men killed by intimate partners declined by almost 40 percent in this period.[25]

> "We have made significant increases in providing shelters, hot lines and restraining orders to protect battered spouses and mandatory arrest for domestic violence incidents," said Professor James Alan Fox of Northeastern University in Boston . . . We've given wives alternatives to feeling like they have to pick up a loaded gun to kill their loaded husbands," Fox said. "Divorce is easier."[26]

Nevertheless, in the year 2000 1,247 women and 440 men were killed by intimate partners; about 33 percent of female murder victims were killed by intimate partners, and 4 percent of male murder victims.

15. *The battered wife "contractor."* While some states have allowed self-defense claims based on battered woman syndrome even if the husband was sleeping at the time of the killing, as yet no states have allowed it in cases where the battered wife hired contract killers. In People v. Yaklich, 833 P.2d 758 (Wash. 1991), the court held that if Donna Yaklich hired two men to kill her husband, her situation lacked the "imminence" of violence necessary for a self-defense claim.

---

24. See Mass. Gen. Laws ch. 278, §8A (1998); N.J. Stat. Ann. §2C:3-4b(2)(b)(i) (West 1998); N.D. Cent. Code §12.1-05-07(2)(b)(1997); the New Jersey Supreme Court, however, has recently urged the legislature to consider amending the statute. State v. Gartland, 694 A.2d 564, 569-71 (N.J. 1997).

25. Bureau of Justice Statistics, Intimate Partner Violence, 1993-2001 (2003).

26. U.S. Reports Big Declines in Domestic Violence, Chicago Tribune, May 18, 2000, at 21.

The court further stated that:

> [W]e cannot overlook the fact that Yaklich's participation in the death of her husband was not merely peripheral. Had it not been for Yaklich, the Greenwells [the two hired men] would not have been involved in the murder. Thus, in our view, we would be establishing poor public policy if Yaklich were to escape punishment by virtue of an unprecedented application of self-defense while the Greenwells were convicted of murder.

Does the court's "public policy" argument make sense? Should we able to punish the Greenwells without punishing Yaklich? (We will examine this aspect of accomplice liability in Chapter 11, *infra*.) If Yaklich had wanted to use a temporary insanity defense, would the court have denied it using the same logic? Alternatively, could the Greenwells, if they had known that Yaklich was a battered woman, have tried to use battered woman's syndrome in their own defense (they needed to protect her from imminent harm)? Are there reasons not to allow this kind of extension of battered woman's syndrome?

What if the "helping killer" is not a paid "contractor?" In State v. Verrinder, 637 A.2d 1382 (Vt. 1994), the defendant befriended one Debra Bullock, who had obtained a "relief-from-abuse" order against her husband, Kenneth Bullock. Debra warned Verrinder that Kenneth had a gun and had threatened to kill him. Alerted that Debra was in Kenneth's car and that Kenneth was screaming at her threateningly, Verrinder followed in his own vehicle. The two vehicles collided, and the two men emerged from their cars and confronted each other at a short distance. As Kenneth shouted threats, Verrinder warned Kenneth to back away, retrieved a gun from his own vehicle, and fatally shot Kenneth, and was charged with first-degree murder. What result? What further facts would help decide? Should defendant have been able to introduce expert BWS evidence?

16. *Make-my-day laws.* Consider the following Colorado statute, C.R.S. 18-1-704.5 (1999), referred to even by the courts as the "make-my-day" law:

> Use of deadly force against an intruder
> (1) The general assembly hereby recognizes that the citizens of Colorado have a right to expect absolute safety within their own homes.
> (2) . . . [A]ny occupant of a dwelling is justified in using any degree of physical force, including deadly physical force, against another person when that other person has made an unlawful entry into the dwelling, and when the occupant has a reasonable belief that such other person has committed a crime in the dwelling in addition to the uninvited entry, or is committing or intends to commit a crime against a person or property in addition to the uninvited entry, and when the occupant reasonably believes that such other person might use any physical force, no matter how slight, against any occupant.
> (3) Any occupant of a dwelling using physical force, including deadly physical force, in accordance with the provisions of subsection (2) of this section shall be immune from criminal prosecution for the use of such force.
> (4) Any occupant of a dwelling using physical force, including deadly physical force, in accordance with the provisions of subsection (2) of this section shall be immune from any civil liability for injuries or death resulting from the use of such force.

Can persons acting under this statute really be said to be acting in self-defense?

17. *Other "battering" syndromes.* At least one state has recognized that the logic behind allowing testimony of battered woman's syndrome to support claims

of self-defense extends to battered children also. In State v. Janes, 822 P.2d 1238 (Wash. App. 1992), the court held that "there is a sufficient scientific basis to justify extending the battered woman syndrome to analogous situations affecting children." Janes shot his abusive stepfather as he walked in the door. Washington State uses what it calls a "subjective standard" in deciding self-defense issues. Is it reasonable to assume that courts using an objective standard would have found that the danger was not "imminent" and not allowed self-defense to be raised? Is danger more "imminent" when an abusive father walks through a door than when an abusive husband is sleeping in his bed? See State v. Nemeth, 82 Ohio St. 202, 694 N.E.2d 1332 (1998) ("battered-child syndrome" evidence by expert admissible to reduce parricide from murder to voluntary manslaughter, though not a categorical defense); but see State v. Mott, 901 P.2d 1221 (Ariz. App. 1995) (battered spouse evidence cannot be used as form of diminished-capacity to negate mental elements for child abuse and child murder).

18. *"Reverse battered wife" expert testimony?* In Brunson v. State, 79 S.W.3d 304 (Ark. 2002), the prosecutor of a man charged with killing his female partner offered purportedly expert psychological evidence that the defendant fit the profile of a battering killer. The witness testified that there were ten "risk factors" comprising the profile: (1) threats of homicide against his spouse or children or threats of suicide; (2) fantasies of homicide or suicide; (3) depression; (4) access to weapons; (5) obsessive behavior about his wife or family; (6) centrality of the battered woman to the batterer's life; (7) rage against the battered woman; (8) drug or alcohol consumption; (9) abuse of the battered woman's pet animal; and (10) access to the battered woman. The State Supreme Court reversed the conviction, holding that the prosecution may not use so-called expert stereotypes or profiles to influence the jury.

19. *Inmate self-defense.* Some courts have recognized one very interesting *limitation* on the right to self-defense: use of force by inmates. In Rowe v. Debruyn, 17 F.3d 1047 (7th Cir. 1994), a prisoner fought off a sexual assault by hitting the aggressor over the head repeatedly with an unheated hot pot. The court held that in a prison setting the state could legitimately deny an inmate the use of the defense of self-defense in furtherance of the state interest in preventing violence in prisons, though the circumstances could be taken into account as mitigation. On the other hand, in one case in Alabama, which does not categorically preclude inmate self-defense, an inmate who killed another in response to a slap-in-the-face assault argued for a somewhat *enhanced* right of inmate self-defense. Peraita v. State [2003 WL 21246440.] (Ala. Crim. App. 2003). He offered a psychologist's testimony about an "institutionalization" effect whereby prisoners may adapt by developing an attitude of "hypervigilance" about danger and insult, including a need for forceful self-assertion to avoid future victimization. The court upheld the exclusion of this evidence, holding that the testimony was too speculative, given the fact-specificity of prisoners' situations and experiences.

3. Reprise on the Reasonable Self-Defender

Recall that the court in *Leidholm* addressed the difference between the so-called subjective and objective standards of reasonableness; it stated that the issue is not whether a reasonable person would have believed something, but rather whether the *defendant* reasonably believed it. But what if the defendant is unreasonably fearful or belligerent? In this context, consider one of the most controversial criminal cases in recent American history.

PEOPLE v. GOETZ
Court of Appeals of New York
68 N.Y.2d 96, 497 N.E.2d 41 (1986)

WACHTLER, CHIEF JUDGE.

. . . On Saturday afternoon, December 22, 1984, Troy Canty, Darryl Cabey, James Ramseur, and Barry Allen boarded an IRT express subway train in the Bronx and headed south toward lower Manhattan. The four youths rode together in the rear portion of the seventh car of the train. Two of the four, Ramseur and Cabey, had screwdrivers inside their coats, which they said were to be used to break into the coin boxes of video machines.

Defendant Bernhard Goetz boarded this subway train at 14th Street in Manhattan and sat down on a bench towards the rear section of the same car occupied by the four youths. Goetz was carrying an unlicensed .38 caliber pistol loaded with five rounds of ammunition in a waistband holster. The train left the 14th Street station and headed toward Chambers Street.

It appears from the evidence before the Grand Jury that Canty approached Goetz, possibly with Allen beside him, and stated "give me five dollars." Neither Canty nor any of the other youths displayed a weapon. Goetz responded by standing up, pulling out his handgun and firing four shots in rapid succession. The first shot hit Canty in the chest; the second struck Allen in the back; the third went through Ramseur's arm and into his left side; the fourth was fired at Cabey, who apparently was then standing in the corner of the car, but missed, deflecting instead off of a wall of the conductor's cab. After Goetz briefly surveyed the scene around him, he fired another shot at Cabey, who then was sitting on the end bench of the car. The bullet entered the rear of Cabey's side and severed his spinal cord.

All but two of the other passengers fled the car when, or immediately after, the shots were fired. The conductor, who had been in the next car, heard the shots and instructed the motorman to radio for emergency assistance. The conductor then went into the car where the shooting occurred and saw Goetz sitting on a bench, the injured youths lying on the floor or slumped against a seat, and two women who had apparently taken cover, also lying on the floor. Goetz told the conductor that the four youths had tried to rob him.

While the conductor was aiding the youths, Goetz headed towards the front of the car. The train had stopped just before the Chambers Street station and Goetz went between two of the cars, jumped onto the tracks and fled. Police and ambulance crews arrived at the scene shortly thereafter. Ramseur and Canty, initially listed in critical condition, have fully recovered. Cabey remains paralyzed, and has suffered some degree of brain damage.

On December 31, 1984, Goetz surrendered to police in Concord, New Hampshire, identifying himself as the gunman being sought for the subway shootings in New York nine days earlier. Later that day, after receiving *Miranda* warnings, he made two lengthy statements, both of which were tape recorded with his permission. In the statements, which are substantially similar, Goetz admitted that he had been illegally carrying a handgun in New York City for three years. He stated that he had first purchased a gun in 1981 after he had been injured in a mugging. Goetz also revealed that twice between 1981 and 1984 he had successfully warded off assailants simply by displaying the pistol.

According to Goetz's statement, the first contact he had with the four youths came when Canty, sitting or lying on the bench across from him, asked, "How are you," to which he replied, "Fine." Shortly thereafter, Canty, followed by one of the other youths, walked over to the defendant and stood to his left, while the other two youths remained to his right, in the corner of the subway car. Canty then said, "Give me five dollars." Goetz stated that he knew from the smile on Canty's face that they wanted to "play with me." Although he was certain that none of the youths had a gun, he had a fear, based on prior experiences, of being "maimed."

Goetz then established "a pattern of fire," deciding specifically to fire from left to right. His stated intention at that point was to "murder [the four youths], to hurt them, to make them suffer as much as possible." When Canty again requested money, Goetz stood up, drew his weapon, and began firing, aiming for the center of the body of each of the four. Goetz recalled that the first two he shot "tried to run through the crowd [but] they had nowhere to run." Goetz then turned to his right to "go after the other two." One of these two "tried to run through the wall of the train, but . . . he had nowhere to go." The other youth (Cabey) "tried pretending that he wasn't with [the others]" by standing still, holding on to one of the subway hand straps, and not looking at Goetz. Goetz nonetheless fired his fourth shot at him. He then ran back to the first two youths to make sure they had been "taken care of." Seeing that they had both been shot, he spun back to check on the latter two. Goetz noticed that the youth who had been standing still was now sitting on a bench and seemed unhurt. As Goetz told the police, "I said '[y]ou seem to be all right, here's another,'" and he then fired the shot which severed Cabey's spinal cord. Goetz added that "if I was a little more under self-control . . . I would have put the barrel against his forehead and fired." He also admitted that "if I had had more [bullets], I would have shot them again, and again, and again." . . .

[Goetz was indicted by a grand jury on charges of attempted murder, assault, and illegal weapons possession. A lower court then quashed the indictment for the attempted murder and assault charges, holding that the prosecutor, in explaining the legal basis for Goetz's claimed justification defense "had erroneously introduced an objective element into this defense by instructing the grand jurors to consider whether Goetz's conduct was that of a 'reasonable man in [Goetz's] situation.'" The state then appealed this ruling and sought to restore the indictment.]

. . . Penal Law §35.15(1) sets forth the general principles governing all such uses of force: "[A] person may . . . use physical force upon another person when and to the extent he *reasonably believes* such to be necessary to defend himself or a third person from what he *reasonably believes* to be the use or imminent use of unlawful physical force by such other person" (emphasis added).

Section 35.15(2) sets forth further limitations on these general principles with respect to the use of "deadly physical force": "A person may not use deadly physical force upon another person under circumstances specified in subdivision one unless (a) He *reasonably believes* that such other person is using or about to use deadly physical force . . . or (b) He *reasonably believes* that such other person is committing or attempting to commit a kidnapping, forcible rape, forcible sodomy or robbery" (emphasis added). . . .

When the prosecutor had completed his charge, one of the grand jurors asked for clarification of the term "reasonably believes." The prosecutor responded by instructing the grand jurors that they were to consider the circumstances of the incident and determine "whether the defendant's conduct was that of a reasonable man in the defendant's situation." It is this response by the prosecutor — and specifically his use of "a reasonable man"— which is the basis for the dismissal of the charges by the lower courts. As expressed repeatedly in the Appellate Division's plurality opinion, because section 35.15 uses the term "*he* reasonably believes," the appropriate test, according to that court, is whether a defendant's beliefs and reactions were "reasonable to *him*." Under that reading of the statute, a jury which believed a defendant's testimony that he felt that his own actions were warranted and were reasonable would have to acquit him, regardless of what anyone else in defendant's situation might have concluded. Such an interpretation defies the ordinary meaning and significance of the term "reasonable" in a statute, and misconstrues the clear intent of the Legislature, in enacting section 35.15, to retain an objective element as part of any provision authorizing the use of deadly physical force.

Penal statutes in New York have long codified the right recognized at common law to use deadly physical force, under appropriate circumstances, in self-defense. These provisions have never required that an actor's belief as to the intention of another person to inflict serious injury be correct in order for the use of deadly force to be justified, but they have uniformly required that the belief comport with an objective notion of reasonableness. . . .

In 1961 the Legislature established a Commission to undertake a complete revision of the Penal Law and the Criminal Code. The impetus for the decision to update the Penal Law came in part from the drafting of the Model Penal Code by the American Law Institute, as well as from the fact that the existing law was poorly organized and in many aspects antiquated. . . . While using the Model Penal Code provisions on justification as general guidelines, however, the drafters of the new Penal Law did not simply adopt them verbatim.

The provisions of the Model Penal Code with respect to the use of deadly force in self-defense reflect the position of its drafters that any culpability which arises from a mistaken belief in the need to use such force should be no greater than the culpability such a mistake would give rise to if it were made with respect to an element of a crime. . . . Accordingly, under Model Penal Code §3.04(2) (B), a defendant charged with murder (or attempted murder) need only show that he "*believe[d]* that [the use of deadly force] was necessary to protect himself against death, serious bodily injury, kidnapping or [forcible] sexual intercourse" to prevail on a self-defense claim (emphasis added). If the defendant's belief was wrong, and was recklessly, or negligently formed, however, he may be convicted of the type of homicide charge requiring only a reckless or negligent, as the case may be, criminal intent (see, Model Penal Code §3.09[2]). . . .

New York did not follow the Model Penal Code's equation of a mistake as to the need to use deadly force with a mistake negating an element of a crime, choosing instead to use a single statutory section which would provide either a complete defense or no defense at all to a defendant charged with any crime involving the use of deadly force. The drafters of the new Penal Law adopted in large part the structure and content of Model Penal Code §3.04, but, crucially, inserted the word "reasonably" before "believes." . . .

We cannot lightly impute to the Legislature an intent to fundamentally alter the principles of justification to allow the perpetrator of a serious crime to go free simply because that person believed his actions were reasonable and necessary to prevent some perceived harm. To completely exonerate such an individual, no matter how aberrational or bizarre his thought patterns, would allow citizens to set their own standards for the permissible use of force. It would also allow a legally competent defendant suffering from delusions to kill or perform acts of violence with impunity, contrary to fundamental principles of justice and criminal law. . . .

Goetz also argues that the introduction of an objective element will preclude a jury from considering factors such as the prior experiences of a given actor and thus, require it to make a determination of "reasonableness" without regard to the actual circumstances of a particular incident. This argument, however, falsely presupposes that an objective standard means that the background and other relevant characteristics of a particular actor must be ignored. To the contrary, we have frequently noted that a determination of reasonableness must be based on the "circumstances" facing a defendant or his "situation" (see, e.g., People v. Ligouri, 284 N.Y. 309, 316, 31 N.E.2d 37).

Such terms encompass more than the physical movements of the potential assailant. As just discussed, these terms include any relevant knowledge the defendant had about that person. They also necessarily bring in the physical attributes of all persons involved, including the defendant. Furthermore, the defendant's circumstances encompass any prior experiences he had which could provide a reasonable basis for a belief that another person's intentions were to injure or rob him or that the use of deadly force was necessary under the circumstances. . . .

. . . The Grand Jury has indicted Goetz. It will now be for the petit jury to decide whether the prosecutor can prove beyond a reasonable doubt that Goetz's reactions were unreasonable and therefore excessive. . . .

Accordingly, the order of the Appellate Division should be reversed, and the dismissed counts of the indictment reinstated.

Notes and Questions

1. *The mugging victim and the battered woman.* Is the New York court's view of the proper state of mind for perfect self-defense the same as that adopted by the court in *Leidholm*? The *Goetz* case eventually went to a New York jury, which acquitted him of all charges except the one for illegal gun possession. Do you think the jury properly followed the "objective" principle mandated by the Court of Appeals? How must the jury have characterized Goetz and the circumstances he found himself in? Should there be a "battered citizen" self-defense doctrine? Could we have expert testimony on this concept?

2. The *Goetz* case may help us reconsider the meaning of the defense claim in *Leidholm*. Was it that battered women have special insight into the risks they face, or that their suffering warrants special mercy? How would the choice of answers bear on *Goetz*? Are the cases different because Leidholm relied on a highly particular understanding of her husband's threats, while Goetz relied on stereo-

typical generalities of the threats from the four young men? But consider the following by Professor Mark Kelman,[27]

> [T]he subway killer claims a great deal of particular knowledge. Of course, he does not know the particular people he shoots, but he claims to interpret perfectly particular gestures; he has been mugged before and he has been with people who have been mugged and asked them what happened, and he has observed many interactions where people are not mugged. Moreover, the battered woman almost surely subjectively relies in part on statistical generalizations (the police don't take domestic violence seriously, protective court orders don't work, men who hit make up and then hit harder), just as much as the subway killer did. . . . Even if the battered woman is *subjectively* a complete localist who does not conceive herself in terms of the socially available categories that make generalization possible (like "battered wife"), her lawyer, attempting to persuade the jury that they too would have been scared in her situation, will *surely* make use of general evidence and will believe that statistical information about the ineffectiveness of police intervention in domestic violence cases or general information about the escalation of violence in the "battering cycle" is germane.
>
> . . . It is most persuasive to me that we reject the subway killer's proffered evidence not because he "inaccurately" assessed risks (though he might well have), but because the consequences of acting as he did, given his perception of risk, are so horrible. This would be true even if his judgment were not in part race based; it is even more dramatically true given the fact that it is.

THE CASE OF PEOPLE v. ABBOTT

Another highly publicized self-defense trial in New York City was that of convict-author Jack Henry Abbott, whom you will recall from Chapter 1. Consider the following summary, compiled by the editors, of the testimony at Abbott's trial in which he was charged with the murder of aspiring actor Richard Adan:

On the evening of July 18, 1981, defendant was residing at a halfway house for men on the Bowery on Manhattan's Lower East Side. Years earlier, while serving a two- to five-year sentence for writing bad checks, he had killed a fellow prison inmate. Convicted of voluntary manslaughter for that killing, Abbott was sentenced to an indeterminate term of up to 20 years, and while serving that term, he escaped and remained a fugitive for six weeks, during which he committed an armed robbery. He was ultimately paroled after serving 17 years on the manslaughter charge, in part because of the intervention of a number of prominent literary figures who were impressed with his talent as a writer. On the night in question, Abbott's book, *In the Belly of the Beast: Letters from Prison,* had recently been published to great acclaim. A highly laudatory review was due to appear in the Sunday New York Times Book Review, on the following morning.

Abbott arranged to celebrate his success with two women he had met through the novelist Norman Mailer, who had employed Abbott as a researcher. Around ten o'clock that night he returned to the halfway house, where he checked in with the guard and tucked a kitchen knife in his pants; shortly thereafter he left the halfway house and met the two women sometime before

27. Reasonable Evidence of Reasonableness, Critical Inquiry, Summer 1991, at 813-14.

midnight at the apartment of one of them. One of the women then observed the knife on his person. Abbott explained that he did not feel safe walking in that neighborhood at night. Abbott and the two women proceeded to a discotheque and then to a bar, where they all had a few drinks. Around five in the morning, the trio arrived for breakfast at the Cafe Binibon on East Fifth Street, a venue frequented by scowling punk rock fans and other black-clad Bohemians.

Abbott testified that after the party sat down he noticed Adan, a waiter, staring at him with what appeared to be intense hostility. He described Adan as muscular and tough-looking, clad in a black T-shirt and with a close-cropped hairstyle of the kind that convicts wear. Abbott rose and approached Adan and asked him if there was anything wrong. At this point, Abbott testified, he was aware of many people staring at them and, not wishing to make a scene, he asked Adan if there was any place such as a cloakroom they could go "to settle this." A second waiter approached and asked Adan if Abbott wanted to use the bathroom. Abbott interjected that he did not, and Adan asked him, "Do you want to go outside?" Abbott replied that that was all right with him. He testified that Adan led him around the corner onto East Fifth Street where there was a dark area behind a garbage Dumpster. Adan then looked up and down Second Avenue as if to assure himself that no one was watching. Then he rapidly approached defendant. Abbott testified that he believed that Adan intended to attack him perhaps with the assistance of others. Abbott withdrew the knife from his pants and stabbed Adan in the chest.

A witness to this stabbing (standing across the street) testified that Abbott then stood over Adan asking, "Do you still want to continue this, motherfucker?" Adan, wounded in the heart, died within seconds. According to the two women, defendant returned to the restaurant, excitedly saying to them "Let's go!" When one of them asked him what was wrong he replied, "I just killed a man. We've got to get out of here."

Upon leaving the restaurant, defendant's companions refused to accompany him further. Abbott disappeared down East Fifth Street. He was apprehended some six weeks later, while working on an oil rig in Louisiana.

The surviving waiter testified that City health regulations prohibited the Cafe Binibon from permitting customers to use the bathroom on the premises. As a consequence, he testified, it was the practice of the restaurant staff to lead male customers behind the Dumpster on East Fifth Street when they wished to urinate.

On redirect, Abbott testified that he now believed that Adan had been staring at one of his companions with admiration rather than at himself with hostility; that Adan had understood defendant to be in need of a bathroom; that Adan had led him outside to that end rather than for the purpose of settling a dispute; that Adan had looked to see that no one was approaching in order to insure Abbott's privacy while urinating, rather than to assure himself that there were no witnesses to an assault; and that he approached Abbott to warn him of the approach of the person who subsequently witnessed the stabbing, rather than in order to attack Abbott. Nevertheless, he claimed, he had been mistaken as to all of these matters at the time of the stabbing.

A psychiatrist testified that Abbott, at the time of the killing, was severely disoriented by the transition from incarceration. Abbott's editor testified that he had been terrified of the people he observed around him on the Bowery, and that he had been completely at a loss in confronting simple transactions like buying a toothbrush, opening a bank account, or using public transportation.

Abbott's book — portions of which were entered into evidence at his trial — detailed his own experience as a "state-raised" prisoner who began periodic incarceration in custodial institutions at age nine, and was almost continuously in custody from age 12 to the time of his parole (at age 37). Abbott claimed to have spent 14 or 15 years in solitary, including two or three years during his juvenile detention. He claimed to have been subjected to a number of other cruel conditions during his confinement including: beating, starvation diet, punitive administration of painful and disorienting drugs, tear gas, shackling, being left hanging from his wrists and ankles, "black-out cells," and "strip cells" (the prisoner is deprived of clothing, furnishings, and running water).

Abbott's book also described the difficulty of managing disputes in a maximum security prison resulting from the confinement together of dangerous, violent men; constant predation by those who establish physical dominance; no meaningful possibility of retreat; and the indifference or ineffectuality of the authorities. Abbott claimed that the most trivial dispute could quickly escalate to murder under these circumstances because prisoners had to strike preemptively or face the continuous threat of ambush.

Notes and Questions

1. Assuming the veracity of Abbott's account, should his experiences in confinement have provided him with a defense in the killing of Richard Adan? If so, what defense? Justified defensive force from the standpoint of the "reasonable state-raised convict"? Insanity? A special excuse based on some sort of "state-raised-convict syndrome"? What about a mistake of law? Consider MPC §3.09:

> (1) The justification afforded by Sections 3.04 to 3.07, inclusive, is unavailable when:
>
> (A) the actor's belief in the unlawfulness of the force or conduct against which he employs protective force or his belief in the lawfulness of an arrest which he endeavors to effect by force is erroneous; and
>
> (B) his error is due to ignorance or mistake as to the provisions of the Code, any other provision of the criminal law or the law governing the legality of an arrest or search.

2. If Abbott was guilty of homicide, homicide of what grade? How should he have been punished? What purpose would reincarcerating him have served? Was Abbott blameworthy? Deterrable? Likely to be incapacitated by prison? Rehabilitated?[28]

4. Defensive Force and Law Enforcement

Aside from self-defense, the most litigated questions involving the use of force in defense arise in the area of law enforcement and the prevention of crime. In some circumstances, persons are privileged to use force against others in order to enforce the law. This "privilege" can be viewed as a justification de-

---

28. Abbott was held by the jury to have established the affirmative defense, under New York law, of extreme emotional disturbance. He was convicted of manslaughter and sentenced as a persistent violent felony offender to a term of 15 years to life.

fense that operates in addition to other justifications for exerting force against the person or property of another.[29]

Originally, in English law, either a peace officer or a private citizen could use force to prevent any felony or breach of the peace or to seize someone who had committed a felony or breach of the peace. On the other hand, neither a public officer nor private citizen could use force to prevent the commission of a misdemeanor that did not breach the peace.

But here we have to distinguish nondeadly from deadly force; the basic rule — that deadly force was permitted to prevent any felony — limited deadly force to preventing dangerous or forcible felonies because almost all felonies fell into those categories. All felonies were, at least in theory, capitally punishable at common law. Most of these common law rules continued into the American states, with or without statutory confirmation.

If it now seems surprising that the common law granted private parties virtually the same privileges as police officers, note that police departments as conceived today hardly existed in Britain or the colonies; private persons were often the primary law enforcers, responsible to join in pursuit of offenders.

In most jurisdictions today, the police may use nondeadly force if it reasonably appears necessary to prevent, or to arrest the perpetrator of, any felony or a misdemeanor threatening public order. As for deadly force, the limitations vary among the states. Some jurisdictions limit the right to use deadly force to law enforcement personnel. Others allow deadly force by anyone in trying to prevent, or arrest the perpetrators of, violent crimes. Other jurisdictions permit the use of deadly force only in the case of dangerous felonies.

The Model Penal Code, which many states now follow on this subject, permits deadly force for law enforcement only when necessary to avoid a substantial risk of death or serious injury to innocent persons. Many municipal governments or police agencies have stiffer rules, often, for example, permitting shooting only where it meets the general criteria for self-defense or defense of others to homicide. The frequent litigation and political controversies over alleged police brutality often reinforce commitment to these restrictions.

Private persons are still accorded the authority to arrest in most jurisdictions, but often not to use deadly force in doing so, and, in most states, the arresting private person must be correct in fact that crime has occurred — reasonable belief is insufficient. But police officers, of course, have broad statutory power to arrest whenever they have probable cause to believe the individual has committed any felony, or even a misdemeanor if committed in the officer's presence. And in those jurisdictions otherwise imposing a duty to retreat, an officer need not retreat before using deadly force in self-defense or to overcome resistance.

An officer may use force to prevent a person's escape from custody, but in some states, where a person tries escaping from a jail or a penal facility, officers may use deadly force. Model Penal Code §3.07(3) allows an officer to use "any force, including deadly force, which he believes to be immediately necessary to prevent the escape of a person from a jail, prison, or other institution for the detention of persons charged with or convicted of a crime," even though the

---

29. For a classic treatment of this subject, see Ronald Boyce, Justification: Law Enforcement, 3 Encyclopedia Crime & Justice 953 (1st ed. 1983).

escaping person may not have originally committed a violent or dangerous felony.

The common law permitted the use of force to suppress riots or civil disorders. Statutes permitted authorities to use deadly force against those resisting public order after due warning. American statutes followed this model, and the fairly typical Model Penal Code rule, §3.07(5), justifies deadly force if "the actor believes that the use of such force is necessary to suppress a riot or mutiny after the rioters or mutineers have been ordered to disperse and warned, in any particular manner that the law may require, that such force will be used if they do not obey."

As is evident from the next case, however, even if a statute or the common law authorizes the use of deadly force, the Constitution may restrict that use further:

TENNESSEE v. GARNER
United States Supreme Court
471 U.S. 1 (1985)

JUSTICE WHITE delivered the opinion of the Court.

This case requires us to determine the constitutionality of the use of deadly force to prevent the escape of an apparently unarmed suspected felon. We conclude that such force may not be used unless it is necessary to prevent the escape and the officer has probable cause to believe that the suspect poses a significant threat of death or serious physical injury to the officer or others. . . .

At about 10:45 P.M. on October 3, 1974, Memphis Police Officers Elton Hymon and Leslie Wright were dispatched to answer a "prowler inside call." Upon arriving at the scene they saw a woman standing on her porch and gesturing toward the adjacent house.[30] She told them she had heard glass breaking and that "they" or "someone" was breaking in next door. While Wright radioed the dispatcher to say that they were on the scene, Hymon went behind the house. He heard a door slam and saw someone run across the backyard. The fleeing suspect, who was appellee-respondent's decedent, Edward Garner, stopped at a 6-feet-high chain link fence at the edge of the yard. With the aid of a flashlight, Hymon was able to see Garner's face and hands. He saw no sign of a weapon, and though not certain, was "reasonably sure" and "figured" that Garner was unarmed. He thought Garner was 17 or 18 years old and about 5 ft. 7 ins. tall.[31] While Garner was crouched at the base of the fence, Hymon called out "police, halt" and took a few steps toward him. Garner then began to climb over the fence. Convinced that if Garner made it over the fence he would elude capture,[32] Hymon shot him. The bullet hit Garner in the back of the head.

---

30. The owner of the house testified that no lights were on in the house, but that a back door light was on. Officer Hymon, though uncertain, stated in his deposition that there were lights on in the house. Record 209.

31. In fact, Garner, an eighth-grader, was 15. He was 5 ft. 4 ins. tall and weighed somewhere around 100 or 110 pounds.

32. When asked at trial why he fired, Hymon stated:

Well, first of all it was apparent to me from the little bit that I knew about the area at the time that he was going to get away because, number 1, I couldn't get to him. My partner then

Garner was taken by ambulance to a hospital, where he died on the operating table. Ten dollars and a purse taken from the house were found on his body.

In using deadly force to prevent the escape, Hymon was acting under the authority of a Tennessee statute and pursuant to Police Department policy. The statute provides that "[i]f, after notice of the intention to arrest the defendant, he either flee or forcibly resist, the officer may use all the necessary means to effect the arrest."[33]

Garner's father . . . brought this action in the Federal District Court for the Western District of Tennessee, seeking damages under 42 U.S.C. §1983 for asserted violations of Garner's constitutional rights. The complaint alleged that the shooting violated the Fourth, Fifth, Sixth, Eighth, and Fourteenth Amendments of the United States Constitution. . . . After a 3-day bench trial, the District Court entered judgment for all defendants.

The District Court found that the statute, and Hymon's actions, were constitutional.

The Court of Appeals reversed and remanded. It reasoned that the killing of a fleeing suspect is a "seizure" under the Fourth Amendment,[34] and is therefore constitutional only if "reasonable." The Tennessee statute failed as applied to this case because it did not adequately limit the use of deadly force by distinguishing between felonies of different magnitudes — "the facts, as found, did not justify the use of deadly force under the Fourth Amendment." Officers cannot resort to deadly force unless they "have probable cause . . . to believe that the suspect [has committed a felony and] poses a threat to the safety of the officers or a danger to the community if left at large."

The State of Tennessee appealed to this Court. . . .

. . . [T]here can be no question that apprehension by the use of deadly force is a seizure subject to the reasonableness requirement of the Fourth Amendment. . . .

. . . To determine the constitutionality of a seizure "[w]e must balance the nature and quality of the intrusion on the individual's Fourth Amendment interests against the importance of the governmental interests alleged to justify the intrusion."

. . . [T]he question [is] whether the totality of the circumstances justifie[s] a particular sort of search or seizure.

. . . The intrusiveness of a seizure by means of deadly force is unmatched. The suspect's fundamental interest in his own life need not be elaborated upon. The use of deadly force also frustrates the interest of the individual, and of society, in judicial determination of guilt and punishment. Against these interests are ranged governmental interests in effective law enforcement. . . . The use of deadly force is a self-defeating way of apprehending a suspect and so setting the criminal justice mechanism in motion. . . . And while the meaningful threat of

---

couldn't find where he was because, you know, he was late coming around. He didn't know where I was talking about. I couldn't get to him because of the fence here, I couldn't have jumped this fence and come up, consequently jumped this fence and caught him before he got away because he was already up on the fence, just one leap and he was already over the fence, and so there is no way that I could have caught him.

33. Although the statute does not say so explicitly, Tennessee law forbids the use of deadly force in the arrest of a misdemeanant. See Johnson v. State, 114 S.W.2d 819 (Tenn. 1938).

34. "The right of the people to be secure in their persons . . . against unreasonable searches and seizures, shall not be violated. . . ." U.S. Const. amend. IV.

deadly force might be thought to lead to the arrest of more live suspects by discouraging escape attempts, the presently available evidence does not support this thesis. The fact is that a majority of police departments in this country have forbidden the use of deadly force against nonviolent suspects. . . . Petitioners and appellant have not persuaded us that shooting nondangerous fleeing suspects is so vital as to outweigh the suspect's interest in his own life. The use of deadly force to prevent the escape of all felony suspects, whatever the circumstances, is constitutionally unreasonable. It is not better that all felony suspects die than that they escape. Where the suspect poses no immediate threat to the officer and no threat to others, the harm resulting from failing to apprehend him does not justify the use of deadly force to do so. It is no doubt unfortunate when a suspect who is in sight escapes, but the fact that the police arrive a little late or are a little slower afoot does not always justify killing the suspect. A police officer may not seize an unarmed, nondangerous suspect by shooting him dead. The Tennessee statute is unconstitutional insofar as it authorizes the use of deadly force against such fleeing suspects.

It is not, however, unconstitutional on its face. Where the officer has probable cause to believe that the suspect poses a threat of serious physical harm, either to the officer or to others, it is not constitutionally unreasonable to prevent escape by using deadly force. Thus, if the suspect threatens the officer with a weapon or there is probable cause to believe that he has committed a crime involving the infliction or threatened infliction of serious physical harm, deadly force may be used if necessary to prevent escape, and if, where feasible, some warning has been given. As applied in such circumstances, the Tennessee statute would pass constitutional muster. . . .

It is insisted that the Fourth Amendment must be construed in light of the common-law rule, which allowed the use of whatever force was necessary to effect the arrest of a fleeing felon, though not a misdemeanant. . . .

It has been pointed out many times that the common-law rule is best understood in light of the fact that it arose at a time when virtually all felonies were punishable by death. . . . Courts have also justified the common-law rule by emphasizing the relative dangerousness of felons.

Neither of these justifications makes sense today. Almost all crimes formerly punishable by death no longer are or can be. And while in earlier times "the gulf between the felonies and the minor offences was broad and deep," today the distinction is minor and often arbitrary. . . . Indeed, numerous misdemeanors involve conduct more dangerous than many felonies.[35]

There is an additional reason why the common-law rule cannot be directly translated to the present day. The common-law rule developed at a time when weapons were rudimentary. Deadly force could be inflicted almost solely in a hand-to-hand struggle during which, necessarily, the safety of the arresting officer was at risk. Handguns were not carried by police officers until the latter half of the last century. As a practical matter, the use of deadly force under the standard articulation of the common-law rule has an altogether different meaning — and harsher consequences — now than in past centuries. . . .

In evaluating the reasonableness of police procedures under the Fourth Amendment, we have also looked to prevailing rules in individual jurisdictions. . . .

35. White collar crime, for example, poses a less significant physical threat than, say, drunken driving. . . .

Nonetheless, the long-term movement has been away from the rule that deadly force may be used against any fleeing felon, and that remains the rule in less than half the States. . . .

Actual departmental policies are important. . . . We would hesitate to declare a police practice of long standing "unreasonable" if doing so would severely hamper effective law enforcement. But the indications are to the contrary. There has been no suggestion that crime has worsened in any way in jurisdictions that have adopted, by legislation or departmental policy, rules similar to that announced today. Amici notes that "[a]fter extensive research and consideration, [they] have concluded that laws permitting police officers to use deadly force to apprehend unarmed, nonviolent fleeing felony suspects actually do not protect citizens or law enforcement officers, do not deter crime or alleviate problems caused by crime, and do not improve the crime-fighting ability of law enforcement agencies." . . .

Nor do we agree with petitioners and appellant that the rule we have adopted requires the police to make impossible, split-second evaluations of unknowable facts. . . . The highly technical felony/misdemeanor distinction is equally, if not more, difficult to apply in the field. An officer is in no position to know, for example, the precise value of property stolen, or whether the crime was a first or second offense. Finally, as noted above, this claim must be viewed with suspicion in light of the similar self-imposed limitations of so many police departments. . . .

The District Court concluded that Hymon was justified in shooting Garner because state law allows, and the Federal Constitution does not forbid, the use of deadly force to prevent the escape of a fleeing felony suspect if no alternative means of apprehension is available. . . .

In reversing, the Court of Appeals accepted the District Court's factual conclusions and held that "the facts, as found, did not justify the use of deadly force." . . . We agree. . . . Hymon did not have probable cause to believe that Garner, whom he correctly believed to be unarmed, posed any physical danger to himself or others. . . .

Notes and Questions

1. Suppose the suspect Garner had been larger, stronger, and slower than Officer Hymon. If Hymon had caught up with Garner and attempted unsuccessfully to wrestle him to the ground, would Hymon have been justified in shooting Garner? What if Garner had struck him? What if Garner had brandished a knife and threatened to stab Hymon if Hymon persisted in chasing him?

2. The court concludes, as a constitutional matter, that Hymon was not justified by a statute allowing police to use any force "necessary" to apprehend a fleeing suspect; and that Hymon's killing of Garner was therefore an unreasonable seizure. Yet the court declines to strike down the statute as inconsistent with the Fourth Amendment prohibition of such seizures. Why?

3. Hymon's killing of Garner gave rise to a civil suit rather than a criminal prosecution. But suppose he had been prosecuted. Would denying him the justification apparently provided by the Tennessee statute have accorded with the due process principles of legality discussed in Chapter 2? Should Hymon have had a defense of reasonable mistake of law in this scenario?

4. Do cases like *Garner* have practical effect? One study concludes that police killings of fleeing felons have decreased since *Garner* by at least 15 percent.[36] One irony, though, is that some states have "overreacted" in the sense that their statutes and rules were already consistent with the *Garner* standard before the *Garner* decision, yet they then responded to the decision by imposing further even more stringent restrictions on police shootings. Does this suggest a misreading of the case? Or does it reflect that court decisions can send cultural signals beyond their strict holdings?

5. *Private citizens.* Should *Garner* now apply to efforts by private citizens to stop fleeing felons, where previously private citizens had been protected by the common law rule? In People v. Couch, 176 Mich. App. 254, 439 N.W.2d 354 (Mich. App. 1989), the facts were as follows:

> On October 15, 1986, at approximately 1:10 P.M., defendant was in his office in Warren, Michigan, when he heard a piercing sound, which he recognized as the burglar alarm on his 1986 Cadillac Seville automobile. He left the office building and walked to the parking lot where he saw a man, later identified as Alphonso Tucker, Jr., sitting in the middle of the front seat of defendant's car. The driver's window of defendant's vehicle had been broken out, with glass shards littering the parking lot. Tucker was bent forward, in the process of stealing the car's radio.
>
> Defendant drew his licensed concealed weapon, a .38 caliber revolver, walked to the rear of the car, held the gun in the air, and said, "Get out of the car and go with me so that I can call the police." Tucker slid over to the passenger door of the car, left the car, and said, "Okay, man, don't shoot." Defendant instructed Tucker to accompany him so he could call the police. Tucker then lunged toward defendant, and defendant fired a single shot. This shot did not strike Tucker. Tucker then began running away, and defendant fired two more shots from a distance of twenty to thirty feet, striking Tucker twice in the back. Tucker later died from the two gunshot wounds.

The court acknowledged that the Fourth Amendment did not itself apply to actions by private citizens, but nevertheless held that if the citizen is to be allowed to substitute for the police, he must obey the same limitations. Would you expect Couch to have a chance at acquittal under *Garner*?

6. *Preventing theft.* An unusual Texas statute, surviving from the frontier era when it applied to horse thieves, reads in part:

> A person is justified in using deadly force against another to protect land or tangible, movable property . . .
>
> (2) when and to the degree he reasonably believes the deadly force is immediately necessary:
>
> (A) to prevent the other's imminent commission of arson, burglary, robbery, aggravated robbery, or *theft during the nighttime* . . . ; and
>
> (3) he reasonably believes that:
>
> (A) the land or property cannot be protected or recovered by any other means; or
>
> (B) the use of force other than deadly force to protect or recover the land or property would expose the actor or another to a substantial risk of death or serious bodily injury. [Tex. Penal Code Ann. §9.42 (Vernon 2003) (emphasis added.)]

36. Abraham N. Tennenbaum, The Influence of the *Garner* Decision on the Police Use of Deadly Force, 85 J. Crim. L. & Criminology 241 (1994).

This statute was cited when a prosecutor declined to prosecute a man who shot to death an automobile repossessor, who was shot in the act of hooking his tow truck to the killer's car, on which payments were overdue. Two trade groups, the Texas Association of Professional Repossessors and the American Recovery Association, responded by lobbying for legislation to protect "repo" men, who are killed on the job at the rate of one or two a year in the United States.[37] In such cases, how plausible would a defendant's claim of mistake as to the identity of the person towing the car be? As construed by the Texas prosecutor in the repo man case, is this statute unconstitutional under Tennessee v. Garner?

Can self-defense be claimed by someone charged with felony murder? In State v. Amado, 756 A.2d 274 (Conn. 2001), the defendant attempted a robbery of a person who, he thought, had taken cocaine from him. A fight ensued in which the victim may have brandished a weapon himself; the defendant shot him to death.

> The defendant argues that a bright line rule that self-defense is not available, based simply on the state's accusation that a defendant committed felony murder, violates the fundamental principle that all defendants are presumed innocent until proved guilty beyond a reasonable doubt. We disagree. Our holding is premised on the fact that a finding, and not an accusation, of felony murder is incompatible with the defense of self-defense. Our rule as to self-defense assumes that the jury concluded that the defendant was in the course of and in furtherance of attempted robbery when the murder occurred. If the jury concluded that the defendant was not committing a felony at the time of the murder, the jury was instructed to find the defendant not guilty of felony murder. Our holding today does not violate the presumption of innocence. . . .
>
> In the present case, the jury reasonably found that the defendant was engaged in the attempted robbery of the victims when the shootings occurred. The evidence indicated that the defendant arrived at the victim's house, armed with a nine-millimeter handgun, with the intention of regaining his cocaine. After the defendant accused the victims of having his cocaine, and both denied having the drugs, the defendant began shooting. The jury could, and did, find that the shootings were in the course of and in furtherance of an attempted robbery. The defendant's testimony that the victims first utilized physical force does not require that he have a defense of self-defense. For purposes of felony murder, "it is immaterial whether the victim of the [felony] or the defendant [first utilizes physical force]." State v. Bell, 450 S.E.2d (N.C. 710) It is inconsistent with the purpose of the felony murder statute to allow a defendant who causes a death in the course of a felony to claim self-defense because the victim attempted to thwart such a felony. [Id. at 283-284.]

Could the defendant have invoked the principle of Gleghorn, p. 394, supra, and claimed that the victim was the initial deadly aggressor?

7. Defensive force against arrest. What about the reverse situation to defensive law enforcement — when may a person use force to resist an illegal arrest? At common law a person could use reasonable, but not deadly force, to resist an illegal arrest. But the definition of "illegal arrest" is not so simple. An arrest is illegal if the officer lacks probable cause to believe the defendant has committed a crime, if the officer uses excessive force, or if the arrest violates some technical requirement (such as obtaining a valid arrest warrant). But some jurisdictions

---

37. See Fear and Anger Follow Killing of a Repo Man, New York Times (March 8, 1994, at A10).

have traditionally limited the right of self-defense to cases where the defendant is aware of the illegality and a reasonable person would have been provoked by the arrest, as in a heat-of-passion case. Moreover, most jurisdictions, recognizing that defendants have increased rights to challenge their arrests in court and that jail conditions have improved, now only allow forceful resistance to arrests that are illegal by virtue of abusive force by the police. See Commonwealth v. Hill, 570 S.E.2d 805 (2002) (reviewing these doctrines and holding that in any event there is no right to resist a detention under an officer's stop and frisk powers that falls short of a full arrest, even if the detention is illegal for lack of reasonable cause to stop).

PEOPLE v. CEBALLOS
Supreme Court of California
12 Cal. 3d 470, 116 Cal. Rptr. 233 (1974)

BURKE, JUSTICE.

Don Ceballos was found guilty by a jury of assault with a deadly weapon. Imposition of sentence was suspended and he was placed on probation. He appeals from the judgment, contending primarily that his conduct was not unlawful because the alleged victim was attempting to commit burglary when hit by a trap gun mounted in the garage of defendant's dwelling and that the court erred in instructing the jury. We have concluded that the former argument lacks merit, that the court did not commit prejudicial error in instructing the jury, and that the judgment should be affirmed.

Defendant lived alone in a home in San Anselmo. The regular living quarters were above the garage, but defendant sometimes slept in the garage and had about $2,000 worth of property there.

In March 1970 some tools were stolen from defendant's home. On May 12, 1970, he noticed the lock on his garage doors was bent and pry marks were on one of the doors. The next day he mounted a loaded .22 caliber pistol in the garage. The pistol was aimed at the center of the garage doors and was connected by a wire to one of the doors so that the pistol would discharge if the door was opened several inches.

The damage to defendant's lock had been done by a 16-year-old boy named Stephen and a 15-year-old boy named Robert. On the afternoon of May 15, 1970, the boys returned to defendant's house while he was away. Neither boy was armed with a gun or knife. After looking in the windows and seeing no one, Stephen succeeded in removing the lock on the garage doors with a crowbar, and, as he pulled the door outward, he was hit in the face with a bullet from the pistol.

Stephen testified: He intended to go into the garage "[f]or musical equipment" because he had a debt to pay to a friend. His "way of paying that debt would be to take [defendant's] property and sell it" and use the proceeds to pay the debt. He "wasn't going to do it [i.e., steal] for sure, necessarily." He was there "to look around," and "getting in, I don't know if I would have actually stolen."

Defendant, testifying in his own behalf, admitted having set up the trap gun. He stated that after noticing the pry marks on his garage door on May 12, he felt he should "set up some kind of a trap, something to keep the burglar out of my home." When asked why he was trying to keep the burglar out, he replied, ". . . Because somebody was trying to steal my property . . . and I don't want to come home some night and have the thief in there . . . usually a thief is pretty desperate . . . and . . . they just pick up a weapon . . . if they don't have one . . . and do the best they can."

When asked by the police shortly after the shooting why he assembled the trap gun, defendant stated that "he didn't have much and he wanted to protect what he did have."

As heretofore appears, the jury found defendant guilty of assault with a deadly weapon. An assault is "an unlawful attempt, coupled with a present ability, to commit a violent injury on the person of another."

Defendant contends that had he been present he would have been justified in shooting Stephen since Stephen was attempting to commit burglary [and] defendant had a right to do indirectly what he could have done directly, and that therefore any attempt by him to commit a violent injury upon Stephen was not "unlawful" and hence not an assault. The People argue . . . that as a matter of law a trap gun constitutes excessive force, and that in any event the circumstances were not in fact such as to warrant the use of deadly force.

This issue of criminal liability . . . where the instrument employed is a trap gun or other deadly mechanical device appears to be one of first impression in this state,[38] but in other jurisdictions courts have considered the question of criminal and civil liability for death or injuries inflicted by such a device.

. . . [I]n England . . . a statute . . . made it a misdemeanor to set spring guns with intent to inflict grievous bodily injury but excluded from its operation a spring gun set between sunset and sunrise in a dwelling house for the protection thereof.

In the United States, courts have concluded that a person may be held criminally liable under statutes proscribing homicides and shooting with intent to injure, or civilly liable, if he sets upon his premises a deadly mechanical device and that device kills or injures another. . . . However, an exception to the rule that there may be criminal and civil liability for death or injuries caused by such a device has been recognized where the intrusion is, in fact, such that the person, were he present, would be justified in taking the life or inflicting the bodily harm with his own hands. . . .

Allowing persons, at their own risk, to employ deadly mechanical devices imperils the lives of children, firemen and policemen acting within the scope of their employment, and others. Where the actor is present, there is always the possibility he will realize that deadly force is not necessary, but deadly mechanical devices are without mercy or discretion. Such devices "are silent instrumentalities of death. They deal death and destruction to the innocent as well as the criminal intruder without the slightest warning. The taking of human life [or infliction of great bodily injury] by such means is brutally savage and inhuman."

It seems clear that the use of such devices should not be encouraged. Moreover, whatever may be thought in torts, the foregoing rule setting forth an exception to liability for death or injuries inflicted by such devices "is inappropriate in penal law for it is obvious that it does not prescribe a workable standard of conduct; liability depends upon fortuitous results." (See Model Penal Code

---

38. The parties have cited no California statute specifically dealing with trap guns, except Fish and Game Code section 2007, which provides: "It is unlawful to set, cause to be set, or place any trap gun. [¶] A 'trap gun' is a firearm loaded with other than blank cartridges and connected with a string or other contrivance contact with which will cause the firearm to be discharged." Even if the Legislature in enacting this section intended merely to regulate the taking of wild life, defendant's attempt to commit a violent injury upon Stephen, as we shall see, was unlawful.

(Tent. Draft No. 8), §3.06, com. 15.) We therefore decline to adopt that rule in criminal cases.

Furthermore, even if that rule were applied here, as we shall see, defendant was not justified in shooting Stephen. Penal Code section 197 provides: "Homicide is . . . justifiable . . . 1. When resisting any attempt to murder any person, or to commit a felony, or to do some great bodily injury upon any person; or, 2. When committed in defense of habitation, property, or person, against one who manifestly intends or endeavors, by violence or surprise, to commit a felony. . . ." (See also Pen. Code, §198.) Since a homicide is justifiable under the circumstances specified in section 197, a fortiori an attempt to commit a violent injury upon another under those circumstances is justifiable.

By its terms subdivision 1 of Penal Code section 197 appears to permit killing to prevent any "felony," but in view of the large number of felonies today and the inclusion of many that do not involve a danger of serious bodily harm, a literal reading of the section is undesirable. [In] People v. Jones, 191 Cal. App. 2d 478, 481, 12 Cal. Rptr. 777, [the court,] rejecting the defendant's theory that her husband was about to commit the felony of beating her (Pen. Code, §273d) and that therefore her killing him to prevent him from doing so was justifiable, stated that Penal Code section 197 "does no more than codify the common law and should be read in light of it." *Jones* read into section 197, subdivision 1, the limitation that the felony be "some atrocious crime attempted to be committed by force." [*Jones*] further stated, "the punishment provided by a statute is not necessarily an adequate test as to whether life may be taken for in some situations it is too artificial and unrealistic. We must look further into the character of the crime, and the manner of its perpetration. When these do not reasonably create a fear of great bodily harm, . . . there is no cause for the exaction of a human life." . . .

Jones involved subdivision 1 of Penal Code section 197, but subdivision 2 of that section is likewise so limited. The term "violence or surprise" in subdivision 2 is found in common law authorities and, whatever may have been the very early common law the rule developed at common law that killing or use of deadly force to prevent a felony was justified only if the offense was a forcible and atrocious crime. "Surprise" means an unexpected attack — which includes force and violence . . . and the word thus appears redundant.

Examples of forcible and atrocious crimes are murder, mayhem, rape and robbery. In such crimes "from their atrocity and violence human life [or personal safety from great harm] either is, or is presumed to be, in peril." . . .

Burglary has been included in the list of such crimes. However, in our opinion it cannot be said that under all circumstances burglary . . . constitutes a forcible and atrocious crime. Where the character and manner of the burglary do not reasonably create a fear of great bodily harm, there is no cause for exaction of human life or for the use of deadly force. . . . The character and manner of the burglary could not reasonably create such a fear unless the burglary threatened, or was reasonably believed to threaten, death or serious bodily harm.

In the instant case the asserted burglary did not threaten death or serious bodily harm, since no one but Stephen and Robert was then on the premises. A defendant is not protected from liability merely by the fact that the intruder's conduct is such as would justify the defendant, were he present, in believing that the intrusion threatened death or serious bodily injury. There is ordinarily the possibility that the defendant, were he present, would realize the true state of affairs and recognize the intruder as one whom he would not be justified in killing or wounding.

We thus conclude that defendant was not justified under Penal Code section 197, subdivisions 1 or 2, in shooting Stephen to prevent him from committing burglary. . . .

In support of his position that had he been present he would have been justified in shooting Stephen, defendant cites Nakashima v. Takase, 8 Cal. App. 2d 35, 46 P.2d 1020, a case in which the decedent's mother was seeking damages. The defendant, a cafe proprietor, suspected a burglary might be committed, returned to the cafe after dark, and hid inside. The decedent and a companion broke into the cafe intending to commit larceny, and after they entered, the defendant, who was secreted in a position where he could not be seen or heard, shot the decedent without warning. *Nakashima,* in reversing the judgment in the plaintiff's favor, concluded that the defendant's act was a justifiable homicide under Penal Code section 197, subdivision 2. That case manifestly differs on its facts from the present one in that, among other things, here no one except the asserted would-be burglar and his companion was on the premises when the gun was fired. . . .

Defendant also does not, and could not properly, contend that the intrusion was in fact such that, were he present, he would be justified under Civil Code section 50 in using deadly force. That section provides, "Any necessary force may be used to protect from wrongful injury the person or property of oneself. . . ." This section also should be read in the light of the common law, and at common law in general deadly force could not be used solely for the protection of property. "'The preservation of human life and limb from grievous harm is of more importance to society than the protection of property.'" (Commonwealth v. Emmons, 157 Pa. Super. 195, 43 A.2d 568, 569. . . .) Thus defendant was not warranted under Civil Code section 50 in using deadly force to protect his personal property. . . .

Notes and Questions

1. How does *Ceballos* differ from the occasions where one is entitled to use deadly force? What if I am a very heavy sleeper and fear that my enemy may come through my window to kill me? Would I be entitled to put up a spring gun at the foot of my bed? If it did kill my enemy as he approached me, hatchet in hand, of what crime, if any, would I be guilty? If it instead killed a burglar merely looking for my wallet, would the answer be different? If nobody was hurt, would I be guilty of attempt?

2. Does California law, as it is set forth in *Ceballos,* reflect a utilitarian or rights-oriented (retributivist) conception of justification? If California law is utilitarian, why should one be able to use deadly force in defense of one's home when one is present? Should one be obliged to retreat? If California law is rights-oriented, why cannot Ceballos use force in defense of his property?

3. Is the court's "non-literal" interpretation of the justification statute convincing? Is it consistent with due process to convict Ceballos when a statute appears to justify his conduct? Should he be able to offer a defense of reasonable mistake of law? What if his mistake of law as to whether his conduct was justifiable was unreasonable, and so negligent? Assuming that assault with a deadly

weapon requires a more culpable mental state than negligence, should Ceballos's unreasonably mistaken belief that he was justified acquit him altogether?

In South Carolina, the State Attorney General recently argued that the typical home-defense law, requiring that a resident may use deadly force to resist an intruder only if her life is reasonably seen to be in danger or the intruder is about to commit some felony, is too restrictive. He then announced he would not prosecute any home occupant who chooses to use deadly force against any unwelcome person. He thus refused to impose the burden of a trial or the obligation to bring a self-defense claim on a woman who got involved in an argument with her boyfriend (who lived some distance away but who kept some clothes and personal possessions in her apartment) and stabbed him to death.[39]

> [Attorney General Charles] Condon said he was tired of seeing homeowners who defended their homes dragged through lengthy investigations and trials before being cleared, when it was obvious to him that they did nothing wrong.
>
> "You don't want to put the homeowner in the position of saying, 'If I use deadly force, I might be cleared after a trial,'" Mr. Condon said. "That's tantamount to saying that people have rights, but there's a huge cross attached to it. Most courts have a laissez-faire attitude about these things, figuring that everything will come out fine after a trial. But I think we need to send the message that the home is sacred ground, period."

B.   CHOICE OF EVILS — NECESSITY

1.   The Moral Issue

THE QUEEN v. DUDLEY & STEPHENS
Queen's Bench Division
14 Q.B.D. 273 (1884)

Indictment for the murder of Richard Parker on the high seas within the jurisdiction of the Admiralty.

At the trial before HUDDLESTON, B., at the Devon and Cornwall Winter Assizes, November 7, 1884, the jury, at the suggestion of the learned judge, found the facts of the case in a special verdict which stated

> that on July 5, 1884, the prisoners, Thomas Dudley and Edward Stephens, with one Brooks, all able-bodied English seamen, and the deceased also an English boy, between seventeen and eighteen years of age, the crew of an English yacht, a registered English vessel, were cast away in a storm on the high seas 1600 miles from the Cape of Good Hope, and were compelled to put into an open boat belonging to the said yacht. That in this boat they had no supply of water and no supply of food, except two 1 lb. tins of turnips, and for three days they had nothing else to subsist upon. That on the fourth day they caught a small turtle, upon which they subsisted

39. David Firestone, Home-Invasion Policy Ignites South Carolina, New York Times (March 16, 2001), at A10.

for a few days, and this was the only food they had up to the twentieth day when the act now in question was committed. That on the twelfth day the remains of the turtle were entirely consumed, and for the next eight days they had nothing to eat. That they had no fresh water, except such rain as they from time to time caught in their oilskin capes. That the boat was drifting on the ocean, and was probably more than 1000 miles away from land. That on the eighteenth day, when they had been seven days without food and five without water, the prisoners spoke to Brooks as to what should be done if no succour came, and suggested that some one should be sacrificed to save the rest, but Brooks dissented, and the boy, to whom they were understood to refer, was not consulted. That on the 24th of July, the day before the act now in question, the prisoner Dudley proposed to Stephens and Brooks that lots should be cast who should be put to death to save the rest, but Brooks refused to consent, and it was not put to the boy, and in point of fact there was no drawing of lots. That on that day the prisoners spoke of their having families, and suggested it would be better to kill the boy that their lives should be saved, and Dudley proposed that if there was no vessel in sight by the morrow morning the boy should be killed. The next day, the 25th of July, no vessel appearing, Dudley told Brooks that he had better go and have a sleep, and made signs to Stephens and Brooks that the boy had better be killed. The prisoner Stephens agreed to the act, but Brooks dissented from it. That the boy was then lying at the bottom of the boat quite helpless, and extremely weakened by famine and by drinking sea water, and unable to make any resistance, nor did he ever assent to his being killed. The prisoner Dudley offered a prayer asking forgiveness for them all if either of them should be tempted to commit a rash act, and that their souls might be saved. That Dudley, with the assent of Stephens, went to the boy, and telling him that his time was come, put a knife into his throat and killed him then and there; that the three men fed upon the body and blood of the boy for four days; that on the fourth day after the act had been committed the boat was picked up by a passing vessel, and the prisoners were rescued, still alive, but in the lowest state of prostration. That they were carried to the port of Falmouth, and committed for trial at Exeter. That if the men had not fed upon the body of the boy they would probably not have survived to be so picked up and rescued, but would within the four days have died of famine. That the boy, being in a much weaker condition, was likely to have died before them. That at the time of the act in question there was no sail in sight, nor any reasonable prospect of relief. That under these circumstances there appeared to the prisoners every probability that unless they then fed or very soon fed upon the boy or one of themselves they would die of starvation. That there was no appreciable chance of saving life except by killing some one for the others to eat. That assuming any necessity to kill anybody, there was no greater necessity for killing the boy than any of the other three men. But whether upon the whole matter by the jurors found the killing of Richard Parker by Dudley and Stephens be felony and murder the jurors are ignorant, and pray the advice of the Court thereupon, and if upon the whole matter the Court shall be of opinion that the killing of Richard Parker be felony and murder, then the jurors say that Dudley and Stephens were each guilty of felony and murder as alleged in the indictment.

From these facts, stated with the cold precision of a special verdict, it appears sufficiently that the prisoners were subjected to terrible temptation, to sufferings which might break down the bodily power of the strongest man, and try the conscience of the best. Other details yet more harrowing, facts still more loathing and appalling, were presented to the jury, and are to be found recorded in my learned Brother's notes. But nevertheless this is clear, that the prisoners put to death a weak and feeble boy upon the chance of preserving their own lives by feeding upon his flesh and blood after he was killed, and with the certainty of depriving him of any possible chance of survival. The verdict finds in terms that "if the men had not fed upon the body of the boy they would probably not have survived," and that "the boy being in a much weaker condition was likely to have died before them." They might possibly have been picked up next day by a passing ship; they might possibly not have been picked up at all; in either case it is obvious that the killing of the boy would have been an unnecessary and profitless act. It is found by the verdict that the boy was incapable of resistance, and, in fact, made none; and it is not even suggested that his death was due to any violence on his part attempted against, or even so much as feared by, those who killed him. Under these circumstances the jury say that they are ignorant whether those who killed him were guilty of murder, and have referred it to this Court to determine what is the legal consequence which follows from the facts which they have found. . . .

The learned judge then adjourned the assizes until the 25th of November at the Royal Courts of Justice. On the application of the Crown they were again adjourned to the 4th of December, and the case ordered to be argued before a Court consisting of five judges.

[The court first discussed certain procedural issues.]

There remains to be considered the real question in the case — whether killing under the circumstances set forth in the verdict be or be not murder. The contention that it could be anything else was, to the minds of us all, both new and strange, and we stopped the Attorney General in his negative argument in order that we might hear what could be said in support of a proposition which appeared to us to be at once dangerous, immoral, and opposed to all legal principle and analogy. All, no doubt, that can be said has been urged before us, and we are now to consider and determine what it amounts to. First it is said that it follows from various definitions of murder in books of authority, which definitions imply, if they do not state, the doctrine, that in order to save your own life you may lawfully take away the life of another, when that other is neither attempting or threatening yours, nor is guilty of any illegal act whatever towards you or any one else. But if these definitions be looked at they will not be found to sustain this contention. . . .

It is . . . clear . . . that the doctrine contended for receives no support from the great authority of Lord Hale. It is plain that in his view the necessity which justified homicide is that only which has always been and is now considered a justification. . . . Lord Hale regarded the private necessity which justified, and alone justified, the taking the life of another for the safeguard of one's own to be what is commonly called "self-defence." (Hale's Pleas of the Crown, i. 478.)

But if this could be even doubtful upon Lord Hale's words, Lord Hale himself has made it clear. For in the chapter in which he deals with the exemption created by compulsion or necessity he thus expresses himself: — "If a man be desperately assaulted and in peril of death, and cannot otherwise escape unless, to satisfy his assailant's fury, he will kill an innocent person then present, the fear and actual force will not acquit him of the crime and punishment of murder, if he commit the fact [*sic*]; for he ought rather to die himself than kill an innocent; but if he cannot otherwise save his own life the law permits him in his own defence to kill the assailant, for by the violence of the assault, and the offence committed upon him by the assailant himself, the law of nature, and necessity, hath made him his own protector. . . ." (Hale's Pleas of the Crown, vol. i. 51.)

But, further still, Lord Hale in the following chapter deals with the position asserted by the casuists, and sanctioned, as he says, by Grotius and Puffendorf, that in a case of extreme necessity, either of hunger or clothing; "theft is no theft, or at least not punishable as theft, as some even of our own lawyers have asserted the same." "But," says Lord Hale, "I take it that here in England, that rule, at least by the laws of England, is false; and therefore, if a person, being under necessity for want of victuals or clothes, shall upon that account clandestinely and animo furandi steal another man's goods, it is felony, and a crime by the laws of England punishable with death." (Hale, Pleas of the Crown, i. 54.) If therefore, Lord Hale is clear — as he is — that extreme necessity of hunger does not justify larceny, what would he have said to the doctrine that it justified murder? . . .

Is there, then any authority for the proposition which has been presented to us? Decided cases there are none. . . . The American cases cited by my Brother Stephen in his Digest, from Wharton on Homicide, in which it was decided [in United States v. Holmes 26 F.Cas. 360, 1 Wall. Jr. 1 (C.C.E.D. Pa. 1842)], correctly indeed, that sailors had no right to throw passengers overboard to save themselves, but on the somewhat strange ground that the proper mode of determining who was to be sacrificed was to vote upon the subject by ballot, can hardly, as my Brother Stephen says, be an authority satisfactory to a court in this country. . . .

The one real authority of former time is Lord Bacon, who . . . lays down the law as follows: — "Necessity carrieth a privilege in itself. Necessity is of three sorts — necessity of conservation of life, necessity of obedience, and necessity of the act of God or of a stranger. First of conservation of life; if a man steals viands to satisfy his present hunger, this is no felony nor larceny. So if divers be in danger of drowning by the casting away of some boat or barge, and one of them get to some plank, or on the boat's side to keep himself above water, and another to save his life thrust him from it, whereby he is drowned, this is neither se defendo nor by misadventure, but justifiable." . . . Lord Bacon was great even as a lawyer; but it is permissible to much smaller men, relying upon principle and on the authority of others, the equals and even the superiors of Lord Bacon as lawyers, to question the soundness of the dictum. There are many conceivable states of things in which it might possibly be true, but if Lord Bacon meant to lay down the broad proposition that man may save his life by killing, if necessary, an innocent and unoffending neighbor, it certainly is not law at the present day. . . .

Now it is admitted that the deliberate killing of this unoffending and unresisting boy was clearly murder, unless the killing can be justified by some well-recognised excuse admitted by law. It is further admitted that there was in this case no such excuse, unless the killing was justified by what has been called "necessity." But the temptation to the act which existed was not what the law has ever called necessity. Nor is this to be regretted.

. . . Though law and morality are not the same, and many things may be immoral which are not necessarily illegal, yet the absolute divorce of law from morality would be of fatal consequence; and such divorce would follow if the temptation to murder in this case were to be held by law an absolute defence of it. It is not so. To preserve one's life is generally speaking a duty, but it may be the plainest and the highest duty to sacrifice it. War is full of duty, in instances in which it is a man's duty not to live, but to die. The duty, in case of shipwreck, of a captain to his crew, of the crew to the passengers, of soldiers to women and children, as in the noble case of the Birkenhead; these duties impose on men the moral necessity, not of the preservation, but of the sacrifice of their lives for others, from which in no country, least of all, it is to be hoped, in England, will men ever shrink, as indeed, they have not shrunk. It is not correct, therefore, to say that there is any absolute or unqualified necessity to preserve one's life. . . . It would be a very easy and cheap display of commonplace learning to quote from Greek and Latin authors, from Horace, from Juvenal, from Cicero, from Euripides, passage after passage, in which the duty of dying for others has been laid down in glowing and emphatic language as resulting from the principles of heathen ethics; it is enough in a Christian country to remind ourselves of the Great Example whom we profess to follow. It is not needful to point out the awful danger of admitting the principle which has been contended for. Who is to be the judge of this sort of necessity? By what measure is the comparative value of lives to be measured? Is it to be strength, or intellect, or what? It is plain what the principle leaves to him who is to profit by it to determine the necessity which will justify him in deliberately taking another's life to save his own. In this case the weakest, the youngest, the most unresisting, was chosen. Was it more necessary to kill him than one of the grown men? The answer must be "No"—

So spake the Fiend, and with necessity, The tyrant's plea, excused his devilish deeds.

It is not suggested that in this particular case the deeds were "devilish," but it is quite plain that such a principle once admitted might be made the legal cloak for unbridled passion and atrocious crime. There is no safe path for judges to tread but to ascertain the law to the best of their ability and to declare it according to their judgment; and if in any case the law appears to be too severe on individuals, to leave it to the Sovereign to exercise that prerogative of mercy, which the Constitution has intrusted to hands fittest to dispense it.

It must not be supposed that in refusing to admit temptation to be an excuse for crime it is forgotten how terrible the temptation was; how awful the suffering; how hard in such trials to keep the judgment straight and the conduct pure. We are often compelled to set up standards we cannot reach ourselves, and to lay down rules which we could not ourselves satisfy. But a man has no right to declare temptation to be an excuse, though he might himself have yielded to it, nor allow compassion for the criminal to change or weaken in any manner the legal definition of the crime. It is therefore our duty to declare that the prisoner's act in this case was wilful murder, that the facts as stated in the verdict are no legal justification of the homicide; and to say that in our unanimous opinion the prisoners are upon this special verdict guilty of murder.[40]

The Court then proceeded to pass sentence of death upon the prisoners.[41]

Notes and Questions

1. Assuming that the three seamen and the cabin boy all would have died if the seamen had not killed and eaten the cabin boy, what reason is there

40. My Brother Grove has furnished me with the following suggestion, too late to be embodied in the judgment but well worth preserving: "If the two accused men were justified in killing Parker, then if not rescued in time, two of the three survivors would be justified in killing the third, and of the two who remained the stronger would be justified in killing the weaker, so that three men might be justifiably killed to give the fourth a chance of surviving."

41. This sentence was afterwards commuted by the Crown to six months' imprisonment.

to prefer four deaths to one? Can there be any argument for the defendants *being justified* if we take a "rights-based" approach? Can a "rights" approach at least allow for an *excuse* defense? What approach does the court take?

2. Is the problem in *Dudley & Stephens* that the seamen did not use a "fair" method to choose the one to die? Would the result have been different if the seamen had drawn straws or cut cards, or held an election, or an auction, rather than simply killed the weakest and youngest? What if Parker had tried to cannibalize the others?

Would the seamen have been justified in basing their choice on principles of social utility? Was it fair to kill the boy on the ground that, because of his weakened condition, he had the shortest life expectancy anyway? If they had all been in the same physical condition, would it have been fair to kill the oldest? Was it relevant that the cabin boy was the only person on board who did not have a family dependent on him? If three cancer researchers were adrift on a lifeboat with a skid-row drunk, would the researchers be justified in killing the drunk to advance social utility?

3. Should we determine whether the defendants were justified from the outcome, or from the perspective and with the information they had before they killed the boy?

4. *Utilitarianism or retributivism.* The judge implies that he himself might have done no better than Dudley and Stephens under the same circumstances. Is it fair for us to blame the sailors for failing "standards we cannot reach ourselves"? Consider the view of Professor George Fletcher: [42]

> The key to Lord Coleridge's unwillingness to countenance an excuse of necessity is his fear that the "legal definition of the crime" would thereby be changed. This is a familiar argument against excusing conditions. The fear is that the public will always interpret an acquittal as a vindication of the deed. . . . The rejection of excusing conditions and the concern for the social impact of the judgment both express a utilitarian philosophy of criminal justice. . . . If Lord Coleridge could embrace utilitarian thinking on these points, one wonders why he recoiled against the prospect of justifying the killing on the grounds of lesser evils. If in fact the killing of one emaciated boy appeared likely to save the lives of two men, then the killing furthered the greater good. . . . The passion of Lord Coleridge runs to a different principle. Though utilitarian in his posture toward excuses and influencing future behavior, Lord Coleridge takes a high moral stand about the unqualified evil of killing the innocent. "[T]he absolute divorce of law from morality," we are told, "would be of fatal consequence." And that absolute divorce would occur "if the temptation to murder in this case were held to be an absolute defense of it." Coleridge did not reject the principle of lesser evils because the probability of death at sea was not sufficiently great. He rejected the idea, root and branch, and delivered himself of a passionate opinion on the Christian duty to die for the sake of principle.
>
> The outcome of the case is Kantian at the level of justification and utilitarian at the level of excuses — the worst possible combination for Dudley and Stephens.

5. *Lesser evils.* The problem is more general than the extreme case of *Dudley & Stephens* might suggest: [43]

> [Justification defenses do not define the harm sought to be prevented or punished by an offense. The harm caused by the justified behavior remains a legally

---

42. Rethinking Criminal Law 824-26 (1978).
43. Paul Robinson, 1 Criminal Law Defenses 83 (1984).

recognized harm that is to be avoided whenever possible. Under the special justifying circumstances, however, that harm is outweighed by the need to avoid an
even greater harm or to further a greater societal interest.

A forest fire rages toward a town of 10,000 unsuspecting inhabitants. The actor burns a field of corn located between the fire and the town; the burned field
then serves as a firebreak, saving 10,000 lives. By setting fire to the field with the
purpose of destroying it, the actor satisfies all elements of the offense of arson.
The immediate harm he has caused — the destruction of the field — is precisely
the harm that the statute serves to prevent and punish. Yet the actor is likely to have
a complete defense, because his conduct and its harmful consequences are
justified. The conduct in this instance is tolerated, even encouraged, by society.

The forest fire case provides an example of the "lesser evils" or "choice of
evils" justification (also called "necessity" when the threat of greater harm stems
from natural forces). This type of justification defense, not always recognized in
American criminal codes, most clearly reflects the general principle of all justification defenses.

6. By the way, did the Crown have any case against Brooks as well? Could
Brooks have used force to defend Parker?

7. *The historical context.* How do we explain the unusual "special verdict"
procedure in this case, whereby the jury merely found the key facts but the question of guilt was then reserved for a five-judge appellate court? How do we
explain the trivial term of imprisonment imposed after the conviction? [44]

44. Some long-obscured history of the Dudley & Stephens case, uncovered by the British his-
torian A.W.B. Simpson, helps provide answers. Cannibalism and the Common Law: The Story of
the Tragic Last Voyage of the Mignonette and the Strange Legal Proceedings to Which It Gave Rise
(1984). Professor Simpson places Dudley & Stephens in the context of a virtual crime wave of maritime cannibalism cases in the mid-nineteenth century that British courts had failed at condemning under a clear legal rule. (In most of these cases, lots were indeed drawn. Indeed, Professor
Simpson reports an oral tradition that Dudley & Stephens were prosecuted solely because they did
not draw lots.) The public rarely viewed these cases as crimes and even occasionally treated them
as journalistic entertainments. Certainly the defendants in this case suffered little public rebuke.
When Dudley, Stephens, and Brooks returned to London, public sympathy lay with them. In fact,
they were regarded virtually as heroes and were instantly released on bail pending trial. At most,
there was grumbling criticism for their failure to draw lots, but even this criticism dissolved when
Dudley almost proudly explained the killing to the public. He noted that Parker, having drunk sea-
water (which sailors of that time equated with poison), was likely to die soon anyway.
In the rare cases where maritime cannibals were brought to trial before 1884, the necessity
claim was not raised. Rather, the defendants claimed self-defense. One of them involved a maritime cannibal recidivist, Alexander Pearce, who was executed for his second act of this sort, but
the evidence there showed that a quarrel, not starvation, originally impelled him to kill. Id. at 147.
In another British case, involving a ship called the Euxine in 1874, government prosecutors
were particularly suspicious of the fact that lots were drawn three times and each time the "ran-
domly" selected victim turned out to be the same person — an Italian boy who spoke little or no
English. Id. at 181. This might have been the case to settle British law, but for the shakiness of the
evidence compounded by bungling procedural blunders by the government. The prosecutors
feared that their weak case might lead to a jury acquittal, which might create the public perception
that the court ratified the custom of maritime cannibalism. Thus, the government decided to drop
the case.
It then befell the Dudley & Stephens case to serve as the official legal declaration that the custom amounted to homicide. This was especially ironic — and risky — given the social standing of
the defendants: Dudley was a gentleman and a professional yacht captain. Brooks and Parker also
belonged to well-born yachting society. Only Stephens, a steamship officer who had been discredited for his negligence in a previous boat disaster, did not.
Hence the Crown feared again an acquittal unless it was headed off by careful legal contrivance. The quick and easy bail reflected assurances given the defendants that they would not suffer severe punishment. The "special verdict" on the facts handed down by the jury was actually
ghostwritten by the trial judge, and it carefully excluded any direct finding of necessity.

8. *Lesser evils in the MPC.* The Model Penal Code contains a general "choice of evils" justification defense:

Section 3.02. Justification Generally: Choice of Evils

(1) Conduct that the actor believes to be necessary to avoid a harm or evil to himself or to another is justifiable, provided that:

(a) the harm or evil sought to be avoided by such conduct is greater than *that* sought to be prevented by the law defining the offense charged; and

(b) neither the Code nor other law defining the offense provides exceptions or defenses dealing with the specific situation involved; and

(c) a legislative purpose to exclude the justification claimed does not otherwise plainly appear.

(2) When the actor was reckless or negligent in bringing about the situation requiring a choice of harms or evils or in appraising the necessity for his conduct, the justification afforded by this Section is unavailable in a prosecution for any offense for which recklessness or negligence, as the case may be, suffices to establish culpability.

The Comment includes this discussion:[45]

1. *Codification of a principle of necessity.* This section accepts the view that a principle of necessity, properly conceived, affords a general justification for conduct that would otherwise constitute an offense. It reflects the judgment that such a qualification on criminal liability, like the general requirements of culpability, is essential to the rationality and justice of the criminal law, and is appropriately addressed in a penal code. Under this section, property may be destroyed to prevent the spread of a fire. A speed limit may be violated in pursuing a suspected criminal. An ambulance may pass a traffic light. Mountain climbers lost in a storm may take refuge in a house or may appropriate provisions. Cargo may be jettisoned or an embargo violated to preserve the vessel. An alien may violate a curfew in order to reach an air raid shelter. A druggist may dispense a drug without the requisite prescription to alleviate grave distress in an emergency. A developed legal system must have better ways of dealing with such problems than to refer only to the letter of particular prohibitions, framed without reference to cases of this kind.

How would the Model Penal Code resolve *Dudley & Stephens*? Does it address the question of how to choose the person to die?

9. *Lesser evils problems.* Model Penal Code section 3.02 gives several hypotheticals to illustrate the position taken in its justification defense:[46]

Suppose, for example, that the actor makes a breach in a dike, knowing that this will inundate a farm, but taking the only course available to save a whole town. If he is charged with homicide of the inhabitants of the farm house, he can rightly point out that the object of the law of homicide is to save life, and that by his conduct he has effected a net saving of innocent lives. The life of every individual must be taken in such a case to be of equal value and the numerical preponderance in the lives saved compared to those sacrificed surely should establish legal justification for the act. So, too, a mountaineer, roped to a companion who has fallen over a precipice, who holds on as long as possible but eventually cuts the rope, must certainly be granted the defense that he accelerated one death slightly but

---

45. Model Penal Code and Commentaries, *supra,* Part I, at 9-14.
46. Model Penal Code and Commentaries, *supra,* at 14-15.

avoided the only alternative, the certain death of both. Although the view is not universally held that it is ethically preferable to take one innocent life than to have many lives lost, most persons probably think a net saving of lives is ethically warranted if the choice among lives to be saved is not unfair. Certainly the law should permit such a choice.

How would the moral position advanced in the passage above resolve the following hypothetical, originally posed by the philosopher Philippa Foot?[47]

A surgeon has five patients who will die without organ transplants. Two need a lung; two need a kidney; one needs a heart. In walks another patient for a check-up, whose blood and tissue remarkably match that of the other five. The surgeon invites this potential donor to sacrifice himself for the other five, but he refuses. The surgeon kills the man and proceeds to transplant the needed organs into the other five patients, thereby saving five lives at the cost of one.

Has the doctor done the "lesser evil"? What if she merely takes one lung and one kidney from the man, thereby saving two lives at the cost of none?

So far, our hypotheticals have involved weighing human lives against one another, or weighing one property value against another. Should we conclude that human life is always more valuable than property? Can you conceive of any property that you could honestly say was more valuable than a human life?

It is generally understood in the heavy construction industry that for roughly every $100 million of heavy construction, one worker will be killed accidentally. Insurance premiums, for instance, are set on such a basis. Why then is not the owner of a construction firm that undertakes the building of a dam or aqueduct, with full knowledge that fatalities will result, guilty of homicide?

10. *United States v. Paolello.* In this case, a man with a criminal record was convicted of violating 18 U.S.C. §922(g)(1), for being a convicted felon in possession of a firearm. United States v. Paolello, 951 F.2d 537 (3d Cir. 1991). With his stepson, Williams, Paollelo went to a bar where he fell into an argument with another patron. Paolello walked out but was followed by the other man, who punched Williams and continued to argue with Paolello. The other man had a gun; he and Paolello struggled over it. Paolello seized the gun and ran away; an officer who had arrived on the scene chased Paolello and demanded that he stop, but Paolello, though he dropped the gun, kept running until the officer apprehended him.

In reversing for failure to give a "justification" defense instruction, the court held there was

a four-part test to determine whether such a defense is available to a particular defendant. This approach requires a defendant to establish that: (1) he was under unlawful and present threat of death or serious bodily injury; (2) he did not recklessly place himself in a situation where he would be forced to engage in criminal conduct; (3) he had no reasonable legal alternative (to both the criminal act and the avoidance of the threatened harm); and (4) there is a direct causal relationship between the criminal action and the avoidance of the threatened harm. . . .

Of course, there is no indication that Paolello was reckless. While the government suggests that he was at fault because he went to a bar "known as a place where 'bad' people hang out in the early morning hours of the day" and that he left the

47. Philippa Foot, "The Problem of Abortion and the Doctrine of Double Effect," Oxford Rev. 5 (1967).

bar even though he had reason to believe there would be trouble if he did that, it seems to us that no reasonable trier of the fact could find that such lawful conduct was "reckless" so as to deprive Paolello of a justification defense which he might otherwise have. Al's Tavern, after all, was a public place of business and, at least as far as the record shows, Paolello went there for legitimate purposes and had no reason to believe that he would be in danger there. . . .

[T]here was sufficient evidence, if believed, to demonstrate that Paolello was subject to a threat of death or serious bodily harm. Williams testified that a man punched him in the face, and that the same man struggled with Paolello. Paolello testified that this man had harassed him while he was in the bar, and that the man had followed him out of the bar, demanding that Paolello buy him a drink. According to Paolello, the man also stated that he could take all of Paolello's money away to buy the drink if he so desired.

Paolello further testified that, after Williams left the bar to join Paolello, he saw this man punch Williams, and at that point noticed that the man had a gun. According to Paolello, he knocked the gun out of the man's hands to keep him from shooting Williams. He then grabbed the gun to avoid being shot himself instead of leaving it on the ground. Further, he testified that he ran away with the gun because he was afraid that the man would send his "friends" after him. . . .

In addition . . . Paolello stated that he grabbed the gun after it had fallen to the ground to avoid being shot or to prevent Williams from being shot. He ran down the alley with the gun because he was afraid the man or his friends would attack him. This testimony indicates that there was no other way for Paolello to take preventive action other than by grabbing the weapon. It is true that Kress testified that he chased Paolello down the alley, ordering him to stop running and identifying himself as a policeman, and that Paolello disobeyed the orders. If Kress's testimony is believed, this would severely undercut Paolello's justification defense because it would appear that Paolello had an opportunity to dispose of the gun and stop running earlier than he did, so that he possessed the firearm longer than absolutely necessary.

Yet Paolello testified that, in contrast to Kress's rendition of the events, he ran down the alley because he was afraid that the man who had punched Williams and had argued with Paolello would instruct his "friends" to chase Paolello. He also testified that as he "was running into the alleyway, I didn't know anybody was behind me. . . . I heard somebody say 'Stop,' you know? And I turned around, and I dropped the gun. . . . He said 'I'm an officer' and I just stopped." Because we must accept in the procedural posture of this case Paolello's version of the facts in the record, it appears that Paolello did not maintain possession of the weapon any longer than absolutely necessary. Thus, even if we find Paolello's testimony unpersuasive, his credibility should be judged by the jury.

11. In United States v. Oakland Cannabis Buyers' Coop, 532 U.S. 485 (2001), the Supreme Court held that federal criminal drug laws preempted a new California law permitting the medical use of marijuana. Though the case involved many issues of federalism and constitutional law, the Buyers' Coop also raised a species of the necessity defense. The Court held:

Under any conception of legal necessity, one principle is clear: The defense cannot succeed when the legislature itself has made a "determination of values." 1 W. LaFave & A. Scott, Substantive Criminal Law §5.4, p. 629 (1986). In the case of the Controlled Substances Act, the statute reflects a determination that marijuana has no medical benefits worthy of an exception (outside the confines of a Government-approved research project). . . . Indeed, for purposes of the Controlled Substances Act, marijuana has "no currently accepted medical use" at all. §811. . . .

The statute divides drugs into five schedules, depending in part on whether the particular drug has a currently accepted medical use. The Act then imposes restrictions on the manufacture and distribution of the substance according to the schedule in which it has been placed. Schedule I is the most restrictive schedule. The Attorney General can include a drug in schedule I only if the drug "has no currently accepted medical use in treatment in the United States," "has a high potential for abuse," and has "a lack of accepted safety for use . . . under medical supervision." §§812(b)(1)(A)-(C). . . .

The Cooperative further argues that use of schedule I drugs generally — whether placed in schedule I by Congress or the Attorney General — can be medically necessary, notwithstanding that they have "no currently accepted medical use." According to the Cooperative, a drug may not yet have achieved general acceptance as a medical treatment but may nonetheless have medical benefits to a particular patient or class of patients. We decline to parse the statute in this manner. It is clear from the text of the Act that Congress has made a determination that marijuana has no medical benefits worthy of an exception. The statute expressly contemplates that many drugs "have a useful and legitimate medical purpose and are necessary to maintain the health and general welfare of the American people," §801(1), but it includes no exception at all for any medical use of marijuana. [Id. at 491-93]

Is there any conceivable argument left for a gravely ill person who asserts that marijuana is the only feasible pain reliever?

2. Escape from Intolerable Prison Conditions

PEOPLE v. UNGER
Supreme Court of Illinois
362 N.E.2d 319 (1977)

RYAN, JUSTICE.

Defendant, Francis Unger, was charged with the crime of escape, and was convicted following a jury trial before the circuit court of Will County. Defendant was sentenced to a term of three to nine years to be served consecutively to the remainder of the sentence for which he was imprisoned at the time of the escape. The conviction was reversed upon appeal and the cause was remanded for a new trial over the dissent of one justice. . . .

We granted leave to appeal and now affirm the judgment of the appellate court.

At the time of the present offense, the defendant was confined at the Illinois State Penitentiary in Joliet, Illinois. Defendant was serving a one- to three-year term as a consequence of a conviction for auto theft in Ogle County. Defendant began serving this sentence in December of 1971. On February 23, 1972, the defendant was transferred to the prison's minimum security, honor farm. It is undisputed that on March 7, 1972, the defendant walked off the honor farm. Defendant was apprehended two days later in a motel room in St. Charles, Illinois.

At trial, defendant testified that prior to his transfer to the honor farm he had been threatened by a fellow inmate. This inmate allegedly brandished a six-inch knife in an attempt to force defendant to engage in [sexual] activities. Defendant was 22 years old and weighed approximately 155 pounds. He testified that he did not report the incident to the proper authorities due to fear of retaliation. Defendant also testified that he is not a particularly good fighter.

Defendant stated that after his transfer to the honor farm he was assaulted and sexually molested by three inmates, and he named the assailants at trial. The attack allegedly occurred on March 2, 1972, and from that date until his escape defendant received additional threats from inmates he did not know. On March 7, 1972, the date of the escape, defendant testified that he received a call on an institution telephone. Defendant testified that the caller, whose voice he did not recognize, threatened him with death because the caller had heard that defendant had reported the assault to prison authorities. Defendant said that he left the honor farm to save his life and that he planned to return once he found someone who could help him. None of these incidents were reported to the prison officials. As mentioned, defendant was apprehended two days later still dressed in his prison clothes.

The State introduced prior statements made by the defendant which cast some doubt on his true reasons for leaving the prison farm. In these statements, defendant indicated that he was motivated by a desire for publicity concerning the sentence on his original conviction, which he deemed to be unfair, as well as fear of physical abuse and death.

Defendant's first trial for escape resulted in a hung jury. The jury in the second trial returned its verdict after a five-hour deliberation. The following instruction (People's Instruction No. 9) was given by the trial court over defendant's objection.

> The reasons, if any, given for the alleged escape are immaterial and not to be considered by you as in any way justifying or excusing, if there were in fact such reasons.

The appellate court majority found that the giving of People's Instruction No. 9 was reversible error. Two instructions which were tendered by defendant but refused by the trial court are also germane to this appeal. Defendant's instructions Nos. 1 and 3 were predicated upon the affirmative defenses of compulsion and necessity. (Ill. Rev. Stat. 1971, ch. 38, pars. 7-11 (compulsion), 7-13 (necessity).) Defendant's instructions Nos. 1 and 3 read as follows:

> It is a defense to the charge made against the Defendant that he left the Honor Farm of the Illinois State Penitentiary by reason of necessity if the accused was without blame in occasioning or developing the situation and reasonably believed such conduct was necessary to avoid a public or private injury greater than the injury which might reasonably result from his own conduct.
> It is a defense to the charge made against the Defendant that he acted under the compulsion of threat or menace of the imminent infliction of death or great bodily harm, if he reasonably believed death or great bodily harm would be inflicted upon him if he did not perform the conduct with which he is charged.

The State contends that, under the facts and circumstances of this case, the defenses of compulsion and necessity are, as a matter of law, unavailable to defendant. . . . Traditionally, the courts have been reluctant to permit the defenses of compulsion and necessity to be relied upon by escapees. This reluctance appears to have been primarily grounded upon considerations of public policy. Several recent decisions, however, have recognized the applicability of the compulsion and necessity defenses to prison escapes. In People v. Harmon (1974), 53 Mich. App. 482, 220 N.W.2d 212, the defense of duress was held to apply in a case where the defendant alleged that he escaped in order to avoid repeated homosexual attacks from fellow inmates. In People v. Lovercamp (1974), 43 Cal. App. 3d 823, 118 Cal. Rptr. 110, a limited defense of necessity was held to be available to two defendants whose escapes were allegedly motivated by fear of [sexual] attacks. . . .

As illustrated by *Harmon* and *Lovercamp,* different courts have reached similar results in escape cases involving sexual abuse, though the question was analyzed under different defense theories. A certain degree of confusion has resulted from the recurring practice on the part of the courts to use the terms "compulsion" (duress) and "necessity" interchangeably, though the defenses are   theoretically distinct. It has been suggested that the major distinction between the two defenses is that the source of the coercive power in cases of compulsion is from human beings, whereas in situations of necessity the pressure on the defendant arises from the forces of nature. (LaFave and Scott, Handbook on Criminal Law 381 (1972).) Also, as noted in the dissenting opinion in the appellate court, the defense of compulsion generally requires an impending, imminent threat of great bodily harm together with a demand that the person perform the specific criminal act for which he is eventually charged. Additionally, where the defense of compulsion is successfully asserted the coercing party is guilty of the crime. LaFave and Scott, Handbook on Criminal Law 380 (1972).

It is readily discernible that prison escapes induced by fear of [sexual] assaults and accompanying physical reprisals do not conveniently fit within the traditional ambits of either the compulsion or the necessity defense. However, it has been suggested that such cases could best be analyzed in terms of necessity. (LaFave and Scott, Handbook on Criminal Law 381-82 n.2 (1972).) One commentator has stated that the relevant consideration should be whether the defendant chose the lesser of two evils, in which case the defense of necessity would apply, or whether he was unable to exercise a free choice at all, in which event compulsion would be the appropriate defense. . . .

In our view, the defense of necessity, as defined by our statute, is the appropriate defense in the present case. In a very real sense, the defendant here was not deprived of his free will by the threat of imminent physical harm which, according to the Committee Comments, appears to be the intended interpretation of the defense of compulsion as set out in section 7-11 of the Criminal Code. Rather, if defendant's testimony is believed, he was forced to choose between two admitted evils by the situation which arose from actual and threatened homosexual assaults and fears of reprisal. Though the defense of compulsion would be applicable in the unlikely event that a prisoner was coerced by the threat of imminent physical harm to perform the specific act of escape, no such situation is involved in the present appeal. We, therefore, turn to a consideration of whether the evidence presented by the defendant justified the giving of an instruction on the defense of necessity.

The defendant's testimony was clearly sufficient to raise the affirmative defense of necessity. That defense is defined by statute (Ill. Rev. Stat. 1971, ch. 38, par. 7-13):

> Conduct which would otherwise be an offense is justifiable by reason of necessity if the accused was without blame in occasioning or developing the situation

and reasonably believed such conduct was necessary to avoid a public or private injury greater than the injury which might reasonably result from his own conduct.

Defendant testified that he was subjected to threats of forced [sexual] activity and that, on one occasion, the threatened abuse was carried out. He also testified that he was physically incapable of defending himself and that he feared greater harm would result from a report to the authorities. Defendant further testified that just prior to his escape he was told that he was going to be killed, and that he therefore fled the honor farm in order to save his life. Though the State's evidence cast a doubt upon the defendant's motives for escape and upon the reasonableness of defendant's assertion that such conduct was necessary, the defendant was entitled to have the jury consider the defense on the basis of his testimony. It is clear that defendant introduced some evidence to support the defense of necessity. As previously mentioned, that is sufficient to justify the giving of an appropriate instruction.

The State, however, would have us apply a more stringent test to prison escape situations. The State refers to the *Lovercamp* decision, where only a limited necessity defense was recognized. In *Lovercamp,* it was held that the defense of necessity need be submitted to the jury only where five conditions had been met. (43 Cal. App. 3d 823, 831, 118 Cal. Rptr. 110, 115.) Those conditions are:

1. The prisoner is faced with a specific threat of death, forcible sexual attack or substantial bodily injury in the immediate future;
2. There is no time for a complaint to the authorities or there exists a history of futile complaints which make any result from such complaints illusory;
3. There is no time or opportunity to resort to the courts;
4. There is no evidence of force or violence used towards prison personnel or other "innocent" persons in the escape; and
5. The prisoner immediately reports to the proper authorities when he has attained a position of safety from the immediate threat.

The State correctly points out that the defendant never informed the authorities of his situation and failed to report immediately after securing a position of safety. Therefore, it is contended that, under the authority of *Lovercamp,* defendant is not entitled to a necessity instruction. We agree with the State and with the court in *Lovercamp* that the above conditions are relevant factors to be used in assessing claims of necessity. We cannot say, however, that the existence of each condition is, as a matter of law, necessary to establish a meritorious necessity defense.

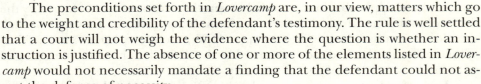

The preconditions set forth in *Lovercamp* are, in our view, matters which go to the weight and credibility of the defendant's testimony. The rule is well settled that a court will not weigh the evidence where the question is whether an instruction is justified. The absence of one or more of the elements listed in *Lovercamp* would not necessarily mandate a finding that the defendant could not assert the defense of necessity.

By way of example, in the present case defendant did not report to the authorities immediately after securing his safety. In fact, defendant never voluntarily turned himself in to the proper officials. However, defendant testified that he intended to return to the prison upon obtaining legal advice from an attorney and claimed that he was attempting to get money from friends to pay for such counsel. Regardless of our opinion as to the believability of defendant's tale, this testimony, if accepted by the jury, would have negated any negative inference which would arise from defendant's failure to report to proper authorities after the escape. The absence of one of the *Lovercamp* preconditions does not alone disprove the claim of necessity and should not, therefore, automatically preclude an instruction on the defense. We therefore reject the contention that the availability of the necessity defense be expressly conditioned upon the elements set forth in *Lovercamp*.

In conclusion, we hold that under the facts and circumstances of the present case the defendant was entitled to submit his defense of necessity to the jury. It was, therefore, reversible error to give People's Instruction No. 9 to the jury and to refuse to give an appropriate instruction defining the defense of necessity, such as the instruction tendered by the defendant. In light of our disposition of this appeal, we need not consider contentions raised by defendant as to the propriety of his sentence. . . .

Notes and Questions

1. Note that while the *Unger* court does not follow *Lovercamp* in treating the inmate's failure to return as an absolute bar to justifying escape, it does treat failure to return as a factor to be considered by the jury. How exactly is this failure to return relevant? Is it possible to justify a failure to return, as well as an initial escape?

2. The *Lovercamp* court requires that the threatened harm be "immediate" as well as requiring that the defendant turn himself in immediately. If the defendant remained at large because he reasonably feared that turning himself in would expose him to the same threat, the *Lovercamp* standard would afford him no defense. Why not? Is the necessity defense made available by *Lovercamp* a form of justification by reason of lesser evils? Is it an excuse, based on the defendant's capacity for choice being overwhelmed by fear? Just what is the nature of the defense afforded by *Unger*?

3. Another of the conditions for the necessity defense defined in *Lovercamp* is the absence of any force or violence against prison personnel. Is this condition always appropriate? Suppose a prison guard is aware that a prisoner has been the victim of sexual assaults and that the prisoner has been threatened with death. Would the guard be justified in using force to impede an otherwise justified escape? If not, would the escaping prisoner be justified in using force to overcome the guard? Does it matter whether we approach the question of justification from a utilitarian or retributivist (i.e., rights-oriented) perspective? How does it change the situation if the guard is unaware of the conditions arguably justifying escape?

3. "Political" Necessity

STATE v. WARSHOW
Supreme Court of Vermont
410 A.2d 1000 (1980)

BARNEY, CHIEF JUSTICE.
The defendants were part of a group of demonstrators that travelled to Vernon, Vermont, to protest at the main gate of a nuclear power plant known as

Vermont Yankee. The plant had been shut down for repairs and refueling, and these protestors had joined a rally designed to prevent workers from gaining access to the plant and placing it on-line.

They were requested to leave the private premises of the power plant by representatives of Vermont Yankee and officers of the law. The defendants were among those who refused, and they were arrested and charged with unlawful trespass.

The issue with which this appeal of their convictions is concerned relates to a doctrine referred to as the defense of necessity. At trial the defendants sought to present evidence relating to the hazards of nuclear power plant operation which, they argued, would establish that defense. After hearing the defendants' offer of proof the trial court excluded the proffered evidence and refused to grant compulsory process for the witnesses required to present the defense. The jury instruction requested on the issue of necessity was also refused, and properly preserved for appellate review.

In ruling below, the trial court determined that the defense was not available. It is on this basis that we must test the issue.

The defense of necessity is one that partakes of the classic defense of "confession and avoidance." It admits the criminal act, but claims justification. . . .

The doctrine is one of specific application insofar as it is a defense to criminal behavior. This is clear because if the qualifications for the defense of necessity are not closely delineated, the definition of criminal activity becomes uncertain and even whimsical. The difficulty arises when words of general and broad qualification are used to describe the special scope of this defense.

In the various definitions and examples recited as incorporating the concept of necessity, certain fundamental requirements stand out:

1. there must be a situation of emergency arising without fault on the part of the actor concerned;
2. this emergency must be so imminent and compelling as to raise a reasonable expectation of harm, either directly to the actor or upon those he was protecting;
3. this emergency must present no reasonable opportunity to avoid the injury without doing the criminal act; and
4. the injury impending from the emergency must be of sufficient seriousness to outmeasure the criminal wrong. . . .

There is no doubt that the defendants wished to call attention to the dangers of low-level radiation, nuclear waste, and nuclear accident. But low-level radiation and nuclear waste are not the types of imminent danger classified as an emergency sufficient to justify criminal activity. To be imminent, a danger must be, or must reasonably appear to be, threatening to occur immediately, near at hand, and impending. . . . We do not understand the defendants to have taken the position in their offer of proof that the hazards of low-level radiation and nuclear waste buildup are immediate in nature. On the contrary, they cite long-range risks and dangers that do not presently threaten health and safety. Where the hazards are long term, the danger is not imminent, because the defendants have time to exercise options other than breaking the law. . . .

Nor does the specter of nuclear accident as presented by these defendants fulfill the imminent and compelling harm element of the defense. The offer does not take the position that they acted to prevent an impending accident. Rather, they claimed that they acted to foreclose the "chance" or "possibility" of accident. This defense cannot lightly be allowed to justify acts taken to foreclose speculative and uncertain dangers. Its application must be limited to acts directed to the prevention of harm that is reasonably certain to occur. . . .

These acts may be a method of making public statements about nuclear power and its dangers, but they are not a legal basis for invoking the defense of necessity. Nor can the defendants' sincerity of purpose excuse the criminal nature of their acts.

Judgment affirmed.

HILL, JUSTICE, concurring. . . .

Both the state of Vermont and the federal government have given their imprimatur to the development and normal operation of nuclear energy and have established mechanisms for the regulation of nuclear power. Implicit within these statutory enactments is the policy choice that the benefits of nuclear energy outweigh its dangers.

If we were to allow defendants to present the necessity defense in this case we would, in effect, be allowing a jury to redetermine questions of policy already decided by the legislative branches of the federal and state governments. This is not how our system of government was meant to operate. . . .

In my opinion the majority puts the cart before the horse. It measures the offer made against the requisite elements of the defense of necessity and concludes that the defendants failed to show a likelihood of imminent danger; yet it reserves judgment on the legislative policy exception to the defense. It is illogical to consider whether the necessary elements of a defense have been shown before determining whether the defense is even available in the particular situation.

The dissent, on the other hand, assumes that defendants' offer was sufficient to show not only imminent danger but also a failure of the regulatory scheme. I cannot agree with this assumption because the offer failed to show a danger not contemplated by the legislative scheme. The legislative framework was set up to deal with the very situation defendants offered to prove "might" happen. But because neither the state legislature nor Congress acted to shut down the power plant based on speculative possibilities does not, in my opinion, give rise to the questionable inference that there was an emergency which the regulatory scheme failed to avert. . . .

Since defendants' defense of necessity was foreclosed by a deliberate legislative policy choice, there was no error on the trial court's part in not allowing the defense to be presented.

BILLINGS, JUSTICE, dissenting. . . .

The majority states that the danger of low-level radiation and nuclear waste, which the defendants offered to prove, are "not the types of imminent danger classified as an emergency sufficient to justify criminal activity." Furthermore, the majority dismisses those portions of the proof dealing with the threat of a nuclear accident by characterizing them as mere "speculative and uncertain dangers." In doing so the majority has decided to so read the evidence as to give credibility only to that evidence offered on the effects of low-level radiation. . . . The defendants also stated that "there was reasonable belief that it would have been an emergency had they started that reactor up. . . . [T]here was a very good chance of an accident there for which there is no insurance coverage or very little." Specifically, the defendants offered to show by expert testimony that there were defects in the cooling system and other aspects of the power plant which they believed could and would result in a meltdown within seven seconds of failure on the start up of the plant. In addition, the defendants went to great lengths to base their defense on the imminent danger that would result from the hazardous radiation emitted from the plant and its wastes when the plant resumed operations.

While the offer made by the defendants was laced with statements about the dangers they saw in nuclear power generally, it is clear that they offered to show that the Vermont Yankee facility at which they were arrested was an imminent danger to the community on the day of the arrests; that, if it commenced operation, there was a danger of meltdown and severe radiation damage to persons and property. . . .

Furthermore, the defendants offered to show that, in light of the imminent danger of an accident, they had exhausted all alternative means of preventing the start up of the plant and the immediate catastrophe it would bring. Under the circumstances of imminent danger arising from the start up of the plant, coupled with the resistance of Vermont Yankee and government officials, which the defendants offered to prove, nothing short of preventing the workers access to start up the plant would have averted the accident that the defendants expected. . . .

I would also dissent from the concurring opinion in so far as it attempts to hide behind inferences that the legislature precluded the courts from hearing the defense of necessity in the instant case. . . . Even assuming that such inferences can be drawn from the regulatory schemes cited, they have no bearing on this case. We were asked to infer under the facts, which the defendants offered to prove (that they were acting to avert an imminent nuclear disaster), that the legislative branch of government would not permit the courts of this state to entertain the defense of necessity because it had legislatively determined nuclear power to be safe. Were the defense raised without any offer to show an imminent danger of serious accident, it might fail both because defendants did not offer evidence on imminent danger and on the basis of legislative preclusion. But, where, as here, the defendants offer to prove an emergency which the regulatory scheme failed to avert, the inference of preclusion is unwarranted. The defendants are entitled to show that although there is a comprehensive regulatory scheme, it had failed to such an extent as to raise for them the choice between criminal trespass and the nuclear disaster which the regulatory scheme was created to prevent. . . .

I am of the opinion that the defendants are entitled to present evidence on the defense of necessity as it exists at common law. To deny them this opportunity is to deny them a fair trial merely because they express unpopular political views. . . .

Notes and Questions

1. The majority opinion holds that a defense of necessity is only available if defendant acts in response to an "emergency . . . so imminent and compelling as to raise a reasonable expectation of harm." Does this imply that we should

only act to avert those harms likely to occur in the very short run? Is this a prudent way to act? What if we know that a distant and unlikely catastrophe can be precluded by a small sacrifice? In determining the lesser evil shouldn't we take into account the gravity of potential harm, as well as its probability and imminence? Indeed, as long as we are confident that one course of action will actually reduce the probability of a grave harm, why should we care whether that harm is imminent?

Given the requirement of imminence, is the defense of "necessity" defined by the court truly a defense of "lesser evils"? Is it a justification or an excuse? The defendants seem to be saying that their offense was a carefully considered act of conscience rather than an expression of fear and desperation. Does the defense of necessity justify this sort of sober decision to take the law into one's own hands? Should it?

2. Does this kind of "political" justification defense raise different issues from those in the cases discussed previously? Do you think that the protesters should have had a justification defense? Should the issue have been submitted to the jury for their decision?

Who is the most "democratic" decisionmaker on questions of nuclear policy: (a) the legislature; (b) the jury; or (c) the legislature, informed by the press coverage and outcomes of jury trials of anti-nuclear protestors?

3. *The Stafford sit-in.* How would you analyze the following case? [48]

Jury Acquits Vt. Protesters of Trespass

Burlington, Vt. — A jury agreed last night with 26 protesters who had argued that their occupation of the Vermont office of U.S. Sen. Robert Stafford (R-Vt.) was an essential part of their campaign against U.S. policies in Central America.

The jury found the protesters innocent of criminal trespass, accepting the so-called necessity defense used by the protesters, which said the trespassing was necessary to prevent the greater evil of U.S. involvement in Central America. . . .

The group had called in a number of national authorities on Central America, including two ex-CIA agents, as defense lawyers sought to prove to the jury of Vermonters that the policies of President Ronald Reagan were wrong.

Judge Frank Mahady had allowed the protesters to use the necessity defense, which is rarely invoked, permitted or used successfully. The prosecutors had dismissed the notion of the necessity defense, charging that the demonstrators broke the law by refusing to leave when asked.

"What one feels about Central America is really not at issue in this case," said Kevin Bradley, state's attorney for Chittenden County. "Senator Stafford had a right to run that office. The question is, was that right violated?" . . .

"We fully intend to use our trial to put the Reagan Administration's Central American war policy on trial," protester Jeanne Keller said when the trial started. "We will show that a state of emergency exists, that our democracy is in jeopardy due to the misinformation campaign out of the White House, that the lives of our brothers and sisters in Central America are in danger and that our alleged criminal act was necessary to bring to light the illegal wars being waged in El Salvador and Nicaragua."

The controversy began in late March when the demonstrators showed up at Stafford's office and staged a peaceful protest against the senator's support of administration policy in Central America.

48. Boston Globe, Nov. 17, 1984, at 21.

The group felt it could pressure Stafford into changing his position for an upcoming vote in the Senate on emergency military aid to El Salvador. The protesters arrived on a Friday and were allowed to remain inside the senator's office complex over the weekend while Stafford's aides went home. On March 26, Stafford's top Vermont aide, Rey Post, asked the group to leave. They refused. . . .

Five of the demonstrators went to trial earlier and were found guilty.

Did Judge Mahady follow the decision in *Warshow*? What should happen to the five protesters who happened to have been tried first and convicted?

As a juror, would your attitude toward the defense depend on your view in the debate over Central American policy? If so, should policy on this issue be decided by the national government or by local juries? Or is the point that this is one way of getting the issue decided by the national government?

How might you have viewed a political justification defense on behalf of protestors in Germany in 1938? Would it matter whether they were objecting to maltreatment of ethnic and religious minorities, or objecting to continued toleration of these minorities?

4. *U.S. v. Kabat.* The federal sabotage statute, 18 U.S.C. section 2155(a), imposes serious felony punishment on "[w]hoever, with intent to injure, interfere with, or obstruct the national defense of the United States, willfully injures, destroys, . . . or attempts to injure [or] destroy . . . any national-defense material." The defendants in United States v. Kabat, 797 F.2d 580 (8th Cir. 1986), were peace activists and included two Roman Catholic priests. They were convicted of sabotage and sentenced from eight to 18 years' imprisonment for breaking into the periphery of an ICBM missile facility and damaging various radar and electrical devices. The total damage was about $30,000; no missile operations were affected in any way. The defendants appealed on the grounds that their goal was not to sabotage national security but rather to enhance the national security by causing it to rest on peace-seeking measures and attitudes instead of military preparedness and confrontation. The Eighth Circuit conceded that section 2155 (a) contained a high "specific intent" requirement that, in effect, amounted to a "motive" requirement. See United States v. Johnson, 15 M.J. 676 (A.F.C.M.R. 1983) (airman not guilty of sabotage where he deliberately damaged airplane engines, since his real motive was to express anger at receiving letter of reprimand). Nevertheless, the court held that despite the defendants' purported patriotic motives, they did indeed exhibit the specific intent to "interfere with what may commonly be taken as the country's activities of national preparedness." 797 F.2d at 587.

Does the court's reading of the sabotage statute effectively bar any possible necessity defense claim in prosecutions under this statute? Should it have mattered that the defendants were perfectly well aware that, given the modest tools they were using, it was physically impossible for them to interfere with the impregnable missile facility itself, so that their vandalism could at best serve symbolic goals? See id. at 595 (Bright, J., dissenting).

5. The prevailing pattern in "political justification" cases is now for judges to allow defendants to make their political case to the jury and — more importantly — the press and the public by presenting evidence of the harms they sought to prevent. Then the judge usually instructs the jury not to consider the evidence. The defendants get the sought-for opportunity to influence policy (or at least public opinion) and sympathetic jurors are given an opportunity to

nullify the law by acquitting, and to thereby "send a message" to public officials. Thus, contemporary judges are often tolerant of efforts to "use" jury trials to stage public debate about controversial issues. Is this an appropriate use of the legal system's strained resources? Recall that the jury trial is a scarce and expensive resource, available in a very small proportion of criminal cases.

6. *Antiabortion sit-ins*. Protestors at abortion clinics frequently raise necessity defenses to criminal charges, arguing that the saving of the life of the unborn outweighs the harm of their crimes. Because Roe v. Wade, 410 U.S. 113 (1973), has given constitutional status to the right to obtain an abortion, lower courts have precluded protestors from even raising necessity as a defense before the jury, certainly where the crime is homicide, see Hill v. State, 688 So.2d 901 (Fla. 1996), and almost universally where the crime is a non-violent trespass illegal under state property law, e.g., Cleveland v. Municipality of Anchorage, 631 P.2d 1073 (Alaska 1981). But applying the simple rule that there can be no necessity defense where the harm to be prevented is in fact a legal right still depends on the level of generality at which the protected activity is examined. In McMillan v. City of Jackson, 701 So.2d 1101 (Miss. 1997), the defendant conceded she had trespassed at an abortion clinic but argued for a necessity defense, not only on the broad ground that she hoped to save unborn fetuses from abortion, but also because she suspected that some abortions done at the clinic were not legally protected by Roe v. Wade. The court rejected this argument, holding that defendants had provided no evidence of such illegal abortions, but the dissent insisted:

> McMillan's counsel indicated that they had evidence and testimony to show that it was reasonable for McMillan to believe that *viable* fetuses were being aborted at the Mississippi Women's Clinic on the day she trespassed. This information is relevant in determining whether the first element has been met since there is no constitutional right to abort a viable fetus. In *Casey*, the United States Supreme Court noted, "[t]he woman's right to terminate her pregnancy *before* viability is the most central principle of *Roe v. Wade*." *Planned Parenthood of Southeastern Pa. v. Casey*, 505 U.S. 833, 871 (1992) (emphasis added). Neither *Roe* nor *Casey* held that any constitutional right to abortion exists once a fetus is viable. On the contrary, any injury or killing of a viable fetus must carry the presumption of illegality. (Id. at 1110, Smith, J. dissenting.)

Should the defendant have been afforded the benefit of the doubt as to the possibility that some viable fetuses were being aborted? Why would the court prefer not to let the jury hear testimony as to that probability? Or as to the defendants' good-faith, if erroneous, belief that this was happening?

C. DURESS

The defense of duress differs from necessity and lesser evils in that it always involves a response to a human threat rather than a natural danger. Duress differs from defensive force because the offense is committed to further rather than to resist the criminal project of the aggressor. Hence duress is clearly an excuse, not a justification; it deflects responsibility for a coerced wrongful act from the perpetrator onto the person who coerced it, and so amounts to a claim that fear rendered the perpetrator blameless or undeterrable. Nevertheless, the defense of duress has traditionally been limited by some considerations of proportionality: The defense fails if the defendant's offense was too great or the threat facing her insufficient. Thus, at common law, the duress defense required that the alleged coercion involved an imminent threat of death or serious bodily harm. Moreover, it would not excuse the killing of an innocent person even if the accused acted in response to immediate threats.

STATE v. CRAWFORD
Supreme Court of Kansas
253 Kan. 629, 861 P.2d 791 (1993)

ALLEGRUCCI, J.

This is a direct appeal by Ace Crawford of his jury convictions of seven counts of aggravated robbery, two counts of aggravated battery, two counts of kidnapping, and four counts of aggravated burglary. He was sentenced to a controlling term of 60 years to life in prison.

Crawford testified that, on February 17, 1991, he traveled from Kansas City to Topeka with Larry Bateman and Bateman's girlfriend. Crawford owed money to Bateman for cocaine which Bateman had supplied to him. Bateman wanted Crawford to commit some robberies in Topeka in order to get money. During the drive, Bateman's girlfriend gave a gun to Crawford. In Topeka they first stopped at the Ramada Inn.

Leaving the Ramada Inn, Bateman drove Crawford to Parkview Hospital. Crawford testified that when Nancy Jo Overholt came out of the hospital, Bateman told him to rob her. As Overholt was putting her seat belt on, Crawford approached her and pointed the gun at her. She grabbed the barrel of the gun, and the two struggled. Crawford pulled the gun from her grasp and hit her with the butt of it. She gave him her wedding rings, and, when she could not get her other ring off, Crawford hit her again with the butt of the gun.

When Crawford walked away from her, Overholt stood and yelled to an approaching man, telling him to run because Crawford had a gun. Overholt's head wounds required sutures, she suffered a concussion, and she spent three days in the hospital.

Crawford approached Mark Monhollon, the man Overholt tried to warn, put the gun in Monhollon's ribs, and told him it was a big gun which would "put a big hole in a big man." At gunpoint, Monhollon got into the driver's seat of his car, and Crawford got in behind him. As Monhollon drove, Crawford kept the gun pressed in Monhollon's side and took Monhollon's wallet and checkbook out of his pockets. Seeing Monhollon's address on his checks, Crawford told him to drive to his residence.

Once inside Monhollon's duplex, Crawford made Monhollon lie face down on the floor, then crawl into the next room where Crawford took Monhollon's ring and the cash from his pockets. While Monhollon was forced to crawl along on the floor, Crawford went from room to room opening storage areas and drawers and pulling or dumping out the contents. Crawford pulled pictures off the walls, tore up photographs, and ripped up the beds.

Crawford changed into Monhollon's clothes and shoes. He ate and drank Monhollon's food and soft drinks. When Crawford made a telephone call, Monhollon heard him say "Steven" or "Stevenson" and "I have transportation." Then Crawford began asking Monhollon about his friends and neighbors as possible sources for another car and valuables.

At gunpoint, Crawford took Monhollon to the back door of the other half of his duplex and instructed him to say his phone was not working. Monhollon's neighbor, Bernice Looka, let him in and Crawford followed him. In the bedroom, Crawford went through Looka's jewelry and dresser drawers. Then Crawford told Looka to take off her clothes and he handcuffed her to the faucet in the bathroom. He made Monhollon wait while he ate Looka's ice cream and cookies.

At gunpoint, Crawford took Monhollon back to his half of the duplex. Crawford went through Monhollon's house a second time, gathering up items he had passed over the first time. Crawford made Monhollon load things into the car and get into the passenger seat.

With Crawford driving, they set out to find an automatic bank teller machine where Crawford could use the bank card he had taken from Monhollon's wallet. Crawford made Monhollon ride on the floor. Crawford then pulled into a residential driveway and said to Monhollon, "We'll walk in here like we own the place."

After they got inside, the homeowner, Nancy Kinney, who had been outside, came into her garage. Crawford pointed the gun at her. When Kinney screamed and tried to run away, Crawford struck her with the gun, and she lost consciousness. When she regained consciousness, Crawford put the gun in her back and forced her into the house where she saw Monhollon lying face down on the floor. Crawford went through the house, looking for money, jewelry, and guns. Kinney got into her purse to get money for Crawford. Crawford then took Kinney to the basement and told her to count to a thousand before coming up.

Crawford told Monhollon to carry the television out to the car. Monhollon got back on the floor of the car, and they drove to an automatic teller machine. With the gun pointed at Monhollon, Crawford gave him the bank card and told him to withdraw his money. Monhollon gave Crawford the money, they drove to what Monhollon believed was the Ramada Inn, and Crawford put Monhollon in the trunk of the car.

Crawford got out of the car to make a phone call, and he warned Monhollon not to do anything. After Crawford returned to the car, Monhollon heard another car drive up, some discussion, and a car drive off. Crawford drove to Lawrence with Monhollon in the trunk. Upon arriving in Lawrence, Crawford stopped at the Holidome. According to Crawford, Bateman was not satisfied with the evening's take and threatened to hurt him and his son if he did not get more. Crawford testified that Bateman instructed him to wait until after midnight and then rob the Holidome. Quite a long time passed while Monhollon remained in the trunk, the car was moved, and the car doors were opened and closed.

After it got quiet around the car, Monhollon kicked the back seat forward so that he could crawl into the interior of the car. He was alone, the keys were in the seat, and he drove from the Holidome parking lot in Lawrence to the turnpike entrance where he told a police officer what had happened.

Lawrence police officers found Crawford underneath a table in the restaurant of the Holidome. Items taken from Crawford by the police included a loaded semiautomatic pistol, a piece of rock cocaine, a glass pipe, some cigarette lighters, and a Holidome room key. . . .

At trial, Crawford testified that when he first began using crack cocaine, he bought it from Bateman. During the months immediately before the occurrences at issue, Bateman informed Crawford that he owed $6,000 and then $10,000 for crack cocaine he had gotten on credit. When Bateman began pressuring him, Crawford went to another supplier. Crawford testified that Bateman and some cronies learned that he had gone to another supplier and threatened him; Crawford believed that Bateman was going to kill him.

After his arrest, Crawford told police that he lived at the Riverview Project in Kansas City. At trial, Crawford testified that he lived in a crack house which Bateman operated and that he was not free to come and go as he pleased. Crawford denied being one of Bateman's "workers," but he stated that "until I could pay him his money off I had to do what he asked me to do," including committing crimes. Crawford testified that Bateman "had me doing a lot of crimes in Kansas City."

When asked on direct examination about how and why he moved into the crack house, Crawford gave the following answer:

> So he got to telling me about I know that he's a member of the Moorish Americans and I know that the type of individuals that he was speaking of were some dangerous people and that it wouldn't be nothing for him to call down there to his friends where my son and mother, the store that she works for and have somebody to set her up while the Ace is with her and possibly burn them up in the house or shoot and kill them.

Crawford testified that Bateman knew about Crawford's son because "he's originally from St. Louis and he knows Anthony Bradley, whom my son's mother works for."

Crawford testified that the Moorish Americans were a religious group who had a branch that "was basically just involved in drug warfare and selling dope and hurting people and stuff like that." Crawford described an instance of revenge killing which he had heard about. Then he was asked the following question and gave the following answer:

Q. Now your knowledge of the St. Louis Moorish American sects have any influence to you as to whether Larry Bateman could in fact hurt your son?
A. Yes, he could, because he was friends with some members down there, the Moor Sciences Temple of America that are still down there, could go do the same thing, driving Cadillacs, got a lot of money.

He gave the following explanation for not going to the police in these circumstances:

A. I just didn't feel that they would believe me with the shape that I was in, and plus I was a junkie. And if they didn't believe me or something and Bateman or somebody found out and get word back to him or something then I didn't have no type of security whatsoever over my son.
Q. What type of security did you have over your son when you were with Bateman?

A.   Because as long as I was doing what he asked and trying to pay him his money that I owed him he wasn't going to do nothing to me or my son. . . .

At trial, Dr. Gilbert Roland Parks, a psychiatrist, testified on behalf of Crawford. Dr. Parks testified that Crawford suffered from chronic drug dependence and use, chronic depression, . . . and an extremely dependent personality disorder. He was of the opinion that Crawford committed the crimes at issue "under the fear" of Bateman.

The first issue asserted on appeal by Crawford is that the district court's instruction on compulsion was erroneous. K.S.A. 21-3209 provides:

> (1) A person is not guilty of a crime other than murder or voluntary manslaughter by reason of conduct which he performs under the compulsion or threat of the imminent infliction of death or great bodily harm, if he reasonably believes that death or great bodily harm will be inflicted upon him or upon his spouse, parent, child, brother or sister if he does not perform such conduct.
> (2) The defense provided by this section is not available to one who willfully or wantonly places himself in a situation in which it is probable that he will be subjected to compulsion or threat. . . .

In the present case, the district court instructed the jurors as follows:

> It is a defense to the charges made against the defendant if he acted under the compulsion or threat of imminent infliction of death or great bodily harm, and he reasonably believed that death or great bodily harm would have been inflicted upon him or upon his child had he not acted as he did.
> Such a defense is not available to one who willfully or wantonly placed himself in a situation in which it was probable that he would have been subjected to compulsion or threat.
> The compulsion or coercion which will excuse the commission of a criminal act must be present, imminent and impending and of such a nature as to induce a well-grounded apprehension of death or serious bodily harm if the act is not done; it must be continuous, and there must be no reasonable opportunity to escape the compulsion without committing the crime. A threat of future injury is not enough, particularly after danger from the threat has passed.

Crawford complains of the district court's addition of the third paragraph, in particular the last sentence. . . .

Crawford argues that there is a real possibility that the jurors would have concluded that he was not guilty due to compulsion had they been correctly instructed. His argument is that, when the legislature used the word "imminent," it was not disallowing the threat of future infliction of death or harm as a defense. He contends that cases such as State v. Myers, 233 Kan. 611, 664 P.2d 834 (1983), and State v. Harrison, 228 Kan. 558, 618 P.2d 827 (1980), which disallow the threat of future harm as a defense are not controlling in the present case where compulsion is not due to the physical presence at the crime scene of a threatening person. . . .

The State contends that the language which the district court added . . . was approved in *Harrison,* 228 Kan. at 560, where State v. Milum, 213 Kan. 581, 516 P.2d 984 (1973), was cited. The State argues that, in any event, the evidence which is relevant to compulsion is extremely thin. . . .

Milum escaped from the Kansas State Penitentiary. The district court refused, on the ground of relevance, to admit his proffered evidence that the deputy warden, on several occasions and in the presence of witnesses, told Milum that he "'had better run off or I will have you shot.'" 213 Kan. at 583. The court noted that the alleged threats were made in June or July and that Milum escaped on August 7, 1970. It concluded:

> It is apparent that the threats, if such there were, were made on several different occasions and thus could not have met the statutory requirement of imminence. At best the threats were aimed at some indefinite time in the future. . . .
> Milum's evidence in its most favorable light would have shown no immediate threat; since it would not establish the supposed defense it was not error to exclude it. 213 Kan. at 583-84, 516 P.2d 894.

In State v. Harrison, Harrison was convicted of aggravated robbery of a convenience store. The district court refused to admit her proffered evidence of compulsion on the ground that it was insufficient as a matter of law to sustain the defense because there was no imminent danger. The substance of Harrison's proffered evidence was that, while she was at the residence of Phil Heath, he "took her into his bedroom, produced a gun, and told her that he would use the weapon on her unless she committed the robbery in question," that attempts to subpoena Heath had been unsuccessful, and that Harrison "was fearful, not only for her own life, but also for the lives of her children if she did not complete the crime as demanded by Heath." 228 Kan. at 559. . . .

This court concluded that the district court had acted properly:

> In our judgment, *Milum* is controlling and dispositive of this case. The general rule followed throughout the country is that in order for the defense of compulsion to be established it must be shown that the accused was without a reasonable opportunity to escape or withdraw from the criminal activity.
> Under the proffered facts here, assuming that they are true, the defendant, having been threatened by Heath, left his house in her own car, drove away, and committed the robbery. There was nothing to prevent her from driving to the police authorities to report the threats made to her. The vague reference to her children is not sufficient to show that there was a present, imminent, and impending threat of direct or serious bodily injury to either herself or her children. She did not propose to testify that the children were in the custody of Heath at his house when she committed the robbery. Such testimony would have changed the factual situation and possibly made the defense of compulsion a factual issue for the jury. 228 Kan. at 560, 618 P.2d 827.

In State v. Myers, Myers was convicted of aggravated burglary, kidnapping, and felony murder. On appeal he argued that the district court had erred in refusing to admit proffered evidence of compulsion and to instruct the jury on the defense. . . .

The evidence showed that in connection with a drug transaction Myers and a man named Axvig entered an apartment occupied by two sisters and Kevin Kitchens, the boyfriend of one of the sisters. Myers proffered evidence that, before entering the apartment, Axvig put a gun to Myers' head, took the clip out of Myers' gun, and said, "'I have your family, do as I tell you or they'll be hurt.'" 233 Kan. at 614. Myers also proffered the testimony that Axvig "stated that there was somebody at the house with Nanette and the kids." 233 Kan. at 614.

The court concluded that the proffered evidence, as a matter of law, would not have established the defense of compulsion. The court reasoned as follows:

> Compulsion, to constitute a defense under K.S.A. 21-3209, must be present, imminent, and impending; it must be continuous; there must be no reasonable opportunity to escape the compulsion without committing the crime. Here, under the proffered evidence, the compulsion was imminent when Myers entered the apartment; thereafter, when Myers was out of the sight and presence of Axvig, it was not imminent. The compulsion was not continuous; Myers and Axvig went their separate ways and operated independently; the compulsion was interrupted time after time. Finally, Myers had abundant opportunities to make his escape, and failed to do so. Myers could have freed the women before or at the time they left the apartment, and he could have made his escape before the murder was committed. 233 Kan. at 616.

The evidence in the present case of Crawford's cocaine addiction and dependence on and indebtedness to Bateman is all that distinguishes it from *Milum, Harrison,* and *Myers.* In other respects, Crawford's evidence of compulsion suffers from the shortcomings discussed in the earlier cases — the required element of an imminent threat is missing, the compulsion is not continuous, and there were opportunities for escape. The question, therefore, is whether circumstances which generally would not constitute compulsion may establish the defense due to the interpersonal dynamics of the defendant and the compelling person.

Crawford contends that he was justified in fearing danger to himself and his son because threats had been made against them by a ruthless drug dealer with ties to a network of violent people. The reasonableness of his apprehension, he argues, should be measured in light of all the evidence of his subservience to Bateman and his perception of his options for escaping from Bateman's control being limited. His chemical dependence and psychological state, he argues, are central to a determination of reasonableness. The next step in the argument appears to be that, as in State v. Hundley, 236 Kan. 461, 693 P.2d 475 (1985), an improper instruction prevented the jury from considering critical factors when determining reasonableness. In *Hundley,* use of the word "immediate" "impermissibly excluded from the jury's consideration the effect on the appellant of the history of violence toward her by the decedent." 693 P.2d. at 480. In the present case, Crawford argues use of the additional paragraph, and in particular the last sentence, impermissibly excluded from the jury's consideration the effect on Crawford of his subservience to and dependence on Bateman. . . .

[T]he weakness in Crawford's theory of defense lies in the indefiniteness of any threat to him or his son. Crawford suggests that this court embrace the position taken by the Ninth Circuit Court of Appeals in [United States v. Contento-Pachon, 723 F.2d 691, 693 (9th Cir. 1984)]. We do not find *Contento-Pachon* to be persuasive. The federal defense which was asserted by Contento-Pachon was duress. Its elements are: "(1) an immediate threat of death or serious bodily injury, (2) a well-grounded fear that the threat will be carried out, and (3) no reasonable opportunity to escape the threatened harm."

Not only are the facts distinguishable from the present case, but the element which the circuit court did not discuss separately is the element of reasonableness of the fear. It is precisely this element which seems most critical in the present case. It also is the element to which the evidence of Crawford's psychological state was directed.

Nor is the federal defense, at least insofar as it is discussed in *Contento-Pachon,* subject to the proviso present in the Kansas statute on compulsion. K.S.A. 21-3209(2) precludes use of the defense by "one who willfully or wantonly places himself in a situation in which it is probable that he will be subjected to compulsion or threat." A strong argument could be made that the defense of compulsion is not available to Crawford due to his placing himself in a position of dependence on and indebtedness to Bateman.

The district court's instruction to the jury on the defense of compulsion is a correct statement of the law. . . . Crawford has not presented facts or arguments which convince this court to depart from our prior decisions. We do not find the instruction to be clearly erroneous. . . .

Notes and Questions

1. The court lays out the criteria for the duress defense in a case involving the very serious crimes of robbery, kidnapping, and aggravated battery. Did it thereby rule that Crawford might have been entitled to weigh the life of his son against the physical safety of, including at least serious risk of death to, innocent strangers? What could justify this balance?

2. Is Crawford's argument based on a retributivist approach or a utilitarian approach? What approach does the court take? Is Crawford arguing that he chose the lesser of two evils? If not, how can he deny liability? Is he arguing that he had no choice? Will decisions like this deter the future Crawfords from committing crimes under these circumstances?

3. Why isn't Monhollon himself liable for robbery? What different set of facts would have given Crawford a plausible duress defense under the Kansas standard? Must he have had a gun held to his back as Monhollon did? Does the decision in *Myers* virtually require just that?

4. *The Model Penal Code standard.* How does the standard for duress in *Crawford* differ from the following in the Model Penal Code? And how much stronger might his duress claim have been under the MPC?

Sec. 2.09 Duress

(1) It is an affirmative defense that the actor engaged in the conduct charged to constitute an offense because he was coerced to do so by the use of, or a threat to use, unlawful force against his person or the person of another, that a person of reasonable firmness in his situation would have been unable to resist.

(2) The defense provided by this Section is unavailable if the actor recklessly placed himself in a situation in which it was probable that he would be subjected to duress. The defense is also unavailable if he was negligent in placing himself in such a situation, whenever negligence suffices to establish culpability for the offense charged.

(3) It is not a defense that a woman acted on the command of her husband, unless she acted under such coercion as would establish a defense under this Section. [The presumption that a woman acting in the presence of her husband is coerced is abolished.]

(4) When the conduct of the actor would otherwise be justifiable under Section 3.02, this Section does not preclude such defense.

Consider the MPC Commentary:[49]

> The standard is not, however, wholly external in its reference; account is taken of the actor's "situation," a term that should here be given the same scope it is accorded in appraising recklessness and negligence. Stark, tangible factors that differentiate the actor from another, like his size, strength, age, or health, would be considered in making the exculpatory judgment. Matters of temperament would not.

Though the MPC, like *Crawford* and all courts, requires at least a threat to personal safety, not to property, as a minimum requirement for the duress defense, the Code commentators also note:

> Beyond this limitation to coercive force or threats against the person, no valid reason was perceived for demanding that the threat be one of death or even of great bodily harm, that the imperiled victim be the actor rather than another or that the injury portended be immediate in point of time. It is sufficient that factors such as these be given evidential weight, along with other circumstances in the application of the statutory standard that a person of "reasonable firmness" would have succumbed to the pressure. They must be weighed, of course, together with other factors, since persons of reasonable firmness surely break at different points depending on the stakes that are involved. It is obvious that even homicide may sometimes be the product of coercion that is truly irresistible, that danger to a loved one may have greater impact on a person of reasonable firmness than a danger to himself, and, finally, that long and wasting pressure may break down resistance more effectively than a threat of immediate destruction.

Is the Code too generous? Too relativistic?

5. *Duress, voluntariness, and mens rea.* Could Crawford have recharacterized his duress claim as something other than an affirmative defense? Could he have said that because of the pressure from Bateman he did not even commit a voluntary act in engaging in the robberies and batteries? That would seem a wildly implausible view of the voluntary act requirement.[50] But might he at least have argued that he lacked the required mens rea for these crimes — that duress deprived him of the capacity to act intentionally? Note that were he able to recharacterize duress as a factor negating mens rea, rather than an affirmative defense, he would shift the burden of proof on this issue to the state. But if duress negates mens rea, why not mistaken duress? Thus, what if the state established that Crawford had exaggerated the risk of harm he had faced from Bateman? Might Crawford then still argue that he had made an honest, if unreasonable, mistake about the gravity and imminence of the threat, and that the prosecution would have to bear the burden of disproving the honesty of that mistake? Courts have rejected any such effort to recharacterize duress as negating the mental element. As stated in People v. King, 1 Cal. 4th 295, 2 Cal. Rptr. 2d 197 (Ct. App. 1991):

---

49. American Law Institute, Model Penal Code and Commentaries, §2.09, Part I, at 372-77 (1985).

50. "A criminal walking to his execution is under compulsion if any man can be said to be so, but his motions are just as much voluntary actions as if he was going to leave his place of confinement and regain his liberty. He walks to his death because he prefers it to being carried." 2 James Stephen, A History of the Criminal Law in England 102 (1883).

One who acts under an honest but unreasonable belief in duress faces an agonizing choice: the defendant simultaneously genuinely perceives the need to defend himself and understands that he can negate the threat to himself by performing a specific unlawful act against an innocent third party. To protect himself, he must both specifically intend to perform the unlawful act and act on that specific intent. There is no inconsistency here but a concurrence of act and intent. [2 Cal. Rptr. 2d 204.]

6. *United States v. Contento-Pachon.* This case, discussed in *Crawford*, concerned the following facts:

[The defendant] is a native of Bogota, Colombia and was employed there as a taxicab driver. He asserts that one of his passengers, Jorge, offered him a job as the driver of a privately owned car. Contento-Pachon expressed an interest in the job and agreed to meet Jorge and the owner of the car the next day.

Instead of a driving job, Jorge proposed that Contento-Pachon swallow cocaine-filled balloons and transport them to the United States. Contento-Pachon agreed to consider the proposition. He was told not to mention the proposition to anyone, otherwise he would "get into serious trouble." Contento-Pachon testified that he did not contact the police because he believes that the Bogota police are corrupt and that they are paid off by drug traffickers.

Approximately one week later, Contento-Pachon told Jorge that he would not carry the cocaine. In response, Jorge mentioned facts about Contento-Pachon's personal life, including private details which Contento-Pachon had never mentioned to Jorge. Jorge told Contento-Pachon that his failure to cooperate would result in the death of his wife and three-year-old child.

The following day the pair met again. Contento-Pachon's life and the lives of his family were again threatened. At this point, Contento-Pachon agreed to take the cocaine into the United States.

The pair met two more times. At the last meeting, Contento-Pachon swallowed 129 balloons of cocaine. He was informed that he would be watched at all times during the trip, and that if he failed to follow Jorge's instruction he and his family would be killed.

After leaving Bogota, Contento-Pachon's plane landed in Panama. Contento-Pachon asserts that he did not notify the authorities there because he felt that the Panamanian police were as corrupt as those in Bogota. Also, he felt that any such action on his part would place his family in jeopardy.

When he arrived at the customs inspection point in Los Angeles, Contento-Pachon consented to have his stomach x-rayed. The x-rays revealed a foreign substance which was later determined to be cocaine. [United States v. Contento-Pachon, 723 F.2d 691, 693 (9th Cir. 1984).]

The trial judge refused to submit the issue of duress to the jury on the ground that the defendant had shown neither the immediacy of the threat nor its inescapability. The court of appeals held that, under the facts, the defendant had presented a jury question as to whether he had been under duress:

Contento-Pachon presented credible evidence that he acted under an immediate and well-grounded threat of serious bodily injury, with no opportunity to escape. Because the trier of fact should have been allowed to consider the credibility of the proffered evidence, we reverse. [Id. at 695.]

Judge Coyle dissented from this view, arguing that

the trial court found that the defendant and his family enjoyed an adequate and reasonable opportunity to avoid or escape the threats of the drug dealers in the weeks before his flight. Until he went to the house where he ingested the balloons containing cocaine, defendant and his family were not physically restrained or prevented from seeking help. The record supports the trial court's findings that the defendant and his family could have sought assistance from the authorities or have fled. Cases considering the defense of duress have established that where there was a reasonable legal alternative to violating the law, a chance to refuse to do the criminal act and also to avoid the threatened danger, the defense will fail. Duress is permitted as a defense only when a criminal act was committed because there was no other opportunity to avoid the threatened danger. [Id. at 697.]

Should the issue of duress have been submitted to the jury? If so, is that because the threat was sufficiently "immediate," or because immediacy should not matter so long as a person of reasonable firmness would have found the threat irresistible?

7. *Placing oneself in danger of duress.* What does it mean for a duress claimant to have "willfully and wantonly" — or, in MPC language, "recklessly" or "negligently" — placed himself in the coercive situation? In Williams v. State, 101 Md. App. 408, 646 A.2d 1101 (1994), the defendant was convicted of attempted robbery with a deadly weapon, on these facts:

The victim, the Reverend Chris Glenn Hale, lived at 8601 Gray Fox Road, Apartment 102, in Randallstown, Maryland, at the time of the incident. On March 1, 1990, at or about 4:45 P.M., Hale heard a knock on his apartment door. He went to the door, looked through the keyhole, and saw Williams standing at the door. Hale asked who was there and Williams answered by mumbling, asking if a certain person resided at Hale's residence. Hale could not understand Williams so he partially opened the door, whereupon four men, including Williams, rushed through. One of the men, not Williams, proceeded to hold a gun to Hale's face. Hale noticed that three of the men were armed, but did not see if Williams was armed.

After the men entered Hale's apartment, they spread out around the apartment to search for other persons, and the apparent leader demanded that Hale divulge the location of "the money" and "the dope." Williams, in the meantime, kept telling the men that the "dope" was in Hale's apartment, that he and Hale were friends, and that he had been in the apartment the previous day where he had used the "dope" with Hale. After searching unsuccessfully for the "dope," Williams was forced to kneel next to Hale, and the three men made more demands of the both of them as to where the money and the dope were located. The men then allowed Williams to get up from the floor to make a telephone call. Williams spoke on the phone for about ten minutes, and when he got off the phone, he walked out of the bedroom with two of the men (including the leader), where they talked for about five minutes. Hale was then tied up and the men, including Williams, left shortly. Nothing was taken from Hale's apartment.

At the trial, Williams testified that he was abducted by the three men because they believed that he knew the whereabouts of the drug stash of one Chuckie Eubanks, a reputed drug dealer. Williams had borrowed money from Chuckie's brother, Rodney, and had been induced to make a drug run to New York in order to help repay his debt. The Eubanks organization required Williams to make a second trip to New York, during which Williams cooperated with the police and obtained the names, phone numbers, addresses, and license tag numbers of the parties involved in the drug deal. Apparently, the three abductors, who were former members of Eubanks's drug organization, knew of Williams's relationship with Eubanks and believed that he would know the location of the stash house. When Williams was abducted by the men, he told them that he did not know the location of the stash house. The men did not believe Williams and threatened to kill him if he did not disclose its location. Williams led the men to Hale's apartment, told them it was the stash house, and knocked on the door. Once inside Hale's apartment, Williams testified that he pretended to participate in the search of the premises. Williams also said that the phone call he made was to his mother and was done at the request of one of the abductors who instructed him to say that "everything was all right," the abductors being concerned because Williams's sister had witnessed the abduction. [Id. at 1103.]

The trial court ruled:

the [Appellant] wants you to believe that he was victimized, that he was taken off the street, and by point of gun, forced to commit an armed robbery. That simply is not true. No one forced him to commit an armed robbery. No one forced him to go to the Reverend's house and demand money. The only thing these three persons wanted was to have the debt repaid, and they didn't care how it was done. The [Appellant] said, I don't care how I repay the debt, I just want to save my own soul, and I will commit an armed robbery to do it, and I will assist in the commission of an armed robbery if that satisfies the debt, if that appeases you and I am safe. [Id. at 1103-1104.]

In rejecting the duress claim, the court cited MPC §2.09 (2) and the Comments to Tentative Draft No. 10:

subsection (2) accepts the view that there should be no exculpation if the actor recklessly placed himself in a situation in which it was probable that he would be subjected to duress. Though this provision may have the effect of sanctioning conviction of a crime of purpose when the actor's culpability was limited to recklessness, we think the substitution is permissible in view of the exceptional nature of the defense. The provision will have its main room for operation in the case of persons who connect themselves with criminal activities, in which case too fine a line need not be drawn.

The court then concluded:

Because Williams's prior conduct contributed mightily to the predicament in which he later found himself, the trial court did not err in concluding that the defense of duress was inapplicable to the instant case. Here, the evidence reveals that Williams voluntarily became involved with the Eubanks's drug organization. It is unrefuted that Williams borrowed money from Rodney Eubanks. Because of his inability to repay promptly, Williams allegedly was forced to make the first drug run up to New York. He also participated in another drug run. In other words, the evidence does not suggest that he was forced to make these runs, he did this of his own volition to help pay off his debt. By becoming involved with this drug ring, Williams through his own recklessness made others aware of his connection with Eubanks, including his abductors. Williams was readily identifiable to those in the organization, including his abductors, and the abductors acted accordingly. This was a situation that would not have occurred but for Williams's association with the drug organization. Considering these facts and the applicable law, we conclude that Williams's assertion that the defense of duress applies is unavailing. [Id. at 1110.]

MPC terms like "recklessly" or "negligently" normally apply to elements of offenses. To what do they apply in *Williams*? What indeed was Williams's actual culpability with respect to the possibility that he would have to commit a dangerous felony against an innocent person? In working for Eubanks did he foresee that he would become a target for others hoping to steal from Eubanks? How would your answer affect, if at all, your determination of his mental state for the crime with which he is now charged? Is the MPC comment too casual about "fine" mens rea distinctions?

8. *The gravity of the offense.* Note that the MPC does not categorically preclude a duress defense to homicide, though the common law did, and most state laws now do. A few states permit a defense of "imperfect duress," lowering murder to manslaughter, and a few others excuse accomplices in felony murders, but not intentional killers. Consider the next case.

STATE v. HUNTER
Supreme Court of Kansas
740 P.2d 559 (1987)

[Hunter was convicted of two counts of felony murder as a result of his participation with Daniel Remeta and others in the kidnapping and killing of Rick Schroeder and Glenn Moore. Hunter had hitched a ride in a pickup truck with Remeta's party. Hunter testified that Remeta then displayed guns, made menacing remarks about killing hitchhikers, and refused to let Hunter out when Hunter requested it. When the truck was pulled over by a police officer, whom Remeta shot him, though not fatally. The truck proceeded to a grain elevator where Remeta shot another person and, apparently with the assistance of Hunter, took Schroeder and Moore hostage. After the hostages were driven some distance, Remeta killed them and left their bodies by the side of the road.]

. . . Hunter contends that the trial court committed reversible error by refusing to instruct the jury on his defense of compulsion. We agree. . . . Defendant's requested instruction, taken from PIK Crim.2d 54.13, stated:

> It is a defense to the charges of Aggravated Battery Against a Law Enforcement Officer, Aggravated Robbery and Aggravated Kidnapping, if the defendant acted under compulsion or threat of immediate infliction of death or great bodily harm, and if said defendant reasonably believed that death or great bodily harm would have been inflicted upon said defendant had he or she not acted as he or she did.

The trial court refused to give the compulsion instruction because the defendant was charged with . . . felony murder. . . . Whether the defense of compulsion is available to a criminal defendant charged with felony murder under K.S.A. 21-3401 is an issue of first impression. Most modern statutes providing for a defense of compulsion evolved from the common-law policy that a person, when faced with a choice between suffering death or serious bodily harm and committing some lesser crime, could not be punished for committing the lesser offense. LaFave and Scott have explained the rationale of this "choice evils" approach as follows:

> One who, under the pressure of an unlawful threat from another human being to harm him (or to harm a third person), commits what would otherwise be a crime may, under some circumstances, be justified in doing what he did and thus not be guilty of the crime in question. . . . The rationale of the defense is not that the defendant, faced with the unnerving threat of harm unless he does an act which violates the literal language of the criminal law, somehow loses his mental capacity to commit the crime in question. Rather it is that, even though he has the mental state which the crime requires, his conduct which violates the literal language of

the criminal law is justified because he has thereby avoided harm of greater magnitude. LaFave and Scott, Handbook on Criminal Law 374 (1972).

However, even early cases refused to recognize any compulsion as sufficient to excuse intentional killing. . . . The rationale is that, when confronted by a choice between two evils of equal magnitude, the individual ought to sacrifice his own life rather than escape by the murder of an innocent. . . . A number of jurisdictions, including Kansas, have incorporated by statute the common law denial of the compulsion defense in crimes of murder. . . . While not all jurisdictions have considered the applicability of these statutes to crimes of felony murder, we note that both Arizona and Missouri have held that defendants are barred from claiming the compulsion defense in felony-murder cases. They reason that the person charged need only have the required intent to commit or participate in the underlying felony and no other mental state on his part need be demonstrated because of the strict liability imposed by the felony-murder rule. . . .

We are not, however, persuaded by the reasoning of these decisions. The better view, consistently adhered to by commentators, is that any limitation to the defense of duress be confined to crimes of intentional killing and not to killings done by another during the commission of some lesser felony. As Lafave and Scott have explained:

> [I]f A compels B at gunpoint to drive him to the bank which A intends to rob, and during the ensuing robbery A kills a bank customer C, B is not guilty of the robbery (for he was justified by duress) and so is not guilty of felony murder of C in the commission of robbery. The law properly recognizes that one is justified in aiding a robbery if he is forced by threats to do so to save his life; he should not lose the defense because his threateners unexpectedly kill someone in the course of the robbery and thus convert a mere robbery into a murder, p. 377. . . .

In a criminal action, a trial court must instruct the jury on the law applicable to the theories of all parties where there is supporting evidence. . . . We must determine whether there was evidence, when viewed in the light most favorable to the defendant, sufficient to require a compulsion instruction.

Hunter testified to the following pertinent facts regarding reasons for his fear of Remeta prior to the incident at the Levant elevator:

(1) On the trip from Wichita to Salina, Remeta fired the .22 three times out of the car window.

(2) When Hunter asked to be let out of the car as they reached Salina, Remeta refused and began to talk about a hitchhiker he wished he had killed.

(3) Remeta then took out two .357 Magnum bullets and asked Hunter if he thought they could kill him (Hunter).

(4) Remeta then told Hunter he had shot a girl five times with one of the weapons.

(5) Later, Remeta fired the .22 in the direction of Hunter while the car was stopped.

(6) Remeta told Hunter he had killed a man for $40 and had killed twelve other people. . . .

There were three versions of the events at the grain elevator in Levant. First, State's witnesses Christie, Sager, and Tubbs all testified that Hunter had played an active role in the kidnapping of Schroeder and Moore and the theft of the pickup truck. Christie and Sager testified that Hunter had a weapon. Second, Hunter testified that he had no weapon at the elevator and that he was ordered by Remeta to go to the other end of the building to watch to see if anyone tried to exit through the back door. According to Hunter he then walked around to the back of the building and stopped there to wait to see what happened, and Remeta then ordered him back around to the other side and into the pickup. Hunter testified that he never felt he had a chance to escape. Third, Remeta testified that he had both guns at all times. He further stated that he asked Hunter to watch Schroeder and Moore at the pickup truck and that he would have shot Hunter if he had not followed orders.

In order to constitute the defense of compulsion, the coercion or duress must be present, imminent, and impending, and of such a nature as to induce a well-grounded apprehension of death or serious bodily injury if the act is not done. The doctrine of coercion or duress cannot be invoked as an excuse by one who had a reasonable opportunity to avoid doing the act without undue exposure to death or serious bodily harm. State v. Milum, 213 Kan. 581, 582, 516 P.2d 984 (1973). In addition, the compulsion must be continuous and there must be no reasonable opportunity to escape the compulsion without committing the crime. State v. Myers, 233 Kan. at 616, 664 P.2d 834.

The only opportunity Hunter would have had for escape would have been when he was out of sight of Remeta at the point when he went around the north side of the building at the Levant elevator. Hunter testified that Remeta came around the building and ordered him to return to the pickup. There was testimony that the total time which elapsed at the grain elevator was approximately five minutes. From the record, it is impossible to tell how long Hunter remained out of sight of Remeta. Viewed in the light most favorable to Hunter, however, and particularly in light of the fact that it was undisputed that Remeta had possession of the .357 Magnum at all times, it cannot be said that Hunter had a reasonable opportunity to escape. [T]he record is replete with testimony that Daniel Remeta was a person to be feared. It was the function of the jury as the exclusive trier of fact to determine if it was believable that Hunter was afraid for his life, if such fear was reasonable, and if such fear justified any criminal acts which Hunter may have performed. When the trial judge refused the requested compulsion instruction, he effectively prevented the jury from considering the evidence presented in Hunter's defense. This denial of the jury's right to determine the facts constitutes reversible error.

Notes and Questions

1. Notice that the *Hunter* court, following Professors LaFave and Scott, explains the rule against excusing murder on grounds of duress by pointing out such murders are not justifiable as the lesser of two evils. Is the duress defense just a special case of justification by reason of lesser evils, or does it have some other basis? Professor Joshua Dressler offers the following critique of the LaFave and Scott position.[51]

What are the arguments for the common law rule that duress does not excuse a murder? Why is a defendant entitled to claim duress if she complies with a gun-to-the-head demand that she steal a car, but the defense is unavailable to her

51. Joshua Dressler, Understanding Criminal Law 279-81 (1995) (notes omitted).

if she kills as the result of precisely the same threat? From a utilitarian perspective, it would seem that the traditional justification for the defense, i.e., that a threat of future punishment would not deter an actor confronted by an immediate deadly threat, applies as much to coerced murders as it does to coerced thefts. . . . The retributivist argument for the no-defense position is also debatable. . . . [T]he no-defense rule supports the moral imperative that, "if a man be desperately assaulted, and in peril of death, and cannot otherwise escape, unless to satisfy his assailant's fury he will kill an innocent person then present . . . he ought rather to die himself than kill an innocent" [quoting Hale]. The difficulty with this argument, is that it supports the proposition that a coerced actor is *unjustified* in taking an innocent life, but it does not necessarily demonstrate that she should not be *excused* for violating the moral imperative. From a retributive perspective, . . . she does not deserve to be treated as a murderer: one who is compelled to kill has no greater (or lesser) opportunity to act freely than one who is ordered to steal a car, assuming that the coercive threat is the same in both circumstances. If a person of reasonable moral strength might comply with a kill-or-be-killed threat (or, perhaps more compellingly, a kill-or-I-will-kill-a-loved-one threat), the case for denying the defense, as a matter of law, is weakened considerably.

　　2. *Nonforcible coercion.* Model Penal Code §2.09 conditions the availability of the defense on the use or threat of unlawful force. Should it? Frieda, an aspiring novelist, has a day job in a jewelry store. Clarice steals the only manuscript copy of the novel Frieda has been working on for seven years, and threatens to destroy it unless Frieda leaves the store's door unlocked and the burglar alarm off so that Clarice can burglarize it (which Clarice proceeds to do). Should Frieda have a defense of duress to accomplice liability for burglary? Might a person of reasonable firmness succumb to such a threat?

　　What about pressures and influences that persons of reasonable firmness succumb to that do not take the form of direct threats? Professor Joshua Dressier poses the following problem concerning the application of Model Penal Code §2.09:[52]

> [S]uppose that by the continued use of unlawful force, persons effectively break down the personality of the actor, rendering him submissive to whatever suggestions they make. They then, using neither force nor threat of force on that occasion, suggest that he perform a criminal act; and the actor does what they suggest. The "brainwashed" actor would not be barred from claiming the defense of duress, since he may assert that he was "coerced" to perform the act by the use of unlawful force on his person. He might also argue that he is responding to earlier threats to use unlawful force that have rendered him submissive to those who made the threats because he still subconsciously fears they will be carried out. Of course, it may be very difficult to persuade a jury that an act willingly performed at the time was truly the product of unlawful force and would have been performed by a person of reasonable firmness subjected to similar conditions, but as framed, the section is broad enough to permit such an argument.

Does Professor Dressler's interpretation of §2.09 require making available a defense of duress for gang-related crime? Professor Richard Delgado evokes the following scenario:

> A youth moves into a ghetto neighborhood dominated by vicious street gangs. To survive, he must join one or the other of the gangs. Membership is achieved

---

52. Model Penal Code and Commentaries, *supra*, at 376.

through intensive indoctrination in gang values, including instant obedience to the gang leaders. The members are required to spend most of their time with the group, returning to the home only for meals and sleep. Violation of gang rules is punished by beatings or expulsion. Gang members are taught a code of conduct that includes robbery, arson, and hatred of adults.[53]

Could either scenario actually fit within MPC §2.09?

What if a defendant is "brainwashed" without the threat of illegal force? In a famous psychology experiment, a psychologist told student subjects that they would be administering test questions to other subjects as part of a learning experiment. The "tester" subjects were told to press a switch each time the "learner" subject gave a wrong answer, and they were told that doing so would administer an electric shock to the learner. This was not in fact true. The "learner" subjects were actors giving scripted responses both to the test questions and the fictitious "shocks." The psychologist induced almost all of his subjects to administer what they thought were increasingly painful and injurious electric shocks past the point where the "learners" protested and demanded to be released. When the subjects hesitated to increase the "voltage" despite the cries from the "learners," the psychologist simply repeated that the experiment required that they continue. Sixty-five percent continued until the highest level of "voltage" was reached. In light of this data it appears that the "person of reasonable firmness" finds even modest psychological pressure from an authority figure difficult to resist.[54] Is this a duress case?

Consider Professor Leo Katz's interesting summary of the facts in United States v. Olsen, 20 C.M.R. 461 (1955), in which psychological pressure played at least as important a role as physical coercion in "brainwashing" the subject:

> Master Sergeant William Olsen was captured during the Korean war by the Communist forces in late 1950 and taken to the Kangye prisoner of war camp. There the Chinese who ran the camp set out to educate him and his fellow prisoners as to the "true" nature of the war, namely, "that they [the prisoners] were the victims of the warmongers and were the aggressors in Korea." The education was in no way haphazard. It was systematic and relentless, involving countless hours of lecturing, group discussion, and interrogation. The Chinese called this treatment of the POWs "lenient policy," because it was short on threats and long on "persuasion." Over the course of the war, it proved remarkably successful. It got American POWs to do things the Germans had never gotten them to do. They informed on each other, frustrated each other's escape attempts, and in one way or another almost all collaborated with the enemy.
>
> The capstone of the Chinese strategy was "start small and build," which the psychologist Robert Cialdini describes thus:
>
>> Prisoners were frequently asked to make statements so mildly anti-American or pro-Communist as to seem inconsequential. ("The United States is not perfect." "In a Communist country, unemployment is not a problem.") But once these minor requests were complied with, the men found themselves pushed to submit to related yet more substantive requests. A man who had just agreed with his Chinese interrogator that the United States is not perfect might then be asked to make a list of these "problems with America" and to sign his name to it. Later he might be asked to read his list

---

53. A Response to Professor Dressler, 63 Minn. L. Rev. 361, 365 (1979).

54. The experiments are described and interpreted in Stanley Milgram, Obedience to Authority (1974).

in a discussion group with other prisoners. "After all, it's what you believe, isn't it?" Still later, he might be asked to write an essay expanding on his list and discussing these problems in greater detail.

The Chinese might then use his name and his essay in an anti-American radio broadcast beamed not only to the entire camp but to other POW camps in North Korea as well as to American forces in South Korea. Suddenly he would find himself a "collaborator," having given aid and comfort to the enemy. Aware that he had written the essay without any strong threats or coercion, many times a man would change his image of himself to be consistent with the deed and with the new "collaborator" label, often resulting in even more extensive acts of collaboration.

On Christmas day 1950 Olsen and his fellow prisoners were assembled for a Christmas party and bullied into making some speeches. Olsen was one of those who spoke. He noted that the Communists were treating their prisoners better than the Germans did theirs during World War II. He also said that the Korean war was a "millionaire's war and that the prisoners had innocent blood on their hands." Later Olsen and some other prisoners were moved to a camp for newly arrived POWs. Olsen would greet the new arrivals by telling them "how to get along with" the Communists, "that escape was impossible, that the Chinese were not guards but were there to protect the prisoners from the Koreans, and [that] they, the prisoners, had been cannon fodder for the imperialists and warmongers." He contributed articles to some POW publications, lauding the Communists' treatment of POWs and saying that America "was engaged in an imperialistic war to fatten certain capitalists and that the blood of innocent victims was on the hands of Americans." After the war, Olsen was charged with aiding the enemy.[55]

Olsen pled insanity unsuccessfully. But should he have been permitted a defense of duress on these facts? Was Olsen coerced to collaborate, or did he simply respond to rational persuasion? In considering whether the Chinese techniques of persuasion should be seen as coercive, bear in mind that Olsen's "offense" consisted merely in assisting the Chinese to persuade others. In determining that Olsen's conduct constituted the offense of "aid[ing] . . . the enemy with arms, ammunition, supplies, money or other thing[s]," the military court concluded that in modern warfare "psychological weapons have become as important as arms, ammunition, and guided missiles. . . . As a result we feel it is unrealistic to say that propaganda [and] the information on which it is based . . . are not 'things' which can aid the enemy." 20 C.M.R. at 462.

10. *Duress and battered-woman syndrome.* An interesting juxtaposition of duress and self-defense law is found when a defendant claims she was brainwashed or intimidated into committing an offense as a result of battered woman syndrome. In In re Romero, 15 Cal. App. 4th 1519, 13 Cal. Rptr. 2d 332 (1992), a California court held that Debra Romero, convicted of robbery and attempted robbery, was denied effective assistance of counsel because her lawyer did not present evidence that her actions were a result of battered woman syndrome. The court held that:

When a woman kills her batterer and pleads self-defense, expert testimony about BWS [battered woman syndrome] is admissible to explain how her particular experiences as a battered woman affected her perceptions of danger and her honest

---

55. Leo Katz, Bad Acts and Guilty Minds, 63-64, 80 (1987) (quoting United States v. Olsen 20 C.M.R. 461, 462 and Robert Cialdini, Influence: The New Psychology of Persuasion, 76 (1984)). The editors have rearranged the order of some of Katz's paragraphs, for ease of exposition.

belief in its imminence and also to rehabilitate her credibility when the prosecutor has attempted to impeach her by urging that her conduct is inconsistent with her claim of self-defense. . . .

If BWS testimony is relevant when a woman kills her batterer, it is a fortiori relevant to her credibility when she participates in robberies at her batterer's insistence. . . . [A] rule permitting testimony about BWS in a self-defense case must necessarily permit it in a case where duress is claimed as a defense.

Is the court right? What reasons might a court give for only accepting a battered woman's syndrome defense in cases in which the woman kills her batterer? At least one court disagrees. In United States v. Willis, 38 F.3d 170 (5th Cir. 1994), Willis, charged with carrying a firearm in connection with a drug crime, wanted to argue that her batterer had placed the gun in her purse against her will. In rejecting her request, the court held that:

in order for a duress defense to criminal liability to succeed, the coercive force of the threat must be sufficient that a person of ordinary firmness would succumb. Additionally there must be no reasonable legal alternative to violating the law. These requirements set out an objective test. To consider battered woman's syndrome evidence in applying that test, however, would be to turn the objective inquiry that duress has always required into a subjective one. The question would no longer be whether a person of ordinary firmness could have resisted. Instead, the question would change to whether this individual woman, in light of the psychological condition from which she suffers, could have resisted. [Id. at 176.]

In light of our earlier examination of self-defense, is the court right about the subjective-objective distinction? Should evidence of battered woman's syndrome be admitted to show whether a person of ordinary firmness would succumb after being victimized repeatedly by violence? Consider the following argument by Prof. Alafair Burke:[56]

. . . Just as Walker's battered woman syndrome theory purports to explain why women who kill their batterers reasonably fear imminent harm, even during nonconfrontational moments, the theory would explain why a battered woman has a "well-grounded" fear of "immediate" harm if she does not commit a crime with her batterer, even if her batterer did not literally hold a gun to her head during the commission of the offense. According to the battered woman syndrome theory, the domestic violence victim's familiarity with her batterer's cycle of violence may have led to a reasonable belief that harm was imminent if she protested his criminal behavior. Moreover, as a result of the cyclical nature of her batterer's violence and her lack of control over the abuse, she may perpetually fear immediate harm.

The battered woman syndrome theory also relates to the third prong of the duress defense, requiring that the defendant have no reasonable opportunity to escape the danger without committing the crime. Walker's version of learned helplessness depicts the battered woman as lacking the cognitive capacity to recognize options for escaping the batterer's abuse. Accordingly, one would expect the battered woman to remain with her batterer, even if he was a criminal who required her to help him. Additionally, Walker's battered woman prioritizes survival skills, so one would expect her to obey any command delivered by her batterer in an attempt — albeit perhaps futile — to avoid further episodes of violence.

56. Burke, *supra,* note 17, at 253-54 (footnotes omitted).

. . . In fact, Walker's theory appears even more applicable to the defense of duress than to self-defense. A primary discrepancy between the law of self-defense and Walker's battered woman syndrome theory is the difficulty explaining how a woman in a constant and heightened fear of danger, who is so helpless that she fails even to appreciate valid escape options, suddenly develops the impulse not just to stop or escape her batterer's abuse, but to end it permanently. In contrast, Walker's theory of learned helplessness, if true, does explain why an abused woman complies with her batterer's requests, even if she apparently has an opportunity to escape him, and even if compliance requires her to commit crimes against third parties.

9

MENTAL ILLNESS AS A DEFENSE

A. INTRODUCTION

Mental diseases and defects are relevant in many types of cases. In the field of trusts and estates, for example, a will may be ineffective if the testator suffered from a mental disease that prevented her from "recognizing the natural objects of her bounty." In family law, a parent whose mental illness makes him incapable of providing for a child's emotional and physical needs may lose his right to custody. Most important outside criminal law, a person whose mental illness leaves her gravely disabled or potentially dangerous to herself or others may face involuntary civil commitment in a mental hospital. In all these cases, of course, establishing legal boundaries around medical criteria for mental disability is a complex matter for courts and legislators.

Mental illness issues arise at various stages of the criminal justice system. A defendant suffering from a mental disease may be deemed incompetent to stand trial if the disease "prevents him from cooperating with his attorney in his defense." A convicted person who becomes insane while in prison may be transferred to a mental institution if he can be "more appropriately treated" there. Traditionally, in states that impose capital punishment, an otherwise properly convicted and sentenced murderer cannot be executed if at his scheduled execution date he suffers from a mental illness that disables him from appreciating the connection between his imminent punishment and his crime.

Our major concern in this chapter, of course, is the question of when a mental defect or illness that the accused suffers at the time of the alleged crime should excuse him from any moral — and legal — responsibility for the crime. We have already seen a line of homicide cases where a state of temporary irrationality induced by certain types of provocation might at least mitigate punishment. See pp. 321-358, *supra*. We have also seen one case in which a mental disease might wholly exculpate an accused — where it might serve to show that he lacked the required mens rea for the crime. See p. 231, *supra*. Thus, we must now grapple with the difficult question of how an accused may possess the required mens rea but nevertheless merit exculpation because of a mental illness.

For centuries, courts and legislatures have struggled to devise precise legal instruments for defining legal insanity. In the previous chapter, we examined the philosophical question whether certain defenses, especially self-defense, were best viewed as justifications or excuses. No such dilemma arises with insanity. The otherwise criminal act of an insane person is indeed wrongful and socially harmful, and we hardly wish to encourage or ratify it. Nevertheless, if the person meets the relevant test of legal insanity, the law finds it unfair to punish him criminally. The question why punishment of the legally insane is unfair or unwise requires us to recur to questions of the purposes of criminal punishment. For example, it may violate notions of retributive justice to punish those who cannot be held morally blameworthy; it may, however, serve the purpose of incapacitation; whether it serves rehabilitation turns on whether the disease is treatable and where treatment is best had; and whether punishment serves general deterrence is, as always, a matter of determining what other persons one is trying to influence.

However one frames the question, the insanity defense differs in one categorical way from necessity, duress, and self-defense: Namely, almost all (of those few) defendants who win acquittal on grounds of insanity are nevertheless immediately diverted into a different system of state incarceration — civil commitment.

Insanity differs from other defenses, and from mitigating excuses like the provocation formula, in another and more subtle way. These other defenses may manifest themselves through mental states, but they all derive in some way from objective or external forces, and are thus limited by the "reasonable person" standard. Though normally we attribute a bad act to a malevolent character, an external excuse offers another explanation. Yet the insanity defense turns, in effect, on an internal cause. Whether we call the cause bad character, defective personality, or mental illness, it is, almost by definition, in the very nature of the insane criminal to commit crimes. Worse yet, the very heinousness of a crime may, to some observers, prove the person must be insane. Indeed, to avoid this circularity problem, one of the formulas for the insanity defense now specifically excludes from the defense any condition chief proof of which is repeated criminality.

The problem, then, is this: We propose to excuse certain people for their crimes because they are not responsible for their inherently dangerous characters or dispositions, but we have no elegant formula for distinguishing those who *cannot* obey the law from those who simply *do not* obey the law. A scientifically rigorous explanation of mental illness — preferably one in the language of biochemistry or neurology — might solve this problem by establishing a source of behavior that is physically internal but morally external — part of the body but not part of the moral phenomenon called character or the self. As we will see, however, psychiatry has hardly succeeded in providing the criminal law with that formula. Moreover, the various legal definitions of insanity over the ages have hardly solved the problem of how lay juries could use any such formula sensibly.

The following introductory case, People v. Serravo, illustrates some of the key issues in the insanity defense, relying on the most venerable and still most widely used test, the famous *M'Naghten* rule. After treating this case, we will turn backward to trace the history of criminal insanity doctrines. The story begins with the original British *M'Naghten* rule and its emphasis on mental cognition, i.e., whether the defendant was so mentally ill that he could not "know" either the nature and quality of his act or its wrongfulness. Then by the 1960s, many

American jurisdictions had replaced *M'Naghten* with the American Law Institute-Model Penal Code ("ALI") test, which broadened the question of "knowledge" to one of whether the defendant had "substantial capacity to appreciate the criminality of his conduct," and, even more significantly, added the alternative so-called volitional question, i.e., whether the defendant, even if he could appreciate the criminality of his act, nevertheless lacked "substantial capacity to conform his conduct to the law." And then, in the 1980s, in the aftermath of the controversial verdict in the John Hinckley case, many (though by no means all) of those ALI states returned to a version of *M'Naghten*. The standard in *Serravo* is typical of this revived *M'Naghten* standard, now in use in the majority of American jurisdictions.

B. THE *M'NAGHTEN* RULE AND COGNITION

PEOPLE v. SERRAVO
Supreme Court of Colorado
823 P.2d 128 (1992)

JUSTICE QUINN delivered the Opinion of the Court.

We granted certiorari to review the decision of the court of appeals in People v. Serravo, 797 P.2d 782 (Colo. App. 1990), in order to determine the meaning of the phrase "incapable of distinguishing right from wrong" in Colorado's statutory definition of insanity codified at section 16-8-101 (1), 8A C.R.S. (1986). The trial court, in the insanity phase of a criminal prosecution, instructed the jury that the phrase "incapable of distinguishing right from wrong" refers to a person who appreciates that his conduct is criminal but, due to a mental disease or defect, believes that the conduct is morally right. The prosecution, pursuant to section 16-12-102(1), 8A C.R.S. (1986), appealed the trial court's ruling on the question of law, and the court of appeals approved the ruling. . . .[1]

I.

Serravo was charged in a multi-count information with crimes of attempt to commit first degree murder after deliberation, assault in the first degree, and the commission of crimes of violence. The charges arose out of the stabbing of his wife, Joyce Serravo, on May 10, 1987. After the charges were filed, Serravo entered a plea of not guilty by reason of insanity and was thereafter examined

---

1. Section 16-12-102(1), 8A C.R.S. (1986), authorizes the prosecution to appeal any decision in a criminal case upon any question of law. [This procedural rule in Colorado explains the unusual posture of this case, i.e., an appeal from a defense victory. Colorado permits the prosecutor to appeal any not guilty verdict on questions of law (not to re-weigh the facts). But the Colorado Supreme Court held in another part of its opinion in this case that double jeopardy forbade any retrial of Serravo, even though, as we will see, the court here overrules one of the trial court's instructional rulings that favored Serravo. Thus, the case can be read as guiding authority to lower courts in Colorado for future insanity cases, but the NGI verdict stands in this one. — EDS.]

by several psychiatrists. The issue of legal insanity was tried to a jury, which returned a verdict of not guilty by reason of insanity.

The evidence at the insanity trial established that the stabbing occurred under the following circumstances. On the evening of May 9, 1987, Serravo, who was a King Soopers union employee, visited striking employees at the King Soopers store near his home. Serravo returned home at approximately 12:30 A.M. on May 10. After sitting in the kitchen and reading the Bible, he went upstairs to the bedroom where his wife was sleeping, stood over her for a few minutes, and then stabbed her in the back just below the shoulder blade. When his wife awoke, Serravo told her that she had been stabbed by an intruder and that she should stay in bed while he went downstairs to call for medical help.

Police officers were later dispatched to the home. Serravo told the officers that he had gone to the King Soopers store and had left the garage door open, that the door leading to the house from the garage was unlocked, that when he returned from King Soopers and was reading the Bible he heard his front door slam, and that he went upstairs to check on his wife and children and saw that his wife was bleeding from a wound in her back. Serravo signed a consent to search his home and gave the police clothes that he was wearing at the time of his discovery of his wife's injury.

Several weeks after the stabbing Serravo's wife found letters written by Serravo. In these letters Serravo admitted the stabbing, stating that "our marriage was severed on Mother's Day when I put the knife in your back," that "I have gone to be with Jehovah in heaven for three and one-half days," and that "I must return for there is still a great deal of work to be done." After reading the letters, Serravo's wife telephoned him in order to confront him about the letters. Serravo told his wife that God had told him to stab her in order to sever the marriage bond. Mrs. Serravo informed the police of these facts and Serravo was thereafter arrested and charged.

The prosecution presented expert psychiatric testimony on Serravo's sanity at the time of the stabbing. Doctor Ann Seig, a resident psychiatrist in training at the University of Colorado Health Sciences Center, examined Serravo pursuant to a court ordered evaluation of his mental state. Serravo gave the doctor a history of having worked on a plan, inspired by his relationship to God, to establish a multi-million-dollar sports complex called Purely Professionals. This facility, according to Serravo, would enable him to achieve his goal of teaching people the path to perfection. On the night of the stabbing, Serravo, according to the history given to Doctor Seig, was excited because he finally believed that he had received some positive encouragement in his endeavor from some King Soopers union members, but he was discouraged by some inner "evil spirits" who kept raising troublesome questions about how he would deal with his wife's lack of encouragement and support. Doctor Seig diagnosed Serravo as suffering either from an organic delusional disorder related to left temporal lobe damage as a result of an automobile accident some years ago or paranoid schizophrenia.[2]

---

2. A standard mental health diagnostic manual published by the American Psychiatric Association, Diagnostic and Statistical Manual of Mental Disorders, Third Edition Revised (1987) (DSM IIIR), defines paranoid schizophrenia as a "major disturbance in the content of thought involving delusions that are often multiple, fragmented or bizarre. . . ." Id. at 188. A preoccupation with grandiose or religious delusions is a symptom of paranoid schizophrenia. Id. The DSM IIIR defines a delusional disorder as the presence of a persistent thematic delusion. A person laboring under a grandiose delusion is convinced that he or she has a great talent or insight, or has a special relationship with a prominent person or deity. Id. at 199-200.

Either diagnosis, in Doctor Seig's opinion, would adequately account for Serravo's delusional belief that he had a privileged relationship with God as the result of which he was in direct communication with God. Doctor Seig testified that Serravo was operating under this delusional system when he stabbed his wife and these delusions caused him to believe that his act was morally justified. Doctor Seig, however, was of the view that Serravo, because he was aware that the act of stabbing was contrary to law, was sane at the time of the stabbing.

Serravo presented four psychiatrists and a clinical psychologist on the issue of his legal insanity. The first psychiatrist, Doctor Frederick Miller, was of the opinion that on the night of the stabbing Serravo was under the psychotic delusion that it was his divine mission to kill his wife and that he was morally justified in stabbing her because God had told him to do so. Doctor Miller was not quite certain whether Serravo's psychotic disorder was paranoid schizophrenia, a paranoid delusional disorder, or an organic delusional disorder. Although uncertain of the exact diagnostic label applicable to Serravo, Doctor Miller was of the opinion that Serravo's mental illness made it impossible for him to distinguish right from wrong even though Serravo was probably aware that such conduct was legally wrong.

Another psychiatrist, Doctor Eric Kaplan, was the attending psychiatrist at the University of Colorado Health Services and a member of the faculty of the medical school. Doctor Kaplan supervised Doctor Ann Seig during her examination of Serravo and also made an independent evaluation of Serravo's mental condition. It was Doctor Kaplan's opinion that Serravo was suffering from paranoid schizophrenia at the time of the stabbing and was laboring under the paranoid delusion that his wife stood in the way of his divine mission of completing the large sports complex, that Serravo believed that the stabbing was the right thing to do, and that Serravo, as a result of his mental illness, was unable to distinguish right from wrong with respect to the stabbing. Two other psychiatrists, Doctor Geoffrey Heron and Doctor Seymour Sundell, offered the opinion that Serravo, at the time of the stabbing, was suffering from paranoid schizophrenia and a paranoid delusion about God which so affected his cognitive ability as to render him incapable of distinguishing right from wrong as normal people would be able to do in accordance with societal standards of morality.

Doctor Leslie Cohen, a clinical psychologist, also testified about Serravo's mental condition at the time of the stabbing. Having conducted extensive psychological testing of Serravo, Doctor Cohen was able to offer an opinion on Serravo's reality testing, his emotional reactivity, and his volition, all of which were relevant to the functioning of his conscience. The doctor was of the opinion that Serravo's conscience was based on a false belief or delusion about his magical powers as a result of his direct communication with God. Serravo, in the doctor's view, was suffering from a psychotic disorder that rendered him incapable of distinguishing right from wrong at the time of the stabbing. Although Doctor Cohen acknowledged that Serravo appeared to cover up his conduct when the police arrived at his home, the doctor explained that conduct as the product of a small part of his still intact reality testing. According to Doctor Cohen, Serravo is "not an incoherent man who can't figure out what's going on," but rather "senses that people don't understand his reasoning very well" and thus apparently believed that the police "wouldn't understand the complex reasoning that went behind the stabbing and that it would be better if he kept it to himself."

At the conclusion of the evidence, the trial court instructed the jury, in accordance with the statutory definition of insanity, that a person "is not accountable who is so diseased or defective in mind at the time of the commission of the act as to be incapable of distinguishing right from wrong, with respect to the act." The court also gave the following jury instruction, to which the prosecution objected, on the meaning of the phrase "incapable of distinguishing right from wrong":

Instruction No. 5

As used in the context of the statutory definition of insanity as a criminal defense, the phrase "incapable of distinguishing right from wrong" includes within its meaning the case where a person appreciates that his conduct is criminal, but, because of a mental disease or defect, believes it to be morally right.

In objecting to the jury instruction, the prosecution stated that it would permit the jury to return an insanity verdict based solely on a purely subjective moral standard rather than a legal standard of right and wrong. The trial court, however, was of the view that, because the statutory definition of insanity was not cast in terms of either legal or moral wrong, it was appropriate to instruct the jury that legal insanity included an incapacity, due to a mental disease or defect, to distinguish right from wrong in a moral sense.

The jury returned a verdict of not guilty by reason of insanity at the time of the commission of the alleged crimes, and the court committed Serravo to the custody of the Department of Institutions until such time as he is found to be eligible for release.[3] The prosecution appealed the district court's ruling on the challenged jury instruction to the court of appeals, which approved the ruling. The court of appeals concluded that the statutory definition of insanity "reflects the General Assembly's intent to define wrong under a societal standard of moral wrong" and that, "as society's moral judgment is usually identical to the legal standard, the test is not broadened much if wrong is determined by a societal moral standard." *Serravo*, 797 P.2d at 783. The court of appeals also concluded that the jury instruction did not apply a subjective moral standard to the defendant's capacity to distinguish right from wrong. Finally, the court adopted the so-called "deific-decree" exception to the societal standard of moral wrong. Based on that exception, the court of appeals determined that, although there was some evidence indicating that Serravo knew the stabbing of his wife was illegal and contrary to societal standards of morality, there was evidentiary support for the insanity verdict because there was expert testimony that Serravo was inspired by an insane delusion that God had decreed the act. Id. at 783. We thereafter granted the People's petition to consider whether the court of appeals correctly interpreted the meaning of the phrase "incapable of distinguishing right from wrong" in the statutory definition of insanity.

---

3. Section 16-8-105(4), 8A C.R.S. (1986), states:

If the trier of fact finds the defendant not guilty by reason of insanity, the court shall commit the defendant to the custody of the department of institutions until such time as he is found eligible for release. The executive director of the department of institutions shall designate the state facility at which the defendant shall be held for care and psychiatric treatment and may transfer the defendant from one institution to another if in the opinion of the director it is desirable to do so in the interest of proper care, custody, and treatment of the defendant or the protection of the public or the personnel of the facilities in question.

II.

We initially consider whether the phrase "incapable of distinguishing right from wrong" should be measured by legal right and wrong, as argued by the People, or instead, should be measured by a societal standard of morality, as determined by the court of appeals. The phrase in question appears in section 16-8-101, 8A C.R.S. (1986), which defines legal insanity as follows:

> The applicable test of insanity shall be, and the jury shall be so instructed: "A person who is so diseased or defective in mind at the time of the commission of the act as to be incapable of distinguishing right from wrong with respect to that act is not accountable. But care should be taken not to confuse such mental disease or defect with moral obliquity, mental depravity, or passion growing out of anger, revenge, hatred, or other motives, and kindred evil conditions, for when the act is induced by any of these causes the person is accountable to the law.

Because Colorado's statutory definition of insanity is based on the right-wrong test of legal insanity articulated in M'Naghten's Case, 8 Eng. Rpt. 718 (1843), our resolution of the issue before us must begin with a review of that case.

A.

In 1843 Daniel M'Naghten shot and killed Edward Drummond, the private secretary to Sir Robert Peel. M'Naghten, believing that Peel was heading a conspiracy to kill him, had intended to kill Peel, but instead shot Drummond because he mistakenly believed Drummond to be Peel. M'Naghten claimed at trial that he was insane and could not be held responsible because his delusion caused him to commit the act. The jury was instructed that it was to decide whether M'Naghten "had or had not the use of his understanding, so as to know that he was doing a wrong or wicked act," and that if the jury found that he "was not sensible, at the time he committed it, that he was violating the laws both of God and man," then the jury should return a verdict of not guilty by reason of insanity. 8 Eng. Rpt. At 719-20. The jury found M'Naghten not guilty by reason of insanity, and the House of Lords thereafter debated the proper standard of legal insanity and posed five questions to the judges of the Queen's Bench in an attempt to better formulate the insanity defense. The judges' answers to these questions, which were appended to the report of the original case, have come to be considered as if they were the law of the case.

The initial question asked of the judges was the following:

> 1st. What is the law respecting alleged crimes committed by persons afflicted with insane delusion, in respect of one or more particular subjects or persons: as, for instance, where at the time of the commission of the alleged crime, the accused knew he was acting contrary to law, but did the act complained of with a view, under the influence of insane delusion, of redressing or revenging some supposed grievance or injury, or of producing some supposed public benefit?

8 Eng. Rpt. at 720. The judges answered that a person under the influence of an insane delusion who believes that the act will redress or revenge a supposed grievance will "nevertheless [be] punishable according to the nature of the crime committed, if he knew at the time of committing such crime that he was

acting contrary to law; by which expression we understand Your Lordships to mean the law of the land." Id. at 722.

The next two questions asked of the judges were answered as one question, and the answer qualifies the reference to "the law of the land" in the first answer. The second and third questions asked in *M'Naghten* were as follows:

> 2d. What are the proper questions to be submitted to the jury, when a person alleged to be afflicted with insane delusion respecting one or more particular subjects or persons, is charged with the commission of a crime (murder, for example), and insanity is set up as a defence?
>
> 3d. In what terms ought the question be left to the jury, as to the prisoner's state of mind at the time when the act was committed?

Id. at 720. The answer to these questions was as follows:

> The jurors ought to be told . . . that to establish a defence on the ground of insanity, it must be clearly proved that, at the time of the committing of the act, the party accused was labouring under such a defect of reason, from disease of the mind, as not to know the nature and quality of the act he was doing; or, if he did know it, that he did not know he was doing what was wrong. The mode of putting the latter part of the question to the jury on these occasions has generally been, whether the accused at the time of doing the act knew the difference between right and wrong: which mode, though rarely, if ever, leading to any mistake with the jury, is not, as we conceive, so accurate when put generally and in the abstract, as when put with reference to the party's knowledge of right and wrong, in respect to the very act with which he is charged. *If the question were to be put as to the knowledge of the accused solely and exclusively with reference to the law of the land, it might tend to confound the jury, by inducing them to believe that an actual knowledge of the law of the land was essential in order to lead to a conviction: whereas the law is administered upon the principle that everyone must be taken conclusively to know it, without proof that he does know it. If the accused was conscious that the act was one which he ought not to do, and if that act was at the same time contrary to the law of the land, he is punishable; and the usual course therefore has been to leave the question to the jury, whether the party accused had a sufficient degree of reason to know that he was doing an act that was wrong: and this course we think is correct, accompanied with such observations and explanations as the circumstances of each particular case may require.*

Id. at 722-23 (emphasis added).

B.

The judges' answer to the second and third questions in *M'Naghten* suggests that a person may be considered legally sane as long as the person commits an act contrary to law and knows that the act is morally wrong without regard to the person's actual knowledge of its legality under positive law. Such an interpretation, in our view, is eminently sound.

We acknowledge that some cases subsequent to *M'Naghten* have interpreted the right-wrong test as limiting the insanity defense to a cognitive inability to distinguish legal right from legal wrong, with the result that a person's simple awareness that an act is illegal is a sufficient basis for finding criminal responsibility. We believe, however, that such an analysis injects a formalistic legalism into the insanity equation to the disregard of the psychological underpinnings of legal insanity. A person in an extremely psychotic state, for example, might be aware that an act is prohibited by law, but due to the overbearing effect of the psychosis may be utterly without the capacity to comprehend that the act is inherently immoral. A standard of legal wrong would render such person legally responsible and subject to imprisonment for the conduct in question notwithstanding the patent injustice of such a disposition. Conversely, a person who, although mentally ill, has the cognitive capacity to distinguish right from wrong and is aware that an act is morally wrong, but does not realize that it is illegal, should nonetheless be held responsible for the act, as ignorance of the law is no excuse. Id.

Construing the term "wrong" as moral wrong finds support in several cases which have basically followed the well-reasoned opinion of the New York Court of Appeals in People v. Schmidt, 216 N.Y. 324, 110 N.E. 945 (N.Y. 1915). The *Schmidt* opinion, written by then Judge Benjamin Cardozo, rejected the view that the term "wrong" means "contrary to the law of the state." 110 N.E. at 946. After a careful analysis of *M'Naghten* and the history of the insanity defense, Judge Cardozo remarked:

> The [*M'Naghten*] judges expressly held that a defendant who knew nothing of the law would nonetheless be responsible if he knew that the act was wrong, by which, therefore, they must have meant, if he knew that it was morally wrong. Whether he would also be responsible if he knew that it was against the law, but did not know it to be morally wrong, is a question that was not considered. In most cases, of course, knowledge that an act is illegal will justify the inference of knowledge that it is wrong. But none the less it is the knowledge of wrong, conceived of as moral wrong, that seems to have been established by that decision as the controlling test. That must certainly have been the test under the older law when the capacity to distinguish between right and wrong imported a capacity to distinguish between good and evil as abstract qualities. There is nothing to justify the belief that the words right and wrong, when they became limited by *M'Naghten's* case to the right and wrong of the particular act, cast off their meaning as terms of morals, and became terms of pure legality.

110 N.E. at 947.

In resolving the ostensible tension between the legal standard of wrong in the answer to the first *M'Naghten* question (i.e., a person is legally responsible if the person acted with knowledge that an act is contrary to the "law of the land") and the moral standard suggested in the answer to the second and third *M'Naghten* questions (i.e., actual knowledge of codified law is not required for a conviction, but rather a person may be punished for conduct if the person knows that the act is one that "he ought not do"), the *Schmidt* opinion stated that the first answer "presupposes the offender's capacity to understand that violation of the law is wrong" and that the offender is sane except for a delusion that his act will redress a supposed grievance or attain some public benefit. 110 N.E.2d at 948. The first *M'Naghten* answer, in other words, "applies only to persons who 'are not in other respects insane.'" Id. The delusion that an act will redress a supposed grievance or result in a public benefit, in Cardozo's words, "has no such effect in obscuring moral distinctions as a delusion that God himself has issued a command," inasmuch as "the one delusion is consistent with knowledge that the act is a moral wrong, [but] the other is not." Id.

Because the delusion emanating from an imagined grievance or public benefit does not obscure moral distinctions — as would an insane belief that

God has issued a command — there is really no conflict between "the commands of law and morals" in a case where a defendant knows that the act is morally wrong but commits the act because he believes that either personal or public good will result. Id. There is an obvious difference in kind, however, between that case and the person who suffers from an insane delusion that virtually destroys the cognitive ability to distinguish the morality or immorality of an act, even though the person may be aware the act is contrary to law. Although in most instances the very same forms of criminal conduct classified as felonies would also be considered violative of basic ethical norms, we are of the view that limiting the definition of "wrong" to "legal wrong" results in stripping legal insanity of a significant part of its psychological components. Various forms of mental diseases or defects can impair a person's cognitive ability to distinguish moral right from moral wrong and yet have no effect whatever on the person's rather sterile awareness that a certain act is contrary to law. To be sure, a person should not be judged legally insane merely because that person has personal views of right or wrong at variance with those which find expression in the law. It is quite another matter, however, to say that a mentally ill person suffering from an insane delusion that overbears the mental capacity to distinguish right from wrong should nonetheless be held criminally responsible for conduct solely because the person was aware that the act charged in the criminal prosecution was contrary to law. Such a result, in our view, proceeds from a narrowly legalistic interpretation that accords little weight to the baneful effects of various forms of mental illness on the cognitive capacity of the human mind. . . .

We thus conclude that the term "wrong" in the statutory definition of insanity refers to moral wrong.

c.

Moral wrong can be measured either by a purely personal and subjective standard of morality or by a societal and presumably more objective standard. We believe that the better reasoned interpretation of "wrong" in the term "incapable of distinguishing right from wrong" refers to a wrongful act measured by societal standards of morality.

The concepts of "right" and "wrong" are essentially ethical in character and have their primary source in the existing societal standards of morality, as distinguished from the written law. A person's awareness and appreciation of right and wrong derive primarily from a variety of experiences and relationships including, but not necessarily limited to, behavioral rules endorsed by the social culture as well as ethical principles transmitted through the family, the community, the formal educational process, and religious associations. . . . Defining "wrong" in terms of a purely personal and subjective standard of morality ignores a substantial part of the moral culture on which our societal norms of behavior are based.

Construing the term "wrong" in accordance with societal standards of morality results in a substantially more objective standard of moral wrong than the purely personal and subjective moral standard, under which an accused could be adjudicated insane even if he knew that the act in question was both forbidden by law and condemned by society, but nonetheless harbored a personal belief that the act *was right*. A personal and subjective standard of morality should not be permitted to exonerate a defendant any more than an ignorance of the law, engendered by a mental illness, should be equated with legal insanity. In sum, the appropriate construction of the term "incapable of distinguishing right from wrong with respect to [the] act" in section 16-8-101 should be measured by existing societal standards of morality rather than by a defendant's personal and subjective understanding of the legality or illegality of the act in question.

D.

We turn then to Jury Instruction No. 5, which stated that the phrase "incapable of distinguishing right from wrong" includes the case of a person who "appreciates that his conduct is criminal but, because of a mental disease or defect, believes it to be morally right." Although the court of appeals concluded that this instruction did not incorporate a "subjective moral standard to the determination of whether defendant understood right from wrong," *Serravo,* 797 P.2d at 782-83, we are of a contrary view. Jury Instruction No. 5 was cast in terms so general that it well could have been interpreted by the jury to incorporate a personal and subjective standard of moral wrong rather than a societal standard of right and wrong. The court of appeals' approval of the instruction, in our view, is inconsistent with its adoption of a societal standard of moral wrong for purposes of legal insanity. . . .

A clarifying instruction on the definition of legal insanity, therefore, should clearly state that, as related to the conduct charged as a crime, the phrase "incapable of distinguishing right from wrong" refers to a person's cognitive inability, due to a mental disease or defect, to distinguish right from wrong as measured by a societal standard of morality, even though the person may be aware that the conduct in question is criminal. Any such instruction should also expressly inform the jury that the phrase "incapable of distinguishing right from wrong" does not refer to a purely personal and subjective standard of morality.

III.

We next consider the relationship between the so-called "deific-decree" delusion and Colorado's test of legal insanity. The court of appeals, after holding that the term "wrong" in the statutory definition of insanity refers not to legal wrong but moral wrong under societal standards of morality, held that the "deific-decree" delusion was an exception to the societal standards of moral wrong. Drawing on the opinion of the Washington Supreme Court in State v. Crenshaw, 98 Wash. 2d 789, 659 P.2d 488 (Wash. 1983),[4] the court of appeals limited the so-called deific-decree exception to those situations "in which a person commits a criminal act, knowing it is illegal and morally wrong according to society's standards but, because of a mental defect, believes that God has decreed the act." *Serravo,* 797 P.2d at 783. This exception, the court of appeals went

___

4. In *Crenshaw,* the Supreme Court of Washington carved out the deific exception from Justice Cardozo's reference in *Schmidt,* 110 N.E. at 949, to a mother insanely obeying God's command to kill her child. The *Crenshaw* court, citing *Schmidt,* stated that although the woman who kills her infant child under an insane delusion that God has ordered the act might know "that the law and society condemn the act, it would be unrealistic to hold her responsible for the crime, since her free will has been subsumed by her belief in the deific decree." 659 P.2d at 494.

on to conclude, must be distinguished from the case "in which a person acts in accordance with a duty imposed by a particular faith." Id. In our view, the "deific-decree" delusion is not so much an exception to the right-wrong test measured by the existing societal standards of morality as it is an integral factor in assessing a person's cognitive ability to distinguish right from wrong with respect to the act charged as a crime.

In discussing the deific-decree delusion in *Schmidt,* the court stated:

> We must not . . . exaggerate the rigor of the rule by giving the word "wrong" a strained interpretation, at war with its broad and primary meaning, and least of all, if in so doing, we rob the rule of all relation to the mental health and true capacity of the criminal. The interpretation placed upon the statute by the trial judge may be tested by its consequences. A mother kills her infant child to whom she has been devotedly attached. She knows the nature and quality of the act; she knows that the law condemns it; but she is inspired by an insane delusion that God has appeared to her and ordained the sacrifice. It seems a mockery to say that, within the meaning of the statute, she knows that the act is wrong. If the definition propounded by the trial judge is right, it would be the duty of a Jury to hold her responsible for the crime. We find nothing either in the history of the rule, or in its reason and purpose, or in judicial exposition of its meaning, to justify a conclusion so abhorrent. . . .
>
> . . . Knowledge that an act is forbidden by law will in most cases permit the inference of knowledge that, according to the accepted standards of mankind, it is also condemned as an offense against good morals. Obedience to the law is itself a moral duty. If, however, there is an insane delusion that God has appeared to the defendant and ordained the commission of a crime, we think it cannot be said of the offender that he knows the act to be wrong.

110 N.E. at 949. If a person insanely believes that "he has a command from the Almighty to kill, it is difficult to understand how such a man can know that it is wrong for him to do it." *Schmidt,* 110 N.E. at 948 (quoting Guiteau's Case, 10 Fed. 161, 182 (1882)). A person acting under such a delusion is no less insane even though the person might know that murder is prohibited by positive law. *Schmidt,* 110 N.E.2d at 948. It thus seems clear to us that a person is legally insane if that person's cognitive ability to distinguish right from wrong with respect to the act has been destroyed as a result of a psychotic delusion that God has commanded the act. We thus conclude that, although the court of appeals mischaracterized the deific-decree delusion as an exception to the right-wrong test for legal insanity, a defendant nonetheless may be judged legally insane where, as here, the defendant's cognitive ability to distinguish right from wrong with respect to the act has been destroyed as a result of a psychotic delusion that God has decreed the act.

IV.

[W]e disapprove the trial court's jury instruction which defined the phrase "incapable of distinguishing right from wrong" in such a general manner as likely to be interpreted by a jury as including a purely subjective and personal standard of morality; we approve of the court of appeals' construction of the phrase "incapable of distinguishing right from wrong" as referring to an incapacity, due to a mental disease or defect, to know that an act is wrong under existing societal standards of morality; and we disapprove of the court of appeals' characterization of the deific-decree delusion as an exception to the right-wrong test for legal insanity rather than as an integral factor in assessing a person's cognitive ability to distinguish right from wrong with respect to the act charged as a crime. The judgment of the court of appeals is accordingly approved in part and disapproved in part.

Notes and Questions

1. What was Serravo's view, at the time he stabbed his wife, of the "wrongfulness" of his conduct? (a) Did he believe stabbing was legal? (b) Did he believe that although stabbing was normally illegal, he had a justification defense (i.e., that killing his wife served a public good)? (c) Did he recognize that he was committing a crime but nevertheless believe that there was a higher moral code that justified his actions — a form of civil disobedience? (d) Or did he recognize that his action was illegal and immoral but nevertheless feel duress from divine command?

Notice how different legal tests of insanity might draw the line between legal insanity and full criminal responsibility at different places along the continuum described above.

According to the court, where should the line be drawn?

2. *Cognition and fact.* Note that the original *M'Naghten* test raised two questions about cognition, the first of which is not addressed by new versions of *M'Naghten* like Colorado's and does not arise in the *Serravo* case anyway: Did the defendant "know the nature and quality of the act he was doing?" Under what facts would that question arise? How often do you think it would arise? If Serravo could win an NGI verdict only if he was so insane as not to realize that knives could harm, would that virtually nullify the insanity defense? See, e.g., Knights v. State, 58 Neb. 225, 78 N.W. 508 (1899) (error to require that a defendant not know that a fire can cause burning before finding insanity in an arson case); People v. Sherwood, 271 N.Y. 427, 3 N.E.2d 581 (1936) (error to require that if mother had known that holding her infant son's head under water meant that he would drown, then she is sane).

3. *Cognition and law.* The court says limiting the cognition question to knowledge that the act is illegal "injects a formalistic legalism into the insanity equation to the disregard of the psychological underpinnings of legal insanity." Why is that so? Does that invite any wrongly based subjective view of morality to serve as a defense? The court adds: "A person in an extremely psychotic state, for example, might be aware that an act is prohibited by law, but due to the overbearing effect of the psychosis may be utterly without the capacity to comprehend that the act is inherently immoral." But are we loath to punish people who simply do not like our laws? Why should it make a difference that the person happens to be insane?

4. In *Schmidt*, discussed in *Serravo*, is Cardozo clearly right that the original *M'Naghten* case did not resolve expressly the law-moral question here? Can you speculate on how the *M'Naghten* judges might have resolved the law-morals issue?

5. *Moral judgment and command hallucinations.* The Colorado Supreme Court treats a "deific decree" as relevant to a defendant's assessment of the conformity of her criminal act with prevailing moral standards. Presumably, in our

society, belief in a morally authoritative supreme being is widespread. But hearing voices in general, and commands in particular, are common psychiatric symptoms. Not all patients suffering from such command hallucinations attribute these voices to a deity. Should the validity of an insanity defense depend on the identity a paranoid schizophrenic ascribes to the voices in her head?

In a widely publicized Texas case, Andrea Yates was convicted of murder after drowning her five children in a bathtub, in answer to "Satan's" command, and also to spare them torment at Satan's hands. Yates had experienced command hallucinations for some time, had suffered repeated bouts of severe postpartum depression, and had twice attempted suicide. The prosecution conceded that she was mentally ill. But Texas, like Colorado, limits insanity to mental diseases that impair the defendant's capacity to distinguish right from wrong. The prosecution expert witnesses emphasized that the deeply religious Yates saw Satan as an evil force, described her killings as sins, and consistently voiced her expectation that she would be punished. For example, the prosecution's direct examination of Dr. Park Dietz contained the following exchange:

Q. Would you explain to the jury the significance of [your] interview in relation to the knowledge of wrongfulness . . . ?

A. Well, the first point is that Mrs. Yates indicates that at the time before the homicide she had the idea of killing her children and she attributed the origin of that idea to Satan. So, of course, the idea comes from her mind, but she is mistakenly thinking Satan put it there. The fact that she regards it as coming from Satan is the first indication of her knowing that this is wrong. Because she recognizes even the idea of killing your children is an evil idea that comes from Satan. She doesn't think this is a good idea that comes from God. She thinks it's an evil idea that comes from Satan and she thought it was Satan who was somehow urging or encouraging or recommending that she do this. So she knows already it's a bad idea.

Q. Now, you found that she concealed these thoughts?

A. Yes . . . . It's not that she kept secret her belief that there were demons and that Satan was trying to do things to people here on earth. What she concealed was the thought of her harming her children and the plan to drown them. That part she didn't share.

Q. Why do you find that significant . . . ?

A. Well, ordinarily, when someone keeps a criminal plan secret, they do it because they know it's wrong. That's why you keep it secret, hide it from other people.[5]

Are these conclusions fair? Does Yates's bizarre interpretation of her own psychiatric symptoms give her crime a moral quality different from Serravo's?

6. Consider this commentary on the *M'Naghten* standard:[6]

Most critics read [*M'Naghten*] as referring to formal cognition or intellectual awareness alone. They distinguish this, the "law's" meaning, from what they describe as the "psychiatric" meaning, which they take to connote a fuller, deeper knowledge, involving emotional as well as intellectual awareness. This fuller knowledge

---

5. Deborah Denno, Who Is Andrea Yates: A Short Story About Insanity, 10 Duke J. Gender L. & Policy 1, 109 (2003).

6. Abraham Goldstein, Insanity, 2 Encyclopedia of Crime and Justice 736 (1983).

can exist only when the accused is able to evaluate his conduct in terms of its actual impact upon himself and others and when he is able to appreciate the total setting in which he is acting. According to the critics, the law's type of knowledge is to be found even in the most serious psychosis. The consequences, the argument continues, are that *M'Naghten* directs jurors to hold many persons responsible who are seriously disturbed and that it makes a successful assertion of the insanity defense virtually impossible.

The assertion that *know* is narrowly defined has been made so often and so insistently that it comes as a surprise to find that very few appellate courts have imposed the restrictive interpretation. In several of the states that use *M'Naghten* as the sole test of insanity, the jury is told that an accused "knows" only if he "understands" enough to enable him to judge "the nature, character, and consequence of the act charged against him" or if he has the "capacity to appreciate the character and to comprehend the probable or possible consequences of his act."

7. Although the Colorado Supreme Court otherwise approves the decision of the court of appeals, it does instruct lower courts to use a rephrased version of the trial court's instruction no. 5. What would that rephrased instruction say? What meaningful change would it make? Is it fair to say that instruction no. 5 invited the jury to exonerate Serravo because of his purely individual and subjective view of morality? Is there any point in asking whether the defendant acted with some notion of an "objective" morality if he was insane in the first place? Is that the very point of requiring proof that he was psychotic?

8. Insanity is almost always designated an affirmative defense. The usual procedure is for the jury to first decide whether the defendant is guilty — i.e., whether the prosecution has proved all the elements, including the required mens rea, beyond a reasonable doubt — and then, if the verdict is guilty, the defendant will initiate a second phase before the same jury in which he will seek an NGI verdict. What goals does this procedure serve? How effectively do you think it works?

In virtually all states, the defendant must bear at least the initial burden of production, i.e., to introduce at least *some* evidence putting his sanity into issue. Although as a matter of federal constitutional law the prosecution must prove each element of a criminal charge beyond a reasonable doubt, the Supreme Court has held that the states may treat insanity as an affirmative defense, and thus a state may constitutionally force the defendant to prove insanity.

Once the defendant carries the initial burden of production, about a fifth of the states will shift the burden of persuasion back to the prosecution to prove the defendant's sanity beyond a reasonable doubt; the majority, however, also require the defense to prove insanity by a preponderance of the evidence, or, in a few cases, by "clear and convincing evidence."

Three states, however, do not have any affirmative defense of insanity: Idaho, Montana, and Utah.[7]

9. *Sanity vs. competence.* Even before a trial begins, the court (not the jury) may have to determine whether the defendant is even mentally competent to stand trial. Though tests used to determine competence vary, all focus on whether the defendant can adequately participate in his defense. For example, under federal criminal law a defendant is incompetent "if there is reasonable

---

7. See Carmen Cirincone & Charles Jacobs, Identifying Insanity Acquittals: Is It Any Easier? 23 L. & Hum. Behavior 487, 489 (1999).

cause to believe that [he] may presently be suffering from a mental disease or defect rendering him mentally incompetent to the extent that he is unable to understand the nature and consequences of the proceedings against him or to assist properly in his defense." 18 U.S.C. §4241 (a). The Supreme Court has stated that the test of competence is "whether [the defendant] has sufficient present ability to consult with his lawyer with a reasonable degree of rational understanding — and whether he has a rational as well as factual understanding of the proceedings against him." Dusky v. United States, 362 U.S. 402 (1960). And although the issue of competence receives much less attention than the insanity defense, it affects many more people: Many times more defendants are found incompetent to stand trial and are sent — unconvicted — to institutions for the "criminally insane" than are acquitted on the grounds of insanity.

The issue of competence poses serious problems for mentally incompetent defendants and their lawyers. While the Constitution, through the Speedy Trial clause of the Sixth Amendment, limits how long an accused can be held pending trial, defendants who raise the competence issue run the risk of prolonged detention for examination, observation, and treatment. Nor will the person confined for incompetence enjoy the protections the federal Constitution affords defendants during a criminal trial or people facing a civil commitment hearing.

In Jackson v. Indiana, 406 U.S. 715 (1972), the Supreme Court held that a defendant

> committed solely on account of his incapacity to proceed to trial cannot be held more than the reasonable period of time necessary to determine whether there is a substantial probability that he will attain that capacity in the foreseeable future. If it is determined that this is not the case, then the state must either institute the customary civil commitment proceeding that would be required to commit indefinitely any other citizen, or release the defendant. [Id. at 720]

But the Court refused to specify any "arbitrary time limits" for these confinements "in light of differing state facilities and procedures." Id. And in the wake of *Jackson,* state laws and practices have varied widely in fleshing out the Court's somewhat vague mandate, and defendants continue to face the possibility of unlimited confinement, e.g., Brown v. Jacquith, 318 So. 2d 856 (Miss. 1975) (nine years). In some states incompetent defendants are treated the same as nondefendants facing civil commitment, but other states do not afford criminal defendants the same rights (such as treatment in the least restrictive alternative manner, or periodic psychiatric reviews, or proof beyond a reasonable doubt of danger to others) as apply in regular civil commitments. Some states make civil commitment automatic upon a finding of incompetence to stand trial.[8] Moreover, most courts deny or revoke bail (or any other form of release) when a pretrial mental examination is ordered. But most remarkably, the states vary widely in terms of how long a defendant declared incompetent to stand trial can be confined. About half the states permit indefinite commitment; a few impose specific limits, ranging from 6 months to 18 months; a few allow confinement up

---

8. Robert Miller, Hospitalization of Criminal Defendants for Evaluation of Competence to Stand Trial or for Restoration of Competence: Clinical and Legal Issues, 21 Behavioral Sciences and the Law 369 (2003).

to the maximum sentence for the crime or crimes charged, or at least some significant fraction of the maximum.[9]

In Sell v. United States, 123 S. Ct. 2174 (2003), the Supreme Court held that the state may, under certain circumstances, compel a defendant to receive treatment necessary to render him competent, even against his will. The Court approved a multi-factor standard for this decision: the government must show that (a) it has an "important" interest in an adjudication of defendant's guilt or innocence (the crime is serious, the defendant is likely to be released from custody much sooner if found incompetent to stand trial than if tried and convicted, the defendant poses a danger of criminality if released); (b) the proposed treatment will render it probable that defendant can understand the proceedings and collaborate with his attorney at trial; (c) the proposed treatment will not have side effects that will preclude a fair trial; and (d) the proposed treatment is "medically appropriate." The Court did not directly confront the most fundamental objection to compelling such "artificial" competence: whether causing the defendant to appear before the jury in a different psychological condition than he was in at the time of the crime inherently prejudices his right to a fair trial.

10. *Disposition after NGI verdicts.* Recall that after his NGI verdict in Colorado, Serravo was to be committed to a state mental health facility under vague criteria of eligibility. Here is one fairly typical post-NGI civil commitment statute:

> (c) If the defendant is found not guilty by reason of insanity under AS 12.47.010 or 12.47.020(b), . . . a hearing shall be held immediately after a verdict of not guilty by reason of insanity to determine the necessity of commitment. The hearing shall be held before the same trier of fact has heard the underlying charge. At the hearing, the defendant has the burden of proving by clear and convincing evidence that the defendant is not presently suffering from any mental illness that causes the defendant to be dangerous to the public. If the court or jury determines that the defendant has failed to meet the burden of proof, the court shall order the defendant committed to the custody of the commissioner of health and social services. If the hearing is before a jury, the verdict must be unanimous.
>
> (d) A defendant committed under (b) or (c) of this section shall be held in custody for a period of time not to exceed the maximum term of imprisonment for the crime for which the defendant was acquitted under AS 12.47.010 or 12.47.020(b) or until the mental illness is cured or corrected as determined at a hearing under (e) of this section. [Alaska Code, §12.47.090]

If found not guilty by reason of insanity, the defendant — though legally not responsible for his crime — may be institutionalized if the court finds that he poses a threat to public safety. As a matter of constitutional law, in a purely civil proceeding a person may be incarcerated indefinitely in a mental hospital only on "clear and convincing evidence" (more than a preponderance) that she is dangerous to herself or others or gravely disabled. Addington v. Texas, 441 U.S. 418 (1979). By contrast, when a criminal defendant has won an NGI verdict where his insanity was proved by a preponderance of the evidence, the NGI verdict itself sufficiently establishes his dangerousness. Moreover, the state may then confine him as long as his illness or dangerousness may require, regardless

---

9. For a detailed survey of state laws, see Grant H. Morris & J. Reid Malloy, Out of Mind? Out of Sight: The Uncivil Commitment of Permanently Incompetent Criminal Defendants, 27 U.C. Davis L. Rev. 1, 79-96 (1993).

of the maximum length of sentence for the crime with which he was originally charged; in some states, the average length of a post-NGI civil confinement is 30 years. (Id. at 494 (noting Connecticut figures)).

In Jones v. United States, 463 U.S. 354 (1983), the Supreme Court upheld a District of Columbia law under which a person acquitted by reason of insanity is automatically committed for 50 days and then may gain release only if he proves by a preponderance of the evidence that he is no longer mentally ill or danger-ous. The court found no constitutional problem in the lack of correlation be-tween the acquittee's civil commitment and the hypothetical maximum sen-tence he could have received if convicted. Justice Powell noted that some acquittees might suffer civil commitment for a shorter time than the hypotheti-cal sentence and others might suffer a longer confinement than the hypotheti-cal sentence. However, he found justification for the law in the different pur-poses underlying civil commitment and criminal imprisonment, the former being concerned with present and future dangerousness, the latter with punish-ment for a completed act. On the other hand, the Court confirmed in Foucha v. Louisiana, 504 U.S. 71 (1992), that a defendant put in civil commitment after an NGI verdict has a constitutional right to release after psychiatrists deter-mined, four years after his confinement began, that he was no longer insane and was not clearly dangerous to himself or others according to the criteria in the civil commitment statute. The state argued that because of a residual personal-ity disorder Foucha remained dangerous, but the Court ruled that the state was bound by the state doctors' opinion that he was no longer mentally ill under the terms of the civil commitment law.

If the burden of proving sanity is placed on the NGI defendant, he may find that burden very difficult to satisfy both because sanity is inherently difficult to "prove" and because, in many jurisdictions, the quantum of sanity required for release is very high. For example, in State v. Maik, 287 A.2d 715 (N.J. 1972), the court ruled that the defendant, who had committed murder during a psychotic episode of schizophrenia, could not be released as long as the "underlying or la-tent personality disorder, and not merely the psychotic episode which emerged from it," continued. Thus, although psychiatrists testified that the defendant's condition was in remission, the court refused to release the defendant absent proof that "the latent personality disorder would not be triggered again into vi-olent expression by reason of some stress defendant could reasonably be ex-pected to experience." Id. at 722.

The difficulty of obtaining release is justified by the need to protect public safety, but concern over the postacquittal behavior of an NGI defendant may well be misplaced. "Studies have shown that persons found not guilty by reason of insanity are far less likely to be re-arrested after release than are convicted felons."[10]

11. *Volition vs. cognition.* What, in the *Serravo* court's view, was wrong with the court of appeals's notion about the deific decree? What is the effect of a deific decree? Consider that a defendant feeling under the sway of a deific decree might say: (a) "The law does not apply to me," or (b) "I am acting illegally but

---

10. Testimony of Leonard S. Rubenstein, Mental Health Law Project, before the House Subcommittee on Criminal Justice (1982), quoted in 6 Mental & Physical Disability L. Rptr. 344, 354-55 (1982) (citing Pantle, Pasewark & Steadman, Comparing Institutionalization Periods and Subsequent Arrests of Insanity Acquittees, 8 J. Psych. & L. 305 (1981)).

according to a moral norm that transcends the law," or (c) "My act is wrong but I feel coerced by a powerful force to act wrongly." Which of these statements would the Colorado Supreme Court attribute to Serravo?

The dissent complains the majority injects into the *M'Naghten* test a "volitional" component that does not belong there, but was added to later versions of the insanity test that Colorado has never adopted. This is a crucial issue, because as we shall see, the presence and meaning of a volitional component helps explain the cyclical history of the insanity doctrine in the last part of this century in the United States. As the dissent in *Serravo* notes, many jurisdictions have adopted the alternative insanity formula devised by the American Law Institute and made part of the Model Penal Code. Ironically, the ALI test is both older and newer than the *M'Naghten* test. The following historical summary explains why.

C. COGNITION AND VOLITION: THE ROAD FROM *M'NAGHTEN* AND BACK

Recall that the *M'Naghten* rule tells jurors simply "that every man is to be presumed to be sane, and . . . that to establish a defense on the ground of insanity, it must be clearly proved that, at the time of the committing of the act, the party accused was laboring under such a defect of reason, from disease of the mind, as not to know the nature and quality of the act he was doing; or if he did know it, that he did not know he was doing what was wrong." In the earlier part of this century, American courts generally used this rule, but offered little interpretation. If expert witnesses testified that the defendant's conduct derived from "mental disease"—usually some form of psychosis—the issue was then to be left to an unguided jury.

By the middle of this century, many of the states added to their *M'Naghten* formulas some version of what came to be known as the "irresistible impulse" rule. By one phrasing or another, these formulas told the jury to acquit by reason of insanity if it found the defendant had a mental disease that kept him from controlling his conduct, even if he knew he was doing something wrong. These rules assumed that there are mental diseases that curtail volition or self-control even while cognition remains unimpaired and that persons suffering from such diseases would not be acquitted under *M'Naghten*. Thus, these "control rules" reflected a reformist effort to bring a supposedly greater psychological sophistication to the criminal law.

These tests often disappointed their proponents because juries tended to interpret them as limiting NGI verdicts to cases of impulsive behavior, and precluding planned behavior. Some critics found them substantively unsatisfactory because they wrongly bifurcated the mind into a cognition component and a will component. Others complained that the control rules might be too broad, since almost anyone with an antisocial or sociopathic or psychopathic personality might claim that he could not control his impulses.

In 1953, responding to criticism of both *M'Naghten* and the control rules, the British Royal Commission on Capital Punishment issued a report concluding that *M'Naghten* should be "abrogated" and the jury left "to determine whether at the time of the act the accused was suffering from disease of the mind (or mental deficiency) to such degree that he ought not to be held responsible." The Commission also generally depicted both the *M'Naghten* and "irresistible impulse" as both narrow and at odds with modern theories of how the mind worked. The Commission's report animated Judge David Bazelon of the D.C. Circuit Court of Appeals to devise yet a new rule in the famous case of Durham v. United States, 214 F.2d 862 (D.C. Cir. 1954). Professor Abraham Goldstein[11] tells the next phase of the story:

> . . . *Durham* took as its basic premise that the mind of man was a functional unit. It followed, therefore, that if the defendant had a mental disease, his mind could not be expected to respond properly to threats of sanction, he was not a "fit" object of anger and blame, and he belonged in a hospital rather than a prison. It would be a mistake, the court reasoned, to try to identify types of malfunctioning or groups of symptoms that would disable a person from complying with the criminal law, because an "integrated personality" could not be only partially diseased and because tests that focused on symptoms would tend to freeze the law in conventional patterns and make it difficult for psychiatric witnesses to appraise new clusters of symptoms that might be equally disabling. The test of insanity should, therefore, be a simple one, patterned on a rule adopted in New Hampshire in 1869 (State v. Pike, 49 N.H. 399 (1869)). In Judge Bazelon's words, "An accused is not criminally responsible if his unlawful act was the product of mental disease or mental defect." Psychiatrists would now be able to "inform the jury of the character of [the defendant's] mental disease" and juries would be "guided by wider horizons of knowledge concerning mental life." Only Maine and the Virgin Islands adopted the *Durham* rule, for a short period. Nevertheless, *Durham* had a tremendous and continuing impact upon the course of the debate.
>
> The principal criticism of *Durham* was that it, like the Royal Commission's first proposal, was really a nonrule. It was said to provide the jury with no standard by which to judge the evidence or direct it to pathological factors relevant to the law's concerns — the impairment of reason and control. The jury was left entirely dependent upon the expert's classification of conduct as the product of mental disease. The court's tacit assumption was that the concept of mental disease would provide a better framework for expert testimony than the earlier tests. It left *mental disease* almost undefined so that the courtroom controversy might shift from the words of the insanity rule to the nature of the particular disease and its relation to the crime.
>
> At the very time *Durham* was decided, the concept of mental disease was being subjected to devastating attack. It emerged as a concept whose content is often affected by the ends for which a diagnosis is made. As a result, when questions arose as to whether psychopathy or neurosis or narcotics addition were mental diseases, the disputes were strikingly reminiscent of those which had previously characterized trials under *M'Naghten*. Psychiatrists for the prosecution classified a given defendant's behavior as not psychotic and, for that reason, not the product of a mental disease. Those testifying for the defense urged that it was psychotic or the product of a lesser mental disorder which nevertheless qualified as mental disease.
>
> By 1962, the District of Columbia court concluded that it was necessary for trial judges to inform juries that mental disease or defect "includes any abnormal condition of the mind which substantially affects mental or emotional processes and substantially impairs behavior controls" (McDonald v. United States, 312 F.2d 847 (D.C. Cir. 1962)). *Durham* had thus traveled a circuitous path toward the conclusion that the jury needed guidance as to the effects of disease which were

---

11. Goldstein, *supra*, fn. 6, at 736-40.

relevant to compliance with the criminal law. Those effects were very much like the ones which were central to the broadened *M'Naghten* and control tests. In United States v. Brawner, 471 F.2d 969 (D.C. Cir. 1972), the court abandoned *Durham* for a rule that would require expert evidence to be framed in a way more meaningful to a lay jury. This rule was the one proposed by the American Law Institute (ALI) in its Model Penal Code.

The ALI rule provides:

> (1) A person is not responsible for criminal conduct if at the time of such conduct as a result of mental disease or defect he lacks substantial capacity either to appreciate the criminality of his conduct or to conform his conduct to the requirements of the law.
>
> (2) As used in this Article, the terms "mental disease or defect" do not include an abnormality manifested only by repeated criminal or otherwise antisocial conduct [Section 4.01].

Proponents noted that by substituting *appreciate* for *know,* the rule expresses a preference for the broader construction of *M'Naghten,* an interpretation that holds that a sane offender must be emotionally, as well as intellectually, aware of the significance of his conduct. By using the word *conform,* the rule tries to divest itself of historical baggage and avoids any implication of "irresistible impulse." By requiring only "substantial" incapacity, it eliminates the risk implicit in the older cases, which sometimes suggested that "complete" or "total" destruction of the defendant's mental capacity was required.

Many legislatures replaced their old *M'Naghten* formulas with the ALI rule, and many judges and scholars praised it as an improvement. According to Chief Judge Haynsworth in United States v. Chandler, 393 F.2d 920, 926 (4th Cir. 1968) (en banc):

> With appropriate balance between cognition and volition, it demands an unrestricted inquiry into the whole personality of a defendant who surmounts the threshold question of doubt of his responsibility. Its verbiage is understandable by psychiatrists; it imposes no limitation upon their testimony and yet, to a substantial extent, it avoids a diagnostic approach and leaves the jury free to make its findings in terms of a standard which society prescribes and juries may apply.

Then, on March 30, 1981, John W. Hinckley Jr. shot and wounded President Ronald Reagan and three others outside a Washington hotel. Hinckley claimed that he shot the president in an attempt to impress movie actress Jodie Foster. He was charged with various offenses, including attempted assassination of the President, assault on a federal officer, and assault with intent to kill, and he pleaded not guilty by reason of insanity. The jury was instructed under the terms of the ALI test, which the federal courts had adopted in the absence of any federal insanity defense statute. There was strong expert testimony on each side, but Hinckley put on persuasive evidence of his psychotic obsession with Foster and was acquitted. Public opinion polls taken immediately after the *Hinckley* verdict was announced indicated that up to 90 percent of those surveyed favored abolishing the insanity defense. While there had been some pressure to modify the insanity defense before the *Hinckley* decision, Hinckley's acquittal captured the public attention and focused lawmakers on the insanity defense to an unprecedented extent. Most of the attention was focused on the so-called volitional prong of the defense in the ALI formulation. Many critics argued that the ALI test made acquittals too easy.

Congress had never before enacted legislation regarding the insanity defense. By the end of 1982, however, its members had introduced more than 40 bills to abolish or substantially reform the insanity defense. Congress ultimately enacted the Insanity Defense Reform Act of 1984, redefining the affirmative defense of insanity to exculpate only those defendants who, "at the time of the commission of the acts constituting the offense, . . . as the result of a severe mental disease or defect, [were] unable to appreciate the nature and quality or wrongfulness of [their] acts."[12] In short, Congress had eliminated the volitional prong of the insanity test of federal criminal law. Three-fourths of the states responded similarly to the *Hinckley* verdict and the resulting anti-insanity defense movement, most reverting to or reaffirming their *M'Naghten*-type rules.

Alaska is one state that, after the *Hinckley* verdict, switched from the ALI test back to a version of *M'Naghten*. The following case, decided during Alaska's ALI phase, helps us examine the degree of difference between ALI and *M'Naghten,* and also illustrates how the ALI test still operates in the notable minority of states that have stuck with the ALI rule.

SMITH v. STATE
Supreme Court of Alaska
614 P.2d 300 (1980)

On September 28, 1977, Allen J. Smith, an army private at Fort Richardson, commandeered a vehicle at gunpoint, left the base and after being chased by the police shot and seriously wounded judicial services officer Leon Jordan. He was charged with shooting with intent to kill, wound, or maim. . . .

Two days before the shooting, Smith purchased the firearm he used, a Colt Commander 9 millimeter pistol. On September 28, Smith was told that he was being processed out of the service on a Chapter 13 discharge as an undesirable. Captain Tucker described Smith as a very apathetic, nonaggressive soldier, who did what he was told most of the time. He had been cited for various disciplinary problems and eventually it was decided that he should be separated from the army. He had been sent to the mental health clinic since he seemed to be continually "spaced out" and "was never actively involved or engrossed in what he was doing."

The testimony of Captain Tucker and other officers in Smith's battalion suggest that they had no knowledge of Smith's prior history of mental illness. Smith had previously been diagnosed as a paranoid schizophrenic. He was hospitalized twice, once in 1973 for approximately 3 1/2 months and once in 1975 in two different facilities for approximately two weeks. The release report in 1975 suggested that no aggressive tendencies were present. His earlier 1973 hospitalization had occurred partly as a result of a violent incident resulting from a depression following the collapse of his marriage. He "jumped on a moving truck pulling off the driver, because he believed that the driver was his father-in-law."

---

12. 18 U.S.C. §17(1986). The act also shifted the burden of proof, placed limits on the admissibility of expert testimony, modified the forms of verdict, and substantially amended the procedures for disposition of mentally ill offenders.

After examination, the mental hygiene unit had originally sent Smith back finding no severe mental problems. When Smith exhibited continued unsatisfactory behavior, he was again sent to the mental hygiene unit. This time they recommended he be processed out of the army. Early on the morning of September 28, Captain Tucker informed Smith that he would be processed out of the military in approximately seven days. Smith showed no noticeable reaction to this information.

At 9:00 A.M., Smith entered the supply room at Fort Richardson and announced he was going to the airport. He pulled a gun and told platoon sergeant Wells that he needed a car. Wells did not have access to a vehicle, but told Smith he knew where a couple of sergeants were who might have one. Wells persuaded Smith to follow him into the bin room where one of the two sergeants present turned over to Smith the keys to his truck. Smith wanted Wells to drive him to the airport, but Wells refused. Keeping a gun trained on Wells and the sergeants, Smith backed out of the room and left with the keys to the pickup.

Smith got in the truck and headed toward downtown Anchorage. Gunfire was exchanged at the Fort Richardson gate. Smith proceeded westward toward the Seward Highway. A general police radio bulletin was issued on Smith, and his vehicle was spotted by several police vehicles. After the vehicle was pinpointed and followed by one police car, several others converged on the area. At that point, Smith accelerated to a high rate of speed and was pursued by several marked and unmarked police vehicles. Smith pulled over to the side of the road, jumped out of his vehicle and went running through a wooded area. One of the officers involved, judicial services officer Leon Jordan, had gone around the block and was standing on the sidewalk. Jordan spotted Smith lying down behind a tree with his gun pointed at Jordan. Jordan yelled at him to freeze and tried to move out of the way. Smith fired twice, hitting Jordan in the chest and shoulder. Jordan got up, took several shots at Smith and hit him once. Jordan then collapsed to the ground and Smith was captured. Smith was found lying on the ground, bleeding from the leg.

Smith subsequently made two statements to the police. In both statements, he admits shooting Jordan. As part of his defense of insanity, Smith was examined by Drs. Robinson, Langdon and Rader. Robinson is a clinical psychologist while Langdon and Rader are both psychiatrists. All three agreed that Smith suffered from chronic schizophrenia. . . . All three agreed that Smith had substantial capacity to tell right from wrong. While Langdon and Robinson thought that Smith lacked capacity to conform his actions to society's norms, Rader concluded that Smith could.

At trial, Smith's only defense was that he was innocent by reason of insanity. The relevant standard and the burden of proof are set forth in AS12.45.083(a) and (b):

> (a) A person is not responsible for criminal conduct if at the time of the conduct, as a result of mental disease or defect, he lacks substantial capacity either to appreciate the wrongfulness of his conduct or to conform his conduct to the requirements of law. . . .

Smith admitted in his statements to the police that what he did was illegal and morally wrong. All three medical experts testified that Smith, even if suffering from a mental illness, could appreciate the wrongfulness of his conduct.

The record contains no contrary evidence. Thus, the focus of our review is on the second prong of the legal responsibility test: whether Smith had substantial capacity to conform his conduct to the requirements of the law when he shot Officer Jordan. . . .

[Dr.] Rader concurred with the basic findings of the other experts that Smith was a schizophrenic. However, he concluded that the conduct that was exhibited on September 28, the shooting of Leon Jordan and its surrounding circumstances, was not a product of that illness. Although Rader's personal examination of Smith revealed characteristics of schizophrenic behavior, Smith also displayed Ganzer syndrome. Ganzer syndrome or prison psychosis is a condition in which one attempts to appear insane, or less sane than one is, for the advantages of being thought insane.

> He malingers his idea of crazy thinking, not appreciating that he in fact does have an underlying thought disorder. His malingering is designed to obscure the fact that his actions and his behavior clearly were intentional, in the service of an identifiable goal (to get out of the service) by unacceptable behavior. His intention was to be more of a problem than he was worth. In this respect he was successful and was being processed from the service.

This malingering partially explains a seemingly ever more fantastic set of tales told by Smith to justify the shooting[13] and a set of test responses given by Smith to Rader that displayed both schizophrenia and an intentional distortion on his part of the results. Rader stated that a medical finding of schizophrenia does not necessarily mean that a person is not legally responsible for his actions. . . . Rader stated that it was important to focus on the "behavior, ideation and motivation of the defendant at the time" of the shooting. His conclusions were as follows:

> In looking at the incident itself, this examiner comes to the conclusion that his behavior was consistent and reasonable in terms of his intention at that time. His intention was to leave the post, to leave Alaska as quickly as possible. In this regard he showed faulty judgment in his decision to leave that day, irrespective of the discharge process. It is felt that he also used poor judgment in expecting to be able to leave Alaska by going toward Seward. Thirdly, it is felt that his judgment was

---

13. Dr. Rader, when testifying and asked to give examples of such behavior, noted:

Well, first of all, he explained as best he could a kind of — of notion of a vendetta that had been going on for some time and seemed to be based partly on a meeting that took place some time in the military. Part of it was based upon that a friend had accosted him before he went in the service and he was an addict and wanted him to do something for him. Part of this — this vendetta idea was based upon the fact that in New Jersey there had been a Ku Klux Klan meeting back in the early '60s and it was a kind of rambling, disjointed scenario that was meant to explain why somebody had a gun on the street looking for him on this particular day that he stole the truck from the military and left the Post without authorization. To me, that's clearly a man that's fabricating things in the service of an idea, that it wasn't to get away from the policeman, to protect himself, to steal a truck, it was something else other than what it obviously was. That I think is unreliable. . . . He said that — again, he said that he was a yeti down in college. When he was asked what this meant he stated that he had been in refrigeration course in college in Wasilla or near Wasilla somewhere and a sergeant threatened to yank him into the college about something. Well, this didn't fit anything I knew about refrigeration school in Wasilla.

Rader later testified that Smith lacked a systemized delusion and seemed to have no emotional investment in any particular explanation.

poor for him to think that he could find shelter in a suburban neighborhood. On the other side, his behavior did seem consistent and reasonable insofar as: One, he was able to collect his personal possessions and have them in order. Second, he was able to impress his peers with his intentions in spite of his having a poor relationship and reputation as being a difficult person. Thirdly, he attempted to procure a driver for the vehicle, which seemed reasonable. Fourthly, he was able to accept refusal of the driver and still proceed with his plan to procure a vehicle. Fifth, he appreciated that the gate could be alerted and was able to successfully negotiate the gate without complications. Sixth, he was able to appreciate imminent capture when confronted by the presence of several police cars. Seventh, he was able to elude search until he was discovered, he discriminated between his captors and picked the person with the handgun over the one with the shotgun and he picked a black person in civilian clothes. Eighth, he was able to surrender without getting killed after having wounded an officer and known to be armed.

. . . Rader was persuaded, beyond a reasonable doubt, that Smith's actions of September 28 were not a product of a delusional paranoid system.

Dr. Langdon's report . . . focused on the existence of delusions ordering Smith's conduct, especially the story that the Mafia were after Smith's girlfriend in New Jersey. When questioned as to the two paragraphs of Dr. Rader's report, quoted *supra,* Langdon stated:

> Those two paragraphs — one of the things that he says here is that these various points along here, they're reasonable. Well, of course they are reasonable in terms of his intention at that time, and my impression is that his intention at the time was based on delusional ideation and that therefore the whole reasonable process thereafter was based on the mental illness.

Langdon thought that all schizophrenics lacked the ability from time to time to conform their conduct to the requirements of the law. . . . Langdon believed that Smith was acting under a delusional framework for the entire period and that most of the time there was no reason to violate societal norms in carrying out his plan, but when they interfered with his delusional plans, Smith would violate these norms. . . .

When asked whether the acts surrounding the shootings could have taken place apart from Smith's mental illness, [Dr.] Robinson responded:

> I really — in trying to turn that over in my mind, I just can't see how, because this man was in a high drive state, his feelings were — really — apparently really mixed up and tense and so how in the world could this man have done this without the presence of thought disorder which seemed to come out in the testing when he was intense? . . . He was able to perform some functions such as driving the car and so forth which you expect schizophrenics to do, but in terms of making big decisions about judgment, how he was going to get to the Lower 48 and so forth, I do not — I do not see that there was any clear judgment there at all.

The appellate court concluded that the trial judge could have reasonably found Dr. Rader's report the most compelling.

The lay testimony in this case also supported Rader's general conclusions as to the lucidity of the actions committed by Smith on September 28. According to his superiors, although Smith showed signs of dissatisfaction, his year in the army was devoid of additional bizarre behavior. . . .

Considering all the evidence, both lay and expert testimony, we conclude that the prosecution presented substantial evidence to prove beyond a reasonable doubt that Smith was legally sane at the moment he shot Officer Jordan. Thus, we affirm Smith's conviction. . . .

BOOCHEVER, JUSTICE, dissenting.

. . . [T]he only doctor who testified that Smith was capable of conforming his conduct to the requirements of law based his conclusion that Smith was not legally insane on a theory that he was motivated by "an identifiable goal (to get out of the service) by unacceptable behavior." In looking at the incident itself, Dr. Rader concluded that Smith intended to leave Alaska as quickly as possible. No rational explanation is even hinted at which would explain the commandeering of a vehicle immediately after Smith had been advised that he was being discharged within seven days. Similarly, the fact that Smith drove toward Seward, a direction which would not serve his purpose of leaving Alaska, is disregarded by Rader as mere "faulty judgment."

It is true that during the course of his wild conduct individual acts could be said to be meaningful, but such actions are not inconsistent with a lack of substantial ability to conform conduct to the requirements of law. In fact, it is well recognized that one may perform intelligent acts in the pursuit of delusionary goals.

Notes and Questions

1. How would Smith have fared under the original *M'Naghten* test? The *Serravo* test?

2. How do experts, and juries, determine whether a person has "substantial capacity . . . to conform his conduct to the requirements of the law"? The experts seem to agree that Smith was schizophrenic, but they disagree as to whether his actions were the product of that schizophrenia. Note Dr. Langdon's view that "all schizophrenics lacked the ability from time to time to conform their conduct to the requirements of the law." Is the disagreement over Smith in particular, or is it a more general conflict within psychiatry as to the nature and consequences of schizophrenia?

3. *Irrationality and insanity.* The court cites Dr. Rader's view that Smith lacked a "systemized delusion" and that Smith could act purposefully at key times. The dissent argues that Smith's behavior was irrational because he would have been released from the army in seven days in any event, and because the road that he took to escape was not the Alaska Highway but a dead end. Are they using different notions of insanity? What is the relation between insanity and irrationality?

If Smith had acted with perfect consistency, would that have strengthened or weakened his claim of insanity under the ALI rule?

4. Ultimately how significant was the change from *M'Naghten* to the ALI rule, and then back to *M'Naghten*? The infamous Hinckley case itself presents an example for consideration. Dr. Alan Stone raises the question whether limiting Hinckley's defense to the cognitive prong would have made any difference.[14]

---

14. Alan Stone, Law, Psychiatry, and Morality 91-92 (1984).

Considering this commentary, if juries rely mostly on evidence of extreme psychotic derangement, does it matter whether they are limited to "cognition" as a test or can look to "volition"?

> . . . Despite the endless attempts of law to define precise tests of criminal responsibility, the ordinary psychiatrist typically asks: is the person psychotic? If the diagnosis is psychosis, particularly schizophrenia, the person is insane. If a personality disorder is diagnosed, the person is sane. The new [American Psychiatric Association] proposal has gone back to that time-honored clinical distinction, noting that we now have 80 percent reliability as to the DSM-III [Diagnostic and Statistical Manual of Mental Disorders, 3d ed.] diagnosis of psychosis. But this new threshold question would have had no impact on the Hinckley testimony since the defense diagnosed schizophrenia and the prosecution diagnosed personality disorder. Hinckley apparently fell into the 20 percent nonreliability category. We should not be surprised by that. Rather, we should expect that in most cases where the prosecution would want to contest an insanity defense, the defendant will not be obviously psychotic. The obviously psychotic defendant can be readily identified even by a prosecutor.
>
> The next part of the APA proposal involves going back to an essentially cognitive test — again in part because psychiatric testimony relevant to cognitive matters such as appreciation and understanding "is more reliable, and has a stronger scientific base" than testimony relevant to volition. Here again the hopes of the APA fail. The defense found ample evidence of thought disorder, including ideas of reference, magical thinking, bizarre ideas, and a break with reality. The prosecution found none of this. Thus testimony limited to the cognitive issue did not prove reliable in the courtroom.
>
> This lack of reliability in diagnosing thought disorder also raises questions about the [American Bar Association's] decision that where the restrictive cognitive test is adopted, the burden of proving beyond a reasonable doubt that the defendant is not insane should remain with the prosecution. Presumably this decision was made on the premise that this burden of proof would be lightened by the narrower test, which would draw brighter lines. The transcript of the trial suggests that this did not happen in the Hinckley case. Given the psychiatric testimony, there would have been reasonable doubt about Hinckley's insanity even as to the narrower cognitive test. If the ABA's decision was made with the Hinckley verdict in mind and intended to produce a different result in similar cases, it fails based on this analysis.
>
> The discrepancies in the psychiatric testimony would be much easier to understand if the defense and prosecution had agreed that there was a thought disorder but disagreed about its extent — for example, whether it was sufficient to be diagnosed psychosis, and whether it was sufficient to negate criminal responsibility. Such agreement would have placed Hinckley in the problem area of psychiatry's familiar nosological disputes. Thus, if both sides had agreed that he was a schizotypal personality or a paranoid personality and the defense said he had gone over into psychosis while the prosecution had insisted he had not, every clinician would have understood the problem. How much thought disorder makes a psychosis? But here the prosecution specifically rejected the diagnoses of schizotypal personality and paranoid personality, the character disorders which suggest a thought disorder. This makes the discrepancies harder to understand and harder to explain to the cynics who believe psychiatrists can be hired to say anything.

Do you conclude from Stone's analysis that the choice of legal standard for insanity ultimately means less than the competition between defense and prosecution psychiatrists over a largely medical question? If most litigated insanity cases lie on the blurry borders of the medical category of psychosis, does that mean that the allocation of the burden of proof is the decisive question?

5. *Compulsion and insanity.* Professor Stephen Morse poses the following challenge to the notion of irresistible impulse:[15]

> Many claim that people with disorders are like mechanisms or that mental disorder generally produces compelled behavior, but the theoretical basis for such claims is problematic and in most cases they are simply factually incorrect. Mental disorders do not turn people into mechanisms. Even the most wildly delusional or hallucinating person retains the ability to act intentionally, to act for reasons.
>
> Compulsive states are marked by allegedly overwhelming desires or cravings, but whether the cravings are produced by faulty biology, faulty psychology, faulty environment, or some combination of the three, a desire is just a desire and satisfaction of it is human action. Even if craving is the symptom of a disease with biological roots, the cause of the desire is immaterial. Consider, for example, a person who suffers from "substance dependence disorder," or, to use the more common term, "addiction." Possessing and using the substance in question is an intentional action. The addict desires either the pleasure of intoxication, the avoidance of the pain of withdrawal or inner tension, or both. Or consider a person suffering from "pedophilia," recurrent, strong desires for sexual contact with children that produce distress or dysfunction. If the person yields and has sexual contact with a child, this, too, is surely intentional action.
>
> . . . [I]magine the following counterexample: a vicious gunslinger follows around the addict and the pedophile and threatens to kill them instantly if they touch drugs or a child. Assume that the addict and the pedophile want to live. . . . Literally no pedophile or addict will yield to the desire.

Are you convinced by his final conclusion? Assuming it is valid, does it undermine the insanity defense?

In light of Morse's commentary, consider a recent and much-publicized New York case. On January 3, 1999, Andrew Goldstein, a 30-year-old man with a record of psychiatric commitment recorded in a 3,500-page file, pushed a young woman to her death onto New York City subway tracks. Twelve hours later Goldstein made a videotaped confession,[16] in which he explained that while he was waiting for a train he felt the onsurge of a psychotic attack:

> "What happened was this train is coming and then it goes away again, and then it comes back again. And then the train is almost there and I said, 'Oh no, it happened.' You know I go into the fit again, like I've done this in the past, and I pushed the woman, not meaning to push her on the tracks, but I shoved her, not knowing which direction I was going, coming or going, and then she fell onto the track and then I went into shock, horror."

The case attracted much publicity because Goldstein's psychiatric history and his record of violence were well known to the mental health system. In just the previous two years, he had been hospitalized 13 times after making unprovoked attacks on 13 individuals. Several times he sought and was denied long-term care because of state budget cuts that especially affected psychotic people

---

15. Craziness and Criminal Responsibility, 17 Behavioral Sciences & the Law 147, 156-57 (1999).

16. Michael Winerip, Oddity and Normality Vie in Killer's Confession, New York Times, Oct. 18, 1999, at A25.

who tended to go off their medication. In taking Goldstein's confession, the police interrogator tried to win Goldstein's concession that he understood the wrongfulness of his act:

> "But you knew," says the interrogator, "that if you pushed her off the platform, she might get . . . "
> "Killed, yeah."
> "And you also knew that if you did that, it would be the wrong thing to do?"
> "Yeah, definitely, I would never do something like that."
> "Well, you did."
> "I know, but the thing is I would never do it on purpose."

But then Goldstein seemed to describe an alien, irresistible impulse:

> "You feel like something is entering you, like you're being inhabited, I don't know, but, and then it's like an overwhelming urge to strike out or push or punch. Now this time, terrific. I grab, bang, zoom, you know, it's right in front of a train."

The interrogator tried one more time, and the colloquy continued:

> "You certainly agree that you knew what you were doing and you knew it was wrong."
> "Uh-huh."
> "When you pushed her onto the tracks to cause her death."
> "I see."
> "No, tell me, did you?"
> "Oh, no. I'm sorry?"
> "Were you really listening to what I was saying?"
> "Oh no."
> "Do you agree or disagree that you knew at the time that you pushed her, that it could cause her death?"
> "I wasn't thinking about anything about pushing. When it happens, I don't think, it just goes whoosh, whoosh, push, you know. It's like a random variable."

Could a jury be reasonably expected to apply the ALI test to this case?

6. *Empirical data on NGI outcomes.* In how many cases does the insanity defense make a difference? Despite its prominence in legal literature and in the media, the frequency with which the insanity defense is asserted varies widely, but is generally quite low. One recent review of research from across the country concludes that only about 1 percent of all defendants invoke the defense, and among those pleading NGI, the success rate varied from 5 percent to 25 percent.[17] One study of several jurisdictions for the year 1985 reported that the ratio of insanity pleas to arrests was, for Colorado 1 in 4,968; for Minnesota 1 in 2,938; for Michigan 1 in 476; for Wyoming 1 in 204; and for Maine 1 in 214.[18]

As for the ratio of successful NGI pleas to arrests, the number was 1 in 2,553 for Missouri; 1 in 5,342 for Maine; 1 in 5,420 for Ohio; and an infinitesimal 1 in 86,674 in Minnesota; and 1 in 49,140 in Utah.

17. Judith Regan, Ann Alderson & William Regan, A Review of the Insanity Defense, 2 Psychiatrist Administrator 66 (2002).

18. Hugh McGinley & Richard Pasewark, National Survey of the Frequency and Success of the Insanity Plea and Alternate Pleas, J. of Psychiatry and the Law (Spring, 1989), at 205, 208-14.

On the other hand, in those relatively rare cases where the defendant pleads NGI, how often is the plea successful? Again, the variation is great: the success rate for NGI pleaders was 44 percent in Colorado, as compared to 7 percent, 4 percent, 3 percent, and 2 percent respectively for Michigan, Maine, Minnesota, and Wyoming.

A recent study by Cirincione and Jacobs[19] counsels that earlier studies may not be wholly reliable, because state correctional and mental health officials are notoriously inconsistent in keeping accurate records of dispositions. In addition, they doubt the accuracy of records on arrests and indictments, and so question studies that determine NGI rates as a function of arrests or indictments. Nevertheless, using the most conservative criteria, the authors infer from a survey of three-fourths of the states that NGI verdicts are indeed quite rare. For example, between 1970 and 1995, the average annual number of NGI verdicts in all of California was 134. When population is accounted for, the number of NGI verdicts per 100,000 ranges from a high of 4.4 in Hawaii to 2.17 in Oregon, to 0.55 in California, to a national average for these 25 years of 0.69. But the study does suggest that changes in the law of the insanity defense may affect NGI rates. The national aggregate figures for NGI verdicts per 100,000 population were about 0.05 in 1970, rose to 0.4 by 1974, and then rose to 0.9 in 1980, before dipping — perhaps as an effect of post-*Hinckley* legal changes — to 0.4 in recent years.[20]

7. *The problem of "expertise."* Note that all insanity tests require that the defendant be suffering from some sort of mental disease. Both the ALI and *Durham* tests, for example, absolve conduct of criminal responsibility only when such conduct is "the result of mental disease or defect"; the *M'Naghten* test has a similar requirement. Thus, the success of an insanity defense turns to a very large extent on what evidence courts will accept as proof of mental disease or defect. With no legal definition of what this term means, however, courts must depend on experts to define it for them. This dependence raises problems of its own. Consider this passage from United States v. Brawner, 471 F.2d 969, 978 (D.C. Cir. 1972):

> In the absence of a definition of "mental disease or defect," medical experts attached to them the meanings which would naturally occur to them — medical meanings — and gave testimony accordingly. The problem was dramatically highlighted by the weekend flip flop case. In re Rosenfield, 157 F. Supp. 18 (D.D.C. 1957). The petitioner was described as a sociopath. A St. Elizabeth's psychiatrist testified that a person with a sociopathic personality was not suffering from a mental disease. That was Friday afternoon. On Monday morning, through a policy change at St. Elizabeth's Hospital, it was determined as an administrative matter that the state of a psychopathic or sociopathic personality did constitute a mental disease.
>
> The concern that medical terminology not control legal outcomes culminated in McDonald v. United States, 114 U.S. App. D.C. 120, 312 F.2d 847, 851 (en banc, 1962), where this court recognized that the term, mental disease or defect, has various meanings, depending upon how and why it is used, and by whom. Mental disease means one thing to a physician bent on treatment, but something

---

19. Carmen Cirincione & Charles Jacobs, Identifying Insanity Acquittals: Is It Any Easier? 23 L. & Hum. Behavior 487 (1999).

20. On the other hand, insanity pleas may affect criminal litigation even when they are not fully adjudicated. One study suggests that because insanity trials can be unusually complex and protracted, they might lead to more frequent and more generous plea bargains. McGinley & Pasewark, *supra*, fn. 18, at 220.

different, if somewhat overlapping, to a court of law. We provided a legal definition of mental disease or defect, and held that it included "any abnormal condition of the mind which substantially affects mental or emotional processes and substantially impairs behavior controls" (312 F.2d at 851). "Thus the jury would consider testimony concerning the development, adaptation and functioning of these processes and controls." Id.

While the *McDonald* standard of mental disease was not without an attribute of circularity, it was useful in the administration of justice because it made plain that clinical and legal definitions of mental disease were distinct, and it helped the jury to sort out its complex task and to focus on the matters given it to decide.

Recall that in People v. Serravo, two of the defense experts testified that in their opinion Serravo's mental illness made it impossible for him to distinguish right from wrong, p. 583, *supra*. Is it their job to offer the jury conclusions in the language of the statute, or merely to supply the jury with information relevant to the statutory standard?

The American Bar Association has taken the view that experts "should not express or be permitted to express an opinion on any question requiring a conclusion of law or a moral or social value judgment properly reserved to a court or jury."[21] Furthermore, a 1984 amendment to the Federal Rules of Evidence, passed as part of the "post-*Hinckley*" revisions of the federal laws on criminal insanity, see pp. 598-600, *infra*, includes a stringent rule explicitly barring experts from testifying on the ultimate issue of guilt:

(a) Except as provided in subdivision (b), testimony in the form of an opinion or inference otherwise admissible is not objectionable because it embraces an ultimate issue to be decided by the trier of fact.

(b) No expert witness testifying with respect to the mental state or condition of a defendant in a criminal case may state an opinion or inference as to whether the defendant did or did not have the mental state or condition constituting an element of the crime charged or a defense thereto. Such ultimate issues are matters for the trier of fact alone. [F.R.E. 704 (P.L. 98-473, Oct. 12, 1984).]

On the other hand, in Ake v. Oklahoma, 470 U.S. 68 (1985), the Supreme Court held that the Sixth Amendment right to counsel and the due process clause guarantee an indigent criminal defendant psychiatric assistance in his defense at public expense if his sanity is a factor in his case.

8. *"Guilty but mentally ill."* Several states have enacted statutes offering juries the option of entering a verdict of guilty but mentally ill in cases where the insanity defense is raised. The statutes are designed to limit the scope of the insanity defense and to ensure that "guilty" defendants are not set free just because they were mentally ill at the time of their crime. Though the "GBMI" verdict is relatively new to this country, England's criminal law had a "guilty but insane" verdict from the time of Queen Victoria until 1964.

When the jury returns a GBMI verdict, the defendant is sentenced as if the verdict were "guilty." However, the statutes provide for treatment of the defendant's mental illness. If a defendant is "cured" during the period of her sentence, she will be transferred to a prison to serve the remainder of her term. For

---

21. II ABA Standards for Criminal Justice 7.3-7.15, 7.294-7.299 (1986).

example, after the John Hinckley verdict, Alaska enacted A.S. 12.47.030, which provides:

> (a) A defendant is guilty but mentally ill if, when the defendant engaged in the criminal conduct, the defendant lacked, as a result of mental disease or defect, the substantial capacity either to appreciate the wrongfulness of that conduct or to conform that conduct to the requirements of law. A defendant found guilty but mentally ill is not relieved of criminal responsibility for criminal conduct and is subject to the provisions of AS 12.47.050 [concerning civil incarceration].

The Alaska GBMI statute is noteworthy for the way it isolates the modern portion of the ALI test from the traditional language of the old *M'Naghten* rule. However, there are other versions of GBMI. Here is the Michigan statute:

> §28.1059. Insanity Defense; Finding of "Guilty but Mentally Ill."
> Sec. 36. (1) If the defendant asserts a defense of insanity in compliance with section 20a, the defendant may be found "guilty but mentally ill" if, after trial, the trier of fact finds all of the following beyond a reasonable doubt:
> (a) That the defendant is guilty of an offense.
> (b) That the defendant was mentally ill at the time of the commission of that offense.
> (c) That the defendant was not legally insane at the time of the commission of that offense.

Thus, a GBMI verdict provides the jury with a "middle ground," as the following commentary explains:[22]

> The most obvious and important function of the GBMI verdict is to permit juries to make an unambiguous statement about the factual guilt, mental condition, and moral responsibility of a defendant. Theoretically, this should allow jurors to feel more comfortable in returning NGRI verdicts in cases where the defendant committed a criminal act but fit the statutory definition of insanity. Conversely, juries should also feel more confident in convicting a mentally ill defendant when appropriate, because they are able to recommend treatment and make a mitigating statement concerning mental illness. In both situations, members of the jury and the public should be satisfied that the issue of moral blameworthiness was resolved by a knowing decision about the relationship between a defendant's misdeeds and illness.
>
> The GBMI verdict further enhances public confidence in the criminal justice system in that it helps eliminate many of the conflicts between legal and medical experts in insanity cases. . . .
>
> This procedure has been highly successful in reducing the public perception that insanity trials are a circus of conflicting psychiatric testimony. Prior to adoption of this plan, fifty percent of those defendants found NGRI and committed to state hospitals were adjudged not to be insane by the doctors who performed their postcommitment examinations. Since GBMI and mandatory forensic center evaluations have been adopted, the rate of such allegedly mistaken NGRI verdicts has dropped to five percent.

Illinois's statute resembles Michigan's but sets out a very specific sequence of decision. If the jury finds the defendant guilty of the crime charged in the first trial phase, it then determines whether he is insane enough to merit an NGI verdict.

---

22. Ira Mickenberg, A Pleasant Surprise: The Guilty but Mentally Ill Verdict Has Both Succeeded in Its Own Right and Successfully Preserved the Traditional Role of the Insanity Defense, 55 U. Cinn. L. Rev. 945, 988-89 (1987).

If it chooses not to issue an NGI verdict, it then proceeds to consider a GBMI verdict. Does this scheme risk confusing juries by suggesting that "mental illness" and "insanity" are mutually exclusive? Does it risk an unfair verdict of GBMI because juries may fear (usually wrongly) that an NGI verdict will not lead to confinement as long as a GBMI verdict? Will juries wrongly infer that "GBMI" denotes a lower level of culpability than an outright conviction? The Illinois Supreme Court has answered these questions in the negative. People v. Lantz, 712 N.E.2d 314 (Ill. 1999). Is it right?

Disposition after GBMI. The Michigan GBMI statute provides that in the event of a GBMI conviction, "the court shall impose any sentence which could be imposed pursuant to law upon a defendant who is convicted of the same offense." The statute further requires that a GBMI defendant will be evaluated and, if necessary, treated by either the department of corrections or the department of mental health. When the treating facility discharges the defendant, the defendant returns to the department of corrections for the balance of her sentence.

Effect of GBMI. Obviously, defense attorneys have feared that the availability of the GBMI verdict would limit the success of traditional NGI pleas. The data bearing on this question remain equivocal. For example, the number of NGI pleas and acquittals in Michigan did not decline after enactment of the GBMI law,[23] although since Michigan had simultaneously adopted the ALI-Model Penal Code standard for NGI pleas, the GBMI law may have prevented what would have been an increased rate of entry and success of NGI claims.[24]

Does the GBMI verdict offer a true alternative, when all jurisdictions already provide mental health treatment to prisoners within the regular prison system? In fact, an admitted shortcoming of the GBMI innovation has been a lack of funding for new treatment programs. Thus, it is frequently the case that a GBMI defendant will be offered exactly the same treatment as a guilty defendant.

In Robinson v. Solem, 432 N.W.2d 246 (S.D. 1988), the defendant argued that his denial of psychiatric treatment after a GBMI verdict was unconstitutional because it amounted to a deprivation of liberty without due process. The Supreme Court of South Dakota denied the appeal, holding:

> In finding a defendant mentally ill under South Dakota's GBMI statute, judge or jury does not find that treatment is needed, but only that the offender has a psychiatric disorder of thought, mood, or behavior which impairs his or her judgment. There is no constitutional right to treatment because of that finding. Once found to be guilty but mentally ill, a defendant who is incarcerated becomes a ward of the executive branch as a prisoner. A prisoner is entitled to treatment only if a mental health provider, exercising ordinary care and skill, concludes with reasonable medical certainty [that treatment is a] medical necessity and not simply treatment which may be considered as merely desirable. . . . [Id. at 249.]

Critique of GBMI. Leonard S. Rubenstein, a former attorney with the Mental Health Law Project, criticizes the GBMI verdict as a prosecutorial sleight-of-hand:[25]

> The "guilty but mentally ill" verdict assuages feelings that the mentally ill defendant is "different" and therefore should be judged differently. It does not, however,

---

23. McGinley & Pasewark, *supra,* fn. 18, at 215.

24. Linda Fentiman, "Guilty but Mentally Ill": The Real Verdict Is Guilty, 26 B.C. L. Rev. 601, 614-15 (1985).

25. Against "Guilty but Mentally Ill," New York Times, Aug. 5, 1982, at 19 (editorial).

ascribe any legal significance to that difference, for a prison sentence would follow conviction just as it does a guilty verdict. It is as if [the legislature] were to enact a law that permitted a verdict of "guilty but from a deprived background" or, for that matter, "guilty but short." The basic problem is that the proposed verdict removes the hard choice that every jury is supposed to make in any criminal case: whether the defendant is to be held responsible for a criminal act.

For all its flaws, the insanity defense forces the jury to make this moral and legal choice when a question is raised about a defendant's mental capacity to commit a crime.

Despite the outcry over the *Hinckley* verdict, it is almost universally recognized that some defendants cannot be held responsible for their actions. Wherever one draws a line on the moral, psychological and legal continuums between individual responsibility (guilt) and compelled behavior (innocence) . . . it must be drawn somewhere. Where to draw the line may be one of the imponderables, yet society and juries should not escape the responsibility for doing it.

The GBMI debate in context. Consider prosecutor Cheryl Coleman's argument for a GBMI option, based on the tragic case of Ralph Tortorici: [26]

Ralph Tortorici was a paranoid schizophrenic SUNY psychology student. For years, he had gone around telling anyone who would listen, including the police, that the government had implanted a microchip in his penis and was sending him messages. . . . He would invariably end up at the Capital District Psychiatric Center where he would always manage to be released after 48 hours, after failing to meet the involuntary commitment criteria.

In December 1994, Ralph, dressed in military fatigues, brought a loaded rifle, a ton of ammo and a knife into a SUNY lecture center, where he terrorized an entire class for hours. Jason McEneaney, a young, handsome student and one of Ralph's hostages, was shot in the groin, catastrophically maimed, his life changed forever.

Within days, Ralph was found incompetent to stand trial and sent to the Mid-Hudson Psychiatric Center. Yet, six weeks later, despite the fact that he had consistently refused medication, the psychiatric "powers that be" there found him competent to stand trial.

This is where I came in. As one of the two prosecutors assigned to prosecute Ralph, I knew two things for sure by the time his case came to trial: (1) Ralph was hugely mentally ill, and (2) Ralph absolutely knew, at the time of his crime, the nature, consequences and wrongfulness of his conduct.

Nor was this a difficult call for the jury, which convicted Ralph, and rejected the insanity defense, in a little over an hour. Despite Ralph's pervasive mental illness, the evidence of premeditation, the secreting of the weapon and a note of apology written to his family beforehand made the actual legal/factual issue, once the jury heard the law, surprisingly non-complex.

As prosecutors, we were satisfied we had done the right thing. We had a totally innocent victim, an incredibly dangerous, albeit insane, defendant, and a law that was clearly on our side. Add to that the fact that if the defendant were to be judged legally non-responsible, either through our acquiescence or by a [not] guilty verdict, the same mental health professionals who had failed to appreciate the depth of his dangerous mental illness before the event, and then returned him to us as "much better" six weeks after the event, would be in charge of deciding when

---

26. Cheryl Coleman, 'Guilty but Mentally Ill' Verdict Needed? YES, N. Y. L. J., September 23, 1999, p. 2.

Ralph was better enough to get day passes, go on furloughs, and then go home. We did not want them making that call. Who could blame us? . . .

Surely, we figured, upon his conviction, Ralph would be placed by the Department of Correctional Services (DOCS) in a prison with a secure mental health facility. . . . Incredibly enough, to the officials at DOCS, the guilty verdict equaled a determination that Ralph was not insane. Nothing, of course, could have been further from the truth.

Into population he went. Within the year, he did a good job hanging himself. He was then transferred to a psychiatric hospital, and subsequently returned to prison. This time, he did a much better job. His death haunts me more than I can explain.

"Guilty but mentally ill?" Why not? . . . It's the law in many states. Defendants found guilty but mentally ill serve their sentence in a secure psychiatric facility until they are successfully treated, and then serve out the remainder of their sentence, if any, in a prison. . . .

It is a law, ultimately, that would save lives. We have heard horror stories about people being killed by the criminally insane who have been either released as no longer dangerous, or furloughed. Now, you have heard Ralph's story. He needed protection from himself as much as we needed protection from him. We need a law that can do both. We need the option of "guilty but mentally ill."

Are you convinced by Coleman's argument that a GBMI option would have saved Tortorici's life? Consider the following rejoinder by Tortorici's appellate advocate:[27]

The tragedy of Ralph's life and death suggests several reforms, but "guilty but mentally ill" is not one of them. In virtually all of the 13 states that have adopted this verdict, there has been no increase whatsoever in access to treatment for mentally ill prisoners. In Illinois, for example, none of the first 44 defendants found guilty but mentally ill received any hospital treatment. And, in Georgia, only three of 150 defendants designated as guilty but mentally ill received inpatient psychiatric care.

Are you convinced by Coleman's claim that, in the absence of a GBMI verdict, she had no option that would lead to Tortorici receiving the care that he needed? Consider that, on the eve of trial, a prosecution psychiatrist examined the defendant and found him severely psychotic and totally unfit to stand trial. The defense attorney, apparently overconfident that a jury would accept the clearly psychotic Tortorici's insanity defense, raised no objection to proceeding to trial. In retrospect, this looks like a strategic blunder. But should the *prosecutor* have urged the court to find Tortorici incompetent to stand trial? Can incompetence be used as a substitute for an ineffective GBMI verdict and an unlikely NGI verdict, as a way to get hospitalization and treatment for insane offenders?

9. *Informing the juries of outcomes.* Should juries be told of the consequences of a not guilty by reason of insanity verdict? Some courts have required such instructions, but the majority position on this question had traditionally been that the disposition of the defendant was irrelevant to his guilt or innocence and hence should not be considered by the jury. In Erdman v. State 553 A.2d 244 (Md. 1989), the defendant had entered a plea of not criminally responsible and

27. Kathryn Kase, 'Guilty but Mentally Ill' Verdict Needed? NO, N. Y. L. J., September 23, 1999, p. 2.

had requested that the jury be told about the consequences of "acquitting" him on that ground. The trial court refused. On appeal, the Maryland Supreme Court reversed, reasoning:

> In our scanning of the cases, we notice that, no matter what the reasons given or the rationale advanced, there is a correlation between the status of the law with respect to the disposition of a defendant found to be not criminally responsible and the determination whether to inform the jury on the matter. It appears that, usually, the instruction is required or permitted in those jurisdictions in which commitment, in practical effect, is automatic, and the eligibility of the committed individual for release is so structured as to give reasonable assurance that he will not be returned to society while still a danger to himself or to the person or property of others. It seems that an instruction as to disposition is looked upon with disfavor in those jurisdictions in which automatic commitment is not mandated, and it is unclear what disposition, in fact, would be made of the defendant found to be not criminally responsible.
>
> . . . We think that, in the light of the [changes made in the criminal insanity] statutes, there is compelling reason to embark on a new course. . . .
>
> . . . The verdict sheet given to the jury to complete contained spaces for the jury to designate "Criminally Responsible" or "Not Criminally Responsible."
>
> The word "responsible" stood naked before the jury. The jury received no indication whatsoever by way of court proceedings as to what happens to a defendant found to be not criminally responsible for his criminal conduct. The curtain was drawn on that matter and no light seeped through officially. All the jury had before it was the test for its determination whether the defendant was "responsible" or not. There was no suggestion as to what effect a finding of not criminally responsible would have. . . .
>
> . . . We lean toward the observation of the ABA that despite instructions cautioning them to consider only the evidence they have heard, jurors who are not informed about dispositional consequences will speculate about the practical results of a nonresponsibility verdict and, in ignorance of reality, will convict persons who are not criminally responsible in order to protect society. Jurors surely know, without being told, what happens to most convicted offenders, as well as defendants who are acquitted outright; the proposed instruction provides the same level of knowledge with respect to the fate of persons acquitted by reason of mental nonresponsibility [insanity]. Commentary to Standard 7-6.8, at 7-345, Criminal Justice Mental Health Standards. . . .
>
> The view that a jury has the need and right to know the consequences of a verdict of not criminally responsible is bottomed on possible prejudice to the defendant. Therefore, we think that the instruction is to be given only when duly requested by the defendant. It may well be that for strategic or tactical reasons or the nature of the evidence, the defendant will not want the instruction. The option is his. [Id. at 250.]

But in Shannon v. United States, 512 U.S. 573 (1994), the Supreme Court held that the federal insanity defense law did not require trial courts to inform the jury that an NGI verdict would result in civil confinement. The Court found no reason to set an exception to the general rule that jurors are not to advert to the punishment consequences of their verdicts. It also cautioned that because the terms and duration of civil commitment could not be determined in advance, any instruction on this subject would fail to give juries reassurance about confinement and might even backfire on the defendant.

What do you think uninstructed jurors assume to be the consequences of an NGI verdict?

10. *Insanity and the death penalty.* One other role of insanity claims in the criminal law concerns the administration — not the adjudication — of the death penalty. An old common law rule held that it was improper to execute an insane prisoner (one who presumably became insane after his crime, or else the insanity defense should have spared him a death sentence in the first place). In Ford v. Wainwright, 477 U.S. 399 (1986), the Supreme Court affirmed this rule as an expression of the Eighth Amendment's ban on cruel and unusual punishments. Speaking for the Court, Justice Marshall noted the various rationales traditionally offered for the rule: that the execution of an insane person simply offends humanity, that it does not serve deterrence or retribution, or that the madness *itself* is its own punishment. Id. at 407-08. Justice Powell added the view that it is unfair to execute a prisoner who cannot appreciate the moral significance of the relationship between his crime and his punishment (and who cannot prepare for his passing). Id. at 422. In *Ford* a plurality of the Court then went on to vacate a Florida death sentence because the Florida scheme, though theoretically ensuring that presently insane prisoners were not executed, did not give the prisoner sufficient procedural and evidentiary rights to prove his present insanity and because it left the final determination wholly within the executive branch.

D.   REPRISE: REASSESSING THE INSANITY DEFENSE

1.   The Continuing Debate over Abolition

Though the courts have declined the invitation to abolish the insanity defense, scholars and commentators have not been deterred. A notable call for abolition came from Professors Norval Morris and Gordon Hawkins,[28] who claim that the professed rationale for the insanity defense "proves too much." In their view, the deterministic assumptions underlying the defense would, with equal force, justify exculpation for such criminogenic factors as suffering poverty or racial prejudice in childhood. They further argued:

> We find it impossible morally to distinguish the insane from others who may be convicted though suffering deficiencies of intelligence, adversities of social circumstances, indeed all the ills to which the flesh and life of man is prey. It seems to us that our approach better accords with the total role of the criminal law in society than does a system which makes a special exculpatory case out of one rare and unusual criminogenic process, while it determinedly denies exculpatory effects to other, more potent processes. In the long run we will better handle these problems, as well as the whole and more complex problem of criminality in the community, if we will recognize that within crime itself there lies the greatest disparity of human wickedness and the greatest range of human capacities for self-control.

28. Norval Morris & Gordon Hawkins, The Honest Politician's Guide to Crime Control 178-85 (1970).

Our perennial perseverations about the defense of insanity impede recognition of this diversity, since they push us to a false dichotomy between the responsible and the irresponsible. They should be abandoned. One occupation for the energies thus released might be suggested, a task in which the psychiatrist has an important role to play: the defining of those categories of psychologically disturbed criminals who are serious threats to the community and to whom special treatment measures should therefore be applied.

Professor Alan Stone, M.D.,[29] answered these objections in a qualified defense of the insanity defense:

. . . So, finally, why not abolish the insanity defense? Who is standing in the way? My answer is the law itself. By the law, I mean those people — lawyers, judges, legislatures, and citizens — who have a profound concern for the morality of the law itself and who believe that the law should reflect our most basic human intuitions of morality. I maintain that every moral philosopher in every culture has realized that morality requires that man has free will. Our legal system and the law are inspired by that moral intuition. At the same time, I maintain that every moral philosopher who has thought about human nature has also concluded that at *some* time in a man's life, he feels he has no choice; he acts without choice. The contradiction between this experience of being without choice and the moral intuition of free will is one of the inescapable contradictions of human existence. That contradiction is expressed and denied by the insanity defense. The insanity defense is the exception that "proves" the rule of law. I bowdlerize the maxim because today the insanity defense does more than test the law, it *demonstrates* that all other criminals had free will — the ability to choose between good and evil — but that they chose evil and therefore deserve to be punished.

It is not psychiatrists, it is not criminals, it is not the insane who need the insanity defense. The insanity defense is the exception that "proves" the rule of free will. It is required by the law itself, and it is this vision of law which has throughout history required resistance to abolition of the insanity defense. It is not for psychiatrists to choose between this vision of law and the new loss of protection to society. . . .

So, in the end, I suggest that it is the law that cannot do without psychiatry. The marriage between law and psychiatry is therefore just like many other marriages in which one hears it said at time of crisis, "I don't know what to do. I can't live with her, and I can't live without her."

The radical psychiatrist Thomas Szasz offered a more fundamental critique of the entire concept of a mental illness defense:[30]

If the defense of insanity [is] raised in a criminal trial, it is considered to be a "matter of fact" for the jury to decide whether the offender suffered from a "mental illness" at the time of the commission of the act with which he is charged.

This is unadulterated nonsense. . . . Disregarding even the most obvious doubt concerning exactly what the expression "mental illness" is supposed to denote, it denotes a *theory* (if it denotes anything) and not a fact. . . .

. . . Yet the jury is supposed to determine, as a matter of *fact,* whether the accused has or has not a "mental illness." Of course, it is quite possible for a group of people (a jury) to decide that someone is "crazy" or "mentally ill." But this is then *their theory* of why he has acted the way he did. . . . To believe that one's own theories are facts is considered by many contemporary psychiatrists as a "symptom" of schizophrenia. Yet this is what the language of the *Durham* decision does. It reifies some of the shakiest and most controversial aspects of contemporary psychiatry (i.e., those

29. 33 Harv. L. Sch. Bull. 21 (Fall 1982).
30. Psychiatry, Ethics, and the Criminal Law, 58 Colum. L. Rev. 183, 190 (1958).

pertaining to what is "mental disease" and the classification of such alleged diseases) and by legal fiat seeks to transform inadequate theory into "judicial fact."

Though most Americans accept the insanity defense on a philosophical level, many distrust it on a practical level. The insanity defense raises concerns about whether we can in fact distinguish between sane and insane offenders. In addition, though we as a society may believe in theory that insane defendants are not culpable and are therefore undeserving of punishment, when we are faced with the results of specific crimes — especially murder — our resolve that insane defendants should go unpunished may weaken.

Because of this ambivalence, society's struggle to define stable moral and practical limits on the insanity defense has been generally unsuccessful. Its contradictory interests and concerns have resulted in a continuing emotional debate and have created a somewhat vague formal legal structure.

Compare the following two cases:

a. Jeffrey Dahmer entered a guilty plea in connection with the murders of 15 men and boys in Milwaukee, Wisconsin. As a result of Wisconsin's bifurcated system, a separate jury trial was held in order to determine whether or not Dahmer was insane at the time he committed the murders. On February 15, 1992, a jury found Dahmer to be legally sane. He was sentenced the next week to 15 consecutive life sentences. That Dahmer committed multiple murders is not the most frightening aspect of the case; rather, it is the gruesome method that he used to kill his victims. Stephen Glynn, a Milwaukee attorney, described it succinctly: "[H]e drill[ed] holes in his living victims' heads, pour[ed] in chemicals to 'zombify' them, ha[d] sex with the corpses' viscera, and ke[pt] some body parts in his refrigerator, occasionally eating them." Those parts that he did not eat, Dahmer either pulverized with a sledge hammer or put into a vat of acid so as to prevent them from being recognized as human.[31]

b. "In a tragic incident on Thanksgiving Day, November 25, 1976, appellant Robert Torsney, a New York City police officer, shot and killed a 15-year-old Black youth. He was indicted and charged with second degree murder. At his trial, held in November 1977, one year after the incident, Torsney interposed as a defense a lack of criminal responsibility for his conduct on the date of the crime charged stemming from a mental disease or defect diagnosed as psychomotor epilepsy. On November 30, 1977, the jury returned a verdict of not guilty by reason of mental disease or defect." Torsney v. Gold, 47 N.Y.2d 667, 668, 420 N.Y. S. 192, 193 (1979). Torsney was briefly committed to a mental hospital and then, on May 5, 1978, he was ordered discharged after a trial court determined that he no longer suffered from a mental disease or defect and was no longer dangerous to himself or others. The Court of Appeals upheld the discharge. Id.

Do you think the outcomes of these two cases can be reconciled?

2. Insanity, the Psychopath, and the Challenge of Biology

Note the following language in the two exemplary insanity defense standards we have examined:

. . . But care should be taken not to confuse such mental disease or defect with moral obliquity, mental depravity, or passion growing out of anger, revenge,

---

31. Anne C. Greshaw, The Insanity Plea: A Futile Defense for Serial Killers? 17 Law & Psychology Review 193 (1993).

hatred, or other motives, and kindred evil conditions, for when the act is induced by any of these causes the person is accountable to the law. [§16-8-101, 8A Colo. Rev. Stat]

(2) As used in this Article, the terms "mental disease or defect" do not include an abnormality manifested only by repeated criminal or otherwise antisocial conduct [MPC §4.01 (ALI test)].

Though the statutory formulas differ, their goal is the same: to deny the insanity defense to people who exhibit what are often called antisocial personalities, or psychopathic or sociopathic behavior. In recent years, many psychological researchers have argued that "antisocial personality" (ASP) is a coherent diagnosis. See Donald Black, Bad Boys, Bad Men (1999).

By Black's reckoning, about 3 percent of the general population suffers from ASP — though the overwhelming majority of people so afflicted are men. ASP is called a mental illness or disorder, but it is nowhere near — or even consistent with — psychosis or schizophrenia. It arguably has a distinct identity — but most of that identity lies in a pattern of continual rule-breaking and callous indifference to the lives or interests of others. And that pattern is very broad: ASPs range on a continuum from the most horrifying killers to burglars and petty thieves to habitual drunks who cannot stay in a job or a marriage but never break the law. In addition, most people with ASP exhibit other nonpsychotic conditions such as alcoholism, Attention Deficit Disorder, depression, or manic depression, and some of the treatments for those conditions — such as Alcoholics Anonymous, Prozac, or lithium carbonate — may alleviate some of the manifestations of ASP.

But skeptics have argued that this diagnosis, however valuable as a descriptive generalization, has no solid scientific basis, and should have no legal consequences. The ultimate concern of the critics, reflected in the statutory formulas quoted, is that defendants who are sane and intelligent will escape criminal responsibility by arguing that they suffer from inherently defective characters or emotional capacities that lead them to choose actions destructive to others' or their own interests.[32]

Now recent psychological research has thrown a weightier challenge back at the skeptics by purporting to find very precise neurobiological sources for some antisocial personalities. Most dramatically, in recent years Prof. Antonio Damasio has offered evidence that prefrontal lobe damage, caused by either external trauma (including physical abuse) or brain tumors, makes it neurologically impossible for the traumatized person to engage in constructive moral reasoning.[33] This research purports to acknowledge the principle of free will, but reconceives free will as including an emotional component that enables normal individuals to invoke constructive and empathetic emotions in making social choices. Damasio's research purports to identify some people as lacking the neurobiological resources to make those choices.

Cognition, in Damasio's view, does not fully describe rationality, nor does it help to artificially separate cognition from volition. Rather, we must take a richer

---

32. In this regard, the psychological debate mirrors a parallel phenomenon in moral philosophy. For a provocative depiction of the psychopath who arguably did not choose his callous character, but who nevertheless seems to make conscious choices to hurt others, see Peter Arenella, Convicting the Morally Blameless: Reassessing the Relationship Between Legal and Moral Accountability, 19 UCLA L. Rev. 1511 (1992).

33. Descartes' Error: Emotion, Reason, and the Human Brain (1994).

view of cognition by seeing it in a deeper emotional context, and to connect that emotional context to its biological roots.[34] These people suffer from "flat affects" and make foolish choices at every turn, not for lack of social knowledge, Damasio argues, but because they can only *use* their social knowledge in the abstract.[35] And when frontal lobe damage occurs, the emotional cues present to guide the instrumental and cognitive part of the brain do not operate.

What effect will this research have on the insanity defense? The science is too young to help predict, but for an argument that the Damasio research should be incorporated into insanity defense standards, see Laura Reider, Toward a New Test for the Insanity Defense: Incorporating the Discoveries of Neuroscience into Moral and Legal Theories, 46 UCLA L. Rev. 289 (1998).

E. "QUASI-INSANITY" DEFENSES

1. Alcohol and Other Drugs

We saw in Chapter 3 on that voluntary intoxication very rarely serves to negate the required mens rea for a crime and by itself cannot serve as an affirmative defense. See pp. 236-242, *supra*. But what happens when alcohol or other drugs interact with mental illness? The general rule is that any mental condition that derives from voluntary intoxication, including permanent psychological damage that mimics the symptoms of insanity, is treated just like the short-term effects of intoxication — it will not exonerate the defendant except in certain cases where it might negate a "specific intent." But how does the following case differ? In State v. Maik, 287 A.2d 715, 60 N.J. 203 (1972), the defendant, a college student, was convicted of second-degree murder. He admitted stabbing his best friend 66 times with a hunting knife but claimed the defense of "temporary insanity." Maik, who had used LSD and hashish during the months preceding the murder, was not under the direct influence of the LSD at the time of the stabbing, but he offered evidence that either the drug use or some other stress combined with an underlying condition and caused him to experience a "true schizophrenic break" at some time before the murder. Maik's mother had been hospitalized for schizophrenia six times, and his brother also suffered from mental illness. However, Maik himself was not diagnosed as having psychotic tendencies until just before the killing, and he had taken LSD and hashish earlier without any violent effects.

The trial judge instructed the jury that if the psychosis was triggered by the voluntary use of LSD or hashish, the defense of insanity could not stand. On appeal, the court considered whether it was error to instruct that a psychosis, precipitated by the use of drugs, could not lead to an insanity acquittal.

> Here defendant seeks to rely upon still another exception to the overall proposition that the voluntary use of such substances will not excuse. That exception is

---

34. Damasio rejects the view that "[u]pstairs in the cortex there is reason and willpower, while downstairs in the subcortex there is emotion and all that weak, fleshy stuff. . . . The apparatus of rationality, traditionally presumed to be *neo*cortical, does not seem to work without that of biological regulation, traditionally presumed to be *sub*cortical." Id. at 128.

35. Id. at xiv-xv.

that if the use of liquor or drugs, though voluntary, results in a fixed state of insanity after the immediate influence of the intoxicant or drug has spent itself, insanity so caused will be a defense if it otherwise satisfies the [insanity] test. The premise is that the specific cause of the medical condition is too remote a consideration, and that the public interest with respect to the threat of further harm can be adequately served by securing the offender so long as that state of insanity persists.

In the case at hand, the medical thesis was somewhat different, for the underlying illness from which the psychotic episode emerged was not caused by the use of drugs. Rather the thesis was that the drugs, acting upon that underlying illness, triggered or precipitated a psychotic state which continued after the direct or immediate influence of the drug had dissipated, and that it was the psychosis, rather than the drug, which rendered defendant unable to know right from wrong at the time of the killing. In other words, defendant urges that when a psychosis emerges from a fixed illness, we should not inquire into the identity of the precipitating event or action. Indeed, it may be said to be unlikely that the inquiry would be useful, for when, as here, the acute psychosis could equally be triggered by some other stress, known or unknown, which the defendant could not handle, a medical opinion as to what did in fact precipitate the psychosis is not apt to rise above a speculation among mere possibilities. We think it compatible with the philosophical basis of *M'Naghten* to accept the fact of a schizophrenic episode without inquiry into its etiology. If protection against further harm can reasonably be assured by measures appropriate for the sickness involved, it would comport with *M'Naghten* to deal with the threat in those terms. [Id. at 722.]

The court ordered a new trial solely on the insanity issue.

Might one argue that Maik was criminally responsible for foreseeing that intoxication might trigger his latent psychotic condition? What if previous drug use had in fact triggered a violent reaction earlier? What if he had had a psychotic episode earlier without any drug use? Compare People v. Decina, p. 121, *supra.*

2.   Specific Disorders

a.   *Post-Traumatic Stress Disorder*

Consider this report, compiled a decade after the end of the Vietnam War:[36]

> The war in Vietnam, which ended for the United States a decade ago, is being recalled with increasing frequency and vividness in courtrooms around the country as veterans charged with crimes cite their traumatic Vietnam experiences as their prime defense.
>
> In the past five years, hundreds of Vietnam veterans, maintaining that war in the rice paddies and jungles of Southeast Asia left them with profound psychological scars, have said they should not be held accountable for such crimes as murder, rape, and drug dealing.
>
> They have maintained, in effect, that they thought they were back in Vietnam when they committed the crimes, that stress induced by the trauma of the war touched off by particular events in this country made them temporarily insane.
>
> Psychiatrists call this condition post-traumatic stress disorder. It achieved legal currency in 1980, when the American Psychiatric Association listed the syndrome

36. David Margolick, New Vietnam Debate: Trauma as Legal Defense, New York Times, May 11, 1985, §1, at 1, col. 3.

in its revised manual of mental disorders. The manual defines the disorder as a condition induced by a traumatic event "outside the range of usual human experience," touched off by conditions resembling or symbolizing the original trauma.

Defense lawyers seized upon the disorder to help those of their clients who were Vietnam veterans, a group long over-represented in the nation's prisons and police blotters.

In the last five years the defense has helped at least 250 Vietnam veterans receive shorter sentences, get treatment instead of incarceration, or win acquittals.

But: the defense has divided judges, psychiatrists and the veterans themselves, and it has encountered growing resistance from juries in the past several years.

For thousands of veterans of America's most unpopular war, particularly those who saw heavy combat, the symptoms of the disorder are painfully familiar. They include nightmares, depression, sleep loss and flashbacks touched off by sights, sounds and smells reminiscent of Vietnam. . . .

Since it is linked so closely to the Vietnam War, the stress disorder defense has permitted lawyers to introduce reminiscences of a struggle a decade or more ago and half a world away. In the process, it has turned dozens of trials into miniature, often painful re-enactments of America's Vietnam experience. . . .

Veterans' rights advocates say that because the stress defense was not officially recognized until 1980, thousands of veterans convicted of crimes in the 1960s and 1970s have not had their day in court. In addition, as the defense has gained legitimacy in veterans' cases, lawyers say that the use of it can be extended to victims of rape, battering and other traumatic experiences, thereby changing ideas about criminal culpability generally. . . .

In the past couple of years, however, juries have rejected an increasing percentage of stress-related defenses.

"It seems there was more receptivity five years ago," said John P. Wilson, a psychologist at Cleveland State University who has testified as a defense expert in more than 50 cases throughout the country. "My batting average was once about .900 but now it's dropped."

Some prosecutors involved in the cases attribute this change to overreaching defense lawyers, who have sought, largely without success, to apply the strategy to conspiratorial crimes like drug dealing instead of to random acts of violence. Even jurors who believe a veteran has the disorder are often unconvinced that he was unable to differentiate between right and wrong at the time of the crime.

Many lawyers and psychologists on both sides of the issue say that the stress defense has been caught in a backlash of sorts against all forms of the insanity defense, fomented by the acquittal of John W. Hinckley, Jr. in the shooting of President Reagan. In addition, because prosecutors have been less prone to try those persons who have bona fide stress defenses, many involved in such cases say that the ones now going to court are generally more tenuous.

Some psychologists also say that the current definition of post-traumatic stress disorder is overly broad and fails to differentiate between those in the process of overcoming their problems and those who are not. Psychologists say that most veterans who do suffer from the stress disorder do so privately, never committing a crime. A 1982 study by Stephen Frye, a psychologist with the Veterans Administration, found that 47 percent of a recent graduating class at the officer training school in Fort Benning, Ga., is afflicted with the disorder. . . .[37]

In some ways post-traumatic stress disorder is just a new label for a condition that has been recognized since ancient times. Virgil wrote about it in the Aeneid.

37. [Some studies claim that as many as 70 percent of Vietnam veterans suffer from some form of PTSD. Id. at 415 (citing Wilson & Zigelbaum, The Vietnam Veteran on Trial: The Relation of Post-Traumatic Stress Disorder to Criminal Behavior, 1 Behav. Sci. & L. 70(1983)).—EDS.]

The traumatized victims of early train wrecks were said to have railway spine. For Union soldiers, the condition was called nostalgia, comparable to the shell shock of World War I and the battle fatigue of World War II. . . .

But many psychologists who have studied the effects of war contend that Vietnam was different. It has been described as America's first teenage war: the average combat soldier was only 19 years old, seven years younger than his World War II counterpart. It was fought for body counts rather than territory. And it evoked opposition among many Americans. In its wake, the psychologists say, the war left thousands whose names will never be carved in granite anywhere, yet are casualties nonetheless.

According to a study by the Ralph Bunche Institute of City University released this year by Mayor Koch's Vietnam Veterans Memorial Commission, for example, 41 percent of the Vietnam veterans in New York have serious employment or financial problems. The rate of divorce or separation for veterans who saw heavy combat was 65 percent, as compared with 39 percent for the veterans of the Vietnam era who served elsewhere. Nearly half of the heavy combat group reported having at least four symptoms of post-traumatic stress in the last year.

A disproportionate number of Vietnam veterans turn to violence. The Federal Government's main study of the effects of the war on veterans, "Legacies of Vietnam," surveyed more than 1,000 veterans in 1981 and found that 24 percent of those who saw heavy combat were later arrested for criminal offenses, as compared to 17 percent of other veterans from the Vietnam era and 14 percent of the nonveterans. . . .

When [the APA included the stress disorder in its diagnostic manual of mental disorders and] the defense became available, lawyers previously frustrated in their attempts to prove that the seemingly random violence of Vietnam veterans was causally related to their wartime experiences quickly seized on it, and scored some impressive victories.

"It's just a matter of educating a jury," said David F. Addlestone of Vietnam Veterans of America Legal Services in Washington. "Once it is all laid out, it's not strange and off-the-wall like most insanity defenses."

What do you think of the last quoted remark? Will this version of the insanity defense become irrelevant as Vietnam veterans age past their crime-committing years?

b. Postpartum Psychosis

Another identifiable subset of insanity cases is made up of prosecutions involving mothers suffering from postpartum psychosis. In a small number of cases, women charged with the murder or attempted murder of their infant children have entered a defense of insanity resulting from this disorder. (Recall that postpartum depression evidence was introduced as part of the insanity claim in the trial of Andrea Yates, p. 592, supra.) Postpartum psychosis, a condition of extreme depression in mothers that can manifest itself in violent, sometimes deadly acts against an infant, is an extreme form of the postpartum depression many women experience following childbirth.

The defense has been successfully raised in a few criminal prosecutions. In late 1988, Sheryl Lynn Massip, a Los Angeles woman who was found guilty by a jury of murdering her infant child, was declared not guilty by reason of insanity by the trial judge.

Massip was accused of repeatedly attempting to murder her child; she allegedly threw the infant into oncoming traffic, struck him with a blunt instrument, and then ran over him in the family car, killing him. Her case took two months to try, and the jury deliberated six and one-half days before declaring her guilty of second-degree murder, subject to a sentence of 15 years to life. Notwithstanding the jury's verdict, however, the trial judge found that Massip was suffering from postpartum psychosis at the time of the killing, that her condition met the legal test of insanity, and that she therefore was innocent.[38]

A postpartum psychosis defense was also successful in the 1988 case of a Manhattan woman accused of murdering one of her children in 1980, a second in 1982, and attempting to murder her third child in 1985, as well as in the 1984 case of a California woman who smothered her infant child.[39]

Defense attorneys arguing the defense of postpartum psychosis often have a difficult task. Because the psychosis lasts for only a short period following childbirth, the defendant may appear totally sane at the time of trial. Trying to convince the jury that the defendant — who appears sane — was so controlled by her disorder that she should not be held responsible for the death of her child can be quite difficult.

c. *Premenstrual Syndrome*

Yet another disorder that arguably could form the basis for an insanity defense involves women suffering from severe premenstrual syndrome (PMS) effects. A number of studies conducted during the last 100 years claim to have demonstrated some link between PMS and criminal activity.[40] To a very limited extent, courts in Britain have accepted PMS as supporting a reduced charge on diminished capacity grounds, and France has legally recognized PMS as a cause of temporary insanity. However, PMS apparently has not yet formed the basis of an outright acquittal on the grounds of temporary insanity and has not yet been accepted by U.S. courts.

Some commentators argue against recognizing these last three categories of disorder as quasi-insanity defenses because they feel that recognition would stigmatize the affected groups (primarily veterans and women), thus causing more harm than good. Do you believe this is likely? If yes, and if you believe the defenses are legally sound, should the possibility of stigmatization cause us to reject the defenses? Or must each defendant be allowed to plead all defenses under which he can make a valid legal claim, whatever the broader social effects of recognizing that defense?

38. See Judge Frees Mother Who Killed Her Child, Chicago Tribune, Dec. 25, 1988, at 29; Nancy Wride & Bill Billiter, Some Jurors in *Massip* Case Express Surprise, Disappointment, L.A. Times, Dec. 24, 1988, pt. 2 at 1, col. 1.

39. See Scott Ladd, Verdict Breaks Ground, Newsday, Oct. 1, 1988, at 3.

40. For example, in an 1894 study of 80 women arrested for "resistance to public officials," 71 were menstruating; in 1945, a study found that 84 percent of all female crimes of violence in Paris were committed during the premenstrual and early menstrual phases of the cycle; a 1953 study of female inmates in a New York prison found that 62 percent of the unpremeditated crimes of violence had been committed during the premenstrual week; and a 1961 study found that, of the 156 women convicted during a six-month period of theft, soliciting, and drunkenness, 49 percent of the crimes were committed during menstruation or premenstruation. Abplanalp, Premenstrual Syndrome, 3 Behav. Sci. & L. 103, 111 (1985).

d. Gambling

Although, as indicated below, the rationales vary slightly among the courts, the virtually unequivocal rule is that a gambling disorder by itself cannot constitute an insanity defense. In United States v. Gould, 741 F.2d 45 (4th Cir. 1984), the defendant, charged with attempted bank robbery (he possessed only a concealed toy gun, and his only overt act was to pass a note to a teller), proffered the following testimony in his effort to get his insanity claim before the jury:

> Gould presented the expert testimony of two psychologists, Jules Moravec, Ph.D., and Robert Rovner, Ph.D., both of whom had evaluated Gould under the ALI standard. Dr. Moravec concluded that on the date of the offense, Gould suffered from a pathological gambling disorder, that this is a mental disease or defect, and that as a result of this disorder, Gould did not have the capacity to refrain from the illegal activity. Dr. Moravec acknowledged that crimes typically associated with pathological gambling, as delineated in DSM-III, included forgery, fraud, embezzlement, and tax evasion, but stated that this list was not all inclusive.
>
> Dr. Rovner testified that Gould was a pathological gambler and that pathological gambling was a disease or defect within the meaning of the ALI test. Dr. Rovner concluded that on the date of the offense, Gould lacked the capacity to conform his conduct to the requirements of the law as a result of the pathological gambling disorder.
>
> Dr. Moravec had studied pathological gambling since 1974 and had evaluated over 300 persons to determine whether they suffered from a pathological gambling disorder. He had testified on behalf of approximately 18 persons with respect to the question of legal responsibility. However, he gave no instance in which another pathological gambler had resorted to attempted bank robbery. Neither did Dr. Rovner identify any instance in which any other pathological gambler had engaged in conduct such as that charged to Gould. [Id. at 52-53.]

The Court of Appeals upheld the trial court's instruction that, as a matter of law, the gambling disorder could not establish criminal insanity under the ALI test. The court noted that it was not deciding the broader issue whether pathological gambling is a "mental disease or defect" under the ALI test, but only whether the linkage between this disorder and the capacity of the person to conform his conduct to the law prohibiting bank robbery had "substantial acceptance" in the relevant discipline. In answering in the negative, the court inferred that gamblers exhibit "a chronic and progressive failure to resist impulses to gamble and gambling behavior that compromises, disrupts, or damages personal, family, or vocational pursuits." It noted:

> Commonly these individuals have the attitude that money causes and is also the solution to all their problems. As the gambling increases, the individual is usually forced to lie in order to obtain money and to continue gambling, but hides the extent of the gambling. There is no serious attempt to budget or save money. When borrowing resources are strained, antisocial behavior in order to obtain money for more gambling is likely. Any criminal behavior — e.g., forgery, embezzlement, or fraud — is typically nonviolent. There is a conscious intent to return or repay the money. [Id. at 51.]

The court inferred a scientific consensus that some criminal activity may be *associated* with pathological gambling, there was no clear consensus that the disorder deprived the gambler of his or her capacity to refrain from such criminal activity as attempted bank robbery. If anything, the court stressed, the associated criminal activity is usually nonviolent.

Does this decision leave any room for making *some* use of a defendant's gambling disorder in establishing an insanity defense? See People v. Lowitzki, 285 Ill. App. 3d 770, 674 N.E.2d 859 (1996) (compulsive gambling no insanity defense to a theft charge related to gambling).

e. *"Multiple Personality" Disorder*

The American Psychiatric Association recognizes the diagnosis of Dissociative Identity Disorder (DID), more commonly known as the phenomenon of "multiple personality."[41] Can DID fall within the criminal law's definition of insanity? Courts have largely been skeptical. In State v. Greene, 984 P.2d. 1024 (Wash. 1999), the defendant, a convicted sex offender placed in a sex offender treatment program, manifested 24 separate identities and several additional identity fragments, and was diagnosed with Dissociative Identity Disorder. Later he sexually assaulted M.S., a counselor in the program.

Greene claimed that "Tyrone," one of his diagnosed alternate personalities, was the prime instigator of the incident with M.S. According to Greene, "Tyrone" was manifesting as a "child, clearly less than seven years of age, and incapable of understanding the nature and quality of his acts or the fact that they were either right or wrong." Greene also claimed at least four other of his alternate personalities exchanged executive control of his body during the incident.

The court held that though DID met the general standard for admissibility of scientific evidence — i.e., it reflected a coherent diagnosis accepted by a consensus of scientists in the relevant field — it was inadmissible in an insanity trial because it would not help a jury determine whether, at the time he committed the acts in question, Greene's mental condition prevented him from appreciating the nature, quality, or wrongfulness of his actions. Expert witnesses on both sides agreed that DID was a coherent and accepted diagnosis, but some noted that the heterogeneity of the so-called "alters" (often varying within an individual by gender, age, race, sexual orientation, etc.) and "their modes of coexisting

---

41. The APA Diagnostic & Statistical Manual of Mental Disorders (4th ed. 1994) (DSM-IV) provides the following diagnostic criteria for DID:

   A. The presence of two or more distinct identities or personality states (each with its own relatively enduring pattern of perceiving, relating to, and thinking about the environment and self).
   B. At least two of these identities or personality states recurrently take control of the person's behavior.
   C. Inability to recall important personal information that is too extensive to be explained by ordinary forgetfulness.
   D. The disturbance is not due to the direct physiological effects of a substance (e.g., blackouts or chaotic behavior during Alcohol Intoxication) or a general medical condition (e.g., complex partial seizures).

DSM-IV at 487. DID is usually linked to childhood trauma (death of a parent/sibling, wartime trauma, etc.) and allows a traumatized individual to "find lifesaving retreat in an altered phenomenal state, in much the way that a hypnotized person is able — not to escape pain — but to disassociate from the experience of pain." George B. Greaves, Multiple Personality 165 Years after Mary Reynolds, 168 J. Nervous & Mental Disease 577, 590 (1980).

with the host (e.g., co-conscious, amnestic, amnestic with "leakage") is extremely varied and defies neat categorization."

The key prosecution expert, though conceding that DID was an accepted medical diagnosis, believed that the identification of personality states is "riddled with all of the same kinds of philosophical and scientific problems as the concept of personality itself," making it difficult to draw the line between where one personality state ends and another begins. "The practical problem for a forensic evaluator is trying to assess the personality states, alters that would have existed at the time of the crime." Id. at 1030. The court stated:

> The various approaches primarily differ on which personality (or personalities) any mental examination should focus. Thus, an approach may focus on the mental condition of the host personality at the time of the offense; or, conversely, on the mental condition of the alter in control at the time of the offense; or, possibly, on the mental condition of each and every alter personality at the time of the crime (under this approach, if any significant alter is not aware of or does not acquiesce in the commission of the crime, such innocent "personlike" entities do not deserve to suffer punishment). According to the testimony and argument in this case, however, none of the various approaches have been accepted as producing results capable of reliably helping to resolve questions regarding sanity and/or mental capacity in a legal sense.
>
> [W]hen a person suffering from DID is charged with a crime, the question becomes, "Who is the proper defendant?" A determination of sanity in this context can be considered only subsequent to the determination of who (which alter personality) should be held responsible for the crime — the host, or possibly one or more of the alters. This, in turn, is related to the scientific possibility of identifying the controlling and/or knowledgeable alters at the time of the crime. [Id. at 1031.]

Is the court too rigid in its application of DID to the legal insanity question?

F.   "DIMINISHED CAPACITY"

The controversial term "diminished capacity" has no distinct meaning in American criminal law. The best one can say in general is that it refers to cases where a defendant who cannot win on an NGI claim nevertheless benefits — through acquittal or mitigation of the charge — from evidence of mental illness or disorder. In United States v. Pohlot, 827 F.2d 889 (3d Cir. 1987), the court nicely summarized the key diverse uses of this contested term:

> The first variant of what courts have called "diminished capacity" defenses inappropriately is the evidentiary doctrine which we have already noted is not a defense at all but merely a rule of evidence; specifically, the admission of evidence of mental abnormality to negate mens rea.
>
> A second strain of diminished capacity permits a defendant to show not only that he lacked the mens rea in the particular case but also that he lacked the *capacity* to form the mens rea. Whether a defendant has the capacity to form mens rea is, of course, logically connected to whether the defendant possessed the requisite mens rea. Commentators have agreed, however, that only in the most extraordinary circumstances could a defendant actually lack the capacity to form

mens rea as it is normally understood in American law. Even the most psychiatrically ill have the capacity to form intentions, and the existence of intent usually satisfies any mens rea requirement. Commentators have therefore argued that permitting evidence and arguments about a defendant's capacity to form mens rea distracts and confuses the jury from focusing on the actual presence or absence of mens rea.

Finally, commentators have identified defenses generally categorized as "diminished responsibility" or "partially diminished capacity." Pure "diminished responsibility" exists in many European countries as a formal defense. It "permits the jury to mitigate the punishment of a mentally disabled but sane offender in any case where the jury believes that the defendant is less culpable than his normal counterpart who commits the same criminal act." [Peter Arenella, The Diminished Capacity and Diminished Responsibility Defenses: Two Children of a Doomed Marriage, 77 Colum. L. Rev. 827, 829 (1977).] . . .

In addition to explicit doctrines of diminished responsibility, commentators have contended that courts may permit juries to excuse a defendant's criminal conduct because of mental abnormality and thereby covertly create a "partially diminished capacity" defense when they admit evidence of mental abnormality that does not truly negate mens rea. In some cases, defendants have attempted to present such theories of defense as the claim that a defendant lacked the mens rea to distribute cocaine because of the psychological domination of her mother. . . . In others, psychiatrists have proved willing to testify that a defendant who planned and executed a murder did not possess the requisite mens rea because of a mental disease such as chronic schizophrenia. . . . Mens rea is generally satisfied, however, by any showing of purposeful activity, regardless of its psychological origins. Such testimony may therefore mislead the jury about the mens rea requirements of a crime.

. . . Notions of intent, purpose and premeditation are malleable and at their margins imprecise. But the limits of these concepts are questions of law. District courts should admit evidence of mental abnormality on the issue of mens rea only when, if believed, it would support a legally acceptable theory of lack of mens rea. In deciding such a question, courts should evaluate the testimony outside the presence of the jury. [Id. at 903-04.]

Pohlot was charged with interstate conspiracy to commit murder for hire. The government proved that Pohlot had arranged a bizarre plot to arrange the contract killing of his wife, after she sued him for divorce and won a court order freezing his assets. Though Pohlot told a government informer that he wanted to secure his money and also suspected his wife of adultery, a defense psychiatrist testified that Pohlot had a "compulsive personality, passive dependent personality and passive aggressive personality" as well as depression. Pohlot himself testified that his wife had physically abused him. The psychiatrist also described a delusion whereby Pohlot expected to rejoin his wife for a happy marriage — after she was murdered. The issue of "diminished capacity" arose for him because his path to an NGI verdict was virtually foreclosed by section 17 (a) of the Insanity Defense Reform Act of 1984, which, as noted *supra*, p. 600, deleted the "volitional prong" of the ALI-Model Penal Code standard for insanity as an affirmative defense.

The court acknowledged that

[b] because admitting psychiatric evidence to negate mens [rea] does not constitute a defense but only negates an element of the offense, §17(a) by its terms does not bar it. Section 17(a) states only that "mental disease . . . does not otherwise constitute a defense;" it does not purport to establish a rule of evidence. . . . [Id. at 897.]

Nevertheless, the court was unconvinced that the defense psychiatric testimony in any way bore on whether Pohlot had "intended" to kill his wife.

Rather than focusing on Pohlot's conscious mind, however, the testimony focused on what Pohlot "really" knew. Pohlot acknowledged that he was attempting "to fight back." Dr. Glass agreed that Pohlot transacted a cash transaction "for the purpose of killing his wife." Similarly, Dr. Glass testified that Pohlot knew in some senses what he was doing, "but he didn't know." Thus, according even to the defense, whatever Pohlot "really" knew and intended, at least a substantial part of his mind knew and intended exactly what were the natural consequences of his plotting. . . .

In the context of the facts, both Pohlot's own testimony and that of Dr. Glass relate clearly not to Pohlot's intent in a legal sense but to Pohlot's meaningful understanding of his actions and their consequences. We often act intending to accomplish the immediate goal of our activity, while not fully appreciating the consequences of our acts. But purposeful activity is all the law requires. When one spouse intentionally kills the other in the heat of a dispute, he or she will rarely at that moment fully appreciate the consequences of the murder. The spouse is guilty of homicide nonetheless.

. . . Pohlot therefore offered his evidence of mental abnormality in support of a legally unacceptable theory of lack of mens rea that amounts covertly to a variation of the partially diminished capacity defense precluded by §17(a). Whether the district court applied this correct analysis or accepted the incorrect broader view advocated by the government, it was correct in instructing the jury under the circumstances not to consider this evidence in deciding whether Pohlot possessed the requisite mens rea. [Id. at 906-07.]

Notes and Questions

1. Recall People v. Hendershott, in Chapter 3, p. 231, *supra*. Clearly Hendershott's "defense" might survive the new trend toward eliminating "partial diminished capacity" defenses. If Pohlot cannot bring a *Hendershott* claim and, under the post-*Hinckley* rules, is not insane, is his bizarre psychological condition of no relevance whatsoever? Given the fine mens rea calibrations of homicide law, would his claim have been stronger had he killed his wife?

2. Is the distinction between mental disorder negating a specific culpable mental state and a disorder negating the defendant's capacity to form that state too subtle to be useful?

3. *Pohlot* probably reflects a general trend toward rejecting "quasi-insanity" defenses on the ground that "Judge and jury ought not be required to identify, classify and evaluate all categories and classifications of human behavior beyond the establishing of the fact of sanity." United States v. Schneider, 111 F.3d 197 (1st Cir. 1997) (evidence of general depression and overmedication is not categorically inadmissible to negate intent in fraud case, but judge should exclude it if its probative value is outweighed by its capacity to mislead jury).

V

ATTRIBUTION OF CRIMINALITY

The criminal law sometimes holds persons or even business entities liable for offenses they have not actually committed. Ada may have tried but failed to commit robbery; if so, she may be liable for the inchoate offense of attempted robbery. We impute or "attribute" to her all or part of the liability she would have faced if successful. Bjorn may have helped someone commit a robbery, perhaps by supplying a gun for use during the crime. Although he did not personally commit the offense, he may well be liable as an accomplice to the crime. We attribute to him all or part of the liability he would have faced had he committed the crime himself. Charlene may have agreed to drive the get-away car after a robbery. Even though she is arrested before the robbery takes place, she may be liable for the inchoate crime of conspiracy to rob. And when the robbery takes place without her help, she may nevertheless be vicariously liable for it. A corporation employs Drew to manage a factory. Drew recklessly permits fire exits to be blocked and as a result a worker dies in a fire. In a sense, the corporation lacks the human mind or body to commit any criminal offense, yet it may well be criminally liable for Drew's act of manslaughter. In some of these cases, an actor is held fully or partially responsible for offenses that were, in a sense, never committed. In others, an actor is held vicariously liable for an offense truly committed by another. The doctrines permitting this extension of liability are generally called doctrines of attribution. We examine attempt liability in Chapter 10, complicity in Chapter 11, conspiracy in Chapter 12, and corporate criminal liability in Chapter 13.

10

ATTEMPT

A. THE PUNISHMENT FOR ATTEMPT

1. Why Punish Attempt?

In Chapter 3, we considered the concept of the strict liability crime, where an actor is held liable for causing or risking proscribed harm without exhibiting any culpable mental state. This controversial concept provokes the question why a person should be held liable for the actual or potential effects of her actions without regard to fault. In Chapter 4, on Causation, we considered the related question why liability for culpable conduct should be conditioned on harmful effects. Punishing attempts raises a new set of dilemmas for criminal jurisprudence.

Liability for attempting — for a *failed* effort to cause harm — poses the complementary problem of punishment for thoughts (first encountered in Chapter 2). To be held liable for attempting crime, the defendant must exhibit mental culpability. And since, in ordinary speech, the term "attempt" implies "intent," usually an intent to cause harm is required. If we thereby condition liability on an unfulfilled desire to cause harm, we provoke the retributivist worry that defendants will be punished without having *done* anything wrong.

The utilitarian might punish the attemptor because the attemptor's action, though harmless, proves that he is dangerous. But failed attempts are, by definition, displays of inept malevolence. And in any case, as we noted in Chapter 1, because of the prevalence of violent assaults among prisoners, incarceration really achieves the retributive aim of segregating the dangerous, rather than the purported utilitarian aim of incapacitating the dangerous.

The retributivist might punish the attemptor because her act manifests bad character. But the retributivist would also insist that punishment must be for wrongdoing, not evil desires. Thus, the retributivist might concede that the offender should not be punished until conscience has been given a reasonable opportunity to check such desires.

The retributivist proponent of attempt liability will ask, "If the defendant does all he can to cause harm, why should the miscarriage of his plan absolve him? This makes his liability turn on a morally irrelevant turn of luck. We would consider it barbaric to decide whom and how much to punish by rolling dice.

But this is what we would be doing if we conditioned punishment exclusively on actual harm."

The retributivist opponent of attempt liability may respond that we take harm into account in other areas of criminal law. We rarely punish harmless negligence or recklessness (charges of "reckless endangerment" are uncommon), and where we do punish harmless risk-taking, we usually expect legislatures to narrowly define the risky conduct that will give rise to liability (as in drunk-driving laws), rather than just proscribing any conduct that poses an unacceptable risk to a particular interest. If we are loath to punish harmless negligence and recklessness, why should we punish harmless malevolence? And if we must punish harmless malevolence, would it not be preferable to do so with more specificity, i.e., to punish "assault with a deadly weapon" or "administration of poison," rather than to punish the vaguely defined conduct of "attempting to kill"?

Utilitarian proponents of attempt liability will argue that punishing attemptors maximizes deterrence. Since deterrence is more effective where punishment is more certain, punishment should not turn on the success or failure of a criminal plan, which will often be a matter of luck. Utilitarian opponents of attempt liability may respond that the vagueness of the conduct giving rise to attempt liability will frustrate the proponents' aim of enhancing the certainty of punishment.

The criminal law offers no elegant resolutions to these dilemmas, because the dilemmas invoke all the fundamental "why punish?" questions we treated in Chapter 1. Instead, the criminal law tends to compromise them by (a) punishing attempts somewhat less than completed crimes, and (b) preventing punishment for "mere thought" or bad character by stressing the need for some significant conduct manifesting the bad thoughts — though, by definition, short of causing proscribed harm.

2.   The Emergence of Attempt Liability

There was a time when the common law did not punish attempts as such. This should not really be surprising when we consider that attempt liability inevitably emphasizes intent, and we saw in Chapter 3 that the view that some form of criminal intent is an element of all crimes did not emerge until the late Eighteenth Century. The practice of deriving attempt liability in a situation where a defendant had failed to consummate a traditionally proscribed crime developed at the same time, and Lord Mansfield was apparently an important exponent of both developments.

GEORGE FLETCHER, RETHINKING CRIMINAL LAW
132, 134-35 (1978)

Liability for an attempted offense is a paradigmatic instance of an inchoate offense. The attempt is inchoate relative to the offense-in-chief. This claim is easily made, for the attempt is defined as an act falling short of the consummated crime. In other contexts, however, it is more difficult to assess whether a defined offense is an "inchoate" or a "consummated" offense. Consider the examples of conspiracy, vagrancy, and disseminating pornography. Are these offenses in the nature of inchoate offenses designed to inhibit a more egregious form of harm? Or is the conspiracy, the occurrence of vagrancy or the dissemination of obscene matter in itself the harm the law seeks to prevent? . . .

Though some arguably inchoate offenses, such as vagrancy and conspiracy, have long been part of the common law, the formal doctrine of attempts did not emerge until the late eighteenth century. . . . [T]he common-law doctrine stems from Rex v. Scofield [Cald. 397 (1784)], decided in 1784; in his opinion, Lord Mansfield noted explicitly that the "completion of an act, criminal in itself, [was not] necessary to constitute criminality." The defendant Scofield was charged with having put a lighted candle among combustible material in a house that was then in his possession, with an intent to burn it. The intended arson was apparently unconsummated, but Lord Mansfield reasoned that a derivative crime of attempting covered the case.

From the outset . . . [t]he intent to commit the offense-in-chief would be the core of the offense, and the function of the act of partial execution would be to demonstrate the firmness of the actor's resolve and perhaps to provide evidence of his intent. Even the opinion in Scofield contains the comment: "The intent may make an act, innocent in itself, criminal . . ." . . . Yet in the course of the nineteenth century, and to some extent in our own time, judges and theorists have been deeply concerned about the potentially unlimited scope of liability of those who intend to commit recognized crimes. . . . Thus [in] the history of liability for attempted offenses . . . [t]he emphasis on the actor's intent as the core of the offense stands in conflict with the emphasis on objective criteria as a condition for liability.

3. The Grading of Attempt

MODEL PENAL CODE
American Law Institute, Model Penal
Code and Commentaries (1985)

Section 5.05. Grading of Criminal Attempt . . .

(1) Grading. Except as otherwise provided in this Section, attempt . . . [is a crime] of the same grade and degree as the most serious offense that is attempted. . . . An attempt . . . to commit a [capital crime or a] felony of the first degree is a felony of the second degree.

Consider the Introduction to Article 5 of the Model Penal Code:

[Attempt is not] the only crime . . . so defined that [its] commission does not rest on proof of the occurrence of the evil that is the object of the law to prevent; many specific, substantive offenses also have a large inchoate aspect. This is true not only with respect to crimes of risk-creation, such as reckless driving, or specific crimes of preparation, like those of possession with unlawful purpose. It is also true, at least in part, of crimes like larceny, forgery, kidnaping and even arson, not to speak of burglary, where a purpose to cause greater harm than that which is implicit in the actor's conduct is an element of the offense. . . .

Since [attempt] always presuppose[s] a purpose to commit another crime, it is doubtful that the threat of punishment for [its] commission can significantly add to the deterrent efficacy of the sanction — which the actor by hypothesis ignores — that is threatened for the crime that is his object. There may be cases where this does occur, as when the actor thinks the chance of apprehension low if he succeeds but high if he should fail in his attempt. . . . These are, however, special situations. General deterrence is at most a minor function to be served in fashioning provisions of the penal law addressed to . . . inchoate crimes; that burden is discharged upon the whole by the law dealing with the substantive offenses.

Other and major functions of the penal law remain, however, to be served. They may be summarized as follows:

First: When a person is seriously dedicated to commission of a crime, a firm legal basis is needed for the intervention of the agencies of law enforcement to prevent its consummation. In determining that basis, there must be attention to the danger of abuse; equivocal behavior may be misconstrued by an unfriendly eye as preparation to commit a crime. It is no less important, on the other side, that lines should not be drawn so rigidly that the police confront insoluble dilemmas in deciding when to intervene, facing the risk that if they wait the crime may be committed while if they act they may not yet have any valid charge.

Second: Conduct designed to cause or culminate in the commission of a crime obviously yields an indication that the actor is disposed towards such activity, not alone on this occasion but on others. There is a need, therefore, subject again to proper safeguards, for a legal basis upon which the special danger that such individuals present may be assessed and dealt with. They must be made amenable to the corrective process that the law provides.

Third: Finally, and quite apart from these considerations of prevention, when the actor's failure to commit the substantive offense is due to a fortuity, as when the bullet misses in attempted murder . . . his exculpation on that ground would involve inequality of treatment that would shock the common sense of justice. Such a situation is unthinkable in any mature system, designed to serve the proper goals of penal law.

These are the main considerations in the light of which the [provisions on attempt have] been prepared. . . .

The Comments to Section 5.05, Part I, at 489-90, explain further:

[Section 5.05 (1)] departs from the law that preceded promulgation of the Model Code by treating attempt . . . on a parity for purposes of sentence and by determining the grade or degree of the inchoate crime by the gravity of the most serious offense that is its object. Only when the object is a capital crime or a felony of the first degree does the Code deviate from this solution, grading the inchoate offense in that case as a felony of the second degree.

The theory of this grading system may be stated simply. To the extent that sentencing depends upon the antisocial disposition of the actor and the demonstrated need for a corrective sanction, there is likely to be little difference in the gravity of the required measures depending on the consummation or the failure of the plan. It is only when and insofar as the severity of sentence is designed for general deterrent purposes that a distinction on this ground is likely to have reasonable force. It is doubtful . . . that the threat of punishment for the inchoate crime can add significantly to the net deterrent efficacy of the sanction threatened for the substantive offense that is the actor's object which he, by hypothesis, ignores. Hence, there is basis for economizing in use of the heaviest and most afflictive sanctions by removing them from the inchoate crimes. The sentencing provisions for second degree felonies, including the provision for extended terms, should certainly suffice to meet whatever danger is presented by the actor.

On the other side of the equation, it is clear that the inchoate crime should not be graded higher than the substantive offense; it is the danger that the actor's conduct may culminate in its commission that justifies creating the inchoate crime.

Why does the Model Penal Code make one exception to its rule that attempts are punished as severely as completed crimes? Is the exception sensible?

Very few states have adopted the Model Penal Code provision on the punishment of attempts. In most states today the punishment for attempt is lower than that for the completed crime. It may be a fixed fraction of the punishment for the completed crime, or, where state law classifies offenses into grades, the next grade below that of the completed crime.

B. THE MENS REA FOR ATTEMPT

STATE v. LYERLA
Supreme Court of South Dakota
424 N.W.2d 908 (1988)

Konenkamp, Circuit Judge.

A jury convicted Gerald K. Lyerla (Lyerla) of second degree murder and two counts of attempted second degree murder. We affirm the second degree murder conviction, but reverse the convictions for attempted second degree murder.

On the night of January 18, 1986, while driving east on Interstate 90 in Haakon County, Lyerla fired three shots with his .357 magnum pistol at a pickup truck carrying three teenage girls. One was killed, the other two were injured. Only one bullet entered the pickup cab, the one that killed seventeen-year-old Tammy Jensen. Another bullet was recovered from the engine block; the third was never found. Lyerla fled the scene, but was later apprehended. He was charged in the alternative with first degree murder or second degree murder for the death of Tammy Jensen and two counts each of attempted first degree murder and alternatively two counts of attempted second degree murder of the two surviving girls.

Before the shooting, the teenagers and Lyerla were traveling in the same direction. The vehicles passed each other a few times. At one point when Lyerla tried to pass the girls, their truck accelerated so that he could not overtake them. Lyerla decided to leave the interstate. When he exited, the Jensen pickup pulled to the side of the road near the entry ramp. Lyerla loaded his pistol, reentered the interstate and passed the Jensen pickup. When the girls attempted to pass him, he fired at the passenger side of their truck.

At his trial, Lyerla told the jury that the teenagers were harassing him to such an extent that he feared for his life and fired the shots to disable their pickup. The two girls gave a different rendition of the events leading up to the shooting, but the prosecutor conceded in closing argument that Tammy Jensen was "trying to play games" with Lyerla by not letting him pass. Both Lyerla's version and that of the girls had a number of discrepancies. We view these inconsistencies to have been resolved by the jury's verdicts. . . . Lyerla argues that it is a legal impossibility to attempt to commit murder in the second degree and his two convictions for this offense should be reversed. . . .

In order to attempt to commit a crime, there must exist in the mind of the perpetrator the specific intent to commit the acts constituting the offense. To attempt second degree murder one must intend to have a criminally reckless state of mind, i.e. perpetrating an imminently dangerous act while evincing a depraved mind, regardless of human life, but without a design to kill any particular person.

Whether there can be such a crime as attempted second degree murder has never been determined in South Dakota. Interpreting a similar statute the Minnesota Supreme Court ruled in State v. Dahlstrom, 276 Minn. 301, 150 N.W.2d 53 (1967):

> We do not conceive of any practical basis upon which the jury could have found defendant guilty of attempted murder in the third degree. Philosophically, it might be possible to attempt to perpetrate an act imminently dangerous to others and evincing a depraved mind regardless of human life within the meaning of the phrase as used in 609.195, defining murder in the third degree. . . . But we cannot conceive of a factual situation which could make such conduct attempted murder in the third degree where the actor did not intend the death of anyone and where no death occurred.

Unlike the *Dahlstrom* case, a death occurred here, but the jury obviously decided that Lyerla did not intend the death of the deceased since he was found guilty of the lesser count of second degree murder. Nor did he intend to kill the other two girls as the verdicts for attempted second degree murder confirm. Other courts have likewise found attempted reckless homicide a logical impossibility. In People v. Perez, 108 Misc. 2d 65, 437 N.Y.S.2d 46, 48 (1981), it was stated:

> However, murder in the second degree under PL 125.25 subdivision 2, involves no intent but instead requires a culpable mental state of recklessness. One may not intentionally attempt to cause the death of another by a reckless act.

The Colorado [Court of Appeals] held:

> An attempt to commit criminal negligent homicide thus requires proof that the defendant intended to perpetrate an unintended killing — a logical impossibility. The words "attempt" and "negligence" are at war with one another; they are internally inconsistent and cannot sensibly co-exist.

People v. Hernandez, 44 Colo. App. 161, 614 P.2d 900, 901 (1980). . . . Stating the rule most succinctly:

> To commit murder, one need not intend to take life; but to be guilty of an attempt to murder, he must so intend. It is not sufficient that his act, had it proved fatal, would have been murder. Merritt v. Commonwealth, 164 Va. 653, 180 S.E. 395 (1935). . . .

Defendant's convictions for attempted second degree murder are reversed.

SABERS, JUSTICE, dissenting.

. . . I agree with the majority that the jury obviously decided that Lyerla did not intend the death of the deceased since he was found guilty of the lesser count of second-degree murder. Nor did he intend to kill the other two girls as the verdicts for attempted second-degree murder confirm. However, had his acts resulted in their deaths, either directly as in the case of Tammy Jensen, or indirectly, through a resulting car accident, he would have been guilty of second-degree murder. Since deaths did not result he was guilty of attempted second-degree murder under South Dakota law.

SDCL 22-4-1 provides:

Any person who attempts to commit a crime and in the attempt does any act toward the commission of the crime, but fails or is prevented or intercepted in the perpetration thereof, is punishable where no provision is made by law for the punishment of such attempt. . . .

SDCL 22-16-7 provides:

Homicide is murder in the second degree when perpetrated by any act imminently dangerous to others and evincing a depraved mind, regardless of human life, although without any premeditated design to effect the death of any particular individual.

This statute deals with "homicide" which is named "murder in the second degree." Neither statute contains an element of specific intent. SDCL 22-16-7 simply requires an act. The act required must be dangerous to others (or stupid) under South Dakota law. If one attempts a "dangerous" or "stupid" act it is sufficient. The only "intent" or "attempt" necessary is a voluntary as opposed to a non-volitional or forced act. In this case, Lyerla clearly attempted the dangerous and stupid act of pulling the trigger and shooting the gun at or near the people or the car in which they were riding. This is sufficient for attempted second-degree murder under South Dakota law. . . .

The majority opinion cites People v. Perez, 437 N.Y.S.2d 46, 48 (1981), and People v. Hernandez, 614 P.2d 900, 901 (Colo. 1980), for the proposition that one cannot intentionally attempt to cause the death of another by a reckless act and for the proposition that the perpetration of an unintended killing is a logical impossibility. Further, these cases are cited to support the proposition that the words "attempt" and "negligence" are at war with one another; that they are internally inconsistent and cannot sensibly co-exist. These cases place emphasis on the word "intentional" contrary to the South Dakota statute on attempt. As previously indicated, the "intent" or "attempt" required under the South Dakota statute is simply to voluntarily act as opposed to an involuntary or forced action. In other words, an attempt to pull the trigger and shoot the gun is enough. This type of "attempt" and the "dangerous" or "stupid" act are not at war with one another; they are internally consistent and can sensibly coexist.

Much of the confusion in this matter results from the use of the word murder, which implies an intent to take life. What we are really dealing with under South Dakota law is homicide, named second-degree murder. To intentionally pull the trigger and shoot a gun in this dangerous manner was not homicide because neither Gropper girl [the other passengers] died, but it was attempted homicide, also known as attempted second-degree murder. Accordingly, attempted second-degree murder is a crime in South Dakota, and Lyerla's convictions for attempted second-degree murder should be affirmed.

Notes and Questions

1. *Attempt without intent.* How can the court reconcile a murder conviction for the death of Tammy Jensen with exculpation for the harm dealt to the other girls? Should the legal concept of "attempt" necessarily involve intent, as does the term "attempt" in ordinary usage? Or should the law use the term to designate any behavior that fulfills the mental element of an offense, without causing the proscribed harm? This question should really be divided into two issues.

First is an issue of policy: *Should* the criminal law punish reckless or negligent risk-taking, even when it does not result in harm?

Suppose a parent abandons an infant in an alley, not caring whether the infant dies of starvation or exposure or is rescued by others. Suppose Billie deliberately pushes Bobbie overboard two miles from shore, not caring whether Bobbie may swim to safety. Suppose Evelyn places one bullet in a five shot revolver, spins the chamber, holds it to Marion's head and fires, to see what happens. If the victims in these situations survive, can the knowing imposition of such a risk of death fairly be described as attempted murder?

Second, there is an issue of legality: *May* the criminal law do so under statutes like SDCL 22-4-1 that proscribe "attempts" to commit crime?

Other states have been virtually unanimous in following the majority holding in *Lyerla.* For example, the court in State v. Coble, 351 N.C. 448, 527 S.E.2d 45 (2000) held:

> [A] charge of attempted second-degree murder is a logical impossibility. Second-degree murder, like felony murder, does not have, as an element, specific intent to kill. Rather, where the element of malice in second-degree murder is proved by intentional conduct, a defendant need only intend to commit the underlying act that results in death. Therefore, . . . a charge of attempted second-degree murder would require a defendant to specifically intend what is by definition not a specifically intended result
>
> . . . *See, e.g., Huitt v. State,* 678 P.2d 415, 419-20 (Alaska Ct. App. 1984) (rejecting offense of attempted second-degree murder where statute did not require specific intent to kill); *Fenstermaker v. State,* 128 Idaho 285, 291, 912 P.2d 653, 659 (Ct. App. 1995) (recognizing crime of attempted second-degree murder where requisite intent for second-degree murder is defined in part as "intent to take life"); *State v. Shannon,* 258 Kan. 425, 429-30, 905 P.2d 649, 652-53 (1995) (rejecting attempted second-degree murder where second-degree murder statute did not require specific intent to kill); *State v. Earp,* 319 Md. 156, 162-67, 571 A.2d 1227, 1230-33 (1990) (rejecting crime of attempted second-degree murder where specific intent to kill is not a necessary element of second-degree murder).[1]

2. *Attempted recklessness.* The appellate court hearing the *Lyerla* case was bound by the jury's interpretation of the facts. If you did not find the facts as given in *Lyerla* compelling with respect to the defendant's lack of intent to kill, what would then be your reaction to the attempt ruling of that case?

---

1. Ironically, one state that has agreed with the dissent in *Lyerla* is Colorado, in a state supreme court decision that came after the *Hernandez* case but still earlier than *Lyerla,* and yet was ignored by both *Lyerla* opinions. People v. Castro, 657 P.2d 832 (1983) (upholding a conviction of attempted extreme indifference murder on the grounds that the conduct risking death was intentional even though there was no intent to cause death).

In each of the following cases the court refused to permit conviction of the defendant on a charge of attempted reckless murder, ruling that such a charge constituted a logical impossibility.

a. In the course of a card game, the defendant got into an argument with a player at the table. He left the room and returned with a pistol concealed in his belt. After reseating himself at the table, he secretly placed the gun on his lap and cocked it. He then requested that the other player, with whom he had been arguing, hand over a knife that was in his possession. The defendant then took the knife, and as he attempted to throw it at a wall across the room, he accidentally brushed the trigger of his gun and it fired a bullet into the abdomen of the other player. State v. Norman, 580 P.2d 237 (1978).

b. The defendant set fire to a duplex in which she knew Dennis Reed was sleeping. It turned out Robert Mapes was also sleeping in the building. There was no evidence offered to show that the defendant had any idea that Mapes was in the building along with Reed. The defendant admitted to having set the fire in an attempt to kill Reed, but in response to questions regarding Mapes, stated she was not angry with Mapes. According to the defendant, "He was just in the wrong place at the wrong time." People v. Hall, 436 N.W.2d 446 (1989).

Do you find either of these sets of facts to compel the charge of attempted reckless murder? Do you have doubts about either defendant's lack of intent to kill? Do you still have any doubts about Lyerla's intent to kill? When courts allow the charge of attempted reckless crimes, are they simply rejecting, in part, the defendant's assertion that the acts were not intentional and allowing the recklessness claimed for the offense to serve as a kind of proxy for intent?[2]

3. *Attempt and circumstance elements.* Consider the Model Penal Code:

Section 5.01. Criminal Attempt

(1) Definition of Attempt. A person is guilty of an attempt to commit a crime if, acting with the kind of culpability otherwise required for commission of the crime, he:

(a) purposely engages in conduct that would constitute the crime if the attendant circumstances were as he believes them to be; or

(b) when causing a particular result is an element of the crime, does or omits to do anything with the purpose of causing or with the belief that it will cause such result, without further conduct on his part; or

(c) purposely does or omits to do anything that, under the circumstances as he believes them to be, is an act or omission constituting a substantial step in a course of conduct planned to culminate in his commission of the crime.

Section 5.01(1) of the Model Penal Code seeks to define the appropriate mens rea for attempt. How would *Lyerla* be decided under section 5.01(1)?

2. The late Prof. John Kaplan was fond of the following classroom hypothetical. A very bad person goes to the roof of a high-rise building, dragging a very heavy potted plant. He pushes the plant over the edge and down to a crowded noontime street, but, by miraculous chance, it does not hit any person. Of what is he guilty? (Extra credit was always given to anyone suggesting "littering.")

The commentary supplementing section 5.01(1) states that subsection (a) addresses the mens rea required with respect to the conduct of the actor or the attendant circumstances of the event, while subsection (b) concerns the mens rea required for the results of the actions taken.[3] Thus, as with the common law, attempt liability would require that the defendant exhibit purpose with respect to any conduct elements of the crime and purpose or possibly knowledge with respect to any result element. But for the circumstance elements, a lower mens rea would be sufficient if recklessness or negligence were otherwise sufficient in the statutory definition of the completed crime. If this interpretation is accepted, Lyerla would be exonerated, because he clearly did not intend or believe that death would result from his actions.

4. *Section 5.01 (1) applied.* Recall the statutory rape cases from Chapter 3. As noted there, a person who purposely has intercourse with a girl under the age of consent may be guilty in some jurisdictions, even if he honestly believed she was over the age of consent. What if a man tries to have intercourse with a girl who is in fact fifteen, and he honestly (and reasonably) thinks she is nineteen, but he is caught or prevented before he actually has intercourse? Is he guilty of attempted statutory rape, even where, from his point of view, he was "attempting" to have intercourse with a female over the statutory age? See Model Penal Code section 5.01(1).

According to the gloss provided by the commentators for section 5.01(1), he would be guilty of attempted statutory rape because section 5.01(1) does not require purpose with respect to attendant circumstances.[4] The mens rea required for those elements of the crime is to be transferred from the underlying substantive crime of statutory rape. Does the conclusion of the commentators follow from the plain language of section 5.01(1)? Which subsection applies to the attempted statutory rape scenario? Is it subsection (a)? If so, will there be attempt liability? What result would application of subsection (c) yield?

5. *Specific intent and attempt.* Many federal courts construing federal criminal statutes continue to use the language of "general" and "specific intent" instead of MPC terms. See the explanation of these terms in Chapter 3, pp. 184-187, *supra.* How does this language address attempt law?

In United States v. Morales-Tovar, 37 F. Supp. 2d 846 (W.D. Tex. 1999), the defendant was charged with violating 8 U.S.C. §1326, which makes it a crime for any deported person to enter, or to attempt to re-enter, the United States without the express permission of the Attorney General. Morales-Tovar, a native of Mexico, had been a permanent resident of the United States for 38 years, and had raised a large family in this country. At the age of 64, he was convicted of a felony drug offense, and, after serving a two-year sentence, he was deported to Mexico. In 1998, in deteriorating health and missing his family, he went to a border port of entry, where he spoke to immigration authorities, whom he showed his Mexican birth certificate and his Mexican labor union card. He said he wanted to replace his resident alien card, which had been lost; he was not asked at that time if he had been previously deported. When a computer check revealed that defendant had been previously deported, he was then patted-down and read his Miranda rights. When asked, the defendant readily admitted that he had previously been deported. The defendant never gave a false name, nor

---

3. American Law Institute, Model Penal Code and Commentaries, Part I, at 299 (1985).
4. Id. at 301.

did he ever present false documents. The District Court, trying the case without a jury, acquitted the defendant:

> The defendant . . . argues that the crime of attempting to re-enter requires specific intent, and that the government failed to show specific intent. That is, the defendant claims that like most attempt-based crimes, he must have specifically intended to violate the law to be convicted. It is determined that *this* argument provides a separate and alternative basis for defendant's acquittal. . . .
>
> In fact, to ignore a defendant's specific intent in an attempt-based case would make 8 U.S.C. §1326 impermissibly self-contradictory. By law, the relevant class of deportees must, in fact, seek permission to apply for re-entry. Without a requirement that a deportee have specific intent to violate the law, any proactive attempt to follow that legally sanctioned and required procedure would actually be illegal "attempt" to re-enter. Such a paradox should not, and cannot, stand. . . . [Id. at 851.]

The Ninth Circuit takes a different view of this issue, ruling that attempt under this statute is a "general intent" crime:

> We do not disagree that most attempts are (and should be) specific intent crimes, whether or not the crime attempted includes an element of specific intent. . . . However, §1326 (a) is different from most ordinary crimes in that it is not based on a common law crime but is instead a "regulatory statute enacted to assist in the control of unlawful immigration by aliens. This offense is a typical mala prohibita offense . . ." Pena-Cabanillas v. United States, 394 F.2d 785 (9th Cir. 1968).

United States v. Gracidas-Ulibarry, 192 F.3d 926, 929 (9th Cir. 1999). Which court has the more sensible view? Would the Ninth Circuit want to punish Morales-Tovar? What class of defendants might it fear would be exonerated were this a "specific intent" crime?

6. *HIV exposure.* In State v. Smith 621 A.2d 495 (N.J. Super. A.D. 1993), a jail inmate who knew he was HIV-positive bit a correctional officer. Upholding his conviction for attempted murder and aggravated assault, the court held there was sufficient evidence that it is possible for the virus to be transmitted through a bite, and that the defendant had been made aware of this possibility. But see Brock v. State, 555 So. 2d 285 (Ala. Cr. App. 1989) (conviction overturned in absence of evidence that defendant believed that HIV virus could be transmitted through a bite). What level of probability of transmission should the state have to prove in such cases? What degree of awareness of the risk of transmission should the state have to prove defendant possessed? What if the defendant knew he had engaged in unsafe sex or unsanitary drug injection but was unaware that he was HIV-positive? What other criminal charges might fit these cases?

Do convictions in these circumstances violate the principle of *Lyerla*? The MPC? In People v. Markowski, LA. Sup. Ct. No. A954578 (1989), the defendant, who was HIV-positive, was charged with assault, attempted murder, and attempted blood poisoning when he tried to sell his blood to a plasma center. Having established that the defendant had not intended any harm to others, the trial court dismissed the assault and attempted murder charges. Could the court have done otherwise? How would Model Penal Code section 5.01 apply here? What sorts of facts about Markowski's condition (or about his understanding of his condition or of the medical consequences of his blood donation) might the prosecution have had to prove to sustain the charges? If the court was right in dismissing those charges, should it necessarily have also dropped the attempted blood poisoning charge? The jury acquitted Markowski on the latter charge, apparently agreeing with his claim that he sold his blood only because he needed money.

7. *Reckless endangerment.* The drafters of the Model Penal Code recognized the gap they had left between a purpose-bound attempt law and the great number of crimes that permit conviction on a lesser mens rea. They tried to fill that gap with a reckless endangerment provision, section 211.2, which provides: "A person commits a misdemeanor if he recklessly engages in conduct which places or may place another person in danger of death or serious bodily injury."

The reckless endangerment approach may result in the conviction of some offenders who would have been acquitted of attempted murder. Moreover, because the term "reckless endangerment" is less condemnatory than a term such as "attempted murder," a jury may be more likely to convict. But the reckless endangerment approach is not without problems. For example, under the Model Penal Code reckless endangerment is a misdemeanor, while an attempt to commit a first degree felony is a second degree felony. Is this sentencing difference defensible? Moreover, the Model Penal Code has no statute on "negligent endangerment." Should it?

C. THE ACTUS REUS OF ATTEMPT

1. Preparation vs. Attempt

PEOPLE v. MURRAY
Supreme Court of California
15 Cal. 159 (1859)

FIELD, C.J., delivered the opinion of the Court.

The evidence in this case entirely fails to sustain the charge against the defendant of an attempt to contract an incestuous marriage with his niece. It only discloses declarations of his determination to contract the marriage, his elopement with the niece for that avowed purpose, and his request to one of the witnesses to go for a magistrate to perform the ceremony. It shows very clearly the intention of the defendant, but something more than mere intention is necessary to constitute the offense charged. Between preparation for the attempt and the attempt itself, there is a wide difference. The preparation consists in devising or arranging the means or measures necessary for the commission of the offense; the attempt is the direct movement toward the commission after the preparations are made. To illustrate: a party may purchase and load a gun, with the declared intention to shoot his neighbor; but until some movement is made to use the weapon upon the person of his intended victim, there is only preparation and not an attempt. For the preparation, he may be held to keep the peace; but he is not chargeable with any attempt to kill. So in the present case, the declarations, and elopement, and request for a magistrate, were preparatory to the marriage; but until the officer was engaged, and the parties stood before him, ready to take the vows appropriate to the contract of marriage, it cannot be said, in strictness, that the attempt was made. The attempt contemplated by the statute must be manifested by acts which would end in the consummation of the particular offense, but for the intervention of circumstances independent of the will of the party. Judgment reversed and cause remanded.

Notes and Questions

1. *Intent and attempt.* The court is convinced that the evidence showed "very clearly the intention of the defendant." Moreover, the defendant took steps in the direction of effectuating his intent. Why, then, should he not be punishable by the law? Can he argue that he did not commit an act, when he committed several acts toward the result he intended? Can he argue that he is not blameworthy where his intent was to violate the law? Why, then, should we draw the distinction between preparation and attempt?

Consider this historical commentary by Prof. George Fletcher:[5]

[Subjective criminality] presupposes a notion of intending that treats intent as a dimension of experience totally distinct from external behavior. Intending is conceived as an event of consciousness, known to the person with the intent, but not to others. Thus, the relationship of intending to action is dualistic rather than monistic. The intent exists in the realm of the mind, the act in the realm of the body.

. . . The criminal law should begin, this theory holds, by identifying interests that are worthy of protection. The next step should be preventing conduct that threatens those interests. The reasons that humans sometimes threaten those interests is either that they intend to do so or that they take risks that subject the protected interests to danger. Therefore the purpose of the criminal law should be to prevent people from embarking on courses of behavior that threaten these worthy interests. The way to deter people from embarking on these courses of conduct is to punish those who intend to violate those interests. The only reason we require offenders to act on their intention is to make sure that the intention is firm and not merely fantasy. . . .

. . . [T]he general thrust of Western legal theory has favored the rise of subjective criminality. . . . The subjective approach is defined by the rejection of the claim that the act of attempting is a distinct dimension of liability. For subjectivists, it is important that the actor take steps to execute his criminal intent, yet no specifically defined act is required for liability. This means that no conviction should ever founder on the ground that there was something wrong with the "act" element of attempting. Of course, a conviction might be barred on the ground that there was insufficient evidence of criminal intent, but never solely on the ground that the "act" did not reveal the objective earmarks of an attempt. . . . Since the late nineteenth century, the principle of subjective criminality has been almost unceasingly ascendant.

Fletcher goes on to argue that the rise of the subjectivist approach denotes a confounding of criminal punishment and civil commitment. As Fletcher notes, confining dangerous persons may be one legitimate goal of the criminal law, but he asks whether the subjectivist approach mistakenly treats that as a sufficient goal of the criminal law and thereby leads us to a realm of preventive detention of dangerous persons who merely may someday commit harmful acts.

5. George Fletcher, Rethinking Criminal Law 118-19, 166-67 (1978).

2. *The preparation/attempt boundary.* Generally, the individual who has engaged only in "preparatory activity" is not criminally liable, while the individual who has gone "beyond mere preparation" may be charged with an attempt. Obviously, then, drawing the line between preparation and attempt becomes an important task. The courts and legislatures have created a great variety of rules for determining when a person has passed from preparation to attempt.

The drafters of the Model Penal Code considered and rejected the following approaches to distinguishing preparation from attempt, as summarized in United States v. Mandujano, 499 F.2d 370, 373 n.5:

(a) The physical proximity doctrine — the overt act required for an attempt must be proximate to the completed crime, or directly tending toward the completion of the crime, or must amount to the commencement of the consummation.

(b) The dangerous proximity doctrine — a test given impetus by Mr. Justice Holmes whereby the greater the gravity and probability of the offense, and the nearer the act to the crime, the stronger is the case for calling the act an attempt.

(c) The indispensable element test — a variation of the proximity tests which emphasizes any indispensable aspect of the criminal endeavor over which the actor has not yet acquired control.

(d) The probable desistance test — the conduct constitutes an attempt if, in the ordinary and natural course of events, without interruption from an outside source, it will result in the crime intended.

(e) The abnormal step approach — an attempt is a step toward crime which goes beyond the point where the normal citizen would think better of his conduct and desist.

(f) The . . . unequivocality test — an attempt is committed when the actor's conduct manifests an intent to commit a crime.

The drafters of the Model Penal Code ultimately agreed that in addition to requiring criminal purpose, attempt would require an act that was a substantial step in a course of conduct designed to accomplish a criminal result, and in order to be substantial such an act must strongly corroborate criminal purpose:

Section 5.01. Criminal Attempt

(1) Definition of Attempt. A person is guilty of an attempt to commit a crime if, acting with the kind of culpability otherwise required for commission of the crime, he: . . .

(c) purposely does or omits to do anything that, under the circumstances as he believes them to be, is an act or omission constituting a substantial step in a course of conduct planned to culminate in his commission of the crime.

(2) Conduct that May Be Held Substantial Step under Subsection (1) (c). Conduct shall not be held to constitute a substantial step under subsection (1) (c) of this Section unless it is strongly corroborative of the actor's criminal purpose. Without negativing the sufficiency of other conduct, the following, if strongly corroborative of the actor's criminal purpose, shall not be held insufficient as a matter of law:

(a) lying in wait, searching for or following the contemplated victim of the crime;

   (b) enticing or seeking to entice the contemplated victim of the crime to go to the place contemplated for its commission;

   (c) reconnoitering the place contemplated for the commission of the crime;

   (d) unlawful entry of a structure, vehicle or enclosure in which it is contemplated that the crime will be committed;

   (e) possession of materials to be employed in the commission of the crime, that are specially designed for such unlawful use or which can serve no lawful purpose of the actor under the circumstances;

   (f) possession, collection or fabrication of materials to be employed in the commission of the crime, at or near the place contemplated for its commission, where such possession, collection or fabrication serves no lawful purpose of the actor under the circumstances;

   (g) soliciting an innocent agent to engage in conduct constituting an element of the crime.

How would *Murray* be decided under the Physical Proximity (or "Last Step"), Dangerous Proximity, Indispensable Element, Probable Desistance, Abnormal Step, and Unequivocality tests? Which of these best describes the test proposed in *Murray*? How would *Murray* be decided under the Model Penal Code's substantial step test?

   3. *Unequivocality.* According to the drafters of the Code, "the object of [the unequivocality] approach is to subject to attempt liability conduct which unequivocally demonstrates that the actor is being guided by a criminal purpose."[6] But how can any action be determined to be unequivocal? Inevitably, in practice, actions will appear "unequivocally" criminal that match widely shared images or stereotypes of criminal behavior.

   It is both the strength and the weakness of the unequivocality test that it links attempt liability to "community" alarm. This is a strength in that it explains why attempts must proceed beyond mere preparation, even where there is overwhelming evidence of criminal purpose. Arguably, we punish attempts not only because they manifest an intent to do harm, but also because they erode the public sense of security. In this sense, attempts are not entirely inchoate crimes — they cause harm. It follows that where an intent to do harm never manifests itself in a way that alarms the public, it should not be punished. The weakness of the test, illustrated by our next case, is that public alarm may be based on nothing more than prejudice.

MCQUIRTER v. STATE
Court of Appeals of Alabama
63 So. 2d 388 (1953)

PRICE, JUDGE.

   Appellant, a Negro man, was found guilty of an attempt to commit an assault with intent to rape, under an indictment charging an assault with intent to rape. The jury assessed a fine of $500.

   About 8 o'clock on the night of June 29, 1951, Mrs. Ted Allen, a white woman, with her two children and a neighbor's little girl, were drinking Coca-Cola at the "Tiny Diner" in Atmore. When they started in the direction of

6. American Law Institute, Model Penal Code and Commentaries, Part I, at 326 (1985).

Mrs. Allen's home she noticed appellant sitting in the cab of a parked truck. As she passed the truck appellant said something unintelligible, opened the truck door and placed his foot on the running board.

Mrs. Allen testified appellant followed her down the street and when she reached Suell Lufkin's house she stopped. As she turned into the Lufkin house appellant was within two or three feet of her. She waited ten minutes for appellant to pass. When she proceeded on her way, appellant came toward her from behind a telephone pole. She told the children to run to Mr. Simmons' house and tell him to come and meet her. When appellant saw Mr. Simmons he turned and went back down the street to the intersection and leaned on a stop sign just across the street from Mrs. Allen's home. Mrs. Allen watched him at the sign from Mr. Simmons' porch for about thirty minutes, after which time he came back down the street and appellant went on home.

Mrs. Allen's testimony was corroborated by that of her young daughter. The daughter testified the appellant was within six feet of her mother as she approached the Lufkin house, and this witness said there was a while when she didn't see appellant at the intersection.

Mr. Lewis Simmons testified when the little girls ran up on his porch and said a Negro was after them, witness walked up the sidewalk to meet Mrs. Allen and saw appellant. Appellant went on down the street and stopped in front of Mrs. Allen's home and waited there approximately thirty minutes.

Mr. Clarence Bryars, a policeman in Atmore, testified that appellant stated after his arrest that he came to Atmore with the intention of getting him a white woman that night.

Mr. W. E. Strickland, Chief of Police of Atmore, testified that appellant stated in the Atmore jail he didn't know what was the matter with him; that he was drinking a little; that he and his partner had been to Pensacola; that his partner went to the "Front" to see a colored woman; that he didn't have any money and he sat in the truck and made up his mind he was going to get the first woman that came by and that this was the first woman that came by. He said he got out of the truck, came around the gas tank and watched the lady and when she started off he started off behind her; that he was going to carry her in the cotton patch and if she hollered he was going to kill her. He testified appellant made the same statement in the Brewton jail.

Mr. Norvelle Seals, Chief Deputy Sheriff, corroborated Mr. Strickland's testimony as to the statement by appellant at the Brewton jail.

Appellant, as a witness in his own behalf, testified he and Bill Page, another Negro, carried a load of junk-iron from Monroeville to Pensacola; on their way back to Monroeville they stopped in Atmore. They parked the truck near the "Tiny Diner" and rode to the "Front," the colored section, in a cab. Appellant came back to the truck around 8 o'clock and sat in the truck cab for about thirty minutes. He decided to go back to the "Front" to look for Bill Page. As he started up the street he saw prosecutrix and her children. He turned around and waited until he decided they had gone, then he walked up the street toward the "Front." When he reached the intersection at the telegraph pole he decided he didn't want to go to the "Front" and sat around there a few minutes, then went on to the "Front" and stayed about 25 or 30 minutes, and came back to the truck.

He denied that he followed Mrs. Allen or made any gesture toward molesting her or the children. He denied making the statements testified to by the officers.

He testified he had never been arrested before and introduced testimony by two residents of Monroeville as to his good reputation for peace and quiet and for truth and veracity.

Appellant insists the trial court erred in refusing the general affirmative charge and in denying the motion for a new trial on the ground the verdict was contrary to the evidence.

"An attempt to commit an assault with intent to rape . . . means an attempt to rape which has not proceeded far enough to amount to an assault." Burton v. State, 8 Ala. App. 295, 62 So. 394, 396.

Under the authorities in this state, to justify a conviction for an attempt to commit an assault with intent to rape the jury must be satisfied beyond a reasonable doubt that defendant intended to have sexual intercourse with prosecutrix against her will, by force or by putting her in fear.

Intent is a question to be determined by the jury from the facts and circumstances adduced on the trial, and if there is evidence from which it may be inferred that at the time of the attempt defendant intended to gratify his lustful desires against the resistance of the female a jury question is presented.

In determining the question of intention the jury may consider social conditions and customs founded upon racial differences, such as that the prosecutrix was a white woman and defendant was a Negro man.

After considering the evidence in this case we are of the opinion it was sufficient to warrant the submission of the question of defendant's guilt to the jury, and was ample to sustain the judgment of conviction.

Defense counsel contends in brief that the testimony of the officers as to defendant's declaration of intent was inadmissible because no attempt or overt act toward carrying that intent into effect had been proven. . . . [But] if any facts are proven from which the jury may reasonably infer that the crime has been committed, proof of the confession is rendered admissible.

We find no reversible error in the record and the judgment of the trial court is affirmed.

Notes and Questions

1. What was McQuirter's act? How did the court determine that the act requirement had been met? According to the court, if there is evidence from which it may be inferred that at the time of the attempt defendant intended to gratify his lustful desires against the resistance of the female, then a jury question is presented. The court must have determined that the evidence met this standard. What was the evidence? The court noted that the jury was free to consider "social conditions and customs" founded on racial differences, particularly the races of the parties. What does that mean? Were those "conditions and customs" in fact the only evidence? What about his "confession"? To what did he confess? What were the likely circumstances of this confession?

2. *Applying contemporary rules.* How would *McQuirter* be decided under the Model Penal Code? Did any of McQuirter's actions "strongly corroborate" criminal purpose as required by section 5.01 (2) of the Code?

Is the *McQuirter* court applying a test of attempt that is similar to the "abnormal step" test that was rejected in the drafting of the Code? Given the cultural and political context of Alabama in the early 1950s, was it sufficiently "abnormal" for a black man to share the sidewalk with a white woman for such an act to be considered evidence of criminal intent? Does *McQuirter* suggest a problem with the "abnormal step" approach?

What about the "unequivocality" test? Is it possible that McQuirter's alleged conduct was "unequivocal" to many white Alabamans in 1953, but would have struck other Americans as equivocal? Is the *McQuirter* court allowing the "social conditions and customs" founded on racial differences to redefine the kind of act required for the conviction of attempted assault with intent to rape?

3. *"Attempted attempts."* McQuirter was convicted of "attempt to commit an assault with intent to rape." Is it fair to say that he was punished for attempting an attempt? If so, is it fair to punish him? Could McQuirter have been prosecuted for attempted rape?

PEOPLE v. RIZZO
Court of Appeals of New York
246 N.Y. 334, 158 N.E. 888 (1927)

CRANE, J.

The police of the city of New York did excellent work in this case by preventing the commission of a serious crime. It is a great satisfaction to realize that we have such wide-awake guardians of our peace. Whether or not the steps which the defendant had taken up to the time of his arrest amounted to the commission of a crime, as defined by our law, is however, another matter. He has been convicted of an attempt to commit the crime of robbery in the first degree, and sentenced to state's prison. There is no doubt that he had the intention to commit robbery, if he got the chance. An examination, however, of the facts is necessary to determine whether his acts were in preparation to commit the crime if the opportunity offered, or constituted a crime in itself, known to our law as an attempt to commit robbery in the first degree. Charles Rizzo, the defendant, appellant, with three others, Anthony J. Dorio, Thomas Milo, and John Thomasello, on January 14th planned to rob one Charles Rao of a pay roll valued at about $1,200 which he was to carry from the bank for the United Lathing Company. These defendants, two of whom had firearms, started out in an automobile, looking for Rao or the man who had the pay roll on that day. Rizzo claimed to be able to identify the man, and was to point him out to the others, who were to do the actual holding up. The four rode about in their car looking for Rao. They went to the bank from which he was supposed to get the money and to various buildings being constructed by the United Lathing Company. At last they came to One Hundred and Eightieth Street and Morris Park Avenue. By this time they were being watched and followed by two police officers. As Rizzo jumped out of the car and ran into the building, all four were arrested. The defendant was taken out from the building in which he was hiding. Neither Rao nor a man named Previti, who was also supposed to carry a pay roll, were at the place at the time of the arrest. The defendants had not found or seen the man they intended to rob. No person with a pay roll was at any of the places where they had stopped, and no one had been pointed out or identified by Rizzo. The four men intended to rob the pay roll man, whoever he was. They were looking for him, but they had not seen or discovered him up to the time they were arrested.

Does this constitute the crime of an attempt to commit robbery in the first degree? The Penal Law, §2, prescribes:

> An act, done with intent to commit a crime, and tending but failing to effect its commission, is "an attempt to commit that crime."

The word "tending" is very indefinite. It is perfectly evident that there will arise differences of opinion as to whether an act in a given case is one tending to commit a crime. "Tending" means to exert activity in a particular direction. Any act in preparation to commit a crime may be said to have a tendency towards its accomplishment. The procuring of the automobile, and searching of the streets looking for the desired victim, were in reality acts tending toward the commission of the proposed crime. The law, however, has recognized that many acts in the way of preparation are too remote to constitute the crime of attempt. The line has been drawn between those acts that are remote and those that are proximate and near to the consummation. The law must be practical, and therefore considers those acts only as tending to the commission of the crime that are so near to its accomplishment that in all reasonable probability the crime itself would have been committed, but for timely interference. The cases that have been before the courts express this idea in different language, but the idea remains the same. The act or acts must come or advance very near to the accomplishment of the intended crime. In People v. Mills, 178 N.Y. 274, 284, 70 N.E. 786, 789 (67 L.R.A. 131), it was said:

> Felonious intent alone is not enough, but there must be an overt act shown in order to establish even an attempt. An overt act is one done to carry out the intention, and it must be such as would naturally effect that result, unless prevented by some extraneous cause.

In Hyde v. U.S., 225 U.S. 347, it was stated that the act amounts to an attempt when it is so near to the result that the danger of success is very great. "There must be dangerous proximity to success." Halsbury in his Laws of England, vol. 9, p.259 says:

> An act in order to be a criminal attempt must be immediately and not remotely connected with and directly tending to the commission of an offense.

Commonwealth v. Peaslee, 177 Mass. 267, 59 N.E. 55, refers to the acts constituting an attempt as coming very near to the accomplishment of the crime.

The method of committing or attempting crime varies in each case, so that the difficulty, if any, is not with this rule of law regarding an attempt, which is well understood, but with its application to the facts. As I have said before, minds differ over the requisite proximity and the nearness of the approach.

How shall we apply this rule of immediate nearness to this case? The defendants were looking for the pay roll man to rob him of his money. This is the charge in the indictment. Robbery is defined in section 2120 of the Penal Law as "the unlawful taking of personal property from the person or in the presence of another, against his will, by means of force, or violence, or fear of injury, immediate or future, to his person"; and it is made robbery in the first degree by section 2124 when committed by a person aided by accomplices actually present. To constitute the crime of robbery, the money must have been taken from Rao by means of force or violence, or through fear. The crime of attempt to commit robbery was committed, if these defendants did an act tending to the commission of this robbery. Did the acts above described come dangerously near to the taking of Rao's property? Did the acts come so near to the commission of robbery that there was reasonable likelihood of its accomplishment but for the interference? Rao was not found; the defendants were still looking for him; no attempt to rob him could be made, at least until he came in sight; he was not in the building at One Hundred and Eightieth Street and Morris Park Avenue. There was no man there with the pay roll for the United Lathing Company whom these defendants could rob. Apparently no money had been drawn from the bank for the pay roll by anybody at the time of the arrest. In a word, these defendants had planned to commit a crime, and were looking around the city for an opportunity to commit it, but the opportunity fortunately never came. Men would not be guilty of an attempt at burglary if they had planned to break into a building and were arrested while they were hunting about the streets for the building not knowing where it was. Neither would a man be guilty of an attempt to commit murder if he armed himself and started out to find the person whom he had planned to kill but could not find him. So here these defendants were not guilty of an attempt to commit robbery in the first degree when they had not found or reached the presence of the person they intended to rob.

For these reasons, the judgment of conviction of this defendant appellant must be reversed and a new trial granted.

A very strange situation has arisen in this case. I called attention to the four defendants who were convicted of this crime of an attempt to commit robbery in the first degree. They were all tried together upon the same evidence, and jointly convicted, and all sentenced to state's prison for varying terms. Rizzo was the only one of the four to appeal to the Appellate Division and to this court. His conviction was affirmed by the Appellate Division by a divided court, two of the justices dissenting, and we have now held that he was not guilty of the crime charged. If he were not guilty, neither were the other three defendants. As the others, however, did not appeal, there is no remedy for them through the courts; their judgments stand, and they must serve their sentences. This, of course, is a situation which must in all fairness be met in some way. Two of these men were guilty of the crime of carrying weapons, pistols, contrary to law, for which they could be convicted. Two of them, John Thomasello and Thomas Milo, had also been previously convicted, which may have had something to do with their neglect to appeal. However, the law would fail in its function and its purpose if it permitted these three men whoever or whatever they are to serve a sentence for a crime [which] the courts subsequently found and declared had not been committed. We therefore suggest to the district attorney of Bronx County that he bring the cases of these three men to the attention of the Governor, to be dealt with as to him seems proper in the light of this opinion.

The judgment of the Appellate Division and that of the county court should be reversed, and a new trial ordered.

CARDOZO, C.J., et al., concur.

Notes and Questions

1. If you were the district attorney, would you take any steps toward securing leniency (by pardon, commutation, or otherwise) for Rizzo's codefendants? If you were the governor, what would be your position on the issue?

2. What do you think the New York police officers involved in this case had to say about the praise lavished upon them by the court of appeals?

3. If precisely the same situation comes up again, what would the police be legally obligated to do?

4. How would *Rizzo* be decided under the Last Step, Dangerous Proximity, Indispensable Element, Probable Desistance, Abnormal Step, Unequivocality, and Substantial Step tests?

5. *A bank robbery hypothetical.* Examine the following series of events:

a. *A* decides to rob a bank (disclosing this intention in his diary and confiding his plan to two friends).

b. He then contracts to buy a new automobile, the down payment for which is due the next day and for which he presently has no funds.

c. He walks past the bank to get the layout of it and to see when it is open for business.

d. He goes to the five-and-ten-cent store and buys a rubber mask.

e. He goes home and draws a map of the interior of the bank.

f. He takes his old gun (possessed legally) from his attic, cleans it and oils it and loads it for the first time in five years.

g. He then writes a note saying "I have a gun — give me all your money."

h. He leaves his house carrying the gun and note.

i. He steals a car from a parking lot.

j. He parks in front of the bank.

k. He gets out of the car.

l. He enters the bank.

m. He walks up to the teller's cage.

n. He pushes the note across toward the teller.

o. The teller slides the money toward him on the counter.

At what point has *A* become guilty of attempted robbery, under each of the seven tests? Is the question whether *A* really intended to commit the robbery? Whether *A* would have backed out? Whether *A* caused any harm? How does one answer these questions? What question does the Model Penal Code ask?

6. *Proving intent to attempt.* Where the steps leading up to a crime are by themselves harmless, if not "innocent," courts may have to rely on contestable forms of evidence to help establish intent.

Informant testimony. In United States v. Jackson, 560 F.2d 112 (2d Cir. 1977), Vanessa Hodges invited Martin Allen and Robert Jackson to join with her in robbing a bank. They planned to enter a particular bank at 7:30 A.M., when the bank manager regularly entered, and steal the weekend deposits. On June 14, Allen and Jackson met Hodges at 7:30 A.M., and all three drove to the bank, carrying a suitcase containing a sawed-off shotgun, toy revolver, masks, and handcuffs in the backseat. They did not arrive at the bank, however, until 8:00 A.M., when it was too late to carry out their intended plan. They drove around briefly and, after stopping for breakfast, returned to the bank. Hodges and Allen peered through the bank window and saw the deposits but decided it was too risky to try the robbery without a fourth participant. They enlisted William Scott, who added another shotgun to the suitcase. The four then returned to the bank. Allen, alone, entered the bank briefly to observe the surveillance system, while Jackson placed a piece of cardboard with a false license number on the car. Several customers were by now inside the bank, so the group decided to postpone the robbery until the following Monday, June 21.

Hodges, in the meantime, was arrested on an unrelated bank robbery charge and immediately informed the government of the events of June 14 and of the plan in place for June 21. On Saturday, at the request of the FBI, Hodges called the defendants to confirm that they were ready to carry out the robbery. She called the next day, but because the defendants had by then heard of her arrest, they informed her that they had decided to abandon the job. In spite of their announced change of plans, the defendants set off for the bank early Monday morning. The FBI surveillance agents were in place at the bank, having doubted the sincerity of the defendants' statements to Hodges. At 7:39 A.M., the agents observed a car fitting the description of the getaway car circling the block on which the bank was located. The car stopped at the side of the bank and one of the occupants got out of the car. He stood near the bank entrance for a short while and then left the area on foot, returning shortly with a cup of coffee. He stood by the bank entrance sipping his coffee and then returned to the car. The car pulled away from the curb and was observed to be parked in several different locations in the vicinity of the bank entrance. At some point, the occupants of the car detected the surveillance agents and left the area. They were overtaken by FBI agents, who ordered the occupants to exit the car. The agents then noticed the suitcase on the backseat; it was partially unzipped, exposing the contents.

Affirming their conviction, the Court of Appeals held that as a matter of law there was sufficient evidence that the defendants had shown the required intent and had committed a "substantial step," because

> [on] two separate occasions, appellants reconnoitered the place contemplated for commission of the crime and possessed the paraphernalia to be employed in the commission of the crime — loaded sawed-off shotguns, extra shells, a toy revolver, handcuffs, and masks — which was specially designed for such unlawful use and which could serve no lawful purpose under the circumstances [Id. at 120.]

Though reliance on "cooperative informant" testimony may strike some as unsavory, courts generally admit it, so long as the defendant has the opportunity to cross-examine the informant for bias or other matters bearing on credibility. If informant testimony such as Hodges's was deemed inadmissible as evidence of the substantive nature of the preparatory actions, how long would police officers have to wait before interrupting suspicious actions?

In United States v. Buffington, 815 F.2d 1292 (9th Cir. 1987), a police informant gave a detailed description of defendants' planned robbery of a bank in a shopping center. The defendants were then observed apparently casing the bank, and one defendant tied a scarf over his face. But the defendants left after the shopping center experienced a power outage, and the bank locked its doors. When arrested they were found with two revolvers. One of them, a man, was dressed as a woman. Another was wearing four or five coats (presumably to disguise his size and weight). The defendants were indicted on a charge of attempted unarmed bank robbery pursuant. In a pretrial ruling, the trial court prohibited the use of any testimony of the police informant and any information given by the informant to the police, because of the government's failure to comply with a discovery order set forth by the court. As a result, the only evidence regarding the charge of attempt presented to the jury was the physical evidence found in the appellant's car and the testimony of the police officers regarding the conduct of the appellants observed in the vicinity of the bank. At the jury trial the appellants were found guilty of attempted federal bank robbery. On appeal the reviewing court held that, "the government's evidence, without the aid and interpretive light of the informant's disclosures, was insufficient as a matter of law to justify the convictions for . . . attempted federal bank robbery." [Id. at 1299.]

Did the actions of the appellants in *Buffington* corroborate their criminal intent any less than those of the appellants in *Jackson*? Is *Buffington* consistent with *Jackson*?

On which of the seven tests do these two cases rely?

Prior crimes as evidence. In some cases, establishing attempt liability may depend on finding exceptions to the general rule of evidence that past bad acts cannot be introduced to prove guilt on a new charge. In Walters v. Maass, 45 F.3d 1355 (9th Cir. 1995), the defendant was convicted of attempted kidnapping and sexual assault on a young girl, whom he tried, unsuccessfully, to lure into his truck by offering her money and saying he needed help finding his lost dog. The prosecution introduced his 1981 conviction for kidnapping and sexual assault in which he used the exact same ploy and completed the crimes. Partly reversing, the Court of Appeals held that the prior crime was properly admitted under an exception to the bar on prior bad act evidence for past crimes used only to show "motive, opportunity, intent, preparation, plan, knowledge, or absence of mistake or accident," rather than simply bad character or a propensity to commit crimes. Id. at 1358. And on that basis the Court held there was sufficient evidence to support the new conviction for attempted kidnapping, but not for the charges of attempted sexual assault. The court held that though the past sexual assault conviction somewhat corroborated his intent to commit sexual assault in the new act, it did not "strongly" corroborate it — he might have been planning some other crime. Is this compromise outcome convincing? Does attempt law overly tempt courts to find exceptions to the bar on past bad act evidence?

7. Consider this call for abolishing all attempt liability for conduct that stops short of the "last act."[7]

> [I]f inchoate criminality is premised on either dangerousness or wickedness of character, and not on culpable acts, then it is in tension with the presumption that defendants freely choose whether they will act dangerously or wickedly. Until the defendant completes an attempt, he is just at one end of a continuum with others who harbor culpable intentions and dangerous beliefs. Until he takes what he believes to be the last step necessary to cause the social harm, he can always reconsider. Whether he will or not — which, together with the probability of other harm-negating events, is the determinant of how dangerous he currently is — is, we presume, a matter over which he has free choice.
>
> . . . Free choice is a bedrock assumption of liberal theories of criminal law. Predictable choice seems to be the bedrock assumption of inchoate criminality. For if it is not, all that is left as a candidate is a wicked state of mind, something that can be quite remote from the socially harmful act to which it is directed and which makes it wicked.
>
> . . . [F]or an act to be culpable, the act must appear to defendant to increase risks to others in a way that is not dependent on defendant's further choices. In

7. Larry Alexander & Kimberly D. Kessler, Mens Rea and Inchoate Crimes, 87 J. Crim. L. & Criminology 1138, 1155, 1169 (1997).

other words, defendant cannot view his own future choices as matters subject to his prediction. Indeed, so long as defendant views himself as having control over any future choices to create risks that will then be beyond his control, it is doubtful that even he, much less the law, can clearly distinguish in terms of risks already present between what he intends on the one hand and his mere wishes or fantasies on the other.

What is the counter-argument, then, for punishing, say, Jackson or Buffington if they are interrupted while they still have an opportunity to abandon their plans?

8. *The economics of attempt and victim incentives.* If you leave your car unlocked on a city street at night, is it your fault if someone steals it? Clearly your failure to lock the car, whether purposeful or not, cannot make you criminally responsible for any theft or mitigate the criminal liability of the thief. But utilitarians often argue that it may be socially efficient in some circumstances to *lower* the punishment for a crime, and to let the populace know that the punishment has been lowered, if the effect is to cause the populace to invest more in security devices or other crime prevention measures. Thus, for example, if our goal is to reduce car theft, rather than to ensure retributive punishment, the proper trade-off between level of punishment and car owners' investment in antitheft devices is an empirical question.[8] And as one commentary has recently argued, the trade-off is even more complex in the area of attempt law, where the punishment and safety investment may influence each other in very subtle ways:[9]

> Precautions against crime taken by potential victims reduce the chances of successful completion of the crime either by increasing the chances that the perpetrator will not complete the activities he plans to commit, or by increasing the chances that, even if the perpetrator completes his plan, the desired consequences of the plan will not be realized. Consequently, crimes directed against more cautious victims are more likely to fail and end up being classified as attempts and punished accordingly. The more potential victims invest in precautions, the more likely they are to be victims of unsuccessful attempts rather than completed crimes.
>
> The very same conclusion is grounded in an additional, independent observation. Precautions taken by potential victims of crime force potential criminals to go through a longer sequence of pre-crime activities. The longer sequence of pre-crime activities exposes the perpetrator to a greater risk of being interrupted before the completion of the crime. Hence, a crime directed against a more cautious victim is more likely to wind up being classified as an attempt than a crime directed against a less cautious victim.
>
> These findings imply that criminals targeting highly cautious victims are more likely to be influenced by sanctions imposed for attempts than criminals operating against less cautious victims because it is the former type of criminal whose actions are likely to result in unsuccessful attempts. As the sanction for attempts decreases relative to the sanction for completed acts, the expected cost of sanctions facing criminals decreases, regardless of the type of victim they target. This expected cost of sanction decreases *more* if the criminal targets an overly cautious victim. Consequently, as the sanction for attempts decreases, cautious victims become more attractive targets. Thus, some criminals are likely, under a rule that exculpates or

---

8. Of course, another factor is the possibility that protecting your car from theft does not reduce car theft at all, but merely diverts the thief to another car.

9. Omri Ben-Shahar & Alon Hare, The Economics of the Law of Criminal Attempts: A Victim-Centered Perspective, 145 U. Penn. L. Rev. 297, 336, 339, 340 (1996) (emphasis in original).

mitigates the sanctions for attempts, to substitute their targets and choose to act against more cautious victims, rather than against less cautious ones. . . .

[Thus], a high level of precaution loses some of its benefits for the victims when the law's treatment of attempts becomes lenient . . .

. . . Under a system that mitigates the sanctions for attempts, victims will find it less profitable to engage in a high level of precaution relative to a system that punishes attempts and completed acts equally.

Are these empirical issues too subtle for criminals or potential victims to ponder? Do they offend retributive principles?

2. Abandonment

PEOPLE v. STAPLES
California Court of Appeal
6 Cal. App. 3d 61, 85 Cal. Rptr. 589 (1970)

REPPY, ASSOCIATE JUSTICE.

Defendant was charged in an information with attempted burglary (Pen. Code, §§664, 459). . . .

In October, 1967, while his wife was away on a trip, defendant, a mathematician, under an assumed name, rented an office on the second floor of a building in Hollywood which was over the mezzanine of a bank. Directly below the mezzanine was the vault of the bank. Defendant was aware of the layout of the building, specifically of the relation of the office he rented to the bank vault. Defendant paid rent for the period from October 23 to November 23. The landlord had 10 days before commencement of the rental period within which to finish some interior repairs and painting. During this prerental period defendant brought into the office certain equipment. This included drilling tools, two acetylene gas tanks, a blow torch, a blanket, and a linoleum rug. The landlord observed these items when he came in from time to time to see how the repair work was progressing. Defendant learned from a custodian that no one was in the building on Saturdays. On Saturday, October 14, defendant drilled two groups of holes into the floor of the office above the mezzanine room. He stopped drilling before the holes went through the floor. He came back to the office several times thinking he might slowly drill down, covering the holes with the linoleum rug. At some point in time he installed a hasp lock on a closet, and planned to, or did, place his tools in it. However, he left the closet keys on the premises. Around the end of November, apparently after November 23, the landlord notified the police and turned the tools and equipment over to them. Defendant did not pay any more rent. It is not clear when he last entered the office, but it could have been after November 23, and even after the landlord had removed the equipment. On February 22, 1968, the police arrested defendant. After receiving advice as to his constitutional rights, defendant voluntarily made an oral statement which he reduced to writing.

Among other things which defendant wrote down were these:

Saturday, the 14th . . . I drilled some holes in the floor of the room. Because of tiredness, fear, and the implications of what I was doing, I stopped and went to sleep.

At this point I think my motives began to change. The actutal [*sic*] commencement of my plan made me begin to realize that even if I were to succeed a fugitive life of living off of stolen money would not give the enjoyment of the life of a mathematician however humble a job I might have.

I still had not given up my plan however. I felt I had made a certain investment of time, money, effort and a certain pschological [*sic*] commitment to the concept.

I came back several times thinking I might store the tools in the closet and slowly drill down (covering the hole with a rug of linoleum square). As time went on (after two weeks or so), my wife came back and my life as bank robber seemed more and more absurd.

Our courts have come up with a variety of "tests" which try to distinguish acts of preparation from completed attempts. "The preparation consists in devising or arranging the means or measures necessary for the commission of the offense; the attempt is the direct movement toward the commission after the preparations are made." (People v. Murray, 14 Cal. 159.) "[T]he act must reach far enough towards the accomplishment of the desired result to amount to the commencement of the consummation." (People v. Miller, 2 Cal. 2d 527, 530, 42 P.2d 308, 309.) ". . . [W]here the intent to commit the substantive offense is . . . clearly established . . . [,] acts done toward the commission of the crime may constitute an attempt, where the same acts would be held insufficient to constitute an attempt if the intent with which they were done is equivocal and not clearly proved." (People v. Berger, 131 Cal. App. 2d 127, 130, 280 P.2d 136, 138.)

None of the above statements of the law applicable to this category of attempts provide a litmus-like test, and perhaps no such test is achievable. Such precision is not required in this case, however. There was definitely substantial evidence entitling the trial judge to find that defendant's acts had gone beyond the preparation stage. Without specifically deciding where defendant's preparations left off and where his activities became a completed criminal attempt, we can say that his "drilling" activity clearly was an unequivocal and direct step toward the completion of the burglary. It was a fragment of the substantive crime contemplated, i.e., the beginning of the "breaking" element. Further, defendant himself characterized his activity as the actual commencement of his plan. The drilling by defendant was obviously one of a series of acts which logic and ordinary experience indicate would result in the proscribed act of burglary.

The instant case provides an out-of-the-ordinary factual situation. . . . Usually the actors in cases falling within [the] category of attempts are intercepted or caught in the act. Here, there was no direct proof of any actual interception. But it was clearly inferable by the trial judge that defendant became aware that the landlord had resumed control over the office and had turned defendant's equipment and tools over to the police. This was the equivalent of interception.

The inference of this nonvoluntary character of defendant's abandonment was a proper one for the trial judge to draw. However, it would seem that the character of the abandonment in situations of this type, whether it be voluntary (prompted by pangs of conscience or a change of heart) or nonvoluntary (established by inference in the instant case), is not controlling. The relevant factor is the determination of whether the acts of the perpetrator have reached such a stage of advancement that they can be classified as an attempt. Once that attempt is found there can be no exculpatory abandonment.

"One of the purposes of the criminal law is to protect society from those who intend to injure it. When it is established that the defendant intended to commit a specific crime and that in carrying out this intention he committed an act that caused harm or sufficient danger of harm, it is immaterial that for some collateral reason he could not complete the intended crime." (People v. Camodeca, 52 Cal. 2d 142, 147, 38 P.2d 903, 906.)

The order is affirmed.

Notes and Questions

1. Did Staples cross the line between preparation and attempt? Did he commit the "last act"? A "substantial step" corroborative of his purpose? If he did, why should his subsequent actions negate his criminal liability? If a thief returns the stolen goods undamaged, is he still guilty of larceny? On the other hand, if we are confident that Staples had renounced any intention to burglarize the bank, why would we want to punish him?

2. *The MPC's "renunciation" rule.* Unlike the *Staples* court, the Model Penal Code does permit a limited defense of abandonment. Section 5.01(4), dealing with "Renunciation of Criminal Purpose," requires

> a complete and voluntary renunciation of his criminal purpose. . . . [R]enunciation is not voluntary if it is motivated in whole or in part, by circumstances, not present or apparent at the inception of the actor's course of conduct, which increase the probability of detection or apprehension or which make more difficult the accomplishment of the criminal purpose. Renunciation is not complete if it is motivated by a decision to postpone the criminal conduct until a more advantageous time or to transfer the criminal effort to another but similar objective or victim.

The Model Penal Code Commentary justifies allowing the defense of voluntary abandonment, explaining that the individual who abandons of his or her own volition early on in the course of an attempt lacks dangerousness of character, and also that permitting the defense for the individual who abandons later will encourage would-be criminals to desist from their unlawful plans.

Why does the Model Penal Code test depend on the reasons for the person's renunciation? What if Staples had read that the government's arrest and conviction rate for bank crimes had gone up dramatically in recent years, and so he decided not to risk a bank burglary?

3. *Abandonment doctrine today.* In practice, the abandonment defense is applied very stringently and there are few reported cases in which the defendant has prevailed on that ground. Of course, some courts dodge the abandonment issue simply by holding that the defendant never crossed the line between preparation and attempt in the first place.

For example, compare the *Staples* case, in which defendant had crossed to the attempt side of the line and was convicted, with Bucklew v. State, 206 So. 2d 200 (Miss. 1968). In *Bucklew* the defendant mayor signed a car repair bill that illegally authorized the city to pay his personal bill. However, he never submitted the bill to a clerk for payment. The court decided he could not be convicted of attempted embezzlement because he abandoned the scheme before taking any overt action and hence had confined himself to preparatory activity.

4. *Good and bad motivation.* In some instances allowing a defense of voluntary abandonment might lead to disturbing results. In Le Barron v. State, 32 Wis. 2d 294, 145 N.W.2d 79 (1966), the defendant voluntarily abandoned his attempt to rape a woman, after assaulting her, only because he found out she was pregnant.

The court rejected the abandonment claim. Would Le Barron have had a defense under the Model Penal Code?

Professor Mark Kelman writes[10]

> [I]t is implausible that a defendant who abandoned his attempted crime because he read a sign, "This Safe Protected by Alarms" could be convicted while one who read a sign, "Safe-crackers Will Be Apprehended and Prosecuted" would be acquitted. Both are simply being informed of the riskiness of their activity. It is simply unwarranted assertive construction to treat these defendants as renouncing larceny because they renounce this larceny. It is not clear how we would ever know that someone is moving on to a more advantageous time and place for his mischief rather than abandoning a life of crime because he has at last understood the social signals about the costs of crime. It is quite plain we cannot know that, because the social signals concerning the propriety of cost-benefit calculation are ambivalent and uninterpretable. We suppress the recognition of this ambivalence by asserting clear cases of total acceptable renunciation and blocking the knowledge that in a world where selfish calculation is acceptable, all renunciations are in significant senses partial.

Do you agree with Kelman that the voluntary/involuntary distinction rests on faulty premises? If so, can you think of a better way to distinguish between situations in which abandonment should be allowed as a defense and situations in which it should not?

5. *Specific abandonment rules.* One possible solution to the logical problem presented by the defense of abandonment is incorporating this defense into the language of the underlying statute. In State v. Andow, 386 N.W.2d 230 (Minn. 1986), the defendant, after being denied custody of her daughter, picked up the child for an approved two-hour visit and took her out of state, leaving a note explaining that she would not be returning. She was convicted of "child snatching" pursuant to section 609.26 of the Minnesota Code, which provides, in part,

> whoever intentionally . . . takes, obtains, retains, or fails to return a minor child from or to the parent or other person having the right to visitation or custody under a court order, where the action manifests an intent substantially to deprive that parent or other person having the right to visitation or custody of his rights to visitation or custody . . . may be charged with a felony. [Id. at 231 n.l.]

Subdivision 5 of section 609.26 further provides,

> A felony charge brought under this section shall be dismissed if the person voluntarily returns the child within 14 days after he takes, detains or fails to return the child in violation of this section. [Id. at 232.]

Does the presence of explicit language regarding abandonment in this statute avoid the conceptual and logical problems associated with abandonment and attempt? Is there any room for attempt liability under this statute? Under section 609.26, could the defendant have been found liable for attempted "child snatching" if she had given up the plan before removing the child?

The defendant in *Andow* was arrested 12 days after she took the child out of the custody of her father. Although the defendant acknowledged that she did not voluntarily abandon her plans to keep the child permanently, she argued

---

10. Kelman, Interpretive Construction in the Substantive Criminal Law, 33 Stan. L. Rev. 591, 630 (1981).

that she was denied the full benefit of the 14-day grace period allowed for abandonment. The appellate court rejected this argument, holding

> that expiration of the 14-day grace period is not an element of the felony offense of "child snatching" under Section 609.26; the offense is a felony from day one, with the charge to be dismissed if the child is voluntarily returned within 14 days. [Id. at 233.]

What effect might the opposite ruling have on child-snatchers? On the police?

6. *The special case of perjury.* Perjury offers a venerable example of a specific renunciation clause in a substantive statute. Consider this New York statute, N.Y. Penal Law §210.25 (McKinney 1999):

> In any prosecution for perjury, it is an affirmative defense that the defendant retracted his false statement in the course of the proceeding in which it was made before such false statement substantially affected the proceeding and before it became manifest that its falsity was or would be exposed.

In the classic case interpreting this statute, People v. Ezaugi, 2 N.Y.2d 439, 141 N.E.2d 580 (N.Y. 1957), the defendant, a detective, testified before a grand jury and falsely denied that he had discussed illegal payments with a police informant. After this testimony, Ezaugi had a conversation with his partner that revealed that the prosecutor knew he was lying. At a later grand jury, Ezaugi admitted that he had lied earlier. The court affirmed his conviction, because his recantation was "not a demonstration of penitence to purge the torments of a guilty conscience, but a calculated effort to escape the dire consequences of admitted false swearing." Id. at 574. Was the crime of perjury complete at the first hearing? Is there any reason why perjury should be treated differently from theft?

The court said it would only allow recantation where it was done promptly, in the same proceeding as the lie, where the lie had not harmed the investigation, and where the perjurer had not been motivated by realizing that his lie had been discovered.

Many states have recantation statutes, some requiring all these criteria, some just requiring one of them. See Peter M. Agulnick: In Search of Truth: A Case for Expanding Perjury's Recantation Defense, 100 W. Va. L. Rev. 353 (1997). Should recantation before the same inquiring body within the same hearing be sufficient as a defense?

If good motive is a criterion, what if the liar recants in the face of harsh and disbelieving cross-examination, but before any factual evidence of her lie becomes apparent?

3.   Solicitation

PEOPLE v. LUBOW

Court of Appeals of New York

29 N.Y.2d 58, 272 N.E.2d 331 (1971)

BERGAN, JUDGE.

. . . The basic statutory definition of criminal solicitation is that, with intent that another person shall "engage in conduct constituting crime," the accused "solicits, requests, commands, importunes or otherwise attempts to cause such other person to engage in such conduct." This basic definitory language is continued through three grades of solicitation, the gravity depending on what crime the conduct sought to be induced would effectuate.

If the conduct would be "a crime" it is criminal solicitation in the third degree, a "violation" (§100.00); if the conduct would be "a felony" it is criminal solicitation in the second degree, a class A misdemeanor (§100.05); and if the conduct would be murder or kidnapping in the first degree it is criminal solicitation in the first degree, a class D felony (§100.10).

As it has been noted, nothing need be done under the statute in furtherance of the communication ("solicits, commands, importunes") to constitute the offense. The communication itself, with intent that the other person engage in the unlawful conduct, is enough. It needs no corroboration.

And an attempt at communication which fails to reach the other person may also constitute the offense, for the concluding clause "or otherwise attempts to cause such other person to engage in such conduct" would seem literally to embrace as an attempt an undelivered letter or message initiated with the necessary intent.

Appellants have been convicted after a trial by a three-judge panel in the Criminal Court of the City of New York of violation of section 100.05, which describes solicitation to commit a felony. The information on which the prosecution is based is made by complainant Max Silverman. It describes the charge as criminal solicitation and states that "defendants attempted to cause deponent to commit the crime of grand larceny" in that they "attempted to induce the deponent to obtain precious stones on partial credit with a view towards appropriating the property to their own use and not paying the creditors, said conduct constituting the crime of larceny by false promise."

Although the Penal Law section number is not stated in the information, it was clearly stated in court before the opening of the trial that the charge was a violation of section 100.05 and the facts alleged that the inducement was to commit grand larceny, a felony, which gave adequate notice of the nature of the offense involved.

The evidence showed that complainant Silverman and both defendants were engaged in the jewelry business. It could be found that defendant Lubow owed Silverman $30,000 for diamonds on notes which were unpaid; that Lubow had told Silverman he was associated with a big operator interested in buying diamonds and introduced him to defendant Gissinger.

It could also be found that in October, 1967, Silverman met the two defendants together at their office, demanded his money, and said that because of the amount owed him he was being forced into bankruptcy.

Silverman testified that in response to this Lubow said "Well, let's make it a big one, a big bankruptcy," and Gissinger said this was a good idea. When Silverman asked "how it is done" he testified that Lubow, with Gissinger participating, outlined a method by which diamonds would be purchased partly on credit, sold for less than cost, with the proceeds pyramided to boost Silverman's credit rating until very substantial amounts came in, when there was to be a bankruptcy with Silverman explaining that he had lost the cash gambling in Puerto Rico and Las Vegas. The cash would be divided among the three men. The gambling explanation for the disappearance of cash would be made to seem believable by producing credit cards for Puerto Rico and Las Vegas. Silverman testified that Lubow said "we would eventually wind up with a quarter of a million dollars each" and that Gissinger said "maybe millions."

Silverman reported this proposal to the District Attorney in October, 1967, and the following month a police detective equipped Silverman with a tape recorder concealed on his person which was in operation during conversations with defendants on November 16 and which tends to substantiate the charge. The reel was received in evidence on concession that it was taken from the machine Silverman wore November 16.

A police detective testified as an expert that a "bust out operation" is a "pyramiding of credit by rapid purchasing of merchandise, and the rapid selling of the same merchandise sometimes 10 and 20 per cent the cost of the merchandise itself, and they keep selling and buying until they establish such a credit rating that they are able to purchase a large order at the end of their operation, and at this time they go into bankruptcy or they just leave."

There thus seems sufficient evidence in the record to find that defendants intended Silverman to engage in conduct constituting a felony by defrauding creditors of amounts making out grand larceny and that they importuned Silverman to engage in such conduct. Thus the proof meets the actual terms of the statute.

The statute itself is a valid exercise of legislative power. Commentators closely associated with the drafting of the Model Penal Code of the American Law Institute, from which the New York solicitation statute stems, have observed:

> Purposeful solicitation presents dangers calling for preventive intervention and is sufficiently indicative of a disposition towards criminal activity to call for liability. Moreover, the fortuity that the person solicited does not agree to commit or attempt to commit the incited crime plainly should not relieve the solicitor of liability.

Solicitation to commit a felony was a misdemeanor at common law (People v. Bush, 4 Hill 133, 135; Rex v. Higgins, 2 East 5). Summarizing this historical fact Judge Cardozo observed: "So at common law, incitement to a felony, when it did not reach the stage of an attempt, was itself a separate crime, and like conspiracy, which it resembled, was a misdemeanor, not a felony" (People v. Werblow, 241 N.Y. 55, 66, 148 N.E. 786, 791, citing Higgins and Rex v. Gregory, L.R. 1 C.C.R. 77).

But as People v. Bush demonstrates, the solicitation in early New York cases was treated as closely related to an attempt. There defendant asked another to burn a barn and gave him a match for that purpose. This principle was followed to some extent but there were fundamental difficulties with it under the concept of attempt and it seems not to have been followed. . . .

In commenting on the criminal solicitation enactment of article 100, two lawyers who were active in the work of the State Commission on Revision of the Penal Law and Criminal Code which prepared the present statute observed that article 100 "closes the gap" for those who believe, as apparently the commission and the American Law Institute did, that "solicitation to commit a crime involves sufficient culpability to warrant criminal sanctions."

There are, however, potential difficulties inherent in this penal provision which should be looked at, even though all of them are not decisive in this present case. One, of course, is the absence of any need for corroboration. The tape recording here tends to give some independent support to the testimony of Silverman, but there are types of criminal conduct which might be solicited where there would be a heavy thrust placed on the credibility of a single witness testifying to a conversation. Extraordinary care might be required in deciding when to prosecute; in determining the truth; and in appellate review of the factual decision.

One example would be the suggestion of one person to another that he commit a sexual offense; another is the suggestion that he commit perjury. The Model Penal Code did not require corroboration; but aside from the need for corroboration which is traditional in some sexual offenses, there are dangers in the misinterpretation of innuendos or remarks which could be taken as invitations to commit sexual offenses. These are discussed by Wechsler-Jones-Korn (61 Col. L. Rev., p.623) with the comment that "it is a risk implicit in the punishment of almost all inchoate crimes." . . .

Another potential problem with the statute is that it includes an attempt to commit unlawful solicitation, i.e., solicits . . . "or otherwise attempts to cause" the conduct. This has the same effect as the Model Penal Code, but the language there is different. The Code spells the purpose out more specifically. . . . "It is immaterial . . . that the actor fails to communicate with the person he solicits to commit a crime if his conduct was designed to effect such communication" (Model Penal Code, §5.02, subd. [2], Tent. Draft No. 10, as analyzed by Wechsler-Jones-Korn, op. cit, p.621). This could be an attempt in the classic sense and might be committed by a telephone message initiated but never delivered. The present Penal Law, stated in different language, has the same effect.

Judgment affirmed.

Notes and Questions

1. The Model Penal Code rule:

Section 5.02. Criminal Solicitation

(1) Definition of solicitation. A person is guilty of solicitation to commit a crime if with the purpose of promoting or facilitating its commission he commands, encourages or requests another person to engage in specific conduct that would constitute such crime or an attempt to commit such crime or that would establish his complicity in its commission or attempted commission.

(2) Uncommunicated solicitation. It is immaterial under Subsection (1) of this Section that the actor fails to communicate with the person he solicits to commit a crime if his conduct was designed to effect such communication.

(3) Renunciation of criminal purpose. It is an affirmative defense that the actor, after soliciting another person to commit a crime, persuaded him not to do so or otherwise prevented the commission of the crime under circumstances manifesting a renunciation of his criminal purpose.

2. *Solicitation vs. attempt.* For purposes of grading punishment, the Code treats solicitation the same way it treats attempt: Soliciting a crime results in the same penalty as completing that particular crime, except that soliciting a felony of the first degree is punishable as a felony of the second degree. §5.05(1). What if a jurisdiction has a sufficiently flexible attempt law, so that a person can be convicted of both solicitation and attempt for the same behavior? The Code position is that the defendant can be punished for either the solicitation or the attempt, but not both. See §5.05(3).

Most state statutes, like the New York statute, are modeled after section 5.02 (and quite a few states now have such statutes). But until recently, most states did not have provisions dealing specifically with solicitation (although solicitation was a separate offense at common law).

If, under the Model Penal Code, solicitation duplicates attempt, does it do so under other legal schemes as well? The answer depends on the scope or definition of attempt in a particular jurisdiction. Consider first the facts in State v. Davis, 6 S.W.2d 609 (Mo. 1928), where the defendant was convicted of attempted murder, but was never charged with solicitation:

> . . . The evidence submitted on the part of the state warrants the finding that defendant and Alberdina Lourie resided in Kansas City. They were seemingly infatuated with each other, planning and arranging to have Edmon Lourie, the husband of Alberdina, killed so that they could obtain the insurance on his life, aggregating $60,000, as well as cohabit. Edmon Lourie was absent from home the greater part of the time, returning at intervals of two or three weeks. In furtherance of their plan, defendant, acting for himself and Alberdina, arranged to have one Earl Leverton obtain for them the services of an ex-convict to murder Edmon Lourie for hire. Leverton, instead of procuring the services of an ex-convict for that purpose, disclosed the plot to Joel L. Dill, a member of the Kansas City police force, who agreed to pose as an ex-convict to that end. Several meetings were had between defendant, Leverton, and Dill, defendant stating that he and Alberdina were in love, and desired Edmon Lourie killed. He agreed to pay for the execution of the plot. Defendant outlined his plan, offering Dill the sum of $600, with the further agreement that Alberdina, who was to be with her husband at the time of the contemplated assault, would wear diamonds of the value of $3,000. He further arranged for Alberdina and Dill to see each other that each might recognize the other on sight. Defendant, Dill, and Leverton, during January and the early part of February, 1926, held prearranged conferences on the subject. Prior to February 11, 1926, defendant arranged for Dill to go to Chicago to kill Edmon Lourie there, defendant making and giving Dill a map or drawing showing where Lourie could be found, as well as two photographs of him. The arrangements contemplated that, if Dill was unable to locate Lourie, Alberdina would go to Chicago to aid him. The trip to Chicago was to be made about February 12th.
>
> However, Edmon Lourie telegraphed Alberdina that he would return to Kansas City on February 13, 1926, defendant thereupon notifying Leverton, who in turn communicated the fact to Dill. Defendant paid Dill $600, advising him that Alberdina would persuade Edmon to accompany her to a place of amusement, and that she planned to leave their home at 8 o'clock P.M. on February 13, 1926. It was further planned that Alberdina was to carry the diamonds on her person, and that Dill was to shoot Lourie either as they left their home or as they returned, and that Alberdina was to be mussed up and the diamonds taken from her, so that it might appear the result of a robbery. Alberdina was to appear to faint, giving Dill time to make his escape. However, on the night of February 13, 1926, Dill, accompanied by three other police officers, proceeded about 8 o'clock P.M. to the home of Edmon Lourie as arranged. Edmon and Alberdina Lourie were there found dressed and ready to leave, with the diamonds on her person. As Dill and the officers entered the room, she turned her face to the wall as planned. Two officers took charge of Edmon and Alberdina; Dill and the other officer going to the home of defendant, where they arrested him. The defendant had previously informed Dill that he would remain at home in order to have an alibi.
>
> Upon his arrest, defendant made and signed a confession in which he stated that he and Alberdina planned to have Edmon Lourie killed. In pursuance of the plan he met Dill, whom he assumed to be an ex-convict and the subject of hire for

the purpose intended. The day before the contemplated murder he gave Dill $200 and he gave him $400 the day the murder was to be consummated, together with a picture of Edmon Lourie. It was arranged that Dill was to go to Chicago to kill Lourie. Lourie, however, unexpectedly arranged to go home, notifying Alberdina of his intention by telegram. Thereupon Alberdina informed defendant of the fact, whereupon he notified Dill, resulting that the scene of the contemplated murder was changed to Lourie's home in Kansas City. The arrangements contemplated that Alberdina was to accompany Lourie that night to a picture show, and Dill was to stage a holdup and kill Lourie. Alberdina agreed to remove the diamond rings from her fingers, giving them to Dill, and he was to retain them as part payment for the murder of Lourie. Lourie masqueraded under different names, among them Lourie, Frank, Payne, and Edmonds, Alberdina telling defendant that she thought he was a master mind among criminals. The confession was made on the night of February 13, 1926. The evidence establishes that all of the acts complained of occurred in Kansas City, Jackson County, Mo., during January and February, 1926.

The evidence on the part of defendant tends to establish that defendant was urged to agree to the arrangement by Dill and Leverton, but that, after paying the money, he abandoned the crime before an overt act was committed. There was also testimony that Alberdina, the coconspirator, abandoned the plot, which abandonment was communicated to Dill and defendant. Defendant was addicted to drink, and had been an inmate of a sanatorium. It was asserted that all these facts were known to Dill and Leverton, who purchased and gave him liquor while persuading him to continue the plot. [Id. at 610-611.]

The court in *Davis* conceded that Davis had solicited the killing, but held that his actions did not cross the line from preparation to attempt:

> The state contends that the arrangement of a plan for the accomplishment of the murder of Lourie and the selecting and hiring of the means or instrumentality by which the murder was to be consummated were demonstrated. We take it that the state means by the foregoing declarations that overt acts were shown. To that we do not agree. The evidence goes no further than developing a verbal arrangement with Dill, the selection of Dill as the one to kill Lourie, the delivery of a certain drawing and two photographs of Lourie to Dill, and the payment of a portion of the agreed consideration. These things were mere acts of preparation, failing to lead directly or proximately to the consummation of the intended crime. In this regard we have found no authority which holds that preparations constitute an overt act. . . .
>
> The employment of Dill as agent to murder Lourie was not tantamount to an attempt. Dill not only had no intention of carrying out the expressed purpose of defendant, but was guilty of no act directly or indirectly moving toward the consummation of the intended crime. He did nothing more than listen to the plans and solicitations of defendant without intending to act upon them. It was not shown that Dill committed an act that could be construed as an attempt. The arrest of Lourie, his wife, and defendant as detailed in the evidence could not be said to have been based upon an act involving the consummation of the crime. . . . [Id. at 612.]

Assuming that Davis could have been convicted of solicitation, does it make any sense to say he was not guilty of attempt? One concurring judge, Justice White, offered the following unusual perspective on the failed criminal:

> In the argument we were directed to the heinous nature of the crime, where one, who is too cowardly to commit the act himself, employs someone else to do it. That is a serious offense, and no doubt many a crime is committed by a hired agent, but the master minds in the criminal world from whom that danger comes never make

mistakes such as Davis made. They know their men, and they employ real killers. Davis was not only a coward, but a fool. The entire plan and preparation showed the want of judgment and discretion. He has no criminal record, and he is not a dangerous criminal. If every person who, at some time in his or her life, entertained a criminal impulse, was put in jail, a small minority of us would be at large. [Id. at 615.]

3. *Uncommunicated solicitation.* In People v. Saephanh, 80 Cal. App. 4th 451, 94 Cal. Rptr. 910 (2001), the defendant conceived a child with a woman named Cassandra. Later, while in prison before the child was born, he sent a friend a letter urging him to attack Cassandra in order to end the pregnancy. A correctional officer read and impounded the letter, according to standard procedure, so that it was never delivered to its intended recipient. An appellate court concluded that such uncommunicated solicitations do not constitute the crime of "soliciting another" under California law. Nevertheless, the court held that Saephanh's undelivered letter constituted "attempted solicitation," and directed that his conviction be reduced to that offense. Although recognizing the doubly inchoate nature of attempted solicitation, the court reasoned that California's general statute on attempts applies to "any crime" as the object of an attempt.

4. *Solicitation and free speech.* By its very nature, the crime of solicitation can raise troublesome political and constitutional issues. What if a person stands on a soapbox in the city park and urges her listeners to take action against the government by refusing to obey unjust laws? When do solicitation laws clash with free speech rights under the First Amendment? See Brandenburg v. Ohio, 395 U.S. 444 (1969) (speech calling for violation of law may be punished only when it is "directed to inciting or producing imminent lawless action and is likely to incite or produce such action").

D. IMPOSSIBILITY

BOOTH v. STATE
Court of Criminal Appeals of Oklahoma
398 P.2d 863 (1964)

Nix, Judge.

John Fletcher Booth, Jr., was charged by information in the District Court of Oklahoma County with the crime of Receiving Stolen Property, and was found guilty of the lesser crime of Attempt to Receive Stolen Property. The jury assessed his penalty at Two Years in the Oklahoma State Penitentiary, and to pay a fine in the amount of $150.00. From said judgment and sentence the defendant appeals.

The record before this Court reveals that this case arose out of a circumstance as testified to by a self-admitted, well-known thief bearing the name of Charley Stanford, whose FBI "rap sheet" covers 8 pages of arrests extending over a period of 15 years. He was obviously braggadocio about his convictions and related from the witness stand that he had been arrested approximately 300 times on everything in the book, short of murder and rape. He admitted serving 4 terms in the penitentiary, and having been committed to a mental institution twice. He testified, in substance, that in the early morning hours he was walking in the parking lot at the YMCA in Oklahoma City and sighted a topcoat in a parked automobile. That he jimmied the window and removed the coat, took it to his home at 308 N.E. 8th Street where he retired until about 7:00, at which time he proceeded down to a pay telephone where he called his attorney (the defendant herein). He testified that he advised him he had the coat he had ordered, and agreed to let him have the coat for $20.00. Arrangements were made for the defendant to meet him at the thief's home at approximately 11:00 A.M., where the transfer was to be made. He returned home, and a friend came by and invited him to go get a drink. He started from his house to his friend's car and was arrested by Lt. Anthony of the Oklahoma City Police Department. He was wearing the stolen coat at the time of his arrest. Lt. Anthony took Stanford to the police station, and asked him where he had gotten the coat and he confessed getting it from the car in the YMCA parking lot.

Lt. Anthony testified, in substance, that he received an anonymous telephone call at approximately 7:00 A.M. on the morning of the day in question, and proceeded to the YMCA and located the owner of the vehicle that had been burglarized. They went then to the vehicle and observed the wing glass had been broken, pried open, and a gray cashmere coat and some shirts were missing. Officer Anthony proceeded to the 300 block on N.E. 8th and saw an ex-convict by the name Charley Stanford leaving his house wearing a gray cashmere coat. Anthony then and there arrested Stanford for Burglary and took him to the police station. He then called Mr. Gothard to the police station, where he identified the coat as his and asked Lt. Anthony for the coat, but was advised that they needed it as evidence. Officer Anthony, Officer Reading and Stanford proceeded to 308 N.E. 8th taking the recovered coat with them. After arriving, they took their position behind a closet door containing "peep-holes" and waited for the arrival of defendant Booth. According to the testimony of Anthony, the following transpired:

A.   We then went back to the 300 block on 8th Street and I concealed myself in the closet and Mr. Stanford stayed in the other part of the house which was a combination of or the apartment was a combination of a kitchen with a divan on the west side of the room. He laid the overcoat on the divan. And in the door of this clothes closet there was small pin holes and I left the door ajar slightly. Shortly after eleven o'clock Mr. John Booth came to the front door. . . .

Q.   May I ask you and interrupt you at this point. Is that person in the courtroom?
A.   Yes sir.
Q.   Would you please point him out to the Court and Jury, Officer?
A.   That person. (Points to defendant, John Booth.)
Q.   Go ahead.
A.   Booth entered the house, and I heard Charlie say —

By the Court.   (Interrupting) Who do you mean by Charlie?
A.   Charlie Stanford.

By Mr. Thomas.
Q.   Then what?
A.   I heard Charlie Stanford say, "John, I got the coat which you wanted. I need the twenty dollars right away." And Mr. Booth said, "This is child support month, Charlie, come to my office later and I will give you a check." There was other conversation. . . .

Q. Officer Anthony, how long was Mr. Booth in the house? With Charlie Stanford?

A. I would judge about ten minutes.

Q. At which time you were in the closet?

A. Yes, sir.

Q. With the door ajar?

A. Yes, sir. But I was looking mostly through the small pin holes.

Q. Were you able to look through the holes?

A. Yes, sir.

Q. Tell us what you observed.

A. They came into this particular room —

Q. Who is "they"?

A. John Booth and Charlie Stanford. They . . . well, Booth picked up the coat in his arms and there was conversation of [*sic*] and he warned him that the thing was "hot."

Q. Who warned who?

A. Charlie Stanford warned John Booth that the thing was "hot."

Q. That the coat was "hot"?

A. Yes, that's the way he termed it.

Q. What did Mr. Booth say?

A. He said, "Well, I know how to handle things like this, don't worry about it, Charlie."

Q. Then what happened? . . .

By Mr. Thomas.

Q. You testified that Charlie Stanford told him the coat was "hot."

A. He warned him the coat was hot, it was criminal talk, hot or stolen.

Q. What did Booth say?

A. Booth said, "I know how to handle these things."

Q. "I know how to handle these things"?

A. Yes, and "Don't worry about it, Charlie."

Q. Then what happened?

A. At this point they went into a restroom and what went on in there, I didn't hear. Then they came back out, and Booth went to his car and put the coat in the turtle-back [*sic*] of his car and then returned to the house and that is about all that occurred.

Q. Altogether then Mr. Booth was in Charlie Stanford's house about how long?

A. About ten minutes.

Q. Did he leave?

A. Yes, he left.

After taking Stanford to the police station, Anthony obtained a search warrant and then maintained a surveillance of Booth's house until he arrived. He then entered the premises, arrested Booth, and again recovered the coat.

Though defendant Booth was charged with Receiving Stolen Property, at the conclusion of the evidence and after the state and defendant had rested their case, the trial judge gave the following instruction:

> You are instructed that under the law of this case you are at liberty to consider only the included offense of whether the defendant John Fletcher Booth may be

guilty of the crime of Attempt to Receive Stolen Property. In this regard you are instructed, an attempt to commit a crime is defined as being the compound of two elements.

(1) The intent to commit a crime.

(2) A direct ineffectual act done towards its commission.

Preparation alone to an attempt to commit a crime is not sufficient.

No doubt this instruction was given based upon the theory that once stolen property has been recovered by the police it loses its character as stolen property. This appears to have been the contention of defense counsel as reflected by the record.

Then the following Motion was made by defense counsel:

> The defendant at this time renews his motion to quash the information for the reason that the evidence introduced in this trial substantially shows that the crime of Receiving Stolen Property could not have been committed under the circumstances of this case, to-wit: The fact that the officers and all of the state's witnesses admitted that the alleged stolen coat had been recovered by the police, that the owner had identified it, that the police checked it and later turned it over to a thief for the purpose of delivery to this defendant.

The trial judge then adjourned court until the following day, stating that there were no guidelines or guideposts in this state and that it would take some little time to prepare the instructions. Thus the prepared instruction number two as heretofore recited was given.

In view of said instruction, we are justified in assuming that the trial judge and all parties concerned were in agreement. That under the testimony in the instant case, the coat had lost its character as stolen property when recovered by the police, and the owner apprised of the recovery and identified the coat as the one taken from him.

The general rule evidently adopted by the trial court is stated in 76 C.J.S., Receiving Stolen Goods §5, pg. 7, as follows:

> In order to convict of receiving stolen goods, the goods in question must have retained their stolen character at the time they were received by accused; if they were stolen, they continue to be stolen goods until they are recovered by their owner or some one for him. Hence, where the actual physical possession of stolen goods has been recovered by the owner or his agent and afterwards carried to the receiver either by the original thief or the instrumentality through which the thief originally intended to convey it, at the express direction of the owner or his agent, for the purpose of entrapping the receiver, his receiving of the goods is not a receiving of stolen goods.

The law seems to be clear on this point, leaving the only question to be decided as whether or not the defendant could be convicted of an attempt to receive stolen property in such cases. It is the defendant's contention that if he could not be convicted of the substantive charge, because the coat had lost its character as stolen property; neither could he be convicted of an attempt because the coat was not in the category of stolen property at the time he received it.

The briefs filed in the case, and extensive research have revealed that two states have passed squarely on the question — New York and California. It is definitely one of first impression in Oklahoma.

The New York Court, in passing upon the question, laid down the following rule in the case of People v. Jaffe, 185 N.Y. 497, 78 N.E. 169, 6 L.R.A., N.S. 263, on the following facts:

> A clerk stole goods from his employer under an agreement to sell them to accused, but before delivery of the goods the theft was discovered and the goods were recovered. Later the employer redelivered the goods to the clerk to sell to accused, who purchased them for about one-half of their value, believing them to have been stolen.
>
> Held, that the goods had lost their character as stolen goods at the time defendant purchased them, and that his criminal intent was insufficient to sustain a conviction for an attempt to receive stolen property, knowing it to have been stolen.

The *Jaffe* case, *supra,* was handed down in 1906, and has prevailed as the law in New York state 58 years without modification.

The State of California has passed upon the question several times and up until 1959, they followed the rule laid down in the *Jaffe* case, *supra.*

In 1959, in the case of People v. Comodeca, 52 Cal. 2d 142, 338 P.2d 903, the California Court abandoned the *Jaffe* rationale that a person accepting goods which he believes to have been stolen, but which was not in fact stolen goods, is not guilty of an attempt to receive stolen goods, and imposed a liability for the attempt, overruling its previous holding to the contrary in the above cited cases. . . .

Though the instant case, insofar as it pertains to the specific crime of attempting to receive stolen property, is one of first impression in Oklahoma, this Court held in Nemecek v. State, 72 Okla. Cr. 195, 114 P.2d 492, 135 A.L.R. 1149, involving attempting to receive money by false pretenses:

> A[n] accused cannot be convicted of an attempt to commit a crime unless he could have been convicted of the crime itself if his attempt had been successful. Where the act, if accomplished, would not constitute the crime intended, there is no indictable attempt.

In the *Nemecek* case, *supra,* the Court quotes with approval In re Schurman, 40 Kan. 533, 20 P. 277; wherein the Kansas Court said:

> With reference to attempt, it has also been said that "if all which the accused person intended would, had it been done, constitute no substantive crime, it cannot be a crime, under the name 'attempt,' to do, with the same purpose, a part of this thing."

. . . The question of "impossibility" was raised for the first time in Regina v. McPherson, Dears. & B. 197, 201 (1857), when Baron Bramwell said:

> The argument that a man putting his hand into an empty pocket might be convicted of an attempt to steal appeared to me at first plausible; but suppose a man, believing a block of wood to be a man who was his deadly enemy, struck it a blow intending to murder, could he be convicted of attempting to murder the man he took it to be?

Subsequently, in Regina v. Collins, 9 Cox C.C. 497, 169 Eng. Rep. 1477 (1864), the Court expressly held that attempted larceny was not made out by proof that the defendant pickpocket actually inserted his hand into the victim's pocket with intent to steal. Chief Justice Cockburn, declaring, at page 499:

> We think that an attempt to commit a felony can only be made out when, if no interruption had taken place, the attempt could have been carried out successfully, and the felony completed of the attempt to commit which the party is charged.

This very broad language, encompassing as it did all forms of "impossibility," was subsequently rejected by the English courts and it was held that the inability of the pickpocket to steal from an empty pocket did not preclude his conviction of an attempted larceny. Regina v. Ring, 17 Cox C.C. 491, 66 L.T. (N.S.) 306 (1892).

In this country it is generally held that a defendant may be charged with an attempt of "physical or factual impossibility," whereas a "legal impossibility" in the completion of the crime precludes prosecution for an attempt.

What is a "legal impossibility" as distinguished from a "physical or factual impossibility" has over a long period of time perplexed our courts and has resulted in many irreconcilable decisions and much philosophical discussion by legal scholars.

The reason for the "impossibility" of completing the substantive crime ordinarily falls into one of two categories: (1) Where the act if completed would not be criminal, a situation which is usually described as a "legal impossibility," and (2) where the basic or substantive crime is impossible of completion, simply because of some physical or factual condition unknown to the defendant, a situation which is usually described as a "factual impossibility."

The authorities in the various states and the text-writers are in general agreement that where there is a "legal impossibility" of completing the substantive crime, the accused cannot be successfully charged with an attempt, whereas in those cases in which the "factual impossibility" situation is involved, the accused may be convicted of an attempt. Detailed discussion of the subject is unnecessary to make it clear that it is frequently most difficult to compartmentalize a particular set of facts as coming within one of the categories rather than the other. Examples of the so-called "legal impossibility" situations are:

(a) A person accepting goods which he believes to have been stolen, but which were not in fact stolen goods, is not guilty of an attempt to receive stolen goods (People v. Jaffe, 185 N.Y. 497, 78 N.E. 169, 9 L.R.A. N.S. 263).

(b) It is not an attempt to commit subornation of perjury where the false testimony solicited, if given, would have been immaterial to the case at hand and hence not perjurious (People v. Teal, 196 N.Y. 372, 89 N.E. 1086. 25 L.R.A. N.S. 120).

(c) An accused who offers a bribe to a person believed to be a juror, but who is not a juror, is not guilty of an attempt to bribe a juror (State v. Taylor, 345 Mo. 325, 133 S.W.2d 336).

(d) An official who contracts a debt which is unauthorized and a nullity, but which he believes to be valid, is not guilty of an attempt to illegally contract a valid debt (Marley v. State, 58 N.J.L. 207, 33 A.208).

(e) A hunter who shoots a stuffed deer believing it to be alive is not guilty of an attempt to shoot a deer out of season (State v. Guffey, 262 S.W.2d 152 (Mo. App.)).

Examples of cases in which attempt convictions have been sustained on the theory that all that prevented the consummation of the completed crime was a "factual impossibility" are:

(a) The picking of an empty pocket (People v. Moran, 123 N.Y. 254, 25 N.E. 412, 10 L.R.A. 109; Commonwealth v. McDonald, 5 Gush. 365 (Mass.); People v. Jones, 46 Mich. 441, 9 N.W. 486).

(b) An attempt to steal from an empty receptacle (Clark v. State, 86 Tenn. 511, 8 S.W. 145) or an empty house (State v. Utley, 82 N.C. 556).

(c) Where defendant shoots into the intended victim's bed, believing he is there, when in fact he is elsewhere (State v. Mitchell, 170 Mo. 633, 71 S.W. 175).

(d) Where the defendant erroneously believing that the gun is loaded points it at his wife's head and pulls the trigger (State v. Damms, 9 Wis. 2d 183, 100 N.W.2d 592, 79 A.L.R.2d 1402).

(e) Where the woman upon whom the abortion operation is performed is not in fact pregnant (Commonwealth v. Tibbetts, 157 Mass. 519, 32 N.E. 910; People v. Huff, 339 Ill. 328, 171 N.E. 261; and Peckham v. United States, 96 U.S. App. D.C. 312, 266 F.2d 34).

In the case at bar the stolen coat had been recovered by the police for the owner and consequently had, according to the well-established law in this country, lost its character as stolen property. Therefore, a legal impossibility precluded defendant from being prosecuted for the crime of Knowingly Receiving Stolen Property.

It would strain reasoning beyond a logical conclusion to hold contrary to the rule previously stated herein, that,

> If all which the accused person intended would, had it been done, have constituted no substantive crime, it cannot be a crime under the name "attempt" to do, with the same purpose, a part of this thing.

If a series of acts together will not constitute an offense, how can it be said that one of the acts alone will constitute an indictable offense? Bishop Crim. Law §747.

The rule is well stated by the English Court in the case of R. v. Percy, Ltd. 33 Crim. App. R. 102 (1949):

> Steps on the way to the commission of what would be a crime, if the acts were completed, may amount to attempts to commit that crime, to which, unless interrupted, they would have led; but steps on the way to the doing of something, which is thereafter done, and which is no crime, cannot be regarded as attempts to commit a crime.

Sayre, 41 Harvard Law Review 821, 853-54 (1928) states the rationale in this manner:

> It seems clear that cases (where none of the intended consequences is in fact criminal) cannot constitute criminal attempts. If none of the consequences which the defendant sought to achieve constitute a crime, surely his unsuccessful efforts to achieve his object cannot constitute a criminal attempt. The partial fulfillment of an object not criminal cannot itself be criminal. If the whole is not criminal, the part cannot be.

The defendant in the instant case leaves little doubt as to his moral guilt. The evidence, as related by the self-admitted and perpetual law violator indicates defendant fully intended to do the act with which he was charged. However, it is fundamental to our law that a man is not punished merely because he has a criminal mind. It must be shown that he has, with that criminal mind, done an act which is forbidden by the criminal law.

Adhering to this principle, the following example would further illustrate the point.

A fine horse is offered to A at a ridiculously low price by B, who is a known horse thief. A, believing the horse to be stolen, buys the same without inquiry. In fact, the horse had been raised from a colt by B and was not stolen. It would be bordering on absurdity to suggest that A's frame of mind, if proven, would support a conviction of an attempt. It would be a "legal impossibility."

Our statute provides that defendant must attempt to Knowingly Receive Stolen Property before a conviction will stand. How could one know property to be stolen when it was not? The statute needs to be changed so it would be less favorable to the criminal.

J. C. Smith, a Reader in Law, University of Nottingham, B.A., Cambridge, 1949, LL. B., 1950, M.A., 1954, said in an article (70 Harvard Law Review 422) supporting the *Jaffe* case, *supra*, and the above reasoning:

> If it appears wrong that the accused should escape unpunished in the particular circumstances, then it may be that there is something wrong with the substantive law and his act ought to be criminal. But the remedy then is to alter the substantive crime. Otherwise "there is no actus reus because 'the accident has turned up in his favour'" and the accused ought to be acquitted. When a man has achieved all the consequences which he set out to achieve and those consequences do not, in the existing circumstances, amount to an actus reus, it is in accordance both with principle and authority that that man should be held not guilty of any crime.

We earnestly suggest that the Legislature revise the law on Attempts in accordance with The American Law Institute for the adoption of a "Model Penal Code," which Article 5.01 defines "Criminal Attempts" in the following manner.

> (1) Definition of Attempt. A person is guilty of an attempt to commit a crime if, acting with the kind of culpability otherwise required for commission of the crime, he:
>
> (a) purposely engages in conduct which would constitute the crime if the attendant circumstances were as he believes them to be; or,
>
> (b) when causing a particular result in an element of the crime, does or omits to do anything with the purpose of causing or with the belief that it will cause such result, without further conduct on his part; or,
>
> (c) purposely does or omits to do anything which, under the circumstances as he believes them to be, is a substantial step in a course of conduct planned to culminate in his commission of the crime.

The Clerk of this Court is requested to send a copy of this decision to the Legislative Council for consideration, as our Court can only adjudicate, it cannot legislate.

In view of our statutory law, and the decisions herein related, it is our duty to Reverse this case, with orders to Dismiss, and it is so ordered. However, there are other avenues open to the County Attorney which should be explored.

Notes and Questions

1. *The conundrum of impossibility: legal vs. factual.* Carefully review the case summaries cited in the *Booth* opinion to illustrate the purported difference between "legal impossibility" (traditionally a good defense) and "factual impossibility" (traditionally no defense). The court heroically tries to explain the common law distinction between "legal impossibility" and "factual impossibility" as follows:

> (1) Where the act if completed would not be criminal, a situation which is usually described as a "legal impossibility," and (2) where the basic or substantive crime is impossible of completion, simply because of some physical or factual condition unknown to the defendant, a situation which is usually described as a "factual impossibility."

Can you perceive relevant distinctions between the two groups of cases? Do these definitions resolve the specific cases listed in the opinion?

A common criticism of common law tests of impossibility is that their application depends on arbitrarily selecting one among many correct descriptions of defendant's act. As an exercise, try to think of two alternative descriptions of the following eight acts — one that would justify exonerating the act as a "legally" impossible attempt under *Booth*, and one that would not:

1. Picking an empty pocket.
2. Shooting an empty bed.
3. Shooting a stuffed deer out of season.
4. Offering a bribe to a nonjuror.
5. Shooting a dead body.
6. Buying talcum powder, believing it is heroin.
7. Receiving recovered property.
8. Selling talcum powder, believing it is heroin.

2. As the *Booth* opinion indicates, some courts have proposed that "factually impossible" attempts should not be punishable. One popular formulation is that an attempt is "factually impossible" if defendant's act does not increase the probability that the offense-in-chief will be completed. Review the eight scenarios listed in the previous note, and try to think of two descriptions for each, one justifying conviction and one justifying acquittal under this "factual impossibility" defense.

3. In United States v. Yang, 281 F.3d 534 (6th Cir. 2002), the defendant was charged with attempting to steal a trade secret, but the arrest was actually made in a sting operation, in which Yang was offered a nonexistent trade secret. The court held:

> ... Here, the purpose of the [Economic Espionage Act] was to provide a comprehensive tool for law enforcement personnel to use to fight theft of trade secrets. To follow the Yangs' reasoning and rule as they ask would eviscerate the effectiveness of the act. The government would be severely limited in its ability to use the assistance of people willing to cooperate to catch and convict thieves of trade secrets. In effect, the Yangs' position would, as the Third Circuit pointed out, force "the government to disclose trade secrets to the very persons suspected of trying to steal them, thus gutting enforcement efforts under the EEA." United States v. Hsu, 155 F.3d 189, 202 (3d Cir. 1998). [Id. at 543].

4. *The "rational motivation" test.* Prof. George Fletcher proposes a "rational motivation" test to resolve the conundrum of "impossible attempts":[11]

> The concepts of "trying" and "attempting" are rooted in English usage and therefore we should probe the semantic rules that generate the boundaries of these concepts. . . .
>
> Let us consider a mundane case of acting under a mistaken belief about the date or the day of the week. Suppose that Paul is trying to fix a leaky faucet on Saturday, and while he is working, he happens mistakenly to think that it is Friday. What is Paul trying to do? To fix a faucet on Friday or simply to fix a faucet? Subjectivist theory, as expressed in the Model Penal Code, suggests that Paul's conduct should be judged according to the circumstances as he takes them to be. Thus his mistaken belief about the day should be incorporated in the description about what he is trying to do. It follows that he is attempting to fix a faucet on Friday. Yet this way of proceeding is not only counterintuitive, it generates absurd results. Suppose Paul were mistaken about any number of other things, such as whether there was life on Mars or whether the president was then at work in the Oval Office. Would we say that he was trying to fix the faucet so long as there was life on Mars or while the president was at work? It is obvious that a mistake about *X* is not sufficient to say that one is trying to do *X*. . . .
>
> There are some cases in which a mistake about the date does bear on an accurate description of what the actor is trying to do. Suppose that a taxpayer is working energetically to finish his income tax forms on Friday in the belief that the date is April 15, and his forms have to be in the mail by midnight on the 15th. In fact it is only April 14. It seems intuitively plausible to say that he is trying to finish his income tax forms by April 15. His mistake about the date proves to be relevant in an account of what he was doing.
>
> On the basis of these examples, we may hazard a general thesis about the relevance of mistakes on attempting. The thesis is this: mistaken beliefs are relevant to what the actor is trying to do if they affect his incentive in acting. They affect his incentive if knowing of the mistake would give him a good reason for changing his course of conduct. If Paul had known that it was Friday rather than Saturday, his being disabused of his mistake presumably would not give him a good reason for postponing his efforts to fix the faucet. Therefore his mistaken belief does not affect his incentive; nor, by like token, his mistaken belief about whether the president is then at work in the Oval Office. On the other hand, if our conscientious taxpayer were told that it was only April 14, he might well decide to relax for the rest of the day and finish the following day. His mistake does bear on his incentive and therefore it should be included in the description of what he is trying to do.
>
> We shall refer to this thesis as the test of rational motivation. Its validity as a theory depends on its providing an account of what ordinary people mean when they talk about "trying" or "attempting" to do something. . . .
>
> Now let us apply the test of rational motivation to [one of the troublesome cases]. . . . In *Jaffe* . . . , the test supports the conclusion of the courts that there is no act of attempting. . . . [I]t seems fairly clear that the fact that the cloth was stolen does not affect the actor's incentive in paying the price at which the cloth was offered to him by the police. If he were told that the goods were not stolen, that would not have provided him with a reason for turning down the offer. If they were not stolen, so much the better. It follows, therefore, that it is inappropriate to describe his conduct as attempting to receive stolen cloth. At least it is no more plausible to say that Jaffe was trying to receive stolen cloth than it is to say that Paul was trying to fix his faucet on Friday. . . . In [this and other] . . . cases, the test

11. George Fletcher, Rethinking Criminal Law 161 (1978).

of rational motivation yields results that are at odds with the subjectivist standard that the circumstances should be taken as the actor believes them to be. On the latter test, Jaffe . . . [is] guilty.

How would Fletcher's "rational motivation" test decide *Booth*? Would knowing that the goods were not stolen deter Booth from buying them at the price paid? If not, could he be exonerated on the "ordinary language" premise that he was not "attempting to buy stolen goods"? If so, Fletcher's test conflicts with the Model Penal Code, which Fletcher criticizes.

Was Booth "attempting to buy a particular good" (which happened to be stolen) or to buy a particular good because that good was stolen? If we are unsure — that is, if Booth's act is equivocal as between an innocent purpose and a guilty one — should Booth be given the benefit of the doubt? Or should his willingness to risk buying stolen goods convict him?

Professor John Hasnas has recently offered a simplified version of Fletcher's rational motivation test.[12] According to Hasnas, courts can reach the same results simply by treating attempts as impossible if any statutorily required attendant circumstance element is absent. Hasnas reasons that an attempt is an effort to achieve a certain result, and that if the result is achieved with no crime being completed, the perpetrator's act is not aptly characterized as a failed attempt to commit a crime. Thus, if property possessed is not stolen, there is no attempt to receive stolen property; if entry is with permission, there is no attempted burglary. In these examples, a rationally motivated actor would not usually care that the proscribed attendant circumstance was absent.

But does this attendant circumstance test "work" for other examples? Consider a statute prohibiting the distribution of pornography over the Internet to a person under 10 years old. Should an attempt to commit this crime be considered impossible when the recipient of pornography is a police officer representing himself as a child under ten? Or, should an attempt to possess 1,000 grams of cocaine be considered impossible if the amount possessed is only 800 grams? The age of a victim and the weight of a drug appear to be attendant circumstances; yet wouldn't a "rationally motivated pedophile" find the age of the victim salient,[13] and a "rationally motivated drug consumer" find the weight of the drug salient?

Hasnas claims that his test is easier to administer than Fletcher's rational motivation test, but is it? Can we always tell whether an element is a circumstance element rather than a result element?

5. *More on the attemptor's motivation.* Reconsider six cases posed above from the standpoint of the Fletcher and Hasnas tests and the Model Penal Code's subjective test:

1. Picking an empty pocket.
2. Shooting an empty bed.
3. Shooting a stuffed deer out of season.
4. Offering a bribe to a nonjuror.
5. Shooting a dead body.
6. Buying talcum powder, believing it is heroin.

12. John Hasnas, Once More Unto the Breach: The Inherent Liberalism of the Criminal Law and Liability for Attempting the Impossible, 54 Hastings L. J. 1, 7-14 (2002).

13. For more on impossible attempts in the context of Internet stings, reconsider the Hasnas test in light of the People v. Thousand case, p. 683, *infra*.

Do the tests yield different results in any of these cases?
Now reconsider two additional cases:

7. Receiving recovered property.
8. Selling talcum powder, believing it is heroin.

Do the tests yield different results in these cases?

6. *Magical attempts.* What about the person who attempts to kill using voodoo? John Henry and Leroy Ivy, two brothers from Tupelo, Mississippi, were charged with conspiracy to commit murder — by voodoo.[14] The two men allegedly planned to kill the judge who previously sentenced one of them to a 40-year prison term for armed robbery. They were arrested when they approached the judge's housekeeper and offered her $100 in exchange for a photograph of the judge and a lock of his hair. These items were allegedly to be sent to a witch doctor so that a hex could be placed on the judge. Local officials claimed that the central issue in the case was the payment of money to have a judge killed and not the voodoo plot. If we believe the voodoo plot is likely to be ineffective, why should the Ivy brothers be charged with conspiracy to commit murder? Is the charge justified because we do not know that these voodoo conspirators will not come around to a more efficacious means of accomplishing their end? Could the court charge the Ivy brothers with attempted murder? What substantial step did they take? If they had sent the items to the witch doctor, would that qualify as a substantial step? See MPC §5.05(2) (allowing mitigation in such cases).

How would Fletcher's "rational motivation" test resolve such attempts to kill by magic? Can it apply at all to conduct that seems inherently irrational?

Now reconsider such cases from the standpoint of the "factual impossibility" standard articulated in note 2 above. Does the "factual impossibility" standard yield a clearer answer in these cases than in the eight cases posed previously? Does it yield a clearer answer than Fletcher's "rational motivation" test?

7. How should we handle the case of the person who attempts to vote, thinking that she is below the appropriate age of 18? In fact, due to a mixup on her birth certificate, she is 19 years old. Is this like the voodoo case? A routine analysis under the Model Penal Code would hold her liable because she thought she was committing a crime and, but for the fact that her age was greater than she thought, would have committed it. On the other hand, if the attempt law is based on some degree of social dangerousness — the view that next time the actor will get it right — we know that she will never be below 18 again. Should it make a difference that, based on her actions, if the law raised the voting age to 21, she then would be likely to violate it? That she might violate some other voting law?

8. *The absent-minded professor's crime.* What about the case where the professor is sitting in the Faculty Club having lunch when it starts raining? He has to go back to class and, rather than getting wet, decides that he will steal from the cloakroom a particularly attractive umbrella. He muses that he has one of the same type at home and that it will keep him very dry and not turn inside-out in the heavy wind. What he does not know is that he left that very umbrella there a week ago when the rain, which had been falling on his way to have lunch,

14. 2 Charged in Voodoo Plot, San Francisco Examiner, Feb. 17, 1989, at A-22; Voodoo Attempt, ABAJ. 48 (Sept. 1989).

suddenly stopped. He marches out with the umbrella and, in an excess of guilt, confesses what he regards as his theft to the nearest police officer. Should he be deemed guilty of an attempt? Would he be guilty under the Model Penal Code? Does your answer reveal a defect in the drafting of the Model Penal Code?

9. *Drug sales and impossibility.* In United States v. Sobrilski, 127 F.3d 669 (8th Cir. 1997), the defendants Sobrilski and Martin arranged to sell some methamphetamine to one Bickers, who was actually an undercover officer. Sobrilski had obtained a large quantity of a powdered substance from Widner and Malthus, who had tried to make the methamphetamine (or "crank") but had botched the process, and instead had produced a harmless substance called phenylacetic acid; this powder has the same odor, appearance and ingredients as amphetamine or methamphetamine, but is not a controlled substance.

After Bickers went through the motions of a purchase, Bickers was arrested, and only later did the government learn that the substance was not actually a controlled one. Sobriliski appealed on the ground that it was an unpunishable impossible attempt.

> At trial, Sobrilski testified that when he sold the substance to Sergeant Bickers, he knew it was not crank because it neither smelled nor tasted like crank and did not give him the "rush" typically associated with crank. He stated that when he broke the flask to remove the quarter pound which he sold to Sergeant Bickers, the substance was wet and Sobrilski knew that crank normally is dry. Sobrilski testified that he intended to sell only a non-controlled substance, and that he would not have tried to steal the officers' money had he known they were police officers. . . .
>
> Ordinarily, legal impossibility is a defense to a charge of attempt, but factual impossibility is not. The line between the two kinds of impossibility frequently is difficult to draw. Legal impossibility occurs when the actions which the defendant performs or sets in motion, even if fully carried out as he desires, would not constitute a crime. Factual impossibility occurs when the objective of the defendant is proscribed by the criminal law but a circumstance unknown to the actor prevents him from bringing about that objective.
>
> It is unnecessary to decide whether the impossibility here involved was legal or factual. That is because we agree with the decision of the Third Circuit in United States v. Everett, 700 F.2d 900 (3d Cir. 1983), that in enacting section 406 of the Comprehensive Drug Abuse and Prevention Control Act of 1970, 21 U.S.C. 846 (1994), the provision under which Sobrilski and Martin were convicted, "Congress intended to eliminate the defense of impossibility." Everett, 700 F.2d at 904.
>
> The Third Circuit . . . concluded that this was "a statute by which Congress intended to punish attempts even when completion of the attempted crime was impossible." Id. at 903. It also discerned such a Congressional intent in the "purpose" of the Drug Act "to strengthen the drug laws." Id. at 906-07. The court concluded that "[i]mpossibility is therefore no defense to the charge of attempted distribution of a controlled substance under 21 U.S.C. 846 (1976)"; and that "[t]he distribution of a non-controlled substance believed to be a controlled substance thus constitutes an attempt to distribute a controlled substance under section 846." Id. at 908.
>
> Sobrilski negotiated to sell what he referred to as drugs, increased the previously negotiated price for what he described as pure "crank" because of its higher quality, and suggested that the buyer dilute it because otherwise people using it could harm themselves; stated that he could provide up to a pound and a half a week on two hours' notice; when he was arrested stated "you got me" and offered to cooperate to secure leniency; during his five-hour automobile ride with the arresting officers to show them where he obtained the drugs, he did not tell them

that the white powder he had attempted to sell to them was not amphetamine; and after his arrest he told Ellison [his partner] that the police had overlooked some drugs in the trailer, which he hoped to sell to raise money for a lawyer.

The evidence showing Martin's participation in the attempt also was sufficient to show that she believed and intended that the substance they were attempting to sell was amphetamine. She told the purchaser that she liked the drug and did not have to pay for it; she retrieved the drug sample that had been left on the kitchen table; and after her arrest told Patty Lowe and Sharon See that the police had overlooked some crank in the trailer, which she intended to sell to raise bond money.[15] [Id. at 673-676.]

How would the common law have handled this case? Is the court's approach better?

10. *A twist: the fraudulent drug seller.* In *Sobrilski,* the prosecution could prove that the defendants thought they were selling controlled substances and, of course, believed their attempt to do so to be culpable and dangerous enough to warrant punishment. But is it also (somewhat) culpable and dangerous for people to sell drugs when they know what they are selling is harmless? The Texas Penal Code had then contained Article 4476-15b, addressing this issue as follows:

§2. DELIVERY PROHIBITED.
    (a) A person commits an offense if the person knowingly or intentionally delivers a simulated controlled substance and the person:
        (1) expressly represents the substance to be a controlled substance (or)
        (2) represents the substance to be a controlled substance in a manner that would lead a reasonable person to believe that the substance is a controlled substance.

Boykin v. State, 818 S.W.2d 782 (Tex. Ct. Crim. App. 1991) overturned a conviction for "expressly" representing a soap derivative as cocaine when the defendant used street slang (a "twenty cent rock") to describe his wares to an undercover police officer. What was the purpose of Article 4476-15b? What danger was the legislature concerned about? Is this an attempt statute?

PEOPLE v. DLUGASH
Court of Appeals of New York
41 N.Y.2d 725, 363 N.E.2d 1155 (1977)

JASEN, JUDGE.

The criminal law is of ancient origin, but criminal liability for attempt to commit a crime is comparatively recent. At the root of the concept of attempt liability are the very aims and purposes of penal law. The ultimate issue is whether an individual's intentions and actions, though failing to achieve a manifest and malevolent criminal purpose, constitute a danger to organized society of suffi-

15. Under the Federal Sentencing Guidelines §2D1.1, a key factor in punishment for a drug sale is the type and volume of the drug sold; and the guideline level for a completed sale also applies to an attempted sale. In *Sobrilski,* the police weighed the powder in the defendants' possession at 2,041 grams; the court then applied the Guideline level for real methamphetamine; and, after looking to other relevant factors, affirmed sentences of 188 and 78 months for the two defendants. 127 F.2d at 676. Can the drafters of the Guidelines have intended this approach?

cient magnitude to warrant the imposition of criminal sanctions. Difficulties in theoretical analysis . . . appear dramatically in reference to . . . the continuing controversy when, if at all, the impossibility of successfully completing the criminal act should preclude liability for even making the futile attempt. The 1967 revision of the Penal law approached the impossibility defense to the inchoate crime of attempt in a novel fashion. The statute provides that, if a person engages in conduct which would otherwise constitute an attempt to commit a crime, "it is no defense to a prosecution for such attempt that the crime charged to have been attempted was, under the attendant circumstances, factually or legally impossible of commission, if such crime could have been committed had the attendant circumstances been as such person believed them to be." (Penal Law, §110.10.) This appeal presents to us, for the first time, a case involving the application of the modern statute. We hold that, under the proof presented by the People at trial, defendant Melvin Dlugash may be held for attempted murder, though the target of the attempt may have already been slain, by the hand of another, when Dlugash made his felonious attempt.

On December 22, 1973, Michael Geller, 25 years old, was found shot to death in the bedroom of his Brooklyn apartment. The body, which had literally been riddled by bullets, was found lying face up on the floor. An autopsy revealed that the victim had been shot in the face and head no less than seven times. Powder burns on the face indicated that the shots had been fired from within one foot of the victim. Four small caliber bullets were recovered from the victim's skull. The victim had also been critically wounded in the chest. One heavy caliber bullet passed through the left lung, penetrated the heart chamber, pierced the left ventricle of the heart upon entrance and again upon exit, and lodged in the victim's torso. Although a second bullet was damaged beyond identification, the bullet tracks indicated that these wounds were also inflicted by a bullet of heavy caliber. A tenth bullet, of unknown caliber, passed through the thumb of the victim's left hand. The autopsy report listed the cause of death as "[m]ultiple bullet wounds of head and chest with brain injury and massive bilateral hemothorax with penetration of [the] heart." Subsequent ballistics examination established that the four bullets recovered from the victim's head were .25 caliber bullets and that the heart-piercing bullet was of .38 caliber.

. . . [During police questioning,] Defendant stated that, on the night of December 21, 1973, he, [Joe] Bush and Geller had been out drinking. Bush had been staying at Geller's apartment and, during the course of the evening, Geller several times demanded that Bush pay $100 towards the rent on the apartment. According to defendant, Bush rejected these demands, telling Geller that "you better shut up or you're going to get a bullet." All three returned to Geller's apartment at approximately midnight, took seats in the bedroom, and continued to drink until sometime between 3:00 and 3:30 in the morning. When Geller again pressed his demand for rent money, Bush drew his .38 caliber pistol, aimed it at Geller and fired three times. Geller fell to the floor. After the passage of a few minutes, perhaps two, perhaps as much as five, defendant walked over to the fallen Geller, drew his .25 caliber pistol, and fired approximately five shots in the victim's head and face. Defendant contended that, by the time he fired the shots, "it looked like Mike Geller was already dead." After the shots were fired, defendant and Bush walked to the apartment of a female acquaintance. Bush removed his shirt, wrapped the two guns and a knife in it, and left the apartment, telling Dlugash that he intended to dispose of the weapons. Bush returned 10 or 15 minutes later and stated that he had thrown the weapons down a sewer two or three blocks away.

After [police detective] Carrasquillo had taken the bulk of the statement, he asked the defendant why he would do such a thing. According to Carrasquillo, the defendant said, "Gee, I really don't know." Carrasquillo repeated the question 10 minutes later, but received the same response. After a while, Carrasquillo asked the question for a third time and defendant replied, "Well, gee, I guess it must have been because I was afraid of Joe Bush."

At approximately 9:00 P.M., the defendant repeated the substance of his statement to an Assistant District Attorney. Defendant added that at the time he shot at Geller, Geller was not moving and his eyes were closed. While he did not check for a pulse, defendant stated that Geller had not been doing anything to him at the time he shot because "Mike was dead."

Defendant was indicted by the Grand Jury of Kings County on a single count of murder in that, acting in concert with another person actually present, he intentionally caused the death of Michael Geller. At the trial, there were four principal prosecution witnesses: Detective Carrasquillo, the Assistant District Attorney who took the second admission, and two physicians from the office of the New York City Chief Medical Examiner. For proof of defendant's culpability, the prosecution relied upon defendant's own admissions as related by the detective and the prosecutor. From the physicians, the prosecution sought to establish that Geller was still alive at the time defendant shot at him. Both physicians testified that each of the two chest wounds, for which defendant alleged Bush to be responsible, would have caused death without prompt medical attention. Moreover, the victim would have remained alive until such time as his chest cavity became fully filled with blood. Depending on the circumstances, it might take 5 to 10 minutes for the chest cavity to fill. Neither prosecution witness could state, with medical certainty, that the victim was still alive when, perhaps five minutes after the initial chest wounds were inflicted, the defendant fired at the victim's head.

The defense produced but a single witness, the former Chief Medical Examiner of New York City. This expert stated that, in his view, Geller might have died of the chest wounds "very rapidly" since, in addition to the bleeding, a large bullet going through a lung and the heart would have other adverse medical effects. "Those wounds can be almost immediately or rapidly fatal or they may be delayed in there, in the time it would take for death to occur. But I would say that wounds like that which are described here as having gone through the lungs and the heart would be fatal wounds and in most cases they're rapidly fatal."

The jury found the defendant guilty of murder. The defendant then moved to set the verdict aside. He submitted an affidavit in which he contended that he "was absolutely, unequivocally and positively certain that Michael Geller was dead before [he] shot him." This motion was denied.[16]

On appeal, the Appellate Division reversed the judgment of conviction on the law and dismissed the indictment. The court ruled that "the People failed

---

16. It should be noted that Joe Bush pleaded guilty to a charge of manslaughter in the first degree. At the time he entered his plea, Bush detailed his version of the homicide. According to Bush, defendant Dlugash was a dealer in narcotic drugs and Dlugash claimed that Geller owed him a large sum of money from drug purchases. Bush was in the kitchen alone when Geller entered and threatened him with a shotgun. Bush pulled out his .38 caliber pistol and fired five times at Geller. Geller slumped to the floor. Dlugash then entered, withdrew his .25 caliber pistol and fired five shots into the deceased's face. Bush, however, never testified at Dlugash's trial.

to prove beyond a reasonable doubt that Geller had been alive at the time he was shot by defendant; defendant's conviction of murder thus cannot stand." Further, the court held that the judgment could not be modified to reflect a conviction for attempted murder because "the uncontradicted evidence is that the defendant, at the time that he fired the five shots into the body of the decedent, believed him to be dead, and . . . there is not a scintilla of evidence to contradict his assertion in that regard."

Preliminarily, we state our agreement with the Appellate Division that the evidence did not establish, beyond a reasonable doubt, that Geller was alive at the time defendant fired into his body. To sustain a homicide conviction, it must be established, beyond a reasonable doubt, that the defendant caused the death of another person. . . . Whatever else it may be, it is not murder to shoot a dead body.

The distinction between "factual" and "legal" impossibility is a nice one indeed and the courts tend to place a greater value on legal form than on any substantive danger the defendant's actions pose for society. The approach of the draftsmen of the Model Penal Code was to eliminate the defense of impossibility in virtually all situations. Under the code provision, to constitute an attempt, it is still necessary that the result intended or desired by the actor constitute a crime. However, the code suggested a fundamental change to shift the focus of analysis to the actor's mental frame of reference and away from undue dependence upon external considerations. The basic premise of the code provision is that what was in the actor's own mind should be the standard for determining his dangerousness to society and, hence, his liability for attempted criminal conduct.

In the belief that neither of the two branches of the traditional impossibility arguments detracts from the offender's moral culpability, the Legislature substantially carried the [Model Penal Code's] treatment of impossibility into the 1967 revision of the Penal Law. Thus, a person is guilty of an attempt when, with intent to commit a crime, he engages in conduct which tends to effect the commission of such crime. (Penal Law, §110.10.) Thus, if defendant believed the victim to be alive at the time of the shooting, it is no defense to the charge of attempted murder that the victim may have been dead.

Turning to the facts of the case before us, we believe that there is sufficient evidence in the record from which the jury could conclude that the defendant believed Geller to be alive at the time defendant fired shots into Geller's head. Defendant admitted firing five shots at a most vital part of the victim's anatomy from virtually point blank range. Although defendant contended that the victim had already been grievously wounded by another, from the defendant's admitted actions, the jury could conclude that the defendant's purpose and intention was to administer the coup de grace.

Defendant argues that the jury was bound to accept, at face value, the indications in his admissions that he believed Geller dead. Certainly, it is true that the defendant was entitled to have the entirety of the admissions, both the inculpatory and the exculpatory portions, placed in evidence before the trier of facts.

However, the jury was not required to automatically credit the exculpatory portions of the admissions. The general rule is, of course, that the credibility of witnesses is a question of fact and the jury may choose to believe some, but not all, of a witness' testimony. . . .

The jury convicted the defendant of murder. Necessarily, they found that defendant intended to kill a live human being. Subsumed within this finding is the conclusion that defendant acted in the belief that Geller was alive. Thus, there is no need for additional fact findings by a jury. Although it was not established beyond a reasonable doubt that Geller was, in fact, alive, such is no defense to attempted murder since a murder would have been committed "had the attendant circumstances been as [defendant] believed them to be." (Penal Law, §110.10.) The jury necessarily found that defendant believed Geller to be alive when defendant shot at him.

The Appellate Division erred in not modifying the judgment to reflect a conviction for the lesser included offense of attempted murder. An attempt to commit a murder is a lesser included offense of murder and the Appellate Division has the authority, where the trial evidence is not legally sufficient to establish the offense of which the defendant was convicted, to modify the judgment to one of conviction for a lesser included offense which is legally established by the evidence. Thus, the Appellate Division, by dismissing the indictment, failed to take the appropriate corrective action.

Notes and Questions

1. *Determining Dlugash's intent.* The court takes the view that in convicting Dlugash of murder, the jury "necessarily . . . found that the defendant had intended to kill a live human being." Is this true? Examine the New York murder statute, p. 301, *supra.* Even assuming that the only basis for murder liability before the jury was intent to kill, could the Court of Appeals logically infer that the jury necessarily found this intent, thus "reconstructing" a conviction of attempted murder? The United States District Court, on a later habeas corpus appeal of Dlugash's attempted murder conviction, answered in the negative.

In Dlugash v. People of State of New York, 476 F. Supp. 921 (E.D.N.Y. 1979), the court reasoned that the "big contention" at trial was whether or not Geller was alive when Dlugash fired the gun. The jury had concluded that Geller was indeed alive and may well have inferred Dlugash's intent to kill Geller by reasoning that Dlugash had intended the natural and probable consequences of his act (causing Geller's death).[17] However, since the New York Court of Appeals ruled the evidence insufficient to establish beyond a reasonable doubt that Geller was indeed alive at the relevant time, the jury's finding of intent to kill may have been an inference based on an unwarranted factual assumption. Thus, the federal court ordered a retrial for Dlugash on the question whether he had in fact intended Geller's death.[18]

2. *Impossibility and mistakes about law.* Consider the following "impossible attempt" case. Sally plans to divorce Fred and then to still claim him as a tax exemption. That would be criminal fraud. She files the divorce papers in February and, thinking the divorce is final in 30 days under state law, files the tax exemption in April (assume you can only claim an exemption for a person who is your spouse at the time you file for the exemption). But Sally has misread the

17. This assumes, of course, that the jury's inference was not based on an instruction that was unconstitutional under Sandstrom v. Montana or Francis v. Franklin, *supra*, pp. 23 and 363-67.
18. Dlugash, in fact, was never retried. Both sides were reluctant to face further appeals or trial proceedings, and Dlugash, who had already been released from prison after serving over three years, pleaded guilty to "attempted reckless manslaughter." Recall the *Lyerla* case, *supra*, p. 635.

divorce laws, which state that a divorce takes place 120 days after the papers are filed.

Under common law, is this "factual" or "legal" impossibility? Under the revised view of "impossibility" in the Model Penal Code, would Sally be guilty?

Now assume the divorce laws make the divorce final 30 days after filing the papers, but Sally believes her divorce will not be final until 120 days after filing. Would this be a "mistake of fact" or "mistake of law" under common law? Under the Model Penal Code, would it make a difference?

Notice that in both scenarios, the Model Penal Code treats mistakes of law of this sort the same way that it treats mistakes of fact.

Now consider another kind of impossible attempt. Ed Emigrant has just moved to Minnesota. He is under the misimpression that the Minnesota Criminal Code contains what he conceives to be a "mopery" law, which, in his view, makes it a misdemeanor to act in a depressed or discouraged fashion on a public highway. Ed wants to engage in an act of civil disobedience in Minnesota, so he purposefully enters a public highway and "mopes."

Is Ed guilty of a crime? What crime? What should his punishment be? This kind of "imaginary crime" is rarely committed — or rather it rarely comes to our attention. Why should the person who commits an imaginary crime be less guilty than the person who "steals" his own umbrella, or someone who "kills" a dead person?

PEOPLE v. THOUSAND
Supreme Court of Michigan
631 N.W.2d 694 (2001)

YOUNG, J.

We granted leave in this case to consider whether the doctrine of "impossibility" provides a defense to a charge of attempt to commit an offense prohibited by law under M.C.L. §750.92. . . . We conclude that the concept of impossibility, which this Court has never adopted as a defense, is not relevant to a determination whether a defendant has committed attempt under M.C.L. §750.92, and that the circuit court therefore erred in dismissing the charge of attempted distribution of obscene material to a minor on the basis of the doctrine of legal impossibility. . . .

Deputy William Liczbinski was assigned by the Wayne County Sheriff's Department to conduct an undercover investigation for the department's Internet Crimes Bureau. Liczbinski was instructed to pose as a minor and log onto "chat rooms" on the Internet for the purpose of identifying persons using the Internet as a means for engaging in criminal activity.

On December 8, 1998, while using the screen name "Bekka," Liczbinski was approached by defendant, who was using the screen name "Mr. Auto-Mag," in an Internet chat room. Defendant described himself as a twenty-three-year-old male from Warren, and Bekka described herself as a fourteen-year-old female from Detroit. Bekka indicated that her name was Becky Fellins, and defendant revealed that his name was Chris Thousand. During this initial conversation, defendant sent Bekka, via the Internet, a photograph of his face.

From December 9 through 16, 1998, Liczbinski, still using the screen name "Bekka," engaged in chat room conversation with defendant. During these exchanges, the conversation became sexually explicit. Defendant made repeated lewd invitations to Bekka to engage in various sexual acts, despite various indications of her young age.[19]

During one of his online conversations with Bekka, after asking her whether anyone was "around there," watching her, defendant indicated that he was sending her a picture of himself. Within seconds, Liczbinski received over the Internet a photograph of male genitalia. Defendant asked Bekka whether she liked and wanted it and whether she was getting "hot" yet, and described in a graphic manner the type of sexual acts he wished to perform with her. Defendant invited Bekka to come see him at his house for the purpose of engaging in sexual activity. Bekka replied that she wanted to do so, and defendant cautioned her that they had to be careful, because he could "go to jail." Defendant asked whether Bekka looked "over sixteen," so that if his roommates were home he could lie.

The two then planned to meet at an area McDonald's restaurant at 5:00 P.M. on the following Thursday. Defendant indicated that they could go to his house, and that he would tell his brother that Bekka was seventeen. Defendant instructed Bekka to wear a "nice sexy skirt," something that he could "get [his] head into." Defendant indicated that he would be dressed in black pants and shirt and a brown suede coat, and that he would be driving a green Duster. Bekka asked defendant to bring her a present, and indicated that she liked white teddy bears.

On Thursday, December 17, 1998, Liczbinski and other deputy sheriffs were present at the specified McDonald's restaurant when they saw defendant inside a vehicle matching the description given to Bekka by defendant. Defendant, who was wearing a brown suede jacket and black pants, got out of the vehicle and entered the restaurant. Liczbinski recognized defendant's face from the photograph that had been sent to Bekka. Defendant looked around for approximately thirty seconds before leaving the restaurant. Defendant was then taken into custody. Two white teddy bears were recovered from defendant's vehicle. . . .

. . . [D]efendant was bound over for trial on charges [including] attempted distribution of obscene material to a minor, M.C.L. §750.92. . . .

Defendant brought a motion to quash the information, arguing that . . . the existence of a child victim was an element of each [this charge], the evidence was legally insufficient to support the charges. The circuit court agreed and dismissed the [charge]. The Court of Appeals affirmed the dismissal of the [charge of] attempted distribution of obscene material to a minor. . . .

We granted the prosecution's application for leave to appeal. . . .

The doctrine of "impossibility" as it has been discussed in the context of inchoate crimes represents the conceptual dilemma that arises when, because of the defendant's mistake of fact or law, his actions could not possibly have resulted in the commission of the substantive crime underlying an attempt charge. . . .

Courts and legal scholars have drawn a distinction between two categories

---

19. Defendant at one point asked Bekka, "Ain't I a lil [sic] old?" Upon Bekka's negative reply, defendant asked, "[Y]ou like us old guys?" Bekka explained that boys her age "act like little kids," and reiterated that she was fourteen years old. Bekka mentioned that her birthday was in 1984 and that she was in ninth grade, and defendant asked when she would be fifteen. Defendant asked whether Bekka was still "pure," to which Bekka responded that she was not, but that she did not have a lot of experience and that she was nervous.

of impossibility: "factual impossibility" and "legal impossibility." It has been said that, at common law, legal impossibility is a defense to a charge of attempt, but factual impossibility is not. However, courts and scholars alike have struggled unsuccessfully over the years to articulate an accurate rule for distinguishing between the categories of "impossibility."

"Factual impossibility," which has apparently never been recognized in any American jurisdiction as a defense to a charge of attempt, "exists when [the defendant's] intended end constitutes a crime but she fails to consummate it because of a factual circumstance unknown to her or beyond her control." Dressler, Understanding Criminal Law (1st ed.), §27.07[C][1], p. 350. An example of a "factual impossibility" scenario is where the defendant is prosecuted for attempted murder after pointing an unloaded gun at someone and pulling the trigger, where the defendant believed the gun was loaded.

The category of "legal impossibility" is further divided into two subcategories: "pure" legal impossibility and "hybrid" legal impossibility. . . .

"*Pure* legal impossibility exists if the criminal law does not prohibit D's conduct or the result that she has sought to achieve." Id., §27.07[D][2], p. 352 (emphasis in original). In other words, the concept of pure legal impossibility applies when an actor engages in conduct that he believes is criminal, but is not actually prohibited by law: "There can be no conviction of criminal attempt based upon D's erroneous notion that he was committing a crime." Perkins & Boyce, Criminal Law (3d ed.), p. 634. . . .

> Most claims of legal impossibility are of the hybrid variety. *Hybrid* legal impossibility exists if D's goal was illegal, but commission of the offense was impossible due to a factual mistake by her regarding the legal status of some factor relevant to her conduct. This version of impossibility is a "hybrid" because, as the definition implies and as is clarified immediately below, D's impossibility claim includes both a legal and a factual aspect to it.
>
> Courts have recognized a defense of legal impossibility or have stated that it would exist if D receives unstolen property believing it was stolen; tries to pick the pocket of a stone image of a human; offers a bribe to a "juror" who is not a juror; tries to hunt deer out of season by shooting a stuffed animal; shoots a corpse believing that it is alive; or shoots at a tree stump believing that it is a human.
>
> Notice that each of the mistakes in these cases affected the legal status of some aspect of the defendant's conduct. . . .
>
> On the other hand, in each example of hybrid legal impossibility D was mistaken about a fact: whether property was stolen, whether a person was a juror, whether the victims were human or whether the victim was an animal subject to being hunted out of season. [Dressler, *supra*, §27.07[D][3][a], pp. 353-354 (emphasis in original).]

As the Court of Appeals panel in this case accurately noted, it is possible to view virtually any example of "hybrid legal impossibility" as an example of "factual impossibility":

> "*Ultimately any case of hybrid legal impossibility may reasonably be characterized as factual impossibility*. . . . [B]y skillful characterization, one can describe virtually any case of hybrid legal impossibility, which is a common law defense, as an example of factual impossibility, which is *not* a defense." [241 Mich.App. at 106, 614 N.W.2d 674 (emphasis in original), quoting Dressler, Understanding Criminal Law (2d ed.), §27.07[D] [3] [a], pp. 374-375.]

It is notable that "the great majority of jurisdictions have now recognized that legal and factual impossibility are 'logically indistinguishable' . . . and have abolished impossibility as a defense." United States v. Hsu, 155 F.3d 189, 199 (C.A.3, 1998).[20] . . .

. . . Finding no recognition of impossibility in our common law, we turn now to the terms of the statute. MCL 750.92 provides, in relevant part:

> Any person who shall attempt to commit an offense prohibited by law, and in such attempt shall do any act towards the commission of such offense, but shall fail in the perpetration, or shall be intercepted or prevented in the execution of the same, when no express provision is made by law for the punishment of such attempt, shall be punished as follows. . . .

Under our statute, then, an "attempt" consists of (1) an attempt to commit an offense prohibited by law, and (2) any act towards the commission of the intended offense. . . .

We are unable to discern from the words of the attempt statute any legislative intent that the concept of "impossibility" provide any impediment to charging a defendant with, or convicting him of, an attempted crime, notwithstanding any factual mistake—regarding either the attendant circumstances or the legal status of some factor relevant thereto—that he may harbor. The attempt statute carves out no exception for those who, possessing the requisite criminal intent to commit an offense prohibited by law and taking action toward the commission of that offense, have acted under an extrinsic misconception.

Defendant in this case is not charged with the substantive crime of distributing obscene material to a minor. It is unquestioned that defendant could not be convicted of that crime, because defendant allegedly distributed obscene material not to "a minor," but to an adult man. Instead, defendant is charged with the distinct offense of attempt, which requires only that the prosecution prove intention to commit an offense prohibited by law, coupled with conduct toward the commission of that offense. . . .

Because the nonexistence of a minor victim does not give rise to a viable defense to the attempt charge in this case, the circuit court erred in dismissing this charge on the basis of "legal impossibility."

Accordingly, we reverse in part, affirm in part, and remand this matter to the circuit court for proceedings consistent with this opinion.

Notes and Questions

1. What result would the Michigan Supreme Court have reached in the *Booth* case? What result would the *Booth* Court have reached on the attempt issue in the *Thousand* case? How would Fletcher's rational motivation test decide the attempt issue in *Thousand*? What about Hasnas's attendant circumstance test?

2. Is it clear that Thousand's e-mailing an obscene picture crossed the line from preparation to attempt? What result on this question under the test used in *Jaffe*? What about under the Model Penal Code's substantial step test?

---

20. Apart from judicial abrogation of this doctrine, many states have done so by legislative enactment. In a 1995 law review article, California Deputy Attorney General Kyle Brodie listed twenty states that had specifically abolished the defense of impossibility by legislative enactment. Brodie, The obviously impossible attempt: A proposed revision to the Model Penal Code, 15 N. Ill. U. L. Rev. 237, n. 39 (1995).

3. *Impossibility exercises.* As an exercise in the many combinations of the law, the facts, and one's idea of the law and the facts, take the case where Congress has forbidden the delivery of obscene materials to someone known to be under the age of 18. Let us then examine the possible situations with respect to the defendant's knowledge and belief. Assume that in all cases the defendant deliverer knows that the material is obscene.

a. First, with respect to the law, let us assume the deliverer knows that the age specified in the statute is 18. Then the possible combinations of his or her (let us say reasonable) belief in the age of the recipient and the actual age of the recipient can be represented by a box with four cells.

Age of recipient in fact is

	17	19
Defendant believes age of recipient is 17	G.	F.I.
Defendant believes age of recipient is 19	N.G.	N.G.

Thus, in the upper left corner where the defendant believes the age of the recipient is 17 and the age of the recipient is in fact 17; the defendant is simply guilty of the offense and the box raises no interesting issue. In the lower lefthand corner, where the defendant thinks the recipient is 19 but he or she in fact is 17, the defendant has made a mistake of fact that prevents him or her from having the mens rea required for the crime; hence under our traditional rules the defendant will be not guilty. In the upper right corner of the box, where the defendant believes the recipient to be 17 but the recipient is in fact 19, we have our classic factually impossible attempt, and since factual impossibility is generally not regarded as a defense, the defendant would be guilty of attempt. And finally, in the lower righthand corner, the defendant, who thinks that the recipient is 19 years old when the recipient is in fact 19 years old, has not committed any crime and has behaved in a perfectly law-abiding way — thus, the box is not interesting.

b. Now, let us assume that the defendant thinks (wrongly) that the law proscribes delivery of the materials (which he or she knows to be obscene) to anyone under the age of 16. Can you fill in the boxes in such a case?

Age of recipient in fact is

	17	19
Defendant believes age of recipient is 17		
Defendant believes age of recipient is 19		

c. Now assume that the defendant believes (again wrongly) that the law makes criminal the delivery of the obscene material to someone under the age of 21.

Age of recipient in fact is

	17	19
17		
19		

Defendant believes age of recipient is

Does the lower left corner of this box reveal an issue that you have not thought of? How should the lower lefthand box be filled in? Do you note anything interesting in comparing the boxes?

11

COMPLICITY

Accomplices are persons held liable for aiding or encouraging the offense of another. It is often said that complicity is not a distinct crime, but a way of committing a crime. Thus complicity always depends on the occurrence of some other offense, whether or not another person is punished for that offense. In this respect complicity differs from conspiracy (Chapter 12), attempt (Chapter 10), and solicitation (Chapter 10), which all can occur absent any other offense. Consider this statement from State v. Foster, 202 Conn. 520, 522 A.2d 277 (1987):

Attempt and conspiratorial liability differ substantially from the liability imposed on an accessory. First, both attempt and conspiracy are offenses in and of themselves, while accessorial liability is not. Attempt is a distinct, inchoate offense and a defendant may be punished for attempting to commit a substantive offense without actually committing the crime. Likewise, conspiracy has been recognized as being a crime distinct from the commission of the substantive offense.

There is, however, no such crime as "being an accessory." The defendant is charged with committing one substantive offense; "[t]he accessory statute merely provides alternate means by which a substantive crime may be committed." State v. Baker, [195 Conn. 598, 489 A.2d 1041 (1985)].

Moreover, because accessorial liability is not a distinct crime, but only an alternative means by which a substantive crime may be committed, it would be illogical to impose liability on the perpetrator of the crime, while precluding liability for an accessory, even though both possess the mental state required for the commission of the crime. Connecticut "long ago adopted the rule that there is no practical significance in being labeled an 'accessory' or a 'principal' for the purpose of determining criminal responsibility. The modern approach 'is to abandon completely the old common law terminology and simply provide that a person is legally accountable for the conduct of another when he is an accomplice of the other person in the commission of the crime. Such is the view taken in the Model Penal Code, which provides that a person is an accomplice of another person in the commission of an offense if, with the purpose of promoting or facilitating the commission of the offense, he solicits the other person to commit it, or aids or agrees or attempts to aid the other person in planning or committing it, or (having a legal duty to prevent the crime) fails to make the proper effort to prevent it.'" LaFave & Scott, Criminal Law (1972) §63, p.501.

To say that complicity is not a crime, but rather a way of committing a crime, is to draw an analogy to commission by omission. Recall from Chapter 2 that an omission in the face of a legal duty to act is simply a way of fulfilling the act element defined by some criminal statutes. Yet omission liability differs from accomplice liability in one key way. In many cases of commission by omission, the defendant is held liable for passively imposing a harm or a risk because of some relationship to the *victim* that establishes the legal duty to act, as in the case of a parent or professional caretaker. In cases of complicity, however, liability for wrongdoing flows from the accomplice's relationship to the *perpetrator*.

It is also helpful to contrast complicity with causation. As we saw in Chapter 4, courts now divide on the issue of whether defendants can cause a proscribed harm by causing the harmful act of another person. But the concept of complicity developed at a time when the common law was still committed to the idea that each person is ordinarily the cause of her own actions. Accordingly, the common law view was that one became responsible for another person's crime by *joining* in it rather than *causing* it. While modern social science has now accustomed us to perceive social causes for individual acts, there remain good reasons to blame and punish those who participate in wrongdoing even when they do not personally cause harm. According to Professor Christopher Kutz:

> The most important and far-reaching harms and wrongs of contemporary life are the products of collective actions, mediated by social and institutional structures. These harms and wrongs are essentially collective products, and individual agents rarely make a difference to their occurrence. So long as individuals are only responsible for the effects they produce, then the result of this disparity between collective harm and individual effect is the disappearance of individual accountability. . . .
>
> The Complicity Principle assumes a different view of collective action. Intuitively, marginally effective participants in a collective harm are accountable for the victims' suffering, not because of the individual differences they make, but because their intentional participation in a collective endeavor directly links them to the consequences of that endeavor. The notion of participation rather than causation is at the heart of both complicity and collective action.[1]

For such reasons, criminal law generally imposes liability when an actor consents to a crime by aiding or encouraging the perpetrator. What conduct constitutes such aid or encouragement is a question we explore in the first section below.

The second subject we will take up is the mens rea for complicity. Here we will encounter a difficulty with the notion of complicity as a way of committing crime. That notion implies that while the accomplice's mode of action act differs from the principal's, she should manifest the same mens rea. Thus, the *Foster* court writes that both perpetrator and accessory "possess the mental state required for the commission of the crime." Yet the court admits that some statutory schemes, including the Model Penal Code, require that accomplices instead act "with the purpose of promoting or facilitating the commission of the offense." If liability as an accomplice involves a distinctive act (aiding or encouraging) and a distinctive mental state (purpose to ease or promote the crime), why is it not in every sense a distinct crime? The chapter's second section will explore this question.

1. Christopher Kutz, Complicity: Ethics and Law for a Collective Age 113, 138 (2000).

A third section will briefly ask you to apply what you have learned by analyzing a controversial homicide committed by members of an angry mob.

A fourth section treats the relationship between the perpetrator and accomplice, a relationship complicated by the premise that the accomplice is guilty because someone else perpetrates an offense. Historically, accomplices could not be convicted before the conviction of a principal. That is no longer the case, but accomplice liability still requires at a minimum proof that another person committed an offense. We consider when an accomplice may be liable without corresponding liability on the part of the perpetrator of the offense; more specifically, we consider how courts sometimes find liability for those who induce unwitting criminal conduct by proximately causing (rather than consenting to) another person's criminal conduct, and how courts reconcile general complicity doctrines with the potentially conflicting definitions of offenses and offenders in specific statutes. This discussion raises the question whether a causal theory of liability for the conduct of others should completely replace complicity.

A. THE ACCESSORIAL ACT

STATE v. OCHOA
Supreme Court of New Mexico
41 N.M. 589, 72 P.2d 609 (1937)

The defendants [Leandro Velarde, Manuel Avitia, and Juan Ochoa] were convicted of murder in the second degree. The victim of the homicide was M.R. Carmichael, sheriff of McKinley county. He was slain while accompanying a prisoner from the office of the local justice of the peace to the county jail.

The homicide occurred about 9:30 o'clock in the forenoon of April 4, 1935. A few days previously one Esiquel Navarro, one Victor Campos, and a Mrs. Lovato had been arrested on warrants charging the unlawful breaking and entering of a certain house [where Campos had previously resided and from which he had recently been evicted]. . . . The preliminary hearing for Navarro, who was confined in jail, was set for 9 A.M., April 4th.

The house in question was located in a section of Gallup known locally as Chiuahuita, largely occupied by former employees of a coal mining company. Considerable excitement had been engendered among them by the eviction proceedings and the approaching trial of Navarro. [The court offered further details on the background of the killing.[2]]

On March 29th, preceding the affray, at a gathering at the home of one Mrs. Conception Aurelio . . . , Leandro Velarde told the group, there gathered, "to prepare for the following day at 8 o'clock in the morning; that they were to be ready at the house of Victor Campos and to be prepared — to be ready and let the officers take their weapons; that they didn't need anything else but a toothpick." Also, he said at this time that the first one they wanted to get hold of was

2. [Some of the subsequent paragraphs of the opinion have been rearranged to place the facts in chronological order. — EDS.]

Carmichael, "because he had a feeling against Carmichael and Carmichael had a feeling against him." He further said, "that he didn't care to die for the poor; that he had a big body and he was going to stick it out for the poor." The meeting planned evidently had to do with restoring Campos to the house from which he had been evicted. . . .

. . . At a mass meeting held in Spanish-American Hall in Gallup on the afternoon of April 3d, . . . a committee was appointed to confer with Sheriff Carmichael regarding Navarro. The committee waited upon the sheriff and demanded Navarro's release. This request was denied. Some members of the committee then asked permission to talk with Navarro. This request likewise was denied by the sheriff, who informed the committee Navarro's trial would take place at 9 A.M. the following day and that they then could see him. . . . Juan Ochoa was chairman of the meeting. . . . Leandro Velarde attended the meeting and was named a member of . . . the committee to see the sheriff. Manuel Avitia also was present at the meeting.

The sheriff, accompanied by several deputies, left the jail with the prisoner, Navarro, shortly before 9 o'clock the morning of April 4th and proceeded to the office of Justice of the Peace William H. Bickel on Coal Avenue, a distance of one and one-half blocks. . . . Soon after they arrived a crowd of approximately 125 people, included in which were many women and children, gathered on the sidewalk and in the street in front of the office of the justice of the peace. . . . The officers, even before leaving the jail with the prisoner, had become apprehensive that an effort might be made to rescue him. So that, when the crowd sought admittance to the justice's chambers which had seating capacity for not more than 25 spectators, none except witnesses were permitted to enter.

The crowd in front grew threatening. They pressed against the plate glass windows to the extent that one of them was cracked; pounded on the windows with their fists; shouted, cursed; and some threatened to kick the door down if they were not admitted. After . . . Navarro's objection that he had no attorney, the hearing of his case was postponed for the purpose of enabling him to secure an attorney to represent him.

Apprehensive of trouble in attempting to make their exit from the office of the justice through the crowd at the front entrance en route back to the jail, the sheriff directed that Navarro should be removed through the rear door . . . [into an alley] thus avoiding the crowd.

About the time it was appreciated by the crowd in front that the prisoner was to be removed through the rear door into the alley, the defendant Leandro Velarde was seen going through the crowd motioning toward the west, the direction to be taken to reach the alley, and he went into the alley practically at the head of the crowd.

The three defendants, Leandro Velarde, Manuel Avitia, and Juan Ochoa, along with certain other defendants acquitted at the trial, were identified as being in the crowd in front of the justice's office and also in the crowd at the rear of the office in the alley after it had hastened there upon discovering that the prisoner, Navarro, was to be removed through the rear door and thence via the alley to the jail. The present defendants, along with Ignacio Velarde and Solomon Esquibel, slain during the affray, were in the forefront of the crowd formed in a semicircle around the rear entrance as the officers prepared to emerge with their prisoner.

Just before they took the prisoner through the rear entrance, former Deputy Fred Montoya, who formed one of the sheriff's party at the justice's office, at the sheriff's request, opened the rear door. He took one step outside. There confronting him among those recognized were Ignacio Velarde, Leandro Velarde, and Solomon Esquibel. Leandro Velarde, clenching his fist and raising it in a threatening manner, said to Montoya: "Now you shall see what happens, disgraced [one]." Solomon Esquibel, reaching his right hand into a partially open blue jacket worn at the time as if to draw a weapon, said: "You move back, leave them to us alone." Montoya being unarmed immediately moved back inside the office of the justice of the peace.

Contemporaneously with Montoya's return to the inside of the office, Sheriff Carmichael and Undersheriff Dee Roberts emerged therefrom with the prisoner. As they did so and started pushing their way out into the alley, the defendant Juan Ochoa, from a distance of about three feet, struck at Undersheriff Dee Roberts with a claw hammer. . . . The officers, nevertheless, succeeded in getting their prisoner into the alley, pushing their way through the crowd. . . . Sheriff Carmichael was . . . holding [the prisoner] by the right arm, and Undersheriff Dee Roberts was . . . holding him by the left arm, walking eastwardly toward the jail. As they proceeded up the alley toward the jail they were surrounded by the crowd. . . . The officers with the prisoner were followed by Deputies E. L. "Bobcat" Wilson and Hoy Boggess. . . .

An unidentified person in the crowd had been heard to shout: "We want Navarro." . . .

When the officers had advanced a short distance up the alley with their prisoner, the defendant Manuel Avitia drew a pistol from his pocket and rushed from the rear through the crowd toward the officers. . . . When they were about forty feet from the rear exit of the justice's office, Deputy Hoy Boggess observed someone, unknown to him, grab at the prisoner as if to take him from the custody of the officers. Thereupon, he raised his arm and hurled a tear gas bomb to the rear and westwardly into the crowd in the alley. . . . After hurling the tear gas bomb, and just before being struck and rendered unconscious, Deputy Boggess observed the defendant Leandro Velarde only a few feet from him on the right; Solomon Esquibel, later slain, not far away; and the defendant Manuel Avitia running toward him (Boggess). When Boggess fell unconscious from a blow on the head delivered by some unidentified person in the crowd, his pistol fell from his belt to the pavement. Two members of the crowd were seen to spring toward same and to be bent over as if to recover it. . . .

While Deputy Boggess was down on the paving . . . , the defendants Avitia and Ochoa, with two or three other persons, were seen beating and kicking him.

. . . Almost simultaneously with the detonation from explosion of the bomb, a shot was fired somewhat to the rear of the officers accompanying the prisoner. Then a second shot followed the first, apparently fired by Ignacio Velarde, a brother of the defendant Leandro Velarde, from a point at the northeast corner of the Independent Building, some fifteen feet from Sheriff Carmichael. This shot struck the sheriff in the left side of the face and passed out of his body on the right side of his neck. The first shot fired had struck the sheriff in the left side, just under the left arm, passed through his chest and out into his right shoulder. He died instantly, his undersheriff, Dee Roberts, catching hold of his right arm and lowering his body to the pavement. The latter then looking to the west observed two men firing toward him. One was on his left at the corner of the Independent Building, perhaps fifteen feet distant. This proved to be Ignacio Velarde. The other was farther down the alley about twenty feet and to his right. This was Solomon Esquibel. Their fire was returned by Undersheriff Roberts, and both Ignacio Velarde and Solomon Esquibel were killed.

In the meantime the firing had become more general, the total number of shots fired during the affray being twelve to fifteen. . . . When the shooting had ceased Avitia ran west out of the alley with a pistol in his hand.

When the firing ceased, besides Sheriff Carmichael and the two others named being killed, Deputy Wilson had been seriously wounded by a bullet which entered his body about an inch below the armpit and was later extracted. Two other members of the crowd had received wounds, a woman by a shot through the leg. Both of these wounded, as well as Deputy Wilson, subsequently recovered.

The pistols with which Ignacio Velarde and Solomon Esquibel were seen firing were never located after the affray. The pistol which dropped from Deputy Boggess' belt when he was knocked unconscious was never recovered. Sheriff Carmichael's pistol was removed from its scabbard on his body after his death. It had never been fired. The bullet which had entered the body of Sheriff Carmichael under the left armpit was later extracted from his right shoulder. The bullet which had wounded Deputy Wilson likewise was later extracted. The pistol which Deputy Boggess lost during the affray and which had not been fired by him when lost was a forty-five Smith and Wesson double action. The bullet removed from the body of Sheriff Carmichael and that extracted from Deputy Wilson were both fired from the same pistol and it was of the same make and caliber as that lost by Deputy Boggess, using the same type of ammunition as that then employed in the Boggess gun.

The defendants were proceeded against by information. Ten were thus accused of the murder of Sheriff Carmichael, of whom seven were acquitted by the jury. The three defendants above named having been convicted of second degree murder, they alone prosecute this appeal. The most serious claim of error is directed at the action of the trial court in submitting to the jury the issue of second degree murder. . . . If this claim be good as to all of the defendants it is decisive. Hence, we give it first consideration. The facts as we have recited them are within the verdicts of guilty returned against defendants. Do they support second degree? That is the issue.

. . . [T]he Attorney General in the State's brief says:

> . . . [W]e . . . have two theories presented by the evidence shown (under) which the jury might find the appellants guilty of second degree murder. First, that one of the appellants actually shot and killed Sheriff Carmichael. Second, that the appellants or any of them aided and abetted the person or persons who actually shot and killed Sheriff Carmichael. . . .

The distinction between an accessory before the fact and a principal and between principals in the first and second degree, in cases of felony, has been abolished in New Mexico and every person concerned in the commission thereof, whether he directly commits the offense or procures, counsels, aids, or abets in its commission, must be prosecuted, tried, and punished as a principal. The evidence of aiding and abetting may be as broad and varied as are the means of communicating thought from one individual to another; by acts, conduct, words, signs, or by any means sufficient to incite, encourage or instigate commission of the offense or calculated to make known that commission of an offense already undertaken has the aider's support or approval. Mere presence, of course, and even mental approbation, if unaccompanied by outward manifestation or expression of such approval, is insufficient.

Before an accused may become liable as an aider and abettor, he must share the criminal intent of the principal. There must be community of purpose, partnership in the unlawful undertaking.

To aid and abet another in a crime one must share the intent or purpose of the principal. If two or more acting independently assault another, and one of them inflicts a mortal wound, the other is not guilty as an aider and abettor. An aider and abettor is a partner in the crime, the chief ingredient of which is always intent. There can be no partnership in the act where there is no community of purpose or intent. . . .

To render one an aider or abettor and, as a consequence, guilty in like degree with the principal in the commission of a crime, there should be evidence of his knowledge of the intention or purpose of the principal to commit the assault. In other words, there must have been a "common purpose" by which is meant a like criminal intent in the minds of Mills and the appellant, to render the latter guilty as charged, and hence authorize the giving of the instruction. State v. Porter, 276 Mo. 387, 207 S.W. 774, 776.

With these preliminary observations, we shall proceed to apply them to the facts of the instant case.

As to the defendant Leandro Velarde there is no evidence which sufficiently connects him with the unlawful design of the slayer of Sheriff Carmichael. The last time seen prior to the hurling of the tear gas bomb and the firing of the first shot, he was in the crowd a few feet removed from Deputy Boggess. There was nothing about his actions when then seen to excite suspicion. If so, it was not testified to by any witness. . . . He is not shown to have taken part in the assault on Deputy Boggess, as were Avitia and Ochoa. . . .

The defendants Avitia and Ochoa are differently situated. After Deputy Boggess hurled the tear gas bomb, he was knocked down and rendered unconscious for a time. Firing from the party of which they formed a part started almost instantly and continued until a total of as many as 12 or 15 shots had been exchanged between members of the two parties. Even if it be assumed that these two defendants were without previous knowledge of the purpose of the slayer or slayers of deceased to make an attempt on his life, the evidence abundantly supports an inference that with the firing of the first shot they became apprised of that purpose. The intent to kill, or to aid and abet in the commission thereof, may be formed at the scene of the crime, even though the accused may have gone there without such intention. If, with knowledge that one of their party was using or was about to use a deadly weapon, they or either of them rendered aid or assistance to him or them engaged in the deadly assault, they are equally guilty as aiders and abettors. The aider under such circumstances adopts the criminal intent of the principal. Both Avitia and Ochoa are identified in the testimony as being still engaged in an assault upon the fallen Boggess after two bullets had entered the body of the deceased. Boggess was a deputy of the slain sheriff and, of course, would be expected to come to the aid of his chief in peril. The fact that they were thus engaged in a vicious assault upon him (Boggess), after firing upon the sheriff's party commenced, left it within the jury's province to infer, if it saw fit, not alone that these defendants shared the intent of the slayer, but also that they aided and abetted him in his unlawful undertaking.

Nor would it seem an unwarranted inference, if the jury should elect so to find, that these defendants saw the sheriff's assailant in the act of drawing or aiming his gun and commenced the assault on Deputy Boggess momentarily before or simultaneously with the first outburst of gunfire. Particularly is this true in view of the fact that the assault on Boggess did not cease when it must have become known to the defendants that a member of their party was firing on the sheriff's party. Such an inference, however, is not essential to sustain the verdicts.

[H]owever free from felonious intent a participant in the combat of opposing parties may have been in the beginning, once it becomes known to him that another member of his party is employing a deadly weapon, he exposes himself to an inference of sharing the latter's intent if, except in necessary defense of his own person, he continues his participation. The question of whether the alleged aider and abettor did share the principal's criminal intent, and whether he knew the latter acted with criminal intent, is one of fact for the jury and may be inferred from circumstances. . . .

It was unnecessary for the State to show who actually fired the fatal shot if the proof was sufficient to warrant the inference as to a given defendant that, if he did not fire it, he aided and abetted him who did. . . . Morally, there never has been a distinction in the degree of culpability. The law long since has ceased to recognize any. All are subject to prosecution, trial, and punishment as principals. The aider and abettor may be tried and convicted even though the actual slayer is never apprehended or has been tried and acquitted.

It follows from what has been said that the judgment of the district court must stand affirmed as to the defendants Avitia and Ochoa. As to the defendant Velarde, it is reversed, with a direction to the trial court to set aside the judgment of conviction pronounced upon him and to discharge the prisoner. . . .

Notes and Questions

1. *Complicity and cause.* Did Leandro Velarde, Avitia, or Ochoa cause the death of Carmichael? Must the state prove their causal role beyond a reasonable doubt? If not, have we altered normal rules of causation where two or more people act in complicity?

Why does the court reverse Leandro Velarde's conviction? Did he make no important contribution to the killing? What inferences might we draw from his statements or actions on March 29? April 3?

How did Avitia and Ochoa aid the sheriff's slayer by their action in attacking the deputy? Would the court have affirmed their convictions if they had attacked the deputy after the sheriff had been killed? Would the court have affirmed their convictions if their attack on the deputy had ended before the shooting began?

2. *Harmony of purpose.* The court states: "Before an accused may become liable as an aider and abettor, he must share the criminal intent of the principal. There must be a community of purpose, partnership in the unlawful undertaking." Notice the ambiguity of the word "share." Assuming that Solomon Esquibel and Ignacio Velarde fired the fatal shots, was it necessary to the court's decision that those men knew that Avitia and Ochoa were trying to help them? If not,

then *sharing* of a purpose is not the same thing as *reciprocal acknowledgment* of help. We will explore the difference in Chapter 12, on conspiracy.

Conversely, what if Avitia and Ochoa, in attacking the deputy, had no idea that others were shooting the sheriff? What if the shooters knew what Avitia and Ochoa were doing, but not vice-versa?

3. *The meaning of "aiding and abetting."* The source of the language of "aiding and abetting" is described in the famous case of State v. Tally, 102 Ala. 25, 15 So. 722 (1894) (whose facts and holding we examine later in this chapter):

> It is said . . . that "the words 'aid' and 'abet' are pretty much the synonyms of each other"; and this has doubtless come to be true in the law, though originally a different meaning attached to each. The legal definition of "aid" is not different from its meaning in common parlance. It means "to assist," "to supplement the efforts of another." Rap. & L. Law Dict. p. 43. "Abet" is a French word, compounded of the two words "a" and "beter" — "to bait or excite an animal;" and Rapalje and Lawrence thus define it: "To abet is to incite or encourage a person to commit a crime. An abettor is a person who, being present or in the neighborhood, incites another to commit a crime, and thus becomes a principal in the offense." Id. p. 4. By the amalgamation of the two words in the meaning — by making synonyms of them — it may be said that to abet has come to mean to aid by presence, actual or constructive, and incitement, and that to aid means not only actual assistance, the supplementing of another's efforts, but also presence for the purposes of such actual assistance as the circumstances may demand or admit of, and the incitement and encouragement which the fact of such presence for such purposes naturally imports and implies.

4. *Principals and accessories.* The *Ochoa* court takes a modern approach to complicity, imposing equal liability for accomplices and principals. The early common law, however, distinguished among parties to a crime, classifying some as "principals" and others as "accessories." Each of these categories, moreover, was subdivided. A principal in the first degree was the actor or actual perpetrator of the criminal act at the scene of the crime. A principal in the second degree was a person who was "present" at the commission of a felony and provided assistance or encouragement to (aided and abetted) the principal in the first degree in the commission of the felony. A principal in the second degree did not actually commit the felony and his or her "presence" could be constructive instead of actual. Thus, someone who acted as a lookout or kept guard, even at some distance from the scene of the crime, could be convicted as a principal in the second degree.

This concept of presence — actual or constructive — distinguished principals from accessories. An accessory before the fact was someone who commanded, counseled, encouraged, or aided the principal in the first degree in committing the felony but who was not actually or constructively present at the scene of the crime. An example would be a person whose only role in the crime was to give the principal a weapon sometime before the crime occurred. By contrast, an accessory after the fact played no role in the preparation or commission of the crime, but rather assisted the felon in eluding capture or destroying evidence. Such assistance had to be an intentional, positive act, rather than a mere failure to notify the authorities.[3]

---

3. Accessories after the fact were recognized only in felonies. In treason, all four categories were treated as principals; and in misdemeanors all except the accessory after the fact were treated as principals and the accessory after the fact was not punishable.

These distinctions resulted in the development of a complex system of rules addressing jurisdiction, pleading, trial, and degree of guilt. Most important was the procedural rule that an accessory could not be tried or convicted before the conviction of the principal in the first degree. This rule prevented trial of an accessory if the principal escaped conviction for any reason, including failure to be identified, escape, death, or acquittal. Only a handful of states retain this rule. Other traditional rules included a requirement that a party to a crime be tried in the jurisdiction where the aid occurred[4] and that a person charged as one type of party could not be convicted as another. This last rule was one device used by judges to reduce the number of executions, since, at early common law, all felonies were punishable by death.

Modern statutes have largely eliminated the common law procedural rules and distinctions. Except for the accessory after the fact, all parties to the crime face prosecution for the substantive crime itself, and thus face the same punishment or range of punishments. For example, the federal statute, 18 U.S.C.A. §2 (2000), provides that

(a) Whoever commits an offense against the United States or aids, abets, counsels, commands, induces, or procures its commission, is punishable as a principal.
(b) Whoever willfully causes an act to be done which if directly performed by him or another would be an offense against the United States, is punishable as a principal.

Model Penal Code section 2.06 has also eliminated the common law distinctions. In most states, however, accessories after the fact still generally receive lesser punishment than other participants.[5]

Generally, accessories can now be convicted regardless of whether the principal is convicted, tried, or even apprehended, although, of course, the state must prove that the acts constituting the crime occurred. The prosecution need not charge a particular type of complicity in order to convict an accomplice, and the jurisdictional complexities have largely vanished.

One type of accomplice recognized at common law was the so-called accessory after the fact, whose offense was often called "misprision of felony." Laws punishing misprision of felony encouraged people to report crimes to the Crown when Britain had no professional police force. Thus, they were a law enforcement mechanism until at least the nineteenth century, when police forces began to emerge. Misprision was essentially defined as the nondisclosure or concealment of a known felony and did not require any affirmative act by the defendant to aid the principal. Some common law jurisdictions required proof that the person affirmatively concealed the crime. Others made passive concealment a misdemeanor under the misprision statute but made "active concealers," like true accomplices, guilty of the same crime as the principal.

4. This rule reduced convictions, since ancient law did not allow the indictment of an accessory if the accessory's actions occurred in one county and the underlying felony took place in another. This limitation was later changed by statute.

5. See, e.g., Va. Code §§18.2-19 (2000) ("In the case of every felony, every accessory after the fact shall be guilty of a Class I misdemeanor").

The United States Code still contains a misprision law, 18 U.S.C.A. §4 (2000):

> Whoever having knowledge of the actual commission of a felony cognizable by a court of the United States, conceals and does not as soon as possible make known the same to some judge or other person in civil or military authority under the United States, shall be fined not more than $500 or imprisoned not more than three years, or both.

Most courts, however, have interpreted the statute to punish only affirmative conduct to conceal the crime or principal from the government. See, e.g., United States v. Davila, 698 F.2d 715 (5th Cir. 1983) (concealment of evidence and of identity of offender establishes for liability).

Even in jurisdictions that have eliminated the crime of misprision or accessory after the fact, a person who takes some active steps to prevent the arrest or prosecution of a criminal may face liability under modern statutory charges. See, e.g., Model Penal Code §242.3 (hindering apprehension or prosecution by harboring a criminal, providing means of escape, destroying evidence or tampering with witnesses, volunteering false information to the police); §242.4 (aiding consummation of a crime by safeguarding proceeds or converting them into negotiable funds); §242.5 (compounding of a crime by accepting money in exchange for refraining from reporting crime to authorities).

5. *"Mere presence."* According to the court in *Ochoa*, "mere presence" and mere "mental approbation" are insufficient to establish liability. Consider Gains v. State, 417 So. 2d 719 (Fla. App. 1982). Michael Gains, Lonnie Williams, and a youth (not tried in this case) entered a bank and committed a robbery:

> As the three robbers left the bank, they walked slowly across the parking lot and calmly got into a car. This car had been parked far away from the bank at the end of the parking lot facing outward. While in the parking lot, the three men were not seen to be carrying guns, the masks worn during the robbery, or money. The driver, Joseph Williams, had not been inside the bank and sat casually in the car as the others got in. The car pulled slowly out of the lot, stopping because of traffic and obeying traffic signals. . . .
>
> When the police tailing the appellants first observed their car, it was not violating any traffic laws. As the police pulled closer, the officer noted that the passengers, Gains, Lonnie Williams, and the juvenile, did something unusual:
>
> > . . . [They] saw me coming down Townsend Boulevard and they turned and starting talking to the driver. At that point, when they'd made a complete turn onto Townsend Boulevard, the two in the back and Lonnie Williams in the front all laid down inside the vehicle as they approached my patrol car, which at that time I was still northbound coming up on them.
>
> At this point, the officer turned on his lights and pulled in front of the car. The driver initially eluded the officer by driving up into a yard, and a chase ensued. This officer never lost sight of the vehicle during the two-minute chase which was concluded when the car being pursued crashed into another car at the intersection of Lone Star and Samontee. During the chase Lonnie Williams fired his pistol at the officer approximately 15 times, and on several occasions reached into the back seat as if getting aid or ammunition.
>
> . . . It is not necessary that the aider or abettor be physically present aiding and abetting his partner or partners in the crime. However, he must be sufficiently near or so situated as to aid or encourage or to render assistance to the actual perpetrator. . . .

... Here, it is apparent that Joseph Williams was not an active participant in the armed robbery. Rather, the prosecution's theory implicitly rests on the assumption that he was the "wheelman" for the crime. The evidence that, as the driver of the car, he was a knowing participant in the crime is circumstantial and thus more is needed than a suspicion or belief that under the circumstances, he knew what was occurring. . . . The mere fact that he fled from the scene after the crime "does not exclude the reasonable inference that [he] had no knowledge of the crime until it actually occurred, and thus that he did not intend to assist in its commission." H. v. State, 370 So. 2d 1219, 1220 (Fla. 3d DCA 1979). . . . Considered in a light most favorable to the state's case, the evidence merely places Joseph Williams in the automobile outside the scene of the crime. There is no evidence that he had seen his companions carrying guns or that he had heard them discussing the crime prior to its inception. There is no evidence that he could see into the bank and thereby have ascertained the apparent intentions of his companions. There is no showing that he acted as a lookout for the trio. . . . He did not attempt to elude the police until, as we can fairly infer from the evidence, his companions informed him of something. . . . Moreover, upon being apprehended, he did nothing to resist arrest. Thus, the evidence in this case just as reasonably supports the inference that, although Joseph Williams may have been in the general vicinity of the crime, he had no knowledge of his companions' intentions and attempted to flee only upon being apprised of their actions while in the bank. . . . [Id. at 722-23]

The court finds, in effect, that no reasonable jury could have inferred from these facts, beyond a reasonable doubt, that Joseph Williams aided in the robbery. Is that inference really so far-fetched as to warrant the unusual step of reversal for insufficiency? How do you think the jury drew that inference? Is it relevant that Joseph Williams apparently kept driving while Lonnie Williams fired his pistol from the car?

If the court is right on these facts, what would it normally take to prove that a true "wheelman" was an intentional partner in the crime if he remained in the car outside the scene of the crime and did nothing but drive the principals away? What if Joseph Williams had been standing at the door of the bank, "sufficiently near or so situated as to aid or encourage or to render assistance to the actual perpetrator"? If the actual perpetrators managed to pull off the robbery with no help from Joseph Williams and if they had run off on their own, what evidence would establish that he was an aider or abettor in this situation?

 6. *Inaction as abetting.* Can a failure to intervene ever be sufficient for a conviction of aiding and abetting another who committed the offense? In State v. Walden, 293 S.E.2d 780 (N.C. 1982), the defendant was convicted of assault with a deadly weapon inflicting serious bodily injury, because she was present when her boyfriend struck her one-year-old son with a belt. At trial, the judge instructed the jury that

a person is not guilty of a crime merely because she is present at the scene. To be guilty she must aid or actively encourage the person committing the crime, or in some way communicate to this person her intention to assist in its commission; *or that she is present with the reasonable opportunity and duty to prevent the crime and fails to take the reasonable steps to do so.* [Id. at 784 (emphasis in original).]

The Supreme Court of North Carolina upheld the convictions:

... [W]e hold that the failure of a parent who is present to take all steps reasonably possible to protect the parent's child from an attack by another person constitutes an act of omission by the parent showing the parent's consent and contribution to the crime being committed. [Id. at 787.]

Note that the court does not reason that the defendant's culpable failure to resist the assault *caused* the child to be assaulted and injured, but rather that the failure of a present parent to resist child abuse *expressed consent* to it. Does it make sense to combine complicity and commission by omission in this way? A Wisconsin statute states:

> A person responsible for [a] child's welfare is guilty of a Class F felony if that person has knowledge that another person intends to cause, is causing or has intentionally and recklessly caused great bodily harm to the child and is physically and emotionally capable of taking action which will prevent the bodily harm from occurring or being repeated [and] fails to take that action and the failure to act exposes the child to an unreasonable risk of great bodily harm by the other person or facilitates the great bodily harm to the child that is caused by the other person. [Wis. Stats. §948.03(4) (2003)]

In State v. Rundle, 500 N.W.2d 916 (Wis. 1993), the defendant was charged with violating the more general criminal statute punishing intentional abuse, by virtue of his failure to stop his wife from beating their child. The prosecutor never charged Rundle under §948.03(4). But the state Supreme Court held that the legislature's passage of §948.03(4) meant that liability for failure to prevent the other parent from abusing a child was *only* to be under §948.03(4) if the alleged accomplice did not act affirmatively to aid the beating. It rejected the following "ingenious argument" offered by the state:

> These cases often involve children who are either too young or too severely injured to provide credible testimony. Consequently, prosecutors must often rely on circumstantial evidence and testimony from one or both parents. In such cases, because the parents are often the only witness to the conduct, the prosecutor is not always able to determine the active or passive role of each of the parents in physical abuse. Therefore, the prosecutor may choose to charge both as parties-to-the-crime. . . . [I]nterpreting sec. 948.03(4) as providing the exclusive means of prosecuting cases involving non-active physical child abuse has the practical effect of preventing prosecutors from permitting juries to determine criminal liability in cases where there is no direct evidence of the active or passive role of each of the parents. . . . [Id. at 924.]

The court rejected this argument, noting that nothing prevented the state from charging Rundle under both statutes. Why might the state have chosen not to take that approach?

7. *Parental nonsupervision as complicity.* Ordinarily, the relationship of complicity is voluntarily undertaken, rather than imputed on the basis of earlier association. Thus, familial intimacy alone cannot render one person complicitous in another's offense. But the *Walden* court's notion of "complicity-by-omission" can get us very close to such guilt by association, requiring only that the legislature or judiciary impose a duty on family members to impede or discourage each other's criminal projects. California, in enacting a new Street Terrorism Prevention Act to combat gang violence, made it a misdemeanor for a parent to fail "to exercise reasonable care, supervision, protection, and control over their [sic] minor child." Cal. Pen. C. §272(a)(2) (Supp. 2003). Suppose that Billy, a child,

becomes involved in a gang under circumstances such that a reasonably vigilant parent would suspect such a possibility, investigate, and take steps to prevent or discourage such an association. Suppose Billy's parents do none of these, and Billy, as part of his initiation as a gang member, robs someone at gunpoint. Should his parents be liable as accomplices to his robbery? If not, is it because their act is insufficient to render them accomplices, or is it only because they do not seem to have enough mens rea?

STATE v. TALLY

Supreme Court of Alabama

102 Ala. 25, 15 So. 722 (1894)

MCCLELLAN, J.[6] Briefly stated, the information in this case contains two charges against John B. Tally, as judge of the ninth judicial circuit. . . . The second count charges complicity on the part of Tally in the murder of R. C. Ross by the hands of [the] Skeltons. Tally was a brother-in-law of all the Skeltons named. . . . The grievance they had against Ross lay in the fact that the latter had seduced, or been criminally intimate with, a sister of three of them and of Mrs. Tally.

[Ross, after a period of hiding from the Skeltons out of town, returned to Scottsboro for a few days. On January 30, 1894, Ross traveled from Scottsboro to Stevenson by carriage. That morning, James Skelton, who lived with the defendant, armed himself and followed by horse, along with Robert and John Skelton. Walter Skelton had already preceded them.] The flight of Ross and the pursuit of the Skeltons at once became generally known in the town of Scottsboro, and was well nigh the sole topic of conversation that Sunday morning. Everybody knew it. Everybody talked about it. Everybody was impressed with the probability of a terrible tragedy to be enacted on the road to Stevenson, or at the latter point. The respondent was soon abroad. He went to the depot, where the telegraph office was. He remained there most of that morning. About nine o'clock that morning Dr. Rorex saw him there, and this, in the language of the witness, passed between them: "I said to Judge Tally that I thought we had better send a hack and a physician to their assistance up the road [referring to the Ross and Skelton parties then on the road to Stevenson]; that these parties might get hurt, and they might need assistance. Judge Tally replied that his folks or friends could take care of themselves. I also said to him that I reckoned we ought to send a telegram to Stevenson and have all of them arrested, to which he made no reply. . . . He said that he was waiting to see if anybody sent a telegram — or words to that effect; waiting and watching, to see if anybody sent a telegram." And he did wait and watch. He was seen there by Judge Bridges just before the passenger train, going west at 10:17, passed. He was seen there after it passed. E. H. Ross, a kinsman of the Ross who had fled, and was being pursued, meeting the telegraph operator, Whitner, at the passenger station, walked with him down to the freight depot, where the telegraph office was. Judge Tally followed them. They went into the telegraph office, and so did he. Ross was sitting at a table, writing a message. It was addressed to R. C. Ross, Stevenson, Ala. Its contents

---

6. [The full opinion in *Tally* would run over 30 pages in casebook type; were it not all true, Justice Thomas McClellan's elegant narrative would rank as one of the finer late Victorian novellas of America. — EDS.]

were: "Four men on horseback with guns following. Look out." Ross handed it to the operator to be sent. Tally either saw this message, or in some way accurately divined its contents. He called for paper, and immediately wrote a message himself. Judge Bridges was still in the office. At this juncture, Tally spoke to him, took him into a corner of the room, and, calling him by his given name, said, "What do you reckon that fellow [the operator] would think if I told him I should put him out of that office before he should send that message?" referring to the message quoted above, which E. H. Ross had just given the operator. Judge Bridges replied: "Judge, I wouldn't do that. That might cause you very serious trouble, and, besides that, might cause the young man to lose his position with the company he is working for." Judge Tally then remarked: "I don't want him to send the message he has, and I am going to send this one." He then showed Judge Bridges a message addressed to William Huddleston, containing these words: "Do not let the party warned get away." This message was signed by Tally. The respondent then handed this telegram to the operator, remarking to him, "This message has something to do with that one you just received"; said he wanted it sent, and paid for it. He then started towards the door, but turned to the operator and said: "Just add to that message, 'say nothing.'" Tally left the office. This message was sent just after that of E. H. Ross to R. C. Ross. The original of it was placed on a file in the office at Scottsboro. . . . These telegrams of Ed Ross and Tally were sent about 10:25 A.M. Tally then, his watch to prevent the sending or delivery of a telegram to R. C. Ross being over, went home.

[When Ross alighted in Stevenson he was shot at by Robert, James, and Walter Skelton. Wounded, Ross ran for cover behind a building, where he was ambushed and shot in the head from behind, by John Skelton. Robert Skelton then telegraphed Tally that Ross was dead and the Skeltons unhurt.]

The second specification charges that the Skeltons "unlawfully, and with malice aforethought, killed Robert C. Ross by shooting him with a gun," and . . . "Tally did aid or abet the said" Skeltons, naming them, "in the commission of the said felony and murder. . . ." These charges of aiding or abetting murder, and of murder direct, which amount to the same thing under our statute (Code, §3704), are, upon considerations to which we have already adverted, to be sustained, if at all, by evidence of the respondent's connection with the homicide after the Skeltons had left Scottsboro in pursuit of Ross, since we do not find any incriminating connection up to that point of time. Being without conviction that Tally knew of the Skeltons' intention to take Ross' life until after they had departed on their errand of death, and there being no evidence or pretense that between this time and the homicide any communication passed between them and Tally, we reach and declare the conclusion that the respondent did not command, direct, counsel, instigate, or encourage the Skeltons to take the life of Ross, and that, in whatever and all that was done by them and him, respectively, there was no understanding, preconcert, or conspiracy between them and him.

This narrows the issues to three inquiries — two of fact and one of law: First (a question of fact), did Judge Tally, on Sunday, February 4, 1894, knowing the intention of the Skeltons to take the life of Ross, and after they had gone in pursuit of him, do any act intended to further their design, and aid them in the taking of his life? If he did, then, second (a question of law), is it essential to his guilt that his act should have contributed to the effectuation of their design — to the death of Ross? And, if so, third (another inquiry of fact), did his act contribute to the death of Ross? There can be no reasonable doubt that Judge Tally knew,

soon after the Skeltons had departed, that they had gone in pursuit of Ross, and
that they intended to take his life. Within a few minutes, he was informed by his
wife that Ross had fled, and that the four Skeltons were pursuing him. He had
seen three of them mounted and heavily armed. He knew the fourth, even
keener on the trail than these, had gone on before. He knew their grievance.
The fact that they intended to wreak vengeance, in the way they did, upon over-
taking Ross, was known to all men in Scottsboro, as soon as the flight and pursuit became known. It was in the minds and on the tongues of everybody there.
Nothing else was thought or talked of. When Dr. Rorex, voicing the universal apprehension, suggested to him that aid be sent up the road to the dead and
wounded, Judge Tally, taking in the full force of the implication that there would
be a fight to the death, with the Skeltons as assailants, and not dissenting therefrom at all, said with the ken of prophecy, as a reason why he would not be a party
to the execution of this humane suggestion, that his folks (the Skeltons) would
take care of themselves. How well they took care of themselves — with what exceeding care they conserved their own safety — is shown by the event, and the
manner in which it was produced. To the other suggestion of Dr. Rorex — resulting from the universal knowledge that, unless something was done, an awful
tragedy would be enacted — that "we telegraph to Stevenson, and have them all
arrested," and thus prevent the catastrophe, if perchance Ross should reach that
point alive, Judge Tally made no direct response; but in the same connection he
said, "I am waiting and watching here to see if anybody sends a telegram." What
he meant by this is most clearly demonstrated by his subsequent shadowing and
following up Ed Ross, and his conversation with Judge Bridges about putting the
operator out of the office before he should send Ed Ross' message of warning to
his kinsman, Robert C. Ross. This was the situation: Ross was in what he supposed to be secret flight from the Skeltons. He was unaware that his early departure had been seen by one of them. He did not know they were all in full pursuit to take his life. Under these circumstances, the pursuers had every
advantage of the pursued. They could come upon him unawares. Being on
horseback, while he was in a vehicle, coming up to him, they could well get beyond and waylay him. This they actually did. Having this tremendous advantage,
accentuated by the fact that they were in no danger from Ross even if he saw
them, unless he was forced to defend himself — that his effort and intent were
to get away, and not to kill — Judge Tally might well feel satisfied with the posture of affairs; he might well feel assured that his folks would take care of themselves, as they did. All he wanted was that this situation, which portended the
death of Ross and the safety of his folks, should not be changed. He would not
agree that it should be changed so as to save Ross' life, even though at the same
time the safety of the Skeltons should be assured, as would have been the result
had the authorities at Stevenson been fully advised, at the time Dr. Rorex suggested the sending of a telegram there, to arrest all parties. He was waiting and
watching there to see that the situation was not changed by advice to Ross which
would or might enable him to escape death at the hands of his folks. He waited
long and watched faithfully, and his patience and vigil were rewarded. He saw Ed
Ross going towards the telegraph office. He at once concluded Ross was going
there to warn his kinsman, and give him a chance for his life. He followed. His
purpose was to stop the message; not to let the warning even start on its journey.
This he proposed to do by overawing the operator, a mere youth, or by brute
force. Judge Bridges dissuaded him from this course, but he adopted another to

destroy this one precarious chance of life which was being held out to Robert C. Ross. It would not do, Bridges advised him, to stop the warning by threatening or overpowering him — the operator. The young man was a newcomer, and a stranger there, and a resort to moral suasion with him was therefore unpromising and hazardous. Not so with the operator at the other end of the line. He was Judge Tally's friend of long standing. [Judge Tally] telegraphed his friend (the operator at Stevenson) not to let Ross get away. His language was, as first written, "Do not let party warned get away." This he handed to the operator to be sent to Stevenson, saying, "This message has something to do with the one you have," referring to Ed Ross' message. What then passed through his mind we are left to conjecture; but upon further thought he added to the message these words, "Say nothing." What was the full import of this completed message, looking at its terms and the circumstances under which it was sent? . . . [I]n short, the substance and effect of what Tally said to Huddleston, taking the two dispatches and all the circumstances into the account, was simply this, no more no less: "Ross has fled in the direction of Stevenson. The four Skeltons are following him on horseback, with guns, to take his life. Ross does not know of the pursuit. An effort is being made to get word to Ross through you that he is thus pursued, in order that he may get away from them. If you do not deliver this word to him, he cannot escape them. Do not deliver that message. Say nothing about it, and thereby prevent his getting away from them." A most careful analysis of the voluminous testimony in this case convinces us beyond a reasonable doubt that this was what Tally intended to convey to Huddleston, and that his message means this, and only this, to all reasonable comprehension. . . .

We therefore find and hold that John B. Tally, with full knowledge that the Skeltons were in pursuit of Ross with the intent to take his life, committed acts, namely, kept watch at Scottsboro to prevent warning of danger being sent to Ross; and, with like purpose, sent the message to Huddleston, which were calculated to aid, and were committed by him with the intent to aid, the said Skeltons to take the life of Ross under the circumstances which rendered them guilty of murder.

And we are next to consider and determine the second inquiry above, namely: Whether it is essential to the guilt of Judge Tally, as charged in the second count of the information, that the said acts, thus adapted, intended and committed by him, should, in fact, have aided the said Skeltons to take the life of the said Ross — should have, in fact, contributed to his death at their hands. . . . To be guilty of murder, therefore, not being a common-law principal, and not being an accessory before the fact — to be concerned in the commission of the offense within the meaning of our statute — he must be found to have aided or abetted the Skeltons in the commission of the offense in such sort as to constitute him at common law a principal in the second degree. A principal in this degree is one who is present at the commission of a felony by the hand of the principal in the first degree, and who, being thus present, aids or abets, or aids and abets, the latter therein. The presence which this definition requires need not be actual, physical juxtaposition in respect of the personal perpetrator of the crime. It is enough, so far as presence is concerned, for the principal in the second degree to be in a position to aid the commission of the crime by others. It is enough if he stands guard while the act is being perpetrated by others to prevent interference with them, or to warn them of the approach of danger; and it is immaterial how distant from the scene of the crime his vigil is maintained, provided it gives some promise of protection to those engaged in its active commission. At whatever distance he may be, he is present in legal contemplation if he is at the time performing any act in furtherance of the crime, or is in a position to give information to the principal which would be helpful to the end in view, or to prevent others from doing any act, by way of warning the intended victim or otherwise, which would be but an obstacle in the way of the consummation of the crime, or render its accomplishment more difficult. . . .

We are therefore clear to the conclusion that, before Judge Tally can be found guilty of aiding and abetting the Skeltons to kill Ross, it must appear that his vigil at Scottsboro to prevent Ross from being warned of his danger was by preconcert with them, whereby they would naturally be incited, encouraged, and emboldened — "given confidence" — to the deed, or that he aided them to kill Ross, contributed to Ross' death, in point of physical fact, by means of the telegram he sent to Huddleston. The assistance given, however, need not contribute to the criminal result in the sense that but for it the result would not have ensued. It is quite enough if the aid merely rendered it easier for the principal actor to accomplish the end intended by him and the aider and abettor, though in all human probability the end would have been attained without it. If the aid in homicide can be shown to have put the deceased at a disadvantage, to have deprived him of a single chance of life which but for it he would have had, he who furnishes such aid is guilty, though it cannot be known or shown that the dead man, in the absence thereof, would have availed himself of that chance; as, where one counsels murder, he is guilty as an accessory before the fact, though it appears probable that murder would have been done without his counsel; and as, where one being present by concert to aid if necessary is guilty as a principal in the second degree, though, had he been absent murder would have been committed, so where he who facilitates murder even by so much as destroying a single chance of life the assailed might otherwise have had, he thereby supplements the efforts of the perpetrator, and he is guilty as [a] principal in the second degree at common law, and is [a] principal in the first degree under our statute, notwithstanding it may be found that in all human probability the chance would not have been availed of, and death would have resulted anyway. We have already said enough to indicate the grounds of the conclusion which we now announce that Tally's standing guard at the telegraph office in Scottsboro to prevent Ross being warned of the pursuit of the Skeltons was not by preconcert with them, and was not known to them. It is even clearer and more certain that they knew neither of the occasion nor the fact of the sending of the message by him to Huddleston; and hence they were not, and could not have been aided in the execution of the purpose to kill by the keeping of this vigil, or by the mere fact of the forwarding of the message to Stevenson, since these facts in and of themselves could not have given them any actual, substantial help, as distinguished from incitement and encouragement, and they could not have aided them by way of incitement and encouragement, because they were ignorant of them; and so we are come to a consideration of the effect, if any, produced upon the situation at Stevenson by the message of Judge Tally to Huddleston, and upon his action in respect of the delivery to Ross of the message of warning sent by Ed Ross. This latter message reached Huddleston for Ross, we suppose, about five minutes — certainly not more than ten minutes — before Ross arrived at Stevenson. Immediately upon the heels of it, substantially at the same time, Tally's message to Huddleston was received by the latter. Ed Ross' message imported extreme urgency in its delivery, and Tally's to Huddleston, though by no means so intended, emphasized the necessity and importance, from the standpoint of duty, for the earliest possible delivery of Ed Ross' message to Robert C. Ross; and it was the manifest duty of Huddleston to deliver it at the earliest practicable moment of time. Huddleston appears to have appreciated the urgency of the case, and at first to have intended doing his duty. Upon receiving the two messages, he went at once without waiting, to copy them, to the Stevenson Hotel, which is located very near the telegraph office, in quest of Ross, upon the idea that he might have already arrived. We are to presume a purpose to do what duty enjoins until the contrary appears; and we therefore shall assume that Huddleston intended to deliver the message to Ross, or to inform him of its contents, had he been in the hotel. Not finding him there (for he had not yet reached Stevenson), Huddleston returned to the door of the depot, upstairs, in which was the telegraph office. By this time the command which Judge Tally had laid upon him had overmastered his sense of duty, and diverted him from his purpose to deliver Ed Ross' message to Robert. Standing there at the door, he saw a hack approaching from the direction of Scottsboro. He said then that he supposed Ross was in that hack. We do not think it was incumbent upon him, inasmuch as the hack was being driven directly to the depot, to go down the road to meet it, though the situation was then more urgent than was indicated by the telegrams, in that the Skeltons were at that time skulking on the flanks of, and immediately behind, the hack; but there is no evidence that Huddleston knew this. But we do not doubt that it was Huddleston's duty to go out to the road along which the hack was being driven, at a point opposite his own position at the depot, and near to it, and there and then have delivered the message or made known its contents to Ross. The only explanation he offers for not then delivering the message or making known its contents to Ross was not that he could not have done it (that was entirely practicable), but that he had not taken a copy of it — a consideration which did not prevent his going to the hotel for the purpose of delivery before he saw Ross appearing, and which, had his original purpose continued, we cannot believe would have swerved him from his plain duty at this juncture. Presuming that he would have done this, because it was his duty to do it — a duty which he at first appreciated — and finding, as a fact, that he did not do it, the reason for his default is found in the injunction laid upon him by Judge Tally. He did not warn Ross, because he did not want Ross to get away, and this because Judge Tally had asked him not to let Ross get away; so that, as he stood there at the door, he mapped out a course of action. He would not deliver the message immediately, if at all, but he would send off for the town marshal, and in the meantime he would call William Tally from over the way, and confer with him as to what should be done: Ross to be the while wholly unadvised of the contents of the message from his kinsman, and wholly ignorant of the pursuit of the Skeltons. So he sends a man in search of the marshal, whose whereabouts, and, of consequence, the time necessary to find and bring whom to the station, were unknown; beckons to William Tally to come to him; then turns and goes upstairs into the telegraph office. He says he went up there to copy Ross' message for delivery to him. If this be true, this was only another factor, so we have seen, in the delay that Judge Tally's message had determined him upon, for while, at first, he was anxious to deliver the message or its contents uncopied to Ross, when he thought Ross might be at the hotel, and went there to find him for that purpose, when Ross was actually in sight of him, and rapidly approaching him, he deemed it most important to copy the message before advising Ross. It was also into this upstairs office that he invited William Tally, and we cannot escape the conclusion that his purpose in going there before delivering the message was to have a consultation with William Tally as to what should be done before advising Ross, and also to give the marshal time to arrive; so that, should they conclude to adopt that course, they could have Ross arrested; and it cannot, we think, be doubted that he then had no purpose whatever of apprising Ross of the contents of the message, if ever, until he had had this conference with the brother of the man who had asked him not to deliver it at all. That this delay was to conserve such ulterior purpose as might be born of this conference, was wholly unwarranted, and was caused by the telegram of Judge Tally to Huddleston, we believe beyond a reasonable doubt.

It remains to be determined whether the unwarranted delay in the delivery of the message to Ross, or in advising him of its contents, thus caused by Judge Tally, with intent thereby to aid the Skeltons to kill Ross, did in fact, aid them or contribute to the death of Ross, by making it easier than it would otherwise have been for the Skeltons to kill him, by depriving him of some advantage he would have had had he been advised of its contents when his carriage stopped, or immediately upon his alighting from it, or by leaving him without some chance of life which would have been his had Huddleston done his duty. The telegram, we have said, should have been delivered, or its contents made known, to Ross at the time the hack came opposite where Huddleston was, and stopped. Huddleston and William Tally were equidistant from this point when the former called to the latter, at which time also Huddleston had seen the hack approaching this point. Tally, going to Huddleston, reached this middle point between them, unhastened, as Huddleston should have been, by the urgency of the message, just as the carriage got there and stopped. It is therefore clear that had Huddleston, instead of calling Tally and going into the depot, himself gone out to the road along which the carriage was approaching, and which was not more than 100 feet from him, he would have gotten there certainly by the time it stopped, and have acquainted Ross with the contents of the message, with the fact that four men were pursuing him with guns to take his life, before Ross alighted from the hack. Being thus advised, and not knowing of the immediate proximity of the Skeltons, it may be that Ross would have alighted as he did, exposed himself to the Skeltons' fire as he did, and been killed as he was. But, on the other hand, the Skeltons were at that time dismounted, and, two of them at least, a long way from their horses, and none of them were in his front up the road, and he had a chance of escape by continued flight in the vehicle. Again, he might then and there have put himself under the protection of Huddleston, as an officer of the law, and had the bystanders, those in the immediate neighborhood, of whom there were several, summoned to help protect him. This might have saved his life; it was a chance that he had. But, if it be conceded that, as he would not have known of the proximity of the Skeltons from mere knowledge that they were in pursuit, he would have alighted precisely as and when he did; yet when the first shot was fired, Ross would have known that the man who fired it was one of the Skeltons, and that three others of them were present in ambush, armed with guns, to take his life. Knowing this, the hopelessness of standing his ground and attempting to defend himself from his enemies, overpowering in number, and secure in their hiding places, while he stood in the open street, would have been at once manifest to him; and instead of standing there as he did, knowing only as he did that some one man, whom he did not know, had fired a gun, and peering and craning his neck to see whence the shot came, and who fired it, he could, and doubtless would, have sought safety by flight in the opposite direction, in which was the Union Hotel, scarce 100 feet away. And in view of the fact that he was hit only once by the numerous shots that were fired at him while he stood there in the open, and that not in a vital or disabling part, it is very probable that, had he attempted that mode of escape as soon as the first shot was fired, he would have reached the hotel in perfect safety. Certain it is that in making that effort he would have gone away from the lurking places of his enemies, and he would not, as he did in his ignorance of the true situation, have placed himself where John Skelton, at close quarter, could and did shoot him to death from behind his back. But whether he would or would not have reached a place of refuge we need not inquire or find. The knowledge that he would have had if the telegram of Ed Ross had been delivered to him, when it could and should have been delivered, of the pursuit of the Skeltons, together with the knowledge which would have been imparted to him by the report of the first gun in connection with the contents of the message, would instantly have advised him of the extent of his danger — a danger which he could not combat, which was deadly in character, and from which he would naturally have been at once impressed the only hope of escape lay in immediate flight. That was a chance for his life that this knowledge would have given him. That was a chance of which the withholding of this knowledge deprived him. Tally's telegram to Huddleston deprived him of that knowledge. Tally, through Huddleston, deprived him of that chance. Again, after having been shot in the legs, and partially disabled by one of the many shots fired at him by Robert, James, and Walter Skelton as he stood fully exposed to their broadside, he, in his crippled condition, made an effort to find protection behind the oil house, the nearest building to him. Only these three men had fired up to that time. He knew of the presence of these three only. The house sheltered him from two of these men and partially also from the third. He got there, and stood facing the direction these three were; and he called aloud for protection from them, meantime keeping a lookout for them, and intending no doubt to protect himself from them if he could. He knew of the presence of these three only. Nobody had seen John Skelton. He did not know that John Skelton was there. Had he gotten Ed Ross' telegram, this he would have known: that there were four of them; that only three had shot at him; that the other was somewhere hidden in the immediate vicinity. And, while seeking to escape from or guard himself from the other three while he was by the side of the oil house, he would also have sought to guard himself against the fourth. He was off his guard as to this fourth man, John Skelton, because he was ignorant of his presence. This ignorance was directly due to Tally's active interference. Tally's aid to the Skeltons by way of preventing Ross being warned enabled John Skelton to come upon Ross from his rear, and shoot him down. Ross went to his death, guarding himself against the other three, and calling for protection from them, without even knowing that the man who killed him was nearer to him than Scottsboro. Can it be doubted that Ross' utter ignorance of John Skelton's presence with the others at Stevenson made it easier for John Skelton to take his life? Can it be doubted that his ignorance of the presence of all four Skeltons when the first gun was fired by Robert Skelton at Bloodwood, when, had he known it, he could have fled in the appreciable time between the time of the firing of the first and other shots — the next one being fired by the same man — made it easier for them to take his life? Can it be doubted in any case that murder by lying in wait is facilitated by the unconsciousness of the victim? Or in any case that the chances of the intended victim would be improved, and his death rendered more difficult of accomplishment, if the first unfruitful shot apprises him of the number and the identity of his assailants, and the full scope and measure of their motive and purposes? We cannot believe otherwise. It is inconceivable to us after the maturest consideration, reflection, and discussion, but that Ross' predicament was rendered infinitely more desperate, his escape more difficult, and his death of much more easy and certain accomplishment by the withholding from him of the message of Ed Ross. This withholding was the work of Judge Tally. An intent to aid the Skeltons to take the life of Ross actuated him to it. The intent was effectuated. They thereby were enabled to take him unawares, and to send him to his death without, we doubt not, his ever actually knowing who sought his life, or being able to raise a hand in defense, or to take an advised step in retreat. And we are impelled to find that John B. Tally aided and abetted the murder of Robert C. Ross, as alleged in the second specification of the second count of the information, and to adjudge that he is guilty as charged in second count; and judgment deposing him from office will be entered on the records of this court.

HEAD, J. (dissenting).

I am of the opinion the respondent should be acquitted of both charges. I do not believe, beyond a reasonable doubt, that respondent intended, in sending the telegram to Huddleston, to aid or abet in the murder of Ross. I do not believe, beyond a reasonable doubt, that the telegram of warning would have been delivered to Ross by Huddleston before the shooting began if the telegram of the respondent had not been sent.

Notes and Questions

1.   What causal role did Tally play in the death of Ross? The court acknowledges that even if Ross had received the warning telegram, he might have been killed. The court speaks of "depriving him of some advantage," but how much deprivation is enough? One chance in a hundred, one in a thousand, or one in a million? Is it crucial to the decision that Ross could conceivably have escaped if Tally had not sent his telegram?

2.   Consider the following variations on Tally:

a.   *Ross's kinsman never sends him a warning telegram. But Tally stands watch at the telegraph office, resolved to interfere, in case anyone tries to warn Ross.*

In this variation, is Tally an accomplice in the later killing? Has he provided aid?

b.   *Ross's relative does send the warning. After Tally sends his telegram, the Skeltons change their minds and make no attempt to kill Ross.*

Assume in this variation that the Skeltons cannot be convicted of any crime. Could Tally be convicted of attempted murder even though no substantive crime was committed? Examine Model Penal Code section 5.01 (3):

Conduct Designed to Aid Another in Commission of a Crime. A person who engages in conduct designed to aid another to commit a crime which would establish his complicity under Section 2.06 if the crime were committed by such other person, is guilty of an attempt to commit the crime, although the crime is not committed or attempted by such other person.

This equation of "attempted complicity" with attempt to perpetrate a substantive offense has been incorporated into the penal codes of about a dozen states. See, e.g., Ariz. Rev. Stat. §13-1001 (A) (3) (2001); N.J.S.A. §2C:5-1 (c) (1995).

> c. *Huddleston ignores Tally's telegram and delivers the warning to Ross, but Ross is killed anyway.*

In this variation is Tally guilty of attempted murder, on the ground that he unsuccessfully attempted to aid a murder? Most jurisdictions reject attempt liability for attempted complicity in a completed crime, on the grounds that (1) attempted complicity in a substantive crime is not an attempt to commit the substantive crime and (2) complicity is not a crime. But under statutes incorporating Model Penal Code section 5.01(3), attempted complicity is an attempt to commit the substantive crime. So Tally's bungled attempt to aid a successful murder becomes attempted murder. Which position makes more sense?

Perhaps, instead of being exonerated or convicted of attempted murder, the superfluous would-be accomplice to a successful murder should be guilty of murder itself. See Model Penal Code §2.06(3) (a) (ii):

> A person is an accomplice of another person in the commission of an offense if:
>> (a) with the purpose of promoting or facilitating the commission of the offense, he . . .
>>> (ii) aids or agrees or attempts to aid such other person in planning or committing it.

What rationale could justify a conviction for murder, given the Model Penal Code makes murder an exception to the rule that attempt is punished as severely as the completed crime?

> d. *Huddleston ignores Tally's telegram and delivers the warning to Ross, who then escapes.*

In this variation, assuming that the Skeltons could be convicted of attempted murder, should Tally be charged with attempting to aid an attempted murder? Is it a stronger case if Huddleston does not deliver the warning but Ross escapes anyway? Even though, in both examples, Tally has done all that he can to thwart Ross's escape?

> e. *Tally changes his mind and sends another telegram, telling Huddleston to ignore his first telegram.*

This variation, of course, raises the issue of whether it is possible for an accomplice to recant in such a manner as to negate his criminal liability. See Model Penal Code section 2.06(6) (c) (i) and (ii):

> Unless otherwise provided by the Code or by the law defining the offense, a person is not an accomplice in an offense committed by another person if: . . .
>> (c) he terminates his complicity prior to the commission of the offense and
>>> (i) wholly deprives it of effectiveness in the commission of the offense; or

(ii) gives timely warning to the law enforcement authorities or otherwise makes proper effort to prevent the commission of the offense.

New York has a similar defense of renunciation, conditioned on a "substantial effort to prevent" the offense, but shifts the burden of proof on to the defendant N.Y. Pen. C. §40.10(1) (1998).

3. *Individual responsibility for collective action: the moral issue.* Should we require proof of causal responsibility for harm before we blame and punish accessories for such harm? Professor Christopher Kutz poses this moral question through a discussion of the allied fire-bombing of Dresden during World War II:[7]

. . . [T]wo principles that are deeply rooted in commonsense moral thinking . . . restrict the object of accountability to individual harms . . . [: The Individual Difference Principle, holding that] . . . I am accountable only for the difference my action alone makes to the resulting state of affairs, and the Control Principle, [holding that] . . . I am accountable only for those harms over whose occurrence I had control.

Let us consider how these principles tend to rule out any substantial notion of complicitous accountability. . . . I will discuss a real example: the Allied strategic bombing of Dresden on February 13-15, 1945. The attack on Dresden involved a series of mainly incendiary bombing raids that combined with meteorological conditions to produce a firestorm that devoured the city's residential sectors. The bombing . . . was seen by many at the time as falling well outside the pale of legitimate warfare. A figure of 35,000 civilians killed is now generally accepted. . . . More significant than the number of deaths was their manner. The firestorm killed through a combination of intense heat and asphyxiation, the latter attacking those who had taken refuge in shelters, when the oxygen was sucked out by the fires. . . . The Dresden firestorm was seen by planners as a welcome, if fortuitous, occurrence — Bomber Command had been trying to repeat its success in the 1943 Hamburg firestorm raid. . . .

[T]he Dresden raids [involved] massive . . . individual participation in a force of destruction as overdetermined as can be imagined. The city was bombed in three raids, and at least 1,000 planes and 8,000 crewmen were directly involved in the raids, in various roles as pilots, navigators, bombers, and gunners. The firestorm was already raging before many crews dropped their bombs. Each crewman's causal contribution to the conflagration, indeed each plane's, was marginal to the point of insignificance. Many thousands further were involved in planning and support at Bomber Command. . . . [Thus, t]he Dresden bombing constitutes an evil that was more inhabited than made, where individuals discovered themselves on the verge or in the course of participation in a great wrong through the flow of obedience and circumstance. . . .

The number of individuals involved in the Dresden bombing and the nature of the destruction license a stipulation close to, if not coincident with, the historical facts. No one rank-and-file individual made a difference to the evil that occurred, and no one could control the devastation that resulted. . . . Even if one (and probably many) of the flyers or planners failed to participate, the firestorm would still have been raised and the massive casualties would still have happened. Therefore, [according to the Individual Difference and Control principles,] there is no basis for holding an individual bomber accountable. . . . We might have contempt for a bomber who reveled in the destruction and killing, but there is nothing he has done for which response is warranted. Each bomber can truly reply to the victims or their survivors, "Why blame me? I have not caused your suffering,

7. Kutz, *supra,* note 1, at 116-124 [some paragraphs have been reordered for ease of exposition — EDS].

nor made you worse off." Since all of the bombers are symmetrically placed, none is accountable for the wrong. Individual accountability has fled the scene of collectively induced suffering.

. . . [Those who think] the Dresden bombing is a great wrong, . . . [and that] each person who participated voluntarily . . . is accountable in some way, . . . are pulled by what I will call the Complicity Principle: I am accountable for what others do when I intentionally participate in the wrong they do or harm they cause . . . , independently of the actual difference I make. . . . The Complicity Principle is well-grounded in our intuitions, ethical practices, and psychologies. But it is clearly inconsistent with the commonsense Individual Difference and Control principles I mentioned earlier.

Should voluntary participants in collective wrongdoing be held responsible for its harms, even when their actions *make no difference?*

B.   MENS REA OF COMPLICITY

One of the most vexing questions in the law of complicity is what kind of culpability a person must exhibit to be guilty as an accomplice. That complicity is merely a way of committing a crime suggests that the mens rea for an accomplice should be the same as it is for a principal — whatever culpable mental states are ordinarily required with respect to the conduct, circumstance and result elements of the offense. Yet there are two obstacles to this approach.

First, the very notion of accomplice liability assumes that the accomplice's conduct is different from the principal's; if so, her culpability with respect to conduct elements may be different as well. For example, a lookout can be an accomplice to burglary without intending to enter a building or to commit a felony therein. On the other hand, the accomplice must have culpability with respect to the conduct elements specifically inherent in complicity — that is, aiding or encouraging. And, as we will see, intent to aid or encourage is a complex mental state, because it necessarily involves some idea of the *perpetrator's* intentions.

Second, as we have seen earlier, we hold accomplices responsible for harmful results even though we may not be sure that they actually have caused such results. What sort of culpability must an accomplice have toward a result element — like a victim's death — in order to share liability with one who does intentionally cause it? Must the accomplice desire or expect this result? Or must the accomplice instead know simply that the principal desires or expects this result?

Thus, in assessing the culpability of one who aids or abets in the commission of a crime, we may wish to consider his or her awareness and attitude with respect to three different factors: the actus reus elements of the principal's offense, the facilitative or encouraging effect of the accomplice's actions, and the principal's intentions. This gives us three different forms of culpability:

- *"Offense culpability"* — culpability with respect to the conduct, circumstance, or result elements of the offense.
- *"Aid culpability"* — culpability with respect to the facilitative or encouraging effect of the accomplice's actions.
- *"Perpetrator culpability"* — culpability with respect to the principal's intentions.

In formulating the culpability required for accomplice complicity, most jurisdictions combine *two* of these three forms of liability.

Thus, for example, because the accomplice's conduct is not the same as the principal's, "offense culpability" by itself is not an adequate standard of liability. One traditional approach replaces it with "perpetrator culpability" and "aid culpability." Yet this approach risks inculpating persons who may participate in crime only to thwart or expose it. Accordingly some jurisdictions substitute "perpetrator culpability" for the conduct part of offense culpability, while retaining the circumstance and result parts of "offense culpability." Jurisdictions influenced by the Model Penal Code employ a combination of "offense culpability" and "aid culpability": they substitute "aid culpability" for culpability with respect to conduct elements, while retaining the normally required culpability with respect to result and, possibly, circumstance elements.

The following subsections explore all three of these two-part standards for accomplice liability.

1. "Perpetrator Liability" and "Aid Culpability"

The following cases and notes focus on the accomplice's mental culpability with respect to the principal's own culpable mental state, and also with respect to the likelihood that the accomplice's actions will encourage or assist the principal in committing her offense. As we will see, the most important issue is whether the accomplice's culpability in this context is "purpose" to aid or "mere knowledge" of facilitative effect.

PEOPLE v. BEEMAN
Supreme Court of California
35 Cal. 3d 547, 199 Cal. Rptr. 60 (1984)

REYNOSO, JUSTICE.

Timothy Mark Beeman appeals from a judgment of conviction of robbery, burglary, false imprisonment, destruction of telephone equipment and assault with intent to commit a felony. . . . Appellant was not present during commission of the offense. His conviction rested on the theory that he aided and abetted his acquaintances James Gray and Michael Burk.

The primary issue before us is whether the standard California Jury Instructions (CALJIC Nos. 3.00 and 3.01) adequately inform the jury of the criminal intent required to convict a defendant as an aider and abettor of the crime.

We hold that instruction No. 3.01 is erroneous. Sound law, embodied in a long line of California decisions, requires proof that an aider and abettor rendered aid with an intent or purpose of either committing, or of encouraging or facilitating commissions of, the target offense. . . .

James Gray and Michael Burk drove from Oakland to Redding for the purpose of robbing appellant's sister-in-law, Mrs. Marjorie Beeman, of valuable jewelry, including a 3.5 carat diamond ring. They telephoned the residence to determine that she was home. Soon thereafter Burk knocked at the door of the victim's house, presented himself as a poll taker, and asked to be let in. When Mrs. Beeman asked for identification, he forced her into the hallway and entered. Gray, disguised in a ski mask, followed. The two subdued the victim, placed tape over her mouth and eyes and tied her to a bathroom fixture. Then they ransacked the house, taking numerous pieces of jewelry and a set of silverware. The jewelry included a 3.5 carat, heart-shaped diamond ring and a blue sapphire ring. The total value of these two rings was over $100,000. In the course of the robbery, telephone wires inside the house were cut.

Appellent was arrested six days later in Emeryville. He had in his possession several of the less valuable stolen rings. He supplied the police with information that led to the arrests of Burk and Gray. With Gray's cooperation appellant assisted police in recovering most of the stolen property.

Burk, Gray and appellant were jointly charged. After the trial court severed the trials, Burk and Gray pled guilty to robbery. At appellant's trial they testified that he had been extensively involved in planning the crime. . . . [They testified that Beeman had supplied them with information about the contents and layout of the house, discussed the method used, made suggestions about how Burk and Gray should dress, and agreed to sell the loot for 20 percent of the proceeds. Gray's testimony did indicate that shortly before the robbery Beeman said he wanted no part of it, and afterward expressed anger that the robbery had been committed and Burk had not disguised himself.]

Appellant Beeman's testimony contradicted that of Burk and Gray as to almost every material element of his own involvement. . . .

Appellant requested that the jury be instructed . . . that aiding and abetting liability requires proof of intent to aid. The request was denied.

After three hours of deliberation, the jury submitted two written questions to the court: "We would like to hear again how one is determined to be an accessory and by what actions can he absolve himself"; and "Does inaction mean the party is guilty?" The jury was reinstructed in accord with the standard instructions, CALJIC Nos. 3.00 and 3.01. The court denied appellant's renewed request that the instructions be modified, explaining that giving another, slightly different instruction at this point would further complicate matters. The jury returned its verdicts of guilty on all counts two hours later.

Penal Code section 31 provides in pertinent part:

All persons concerned in the commission of a crime, . . . whether they directly commit the act constituting the offense, or aid and abet in its commission, or, not being present, having advised and encouraged its commission, . . . are principals in any crime so committed.

Thus, those persons who at common law would have been termed accessories before the fact and principals in the second degree as well as those who actually perpetrate the offense, are to be prosecuted, tried and punished as principals in California. The term "aider and abettor" is now often used to refer to principals other than the perpetrator, whether or not they are present at the commission of the offense.

CALJIC No. 3.00 defines principals to a crime to include

Those who, with knowledge of the unlawful purpose of the one who does directly and actively commit or attempt to commit the crime, aid and abet in its commission . . . or . . . who, whether present or not at the commission or attempted commission of the crime, advise and encourage its commission.

CALJIC No. 3.01 defines aiding and abetting as follows:

> A person aids and abets the commission of a crime if, with knowledge of the unlawful purpose of the perpetrator of the crime, he aids, promotes, encourages or instigates by act or advice the commission of such crime. . . .

Appellant asserts that the current instructions, in particular CALJIC No. 3.01, substitute an element of knowledge of the perpetrator's intent for the element of criminal intent of the accomplice, in contravention of common law principles and California case law. He argues that the instruction given permitted the jury to convict him of the same offenses as the perpetrators without finding that he harbored either the same criminal intent as they, or the specific intent to assist them, thus depriving him of his constitutional rights to due process and equal protection of the law. Appellant further urges that the error requires reversal because it removed a material issue from the jury and on this record it is impossible to conclude that the jury necessarily resolved the same factual question that would have been presented by the missing instruction.

The People argue that the standard instruction properly reflects California law, which requires no more than that the aider and abettor have knowledge of the perpetrator's criminal purpose and do a voluntary act which in fact aids the perpetrator. . . . The People further contend that defendants are adequately protected from conviction for acts committed under duress or which inadvertently aid a perpetrator by limitation of the liability of an aider and abettor to those acts knowingly aided and their natural and reasonable consequences [and] because proof of intentional aiding in most cases can be inferred from aid with knowledge of the perpetrator's purpose. Thus, respondent argues, it is doubtful that the requested modification would bring about different results in the vast majority of cases. . . .

There is no question that an aider and abettor must have criminal intent in order to be convicted of a criminal offense. . . . The act of encouraging or counseling itself implies a purpose or goal of furthering the encouraged result. "An aider and abettor's fundamental purpose, motive and intent is to aid and assist the perpetrator in the latter's commission of the crime."

The essential conflict in current appellate opinions is between those cases which state that an aider and abettor must have an intent or purpose to commit or assist in the commission of the criminal offenses, and those finding it sufficient that the aider and abettor engage in the required acts with knowledge of the perpetrator's criminal purpose. . . .

The facts from which a mental state may be inferred must not be confused with the mental state that the prosecution is required to prove. Direct evidence of the mental state of the accused is rarely available except through his or her testimony. The trier of fact is and must be free to disbelieve the testimony and to infer that the truth is otherwise when such inference is supported by circumstantial evidence regarding the actions of the accused. Thus, an act which has the effect of giving aid and encouragement, and which is done with knowledge of the criminal purpose of the person aided, may indicate that the actor intended to assist in fulfillment of the known criminal purpose. However . . . the act may be done with some other purpose which precludes criminal liability.

If the jury were instructed that the law conclusively presumes the intention of the accused solely from his or her voluntary acts, it would "effectively eliminate intent as an ingredient of the offense" and would "conflict with the overriding presumption of innocence with which the law endows the accused and which extends to every element of the crime." (Sandstrom v. Montana (1979) 442 U.S. 510, 522, quoting from Morissette v. United States (1952) 342 U.S. 246, 274-75; original emphasis omitted.) . . .

Thus, we conclude that the weight of authority and sound law require proof that an aider and abettor act with knowledge of the criminal purpose of the perpetrator and with an intent or purpose either of committing, or encouraging or facilitating commission of, the offense.

When definition of the offense includes the intent to do some act or achieve some consequence beyond the actus reus of the crime . . . the aider and abettor must share the specific intent of the perpetrator. By "share" we mean neither that the aider and abettor must be prepared to commit the offense by his or her own act should the perpetrator fail to do so, nor that the aider and abettor must seek to share the fruits of the crime. Rather, an aider and abettor will "share" the perpetrator's specific intent when he or she knows the full extent of the perpetrator's criminal purpose and gives aid or encouragement with the intent or purpose of facilitating the perpetrator's commission of the crime. The liability of an aider and abettor extends also to the natural and reasonable consequences of the acts he knowingly and intentionally aids and encourages.

CALJIC No. 3.01 inadequately defines aiding and abetting because it fails to insure that an aider and abettor will be found to have the required mental state with regard to his or her own act. . . . We suggest that an appropriate instruction should inform the jury that a person aids and abets the commission of a crime when he or she, acting with (1) knowledge of the unlawful purpose of the perpetrator, and (2) the intent or purpose of committing, encouraging, or facilitating the commission of the offense, (3) by act or advice aids, promotes, encourages or instigates, the commission of the crime. . . .

Respondent urges that any instructional error was harmless. . . .

Appellant did not deny that he had given information to Burk and Gray which aided their criminal enterprise, but he claimed his purposes in doing so were innocent. Appellant admitted that he was at some time made aware of his friends' intent to rob Mrs. Beeman, but insisted that he wanted nothing to do with a robbery of his relatives.

He testified that he didn't think Burk would really go through with the robbery or that Gray would help. Two days before the incident, he again told Gray that he didn't want to be involved. Gray's testimony confirmed that appellant had twice said he did not want to be involved. Finally, appellant claimed to have taken possession of the jewelry and feigned attempts to sell it in order to recover the property and return it to the victims. Thus, the essential point of his defense was that although he acted in ways which in fact aided the criminal enterprise, he did not act with the intent of encouraging or facilitating the planning or commission of the offenses. . . .

Under these circumstances, where the defense centered on the very element as to which the jury was inadequately instructed and the jurors' communication to the court indicated confusion on the same point, we cannot find the error harmless.

The convictions are reversed.

Notes and Questions

1. If Beeman's testimony were accepted, what would be his mens rea for the crimes? If it were knowledge rather than purpose, should that make him less culpable than the principals? Recall the discussion of purpose and knowledge in the introduction to mens rea in Chapter 3, p. 191, *supra.*

The court rejects automatic criminal liability for "an act which has the effect of giving aid and encouragement, and which is done with the knowledge of the criminal purpose of the person aided." It states that "the act may be done with some other purpose which precludes criminal liability." What could these other purposes have been in Beeman's case?

2. *"True purpose."* For decades, the American courts and legislatures have debated whether knowledge or "true purpose" should be the required mens rea for accomplice liability. Judge Learned Hand authored the definitive opinion adopting the purpose requirement. In United States v. Peoni, 100 F.2d 401, 402 (2d Cir. 1938), the defendant had sold counterfeit money to Regno, who in turn had sold the counterfeit money to Dorsey. Peoni was charged as an accessory to Dorsey's possession of the counterfeit money. Though Peoni had reason to know that Regno would sell the money to a third party, the prosecution could not show that Peoni intended or desired that Regno would sell the counterfeit money again. In reversing the conviction, Judge Hand rejected the government's argument that "the possession of the second buyer was a natural consequence of Peoni's original act, with which he might be charged." Instead, the complicity doctrine required that the defendant "in some sort associate himself with the venture, that he participate in it as something that he wishes to bring about, that he seek by his action to make it succeed. All the words used — even the most colorless 'abet' — carry an implication of purposive attitude towards it."

Even if Judge Hand is right in principle, is it clear that Peoni did not "want" Regno to resell the money? What if Peoni knew Regno always served as middleman in counterfeit transactions?

The famous contrast to *Peoni* is Backun v. United States, 112 F.2d 635, 637 (4th Cir. 1940), where the defendant knowingly sold stolen silverware to a third person, Zucker, in New York, and Zucker then transported the silverware to North Carolina to sell it. Backun wanted Zucker to sell the silverware and knew Zucker would go out of state to do so, but he did not specifically desire that Zucker leave the state. Judge Parker nevertheless upheld Backun's conviction of interstate transportation of stolen merchandise, using the "knowledge" test:

> Guilt as an accessory depends, not on "having a stake" in the outcome of crime . . . but on aiding and assisting the perpetrators; and those who make a profit by furnishing to criminals, whether by sale or otherwise, the means to carry on their nefarious undertakings aid them just as truly as if they were actual partners with them, having a stake in the fruits of their enterprise. To say that the sale of goods is normally a lawful transaction is beside the point. The seller may not ignore the purpose for which the purchase is made if he is advised of that purpose, or wash his hands of the aid that he has given the perpetrator of a felony by the plea that he has merely made a sale of merchandise. One who sells a gun to another knowing that he is buying it to commit a murder, would hardly escape conviction as an accessory to the murder by showing that he received full price for the gun; and no difference in principle can be drawn between such a case and any other case of a seller who knows that the purchaser intends to use the goods which

he is purchasing in the commission of a felony. In any such case, not only does the act of the seller assist in the commission of the felony, but his will assents to its commission, since he could refuse to give the assistance by refusing to make the sale.

The majority of jurisdictions have adopted the Hand approach over Parker's analysis in *Backun*, requiring a showing of purpose. The Model Penal Code has also adopted a purpose requirement:

Section 2.06.   Liability for Conduct of Another; Complicity

(3) A person is an accomplice of another person in the commission of an offense if:

(a) with the purpose of promoting or facilitating the commission of the offense he

(i) solicits such other person to commit it; or

(ii) aids or agrees or attempts to aid such other person in planning or committing it. . . .

3. *"Willful ignorance" and "true purpose."* In United States v. Giovanetti, 919 F.2d 1223 (7th Cir. 1990), Janis owned a house which he rented to Orlando, who ran a voluminous gambling business. Janis, prosecuted for aiding and abetting the gambling ring, denied that he knew that the house was being used for gambling, though government witnesses testified that Janis knew enough about Orlando to infer that Orlando would only have wanted the house to run his gambling trade. The trial court gave the jury the following so-called "willful ignorance" or "ostrich" instruction, drawn from the case of United States v. Jewell in Chapter 3, *supra*, p. 193:

> You may infer knowledge from a combination of suspicion and indifference to the truth. If you find that a person had a strong suspicion that things were not what they seemed or that someone had withheld some important facts, yet shut his eyes for fear that he would learn, you may conclude that he acted knowingly.

The Court of Appeals reversed, with Judge Richard Posner explaining why the "ostrich" instruction was improper in this case:

> Now it is not the law that every time a seller sells something that he knows will be used for an illegal purpose he is guilty of aiding and abetting, let alone of actual participation in the illegal conduct. . . . It is not the purpose of the ostrich instruction to tell the jury that it does not need direct evidence of guilty knowledge beyond a reasonable doubt. Still less is it to enable conviction of one who merely suspects that he may be involved with wrongdoers . . . Aider and abettor liability is not negligence liability. The aider and abettor must know that he is assisting an illegal activity.
>
> The most powerful criticism of the ostrich instruction is, precisely, that its tendency is to allow juries to convict upon a finding of negligence for crimes that require intent. The criticism can be deflected by thinking carefully about just what it is that real ostriches do (or at least are popularly supposed to do). They do not just fail to follow through on their suspicions of bad things. They are not merely *careless* birds. . . . They *deliberately* avoid acquiring unpleasant knowledge. The ostrich instruction is designed for cases in which there is evidence that the defendant, knowing or strongly suspecting that he is involved in shady dealings, takes steps to make sure that he does not acquire full or exact knowledge of the nature and extent of those dealings.

The government points out that the rented house in Bridgeview was a short way down a side street from the thoroughfare on which Janis commuted to work daily. It would have been easy for him to drive by the house from time to time to see what he was doing, and if he had done so he might have discovered its use as a wireroom. He did not do so. But this is not the active avoidance with which the ostrich doctrine is concerned. It would be if the house had been *on* the thoroughfare, and Janis, fearful of what he would see if he drove past it, altered his commuting route to avoid it. Janis failed to display curiosity, but he did nothing to prevent the truth from being communicated to him. He did not act to avoid learning the truth. [919 F.2d at 1227-28 (emphasis in original)]

Is Judge Posner's distinction too generous to Janis? Is it too subtle for future trial courts to use?

4. *Dual crime cases.* In some jurisdictions a purposive accomplice to one crime can become liable for a second crime committed by a principal or co-accomplice where she is merely negligent with respect to the possibility of that second crime. For example, Title 17-A, Section 57(3)(A), of the Maine Revised Statutes (1983) provides:

A person is an accomplice of another person in the commission of a crime if:

A. With the intent of promoting or facilitating the commission of the crime, he solicits such other person to commit the crime, or aids or agrees to aid or attempts to aid such other person in planning or committing the crime. A person is an accomplice under this subsection to any crime the commission of which was a reasonably foreseeable consequence of his conduct.

Thus, even in the absence of a felony-murder doctrine, an accomplice could be held liable for an unforeseen killing committed by the principal during an armed robbery. He would not escape liability even if he did not participate in the actual killing but waited outside as a lookout. For example, in People v. Kessler, 57 Ill. 2d 493, 315 N.E.2d 29 (1974), the defendant

waited in an automobile outside a tavern while his two unarmed companions entered the building to commit burglary. While inside the tavern, they were surprised by the owner, and one of the burglars shot and wounded him with a gun taken during the burglary. Later while defendant's companions were fleeing on foot, one of them fired a shot at a passing police officer. At that time defendant was sitting in an automobile. [315 N.E.2d at 30]

The defendant's conviction for attempted murder was reversed by the appellate court on the ground that the defendant did not intend the crime to occur. The Supreme Court of Illinois reinstated the conviction, stating that

where one aids another in the planning or commission of an offense he is legally accountable for the conduct of the person he aids; and . . . the word "conduct" encompasses any criminal act done in furtherance of the planned and intended act. [Id. at 32]

Therefore, because the defendant intended to take part in the burglary he is criminally liable for the attempted murder committed by his companions in connection with that crime.

Similarly, in State v. Carson, 950 S.W.2d 951 (Tenn. 1997), Carson, along with Gary and Stover, decided to rob a television repair store. Carson, who had been in the store before, described to his co-robbers the layout, and gave each a handgun. Then Carson waited in the car while Gary and Stover entered the store under the pretense of seeking repair advice. Gary and Stover then held two employees at gunpoint, and then, as they left with their loot, fired three shots. All three were charged with aggravated robbery and aggravated assault. Affirming the conviction, the court stated the relevant rule:

> "If two persons join in a purpose to commit a crime, each of them, if actually or consecutively present, is not only guilty as a principal, if the other commits that particular crime, *but he is also guilty of any other crime committed by the other in pursuance of the common purpose, or as a natural and probable consequence thereof.*" [Id. at 954, quoting Key v. State, 563 S.W.2d 184, 186 (Tenn. 1978) (emphasis by *Carson* court).]

5. *Facilitation.* New York has taken a slightly different approach to accomplice liability. Although it strictly adheres to the true purpose test for accomplice liability, it has also adopted the lesser included crime of "criminal facilitation." New York Penal Law section 115.05 (1998) states,

> A person is guilty of criminal facilitation in the second degree when, believing it is probable that he is rendering aid to a person who intends to commit a class A felony, he engages in conduct which provides such person with means or opportunity for the commission thereof and which in fact aids such person to commit such class A felony. . . . Criminal facilitation in the second degree is a class C felony.

Is this a sensible compromise? Is its goal to offer a trade-off between the accomplice's culpability and the court's or jury's reluctance to punish an accomplice as severely as it does the principal? How much of a sentencing differential between the two classes of felonies would make that trade-off optimal?

Another way of looking at "facilitation" is to contrast it with complicity, treating facilitation as a crime of risk-taking and complicity as a form of liability for actual harm.[8] One statute reflecting such an approach is the following Colorado statute, punishing one very specific form of criminal facilitation as a felony:

> Any person who intentionally, knowingly, or recklessly provides a handgun with or without remuneration to any person under the age of eighteen years . . . commits the crime of unlawfully providing or permitting a juvenile to possess a handgun. [Colorado Stats. §18-12-108.7] (1) (a) (Supp. 2003).

This statute was applied in the following situation:

Man Admits Selling Gun Used in U.S. School Massacre[9]

A 22-year-old computer programmer pleaded guilty Wednesday to providing two teenagers with the assault weapon they used to shoot up Columbine High School last April, killing 13 people before taking their own lives.

In the first guilty plea connected to the massacre, Mark Manes also admitted to selling one of the gunmen, Eric Harris, 100 rounds of 9mm ammunition for $25 the night before the April 20 attack . . .

---

8. See Daniel B. Yeager, Dangerous Games and the Criminal Law, Criminal Justice Ethics, Winter/Spring 1997, at 3, 10.

9. Reuters, Aug. 18, 1999.

Manes's attorney Robert Ransome said his client asked Harris if he was going to go shooting that night and he said Harris answered no, but that he was going shooting the next day.

Manes also pleaded guilty to handling two sawed-off shotguns that he used at a shooting range with the two gunmen several weeks before the attack. . . .

Harris, who turned 18 just before the shooting and his friend Dylan Klebold, 17, killed 12 fellow students and a teacher at the school in Littleton, Colo., before turning the guns on themselves.

According to court records, Manes sold the gunmen the assault weapon used in the rampage for $500. Ransome said his client had no idea the TEK-DC9 assault pistol would be used in the attack and that Manes pleaded guilty because he wanted to spare the community a trial.

"Even though Mark had no idea about what was going to happen at Columbine — just the fact that he played a part in the chain of events and was involved with the handgun — the entire family felt strongly that he needed to take responsibility," Ransome said after the hearing.

Then on Nov. 12, 1999, Manes was sentenced to six years in prison (out of a maximum possible 18 years) for the gun-transfer crime. At the sentencing hearing, the judge was informed that Manes had met the killers months before the killings at a gun show, where he bought them a semiautomatic handgun. Later, Manes accompanied them to a target-practice range. In Manes's presence, Harris shot at a tree trunk and said, "Imagine that in someone's [expletive] brain." Manes also supplied them with ammunition the day before the killings. Finally, the judge heard a transcript of a videotape made by the two teenage killers shortly after the gun purchase from Manes and before the killings. In the tape, Klebold thanked Manes and another man involved in the sale, Philip Duran, who was awaiting prosecution himself: "Oh, I'd like to make a thank you to Mark and Phil. . . . Very cool. You helped us do what we needed to do. Thank you." But then Klebold added, "Let me tell you this much, they have no clue. So don't blame them and arrest them for what we did." Harris added, "Yeah, you know it's not their fault . . . We would have found someone else."[10]

Without this statute, could Manes have been charged as an accomplice in the Columbine killings? Should the availability of the statute preclude a prosecution for his role in the killings?[11]

2.   "Perpetrator Culpability" and "Offense Culpability"

As noted earlier, a problem with relying on the combination of "perpetrator liability" and "aid culpability" is that it risks imposing criminal punishment on a person whose clear goal is to thwart or expose the crime. The following famous case illustrates the problem of the "accomplice" who "wants" the crime to happen — in order that the "principal" get caught.

10. Michael Janofsky, Columbine Killers, on Tape, Thanked 2 for Gun, New York Times, Nov. 13, 1999, at A1.

11. The other gun provider, Philip Duran, also went to prison for his role. Duran, then 22, who knew Klebold and Harris from a pizza shop they had all worked in, introduced the two to Manes, and received 4½ years for helping minors to obtain a handgun. Howard Pankratz, Duran Gets 4½ Year Term, Denver Post, June 24, 2000.

WILSON v. PEOPLE
Supreme Court of Colorado
100 Colo. 441, 87 P.2d 5 (1939)

OTTO BOCK, JUSTICE.

Plaintiff in error was charged and convicted under two counts of having unlawfully and feloniously aided, abetted and assisted one Dwight J. Pierce in the commission of a burglary and larceny. One of his defenses was the absence of felonious intent on his part to commit the crimes in question, because he acted solely as a decoy to detect the commission of the crime and to report it to the proper officers, so that Pierce might be apprehended. Plaintiff in error will hereinafter be referred to as Wilson.

The facts, substantially, are as follows:

On the night of February 19, 1938, Wilson, son of the deputy district attorney of the thirteenth judicial district, and employed by him for several months prior thereto, was in Johnson's Cafe in Sterling, Colorado. Some time after 10 o'clock P.M. Pierce entered. Pierce had been drinking and was looking for a place where he could purchase more liquor. Without previous arrangement, Pierce approached Wilson and prevailed upon him to make an effort to find such a place. The two left the cafe and went to the Commercial Hotel, where Pierce borrowed some money. Wilson left and came back to report to Pierce that no whiskey could be had, but he could get a pint of sloe gin. This was satisfactory to Pierce, and Wilson procured a bottle of the gin which he delivered to Pierce, and both returned to the Johnson Cafe, where they drank some of the liquor. During that time a wristwatch which Wilson had been wearing disappeared while he was in the company of Pierce. When Wilson missed his watch he immediately accused Pierce of taking it. He continued to make the accusation through the evening, and at one time threatened to fight Pierce because of the alleged theft. Pierce denied the theft. The argument about the wristwatch became so noisy that the participants were asked to leave the cafe. They then went to another cafe and Wilson bought Pierce a cup of coffee, and the argument concerning the watch was resumed until Pierce, as he testified, thought they would be thrown out there.

While drinking the liquor at the Johnson Cafe, Pierce first commenced to talk about jobs that he had done and specifically mentioned his burglary of the Wheat Growers Cafe. This talk came up in connection with the disappearance of Wilson's wristwatch. Finally they reached the Commercial Hotel, where Pierce was a janitor, and in the furnace room the conversation about burglaries continued between them. There also was some talk concerning tools, and Pierce procured a piece of paper and wrote down a list of tools that would be needed, not that night, but at some future time, and Wilson said that he could get them for him. The subject of the watch again came up in the furnace room, and Pierce again denied taking it. Wilson suggested that they go to his father's office, to which he had the keys, to start on the jobs, and they there conceived the idea of breaking into Hecker Brothers' Drugstore. Wilson did not first propose the burglarizing, the idea originating with Pierce, and after the latter had told Wilson that he had burglarized the Wheat Growers Cafe several days before. There is some conflict in the evidence as to who first suggested breaking into Hecker Brothers' Drugstore, but they proceeded to the building in which it was located, tried several doors, finally going outside, and effecting an entry through the front transom. After Wilson had boosted Pierce up so that he could break the glass in the transom, and after looking around to see if anyone had heard them, Wilson again lifted Pierce and the latter handed the broken glass to Wilson, who dropped it on the cement. Thereupon Wilson again lifted Pierce up so that he could crawl through the transom. Pierce then proceeded to the cash register. Immediately after Pierce was inside the store Wilson ran to his father's office and telephoned the police to come to Hecker Brothers' Drugstore. He then returned to where the entry had been effected, and a few moments before the police arrived, Pierce handed to Wilson, through the transom, two or three bottles of liquor which he placed on the cement. Pierce noticed after he entered the store that Wilson had disappeared. Immediately after arrival of the police Wilson told them that Pierce was inside, designating him as "that guy from the Commercial Hotel." The police officer asked him how he knew, and he replied, "I boosted him in." Pierce escaped through the back door and Wilson immediately volunteered to track him down, and did so by going to Pierce's room at the Commercial Hotel, where he identified Pierce as the burglar in the presence of the police authorities. Wilson told the police, shortly after the apprehension of Pierce, that his connection with the burglary was for the purpose of getting even with Pierce for taking his watch, and that that was the only way he hoped to recover it. He also stated later that evening that he wanted to apprehend Pierce and turn him over to the authorities — he wanted to catch him in the act.

The record indicates that Wilson was sincere in his belief that Pierce had taken his watch. Moreover, there is evidence in the people's case that tends to support his defense that he acted only as a decoy to apprehend Pierce in the act of committing the crime. Wilson's testimony at the trial substantially supported his defense that he had no criminal intent to feloniously burglarize or steal. . . .

Instruction No. 10, to the giving of which defendant assigns error, reads as follows:

> One may not participate in the commission of a felony and then obtain immunity from punishment on the ground that he was a mere detective or spy. One who attempts to detect the commission of crime in others must himself stop short of lending assistance, or participation in the commission of the crime.

Defendant contends that this instruction is erroneous because it left no question of fact for the determination of the jury on his defense of decoy and detection. Wilson did assist Pierce in entering the drugstore. This he never denied and immediately revealed to the police his part in the transaction when they arrived in response to his call. The instruction inferentially placed guilt upon Wilson, because he did not "stop short of lending assistance," but actually gave assistance. We find the following language in 16 Corpus Juris at page 128, section 115:

> For one to be guilty as principal in the second degree, it is essential that he share in the criminal intent of the principal in the first degree; the same criminal intent must exist in the minds of both.

And on page 129:

> One who participates in a felony as a feigned accomplice, in order to entrap the other, is not criminally liable, and he need not take an officer of the law into his confidence to avoid an imputation of criminal intent.

In this connection we cite also Wharton's Criminal Law (12th ed.) volume 1, section 271, which reads in part as follows: "A detective entering apparently into a criminal conspiracy already formed for the purpose of exploding it is not an accessory before the fact."

It may be that the jury in the instant case placed more stress on the motives that actuated Wilson in his participation in the transaction than they did on the necessity of determining his felonious intent under the circumstances.

Reverting to Instruction No. 10, by judicial fiat this instruction makes any assistance in the perpetration of an offense criminal, whether felonious or not. The determination of whether the assistance by Wilson under the evidence in this case was given with felonious intent was solely the province of the jury, and this instruction erroneously invaded that province. There may be offenses and circumstances when any assistance rendered may make a participant guilty of a criminal offense; but here we are concerned only with the facts, circumstances and defenses in this case. . . . The giving of Instruction No. 10 constituted prejudicial error.

The judgment is reversed and the cause remanded for new trial.

Notes and Questions

1. Assuming that Pierce was guilty of burglary, was Wilson's conduct enough to qualify him as an aider and abettor under the mens rea standard employed in *Beeman*?

If Wilson was aware of Pierce's criminal purpose and had the purpose of aiding him, can he be acquitted simply because he has a good motive? Was his motive to ensure that Pierce committed burglary? Did Wilson have the requisite mental state with regard to the elements of the burglary?

2. *Stings and complicity.* In State v. Hohensee, 650 S.W.2d 268 (Mo. App. 1982), state police retained the services of one undercover police officer, Roberts, and two known burglars, Bressie and Yarberry, who were instructed to burglarize a building. The purpose of the plan was to secure the conviction, on a theory of accomplice liability, of a fourth burglar who had agreed to stand lookout for the other three. Id. at 268-70. The court held that the government's involvement in the break-in was "outrageous" and that due process barred the conviction of the defendant for burglary. Id. at 274. The court distinguished the case from those in which convictions had been sustained notwithstanding some police involvement in the criminal enterprise carried out by the defendants. The court noted:

> In [those cases] the defendant himself participated in the illegal entry. . . . If the conduct of Bressie, Yarberry and Officer Roberts, each acting as a salaried agent of the police department, is subtracted from the . . . break-in, what remains of that midnight enterprise is a lone figure, sitting in a parking lot ½ block away. It is true that defendant had criminal intent but his conduct, standing alone, represented no more of a threat to society than that of a stargazer, similarly situated, contemplating Polaris. It is difficult to conceive a situation where the government's involvement could be greater or the defendant's could be less, and the conduct of the latter still be a likely subject for prosecution. The break-in was accomplished by the government agents, whether or not defendant was in the vicinity. If the

government agents had not been there, doing their illegal acts, defendant's conduct would not be illegal.[12]

3. *Reverse traps*. Assume the precise facts of *Wilson*, except reverse the roles: Wilson agrees to help Pierce burgle the store, only it is Pierce who assists Wilson in climbing through the window. Would the result be different? Would Wilson be guilty of burglary? If the court would still hold Wilson not liable, could it hold Pierce liable as an accomplice? How could he be an accomplice to a person who committed no crime? In State v. Hayes, 105 Mo. 76, 16 S.W. 514 (1891), Hill feigned interest in a burglary proposed by Hayes. Hayes assisted Hill in entering a store to steal bacon, and after Hill handed Hayes the bacon, he helped the police apprehend Hayes. The court reversed Hayes's conviction, finding no common design to support complicity in burglary, but suggested that Hayes could still be guilty of larceny of the bacon. Again, many states might disagree.

3. "Offense Culpability" and "Aid Culpability"

Most jurisdictions requiring "offense culpability" have combined it with "aid culpability." For example, the New York Penal Law provides that "When one person engages in conduct which constitutes an offense, another person is criminally liable for such conduct when, acting with the mental culpability required for the commission thereof, he . . . intentionally aids such person to engage in such conduct." N.Y. Pen. Law §20.00 (1998). But this approach creates another problem: In the case of a "result" crime, if the accomplice need only share the principal's culpable mental state with respect to a harmful result, and need not act with the potentially more culpable mental state of "purpose," then we permit accomplice liability for crimes of negligence.

STATE v. ETZWEILER
Supreme Court of New Hampshire
125 N.H. 57, 480 A.2d 870 (1984)

BATCHELDER, JUSTICE: . . . On July 30, 1982, the defendants, Mark Etzweiler and Ralph Bailey, arrived in Etzweiler's automobile at the plant where both were

---

12. [It is tempting to treat these cases as "entrapments." The doctrine barring prosecution by entrapment has considerable moral appeal: "Entrapment is the conception and planning of an offense by an officer, and his procurement of its commission by one who would not have perpetrated it except for the trickery, persuasion, or fraud of the officer." Sorrells v. United States, 287 U.S. 335 (1932). However, though entrapment is beyond the scope of this book, we note that in both the state and federal courts, the entrapment defense is very limited. The federal courts and most state courts use a so-called "subjective" approach, asking both whether a government agent induced the offense and whether the defendant was "ready and willing to commit the crimes . . . whenever opportunity was afforded." 1 E. Devitt & C. Blackmar, Federal Jury Practice and Instructions, §13.09 (3d. ed. 1977). Commentators and some courts favor the "objective" approach, asking whether the offense was encouraged by "methods of persuasion or inducement which create a substantial risk that such an offense will be committed by persons other than those who are ready to commit the offense." E.g., MPC §2.13. Under either approach, the entrapment defense is rarely successful. Moreover, it is disfavored by many defense counsel, because it permits the prosecution to rebut the claim with much previous bad conduct by the defendant, and it normally precludes the defendant from denying that he committed the offense per se. See W. LaFave & A. Scott, Criminal Law, §5.2. In addition, the Model Penal Code and other statutes bar the defense in cases of conduct causing or threatening bodily injury to an innocent person. MPC 2.13(3). —EDS.]

employed. Bailey had been drinking alcoholic beverages and was, allegedly, intoxicated. Etzweiler, allegedly knowing that Bailey was intoxicated, loaned his car to Bailey and proceeded into the plant to begin work. Bailey drove Etzweiler's car away. Approximately ten minutes later, Bailey, driving recklessly, collided with a car driven by Susan Beaulieu. As a result of the accident, two passengers in the Beaulieu car, Kathryn and Nathan Beaulieu, were killed.

On August 26, 1982, the grand jury handed down two indictments charging Etzweiler with negligent homicide. Subsequently, on April 6, 1983, the grand jury issued two additional indictments charging Etzweiler with negligent homicide as an accomplice.

Etzweiler filed motions to quash all indictments against him, and the Superior Court (Pappagianis, J.) transferred to this court the questions of law raised by the motions. . . . We dismiss all indictments against Etzweiler and affirm the denial of Bailey's motion to dismiss. . . .

The requisites of the negligent homicide statute are met if a defendant negligently causes death. RSA 630:3, I. The State must establish that the defendant failed to become aware of a substantial and unjustifiable risk that his or her conduct may cause the death of another human being. "The risk must be of such a nature and degree that his [or her] failure to become aware of it constitutes a gross deviation from the conduct that a reasonable person would observe in the situation." Id.

In this case, however, death resulted not from the conduct of Etzweiler but from the conduct of Bailey, and the accountability of Etzweiler therefore must rest on the complicity of Etzweiler in Bailey's conduct.

At common law, an individual, who did not actually engage in the felonious conduct, could be held criminally liable as a principal if he or she were present during the commission of the crime, aiding and abetting the perpetrator. Thus, the owner of an automobile who lent his or her car to an intoxicated individual, sat by that individual and permitted him to operate the vehicle, may be convicted as a principal to manslaughter if death results from the operation of the vehicle. At common law, Etzweiler could not have been guilty as a principal. He was not actually or constructively present during the commission of the offense, a necessary prerequisite.

In 1973, the legislature enacted the Criminal Code and created RSA 626:8, the accomplice liability statute. That statute abrogated the common-law distinction between principals and accessories and narrowly defined those situations in which an individual could be held criminally liable for the conduct of another. Etzweiler's conduct, in lending his automobile to Bailey, must be measured against the standards set forth in the statute. . . .

The second indictments charge Etzweiler with the offense of negligent homicide as an accomplice.

RSA 626:8, III, provides: "A person is an accomplice of another person in the commission of an offense if: (a) with the purpose of promoting or facilitating the commission of the offense, he aids . . . such other person in planning or committing it. . . ."

Section IV sets forth the elements of the substantive offense that the State has the burden of establishing against the accomplice. "When causing a particular result is an element of an offense," the accomplice must act "with the kind of culpability, if any, with respect to that result that is sufficient for the commission of the offense."

Our interpretation of the accomplice liability statute effectuates the policy that an accomplice's liability ought not to extend beyond the criminal purposes that he or she shares. Because accomplice liability holds an individual criminally liable for actions done by another, it is important that the prosecution fall squarely within the statute. . . .

The State has alleged that, with the purpose of promoting or facilitating the offense of driving under the influence of alcohol, Etzweiler aided Bailey in the commission of that offense. However, under our statute, the accomplice must aid the primary actor in the substantive offense with the purpose of facilitating the substantive offense — in this case, negligent homicide. Therefore, the indictments against Etzweiler must be quashed. . . .

To satisfy the requirements of RSA 626:8, III, the State must establish that Etzweiler's acts were designed to aid Bailey in committing negligent homicide. Yet under the negligent homicide statute, Bailey must be unaware of the risk of death that his conduct created. . . . We cannot see how Etzweiler could intentionally aid Bailey in a crime that Bailey was unaware that he was committing. Thus, we hold, as a matter of law, that, in the present context of the Criminal Code, an individual may not be an accomplice to negligent homicide.

Notes and Questions

1. Etzweiler intentionally facilitated conduct that caused death, while negligent of the foreseeable risk that death would result. If complicity were indeed simply a way of committing the conduct element of a crime, but not a distinct crime itself, then would it not be perfectly logical to make Etzweiler an accomplice to negligent homicide?

Why does the court refuse to treat this as a case of "direct" negligent homicide on Etzweiler's part? Is its reason convincing? Is its focus on "presence" useful?

2. *Abetting negligence.* The provisions of the New Hampshire complicity statute discussed in *Etzweiler* are based on Model Penal Code §§2.06(3)(a) and 2.06(4):

> (3) A person is an accomplice of another person in the commission of an offense if:
>
> (a) with the purpose of promoting or facilitating the commission of the offense, he
>
> (i) solicits such other person to commit it: or
>
> (ii) aids or agrees or attempts to aid such other person in planning or committing it. . . .
>
> (4) When causing a particular result is an element of an offense, an accomplice in the conduct causing such result is an accomplice in the commission of that offense, if he acts with the kind of culpability, if any, with respect to that result, that is sufficient for the commission of the offense.

What is meant by the statutory requirement that accomplices have the "purpose of promoting or facilitating the commission of an offense"? Does the "offense" mean only the conduct element, or does it also include the mens rea? If the latter, then accomplice mens rea with respect to the facilitative effect of aid implies accomplice mens rea with respect to the principal's mens rea. What does it mean to purposefully promote or facilitate an offense involving negligence? Arguably, §2.06(4) is an effort to solve this conundrum by requiring that an accomplice purposefully assist or encourage the principal's act, while having whatever culpable mental state with respect to the result is required for liability as a principal. Is the *Etzweiler* court faithfully interpreting the statutory language by reading it to require that the accomplice have purpose with respect to the result of the principal's conduct?

3. Can *Etzweiler* be reconciled with State v. Foster, 202 Conn. 520, 522 A.2d 277 (1987)? Foster and a friend, Cannon, sought out one Middleton, who was suspected of an attack on Foster's girlfriend. They found and seized Middleton; Foster briefly left to bring his girlfriend to the scene to identify Middleton, first, however, giving Cannon a knife with which to guard Middleton. Before Foster returned, Cannon and Middleton fought, and Cannon stabbed Middleton to death.

> General Statutes §53a-8 provides in relevant part that "[a] person, acting with the mental state required for the commission of an offense, who . . . intentionally aids another person to engage in conduct which constitutes an offense shall be criminally liable for such conduct . . . as if he were the principal offender." We have previously stated that a conviction under §53a-8 requires proof of a dual intent, i.e., "that the accessory have the intent to aid the principal and that in so aiding he intend to commit the offense with which he is charged." State v. Harrison, 178 Conn. 689, 694, 425 A.2d 111 (1979).
>
> Citing this "dual intent" requirement, the defendant argues that a person cannot be convicted as an accessory to criminally negligent homicide. He reasons that because accessorial liability requires an accused, in aiding a principal, to "intend to commit the offense with which he is charged" and because criminally negligent homicide requires that an unintended death occur, the crime of being an accessory to criminally negligent homicide is a logical impossibility in that it would require a defendant, in aiding another, to intend to commit a crime in which an unintended result occurs. . . .
>
> Section 53a-8, however, is not limited to cases where the substantive crime requires the specific intent to bring about a result. General Statutes §53a-8 merely requires that a defendant have the mental state required for the commission of a crime while intentionally aiding another. "When the commission of an offense . . . or some element of an offense, requires a particular mental state, such mental state is ordinarily designated . . . by the use of the terms 'intentionally,' 'knowingly,' 'recklessly,' or 'criminal negligence.' . . . " General Statutes §53a-5. Accordingly, an accessory may be liable in aiding another if he acts intentionally, knowingly, recklessly or with criminal negligence toward the result, depending on the mental state required by the substantive crime. When a crime requires that a person act with criminal negligence, an accessory is liable if he acts "with respect to a result or to a circumstance described by a statute defining an offense when he fails to perceive a substantial and unjustifiable risk that such result will occur or that such circumstance exists." General Statutes §53a-3(14).
>
> . . . From the evidence presented, the jury could reasonably have found that the defendant intentionally had aided Cannon by giving him the knife. Additionally, the jury could reasonably have inferred that the defendant had failed to perceive a substantial and unjustifiable risk that death would occur by handing Cannon the knife to prevent Middleton from escaping. Contrary to the defendant's claim, there was sufficient evidence to support the conviction.

4. *Crimes of purpose. Foster* shows how the addition of a requirement that an accomplice have the mens rea required for the substantive crime can paradoxically *ease* conviction by reducing the culpability required to show purposeful

aid or encouragement of an offense. This can occur where the substantive offense has a mens rea of negligence or recklessness. But where the substantive offense requires purpose or, as it is sometimes called, "specific intent," the additional requirement that an accomplice have the mens rea required for the substantive offense can make it *harder* to convict an accomplice of crimes if she foreseeably facilitated these crimes but did not necessarily intend them. Consider United States v. Short, 493 F.2d 1170 (9th Cir. 1974):

> . . . A federally insured bank in San Francisco was robbed by one John Seymour who used a gun during the robbery. Short drove Seymour to the vicinity of the bank and parked his car a block from the bank. During the robbery the hood of Short's car was up and he was apparently repairing it. While he was waiting for Seymour, Short met one Gloria Quails, who became the key government witness, and offered her a ride. After the robbery Seymour returned to the car, whereupon Short closed the hood and drove off with Seymour and Quails in the car. Short dropped Seymour off at Seymour's residence and shortly thereafter Short and Quails returned to the residence. After a short stay at the house during which Short and Seymour conferred privately with a third person, all four persons in the house went to a bar. Later, Short and Quails left the bar and drove to a parking lot where they waited until the time that Short was to meet with Seymour again. At the parking lot Short complained to Quails that he knew that he had not gotten his fair share of the money that was taken. There was no direct evidence that Short knew that Seymour had a gun or that Seymour intended to use it. . . .
>
> [Short was convicted of armed bank robbery. The jury was instructed on aiding and abetting, as follows:] "Now, in light of the instructions and the government's case and status of the evidence here that Short's participation, if any, was an aider and abettor, I would further instruct you that it is not necessary that Mr. Short had to have known the exact or precise details by which Mr. Seymour was going to accomplish the bank robbery or what methods he was going to use. What is necessary is that Mr. Short knew that a bank robbery was going to be attempted or accomplished by Mr. Seymour and then that Mr. Short did some affirmative act to attempt to help, attempt to carry that conduct out with the intent that the bank robbery should be successfully accomplished and so, therefore, whatever occurred in the bank, whether or not he knew that Mr. Seymour was armed or what he was armed with or not, is not necessary, not a necessary element to the crime, if in fact Seymour did use, commit the bank robbery by the use of a weapon which would put it in the classification of being an armed bank robbery and so it is essential that you bear in mind that Seymour had to have done these acts." . . .
>
> This instruction is erroneous because it fails to require the jury to find an essential element of the crime of armed bank robbery as a prerequisite to conviction. It is the aider and abettor's state of mind, rather than the state of mind of the principal, that determines the former's liability. . . . It is true that the prosecution is not required to prove that the aider and abettor was aware of all of the details of the planned offense. It is also true that the aider and abettor may be liable for the natural and probable consequences of the crime that he aided and abetted.
>
> However, here Congress has specifically provided for an increased penalty for aggravated forms of bank robbery. An essential element of armed bank robbery as charged here is that the principal was armed and used the weapon to jeopardize the life of the teller. It is this conduct that Short must be shown to have aided and abetted. "[An] aider and abettor is made punishable as a principal . . . and the proof must encompass the same elements as would be required to convict any other principal." . . . Thus the jury must be told that it must find that Short knew that Seymour was armed and intended to use the weapon, and intended to aid him in that respect. [Id. at 1171-72.]

C. ACT AND MENS REA: AN EXERCISE

Once a case is in the hands of the jury, it is difficult to predict how a complicity charge will be decided. Consider the following summary of facts, compiled by the editors from newspaper sources, of a famous racially charged case that dominated the attention of New York City in 1989 and 1990.

THE KILLING OF YUSUF HAWKINS

Like other neighborhoods in Brooklyn, Bensonhurst is a distinctive enclave. There are approximately 150,000 residents, half of them immigrants from Italy, most coming from Sicily and Northern Italy, with a majority of the other half made up of second or third generation Italian-Americans. The minority population is very small. Street signs and store windows are often in Italian, and inside the many private social clubs one can find elderly men sipping small cups of darkly brewed espresso. Many of the younger men and teenagers gather in the evenings on street corners, where they smoke, drink, and talk.

Each night a group of young men would meet outside a candy store at the corner of 68th Street and 20th Avenue. One of the leaders of this group was Keith Mondello, a 19-year-old who had spent all his life in the neighborhood. Others who hung out on the corner and whose names would later become familiar to most New Yorkers were 18-year-old Joseph Fama, 21-year-old John Vento, and 19-year-old Joseph Serrano. In an apartment above the candy store lived 18-year-old Gina Feliciano and her mother, Phyllis D'Agata. Gina was disliked by many of the neighborhood residents because she dated black men as well as dark-skinned Latino men.

On August 23, 1989, Gina Feliciano and Keith Mondello had a conversation in which, according to Keith Mondello, Gina threatened to call a group of her black and Puerto Rican friends to fight the men who hung out outside the candy store under her apartment. According to Feliciano, Mondello told her during this same conversation that he would "blow the heads off the nigger bastards," and that "I should spit in your face, you nigger-lover." Although Mondello and Feliciano disagreed about this conversation, what happened next is indisputable. Mondello, perceiving a threat, gathered most of his friends and handed out baseball bats and other weapons. The armed group consisted of at least 30 people, and at least one person had a handgun.

Although no gang ever arrived to fight the neighborhood youths, disaster occurred that evening when Yusuf K. Hawkins, a 16-year-old African-American boy from another Brooklyn neighborhood, arrived in Bensonhurst with three of his friends in order to see a used car he was thinking of buying. Hawkins and his friends were not friends of Feliciano, and were clearly not the gang she may have referred to. Nevertheless, when Mondello, Fama, and his friends saw the four young black men, they verbally abused them and began to chase them. Hawkins and his friends ran and were trapped near a doorway at 20th Avenue and Bay Ridge Avenue, where a fight broke out that ended abruptly when at least three shots rang out. All the youths fled, leaving Yusuf Hawkins bleeding, two bullets in his chest. Hawkins died soon after.

The killing shocked the city. Brooklyn District Attorney Elizabeth Holtzman publicly declared that it would be the priority of her office to catch those who participated in the mob that evening. The killing became politicized when the Reverend Al Sharpton was hired as an advisor to the slain boy's parents. Widely publicized marches by African-Americans were led through the streets of Bensonhurst. Almost 300 local residents subjected the marchers to racist taunts, while others waved watermelons at the marchers. Meanwhile, investigators met with an almost total wall of silence when they interviewed local residents. Although many people must have either seen the chase or heard the screams, few were willing to tell the police anything.

Within several days the police learned the names of some of the participants. A break in the case came when John Vento, a participant in the mob that chased Yusuf Hawkins, agreed to testify before the grand jury and at trial in exchange for immunity from prosecution. Relying in great part on his testimony, a grand jury indicted Joseph Fama, whom Vento identified as the shooter, on charges of second degree murder with intent to kill, second degree murder with a depraved indifference to human life, and various other assault, rioting and weapons charges. Keith Mondello was identified by Vento as the leader of the group, and was charged with basically the same crimes as Fama, under the theory that he aided and abetted the murder and shared the intent to kill. Eventually six others would be charged as accomplices in the killing. New York law holds that a person is criminally liable for the actions of another if, with the accompanying mens rea, that person "solicits, requests, commands, importunes or intentionally aids" the actions. Five others were also charged as accomplices in the killing: Joseph Serrano, Pasquale Raucci, James Patino, Charles Stressler, and Steven Currier.

As the time for trial approached, the prosecution was dealt a blow when John Vento fled. Prosecutors requested and were granted a delay while they searched for him, and in April of 1990 Vento turned himself in to an FBI office in Ohio. Upon his return to New York he was told that he could still have immunity if he testified truthfully, but he refused, citing a fear of retaliation from organized crime. He was then indicted for the killing of Yusuf Hawkins.

Judge Thaddeus Owens, who had been selected to handle all the trials because of his experience with highly publicized cases, severed most of the trials of the defendants since they might testify against each other. He ruled that the trials of Mondello and Fama would come first, and that they would be tried together, although with different juries. After a lengthy jury selection, two racially mixed juries were chosen. As the trials began, most commentators felt that the case against Mondello was far stronger than the case against Fama. Without the testimony of Vento, all the state had against Fama were the statements of witnesses of questionable reliability, including Gina Feliciano (who not only had not seen the shooting but had checked herself into a drug rehabilitation clinic shortly before the trial); two not particularly reliable jailhouse snitches who claimed that Fama had admitted shooting Hawkins (one was mentally unstable while the other had on many previous occasions offered to tell the authorities that inmates had confessed to crimes in exchange for a reduction in his sentence); and purported eyewitness Franklin Tighe (who had a history of hallucinations).

The case against Mondello was thought to be stronger, and would be based mostly on his own statements after the incident. Mondello had given a detailed statement to the police, which he signed on five occasions, admitting that he had distributed the baseball bats (he also claimed that Fama was the shooter, although this statement was ruled inadmissible against Fama). Despite his later protests that the statement was coerced, and his claim that he never read it before signing it, the judge admitted it in its entirety. Mondello made similar statements in an interview with a local television station five days after the killing. The jury was shown a videotape of this interview.

The trial was highly charged and tense. On one side of the visitors gallery sat the parents of Yusuf Hawkins and their supporters, while on the other side sat the family and friends of Keith Mondello and Joseph Fama. The pretrial conjecture about the strength of the respective cases against Fama and Mondello seemed to run true to form. The jury heard Mondello's self-incriminating statements, and saw similar statements on video. Another witness testified that a group of up to 40 whites ran past her chasing four black men, with Fama and Mondello at the head of the pack. She testified that Mondello had a bat, while Fama was "holding his left side," with his hand at his waist. Gina Feliciano and her mother both testified. Gina repeated Mondello's statements on the day of the murder. Defense attorneys attacked both as drug addicts and liars who had smoked marijuana shortly before the events about which they testified. The two jailhouse snitches did not give convincing performances on the stand, and one juror in the Fama case later described their testimony as "totally discredited." Franklin Tighe said that he saw Fama shoot Yusuf Hawkins, but the defense attacked his testimony by asking him about his mental history. Within days he attempted to recant his testimony, but Judge Owens refused to allow him to do so, stating that the defendants could appeal if they were convicted.

The two juries retired on the same day to deliberate separately, and New York City was swept up into a frenzy of speculation as residents debated who, if anyone, would or should be convicted. Some thought that if one defendant was convicted of murder, both would be, while others contended that without the testimony of John Vento, the prosecution had been left with almost nothing, and that neither Fama nor Mondello would be convicted. After nine days of deliberation, the Fama jury returned its verdicts first. To the first charge, second degree murder with intent to kill, the verdict was not guilty. Fama's pleasure was short-lived, however, for the verdict on second degree murder with depraved indifference to human life was guilty, as were the verdicts on the other 12 counts of the indictment.

The next day the jury returned its verdicts against Keith Mondello. With most observers believing that he would also be found guilty of murder, the jury shocked the city by finding Mondello not guilty on both second degree murder counts. Like Fama, Mondello was convicted on 12 lesser counts, many of them serious felonies such as assault and rioting.

The astonishing nature of the verdicts and the complexity of proving complicity was revealed when the press interviewed members of the juries, and the public discovered how two groups of 12 citizens hearing mostly the same evidence could interpret it in completely different ways. Statements made by the jurors in the Fama case revealed that they were not convinced that he was the shooter. Fama was acquitted of the charge he actually shot Hawkins. One juror was quoted as saying, "We believe that Joey went from 68th to 69th Street. If he wasn't an active participant, he would have gone home." The jury had convicted him of aiding, abetting, and encouraging the murder of Yusuf Hawkins.

The Mondello jury, which was not presented with the theory that he was the shooter, but with stronger evidence that Mondello was responsible for forming and inciting the mob, declined to find that he aided or abetted the killing.

Many people believe that the two verdicts can be explained through the questions the two juries asked of the judge while deliberating. The Fama jury asked the judge several times whether it could convict someone of murder who did not know that an accomplice had a gun and intended to use it. Judge Owens said yes. The Mondello jury never asked this question, and thus never received this instruction from the judge. Several jurors in the Fama trial also said that they were influenced by the judge's analogies concerning complicity, which ranged from the Met to the Mets. The judge told the jurors that just as the cymbal player in a large orchestra acts in concert with the orchestra even if he only sounds the final note, they could find Fama guilty if they believed he acted in concert with the gang of youths. Similarly, he told them that if baseball player McReynolds throws to Jefferies who throws to Lyons who tags a runner out, Lyons gets the put-out, but McReynolds and Jefferies were acting in concert with him.

When it came time for sentencing, Judge Owens was not sympathetic to pleas for leniency. He sentenced Joseph Fama to 32 years to life in prison, the maximum sentence. Fama would only be eligible for parole in 32 years. Keith Mondello received consecutive sentences for each of his convictions, a total of 5 years, 4 months, to 16 years. In denying the defense lawyer's request that the sentences run concurrently, Judge Owens said that "without Mr. Mondello, there would not have been the death of anyone," which perhaps expressed his own belief that the jury reached the wrong verdict on the murder charges.

Several other trials followed the Fama and Mondello trial. None of the other six defendants was found guilty of complicity in the murder of Yusuf Hawkins. John Vento was convicted of lesser charges and sentenced to two-and-two-thirds to eight years in prison. Pasquale Raucci was convicted only of lesser charges, while Charles Stressler was acquitted on all counts. Joseph Serrano and James Patino were acquitted on almost all charges. Interestingly, both had agreed to plea bargains which would have sent them to prison, but Charles Hynes, who by this time was the District Attorney, rescinded the plea offers when the Hawkins family asked that the two be brought to trial. Afterward, the prosecution was condemned by Al Sharpton and the Hawkins family for only getting one murder conviction (and indeed for only arresting eight people out of a group of at least 30).

Notes and Questions

1. Consider how you would have voted on each of the juries, relying on the act and mens rea requirements laid out in this chapter.

2. As a variation, to help the analysis of complicity liability in this troubling case, make two simplifying assumptions: First, assume that all defendants are charged only with "depraved indifference" murder, requiring that defendant "under circumstances evincing a depraved indifference to human life, . . . recklessly engages in conduct which creates a grave risk of death to another person, and thereby causes the death of another person." Second, suppose that instead of being shot, Yusuf Hawkins had died from the effects of a severe beating.

On these modified facts, could persons proved to have chased Hawkins and stood by while he was beaten be said to have aided the crime? Encouraged it? Would Mondello's organizing and inciting the mob constitute encouragement? Would his distribution of baseball bats constitute aid?

Would chasers and bystanders have the requisite mens rea for complicity in "depraved indifference" murder? Would they have shown recklessness and depraved indifference to human life? Would they necessarily have known that Hawkins's batterers were acting with depraved indifference to human life? Assuming that chasing Hawkins and standing by while he was beaten would have the effect of aiding or encouraging his killing, would participants in the mob *necessarily* have known this?

When Mondello organized, armed, and incited the mob, did he hope or know that its members would act with depraved indifference to human life?

3. Now return to the facts as they occurred, culminating in the shooting of Yusuf Hawkins. Assume no one could be proved to have known that anyone in the crowd had a gun. Does the shooting change the complicity analysis? Assuming the participants in the mob believed they were aiding and encouraging the depraved and reckless act of beating Hawkins with bats when they chased and cornered him, did they necessarily intend the different (and arguably even more) depraved and reckless act of shooting him? If not, should this make any difference to their liability as accomplices? If participants in the mob intended to aid a depraved and reckless act, and ended up aiding an intentional killing, can they still be held liable for complicity in a depraved and reckless killing? Similarly, if Mondello incited and organized a depraved and reckless mob beating, can he be liable as an accomplice to a depraved and reckless killing if the perpetrator shot Hawkins with intent to kill?

4. Are the *Fama* and *Mondello* jury verdicts reconcilable? Consider the possibility that both juries sought "rough justice" in the case, according to the following principles:

a. All of the mob participants were accomplices to the murder.
b. But it is unjust to punish accomplices as murderers (although perhaps they should be punished for a lesser offense).
c. But it would also be unjust to acquit someone of murder if there is a substantial possibility that he committed murder.
d. While it was not proven that Fama pulled the trigger, he probably did.

If Fama was convicted of complicity in a "depraved indifference" murder on the basis of such reasoning, did the jury act legally?

D. RELATIONS OF PARTIES

Can an accomplice be guilty of a crime even if there is no (guilty) principal? As a general matter, accomplice liability requires only that the accomplice have encouraged or aided the commission of a wrongful offense. It is not necessary that another person be found guilty of that offense.

In contemporary American jurisdictions an accomplice may be convicted even if the principal is dead, immune from prosecution (e.g., due to diplomatic status), not charged (e.g., in return for testimony against an accomplice deemed a greater threat to the public), or not identified (provided it is clear that some unidentified person perpetrated an offense). Section 20.05 (1998) of the New York Penal Law provides that

> In any prosecution for an offense in which the criminal liability of the defen-dant is based upon [complicity]. . . . it is no defense that: . . .
>   2. Such other person has not been prosecuted for or convicted of any of-fense based upon the conduct in question, or has previously been acquitted thereof, or has legal immunity from prosecution therefor. . . .

What if the perpetrator is demonstrably innocent? Whether one may be an ac-complice to an innocent perpetrator may depend on the grounds for the per-petrator's innocence.

1.   The Perpetrator Is Excused

American law exhibits a general consensus that an accomplice may be guilty even if the principal is excused — say on grounds of insanity, duress, or reason-able mistake of law — unless the accomplice can avail herself of the same ex-cuse. New York law provides that it is no defense to accomplice liability for the conduct of another that:

> Such other person is not guilty of the offense in question owing to criminal irre-sponsibility or other legal incapacity or exemption, or to unawareness of the crim-inal nature of the conduct in question or of the defendant's criminal purpose or to other factors precluding the mental state required for the commission of the offense in question. [N.Y. Pen. C. §20.05 (1998).]

It would follow that if a principal's liability is mitigated by a partial excuse like provocation, an accomplice could be liable for a more serious crime (murder) than would the principal she assisted or encouraged (who would be liable only for manslaughter). At common law, accessories and principals could only be convicted of the same degree offense, but modern law has eliminated this re-striction, as some defendants have discovered to their dismay. In Pendry v. State, 367 A.2d 627 (Del. Supr. 1976), brothers Timothy and Kenneth Pendry were convicted of first-degree murder, on the following evidence:

> Clifford Faulkner (the victim) was shot and killed by Timothy Pendry follow-ing an argument between the victim and defendants concerning defendants' sis-ter, who had lived intermittently with the victim in a stormy relationship, and was, at the time, being held by the victim in her trailer against her will. The defendants went to their sister's trailer, and after some discussion with her, confronted the vic-tim, ordering him to leave the trailer. They testified that the victim refused to leave, and picked up a whiskey bottle, threatening to kill them. Timothy left the trailer, returned with a shotgun, and fired the three shots which killed the victim. [Id. at 629.]

The Supreme Court of Delaware reduced Timothy's conviction to man-slaughter because he "presented some credible evidence of extreme emotional distress at the time of the shooting." Kenneth, however, presented no such evidence because his lawyer believed that the accomplice could not be convicted of a greater offense than the principal. The court upheld Kenneth's conviction for first-degree murder, citing Title 11 §272 of the Delaware Code (2001), which contains language identical to that found in §20.05 of the New York Penal Law. Title 11 §272 also adds that it is no defense that the principal "has been convicted of a different defense or in a different degree."

Was the Pendry brothers' disparate liability based on differential *responsibility* or on differential *mens rea?* The defense of "extreme emotional distress" was an affirmative defense provable by a preponderance of the evidence, similar in design to the New York affirmative defense of "extreme emotional disturbance" the Supreme Court subsequently approved in Patterson v. New York, 432 U.S. 197 (1977). (See Introduction, *supra,* p. 18.) Recall that the Supreme Court permitted burden-shifting only if the defense was an excuse rather than a negation of the mental element of murder.

Some courts take the view that a defendant who knowingly exploits a perpetrator's excusing condition to induce the perpetrator to commit the crime is guilty as a principal. One who manipulates a child or a lunatic into committing a crime, or forces an otherwise responsible person to commit a crime under duress, may be characterized as a "perpetrator-by-means." Nevertheless, the general view is that it is possible to be liable as an accomplice to an excused offense. Indeed, recall from our discussion of felony murder in Chapter 6, *supra,* pp. 406-410, that under certain circumstances, a robber could be guilty of first-degree murder, where the victim is (excusably) killed by a police officer.

2. The Perpetrator Is Justified

What if the principal is justified? If Alice, walking down the street, sees Bert brutally attacking Carl, then Alice is probably justified if she assists Carl in using deadly force against Bert. But the legal situation is different if the bystander intervenes not in support of *justified* force, but in support of *wrongful* force that happens to be *excusable.* Thus, if Jones, a sane person, aids Smith, an insane person, when Smith is irrationally attacking Green, Jones certainly cannot escape liability simply because Smith is excused on grounds of insanity. The difficulty is that many American jurisdictions condition defenses of "justification" on the defendant's reasonable beliefs rather than the actual results of defendant's conduct. See State v. Menilla, 177 Iowa 283, 158 N.W. 645 (1916) (defendant killed her husband wrongly but reasonably believing that the husband was about to kill their son unless she attacked first; the son knew he was in no danger and could not have himself legally attacked his father).

Suppose a county social worker tries to execute a court order removing an abused child from the home. The child's parent, saying nothing about the court order, tells a neighbor the child is being kidnapped and asks the neighbor to get a gun. The neighbor threatens the social worker with a gun, relenting only on being shown the court order. The neighbor has committed an assault (see Model Penal Code §211.1 (1) (c)) but she may argue that her offense is "justified" by her honest and reasonable belief that it was necessary to prevent a kidnapping (see Model Penal Code §§3.04(1), 3.04(2) (b), and 3.05(1)). Should the parent, who abetted the assault and knew that it was not necessary to prevent a kidnapping, be guilty of assault? As an accomplice? As a perpetrator by means?

3. The Perpetrator Lacks Mens Rea

May one be liable as an accomplice if the principal lacks mens rea? Here we really confront the question of whether, strictly speaking, complicity even requires a "principal."

Suppose that Anna supplies Paula with a ladder and falsely tells her that Felice does not mind if anyone picks her apples. Paula takes several bushels of Felice's apples, but lacks the mens rea for theft. Is Anna guilty of theft? Traditionally it was held that she could not be liable because there was no offense. Can Anna be held liable as a "perpetrator-by-means"? Traditionally, courts restricted the doctrine of perpetration-by-means to cases where the perpetrator lacks responsibility (i.e., is excusable). Recall State v. Hayes, *supra*, p. 726, in which the court overturned Hayes's conviction as an accomplice to burglary because his principal, Hill, had acted with no mens rea.

But courts now incline toward a different outcome, exemplified by Muni v. United States, 668 F.2d 87 (2d Cir. 1981). Muni, a New York merchant, charged over $90,000 of spurious purchases on counterfeit credit cards. Chemical Bank's credit card authorization center made standard electronic inquiries on these charges to computer centers in Virginia and Missouri. Convicted of wire fraud in interstate commerce, Muni denied that the interstate transmissions could be imputed to him. But because Muni caused the operator to make these inquiries and could reasonably foresee that she would do so, the court affirmed the conviction. Thus, when the actor is both the "but for" and the proximate cause of proscribed conduct, the law will impute criminal liability to one person for the innocent actions of another. Note that when the law does so, it holds the defendant liable as a principal, under the doctrine of "perpetration-by-means," rather than as an accomplice.

Model Penal Code section 2.06(2) (a) states

> A person is legally accountable for the conduct of another person when: (a) acting with the kind of culpability that is sufficient for the commission of the offense, he causes an innocent or irresponsible person to engage in such conduct.

Would Muni be convicted under this provision? Would Hayes? Would Anna?

How would this provision resolve these two cases:

a. The defendant, a Mansonesque figure, instructs a drug-dependent follower, incapable of forming intent, to shoot the victim for allegedly smashing the defendant's car window. The follower obediently performs her task, with a gun provided by the defendant. See State v. McCarthy, 179 Conn. 1, 475 A.2d 924 (1979).

b. Defendant packs a bomb in his wife's suitcase in their home and drives her to the airport where she boards an airplane. The bomb is not discovered until she unpacks her suitcase after the airplane has landed. The defendant is charged with willfully causing an explosive device to be placed in an aircraft. The defendant's wife was totally unaware of the bomb's presence. See United States v. Bradley, 540 F. Supp. 690 (D. Md. 1982).

The New York and Delaware statutory provisions discussed above make no distinction between principals who lack responsibility and those who lack mens rea. They apparently preclude defenses to accomplice liability based on the innocence of the principal, if that innocence results from any factor "precluding the mental state required for commission of the offense." (Del. Code 11 §272 (2001); N.Y. Pen. L. §20.05(1) (1998)). Consider how such a statutory provision would apply to the following hypothetical:

> Although married to Desmond, Olivia has been having an affair with Ian. Ian urges Olivia to kill Desmond and leaves a loaded gun with her. Olivia, however, has no intention of killing Desmond. After Ian leaves, she attempts to unload the gun. Desmond returns home, startling her. Olivia drops the gun and it goes off, killing Desmond. Is Ian liable for murder as an accomplice to this accidental killing under the New York and Delaware statutes?

Many jurisdictions require that accomplices know of the mens rea or criminal purpose of the principal. Would the latter mens rea requirement be compatible with a rule that the principal's lack of mens rea is no defense to liability as an accomplice?

4. Discrepant Mens Rea

Even if a jurisdiction precludes accomplice liability for assisting actors who *lack* mens rea, should it nevertheless permit differential liability based on *differential* mens rea? In Regina v. Howe, (1987) 85 Cr. App. R. 32, the House of Lords thought so, invoking the following hypothetical:

> A hands a gun to D informing him that it is loaded with blank ammunition only and telling him to go and scare X by discharging it. The ammunition is in fact live, as A knows, and X is killed. D is convicted only of manslaughter, as he might be on those facts. It would seem absurd that A should thereby escape conviction for murder. [Id. at 65.]

And the trend in American cases has been to permit discrepant liability based on differential mens rea where the evidence warrants it. In People v. McCoy, 25 Cal. 4th 1111, 108 Cal. Rptr. 2d 188, 24 P.3d 1210 (2001), the facts were these:

> Codefendants Ejaan Dupree McCoy and Derrick Lakey were tried together and convicted of crimes arising out of a drive-by shooting in Stockton in 1995. McCoy drove the car and Lakey was in the front passenger seat, with others in the back. The car approached four people standing on a street corner. McCoy leaned out of the window and shouted something. A flurry of shots was fired from the car toward the group. Witnesses saw both McCoy and Lakey shooting handguns. Two of the group were shot, one fatally. The other two escaped injury. Someone from outside the car returned fire, wounding Lakey. The evidence showed that McCoy fired the fatal bullets.

At trial, McCoy but not Lakey testified. McCoy admitted shooting but claimed he did so because he believed he would be shot himself. He said that earlier that day, he had driven by that same intersection, and someone fired shots in his direction. He decided to seek out a friend who might be able to help him determine who had fired at him. McCoy brought his gun for protection and picked up Lakey, who also had a gun. Across the street from his friend's house, McCoy saw three men standing near a tree. Thinking that one of them might be his friend, McCoy drove slowly toward the group, stopped, and called out to get their attention. McCoy then saw that the man was not his friend and that he held a "dark something" that appeared to be a gun. Believing that the man was going to shoot him, McCoy grabbed his own gun and fired until the gun was empty. Lakey also fired his gun out the car window. [25 Cal. 4th at 1115.]

Both men were convicted of murder, but the Court of Appeals reversed and remanded McCoy's case because he had not received the correct instruction on imperfect self-defense, which negates the malice required for murder in California. As a result, the Court of Appeals concluded, he was unfairly denied a chance for reduction to voluntary manslaughter. The State Supreme Court held, however, that the court of Appeal was wrong to conclude that it also had to reverse Lakey's murder conviction:

The statement that an aider and abettor may not be guilty of a greater offense than the direct perpetrator, although sometimes true in individual cases, is not universally correct. Aider and abettor liability is premised on the combined acts of all the principals, but on the aider and abettor's own mens rea. If the mens rea of the aider and abettor is more culpable than the actual perpetrator's, the aider and abettor may be guilty of a more serious crime than the actual perpetrator.

Moreover, the dividing line between the actual perpetrator and the aider and abettor is often blurred. It is often an oversimplification to describe one person as the actual perpetrator and the other as the aider and abettor. When two or more persons commit a crime together, both may act in part as the actual perpetrator *and* in part as the aider and abettor of the other, who also acts in part as an actual perpetrator. Although Lakey was liable for McCoy's actions, he was an actor too. He was in the car and shooting his own gun, although it so happened that McCoy fired the fatal shots. Moreover, Lakey's guilt for *attempted* murder might be based entirely on his own actions in shooting at the attempted murder victims. . . .

As applied here, Lakey and McCoy were to some extent both actual perpetrators and aiders and abettors. Both fired their handguns, although McCoy's gun inflicted the fatal wounds. Once the jury found, as it clearly did, that Lakey acted with the necessary mental state of an aider and abettor, it could find him liable for both his and McCoy's acts, without having to distinguish between them. But Lakey's guilt was also based on his own mental state, not McCoy's. McCoy's unreasonable self-defense theory was personal to him. A jury could reasonably have found that Lakey did not act under unreasonable self-defense even if McCoy did. Thus, his conviction of murder and attempted murder can stand, notwithstanding that on retrial McCoy might be convicted of a lesser crime or even acquitted. [Id. at 1120-22 (emphasis in original).]

Should discrepant liability be allowed where it results from a plea bargain rather than differential culpability? In People v. Hines, 28 Ill. App. 3d 976, 329 N.E.2d 903 (1975), an aider and abettor was convicted of murder even though the killer he hired pled to the lesser charge of conspiracy to murder. Is such a result unfair?

5. One of the Parties Lacks a Required Status for the Crime

Many crimes condition liability on the circumstance element that the perpetrator occupies a certain status. What if a person of such a status commits the crime in concert with another person who lacks that status? As this section shows, sometimes courts face this problem when the person lacking the status required by the criminal definition is the principal and sometimes when that person is the accomplice.

The parental kidnapping example. One recurring situation raising this problem is the kidnapping of children in custody battles. In State v. Simplot, 180 Wisc. 383, 509 N.W.2d 338 (1993), the defendant participated in an armed kidnapping of his sister's three children, who had been living with her ex-husband. The sister, Lisa Oliver, had legal custody of the children, and thus under state law was immune from a kidnapping charge. Simplot maintained that he could not be convicted of aiding and abetting a kidnapping since he was acting on behalf of the children's mother, and therefore had a (vicarious) legal right to take them. The appellate court stated that the prosecutor's argument for holding the agent liable for kidnapping despite the parent's immunity

> finds support in the decisions of several courts which have held agents guilty of kidnapping while exempting the parent at whose instance the taking occurred. The distinction rests on the presumption that the danger to the child is substantially less where the person doing the taking is a parent likely to have the best interests of the child in mind. Further, the parent from whose custody the child is taken will recognize the taker, thereby lessening that parent's mental anguish and reducing the likelihood of breaches of the peace inherently probable where the child is taken by an unrecognized, alleged agent of the parent. [Quoting State v. Edmiston, 602 P.2d 282, 283 (Or. 1979).]
>
> We thus adopt the so-called "minority" view which refuses to extend the parent's immunity to an agent in cases such as this. In doing so, we realize that many such takings may be undertaken peaceably by a relative known to the child acting on behalf of a parent entitled to custody. We cannot escape the conclusion, however, that adoption of a rule that would immunize conduct such as that exhibited by Simplot and his associates in this case would be contrary to Wisconsin's historic commitment to the rule of law and the protection and promotion of the best interests of its children. [509 N.W.2d at 343.]

In this case, some of the other "aiders and abettors," who were not related to the children, actually threatened, beat, and injured the children's father and participated in taking the children from the home. Afraid of being recognized, Simplot stood watch out of sight. Does it make more sense to view Simplot as an accomplice to the exempt Lisa Oliver, or to view him as an accomplice to these other nonexempt actors? Suppose an accomplice to a parental kidnapping merely distracts the parent with whom the children reside while the other parent surreptitiously removes a child. In State v. Stocksdale, 350 A.2d 539 (N.J. Super. Ct. Law Div. 1975), a private detective was held liable for kidnapping under such circumstances, despite the fact that the parent who actually took the children was exempt. How could Stocksdale be an accomplice if he did not facilitate a criminal offense? On the other hand, could Stocksdale be considered the kidnapper himself on a theory of perpetration by means? The difficulty with this approach is that the parent who hired him, and who actually took the children, was a responsible, purposive actor.

Perhaps cases like *Stocksdale* are best understood neither as complicity cases nor as traditional perpetration-by-means cases. Perhaps Stocksdale is being held liable for proximately causing a child to be kidnapped, on the assumption that the act of another does not break the chain of causation if the defendant anticipated the kidnapping with the requisite culpability. In this case, Stockdale's very purpose in distracting one parent was to facilitate kidnapping by the other, so he may be said to have proximately caused the kidnapping.

Arguably, the function of accomplice liability in the common law was to permit liability for causing the criminal act of another notwithstanding the intervening actor limitation on causation. As courts increasingly abandon the intervening actor rule in favor of proximate cause, is accomplice liability still necessary? On the other hand, if we restrict liability for the criminal acts of others to situations in which the defendant has proximately caused the criminal act of another, do we still get liability in cases like *Ochoa* and *Tally*? Should we?

The perjury example. In People v. Sadacca, 128 Misc. 2d 494, 489 N.Y.S.2d 824 (1985), the defendant, Martin Sadacca, was originally charged with grand larceny. Sadacca had swindled a jeweler out of over a million dollars worth of diamonds by pretending to be an intermediary for a fictitious buyer named Whitney Biddle. At trial, however, Sadacca argued that he himself had been duped by his alleged accomplice, businessman David Latner. Sadacca produced a witness, Benoit, who was a casual acquaintance. Benoit testified to having met Sadacca at a Manhattan restaurant. They were joined by two men who identified themselves as Latner and Biddle. The witness testified that he saw Latner introduce Biddle to the defendant. In fact, such a meeting had taken place but was staged by Sadacca, who had two confederates pose as Latner and Biddle. Benoit never saw the real Latner at the trial, so he testified under oath fully believing that the meeting had taken place as described. Sadacca was acquitted. When Benoit later saw the real Latner, he realized that his testimony had been false, and Sadacca was subsequently convicted of perjury, even though perjury requires that the perpetrator lie under oath.

The New York Court of Appeals upheld the conviction. The court found the requisite causation factor was satisfied by Sadacca's use of an innocent agent to commit the crime and then addressed the question of the imputation of perjury:

> . . . Perjury is not unlike other crimes which by definition can only be committed by persons of a designated class (such as bribe receiving; see e.g., People v. Brody, 298 N.Y. 352, 83 N.E. 2d 676 (1949)). As to such crimes, the revised penal law expressly provides that it is no defense that the alleged accomplice is not a member of the definitional class of those with whom he acted. The facts of the instant case are, if anything, more compelling, since the defendant placed the unwitting accomplice within the definitional class by means of a subpoena ad testificandum.
>
> . . . Federal courts have held persons who cause members of a definitional class unwittingly to commit status crimes liable for those crimes as if the members had been willing accomplices. [The underlying principles] are that no one should avoid criminal liability by virtue of factors having no bearing upon his culpability. The legislative judgment is often to enhance punishment for those who attempt to obtain vicarious immunity by using innocent agents to commit crimes. The defendant in the instant case directly caused the innocent agent to engage in conduct

which constituted the actus reus of the crime of perjury, and incidentally, to assume the status necessary to commission of the crime. [Id. at 829.]

But what about the complementary problem, in which the aider and abettor is exempt but the principal is not? Consider the following provision of the Oregon criminal code (Supp. 1998):

§161.160. *Defense to criminal liability for conduct of another.* In any prosecution for a crime in which criminal liability is based upon the conduct of another person pursuant to ORS §161.55, it is no defense that . . .
   (2) The crime, as defined, can be committed only by a particular class or classes of persons to which the defendant does not belong, and the defendant is, for that reason legally incapable of committing the crime in an individual capacity.

Is this rule compatible with the view that complicity is just another way of perpetrating an offense? If we are punishing the aider and abettor for consenting to another's offense, arguably it should not matter that the aider and abettor is incapable of committing the criminal act personally. But if we are trying to punish the aider and abettor for perpetrating the offense through a passive agent, should the aider and abettor's exemption indeed serve to exempt her? In fact, ORS §161.55, the complicity provision referred to, does not make aiders and abettors vicariously liable on the basis of "perpetration-by-means."

By contrast, we have seen that New York Penal Law §20.05(1) allows culpable accomplices to be liable for the acts of nonculpable perpetrators. Section 20.05(3) allows accomplices to be vicariously liable for crimes they are personally exempt from committing. Combining these two provisions, a court may hold an aider and abettor liable as perpetrator-by-means of a crime he could not personally commit.

The Model Penal Code tries to address the problem of complicity rules potentially clashing with the specific definitions and exclusions of offenders under specific criminal statutes in section 2.06:

   (5) A person who is legally incapable of committing a particular offense himself may be guilty thereof if it is committed by the conduct of another person for which he is legally accountable, unless such liability is consistent with the purpose of the provision establishing his incapacity . . .
   (6) Unless otherwise provided by the Code or by the law defining the offense, a person is not an accomplice in an offense committed by another person if:
      (a) he is a victim of that offense; or
      (b) the offense is so defined that his conduct is inevitably incident to its commission. . . .

Now consider some test cases for this principle of interpretation:

The official misconduct example. Can a private citizen be liable for official misconduct? In United States v. Ruffin, 613 F.2d 408 (2d Cir. 1979), the court upheld the conviction of William Ruffin under 42 U.S.C. 2703 for fraudulently obtaining federal funds while an officer or employee of a federally financed agency — even though he was not such an officer or employee. The funds, about $115,000, were paid to Ruffin as rent for an uninhabitable building, by his friend Olga Defreitas, executive director of the federally financed social service agency in question. Although charged under the same statutory provision, and despite evidence that she received a $30,000 kickback, Defreitas was acquitted. Judge Mansfield wrote for the court:

> The central issue raised on this appeal is whether a person incapable of personally committing a specified crime (in this case because he was not an officer, director, agent or employee of an agency receiving federal financial assistance) who causes an innocent agent meeting the capacity requirements to engage in the proscribed conduct may be punished as a principal under 18 U.S.C. §2. We hold that he may and affirm. . . .
>
> To the extent that Ruffin was charged under 18 U.S.C. §2(a) as an "aider" and "abettor" of Defreitas' alleged criminal conduct, he could not be found guilty unless Defreitas as a principal had violated 42 U.S.C. §2703. It is hornbook law that a defendant charged with aiding and abetting the commission of a crime by another cannot be convicted in the absence of proof that the crime was actually committed. . . . [T]he acquittal of Defreitas by the same jury which convicted Ruffin precludes a finding under 18 U.S.C. §2(a) that Ruffin aided and abetted her commission of the alleged crime, since the jury's verdict amounts to a finding that she had not been proven beyond a reasonable doubt to have knowingly and wilfully committed it.
>
> Had Ruffin acted alone, without using Defreitas as an intermediary, he obviously could not have been found guilty of violating 42 U.S.C. §2703, since he was never an "officer, director, agent or employee of, or connected in any capacity with, any agency receiving financial assistance," the only category of persons to whom the criminal sanction of §2703 directly applies. However, the record in this case would permit an inference that Ruffin caused Defreitas, a person within this category, to engage in the alleged criminal conduct. . . . We are persuaded that such a "causer" may be found guilty under §2(b).
>
> One purpose of 18 U.S.C. §2 is to enlarge the scope of criminal liability under existing substantive criminal laws so that a person who operates from behind the scenes may be convicted even though he is not expressly prohibited by the substantive statute from engaging in the acts made criminal by Congress. Where the principal is found guilty of a criminal offense, for instance, it is undisputed that a person may be convicted as an aider and abettor under 18 U.S.C. §2(a) even though he may lack the capacity to violate the substantive criminal statute. We see no logical reason why a person who causes an innocent agent having the capacity to commit a criminal act to do so should not likewise be held criminally responsible under 18 U.S.C. §2(b) even though the causer lacks the capacity. . . .
>
> The evidence, moreover, justifies the conclusion that the jury properly applied §2(b) to the evidence and that there was no inconsistency in its acquittal of Defreitas and its conviction of Ruffin. Concededly the proof against Defreitas, at least on paper, appears to have been strong, warranting a conviction of her. On the other hand, there was evidence indicating that she may have been dominated or manipulated by her close friend Ruffin, that the fraudulent plan was his idea rather than hers, that he may have known more than she did about the lack of any real prospect for the renovation of the 1402 Bedford Avenue building, and that he received and personally retained most of the fraudulently obtained rentals totalling some $115,000 under the leases. This evidence would permit the jury to have concluded that Ruffin was guilty beyond reasonable doubt but that Defreitas lacked the necessary criminal intent. . . . [Id. at 416-17.]

Judge Wyatt argued in dissent that the majority's position impermissibly mingled a complicity theory of liability, under which Ruffin could have been guilty of assisting Defreitas's offense, and a perpetration-by-means theory, under which only an employee or officer of a federally financed agency could be guilty. Judge Wyatt wrote:

> It seems entirely clear to me that a person who lacks the capacity to commit a substantive offense may be prosecuted as an "aider and abettor" under Section 2(a) if there is proof that a principal who did have the capacity was guilty of the offense. At the same time, a person who lacks the capacity to commit a substantive offense may not be prosecuted as a causer under Section 2(b) using an innocent intermediary who does have the capacity. This is not so "incongruous" as the majority thinks. On the contrary, it is the reasonable and logical consequence of settled rules of criminal law, deriving from the classification at common law of parties to crimes and the reasons for that classification.
>
> Before there can be any conviction for any felony offense, there must be at least one guilty principal in the first degree. Where the substantive offense is limited to a specified class agency employees in the case at bar, bank officers, etc. in 18 U.S.C. §656 and the like and an outsider is indicted as an aider and abettor under 18 U.S.C. §2(a), it is essential for the government to prove that the offense was committed by a principal who, by definition, had the capacity to be such. . . . Where the substantive offense is limited to a specified class, and the causer is not a member of the class, but the innocent intermediary is a member of the class, there can be no conviction of the causer as a principal, by the use of Section 2(b) together with the substantive statute. The causer cannot be a principal because of lack of capacity. The intermediary cannot be a principal because, though possessing capacity, he or she is innocent. Without a principal there can be no violation of the substantive statute. [Id. at 426.]

Who has the better of this argument?

The victim as accomplice. One clash of complicity doctrine and a specific offense definition should have an obvious solution. If the underage female in a case of statutory rape arguably "consents" to having sexual relations with the offender (assuming that "consent" is a meaningful concept under statutory rape laws), then it hardy seems within the legislature's intent to punish the female as an accomplice. See the famous case of Queen v. Tyrell (1893) 1 Q.B. 710.

But sometimes a statute leaves "victim status" ambiguous. In United States v. Spitler, 800 F.2d 1267 (4th Cir. 1986), Carpenter, a state highway official, demanded and received bribes from Spitler, head of a contracting firm, for award of a contract to provide highway services. Both were charged with violating the Hobbs Act, 18 U.S.C. §1951, which punishes the "obtaining of property from another, with his consent, induced by wrongful use of actual or threatened force, violence, of fear, or under color of official right." The language of the Hobbs Act suggests forceful or coercive extortion, but the statute has traditionally punished bribery where the official takes advantage of his official power but where the other party seems to act quite consensually. Spitler argued that as a victim of the extortion, he could not be charged as an accomplice, unless he actively initiated the illegal transaction. The court rejected this argument, finding that after an initial "shakedown" by Carpenter, Spitler took affirmative steps to repeat these transactions, and thus that the Spider-Carpenter relationship was a "symbiotic" one in which Spitler "provided the necessary lubrication." Id. at 1278.

E. THE "STRAW MAN" GUN PURCHASE: A CLOSING EXERCISE ON COMPLICITY

Consider the following news report:

Feds Indict Gun Sellers[13]

Opening a new front in the war on gun violence, federal prosecutors announced indictments today against suburban gun sellers accused of helping put firearms in the hands of drug-selling street gangs.

Federal officials said "Operation Surefire," in which federal agents cooperated with Chicago police, represented the first concerted attack on suburban gun shops that furnish arms to city-based gangs responsible for hundreds of homicides.

"The message is simple — if you violate the gun laws, you're going to prison," U.S. Attorney Scott Lassar said in announcing the charges.

Owners and employees of five suburban gun shops were charged with avoiding state laws designed to keep guns out of the hands of criminals by selling guns to "straw purchasers" — people with clean records who turn the weapons over to gang members convicted of past crimes.

The indictments follow a $433 million lawsuit filed by the city of Chicago against suburban gun dealers and the firearms industry.

The most dramatic recent example of what might be called a "specific facilitation law" is the frequent application of the federal gun statutes, and particularly this "straw man" doctrine.

The federal law, in 18 U.S.C. §922(b), makes it a crime for a licensed firearms dealer to sell or deliver any firearm or ammunition to any ineligible person; ineligible buyers include, among other categories, (1) minors; (2) persons by whom the purchase would violate applicable state law; (3) nonresidents of the state where the dealer operates; and (4) persons indicted for or convicted of felonies. In addition, 18 U.S.C. §922(a)(6) (2000) makes it a federal offense

> for any person in connection with the acquisition of any firearm or ammunition from a license importer, licensed manufacturer, licensed dealer, or licensed collector, knowingly to make any false, fictitious, or misrepresented identification, intended or likely to deceive such importer, manufacturer, dealer or collector with respect to the lawfulness of the sale or other disposition of such firearm or ammunition. . . .

The confluence of these provisions creates the "straw man" situation, and it can produce liability for either a seller, or a buyer, or both. Thus, in United States v. Straach, 987 F.2d 232 (5th Cir. 1993), the court affirmed the conviction of a Texas gun dealer who negotiated the sale of guns to one Albritton, who identified himself as an out-of-state resident who was going to sell them right away in Oklahoma. Once they settled on the items for purchase, Albritton had one Bishop, an otherwise silent companion in the transaction, present a Texas driver's license and complete the sales paperwork in his own name. (Albritton and Bishop were actually undercover "sting" police.) Then Bishop handed the receipts and guns to Albritton as they left. Conversely, in United States v. Howell, 37 F.3d

13. Associated Press, Chicago, Aug. 18, 1999.

1197 (7th Cir. 1994), the government employed a gun dealer in a sting operation where a man and wife entered his gun shop, and the husband did all the negotiation for the purchase and made all the inquiries about the gun (including fitting the gun to his own hand size), and then had his wife sign the paperwork and provide identification. The husband was a convicted felon. The Court of Appeals affirmed the conviction of the husband for being a felon in illegal possession of a gun, and of the wife for violating the false statement provision of 18 U.S.C. §922(a)(6).

Thus, the straw-man doctrine enables the federal gun laws to operate as a specific facilitation statute: They punish either the dealer or the straw-man buyer for creating the risk that an ineligible user of the gun will commit violent crimes with the gun. But since liability is for the specific straw-man transaction, it does not require any proof of the defendants' mental state with respect to the ultimate crime.

Given the range of crimes that an ineligible user could conceivably commit with the gun, what is an appropriate level of punishment for defendants in a straw-person case? Where the ultimate user does commit a dangerous crime, should the dealer or straw buyer's liability for the federal gun crime preempt any conviction as an accomplice in the ultimate crime? Should the ultimately harmful result of the forbidden transaction be used as a sentencing factor, to increase punishment for the transactor to the level of a participant in the ultimate crime?

The case of United States v. Moore, 109 F.2d 1456 (9th Cir. 1997) (en banc) presents one of the most striking examples of a straw-man purchase case, and raises a panoply of complicity questions.

> On September 2, 1993, fourteen-year-old Bobby Moore saw a .25 caliber handgun in a pawnshop which had a federal license to sell firearms. When he showed interest in the weapon, a clerk shooed him off the premises because his age rendered him ineligible under federal law to buy it. Undaunted, Bobby set out to find a way to acquire the handgun for himself. He approached his mother to buy it for him, but she turned him down. Bobby's friend Jason Marks witnessed this discussion. Jason's unchallenged testimony about the discussion established not only that Mrs. Moore refused to buy the gun on behalf of her son, but that she explicitly told him he would have to "get someone else" to get it for him because she "didn't want her name on the papers."

> *Q.* When [Bobby] first talked to Mrs. Moore, he was there looking for something to sell, looking at the boom box. When he first talked to his mom, what did he say? What did he ask her?
> *A.* He asked if she would pawn this for him, and she said, no, and they got in an argument. . . .
> *Q.* Did [Bobby] ask her to pawn it or hawk it for anything in particular?
> *A.* Yeah, for the gun . . . and Bob's mom said she didn't want to do it because she didn't want her name on the papers and he could hurt somebody and she didn't think he needed a gun. But Bob has a way of talking people into things, and so he kind of threw a tantrum and got all mad, and finally his mom said that she would do it . . . *Just pawn the CD player and he would have to figure out a different way of getting the gun because she didn't want her name on the papers.*

Mrs. Moore then pawned Bobby's CD player and gave him the cash she received from the transaction. She did so knowing that he intended to use it to purchase a firearm.

The next day, Bobby went looking for someone else to help him acquire the weapon, as suggested by his mother. He took the cash to [neighbor Lee Roy] Wiley's residence to see if Wiley would assist him. The neighborhood knew Wiley as "Grandpa," and he frequently did favors for the children. The record reflects that Wiley is a man of limited intelligence. Wiley was neither Bobby's parent nor guardian, nor was he related to him in any respect whatsoever.

Wiley balked at first, but Bobby persisted; and with the promise of money as a sweetener, Wiley relented and agreed to purchase the gun on Bobby's behalf.

Mrs. Moore then drove Wiley, Bobby, and Jason to the pawnshop. During this trip, Wiley asked Mrs. Moore if the purchase of the gun was all right with her, to which she replied that it was fine.

When the group arrived at the pawnshop, Mrs. Moore waited in the car while Wiley, Bobby, and Jason went inside. Wiley asked the clerk to see the handgun Bobby had spotted on his earlier visit. Because the two boys were present, the clerk inquired for whom Wiley wanted to purchase the gun. Wiley responded that the gun was for Bobby, but that he was Bobby's grandfather, and that he was going to hold it for Bobby until Bobby was 21 years of age. . . .

The clerk responded to Wiley's representations with an inquiry about Bobby's parents and whether they knew about this purchase. Bobby said that his mother was outside, and he went to get her. In short order, Mrs. Moore appeared briefly in the doorway, and, without prompting by Wiley, said to the clerk, "His grandfather is buying a gun for him. He's going to hold it until he's 21, and everything is fine with me."

Satisfied by Mrs. Moore's representations, the clerk had Wiley sign BATF form 4473 as the "transferee (buyer)," accepted the cash Bobby had given Wiley for the transaction, and turned the gun over to Wiley. Back in the car, and contrary to the intentions he expressed to the clerk, Wiley gave the gun to Mrs. Moore, expecting that it would go to Bobby. As Bobby intended from the start, he then took the firearm as his own possession.

Mrs. Moore's reluctance to buy this weapon for her son and to put her name on the papers was well founded, and her worry about Bobby hurting someone with it was prescient. On January 20, 1994, Bobby used the gun to shoot Ronald Wade Feldner, a New Plymouth, Idaho, police officer, in the face. Officer Feldner died, leaving behind a wife and minor children.

An Idaho law at the time of the sale permitted the sale of a firearm to a minor so long as the minor had the consent of a parent or guardian. Idaho Code §18-2202A (1990). Nevertheless, the court affirmed Wiley's conviction for making a false statement under 18 U.S.C. §922(a)(6) and Mrs. Moore as accomplice to that crime.

Was the court right?

Should Wiley or Mrs. Moore face any liability for the killing of Officer Feldner?

Should the gun dealer have faced some liability in this case?

12

CONSPIRACY

Perhaps no common law crime is so mysterious and vexing as conspiracy. Conspiracy has two very different aspects: First, it is an *inchoate* crime — like attempt, it punishes anticipatory action that aims at, but does not necessarily ever reach, a criminal object. Second, it is a doctrine of *accessorial liability* that implicates all the coconspirators in each other's acts. Consider the following historical perspective:[1]

> Ironically, conspiracy was initially directed neither at preparatory activity nor at group crime in general. Rather, it was a narrowly circumscribed statutory remedy designed to combat abuses against the administration of justice. According to Edward Coke, it consisted of "a consultation and agreement between two or more to appeal or indict an innocent man falsely and maliciously of felony, whom accordingly they cause to be indicted and appealed; and afterward the party is lawfully acquitted." A writ of conspiracy would lie only for this particular offense, and only when the offense (including acquittal of the falsely indicted party) had actually taken place. However, in 1611 the Court of Star Chamber extended the law by upholding a conspiracy conviction even though the falsely accused party was not indicted (Poulterers' Case, 77 Eng. Rep. 813 (KB. 1611) (Coke)). The court reasoned that the confederating together, and not the false indictment, was the gist of the offense. The ramifications of this decision were twofold. First, if it was not necessary that the intended injury occur, then conspiracy punished the attempted crime. Second, if the agreement and not the false indictment was the target of conspiracy law, then conspiracy was loosed from its mooring: subsequent decisions logically could and in fact did hold that agreement to commit any unlawful act was criminal conspiracy.

The following case illustrates the relationship between the two key aspects of conspiracy.

---

1. James Burke, Sanford Kadish & Dan M. Kahan, Conspiracy, 1 Encyclopedia of Crime and Justice 241-42 (2d ed. 2002).

A. THE NATURE OF CONSPIRACY

STATE v. VERIVE
Court of Appeals of Arizona
128 Ariz. 70, 627 P.2d 721 (1981)

HAIRE, PRESIDING JUDGE.

This is an appeal by Charles Anthony ("Carl") Verive (hereinafter "defendant") from his convictions on charges of attempting to dissuade a witness and conspiracy to dissuade a witness. . . .

The underlying facts may be stated simply. Howard Woodall had filed a false affidavit with a trial court in relation to civil litigation. Lee Galvin filed an affidavit exposing Woodall's perjury. Upon learning of Galvin's cooperation with authorities in regard to exposing the perjury, Woodall and defendant agreed that defendant would go to Galvin's home and beat Galvin in an effort to dissuade him from becoming a witness against Woodall. In return for this beating, defendant would receive from Woodall $900 and a motorcycle. On December 3, 1973, defendant drove to Galvin's home accompanied by one Mr. Baugh with whom defendant had been drinking. Defendant confronted Galvin in the doorway of the house, saying: "Do you know Howard Woodall? Well, he sent us." Defendant then proceeded to beat Galvin. In response to the scuffle, Galvin's wife started screaming and his son intervened to rescue him. . . .

In 1978, Woodall became willing to testify against defendant, after having secured his own immunity from prosecution. . . .

The grand jury indictment against defendant charged him with two counts:

(1) Conspiracy, second degree . . .
(2) Attempt to dissuade a witness . . .

We first consider whether the two convictions violated A.R.S. §13-1641, which provides as follows:

> An act or omission which is made punishable in different ways by different sections of the laws may be punished under either, but in no event under more than one. An acquittal or conviction and sentence under either one bars a prosecution for the same act or omission under any other.

. . . The statute's purpose is to preclude attaching more than one punishment to one act. The test for determining whether one act of the defendant has been punished more than once was established in State v. Tinghitella, 108 Ariz. 1, 491 P.2d 834 (1971). Denominated as the "identical elements test," it requires that, after eliminating the evidence necessary to support one of the charges, the remaining evidence must be sufficient to support the remaining charge. The test focuses upon the evidence actually presented at the trial, to establish that each punishment could have related to a different act. That the punishable acts occur within a very short time span is not material to the application of this test.

To apply this test one must determine what elements must be proven to satisfy each charge and whether each charge can be supported without using the same act to prove more than one charge. An essential element of conspiracy is an unlawful agreement with one or more persons to engage in the commission of a felony or to cause the commission of a felony. Also essential to a conviction for a second degree conspiracy is proof of some overt act to effect the object of the conspiracy. At least one overt act must be expressly alleged in the indictment and proved.

Defendant argues that the state relied upon the same overt act to prove both the attempt and the conspiracy. If only one overt act were alleged in the conspiracy indictment, this same act could not be used to establish an essential element of any other charge. However, two overt acts were specifically alleged in support of the conspiracy charge:

(1) CARL VERIVE aka CHARLES ANTHONY VERIVE struck LERLIA LEE GALVIN with his fist on or about the 1st day of DECEMBER, 1973;

(2) CARL VERIVE aka CHARLES ANTHONY VERIVE or JAMES A. ROBISON went to 948 West 10th Street, Mesa, Arizona.

Either of these acts was sufficient to support the conspiracy charge; only one was required. The conspiracy charge was supported by proof that defendant Verive went to Galvin's home pursuant to the agreement to dissuade Galvin from testifying. Eliminating this evidence, there remained evidence of an overt act sufficient for a conviction of attempt. This meets the *Tinghitella* test. Therefore, we find no violation of A.R.S. §13-1641.

This, however, does not end our inquiry. Defendant has also asserted that to convict him of both attempt to dissuade a witness and conspiracy to dissuade a witness violates his rights under the double jeopardy clause of the fifth amendment to the United States Constitution, which provides:

[N]or shall any person be subject for the same offense to be twice put in jeopardy of life or limb.

. . . In this single trial context, our concern is limited to whether the charges upon which the defendant is convicted are really the same offense, or, of equal importance, whether one of the charges is a lesser included offense of another. . . .

The established test for determining whether two offenses are sufficiently distinguishable to permit the imposition of cumulative punishment was stated in Blockburger v. United States, 284 U.S. 299, 304 (1932):

The applicable rule is that where the same act or transaction constitutes a violation of two distinct statutory provisions, the test to be applied to determine whether there are two offenses or only one, is whether each provision requires proof of an additional fact which the other does not. [Brown v. Ohio, 432 U.S. 161, 166 (1977).]

. . . [T]he Court's application of the test focuses on the statutory elements of the offense. If each requires proof of a fact that the other does not, the *Blockburger* test is satisfied, notwithstanding a substantial overlap in the proof offered to establish the crimes.

. . . [H]ere, both of defendants' offenses were inchoate. Successful accomplishment of the intended result (i.e., dissuasion) was not required by either. . . . The elements of attempt to dissuade a witness are: (1) the intent to dissuade the witness, and (2) an overt act in furtherance of that intent. Conspiracy to dissuade a witness, second degree, requires: (1) the intent to dissuade the witness, (2) an overt act, and (3) an agreement between two or more people. Unless the overt act required to establish an attempt is significantly different than [sic] the act required to establish a conspiracy, attempt to dissuade a witness would be a lesser included offense of conspiracy to dissuade a witness.

Without determining the exact parameters of the overt act requirement of conspiracy and attempt, we conclude that an act which would support a conspiracy conviction would not necessarily be sufficient to support an attempt conviction. Therefore, the attempt is not a lesser included offense of conspiracy. A conspiracy to dissuade can be committed without committing an attempt to dissuade.

The primary focus of the crime of conspiracy is the agreement itself, the collusion, the secrecy and the resulting threat to society that such criminal liaisons create. The act is required as a method of showing that some step has been taken toward executing the illicit agreement. Any action sufficient to corroborate the existence of the agreement and to show that it is being put into effect is sufficient to support the conspiracy. In contrast, the crime of attempt focuses more directly upon the unequivocal nature of the steps taken toward consummating the intended crime. In attempt, the act for which the defendant is held criminally responsible must be more than preparatory. Perkins, in his treatise on criminal law, concludes that the "overt act" in a conspiracy "need not amount to an attempt to commit the crime which is the object of the combination." Perkins, Criminal Law, 618 (2d ed. 1968).

That the overt act required for a conspiracy is different than [sic] that required for an attempt has been recognized in Arizona. In State v. Celaya, 27 Ariz. App. 564, 556 P.2d 1167 (1976), the court stated:

> Care must be taken not to equate the overt act required by conspiracy with the overt act required in the crime of attempt. Whereas under the crime of attempt, mere preparation does not constitute an overt act, this is not true when dealing with the overt act required by conspiracy. The overt act may be merely a part of preliminary arrangements for commission of the ultimate crime. It need amount to no more than an act showing that the conspiracy has gone beyond a mere meeting of the minds upon the attainment of an unlawful object and that action between conspirators as such has begun. . . .

We conclude that conspiracy to dissuade a witness and attempt to dissuade a witness are separate and distinct offenses. Each offense requires proof of an element that is not required to prove the other. Conspiracy requires an agreement. Attempt requires an act beyond mere preparation. Neither is a lesser included offense of the other. We find no constitutional or statutory infirmity in the convictions or sentences imposed.

The judgment and sentences of the trial court are affirmed.

Notes and Questions

1. *Conspiracy vs. attempt.* Conspiracy, as we see, is an inchoate, or preparatory, crime. Though it resembles attempt and solicitation in this respect, conspiracy differs from the other preparatory crimes in important ways. It requires more than attempt, because it requires at least two participants. Yet,

it requires less than attempt, because it pushes the line between preparation and criminal liability farther back than attempt law does.

Although the court in *Verive* does not treat conspiracy as a lesser included offense within attempt, some jurisdictions disagree. In State v. Burleson, 50 Ill. App. 3d 629, 365 N.E.2d 1162 (1977), the defendant and his ally, Brown, met on September 11 to plan a bank robbery for September 13. On reaching the bank on the 13th, they noticed too many people nearby, so they decided merely to make a practice run of their approach to and escape from the bank, and then to try again on September 16. On September 16, Burleson and Brown arrived at the bank wearing disguises and carrying a shotgun and suitcase. As they approached the door of the bank, a man bolted the door from the inside. Burleson and Brown escaped by car but were later arrested.

Burleson was convicted of conspiracy to commit armed robbery for his actions on September 13 and for both conspiracy and attempt for his actions on September 16. The appellate court partly affirmed and partly reversed:

> [T]he State has not relied on the same conduct of the defendant to establish the conspiracy to rob the bank on September 13, 1975, and the attempt to rob which was committed on September 16, 1975. We do not view the conspirators' actions in terms of a single course of conduct. Rather, the conspirators' actions originate in separate agreements or impulses to rob the bank on separate dates. With their attempt to rob the bank on September 13, 1975, the conspirator[s'] first agreement to rob the bank came to an end. The attempt of September 16, 1975, was not the result of the original agreement, but of a fresh agreement which was entered into after the attempt of September 13, 1975. Since [the] aforementioned offenses arise from separate courses of conduct, we, accordingly, affirm the defendant's convictions for the conspiracy of September 13, 1975, and for the attempted armed robbery of September 16, 1975. In addition, we reverse defendant's conviction for the conspiracy of September 16, 1975, because it is a lesser included offense of attempt.

Could Burleson also have been convicted of attempt on September 13? Could he have been convicted of conspiracy on September 11, even if he could not have been convicted of attempt on that date?

2. *Varying rules on double punishment.* One commentator describes the state of the law on the issue of multiple convictions for attempt and conspiracy as follows:[2]

> . . . [A] problem emerges when conspirators attempt to commit the crime which is their object, but fail. May they then be convicted of both conspiracy and attempt? Thirteen states and the MPC answer in the negative. The Hawaii Code Comments offer a concise explanation for this prohibition of multiple inchoate convictions.
>
> > . . . [T]he danger which is represented by inchoate crimes lies in the possibility that the substantive [crime] will be carried to fruition because of [the criminal] disposition of the defendant. Hence any number of stages preparatory to the commission of a given offense, if taken together, still constitute a single danger: that the crime contemplated will be committed. Such a rationale precludes cumulating convictions of attempt . . . and a conspiracy to commit the same offense.

2. Note, Conspiracy: Statutory Reform Since the Model Penal Code, 75 Colum. L. Rev. 1122, 1182-83 (1975).

Five additional states occupy the somewhat incongruous position of specifically precluding conviction of both conspiracy and a substantive offense, but remaining silent on multiple inchoate convictions. Almost undoubtedly, convictions of both conspiracy and attempt will not be sanctioned in these jurisdictions either. Where such dual judgments *are* rendered, criminal codes which reject consecutive sentences when several offenses arise out of a single criminal episode, or when one offense is only a conspiracy to commit the other, would require concurrent terms. Many state statutes have not considered the question of multiple inchoate convictions, but the reasoning displayed in the Hawaii Comment above may very well be persuasive, even where conviction of both conspiracy and substantive crime is acceptable.

Can one argue that a conspiracy should not be regarded as a lesser included offense within attempt, on the ground that group pressures among the conspirators increase the likelihood that they will not back down from the ultimate crime? That is, might the presence of more than one actor make the attempt less likely to be abandoned, and the division of labor among the conspirators make it more likely that the attempt will succeed?

3. *Overt acts.* What was the significance of the two "overt acts" that the court attributes to Verive? Are they sufficient to push him across the preparation/ attempt line under any of the tests examined in Chapter 10? If not, how do they establish Verive's criminal liability? Why does the presence of an ally make a difference?

Is an overt act always required? In *Verive,* the court applied the traditional requirement that the prosecution prove at least one "overt act" committed by at least one alleged co-conspirator. The "overt act" requirement is not onerous. The act may be fairly trivial, far short of the actus reus necessary for an attempt; moreover, one overt act committed by one conspirator is sufficient to confirm the conspiracy charge against all. Furthermore, the overt act requirement is not universal: At least under federal law, it only applies it where the conspiracy law at issue explicitly so states. In United States v. Shabani, 513 U.S. 10 (1994), the Court noted that whereas the general federal conspiracy law, 18 U.S.C. §371, requires that a conspirator "do any act to effect the object of the conspiracy," Shabani was prosecuted under the more specific law proscribing conspiracy to distribute cocaine, 18 U.S.C. §846, which did not require that any overt act be mentioned in the indictment or proved at trial. To the argument that without an overt act the legislature would be punishing mere thought, the Court responded that "the criminal agreement itself is the actus reus." Id. at 16.

4. *Other overlaps with conspiracy.* Under *Blockburger,* the key element in conspiracy that is not included in attempt is the involvement of at least two people. In the case of other substantive crimes that do require more than one actor, the courts have followed *Blockburger* to forbid double punishment. For example, 21 U.S.C. §848 makes it a special "continuing criminal enterprise crime" for a person to commit any of several drug-related crimes "in concert with five or more persons with respect to whom such person occupies a position of organizer, a supervisory position, or any other position of management." Is it possible to violate §848 and *not* violate §846? In Rutledge v. United States, 517 U.S. 292 (1996), the Supreme Court held that the defendant could not suffer separate judgments for both general drug conspiracy crime under 18 U.S.C. §846 and a "continuing criminal enterprise" crime arising from the same transaction, even if sentences were concurrent. The Court concluded that the §846 generic

conspiracy was a lesser included offense of the §848 crime. Could the term "in concert" indicate anything other than "in conspiracy"?

5. *Punishment for conspiracy and the completed offense.* In addition to the in-choate aspect of conspiracy law, conspiracy seems also to be an aggravating factor in a substantive crime. The criminal law assumes that a group planning to commit a crime poses a special danger to the public welfare. The support and cooperation of co-conspirators supposedly increase the probability of criminal conduct on the part of each participant, increase the social damage the members can do, and make it harder for the police to apprehend them. Thus, under federal criminal law, even where the conspirators achieve their criminal objective, they may be punished for both the conspiracy *and* the substantive crime. In Callanan v. United States, 364 U.S. 587 (1961), the defendant was convicted of a conspiracy to obstruct commerce by extorting money, as well as the substantive offense of obstructing commerce by extortion, and was sentenced to consecutive terms of 12 years on each count. Affirming the consecutive sentences, the court, through Justice Frankfurter, explained:

> Under the early common law, a conspiracy — which constituted a misdemeanor — was said to merge with the completed felony which was its object. This rule, however, was based upon significant procedural distinctions between misdemeanors and felonies. The defendant in a misdemeanor trial was entitled to counsel and a copy of the indictment; these advantages were unavailable on trial for a felony. Therefore no conviction was permitted of a constituent misdemeanor upon an indictment for the felony. When the substantive crime was also a misdemeanor, or when the conspiracy was defined by statute as a felony, merger did not obtain. As these common-law procedural niceties disappeared, the merger concept [assumed] less significance, and today it has been abandoned.
>
> . . . Unlike the merger doctrine, petitioner's position does not question that the Government could charge a conspiracy even when the substantive crime that was its object had been completed. His concern is with the punitive consequences of the choice thus open to the Government; it can indict for both or either offense, but, petitioner contends, it can punish only for one.
>
> The distinctiveness between a substantive offense and a conspiracy to commit is a postulate of our law. . . .
>
> . . . Concerted action both increases the likelihood that the criminal object will be successfully attained and decreases the probability that the individuals involved will depart from their path of criminality. Group association for criminal purposes often, if not normally, makes possible the attainment of ends more complex than those which one criminal could accomplish. Nor is the danger of a conspiratorial group limited to the particular end toward which it has embarked. Combination in crime makes more likely the commission of crimes unrelated to the original purpose for which the group was formed. In sum, the danger which a conspiracy generates is not confined to the substantive offense which is the immediate aim of the enterprise. [Id. at 589-94.]

A defendant therefore can receive a sentence in excess of the allowable maximum sentence for the substantive crime. Is this result fair? Does the maximum sentence for the substantive crime provide enough deterrence? Does an extra sentence for conspiracy add more deterrence? If not, can the conspiracy sentence be justified?

6. *Sentences for conspiracy.* Punishment schemes in conspiracy statutes vary widely among jurisdictions. Before the influence of the Model Penal Code

spread, the variation was even greater. Under some statutes, conspiracy was a misdemeanor. See, e.g., Ark. Stat. Ann. §41-1201 (1947). Others provided a permissible maximum sentence, regardless of the conspiratorial objective. See, e.g., Ariz. Rev. Stat. §13-331 (1956). In still others, the maximum sentence depended on whether the objective of the conspiracy amounted to a misdemeanor or a felony. See, e.g., 18 U.S.C. §371 (1976). (Section 371 is still in effect today.) Because these conspiracy statutes usually did not provide for a maximum sentence related to the maximum penalty permitted for the substantive crime objective, the penalty for the conspiracy was often greater than the permissible penalty for the crime that was its object. See, e.g., Clune v. United States, 159 U.S. 590 (1895) (two-year sentence for conspiracy to steal from mails permissible even where maximum penalty for target crime was $100 fine).

The Model Penal Code authors criticized these statutes, stating that "there is likely to be little difference in the gravity [of the actor's offense if the plan is consummated or fails]." Section 5.05 of the Code fixes the maximum sentence for the conspiracy equal to the maximum penalty for the criminal objective. The Code influenced a number of states to revise their conspiracy statutes to provide for a maximum sentence that is either equivalent to the maximum sentence for the object of the conspiracy or is a fraction of the maximum sentence. See, e.g., Ariz. Rev. St. Ann. §13-1003 (2001); Mo. Ann. Stat. §564.016 (Vernon 1999). Is this change an improvement?

Section 1.07 of the Model Penal Code provides:

(1) *Prosecution for Multiple Offenses.* . . . [W]hen the same conduct of a defendant may establish the commission of more than one offense, the defendant may be prosecuted for each offense. He may not, however, be convicted of more than one offense if: . . .

(b) one offense consists only of a conspiracy or other form of preparation to commit the other. . . .

7. *Criminally conspiring to commit a noncriminal act.* One of the most remarkable aspects of conspiracy at common law was the rule that the object of the conspiracy need not be a crime itself, or even an unlawful act.

In Commonwealth v. Donoghue, 250 Ky. 343, 63 S.W.2d 3 (1933), the court upheld an indictment charging conspiracy to violate the usury laws, even though Kentucky's usury law was noncriminal and provided as its sole sanction that the lender remit the excessive interest:

According to the overwhelming weight of authority the objects of the conspiracy need not be an offense against the criminal law for which an individual could be indicted or convicted, but it is sufficient if the purpose be unlawful. That term "unlawful" in this connection has been expanded beyond its original limits of being only some act punishable as a crime. It is now understood and regarded as covering an act not embraced in the crime of conspiracy as it originally existed. It cannot be said, however — and care must ever be exercised in the application, as all courts recognize — that the term "unlawful" includes every act which violates legal rights of another or such as may create a right of action. . . . There is a series of acts which have the essence but not the form of crime (e.g., immoral acts, unindictable cheats), which, wanting the necessary objective constituents, escape judicial cognizance as being intrinsically criminal, but which are held to be invested by conspiracy with a garb that exposes them to the penalties of the law. Without the combination of men attempting to accomplish the objects, they had only the essence of crime, but, by means of the conspiracy, an unfair and mischievous advantage of the aggressors is recognized, and the acts are presented in such definiteness that they can be taken hold of and punished. Of this character is a conspiracy to use violence, as a riot, which derives its indictability from the plurality of persons concerned and to conspiracy to injuriously affect the body politic. Another series of acts which become cognizable by reason of the plurality of men or union of forces are those which prejudice the public or the government generally, such as unduly elevating or depressing wages, the price of the necessities of life, or impoverishing a class of individuals. The gist of conspiracies of this class is the unlawfulness of the means used. . . .

One commentator[3] discusses the state of the law on this topic:

> [T]he ALI drafters refused to approve the imposition of criminal sanctions on agreements directed toward the performance of conduct which, if achieved, would not itself constitute a penal violation. With only one exception, each new statute, adopted or proposed, has reflected this conclusion by making criminal only those conspiracies whose objective is the commission of a crime (or, in some states, an offense) as defined elsewhere in the jurisdiction's penal code.
>
>   A number of states have gone even further. For an agreement to be criminal in Oregon, either a felony or a class A misdemeanor must be included among its objectives. The laws of New Mexico, Texas, and Virginia do not prohibit conspiracies to commit any sort of misdemeanor; they subject agreements to criminal sanctions only where the goal sought constitutes a felony. Ohio has chosen the most drastic approach of all, making criminal only conspiracies designed to achieve one or more of certain enumerated criminal ends, including murder, kidnapping, compelling or promoting prostitution, arson, robbery, burglary, and felonious use of a vehicle. . . .
>
>   On the other hand, Massachusetts, even in its proposed new provision, clings stubbornly to a definition of conspiracy which includes among the possible objectives of a criminal agreement "conduct . . . which . . . the defendant knows to be substantially and clearly unlawful [but not necessarily criminal], and likely to cause such significant harm to an individual or to the general public as to be seriously contrary to the public interest." The contours of this additional set of conspiratorial goals are derived from the 1966 case of Commonwealth v. Bessette [351 Mass. 148, 217 N.E.2d 893]. That controversy concerned an alleged unauthorized exchange, between private companies, of publicly awarded contracts, in violation of the "Standard Specifications" of the Massachusetts Department of Public Works.

Lieutenant Colonel Oliver North, the former deputy National Security Advisor to President Reagan, was charged with conspiring to violate the Boland Amendment to the 1983 Department of Defense Appropriations Act, Pub. L. No. 97-377, S793 (1982), which stated,

> None of the funds provided in this Act may be used by the Central Intelligence Agency or the Department of Defense to furnish military equipment, military training or advice, or other support for military activities, to any group or individual, not part of a country's armed forces, for the purpose of overthrowing the Government of Nicaragua or provoking a military exchange between Nicaragua and Honduras.

In effect, North was charged with conspiring to violate the intent of Congress by assisting the Nicaraguan rebels (the Contras), through unlawful covert operations to overthrow the Sandinista government. The Boland Amendment provided no criminal sanctions. Nevertheless, Lawrence Walsh, the special prosecutor in the North case, claimed that North violated federal conspiracy law through a

---

3. Note, Conspiracy: Statutory Reform Since the Model Penal Code, 75 Colum. L. Rev. 1122, 1129-32 (1975).

"deceitful interference" with the function of the government. The Justice Department, on the other hand, filed a brief in support of North, asserting:

> Conduct by executive branch officials cannot be made criminal simply because it interferes with some general, unenacted intent of Congress. . . . [This charge] threatens the constitutional system of separation of power by suggesting that the pursuit of executive branch officials of policies which differ from those of Congress constitutes a criminal conspiracy.[4]

United States District Judge Gerhard Gesell upheld the charges against North in his order of November 29, 1988, 708 F. Supp. 375 (D.D.C. 1988):

> Count 1 clearly states all elements of a conspiracy to defraud the United States, and contrary to his assertions in Motion #42, North had fair notice that the conduct charged was subject to criminal charges. In 1924, the Supreme Court described defrauding the United States in terms that clearly encompass North's conduct as alleged. Chief Justice Taft said:
>
> > To conspire to defraud the United States means primarily to cheat the Government out of property or money, but it also means to interfere with or obstruct one of its lawful government functions by deceit, craft or trickery, or at least by means that are dishonest. It is not necessary that the Government shall be subjected to property or pecuniary loss by the fraud, but only that its legitimate official action and purpose shall be defeated by misrepresentation, chicane or the overreaching of those charged with carrying out governmental intention. [Id. at 376-77, quoting Hammerschmidt v. United States, 265 U.S. 182, 188 (1924).]

The Court also refuses to strike references to Executive Order 12333 and National Security Decision Directive 159 and to preclude evidence relating to these provisions, as North urges in Motion #41. These orders form part of the framework of laws and regulations which North is alleged to have conspired to circumvent and impair. That they themselves do not carry criminal penalties is of no consequence. These are counts alleging conspiracy to defraud the United States and defeat its lawful governmental functions.[5]

B.   THE AGREEMENT

1.   Proof of formation

GRIFFIN v. STATE
Supreme Court of Arkansas
455 S.W.2d 882 (1970)

FOGLEMAN, JUSTICE.
. . . Evidence upon behalf of the State was as follows:
Appellant's automobile overturned in a ditch. The police were called. Officers Harold Vines and David Ederington arrived at the scene, and saw a

---

4. As quoted in the New York Times, Nov. 19, 1988, at 9.

5. The conspiracy charge against North was later dropped when the government chose to sacrifice it in order to maintain secrecy for classified evidence of other covert operations — evidence that North could have used in his defense.

crowd of people gathered there. The officers got out of the police car and Vines asked if anyone was hurt. Upon receiving a negative response from an unidentified person, Vines then asked who was driving the vehicle. Appellant, who was standing beside his vehicle, stepped forward, said "I was, I'm not scared, I've been in the war. I wasn't killed over there. I'm not going to be killed here. Take me G —— d —— you, if you can," and started toward Vines with his fists. Vines attempted to halt Griffin by use of chemical mace, to no avail. Griffin started hitting the officer, who then attempted to defend himself by striking appellant twice with a "slapper." A group . . . then "swarmed" him. Vines observed that some of the crowd had Ederington down in the street. Griffin was immediately in front of Vines, swinging at and striking him, while the others came up behind the officer and to his side. They knocked Vines down in the ditch, with all of the participants on top of him. Griffin was then on top of Vines, and the others at his side. Griffin was beating the officer with his fists and kicking him and "hollering" all the while. At the same time, the other participants were kicking the policeman about his arms and legs, and striking him about his face, nose, and side. They were also "hollering." Vines, feeling that he and his companion were about to be killed, drew his pistol and fired at appellant, who was still kicking and beating the officer. Griffin was struck about his chest and backed away, as did the others. Vines said, however, that they were all still "hollering" at the police officers, cursing them and saying "that they were going to get us."

As Ederington went to assist Vines, after having heard Griffin's statement to the officer when that officer and Griffin started "scuffling," he was "jumped" by two or three persons from the crowd, and knocked to the street. After he had "scuffed around" with them for three or four seconds he heard the report of a gun and saw everyone start backing away. From his position on the ground, he then saw Vines leaning against a fence over in the ditch with his nose bleeding. Ederington saw Griffin standing about five feet from Vines. He heard Vines "holler" at the people standing around that if they didn't want Griffin shot again they had better come get him. At that time Griffin was still trying to advance toward officer Vines. Appellant's father then came and tried to hold him back. . . .

Appellant seems to take the position that there must be direct evidence of a conspiracy, common design or purpose, and of the intent of the conspirators or joint actors to engage therein. In this he is mistaken. We have long recognized in Arkansas that it is not necessary that an unlawful combination, conspiracy or concert of action to commit an unlawful act be shown by direct evidence, and that it may be proved by circumstances. . . . It may be inferred, even though no actual meeting among the parties is proved, if it be shown that two or more persons pursued by their acts the same unlawful object, each doing a part, so that the acts, though apparently independent, were in fact connected. . . . Where the testimony shows a concert of action, between the persons alleged to have jointly committed a crime, or the person charged and another, it has been held sufficient to establish the necessary common object and intent. . . .

In a murder prosecution, the mere fact that two persons separately approached a third, within a few hours for the purpose of prevailing upon him to kill a fourth person, was held sufficient evidence from which to infer a conspiracy among the three to take the life of the victim. Decker v. State, 185 Ark. 1085, 51 S.W.2d 521. The fact that each of two parties was found to possess portions of stolen goods taken in the same larceny was itself held competent to establish a conspiracy to take the goods and implicate both in the commission of the crime. Wiley v. State, 93 Ark. 586, 124 S.W. 249.

We find that the circumstances shown by the testimony presented by the state were sufficient to pose a jury question as to whether the parties involved in the assault on the officers did so with a common intent and object pursuant to a common plan. It would be extremely difficult, if not impossible, to ever produce direct evidence of a conversation or meeting among the assaulters during the period intervening between the call to the officers and the alleged challenge given them by Griffin, unless one of the participants elected to tell of it. This very problem, arising from the secrecy usually surrounding such understandings, gave rise to the rule . . . often cited by this court, that the existence of the necessary assent of minds may be, and usually must be, inferred from proof of facts and circumstances which, taken together, apparently indicate that they are mere parts of some complete whole. . . .

The judgment is affirmed.

Notes and Questions

1. *Tacit agreements.* Recall the facts of *Ochoa* and *Tally* in Chapter 10 on complicity. Did Ochoa, Avitia, or Leandro Velarde conspire with the killers of the sheriff? Did Tally conspire with the Skeltons? The issue of just what we mean by an "agreement" has caused considerable confusion. One commentator[6] attempts to explain why:

> [T]o aid and abet a crime it is necessary not merely to help the criminal, but to help him in the commission of the particular offense. A person does not aid and abet a conspiracy by helping the "conspiracy" to commit a substantive offense, for the crime of conspiracy is separate from the offense which is its object. It is necessary to help the "conspiracy" in the commission of the crime of conspiracy, that is, in the commission of the act of agreement. Only then is it justifiable to dispense with the necessity of proving commission of the act of agreement by the defendant himself. In all other cases, to convict the defendant of conspiracy it is necessary to prove not only knowledge on his part that he was helping in a wrongful enterprise, but also knowledge on another's part that he intended to do so, and at least a tacit agreement to give and accept such help.

2. *Proving the agreement by inference.* In United States v. Cepeda, 768 F.2d 1515 (2d Cir. 1985), the defendant was convicted of conspiring "with others unknown" to distribute, or to possess with intent to distribute, cocaine, on the following facts:

> The overt acts cited in the indictment to support the conspiracy charge are possession of 0.41 grams ($^{13}/_{1000}$ ounce) of cocaine; residue traces of cocaine on two clear plastic bags, on two metal and plastic kitchen strainers, and on a playing card (the six of clubs); and a clear plastic bag containing 6.8 grams (less than one-quarter ounce) of lactose (also known as "cut"), a clear capped bottle containing 18.8 grams (two-thirds of an ounce) of lactose, two "Ohaus" brand triple beam scales, two boxes of plastic ziplock-type sandwich bags, and one empty green cardboard

6. Developments — Conspiracy, 72 Harv. L. Rev. 933-35 (1959).

box inscribed "Deering Grams Scale." In addition to the above, four metal measuring spoons, $1,151 in cash, a wallet with identification for someone named Saul Lora, seven color photographs (some depicting Cepeda and other, unidentified persons), a telephone beeper, four telephone address diaries, and various bills and receipts were found and seized, pursuant to an oral search warrant, at the West 93rd Street apartment concededly occupied by Cepeda and her twelve-year-old son.

The sole witness for the prosecution was a New York state trooper and narcotics investigator, Lawrence McDonald, who participated in the raid and gave expert testimony that among the seized items were the tools of a cocaine cutting mill, where relatively pure cocaine is "cut" with lactose and repackaged for sale by a middle-level distributor, that a tinfoil containing .36 grams ($\frac{13}{1000}$ ounce) of cocaine of 92.6% purity found in a dresser was characteristic of a seller's sample to a prospective buyer; and, from personal knowledge, that Cepeda when arrested had acknowledged her possession of "cut." The trooper/investigator also testified, however, that Cepeda claimed the Ohaus scales had been given to her by an unidentified person, and that the $1,151 were earnings made "off the books" at a beauty shop and as gambling winnings for herself and her sister. He further testified that the playing card is an item associated with personal use of cocaine, and that Cepeda stated that she and her twelve-year-old son had lived in the apartment for ten years. After a two-day jury trial, Cepeda was convicted and sentenced to probation for two years on condition that she engage in drug or psychiatric counseling if directed by the probation department and perform 150 hours of community service. Thus do the mighty engines of federal law enforcement grind. [Id. at 1515-16.]

The court overturned the conviction:

Here there was not even evidence of a sale. Nor can appellant's intent to enter into a conspiracy be inferred from the presence and her mere possession of paraphernalia usable, or inferably previously used, in drug-cutting. . . .

. . . Having the paraphernalia in the apartment is as consistent with someone's having left it there, with personal use, future intent, or even some single sale in the past as it is with conspiracy on or about the date of the indictment, especially since the trooper/investigator testified that there was no way to know when the paraphernalia had arrived or been used. In addition, the quantity of cocaine found in Cepeda's apartment was not inconsistent with personal use; and, to the contrary, the presence of the six of clubs *suggested* personal use. To be sure, there was the supposed "sample," the $\frac{13}{100}$ of an ounce of cocaine, and there were the fractions of an ounce of "cut," but such quantities are also consistent with personal use.

As for the unexplained "wealth," . . . [w]e do not think $1,151, even in an apartment at West 93rd Street, indicative of very much,[7] and it was at least accompanied by an explanation (working "off the books" at the beauty shop — tips?; gambling — numbers?). [Id. at 1517-18.]

What do you think of the court's view of permissible inferences from the facts?

Might a jury benefit in cases like these from police testimony about the customs and practices of the illegal drug trade? In People v. Colon, 238 A.D.2d 18, 667 N.Y.S.2d 692 (1997), an undercover officer testified that

---

7. For example, the presence of $1,151 in cash in an apartment on West 93rd Street might well reflect the difficulties encountered by low-income families seeking basic banking services in this day of banking deregulation. See, e.g., Deregulating Away the Little Guy, New York Times, Feb. 19, 1984, §3, at 12, col. 3, New York Times, Feb. 13, 1984, at D1, col. 6.

after observing defendant pass a glassine envelope to a woman, he approached the defendant and said "uno," whereupon defendant, in exchange for a marked ten dollar bill, handed him a glassine envelope. Immediately after this sale, a description of the seller was transmitted by the undercover to the officer who, minutes later, arrested defendant. Contrary to the expectation naturally arising from the undercover officer's testimony, however, the arresting officer testified that a search of the defendant incident to his arrest disclosed only ten dollars in unmarked currency; neither drugs nor buy money was recovered.

To the aforementioned testimony, the prosecutor added the testimony of a third police officer, who was presented to the jury as an expert in street-level narcotics transactions. This officer's lengthy testimony, spread out over some 17 pages of the record, went into considerable detail about how street-level conspiracies to sell drugs were typically structured; a "steerer" directed customers to a "pitcher," who would obtain the drugs to be sold on an as-needed basis from a "stash man" and pass them to the buyer. The proceeds of such transactions were delivered with some frequency to a "money man" and might thereafter be laundered at stores "fronting" for the conspiracy. All of this activity was safeguarded by "lookouts" and supervised by "managers" or "owners," who would periodically replenish the street-level operation's supply of product. This particular division of labor was employed, according to the expert, to minimize the risk of detection and successful prosecution by reducing the probability that the most exposed members of the conspiracy would, if apprehended, be found in possession of either drugs or money. [Id. at 692-93.]

The court held that this expert testimony was wrongly admitted, ruling that it could only be offered to the jury after the state otherwise established a factual basis for the conspiracy. How might the prosecutor do so in this sort of case? What role would the expert testimony then play? Did the alleged conspirators here conceive the "perfect crime"?

3. *Conspiracy and political terrorism.* Throughout American history many political organizations have been accused of being criminal conspiracies. Whenever some criminal acts appear to result at least indirectly from the organization's activities, the line between constitutionally protected political speech and criminal agreement becomes blurry, and two related questions of conspiracy law doctrine arise.

First, when does a political leader's encouragement or coordination of political action make him a conspirator with members of an organization that ultimately commit crimes to achieve goals they would impute to the leader's exhortations?

The federal seditious conspiracy law, 18 U.S.C. §2384, makes it a crime where

two or more persons . . . conspire to overthrow, put down, or destroy by force the Government of the United States, or to levy war against them, or to oppose by force the authority thereof, or by force to prevent, hinder, or delay the execution of any law of the United States, or by force to seize, take, or possess any property of the United States contrary to the authority thereof . . .

In United States v. Rahman, 189 F.3d 88 (2d Cir. 1999),

the Government sought to prove that the defendants and others joined in a seditious conspiracy to wage a war of urban terrorism against the United States and forcibly to oppose its authority. . . . The Government alleged that members of the conspiracy (acting alone or in concert) took the following actions, among others, in furtherance of the group's objectives: the attempted murder of [Egyptian President] Hosni Mubarak, the provision of assistance to the bombing of the World Trade Center in New York City on February 26, 1993, and the Spring 1993 campaign of attempted bombings of buildings and tunnels in New York City. . . .

The Government adduced evidence at trial showing the following: Rahman, a blind Islamic scholar and cleric, was the leader of the seditious conspiracy, the purpose of which was *"jihad,"* in the sense of a struggle against the enemies of Islam. Indicative of this purpose, in a speech to his followers Rahman instructed that they were to "do *jihad* with the sword, with the cannon, with the grenades, with the missile . . . against God's enemies." Rahman's role in the conspiracy was generally limited to overall supervision and direction of the membership, as he made efforts to remain a level above the details of individual operations. However, as a cleric and the group's leader, Rahman was entitled to dispense "fatwas," religious opinions on the holiness of an act, to members of the group sanctioning proposed courses of conduct and advising them whether the acts would be in furtherance of *jihad.*

. . . In July 1989, on three successive weekends, FBI agents observed and photographed members of the *jihad* organization . . . shooting weapons, including AK-47s, at a public rifle range on Long Island. Although Rahman was in Egypt at the time, Nosair and Abouhalima called him there to discuss various issues including the progress of their military training, tape-recording these conversations for distribution among Rahman's followers. Nosair told Rahman "we have organized an encampment, we are concentrating here." [Id. at 104-05.] . . .

. . . Rahman asserts that he had limited contact with most of the other defendants, that he was physically incapable, due to his blindness, of participating in the "operational" aspects of the conspiracies, and that there was little direct evidence of his knowledge of many of the events in question. We find Rahman's claims unavailing.

. . . While there is no evidence that Rahman personally participated in the performance of the conspiracy, when conspiracy is charged, the Government is not required to show that the defendant personally performed acts in its furtherance: it is sufficient for the defendant to join in the illegal agreement. The evidence showed that Rahman was in constant contact with other members of the conspiracy, that he was looked to as a leader, and that he accepted that role and encouraged his co-conspirators to engage in violent acts against the United States. . . .

Siddig Ali [another indicted conspirator] told Salem [an FBI informant who had infiltrated the organization] that Rahman had referred to the Spring 1993 bombing campaign as a "must" and a "duty." Siddig Ali also told Salem that he was free to discuss the plot with Rahman, but to do so in general terms so as to keep Rahman insulated. Although Rahman did advise against making the United Nations a bombing target because that would be bad for Muslims, he advised Salem to seek a different target (U.S. military installations) for the bombings, and to plan for them carefully. . . . [Id. at 123-24.]

At what point did Rahman's exhortations move from protected speech to conspiratorial agreement? Would Rahman have been guilty of conspiracy if he had spoken only generally about the need to punish the United States, without referring to specific violent actions? If a conspiracy is a manifest agreement to commit an illegal act, conspiracy law may apply to people who exercise their freedom of speech and association — or religion — to take *anti-government* political action that could indirectly lead to *unlawful* action. While the state may not criminalize the expression of views — even the view that violent overthrow of the government is desirable — it may nonetheless outlaw encouragement, inducement, or conspiracy to take violent action. In Brandenburg v. Ohio, 395 U.S. 444, 447 (1969) (per curiam), the Court held that a state may proscribe subversive advocacy only when it is directed toward, and is likely to result in, "imminent lawless action." The Second Circuit found the conspiracy charge against Rahman consistent with that principle:

> Rahman also protests the Government's use in evidence of his speeches, writings, and preachings that did not in themselves constitute the crimes of solicitation or conspiracy. He is correct that the Government placed in evidence many instances of Rahman's writings and speeches in which Rahman expressed his opinions within the protection of the First Amendment. However, while the First Amendment fully protects Rahman's right to express hostility against the United States, and he may not be prosecuted for so speaking, it does not prevent the use of such speeches or writings in evidence when relevant to prove a pertinent fact in a criminal prosecution. The Government was free to demonstrate Rahman's resentment and hostility toward the United States in order to show his motive for soliciting and procuring illegal attacks against the United States and against President Mubarak of Egypt. [Id. at 116-18.] [8]

The Moussaoui case. A second problem of conspiracy law raised by prosecutions of political organizations focuses on the often disparate members of the organization. Such members often act in parallel with each other but only through indirect or tacit communication, and in response to the same general exhortations from organization leaders. At what point, then, do their individual actions, not illegal in themselves, establish the act of agreeing with the illegal acts or plans of others? Consider the charges against Zacharias Moussaoui, the only person prosecuted for involvement in the September 11, 2001 hijackings.

Below are the key paragraphs of the grand jury indictment against Moussaoui, charging him with conspiracy to commit the four hijackings and the killings of all the passengers and the thousands of victims at the World Trade Center and the Pentagon. (Where any of the actual hijackers, including their alleged leader, Mohammed Atta, are mentioned, they are designated by the flight number of the planes they hijacked. The deleted paragraphs lay out the general goals and operations of al Qaeda, as well as the facts of the hijackings themselves.)

UNITED STATES v. ZACARIAS MOUSSAOUI
(Superseding Indictment, E.D. Va., Crim. No. 01-455-A, July 2002)

THE DEFENDANT

13. ZACARIAS MOUSSAOUI, a/k/a "Shaqil," a/k/a "Abu Khalid al Sahrawi," was born in France of Moroccan descent on May 30, 1968. Before 2001 he was a resident of the United Kingdom. MOUSSAOUI held a masters degree from Southbank University in the United Kingdom and traveled widely.

---

8. For example, Rahman told Salem he "should make up with God . . . by turning his rifle's barrel to President Mubarak's chest, and kill[ing] him." Tr. 4633.

MOUSSAOUI'S SUPPORTING CONSPIRATORS

14. Ramzi Bin al-Shibh, a/k/a "Ahad Sabet," a/k/a "Ramzi Mohamed Abdellah Omar," was born in Yemen on May 1, 1972. He entered Germany in or about 1995 and afterwards lived in Hamburg, where he shared an apartment with hijacker Mohammed Atta (#11) in 1998 and 1999. Bin al-Shibh also was employed with Atta as a warehouse worker at a computer company in Hamburg....

OVERT ACTS

In furtherance of the conspiracy, and to effect its objects, the defendant, and others known and unknown to the Grand Jury, committed the following overt acts:

13. In or about April 1998, ZACARIAS MOUSSAOUI was present at the al Qaeda-affiliated Khalden Camp in Afghanistan.

14. Beginning in and about 1998, Ramzi Bin al-Shibh, Mohammed Atta (#11), Marwan al-Shehhi (#175), and Ziad Jarrah (#93), and others, formed and maintained an al Qaeda terrorist cell in Germany.

21. On or about July 26, 2000, in Germany, Ramzi Bin al-Shibh wired money to Marwan al-Shehhi (#175) in Florida.

24. On or about September 17, 2000, $70,000 was wired from UAE into a Florida SunTrust bank account in the names of Mohamed Atta (#11) and Marwan al-Shehhi (#175).

25. In or about August 2000, Ziad Jarrah (#93) attempted to enroll Ramzi Bin al-Shibh in a flight school in Florida.

28. On or about August 14, 2000, in Yemen, Ramzi Bin al-Shibh arranged to wire money from his account in Germany to the account of a flight training school in Florida.

29. On or about September 15, 2000, in Yemen, Ramzi Bin al-Shibh applied for a visa to travel to the United States, listing a residence in Hamburg, Germany. This visa application was denied in September 2000.

32. On or about September 29, 2000, ZACARIAS MOUSSAOUI contacted Airman Flight School in Norman, Oklahoma using an e-mail account he set up on September 6 with an internet service provider in Malaysia.

33. In or about October 2000, ZACARIAS MOUSSAOUI received letters from Infocus Tech, a Malaysian company, stating that MOUSSAOUI was appointed Infocus Tech's marketing consultant in the United States, the United Kingdom, and Europe, and that he would receive, among other things, an allowance of $2500 per month.

35. Between on or about December 2 and December 9, 2000, Ramzi Bin al-Shibh traveled from Hamburg, Germany to London, England.

36. On or about December 9, 2000, ZACARIAS MOUSSAOUI flew from London, England to Pakistan.

41. On or about February 7, 2001, ZACARIAS MOUSSAOUI flew from Pakistan to London, England.

42. On or about February 23, 2001, ZACARIAS MOUSSAOUI flew from London, England to Chicago, Illinois, declaring at least $35,000 cash on his Customs declaration, and then from Chicago to Oklahoma City, Oklahoma.

43. On or about February 26, 2001, ZACARIAS MOUSSAOUI opened a bank account in Norman, Oklahoma, depositing approximately $32,000 cash.

44. Between on or about February 26, 2001, and on or about May 29, 2001, ZACARIAS MOUSSAOUI attended the Airman Flight School in Norman, Oklahoma, ending his classes early.

49. On or about May 23, 2001, ZACARIAS MOUSSAOUI contacted an office of the Pan Am International Flight Academy in Miami, Florida via e-mail.

53. On or about June 20, 2001, ZACARIAS MOUSSAOUI purchased flight deck videos for the Boeing 747 Model 400 and the Boeing 747 Model 200 from the Ohio Pilot Store.

58. On or about July 10 and July 11, 2001, ZACARIAS MOUSSAOUI made credit card payments to the Pan Am International Flight Academy for a simulator course in commercial flight training.

63. Between on or about July 29 and August 2, 2001, in Norman, Oklahoma, ZACARIAS MOUSSAOUI made several telephone calls from public telephones to a number in Duesseldorf. . . .

65. On or about August 1 and 3, 2001, Ramzi Bin al-Shibh, using the name "Ahad Sabet," wired approximately $14,000 in money orders to ZACARIAS MOUSSAOUI in Oklahoma from train stations in Dusseldorf and Hamburg, Germany.

66. On or about August 3, 2001, ZACARIAS MOUSSAOUI purchased two knives in Oklahoma City, Oklahoma.

68. On or about August 9 and August 10, 2001, ZACARIAS MOUSSAOUI was driven from Oklahoma to Minnesota.

69. On or about August 10, 2001, in Minneapolis, Minnesota, ZACARIAS MOUSSAOUI paid approximately $6,300 in cash to the Pan Am International Flight Academy.

70. Between August 13 and August 15, 2001, ZACARIAS MOUSSAOUI attended the Pan Am International Flight Academy in Minneapolis, Minnesota, for simulator training on the Boeing 747 Model 400.

71. On or about August 16, 2001, ZACARIAS MOUSSAOUI possessed, among other things:

> two knives; a pair of binoculars; flight manuals for the Boeing 747 Model 400; a flight simulator computer program; fighting gloves and shin guards; a piece of paper referring to a handheld Global Positioning System receiver and a camcorder; software that could be used to review pilot procedures for the Boeing 747 Model 400; a notebook listing German Telephone #1, . . . , and the name "Ahad Sabet;" letters indicating that MOUSSAOUI is a marketing consultant in the United States for Infocus Tech; a computer disk containing information related to the aerial application of pesticides; and a hand-held aviation radio.

72. On or about August 17, 2001, ZACARIAS MOUSSAOUI, while being interviewed by federal agents in Minneapolis, attempted to explain his presence in the United States by falsely stating that he was simply interested in learning to fly.

86. On or about September 5, 2001, Ramzi Bin al-Shibh traveled from Dusseldorf, Germany, to Madrid, Spain, and did not return to Germany.

Granted that an indictment need not put forth all the evidence the prosecution may introduce at trial, how well do the facts alleged in the indictment support the inference that Moussaoui was in a conspiracy with the actual hijackers? Note the important role of Ramzi Bin al-Shibh, who, says the government, was trying to enter the United States with the goal of participating in the hijackings. Does Moussaoui's link to him "connect the dots" to the conspiracy with the hijackers?[9]

2. Termination of the Agreement

UNITED STATES v. RECIO
Supreme Court of the United States
270 U.S. 537 (2003)

JUSTICE BREYER delivered the opinion of the Court.

We here consider the validity of a Ninth Circuit rule that a conspiracy ends automatically when the object of the conspiracy becomes impossible to achieve — when, for example, the Government frustrates a drug conspiracy's objective by seizing the drugs that its members have agreed to distribute. In our view, conspiracy law does not contain any such "automatic termination" rule. . . .

On November 18, 1997, police stopped a truck in Nevada. They found, and seized, a large stash of illegal drugs. With the help of the truck's two drivers, they set up a sting. The Government took the truck to the drivers' destination, a mall in Idaho. The drivers paged a contact and described the truck's location. The contact said that he would call someone to get the truck. And three hours later, the two defendants, Francisco Jimenez Recio and Adrian Lopez-Meza, appeared in a car. Jimenez Recio drove away in the truck; Lopez-Meza drove the car away in a similar direction. Police stopped both vehicles and arrested both men.

A federal grand jury indicted Jimenez Recio, Lopez-Meza, and the two original truck drivers, charging them with having conspired, together and with others, to possess and to distribute unlawful drugs. A jury convicted all four. But the trial judge then decided that the jury instructions had been erroneous in respect to Jimenez Recio and Lopez-Meza. The judge noted that the Ninth Circuit, in United States v. Cruz, 127 F.3d 791 (1997), had held that the Government could not prosecute drug conspiracy defendants unless they had joined the conspiracy before the Government seized the drugs. That holding, as applied here, meant that the jury could not convict Jimenez Recio and Lopez-Meza unless the jury believed they had joined the conspiracy before the Nevada police stopped the truck and seized the drugs. The judge ordered a new trial where the jury would be instructed to that effect. The new jury convicted the two men once again.

Jimenez Recio and Lopez-Meza appealed. They pointed out that, given Cruz, the jury had to find that they had joined the conspiracy before the Nevada stop, and they claimed that the evidence was insufficient at both trials to warrant any such jury finding. . . .

_____

9. As of early 2004, the trial of Moussaoui was still delayed because of contentious procedural and evidentiary issues, including whether the defendant could subpoena classified national security information.

In *Cruz,* the Ninth Circuit held that a conspiracy continues "'until there is affirmative evidence of abandonment, withdrawal, disavowal or defeat of the object of the conspiracy.'" 127 F.3d, at 795 [quoting United States v. Castro, 972 F.2d 1107, 1112 (1992)]. The critical portion of this statement is the last segment, that a conspiracy ends once there has been "defeat of [its] object." The Circuit's holdings make clear that the phrase means that the conspiracy ends through "defeat" when the Government intervenes, making the conspiracy's goals impossible to achieve, even if the conspirators do not know that the Government has intervened and are totally unaware that the conspiracy is bound to fail. In our view, this statement of the law is incorrect. A conspiracy does not automatically terminate simply because the Government, unbeknownst to some of the conspirators, has "defeat[ed]" the conspiracy's "object."

[T]he Ninth Circuit's rule is inconsistent with our own understanding of basic conspiracy law. The Court has repeatedly said that the essence of a conspiracy is "an agreement to commit an unlawful act." Iannelli v. United States, 420 U.S. 770, 777 (1975). That agreement is "a distinct evil," which "may exist and be punished whether or not the substantive crime ensues." Salinas v. United States, 522 U.S. 52, 65 (1997). The conspiracy poses a "threat to the public" over and above the threat of the commission of the relevant substantive crime — both because the "[c]ombination in crime makes more likely the commission of [other] crimes" and because it "decreases the probability that the individuals involved will depart from their path of criminality." Callanan v. United States, 364 U.S. 587, 593-594 (1961). Where police have frustrated a conspiracy's specific objective but conspirators (unaware of that fact) have neither abandoned the conspiracy nor withdrawn, these special conspiracy-related dangers remain.

. . . No other Federal Court of Appeals has adopted the Ninth Circuit's rule. Three have explicitly rejected it. In United States v. Wallace, 85 F.3d 1063, 1068 (CA2 1996), for example, the court said that the fact that a "conspiracy cannot actually be realized because of facts unknown to the conspirators is irrelevant." And the American Law Institute's Model Penal Code §5.03, p. 384 (1985), would find that a conspiracy "terminates when the crime or crimes that are its object are committed" or when the relevant "agreement . . . is abandoned." It would not find "impossibility" a basis for termination.

The *Cruz* majority argued that the more traditional termination rule threatened "endless" potential liability. To illustrate the point, the majority posited a sting in which police instructed an arrested conspirator to go through the "telephone directory . . . [and] call all of his acquaintances" to come and help him, with the Government obtaining convictions of those who did so. 127 F.3d, at 795, n. 3. The problem with this example, however, is that, even though it is not necessarily an example of entrapment itself, it draws its persuasive force from the fact that it bears certain resemblances to entrapment. The law independently forbids convictions that rest upon entrapment. See Jacobson v. United States, 503 U.S. 540, 548-49 (1992). And the example fails to explain why a different branch of the law, conspiracy law, should be modified to forbid entrapment-like behavior that falls outside the bounds of current entrapment law. At the same time, the *Cruz* rule would reach well beyond arguable police misbehavior, potentially threatening the use of properly run law enforcement sting operations. See Lewis v. United States, 385 U.S. 206, 208-209 (1966) (Government may "use decoys" and conceal agents' identity). . . .

The judgment of the Ninth Circuit is reversed. . . .

Notes and Questions

1. Can the defendants argue that their combination no longer posed any public danger once the government agents were in control? The Court is confident that the independently available entrapment defense will check government abuses in this situation. But as noted in the context of complicity, an entrapment claim is almost an insuperable challenge for defendants. See p. 726, *supra,* note 12. Is the Court too confident here?

2. If *Recio* were an attempt, rather than a conspiracy case, would it be treated as an instance of "factual" or "legal impossibility"? We saw in Chapter 10 that though courts have struggled with that distinction, the general trend is toward expanding the former category, that is, to reduce the availability of impossibility defense. Should the rule be different in conspiracy? Though *Recio* deals with a conspiracy that was once attainable but then was thwarted by the government, the Court's assertion that "impossibility" is no defense to a conspiracy has generally extended to cases where the object was never attainable. Typical is United States v. LaBudda, 882 F.2d 244, 248 (7th Cir. 1989), upholding a conviction even though the conspiracy's object was "unattainable from the very beginning" because of a government sting operation. This very situation is also addressed under the separate doctrinal rubric called "unilateral conspiracy." See pp. 791-92, *infra.*

3. *Withdrawal from a conspiracy.* Even where a conspiracy has undoubtedly occurred and even partially succeeded, particular co-conspirators may claim that they terminated their participation sufficiently to escape liability. Recall from Chapter 10, p. 657 *supra,* that a few jurisdictions permit the defense of having "renounced" a criminal attempt, and from Chapter 11, pp. 711-12, *supra,* that one can, in theory, terminate one's complicity in a crime. Similarly, the issue of withdrawal sometimes arises in conspiracy cases. How can one withdraw from a conspiracy? In United States v. Read, 658 F.2d 1225 (7th Cir. 1981), defendants were convicted of conspiracy to commit securities fraud and mail fraud for artificially inflating their company's year-end inventory (to show higher profits) over a five-year period. One of the defendants, Ronald Spiegel, claimed he withdrew from the conspiracy more than five years before the indictment was filed and hence that the statute of limitations had run.

The trial court in its instruction to the jury gave the following definition of withdrawal:

> A defendant may withdraw by notifying co-conspirators that he will no longer participate in the undertaking. A defendant may also withdraw from a conspiracy by engaging in acts inconsistent with the objects of the conspiracy. These acts or statements need not be known or communicated to all other co-conspirators as long as they are communicated in a manner reasonably calculated to reach some of them. To withdraw from a conspiracy there is no requirement that a conspirator try to convince the other co-conspirators to abandon their undertaking or that he go to public authorities or others to expose the conspiracy or to prevent the carrying out of an act involved in the conspiracy. But a withdrawal defense requires that a defendant completely abandon the conspiracy and that he do so in good faith. [Id. at 1231.]

Spiegel claimed that (1) he instituted a computer program that would improve, not worsen, inventory control; (2) he refused to meet defendant Read's projections for inflating inventory; and (3) he was terminated because he was "not going to go along with more inflation." Do any of these acts alone constitute withdrawal? What about all the acts together?

But as the court noted, a conspirator gains only partial exoneration by withdrawing:

> Withdrawal marks a conspirator's disavowal or abandonment of the conspiratorial agreement. By definition, after a defendant withdraws, he is no longer a member of the conspiracy and the later acts of the conspirators do not bind him. The defendant is still liable, however, for his previous agreement and for the previous acts of his co-conspirators in pursuit of the conspiracy. Withdrawal is not, therefore, a complete defense to the crime of conspiracy. Withdrawal becomes a complete defense only when coupled with the defense of the statute of limitations. A defendant's withdrawal from the conspiracy starts the running of the statute of limitations as to him. If the indictment is filed more than five years after a defendant withdraws, the statute of limitations bars prosecution for his actual participation in the conspiracy. He cannot be held liable for acts or declarations committed in the five years preceding the indictment by other conspirators because his withdrawal ended his membership in the conspiracy. It is thus only the interaction of the two defenses of withdrawal and the statute of limitations which shields the defendant from liability.
>
> Withdrawal, then, directly negates the element of membership in the conspiracy during the period of the statute of limitations. . . . [T]he government should disprove the defense of withdrawal beyond a reasonable doubt. [1232-33.]

Some commentators feel that withdrawal should be a full affirmative defense to the crime of conspiracy. In fact, the Model Penal Code in §5.03(6) states that withdrawal is an affirmative defense, but only when the defendant has "thwarted the success of the conspiracy, under circumstances manifesting a complete and voluntary renunciation of his criminal purpose." Why is this requirement so strict? Is it because one conspirator's withdrawal usually will not prevent her co-conspirators from pursuing the objective of the conspiracy?

C. THE MENS REA OF CONSPIRACY

PEOPLE v. LAURIA
California Court of Appeal
251 Cal. App. 2d 471, 59 Cal. Rptr. 628 (1967)

FLEMING, J.

In an investigation of call-girl activity the police focused their attention on three prostitutes actively plying their trade on call, each of whom was using Lauria's telephone answering service, presumably for business purposes.

On January 8, 1965, Stella Weeks, a policewoman, signed up for telephone service with Lauria's answering service. Mrs. Weeks, in the course of her conversation with Lauria's office manager, hinted broadly that she was a prostitute concerned with the secrecy of her activities and their concealment from the police. She was assured that the operation of the service was discreet and "about as safe as you can get." It was arranged that Mrs. Weeks need not leave her address with the answering service, but could pick up her calls and pay her bills in person.

On February 11, Mrs. Weeks talked to Lauria on the telephone and told him her business was modelling and she had been referred to the answering service by Terry, one of the three prostitutes under investigation. She complained that because of the operation of the service she had lost two valuable customers, referred to as tricks. Lauria defended his service and said that her friends had probably lied to her about having left calls for her. But he did not respond to Mrs. Weeks' hints that she needed customers in order to make money, other than to invite her to his house for a personal visit in order to get better acquainted. In the course of his talk he said "his business was taking messages."

On February 15, Mrs. Weeks talked on the telephone to Lauria's office manager and again complained of two lost calls, which she described as a $50 and $100 trick. On investigation the office manager could find nothing wrong, but she said she would alert the switchboard operators about slip-ups on calls.

On April 1, Lauria and the three prostitutes were arrested. Lauria complained to the police that this attention was undeserved, stating that Hollywood Call Board had 60 to 70 prostitutes on its board while his own service had only 9 or 10, that he kept separate records for known or suspected prostitutes for the convenience of himself and the police. When asked if his records were available to police who might come to the office to investigate call girls, Lauria replied that they were whenever the police had a specific name. However, his service didn't "arbitrarily tell the police about prostitutes on our board. As long as they pay their bills we tolerate them." In a subsequent voluntary appearance before the Grand Jury, Lauria testified he had always cooperated with the police. But he admitted he knew some of his customers were prostitutes, and he knew Terry was a prostitute because he had personally used her services, and he knew she was paying for 500 calls a month.

Lauria and the three prostitutes were indicted for conspiracy to commit prostitution, and nine overt acts were specified. Subsequently the trial court set aside the indictment as having been brought without reasonable or probable cause. The People have appealed, claiming that a sufficient showing of an unlawful agreement to further prostitution was made.

To establish agreement, the People need show no more than a tacit, mutual understanding between co-conspirators to accomplish an unlawful act. Here the People attempted to establish a conspiracy by showing that Lauria, well aware that his codefendants were prostitutes who received business calls from customers through his telephone answering service, continued to furnish them with such service. This approach attempts to equate knowledge of another's criminal activity with conspiracy to further such criminal activity, and poses the question of the criminal responsibility of a furnisher of goods or services who knows his product is being used to assist the operation of an illegal business. Under what circumstances does a supplier become a part of a conspiracy to further an illegal enterprise by furnishing goods or services which he knows are to be used by the buyer for criminal purposes?

The two leading cases on this point face in opposite directions. In United States v. Falcone, 311 U.S. 205, the sellers of large quantities of sugar, yeast, and cans were absolved from participation in a moonshining conspiracy among distillers who bought from them, while in Direct Sales Co. v. United States, 319 U.S. 703, a wholesaler of drugs was convicted of conspiracy to violate the federal narcotic laws by selling drugs in quantity to a codefendant physician who was supplying them to addicts. The distinction between these two cases appears primarily based on the proposition that distributors of such dangerous products as drugs are required to exercise greater discrimination in the conduct of their business than are distributors of innocuous substances like sugar and yeast.

In the earlier case, *Falcone,* the sellers' knowledge of the illegal use of the goods was insufficient by itself to make the sellers participants in a conspiracy with the distillers who bought from them. Such knowledge fell short of proof of a conspiracy, and evidence on the volume of sales was too vague to support a jury finding that respondents knew of the conspiracy from the size of the sales alone.

In the later case of *Direct Sales,* the conviction of a drug wholesaler for conspiracy to violate federal narcotic laws was affirmed on a showing that it had actively promoted the sale of morphine sulphate in quantity and had sold codefendant physician, who practiced in a small town in South Carolina, more than 300 times his normal requirements of the drug, even though it had been repeatedly warned of the dangers of unrestricted sales of the drug. The court contrasted the restricted goods involved in *Direct Sales* with the articles of free commerce involved in *Falcone:* "All articles of commerce may be put to illegal ends," said the court. "But all do not have inherently the same susceptibility to harmful and illegal use. . . . This difference is important for two purposes. One is for making certain that the seller knows the buyer's intended illegal use. The other is to show that by the sale he intends to further, promote and cooperate in it. This intent, when given effect by overt act, is the gist of conspiracy. While it is not identical with mere knowledge that another proposes unlawful action, it is not unrelated to such knowledge. . . . The step from knowledge to intent and agreement may be taken. There is more than suspicion, more than knowledge, acquiescence, carelessness, indifference, lack of concern. There is informed and interested cooperation, stimulation, instigation. And there is also a 'stake in the venture' which, even if it may not be essential, is not irrelevant to the question of conspiracy." (319 U.S. at 710-13.)

While *Falcone* and *Direct Sales* may not be entirely consistent with each other in their full implications, they do provide us with a framework for the criminal liability of a supplier of lawful goods or services put to unlawful use. Both the element of *knowledge* of the illegal use of the goods or services and the element of *intent* to further that use must be present in order to make the supplier a participant in a criminal conspiracy.

Proof of *knowledge* is ordinarily a question of fact and requires no extended discussion in the present case. The knowledge of the supplier was sufficiently established when Lauria admitted he knew some of his customers were prostitutes and admitted he knew that Terry, an active subscriber to his service, was a prostitute. In the face of these admissions he could scarcely claim to have relied on the normal assumption an operator of a business or service is entitled to make, that his customers are behaving themselves in the eyes of the law. Because Lauria knew in fact that some of his customers were prostitutes, it is a legitimate inference he knew they were subscribing to his answering service for illegal business purposes and were using his service to make assignations for prostitution. On this record we think the prosecution is entitled to claim positive knowledge by Lauria of the use of his service to facilitate the business of prostitution. . . .

The more perplexing issue in the case is the sufficiency of proof of *intent* to further the criminal enterprise. The element of intent may be proved either by direct evidence, or by evidence of circumstances from which an intent to further a criminal enterprise by supplying lawful goods or services may be inferred. Direct evidence of participation, such as advice from the supplier of legal goods or services to the user of those goods or services on their use for illegal purpose . . . , provides the simplest case. When the intent to further and promote the criminal enterprise comes from the lips of the supplier himself, ambiguities of inference from circumstance need not trouble us. But in cases where direct proof of complicity is lacking, intent to further the conspiracy must be derived from the sale itself and its surrounding circumstances in order to establish the supplier's express or tacit agreement to join the conspiracy.

In the case at bench the prosecution argues that since Lauria knew his customers were using his service for illegal purposes but nevertheless continued to furnish it to them, he must have intended to assist them in carrying out their illegal activities. Thus through a union of knowledge and intent he became a participant in a criminal conspiracy. Essentially, the People argue that knowledge alone of the continuing use of his telephone facilities for criminal purposes provided a sufficient basis from which his intent to participate in those criminal activities could be inferred.

In examining precedents in this field we find that sometimes, but not always, the criminal intent of the supplier may be inferred from his knowledge of the unlawful use made of the product he supplies. Some consideration of characteristic patterns may be helpful. . . .

1. Intent may be inferred from knowledge, when the purveyor of legal goods for illegal use has acquired a stake in the venture. (United States v. Falcone, 2 Cir., 109 F.2d 579, 581.) For example, in Regina v. Thomas [1957], 2 All E.R. 181, 342, a prosecution for living off the earnings of prostitution, the evidence showed that the accused, knowing the woman to be a convicted prostitute, agreed to let her have the use of his room between the hours of 9 P.M. and 2 A.M. for a charge of £3 a night. The Court of Criminal Appeal refused an appeal from the conviction, holding that when the accused rented a room at a grossly inflated rent to a prostitute for the purpose of carrying on her trade, a jury could find he was living on the earnings of prostitution.

In the present case, no proof was offered of inflated charges for the telephone answering services furnished the codefendants.

2. Intent may be inferred from knowledge, when no legitimate use for the goods or services exists. The leading California case is People v. McLaughlin, 111 Cal. App. 2d 781, 245 P.2d 1076, in which the court upheld a conviction of the suppliers of horse-racing information by wire for conspiracy to promote bookmaking, when it had been established that wire service information had no other use than to supply information needed by bookmakers to conduct illegal gambling operations.

In Rex v. DeLaval, [1763] 3 Burr. 1434, 97 E.R. 913, the charge was unlawful conspiracy to remove a girl from the control of Bates, a musician to whom she was bound as an apprentice, and place her in the hands of Sir Francis Drake for the purpose of prostitution. Lord Mansfield not only upheld the charges against Bates and Sir Francis, but also against Fraine, the attorney who drew up the indentures of apprenticeship transferring custody of the girl from Bates to Sir Francis. Fraine, said Lord Mansfield, must have known that Sir Francis had no facilities for teaching music to apprentices so that it was impossible for him to have been ignorant of the real intent of the transaction.

In Shaw v. Director of Public Prosecutions, [1962] A.C. 220, the defendant was convicted of conspiracy to corrupt public morals and of living on the earnings of prostitution, when he published a directory consisting almost entirely of advertisements of the names, addresses, and specialized talents of prostitutes. Publication of such a directory, said the court, could have no legitimate use and serve no other purpose than to advertise the professional services of the prostitutes whose advertisements appeared in the directory. The publisher could be deemed a participant in the profits from the business activities of his principal advertisers.

Other services of a comparable nature come to mind: the manufacturer of crooked dice and marked cards who sells his product to gambling casinos; the tipster who furnishes information on the movement of law enforcement officers to known lawbreakers. (Cf. Jackson v. State of Texas, 164 Tex. Cr. R. 276, 298 S.W.2d 837 (1957), where the furnisher of signaling equipment used to warn gamblers of the police was convicted of aiding the equipping of a gambling place.) In such cases the supplier must necessarily have an intent to further the illegal enterprise since there is no known honest use for his goods. . . .

However, there is nothing in the furnishing of telephone answering service that would necessarily imply assistance in the performance of illegal activities. Nor is any inference to be derived from the use of an answering service by women, either in any particular volume of calls, or outside normal working hours. Nightclub entertainers, registered nurses, faith healers, public stenographers, photographic models, and freelance substitute employees provide examples of women in legitimate occupations whose employment might cause them to receive a volume of telephone calls at irregular hours.

3. Intent may be inferred from knowledge, when the volume of business with the buyer is grossly disproportionate to any legitimate demand, or when sales for illegal use amount to a high proportion of the seller's total business. In such cases an intent to participate in the illegal enterprise may be inferred from the quantity of the business done. For example, in *Direct Sales, supra,* the sale of narcotics to a rural physician in quantities 300 times greater than he would have normal use for provided potent evidence of an intent to further the illegal activity. In the same case the court also found significant the fact that the wholesaler had attracted as customers a disproportionately large group of physicians who had been convicted of violating the Harrison Act. In Shaw v. Director of Public Prosecutions, [1962] A.C. 220, almost the entire business of the directory came from prostitutes.

No evidence of any unusual volume of business with prostitutes was presented against Lauria.

Inflated charges, the sale of goods with no legitimate use, sales in inflated amounts, each may provide a fact of sufficient moment from which the intent of the seller to participate in the criminal enterprise may be inferred. In such instances participation by the supplier of legal goods to the illegal enterprise may be inferred because in one way or another the supplier has acquired a special interest in the operation of the illegal enterprise. His intent to participate in the crime of which he has knowledge may be inferred from the existence of his special interest. . . .

Yet there are cases in which it cannot reasonably be said that the supplier has a stake in the venture or has acquired a special interest in the enterprise, but in which he has been held liable as a participant on the basis of knowledge alone. Some suggestion of this appears in *Direct Sales, supra,* where both the knowledge of the illegal use of the drugs and the intent of the supplier to aid that use were inferred. In Regina v. Bainbridge [1959], 3 W.L.R. 656 (CCA 6), a supplier of oxygen-cutting equipment to one known to intend to use it to break into a bank was convicted as an accessory to the crime. . . . It seems apparent from these cases that a supplier who furnishes equipment which he *knows* will be used to commit a serious crime may be deemed from that knowledge alone to have intended to produce the result. Such proof may justify an inference that the furnisher intended to aid the execution of the crime and that he thereby became a participant. For instance, we think the operator of a telephone answering service with positive knowledge that his service was being used to facilitate the extortion of ransom, the distribution of heroin, or the passing of counterfeit money who continued to furnish the service with knowledge of its use, might be chargeable on knowledge alone with participation in a scheme to extort money, to distribute narcotics, or to pass counterfeit money. The same results would follow the seller of gasoline who knew the buyer was using his product to make Molotov cocktails for terroristic use.

Logically, the same reasoning could be extended to crimes of every description. Yet we do not believe an inference of intent drawn from knowledge of criminal use properly applies to the less serious crimes classified as misdemeanors. The duty to take positive action to disassociate oneself from activities helpful to violations of the criminal law is far stronger and more compelling for felonies than it is for misdemeanors or petty offenses. In this respect, as in others, the distinction between felonies and misdemeanors, between more serious and less serious crime, retains continuing vitality. In treason, historically the most serious felony, an individual with knowledge of the treason can be prosecuted for concealing and failing to disclose it. In other felonies, both at common law and under the criminal laws of the United States, an individual knowing of the commission of a felony is criminally liable for concealing it and failing to make it known to proper authority. But this crime, known as misprision of felony, has always been limited to knowledge and concealment of felony and has never extended to misdemeanor. A similar limitation is found in the criminal liability of an accessory, which is restricted to aid in the escape of a principal who has committed or been charged with a *felony*. We believe the distinction between the obligations arising from knowledge of a felony and those arising from knowledge of a misdemeanor continues to reflect basic human feelings about the duties owed by individuals to society. Heinous crime must be stamped out, and its suppression is the responsibility of all. Venial crime and crime not evil in itself present less of a danger to society, and perhaps the benefits of their suppression through the modern equivalent of the posse, the hue and cry, the informant, and the citizen's arrest, are outweighed by the disruption to everyday life brought about by amateur law enforcement and private officiousness in relatively inconsequential delicts which do not threaten our basic security. The subject has been summarized in an English test on the criminal law:

> Failure to reveal a felony to the authorities is now authoritatively determined to be misprision of felony, which is a common-law misdemeanor; misprision of treason is punishable with imprisonment for life. . . . No offence is committed in failing to disclose a misdemeanor. . . .
> To require everyone, without distinction as to the nature and degree of the offence, to become an accuser, would be productive of inconvenience in exposing numbers to penal prosecutions, multiplying criminal charges, and engendering

private dissension. It may sometimes be more convenient that offences should be passed over, than that all should indiscriminately be made the subject of prosecution; and a law would be considered to be harsh and impolitic, if not unjust, which compelled every party injured by a criminal act, and, still more so, to compel everyone who happened to know that another had been so injured, to make a public disclosure of the circumstances. Here, therefore, there is reason for limiting the law against mere misprisions to the concealment of such crimes as are of an aggravated complexion. . . . (Criminal Law, Glanville Williams (2d ed.) p. 423.)

With respect to misdemeanors, we conclude that positive knowledge of the supplier that his products or services are being used for criminal purposes does not, without more, establish an intent of the supplier to participate in the misdemeanors. With respect to felonies, we do not decide the converse, viz., that in all cases of felony, knowledge of criminal use alone may justify an inference of the supplier's intent to participate in the crime. The implications of *Falcone* make the matter uncertain with respect to those felonies which are merely prohibited wrongs. See also Holman v. Johnson, 98 E.R. 1120 (1775) (sale and delivery of tea at Dunkirk known to be destined for smuggling into England not an illegal contract). But decision on this point is not compelled, and we leave the matter open. . . .

From this analysis of precedent we deduce the following rule: the intent of a supplier who knows of the criminal use to which his supplies are put to participate in the criminal activity connected with the use of his supplies may be established by (1) direct evidence, (2) through an inference that he intends to participate based on, (a) his special interest in the activity, or (b) the aggravated nature of the crime itself. . . .

When we review Lauria's activities in the light of this analysis, we find no proof that Lauria took any direct action to further, encourage, or direct the call-girl activities of his codefendants and we find an absence of circumstances from which his special interest in their activities could be inferred. Neither excessive charges for standardized services, nor the furnishing of services without a legitimate use, nor an unusual quantity of business with call-girls, are present. The offense which he is charged with furthering is a misdemeanor, a category of crime which has never been made a required subject of positive disclosure to public authority. Under these circumstances, although proof of Lauria's knowledge of the criminal activities of his patrons was sufficient to charge him with that fact, there was insufficient evidence that he intended to further their criminal activities, and hence insufficient proof of his participation in a criminal conspiracy with his codefendants to further prostitution. Since the conspiracy centered around the activities of Lauria's telephone answering service, the charges against his codefendants likewise fail for want of proof.

In absolving Lauria of complicity in a criminal conspiracy we do not wish to imply that the public authorities are without remedies to combat modern manifestations of the world's oldest profession. Licensing of telephone answering services under the police power, together with the revocation of licenses for the toleration of prostitution, is a possible civil remedy. The furnishing of telephone answering service in aid of prostitution could be made a crime. (Cf. Pen. Code §316, which makes it a misdemeanor to let an apartment with knowledge of its use for prostitution.) Other solutions will doubtless occur to vigilant public authorities if the problem of call-girl activity needs further suppression. The order is affirmed.

Notes and Questions

1. Entirely apart from his mens rea, do Lauria's actions satisfy the requirement of an agreement for conspiracy?

According to the court, what mens rea does one need to become a member of a conspiracy? What does the court mean by intent? Why should we allow the inference of intent when a defendant exhibits knowledge of a serious crime but not knowledge of a less serious crime? What does the court mean by a "heinous" crime — any felony? If not, which felonies?

Is *Lauria*'s test for conspiracy the same as the test we saw under the MPC and the *Beeman* case for complicity (see pp. 714-19, *supra*)? What might justify any difference?

2. *Mens rea of conspiracy for multi-element crimes.* In United States v. Gallishaw, 428 F.2d 760 (2d Cir. 1970), the defendant was convicted of conspiracy to rob a bank for lending the would-be bank robber the machine gun actually used in the robbery. The evidence included this conversation:

> Mr. Gallishaw said, "Make sure you bring it back," and Thomas said that he will be sure that he will bring it back and if he didn't pull the bank job, "I will pull something else to give him the money."

During its deliberations the jury asked whether it mattered that Gallishaw may not have known exactly how or where the gun would be used. The judge responded that it was sufficient that Gallishaw knew Thomas planned to "do something wrong." The court of appeals reversed the conviction, first noting that for Gallishaw to be guilty of the substantive crime of bank robbery the government would need to show that he knew the gun was to be used specifically at a bank, and then noting that he was charged specifically with conspiracy to rob a bank, not some more general conspiracy (which might not even have been a federal crime). Since, the court held, the conspiracy charge required at least the level of mens rea necessary for the substantive charge, the trial judge had misinstructed the jury. Would *Lauria* have supported the result here?

We saw in Chapter 3 on culpability that the legislature can assign requirements of different mental states for different elements of a crime. *Gallishaw* seems to require that the mental state needed for conspiracy not be less than the mental state needed for the substantive crime. This, of course, raises the issue of whether conspiracy requires a *more* culpable mental state than does the substantive crime.

In United States v. Feola, 420 U.S. 671 (1974), Feola and his confederates arranged for a sale of heroin to buyers who turned out to be undercover federal drug agents. The group planned to palm off on the purchasers, for a substantial sum, a form of sugar in place of heroin and, should that ruse fail, simply to surprise their unwitting buyers and relieve them of the cash they had brought along for payment. The plan failed when one agent, his suspicions having been aroused,[10]

> drew his revolver in time to counter an assault upon another agent from the rear. Instead of enjoying the rich benefits of a successful swindle, Feola and his

---

10. [In the Manhattan apartment where the sale was to have taken place, the agent opened a closet door and observed a man on the floor, bound and gagged. — EDS.]

associates found themselves charged, to their undoubted surprise, with conspiring to assault, and with assaulting, federal officers. [Id. at 674-75.]

The Supreme Court first had to determine the required mens rea for the substantive crime of assault on a federal officer — an issue never before resolved. The statute required purpose with respect to the act element of assault, but the Court held that the attendant circumstance — the identity of the victim as a federal agent — was a strict liability element: If the defendants purposely assaulted the victims, it was no defense under the federal assault statute that they did not know, or did not or even could not reasonably foresee, that their victim was a federal officer.

The Court then decided that the identity of the victim remained a strict liability element even on a charge of conspiracy to assault a federal officer. The Court found nothing in the principles of conspiracy that warranted changing the mens rea requirements established for the substantive offense.

When the defendants are unaware and have no reason to know that their victim is other than a private citizen, can it be said that they "conspired to assault a federal officer"?

How far might this notion of conspiracy extend? Assume we have a statutory rape law that requires purpose for the act of intercourse but sets strict liability as the mens rea for the circumstance element of the girl's age. Hence, a mistake of fact about age will not exculpate. Two boys agree to go to a 15-year-old's house to persuade her to have intercourse with one or both of them. Both boys mistakenly think the girl is nineteen. On the substantive statutory rape charge, their mistake will not exonerate them, but if they are caught before any sex act occurs, can they be convicted of conspiracy? Some courts have held no, taking the word "conspire" to connote very specific purpose or motive: In effect they deny that someone "conspires" to have intercourse with a fifteen-year-old when he thinks she is nineteen. By now you should be familiar with this dilemma in framing a mens rea question. The emerging view, consistent with *Feola,* above, is to require no more than that the mens rea of the conspirators have symmetry with the substantive crime's mens rea requirement. But the drafters of the Model Penal Code said:

> Although the agreement must be made with "the purpose of promoting or facilitating the commission of the crime," [MPC §5.03(1)] it is arguable, though by no means certain, that such a purpose may be proved although the actor did not know of the existence of a circumstance, which did exist in fact, when knowledge of the circumstance is not required for the substantive offense. Rather than press the matter further in this section, the Institute deliberately left the matter to interpretation in the context in which the issue is presented.[11]

Why would the drafters decide not to decide this particular issue?

D. SPECIAL MENS REA PROBLEMS OF CONSPIRACY

1. *Mistake of law.* Some courts have enunciated what is called the "corrupt motive" doctrine. This means that a mistake about the law defining the offense,

---

11. American Law Institute, Model Penal Code and Commentaries, Part I, at 413-14 (1985).

see Chapter 3, p. 218, *supra,* would exculpate one of a charge of conspiracy even where it did not exculpate one of the substantive crime itself.

In People v. Powell, 63 N.Y. 88, 92 (1875), the defendants were municipal officials charged with conspiring to purchase supplies without advertising for bids. Their defense was that they were unaware of the criminal statute requiring them to solicit bids. The court reversed their convictions, holding that it was implied in the meaning of the word "conspiracy" that "the agreement must have been entered into with an evil purpose, as distinguished from a purpose to do the act prohibited, in ignorance of the prohibition." Later cases followed the "corrupt motive" doctrine, e.g., Landen v. United States, 299 F. 75 (6th Cir. 1924) (druggists not guilty of conspiracy to violate the prohibition laws where they honestly believed those laws did not apply to their selling methods), some of them applying the doctrine only to preclude charges of conspiracy to violate so-called malum prohibitum statutes. But the modern trend is to reject the "corrupt motive" doctrine and to equate the mens rea requirements for a conspiracy with those for the substantive crime.

The Model Penal Code Commentary provides:[12]

> The *Powell* rule, and many of the decisions that rely upon it, may be viewed as a judicial endeavor to import fair mens rea requirements into statutes creating regulatory offenses that do not rest upon traditional concepts of personal fault and culpability. This should, however, be the function of the statutes defining such offenses. Section 2.04(3) specifies the limited situations where ignorance of the criminality of one's conduct is a defense in general. . . . There is no good reason why the fortuity of concert should be used as the device for limiting criminality in this area, just as there is no good reason for using it as a device for expanding liability through imprecise formulations of objectives that include activity not otherwise criminal.

2. *"Nonpurposeful conspiracy."* Recall our problems with "attempted recklessness" in Chapter 10, pp. 638-39, *supra.* Assume two people agree to hold a drag race, knowing it to be dangerous. If a bystander or someone else is killed, one or both of the racers may be guilty of involuntary manslaughter, on a recklessness or negligence theory. But what of their conspiracy liability at the point of the original agreement to hold the race? Can we charge them with conspiracy to commit involuntary manslaughter? With respect to the crime's element of requiring *result,* as in homicide, it would seem no conspiracy exists unless the parties have purpose or at least knowledge with respect to result. However, if reckless driving is itself a crime, could they be guilty of conspiracy to commit *that* crime?

3. *Conspiracy in the heat of passion.* Bill and John are brothers. They both hear that Fred has attacked their sister. In the heat of passion, they agree to kill Fred. Whether or not they succeed, are they guilty of conspiracy to commit murder? If they succeed, the substantive charge might be reduced to voluntary manslaughter because of provocation. Assuming the punishment for conspiracy can be calibrated according to the severity of the object crime, it makes a considerable difference whether they are charged with conspiracy to commit murder or conspiracy to commit voluntary manslaughter. One view is that as long as they have the mens rea of purpose for the act of agreement, they should be guilty of conspiracy to murder: Provocation diminishes culpability for the killing, but not

12. Id. at 417-18.

for the agreement. In People v. Horn, 12 Cal. 3d 290, 524 P.2d 1300 (1974), the California Supreme Court rejected that view and held that the conspiracy charge can be reduced in the same way the substantive crime charge would be.

4. *Spontaneous conspiracy?* Can there be conspiracy to commit second-degree murder? Or does conspiracy entail the kind of planning that necessarily establishes premeditated first-degree murder? In Mitchell v. State, 767 A.2d 844 (Md. App. 2001), three men, apparently with robbery in mind, tricked the victim into leaving his apartment by paging him, knowing that he had no phone in his house, and then shot him in the back. The lower court had held "that it was legally and factually possible for a person to conspire to commit an unpremeditated murder" because the agreement could be arrived at "virtually instantaneously with the commission (or attempt) of that crime"— and thus spontaneity was not inconsistent with conspiracy. But the appellate court rejected the "metaphysical physical analysis" by which some courts had found impulse and conspiracy compatible:

> The problem may be in confusing the nature and effect of impulse. . . . Although it is true that murder committed solely on impulse — the "immediate offspring of rashness and impetuous temper"— is not one committed with deliberation and premeditation, the law does not require that deliberation and premeditation be the product of clear and rational thought; it may well be from anger and impulse. The test for first degree murder is whether there was the deliberation and premeditation — sufficient time to reflect — not the quality or rationality of the reflection or whether it may have been emotionally based. [Id. at 855.]

Does the court's distinction between quantity and quality here square with the definitions of premeditation discussed in Chapter 5, *supra?*

E.   THE INCIDENTS OF CONSPIRACY

UNITED STATES v. DIAZ
United States Court of Appeals, Seventh Circuit
864 F.2d 544 (1988)

RIPPLE, CIRCUIT JUDGE.

. . . After a jury trial, the appellant, Reynaldo Diaz, was convicted of conspiracy to distribute cocaine, possession and distribution of cocaine, and use of a firearm in relation to the commission of a drug trafficking crime.

. . . Mr. Diaz alleges that his conviction for use of a firearm was based improperly on his conviction on the conspiracy charge. . . .

The testimony at trial revealed the following. A DEA agent purchased cocaine from Carmen Diaz (no relation to the appellant) and Perez on July 23, 1987. There was no testimony that Reynaldo Diaz was involved in this sale. Perez was just beginning to deal in drugs and contacted Rodriguez in an effort to find a supplier of cocaine. Rodriguez testified that he knew somebody who could "help [Perez] out" and arranged a meeting between himself, Perez, and Mr. Diaz. Rodriguez had known Mr. Diaz since 1977. After the meeting, Mr. Diaz agreed to supply drugs to Perez.

On August 21, 1987, and again on September 3, 1987, Perez sold two ounces of cocaine to DEA Agent Patricia Collins. Perez testified that he obtained these drugs from Mr. Diaz. Although Mr. Diaz was not present for either sale, Perez testified that the second sale occurred a half-block from Mr. Diaz's house so that Mr. Diaz could see the buyer. Rodriguez and Perez also testified that they dropped the money off at Mr. Diaz's house after the second sale. . . .

On September 9, 1987, Perez and Rodriguez went to a designated location; they were to meet with Mr. Diaz to sell one kilogram of cocaine to Agent Collins. Upon their arrival, Mr. Diaz was not present. Telephone records introduced at trial corroborated that Perez and Rodriguez telephoned Mr. Diaz. Testimony of Perez and Rodriguez at trial revealed that Mr. Diaz thought the deal was going to take place closer to his home but agreed to join the men in ten to fifteen minutes. Approximately five minutes after Mr. Diaz arrived, Peirallo arrived. Peirallo had brought the kilogram of cocaine from Miami, Florida, to Chicago, Illinois, earlier that same day.

The parties waited an hour for Agent Collins. Peirallo became impatient and decided to leave the scene. He asked to be paged telephonically when Agent Collins arrived. Almost as soon as Peirallo left, Agent Collins arrived. Telephone records and testimony confirmed that Mr. Diaz telephoned Peirallo's pager. Perez joined Agent Collins in her car, counted the money, and then met with Mr. Diaz to confirm that Peirallo was on his way. Perez returned to Agent Collins' car to await Peirallo's arrival. Almost immediately, Mr. Diaz sent Rodriguez to Agent Collins' car to announce that Peirallo was arriving. After Peirallo had arrived and parked, the cars were lined up so that Peirallo's was first in line, Mr. Diaz's was the middle car and Agent Collins' car was the last car parked in line.

The officers engaged in surveillance testified that there was a great deal of movement and conversation among Mr. Diaz, Peirallo, and Rodriguez. When Peirallo arrived, Mr. Diaz and Rodriguez moved to Mr. Diaz's car; Mr. Diaz opened the hood of his car. The government and the appellant have conflicting theories about why the hood of the car was opened. Mr. Diaz claims the hood was opened because he was having car trouble. The government, in contrast, asserts that opening a car hood is a standard method by which drug dealers prevent their buyers from seeing the supplier of the drugs. Around the time the hood was raised, Perez left Agent Collins' car and went to Peirallo's car. Peirallo told Perez that he had a gun which he intended to use if anyone tried to steal the drugs. While Perez was with Peirallo, Mr. Diaz and Rodriguez continued to stand by Mr. Diaz's car watching Agent Collins. Perez took the drugs to Agent Collins. Agent Collins then gave the arrest signal. . . .

Mr. Diaz was convicted of using and carrying a firearm during and in relation to the commission of drug trafficking crimes.[13] As a result of this conviction, Mr. Diaz was sentenced to an additional five years in prison. The government did not submit evidence at trial that Mr. Diaz was armed. Rather, it contended that Peirallo's carrying of a firearm could be imputed to Mr. Diaz because of their joint membership in the conspiracy. . . .

---

13. Mr. Diaz was convicted under section 924(c)(1) of title 18 of the United States Code. The statute reads as follows:

(c) (1) Whoever, during and in relation to any crime of violence or drug trafficking crime, [sic] including a crime of violence or drug trafficking crime, which provides for an enhanced punishment if committed by the use of a deadly or dangerous weapon or device, for which he may be prosecuted in a court of the United States, uses or carries a firearm, shall, in addition to the punishment provided for such crime of violence or drug trafficking crime, [sic] be sentenced to imprisonment for five years. . . .

The firearm violation under section 924(c)(1) may be imputed to other members of the conspiracy, including Mr. Diaz, under Pinkerton v. United States, 328 U.S. 640 (1946). In *Pinkerton,* the Supreme Court held that a party to a continuing conspiracy may be responsible "when the substantive offense is committed by one of the conspirators in furtherance of the [conspiracy]," even though he does not participate in the substantive offense or have any knowledge of it. Id. at 647. . . . The jury was instructed that:

> To sustain the charge in Count Six as to defendant Reynaldo Diaz, of using and carrying a firearm during and in relation to a drug trafficking crime, the government must prove the following propositions:
>
> First, the defendant David Peirallo is guilty of the offense charged in Count Six of the indictment;
>
> Second, the defendant David Peirallo committed the offense charged in Count Six in furtherance of or as a natural and foreseeable consequence of the conspiracy charged in Count One [*sic*] of the indictment; and
>
> Third, defendant Reynaldo Diaz was a member of the conspiracy at the time defendant David Peirallo committed the offense charged in Count Six.
>
> If you find from your consideration of all the evidence that each of these propositions has been proved beyond a reasonable doubt, then you should find the defendant Reynaldo Diaz guilty of Count Six of the indictment.
>
> If, on the other hand, you find from your consideration of all the evidence that any of these propositions has not been proved beyond a reasonable doubt, then you should find defendant Reynaldo Diaz not guilty of Count Six.

This circuit has interpreted "*Pinkerton* to mean that each conspirator may be liable for 'acts of every other conspirator done in furtherance of the conspiracy.'" [United States v. Gironda, 758 F.2d 1201, 1211 (7th Cir. 1985)] (quoting United States v. Read, 658 F.2d 1225, 1230 (7th Cir. 1981)). Therefore, Peirallo's possession of a gun during the cocaine sale may be imputed to Mr. Diaz. . . .

There is, of course, one established exception to the *Pinkerton* doctrine. A conspirator may be found guilty of a substantive crime *unless* that crime "could not be reasonably foreseen as a necessary or natural consequence of the unlawful agreement." *Pinkerton,* 328 U.S. at 648. However, the illegal drug industry is, to put it mildly, a dangerous, violent business. When an individual conspires to take part in a street transaction involving a kilogram of cocaine worth $39,000, it certainly is quite reasonable to assume that a weapon of some kind would be carried. . . .

Affirmed.

Notes and Questions

1. *The* Pinkerton *rule.* In *Pinkerton,* two brothers were convicted of conspiracy to violate the Internal Revenue Code. Both brothers were also convicted of a number of substantive offenses — namely, removing, depositing, and concealing a large quantity of distilled spirits without paying the appropriate tax. At the time some of the substantive offenses were committed, the defendant was in the penitentiary (apparently for violating the liquor laws) and he contended that because of this he could not be implicated in these offenses. The court held, though, that since his brother (a co-conspirator) had committed these crimes in furtherance of the conspiracy of which the defendant was a member, the defendant was liable for them, especially since he had made no effort to withdraw

from the conspiracy. In *Pinkerton* the brothers lived next to each other, bailed each other out of jail, and helped each other when questioned by the county sheriff. Should the same rule apply in *Diaz* where there arguably was never any agreement with respect to firearms?

Without the *Pinkerton* rule, could Diaz have been held liable for the gun offense? Under what other legal doctrine? Once Diaz had joined the conspiracy to deal in drugs, is there anything he could have done to avoid being liable for a co-conspirator's use of a gun? Does the traditional concern about the special dangers of concerted action bear on this issue? Does the fact of criminal combination itself greatly increase the risk of secondary crimes?

2. *The "Pinkerton rule" in practice.* What if Peirallo had killed someone with the gun? Would the *Pinkerton* rule have made Diaz guilty of homicide? In United States v. Alvarez, 755 F.2d 830 (11th Cir. 1985), an undercover federal agent named Rios, posing as a buyer of cocaine, was shot to death by one of the drug dealers, Simon, who fired when he realized that the police were closing in. Simon's coconspirators in the drug deal, Portal, Concepcion, and Hernandez, were convicted of second-degree murder for the death of Rios by virtue of the *Pinkerton* rule. The court upheld the convictions as follows:

> . . . First, the evidence clearly established that the drug conspiracy was designed to effectuate the sale of a large quantity of cocaine. The conspirators agreed to sell Agents Rios and D'Atri three kilograms of cocaine for a total price of $147,000. The transaction that led to the murder involved the sale of one kilogram of cocaine for $49,000. In short, the drug conspiracy was no nickel-and-dime operation; under any standards, the amount of drugs and money involved was quite substantial.
>
> Second, based on the amount of drugs and money involved, the jury was entitled to infer that, at the time the cocaine sale was arranged, the conspirators must have been aware of the likelihood (1) that at least some of their number would be carrying weapons, and (2) that deadly force would be used, if necessary, to protect the conspirators' interests. . . .
>
> . . . In addition, we note . . . that at least two of the conspirators were extremely nervous about the possibility of a rip-off or a drug bust. During a lull in the negotiations, Alvarez observed, "In this business, you have to be careful. It's a dangerous business. You have to watch out for rip-offs and Federal agents." Alvarez also stated that he would never go back to prison, and that he would rather be dead than go back to prison. Alvarez's statements clearly implied that he contemplated the use of deadly force, if necessary, to avoid a rip-off or apprehension by Federal agents. The evidence also indicated that, immediately prior to the shoot-out, Simon looked nervously out the window while fidgeting with a leather pouch that was suspected to contain a weapon. The jury properly could take this additional evidence into account in reaching its conclusion about the foreseeability of the murder. [Id. at 848-49.]

Moreover, the court went on to assess the individual culpability each of the three defendants exhibited with regard to the death of Rios:

> . . . [I]n a typical *Pinkerton* case, the court need not inquire into the individual culpability of a particular conspirator, so long as the substantive crime was a reasonably foreseeable consequence of the conspiracy.[14]

---

14. A typical *Pinkerton* case falls into one of two categories. The first and most common category includes cases in which the substantive crime that is the subject of the *Pinkerton* charge is also one of the primary goals of the alleged conspiracy. See, e.g., United States v. Harris, 713 F.2d 623, 626

We acknowledge that the instant case is not a typical *Pinkerton* case. Here, the murder of Agent Rios was not within the originally intended scope of the conspiracy, but instead occurred as a result of an unintended turn of events. We have not found, nor has the government cited, any authority for the proposition that all conspirators, regardless of individual culpability, may be held responsible under *Pinkerton* for reasonably foreseeable but originally unintended substantive crimes. Furthermore, we are mindful of the potential due process limitations on the *Pinkerton* doctrine in cases involving attenuated relationships between the conspirator and the substantive crime.

Nevertheless, these considerations do not require us to reverse the murder convictions of Portal, Concepcion, and Hernandez, for we cannot accept the three appellants' assessment of their individual culpability. All three were more than "minor" participants in the drug conspiracy. Portal served as a look-out in front of the Hurricane Motel during part of the negotiations that led to the shoot-out, and the evidence indicated that he was armed. Concepcion introduced the agents to Alvarez, the apparent leader of the conspiracy, and was present when the shoot-out started. Finally, Hernandez, the manager of the motel, allowed the drug transactions to take place on the premises and acted as a translator during part of the negotiations that led to the shoot-out.

In addition, all three appellants had actual knowledge of at least some of the circumstances and events leading up to the murder. The evidence that Portal was carrying a weapon demonstrated that he anticipated the possible use of deadly force to protect the conspirators' interests. Moreover, both Concepcion and Hernandez were present when Alvarez stated that he would rather be dead than go back to prison, indicating that they, too, were aware that deadly force might be used to prevent apprehension by Federal agents. [Id. at 849-51.]

Is this last phase of the court's holding gratuitous in light of *Pinkerton*? Does it suggest that the court does not truly want to apply *Pinkerton*?

3. *Acts in furtherance of conspiracy.* Jurisdictions that follow the *Pinkerton* rule have three means of making a person vicariously liable for the act of another. One is the *Pinkerton* rule; another is complicity; and the third is the felony murder rule. Note that the felony murder rule is a rule of accessorial liability, in that it could, for example, make a person who is guilty of a robbery also guilty of murder, if an accomplice in the robbery performed an act that resulted in a death.

The *Pinkerton* rule is often phrased in terms of making each conspirator liable for any secondary crimes committed by a co-conspirator "in furtherance" of the conspiracy or the primary object crime. Recall the parallel rule for accomplice liability discussed in relation to the *Kessler* case, *supra,* p. 720. That rule would make one person liable for secondary crimes committed by an accomplice that, though unintended by the first person, were nevertheless "reasonably foreseeable" results of the common criminal design. The *Pinkerton* rule is usually thought to impose much wider liability. However, given the vagueness of such phrases as "in furtherance" and "reasonably foreseeable," judges and juries may

---

(11th Cir. 1983) (conspiracy to distribute cocaine; substantive crimes of possession and distribution of cocaine); United States v. Tilton, 610 F.2d 302, 309 (5th Cir. 1980) (conspiracy to commit mail fraud; substantive crime of mail fraud).

The second category includes cases in which the substantive crime is not a primary goal of the alleged conspiracy, but directly facilitates the achievement of one of the primary goals. See, e.g., Shockley v. United States, 166 F.2d 704, 715 (9th Cir. 1948) (conspiracy to escape by violent means from federal penitentiary; substantive crime of first degree murder of prison guard).

In either of these two categories, *Pinkerton* liability can be imposed on all conspirators because the substantive crime is squarely within the intended scope of the conspiracy.

have enough leeway to achieve similar results under the two doctrines. Would the results in *Diaz* or *Alvarez* have been different under the *Kessler* approach?[15]

4. *The Oklahoma City conspiracy.* The infamous Oklahoma City bombing of 1995 provided a searching test of co-conspirator liability and also demonstrated how the federal *Pinkerton* rule interacts with several other legal phenomena: jury discretion, prosecutorial discretion, and the special rules of the federal sentencing guidelines.

The McVeigh-Nichols conspiracy. Timothy McVeigh alone took the bomb to the federal building and set it off, and he himself was sentenced to death and ultimately executed for crimes including using a weapon of mass destruction, 18 U.S.C. §2332a, destruction by explosives, §844(f), and first-degree murder, §§1111, 1114, as well as conspiracy to commit these crimes. United States v. McVeigh, 153 F.3d 1166 (10th Cir. 1998).

McVeigh's old army friend Terry Nichols had shared McVeigh's distrust of the federal government and anger over the 1992 government siege of the Branch Davidian compound in Waco, Texas. Nichols, facing capital murder charges in a separate trial, helped McVeigh by committing a robbery to finance the construction of the bomb and by acquiring and helping assemble parts for it, and the prosecution also offered evidence that Nichols drove McVeigh to Oklahoma City three days before the bombing so McVeigh could drop off his escape car. But Nichols was at home alone in Kansas when the explosion occurred; he called authorities right after the explosion once he heard his name linked to McVeigh, and defense witnesses testified that Nichols's antigovernment views were not as virulent as McVeigh's.

The trial jury found Nichols guilty of conspiring to use a weapon of mass destruction, but it acquitted him on the substantive counts of which McVeigh was convicted, and spared him the death penalty. United States v. Nichols, 169 F.3d 1255 (10th 1998).

By what logic could the jury convict Nichols of the conspiracy but acquit him of the murder charges and the death penalty? Does the approach in United States v. Alvarez, *supra,* offer any guidance? Or do you infer that the jury partly "nullified" in Nichols's favor?

On the other hand, though Nichols was thereby spared the death penalty, the trial court recognized that under the sentencing guidelines it could look to the actual conduct proved by the prosecution, regardless of the formal definitions of the counts on which he was convicted. Holding that the facts underlying the conspiracy effectively established his culpability of the substantive crimes, the court was able to look to the sentencing levels at least for noncapital first-degree murder, and sentenced him to life imprisonment. 169 F.3d at 1272-76.

The Fortier-McVeigh conspiracy. Parallel, and more mysterious, was the sentencing of Michael Fortier, another old army friend of McVeigh, who became involved with McVeigh and Nichols before the fatal bombing, as follows:

> Mr. Fortier first learned of the bombing conspiracy in September 1994, when McVeigh, the primary agent provocateur, tried to recruit him by letter. The letter

15. Here is an unusual twist on *Diaz:* What if the head of a conspiracy provides his fellow conspirators with guns to use in a planned robbery, but the plan is thwarted by the police just after the agreement is made? In United States v. Phan, 121 F.3d 149 (4th Cir. 1997), the court held that the "active use" element of 924(c) applied to a conspiracy as well as a completed crime and affirmed the 924(c) conviction against the ringleader. Would his co-conspirators also face the 924(c) penalty if they willingly received, but never used, the guns?

told the defendant that McVeigh and Nichols, both of whom Mr. Fortier knew from their service together in the United States Army, had decided to take some type of positive offensive action against the federal government. Mr. Fortier did not reject the solicitation but instead wrote back asking what McVeigh had meant by taking action. At a subsequent meeting in Mr. Fortier's home in Arizona, McVeigh explained that he and Nichols planned to blow up a federal building. With these details on the table, McVeigh renewed the invitation to join the conspiracy, but Mr. Fortier declined.

McVeigh later informed Mr. Fortier that he and Nichols had stolen some explosives and intended to use them to bomb the federal building in Oklahoma City on the two-year anniversary of the destruction of the Branch Davidian compound in Waco, Texas. . . . Mr. Fortier expressed concern about the innocent people who would be killed by the bomb, but McVeigh dismissed them as persons who had to die because they served an evil system.

In late October 1994, McVeigh then told Mr. Fortier about a plan to rob an Arkansas gun collector as a means of funding the conspiracy. Nichols had grown tired of paying his and McVeigh's expenses. The robbery, which McVeigh characterized as a "fund-raiser," was designed to solve the problem. Soon thereafter, Nichols executed the plan and robbed Roger Moore of 78 firearms, cash, precious metals, and other valuables.

One month later, in mid-December, McVeigh asked Mr. Fortier to accompany him to Kansas; in exchange, McVeigh promised to give Mr. Fortier some of the stolen firearms. The defendant agreed and took some time off from work for what he understood was probably a "shady deal" involving the stolen guns. On the way to Kansas, McVeigh drove by the Murrah Federal Building in Oklahoma City, gesturing that the edifice was the intended target. McVeigh further explained the details of the bombing to include placing the bomb in a Ryder truck to be parked in front of the building. He asked Mr. Fortier if such a large truck would fit in the driveway in front of the building; Mr. Fortier opined that it would. McVeigh then drove into an alley to point out a parking spot where Nichols would either drop off a getaway car ahead of time or else wait for McVeigh on the day of the bombing. Mr. Fortier and McVeigh then left Oklahoma City for Kansas.

Soon after, the men arrived in Council Grove, Kansas. The two stopped at a storage unit where McVeigh had stored the firearms stolen from Roger Moore. McVeigh removed several of the guns, and the two then spent the night at a hotel. The following day, Mr. Fortier rented a car and he and McVeigh returned to the storage locker. McVeigh selected 20 to 25 guns from the locker and loaded them into the defendant's rental car. Mr. Fortier then drove back alone to Arizona. Once home, he moved the weapons into his house.

Mr. Fortier next saw McVeigh in January 1995, at a hotel in Kingman, Arizona. McVeigh asked the defendant if he had sold any of the stolen weapons. Mr. Fortier responded that he had not, and McVeigh became upset. McVeigh then arranged for the defendant to sell the firearms at various gun exhibitions. The first of these, which both Mr. Fortier and McVeigh attended, was in Reno, Nevada, in early February 1995. Mr. Fortier made approximately $2,100 from sales of firearms at that show. After the exhibition, McVeigh informed Mr. Fortier that Nichols was angry because McVeigh had given the defendant some of the stolen weapons; Nichols wanted $2,000 in return. Mr. Fortier immediately gave McVeigh $1,000 with the understanding it would then be sent to Nichols. After attending two more gun shows in February and March 1995 — during one of which he was again accompanied by McVeigh — Mr. Fortier gave McVeigh an additional $1,000.

During the months of February and March 1995, McVeigh again sought to recruit Mr. Fortier's participation in the larger conspiracy to destroy the Murrah Federal Building. Specifically, he wanted the defendant to mix the bomb components and assist in the post-bombing escape plan. Mr. Fortier declined both requests.

The defendant saw McVeigh for the last time on April 12, 1995, when Mr. Fortier and his wife Lori went to McVeigh's hotel room to return some books McVeigh had loaned them several days earlier. The meeting was tense, and McVeigh told the defendant that they were on very different paths in life and could no longer be friends. The Fortiers left and did not see McVeigh again until the trial. One week later, at 9:02 in the morning, a massive explosion tore apart the Murrah Federal Building killing 168 people and injuring hundreds more. [United States v. Fortier, 180 F.3d 1217 (10th Cir. 1999).]

Fortier was allowed to plead guilty to charges including conspiring to transport stolen firearms, making a materially false statement to the FBI, 18 U.S.C. §1001, and misprision of a felony, 18 U.S.C. §4. Did these facts bar the government from implicating Fortier in the bombing itself?

At sentencing the trial court heavily relied on Fortier's cooperation with the government in the cases against McVeigh and Nichols. It also relied on the following stipulated facts:

The United States has no evidence that when Fortier received the firearms from McVeigh [in December 1994] there was any agreement, promise or condition that Fortier would sell the firearms and return part of the proceeds to McVeigh and/or Nichols. . . .

The United States has no evidence tracing to any bombing expenditure . . . the $2,000 given to McVeigh by Fortier for Nichols. The United States also has no direct evidence that Michael Fortier had actual knowledge that this $2,000 would be or was used to further or facilitate the bombing conspiracy. [Id. at 1221-22.]

Did these stipulations necessarily preclude charging Fortier with the bombing under *Pinkerton*? If not, why was Fortier spared the capital murder charge?

Again relying on the facts underlying Fortier's involvement, rather than just the formal charges of which he was convicted, the trial court decided that Fortier had effectively exhibited criminal negligence or recklessness in regard to the possible death of the victims, and sentenced him to 144 months of imprisonment.

Do the discretion residing in juries and prosecutors and the flexibility of the sentencing guidelines offer a fair and practical way of fine-tuning the otherwise harsh federal conspiracy law? Or do they undermine or capriciously tinker with the principles of conspiracy law?

5. *The MPC rejects* Pinkerton. The *Pinkerton* rule has come under considerable attack and has been rejected wholesale by the Model Penal Code. According to one commentator:[16]

The MPC position . . . is that a conspirator should be measured by the same standard of legal accountability for conduct applicable to any other individual. Therefore, the Code departs from prevailing law in several jurisdictions and establishes no special complicity rules for conspirators. "[L]iability for a substantive crime as an accomplice cannot be predicated on the sole fact of having been a party to a conspiracy; further inquiry must examine a person's real culpability with respect to the substantive offense."[17] . . . [E]ven when this limitation is added to

16. Note, Conspiracy: Statutory Reform Since the Model Penal Code, 75 Colum. L. Rev. 1122, 1149-53.
17. See, e.g., the illuminating comments of the Kentucky Criminal Law Revision Committee:

The question to be faced by the decision makers in deciding whether to impute liability through a conspiracy is not whether the defendant was a party to the conspiracy; instead, it is

the "in furtherance of the agreement" prerequisite, the embrace of vicarious liability under federal law remains unjustifiably broad. The vast majority of criminal codes drafted or adopted since the promulgation of the MPC have, it seems, chosen to make accountability for substantive crimes entirely independent of conspiracy as such. . . .

. . . Probably the most peculiar provision, in form if not in effect, is contained in the Texas complicity section. This statute determines conspirator responsibility for an *object* offense by reference to complicity tests of general applicability (i.e., not dependent on conspiracy membership). Simultaneously, §7.02(b) makes all conspirators vicariously liable for *non-object* offenses which are committed "in furtherance of the unlawful purpose" and which "should have been anticipated as a result" of the agreement's implementation. Thus, where special conspirator accountability for a substantive crime would be most easily defensible, Texas invokes ordinary complicity measures. On the other hand, where questions of intent and causality are most serious, a *Pinkerton*-type rule is imposed.

For an example of a state court favoring the MPC rule over the federal *Pinkerton* rule, see Evanchyk v. Stewart, 47 P.3d 1114 (Ariz. 2002) (defendant who conspired to commit robbery could not be charged with conspiracy to commit first-degree murder where killing itself was not premeditated but was charged as first-degree solely because of felony murder rule).

6. *Hearsay and conspiracy.* The hearsay rule forbids, subject to various exceptions, the admission of evidence given by a witness on the stand as to what someone said off the stand, when the probative value of that evidence depends on the credibility of the out-of-court declarant (the person who made the statement that the witness is repeating). Thus, a witness's statement on the stand that "my brother-in-law told me he saw the defendant break into the building" would be hearsay. The theory is that the witness's brother-in-law, the person who allegedly observed the defendant, is not in court to be cross-examined. Such cross-examination might reveal defects in his perception, memory, or honesty.

One of the most important exceptions to the hearsay rule is that an out-of-court statement made by one co-conspirator in furtherance of the conspiracy may be admissible against another co-conspirator, just as a person's own statements are admissible against her (whether formal confessions or unintentionally overheard inculpatory "admissions"). The law has created the fiction that statements made by a conspirator in the course of or in furtherance of the conspiracy are authorized by all of his or her co-conspirators, and are therefore admissible against them as admissions, so long as the trial judge is satisfied by a preponderance of the evidence that a conspiracy does exist. Thus, if Lefty, Righty, and Crook are in a conspiracy, and Lefty says to Righty, "Join our burglary ring. We've got Crook as our safe-cracker," and if Bystander overhears this, Lefty's statement could be admissible against Crook (or Righty) if Bystander reports it to the jury. (Of course, the irony is that the government will make a preliminary

---

whether he aided, counseled, agreed to aid or attempted to aid in the planning or commission of the offense committed. Justification for this approach was put this way in the Model Penal Code: "Conspiracy may prove command, encouragement, assistance or agreement to assist, etc.; it is evidentially important and may be sufficient for that purpose. But whether it suffices ought to be decided by the jury; they should not be told that it establishes complicity as a matter of law." Model Penal Code §2.04(3), Comment (Tent. Draft No. 1 1953).

Ky. Penal Code, Final Draft (1971), Comment to §310, at 29-30.

showing, based on other evidence, that a conspiracy existed, in order to use the admission to show the conspiracy.)[18]

7. *Joinder.* Another incident of conspiracy relates to the likelihood of joint trial. Though the rules of procedure often permit joinder of defendants in situations that do not depend on the existence of a conspiracy, in practice it is far easier to try defendants together if they are accused of conspiracy. Trying the defendants together gives the prosecutor certain important advantages. If some of the defendants are clearly guilty, the jury may look at the rest and decide that "birds of a feather flock together." Evidence that is admissible against one defendant may be heard by the jury and "informally" considered against another defendant, even though, for one reason or another, the evidence is technically inadmissible against the second defendant. A defendant's privilege against self-incrimination may be impaired if his failure to take the stand is emphasized by the fact that his codefendants do testify. The prosecutor may even be able to arrange to have each of the defendants accuse the other — while she sits back and argues that they are all correct. Finally, a prosecutor saves resources by having to pick a jury and present witnesses only once in a large trial, rather than often in many small trials.

The defendant dislikes joint trials for all the reasons that the prosecutor likes them. In addition, defending a case where there are many other defendants requires more resources, because the defendant's attorney in a joint trial will have to sift through far more evidence than concerns her client directly. The very number of defendants may confuse the jury. This is not to say that in all cases joinder favors the prosecution. A defendant who is technically guilty but not very deeply involved in a conspiracy may benefit from comparison with those who are much more deeply involved, and the jury may acquit him either because he looks innocent compared to the others, or because it wishes to maintain an appearance of balance by not convicting everyone.

8. *Venue.* The rules as to venue — where a prosecution may be brought — are another incident of conspiracy. As the Commentary to the Model Penal Code §5.03 points out:[19]

> The sixth amendment of the Federal Constitution states that in "all criminal prosecutions, the accused shall enjoy the right to a speedy and public trial, by an impartial jury of the State and district wherein the crime shall have been committed." The rule is well settled that venue in a conspiracy prosecution may be laid, consistently with these provisions, in any county or district in which the agreement was formed or in which an overt act by any of the conspirators took place. . . . The protection of the constitutional provisions has been seriously diluted, however, because of loose present approaches toward unity and scope of a conspiracy. In the words of Justice Jackson, "the leverage of a conspiracy charge lifts this limitation from the prosecution and reduces its protection to a phantom."

18. Incidentally, the hearsay exception should only apply if the co-conspirator's statement is made *before* the conspirators have achieved their central objective. For example, in State v. Rivenbark, 533 A.2d 271 (Md. 1987), Rivenbark and Johnson allegedly conspired to commit a burglary, which ended in the death of the owner of the burgled home. Six months after the crime, Johnson apparently told his girlfriend, Wilson, that he and Rivenbark had committed the burglary and also gave Wilson instructions on disposing of evidence. Rivenbark was tried separately for murder and burglary, and Wilson's testimony as to Johnson's statements was admitted against Rivenbark. The court reversed the convictions, rejecting the state's claim that Johnson's statements to Wilson were in furtherance of the Johnson-Rivenbark conspiracy as part of an "implied, subsidiary conspiracy" to conceal the crime. The court reasoned that automatically inferring such a conspiracy to conceal, especially so long after the crime, would extend this exception to the hearsay rule too far.

19. Model Penal Code and Commentaries, *supra,* at 449-50.

In The Best Defense 155-74 (1982), Professor Alan Dershowitz describes how his client, Harry Reems, star of the pornographic movie *Deep Throat*, faced federal conspiracy charges in Memphis, Tennessee, even though Reems had never been in Memphis nor had the movie ever played there. According to Dershowitz, a zealous Assistant United States Attorney charged Reems and others with conspiracy to distribute the film throughout the United States and persuaded a federal judge that venue could lie in any place where the film *could* have been shown.

Sometimes a state court may be uncertain whether it even has jurisdiction over a conspiracy that arguably takes place elsewhere. In People v. Morante, 20 Cal. 4th 403, 975 P.2d 1071, 84 Cal. Rptr. 665 (1999), the defendants conducted conversations in California about conducting a drug transaction in another state, and also engaged in overt acts in California. The defendants argued that they could not be punished in California unless their actions in California at least met the standard of a "substantial step" sufficient to establish attempt liability, but the court rejected that argument:

> We logically cannot hold that those elements of the offense are sufficient to attach criminal liability to the conspirators when they intend to accomplish the criminal objective — even if they do not meet that objective, within the state — but are not sufficient, and must be accompanied by an attempt within the state to commit the crime, when the conspirators intend to consummate the criminal objective outside the state. [20 Cal. 4th at 424.]

In a different context, determining the location of an unfulfilled conspiracy required a California court to identify the substantive harms caused by a still inchoate agreement in the place where some parties agree. California, like many jurisdictions, enhances the punishment for a drug crime if the crime occurs in a public place within 1,000 feet of a school. In People v. Marzet, 57 Cal. App. 4th 329, 67 Cal. Rptr. 2d 83, the defendants stood physically within 1,000 feet of a school when they negotiated the sale of drugs, but the drugs themselves were in a private home, and the actual sale and delivery were to take place in that home. Nevertheless, because the agreement was made, and overt acts committed, within the statutory distance, the court affirmed the sentence enhancement. It held that the conspiratorial actions "exposed school-age children to the dangerous and potentially influential conduct of drug dealers and buyers as surely as if the children had witnessed the transaction itself." Id. at 88.

9. *Statute of limitations.* The overt act in furtherance of a conspiracy is crucial to the running of the statute of limitations. Most jurisdictions provide that the statute of limitations on conspiracy runs not from the time of the agreement, but from the time of the last overt act in furtherance of that agreement.

F.   THE PARTIES TO AND OBJECTS OF CONSPIRACY

1.   Bilateral and Unilateral Conspiracies

What is the sound of one (conspiratorial) hand clapping? In abstract logic, a conspiracy by definition requites two people agreeing, but courts have faced innumerable subsidiary questions about whether a single person can be charged with conspiracy when some fact or legal rule negates the liability of the other supposed conspirator(s).

The problem of the single conviction. In United States v. Fox, 130 F.2d 56 (3d Cir. 1942), Fox, Davis, and Kaufman were charged with conspiracy to obstruct justice and to defraud the United States. Fox pleaded guilty and testified for the government, but after two juries tried without success to reach a verdict, the government entered a nolle prosequi against Davis and Kaufman. Fox then moved for leave to withdraw his plea of guilty, but the court refused. The court acknowledged that in a single trial of the alleged parties to a conspiracy, the acquittal of *all* but one of the defendants on the merits would require a directed acquittal of the last. But other possible permutations of outcome would not forbid conviction of one conspirator, because they would not be inconsistent with a particular court or jury finding that there was indeed an illegal agreement:

> . . . The conviction of some alleged conspirators does not fall because others named are acquitted, even though the conviction of the others is logically required for the finding of guilty of those held. Nor is the conviction of one alleged conspirator vitiated because of the possible later acquittal of co-defendants not yet tried or even apprehended. Furthermore, one may be convicted and punished for a conspiracy even though his fellow conspirators may be immune from prosecution because of the immunity attaching to representatives of foreign governments. . . . "The rule that the acquittal of all save one of alleged conspirators results in the acquittal of all applies to acquittals on the merits." [quoting Farnsworth v. Zerbst, 98 F.2d 541, 544 (5th Cir. 1938).]
>
> We think that to treat a convicted conspirator whose fellow conspirator's case has ended by a nolle prosequi like the case where one is convicted and the other is acquitted goes too far. The analogy overlooks the difference between an acquittal and a nolle prosequi. The courts seem to have treated the acquittal in this connection as though the jury had expressly found that the defendant did not participate in the conspiracy charged. Therefore, the defendant who is convicted stands in the situation of having been found to conspire by himself, a manifest impossibility by the definition of conspiracy. One may criticize that rule as being founded upon a false premise, for a not guilty verdict is not necessarily a declaration of innocence by the jury, but simply an indication of lack of proof beyond a reasonable doubt. Be that as it may, the acquittal of the alleged conspirator does free the accused from further prosecution for the offense charged. The nolle prosequi does not. [Id. at 58.]

Does the *Fox* rule raise concerns about equity? Does it subject a conspiracy defendant to the possibly irrational actions of a jury?

Under the rules of criminal procedure, two parties to the same crime usually will be tried together, but, may, under certain circumstances, be given separate trials. See, e.g., Fed. R. Crim. Proc. 14 (otherwise properly joined trials may be severed if single trial prejudicial to a party). In State v. Colon, 778 A.2d 875, 257 Conn. 587 (2001), the Connecticut Supreme Court held that even a jury acquittal of a defendant's sole co-conspirator will not, as a matter of law, bar conviction of conspiracy, where the parties receive separate trials. What practical reasons might underlie this principle?

Unilateral conspiracies. Fox deals with the case where not all of the alleged conspirators turn out to be convicted. But what if, by the very nature of the case, only one of them *could* be convicted? Is there still an illegal agreement in the first place?

Jim and Mike agree to commit a crime. Mike is not convicted of conspiracy because (1) he is an undercover policeman; or (2) he is a private citizen, but never intended that the crime be committed; or (3) he has some special excuse — he is insane, underage, or a foreign ambassador, not subject to the criminal law of the United States. Can Jim be guilty? Can he "agree" by himself? Should it matter *why* Mike is not guilty?

The common older view of the courts, and the one still often followed by the federal courts, is the "bilateral" view:

> Conspiracy is the agreement of two or more to effect an unlawful purpose. Two people cannot agree unless they both intend to carry out the purpose which is stated to be the object of their combination. Therefore there is no agreement, and consequently no conspiracy, where one of the two never intends to carry out the unlawful purpose.[20]

Hence, if there were no one who could be legally responsible for agreeing with Jim, he *could not be guilty of conspiracy*. However, some have proposed a unilateral view of conspiracy has been emerging, reasoning that

> [t]he fact that, unknown to a man who wishes to enter a conspiracy to commit some criminal purpose, the other person has no intention of fulfilling that purpose, ought to be irrelevant as long as the first man does intend to fulfill it if he can because a man who believes he is conspiring to commit a crime and wishes to conspire to commit a crime has a guilty mind and has done all in his power to plot the commission of an unlawful purpose.[21]

The Model Penal Code, in section 5.03(1), adopted the unilateral approach:

> A person is guilty of conspiracy with another person or persons to commit a crime if with the purpose of promoting or facilitating its commission he
>
> (a) agrees with such other person or persons that they or one or more of them will engage in conduct which constitutes such crime or an attempt or solicitation to commit such crime; or
> (b) agrees to aid such other person or persons in the planning or commission of such crime or of an attempt or solicitation to commit such crime.

Is the unilateral approach consistent with the purposes of conspiracy law? To what extent has Jim's chance of success in carrying out a criminal act been increased by the agreement? See Miller v. State, 955 P.2d 892 (Wyo. 1998) (adopting unilateral theory, where defendant unaware that his supposed co-conspirator in a kidnapping was a government agent).

Statutory exclusion of liability for one party. In certain cases, one of the persons who agrees to commit a crime is a protected party and not subject to prosecution. For example, under many state statutes, a "bookie," the person who accepts bets, commits a crime but his clients do not. Of course, a man who has intercourse with a female under the age of consent is guilty of statutory rape, while the female is not. And, the old rule, still operative in some states, is that a prostitute commits a crime if she offers sex for sale, but the "john" who is her customer does not.

---

20. G.H.L. Fridman, Metis Rea in Conspiracy, 19 Mod. L. Rev. 276 (1956).
21. Id. at 282, 283.

Though we encountered a parallel problem under the law of complicity (see pp. 741-43, *supra*), conspiracy law presents some special ways of addressing these cases.

In Gebardi v. United States, 287 U.S. 112 (1932), the following occurred:

> . . . [A] man and a woman, not then husband and wife, were indicted for conspiring together to transport the woman from one state to another for the purpose of engaging in sexual intercourse with the man. At the trial without a jury there was evidence from which the court could have found that the petitioners had engaged in illicit sexual relations in the course of each of the journeys alleged; that the man purchased the railway tickets for both petitioners for at least one journey, and that in each instance the woman, in advance of the purchase of the tickets, consented to go on the journey and did go on it voluntarily for the specified immoral purpose.

Section 2 of the Mann Act (violation of which was charged as the object of the conspiracy) states:

> Any person who shall knowingly transport or cause to be transported, or aid or assist in obtaining transportation for, or in transporting in interstate or foreign commerce . . . any woman or girl for the purpose of prostitution or debauchery or for any other immoral purpose [commits a punishable act].

The Supreme Court held that the female defendant only "consented to," but did not "aid or assist" in obtaining her transportation, and that Congress had not intended for her to be punished under the act. Thus, she also could not be convicted for conspiracy, leaving no one for the man to conspire with. "The criminal object [involved] the agreement of the woman to her transportation by the man, which [was] the very conspiracy charged." Thus, the male defendant though guilty of violating of the Mann Act itself was not guilty of conspiracy.

Could a prostitute be found guilty of conspiring with a client to commit prostitution? If an unmarried person consented to adultery with a married person, where the latter alone is guilty of the substantive offense, can either or both be guilty of conspiracy to commit adultery? What does *Gebardi* say? Does it seem right that a person is not guilty of conspiracy if her co-conspirator is a protected party? Notice that under the unilateral approach, many of these problems disappear.

Wharton's Rule. An important exception to the principle that a conspiracy is a distinct crime from the target substantive offense is the so-called Wharton's Rule. As stated by the scholar after whom it is named,

> [W]hen, to the idea of an offense, plurality of agents is logically necessary, conspiracy, which assumes the voluntary accession of a person to a crime of such a nature that it is aggravated by a plurality of agents, cannot be maintained.[22]

Thus, the two parties to a crime of adultery, incest, bigamy, or duelling cannot be convicted of both the substantive crime and the conspiracy: The definition of the substantive crime assumes that at least two people will agree to commit it, so it would be unfair "double-counting" for the state to charge conspiracy as well.

---

22. Francis Wharton, Criminal Law §1604 (12th ed. 1932).

But what if, for example, the alleged conspiracy consists of more than the number of parties needed to commit the target offense, as where *A, B, C,* and *D* succeed in arranging a duel between *A* and *B*? Consider the following facts:

> Each of eight petitioners was charged with conspiring to violate and violating a federal gambling statute making it a crime for five or more persons to conduct, finance, manage, supervise, direct, or own a gambling business prohibited by state law. Each petitioner was convicted of both the conspiracy and the substantive offense. On appeal the petitioners argued that the conspiracy should merge into the substantive offense because the substantive offense necessarily requires the participation of a number of petitioners for its commission.

The Supreme Court, in Iannelli v. United States, 420 U.S. 770 (1975), held that Wharton's Rule did not apply to these facts, stating,

> The conduct proscribed by [the federal statute] is significantly different from the offenses to which the Rule traditionally has been applied. Unlike the consequences of the classic Wharton's Rule offenses, the harm attendant upon the commission of the substantive offense is not restricted to the parties to the agreement. Large-scale gambling activities seek to elicit the participation of additional persons — the bettors — who are parties neither to the conspiracy nor to the substantive offense that results from it. Moreover, the parties prosecuted for the conspiracy need not be the same persons who are prosecuted for commission of the substantive offense. An endeavor as complex as a large-scale gambling enterprise might involve persons who have played appreciably different roles, and whose level of culpability varies significantly. It might, therefore, be appropriate to prosecute the owners and organizers of large-scale gambling operations both for the conspiracy and for the substantive offense but to prosecute the lesser participants only for the substantive offense. Nor can it fairly be maintained that agreements to enter into large-scale gambling activities are not likely to generate additional agreements to engage in other criminal endeavors. [Id. at 784.]

Do you agree? Would petitioner's argument have been stronger if they had been only five in number?

In People v. Sesi, 300 N.W.2d 535 (Mich. App. 1981), the court followed *Iannelli* in upholding a conviction of three men for conspiracy to suborn perjury, notwithstanding Wharton's Rule, since it only requires two people, the suborner and the subornee, to commit perjury.

Uneven penalties. What if, unlike the previous few cases, the substantive criminal law would indeed punish both parties to the proscribed transaction, but with highly disparate penalties? Would a conspiracy charge be improper here as well? In State v. Pinkerton, 628 N.W.2d 159 (Minn. App. 2001), the police arranged a controlled purchase of cocaine from the defendant, who was then convicted of both the substantive charge of selling the cocaine and conspiracy to commit a controlled-substance crime. Minnesota law permitted double punishment of a target crime and a conspiracy; moreover, it permitted punishment of a "unilateral" conspiracy, where one of the co-conspirators is actually an undercover agent. But Pinkerton had another argument, which the court accepted.

> . . . Under the current version of the act, a person who sells cocaine with a total weight of three grams or more within a 90-day period is guilty of controlled-substance crime in the second degree and is subject to imprisonment for 25 years,

a fine of $500,000, or both. But a person who possesses the same amount of co-caine is guilty of a lesser degree of controlled-substance crime and is subject to a lesser penalty. . . .

. . . If an agreement solely between a seller and a buyer of controlled substances can constitute conspiracy, the seller and buyer would, as co-conspirators, be subject to the same penalty. But to the extent that the buyer is, at most, guilty of a crime of possession, the legislature would not intend that a seller and a buyer of controlled substances could be subject to the same penalty. We conclude that an agreement solely between a seller and a buyer of controlled substances cannot constitute a conspiracy under Minn. Stat. §152.096.

. . . The evidence shows that during the April 16 drug buy, an unknown person was in the car with Pinkerton when he sold cocaine to Kowalewski. During the April 20 drug buy, a person identified as Lay-Low was in the car with Pinkerton when he sold cocaine to Fenske. For both occasions, the record contains no evidence that there was any interaction between the person in the car and Pinkerton, Kowalewski, or Fenske. Nor does the record contain any evidence that any other third party was involved with Pinkerton. Pinkerton argues that a jury could not reasonably conclude that an agreement to sell controlled substances existed between Pinkerton and any person but the informant-purchasers, Kowalewski and Fenske. We agree.

. . . The bare fact that a person is present in a vehicle during a controlled-substance transaction, without more, does not support a finding of a conspiratorial agreement. . . . [Id. at 163-64.]

Does it make sense that under conspiracy law, a huge difference in sentence might rest on the question whether Pinkerton had an ally in the sale? Conversely, should Pinkerton, a seller, benefit from a legislative decision that a buyer should receive a lower sentence?

Spouses. At common law a husband and wife could not be charged as conspirators with each other. The reason was that a husband and wife were seen as one person in law, having one will, while conspiracy required at least two people. But the Supreme Court held that federal law was otherwise, in United States v. Dege, 364 U.S. 51 (1960), where a husband and wife were indicted for conspiring to bring goods into the United States illicitly:

> For this Court now to act on . . . the medieval view that husband and wife "are esteemed but as one Person in Law, and are presumed to have but one Will" would indeed be "blind imitation of the past." It would require us to disregard the vast changes in the status of woman — the extension of her rights and correlative duties — whereby a wife's legal submission to her husband has been wholly wiped out, not only in the English-speaking world generally but emphatically so in this country. . . .
>
> . . . Suffice it to say that we cannot infuse in the conspiracy statute a fictitious attribution to Congress of regard for the medieval notion of woman's submissiveness to the benevolent coercive powers of a husband in order to relieve her of her obligation of obedience to an unqualifiedly expressed Act of Congress by regarding her as a person whose legal personality is merged in that of her husband, making the two one. [Id. at 54.]

Chief Justice Warren, in dissent, argued that the traditional rule was sound:

> A wife, simply by virtue of the intimate life she shares with her husband, might easily perform acts that would technically be sufficient to involve her in a criminal conspiracy with him, but which might be far removed from the arm's-length

agreement typical of that crime. It is not a medieval mental quirk or an attitude "unnourished by sense" to believe that husbands and wives should not be subjected to such a risk, or that such a possibility should not be permitted to endanger the confidentiality of the marriage relationship. [Id. at 57-58.]

Is the dissent attempting to protect the husband, the wife, or the marriage?

2.   The Scope of the Conspiracy

a.   *Single vs. Multiple Conspiracies*

Far more litigated than the issue of whether a particular person can be guilty of conspiracy on the basis of her agreement is the problem of determining the extent of the conspiratorial relation — both as to its objectives, where more than one crime is to be committed, and as to its membership, where different people participate in the commissions of different crimes.

One commentator has laid out the problems faced by law enforcement in grappling with the amorphous law on this issue.

JEROME CAMPANE,
CHAINS, WHEELS, AND THE SINGLE CONSPIRACY
50 FBI Law Enforcement Bulletin 24-31
(Aug./Sept. 1981)

Suppose *A* and *B* steal an automobile and sell it to *C*, the owner of a chop-shop that fronts as a legitimate automotive repair business. Then a week later, *B* and *D* burglarize a home and sell stolen jewelry to *C*. In addition to the substantive offenses of motor vehicle theft and burglary, does this activity constitute one criminal conspiracy among all three thieves and the fence, or two separate conspiracies, with *A*, *B*, and *C* participating in a stolen auto conspiracy, and *B*, *C*, and *D* participating in a burglary conspiracy? From a conspiratorial point of view, does it matter whether the evidence tends to establish one large conspiracy, as opposed to two smaller ones? If it does matter, how does an investigator gather evidence showing one large conspiracy?

The single vs. multiple conspiracy issue raised by these questions is one of the most perplexing problems facing courts in criminal conspiracy cases. The investigation of this crime can be particularly cumbersome when the evidence establishes a large criminal organization with several persons actively participating in a variety of unlawful acts, while others appear only on the periphery of the enterprise. . . .

The evidence may suggest one overall conspiracy, while proof at trial establishes the existence of two or more. It has long been held that in such a case, the variance between the charge and the proof may "affect the substantial rights" of the accused. . . .

[I]n 1946, the Supreme Court identified [a] . . . constitutional guarantee available to attack single conspiracy prosecutions. . . . [T]he leading conspiracy case of Kotteakos v. United States[, 328 U.S. 750 (1946)], [involved] 32 defendants [who] were charged in a single conspiracy prosecution for defrauding the Federal Government. The defendants used the same loan broker to assist them to induce various financial institutions and the Federal Housing Administration to grant credit, loans, and advances for housing renovation and modernization. . . . [T]he loan applications contained false and fraudulent information because the proceeds were intended to be used for purposes other than [those] required by the National Housing Act. Seven defendants were eventually found guilty.

The Circuit Court of Appeals believed the trial judge was plainly wrong in supposing that upon the evidence there could be a single conspiracy, for no connection was shown between any of the defendants other than their mutual use of the same loan broker. The appellate court believed the trial judge should have dismissed the indictment for this material variance between the proof shown and the pleadings, but nevertheless held the error to be nonprejudicial, since guilt was so manifest that it was "proper" to join the conspiracies, and "to reverse the conviction would be a miscarriage of justice." . . .

The Supreme Court disagreed with the lower court and reversed the convictions because due process required the defendants' guilt be proved individually and personally. . . .

The court recognized that when many conspire, they invite mass trial, but in such cases every effort must be made to individualize and safeguard each defendant in his relation to the mass. The Court pointed out:

The dangers of transference of guilt from one to another across the line separating conspiracies, subconsciously or otherwise, are so great that no one really can say prejudice to substantial rights has not taken place. . . . That right, in each instance, was the right not to be tried en masse for the conglomeration of distinct and separate offenses committed by others as shown by this record. . . .

In a more recent case, the Second Circuit Court of Appeals in United States v. Bertolotti [529 F.2d 149 (2d Cir. 1975)] reversed the single conspiracy conviction of seven individuals for prejudicial variance when it held that the evidence proved multiple conspiracies. The court cited one item of evidence as a specific example of prejudice suffered by the defendants, as well as an illustration of the inherent dangers of combining unrelated criminal acts under the roof of an alleged single conspiracy. As a part of its investigation, the district attorney's office placed a court-authorized wiretap on the telephone of one suspect. Tapes of 55 intercepted calls were played to the jury and introduced as evidence of narcotics negotiations between two defendants. None of the remaining defendants either participated or was mentioned in any of the 55 taped conversations. As a result, the court stated:

The prejudicial effect, however, of requiring the jury to spend two entire days listening to obviously shocking and inflammatory discussions about assault, kidnapping, guns and narcotics cannot be underestimated. No defendant ought to have a jury which is considering his guilt or innocence hear evidence of this sort absent proof connecting him with the subject matter discussed.

After a review of the evidence as [a] whole, the court concluded:

The possibilities of spill-over effect from testimony of these transactions are patent when the number of defendants and the volume of evidence are weighed against the ability of the jury to give each defendant the individual consideration our system requires. . . .

[P]rosecution for multiple conspiracies in successive trials or multiple counts in one trial, presents equally hazardous constitutional problems. . . .

United States v. Palerma [410 F.2d 468 (7th Cir. 1969)] is a case in point. Joseph Amabile was associated with Melrose Park Plumbing, a subcontractor for the Riley Management Company which built various apartment building complexes in suburban Chicago from 1962 to 1965. He was tried and convicted in Federal court for conspiring to extort $48,500 from the management company by threatening Riley with work stoppages and physical violence, and in doing so, interfering with interstate shipments of construction materials.

In a second prosecution, Amabile was tried and convicted for extorting an additional $64,000 from Riley on a later subcontracted construction project in which Amabile conspired with others, including various public officials in Northlake, Ill. On appeal, Amabile successfully argued his participation in one continuous agreement to extort money from Riley whenever his company was Riley's plumbing subcontractor. The Court held:

> Although the methods of obtaining money from Riley on the various projects may have been different, the overall objective was the same. . . . Even though the incident occurred over a period of years, the overall agreement constituted a continuing conspiracy against Riley. Since Amabile has already been tried and convicted of conspiring to extort money from Riley, Amabile's Fifth Amendment rights were violated by placing him in jeopardy twice for the same criminal act. . . .

Another form of fragmentation occurs in conspiracy prosecutions when a defendant is charged at one trial with multiple counts of conspiracy and the proof establishes a lesser number, or only one. The principal vice of this procedure is that it, too, may result in multiple punishment for participation in a single conspiracy. . . .

The common remedy for such unconstitutional fragmentation is fortunately less severe than the outright bar to the subsequent prosecution required in multiple trial fragmentation. The court will generally let the trial proceed and ignore the number of charges on which a defendant is subsequently convicted, and impose but a single sentence for the one conspiracy.

One difficulty with analyzing the evidence in conspiracy cases stems from the common law notion that the substance of the offense was the making of an agreement to commit a readily identifiable crime, such as robbery or murder. From this perspective, some courts are inclined to focus on what the individual co-conspirators agreed to. . . .

As a result . . . , a successful conspiracy prosecution may depend on the ability of the prosecutor to fashion the proof in such away as to shift the court[s] and the jury's examination of the evidence away from the agreement of each participant and toward the organization formed to commit the crime. Many courts are willing to accept the bilateral approach and charge the jury to recognize the continuance of a single dominant plan, despite changes in personnel, location, victims, or methods of operation. This shift in focus is often accomplished successfully when the evidence is presented in a form that structures the group's activity as either a chain or wheel conspiracy.

Kotteakos v. United States[, *supra*,] decided in 1946, and *Blumenthal,* decided a year later, are the two Supreme Court cases which are generally recognized for their acceptance of such structural metaphors to distinguish the single from the multiple conspiracy.

When a number of persons (the spokes) are engaged in a criminal conspiracy with the same individual or group (the hub), a successful single conspiracy prosecution will depend upon whether the spokes can be drawn together (rim around the wheel) into a single agreement.

The hub generally views his dealings with the spokes as part of a single enterprise, but a spoke may be concerned merely with his own actions, unless it can be shown that the existence and cooperation of other spokes were or should have been known to him. Failing such proof, a court will hold that the other spokes remain individual members of multiple conspiracies. Crimes such as bribery, theft, and fraud particularly lend themselves to a wheel analysis.

In *Kotteakos,* the president of a lumber company, one Brown, having experience in obtaining loans under the National Housing Act (NHA), undertook to act as a broker for others who fraudulently applied to various financial institutions for NHA modernization loans. The undisputed proof showed separate and independent unlawful agreements between eight applicants and Brown. The applicants' only connection with each other was their mutual use of the same broker.

The Federal Government claimed the conspiratorial pattern was that of separate spokes meeting at a common center, but the Supreme Court agreed with the Federal appellate court that without the rim of the wheel to enclose the spokes, the proof made out a case of several conspiracies, notwithstanding [the fact that] only one was charged in the indictment. (See Figure 1.)

Kotteakos . . . suggest[s] that the nature of the crime itself generally precludes a wheel analysis. A year later, explaining its conclusion in *Kotteakos,* the Supreme Court pointed out that no two of the fraudulent loan agreements were tied together as stages in the formation of a larger all-inclusive combination, and no spoke gained from the fact that others were involved. Because each loan

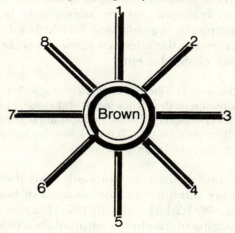

FIGURE 1. The Rimless Wheel
No single conspiracy (*Kotteakos*)

FIGURE 2. The Classic Chain Conspiracy (*Blumenthal*)

was an end in itself, the co-conspirators did not know or need to know of each other's existence or involvement:

> The conspiracies therefore were distinct and disconnected, not parts of a larger general scheme. . . . There was no drawing of all together in a single, overall comprehensive plan.

Conspiracies suggested by the chain configuration relate to agreements between sellers, middlemen, wholesalers, retailers, and ultimate purchasers. Whether the purpose of the conspiracy is the sale of such commodities as narcotics, counterfeit money, or liquor, the object is to place the goods into the hands of the paying consumer. No one in the chain profits unless each does his part (connects the links) to supply the buyer. (See Figure 2.)

In *Blumenthal*, two whiskey distributors and three of their salesmen were convicted in a single conspiracy prosecution for selling 2,000 cases of whiskey at prices in excess of the ceiling set by the Federal Office of Price Administration. The two distributors operated the Francisco Company as a front for a hidden owner. The three company salesmen sold the whiskey to tavern owners at a price barely above cost, plus a kickback shared by the salesmen, distributors, and hidden owner. The price for product and kickback combined exceeded the mandated ceiling.

Although evidence [at] trial proved an unlawful agreement between the hidden owner and distributors, the three salesmen claimed they did not know of the unknown owner's existence or his part in the plan. The government's case, they argued, proved one conspiracy between the owner and distributors and one between the salesmen and distributors. As such, testimony about the conspiracy between the owner and distributors was inadmissible against them as this was evidence of a conspiracy for which they were not charged.

The Court disagreed, however, and upheld the conviction. It was scarcely conceivable, the Court reasoned, for the salesmen to believe the unknown owner of Francisco Company was giving away his whiskey. It was more appropriate to draw the inference that the salesmen knew an owner, unknown to them, contemplated the entire chain of events:

> All intended to aid the owners, whether Francisco or another, to sell the whiskey unlawfully. . . . All by reason of their knowledge of the plan's general scope, if not its exact limits, sought a common end to aid in disposing of the whiskey. True, each salesman aided in selling only his part. But he knew the lot to be sold was larger and thus that he was aiding in a larger plan.

Complex conspiratorial plans do not easily lend themselves to chain or wheel structures and are oftentimes a combination of both. For example, in United States v. Perez[, 489 F.2d 51 (5th Cir. 1973)], a statewide, get-rich-quick scheme involved the staging of fraudulent automobile accidents for the purpose

FIGURE 3. A Classic Chain (*Perez*)

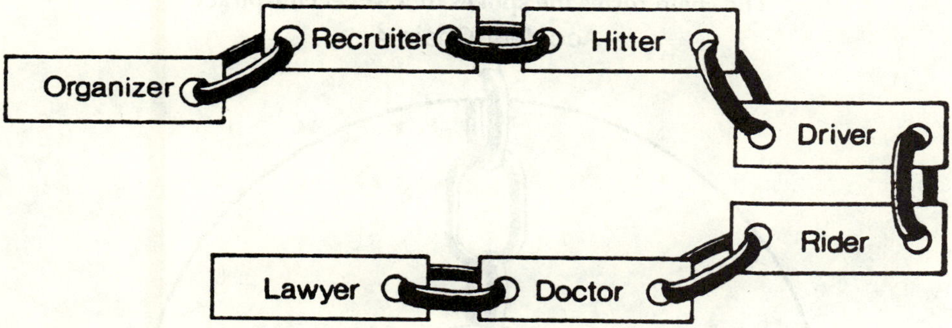

of creating false personal injury claims. Twelve individuals appealed from their convictions in a single mail fraud conspiracy. Each of many phony accidents was organized the same way. "Recruiter" located willing "hitters," who would be liable for a contrived accident with a "target" vehicle. The occupants of the target were "drivers" and "riders" participating in the scheme. The rider would feign injury and be sent to cooperative doctors and lawyers. They, in turn, would contrive to document a bogus medical history in support of a personal injury claim mailed to an insurance company. The rider claimant would then pass the insurance proceeds back through the claim for proportionate disbursement to each cooperating participant. The court held that because each conspirator performed a separate function in a scheme where every participant's cooperation was necessary for the plan to succeed, a classic chain had been drawn. (See Figure 3.)

[The] court believed that each participant, after cooperating in a second phony accident with a similar modus operandi, rimmed the wheel because each knew or should have known that there had to be someone organizing a larger scheme. And . . . the court appeared impressed with the identity of certain defendants. It believed the participants in each accident must have known that there had to be a series of accidental phony accidents to create rewards high enough to compensate for the risk of loss of professional status for the participating doctors and lawyers. The court therefore concluded that all the defendants were co-conspirators in a single common scheme to use the mails to defraud the insurance companies. (See Figure 4.) It observed:

> From an operational sense this was not a series of little concoctions to set up a particular collision. . . . It was one big and hopefully profitable enterprise, which looked toward successful frequent, but nonetheless discreet, repetitions, and in which each participant was neither innocent nor unrewarded.

The case of United States v. LaVechia[, 513 F.2d 1210 (2d Cir. 1975),] supports the importance of evidence indicating multiple and voluminous sales. A Federal court upheld a single conspiracy among counterfeiters and distributors because it thought the amount of money printed ($450,000) was so large that the success of the conspiracy must have depended on distribution by others. Remote purchasers were also linked to the counterfeiters because the evidence showed: (1) Large ($10,000) purchases suggested a larger operation, (2) the purchasers' negotiations in terms of "points" suggested familiarity with the counterfeit business, and (3) the purchasers' knowledge that additional buys

FIGURE 4. The Chain-Wheel (*Perez*)
The chain forms the spokes of a wheel conspiracy.

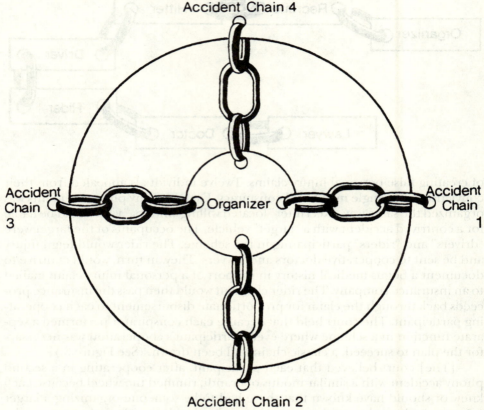

could be made suggested a large-scale operation. In structural form, the counterfeiters should have known they were part of a chain of distribution, and the independent remote purchasers should have suspected that additional chains were working with the same distributors. Evidence regarding the volume of sales, however, was the key to pull the rim around these chains and thus create a wheel conspiracy.

G.   THE RICO STATUTE AND THE FRONTIER OF CONSPIRACY

1.   The Statute

In 1970 Congress passed the Racketeer Influenced and Corrupt Organization Act (RICO). The avowed purpose of the act was "to seek the eradication of organized crime in the United States by strengthening the legal tools in the evidence-gathering process, by establishing new penal prohibitions, and by providing enhanced sanctions and new remedies to deal with the unlawful activities of those engaged in organized crime." The Statement of Findings and Purpose attached to the RICO statute reads as follows:

> The Congress finds that (1) organized crime in the United States is a highly sophisticated, diversified, and widespread activity that annually drains billions of dollars from America's economy by unlawful conduct and the illegal use of force, fraud, and corruption; (2) organized crime derives a major portion of its power through money obtained from such illegal endeavors as syndicated gambling, loan sharking, the theft and fencing of property, the importation and distribution of narcotics and other dangerous drugs, and other forms of social exploitation; (3) this money and power are increasingly used to infiltrate and corrupt legitimate business and labor unions and to subvert and corrupt our democratic processes; (4) organized crime activities in the United States weaken the stability of the Nation's economic system, harm innocent investors and competing organizations, interfere with free competition, seriously burden interstate and foreign commerce, threaten the domestic security, and undermine the general welfare of the Nation and its citizens; and (5) organized crime continues to grow because of defects in the evidence-gathering process of the law inhibiting the development of the legally admissible evidence necessary to bring criminal and other sanctions or remedies to bear on the unlawful activities of those engaged in organized crime and because the sanctions and remedies available to the Government are unnecessarily limited in scope and impact.

> It is the purpose of this Act to seek the eradication of organized crime in the United States by strengthening the legal tools in the evidence-gathering process, by establishing new penal prohibitions, and by providing enhanced sanctions and new remedies to deal with the unlawful activities of those engaged in organized crime. [Public Law 91-452; 84 Stat. 922.]

What aspects of crime do you think Congress was after? How far should this statute reach?

Presumably, the RICO statute was meant, first and foremost, to combat organized crime in its original sense, the Mafia, whose range of criminal activities typically included loan sharking, extortion against employers through manipulation of labor union power, prostitution and drug rings, and, where necessary to enhance any of these crimes, murder of competitors or disloyal members of the organization. As we will see, whatever the legislative intention underlying RICO, federal prosecutors have applied it far beyond the Mafia context. Before we examine the breadth of its application to wider contexts, we turn to a systematic analysis of the elements of a RICO crime.

§1961. Definitions

As used in this chapter—

(1) "racketeering activity" means (A) any act or threat involving murder, kidnaping, gambling, arson, robbery, bribery, extortion, or dealing in narcotic or other dangerous drugs, which is chargeable under State law and punishable by imprisonment for more than one year; (B) any act which is indictable under any of the following provisions of title 18, United States Code [including bribery, counterfeiting, theft from interstate shipment, embezzlement from pension and welfare funds, extortionate credit transactions, transmission of gambling information, mail fraud, wire fraud, obstruction of justice, obstruction of criminal investigations, obstruction of State or local law enforcement, interstate transportation of wagering

paraphernalia, unlawful welfare fund payments, interstate transportation of stolen property, trafficking in contraband cigarettes, white slave traffic, payments and loans to labor organizations, embezzlement from union funds,] fraud in the sale of securities, or felonious manufacture, importation, receiving, concealment, buying, selling, or otherwise dealing in narcotic or other dangerous drugs, punishable under any law of the United States; . . .

(4) "enterprise" includes any individual, partnership, corporation, association, or other legal entity, and any union or group of individuals associated in fact although not a legal entity;

(5) "pattern of racketeering activity" requires at least two acts of racketeering activity, one of which occurred after the effective date of this chapter and the last of which occurred within ten years (excluding any period of imprisonment) after the commission of a prior act of racketeering activity. . . .

RICO prohibits three types of substantive criminal activities (sections 1962(a)-(c)) as well as the inchoate crime of conspiring to violate one of the substantive provisions (section 1962(d)). Each of the three substantive provisions requires proof of (1) a pattern of racketeering activity and (2) involvement in an enterprise that is engaged in or affects interstate commerce. The nature of the relationship of the pattern to the enterprise determines which substantive subsection of RICO is at issue.

2.   RICO Penalties

RICO violations may lead to severe fines and to terms of imprisonment up to 20 years for each violation. In addition, section 1963(a) provides that an individual violating RICO may be forced to forfeit all her property interest in, or proceeds from, a RICO enterprise. Finally, there is a private civil side to RICO: Section 1964(c) states that "any person injured in his business or property by reason of a violation of section 1962" can sue for "treble damages" against any person liable for that violation. Though the particulars of "civil RICO" law go beyond the scope of our criminal law concerns here, one result of these civil provisions is that some purely civil RICO decisions, including several noted below, by interpreting such core RICO elements as "enterprise," may logically apply to criminal cases.

a.   Section 1962(a) Violations

Section 1962(a) provides in part that

[i]t shall be unlawful for any person who has received any income derived . . . from a pattern of racketeering activity . . . to use or invest any part of such income . . . in acquisition of any interest in . . . any enterprise which is engaged in . . . interstate or foreign commerce.

In other words, this subsection forbids the investment or "laundering" of racketeering profits in interstate commercial businesses, where the business itself has a legitimate purpose wholly independent of racketeering activity. Thus, in United States v. Cauble, 706 F.2d 1322 (5th Cir. 1983), the defendant, Rex Cauble, a wealthy Texas businessman, was charged with being the "range boss" of the highly publicized "Cowboy-Mafia," a loosely knit group responsible for importing and distributing over 147,000 pounds of marijuana from 1976 to 1978. The group used shrimp boats and small airplanes to bring the marijuana into this country and then used Cauble's ranches as distribution headquarters. Profits of the business apparently ended up in Cauble's regular business entity, a limited partnership called Cauble Enterprises.

b. Section 1962(b) Violations

Section 1962(b) of RICO provides in part that

> [i]t shall be unlawful for any person through a pattern of racketeering activity . . . to acquire or maintain . . . any interest in or control of any enterprise which is engaged in . . . interstate or foreign commerce.

This subsection prohibits racketeering directly aimed at acquiring an otherwise legitimate business enterprise, as opposed to the presumably passive laundering investment of racketeering profits prohibited by section 1962(a). Thus, RICO bars the infiltration of legitimate enterprises by means of bribery, extortion, or other predicate acts. In United States v. Local 560, International Brotherhood of Teamsters, Chauffeurs, Warehousemen, and Helpers of America, 581 F. Supp. 279 (D.N.J. 1984), the charge was that individual defendants associated under the leadership of defendant Anthony Provenzano unlawfully acquired and maintained the Teamsters Local 560 "enterprise" through a pattern of racketeering activity involving murder and extortion.

c. Section 1962(c) Violations

Section 1962(c) provides in part that

> [i]t shall be unlawful for any person employed by or associated with any enterprise engaged in . . . interstate or foreign commerce . . . to conduct or participate . . . in the conduct of such enterprise's affairs through a pattern of racketeering activity. . . .

This section prohibits racketeering activity that springs from the business affairs of an enterprise; that is, it applies where a person first becomes associated with an enterprise and then begins to conduct the affairs of that enterprise through actions that constitute predicate acts of racketeering. Thus, section 1962(c) aims at corruption of the enterprise from within. Though obviously most section 1962(c) prosecutions involve commercial enterprises, the "enterprise" concept has proved remarkably malleable. For one thing, the enterprise subject to corruption under section 1962(c) need not be a commercial entity at all. In one of the most strikingly creative uses of RICO, the federal government charged United States District Judge Robert Aguilar with a RICO violation. Judge Aguilar was accused of a pattern of racketeering activity including obstructing justice by assisting a fugitive to avoid arrest by the United States Marshal, by interceding with other judges in behalf of criminal defendants whom he knew personally, by counseling a grand jury witness to lie, and by interfering with an FBI wiretap.

The "enterprise" Judge Aguilar was accused of corrupting was the United States District Court for the Northern District of California. See Indictment, United States v. Aguilar (Crim. 89-0365) (N.D. Cal. 1989). (Judge Aguilar was eventually convicted on several counts.) [23]

While RICO enterprises can include both otherwise legitimate white-collar financial organizations and non-commercial enterprises, the Supreme Court was forced by the wording and premises of the RICO statute to examine the question whether RICO applied where there was *no* legitimate enterprise whatsoever for the racketeers to corrupt. In United States v. Turkette, 452 U.S. 576 (1981), the Court held that under RICO the term "enterprise" includes purely criminal organizations, as well as legitimate businesses. Turkette had committed the predicate racketeering offenses of trafficking in narcotics, arson, and bribery. His "enterprise," however, consisted of a handful of various confederates who participated in some of the crimes. There was no legitimate enterprise; such organization as there was existed solely for criminal purposes. Turkette argued that since congressional intent in passing RICO had been to protect against infiltration of legitimate businesses by organized crime, purely criminal enterprises were beyond the reach of RICO.

The Court admitted that "the legislative history forcefully supports the view that the major purpose of [RICO] is to address the infiltration of legitimate business by organized crime," but it denied the "negative inference that [RICO] did not reach the activities of enterprises organized and existing for criminal purposes." Failing to apply RICO to criminal organizations, the Court argued, would eliminate many possible remedies and preventive actions under RICO and would prevent the statute from reaching some organized crime activity.

Why might Congress have wanted to provide enhanced penalties for the infiltration of legitimate business by organized crime? Compare Turkette to a criminal who commits the same substantive crimes but without the aid of an enterprise. Should Turkette be subject to enhanced penalties? Note that without RICO the narcotics offenses would probably have had to be tried separately from the arson offenses.

The Court in *Turkette* emphasized that at trial the "evidence focused upon . . . the professional nature of this organization." Does this matter? If Turkette had been amateurish, should he have been able to escape RICO charges? In United States v. Patrick, 248 F.3d 11 (1st Cir. 2001), the court faced the question of how "organized" a group must be to face RICO liability.

Samuel Patrick and Jason Arthur were each convicted on over six counts of a criminal RICO indictment arising out of their membership in the Intervale Posse (IVP), a gang that distributed crack cocaine from 1990 to 1996 in the Dorchester neighborhood of Boston. Arthur was also convicted of the 1992 murder of a rival drug dealer. One of their defenses was that the IVP was simply a loose connection of individual, young drug entrepreneurs, one competing with another. RICO, they say, was meant to counter organized crime, and there was nothing particularly "organized" about the crimes committed by the IVP. . . .

_____

23. Moreover, the enterprise can be a sole proprietorship, McCullough v. Suter, 757 F.2d 142 (7th Cir. 1985), or single-owner corporation, Cedric Kushner Promotions, Ltd. v. King, 533 U.S. 158 (2001), even when the "person" charged with the RICO crime is the owner and hence arguably not really separate from the "enterprise."

. . . During the 1990s, members of the IVP sold crack cocaine in the Intervale neighborhood of Dorchester, an area of Boston. The IVP was the successor to an earlier gang, known as "Adidas Park." The gang gave a new spin to the concept of brand identification. IVP members wore Adidas clothing, identified themselves and referred to the gang by signifying the Adidas brand logo (a sign of three fingers signifying the three stripes on Adidas products), and, in a few instances, owned mirrors painted with their nicknames and the IVP logo. Members referred to one another as family. Younger members, often teenagers, "pumped" (or sold) drugs for the older members, although some younger members also operated on their own.

Patrick held the supplier's role within the IVP. He decided who could sell on IVP territory, set the prices for the IVP's crack, and directed sales by younger members. Patrick also determined when the gang would eliminate rivals. Arthur supplied crack to the IVP and also bought crack from Patrick. In addition, Arthur helped keep order in the IVP, reprimanding younger members for risky behavior that attracted police attention.

As part of the IVP's operating procedures, IVP members would page suppliers like Patrick and Arthur to deliver drugs to a customer's house. At the house, the crack was "cut" and "bagged" in smaller amounts for resale on the street, and the customer was paid in crack or money for use of the house. Although IVP members competed with one another for individual customers, they all profited from increased sales overall in the neighborhood. Only IVP members could sell on the IVP's "turf," and the gang used actual and threatened violence to deter rivals. Members held "sessions" (or meetings) where they discussed rival drug operations as well as problems with police. . . . [Id. at 15-16.]

The court held that the trial judge had rightly refused to instruct the jury that RICO required proof of some "ascertainable structure" that guided the group's decisions, whether it be "hierarchical or consensual."

. . . While "enterprise" and "pattern of racketeering activity" are separate elements of a RICO offense, proof of these two elements need not be separate or distinct but may in fact "coalesce." Turkette, 452 U.S. at 583. . . . Here, on the issue of structure and its ascertainability, the slope is slippery, and the district court appropriately avoided the slope's edge. Since Congress intended the term "enterprise" to include both legal and criminal enterprises, and because the latter may not observe the niceties of legitimate organizational structures, we refuse to import an "ascertainable structure" requirement into jury instructions.

Defendants also argue that there was insufficient evidence of any enterprise. Not so. The gang was ongoing and identifiable: it changed its name from Adidas to the IVP, it had colors and signs, it had older members who instructed younger ones, its members referred to the gang as family, and it had "sessions" where important decisions were made, including decisions about taking action against rival drug dealers.

Defendants protest that the IVP is just a motley crew of young criminals and that it hardly constitutes the type of highly sophisticated organized crime that spurred Congress to enact RICO. Even if the IVP were a fledgling criminal organization, we doubt that Congress meant to give a pass to such fledgling organizations. [Id. at 19.]

Non-economic racketeering. Even in the area of wholly criminal organizations, RICO is not limited to enterprises formed for financial gain. In United States v. Bagaric, 706 F.2d 42 (2d. Cir. 1983), a Croatian group seeking independence from Yugoslavia was convicted under RICO for various terrorist activities, including such predicates as murder, bombings, and extortion. The defendants argued that their non-economic goals put them outside the intended scope of a RICO enterprise. The court, however, noted that the gang raised its money by extorting funds from other Croatians through threats and violence and found sufficient financial motive in the extortion activities to qualify the organization as an enterprise under RICO. But that finding by the *Bagaric* court would now be unnecessary: A unanimous Supreme Court ruled in N.O.W. v. Scheidler, 510 U.S. 249 (1994), that "Congress has not either in the definitional section or in the operative language, required that an 'enterprise' in 1962(c) have an economic motive." There, an organization dedicated to opposing abortion rights was held to be an "enterprise" for civil RICO purposes, and by necessary implication for criminal RICO as well. Justice Souter, concurring, explained why the economic motive requirement was neither necessary nor desirable to ensure that RICO did not infringe on constitutionally protected speech:

> But an economic motive requirement would protect too much with respect to First Amendment interests, since it would keep RICO from reaching ideological entities whose members commit acts of violence we do not fear chilling. An economic motive requirement might also prove underprotective, in that entities engaging in vigorous but fully protected expression might fail the proposed economic motive test (for even protest movements need money). . . .
>
> An economic-motive requirement, finally, is unnecessary, because legitimate free-speech claims may be raised and addressed in individual RICO cases as they arise. . . . See NAACP v. Claiborne Hardware Co., 458 U.S. 886, 917 (1982) (holding that a state common-law prohibition on malicious interference with business could not, under the circumstances, be constitutionally applied to a civil-rights boycott of white merchants). [Id. at 263-64.]

Conduct and participation. Finally, what does it mean for an individual to "conduct or participate" in the conduct of the enterprise? Does the phrase suggest active managerial control? In United States v. Oreto, 37 F.3d 739 (1st Cir. 1994), where the enterprise was a loan-sharking operation and the "employee" was a "bill collector," the court held that even a low-level employee of the enterprise violated RICO so long as his work was necessary to the enterprise's operations. But cf. Reves v. Ernst & Young, 507 U.S. 170 (1993) (outside accounting firm contracting with enterprise held outside reach of RICO).

Must the conduct *benefit* the enterprise, or merely be associated with it? In United States v. Marino, 277 F.3d (1st Cir. 2002), drug dealers who were members of one of two disputing factions within the Patriarca crime "family" used a clubhouse owned by other Patriarca members and supplied free cocaine to family members to reward them for shootings; in addition, they invoked the name of Patriarca to frighten a third party to pay a debt. The court made clear that there was sufficient nexus between the predicate racketeering crimes and the enterprise here where the defendants used the resources, property, facilities, or their position in an enterprise to commit their crimes, even if they did not intend the crimes to benefit the enterprise. The court rejected the argument that the RICO charge required proof that the defendants plowed their profits back into the enterprise or somehow affected the overall operations of the enterprise.

3. The "Pattern" Requirement

Just what is a "pattern of racketeering activity" under 18 U.S.C. §1961(5)? The RICO statute requires "at least two acts of racketeering . . . the last of which occurred within ten years after the commission of a prior act of racketeering activity." Nevertheless, the Supreme Court has noted "that while two acts are necessary, they may not be sufficient" to establish the requisite pattern. Sedima v. Imrex, 473 U.S. 479, 496 n.14 (1985). As the Court stated,

> [t]he legislative history supports the view that two isolated acts of racketeering activity do not constitute a pattern. As the Senate Report explained: "The target of [RICO] is thus not sporadic activity. The infiltration of legitimate business normally requires more than one 'racketeering activity' and threat of continuing activity to be effective. It is this factor of continuity plus relationship which combines to produce a pattern." S. Rep. No. 91-617, p. 158 (1969) . . .

The vagueness of the "pattern" doctrine as delineated by Congress and Sedima has led to some uncertainty as to the criteria for establishing an illegal "pattern." In United States v. Indelicato, 865 F.2d 1370 (2d. Cir. 1989), these were the key facts:

> In 1979, the boss of the Bonanno family was Carmine Galante. Indelicato was a member of the family; his father was a capo; and an uncle, J.B. Indelicato, was a member. As part of an overall plan to end the factional disputes within the Bonanno family and to realign its leadership, the Commission planned and implemented the murder of Galante and two of his close associates.
>
> On July 12, 1979, Indelicato and two other men, all wearing ski masks, entered a restaurant in Brooklyn, New York, where Galante, his cousin Giuseppe Turano, and Galante's friend and associate Leonard Coppola were having lunch. . . . Indelicato and his two companions shot and killed Galante, Turano, and Coppola. The victims were shot numerous times at close range with several weapons. The evidence also showed that two other men, including Bonventre, who had accompanied Coppola to lunch and were uninjured in the shootings, had joined in shooting Coppola, Turano, and Galante. . . .
>
> The three murders were the only RICO predicate acts alleged against Indelicato. [Id. at 1372.]

The court said:

> We recognize that to the extent relatedness is to be shown by the acts' temporal proximity, there may well be a tension between relatedness and continuity, for obviously the shorter the elapsed time between the two acts, the less it can be said that the activity is continuing. Nonetheless . . . where the virtual simultaneity of two acts suggests that they are related, the timing does not negate the existence of a pattern; rather, evidence of continuity or the threat of continuity will simply have to come from facts external to those two acts. . . .
>
> . . . While temporal separation of events is a common feature of a pattern of action, it is not an essential; such a pattern may be found, for example, in the simultaneous commission of like acts for similar purposes against a number of victims. Nor, with respect to the requirement of continuity or threat of continuity, do we see any basis in RICO or its legislative history for the proposition that a RICO violation cannot be established without proof of more than one scheme, episode, or transaction, or without proof that the scheme pursuant to which the racketeering acts were performed is a scheme with no apparent termination date. . . . There

is no mention of schemes, episodes, or transactions. We doubt that Congress meant to exclude from the reach of RICO multiple acts of racketeering simply because they achieve their objective quickly or because they further but a single scheme. . . .

. . . To the extent, therefore, that the relationship between acts necessary to establish a pattern depends on the relationships between individual acts and the enterprise, there will often be some overlap of proof and analysis. The degree of overlap will vary depending in part on the substantive RICO subsection at issue. The establishment of a subsection (a) violation, for example, will likely entail less overlap, since the acts by which the tainted income is acquired need have no logical relationship to the enterprise in which investment will thereafter be made. In contrast, establishment of a subsection (c) violation will often entail overlap, for each act of racketeering activity will be related to the enterprise since the latter's affairs are by hypothesis conducted through a pattern of such acts. The differences and overlap are simply a consequence of Congress's use of the same defined terms in fashioning different substantive prohibitions. . . . Under these standards, we have little difficulty in concluding that Indelicato's participation in the three Bonanno family murders as a representative of the Commission constituted a pattern of racketeering activity within the meaning of RICO. There were three persons targeted for assassination. Though the murders were virtually simultaneous, they plainly constituted more than one act. Further, the three murders were indisputably related since the purpose for each was facilitation of the desired change in leadership of the Bonanno crime family. Though the murders themselves were quickly completed, both the nature of the Commission, which was the alleged RICO enterprise, and the criminal nature of the Bonanno family, control of which the murders were designed to achieve, made it clear beyond peradventure that there was a threat of continuing racketeering activity. The evidence was plainly ample to permit the jury to infer that the murders were part of a RICO pattern. [Id. at 1381-85.]

Is the court successful in reconciling the concepts of relatedness and continuity? Is it successful in distinguishing the criteria for establishing an enterprise from the criteria for establishing a pattern of racketeering activity? Beyond the specific conventional homicide crimes of which the defendants are certainly guilty, what is the larger harm they pose to society through the enterprise and pattern elements? What relationship does this harm bear to the harm punished by conventional conspiracy law?

The United States Supreme Court tried to settle the definition of the "pattern" requirement in H.J., Inc. v. Northwestern Bell Telephone Co., 492 U.S. 229 (1989). Rejecting an Eighth Circuit decision requiring a RICO complaint to allege multiple schemes of racketeering, the Supreme Court adopted a position essentially affirming the approach taken in *Indelicato*:

A RICO pattern may surely be established if the related predicates themselves involve a distinct threat of long-term racketeering activity, either implicit or explicit. Suppose a hoodlum were to sell "insurance" to a neighborhood's storekeepers to cover them against breakage of their windows, telling his victims he would be reappearing each month to collect the "premium" that would continue their "coverage." Though the number of related predicates involved may be small and they may occur close together in time, the racketeering acts themselves include a specific threat of repetition extending indefinitely into the future, and thus supply the requisite threat of continuity. In other cases, the threat of continuity may be established by showing that the predicate acts or offenses are part of an ongoing entity's regular way of doing business.

Does *Bell* resolve the "pattern" problem? Though "multiple schemes" are not required, is it clear what *is* required? Is the "pattern" requirement unconstitutionally vague? That is, can a reasonable person fully appreciate and anticipate what is unlawful under RICO?

4. RICO Conspiracies

As should be apparent, the "enterprise" and "pattern" elements of the substantive RICO provisions are an important prosecutorial adjunct to conspiracy law. Nevertheless, RICO contains its own special conspiracy provision as well in section 1962(d): "It shall be unlawful for any person to conspire to violate any of the provisions of subsection (a), (b), or (c) of this section." Thus, though even a "substantive" RICO violation under §1962(a)-(c) resembles a big conspiracy, the government can also invoke §1962(d) to charge a conspiracy to violate RICO.

UNITED STATES v. NEAPOLITAN
United States Court of Appeals, Seventh Circuit
791 F.2d 489 (1986)

FLAUM, CIRCUIT JUDGE.

. . . Robert Neapolitan, along with his two co-defendants, Robert Cadieux and Ronald Sapit, was employed as an investigator for the Cook County Sheriff's Police Department until his indictment in 1984 on five counts of mail fraud and one count of racketeering conspiracy. The indictment, in conjunction with the evidence adduced at trial, presents a picture of police corruption in which Officers Cadieux and Sapit at once encouraged known car thieves to supply them with automobiles and establish a "chop shop," while also soliciting bribes in the form of auto parts and cash in exchange for police protection. The evidence linking Neapolitan to the scheme shows that he entered the arrangement after its establishment and that his involvement was limited.

Neapolitan was named in four of the five alleged acts of mail fraud but was acquitted of all the mail fraud counts by the district judge. Neapolitan then went to trial as the sole defendant charged only with the RICO conspiracy — both Sapit and Cadieux pleaded guilty earlier. The government's theory under section 1962(d) can be summarized briefly. Sapit, Cadieux, and Neapolitan were alleged to have conspired to conduct the affairs of the sheriff's office, the RICO "enterprise" for purposes of this case (see U.S.C. §1961(4)), through a pattern of racketeering activity. The predicate acts constituting the pattern under 18 U.S.C. §1961(5) were the four alleged acts of mail fraud and eleven specified acts of bribery in violation of Ill. Rev. Stat. ch. 38, §33-1(d), (e). Of the listed acts of bribery, Neapolitan was identified as having been involved in only one. Thus, with the dismissal of the mail fraud counts against him, Neapolitan's involvement in the conspiracy, as it is sketched in the indictment, is limited to the solicitation of one cash bribe. . . .

. . . [T]he district court did not require that the defendants agreed personally to commit two predicate acts in a context that implicates RICO. It was sufficient for the defendant to join a conspiracy, the goal of which was the conduct of or participation in the affairs of an enterprise through a pattern of racketeering activity. Neapolitan and those defendants [in a companion case] who were acquitted of the non-RICO counts take issue with the district court's characterization of a RICO conspiracy. They contend that section 1962(d) is implicated only when a defendant agrees personally to commit two predicate acts. . . .

As an analytical starting point for divining the meaning of this aspect of the RICO statute, the defendants in both cases were charged with conspiring, as proscribed by section 1962(d), which provides:

> It shall be unlawful for any person to conspire to violate any of the provisions of subsections (a), (b), or (c) of this section,

to violate section 1962(c), which provides:

> It shall be unlawful for any person employed by or associated with any enterprise engaged in, or the activities of which affect, interstate or foreign commerce, to conduct or participate, directly or indirectly, in the conduct of such enterprise's affairs through a pattern of racketeering activity or collection of unlawful debt. . . .

. . . Under classic conspiracy law, agreeing to the commission of the conspiracy's illegitimate objectives constitutes the crime. The goal of a RICO conspiracy, as defined by section 1962(d), is a violation of RICO. The defendant need only agree to a single violation of RICO; he need not agree personally to violate the statute. . . .

. . . Section 1962(d) explicitly prohibits conspiracies to violate RICO. The natural reading of that phrase is the proscription of any agreement the object of which is the conducting of or participation in the affairs of an enterprise through a pattern of racketeering activity. In other words, rather than creating a new law of conspiracy, RICO created a new objective for traditional conspiracy law — a violation of sections 1962(a), (b), or (c). Requiring an agreement personally to commit two predicate acts would establish a new form of conspiring in contradistinction to section 1962(d)'s base in traditional conspiracy law. Under the defendants' theory, section 1962(d) would require not only an agreement to join in the conspiracy's objective, a RICO violation, but also an agreement to personally commit the underlying offense through the commission of two predicate acts. This involves a degree of involvement in the affairs of the conspiracy that is not required in any other type of conspiracy, where agreeing to a prescribed objective is sufficient.

Nothing on the face of the statute or its legislative history supports the imposition of a more stringent level of personal involvement in a conspiracy to violate RICO as opposed to a conspiracy to violate anything else. In fact, it seems more likely that Congress, in search of means to prosecute the leaders of organized crime, intended section 1962(d) to be broad enough to encompass those persons who, while intimately involved in the conspiracy, neither agreed to personally commit nor actually participated in the commission of the predicate crimes.

> The crime leaders are experienced, resourceful, and shrewd in evading and dissipating the effects of established procedures in law enforcement. Their operating methods, carefully and cleverly evolved during several decades of this century,

generally are highly effective foils against diligent police efforts to obtain firm evidence that would lead to prosecution and conviction.

The crime chieftains, for example, have developed the process of "insulation" to a remarkable degree. The efficient police forces in a particular area may well be aware that a crime leader has ordered a murder, or is an important trafficker in narcotics, or controls an illegal gambling network, or extorts usurious gains from "shylocking" ventures. Convicting him of crimes, however, is usually extremely difficult and sometimes is impossible, simply because the top-ranking criminal has taken the utmost care to insulate himself from any apparent physical connection with the crime or with his having to commit it.

Permanent Subcommittee on Investigations of the Senate Committee on Government Operations, Organized Crime and Illicit Traffic in Narcotics, S. Rep. No. 72, 89th Cong., 1st Sess. 2 (1965). . . . It is important to emphasize two aspects of the 1962(d) conspiracy that serve to limit the scope of the theory: (1) the nature of the agreement required and (2) the necessity of proving the existence of an enterprise.

. . . From a conceptual standpoint a conspiracy to violate RICO can be analyzed as composed of two agreements (in reality they would be encompassed by the same manifestations of the defendant): an agreement to conduct or participate in the affairs of an enterprise and an agreement to the commission of at least two predicate acts. Thus, a defendant who did not agree to the commission of crimes constituting a pattern of racketeering activity is not in violation of section 1962(d), even though he is somehow affiliated with a RICO enterprise, and neither is the defendant who agrees to the commission of two criminal acts but does not consent to the involvement of an enterprise. If either aspect of the agreement is lacking then there is insufficient evidence that the defendant embraced the objective of the alleged conspiracy. Thus, mere association with the enterprise would not constitute an actionable 1962(d) violation. In a RICO conspiracy, as in all conspiracies, agreement is essential. . . .

There is substantial circumstantial evidence that taken as a whole supports an inference that Neapolitan agreed to conduct the affairs of the sheriff's office through a pattern of racketeering activity and, more specifically, that he agreed to the commission of at least two of the predicate crimes listed in the indictment. First, statements were made by his alleged co-conspirators, Officers Sapit and Cadieux, to a government informant that identified Neapolitan as having been involved with the corruption in the sheriff's office arising out of the auto theft operation. Second, at the time Neapolitan received the bribe specified in the indictment, he made numerous statements, all of which were recorded, indicating that he was associated with others rather than working on his own. Third, while Neapolitan was taking his bribe, Officer Cadieux was also present to receive a payoff. There was also testimony to the effect that Cadieux arranged the meeting. This provides further evidence that Neapolitan was associated with Sapit and Cadieux and was aware of their activities. Fourth, the evidence of other crimes, while irrelevant for purposes of establishing predicate acts, is evidence of Neapolitan's link to the other officers because all these alleged crimes involved all three officers. At a minimum, this evidence establishes that Cadieux's presence at Neapolitan's bribe was not coincidence but part of an on-going relationship. Finally, it should be noted that even if one were to assume that the bribe to Neapolitan marked the commencement of his involvement, the indictment lists two other bribes, including the concurrent bribe to Cadieux, that would have occurred during Neapolitan's participation. On this record, there is sufficient evidence for a rational jury to infer that Neapolitan agreed to the commission of two of the predicate crimes that appeared in the indictment. The introduction of any non-indicted crimes for purposes of establishing a pattern of racketeering cannot, under the circumstances of this case, be deemed prejudicial. . . .

Notes and Questions

1. What scope for prosecution did the RICO conspiracy law give the government here that conventional (and very broad) federal conspiracy law does not itself provide? Does the "substantive" RICO crime itself so much resemble a conspiracy that it is "double-counting" to punish a conspiracy to violate RICO?

2. *The one-act RICO conspirator.* Though Neapolitan could not be convicted of the minimum two predicate acts, he "agreed" that an enterprise pattern of crime occurred. Some federal circuit courts held, contrary to the 7th circuit, that this one-act participant could not be guilty of RICO conspiracy, but in Salinas v. United States, 522 U.S. 52 (1997), the Supreme Court affirmed the position taken by the *Neapolitan* court:

> A conspiracy may exist even if a conspirator does not agree to commit or facilitate each and every part of the substantive offense. The partners in the criminal plan must agree to pursue the same criminal objective and divide up the work, yet each is responsible for the acts of each other. If conspirators have a plan which calls for some conspirators to perpetrate the crime and others to provide support, the supporters are as guilty as the perpetrators. As Justice Holmes observed: "[P]lainly a person may conspire for the commission of a crime by a third person." United States v. Holte, 236 U.S. 140, 144 (1915). A person, moreover, may be liable for conspiracy even though he was incapable of committing the substantive offense. . . .

> A conspirator must intend to further an endeavor which, if completed, would satisfy all of the elements of a substantive criminal offense, but it suffices that he adopt the goal of furthering or facilitating the criminal endeavor. He may do so in any number of ways short of agreeing to undertake all of the acts necessary for the crime's completion. . . .

> . . . True, though an "enterprise" under 1962(c) can exist with only one actor to conduct it, in most circumstances it will be conducted by more than one person or entity; and this in turn may make it somewhat difficult to determine just where the enterprise ends and the conspiracy begins. In some cases, the connection the defendant had to the alleged enterprise or to the conspiracy to further it may be tenuous enough so that his own commission of two predicate acts may become an important part of the Government's case. [Id. at 63-67.]

3. *RICO and enlargement of conspiracies.* The other enhancement RICO lends to conspiracy law is the government's power to "rim the wheel" of the sort of conspiracy seen earlier in Kotteakos v. United States, 328 U.S. 750 (1946), where the Court had discredited the "rimless wheel" theory of conspiracy. Thus, before RICO, where the only common element in several conspiracies was one criminal who had contact with several co-conspirators, the prosecution could not charge a single conspiracy. In United States v. Elliot, 571 F.2d 880 (5th Cir. 1978), six defendants and 37 unindicted co-conspirators were implicated in more than 20 different criminal endeavors, but the prosecution only charged a single conspiracy to violate RICO. The predicate crimes in *Elliot,* committed

between 1970 and 1976, included arson, dealing in narcotics, car theft, murder, jury tampering, and dealing in stolen meat. The common thread of all predicate crimes was ringleader J.C. Hawkins; indeed, for some of the crimes he was the only connecting thread. For example, to run the car theft ring, which operated from 1971 to 1974, Hawkins supplied counterfeit titles to codefendants Ervin Delph and John Taylor, who then marketed the car titles to car thieves. The arson element of the conspiracy, on the other hand, arose out of an unrelated incident in 1970 when codefendant William Foster hired Hawkins and his brother, codefendant Recea Hawkins, to burn a nursing home that Foster's construction company had just completed. Because these and other predicate crimes seemed unrelated, the defendants argued on appeal that the prosecution could not establish a single conspiracy to violate RICO. At first blush, the conspiracy in *Elliot* looked more like a rimless wheel than a chain. However, as the court explained:

> [W]e are convinced that, through RICO, Congress intended to authorize the single prosecution of a multifaceted, diversified conspiracy by replacing the inadequate "wheel" and "chain" rationales with a new statutory concept: the enterprise. . . .
>
> [T]he object of a RICO conspiracy is to violate a substantive RICO provision — here, to conduct or participate in the affairs of an enterprise through a pattern of racketeering activity. The gravamen of the conspiracy charge in this case is not that each defendant agreed to commit arson, to steal goods from interstate commerce to obstruct justice, and to sell narcotics; rather, it is that each agreed to participate, directly and indirectly, in the affairs of the enterprise by committing two or more predicate crimes. Under the statute, it is irrelevant that each defendant participated in the enterprise's affairs through different, even unrelated crimes, so long as we may reasonably infer that each was intended to further the enterprise's affairs. [Id. at 902.]

Elliot has established that RICO conspiracies cut a wider swath than standard conspiracy law. Does this wider swath represent a clear departure from former law, or just an expansion of the incidents of conspiracy previously discussed? Has conspiracy law reached its limit?

13

CRIMINAL LIABILITY OF CORPORATIONS

This chapter addresses when and how the actions of individual officers, directors, or employees within a business enterprise might make the enterprise itself criminally liable. Although in our legal system the business enterprise — most often a corporation — is theoretically a distinct legal entity, its "behavior" must obviously consist of the behavior of individuals within the enterprise. Thus, the criminal liability of the enterprise is, in effect, a form of accomplice liability. If, as we have shown in Chapter 11, the law of complicity attributes to one person the acts of another whose crimes she consents to, encourages, or abets, then corporate criminal liability similarly attributes to the corporate "person" the criminal acts of individual persons who are a part of, or act in behalf of, that entity. The relationship of individual to corporate behavior under the criminal law is a complex one that provides an interesting supplement to the larger issue we examined in Chapter 11 — the relative liability of multiple parties to a crime.

The first section of this chapter establishes how the ancient doctrine of respondeat superior — the vicarious liability of a party for unlawful actions taken by the party's employee or agent — provides the foundation for the criminal liability of the corporation for the acts of its owners, managers, or employees. The second section examines how courts and legislatures, adapting this form of vicarious liability to the modern complex business organization, have derived workable models of the "mens rea of the corporation" from the various acts and mental states of corporate agents. The last section applies these concepts to an emerging and vexing area — corporate criminal liability for homicide.

A. RESPONDEAT SUPERIOR AND THE PREMISES OF CORPORATE LIABILITY

STATE v. CHRISTY PONTIAC-GMC, INC.
Supreme Court of Minnesota
354 N.W.2d 17 (1984)

SIMONETT, JUSTICE.
We hold that a corporation may be convicted of theft and forgery, which are crimes requiring specific intent, and that the evidence sustains defendant corporation's guilt.

In a bench trial, defendant-appellant Christy Pontiac-GMC, Inc., was found guilty of two counts of theft by swindle and two counts of aggravated forgery, and was sentenced to a $1,000 fine on each of the two forgery convictions. Defendant argues that as a corporation it cannot, under our state statutes, be prosecuted or convicted for theft or forgery and that, in any event, the evidence fails to establish that the acts complained of were the acts of the defendant corporation.

Christy Pontiac is a Minnesota corporation, doing business as a car dealership. It is owned by James Christy, a sole stockholder, who serves also as president and as director. In the spring of 1981, General Motors offered a cash rebate program for its dealers. A customer who purchased a new car delivered during the rebate period was entitled to a cash rebate, part paid by GM and part paid by the dealership. GM would pay the entire rebate initially and later charge back, against the dealer, the dealer's portion of the rebate. Apparently it was not uncommon for the dealer to give the customer the dealer's portion of the rebate in the form of a discount on the purchase price.

[The evidence showed that employees of Christy Pontiac twice forged customers' signatures to obtain and to pocket for the dealership the customers' share of the rebate. One of the salesmen who did the forgeries, Phil Hesli, was convicted of theft in a separate trial.]

Christy Pontiac argues on several grounds that a corporation cannot be held criminally liable for a specific intent crime. . . . This should be so, argues defendant, because the legislature has defined a crime as "conduct which is prohibited by statute and for which the actor may be sentenced to imprisonment, with or without a fine," Minn. Stat. §609.02, subd. 1 (1982), and a corporation cannot be imprisoned. Neither, argues defendant, can an artificial person entertain a mental state, let alone have the specific intent required for theft or forgery.

We are not persuaded by these arguments. . . . The legislature has not expressly excluded corporations from criminal liability and, therefore, we take its intent to be that corporations are to be considered persons within the meaning of the Code in the absence of any clear indication to the contrary. . . . Interestingly, the specific statutes under which the defendant corporation was convicted, sections 609.52 (theft) and 609.625 (aggravated forgery), expressly state that the sentence may be either imprisonment or a fine.

Nor are we troubled by any anthropomorphic implications in assigning specific intent to a corporation for theft or forgery. There was a time when the law, in its logic, declared that a legal fiction could not be a person for purposes of criminal liability, at least with respect to offenses involving specific intent, but that time is gone. If a corporation can be liable in civil tort for both actual and punitive damages for libel, assault and battery, or fraud, it would seem it may also be criminally liable for conduct requiring specific intent. Most courts today recognize that corporations may be guilty of specific intent crimes. . . . Particularly apt candidates for corporate criminality are types of crime, like theft by swindle and forgery, which often occur in a business setting. . . .

. . . In what sense, then, does a corporation "do" something for which it can be convicted of a crime? . . . If a corporation is to be criminally liable, it is clear that the crime must not be a personal aberration of an employee acting on his own; the criminal activity must, in some sense, reflect corporate policy so that it is fair to say that the activity was the activity of the corporation. There must be, as Judge Learned Hand put it, a "kinship of the act to the powers of the officials, who commit it." United States v. Nearing, 252 F. 223, 231 (S.D.N.Y. 1918).

We believe, first of all, the jury should be told that it must be satisfied beyond a reasonable doubt that the acts of the individual agent constitute the acts of the corporation. Secondly, as to the kind of proof required, we hold that a corporation may be guilty of a specific intent crime committed by its agent if: (1) the agent was acting within the course and scope of his or her employment, having the authority to act for the corporation with respect to the particular corporate business which was conducted criminally; (2) the agent was acting, at least in part, in furtherance of the corporation's business interests; and (3) the criminal acts were authorized, tolerated, or ratified by corporate management.

This test is not quite the same as the test for corporate vicarious liability for a civil tort of an agent. The burden of proof is different, and, unlike civil liability, criminal guilt requires that the agent be acting at least in part in furtherance of the corporation's business interests. . . . Moreover, it must be shown that corporate management authorized, tolerated, or ratified the criminal activity. Ordinarily, this will be shown by circumstantial evidence, for it is not to be expected that management authorization of illegality would be expressly or openly stated. Indeed, there may be instances where the corporation is criminally liable even though the criminal activity has been expressly forbidden. What must be shown is that from all the facts and circumstances, those in positions of managerial authority or responsibility acted or failed to act in such a manner that the criminal activity reflects corporate policy, and it can be said, therefore, that the criminal act was authorized or tolerated or ratified by the corporation.

. . . The evidence shows that Hesli, the forger, had authority and responsibility to handle new car sales and to process and sign cash rebate applications. Christy Pontiac, not Hesli, got the GM rebate money, so that Hesli was acting in furtherance of the corporation's business interests. Moreover, there was sufficient evidence of management authorization, toleration, and ratification. Hesli himself, though not an officer, had middle management responsibilities for cash rebate applications. When the customer Gores asked Mr. Benedict, a salesman, about the then discontinued rebate, Benedict referred Gores to Phil Hesli. Gary Swandy, a corporate officer, signed the backdated retail buyer's order form for the Linden sale. James Christy, the president, attempted to negotiate a settlement with Gores after Gores complained. Not until after the Attorney General's inquiry did Christy contact divisional GM headquarters. As the trial judge noted, the rebate money "was so obtained and accepted by Christy Pontiac and kept by Christy Pontiac until somebody blew the whistle. . . ." We conclude the evidence establishes that the theft by swindle and the forgeries constituted the acts of the corporation.

We wish to comment further on two aspects of the proof. First, it seems that the state attempted to prosecute both Christy Pontiac and James Christy, but its prosecution of Mr. Christy failed for lack of evidence. We can imagine a different situation where the corporation is the alter ego of its owner and it is the owner who alone commits the crime, where a double prosecution might be deemed fundamentally unfair. Secondly, it may seem incongruous that Hesli, the forger, was acquitted of three of the four criminal counts for which the corporation was convicted. Still, this is not the first time different trials have had different results. We are reviewing this record, and it sustains the convictions.

Notes and Questions

1. The court states the basic premise of corporate criminal liability — that under certain circumstances "the acts of the individual agent constitute the acts of the corporation." To understand why and when that is so, consider the following excerpt: [1]

Respondeat Superior. — The respondeat superior doctrine of corporate criminal liability, derived from agency principles of tort law, is the common law rule in the federal courts and in most state courts today. . . . Proving specific intent should be the same for a corporation as for an individual defendant, because under respondeat superior, the intent of the offending agent is imputed directly to the corporation. However, since the corporation is perceived as an aggregation of its agents, it is not necessary to prove that a specific person acted illegally, only that *some* agent of the corporation committed the crime. Thus, proving that a corporate defendant committed the illegal act is in practice substantially easier than an individual prosecution.

Courts have also found the requirement of corporate criminal intent satisfied where no agent's criminal intent has been shown. Corporations have been convicted of crimes requiring knowledge on the basis of the "collective knowledge" of the employees as a group, even though no single employee possessed sufficient information to know that the crime was being committed. For example, in United States v. T.I.M.E.-D.C., Inc., [381 F. Supp. 730 (W.D. Va. 1974),] a trucking company was found guilty of knowingly violating an ICC regulation which forbade truckers from driving when ill. One employee, a dispatcher, knew that the driver in question had telephoned to say he could not work, and then changed his mind after learning of the company's new absentee policy. Corporate officers, the court found, knew that the harsh new policy was likely to encourage truckers to drive despite being ill. Through the collective knowledge of the dispatcher and the officers, the corporation was found to have known that the driver was unfit to drive under the ICC regulation. . . .

Second, to establish corporate liability under the doctrine of respondeat superior, the prosecution must show that the illegal act was committed within the agent's scope of employment. The traditional agency definition limits scope of employment to conduct that is authorized, explicitly or implicitly, by the principal or that is similar or incidental to authorized conduct. However, courts generally find conduct to fall within the scope of employment even if it was specifically forbidden by a superior and occurred despite good faith efforts on the part of the corporation to prevent the crime. Thus, scope of employment in practice means little more than the act occurred while the offending employee was carrying out a job-related activity. This extension is essential, for if scope of employment were limited to authorized conduct under the doctrine of respondeat superior, a corporation could too easily evade criminal liability. The board of directors, for example, could protect a corporation from liability for the acts of all officers and employees through a simple prohibition of illegal conduct, thus placing such conduct outside the scope of employment.

Third, it must be proved that the agent committed the crime with the intent to benefit the corporation. The corporation may be held criminally liable even if it received no actual benefit from the offense, although the existence or absence of benefit is relevant as evidence of an intent to benefit.

1. Note, Developments in the Law — Corporate Crime: Regulating Corporate Behavior Through Criminal Sanctions, 92 Harv. L. Rev. 1227, 1247-51 (1979).

The requirements of scope of employment and intent to benefit the corporation can also be met through ratification. When an employee commits a crime with no intent to benefit the corporation, or while acting outside the scope of his employment, subsequent approval of the act by his supervisor will be sufficient to hold the corporation liable for the employee's criminal act. In a sense, under the doctrine of ratification, a corporation is culpable for approving the criminal act, rather than committing it.

As summarized in this commentary, vicarious liability of a corporation for the acts of its agents is *not* limited to so-called malum prohibitum crimes, while such a limitation on the vicarious liability might apply to an employer who is a natural person. Is the distinction sound, on the theory that we cannot feel much empathy for a corporation?[2]

2. By what reasoning did the jury acquit Hesli of several of the criminal counts? Why might the prosecution of James Christy have failed? Consider this comment on the relationship between individual and corporate liability:[3]

. . . A number of appellate opinions reveal situations in which juries have held the corporate defendant criminally liable while acquitting the obviously guilty agents who committed the criminal acts.

This may reflect more than faulty or capricious judgment on the part of the juries. It may represent a recognition that the social consequences of a criminal conviction may fall with a disproportionately heavy impact on the individual defendants where the conduct involved is not of a highly immoral character. It may also reflect a shrewd belief that the violation may have been produced by pressures on the subordinates created by corporate managerial officials even though the latter may not have intended or desired the criminal behavior and even though the pressures can only be sensed rather than demonstrated. . . .

. . . In [these cases], the jury had corporate liability available as an alternative to acquittal of all of the defendants. Conceivably, if that alternative had not been available, verdicts against the individuals in some of the cases might have been returned. Thus, it is at least possible that corporate liability encourages erratic jury behavior. It may be true that the complexities of organization characteristic of large corporate enterprise at times present real problems of identifying the guilty individual and establishing his criminal liability. It would be hoped, however, that more could be pointed to in justification of placing the pecuniary burdens of criminal fines on the innocent than the difficulties of proving the guilt of the culpable individual. Where there is concrete evidence that the difficulties are real, however, the effectuation of regulatory policy may be thought to justify the means. . . .

---

2. State and federal courts have construed a wide variety of criminal statutes to impose liability on corporations as well as individual persons. Here is a list helpfully supplied by one court, Commonwealth v. McIlwain School Bus Lines, 423 A.2d 413 (Pa. Supr. 1980): See, e.g., United States v. Johns-Manville Corporation, 231 F. Supp. 690 (E.D. Pa. 1964) (antitrust, conspiracy); People v. Schomig, 74 Cal. App. 109, 239 P. 413 (1925) (violation of legislation regulating real estate brokerages); West Valley Estates, Inc. v. Florida, Fla. App., 286 So. 2d 208 (1973) (violation of statute proscribing dredging of lands); State v. Adjustment Dept. Credit Bureau, Inc., 94 Idaho 156, 483 P.2d 687 (1971) (extortion); People v. Duncan, 363 Ill. 495, 2 N.E.2d 705 (1936) (violation of Motor Fuel Tax Act); G. & H. Cattle Co. v. Commonwealth, 312 Ky. 315, 227 S.W.2d 420 (1950) (nuisance, pollution); Telegram Newspaper Co. v. Commonwealth, 172 Mass. 294, 52 N.E. 445 (1898) (criminal contempt); People v. Canadian Fur Trappers' Corp., 248 N.Y. 159, 161 N.E. 455 (1928) (larceny); Commonwealth v. American Baseball Club of Philadelphia, 290 Pa. 136, 138 A. 497 (1927) (violation of Sunday laws); Vulcan Last Co. v. State, 194 Wis. 636, 217 N.W. 412 (1928) (attempt to influence votes of employees in referendum election).

3. Model Penal Code and Commentaries, Part I, American Law Institute, at 333-34 (1985).

3. *The Arthur Andersen trial and the elements of vicarious liability.* Under the principle of respondeat superior, what happens if all the jurors in a criminal prosecution of the company agree that a company employee, acting within the scope of her duty, committed a crime, but the jurors cannot agree on which particular employee was the violator? Would a unanimous vote for conviction actually fail to meet the requirement of a unanimous jury verdict?

This very question arose in the criminal prosecution of the Arthur Andersen accounting firm, in the first completed criminal trial to arise from the Enron scandal. In United States v. Arthur Andersen, LLP, one of the nation's largest accounting firms (technically a partnership, not a corporation), was prosecuted for obstruction of justice, on the theory that a company employee had destroyed documents that might be sought in proceedings against Andersen or Enron. At a dramatic point during jury deliberations, the jurors sent the following note to Judge Melinda Harmon of the United States District Court in Houston. "If each of us believes that one Andersen agent acted knowingly and with corrupt intent, is it [necessary] for all of is to believe it was the same agent? Can one believe it was agent A, another believe it was agent B, and another believe it was agent C?" After hearing argument on this question, Judge Harmon lamented, "If someone knows of a case that's directly on point, I would really urge you to give me [the citation] right now so I don't make a mistake and rule incorrectly."[4]

Ultimately, Judge Harmon sided with the government and instructed the jurors that so long as each individual juror believed that some company agent had acted with the required specific intent to destroy evidence, then there need be no jury consensus on the identity of the culpable agent. The issue became moot when the jurors all agreed that one named company employee was the violator. Nevertheless, it provoked discussion of whether Judge Harmon had implicitly expanded the scope of enterprise liability.[5]

Would the instruction have allowed the jurors to convict where they were divided on whether a required element of the crime had been proved? Or was any uncertainty about the identity of the violator merely a matter of the *means* by which the crime was done, rather than whether the elements had been proved? Consider two polar cases. First, a defendant is prosecuted for illegally possessing an unlicensed firearm; the jurors agree that she possessed an unlicensed gun, but disagree on which of several guns introduced in evidence was the one she possessed. Second, the Continuing Criminal Enterprise law, 18 U.S.C. §848, augments penalties for drug criminals who engage in a "continuing series of violations." In convicting a defendant, need the jurors agree on which specific predicate offenses the defendant had committed, so long as they unanimously agree that he committed three? In the former case, the verdict is proper. See United States v. Verrechia, 196 F.3d 294 (1st Cir. 1999). In the latter, it is not. Richardson v. United States, 526 U.S. 813 (1999). What concern might explain the difference in the two holdings? Which holding should apply to the instruction in *Andersen*? How does the particular context of corporate criminal liability bear on which holding should apply?

4. The court in *Christy Pontiac* suggests, in dictum: "Indeed, there may be instances where the corporation is criminally liable even though the criminal activity has been expressly forbidden." The next case tests that proposition.

---

4. Kurt Eichenwald, Andersen Jury Startles Court with Question, N.Y. Times, June 14, 2002, at C1.

5. See Elkan Abramowitz & Barry Bohrer, Andersen Jury Instruction; A New Collective Corporate Liability?, N.Y.L.J. 3 (July 2, 2002).

UNITED STATES v. HILTON HOTELS CORP.
United States Court of Appeals, Ninth Circuit
467 F.2d 1000 (1972)

BROWNING, CIRCUIT JUDGE.

This is an appeal from a conviction under an indictment charging a violation of section 1 of the Sherman Act, 15 U.S.C. §1.

Operators of hotels, restaurants, hotel and restaurant supply companies, and other businesses in Portland, Oregon, organized an association to attract conventions to their city. To finance the association, members were asked to make contributions in predetermined amounts. Companies selling supplies to hotels were asked to contribute an amount equal to one percent of their sales to hotel members. To aid collections, hotel members, including appellant, agreed to give preferential treatment to suppliers who paid their assessments, and to curtail purchases from those who did not.

The jury was instructed that such an agreement by the hotel members, if proven, would be a per se violation of the Sherman Act. Appellant argues that this was [an] error. . . .

Appellant's president testified that it would be contrary to the policy of the corporation for the manager of one of its hotels to condition purchases upon payment of a contribution to a local association by the supplier. The manager of appellant's Portland hotel and his assistant testified that it was the hotel's policy to purchase supplies solely on the basis of price, quality, and service. They also testified that on two occasions they told the hotel's purchasing agent that he was to take no part in the boycott. The purchasing agent confirmed the receipt of these instructions, but admitted that, despite them, he had threatened a supplier with loss of the hotel's business unless the supplier paid the association assessment. He testified that he violated his instructions because of anger and personal pique toward the individual representing the supplier.

Based upon this testimony, appellant requested certain instructions bearing upon the criminal liability of a corporation for the unauthorized acts of its agents. These requests were rejected by the trial court. The court instructed the jury that a corporation is liable for the acts and statements of its agents "within the scope of their employment," defined to mean "in the corporation's behalf in performance of the agent's general line of work," including "not only that which has been authorized by the corporation, but also that which outsiders could reasonably assume the agent would have authority to do." The court added:

> A corporation is responsible for acts and statements of its agents, done or made within the scope of their employment, even though their conduct may be contrary to their actual instructions or contrary to the corporation's stated policies.

Appellant objects only to the court's concluding statement. . . .

The intention to impose such liability is sometimes express, but it may also be implied. The text of the Sherman Act does not expressly resolve the issue. For the reasons that follow, however, we think the construction of the Act that best achieves its purpose is that a corporation is liable for acts of its agents within the scope of their authority even when done against company orders. . . .

Because of the nature of Sherman Act offenses and the context in which they normally occur, the factors that militate against allowing a corporation to disown the criminal acts of its agents apply with special force to Sherman Act violations.

Sherman Act violations are commercial offenses. They are usually motivated by a desire to enhance profits. They commonly involve large, complex, and highly decentralized corporate business enterprises, and intricate business processes, practices, and arrangements. More often than not they also involve basic policy decisions, and must be implemented over an extended period of time.

Complex business structures, characterized by decentralization and delegation of authority, commonly adopted by corporations for business purposes, make it difficult to identify the particular corporate agents responsible for Sherman Act violations. At the same time, it is generally true that high management officials for whose conduct the corporate directors and stockholders are the most clearly responsible, are likely to have participated in the policy decisions underlying Sherman Act violations, or at least to have become aware of them.

Violations of the Sherman Act are a likely consequence of the pressure to maximize profits that is commonly imposed by corporate owners upon managing agents and, in turn, upon lesser employees. In the face of that pressure, generalized directions to obey the Sherman Act, with the probable effect of [forgoing] profits, are the least likely to be taken seriously. And if a violation of the Sherman Act occurs, the corporation, and not the individual agents, will have realized the profits from the illegal activity.

In sum, identification of the particular agents responsible for a Sherman Act violation is especially difficult, and their conviction and punishment is peculiarly ineffective as a deterrent. At the same time, conviction and punishment of the business entity itself is likely to be both appropriate and effective.

For these reasons we conclude that as a general rule a corporation is liable under the Sherman Act for the acts of its agents in the scope of their employment, even though contrary to general corporate policy and express instructions to the agent.

Thus the general policy statements of appellant's president were no defense. Nor was it enough that appellant's manager told the purchasing agent that he was not to participate in the boycott. The purchasing agent was authorized to buy all of appellant's supplies. Purchases were made on the basis of specifications, but the purchasing agent exercised complete authority as to source. He was in a unique position to add the corporation's buying power to the force of the boycott. Appellant could not gain exculpation by issuing general instructions without undertaking to enforce those instructions by means commensurate with the obvious risks. . . .

Affirmed.

Notes and Questions

1. Does the court's rejection of Hilton's defense raise the concern that vicarious criminal liability for an employer may leave nothing an employer can do to protect himself? Or was the court right in suggesting that Hilton could have taken steps to enforce its policy? In any event, is there any legal significance in a corporation's having established a policy against criminal activity by its employees, given the general presumption in our jurisprudence that all citizens know the criminal law?

Assume that the XYZ Corporation owns 15,000 stores around the country, each operated by a corporation employee (not a franchisee). Assume that the corporation president regularly sends to all store operators vigorous messages reminding the operators that they must comply with all local health and safety codes, adding that the company will fire any operator who is fined or punished for violating a local law. Assume that, in addition, the company sends inspectors to visit each store at least four times a year to ensure that the stores are complying with local laws. If one store operator nevertheless violates a local health law just after one of the company inspections, is the corporation criminally liable? What if the store operator bribes a police officer not to ticket customers?

2. Some recent cases have softened the holding of *Hilton*. In United States v. Beusch, 596 F.2d 871 (9th Cir. 1981), Deak & Company, a foreign currency exchange dealer, was convicted of 377 misdemeanor violations when its vice-president, Beusch, failed to make federally required reports of large transactions. The court confirmed that "a corporation *may* be liable for acts of its employees done contrary to express instructions and policies . . . but the existence of such instructions and policies may be considered in determining whether the employee in fact acted to benefit the corporation." [Id. at 877 (emphasis in original).]

3. *The liquidated defendant.* What if a corporate defendant has gone out of business before the trial? See United States v. Central National Bank, 705 F. Supp. 336 (S.D. Tex. 1988) (any successor corporation, as in a merger, which is obligated on the earlier firm's commercial liabilities can also be criminally prosecuted).

4. *Other entities.* Can a partnership be prosecuted in the same way as a corporation? New York says it can. People v. Lessoff & Berger, 608 N.Y.S.2d 54, 159 Misc. 2d 1096 (1994) (law partnership can be liable for crime committed by one partner).

B.   THE MPC AND THE "CORPORATE MIND"

The Model Penal Code contains a complex provision establishing when a corporation is criminally liable for the act of a corporate agent. But the key significance of the MPC in this area is that for certain categories of crime, it modifies the traditional notion of respondeat superior by requiring some manifest level of culpability on the part of high enterprise officials. Thus, the MPC moves at least partly toward identifying actual human decisionmakers to represent the "corporate mind," and on whom to focus efforts at deterrence.

MODEL PENAL CODE
American Law Institute

Section 2.07. Liability of Corporations, Unincorporated Associations and Persons Acting, or Under a Duty to Act, in Their Behalf

(1) A corporation may be convicted of the commission of an offense if:

(a) the offense is a violation or the offense is defined by a statute other than the Code in which a legislative purpose to impose liability on corporations plainly appears and the conduct is performed by an agent of the corporation acting in behalf of the corporation within the scope of his office or employment, except that if the law defining the offense designates the agents for whose conduct the corporation is accountable or the circumstances under which it is accountable, such provisions shall apply; or

(b) the offense consists of an omission to discharge a specific duty of affirmative performance imposed on corporations by law; or

(c) the commission of the offense was authorized, requested, commanded, performed or recklessly tolerated by the board of directors or by a high managerial agent acting in behalf of the corporation within the scope of his office or employment.

(2) When absolute liability is imposed for the commission of an offense, a legislative purpose to impose liability on a corporation shall be assumed, unless the contrary plainly appears. . . .

(4) As used in this Section: . . .

(b) "agent" means any director, officer, servant, employee or other person authorized to act in behalf of the corporation or association and, in the case of an unincorporated association, a member of such association;

(c) "high managerial agent" means an officer of a corporation or an unincorporated association, or, in the case of a partnership, a partner, or any other agent of a corporation or association having duties of such responsibility that his conduct may fairly be assumed to represent the policy of the corporation or association.

(5) In any prosecution of a corporation or an unincorporated association for the commission of an offense included within the terms of Subsection (1)(a) or Subsection (3)(a) of this Section, other than an offense for which absolute liability has been imposed, it shall be a defense if the defendant proves by a preponderance of evidence that the high managerial agent having supervisory responsibility over the subject matter of the offense employed due diligence to prevent its commission. This paragraph shall not apply if it is plainly inconsistent with the legislative purpose in defining the particular offense.

MODEL PENAL CODE AND COMMENTARIES
Part I, American Law Institute, at 333-34 (1985)

Subsection (1)(a) . . . recognizes corporate responsibility for the commission of violations, whether defined by the Code or by other statutes. The term "violation," defined in Section 1.04(5), refers generally to those minor offenses that are not classified as crimes and that are punishable only by fine. Subsection (1)(a) is thus a reflection of the judgment that liability for the more serious offenses defined by a criminal code — misdemeanors and felonies — should be ascribed to corporations only after the satisfaction of a more rigorous standard than the one it sets forth. Accordingly, unless the offense is a violation or the offense is defined by a statute other than the criminal code and plainly reflects a legislative purpose to impose liability on corporations, corporate criminal liability will be measured by the standard established in Subsection (1)(c).

. . . Subsection (1)(b) deals with a situation where the criminal law speaks explicitly to corporations, and thus like Subsection (1)(a) leaves the question of more general liability to Subsection (1)(c). The reference to a "specific" duty imposed on corporations by law is designed to make it clear that the provision does not govern in such a case as negligent homicide, where the duty violated is one that the law imposes generally. Rather, the section will apply when there is a failure, for example, to file a report of a kind that the corporation is specifically required to file, or to maintain records that the corporation is required by law to keep. Virtually all revisions with provisions for corporate liability have a similar provision.

. . . Subsection (1)(c) governs the general liability of corporations for crimes defined by the criminal code. In essence, it defines the types of conduct engaged in by corporate officials that will result in charging the offense to the entity.

. . . The direct burden of a corporate fine is visited upon the shareholders of the corporation. In most cases, the shareholders have not participated in the criminal conduct and lack the practical means of supervision of corporate management to prevent misconduct by corporate agents. This is not to say, of course, that all the policy considerations at issue in imposing vicarious responsibility on a human principal are present to the same degree in the corporate cases. Two fundamental distinctions should be noted. First, the fact that the corporation is the party nominally convicted means that the individual shareholders escape the opprobrium and incidental disabilities that normally follow a personal conviction or even indictment. Second, the shareholder's loss is limited to his equity in the corporation. His personal assets are not ordinarily subject to levy and the conviction of the corporation will not result in loss of liberty to the stockholders. Nevertheless, the fact that the direct impact of corporate fines is felt by a group ordinarily innocent of criminal conduct underscores the point that such fines ought not to be authorized except where they clearly may be expected to accomplish desirable social purposes. To the extent that shareholders participate in criminal conduct, or to the extent that there are unlawful transactions involving the shareholders' holdings, they may be reached directly through application of the ordinary principles of criminal liability.

It would seem that the ultimate justification of corporate criminal responsibility must rest in large measure on an evaluation of the deterrent effects of corporate fines on the conduct of corporate agents. Is there a reason for anticipating a substantially higher degree of deterrence from fines levied on corporate bodies than can fairly be anticipated from proceeding directly against the guilty officer or agent or from other feasible sanctions of a noncriminal character?

It may be assumed that ordinarily a corporate agent is not likely to be deterred from criminal conduct by the prospect of corporate liability when, in any event, he faces the prospect of individually suffering serious criminal penalties for his own act. If the agent cannot be prevented from committing an offense by the prospect of personal liability, he ordinarily will not be prevented by the prospect of corporate liability.

Yet the problem cannot be resolved so simply. For there are probably cases in which the economic pressures within the corporate body are sufficiently potent to tempt individuals to hazard personal liability for the sake of company gain, especially where the penalties threatened are moderate and where the offense does not involve behavior condemned as highly immoral by the individual's associates. . . .

The approach of Subsection (1)(c) is to provide for a more restricted basis of liability for all cases not included within the terms of Subsections (1)(a) and (1)(b). The general respondeat superior approach of Subsection (1)(a) is rejected for these cases, and corporate liability is confined to situations in which the criminal conduct is performed, participated in or recklessly tolerated by the board of directors or by corporate officers or agents sufficiently high in the hierarchy to make it reasonable to assume that their acts are in some substantial sense reflective of the policy of the corporate body. The agents having such power to make the corporation criminally liable are described by the terms of Subsection (1)(c) as the board of directors or any "high managerial agent acting in behalf of the corporation within the scope of his office or employment." The phrase "high managerial agent" is defined in Subsection (4)(c). Given the wide variations in corporate structure, these criteria are necessarily very general. But taken with Subsection (4)(c), they are considerably more precise than those enunciated by many courts as a matter of decisional law. . . .

In practical effect, Subsection (1)(c) would result in corporate liability for the conduct of the corporate president or general manager but not for conduct of a foreman in a large plant or of an insignificant branch manager in the absence of participation at higher levels of corporate authority. The provision thus works a substantial limitation on corporate responsibility in cases in which the deterrent effects of corporate fines are most dubious but preserves it in cases in which the shareholders are most likely to be in a position to bring pressures to bear to prevent corporate crime. . . .

Notes and Questions

1. *The MPC cuts back vicarious liability.* The Code clearly intends to narrow the scope of respondeat superior liability imposed in many federal and state courts. The most controversial part of section 2.07 is subsection (1)(c), which greatly limits the liability of the corporation for "true crimes" (or common law offenses or malum in se crimes), by requiring proof that the board of directors or a high managerial agent "authorized, requested, commanded, performed or recklessly tolerated" the offense.

Under section 2.07, if in *Hilton Hotels,* the purchasing agent's purposeful antitrust violation was the sort of crime covered by section 2.07(1)(c), would the Hilton corporation have been liable? Could the corporation rely on its express policy against illegal "refusals to deal" to invoke the "due diligence" defense of section 2.07(5)?

Is subsection (2) a fair compromise on strict liability? Is subsection (5) too generous a defense?

2. One commentator[6] vigorously applauds the principle of corporate liability for the acts of directors, officers, or high managerial agents on the ground that this principle alone contains a coherent notion of the mens rea of an abstract entity:

> . . . [I]f a non-elected high managerial agent shows signs of dereliction, the shareholders will, or ought to, exert pressure in order to cause his removal from a position of command, or at least to restrain him from wrongdoing. Thus, we can call all those officers, whether elected or appointed, who direct, supervise and manage the corporation within its business sphere and policy-wise, the "inner circle." They are the *mens,* the mind or brain, of the corporation. . . .
>
> . . . Likening a corporation to a natural person for the purpose of criminal law administration is not an outgrowth of the "psychological tendency toward personification," as Machen suggested,[7] but is a rational interpretation of the theory

6. Gerhard Mueller, Mens Rea and the Corporation, 19 U. Pitt. L. Rev. 21, 40-41 (1957).
7. Arthur Machen, Corporate Personality, 24 Harv. L. Rev. 253, 347 (1911).

of the corporate fiction for purposes of the application of a rational theory of corporate criminal liability on the basis of the guilt-deterrence orientation of the common law of crimes.

On the same principle, Mueller goes on to denounce vicarious corporate liability for the acts of lower-level corporate agents:

> As far as discussed in the previous section, the Code is entirely in keeping with orthodox principles of criminal liability. But when the Code goes further, as it does in section 2.07(1)(a), and extends criminal liability of the corporation to independent acts of inferior employees, i.e., not those who are members of the inner circle, it subjects the corporation to liability for acts which "it" (as represented by the inner circle) has not willed, not directed, not authorized. In such a case not only does the corporation lack *mens rea*, it even lacks mental self-direction. Here the hand has moved without order from the brain. To impose liability for such a movement of the corporate hand would be analogous to subjecting an epileptic to criminal liability for the harm done by a motion of his hand, not willed, but solely the reflex of an epileptic fit.

Hyperbole aside, is Mueller's analogy overdone in substance?

3. *Imputing corporate liability back to the individual.* Since MPC §2.07(1)(c) requires the equivalent of recklessness on the part of high corporate agents as a predicate for corporate liability for serious crimes, it may have implications for the individual liability of those agents. If a company is charged under that provision, should it follow that an agent be charged as well? One would think that the government would have to prove that the individual agent possessed the mens rea normally required for individual liability under the statute. But note another provision of the MPC:

> §2.07(6)(a). A person is legally accountable for any conduct he performs or causes to be performed in the name of the corporation or an unincorporated association or in its behalf to the same extent as if it were performed in his own name or behalf.
>
> (b) Whenever a duty to act is imposed by law upon a corporation or an unincorporated association, any agent of the corporation or association having primary responsibility for the discharge of the duty is legally accountable for a reckless omission to perform the required act to the same extent as if the duty were imposed by law directly upon himself.
>
> (c) When a person is convicted of an offense by reason of his legal accountability for the conduct of a corporation or an unincorporated association, he is subject to the sentence authorized by law when a natural person is convicted of an offense of the grade and the degree involved.

If the corporation is charged with a crime requiring purpose with respect to key elements, does this rule effectively modify the normal mens rea requirements for the individual liability of the official? Is it consistent with the principles of the mens rea for complicity we saw in Chapter 11?

Some commentators have suggested that the special challenge of deterring criminal conduct within large corporations and the difficulty of piercing the corporate veil to prove that an official acted purposefully or knowingly require a compromise standard based on recklessness or even negligence. Thus, says one, a corporate official should face individual criminal liability "whenever [he or she] knew or should have known of a substantial risk that an illegal act was occurring or would occur within [his or her] realm of authority, and failed to take reasonable steps to prevent the offense." Developments — Corporate Crime, [92 Harv. L. Rev. 1270 (1979)]. On the other hand, should a clear legislative intent to punish the corporation be construed to *limit*, rather than expand, the liability of an official? See United States v. Doig, 950 F.2d 411 (7th Cir. 1991) (manager of tunnel project in which violations caused explosion that killed three employees not liable because "affirmative legislative policy placing the onus of workplace safety upon employers precludes finding that an employee may aid and abet his employer's criminal OSHA violation.")

4. *The persistence of respondeat superior.* For an example of continuing resistance to the MPC rule's alteration of respondeat superior, consider Commonwealth v. Beneficial Finance Co., 360 Mass. 188, 275 N.E.2d 33 (1971). Three loan companies, along with several of their employees, were convicted of bribery and conspiracy to commit bribery, after the employees, hoping to influence officials to set a high maximum interest rate on consumer loans, offered money to state officials. In affirming the convictions of the corporations, the Supreme Judicial Court of Massachusetts refused to adopt the MPC position that the state had to prove that high managerial agents had authorized the bribes.

> . . . [C]riminal conspiratorial acts are not performed within the glare of publicity, nor would we expect a board of directors to meet officially and record on the corporate records a delegation of authority to initiate, conduct or conclude proceedings for the purpose of bribing a public official. Of necessity, the proof [of] authority to so act must rest on all the circumstances and conduct in a given situation and the reasonable inferences to be drawn therefrom.
>
> Additional factors of importance are the size and complexity of many large modern corporations which necessitate the delegation of more authority to lesser corporate agents and employees. As the judge pointed out: "There are not enough seats on the Board of Directors, nor enough offices in a corporation, to permit the corporation engaged in widespread operations to give such a title or office to every person in whom it places the power, authority, and responsibility for decision and action." This latter consideration lends credence to the view that the title or position of an individual in a corporation should not be conclusively determinative in ascribing criminal responsibility. In a large corporation, with many numerous and distinct departments, a high ranking corporate officer or agent may have no authority or involvement in a particular sphere of corporate activity, whereas a lower ranking corporate executive might have much broader power in dealing with a matter peculiarly within the scope of his authority. Employees who are in the lower echelon of the corporate hierarchy often exercise more responsibility in the *everyday operations* of the corporation than the directors or officers. Assuredly, the title or office that the person holds may be considered, but it should not be the decisive criterion upon which to predicate corporate responsibility. . . .
>
> To permit corporations to conceal the nefarious acts of their underlings by using the shield of corporate armor to deflect corporate responsibility, and to separate the subordinate from the executive, would be to permit "endocratic" corporations to inflict widespread public harm without hope of redress. It would merely serve to ignore the scramble and realities of the market place.[8] [Id. at 82-84 (emphasis in original).]

---

8. The term "endocratic" was coined by Prof. Eugene Rostow and means a "large, publicly held corporation, whose stock is scattered in small fractions among thousands of stockholders." Note, Increasing Community Control over Corporate Crime — A Problem in the Law of Sanctions, 71 Yale L.J. 280, 281, n.3.

5. *What "corporate person" is the target of deterrence?* Any effort to define the nature of the "corporate mind" that should be the focus of criminal law must reckon with the economic realities of deterrence in large corporations. Prof. John Coffee argues that neglect of those realities helps explains why corporate crime is especially hard to deter.[9] Coffee asserts that because the financial penalty imposed on a corporation typically ends up resting on such disparate, nonculpable parties as stockholders, bondholders and other creditors, low-level employees, and consumers, judges often resist imposing huge fines. He adds that the career-enhancing incentives of individual managers may offer enough benefits to outweigh any expected cost likely to be imposed on them personally, especially when one factors in the difficulty the government has in proving corporate crime, and the difficulty victims have of even detecting their injuries in such areas as price-fixing and pollution.

To mitigate these constraints on punishing corporations, Coffee recommends as a penalty an "equity fine."[10] That is, the stockholders will have to give up a certain percentage of their equity to a trustee, who may represent the government or some class of victims. Thus, all stockholders suffer a "negative stock split," but the net worth of the corporation is unchanged and presumably bondholders and other creditors face no greater default risk, nor should employees fear layoffs. Stockholders, to be sure, may innocently lose a share of the stock value, but, Coffee argues, where most stockholders have diverse portfolios, this loss is far more diffuse than an employee's loss of her job. Moreover, because what high-level managers fear most is a move by owners to replace them, introducing this equity holder (who may, of course, proceed to sell its share on the market) may properly cause managers to align their personal interests with those of the corporation.

Does Coffee underestimate the indirect harm the equity fine may cause those he wishes to protect?

6. *Federal sentencing of "organizational defendants."* Perhaps in reaction to the savings and loan crisis, in 1991 new federal Sentencing Guidelines went into effect for corporate crimes, allowing vastly increased fines. Under the new system, courts can impose fines of hundreds of millions of dollars on corporations, with enhancements for such factors as involvement of top management, prior convictions, or bribery of officials, and mitigation for corporations in which senior managers had acted to prevent criminal behavior, in which a compliance program was in effect, or for corporations that had turned themselves in.

The main variables in setting the fine will be the greatest of a fixed base amount for the category of crime, the pecuniary gain to the organization from the offense; or the pecuniary loss from the offense caused by the organization, to the extent the loss was caused intentionally, knowingly, or recklessly; the size of the organization; and the place in the hierarchy of a culpable individual, i.e., the bigger the organization and the higher in the hierarchy was an individual who participated in, condoned, or was willfully ignorant of the offense, the higher the fine.[11]

9. John C. Coffee, Jr., Making the Punishment Fit the Corporation: The Problems of Finding an Optimal Corporation Criminal Sanction, 1 North. Ill. L. Rev. 1, 6-11 (1980).

10. Id. at 14-21.

11. Subsection (a)(6) provides that the court, in setting the fine within the guideline fine range, should consider any prior criminal record of an individual within high-level personnel of the organization or a unit of the organization. Since an individual within high-level personnel either exercises substantial control over the organization or a unit of the organization or has a sub-

Compliance and prevention. A key factor in sentencing is whether the defendant had a compliance program in Section 8C2.5:

(k)   An "effective program to prevent and detect violations of law" means a program that has been reasonably designed, implemented, and enforced so that it generally will be effective in preventing and detecting criminal conduct. Failure to prevent or detect the instant offense, by itself, does not mean that the program was not effective. The hallmark of an effective program to prevent and detect violations of law is that the organization exercised due diligence in seeking to prevent and detect criminal conduct by its employees and other agents. Due diligence requires at a minimum that the organization must have taken the following types of steps:

   (1)   The organization must have established compliance standards and procedures to be followed by its employees and other agents that are reasonably capable of reducing the prospect of criminal conduct.
   (2)   Specific individual(s) within high-level personnel of the organization must have been assigned overall responsibility to oversee compliance with such standards and procedures.
   (3)   The organization must have used due care not to delegate substantial discretionary authority to individuals whom the organization knew, or should have known through the exercise of due diligence, had a propensity to engage in illegal activities.
   (4)   The organization must have taken steps to communicate effectively its standards and procedures to all employees and other agents, e.g., by requiring participation in training programs or by disseminating publications that explain in a practical manner what is required.
   (5)   The organization must have taken reasonable steps to achieve compliance with its standards, e.g., by utilizing monitoring and auditing systems reasonably designed to detect criminal conduct by its employees and other agents and by having in place and publicizing a reporting system whereby employees and other agents could report criminal conduct by others within the organization without fear of retribution.
   (6)   The standards must have been consistently enforced through appropriate disciplinary mechanisms, including, as appropriate, discipline of individuals responsible for the failure to detect an offense. Adequate discipline of individuals responsible for an offense is a necessary component of enforcement; however, the form of discipline that will be appropriate will be case specific.
   (7)   After an offense has been detected, the organization must have taken all reasonable steps to respond appropriately to the offense and to prevent further similar offenses — including any necessary modifications to its program to prevent and detect violations of law.

However, mitigation for a program designed to prevent and detect violations will not be available

   if an individual within high-level personnel of the organization, a person within high-level personnel of the unit of the organization within which the offense was committed where the unit had 200 or more employees, or an individual

---

stantial role in the making of policy within the organization or a unit of the organization, any prior criminal misconduct of such an individual may be relevant to the determination of the appropriate fine for the organization.

responsible for the administration or enforcement of a program to prevent and detect violations of law participated in, condoned, or was willfully ignorant of the offense. Participation of an individual within substantial authority personnel in an offense results in a rebuttable presumption that the organization did not have an effective program to prevent and detect violations of law. [§8C2.5(f)]

Finally, a key innovation of the Guidelines, in section 8D1.1, is corporate probation (which can be imposed for a term of up to five years), where, for example, probationary monitoring would be necessary where a fine is to be paid out in installments, or where a company is given time to set up a required compliance program. In addition, the court may, if feasible, require the organization to create a trust fund sufficient to address any future harm, §8B1.2, or to impose on the corporation "community service" that is "reasonably designed to repair the harm caused by the offense." §8B1.3. Under Section 8D1.3(a), "any sentence of probation shall include the condition that the organization not commit another federal, state, or local crime during the term of probation." Finally, according to the Policy Statement for Section 8D1.4(a):

> The court may order the organization, at its expense and in the format and media specified by the court, to publicize the nature of the offense committed, the fact of conviction, the nature of the punishment imposed, and the steps that will be taken to prevent the recurrence of similar offenses.

In the coming years, scholars are likely to argue whether the guidelines give courts subtle and sophisticated guidance, virtually unlimited discretion, or a fantastic illusion of economic precision. One commentary[12] employing a law-and-economics approach gives the Sentencing Commission a mixed review for its efforts to design an optimal deterrent for organizations, praising the Organization Guidelines for sensibly mixing opportunities for mitigation through self-reporting and investigation with residual liability, but noting:

> The amount of mitigation firms receive for monitoring, investigating, and reporting is not necessarily sufficient to induce optimal policing. . . . [T]he proportional amount of mitigation granted for monitoring, investigating, or reporting "promptly" depends on the size of the firm and the seniority of the individual wrongdoer. By contrast, as we show, the mitigation amount should be larger the greater the benefit to society of implementing optimal policing measures — or more specifically, the greater the impact of optimal policing measures on the probability of detection. The amount of mitigation must increase with the impact of policing on the probability of detection to ensure that policing does not increase the firm's expected liability for wrongdoing. To induce optimal policing, therefore, the Commission must abandon its goal of standardizing fines for all similar crimes, and attempt to take into account the impact of policing measures on the probability of detection.
>
>   . . . The Sentencing Guidelines provide that a firm that reports, cooperates, and accepts full responsibility for a wrong is eligible for mitigation of five points. For a larger firm this may only result in a 50% reduction in the fine if it reports, investigates, and cooperates. This mitigation provision will induce reporting, therefore, only if a firm that detects and does not report faces at least a 50% chance of getting caught. . . .

---

12. Jennifer Arlen & Reinier Kraakman, Controlling Corporate Misconduct: An Analysis of Corporate Liability Misconduct Regimes, 72 N.Y.U. L. Rev. 687, 746-49 (1997).

834 13. Criminal Liability of Corporations

> In addition . . . firms are ineligible for mitigation based on their monitoring efforts whenever misconduct is committed by certain managerial employees. . . . This means that a firm cannot earn mitigation for programs designed to deter wrongdoing by directors, executives, officers, and supervisors of major units, even though such programs may be worthwhile. . . .
>
> The Sentencing Guidelines also provide that a firm is not eligible for mitigation for reporting or cooperating in a investigation unless it accepts responsibility for the offense. The guidelines state that only in "rare situations" will a firm be able to satisfy this requirement without pleading guilty. This requirement, in combination with the requirement that firms report detected wrongdoing "promptly" to be eligible for mitigation, may force firms to report — and even plead guilty to — suspected wrongdoing before they can determine whether their agents committed wrongs.

Does this critique demand a plausible degree of precision? Is it right that guidelines of this level of detail be prescribed by a congressionally mandated agency? Should these questions be left to judicial discretion?

7. *The corporate mens rea and the concept of "good faith."* So long as the corporate liability rules, like that of the MPC, lean toward some notion of an actual decision-making "corporate mind" as the culpable party, the fit between conventional mens rea principles and the corporate defendant may prove challenging. This is especially true where penalty schemes like that of the Sentencing Guidelines aim to credit the corporation as a whole for such "good faith" efforts as setting up compliance programs. Does approval of these schemes suggest that there are mental processes and moral qualities that can be imputed to the corporation?

In United States v. Ladish Malting Co., 135 F.3d 484 (7th Cir. 1998), the corporate defendant was charged with criminal violation of an OSHA safety regulation when a rickety fire escape platform collapsed, killing a worker. Judge Frank Easterbrook's opinion holds:

> Ladish contends that it was entitled to an instruction under which the jury would acquit if it found that Ladish made good faith efforts to maintain a safe work place. The magistrate judge refused to give such an instruction, and properly so. There is no generic "good faith" defense in federal criminal law in general, or for violations of the Occupational Safety and Health Act in particular. . . . Safety programs reduce not only the number of injuries but also the likelihood that the prosecutor will press criminal charges if a death nonetheless occurs. But complying with the law 99.99% of the time is not a defense to disobedience the other 0.01%. Wilfulness is different in this regard from purpose; only when the statute requires the prosecution to show that the defendant acted "purposely"— that is, that the defendant wanted to produce the consequences that the statute forbids — would "good faith" be relevant, because it would tend to show that the defendant did not have the forbidden purpose. But §666(e) calls for proof of knowledge of the safety hazard, not proof that the firm set out to kill an employee or had another evil motive. Because we interpreted §666(e) in *Union Oil* to require proof that the employer knew of its legal obligation to abate safety hazards, something that a lay person may think of as good faith has some role to play: "[a] violation is not willful when it is based on a nonfrivolous interpretation of OSHA's regulations." [McLaughlin v. Union Oil, 869 F.2d 1039, 1047 (7th Cir. 1989).] But Ladish does not contend that it interpreted the rules and regulations in a way that permitted it to maintain tumbledown fire escapes. It would divert attention from the big issue — the state of its knowledge of the facts — to give an instruction implying that an employer with a well-organized safety program cannot be convicted under §666(e) even if it knows about and ignores a life-threatening hazard. . . .

Next Ladish contends that the jury should have been told that corporations, like natural persons, can be forgetful, so that even if Ladish knew at one time that the platform was about to give way, it did not necessarily know this at the time of the violation. Again the magistrate judge made a sound decision not to give such an instruction. Corporate crime and collective knowledge are both problematic constructs, but Congress has concluded that corporations can "know" and "intend" things, and may be punished as if they were natural persons. Although the rules of law under §666(e) are the same for corporate and human employers, other vital things differ. Persons forget because the chemical connections in their brains change over time. Corporations do not record knowledge in neural pathways; they record it in file cabinets (and increasingly on computer disks). File cabinets do not "forget." Files may be destroyed, and people may forget about data in file cabinets, but a memorandum saying "platform X is unsound and must be repaired" remains in the corporation's knowledge as long as the memo itself continues to exist (and, even after its destruction, as long as a responsible employee remembers it).

There is a second reason, applicable to both persons and corporations, why Ladish is not entitled to a "forgetfulness" instruction. The premise of this instruction is that the employer's knowledge must be contemporaneous with the injury. But this cannot be right. Suppose an employer learns in January 1991 as a result of an inspection that a fire escape is verging on collapse but, wilfully violating its duties under the statute and regulations, decides not to fix the platform (or even to seal the door and direct workers to other escape routes). Six years pass; no one uses the fire escape, so there is no injury. Then in January 1997 a worker ventures onto the platform, which gives way. The death comes as a shock to current employees; the inspection team no longer remembers its recommendations of years before; managers in charge of safety in 1991 have left the firm, and the new managers never discover what their predecessors knew. Still, the employer knew of the safety hazard, and delaying repairs so long that the people with knowledge quit or forget does not reduce the employer's culpability. The statute required the employer to act in January 1991, not after the death; the wilful violation for purposes of §666(e) occurs when the employer knows of the noncompliance but allows the lethal condition to continue. This may long precede the accident. Death is a condition of criminal liability but is distinct from and need not be contemporaneous with the "willfulness" element.

Finally, there is a dispute about whose knowledge counts. . . . As for the argument that only supervisors' knowledge counts: why? Corporations "know" what their employees who are responsible for an aspect of the business know. Doubtless the knowledge of a worker who trips over a safety hazard but does not understand or report what he has found does not count. Most federal statutes that make anything of corporate knowledge also require the knowledge to be possessed by persons authorized to do something about what they know. But what's so special, for this purpose, about supervisors? The magistrate judge told the jury to consider the knowledge of Ladish's "officers, directors, and authorized agents" provided "that supervisor or employee has some duty to communicate that knowledge to someone higher up in the corporation." This definition, which asks whether a particular person has been given responsibility over safety (perhaps by being placed on an inspection team), makes more sense than asking whether someone is a supervisor — a status that refers to the power to hire and fire others but that may be unrelated to workplace safety. Following the ordinary law of agency, the instructions told the jury that employers may decide for themselves who is "authorized" to inspect the plant for safety hazards, who is to receive and respond to safety complaints, and who is to report to the persons with authority to make decisions. If "authorized agents" with reporting duties acquire actual knowledge, it is entirely sensible to say that the corporation has acquired knowledge. Ladish could not, by delegating all safety inspection and reporting functions to non-supervisors, shield itself from knowledge of the hazards.

Has Judge Easterbrook properly distinguished the mentality of a corporation from that of an individual? Or has he failed to give due credit to actual thought processes or moral values of company officials that, if difficult to discern, nevertheless likely animate company conduct?

8. Professor Brent Fisse speaks of "strategic" or "reactive" mens rea as the key to corporate liability:

> Consider the well-known Kepone case, United States v. Allied Chemical Corporation, [420 F. Supp. 122 (E.D.Va. 1976),] in which Allied Chemical pled no contest to 940 counts of water pollution resulting from the escape of the pesticide Kepone into the waterways of Virginia. Because Allied was convicted under a statute that imposed strict responsibility, fault was relevant only to gravity of sentence. In the opinion of District Judge Merhige, Allied had been at fault at the time of the actus reus: "I disagree with the defendant's position that all of this was so innocently done, or inadvertently done. I think it was done because of what it considered to be business necessities, and money took the forefront." Yet it is not clear that the *corporation* intentionally or recklessly committed illegal acts of pollution. A few middle managers may have possessed mens rea, but, as we have seen, managerial mens rea alone does not indicate genuinely *corporate* blameworthiness.
>
> Suppose, however, that upon proof of the actus reus of the pollution offenses charged, the court had required Allied to prepare a compliance report detailing a program of preventive and restitutionary measures which the company proposed to undertake in response to the violations. Suppose further that the compliance report was unsatisfactory to the court, or bent upon scapegoating rather than reforming. In this situation, public attitudes toward Allied's conduct would focus on its compliance program in response to the prosecution rather than on what it intended at or before the time the actus reus was committed. Moreover, if notice were given to the company that its compliance report would be treated as a record of top-level corporate policy, public attitudes would focus on *corporate* intent, rather than on the individual states of mind of one or more middle managers.
>
> If the reactive strategies of corporations represent corporate policy in this way, then unsatisfactory reactive strategies would display strategic mens rea and thus, in absence of good excuse, corporate blameworthiness. In other words, if society looks to a corporate defendant to generate a reactive prevention and cure strategy, then an unsatisfactory response would tend to indicate a noncompliant corporate policy and hence arouse attitudes of resentment and blame toward the corporation.
>
> The concept of reactive mens rea reflects very sharply the organizational reality of management by exception. An axiom of orthodox management is that routine tasks should be delegated, leaving managers to use their creativity and leadership to the greatest possible corporate advantage. In the normal course of corporate business, top management assumes that compliance with the law is routine. Management typically issues policy directives from time to time, which are implemented by means of standard operating procedures. Only when an "exceptional" event occurs, as when the corporation is alleged to have committed an offense, are questions of compliance referred upwards to managers. For instance, in the Kepone case, there is reason to believe that top managers at Allied Chemical had not even heard of Kepone before the disaster became public news, but, once the problem had surfaced, a program of corrective action was initiated as a matter of high managerial priority.[13]

---

13. Fisse, Reconstructing Corporate Criminal Law Deterrence, Retribution, Fault, and Sanctions, 56 S. Cal. L. Rev. 1141, 1197-1200 (1983).

Is Fisse's reconciliation of mens rea concepts with corporate structure consistent with Easterbrook's? Is it more or less plausible?

9. *Conspiracy and the corporation.* If corporate criminal liability can result from the converging actions of individuals within the entity, does conspiracy law have any role in *intracorporate* crime? If agents of the corporation take overt acts toward a criminal goal but fall way short, may the corporation itself be viewed as a conspirator? Is this stretching too far the notion of the corporation as a distinct person? These cases can arise in any of several ways: The corporation could be charged with conspiring with one of its agents or with a related corporation, such as a subsidiary; or the corporation could be charged with conspiracy where two of its agents conspired with each other. For a skeptical look at the federal courts' willingness to approve these conspiracy prosecutions, see Shaun Martin, Intracorporate Conspiracies, 50 Stan. L. Rev. 399, 410 (1998).

Ultimately, do you feel that a criminal conviction has the same meaning for a corporation as for an individual? Given the rules about corporate liability, should the two kinds of liability bear the same stigma? Should the rules be changed so that they do? How?

C.   CORPORATE HOMICIDE

COMMONWEALTH v. MCILWAIN SCHOOL BUS LINES
Superior Court of Pennsylvania
423 A.2d 413 (1980)

SPAETH, JUDGE.

This is an appeal by the Commonwealth from an order quashing an information. The principal issue is whether a private corporation may be held criminally liable for homicide by vehicle. On April 3, 1978, a school bus owned by the McIlwain School Bus Lines, Inc. (hereinafter, the corporation) and operated by one of its employees, ran over and killed 6-year-old Lori Sharp; she had just gotten off the bus and was walking in front of it when she was run over. On May 26, 1978, the corporation was charged with homicide by vehicle. The corporation waived its right to a preliminary hearing, but subsequently filed a motion to quash the information against it. One ground of the motion was that by definition, the offense could only be committed by a natural person, not by a corporation. . . .

. . . The statute provides:

> Any person who unintentionally causes the death of another person while engaged in the *violation of any law of the Commonwealth or municipal ordinance* applying to *the operation or use of a vehicle or to the regulation of traffic* is guilty of homicide by vehicle, a misdemeanor of the first degree, when the violation is *the cause of death.* 75 P.S. §3732. (Emphasis added.)

[T]he corporation filed a request for a bill of particulars, asking that the Commonwealth "[p]lease specify the law of this Commonwealth or municipal ordinance which the Defendant was violating which caused the death of Lori Sharp." The Commonwealth answered as follows:

> Sections 4551, 4552 of the Pennsylvania Vehicle Code require the Department of Transportation to promulgate rules and regulations pertaining to the equipment required on school buses.
>
> Specifically the rules and regulations require that a mirror be placed on the front of the bus which will permit the operator to see any pedestrian in front of the bus. This mirror was missing.
>
> Also the bus is required to be equipped with a rearview mirror to provide the operator with a proper view to the rear and side of the bus.
>
> The rearview mirror was not properly positioned to afford the operator proper view of the area. [Violations of regulations under section 4551 are punishable by fines of $50 to $100.]

The criminal law has not always regarded a corporation as subject to criminal liability. Indeed, it was once widely accepted that a corporation was incapable of committing a criminal offense:

> This doctrine of nonliability for crime arose from the theory that a corporation, being an intangible entity, could neither commit a crime nor be subjected to punishment, because any illegal act of a corporate agent was done without authority of the corporation and ultra vires.

Today, however, it is generally recognized that a corporation may be held criminally liable for criminal acts performed by its agents on its behalf.

. . . It is true that Section 3732 does not use the word "corporation." However, given the definition of the word "person," there is no need for it to do so. It is also true — at least so far as we know — that no court in Pennsylvania has applied Section 3732 to a corporation; the present case appears to be of first impression. However, given the fact that the section did not become effective until July 1, 1977, the fact that no case other than this one has been brought against a corporation for homicide by vehicle is hardly conclusive proof that the section may not be so applied. Neither are we persuaded by the next two reasons of the lower court — that since a corporation cannot be put in jail or have its license revoked, Section 3732 does not apply to corporations.

The offense of homicide by vehicle is a misdemeanor of the first degree. 75 Pa. C.S.A. §3732. It is true that one of the punishments that may be imposed for committing a misdemeanor of the first degree is a term of imprisonment [for not more than five years, 18 Pa. C.S.A. §1104]. . . .

It is also true that another possible punishment for homicide by vehicle is the revocation of one's driver license [Pa. C.S. §1532(a)(3)]. . . .

However, a third possible punishment is the imposition of a fine [for a first-degree misdemeanor, not to exceed $10,000. 18 Pa. C.S.A. §1101]. . . .

Where alternate punishments are provided for a crime, the court may in appropriate circumstances impose the fine only:

> *Fine only.* — The court may, as authorized by law, sentence the defendant only to pay a fine, when, having regard to the nature and circumstances of the crime and to the history and character of the defendant, it is of the opinion that the fine alone suffices. 18 Pa. C.S. §1326(a). . . .

. . . [W]e are unable to accept the lower court's conclusion that §3732 "is strictly natural person solely operational driver oriented." For the reasons we have given, it appears to us equally to include corporations.

Reversed.

Notes and Questions

1. *Can a corporation alone commit a homicide?* If a corporation can be guilty of homicide, does that mean that some individual working for the corporation must also be guilty? How should we handle the situation where a corporation releases a toxic chemical that causes a death under the following conditions:

> Engineer *A* knows that the chemical is toxic but does not know that it is being released. Engineer *B* knows that he is releasing the chemical by twisting a valve but is under the impression that the chemical is harmless.

If neither *A* nor *B* is negligent, who should be criminally liable? Or is civil liability enough? Might it be that no individual agent of the corporation knows both that the material is toxic and that it is being released? Can you conceive of circumstances under which no individual would even be negligent in lacking such knowledge? In such a case should no individual be criminally liable? What about the person who designed the system under which this could happen? Could the corporation nonetheless be criminally liable anyway? Why?

Is it a fair objection to imposing manslaughter liability on a corporation that the only sensible penalty is a fine rather than imprisonment? Remembering that imposing any sort of sanction on individual corporate officers is an entirely independent matter, can you devise any "punishment" for a corporation that is usefully analogous to imprisonment of an individual? Does forcing dissolution of the business in bankruptcy make any sense? One court, in a nonhomicide case (in fact, a price-fixing case under the Sherman antitrust law) has imposed "imprisonment" on a company in the form of directing the United States Marshal to seize all corporate assets and monitor all business activities in an appropriate manner. United States v. Allegheny Bottling Co., 695 F. Supp. 856 (E.D. Va. 1989), aff'd in part & rev'd in part, 870 F.2d 655 (4th Cir. 1989).

2. *The Dalkon Shield deaths.* Who, if anyone, should be criminally liable in the following case?[14]

> In the late 1960s, the hot technology was birth control [especially the Pill]. . . . But there was another means of birth control becoming available, the intrauterine device, or IUD. . . . The first IUD . . . was already widely used when A.H. Robins Co. decided to jump into the business. . . .
>
> The problem was, Robins didn't have an IUD. . . . Robins was best known for its nonprescription products, Sergeant's Flea and Tick collars, Robitussin cough medicine, and Chap Stick lip balm. When Robins first decided to enter the IUD market, it did not have a single obstetrician or gynecologist on its staff. After Robins acquired the rights to an IUD, the Dalkon Shield, from inventor Irwin S. Lerner and Lerner's company, the Dalkon Corp., in June 1970, it assigned assembly of the Shield to its Chap Stick division.

14. Subrata Chakravarty, Tunnel Vision, Forbes 214, 218 (May 21, 1984).

Without the requisite knowledge or experience, Robins appears to have handled the Shield improperly, almost from the beginning. In good science, for example, research should be categorically confirmed by an outside disinterested party. For sales literature on the Shield's effectiveness, however, Robins relied on a report by Dr. Hugh J. Davis of Johns Hopkins University. Robins knew, but others did not, that Davis was one of the co-owners of Dalkon Corp. Robins ignored an internal company memo, written within days of the Shield's acquisition, that cited evidence from inventor Lerner himself that pregnancy rates with the Dalkon Shield were considerably higher than Dr. Davis had reported, and emphasized that more research was needed. Eager to get to the market before competitors piled in, Robins was selling Dalkon Shields nationally six months after the rights were acquired.

That the Shield was not as effective as touted was no problem,[15] but when the device failed, severe infections developed in scores of cases, leading to miscarriages midway during the unwanted pregnancies. A Robins internal memo of October 1975 cites 248 cases among Shield users in the U.S. of infection-caused miscarriages; compared with only 55 for users of all other IUDs. Even more serious, some Shield users developed pelvic inflammatory disease (PID), which can lead to sterility, removal of a woman's reproductive organs or even death. At least 20 women have died in the U.S. from Shield-related complications.

What did Robins do about the problem? The company insisted, and continues to insist to this day, that it was not responsible. . . .

. . . [T]o take the Dalkon Shield off the market would be to kill an extremely promising — and profitable — new product. Shields generated operating margins of over 40 percent in the U.S. and over 70 percent overseas. . . . From January 1971 until sales were suspended in the U.S. in June 1974, at the request of the Food & Drug Administration, and overseas in April 1975, Robins sold some 4.6 million Shields worldwide, making them the largest-selling IUDs in the world. . . .

[Internal memoranda at Robins reported that the Dalkon Shield had a feature likely to cause pelvic inflammatory disease.] Neither memo was provided to the FDA when it investigated the Shield's problems in 1974. . . .

The company's executives have been publicly chastised. [The president, general counsel, and director of research] were forced to endure an extraordinary public rebuke at the hands of Miles Lord, chief judge for the Federal District Court of Minnesota. Following the Minneapolis settlements, Judge Lord excoriated . . . [them, saying] in part: "You have taken the bottom line as your guiding beacon and the low road as your route."[16]

The Fourth Circuit Court of Appeals ultimately approved a reorganization plan for A.H. Robins Co., as a result of Dalkon Shield litigation. The plan provided that $700 million in assets would go to stockholders (not the traditional

---

15. [No problem to whom? — EDS.]

16. [The trial judge was subsequently reprimanded by the court of appeals for his remarks:

[T]he officers' personal liberty interests were infringed when the judge directed each officer to appear in his court . . . even though the officers were not parties to the litigation pending. . . . Such intimidation of private citizens who are not parties to proceedings before the district court is antithetical to our notions of fundamental fairness and the proper functioning of our judicial system.

. . . The record is clear that, at the time he issued the reprimand, Judge Lord had decided the merits of the underlying dispute against Robins, even though there had been no trial. . . . Judge Lord stated that he believed the truth of the plaintiffs' allegations, adding that he had become an advocate for plaintiffs and that he was, in fact, prejudiced. Gardiner v. A.H. Robins Co., Inc., 747 F.2d 1180, 1191-92 (8th Cir. 1984) — EDS.]

approach to bankruptcy; members of the Robins family would receive $350 million of that amount). Plaintiffs in the Dalkon Shield cases would be allocated $2.47 billion — at the time the largest mass tort award in American history, yet arguably inadequate. The figures for the "value" of injuries come from averaging the awards and settlements received by plaintiffs at trial and through out-of-court settlements. Those numbers are skewed, however, because for years Robins withheld evidence of its knowledge of the Shield's harm. Dollar values for liability were lower when this evidence was suppressed. As of 1995, the final distribution of the surplus of the trust was in sight, with all but 6,000 of 192,000 claimants still pending.[17]

In the late 1980s, federal prosecutors pursued possible criminal charges in connection with the Dalkon Shield, but only for perjury, obstruction of justice, and fraud — not for homicide. Even those charges were dropped in 1990, and the government never pursued indictments against Robins any further.

3. *The Pinto deaths.* In 1978, the Ford Motor Company became the first automaker to face criminal homicide liability:[18]

. . . [The] Ford Motor Company [sold] some one and a half million Pintos, vintage 1971-1976, *knowing* that its gas tank posed a dangerous risk of fuel leakage and explosion. The company made no attempt to fix or redesign the gas tank, nor to warn its customers of the hazards until forced to do so by the federal government. The results were tragic.

. . . [A] van smashed into the back of a 1973 Ford Pinto traveling on U.S. 33 toward Goshen, Indiana. The gas tank impacted against the differential, ripping it open on four protruding bolts; gasoline splashed into the passenger compartment, igniting and engulfing the interior of the car in flames. The two girls trapped inside the Pinto were incinerated; a third girl partially thrown from the vehicle, received burns over ninety percent of her body and died six hours later.

Elkhart County prosecutor Michael Cosentino brought Ford Motor Company to trial on three reckless homicide charges; he claimed the three girls [in that car] died as a result of a high-level corporate decision to risk human life for greater company profit. . . . [The prosecutor brought] the case on a new and unchallenged Indiana statute permitting criminal prosecution of a corporation. . . . Previously, corporations faced criminal sanctions in antitrust, environmental, and securities laws, but never before ha[d] manufacturers been criminally indicted for the reckless design of their products.

Indiana's Pinto Case raised for the first time in a legal setting the fascinating issue of whether or not a corporation is capable of committing homicide through the reckless design of its products. It was Ford's contention that the legislature did not intend to charge reckless homicide to a corporation. Instead, they argued the statutes were intended only to prevent *people* from killing other *people*. The prosecutor found fault with Ford's analysis, stating that it "patently exploits the corporate fiction." [While the state] "does not desire to chill manufacturing generally, it does desire to deter outrageous decisions to sacrifice human life for private profit."

Although one of the most bitter and highly publicized trials in product liability history, its ultimate precedential value remains . . . the victim of a judicial stalemate. For the first time, a court of law has ruled that a corporation can be indicted for the reckless design of a product, opening the door to new theories of corporate liability. Whether this fact is construed as achievement or legal extremism, it

17. Wall Street Journal, Oct. 3, 1995, at B16.
18. Note, Corporate Homicide: The Stark Realities of Artificial Beings and Legal Fictions, 8 Pepperdine L. Rev. 367, 367-70, 372-74, 404-08 (1981) (emphasis in original).

is counteracted by the additional fact that Ford Motor Company today stands acquitted of all criminal charges — hence the stalemate. . . .

Ford Motor Company made a decision to place on the market a car whose gas tank design was fully expected to injure and kill a substantial number of people. The charge is supported by evidence, much of which comes from Ford's own company documents. One of those documents . . . was prepared for the company in its efforts to lobby the federal government to reduce its fuel tank standards. The heart of that document reveals a typical cost-benefit analysis, which resulted in a company decision not to redesign the Pinto gas tank, despite having the technology to do so. . . .

The [Pinto had been] tested on five separate occasions by running it into a stationary barrier at speeds of around nineteen and a half miles per hour. The Pinto leaked gas on all five occasions. Ford put the car into production, knowing that it had never passed a fuel tank test. . . .

Opponents of corporate criminal liability advance several justifications for retaining the limited scope of this liability. One reason is the resulting inequity to innocent parties. Shareholders are one such group, who in the final analysis feel the sting of any verdict against a corporation. Yet they are most likely innocent of personal wrongdoing and incapable of exerting any effective control over actions of the corporate agents. . . .

. . . If it is true [however] that decisions to market "defective products in flagrant disregard of excessive dangers spring from the intensity of the profit motive rather than from animus toward consumers," then such behavior could be impliedly consented to and authorized by the shareholder who seeks a high return on . . . investment. Moreover, any impact upon the shareholder is minimized . . . [because] shareholder losses are limited only to the amount of individual capital investment [and corporations may pass along the cost of fines to consumers through increased prices].

Another concern is the impact of placing criminal liability on unknowing corporate directors, on the theory that the wrongful activity occurred as a result of the principal's failure to exercise due care and attention to corporate affairs. Directors who are primarily concerned about long term planning and company goal setting may never become aware that the product they recently marketed had failed all its safety tests or for some reason is dangerously defective. . . . [E]xpanded liability of directors has stopped many able businessmen from accepting directorships in large companies. . . .

Yet . . . corporations do not commit crimes — people do, and thus it would seem to be more appropriate to proceed directly against the individual perpetrator than the corporation as a whole. [Of course, there is the difficulty of identifying the guilty person(s) to be jailed.]

. . . [C]orporate diversity and complexity [have now] necessitated the expansion of corporate liability to the point where a court has held a corporation guilty of manslaughter. There is even scholarly support for the concept of corporate murder. . . .

The economic pressures which ferment within the corporate structure are sometimes strong enough to cause employees to risk their own liability for the sake of corporate gain. "[I]f the penalty for corporate wrongdoing were punishment of the corporation the punishment would ipso facto fall upon the true logical wrongdoer."

What does it mean to say, as does this excerpt, that the corporation *knew* that its gas tank posed a dangerous risk of explosion? Could one design an automobile that posed virtually no risk of danger to those inside? Why do we not require all our automobiles to be built this way?

Are you surprised that Ford was able to win a jury acquittal? Consider some of the evidence at trial. On the one hand, the prosecution offered evidence that Ford officials had done cost-benefit analyses on the economic efficiency of improving the safety of the tank. For example, Ford calculated that to protect the fuel tank from explosion in a rollover, the cost to repair all Pintos then on the road was about $11 per car, multiplied by about 12.5 million cars, to produce a cost of about $137 million; on the other hand, it predicted that this improvement would prevent about 180 deaths and 180 cases of severe nonfatal burns, and used a figure of $200,000 per human life lost and $67,000 for a seriously burned victim to yield a likely savings of about $49.5 million.[19] On the other hand, the $200,000 per life figure was devised by the government itself; moreover, Ford offered evidence that during two key years in question, 1975-76, 1.9 percent of all fire-accompanied passenger fatalities involved Pintos — the exact same percentage as the Pinto's share of the cars on the road. How would this evidence affect a jury instructed in the normal principles of reckless or negligent manslaughter? To what extent might a jury's view of this evidence change when the defendant is a corporation?

4. What about "corporate murder"? The facts in People v. O'Neil, 194 Ill. App. 3d 79, 550 N.E.2d 1090 (1990), were as follows:

Following a joint bench trial, individual defendants Steven O'Neil, Charles Kirschbaum, and Daniel Rodriguez, agents of Film Recovery Systems, Inc. (Film Recovery), were convicted of murder in the death of Stefan Golab, a Film Recovery employee, from cyanide poisoning stemming from conditions in Film Recovery's plant in Elk Grove Village, Illinois. . . .

In 1982, Film Recovery occupied premises at 1855 and 1875 Greenleaf Avenue in Elk Grove Village. Film Recovery was there engaged in the business of extracting, for resale, silver from used x-ray and photographic film. Metallic Marketing operated out of the same premises on Greenleaf Avenue and owned 50% of the stock of Film Recovery. The recovery process was performed at Film Recovery's plant located at the 1855 address and involved "chipping" the film product and soaking the granulated pieces in large open bubbling vats containing a solution of water and sodium cyanide. The cyanide solution caused silver contained in the film to be released. A continuous flow system pumped the silver laden solution into polyurethane tanks which contained electrically charged stainless steel plates to which the separated silver adhered. The plates were removed from the tanks to another room where the accumulated silver was scraped off. The remaining solution was pumped out of the tanks and the granulated film, devoid of silver, shovelled out.

On the morning of February 10, 1983, shortly after he disconnected a pump on one of the tanks and began to stir the contents of the tank with a rake, Stefan Golab became dizzy and faint. He left the production area to go rest in the lunchroom area of the plant. Plant workers present on that day testified Golab's body had trembled and he had foamed at the mouth. Golab eventually lost consciousness and was taken outside of the plant. Paramedics summoned to the plant were unable to revive him. Golab was pronounced dead upon arrival at Alexian Brothers Hospital. [Id. at 1091-92.]

The verdicts in the *O'Neil* case were considered a landmark in the application of state homicide law to the commercial workplace. However, the Supreme Court of Illinois overturned them on grounds of inconsistency: The jury had

19. Id. at 369.

found O'Neil, Kirschbaum, and Rodriguez guilty of Illinois's equivalent of "abandoned and malignant heart" murder, and the corporation and other individuals guilty of reckless manslaughter. Since the corporation's liability essentially derived from the actions of its principals, said the court, the jury had imputed to O'Neil, Kirschbaum, and Rodriguez two inconsistent mental states: (1) knowing creation of a strong probability of death and (2) reckless causation of harm. Id.[20]

Putting aside this technical question, do the facts support a murder charge against the principals? If so, could the prosecutors have finessed the inconsistency problem by charging the *corporation,* as well as the principals, with second-degree murder? Does this stretch corporate homicide doctrine too far?

5. Perhaps surprisingly, corporate homicide prosecutions have been very infrequent in recent years in the United States, yet there has been a trend toward them in other countries, especially the United Kingdom. In 1994, a British leisure activity corporation named OLL, Ltd. was convicted of manslaughter for the death of four youths who had gone on a canoe trip run by the company. The prosecutor proved the company had not given the youths proper instruction or safety equipment, and two of its instructors had quit after protesting their employer's lack of safety planning.[21] A commentator notes:

> One abiding difficulty in this area of law, and possibly one of the chief reasons why to date so few companies in the UK have been convicted of manslaughter, is the rule against "aggregation of fault". Thus, if several directors were each aware of a few jigsaw pieces in the overall picture of an "obvious risk", the company cannot be blamed. . . .
>
>   . . . The [OLL] case was, however, arguably atypical of corporate homicide scenarios. The company was small (Kite and Stoddart were the only people with directorial managerial control over the company's affairs). Therefore it was relatively easy to find the "controlling minds".[22]

How might this prosecution have fared under American law?

---

20. All three ultimately pleaded guilty to involuntary manslaughter and received short prison sentences. The company is now defunct. See Chicago Sun-Times, Sept. 10, 1993, p.18.

21. See Gary Slapper, Corporate Manslaughter: The Changing Legal Scenery, 10 Asia Pacific L. J. 161 (2002).

22. Id. at 165-66. To expand corporate liability major new bills have been introduced in Parliament under such names as Corporate Homicide and Corporate Killings laws.

VI

ADDITIONAL OFFENSES

This part explores two sets of criminal offenses — theft offenses and various forms of sexual assault — that may seem to lack any common denominator. Certainly theft cannot be compared with rape in terms of the nature and severity of harm to the victim. Nevertheless, these crimes pose some similar conceptual problems. In both types of offenses there is an element of conduct — the acquisition of property on the one hand, and intimate sexual contact on the other — that can also be engaged in innocently. These acts both become criminal when an additional element is added, the violation of a victim's consent. Thus, a major doctrinal issue in both theft law and rape law is how to define the requisite nonconsent. Moreover, consent can be violated in many different ways: by violence, by threats of violence, by threats of nonphysical harm, by fraud, by exploitation of a victim's incapacity based on infancy, insanity, or unconsciousness. Should the law criminalize all of these violations of consent for each offense? Some but not others? Should it grade and punish some of these violations more severely than others? Should it require separate proof of nonconsent as well as, say, force or threat?

These problems are particularly troubling in the context of rape and sexual assault. Here the criminal law has traditionally condemned forcible rape severely while seeming to condone rapes achieved by threat and fraud. Yet some reformers have posed the question, how can rape — which by definition involves invasive physical contact — be nonforcible? Unlike theft, rape necessarily involves a physical assault. It is much more likely than simple theft to involve physical injury and to place the victim in fear of death or maiming. Yet the criminal law traditionally defined force in the context of rape as requiring physical resistance on the part of the victim, while imposing no such requirement for theft or robbery. This has prompted some reformers to suggest that the law of rape be made more like the law of theft.

Chapter 14 explores the historical development and contemporary form of such theft offenses as larceny, embezzlement, fraud, and extortion, and includes brief notes on robbery and burglary. Chapter 15 examines the elements of rape and related forms of sexual abuse, as well as the continuing policy debate about whether and how best to increase the scope and effectiveness of rape proscriptions.

ADDITIONAL OFFENSES

14

THEFT OFFENSES

A. THEFT

1. The Meaning of Theft

COMMONWEALTH v. MITCHNECK

Superior Court of Pennsylvania
130 Pa. Super. 433, 198 A. 463 (1938)

Keller, P. J.

The appellant was convicted of the offense of fraudulently converting the money of another person to his own use. . . .

The evidence produced on the part of the commonwealth would have warranted the jury in finding that the defendant, Mitchneck, operated a coal mine in Beaver township, Columbia county; that he employed certain persons, Hunsinger, Derr, Steeley, and others, as workers in and about his mine; that these employees dealt at the store of A. Vagnoni and signed orders directing their employer to deduct from their wages the amounts of their respective store bills and pay the same to Vagnoni; that the defendant agreed to do so, and pursuant to said agreement deducted from the wages due the eleven workmen, named in the indictment, an aggregate of $259.26, which he agreed to pay Vagnoni, but had failed and neglected to do so.

We are of the opinion that the evidence was insufficient to support a conviction under the Fraudulent Conversion Act of 1917, and that the court erred in refusing the defendant's point for a directed verdict of acquittal.

The gist of the offense of fraudulent conversion is that the defendant has received into his possession the money or property of another person, firm, or corporation, and fraudulently withholds, converts, or applies the same to or for his own use and benefit, or to the use and benefit of any person other than the one to whom the money or property belonged. If the property so withheld or applied to the defendant's use and benefit, etc., did not belong to some other person, etc., but was the defendant's own money or property, even though obtained by borrowing the money, or by a purchase on credit of the property, the offense has not been committed. "Whatever may have been the intention of the legislature in the enactment of the statute under which the indictment in this case was drawn, it was clearly not intended to make criminal the act of one who sells his own property, and it is not to be so applied as to make it an effective substitute for an action at law in the collection of a debt." Com. v. Hilpot, [84 Pa. Super. 424, 458]. . . .

The defendant in the present case had not received, nor did he have in his possession, any money *belonging* to his employees. True he owed them money, but that did not transfer to them the title to and ownership of the money. His deduction from their wages of the amounts of the store bills which they had assigned to Vagnoni did not change the title and ownership of the money thus withheld, nor did his agreement to pay to Vagnoni the amounts thus deducted constitute the latter the owner of the money. It effected only a change of creditors. The money, if Mitchneck actually had it, of which there was no proof, was still his own, but, after he accepted the assignments, he owed the amount due his employees to Vagnoni instead of to them. A novation had been effected. The defendant had been discharged of his liability to his employees by contracting a new obligation in favor of Vagnoni. But failure to pay the amount due the new creditor was not fraudulent conversion within the Act of 1917. Otherwise, it would be a very dangerous thing to agree to a novation. Defendant's liability for the unpaid wages due his employees was, and remained, civil, not criminal. His liability for the amount due Vagnoni after his agreement to accept or honor the assignments of his employees' wages was likewise civil and not criminal. . . .

The judgment is reversed, and the appellant is discharged.

Notes and Questions

1. See Model Penal Code §223 in Appendix B. Of what form of theft did the lower court convict Mitchneck? What provisions of the Model Penal Code could it have invoked? Section 223.2? Section 223.3? Section 223.8? Would Mitchneck have been found guilty under Model Penal Code §223.8? Would he be more clearly guilty if the word "retains" were added after the word "obtains"?

Would the result in the case have been the same if Mitchneck's employees had drawn their pay and immediately handed the money back to Mitchneck to pay their store bills to Vagnoni? *Should* the case turn on the fact that the employees did *not* do so? Is that too subtle or formal a distinction? Did Mitchneck in any event unlawfully deprive the employees of their property?

2. *Debt vs. crime.* Should creditors be given the power of the state, including the power to imprison, in enforcing contract obligations? If Mitchneck were criminally liable, would criminal liability also extend to every consumer installment buyer who fails to make her payments? To employees who abscond before working off an advance against wages? Would it make a difference that Mitchneck agreed to make payments on behalf of others, to whom he owed money?

2. The Development of Theft Offenses

Why does the Code need any theft provision other than §223.2? To get a sense of the complex historical answer to this reasonable question, consider the three brief but famous cases reproduced below. As you read them, pay particular attention to one issue of great importance in the common law of larceny: timing. The common law required a temporal "concurrence" of act and intent for criminal liability (where intent was required at all).

The elements of common law larceny that had to concur were (1) a "trespassory" taking and carrying away of property; (2) from the possession of another; with (3) the intent to permanently deprive the owner of that property.

The requirement that goods be taken from the *possession* implied that once a thief acquired possession, he could forcibly defend the goods, with the intent to retain them, without being guilty of *larceny*. The owner of the property would have to proceed civilly to vindicate his rights in the property. Thus the moment possession passed to the thief was crucial in determining the thief's criminal liability. In reading the cases below, pay attention to the moment possession passes and the moment when the thief displays an intention to make off with the property. Do they concur?

What was meant by the requirement that the taking be "trespassory"? The meaning of this slippery term appears to have changed over time. One answer is that the taking had to be one that could justify a civil action of trespass against the taker. But this does not mean that any trespassory acquisition of goods was larceny, since the civil action of trespass did not require that all its elements concur in time. At the very least, a trespassory taking was a taking without the consent of the owner. But it appears that "trespass" originally had other connotations: either force or stealth. Thus, though larceny required the taking of moveable property, it typically violated another of the victim's rights — involving either an attack against his person or an invasion of his real property. Thus, it was essentially a robbery or a burglary that "manifested" the thief's dishonest purpose.[1]

The cases that follow, however, all depart from this core image of the thief as robber or burglar. The thief gets possession without forcibly invading the victim's person or premises. Indeed, the victim appears to consent to the thief's possession.

> An owner voluntarily hands over his goods to *D*, whose stated purpose is to use them for a limited time. *D* might plan to return the goods to the owner, or he might plan to deliver them to a third party. At a subsequent time, as things turn out, *D* uses the goods in a manner inconsistent with the owner's rights. He might sell the goods to a stranger, or he might remove the contents of the package he is supposed to deliver. In any case, he converts the goods to his own use.[2]

The thief appears to acquire possession innocuously, so the "trespass" must come later. How, in these cases, do the courts manage to reconcile this form of dishonesty with the traditional requisites of larceny?

THE CASE OF THE CARRIER WHO BROKE BULK
ANON v. THE SHERIFF OF LONDON
Star Chamber (1473)
YB. Pasch. 13 Edw. IV, f. 9, pl. 5 (1473), 64 Selden Soc. 30 (1945)

Before the King's Council in the Star Chamber the matter shown and debated was how a man had made a bargain with another to carry certain bales of

---

1. George Fletcher, The Metamorphosis of Larceny, 89 Harv. L. Rev. 469 (1976).
2. George Fletcher, Manifest Criminality, Criminal Intent, and the Metamorphosis of Lloyd Weinreb, 90 Yale L.J. 319 (1980).

woad [a type of dye] and other things to Southampton, and he took them and carried them to another place, and broke open the bales and took the goods contained in the same feloniously and converted them to his own use, and concealed them. And the case was whether this could be called felony or not.

BRYAN [C.J.C.P]. It seems not, for where they aver that the party has possession by bailment and lawful delivery, there cannot afterwards be said to be felony or trespass touching this; and there can be no felony except with violence and *vi et armis*. But such things as he himself holds, he cannot take *vi et armis* nor against the peace; therefore in cannot be said to be felony or trespass, for there can be no action for these goods except action of detinue etc....

CHOKKE [J.C.P.] It seems that where a man has goods in his possession by reason of a bailment, he cannot take them feloniously when he is in possession, but yet it seems that it is felony, for here the things which were in the bale were not given to him, but the bales as chose entire were delivered *ut supra* to carry etc. in which case if he had given away the bales or sold them, it would not be felony, but when he broke open and took out what was inside, he did this without warrant. Thus if a man is given a tun of wine to carry, if he sells the tun, it is not felony or trespass, but if he took out twenty pints it is felony, for the twenty pints were not given to him, and peradventure he had no knowledge of it at the time of the bailment. So it is if I give the key of my chamber to anyone, if he takes my goods in this chamber, it is felony for they were not given to him....

THE CHANCELLOR... And the matter of felony was argued before the justices in the Exchequer Chamber. And all except Nedeham held that where goods are given to a man he cannot take them feloniously. But Nedeham [J.K.B.] holds the contrary, for he can take them feloniously just as any other man can, and he says that it has been held that a man can take his own goods feloniously. For instance, if I give goods to a man to take care of, and I come secretly like a felon, because I want to recover damages against him by a writ of detinue, and I take the goods secretly like a felon, it is felony. And it was held that where a man has possession and it is determined, it may be felony. For example, if I gave a man goods to carry to my house and he took them there and then took them out of it, this is felony, for when they were in the house his possession is determined etc. But if a taverner serves a man with a drinking cup and he takes it away, this is felony, for he shall not have possession of this drinking cup, for it was put on the table to enable him to drink. And so it is in my house with my butler or my cellarer; they are only servants to do me service, if they carry off etc. it is felony, for they have not possession, but possession is always mine. It would be otherwise if they were given to the servants, peradventure then it may be that they are not felons etc....

REX v. CHISSER
Court of King's Bench (1678)
T. Raym 275, 83 Eng. Rep. 142

Upon a special verdict the jury find that on the day, and at the place in the indictment mentioned, Abraham Chisser came to the shop of Anne Charteris... and asked to see two crevats in the indictment mentioned, which she shewed to him, and delivered them into his hands, and thereupon he asked the price of them, to which she answered 7s, whereupon the said Abraham Chisser offered her 3s and immediately run out of the said shop, and took the said goods openly in her sight, but whether this is felony, or not, is the question. . . .

And I am of the opinion, that this act of Chisser is felony; for that, 1. He shall be said to have taken these goods *felleo animo;* for the act subsequent, viz. his running away with them, explains his intent precedent . . . 2. Although these goods were delivered to Chisser by the owner, yet they were not out of her possession by such delivery, till the property should be altered by the perfection of the contract, which was but inchoated and never perfected between the parties; and when Chisser run away with the goods, it was as if he had taken them up, lying in the shop, and run away with them. . . .

THE KING v. PEAR
I Leach 211, 168 Eng. Rep. 208 (1779)

This case was reserved by MR. JUSTICE ASHHURST, at the Old Bailey in September Session 1779.

The prisoner was indicted for stealing a black horse, the property of one Samuel Finch. It appeared in evidence that Samuel Finch was a Livery-Stable-keeper in the Borough; and that the prisoner, on the 2d of July 1779, hired the horse of him to go to Sutton, in the county of Surry, and back again, saying on being asked where he lived, that he lodged at No. 25 in King-street, and should return about eight o'clock the same evening. He did not return; and it was proved that he had sold the horse on the very day he had hired it, to one William Hollist, in Smithfield Market; and that he had no lodging at the place to which he had given to the prosecutor.

The learned Judge said: There had been different opinions on the law of this class of cases; that the general doctrine then was that if a horse be let for a particular portion of time, and after that time is expired, the party hiring, instead of returning the horse to its owner, sell it and convert the money to his own use, it is felony, because there is then no privity of contract subsisting between the parties; that in the present case the horse was hired to take a journey into Surry, and the prisoner sold him the same day, without taking any such journey; that there were also other circumstances which imported that at the time of the hiring the prisoner had it in intention to sell the horse, as his saying that he lodged at a place where he was not known. He therefore left it with the Jury to consider, Whether the prisoner meant at the time of the hiring to take such journey, but was afterwards tempted to sell the horse? For if so he must be acquitted; but that if they were of opinion that at the time of the hiring the journey was a mere pretence to get the horse into his possession, and he had no intention to take such journey but intended to sell the horse, they would find that fact specially for the opinion of the Judges.

The Jury found that the facts above stated were true; and also that the prisoner had hired the horse with a fraudulent view and intention of selling it immediately.

The question was referred to the Judges, Whether the delivery of the horse by the prosecutor to the prisoner, had so far changed the possession of the property, as to render the subsequent conversion of it a mere breach of trust, or whether the conversion was felonious?

The Judges differed greatly in opinion on this case; and delivered their opinion *seriatim* upon it at Lord Chief Justice De Gray's house on 4th February 1780 and on the 22nd of the same month Mr. Baron Perryn delivered their opinion on it. The majority of them thought, That the question, as to original intention of the prisoner in hiring the horse, had been properly left to the jury; and as they had found, that his view in so doing was fraudulent, the parting with the property had not changed the nature of the possession, but that it remained unaltered in the prosecutor at the time of the conversion; and that the prisoner was therefore guilty of felony.

Notes and Questions

1. Why would the courts have even hesitated to punish the Carrier, Chisser, and Pear for larceny? Are the concerns merely "metaphysical"?

2. *Possession, intent, and larceny.* The history of theft law begins with the common law courts' concern for protecting society against violent breaches of peace. The courts progressed to punishing as larceny all taking of another's property from his possession without his consent, even without force. Professors LaFave and Scott explain:[3]

> The principal factor which limited the scope of larceny was the requirement that the thief must take it from the victim's possession; larceny requires a "trespass in the taking," as the matter is often stated. The judges who determined the scope of larceny (including its limitations) apparently considered larceny to be a crime designed to prevent breaches of the peace rather than aimed at protecting property from misappropriation. The unauthorized taking of property, even by stealth, from the owner's possession is apt to produce an altercation if the owner discovers the property moving out of his possession in the hands of the thief. But when the wrongdoer already has the owner's property at the time he misappropriates (today's embezzlement) or when he obtains the property from the owner by telling him lies (now the crime of false pretenses) there is not the same danger of an immediate breach of the peace.

Because the requirement of a trespassory taking made larceny an offense against possession, a person such as a bailee who had rightfully obtained possession of property from its owner could not be guilty of larceny even if she used the property in a manner against the owner's expectations.

To fill this gap, the courts began manipulating the concept of possession to cover misappropriation by a person who with the consent of the owner already had physical control over the property. Professor Fletcher explains the importance of the Carrier's Case:[4]

> The Carrier's Case, decided in the Star Chamber in 1473, was a major event in the history and theory of larceny. It was the first and only judicial effort to pierce the veil of possessorial immunity and subject a bailee to liability for larceny. The rule of the case, namely, that a bailee is liable if he "breaks bulk" in taking the goods in

---

3. Wayne R. LaFave & Austin W. Scott, Criminal Law 919-920 (2003).
4. George Fletcher, Rethinking Criminal Law 68 (1978).

his possession, has taxed the explanatory powers of commentators for nearly five centuries. . . .

In all of the above cases, the courts implicitly distinguished "possession" from "custody," so that an employer temporarily entrusting his goods to an employee or customer still retained "possession" over the goods until a sale was completed. These fine distinctions, the foundations of the modern statutory offense of theft, enabled the courts to find larceny when the customer, after receiving "custody" of goods, intentionally converted the property to his own use and thereby constructively committed a "trespassory taking."

As the law of theft developed further, the intent element came to dominate the "trespassory taking" requirement. In *Pear*, "larceny by trick" was born when the judges decided that intent to steal overcame the immunity provided by rightfully acquiring possession. The judges reasoned that if Pear's intention was fraudulent from the start, he never acquired legal possession, and so the conversion of the horse (at the time of the sale) was equivalent to the taking and carrying away under common law larceny. Later commentators reinterpreted the effect of Pear's fraudulent intent. They held that Pear's fraudulent intent supplied the element of trespass *at the time of Pear's initial hiring of the horse*. Rather than preventing "possession" from transferring, the fraud meant that possession transferred nonconsensually, and nonconsent was sufficient for trespass. Hence, the larceny took place at the time of the hiring of the horse rather than at the later moment of conversion. We can "modernize" *The Case of the Carrier* and *Chisser* in the same way, by shifting the larceny backward to the moment of apparent consensual delivery. To do so, (1) we must impute to the thieves fraudulent intent at the time they first laid hands on the goods; (2) we must hold that fraud is consistent rather than inconsistent with acquiring possession; and (3) we must hold that fraudulent acquisition of possession is a method of "taking." On this view, the crime is complete as soon as the Carrier, Chisser, or Pear touches the goods.

Following this interpretation, courts gradually took the position that the actor's wrong had less to do with the manner of acquiring physical control over the object than with the intent of the actor as evidenced by his unauthorized exercise of control over the property. Professor Fletcher has argued that this reinterpretation of larceny reflected a larger shift in the law's conception of crime that roughly coincided with the nineteenth century's legislative codification of criminal law, the development of professional police forces, and the shift from corporal and capital punishment of crime to reliance on incarceration in penitentiaries. The common theme is an increasing emphasis on psychology. Just as punishment increasingly aimed at reforming the character of the offender, criminal liability increasingly turned on the actor's subjective intent.

> . . . Under . . . [the subjective] conception, the intent to violate a legally protected interest constitutes the core of the crime. . . . The critical implication of subjective criminality is that an act "quite innocent on its face" may qualify as a criminal act. It does not matter whether mounting the horse[, picking up the cravats, or receiving the bails] . . . incriminates the actor. We trust the police to elicit other forms of evidence to establish the required intent. Confessions are good evidence, as are admissions to friends of the suspect. Prior convictions will do, as will secretive conduct after the incident. . . . [By contrast, the older] principle of manifest criminality rejects the possibility of convicting someone of larceny . . . on the basis

of an act not incriminating on its face. The requirement of a criminal act takes on a different meaning under this conception of criminal behavior: the act must permit an inference of criminal intent.[5]

3. *Trespass and staged larceny.* The requirement of a trespassory taking remained an element of larceny into the twentieth century and played a role in the "staged larceny" case of Topolewski v. State, 130 Wis. 244, 109 N.W. 1037 (1906). The evidence showed that

> . . . The Plankinton Packing Company suspected the accused of having by criminal means possessed himself of some of its property and of having a purpose to make further efforts to that end. A short time before the 14th day of October, 1905, one Mat Dolan, who was indebted to the accused in the sum of upwards of $100.00, was discharged from the company's employ. Shortly therefore the accused pressed Dolan for payment of the aforesaid indebtness and the latter, being unable to respond, the former conceived the idea of solving the difficulty by obtaining some of the company's meat products through Dolan's aid and by criminal means, Dolan to participate in the benefits of the transaction by having the value of the property credited upon his indebtness. . . . [T]he accused proposed that Dolan should procure some packages of the company's meat to be placed on their loading platform, as was customary in delivering meat to customers, and that he should drive to such platform, ostensibly as a customer, and remove such packages. Dolan agreed to the proposition and it was decided that the same should be consummated early the next morning, all of which was reported to [Dolan's supervisor,] Mr. Layer. He thereupon caused four barrels of meat to be packed and put in the accustomed condition for delivery to customers and placed on the platform in readiness for the accused to take them. He set a watch over the property and notified the person in charge of the platform, who was ignorant of the reason for so placing the barrels, upon his inquiring what they were there for, to let them go; that they were for a man who would call for them. About the time appointed for the accused to appear he drove to the platform and commenced putting the barrels in his wagon. The platform boss supposing, as the fact was, that the accused was the man Mr. Layer said was to come for the property, assumed the attitude of consenting to the taking. He did not actually help load the barrels on the wagon, but he was by, consented by his manner and when the accused was ready to go, helped him arrange his wagon and inquired what was to be done with the fourth barrel. The accused replied that he wanted it marked and sent up to him with a bill. He told the platform boss that he ordered the stuff the night before through Dolan. He took full possession of the three barrels of meat with intent to deprive the owner permanently thereof and without compensating it therefor, wholly in ignorance, however, of the fact that Dolan had acted in the matter on behalf of such owner and that it knowingly aided in carrying out the plan of obtaining the meat. [Id. 109 N.W. at 1038.]

Reversing the conviction, the court held:

> It will be noted that the plan for depriving the packing company of its property originated with the accused, but that it was wholly impracticable of accomplishment without the property being placed on the loading platform and the accused not being interfered with when he attempted to take it. When Dolan agreed to procure such placing the packing company in legal effect agreed thereto. Dolan

5. Fletcher, 90 Yale L.J. at 338-40.

did not expressly consent nor did the agreement he had with the packing company authorize him to do so, to the misappropriation of the property. Did the agreement in legal effect with the accused to place the property of the packing company on the loading platform, where it could be appropriated by the accused . . . constitute consent to such appropriation?

The case is very near the border line, if not across it, between consent and nonconsent to the taking of the property. Reg. v. Lawrence, 4 Cox C.C. 438, it was held that if the property was delivered by a servant to the defendant by the master's direction the offense cannot be larceny, regardless of the purpose of the defendant. In this case the property was not only placed on the loading platform, as was usual in delivering such goods to customers, with knowledge that the accused would soon arrive, having a formed design to take it, but the packing company's employee in charge of the platform, Ernst Klotz, was instructed that the property was there for a man who would call for it. . . . [Klotz's conduct] amounted, practically, to a delivery of the three barrels to the accused. . . .

We cannot well escape the conclusion that this case falls under the condemnation of the rule that where the owner of property by himself or his agent, actually or constructively, aids in the commission of the offense, as intended by the wrongdoer, by performing or rendering unnecessary some act in the transaction essential to the offense, the would-be criminal is not guilty of all the elements of the offense. . . .

The logical basis for the doctrine above discussed is that there can be no larceny without trespass. So if one procures his property to be taken by another intending to commit larceny, or delivers his property to such other, the latter purposing to commit such crime, the element of trespass is wanting and the crime not fully consummated however plain may be the guilty purpose of the one possessing himself of such property. That does not militate against a person's being free to set a trap to catch one whom he suspects of an intention to commit the crime of larceny, but the setting of such trap must not go further than to afford the would-be thief the amplest opportunity to carry out his purpose, formed without such inducement on the part of the owner of the property, as to put him in the position of having consented to the taking. . . . [Id. at 1039-41.]

Why did not Topolewski's fraudulent intent vitiate the packing company's consent to his possession?

4. *Embezzlement.* While the English courts expanded the concept of trespassory taking to include obtaining by fraud, they did not eliminate the requirement of a taking from possession. In Bazeley's Case, 2 East P.C. 571 (Cr. Cas. Res. 1799), a bank teller was charged with larceny after pocketing a hundred pounds presented by a customer for deposit in his account, and then using it to pay a bill owed by another business in which he was involved. Defense counsel argued that "To constitute the crime of larceny, the property must be taken from the possession of the owner. . . . The Prosecutors in the present case had only a right or title to possess the note, and not the . . . possession of it. It was never in their custody or control." The court agreed. Parliament responded by creating the statutory offense of embezzlement, defined as the fraudulent conversion of money or goods received by an employee for his employer (39 Geo. III, c. 85 (1799)).

5. *False pretenses.* Pear purported to rent the horse, a transaction that confers possession but not title. Suppose he had instead induced Samuel Finch to sell him the horse on credit, by giving a false name and address, perhaps pretending to be a clergyman related to a local squire. He would have been guilty of the offense of obtaining (title to) property by false pretenses, created by statute in 1757 (30 Geo. II, c. 24). The false pretense would have been his false

claims as to his identity rather than his false promise to pay. The offense of false pretenses depended upon a material misrepresentation of fact, not an insincere promise or expression of opinion. If Pear had gained title to the horse by using a forged letter or draft, he would have been guilty of the still older statutory offense of obtaining property by false token (33 Hen. VIII, c. 1 (1541)).

6. *The forms of theft.* The emerging typology of theft had three key categories: larceny, embezzlement, and false pretenses or fraud. Consider the following comments by Professor Fletcher:[6]

> In general terms, we could identify the voluntary participation of the victim as the source of the distinctions among these three classic offenses. Larceny is committed against an involuntary victim. Embezzlement is committed against a victim who voluntarily entrusts possession of his goods to the defendant, but who is an involuntary victim of the defendant's subsequent appropriation. The crime of obtaining property by false pretenses is committed against a victim who nominally consents to the transfer of his goods to the defendant. Yet his nominal consent is induced by fraud and therefore does not reflect the owner's true preference. In a fourth type of offense, extortion, the owner again nominally consents to the surrender of property. But in this variation the consent is induced by improper threats rather than fraud. . . .
>
> In English legal history, embezzlement is engrafted onto the crime of larceny in a series of eighteenth-century statutory enactments, which typically took the form of extending larceny to encompass cases now called embezzlement. In the nineteenth century, the English courts began to hold that the most far-reaching of these eighteenth-century statutes, that of 39 George III (1799), created a new offense of embezzlement. . . . [E]mbezzlement is a creature of legislative will that varies from jurisdiction to jurisdiction. The legislative schemes typically require (1) that the offender has been entrusted with the object by the owner, or at least have possession at the time of the offense, and (2) a subsequent act of deprivation, usually termed conversion or fraudulent appropriation. The differences among legislative schemes turn primarily on whether they are comprehensive or whether they are limited to specified relationships of trust. The generative English Statute of 1799 was limited to "servants and clerks". . . . Yet the inclusion of some and the exclusion of others . . . has never seemed to be backed by convincing arguments of principle, and therefore the historical pattern has been to expand the categories of persons subject to liability. . . .
>
> [T]he eighteenth-century English courts found that a necessary condition for the crime of fraud was that the defendant's false pretense induce the victim to part with title in his goods. Thus in this judicial refinement, the offense does not apply where the pretense merely induces the owner to part with possession, but not title — as in a transaction of lease or pledge. This restriction of the offense, coupled with the expansion of larceny, has generated particular difficulties in distinguishing larceny from the crime of false pretenses. A good example is Graham v. United States[, 187 F.2d 87 (D.C. Cir. 1950)], in which the victim gave the defendant, a lawyer, $2,000 that this lawyer was to use in bribing the police on the victim's behalf. In fact, the defendant was honest about bribing but not about stealing; he kept the money for himself. On appeal from the defendant's conviction for larceny, the dispute was whether the victim had parted with title or merely possession in the sum of money. The appellate court affirmed the conviction on the ground that the owner had not intended to part with title, but merely possession and that therefore, the appropriate charge was larceny rather than false pretenses.

6. Fletcher, Rethinking Criminal Law at 3-9 (1978).

It is obvious that one could have maintained that the victim had parted with the $2,000 with no intention of ever seeing it again, and that is an intent to pass title if anything is.

. . . Contemporary efforts at law reform in Anglo-American jurisdictions point . . . toward looser boundaries in the law of false pretenses. The English Theft Law of 1968 casts the net of fraud wide enough to include anyone who obtains "ownership, possession or control" of property by a fraudulent deception. This definition would obviously include *Graham* as well as many other cases of larceny. The Model Penal Code takes a more conservative line, insisting upon transfer of "property" as an element in theft by deception.

Another area in which the Anglo-American law of false pretenses is enjoying a relaxation of earlier restraints is in the requirement of pretense itself. The earlier rule was that the actor had to induce the victim to transfer title by deception about the external world — about, say, the defendant's credit status or the quality of goods offered for sale. In the 1954 case of People v. Ashley, 267 P.2d 271 (1954), the California Supreme Court boldly swept aside the requirement of an objective misrepresentation and held that a misrepresentation about one's intention could be a false pretense. That precedent has not garnered a following in other common-law courts. But the trend of contemporary legislation is to drop the traditional requirement of an objective, documentable lie and embrace the potential punishability of routine credit transactions. It is now possible to commit the crime of false pretenses in many jurisdictions by borrowing money with the intent not to repay it. . . . Though the borrower falsely promises to repay the loan, he engages in no deception about the external world that is subject to proof at the time of his act. His deception, if any, is about his plans for the future, and the best evidence of that is what he does when the debt falls due. Though the crime is technically committed at the time the loan is received, the critical evidence of liability is furnished by his failure to repay at some future time. . . .

7. *The need for consolidation.* The existence of three such similar crimes, divided by the thin and hazy lines between title, possession, and custody, could produce very awkward results, as illustrated by the case of Commonwealth v. O'Malley, 97 Mass. 584 (1867), in which the victim handed the defendant a wad of bills to count and from which she authorized him to take a dollar as a loan. O'Malley, however, ran off with the entire amount. O'Malley was initially tried for larceny and acquitted, apparently on the ground that he might have formulated the intent to steal the bills only after receiving possession of them. O'Malley was then indicted and convicted of embezzlement. He successfully appealed:

HOAR, J. We are of opinion that there was no evidence to sustain the indictment for embezzlement, and that the conviction was wrong. The defendant had been previously acquitted of larceny upon proof of the same facts; and it is therefore of great importance to him, if the offence committed, if any, was larceny, that it should be so charged.

To constitute the crime of embezzlement, the property which the defendant is accused of fraudulently and feloniously converting to his own use, must be shown to have been entrusted to him, so that it was in his possession, and not in the possession of the owner. But the facts reported in the bill of exceptions do not show that the possession of the owner of the money was ever divested. She allowed the defendant to take it for the purpose of counting it in her presence, and taking from it a dollar, which she consented to lend him. The money is alleged to have consisted of two ten-dollar bills, three five-dollar bills, a two-dollar bill, and a one-dollar bill, amounting in all to thirty-eight dollars. The one dollar he had a right to retain, but the rest of the money he was only authorized to count in her presence and hand back to her. He had it in his hands, but not in his possession, any more than he would have had possession of a chair on which she might have invited him to sit. The distinction pointed out in the instructions of the court between his getting it into his hands with a felonious intent, or forming the intent after he had taken it, was therefore unimportant. The true distinction, upon principle and authority, is that . . . if the owner puts his property into the hands of another, to use it or do some act in relation to it, in his presence, he does not part with the possession, and the conversion of it, *animo furandi*, is larceny. [Id. at 586-87.]

Just as it may be difficult to distinguish larceny from embezzlement, as in *O'Malley,* and larceny from false pretenses, as in *Graham,* it may also be difficult to distinguish false pretenses from extortion, as pointed out in the Model Penal Code Commentaries:[7]

In Norton v. United States, 92 F.2d 753 (9th Cir. 1937), the defendant was convicted under the mail-fraud statute of scheming to defraud Clark Gable by representing in letters to him that as a result of illicit relations with him she had given birth to a child for whom she sought support. The indictment charged that the representations were false in that no such relations had ever occurred and that Gable had not even been in England during the year in which they were alleged to have occurred. Conviction was reversed on the ground that although the scheme employed a false pretense, and although no threat to make the charge public was involved, the method employed was a resort to coercion or fear rather than trickery or deception.

8. *Consolidation schemes.* Many jurisdictions have responded to these difficulties by adopting consolidated theft statutes, which combine larceny, embezzlement, false pretenses, and perhaps extortion in a single offense of "theft." The following Ohio provision is typical:

2913.02. *Theft.*

(A) No person, with purpose to deprive the owner of property or services, shall knowingly obtain or exert control over either the property or services in any of the following ways:

(1) Without the consent of the owner or person authorized to give consent;

(2) Beyond the scope of the express or implied consent of the owner or person authorized to give consent;

(3) By deception;

(4) By threat.

(B) Whoever violates this section is guilty of theft.

The Model Penal Code's Article 223 involves a somewhat more elaborate scheme explained in the following comment:[8]

Article 223 recognizes the substantive problems inherent in the different forms of theft by dealing in Sections 223.2 through 223.8 with different methods

7. Model Penal Code and Commentaries Part II, at 134, n.9 (Official Draft and Revised Comments 1980).

8. Id. at 136-37.

of acquisitive behavior. Section 223.1(1), however, creates the single offense of "theft" which is committed by violation of any one of the succeeding sections. . . .

The second sentence of Subsection (1) provides that an accusation of theft may be supported by evidence that it was committed in any manner that would be theft under Article 223, even though a different manner was specified in the indictment or information. The defendant is thus foreclosed from defending on the basis that his conduct was not larceny as charged but extortion. These offenses are abolished as separate categories of crime and are to be charged as the single theft offense created by this article.

There is, however, the problem of fair notice to the defendant. . . . [A]ccount must be taken of the possibility that too great a variance between charge and proof may render an indictment or information insufficient to apprise the defendant of the case he must meet. Accordingly, the last clause of Subsection (1) refers to the inherent power of the court to ensure a fair trial by granting a continuance or other appropriate relief where the conduct of the defense would be prejudiced by lack of fair notice or by surprise.

9. *Intent to deprive.* The Model Penal Code and the Ohio Code both condition the consolidated theft offense on intent to "deprive." Does this require an intent to deprive permanently? Entirely? Certainly? Model Penal Code §223.0(1) further defines "deprive" as "(a) to withhold property from another permanently or for so extended a period as to appropriate a major portion of its economic value, or with intent to restore only upon payment of reward or other compensation; or (b) to dispose of the property so as to make it unlikely that the owner will recover it." The Ohio statute defines "deprive" similarly, but adds accepting property or money "with purpose not to give proper consideration in return." (§2913.01(c)(3) (2004).)

In State v. Bautista, 86 Hawaii 207, 948 P.2d 1048 (1997), the defendant bought a new truck and paid by check, but the check bounced. He then returned the truck as requested, but with 592 miles on the odometer, so the truck could not be sold as new. The evidence showed that the defendant's plan all along was to have the car for the weekend. The statute said it was theft "to withhold property or cause it to be withheld from a person permanently or for so extended a period of time or under such circumstance that a significant portion of its economic value, or the use and benefit thereof, is lost to him," but the court reversed the conviction of theft in the first degree (taking the property of $20,000 or more) for want of sufficient evidence of significant deprivation. Did Bautista "steal" a lesser amount?

The intent to deprive another of property implies knowledge that the property in question belongs to another or that another is entitled to possess it. In Chapter 3 we saw the Supreme Court requiring such a mental element for a federal theft offense in Morissette v. United States (p. 166, *supra*). This requirement of knowledge that another owns or is entitled to possess the property has traditionally been referred to as the absence of a "claim of right." Model Penal Code §223.1(3) provides:

(3) *Claim of Right.* It is an affirmative defense to prosecution for theft that the actor:
(a) was unaware that the property or service was that of another; or
(b) acted under an honest claim of right to the property or service involved or that he had a right to acquire or dispose of it as he did; or

(c) took property exposed for sale, intending to purchase and pay for it promptly, or reasonably believing that the owner, if present, would have consented.

10. *The object of theft.* Traditionally, larceny was restricted to the theft of tangible, movable property. Consider Lund v. Commonwealth, 232 S.E.2d 745 (Va. 1977):

Defendant, Charles Walter Lund, was charged in an indictment with the theft of keys, computer cards, computer printouts and using "without authority computer operation time and services of Computer Center Personnel at Virginia Polytechnic Institute . . . with intent to defraud, such property and services having a value of one hundred dollars or more." . . . He was found guilty of grand larceny and sentenced to two years in the State penitentiary. . . .

Defendant was a graduate student in statistics and a candidate for a Ph.D. degree. . . . The preparation of his dissertation on the subject assigned to him by his faculty advisor required the use of computer operation time and services of the computer center personnel at the University. His faculty advisor neglected to arrange for defendant's use of the computer, but defendant used it without obtaining the proper authorization. . . .

An account is established when a duly authorized administrator or "department head" fills out a form allocating funds to a department of the University and an individual. When such form is received, the computer center assigns an account number to this allocation and provides a key to a locked post office box which is also numbered to the authorized individual and department. The account number and the post office box number are the access code which must be provided with each request before the computer will process a "deck of cards" prepared by the user and delivered to computer center personnel. The computer printouts are usually returned to the locked post office box. . . .

Defendant came under surveillance on October 12, 1974, because of complaints from various departments that unauthorized charges were being made to one or more of their accounts. When confronted by the University's investigator, defendant initially denied that he had used the computer service, but later admitted that he had. He gave to the investigator seven keys for boxes assigned to other persons. One of these keys was secreted in his sock. He told the investigating officer he had been given the keys by another student. A large number of computer cards and printouts were taken from defendant's apartment.

The director of the computer center testified that the unauthorized sum spent out of the accounts associated with the seven post office box keys amounted to $5,065. He estimated that on the basis of the computer cards and printouts obtained from the defendant, as much as $26,384.16 in unauthorized computer time had been used by the defendant. He said, however, that the value of the cards and printouts obtained from the defendant was "whatever scrap paper is worth."

Defendant testified that he used the computer without specific authority. He stated that he knew he was a large computer user, but, because he was doing work on his doctoral dissertation, he did not consider this use excessive or that "he was doing anything wrong." . . .

The Commonwealth concedes that the defendant could not be convicted of grand larceny of the keys and computer cards because there was no evidence that those articles were stolen and that they had a market value of $100 or more. The Commonwealth argues, however, that the evidence shows the defendant violated the provisions of §18.1-118 when he obtained by false pretense or token, with intent to defraud, the computer printouts which had a value of over $5,000.

Under the provisions of Code §18.1-118, for one to be guilty of the crime of larceny by false pretense, he must make a false representation of an existing fact with knowledge of its falsity and, on that basis, obtain from another person money or other property which may be the subject of larceny, with the intent to defraud. . . .

. . . The phrase "goods and chattels" cannot be interpreted to include computer time and services in light of the often repeated mandate that criminal statutes must be strictly construed. . . .

At common law, labor or services could not be the subject of the crime of false pretense because neither time nor services may be taken and carried away. It has been generally held that, in the absence of a clearly expressed legislative intent, labor or services could not be the subject of the statutory crime of false pretense. . . . We have no such provision in our statutes.

Furthermore, the unauthorized use of the computer is not the subject of larceny. Nowhere in Code §18.1-100 or §18.1-118 do we find the word "use." The language of the statutes connotes more than just the unauthorized use of the property of another. It refers to a taking and carrying away of a certain concrete article of personal property. . . .

The Commonwealth argues that even though the computer printouts had no market value, their value can be determined by the cost of the labor and services that produced them. We do not agree.

The cost of producing the printouts is not the proper criterion of value for the purpose here. Where there is no market value of an article that has been stolen, the better rule is that its actual value should be proved. . . . Here the evidence shows that the printouts had no ascertainable monetary value to the University or the computer center. Indeed, the director of the computer center stated that the printouts had no more value than scrap paper. Nor is there any evidence of their value to the defendant, and the value to him could only be based on pure speculation and surmise. Hence, the evidence was insufficient to convict the defendant of grand larceny under either Code §18.1-100 or §18.1-118. . . . [Id. at 746-48.]

By contrast to the theft statutes applied in *Lund,* the Model Penal Code criminalizes theft of services. (§223.7.) The Code also defines property as "anything of value, including real estate, tangible and intangible personal property, contract rights, choses-in-action and other interests in or claims to wealth, admission or transportation tickets, captured or domestic animals, food and drink, electric or other power." (§223.0(7).)

B. FRAUD

1. False Pretenses

PEOPLE v. SATTLEKAU
Supreme Court of New York, Appellate Division
120 App. Div. 42, 104 N.Y.S. 805 (1907)

CLARKE, J. The defendant was indicted and convicted of the crime of grand larceny in the first degree for obtaining by false pretenses the sum of $1,000 from Rosa Kaiser, a lady's maid and seamstress. The defendant first met the complaining witness near the flower stand at the Grand Central Depot on April 20, 1906, through an advertisement inserted by him in the New York Herald, signed "Bachelor," and which, according to his testimony, read:

> Good woman wanted. Practical housekeeper for hotel purposes. Possibility of matrimony.

The witness answered this advertisement by letter, giving her name and address, and stating:

> If gentleman would correspond with reference to the letters, I would like to get particulars.

In reply she received from the defendant a letter, signed "E. Paul," upon a paper bearing the heading: "Uncle Sam Hotel, E. Paul, Prop. Rates $2 per day; special by the week, Millville, Pa." — arranging for an interview at the Grand Central Depot. The defendant met her, stated to her that he was Ernest Paul (although his real name was Sattlekau), asked whether she was Miss Kaiser and whether she had received his letter, and upon receiving an affirmative answer asked her to take a walk. They went to the Terrace Garden, heard the music, and had a long talk. Subsequently she had eight or nine interviews with him, during the course of which he made to her the following representations, as set out in the indictment: That he was then and there a single and unmarried man, and then and there in a condition and able to intermarry with her; that he was then the owner and proprietor or of a certain hotel, called "Uncle Sam Hotel," situated at the town of Millville, in the state of Pennsylvania, and that a certain man named Morgan, at Millville, Pa., had heretofore offered, and was then and there ready and desirous, to purchase the said hotel from him for the sum of $6,000; that he then and there had an option for the lease for the period of 15 years, for the sum of $20,000, of a certain hotel, called the "Studio," situated on the east side of Sixth avenue, and that he was desirous of procuring from her, the said Rosa Kaiser, the sum of $1,000 for the purpose of enabling him to lease the said hotel; and that he desired to lease the said hotel for the purpose, among other things, of making the same a home for her and himself, to be occupied by them upon their marriage. He had made other false statements, not set out in the indictment, but proved upon the trial. On the 19th of April, 1906, he wrote to her the following letter:

> My Dear Rosa:
>
> I have been hustling things here to stay in great shape. Saw the bank cashier, and as a personal favor he will increase the loan to $3,000, instead of $2,000. I can have the loan for years, as long as I pay the interest. Then I called Morgan, the man who wants the Uncle Sam Hotel, and told him I was ready to do business. He promptly got out a bank deposit certificate for $4,000; but the other $2,000 he cannot pay till the 15th of May. He has the money for the mortgage. From the banker I learned that the party who owes Morgan the money has more than $2,000 in bank, and that the money will be promptly paid on the 15th. Of course, until Morgan pays the $2,000, I do not turn the place over to him, so that I will get another 15 days out of the place here. Business is good, and as I am not buying any stock

now, I can figure on some $300, to go to me in these 15 days. You will see now that I have all the $18,000 I need for the New York business.

My bank balance is some	$ 8,700
Until the 15th I will take in	300
Total bank balance	$ 9,000
Received from Morgan on account of the sale	
of the hotel	4,000
	$13,000
Loan from the bank	3,000
	$16,000
To be paid by Morgan on the 15th of May	2,000
	$18,000

If I could wait until the 15th now, to buy the New York place, I would be all right; but the man told me Saturday that he could not hold the place for her after Monday noon, as there are two other parties after it. So I will have to find $2,000 on Monday morning, $1,000 I can get from the whisky firm I told you about, and the other $1,000 I want you to furnish, if you will. I will pay it back on the 15th, when get Morgan's $2,000, and for the two weeks I will pay you 6 per cent, interest, same as I pay my bank for the $3,000. I will give you a judgment note for the $1,000, and that is the only judgment note I have to give. All the $18,000 I own will stand as security for your transaction, even if you do not consider the fact that you are helping the man who is going to be your husband in a month, and that by helping him, of course, you are helping yourself. I expect to reach the Ashland House, Fourth avenue, near Twenty-Third street, on Monday morning about 10 o'clock, and would like you to meet me there and go to the bank with me and get the $1,000. Tell your lady you must get off for an hour to attend some important business. If she kicks, tell her to take the job, and you take a rest for a month, until we get married. I am giving this letter to a man who is going to New York on the next train, and who will mail it on his arrival there, so it will reach you Monday first mail. With kindest regards,

Yours sincerely,
Ernest

On the 1st of May, 1906, complainant testified that she met the defendant, at his request, at a hotel in this city, and that he said to her:

"We must hasten. I want to finish this deal about the hotel, and I must have the money. You must go to the bank and get it, and I will go with you."

She testified that she drew $1,000 from the bank, and they went back to the hotel, where the defendant said: "'I want you to give me the money now.' He said that I was perfectly safe, as he was the owner of the Uncle Sam Hotel, and he said he was a wealthy man, and I was perfectly secure about the money, and I would get it back"— and that, believing his statements to be true and relying upon them, she gave him the $1,000; and then he said, "Now I must go and finish up this deal," that he said, "I will meet you at 5 o'clock at the hotel again"; that she was there and waited, but instead of seeing the defendant again she received from him a telegram. The telegram was:

Hoboken Depot, N.J., 21st. To Mrs. E. Paul: Telegram Millville place afire, leaving next train. Will wire tomorrow. Do not worry. Ernest.

Subsequently, she received a letter, written on paper with the same heading as that on which his first letter was written — that is, "Uncle Sam Hotel. E. Paul, Proprietor" — reading:

Millville, Pa. May 1st, 1906

My Dear Rosa:

Got telegram about fire just after you left. Stopped the deal in New York, because, if damage is heavy, it will cripple me financially, as I will have to pay back the $4,000, and won't have any place to sell. Will write you in a day or so how bad the fire was. Do not worry. You will not lose anything, only you will have to wait for me a little.

Yours ever,
Ernest

These were the only communications that she received from the defendant after giving him the $1,000, and she did not see him again until after his arrest, The defendant was arrested on July 13, near the flower stand at the Grand Central Station, just as he was bowing to and addressing another woman who had some flowers in her hand. In his first letter to the complaining witness, arranging for the interview, he has said, "For recognition, please carry a few violets in your hand." He admitted that he was a married man, and that he had received probably a hundred answers to similar advertisements he had put in the newspapers, and he had in his possession a list of the names and addresses of his correspondents,

The defendant was a witness in his own behalf and was examined at great length. He called no other witnesses to substantiate his story, which in essential details corroborated that of the complaining witness, and where it contradicted her was self-contradictory and not credible. The jury properly found a verdict of guilty. The evidence was sufficient to justify the finding that the presentation that defendant was the owner of the Uncle Sam Hotel was the representation of an existing fact, that said representation was false, that the complaining witness believed it to be true, and that in reliance upon its truth she gave the defendant $1,000. There was no Uncle Sam Hotel at Millville, Pa., and the defendant was not the proprietor of it. It was not burned on the day he got her $1,000. The deliberate intention to defraud, the falsity of the pretenses made, and the reliance by the complaining witness thereon were fully established. If there were such a crime as obtaining money under false pretenses, this is that case. The defendant was a clever swindler of confiding women.

The appellant urges that the indictment is defective, because it does not contain an allegation to the effect that the complainant relied upon the representations alleged in the indictment to have been made by the defendant to her, and that such an allegation is absolutely necessary to the validity of an indictment for grand larceny by false pretenses. . . . [In People v. Baker, 96 N.Y. 340, the court held:]

In order to constitute the crime of obtaining property by false pretenses, it is not sufficient to prove the false pretenses and that property was obtained thereby; but it must be proved that the false pretenses were made with intent to cheat and defraud another.

Here [the] intent to cheat and defraud were abundantly proved. . . . Again:

> Another essential element of the crime . . . is that the money was paid or the property parted with in reliance upon or under the inducement of the false pretenses alleged.

Here the people did establish that the money was paid in reliance upon the false pretenses alleged.

The appellant further alleges that the indictment is also defective in that it does not allege that complainant believed to be true the representations alleged to have been made, or that they were the inducing cause of the complainant's parting with her money. . . .

> By color and by aid of which said false and fraudulent representations the said Ernest Paul did then and there feloniously and fraudulently obtain from the possession of the said Rosa Kaiser the sum of $1,000, with intent to deprive and defraud the said Rosa Kaiser of the same and of the use and benefit thereof, and to appropriate the same to his own use.

This is equivalent to alleging that Rosa Kaiser, in parting with her property, relied upon that pretense.

The appellant further urges that the indictment is also defective because the representations alleged therein are not all of existing facts; that some representations express the defendant's desires, wishes, or hopes, others refer to his means or ability to pay debts, others as to promises or intentions to do things in the future; . . . In the case at bar, the people proved that between April 20th and May 1st, the date when the defendant obtained the money from Rosa Kaiser, defendant made, not only the representations as to the existing facts mentioned in the indictment, but also other representations. Proof of these other representations was clearly competent as part of the res gestae. . . . "It is not necessary, to sustain a conviction, that such pretense should be the sole inducement to the act of the party defrauded." People ex rel. Phelps v. Court of Oyer and Terminer, 83 N.Y. 436. . . .

The judgment, therefore, should be affirmed.

Notes and Questions

1. *Elements of false pretenses.* The court states the three key elements of the crime — intent to defraud, a material misrepresentation of fact, and the victim's reliance upon that misrepresentation in deciding to part with her property. Would it have been any less "fraudulent" if the sole "misrepresentation" of the defendant had been as to his intentions or promises, rather than as to an existing fact? Is the reason for distinguishing these two types of misrepresentation rooted in some moral difference, or is it just a matter of difficulties of proof?

2. Was Rosa Kaiser wise to entrust her savings to a man she had recently met through a newspaper ad? If she relied on his claims to wealth unreasonably, was "the inducing cause" of her loss really the defendant's fraud rather than her own gullibility? Courts have traditionally conditioned the offense of false pretenses on actual rather than reasonable reliance.

3. The traditional elements of false pretenses — especially the requirement of actual reliance by the victim on the defendant's deceit — have persisted in contemporary criminal law, even in the modern regulatory state. For example, in People v. Levitas, 40 Misc. 2d 331, 243 N.Y.S.2d 234 (1963), the defendant landlord Jakubovitz was convicted of larceny by fraud when he falsified claims of repair to the rent control board and thereby won permission for unmerited rent increases. The court reversed the conviction because it was the rent control board that received the false statements, yet it was only the blissfully innocent tenants who paid the extra money. Could the court have managed to identify reliance here?

2. Scheme to Defraud in Federal Law

For over a century, federal prosecutors have had in their arsenal the powerful and versatile weapon known as the mail fraud statute. This statute is one of a number of criminal statutes passed pursuant to Congress's Article 1, Section 8 powers to regulate the mails and to prevent criminals from exploiting so-called instrumentalities of interstate commerce — especially the telephone and other wire or electronic communications. Many federal fraud offenses are formulated as "inchoate" or anticipatory crimes. Thus the offense punished by the mail fraud statute is not obtaining property by false pretenses, but the distinct offense of scheme to defraud. In current form, the statute reads as follows:

18 U.S.C. §1341. Frauds and Swindles

Whoever, having devised or intending to devise any scheme or artifice to defraud, or for obtaining money or property by means of false or fraudulent pretenses, representations, or promises, . . . for the purpose of executing such scheme or artifice . . . places in any post office or authorized depository for mail matter, any matter or thing whatever to be sent or delivered by the Postal Service, or deposits or causes to be deposited any matter or thing whatever to be sent or delivered by any private or commercial interstate carrier, . . . shall be fined not more than $1,000 or imprisoned not more than five years, or both. If the violation affects a financial institution, such person shall be fined not more than $1,000,000 or imprisoned not more than 30 years, or both.[9]

DURLAND V. UNITED STATES
Supreme Court of the United States
161 U.S. 306 (1896)

[The indictment charged Durland with running a dishonest "tontine" (a group investment plan) called the Provident Bond and Investment Company, whereby he would trick individuals into "investing" such small amounts of

---

9. The parallel "wire fraud" statute, 18 U.S.C. §1343, equally punishes schemes where the accused "transmits or causes to be transmitted by means of wire, radio, or television communication in interstate or foreign commerce, any writings, signs, signals, pictures, or sounds for the purpose of executing such scheme or artifice."

money as five dollars a month and promising them large returns. The rate of return would increase the longer that the investors left their money with Durland, ultimately running as high as 50 percent over six months.] A brochure advertising the bond plan stated:

A Nut for Lottery Cranks to Crack

We give below our graduatory scale of redemption values, which is a complete refutation of the charge that a "lottery" element enters into the methods of the Provident Bond and Investment Company. It will be observed that a steadily increasing cash value applies to every bond in force from its issue to redemption; that every bond of equal age has the same cash value.

It is a further fact that every bond is nonforfeitable and interest bearing, having both "cash surrender" and loan values. Where does the lottery element come in?

MR. JUSTICE BREWER . . . delivered the opinion of the court.

Inasmuch as the testimony has not been preserved, we must assume that it was sufficient to substantiate the charges in the indictments; that this was a scheme and artifice to defraud; and that the defendant did not intend that the bonds should mature, or that, although money was received, any should be returned, but that it should be appropriated to his own use. In other words, he was trying to entrap the unwary, and to secure money from them on the faith of a scheme glittering and attractive in form, yet unreal and deceptive in fact, and known to him to be such. So far as the moral element is concerned, it must be taken that the defendant's guilt was established.

But the contention on his part is that the statute reaches only such cases as, at common law, would come within the definition of "false pretenses," in order to make out which there must be a misrepresentation as to some existing fact, and not a mere promise as to the future. It is urged that there was no misrepresentation as to the existence or solvency of the corporation the Provident Bond & Investment Company, or as to its modes of doing business; no suggestion that it failed to issue its bonds to any and every one advancing the required dues; or that its promise of payment according to the conditions named in the bond was not a valid and binding promise. And then as counsel say in their brief, "it [the indictment] discloses on its face absolutely nothing but an intention to commit a violation of a contract. If there be one principle of criminal law that is absolutely settled by an overwhelming avalanche of authority, it is that fraud either in the civil courts or in the criminal courts must be the misrepresentation of an existing or a past fact, and cannot consist of the mere intention not to carry out a contract in the future."

The question thus presented is one of vital importance, and underlies both cases. We cannot agree with counsel. The statute is broader than is claimed. Its letter shows this: "Any scheme or artifice to defraud." Some schemes may be promoted through mere representations and promises as to the future, yet are none the less schemes and artifices to defraud. Punishment because of the fraudulent purpose is no new thing. As said by Mr. Justice Brown, in Evans v. U.S., 153 U.S. 584, 592, 14 Sup. Ct. 934: "If a person buys goods on credit in good faith, knowing that he is unable to pay for them at the time, but believing that he will be able to pay for them at the maturity of the bill, he is guilty of no offense, even if he be disappointed in making such payment. But if he purchases them knowing that he will not be able to pay for them, and with an intent to cheat the vendor, this is a plain fraud, and made punishable as such by statutes in many of the states."

But beyond the letter of the statute is the evil sought to be remedied, which is always significant in determining the meaning. It is common knowledge that nothing is more alluring than the expectation of receiving large returns on small investments. Eagerness to take the chances of large gains lies at the foundation of all lottery schemes, and, even when the matter of chance is eliminated, any scheme or plan which holds out the prospect of receiving more than is parted with appeals to the cupidity of all.

In the light of this the statute must be read, and, so read, it includes everything designed to defraud by representations as to the past or present, or suggestions and promises as to the future. The significant fact is the intent and purpose. The question presented by this indictment to the jury was not, as counsel insist, whether the business scheme suggested in this bond was practicable or not. If the testimony had shown that this Provident Company, and the defendant, as its president, had entered in good faith upon that business, believing that out of the moneys received they could, by investment or otherwise, make enough to justify the promised returns, no conviction could be sustained, no matter how visionary might seem the scheme. The charge is that, in putting forth this scheme, it was not the intent of the defendant to make an honest effort for its success, but that he resorted to this form and pretense of a bond without a thought that he or the company would ever make good its promises. It was with the purpose of protecting the public against all such intentional efforts to despoil, and to prevent the post office from being used to carry them into effect, that this statute was passed; and it would strip it of value to confine it to such cases as disclose an actual misrepresentation as to some existing fact, and exclude those in which is only the allurement of a promise. This, which is the principal contention of counsel, must be overruled. . . .

We do not wish to be understood as intimating that, in order to constitute the offense, it must be shown that the letters so mailed were of a nature calculated to be effective in carrying out the fraudulent scheme. It is enough if, having devised a scheme to defraud, the defendant, with a view of executing it, deposits in the post office letters which he thinks may assist in carrying it into effect, although, in the judgment of the jury, they may be absolutely ineffective therefor.

. . . [T]he judgment in each of these cases is affirmed.

Notes and Questions

1. *An inchoate crime.* As *Durland* establishes, the key distinction between common law criminal fraud and federal mail (or wire) fraud is that the latter's notion of a "scheme to defraud" amounts to an inchoate crime, not requiring actual reliance or transfer of property by any victim. In United States v. King, 860 F.2d 54 (2d Cir. 1988), the facts were:

> Roger King, a Vice-President of J.J. King, a distributor of highway maintenance equipment . . . participated in a scheme in which the prices of various equipment offered for sale to two municipalities were inflated. Under the scheme, King broke the offering price down into several separate components so that corrupt

municipal purchasing agents could evade competitive bidding requirements applicable to higher priced items. The total of these prices was then inflated in order to obtain money to pay kickbacks to those agents. [Id. at 54.]

The defense presented evidence that, in the case of one municipality, the equipment in question was worth the total purchase price and, in the case of the other, the transaction was frustrated before completion. King therefore argued that the prosecutor failed to prove that the municipalities were defrauded of money or property, but the court nevertheless held that

> the validity of a mail fraud conviction does not hinge upon a showing of actual loss by the intended victim. . . . It is enough that appellant knowingly devised a scheme to defraud and caused the use of the mails in furtherance of the scheme. In the case of the first municipality, appellant misled it as to the true sale price by evading competitive bidding requirements and inflating the total to include a kickback. This was fraud whether or not the municipality got fair value because of some bizarre circumstances unexplained by King's expert. In the case of the second municipality, the frustration of the sale is irrelevant because ultimate success is not an element of the crime. [Id. at 55.]

2. *The "cheat" background.* One commentator suggests that though federal mail fraud differs from common law criminal fraud in dropping any requirement of actual reliance, mail fraud nevertheless has a source in one particular form of common law larceny, the law of cheat or false token:[10]

> At common law, a cheat was a fraud perpetrated by some false symbol or token that injured another's property interest. The judges reasoned that a token, such as a counterfeit letter, gave "effect, character, and credibility to the verbal falsehood." Thus, a scheme perpetrated without the use of such a token was not indictable even if it included fraudulent misrepresentations of fact that were a substantial departure from the truth and that deceived another into parting with the title to his chattel.
>
> . . . [A] mere lie did not qualify as a token. Rather, a token signified something "real" and "visible" such as a ring, key, a seal or other mark, or some writing. A false measure, for example, qualified as a token. . . . The rationale underlying the distinction between a mere lie and a false measure was that in the case of a lie, "it [was] in everybody's power to prevent this sort of imposition; whereas a false measure [was] a general imposition upon the public which cannot be well discovered." . . .
>
> A conspiracy to defraud was also indictable at common law. But, it was not indictable for a person to obtain another's property by a mere lie, or by a promise that he did not intend to perform, or by other practices not affecting the public because these acts were considered private fraud. . . . For a cheat to be indictable, it must potentially affect the public at large and not merely a single individual.

3. *Materiality.* Although the government does not have to prove actual injury, it must at least prove that defendants *contemplated* some harm or injury to their victims. Thus in United States v. Regent Office Supply, Inc., 421 F.2d 1174 (2d Cir. 1970), the defendant's hyperaggressive salesmen falsely represented that they had been referred by customers' friends and that they were offering a

---

10. Note, Whatever Happened to *Durland*?: Mail Fraud, RICO, and Justifiable Reliance, 68 Notre Dame L. Rev. 333, 344-47 (1992).

good price because they had a huge inventory to dispose of. Nevertheless, the salesmen delivered the requested goods in acceptable form at the stated (and acceptable) price. The court held that because these facts were collateral to the sale and did not concern the quality or nature of the goods, the lies did not go to the basis of the bargain, and so the government had failed to allege that the defendants had intended actual injury. An intent to deceive and even successful deception in inducing customers to enter the transaction were not enough to establish mail fraud.

4. *Intended reliance.* In light of *Regent Office Supply*, some courts go to extreme lengths to limit the statute by holding that the defendant did not intend any victim to part with property in reliance on the defendant's misrepresentations. In United States v. Starr, 816 F.2d 94 (2d Cir. 1987), the owners of a bulk mailing service pulled off the following scheme: They charged customers various rates for different classes of mail; they then deceived the post office by burying higher-class mail in large bags of lowest-class mail, paying the lowest rate for all the mail in the bag; and they pocketed the difference between the lowest-class mail rate (which they paid the postal service) and the higher rates they charged their customers. None of the customers knew about this scheme, and of course all said that they had been satisfied with the service because all their mailings had arrived at the expected time. Conceding that the defendants had cheated the United States Postal Service, the court nevertheless reversed the conviction on the mail fraud charge.

Citing *Regent Office Supply*, the court stated that the defendants had not evinced any intent to harm the customers, even though they certainly deceived the customers by representing that all the customers' payments for postal costs would indeed be paid to the postal service. In addition, the defendants had sent fraudulent postal receipts to their customers to avoid detection.

Nevertheless, the court could find no evidence that defendants had intended any harm to their customers. Since all the customers' mailings arrived at the expected time, the customers suffered no misrepresentation as to the nature or quality of the service. It identified any intended harm as "metaphysical." It noted, ironically, that the customers were not entitled to the extra money pocketed by the defendants, because they would have then owed that money to the postal service.

5. *Cheating without obtaining.* In United States v. Walters, 997 F.2d 1219 (7th Cir. 1993), the facts were these:

> Norby Walters, who represents entertainers, tried to move into the sports business. He signed 58 college football players to contracts while they were still playing. Walters offered cars and money to those who would agree to use him as their representative in dealing with professional teams. Sports agents receive a percentage of the players' income, so Walters would profit only to the extent he could negotiate contracts for his clients. The athletes' pro prospects depended on successful completion of their collegiate careers. To the NCAA, however, a student who signs a contract with an agent is a professional, ineligible to play on collegiate teams. To avoid jeopardizing his clients' careers, Walters dated the contracts after the end of their eligibility and locked them in a safe. He promised to lie to the universities in response to any inquiries. . . .
>
> Having recruited players willing to fool their universities and the NCAA, Walters discovered that they were equally willing to play false with him. Only 2 of the 58 players fulfilled their end of the bargain; the other 56 kept the cars and

money, then signed with other agents. They relied on the fact that the contracts were locked away and dated in the future, and that Walters' business depended on continued secrecy, so he could not very well sue to enforce their promises. When the 56 would neither accept him as their representative nor return the payments, Walters resorted to threats. One player, Maurice Douglass, was told that his legs would be broken before the pro draft unless he repaid Walters' firm. A 75-page indictment charged Walters and his partner Lloyd Bloom with conspiracy, RICO violations (the predicate felony was extortion), and mail fraud. The fraud: causing the universities to pay scholarship funds to athletes who had become ineligible as a result of the agency contracts. The mail: each university required its athletes to verify their eligibility to play, then sent copies by mail to conferences such as the Big Ten. [Id. at 1221.]

Judge Easterbrook identified a key flaw in the government's case:

> . . . The United States tells us that the universities lost their scholarship money. . . . Walters emphasizes that the universities put his 58 athletes on scholarship long before he met them and did not pay a penny more than they planned to do. But a jury could conclude that had Walters' clients told the truth, the colleges would have stopped their scholarships, thus saving money. So we must assume that the universities lost property by reason of Walters' deeds. Still, they were not out of pocket to Walters; he planned to profit by taking a percentage of the players' professional incomes, not of their scholarships. Section 1341 condemns "any scheme or artifice to defraud, or for obtaining money or property" (emphasis added). If the universities were the victims, how did he "obtain" their property, Walters asks.
>
> According to the United States, neither an actual nor a potential transfer of property from the victim to the defendant is essential. It is enough that the victim lose; what (if anything) the schemer hopes to gain plays no role in the definition of the offense. We asked the prosecutor at oral argument whether on this rationale practical jokes violate §1341. A mails B an invitation to a surprise party for their mutual friend C. B drives his car to the place named in the invitation. But there is no party; the address is a vacant lot; B is the butt of a joke. The invitation came by post; the cost of gasoline means that B is out of pocket. The prosecutor said that this indeed violates §1341, but that his office pledges to use prosecutorial discretion wisely. Many people will find this position unnerving (what if the prosecutor's policy changes, or A is politically unpopular and the prosecutor is looking for a way to nail him?). [Id. at 1224.]

Is Judge Easterbrook's "practical joke" hypothetical really analogous to this case? Does the joker have the intent to deprive the victim of property? Wouldn't there be a much stronger case against a joker who deliberately deceived a victim into throwing away cash or burning his own car?

Could the individual athletes have been charged with using the mails for the purpose of executing schemes to defraud their colleges? Can a "scheme" to defraud contemplate only a single victim? Does it matter to the liability of the athletes that the schemes were suggested by Walters? If the athletes could have been charged with schemes to defraud, could not Walters have been charged as their accomplice?

6. *The "mail" nexus.* In addition to the other problems with charging Walters, Judge Easterbrook held there was insufficient nexus to the mail because Walters would have been indifferent to, and possibly ignorant of, the universities' obligation to mail athletes' verification forms to the NCAA. Is this result consistent

with the Supreme Court's holding in Schmuck v. United States, 489 U.S. 705 (1989)? The facts were these:

> . . . Schmuck purchased used cars, rolled back their odometers, and then sold the automobiles to Wisconsin retail dealers for prices artificially inflated because of the low-mileage readings. These unwitting car dealers, relying on the altered odometer figures, then resold the cars to customers, who in turn paid prices reflecting Schmuck's fraud. To complete the resale of each automobile, the dealer who purchased it from Schmuck would submit a title-application form to the Wisconsin Department of Transportation on behalf of his retail customer. The receipt of a Wisconsin title was a prerequisite for completing the resale; without it, the dealer could not transfer title to the customer and the customer could not obtain Wisconsin tags. The submission of the title-application form supplied the mailing element of each of the alleged mail frauds.
>
> Before trial, Schmuck moved to dismiss the indictment on the ground that the mailings at issue — the submissions of the title-application forms by the automobile dealers — were not in furtherance of the fraudulent scheme and, thus, did not satisfy the mailing element of the crime of mail fraud. . . . [Id. at 707-08.]

The Court held:

> . . . To be part of the execution of the fraud, however, the use of the mails need not be an essential element of the scheme. It is sufficient for the mailing to be "incident to an essential part of the scheme," or "a step in [the] plot."
>
> Schmuck . . . argues that mail fraud can be predicated only on a mailing that affirmatively assists the perpetrator in carrying out his fraudulent scheme. The mailing element of the offense, he contends, cannot be satisfied by a mailing, such as those at issue here, that is routine and innocent in and of itself, and that, far from furthering the execution of the fraud, occurs after the fraud has come to fruition, is merely tangentially related to the fraud, and is counterproductive in that it creates a "paper trail" from which the fraud may be discovered. . . .
>
> . . . Schmuck's was not a "one-shot" operation in which he sold a single car to an isolated dealer. His was an ongoing fraudulent venture. A rational jury could have concluded that the success of Schmuck's venture depended upon his continued harmonious relations with, and good reputation among, retail dealers, which in turn required the smooth flow of cars from the dealers to their Wisconsin customers.
>
> . . . Schmuck's scheme would have come to an abrupt halt if the dealers either had lost faith in Schmuck or had not been able to resell the cars obtained from him. . . . Thus, although the registration-form mailings may not have contributed directly to the duping of either the retail dealers or the customers, they were necessary to the passage of title, which in turn was essential to the perpetuation of Schmuck's scheme. [Id. at 710-12.]

7. *Mail fraud and intangible property.* The case of Carpenter v. United States, 484 U.S. 19 (1987), concerned a reporter named Winans who wrote the influential "Heard on the Street" column for the *Wall Street Journal,* which often drove up the price of stocks reported on. According to the Court:

> The official policy and practice at the *Journal* was that prior to publication, the contents of the column were the *Journal's* confidential information. Despite the rule, with which Winans was familiar, he entered into a scheme in October 1983 with Peter Brant and petitioner Felis, both connected with the Kidder Peabody brokerage firm in New York City, to give them advance information as to the timing and contents of the . . . column. This permitted Brant and Felis and another conspirator,

David Clark, a client of Brant, to buy or sell based on the probable impact of the column on the market. Profits were to be shared. The conspirators agreed that the scheme would not affect the journalistic purity of the "Heard" column, and the District Court did not find that the contents of any of the articles were altered to further the profit potential of petitioners' stock-trading scheme. . . . Over a 4-month period, the brokers made prepublication trades on the basis of information given them by Winans about the contents of some 27 "Heard" columns. The net profits from these trades were about $690,000. . . .

Petitioners assert that their activities were not a scheme to defraud the *Journal* within the meaning of the mail and wire fraud statutes; and that in any event, they did not obtain any "money or property" from the *Journal*, which is a necessary element of the crime under our decision last Term in McNally v. United States, 483 U.S. 350 (1987). . . .

We held in *McNally* that the mail fraud statute . . . is "limited in scope to the protection of property rights." Id., at 360. Petitioners argue that the *Journal's* interest in prepublication confidentiality for the "Heard" columns is no more than an intangible consideration outside the reach of §1341; nor does that law, it is urged, protect against mere injury to reputation. . . . [However,] the *Journal*, as Winans' employer, was defrauded of much more than its contractual right to his honest and faithful service, an interest too ethereal in itself to fall within the protection of the mail fraud statute. . . . Here, the object of the scheme was to take the *Journal's* confidential business information — the publication schedule and contents of the "Heard" column — and its intangible nature does not make it any less "property" protected by the mail and wire fraud statutes. . . .

. . . "Confidential information acquired or compiled by a corporation in the course and conduct of its business is a species of property to which the corporation has the exclusive right and benefit, and which a court of equity will protect through the injunctive process or other appropriate remedy." 3 W. Fletcher, Cyclopedia of Law of Private Corporations §857.1, p.260 (rev. ed. 1986). . . .

Petitioners' arguments that they did not interfere with the *Journal's* use of the information or did not publicize it and deprive the *Journal* of the first public use of it . . . miss the point. The confidential information was generated from the business, and the business had a right to decide how to use it prior to disclosing it to the public. . . . [I]t is sufficient that the *Journal* has been deprived of its right to exclusive use of the information, for exclusivity is an important aspect of confidential business information and most private property for that matter. . . .

. . . Winans' undertaking at the *Journal* was not to reveal prepublication information about his column, a promise that became a sham when in violation of his duty he passed along to his co-conspirators confidential information belonging to the *Journal*, pursuant to an ongoing scheme to share profits from trading in anticipation of the "Heard" column's impact on the stock market. . . . As the New York courts have recognized: "It is well established, as a general proposition, that a person who acquires special knowledge or information by virtue of a confidential or fiduciary relationship with another is not free to exploit that knowledge or information for his own personal benefit but must account to his principal for any profits derived therefrom." Diamond v. Oreamuno, 24 N.Y.2d 494, 497, 301 N.Y.S.2d 78, 80, 248 N.E.2d 910, 912 (1969). . . .

We have little trouble in holding that the conspiracy here to trade on the *Journal's* confidential information is not outside the reach of the mail and wire fraud statutes. . . . [Id. at 23-28.]

Does this opinion convince you that Winans committed a form of theft? Whom exactly did Winans steal from? Under the "scheme to defraud" theory of liability, does there need to be an identifiable victim?

C. EXTORTION

PEOPLE v. DIOGUARDI
Court of Appeals of New York
8 N.Y.2d 260, 203 N.Y.S.2d 870 (1960)

FROESSEL, JUDGE.

The Appellate Division has reversed defendants' convictions for extortion and conspiracy to commit extortion, dismissed the indictment and discharged them from custody. In addition to the conspiracy count, the indictment charged defendants with extorting $4,700 from the officers of two corporations. Said corporations were nonunion, conducted a wholesale stationery and office supply business in Manhattan, did an annual business of several million dollars, and their stock was wholly owned by a family named Kerin. Anthony Kerin, Sr., president and "boss" of the Kerin companies, made all the important corporate policy decisions. The other two corporate officers were his son Kerin, Jr., and one Jack Shumann.

Defendant [John] McNamara, the alleged "front man" in the extorsive scheme, was an official of Teamster Local 295 and 808, as well as a member of the Teamsters Joint Council. Defendant Dioguardi, the immediate beneficiary of the payments and the alleged power behind the scene, was sole officer of Equitable Research Associates, Inc. — a *publishing house,* according to its certificate of incorporation, a *public relations concern,* according to its bank account and the Yellow Pages of the telephone directory, a *labor statistics concern,* according to its office secretary and sole employee, and a *firm of labor consultants,* according to its business card and alternate listing in the aforesaid directory. . . .

Between November 1955 and mid-January 1956, the Kerin companies were confronted with organizational activities on the part of four unions. A CIO local first contacted management by letter. Two visiting representatives from Teamster Local 210 then threatened to organize the companies by "putting pickets out" and "stopping shipments" if management did not agree to organize the employees on behalf of their local. Some six weeks later a picket appeared at the delivery and shipping entrance in the rear of the Kerin premises, carrying a placard reciting that one of the Kerin companies was unfair to members of Teamster Local 138. No representative from that local ever contacted management, and all its officials testified that they had not authorized a picket line at the premises.

Finally, during the week in which the picket was parading at the rear, two organizers from Local 1601 of the Retail Clerks International Association appeared in the front lobby distributing literature to the companies' employees. . . .

The appearance of the picket line — which truck drivers from two companies refused to cross — thoroughly alarmed the Kerin officers, since they were in an "extremely competitive business," and a cessation of incoming or outgoing truck deliveries for as short a period as two weeks would effectively force them out of business. Their attorney, William Coogan, advised them that filing a petition with the National Labor Relations Board (NLRB) for an election among the competing unions would not constitute a solution, since such proceeding might take anywhere from two weeks to three months, and peaceful picketing could not be enjoined before, during, or even after the election. He felt that a *consent* election was the best way to settle the matter, and informed them that he might be able to meet with a prominent teamster official on a higher level, who would call a halt to the "ridiculous" situation of two teamster locals competing with each other.

Coogan had previously been in touch with his brother-in-law, William White, a labor law professor who had met McNamara socially and, after the Kerin management agreed, White contacted McNamara and arranged a meeting with him and Coogan. At the meeting, McNamara was generally discouraging as to the feasibility of a consent election. However, after joining Coogan in a men's room, McNamara suggested privately "that something might be done, but that it would be expensive . . . it could run five to ten thousand dollars." After Coogan vetoed that possibility, and McNamara made several phone calls, the three adjourned to a Chinese restaurant recommended by McNamara for dinner, during the course of which one Milton Holt approached the table and was introduced by McNamara as an attorney, although, in fact, he was an officer of Teamster Local 805 and not a member of the Bar. After Holt was apprised of the labor difficulties confronting the Kerin companies, McNamara stated: "This looks to me to be the kind of a situation which Equitable can help out," to which Holt nodded an affirmative. Neither White nor Coogan had ever heard of Equitable before that day, and they neither sought nor received enlightenment.

The following morning Coogan reported to the Kerin officers that he had had "a very rough evening" with McNamara — whom he described as a "tough-talking man" who "was obviously a high official in the labor movement," "had a grasp of the whole situation," and "knew what was going on" — and that "the gist of the conversation was that . . . for a payment of ten thousand, the whole matter could be settled, and settled almost immediately." [Kerin, Sr., "furiously" rejected this proposal.]

On Friday afternoon, January 20, 1956, McNamara, accompanied by Holt — whom he again introduced as his attorney — met with the three Kerin officers in a private dining room at the Manhattan Club. Holt soon suggested that Kerin, Sr., and McNamara "step outside and have a chat" and, after adjourning to another room, McNamara assured Kerin, Sr., that his troubles could be ended, and *would be,* if he did three things: (1) "joined up" with McNamara's local 295, (2) paid $3,500 to Equitable to defray the "out-of-pocket" expenses incurred by the various unions that had sought to organize the companies, and (3) retained Equitable as labor consultant at $100 per month for each company for the period of the collective bargaining contract to be signed with Local 295, for which the companies "would get counsel and advice . . . in any matter that was pertinent or related to labor or labor relationships." McNamara repeatedly assured Kerin, Sr., that the picketing would stop immediately and the companies would be guaranteed labor peace if his program were accepted.

Kerin, Sr., stated that he was not adverse to having his employees organized by Local 295, if it was a good honest union, and that he could "accept the idea of a hundred dollars a month as a retainer fee for labor counsel and advice." He protested against the proposed payment of $3,500, however, as an "extraordinary charge" that sounded "like a hold-up," to which McNamara replied: "'It may seem that way to you, Mr. Kerin, but that is the amount of money that these unions that have sought to organize you . . . have expended, and *if we are going to avoid further trouble and further difficulties, it is my suggestion that you pay that to the*

Equitable Associates. If you don't pay it, we can't go through with the program.'" . . . (Emphasis supplied.) Kerin, Sr., finally agreed, . . . [and] Kerin, Jr., and Shumann assented to the program. . . .

. . . The Kerin companies continued to pay Equitable $200 a month until July, 1956, when they were instructed by the District Attorney's office to discontinue the payments. A total of $4,700 had been paid to Equitable, which was the amount defendants were charged in the indictment with extorting. . . .

Upon the proof in this record, a jury could properly conclude that defendants were guilty of extortion — cleverly conceived and subtly executed, but extortion nonetheless. The essence of the crime is obtaining property by a wrongful use of fear, induced by a threat to do an unlawful injury (Penal Law, Consol. Laws, c.40, §§850, 851). It is a well-settled law in this State that fear of *economic loss or harm* satisfies the ingredient of fear necessary to the crime.

Moreover, it is not essential that a defendant *create* the fear existing in the mind of his prospective victim so long as he succeeds in persuading him that he possesses the power to remove or continue its cause, and instills a new fear by threatening to misuse that power as a device to exact tribute. Our statute, as well as the Hobbs or Federal Anti-Racketeering Act (U.S. Code, tit. 18, §1951, subd. [b], par. [2]) which was patterned after it, talks in terms of a wrongful *use of fear,* and the ultimate issue "'is not so much the cause of the victim's fear, as it is whether or not defendants played upon that fear, in other words, made use of that fear to extort money or property'" (Callanan v. United States, 8 Cir., 223 F.2d 171, 174, *supra*).

The Kerin management unmistakably feared that the continued existence of the picket line and the perpetuation of the ostensible organizational struggle between competing locals would put their companies out of business. The failure to establish that this fear was *initially* induced by or attributable to either defendant, or someone acting in concert with them, is not determinative, so long as there was proof that defendants "seized upon the opportunity presented by" that fear "to line their own pockets by implanting in the minds of the company officials the idea that unless and until the tribute demanded was paid the defendants," the picketing and labor war would continue. . . .

As to the element of a *threat,* the crux of defendant's position is that McNamara was under no duty to intervene to alter the existing situation, and a threat to do nothing to aid the Kerin management if they did not assent to the terms of his proposal is not tantamount to a threat to do an unlawful injury within the contemplation of the statute. However, section 858 of the Penal Law expressly makes it "immaterial" to the crime of extortion "whether a threat . . . is of things to be done *or omitted* by the offendor, or by any other person" (emphasis supplied), and we long ago held: "No precise words are needed to convey a threat. *It may be done by innuendo or suggestion.* To ascertain whether a letter [or oral proposal] conveys a threat, all its language, together with the circumstances under which it was written [or spoken], and the relations between the parties may be considered, and if it can be found that *the purport and natural effect* of the letter [or oral proposal] is to convey a threat, then the mere form of words is unimportant." People v. Thompson, 97 N.Y. 313, 318. (Emphasis supplied.) If McNamara, acting for himself and Dioguardi's alter ego, Equitable, professed to have control over the labor problems besetting the Kerin companies, i.e., if he instilled the belief in the minds of the Kerin officers that the continuance or discontinuance of the picket line and the labor war rested with him and Equitable, and he demanded tribute for the exercise of that control, then he effectively conveyed a threat to do an unlawful injury, and he and those acting in concert with him could properly be convicted of extortion.

Local 210, which threatened to organize the Kerin companies by picket lines if necessary, and Local 138, which ostensibly commenced the potentially ruinous picket line, were both teamster unions and from the beginning McNamara was pictured to Coogan, and, in turn, to the Kerin management, as a powerful and high-ranking figure in the teamster organization. McNamara effectively heightened this image by displaying to Coogan a familiarity with the labor difficulties faced by his client, and by suggesting that the matter could be "settled almost immediately" by the payment of as much as $10,000. He discouraged resort to a consent election, since Locals 210 and 138 were "old-line unions" who would press their organizational efforts to the utmost, and not willingly forgo their investment in organizational expenses. He further darkened the picture by informing Coogan that it was "entirely probable" that other unions would respect the organizational picket line, and there was no "real hope" that even partial deliveries would continue. There is also evidence that McNamara left Coogan with the impression — thereafter conveyed to the Kerin officers — that he had the power to intensify the picket line by having the Joint Council issue orders to all teamster locals to make the picket line 100 percent effective, with the necessary result of putting the Kerin companies out of business.

It seems clear, at all events, that the "furious" Kerin, Sr., as well as the other two corporate officers, agreed to meet with McNamara because they believed he possessed the power to cure the labor situation which threatened their business with potential ruin. During the private chat suggested by the bogus attorney Holt, McNamara confidently assured Kerin, Sr., that his troubles not merely "could be ended" but "would be ended" if his (McNamara's) package deal were accepted. McNamara flatly stated that the picket "would be out of there by Monday morning" and, if any other union attempted to organize, "all we had to do was tell them that we were members of his local, and that that should be enough for them, and advise the Equitable Research Associates of our problem." All the Kerin officers testified, in substance, that McNamara induced them to believe that they would be guaranteed labor peace if they made the suggested payments. . . .

. . . The picketing here . . . may have been perfectly lawful in its inception (assuming it was part of a bona fide organizational effort) and may have remained so — despite its potentially ruinous effect on the employer's business — so long as it was employed to accomplish the legitimate labor objective of organization. Its entire character changed from legality to criminality, however, when it was used as a pressure device to exact the payment of money as a condition of its cessation. . . . The fact that McNamara . . . was not an official of the particular local engaging in the injurious activity is immaterial, so long as he and Equitable professed to have power to eliminate or continue it, and used that purported power as a lever to exact tribute. Although McNamara "did not *expressly* represent that he controlled" the picket and Kerin, Sr., "did not *expressly* testify that he believed that the defendant would keep the [picket line going] unless his demands were acceded to," the evidence [fairly warranted the jury in finding those facts]. . . . The power to remove a picket clearly implies the power to maintain it. The jury could properly infer that the substance of McNamara's proposal was: "You have got to pay Equitable $3,500 down and $200 a month to have the picket removed and labor peace guaranteed." . . .

Moreover, in the present case, we have not only "the pretense of control," but clear evidence of *actual* control. On the business day next following the Manhattan Club meeting, *before any money was paid* and before any written contract with Equitable had been signed by management, no picket or organizer appeared at the Kerin premises. McNamara promptly reminded management to notice "you have no more picket," and, so long as the monthly payments to Equitable continued, labor peace ensued. Any doubt concerning the "control" flavor of the entire transaction seems dissipated by the necessity of $200 monthly payments to the labor consultant who never advised and was never consulted. As the People contend, the jury could reasonably infer that the Kerin companies continued to make these payments "because of a plain implication that [Equitable's] demonstrated influence and control could and doubtless would be exerted to restore and even intensify the labor predicament just as readily as it could be and was employed to terminate it." . . .

The orders appealed from should be reversed, the indictments reinstated, and a new trial ordered.

Notes and Questions

1. The court makes much of the fact that the defendants claimed to be able to remove the picket line and were able to do so. Why is this relevant? The court also implies that there was no proof that the picket line was initiated by the defendants or by a confederate of theirs. If so, what distinguishes the defendants' conduct from normal fee-for-service negotiations? Is the conduct in this case different from that of a doctor who threatens to let a patient die unless the patient pays the doctor a fee? Isn't there a difference between a threat to commit an injurious act and a threat not to come to another's aid?

Should it matter that the complainants approached the defendants first and requested their aid in ending the picket line?

2. *Common law and statutory extortion.* At common law, extortion was the corrupt collection of an unlawful payment by an official under color of office. Neither threat nor coercion was an element of the offense. Statutory extortion, also sometimes referred to as blackmail, is a broader offense. A person is guilty of statutory extortion if she obtains, or attempts to obtain, the property of another by means of a threat.

3. *Nature of the threat.* The act threatened by the extortionist need not itself be illegal. Indeed, the actor may be privileged or even required to perform the threatened act. For example, a police officer is guilty of extortion if he threatens to arrest a person whom he has caught committing a crime unless that person pays $100 to the officer. Nor need the threat involve a commission by the actor; as *Dioguardi* demonstrates, omissions and refusals to act are also included.

The wide scope of actionable threats under the extortion statutes creates a number of potential problems in distinguishing extortion from tolerable, or even desirable, behavior. A merchant who is unable to collect a debt owed by a customer should, for example, be allowed to threaten suit if payment is not made, even though the suit would tend to impair the credit of the customer. Extortion statutes like the one in the Model Penal Code eliminate many of these difficulties by creating an affirmative defense where the defendant "honestly" claims the property sought as restitution for harm done "in the circumstances to which such accusation, exposure, lawsuit or other official action relates" (MPC §223.4). Thus, an employer who discovers that one of his employees has been stealing from him is not guilty of extortion for threatening to bring theft charges unless the employee pays restitution. State v. Burns, 161 Wash. 362, 297 P. 212 (1931). However, if the employer demands an amount greater than that stolen by the employee, he may be guilty of extortion. People v. Fichtner, 281 App. Div. 159, 118 N.Y.S.2d 392 (1952). Nonetheless, distinguishing extortion from lawful, consensual exchanges can sometimes be difficult, particularly when the threatened act is not in itself unlawful.

4. *Threats to reveal secrets.* The defendant in State v. Harrington, 128 Vt. 242, 260 A.2d 692 (1969), was convicted of extortion because he had threatened to use incriminating photos in a divorce action. Harrington had obtained the photos on behalf of his client, Mrs. Morin, who wished to divorce her husband. Harrington hired a woman, Mrs. Mazza, who was instructed to make herself "'receptive and available' but not aggressive" to the advances of Mr. Morin. Harrington and his associates were subsequently able to take several photographs of Mr. Morin and Mrs. Mazza undressed and in bed. Harrington then contacted Mr. Morin and informed him that Mrs. Morin desired a divorce and $175,000 in alimony. In return, she would relinquish all her other marital rights. Mr. Morin was told that if he did not consent to these terms, Mrs. Morin would sue him for divorce on grounds of adultery and introduce the photos as evidence. In upholding Harrington's conviction, the court emphasized that the incriminating evidence was "willfully contrived and procured." Should this be relevant? What purpose is served by punishing as extortion threats to reveal essentially accurate information of wrongdoing? For an argument that such threats constitute a desirable sanction against misconduct, see George Stigler, An Introduction to Privacy in Economics and Politics, 9 J. Legal Studies 623, 643-44 (1980).

5. *Blackmail.* The crime of blackmail has spawned a rich literature trying to define the theoretical underpinnings of its definition. Professor James Lindgren describes the paradox of blackmail:[11]

> Most crimes do not need theories to explain why the behavior is criminal. The wrongdoing is self-evident. But blackmail is unique among major crimes: no one has yet figured out why it ought to be illegal. Recognizing the magnitude of the problem, one theorist wondered whether we can find "a principled distinction (or indeed any interesting distinction)" between blackmail and permissible behavior that is not blackmail.
>
> In blackmail, the heart of the problem is that two separate acts, each of which is a moral and legal right, can combine to make a moral and legal wrong. For example, if I threaten to expose a criminal act unless I am paid money, I have committed blackmail. Or if I threaten to expose a sexual affair unless I am given a job, once again I have committed blackmail. I have a legal right to expose or threaten to expose the crime or affair, and I have a legal right to seek a job or money, but if I combine these rights it is blackmail. If both a person's ends — seeking a job or money — and his means — threatening to expose — are otherwise legal, why is

11. James Lindgren, Unraveling the Paradox of Blackmail, 84 Colum. L. Rev. 670. 670-72 (1984).

it illegal to combine them? Therein lies what has been called the "paradox of blackmail."

. . . Most [blackmail] statutes broadly prohibit behavior that no one really believes is criminal and then rely on the good judgment of prosecutors not to enforce the statute as written. It is unlikely that anyone will be able to bring order out of this confusion until we discover a theory of blackmail that explains the illegality of the paradoxical case.

Lindgren offers his own theory for distinguishing legitimate from illegitimate threats:

In brief, I argue that the key to the wrongfulness of the blackmail transaction is its triangular structure. The transaction implicitly involves not only the blackmailer and his victim but always a third party as well. This third party may be, for example, the victim's spouse or employer, the authorities or even the public at large. When a blackmailer tries to use his right to release damaging information, he is threatening to tell others. If the blackmail victim pays the blackmailer, it is to avoid the harm that those others would inflict. Thus blackmail is a way that one person requests something in return for suppressing the actual or potential interests of others. To get what he wants, the blackmailer uses leverage that is less his than someone else's. Selling the right to go to the police involves suppressing the state's interests. Selling the right to tell a tort victim who committed the tort involves suppressing the tort victim's interests. And selling the right to inform others of embarrassing (but legal) behavior involves suppressing the interests of those other people.

Noninformational blackmail involves the same misuse of a third party's leverage for the blackmailer's own benefit. For example, when a labor leader threatens to call a strike unless he is given a personal payoff, he is using the leverage of third parties to bargain for his own benefit. Thus the criminalization of informational and noninformational blackmail represents a principled decision that advantages may not be gained by extra leverage belonging more to a third party than to the threatener. Recognizing the triangular structure of the blackmail transaction makes clear the parasitic nature of the blackmailer's conduct. Once this structure is understood, it becomes easier to find in blackmail the kind of behavior that concerns the other theorists: immorality, invasiveness, and economic waste.[12]

An economic defense for the criminalization of blackmail is offered by Professors William Landes and Richard Posner:

. . . Blackmail may be defined as the sale of information to an individual who would be incriminated by its publication, and at first glance appears to be an efficient method of private enforcement of the law (the moral as well as the positive law). The value of the information to the blackmailed individual is equal to the cost of the punishment that the individual will incur if the information is communicated to the authorities as a result, and so he will be willing to pay up to that amount to the blackmailer for the information. The individual is thereby punished, and the punishment is the same as if he had been apprehended and convicted for the crime that the blackmailer has discovered, but the fine is paid to the blackmailer rather than to the state.

Why then is blackmail a crime? . . .

12. Id. at 672.

A[n] explanation of why blackmail is a crime is that the decision to discourage blackmail follows directly from the decision to rely on a public monopoly of law enforcement in some areas of enforcement, notably criminal law. Were blackmail, a form of private enforcement, lawful, the public monopoly of enforcement would be undermined. Overenforcement of the law would result if the blackmailer were able to extract the full fine from the offender. Alternatively, the blackmailer might sell his incriminating information to the offender for a price lower than the statutory cost of punishment to the criminal, which would reduce the effective cost of punishment to the criminal below the level set by the legislature. . . .[13]

Professor Leo Katz offers the following solution to the "paradox of blackmail."[14]

The blackmailer puts the victim to a choice between a theft . . . and some other minor wrong. The execution of the theft then carries with it the level of blameworthiness of a theft. To be sure, the wrong must not be too minor. The mere threat to be nasty or unpleasant won't suffice; the immorality has to be more substantial than that. But it need not . . . be an immorality that comes anywhere close to being criminal. . . .

. . . Busybody . . . extracts $10,000 from Philanderer by threatening to reveal infidelities to his wife. Busybody is putting Philanderer to a choice between two wrongs. Busybody will either commit the theft — the unconsented to taking of $10,000 — or the revelation of Philanderer's infidelities. Why is the payment of $10,000 unconsented to, given that Philanderer is paying voluntarily? It is unconsented to because it is made with the threat of something wrongful, the revelation. But how is the revelation something wrongful, when it is not in fact prohibited by the criminal law? It is wrongful because it is immoral, even though not criminal or even tortious. To be sure, it is not a major immorality by any means, but simply "swinishness." Indeed, it wouldn't even be immoral if it had been done out of friendship with the cheated wife. It is immoral only because, if it were done, it would be done for purely retaliatory reasons — retaliating for Philanderer's refusal to pay. But now comes the most formidable objection: *If revealing the infidelities is only a minor immorality, then how can the taking of the money which the victim prefers to that minor immorality be anything more than a minor immorality itself?* [The answer is that in the criminal law, we often judge harm objectively rather than subjectively.] *[W]hen the defendant has the victim choose between either of two immoralities which he must endure, the gravity of defendant's wrongdoing is to be judged by what he actually did (or sought to achieve), not by what he threatened to do.*

Were I to put my argument in the tiniest of nutshells, it would go like this: The essence of blackmail resides in a strange anomalous-looking act. The defendant manages to leverage the threat of a mild wrong into a substantial advantage and this leveraging is deemed by us a very major wrong. . . . [B]ut this fact is not so strange and anomalous after all. It is a natural, but somewhat counterintuitive, consequence of the fact that blameworthiness is also a function not merely of how much the victim hates the wrong being done to him, but is also a function of other attributes of the wrong, such as mens rea, actus reus, and so on. The fact that blameworthiness depends on these other attributes implies that situations will arise in which the victim will prefer to be subjected to a greater rather than a lesser wrong; which, in turn, implies that a defendant who persuades his victim to accept

13. William M. Landes & Richard A. Posner, The Private Enforcement of Law, 4 J. Legal Stud. 1, 42 (1975).

14. Leo Katz, Blackmail and Other Forms of Arm-Twisting, 141 U. Pa. L. Rev. 1567, 1597-98, 1615 (1993) (emphasis in original).

a bigger wrong in lieu of a smaller wrong, should in fact be deemed guilty of a bigger wrong. This is exactly what the blackmail doctrine does.

Has Katz indeed identified the "most formidable objection"? For Katz, the immorality of revealing Philanderer's philanderings inheres in the motive — "retaliation" for not paying Busybody off. But how does this "immoral" motive distinguish Busybody's act from the refusal of any vendor to part with goods or perform services in "retaliation" for a potential customer's refusal to pay? How, in short, does Katz distinguish blackmail from any ordinary market transaction?

6. Bribery of public officials seems so obviously dishonest and corrupt that it should be a straightforward matter for legislatures to make it a crime. But as the following case shows, the effort to place bribery within the traditional definition of extortion has proved a major problem for American law.

MCCORMICK v. UNITED STATES
Supreme Court of the United States
500 U.S. 257 (1991)

JUSTICE WHITE delivered the opinion of the Court.

This case requires us to consider whether the Court of Appeals properly affirmed the conviction of petitioner, an elected public official, for extorting property under color of official right in violation of the Hobbs Act, 18 U.S.C. §1951. . . .

Petitioner Robert L. McCormick was a member of the West Virginia House of Delegates in 1984. He represented a district that had long suffered from a shortage of medical doctors. For several years, West Virginia had allowed foreign medical school graduates to practice under temporary permits while studying for the state licensing exams. Under this program, some doctors were allowed to practice under temporary permits for years even though they repeatedly failed the state exams. McCormick was a leading advocate and supporter of this program.

In the early 1980s, following a move in the House of Delegates to end the temporary permit program, several of the temporarily licensed doctors formed an organization to press their interests in Charleston. The organization hired a lobbyist, John Vandergrift, who in 1984 worked for legislation that would extend the expiration date of the temporary permit program. McCormick sponsored the House version of the proposed legislation, and a bill was passed extending the program for another year. Shortly thereafter, Vandergrift and McCormick discussed the possibility of introducing legislation during the 1985 session that would grant the doctors a permanent medical license by virtue of their years of experience. McCormick agreed to sponsor such legislation.

During his 1984 reelection campaign, McCormick informed Vandergrift that his campaign was expensive, that he had paid considerable sums out of his own pocket, and that he had not heard anything from the foreign doctors. Vandergrift told McCormick that he would contact the doctors and see what he could do. Vandergrift contacted one of the foreign doctors and later received from the doctors $1,200 in cash. Vandergrift delivered an envelope containing nine $100 bills to McCormick. Later the same day, a second delivery of $2,000 in cash was made to McCormick. During the fall of 1984, McCormick received two more cash payments from the doctors. McCormick did not list any of these payments as campaign contributions, nor did he report the money as income on his 1984 federal income tax return. And although the doctors' organization kept detailed books of its expenditures, the cash payments were not listed as campaign contributions. Rather, the entries for the payments were accompanied only by initials or other codes signifying that the money was for McCormick.

In the spring of 1985, McCormick sponsored legislation permitting experienced doctors to be permanently licensed without passing the state licensing exams. McCormick spoke at length in favor of the bill during floor debate, and the bill ultimately was enacted into law. Two weeks after the legislation was enacted, McCormick received another cash payment from the foreign doctors.

Following an investigation, a federal grand jury returned an indictment charging McCormick with five counts of violating the Hobbs Act,[15] by extorting payments under color of official right. . . . At the close of a 6-day trial, the jury was instructed that to establish a Hobbs Act violation the Government had to prove that McCormick induced a cash payment and that he did so knowingly and willfully by extortion. . . .

The jury convicted McCormick of the first Hobbs Act count (charging him with receiving the initial $900 cash payment) . . . but could not reach verdicts on the remaining four Hobbs Act counts. The District Court declared a mistrial on those four counts.

The Court of Appeals affirmed, observing that nonelected officials may be convicted under the Hobbs Act without proof that they have granted or agreed to grant some benefit or advantage in exchange for money paid to them and that elected officials should be held to the same standard when they receive money other than "legitimate" campaign contributions, 896 F.2d 61 (CA4 1990). After stating that McCormick could not be prosecuted under the Hobbs Act for receiving voluntary campaign contributions, the court rejected McCormick's contention that conviction of an elected official under the Act requires, under all circumstances, proof of a quid pro quo, i.e., a promise of official action or inaction in exchange for any payment or property received. Rather, the court interpreted the statute as not requiring such a showing where the parties never intended the payments to be "legitimate" campaign contributions. . . . The court concluded:

> Under these facts, a reasonable jury could find that McCormick was extorting money from the doctors for his continued support of the 1985 legislation. Further, the evidence supports the conclusion that the money was never intended by any of the parties to be a campaign contribution. Therefore, we refuse to reverse the jury's verdict against McCormick for violating the Hobbs Act. . . .

Because of disagreement in the Courts of Appeals regarding the meaning of the phrase "under color of official right" as it is used in the Hobbs Act, we granted certiorari. We reverse and remand for further proceedings. . . .

15. The Hobbs Act, 18 U.S.C. §1951, provides in relevant part as follows:

(a) Whoever in any way or degree obstructs, delays, or affects commerce . . . by robbery or extortion . . . in violation of this section shall be fined not more than $10,000 or imprisoned not more than twenty years, or both.

(b) As used in this section — . . .

(2) The term "extortion" means the obtaining of property from another, with his consent, induced by wrongful use of actual or threatened force, violence, or fear, or under color of official right.

Serving constituents and supporting legislation that will benefit the district and individuals and groups therein is the everyday business of a legislator. It is also true that campaigns must be run and financed. Money is constantly being solicited on behalf of candidates, who run on platforms and who claim support on the basis of their views and what they intend to do or have done. Whatever ethical considerations and appearances may indicate, to hold that legislators commit the federal crime of extortion when they act for the benefit of constituents or support legislation furthering the interests of some of their constituents, shortly before or after campaign contributions are solicited and received from those beneficiaries, is an unrealistic assessment of what Congress could have meant by making it a crime to obtain property from another, with his consent, "under color of official right." To hold otherwise would open to prosecution not only conduct that has long been thought to be well within the law but also conduct that in a very real sense is unavoidable so long as election campaigns are financed by private contributions or expenditures, as they have been from the beginning of the Nation. It would require statutory language more explicit than the Hobbs Act contains to justify a contrary conclusion. . . .

This is not to say that it is impossible for an elected official to commit extortion in the course of financing an election campaign. Political contributions are of course vulnerable if induced by the use of force, violence, or fear. The receipt of such contributions is also vulnerable under the Act as having been taken under color of official right, but only if the payments are made in return for an explicit promise or undertaking by the official to perform or not to perform an official act. . . .

We thus disagree with the Court of Appeals' holding in this case that a quid pro quo is not necessary for conviction under the Hobbs Act when an official receives a campaign contribution. By the same token, we hold, as McCormick urges, that the District Court's instruction to the same effect was error. . . .

Accordingly we reverse the judgment of the Court of Appeals and remand the case for further proceedings consistent with this opinion.

So ordered.

Notes and Questions

1. Why would Congress and the courts treat bribery under the somewhat inapt category of extortion? Concurring in *McCormick,* Justice Scalia notes that this understanding of extortion is a legacy of the common law conception of extortion as official corruption, but doubts that the language of the Hobbs Act supports such an interpretation:

> When, in the 1960s, it first occurred to federal prosecutors to use the Hobbs Act to reach what was essentially the soliciting of bribes by state officials, courts were unimpressed with the notion. They thought that public officials were not guilty of extortion when they accepted, or even when they requested, *voluntary* payments designed to influence or procure their official action. . . . United States v. Addonizio, 451 F.2d 49, 72 (CA3 1971) ("[W]hile the essence of bribery is voluntariness, the essence of extortion is duress"). . . . Not until 1972 did any court apply the Hobbs Act to bribery. See United States v. Kenny, 462 F.2d 1205, 1229 (CA3 1972) ("kickbacks" by construction contractors to public officials established extortion "under color of official right," despite absence of "threat, fear, or duress"). . . .

It is acceptance of the assumption that "under color of official right" means "on account of one's office" that brings bribery cases within the statute's reach, and that creates the necessity for the reasonable but textually inexplicable distinction the Court makes today. That assumption is questionable. "The obtaining of property . . . under color of official right" more naturally connotes some false assertion of official entitlement to the property. This interpretation might have the effect of making the §1951 definition of extortion comport with the definition of "extortion" at common law. One treatise writer, describing "extortion by a public officer," states: "At common law it was essential that the money or property be obtained under color of office, that is, under the pretense that the officer was entitled thereto by virtue of his office. The money or thing received must have been claimed or accepted in right of office, and the person paying must have yielded to official authority." 3 R. Anderson, Wharton's Criminal Law and Procedure 790-91 (1957). . . .
[500 U.S. at 276-80.]

2. What if the allegedly extorsive transaction is initiated by a private person who offers the government official a thing of value? In Evans v. United States, 504 U.S. 255 (1992), the Supreme Court held that the Hobbs Act could apply in this situation as well, even without affirmative inducement by the official to initiate the deal, so long as the official's "acceptance of the bribe constituted an implicit promise to use his official position to serve the interests of the bribegiver." Id. at 257. Does this eliminate the distinction between bribery and extortion?

3. *Limits of the Hobbs Act: fair exchanges of political favors.* Can extortion by a private party, in a political context, occur even if the payor receives a "thing of value" to which he was not otherwise entitled? Consider United States v. Albertson, 971 F. Supp. 837 (D. Del. 1997). Corrado wanted to develop 80 acres of land for tract housing and sought rezoning. The local opposition was huge, and one of its leaders was Albertson. Albertson helped elect antidevelopment candidates as mayor and councilmen, and Corrado's plan was stymied by officials.

This was essentially how matters stood until October 30, 1996, when Albertson telephoned Corrado at work with a surprising proposition: sponsor Albertson's newly acquired semi-pro football team, the Dover Destroyers, in the form of a $20,000 donation, and Albertson would drop his opposition to the Applewood Farms development. At trial, Corrado related the conversation as follows:

PROSECUTOR: How did the conversation go?
CORRADO: Well, I picked up the phone and said, Hello. And Mr. Albertson said, Do you know who this is?
And I said, Yes, I do.
He said to me — he said, I have a proposition for you.
And I said, Oh, what was that, or what is that?
And he said, I'd like you to consider that for removing opposition to your project, would you contribute $20,000 to my football team?
And I guess I was silent for several seconds and I said to him, Well, I can't give you an answer now. I'll have to talk to my partners and I'll have to get back to you.

As he walked out of his office following his conversation with Albertson, a shocked Corrado told his administrative assistant, "I think I've just been bribed."
. . . Corrado initiated and recorded a telephone conversation with Albertson on November 20, 1996. During that conversation, Albertson informed Corrado he was "serious about the cause," but had "another thing that has risen up [i.e., his football team]." Albertson told Corrado he was "pretty excited" about the semi-pro football team, and advised Corrado a $20,000 donation would "show possibly good intentions on your side in the community." Curious about what he would receive

in return, Corrado prodded Albertson further by stating, "Um, you know, you said you could fix things and take away all the opposition. . . ."

. . . At [a] restaurant on November 20th, Albertson explained his position to Corrado:

> I controlled all the meetings. I put all the people in, I didn't personally put them in, the people voted them in, but I gave the people something to vote for. . . . I've got 800 more fliers sitting out there ready to go to town. Cause you've got these elections coming up, you've got four people on the council that are opposed to you, your chances start getting slimmer all the way down the line. You know, like I said, I don't think it's good idea. . . . I'm truly 100% against it. But, if you do what you're going to do and sponsor my football team, I'll not stand in your way anymore. . . . [Id. at 839-40.]

Corrado then arranged for arresting officers to be present when he gave Albertson a check for the money.

At trial, Albertson requested this instruction:

> The use of fear, in and of itself, is not "wrongful" within the meaning of the statute. If Joseph Corrado or the business entities with which he was associated, in exchange for money paid to the defendant, were to receive something of substantial value which they otherwise were not entitled to receive, the defendant would not be acting in a "wrongful" manner.

Denying the instruction, the trial court said:

> Please keep in mind, however, that the defendant did not act wrongfully merely by requesting and receiving money in exchange for settling litigation and/or merely by seeking contribution or sponsorship for his football team, despite the fact that he did not have a claim of right to that contribution or sponsorship. Also, keep in mind Mr. Corrado had no right to be free from opposition to its development pro-ject. Therefore, the defendant also did not act wrongfully by actively opposing Mr. Corrado's project — all of us have the right to participate in the political process and oppose real estate projects of developers. The defendant only acted wrongfully if, for the purpose of exploiting Mr. Corrado's fear of economic loss, he threatened to continue opposition to Mr. Corrado's project so that the defendant might gain sponsorship and/or contribution for his football team. [Id. at 842.]

The trial court was ultimately persuaded to grant a judgment of acquittal. It found that Albertson's "proposition" was "disgraceful, offensive, and ethically repugnant." But it concluded that the government had failed to establish the wrongful use of economic fear because

> a payor must be deprived of a "level playing field" to be the victim of a Hobbs Act violation. In other words, if the payor is paying the defendant for the opportunity to compete like everybody else, then the payor is a "victim" under the Hobbs Act; while he has received something for his money, it was something to which he was otherwise entitled — a level playing field — and therefore what was received was "imposed, unwanted, or superfluous." On the other hand, if a payor willingly transfers property to the defendant in an effort to gain an advantage and will not suffer more than anybody else for not making the payment, then there is no Hobbs Act violation. What Albertson offered Corrado was the opportunity to make considerable headway on an already-level playing field, an opportunity from which Corrado was free to walk away with impunity. [Id. at 845.]

Was Corrado deprived of an entitlement to Albertson's continuing to act on political principle? Even if Albertson's acting on principle would have made Corrado worse off?

D.   ROBBERY

LEAR v. STATE
Supreme Court of Arizona
39 Ariz. 313, 6 P.2d 426 (1931)

Ross, J. The appellant was convicted of robbery. He appeals and assigns as error the insufficiency of the evidence to sustain the conviction. . . .

The prosecuting witness, George Gross, testified that around 7 o'clock on the morning of August 12, 1931, he opened the Campbell Quality Shop, located in Buckeye, Maricopa county; that just about that time appellant entered the store and inquired about purchasing some shirts and shoes; that in the meantime he had taken a box of currency and a bag of silver out of the store safe; had placed the currency in the cash register and the bag of silver on the counter; that, while he was in the act of untying or unrolling the bag of silver, and while it was on the counter, appellant grabbed it from his hands and ran out of the back door; that appellant said no word at the time, exhibited no arms, and used no force other than to grab the bag as stated above. Appellant admitted taking the bag of silver and that it contained $33.

It was the contention of appellant at the trial, and is his contention here, that the facts do not show that he committed the crime of robbery. This crime is defined by our statute, section 4602, Revised Code of 1928, as follows:

"Robbery is the felonious taking of personal property in the possession of another, from his person or immediate presence and against his will, accomplished by means of force or fear. The fear may be either of an unlawful injury to the person or property of the person robbed, or of a relative or member of his family; or of an immediate and unlawful injury to the person or property of any one in the company of the person robbed at the time of the robbery."

The crimes of robbery and larceny are not the same. The former is classified as a crime against the person and the latter as a crime against property. In robbery there is, in addition to a felonious taking, a violent invasion of the person. If the person is not made to surrender the possession of the personal property by means of force or fear, the dominant element of robbery is not present. The mere taking of property in possession of another, from his person or immediate presence and against his will, is not robbery. Such taking must be accomplished by force or fear to constitute robbery.

The element of fear is not in the case. Appellant made no threat or demonstration. He simply grabbed the bag of silver from the hands of the prosecuting witness and ran away with it. There was no pulling or scrambling for possession of the bag. Was the force employed by appellant the kind of force necessary to constitute robbery? We think not. As we read the cases and text-writers, "the force used must be either before, or at the time of the taking, and must be of such a nature as to show that it was intended to overpower the party robbed, and prevent his resisting, and not merely to get possession of the property stolen." Rex v. Gnosil, (1824) 1 Car. & P. 304, 171 Eng. Reprint 1206. . . . Bishop on Criminal Law, ninth edition, volume 2, page 864, section 1167, states the force necessary for robbery as follows: "Snatching — which is sufficient asportation in simple larceny, may or may not carry with it the added violence of robbery, according as it is met or not by resistance. . . . The true distinction is that in the absence of active opposition, it will be robbery if the article is so attached to the person or clothes as to create resistance however slight."

In Ramirez v. Territory, 9 Ariz. 177, 80 Pac. 391, the prosecuting witness testified that he felt somebody come up behind him and run his hands in his pockets and then run off. The conviction of the defendant was set aside; the court holding that the mere taking of money by stealth from the person of another did not constitute robbery. . . .

The Attorney General, while expressing doubt as to whether the facts shown constitute robbery, calls our attention to the case of Brown v. State, 34 Ariz. 150, 268 Pac. 618, as authority that possibly robbery was committed. In that case the defendant and one Jefferson had gone to the home of the prosecuting witness, and, after she had sold them some beer, represented to her that they were prohibition officers, and that they were going to "throw her in" for violation of the prohibition law. Jefferson seized her and started towards the door. Brown intervened and suggested that, if she paid him $150, the matter could be "fixed up." The prosecuting witness went to her bedroom, obtained her purse, and dumped its contents in her lap, and while she was counting the money Brown snatched the roll of bills from her and left the premises. We held this constituted robbery. We think the *Brown* case falls within the rule announced by many courts to the effect that threats to accuse, arrest, or prosecute, when supplemented by force, actual or constructive, will support a charge of robbery. In the *Brown* case the defendants actually took hold of the prosecuting witness and started with her towards the door as though they would place her in jail. This demonstration of force no doubt put her in fear. . . .

The judgment of the lower court is reversed and the cause remanded for such further action as may seem advisable. . . .

Notes and Questions

1. How do the circumstances in *Brown* supply the force or fear missing in *Lear* and *Ramirez*? That Jefferson and Brown impersonated law enforcement officers suggests fraud; that they demanded a bribe for not arresting her suggests extortion. But what about this situation carries it across the line into robbery? Is it the force involved in briefly "seizing" the victim? Is it the threat of future imprisonment for crime? Yet threats of force only suffice for robbery if they are immediate: more remote threats trigger extortion liability. Is it the threat of being held in jail?

2. Examine Model Penal Code §222.1:

(1) *Robbery Defined.* A person is guilty of robbery if, in the course of committing a theft, he:

(a) inflicts serious bodily injury upon another; or

(b) threatens another with or purposely puts him in fear of immediate serious bodily injury; or

(c) commits or threatens immediately to commit any felony of the first or second degree.

An act shall be deemed "in the course of committing a theft" if it occurs in an attempt to commit theft or in flight after the attempt or commission.

(2) *Grading.* Robbery is a felony of the second degree, except that it is a felony of the first degree if in the course of committing the theft the actor attempts to kill anyone, or purposely inflicts or attempts to inflict serious bodily injury.

Note this section stresses that the harmful or intimidating acts committed by the robber must, if not qualifying as felonies in the first or second degree, involve "serious bodily harm" or the threat of "serious bodily injury" to the victim. Does the *Brown* case involve the threat of "serious bodily injury"? Does Bishop's "resistance however slight" test comport with this requirement of "serious bodily injury"? Most state statutes do not follow the Model Penal Code in setting such a high standard of harm or threatened harm in robbery. But does the high standard make sense on the ground that the law should clearly distinguish robbery from theft, given the increased penalties associated with robbery? In addition, "The elements of force and fear — of violence and intimidation — are alternatives: if there is force, there need be no fear, and *vice versa*. (Thus, all modern codes define robbery in terms of actual or threatened injury.)"[16]

3. Normally, the force or intimidation of a robbery must occur in the course of the commission of the theft. Common law courts often interpreted this rule narrowly to require that the harmful or threatening behavior occur during the actual "taking" and, further, that the taking be successfully completed. In contrast, section 222.1 of the Model Penal Code has interpreted this requirement broadly to include force or intimidation occurring during an attempted theft or during flight from a completed or attempted crime. The commentators of the Model Penal Code have justified their reliance on such a broad time span on the grounds that, with a robbery, "primary concern is with the physical danger or threat of danger to the citizen and not the property aspects of the crime."[17] Thus, under the Code a person may commit a robbery even if he fails to take the property of the victim. Are the commentators correct to make the primary issue for robbery the violence or threat of violence? In support of their expansion of "in the course of the commission of the theft" to include flight, the commentators assert that "the thief's willingness to use force against those who would restrain him in flight suggests that he would have employed force to effect the theft had the need arisen."[18] Is this sound logic?

A similar approach was taken by the Indiana Supreme Court in Coleman v. State, 653 N.E. 2d 481 (Ind. 1995), affirming a conviction and 12-year sentence on the following facts:

Coleman entered a Marsh supermarket in Muncie and proceeded to the video rental counter. At the counter, Coleman instructed a customer, Joe Williamson, to keep quiet while he pocketed five rolls of film. As Coleman was leaving the store, Williamson told a salesperson what had happened, and the salesperson alerted one of the store's comanagers, Max Smith. Smith followed Coleman just outside the store, where Coleman was still standing at the store's entrance. Seeing the film

16. LaFave & Scott, *supra,* at 1005.
17. American Law Institute, Model Penal Code and Commentaries, Part I, at 100 (1985).
18. Id. at 104.

protruding from Coleman's pocket, Smith asked Coleman if he had forgotten to pay for anything. Coleman then pulled a knife and threatened Smith, saying "do you want some of this." Fearing that Coleman would stab him, Smith retreated into the store. . . .

Do the facts established at Coleman's trial constitute robbery? The Indiana Code defines robbery as follows:

> A person who knowingly or intentionally takes property from another person or from the presence of another person:
> (1) by using or threatening the use of force on any person; or
> (2) by putting any person in fear;
> commits robbery, a Class C felony. However, the offense is a Class B felony if it is committed while armed with a deadly weapon or results in bodily injury to any person other than a defendant. . . . [Ind. Code Ann. §35-42-5-1 (2004).]

The court concluded:

> We agree with Coleman that if the "taking" was completed before Smith confronted him in front of the store, then he did not commit robbery as defined by our statute. At most, Coleman would be guilty of theft, which requires only the unauthorized exertion of control over the property of another with intent to deprive that person of the property, and perhaps an additional offense for threatening Smith with the knife.
> We have previously held, however, that a "taking" is not fully effectuated if the person in lawful possession of the property resists before the thief has removed the property from the premises or from the person's presence. . . . Coleman could not have perfected the robbery without eluding Smith. Smith confronted Coleman before he left the premises and thus presented an obstacle to the taking itself. . . . As such, Coleman's use of force was necessary to accomplish the theft of the film and was thus part of the robbery. [Id. at 482.]

Are you convinced by the court's argument that the threat was necessary to Coleman's successful completion of the theft? Could Coleman have been convicted of theft as soon as he left the store with the tapes?

E.   BURGLARY

Burglary at common law was a breaking and entering of a dwelling house at night, with the intent to commit a felony therein. Felonies were limited in number and were potentially punishable with death. Modern burglary statutes typically substitute the violation of consent for an actual breaking, or eliminate this element altogether. They typically apply to all buildings, and sometimes vehicles, while sometimes treating the traditional "dwelling" and "nighttime" elements as aggravators. The category of "felonies" has expanded to include any offense punishable by more than a year in prison, and, in any case, often the burglar must merely intend a "crime," not necessarily a felony. Burglary itself is no longer capitally punishable, but it continues to be punished with great severity. The following case illustrates some of the legal and policy issues raised by burglary today.

STATE v. COLVIN
Supreme Court of Minnesota
645 N.W.2d 449 (2002)

LANCASTER, JUSTICE.

This appeal presents the question of whether a criminal defendant's violation of an order for protection (OFP) is sufficient to establish first-degree burglary, absent the commission of or intent to commit a crime other than a violation of the order for protection. . . .

Michelle Colvin applied for and obtained an emergency (ex parte) OFP pursuant to Minn. Stat. §518B.01 (2000), against her ex-husband, Peter Colvin, on October 14, 1998. The order, which was valid for one year and was served on Colvin on the date obtained, provided that "Respondent [Colvin] must not enter Petitioner's [Michelle Colvin's] residence located at [address] or any future residence. . . ." The order also provided that Colvin could not commit acts of domestic abuse against Michelle Colvin, have any contact with her, or enter or call her workplace.

On February 25, 1999, Michelle Colvin telephoned the Rochester Police Department to report a violation of the OFP. According to the police report, a fifteen-year-old girl, A.M.E., who was staying with Michelle Colvin, returned to their home in Rochester that evening at 6:10 P.M. A.M.E. found Colvin inside the residence, watching television and drinking a beer. A.M.E. asked Colvin to leave, and he complied. . . .

As a result of the events of February 25, 1999, Colvin was charged with first-degree burglary in violation of Minn. Stat. §609.582, subd. 1(a) (2000), and violation of an OFP in violation of Minn. Stat. §518B.01, subd. 14(d)(1). Because Colvin had been convicted of two prior order for protection violations in the past five years, this OFP violation was charged at the felony level. . . . [T]he parties stipulated to the facts as represented in the police report and complaint and further agreed that there was no allegation that Colvin committed or attempted to commit any crime independent of the OFP violation. . . .

On April 10, 2000, the district court found Colvin guilty of first-degree burglary. The court made written findings of guilt, specifically finding: That Colvin entered a building; that he did so without consent; that the building was a residence; that another person, not an accomplice, was present in the building during some of the time Colvin was present; and that in entering the building Colvin intended to commit and did commit the crime of violating the valid October 14, 1998, OFP.

. . . The court of appeals affirmed the district court. . . . On appeal to this court, Colvin raises only the question of whether intent to violate an OFP is sufficient to establish burglary, absent the commission of or intent to commit a crime other than the OFP violation. . . .

Colvin was charged with first-degree burglary in violation of Minn. Stat. §609.582, subd. 1(a). Subdivision 1 provides:

> Whoever enters a building without consent and with intent to commit a crime,
> or enters a building without consent and commits a crime while in the building,

either directly or as an accomplice, commits burglary in the first degree and may
be sentenced to imprisonment for not more than 20 years or to payment of a fine
of not more than $35,000, or both, if:

(a) the building is a dwelling and another person, not an accomplice, is present in it when the burglar is in the building.

For a burglary conviction to stand, the state must prove that a defendant intended to commit some independent crime other than trespass. State v. Larson,
358 N.W.2d 668, 670 (Minn. 1984). . . .

Violation of an OFP, however, can be accomplished in many ways. It is the
nature of the OFP violation that will determine whether the OFP violation constitutes an independent crime under the burglary statute. For example, the OFP
in this case prohibited Colvin from: (1) committing acts of domestic abuse
against his ex-wife; (2) having any contact with his ex-wife; (3) entering her residence; and (4) entering or calling her workplace. If Colvin had acted in contravention of either the first, second, or fourth provision, his conduct would not
resemble trespass, while violation of the no-entry provision clearly does bear
such a resemblance.

The state argues that Colvin committed two violations of the OFP — by entering his ex-wife's residence, he violated the no-entry prohibition in the order,
and evidence of this conduct satisfied the illegal entry element of burglary. Second, by intending to contact his ex-wife in violation of the order's prohibition
against "any contact" with his ex-wife, Colvin violated the order a second time.
Evidence of this second method of violating the OFP, the state contends, satisfies
the intent to commit an independent crime element of burglary.

We disagree, because the district court's findings and the stipulated facts
fail to support the state's allegation that Colvin intended to contact his ex-wife
in violation of the OFP. The district court in its written findings of guilt specifically found that the independent crime committed by Colvin was violation of
the no-entry part of the OFP. The district court stated: "In entering the building, [Colvin] intended to and did commit a crime — specifically violation of
the October 14, 1998 Order for Protection which excluded [Colvin] from
that building. . . ." The district court made no other finding related to the no-
contact provision of the order. Further, nothing in the stipulated facts . . . establishes that Colvin intended to contact Michelle. . . .

Accordingly, the narrow issue presented is whether Colvin's violation of the
no-entry provision of the OFP is sufficient to establish the independent crime
element of burglary.

In *Larson*, this court held that trespass cannot serve as the crime committed
or intended to be committed to establish burglary. 358 N.W.2d at 670. We explained: "To allow an intent to commit a trespass to satisfy the requirement of
intent to commit a crime would mean that a mere trespasser who had no intent
other than to enter or remain in a building without the consent of the owner
could be convicted of burglary." Id. . . .

We conclude that violation of a no-entry provision of an OFP, like trespass,
is excluded from the crimes that can be the bases for the independent crime
element of burglary. Both offenses are designed to protect the interests that are
invaded by the unauthorized entry that the burglar makes. Thus both trespass
and violation of the no-entry provision of an OFP satisfy the illegal entry
element of burglary. Further, both offenses are complete upon entry. But we

conclude that the same entry is insufficient to satisfy both the illegal entry element of the burglary statute and the independent-crime requirement. . . .

Finally, we note that the legislature has created a statutory scheme to address the serious problem of domestic abuse. Minn. Stat. ch. 518B (2000). Among other remedies, the statutes address the significant danger inherent in domestic abuse by ratcheting up the penalties for repeat violations. *See* Minn. Stat. §518B.01, subd. 14(c), (d). Unlike the crime of trespass, repeat violations of orders for protection are designated as felonies. Id., subd. 14(d). A defendant convicted of violating three orders for protection in five years — such as the defendant here — is guilty of a felony level offense carrying a presumptive prison sentence. Id. Had the defendant been convicted of simple trespass for a third time, the crime would be a misdemeanor. Minn. Stat. §609.605 (2000). Such disparate treatment of domestic abuse based on unauthorized entry as compared to trespass underscores the legislature's intent to treat domestic abuse seriously and severely. If the legislature chooses to sanction violation of an OFP based solely on entering a home similarly to first-degree burglary — with a presumptive sentence of 48 months for a first-time offender — it can do so by amending the appropriate statutes. . . .

Reversed.

ANDERSON, RUSSELL A., JUSTICE (dissenting)

. . . I suspect the majority's true concern, a valid one, is whether a burglary charge, a severity level 6 offense, should be charged when the perhaps more accurate characterization of the offense is felony violation of the order for protection, a severity level 4 offense. However, if the state has misused its charging authority given the facts in this case, that action should be addressed directly rather than through a strained interpretation of the district court's straightforward ruling. . . . [T]he district court found that the felony underlying the burglary charge was violation of the order for protection and not the *"no-entry part"* of the OFP. . . .

I would affirm.

Notes and Questions

1. Peter Colvin *entered* his ex-wife's *dwelling without consent,* thereby committing the *crime* of violating an order for protection, and apparently *intending* to do so. He also encountered *another person* there. Why, then, does he not satisfy all the elements of first-degree burglary, according to the court? What result would the court have reached if the facts had more clearly established that his purpose in entering the apartment was to see his ex-wife? Suppose that Colvin had, without permission, entered the apartment of his ex-wife's friend, mistakenly believing that he would find his ex-wife there? Would he have been guilty of first degree burglary for this failed attempt to violate the order for protection?

2. Of what offense would Colvin have been guilty had there been no order of protection? How severely do you think such an offense is punished? Notice that the maximum penalty for first degree burglary in Minnesota is a twenty-year sentence and that, under Minnesota's sentencing guidelines, a first-offender convicted of first degree burglary would probably receive four years in prison. As the majority points out, domestic assaults are serious offenses justly subject to

increasingly severe penalties. But are sentences in the range of four to twenty years appropriate penalties for a nonviolent violation of an order of protection, or a failed attempt to violate an order of protection?

Notice that in Minnesota's statute, the crime intended need not be a felony, or a violent offense. This is typical of many modern burglary statutes. For example, Connecticut General Statutes section 53a-103 (2001) defines third degree burglary merely as "enter[ing] or remain[ing] unlawfully in a building with intent to commit a crime therein." In State v. Wallace, 745 A. 2d 216 (Conn., App. 2000) an employee of a New Haven private club confronted the defendant in the club parking lot, near some cars that had been broken into. When defendant ran, police were called and pursued him through a residential neighborhood. Defendant broke into an apartment and hid in the bathtub, and was ultimately convicted of burglary. He was found to have intended to commit the crime of "interfering with an officer," by hiding in the apartment. On appeal, the Appellate Court of Connecticut held that this offense satisfied the requirement of intending to commit a crime "therein," even though the police were not in the apartment when he hid there. The Court reasoned that

> "the basic rationale underlying the enactment of our burglary statutes was protection against the type of invasion of premises likely to terrorize occupants." (State v. Belton, 461 A.2d 973 (1983)) Entering a residence unlawfully to evade the police is very likely to terrorize the occupants of the residence. It would, therefore, frustrate the purpose of the statute to hold that simply because the "crime therein" is not specifically against people or property inside, a burglary has not been committed. In the present case, the defendant was allegedly breaking into residences to hide from the police who were chasing him. Because interfering with the police is a crime and because defendant entered the homes unlawfully to commit this crime, we hold that interfering with the police is a valid predicate offense in this case. [Id. at 220.]

Do you find this reasoning convincing? The penalty for interfering with an officer in Connecticut is up to a year, and for criminal trespass is up to six months, whereas the penalty for third degree burglary is one to five years. Notice that third degree burglary in Connecticut has no requirement that the building be a dwelling or be occupied by a person who might be "terrorized."

3. Professor Wayne LaFave offers the following critique of the offense of burglary:[19]

> Burglary is in fact a rather unique type of attempt law, as all the required elements merely comprise a step taken toward the commission of some other offense. . . . [I]t is doubtful that the offense is any longer required to punish or deter such preliminary conduct. An expanded law of attempts is now available to reach such conduct.
>
> The one feature of burglary which separates it from other attempts . . . is the punishment inflicted upon the offender. Unlike the usual attempt, burglary is generally held not to merge into a completed offense, thus allowing punishment for the offense committed and also for attempting to commit it in this particular way. The punishment for burglary itself is usually far greater than for most of the offenses which might actually be committed within the structure. This might

_____

19. LaFave, *supra,* at 1027.

suggest that the best way to deal with the offense of burglary would be to abolish it. . . . [M]odern laws of attempt would better serve in punishing the conduct, as this would better ensure a punishment rationally connected to the grievousness of the offense which was being attempted; an attempted petty theft would no longer be punishable as severely as an attempted murder.

4. Examine Model Penal Code §221.1:

(1) *Burglary Defined.* A person is guilty of burglary if he enters a building or occupied structure, or separately secured or occupied portion thereof, with purpose to commit a crime therein, unless the premises are at the time open to the public or the actor is licensed or privileged to enter. It is an affirmative defense to prosecution for burglary that the building or structure was abandoned.

(2) *Grading.* Burglary is a felony of the second degree if it is perpetrated in the dwelling of another at night, or if, in the course of committing the offense, the actor:

(a) purposely, knowingly or recklessly inflicts or attempts to inflict bodily injury on anyone; or

(b) is armed with explosives or a deadly weapon.

Otherwise, burglary is a felony of the third degree. An act shall be deemed "in the course of committing" an offense if it occurs in an attempt to commit the offense or in flight after the attempt or commission.

(3) *Multiple Convictions.* A person may not be convicted both for burglary and for the offense which it was his purpose to commit after the burglarious entry or for an attempt to commit that offense, unless the additional offense constitutes a felony of the first or second degree.

Does this formulation of the offense resolve the problems LaFave points to? Consider the following official comments. Do they justify the retention of burglary as a distinct offense?[20]

In view of the difficulties with the burglary offense in prior law, it is right to ask whether there remains a need for a separate burglary provision in a modern penal code. The Model Penal Code remedies the defects of attempt law that may have led to the development of the burglary offense, both by moving the point of criminality back into the area of preparation to commit a crime and by assimilating the penalty for the attempt to the penalty for the completed offense. The case for an independent burglary offense must rest on the gains that are perceived from aggravated grading of offenses that under ordinary circumstances would be punished adequately by other provisions of the Code. It is noteworthy that the civil-law countries know of no such offense, being content to penalize crimes involving intrusion by adding a minor term of imprisonment for criminal trespass to the appropriate sentence for the other crime committed or attempted. This approach could be pursued, or other offenses could be graded more severely in cases where they are accompanied by an intrusion of the sort that burglary offenses normally reach. With the crime of theft, for example, an intrusion into home or office could be made an element of aggravation, or a robbery-burglary section could be drafted to deal with the circumstances of violence or potential violence that should raise theft from a third- to a second-degree felony. Although rape, kidnapping, and infliction of serious bodily harm are already graded as first- or second-degree felonies and attempts to commit these offenses are graded as second-degree

20. American Law Institute, Model Penal Code and Commentaries, Part II, §221.1, at 62-76 (1980).

felonies, the imposition of extended sentences could be authorized for these offenses in situations where they are accomplished by intrusion.

It may be, therefore, that burglary could be eliminated as a distinct offense and the issues that are raised could be pursued as a grading matter, perhaps with the addition of a relatively minor criminal trespass provision to take account of the less serious cases. Centuries of history and a deeply imbedded Anglo-American conception such as burglary, however, are not easily discarded. . . .

15

RAPE

A. INTRODUCTION

1. Defining Rape

The problem of defining the elements. To set out the conventional elements of rape, at least under the common law, is deceptively straightforward. Blackstone defined rape as "carnal knowledge of a woman forcibly and against her will." A typical common-law–based statute would define rape as sexual intercourse "by means of force, against the will of the woman and without her consent." These would constitute the act and perhaps circumstance elements of the offense.[1] Whether the offense required any mens rea beyond awareness of the sexual intercourse was rarely specified.

Thus the conventional definition really explains very little. What is force? What is nonconsent? Can there be force without nonconsent? Can there be nonconsensual physical contact without force? Can an offender use force to overcome the will of a victim without being culpably aware of her nonconsent? It is very hard to distinguish these different elements in practice, and often the same evidence must be used to prove them all.

Any effort to delineate distinct elements of the crime of rape must also confront the distinction that factfinders often draw between "stranger" and "acquaintance" rapes. As a practical matter, in stranger-rape cases, factfinders tend to presume nonconsent and even force. Such cases are often litigated only on the question whether the victim has misidentified the perpetrator. By contrast, in many cases of sexual encounter between nonstrangers, the defendant may not use or threaten violent force unless he encounters resistance. Here prosecutors may find it more difficult to persuade factfinders that the defendant used force or even that the complainant did not consent. Thus, these cases underscore the particular difficulty of separating out resistance, force, nonconsent, and culpability with respect to nonconsent.

---

1. As we will see later in this chapter, rape law generally also proscribes intercourse where the victim is unconscious, heavily intoxicated, mentally incompetent, or underage. These situations fall under the general rape law or under special statutes.

What rape law should protect. The distinction between stranger and "non-stranger" or "acquaintance" rapes is generally a descriptive, not a legal one, and violent force and severe physical injury can occur in the latter category as well. Nevertheless, as legislatures and courts in recent years have given increasing attention to nonstranger rapes, commentators have offered broader views of the proper goal of rape law to protect victims from harm beyond the obvious need to protect people from the physical injury caused by violent attack. Professor Stephen Schulhofer has argued that rape law should focus on the value of "sexual autonomy":[2]

> Respect for sexual autonomy . . . requires that the law protect our freedom to seek emotional intimacy and sexual fulfillment with willing partners. . . . What is at stake is nothing less than women's bodily security and every person's right to control the boundaries of his or her own sexual experience.
>
> Existing criminal law resolves the dilemmas of sexual autonomy by making almost no effort to control abuses that are not physically violent. This "solution" implicitly places an imprimatur of social permission on virtually all pressures and inducements that can be considered nonviolent. . . .
>
> Sexual autonomy . . . has three distinct dimensions. The first two are mental — an internal capacity to make reasonably mature and rational choices and an external freedom from impermissible pressures and constraints. The third dimension is equally important. The core concept of the person, long protected by the common law, implies a physical boundary, the bodily integrity of the individual. Autonomy, therefore, is not only mental and intellectual, not only the capacity for meaningful, unconstrained choice. It is also physical, the separateness of the corporeal person. Even without making threats that restrict the exercise of free choice, an individual violates a woman's autonomy when he engages in sexual conduct without ensuring that he has her valid consent.

On a related dimension, Prof. Samuel Pillsbury argues:[3]

> But as with stranger rapes, the central injury of forced sex is a harm to the spirit. Here the effect of a prior relationship and the nature of that relationship must be considered aggravating factors. Forced sex [by a non-stranger] involves a betrayal of the personal human bond. A man assumed to be trustworthy, at least to the extent of fundamental respect for physical integrity, proves to be entirely untrustworthy. A person thought to be a friend, or at least friendly, becomes for a critical time, an enemy.

2.   Some Facts About Rape in the United States

Frequency of rape. Though disputes over definition, great underreporting, and the general inaccuracy of statistics make any number hopelessly speculative, one recent government study suggests that 500,000 women per year are victims of rape or other criminal sexual assault and that as many as 15 million women

---

2. Stephen Schulhofer, Unwanted Sex: The Culture of Intimidation and the Failure of Law 15, 111 (1998).

3. Crime Against the Heart: Recognizing the Wrongs of Forced Sex, 35 Loy. L.A. L. Rev. 845, 897 (2002).

in America have been so victimized at least once in their lives,[4] while some estimates are even higher.

In terms of rapes reported to the police, in 1995 police received complaints
of about 100,000 forcible rapes, reflecting a modest decreasing pattern in recent
years (and 14 percent lower per capita than the peak year of 1976).[5] In terms of
surveys of victims 12 years of age or older, there were about 260,000 attempted
or completed rapes and almost 100,000 threatened or completed sexual assaults
other than rape. About one woman in 625 was the victim of some kind of sexual
assault, about 1 in 1400 the victim of a forcible rape. On the whole, the ratio between rapes and sexual assaults reported to the police and those indicated on
victim surveys has grown in recent years. Many credit this apparent increase in
the ratio of reports to actual crimes to legal reforms that have made prosecutions more feasible and hence increased incentives to report, but many also attribute the change to changes in social attitudes about rape independent of legal reforms.[6]

In terms of law enforcement response, there were about 35,000 arrests for
forcible rape, reflecting a clearance rate of about 50 percent of reported
forcible rapes. There were about 100,000 arrests for other sex offenses. Of
people arrested for rape or sexual assault, 99 percent were male and about 60
percent Caucasian; the average age of arrestees was in the early thirties. About
90 percent of the victims of reported rapes and sexual assaults were female.

Though rape occurs throughout society, some groups appear to be exceptionally at risk; just as lower-income and urban people tend to be disproportionately victimized by crime generally, women in lower-income urban environ-
ments are more likely than others to be raped, and studies also suggest that
college students are a very vulnerable population.[7]

Relationship of rapist to victim. The consensus of research is that the great majority of rape victims are attacked by nonstrangers. A typical survey revealed that
only 22 percent of rape victims had been raped by total or virtual strangers; 9
percent by husbands or ex-husbands; 11 percent by fathers or stepfathers; 10
percent by boyfriends or ex-boyfriends; 16 percent by other relatives; 29 percent
by other acquaintances or neighbors.[8] About 60 percent of rape or sexual assault
incidents were reported in 1995 to have occurred at the home of the victim or
at the home of a relative, neighbor, or friend. In 75 percent of the cases the
complainant and the accused had some prior relationship as family member, intimate, or acquaintance.

Reporting and "attrition" rates. As suggested by the numbers above, the approximately 100,000 rapes reported to the police each year may be as small a

---

4. Bureau of Justice Statistics, Violence Against Women: Estimates from the Redesigned Survey 1 (1995).

5. All 1995 figures come from the most comprehensive recent government compilation from
the Bureau of Justice Statistics, Lawrence A. Greenfield, Sex Offenses and Offenders: An Analysis
of Data on Rape and Sexual Assault (1997).

6. For a skeptical view of the link between reforms and reporting rates, see David Bryden & Sonja
Lengnick, Rape in the Criminal Justice System, 87 J. Crim. L. & Criminology 1194, 1218-30 (1997).

7. See Mary Koss et al., The Scope of Rape: Incidence and Prevalence of Sexual Aggression
and Victimization in a National Sample of Higher Education Students, 55 J. Consulting & Clinical
Psycholo. 162, 66 (1987) (25 percent of college men surveyed reported engaging in coercive sex).
For a discussion of rape in college settings, see Katherine Baker, Sex, Rape, and Shame, 79 B.U. L.
Rev. 663 (1999).

8. Crime Victims Research and Treatment Center, Rape in America 4 (1992).

fraction as one-fifth of actual offenses,[9] and in any event only about 35 percent of the reported cases lead to arrest. This apparently high "attrition" rate may well be due to the perceived hostility or indifference of police and prosecutors toward rape law enforcement or rape victims, though the attrition rate for rape cases, while much higher than for homicide, is probably much lower than that for robbery and burglary.[10] In any event, a major factor in the attrition rate is that so high a percentage of rape cases involve acquaintances or relatives where the complainant declines to pursue justice in the courts.

Case outcomes. Conviction/acquittal ratios in rape cases vary widely among jurisdictions (and depend heavily on the percentage of investigated cases that are brought to trial), though in most jurisdictions convictions are much more likely in stranger cases. Overall, about two-thirds of rape arrests lead to convictions of some serious charge.[11] About two-thirds of convicted rape defendants receive prison sentences, with the average term imposed about 14 years, and the average time served about 5 (these numbers are about twice the numbers for sexual assault other than rape). Since 1980, while prison populations generally have risen about 7.6 percent annually, the number imprisoned for sexual assault other than rape has grown annually at about 15 percent — the highest rate for any category of violent crime.

3.   The Evolution of Rape Rules

The modern story of rape law in the United States has largely been one of efforts over the last few decades to address the problem, widely acknowledged, that rape laws are drastically underenforced. Of course, there is a complex counter-story rooted deep in American history of the disproportionately heavy and unjust application of rape laws in one context: the story of black men accused of raping white women.[12] Moreover, the rape laws have traditionally set extremely high punishments, at least in theory,[13] for those convicted of rape. In

9. Other estimates of the fraction range from one-tenth to three-fifths; see Bryden & Lengnick, *supra,* at 1220.

10. Michael R. Gottfredson & Don M. Gottfredson, Decision-Making in Criminal Justice: Toward the Rational Exercise of Discretion 154, 331 (1980).

11. The general perception that juries are even more acquittal-prone in rape cases than are judges in bench trials finds some support in the classic study, Harry Kalven, Jr. & Hans Zeisel, The American Jury (1966). That study's conclusions on rape cases may be outdated because they preceded modern reforms in jury composition, though the conclusion that juries are differentially lenient toward defendants in acquaintance rape cases may stand. Bryden & Lengnick, *supra,* at 1263.

12. For a study of race prejudice in the administration of rape laws in colonial and antebellum Virginia, see Leon Higginbotham & Anne F. Jacobs, The "Law Only as an Enemy": The Legitimization of Racial Powerlessness Through the Colonial and Antebellum Criminal Laws of Virginia, 70 N.C. L. Rev. 969, 1057 (1992). For a major treatment of the dynamics of both race and gender in the disparate treatment of both rape defendants and rape victims by virtue of their race, see Kimberle Crenshaw, Mapping the Margins: Intersectionality, Identity Politics, and Violence against Women of Color, 43 Stan. L. Rev. 1241, 1265-82 (1991); see also Andrew Taslitz, Race, and Two Concepts of the Emotions in Date Rape, 15 Wisconsin Women's L.J. 3, 39-40 (2000) (arguing that disparate punishment of black men accused of raping white women reflected greater concern with insult to white domination than to women's autonomy). Finally, for a modern empirical study cautiously finding some evidence of continuing disparate treatment of rape cases on account of the race of both accused and complainant, see Gary LaFree, Rape and Criminal Justice: The Social Construction of Sexual Assault (1989).

13. The laws on the statute books create extremely severe punishments for rape, generally setting maximums for a state's highest degree of forcible rape at life (Mich. Comp. Stat. Ann. §750.520b) (2003) or 25 years (N.Y. Pen. Code §70.00) (2004) though even where prosecutors are

addition, so-called sexual psychopath laws that stigmatize and curtail the liberties for those convicted of rape or otherwise identified as sexual offenders trace back well before the era of rape law reform. Moreover, in light of renewed social fear of child molesters in particular, sex offender registration and other laws aimed at isolating or incapacitating offenders have gotten more severe in recent years.[14] Nevertheless, the clear consensus among courts, legislators, and commentators in the past few decades has been that because of outdated laws and gender biases, rape defendants have enjoyed undeserved leniency in the criminal justice process, while too often complainants are neither believed nor respected by the prosecutorial and trial systems. Hence, over the last few decades, most jurisdictions have significantly reformed their rape law schemes in an effort to increase the prosecutor's ability to win convictions, and thereby to provide better protection for rape victims and to induce more of them to be willing to report and help prosecute the crimes.

These reform efforts have been of three kinds. First, evidentiary barriers to rape prosecution have been lowered. Traditionally, most jurisdictions have had some special requirements for rape prosecutions. These rules have included: (1) a rule that no rape defendant can be convicted solely on the basis of a victim's uncorroborated testimony; (2) a requirement that the complainant made a "prompt complaint" to the police; (3) rules of evidence deeming the complainant's past sexual conduct or reputation for chastity relevant to her credibility or her consent to sexual intercourse; (4) the requirement of a cautionary instruction to all juries, alerting them that rape complaints are easy to fabricate. In almost all jurisdictions, these rules have been eliminated or weakened, and many credit these reforms with increased success in rape prosecutions and an increased willingness of victims to report rapes.

Next, many jurisdictions have effected substantive reforms that frame the crime of rape very generally. Substantive changes include: making the crime gender neutral for both perpetrator and victim; removing the traditional "marital exemption" that made it legally impossible for a husband to be charged with raping his wife (see pp. 966-70, *infra*); and broadening the definition of the rape act beyond penile-vaginal intercourse; changing the name of the crime from "rape" to such terms as "criminal sexual assault," either with the goal of altering social conceptions of the crime from one of sexual desire to violence, or of making it less stigmatic so as to induce juries to convict more often.

But most significant, as we will examine in the rest of this chapter, is an effort to redefine the core elements of force and nonconsent. The general direction of change is clear: Many jurisdictions have lowered or even eliminated the state's obligation to prove resistance as part of proving force or nonconsent; many have broadened the criteria for establishing force, by including indicia beyond aggravated physical injury or threats thereof; some states have purported to eliminate even any need to prove force at all, making the fact of nonconsent the gist of the crime; a few others have made the absence of an affirmative manifestation of consent the core of the crime.

---

rigorous in pursuing rape cases the maximum is rarely reached unless the crime involves great violence beyond the rape itself.

14. For a critical treatment of these laws, ascribing them to historically fluctuating psychological stereotypes of offenders and to "panics" cased by the media, see Deborah H. Denno, Life Before the Modern Sex Offender Statutes, 92 Northwestern U. L. Rev. 1317 (1998).

As the requirements of physical force and resistance have been weakened or eliminated, the actus reus of rape has increasingly come to be seen simply as nonconsensual sexual intercourse; and this change has had two consequences. First, courts have had to consider nonforcible invasions of sexual autonomy, such as sexual acts committed by means of fraud or extortion. Second, a simpler actus reus has caused courts and scholars to reconsider the mental element. Requiring the prosecutor to prove violent force or resistance tended to obviate any need for an independent inquiry into the attacker's mental state. But if the gist of rape is now the fact of nonconsent, then the criminal law may have to determine the required mental culpability with respect to nonconsent. Must the defendant be aware of the victim's nonconsent? Reckless as to nonconsent? Negligent? And what kind of evidence suffices to establish these mental states?

As we begin to review the traditional elements of rape, a roadmap is useful. Professor David Bryden offers a useful chart of the possible elements of rape:[15]

[I]magine for a moment that you are free to adopt any definition of rape. Here are some possibilities:

MENS REA	ACT
	Penetration, plus
1. Intentional	1. Force and Nonconsent
2. At Least Reckless	2. Nonconsent (Subjective)
3. At Least Grossly Negligent	3. Nonconsent Manifested by Either
4. At Least Negligent	Verbal or Physical Resistance
5. Strict Liability	4. Lack of Affirmative Expression of
	Consent

By combining one of the mental states from the left column with one of the acts from the right column, we can create a definition of rape to suit nearly anyone. Of all the possible combinations of a mens rea and an act, the most advantageous to the prosecution would be strict liability combined with subjective nonconsent. The most favorable to the defense would be intent (to have nonconsensual intercourse) combined with force and nonconsent.

We would add to Bryden's taxonomy a fifth act definition, employed by Model Penal Code §213.1(1)(a): penetration plus force.

B. THE REQUIREMENT OF "UTMOST RESISTANCE"

Traditionally, to win a rape prosecution the state would have to prove very overt force. In many cases involving encounters between complete strangers, force was easy to establish, since the defendant often would use a weapon or assaulting physical violence. Factfinders and appellate judges were far readier to believe that victims did not consent to sex with a stranger and that a stranger was willing to achieve his aim by violence. Thus, the resistance requirement, however

15. Redefining Rape, 2 Buff. Crim. L. Rev. 101, 208-09 (1999).

strong in theory, might be obviated in stranger cases. But once we move into the area of nonstranger rapes, which probably are the majority, we find courts looking to the victim's resistance as an indicator of the assailant's force and the victim's nonconsent. Thus, the key factor in many famous common law cases was the amount of resistance "required" of the complainant.

BROWN v. STATE
Supreme Court of Wisconsin
127 Wis. 193, 106 N.W. 536 (1906)

The information alleged that: "On the 27th day of October, in the year 1904, . . . Grant Brown did ravish and carnally know one Edna Nethery, a female of age of 14 years or more, by force and against her will. . . ." The two parties were children of neighboring farmers who had known each other all their lives. The accused was 20 years old and the prosecutrix 16. . . . [T]he prosecutrix went by a usual path across fields to her grandmother's house for the purpose of having an aunt try on certain clothing being made for her. Such path passed by and over part of the farm of the defendant's father. Defendant was in the field driving out hogs and repairing a fence, and, as prosecutrix reached a stile, he was close thereto, so engaged. She addressed him in a playful way with reference to his work, and he suspended same and came up to her. Her story is that he at once seized her, tripped her to the ground, placed himself in front and over her, unbuttoned her underclothing, then his own clothing, and had intercourse with her; that the only thing she said was to request him to let her go, and, throughout the description of the event, her only statement with reference to her own conduct was, repeatedly: "I tried as hard as I could to get away. I was trying all the time to get away just as hard as I could. I was trying to get up; I pulled at the grass; I screamed as hard as I could, and he told me to shut up, and I didn't, and then he held his hand on my mouth until I was almost strangled." . . . She makes no mention of any use of her hands or her lower limbs. After the completion of the intercourse she says he made her promise not to tell, and, upon her doing so, allowed her to arise. She says she made the promise because she was afraid of him. . . . The defendant's story differed only in details and in the denial of any resistance. . . . There were no marks upon his face, hands, or clothing of any struggle. . . .

[P]laintiff in error urges, with great force, that there was not evidence sufficient to satisfy any reasonable mind, beyond reasonable doubt, of such resistance as the law makes sine qua non to the crime of rape. We need not reiterate these considerations of the ease of assertion of the forcible accomplishment of the sexual act, with the impossibility of defense save by direct denial, or the proneness of the woman when she finds the fact of her disgrace discovered or likely of discovery, to minimize her fault by asserting vis major. . . . Not only must there be the entire absence of mental consent or assent, but there must be the most vehement exercise of every physical power to resist the penetration of her person, and this must be shown until the offense is consummated. We need not mention the exception where the power of resistance is overcome by unconsciousness, threats, or exhaustion, for in this case, there is no proof of any of those things. . . . Turning to the testimony of the prosecutrix, we find it limited to the general statement, often repeated, that she tried as hard as she could to get away. Except for one demand, when first seized, to "let me go," and

inarticulate screams, she mentions no verbal protests. While we would reasonably recognize the limitations resting on many people in attempting expression
and description, we cannot conceive it possible that one whose mind and exer-
tions had, during an encounter of this sort, been set on resistance, could or
would in narrative mention nothing but escape or withdrawal. . . . It is hardly
within the range of reason that a man should come out of so desperate an encounter as the determined normal woman would make necessary, without signs
thereof upon his face, hands, or clothing. . . . Resistance is opposing force to
force, not retreating from force.

[Judgment reversed.]

Notes and Questions

1. Why does the court demand so much of the "prosecutrix"? Does it suspect that in the absence of greater resistance, she must have desired to have sex
with Brown? Or is it implying that even if she refused to consent to sex, she had
some legal or moral obligation to fight harder, so that strong resistance is an element of the crime even if it is clear the victim did not consent? Or is it suggesting that she refused at first to consent but, given the absence of injuries on
Brown, she must have ultimately "consented"?

2. For another famous example of the requirement of utmost resistance,
consider People v. Dohring, 59 N.Y. 374, 384 (1874). The defendant locked the
14-year-old complainant in a barn.

> The resistance must be up to the point of being overpowered by actual force, or of
> inability from loss of strength longer to resist, or from the number of persons at-
> tacking resistance must be dangerous or absolutely useless, or there must be fear
> of duress or death. . . .
>
>   . . . Certainly, if a female, apprehending the purpose of a man to be that of
> having carnal knowledge of her person, and remaining conscious, does not use all
> her own powers of resistance and defence, and all her powers of calling others to
> her aid, and does yield before being overcome by greater force, or by fear, or be-
> ing surrounded by hostile numbers, a jury may infer that, at some time in the
> course of the act, it was not against her will.
>
>   . . . Can the mind conceive of a woman . . . revoltingly unwilling that this deed
> should be done upon her, who would not resist so hard and long as she was able?
> And if a woman, aware that it will be done unless she does resist, does not resist to
> the extent of her ability on the occasion, must it not be that she is not entirely
> reluctant?

As an alternate statement of the common law, does *Dohring* cast light on *Brown*?

3. *Utmost resistance in historical perspective.* The common law doctrine of utmost resistance reflected in *Brown* may make more historical sense if we consider
the following perspective offered by Professor Anne M. Coughlin.[16]

> . . . [W]e cannot understand rape law unless we study the doctrine, not in iso-
> lation, but in conjunction with the fornication and adultery prohibitions with
> which it formerly resided. . . . When we recall that the contemporary definition of
> rape emerged from a system that outlawed these forms of consensual heterosexual

16. Sex and Guilt, 84 Va. L. Rev. 1, 6-9, 45 (1998).

intercourse, it seems clear that the official purposes of rape law . . . did not include the protection of sexual autonomy. Contrary to the assumptions of the modern rape critique, influential institutions within that former system decreed that sexuality was a force so dangerous that it could not safely be left to self-regulation, but rather should be closely confined, by state law, within marital relationships. Far from being positively valued and protected, therefore, the exercise of sexual autonomy was something to be discouraged, even criminalized. . . .

. . . How would judges who believed that consensual nonmarital intercourse was a crime define rape? . . . By unearthing our ancestors' belief that all nonmarital intercourse should be criminalized, we may begin to understand, even as we reject, the inclination of courts to approach rape complaints with deep suspicion. Since, under our ancestors' system, the underlying sexual activity in which a rape complainant engaged (albeit, by her own testimony, unwillingly) was criminal misconduct, her complaint logically could be construed as a plea to be relieved of responsibility for committing that crime. A court would be receptive to such a plea only if the woman could establish that, although she had participated in a sexual transgression, she did so under circumstances that afforded her a defense to criminal liability. Significantly, careful examination of rape doctrine reveals that the elements of the rape offense (almost) are a mirror image of the defenses we would expect from women accused of fornication or adultery. Such traditional defensive strategies would include the claim that the woman had committed no actus reus, that she lacked the mens rea for fornication or adultery, or that she had submitted to the intercourse under duress. For example, just as courts allowed perpetrators of nonsexual crimes to interpose a duress defense, so we must assume that they would be willing to excuse those women suspected of fornication or adultery who could prove that their accomplices had forced them to offend under threat of death or grievous bodily harm. According to this account, the features of rape law to which the critics most strenuously object — namely, the peculiar definitions of the nonconsent and force elements of the crime — are better understood as criteria that excuse the woman for committing an illegal sexual infraction, than as ingredients of the man's offense. . . .

. . . For most contemporary observers, the gulf between the Puritan world and our own must seem impassable, and properly so: There simply is and should be no way to reconcile our world's official laissez-faire approach to sexuality with the Puritan preference for official interference in the sexual domain. The problem for women today is that we seem to inhabit neither of these two worlds; rather, we live in a world that combines the worst features of both. . . . [W]hen women bring a rape complaint in order to vindicate their interest in heterosexual autonomy, they discover that [the] movement towards decriminalizing nonmarital sexuality has been far from complete insofar as they are concerned. Though our system no longer punishes anyone directly for fornication or adultery, the substantive elements of rape still are calibrated so as to require women to prove — as a condition for convicting the men who violated their interest in sexual self-determination — that they should not be held responsible for one of those offenses.

C. "REASONABLE" OR "EARNEST" RESISTANCE

As courts began to reform rape law to eliminate the requirement of utmost resistance, they hardly eliminated the resistance requirement altogether. Rather, expanding the exception already immanent in the older rules for cases where resistance would be futile, they redefined the required resistance as reasonable or earnest, and became far more willing to accept arguments of futility.

PEOPLE v. DORSEY
New York State Supreme Court
429 N.Y.S.2d 828 (1980)

SCHACKMAN, JUSTICE. On August 27, 1979, the complainant, a forty-one-year-old woman, who was five feet tall and weighed 130 pounds, entered the lobby of her apartment building at about 6:00 P.M., returning home from work. When an elevator arrived, the complainant entered and pressed the button for the tenth floor, on which her apartment was located. A young male entered the elevator with her and pressed the button for another floor.

The next thing the complainant noticed was the elevator stopping. Upon looking up to see if it was her floor, she saw the defendant standing by the elevator buttons, manipulating them. She also saw that the elevator was stopped between floors, with the door to the elevator shaft being open. However, the alarm bell of the elevator did not go off.

The complainant testified that the defendant, a fifteen-year-old male approximately five feet seven inches tall and weighing in excess of two hundred pounds, turned around and told her to take her clothes off. . . . When the complainant did not respond the defendant repeated his demand. The complainant then complied and was subjected to acts of sexual intercourse and sodomy during the next ten to fifteen minutes.

Following this, the defendant told the complainant to get dressed, and he started the elevator back up, eventually getting off at the twenty-second floor. The complainant testified that she was then able to get the elevator back down to her floor, where she got out, went into her apartment, and called the development's security police force. They then contacted the New York City Police Department. The defendant was identified by the complainant later that evening at the security police offices, and he was then arrested.

The complainant testified that she had not attempted to scream at any time before or during the incident because she felt that no one outside the elevator could have heard her, or helped her. She also testified that the defendant did not use any overt physical force against her, either before or during the incident, other than what was necessary for the completion of the sexual acts. She further testified that the only express threat made by the defendant came after completion of the incident, as he was leaving the elevator, in which he stated that if anything "happened" to him in the next couple of days, his friends would "get her."

Since 1965, New York's statutes dealing with nonconsensual sex offenses that were committed by forcible compulsion have spoken in terms of the use by the perpetrator of either a sufficient amount of physical force or of threats. In addition, the courts were also required to judge the sufficiency of the resultant behavior and emotions of the victim. Therefore, where physical force was used by the defendant, the question was whether the resistance of the victim was sufficient to indicate lack of consent, and when the defendant resorted to the use of threats, either express or implied, the question was whether the victim sustained a sufficient degree of fear, either of death, serious physical injury or of being kidnapped.

Many jurisdictions have similar forcible rape and sodomy statutes, and many of them have had as much difficulty applying them to the changing societal standards and viewpoints as New York has had. "As might be expected, the use of the outward manifestation of the subjective state of mind of the victim has proved an unsure index to the conduct of rapists. How much resistance indicates nonconsent? Some states require resistance to the utmost, an unenlightened attitude that has been repudiated elsewhere. Where utmost resistance is not required, great confusion exists. Some cases seem to impose a reasonableness standard, while others emphasize the decision by the woman without requiring that her fears be reasonable. . . . Still other cases require sufficient resistance to make nonconsent reasonably manifest. The amount of resistance required depends on all of the circumstances of the case." (The Resistance Standard in Rape Legislation, 18 Stanford L. Rev. 680, 682-83.)

The cases in New York seemed to fluctuate on a case-by-case basis, each judge and jury having to decide for themselves whether or not the resistance offered by the victim was sufficient. Many cases used the "reasonable resistance" standard, in which the judge and jury decided whether or not the resistance of the woman in each case was of a type which reasonably indicated, in light of all the circumstances of the incident, that she did not consent to the sexual advances of the man. . . . The use in New York of the "reasonable resistance" standard seemed to come to a definitive end, however, when the Appellate Division, First Department, issued a pronouncement that "Rape is not committed unless the woman opposed the man to the utmost limit of her power. . . ." (People v. Yanik, 55 A.D.2d 164, 167.)

Many civil rights and women's rights groups . . . [responded by arguing] that awareness of women's rights was rapidly changing in today's society, and it was time to discard the anachronistic concept that women who are raped had probably "asked for it," a concept which held them to be equally guilty in the eyes of many. Many women's groups sought changes in the law in order "to focus attention exclusively on the actor's conduct. In every other crime except a sex crime the only factor that is considered important is the behavior of the defendant. It is only in sex crimes that the victim has had to 'prove' himself or herself, and in many cases the victim has been, effectively, put on trial along with the defendant to have his or her conduct judged." (Snyder, Reform of New York's Rape Law Proposed, N.Y.L.J., Dec. 14, 1978, p. 4, col. 2.)

The New York State Legislature did not delay long in taking action to remedy this situation. The legislators realized that "the existing law places women in a cruel dilemma, forcing them to choose to follow either the advice of law enforcement experts not to resist where personal safety would be jeopardized, on the one hand, or [to follow] the legal resistance mandate on the other." (An act to amend the Penal Law, in relation to the definition of "forcible compulsion" in sex offenses: Memorandum in Support, New York State Senate, June, 1977.) They realized that women in New York were faced with a decision, not to resist in order to save their lives, but destroying any possibility of obtaining a rape conviction against their assailants. This was not demanded of the victim of any other crime.

Therefore, barely six months after the decision by the Appellate Division, First Department, in *Yanik* (55 A.D.2d 164, *supra*), the New York State Legislature passed a law amending subdivision 8 of section 130.00 of the New York Penal Law, the definition of forcible compulsion, by explicitly stating that a woman has to exert only "earnest resistance," and that earnest resistance does not mean utmost resistance. Rather, earnest resistance means "resistance of a type reasonably to be expected from a person who genuinely refuses to participate in sexual intercourse, deviate sexual intercourse or sexual contact, under all the attendant circumstances." (L. 1977, ch. 692, §2.) The intent behind this legislation was set forth in the preamble of the new law, in which it was decreed that: "It is the legislature's intention to modify the resistance requirement in the definition of forcible compulsion so that the victim need only offer so much resistance as is reasonable under the circumstances." (L. 1977, ch. 692, §1.)

The Legislature had clearly decided to modify "the requirement in forcible rape cases so that the amount of resistance must be proportional to the circumstances of the attack, [taking into account factors] such as the relative strength of the parties, and the futility of resistance. Under [this] standard, the perpetrator of a sex crime would no longer be excused from culpability because his victim, in fear of death or serious physical injury, had ceased to resist, and had therefore survived." (Senate Mem.) Some states, such as Michigan (Mich. Comp. Laws Ann., §750.5201) and Ohio (Ohio Rev. Code Ann., §2907.02) have gone further and recently passed statutes relieving the prosecution of the need to show any resistance as proof of nonconsent, an enlightened viewpoint which would eliminate this problem altogether. However, New York was brought in line with the majority of other states, such as California, of whose law it was written: "The resistance must be such as might be expected from 'a' woman in the victim's circumstances. This plus the reasonableness required removes the victim's opinion from the case. The concern is not with what she thought was necessary but what would reasonably appear necessary to a woman in her position. The reasonable-under-the-circumstances approach, with language to make clear that the woman need not incur serious risk of death or serious bodily injury, is as low as the standard can be set and remain consistent with fair treatment of defendants." (Stanford L. Rev. 680, 685.)

. . . The issue before this court is [to] determine from the facts of this case whether the defendant either exerted physical force capable of overcoming this complainant's reasonable, earnest resistance, or whether the complainant was overcome by fear of immediate death or serious physical injury due to threat from the defendant. Both of these questions must be measured by all of the attendant circumstances of this case.

Taking the latter question first, it is clear that there was no express threat issued by the defendant. It is just as clear to this court, however, that there was a definite implied threat from the defendant to the complainant, from which she could reasonably have concluded that she was faced with immediate death or serious physical injury. The defense argued that the defendant never once threatened her expressly, and that there was also no implied threat, because the defendant did not mention or display any gun, knife or other weapon. How then could the complainant have been put in fear of immediate death or serious physical injury?

The answer, in part, is that it is a well-settled point of law that a threat can be implied, as well as being express. . . . Here, instead of being faced with four big men in a lonely place, the complainant was faced with a husky teenager, who was seven inches taller and who outweighed her by over 70 pounds. She was trapped in a stalled elevator, between floors, with no place to retreat to, or from which help could arrive. The law, and common sense, did not require that she ascertain what the defendant would do to her if she refused to take off her clothes. Nor does it take but a brief recognition of the everyday events in this city to reasonably conclude that a gun, knife or other deadly weapon might quickly and savagely be used if she did not yield to the defendant. Therefore, this court finds, as a matter of law, that the People presented sufficient trial evidence from which the jury could conclude, beyond a reasonable doubt, that the defendant engaged in sexual acts with the complainant by means of forcible compulsion, in that there was an implied threat which placed the complainant in fear of immediate death or serious physical injury.

Although this alone would be enough to deny the defendant's motion, the "physical force" aspect of this case would lead this court to the same conclusion. While the defendant did not actually grab or hit the complainant, his act of manipulating the elevator to stop it between floors was certainly a physical act directed against the complainant. That act, plus the physical advantages that the defendant enjoyed, constituted the use of physical force which is capable of overcoming earnest resistance.

There are many instances where no resistance could reasonably be expected from a person who genuinely refuses to participate in sexual activities, and it is difficult for this court to imagine one clearer than the case at hand. The fact that the defendant would have inevitably succeeded in forcing himself on the complainant, able to overcome any possible resistance she could have offered, plus the fact that she was totally at his mercy in the stalled elevator, clearly indicates to this court, under all the attendant circumstances, that total compliance by the complainant was all that earnest resistance could reasonably require. . . .

Therefore, this court finds, as a matter of law, that the People presented sufficient trial evidence from which the jury could conclude, beyond a reasonable doubt, that the defendant engaged in sexual acts with the complainant by means of forcible compulsion, in that he used physical force capable of overcoming the earnest resistance of the complainant. . . . As mentioned previously, the jury returned a guilty verdict on both counts of the indictment, and this court finds no grounds to set aside that verdict. Wherefore the defendant's motion to dismiss the indictment, on the ground that the trial evidence was not legally sufficient to establish the offenses charged therein, is denied.

Notes and Questions

1. What would have been the outcome of State v. Brown, *supra,* under the *Dorsey* standard? What would have been the outcome in *Dorsey* under the old *Brown* standard? Try to articulate the difference in the standards. Are the different outcomes explained by the different standards or by the different assumptions the courts make in applying those standards?

2. *Is resistance an independent element?* The New York statute defines forcible compulsion as force that overcomes reasonable resistance. Does this mean that resistance is not required if there is other evidence of force or threat? In State v. Powell, 438 So. 2d 1306 (La. App. 1983), a Louisiana court construed a similar statute. The facts were these:

The alleged offense occurred on the evening of November 22, 1980, at approximately 8:15 P.M., when the victim, Cassandra Weeks Sylvester (Weeks), was standing on the corner of Havana Street in Leesville, waiting for a ride to Fort Polk. She related the following account of the incident. As she was waiting for her cousin to pick her up, the defendant, Clyde Powell, drove past her in an early 1970s model car. The defendant noticed the victim, stopped his car and parked not far from where she was standing. Shortly thereafter the victim, Weeks, approached defendant's car inquiring about his reasons for stopping. At trial she admitted having met the defendant earlier that evening and testified that she voluntarily went over and entered his car to talk for a while. From this point the facts are highly disputed.

Weeks testified that she entered defendant's car after he agreed to bring her to her cousin's residence, located nearby. The defendant then allegedly brought Weeks to a secluded area and threatened to kill her when she refused to have sexual intercourse with him. Weeks stated that defendant slapped her in the face three or four times while threatening to kill her. He allegedly threatened to use a weapon which, he had indicated, was under the seat of the car. Weeks admitted that she never saw the weapon or an object of any type which defendant threatened to kill her with. Following these incidents the victim testified that they each removed their own pants and defendant had intercourse with her on the front seat of the car. Thereafter, defendant brought Weeks to where she initially approached him that evening and the victim sought help from nearby friends who in turn contacted the police. [Id. at 1306-07.]

The court held that there was sufficient evidence for the jury to find that the complainant had not consented to intercourse. Nevertheless:

There was no showing, however, of resistance on the part of the victim and very little evidence that she was prevented from resisting by force or threats of physical violence under the circumstances. Construing the evidence in a light most favorable to the prosecution, we do not feel that any rational trier of fact could find beyond a reasonable doubt that there was force or threats of physical violence where the victim reasonably believed that resistance to the act would be to no avail. . . .

Certainly, the victim was afraid, but she also testified that the defendant said he would not hurt her. It is important to note that all of the witnesses who saw the victim immediately after the alleged rape testified that they did not see any cuts, bruises or evidence of any physical attack. Her own testimony indicates that she did not make any efforts to resist. The victim asserted at trial that the defendant threatened to kill her, yet, he did nothing to warrant a reasonable person in these circumstances to believe that resistance would not prevent the rape. The victim testified that she took her own pants off while defendant disrobed. She admitted that she never saw the object under the seat which defendant allegedly threatened to kill her with.

After a thorough review of the record we find that the evidence is insufficient to convince a reasonable fact finder beyond a reasonable doubt that the victim was prevented from resisting the act by threats of force or physical violence under the circumstances. . . . [Id. at 1308.]

The court therefore ordered an acquittal. Judge Stoker dissented:

The resistance standard (not resistance in fact) required for forcible rape is contained in the definition of the crime set forth in LSA-R.S. 14:42.1:

Forcible rape is a rape committed where the . . . intercourse is deemed to be without the lawful consent of the victim because the victim *is prevented from resisting the act by force or threats of physical violence under circumstances where the victim reasonably believes that such resistance would not prevent the rape.*

. . . In forcible rape the victim is not required to actually resist. It is necessary only that the victim be prevented from resisting either from (1) force or (2) threats of physical violence justifying the victim in believing that resistance will not prevent the rape. All that is required is a reasonable belief. . . .

Under the circumstances, . . . I believe the jury could have reasonably concluded that the victim in this case was prevented from resisting the act of rape because of defendant's threats to kill her if she did not cooperate and submit combined with his statement that he had something under the seat with which he could kill her. The jury could reasonably have concluded that the victim did believe, and believed reasonably, that resistance would not prevent rape. . . .

The victim in this case stated that she submitted because the defendant threatened to kill her if she did not. Although she did not state in so many words that she did not resist because she believed that resistance would not prevent the rape, that is the clear meaning of her testimony. If that meaning is not given to her testimony, it is tantamount to requiring a person threatened with rape to either be faced with a dangerous weapon or to resist to the utmost and, in either case, subject themselves to the possibility of great physical harm or death. . . . [Id. at 1309-10 (emphasis in original).]

Since the court seems to accept the jury's conclusion that the victim did not consent to intercourse, why does it still fault the prosecution for failing to establish resistance? How would the *Powell* court treat the facts in *Dorsey*? How would the *Dorsey* court treat the facts in *Powell*?

3. *"Reasonable resistance" and stranger rapes. Dorsey* is clearly an instance of a "stranger" rape. Should it have been necessary at all to even raise the issue of resistance, if resistance is not an independent requirement, but a means of establishing that sex was obtained through force and against the victim's consent?

In this regard, consider People v. Warren, 446 N.E.2d 591 (Ill. 1983):

[The complainant] rode her bicycle to Horstman's Point which overlooks the Carbondale City Reservoir in Carbondale. While complainant was standing alone at Horstman's Point, defendant approached her and initiated and engaged in a conversation with her. Although complainant did not know defendant, she responded to his conversation which was general in nature.

Complainant started to walk away from the lake in the direction of her bicycle which was at the top of the hill. While she walked up the hill, defendant continued talking as he walked alongside of her. Complainant testified that when she got on her bicycle defendant placed his hand on her shoulder. At this time, complainant stated, "No. I have to go now," to which defendant responded, "This will only take a minute. My girlfriend doesn't meet my needs." Defendant also told her that "I don't want to hurt you."

According to complainant, defendant then lifted her off the ground and carried her into a wooded area adjacent to the reservoir. Upon entering the woods, defendant laid complainant on the ground and told her to put her head on his backpack. Defendant then told her to take her pants down which she did part of the way. [Defendant then undressed himself, and complainant performed oral sex on him.] Defendant testified that complainant asked him, "Is that all?" to which he answered "Yes." [Complainant then immediately reported the incident to the police and was able to identify defendant later.] [Id. at 592.]

The court noted:

At the outset, we note that there are no significant inconsistencies in the testimony of the two parties. Instead, we are faced with facts which are susceptible of more than one reading. Defendant admits that he performed the acts upon which the deviate sex charges are based. He contends, however, that the acts complained of were performed without force or threat of force. [Id. at 592.]

Should the court have expected the defense to proffer some explanation of how, on the facts agreed on, one can infer that the complainant might have consented?

Ultimately, the court reversed the conviction for lack of evidence that the complainant made any reasonable effort to resist. Noting that the defendant did not brandish a weapon or strike complainant, it added:

> Furthermore, complainant did not attempt to flee or in any meaningful way resist the sexual advances of defendant.
>   . . . [T]he State offers complainant's statement that she did not attempt to flee because, "it was like the middle of the woods and I didn't feel like I could get away from him and I thought he'd kill me." Moreover, complainant stated that she did not yell or scream because the people she had seen in the area were too far away and that under the circumstances she felt that screaming ". . . would be bad for me." [Id. at 593.]

The court concluded that in the absence of greater protest or resistance, the conviction could not stand. "Complainant's failure to resist when it was within her power to do so conveys the impression of consent and removes from the act performed an essential element of the crime." Id. at 594.

Does this case show that courts are willing to apply the resistance requirement even in stranger rape cases?

D. FORCE

Many states have gone a step further, formally eliminating any requirement of resistance, so that the elements of rape become the combination of force and nonconsent. Though resistance might help establish force, it is not necessary to it.

PEOPLE v. BARNES
Supreme Court of California
42 Cal. 3d 284, 228 Cal. Rptr. 228 (1986)

BIRD, CHIEF JUSTICE.

Was the Court of Appeal correct in relying on a rape complainant's lack of "measurable resistance" to overturn convictions of rape and false imprisonment as unsupported by sufficient evidence?

I

Since the sufficiency of evidence to support the convictions is in issue, it is necessary to present a somewhat detailed statement of the factual circumstances of this case.

Marsha M. had known appellant about four years as of May of 1982. They were neighbors and acquaintances. She had been to his house briefly once before to buy some marijuana. A couple of weeks before the present incident, they had drunk wine together at her house.

Around 10 P.M. on May 27, 1982, appellant called Marsha and invited her over for some drinks to celebrate his parents' having come into a sum of money. Marsha was undecided and told appellant to call back or she would call him.

Over the next two hours, appellant called twice to see what Marsha had decided to do. She finally told him she would come over and that she wanted to buy a little marijuana from him. She asked him to meet her outside his house.

Marsha arrived at appellant's house around 1 A.M. Appellant was waiting for her outside the front gate. It was cold. Appellant suggested they go inside and smoke some marijuana. At first Marsha refused. She told appellant she had to get up early and wanted to buy the marijuana and go home. However, after a couple of minutes, appellant persuaded her to come inside.

Marsha followed appellant through the house to a room off the garage.[17] At first, they carried on a conversation which Marsha described as "normal chatter." Appellant provided some marijuana and they both smoked it. Appellant offered some cocaine, but she refused. She kept telling appellant she wanted to hurry up and leave.

After 10 or 15 minutes, appellant began to hug Marsha. She pushed him away and told him to stop. She did not take him seriously as he was "just coming on."

Appellant continued his advances despite Marsha's insistence that she only wanted to buy marijuana and leave. . . . Appellant told her he did not want her to leave. Marsha finally said good-bye and walked out of the room. Until this point, things between them had been "decent and friendly."

As Marsha approached the front gate, appellant, who was behind her and appeared angry, stated, "No, you don't go leaving. You don't just jump up and leave my goddamn house." He began "ranting and raving" and arguing with her. He wanted to know why she was "trying to leave." He told her that she made him feel as if she had stolen something; that she was acting like he was "a rapist or something." Marsha characterized appellant's behavior as "psychotic."

When she reached the front gate, Marsha did not try to open it because she did not know how. She asked appellant to open it, but he just stood looking at her. This behavior made her nervous. When she asked appellant what was wrong, he "reared back" as if he were going to hit her.[18]

They argued at the gate for about 20 minutes.[19] Marsha told appellant she did not understand what he was arguing with her about and that he seemed to be trying to find a reason to be angry with her. She told him, "I came to your house to get some grass. Now, I want to leave. You won't let me leave."

Appellant replied that he was going to let her leave but needed to put his shoes on first. He then returned to the room and Marsha followed. She said she

---

17. Marsha described the house where appellant lived as having an iron gate that had to be opened in order to reach the front door. Once inside the house, a door to the right opened to some stairs, which led to a room off the garage.

18. Marsha testified that several times appellant reared back with fists raised and "balled up." She felt threatened by these gestures and believed he was going to hit her. The first time he "reared back" was during the argument at the front gate. She testified she did not think his fist was raised during this instance, but that he did "rear back" and look at her.

19. During this argument, Marsha asked appellant several times to open the gate.

returned to the room because she felt she could not get out the front gate by herself.

As she was following appellant, the door leading to the stairs closed behind her, prompting him to shout that she was "slamming the goddamn door" in his house. After they entered the room, appellant closed the door behind them. He was "fussing" at Marsha, talking and "carrying on" the whole time he was putting on his shoes. He stated, "I don't know what the hell you bitches think you want to do." Marsha was confused and concerned about what was happening and about what appellant was going to do. Several times, appellant stopped talking and looked at her "funny."

Appellant then stood up and began to "lecture" Marsha. He was angry. He began to threaten her, telling her he was a man and displaying the muscles in his arms. He grabbed her by her sweater collar and told her he could pick her up with one hand and throw her out. Flexing his muscles, he stated, "You see this? I am a man. You respect me like a man. I am no kid." . . .

At one point appellant said, "You're so used to see [sic] the good side of me. Now you get to see the bad." Then he became quiet and stared at her. This statement again made Marsha believe he was going to hit her.

Marsha asked appellant whether he wanted to hit her. She told him she could not fight him. Appellant responded by lecturing her. Marsha began to move toward the door. When appellant noticed her, he said, "I don't know why you're standing by the door. What are you looking at the door for?" Marsha thought appellant pushed the door closed a little tighter.

Appellant continued talking but then suddenly turned and started hugging Marsha "affectionately." He told her he did not mean to "fuss" at her. By now, Marsha felt she was in the room with a "psychotic person" who had again changed personalities. Approximately 40 minutes had elapsed since they entered the room a second time. It was at this juncture that Marsha began to "play along" and feign compliance with appellant's desires.

In an effort to get out of appellant's house, Marsha suggested they go to her house where they could be alone. Appellant told her not to worry about his parents coming home. He continued to hug and talk to her. After a few minutes, appellant stated, "I have to have some of this right now," and told Marsha to remove her clothes. Marsha refused. Appellant reacted by telling her she was going to upset him and by making some type of gesture. In response, Marsha removed her clothes. An act of sexual intercourse ensued which lasted about one hour and included the exchange of kisses. Afterward, both appellant and Marsha fell asleep.

Marsha testified she engaged in sexual intercourse with appellant because she felt if she refused he would become physically violent. She based this assessment on appellant's actions and words, including his statements that she was about to "see the bad side" of him and that he could throw her out if he wanted.

Marsha awoke around 4 A.M. She cajoled appellant into walking her to the front gate and opening it so she could leave. She returned home and immediately called Kaiser Hospital to request an examination. She was eventually referred to the sexual trauma center and examined for venereal disease.

Marsha did not report the incident to the police that day because she was confused and felt "it was my word against his." She had been told at the sexual trauma center that she had three days within which to make a report. After discussing the incident with a coworker, she reported it to the police the following day.

Appellant telephoned Marsha the morning of the incident and a couple of days later. On both occasions she hung up on him.

The defense was consent. Appellant's testimony was substantially similar to Marsha's regarding the events prior to her arrival at his house. However, the versions differed markedly as to the subsequent events.

Appellant testified that the first time they were in the room together he gave Marsha some marijuana and refused payment for it. They smoked some marijuana. Appellant told Marsha he had "feelings for her," he was sexually attracted to her and did not want her to leave so quickly. According to appellant, they did not argue over anything. He was surprised that she was in such a rush to leave.

At the front gate, they continued to talk. He again expressed feelings of sexual attraction for her. According to appellant, it was Marsha who first returned to the room. There, she told him she would stay a little while longer. Then, without being asked, she started removing her clothes. Consensual sexual intercourse ensued during which Marsha returned appellant's hugs and kisses. Appellant testified he did not threaten Marsha in any way, make gestures toward her, display his muscles or force her to stay. He confirmed the fact that he had telephoned Marsha twice afterwards. However, he testified they talked briefly each time. . . .

II

Until its amendment in 1980, former section 261, subdivisions 2 and 3, defined rape as an act of sexual intercourse under circumstances where the person resists, but where "resistance is overcome by force or violence" or where "a person is prevented from resisting by threats of great and immediate bodily harm, accompanied by apparent power of execution. . . ."

The Legislature amended section 261 in 1980 to delete most references to resistance. In pertinent part, the statute now defines rape as "an act of sexual intercourse accomplished with a person not the spouse of the perpetrator, under any of the following circumstances: . . . (2) Where it is accomplished against a person's will by means of force or fear of immediate and unlawful bodily injury on the person or another."

The events in this case occurred on May 28, 1982. Therefore, appellant was charged, tried and convicted under section 261, subdivision (2), as amended in 1980. In the Court of Appeal, appellant argued that the evidence was insufficient to sustain his conviction of rape under that statute. Inexplicably, the Court of Appeal quoted and relied upon the language from People v. Nash, (1968) 261 Cal. App. 2d 216, 224, 67 Cal. Rptr. 621, which reiterated the requirements of rape prior to the 1980 amendment to section 261: "The offense of rape is committed when the victim resists the act, but her resistance is overcome by force or violence. (Pen. Code, §261, subd. 3.) Although she must resist in fact, an extraordinary resistance is not required. The amount of resistance need only be such as to manifest her refusal to consent to the act." . . . On this basis, the Court of Appeal reversed appellant's conviction of rape.

It is undisputed that the Court of Appeal erred in applying the requirements of former section 261 to the facts of this case. . . .

. . . [I]nsight into the purpose of Assembly Bill No. 2899[, which enacted the 1980 amendment to section 261,] can be garnered from the analysis by the Assembly Committee on Criminal Justice (now called the Assembly Committee on Public Safety): "The main purpose of this bill is to eliminate the 'resistance' requirement in rape. Under current law, a woman must either resist or be prevented from resisting because of threats. According to the proponents, victims who resist are injured by the rapist twice as often as victims who don't resist. The proponents also indicate that prosecutors are unable and unwilling to file cases when the victim does not resist." . . .

Recently, however, the entire concept of resistance to sexual assault has been called into question. It has been suggested that while the presence of resistance may well be probative on the issue of force or nonconsent, its absence may not.

For example, some studies have demonstrated that while some women respond to sexual assault with active resistance, others "freeze." One researcher found that many women demonstrate "psychological infantilism"— a frozen fright response — in the face of sexual assault. (Symonds, The Rape Victim: Psychological Patterns of Response, 36 Am. J. Psychoanalysis at p. 30.) . . . The "frozen fright" response resembles cooperative behavior. Indeed, as Symonds notes, the "victim may smile, even initiate acts, and may appear relaxed and calm." (Ibid.) Subjectively, however, she may be in a state of terror. (Ibid.) Symonds also reports that the victim may make submissive signs to her assailant and engage in propitiating behavior in an effort to inhibit further aggression. (Id., at pp. 30-31.) These findings belie the traditional notion that a woman who does not resist has consented. They suggest that lack of physical resistance may reflect a "profound primal terror" rather than consent.

Additionally, a growing body of authority holds that to resist in the face of sexual assault is to risk further injury. . . .

In a 1976 study of rape victims and offenders, the Queen's Bench Foundation found that over half of the sexual assault offenders studied reported becoming more violent in response to victim resistance. [Queen's Bench Foundation, Rape Prevention and Resistance 85 (1976).] Injury as reported by victims correlated with some form of resistance, including verbal stalling, struggling and slapping. (Id., at p. 108.) Those victims who resisted during coitus suffered increased violence as the assailant forced compliance. (Id., at p. 84.) Victim resistance, whether passive or active, tended to precede an increase or intensification of the assailant's violence. (Id., at p. 85; accord Amir, Patterns in Forcible Rape, 971 164-65, 169-71 [victim resistance in some instances serves to provoke more physical brutality and sexual humiliation].)

On the other hand, other findings indicate that resistance has a direct correlation with *deterring* sexual assault. (QBF, *supra*, at p. 105.) Of the 75 convicted rapists the Queen's Bench Foundation questioned, half believed that their sexual assaults could have been deterred by active victim resistance. (Id., at p. 109.) Brownmiller argues that submissive behavior is *not* necessarily helpful to a rape victim and suggests that strong resistance on the part of women can thwart rape. [Susan Brownmiller, Against Our Will: Men, Women and Rape 357, 360-61 (1975).] She suggests it would be well for women to undergo systematic training in self-defense in order to fight back against their attackers. (Id., at pp. 403-04.) . . .

In sum, it is not altogether clear what the absence of resistance indicates in relation to the issue of consent. Nor is it *necessarily* advisable for one who is assaulted to resist the attack. It is at least arguable that if it fails to deter, resistance may well increase the risk of bodily injury to the victim. This possibility, as well as the evolution in societal expectations as to the level of danger a woman should risk when faced with sexual assault, are reflected in the Legislature's elimination of the resistance requirement. In so amending section 261, subdivision (2), the Legislature has demonstrated its unwillingness to dictate a prescribed response to sexual assault. For the first time, the Legislature has assigned the decision as to whether a sexual assault should be resisted to the realm of personal choice. . . .

By removing resistance as a prerequisite to a rape conviction, the Legislature has brought the law of rape into conformity with other crimes such as robbery, kidnapping and assault, which require force, fear, and nonconsent to convict. In these crimes, the law does not expect falsity from the complainant who alleges their commission and thus demand resistance as a corroboration and predicate to conviction. Nor does the law expect that in defending oneself or one's property from these crimes, a person must risk injury or death by displaying resistance in the face of attack. . . .[20]

For these reasons, the Court of Appeal's reliance upon any absence of resistance by Marsha was improper.

III

. . . Although resistance is no longer the touchstone of the element of force, the reviewing court still looks to the circumstances of the case, including the presence of verbal or nonverbal threats, or the kind of force that might reasonably induce fear in the mind of the victim, to ascertain sufficiency of the evidence of a conviction under section 261, subdivision (2). Additionally, the complainant's conduct must be measured against the degree of force manifested or in light of whether her fears were genuine and reasonably grounded. . . .

Marsha's testimony constitutes substantial evidence of rape by means of force or fear of immediate and unlawful bodily injury under the provisions of section 261, subdivision (2). From the moment she arrived at appellant's house, she communicated to him that she did not want to stay and intended to leave after purchasing marijuana. She initially refused appellant's suggestion that they go inside, but ultimately agreed so that she could obtain the marijuana. Once inside, she repeated her desire to proceed with the drug transaction so she could leave. She rebuffed the first round of appellant's physical advances by pushing him away and telling him to stop. When appellant disregarded this rebuff and continued his advances, Marsha left the room and went to the front gate. At this point, appellant's demeanor changed markedly. He cursed and berated Marsha for leaving, apparently in an effort to intimidate her.

At the front gate, Marsha repeatedly requested that appellant "let me leave," a plea which fell on deaf ears. Significantly, on at least one such occasion, appellant "reared back" — a gesture which made Marsha believe he was going to hit her. Appellant created the impression, even if it were untrue, that the outside gate was locked and that Marsha would not be able to open it. He reinforced this impression by telling her he would *let* her leave after he returned to the room for his shoes.

---

20. The statutory change does not mean that when resistance does exist it is irrelevant to nonconsent. Absence of resistance may also continue to be probative of whether the accused honestly and reasonably believed he was engaging in consensual sex.

Back in the room, appellant shouted at Marsha, cursing the fact she had caused the door to slam. He interrupted his angry, verbal onslaught only to stop all activity and look at Marsha in a "funny" manner. He threatened her by displaying his muscles, grabbing her by the collar, and claiming he could pick her up with one hand and throw her out.

Most importantly, he ominously informed her he could make her do "anything he wanted" and that she was about to see the "bad side" of him. These statements were made in conjunction with his boasting of having had other women perform sex acts upon him and with Marsha's statement to him that she could not fight him. Appellant's response of pressing the door closed when he saw Marsha's movement toward it also suggested coercion. Finally, when Marsha initially refused to remove her clothes, appellant warned her — both physically and verbally — that her refusal "was going to make him angry."

In light of the totality of these circumstances, the jury, having observed the witnesses and their demeanor, could reasonably have concluded that Marsha's fear of physical violence from appellant if she did not submit to sexual intercourse was genuine and reasonable. Under these facts, a reasonable juror could have found that Marsha's subsequent compliance with appellant's urgent insistence on coitus was induced either by force, fear, or both, and, in any case, fell short of a consensual act. . . .

Marsha . . . explained that she pretended to be a willing partner and to invite appellant to her house in an attempt to extricate herself from the situation. She testified that she engaged in sexual intercourse to avoid physical violence. A reasonable juror could have concluded that her subsequent act of exchanging kisses was part of a similar effort to avoid physical violence by simulating reciprocation. Marsha was not required to display either active or passive resistance in order to save her testimony from inherent improbability, or to "develop corroborative evidence." . . .

Under these circumstances, this court holds that the evidence was sufficient to sustain appellant's conviction of rape. . . .

Notes and Questions

1. In light of *Barnes,* what are the act and circumstance elements of rape in California? Have they changed significantly? Consider two possibilities:

(1) The key element has always been sexual intercourse by force, without the woman's consent. The 1982 law merely removed an *evidentiary* requirement — that the woman have manifested resistance as a way of establishing the force and nonconsent.

(2) The 1982 law effected a substantive change in the elements of rape. Resistance was once essentially an element — that is, the defendant had to have used his force to overcome manifest resistance, but that requirement has now been removed.

Note that under either possibility, a jury under the earlier law was not free to convict the defendant of rape unless the judge found sufficient resistance to even give the rape charge to the jury. Now, however, resistance is neither an evidentiary requirement nor an element — it is simply one possible type of evidence that goes to establish nonconsent or, implicitly, force, so that a jury could find these elements beyond a reasonable doubt on the basis of evidence other than resistance.

2. But what other evidence would suffice? What evidence did the court find sufficient here?

3. How does the *Barnes* standard differ from that in *Dorsey*? Would Barnes's conviction have been upheld under *Dorsey*?

4. *The Model Penal Code.* Review the Model Penal Code's substantive provisions on rape:

Section 213.1. Rape and Related Offenses

(1) *Rape.* A male who has sexual intercourse with a female not his wife is guilty of rape if:

(a) he compels her to submit by force or by threat of imminent death, serious bodily injury, extreme pain or kidnapping, to be inflicted on anyone; or

(b) he has substantially impaired her power to appraise or control her conduct by administering or employing without her knowledge drugs, intoxicants or other means for the purpose of preventing resistance; or

(c) the female is unconscious; . . .

Rape is a felony of the second degree unless (i) in the course thereof the actor inflicts serious bodily injury upon anyone, or (ii) the victim was not a voluntary social companion of the actor upon the occasion of the crime and had not previously permitted sexual liberties, in which cases the offense is a felony of the first degree.

(2) *Gross Sexual Imposition.* A male who has sexual intercourse with a female not his wife commits a felony of the third degree if:

(a) he compels her to submit by any threat that would prevent resistance by a woman of ordinary resolution; or

(b) he knows that she suffers from a mental disease or defect which renders her incapable of appraising the nature of her conduct. . . .

Note that the MPC uses the term "by force" but has no term for nonconsent, and distinguishes force from "threat of imminent death, serious bodily injury, extreme pain or kidnapping." How do we then construe "force"?

Note also that the MPC makes it a lower grade of felony to commit "gross sexual imposition" by compelling the woman to submit to intercourse "by any threat that would prevent resistance by a woman of ordinary resolution." Does that mean that "force" under §(1)(a) might mean threat of physical harm to distinguish it from compulsion to submit under §2(a)? Does the MPC make it easier for the jury to compromise in cases like *Barnes* by convicting on a somewhat lesser charge?

A number of components of the MPC rape law quoted above now seem startlingly anachronistic in light of modern rape law reform, and have been left unchanged since the drafting of the MPC almost half a century ago. What explains these anachronisms? Some commentators suggest that progressive motives in an earlier legal and political context had unintended consequences. The MPC drafters feared that excessive punishments in cases not involving strangers or severe bodily harm had two perverse effects. The perception that these penalties were too severe led to underenforcement and false acquitals, but also served to exacerbate the problem of racially motivated prosecutions of black men accused of raping white women. Hence the drafters created a lesser crime for that category, explicitly for sex between "voluntary social companions" and where the complainant had "previously permitted [the defendant] sexual liberties." And it was only after great debate that they reluctantly excluded any explicit reference to nonconsent out of the elements of rape, fearing that the consent issue would end up reinforcing the problem of putting the victim's conduct and psyche on trial instead of the defendant's.[21] But the drafters' failure to address the matter of nonconsent in acquaintance rapes is reflected in their inadvertently telling assertion that rape law must draw "a line between forcible rape on the one hand and reluctant submission on the other."[22] Though these substantive provisions, along with a number of outdated evidentiary rules in the MPC (cf. pp. 961-64 *infra*), no longer reflect the state of American rape law, Professor Deborah Denno argues that because they are still widely cited, they remain important and need to be revised.[23]

5. *The risks of resisting.* The *Barnes* court reviews new research on the common — and advisable — responses of women to sexual attacks. What is the relevance of this research? Does the court want to define rape in such a way as to better protect women from violent retaliation by rapists? Or is the court using this research to clarify when and whether an illegal sexual attack has taken place in the first place? In this light, Professor Michelle Anderson argues for retaining the resistance element:[24]

> Because resistance can deter rape, a passive woman is trading the increased risk of being raped for the decreased risk of sustaining extrinsic injury. That trade only makes sense if the extrinsic injury she might suffer is significantly worse than having been raped. According to the Bureau of Justice Statistics, about 40% of rapes involve extrinsic injury. Only 5% of rapes involve serious, extrinsic injuries, such as broken bones or teeth, loss of consciousness, severe lacerations, or wounds that require hospitalization, however. In 95% of completed rapes, then, the extrinsic injury a woman sustains is not serious and is less severe than the injury of having been raped itself. Therefore, in 95% of rape situations it would be unwise for a woman to trade completion for extrinsic injury reduction because the extrinsic injury she might avoid would be less harmful to her than enduring the rape itself. . . .
>
> Despite the fact that resistance substantially decreases the risk of rape completion and does not increase the risk of serious injury, [t]he mass media's focus on the most violent rapes alters popular perception of the crime. . . . This popular perception has shifted many women's attention when faced with sexual attacks from avoiding rape to avoiding mutilation or death. During rape attempts, most rape avoiders thought about avoiding the rape, whereas most rape victims thought about avoiding death.

Moreover, perhaps the most comprehensive study suggests that victim resistance does not increase physical injury, once one controls for situational danger and offender aggression.[25] Further, some of the statistics purporting to prove increased danger rely disproportionately on stranger rapes — where there are the most convictions and thus more data — and some studies may invert cause and effect — i.e., sometimes women resist more forcefully after they have been injured.[26]

21. Schulhofer, Unwanted Sex, *supra*, at 20-24.

22. Model Penal Code and Commentaries, at 303.

23. Why the Model Penal Code's Sexual Offense Provisions Should Be Pulled and Replaced, 1 Ohio St. J. Crim. L. 207, 208 (2003).

24. Professor Michelle Anderson, Reviving Resistance in Rape Law, 1998 U. Ill. L. Rev. 953.

25. Sarah Ullman & Raymond Knight, a Multivariate Model for Predicting Rape and Physical Injury Outcomes During Sexual Assaults, 59 J. Consulting Clinical Psychol. 724 (1991).

26. Bryden, Redefining Rape, *supra* at 150-53.

6. *Prior violence in sexual relationship.* In State v. Alston, 312 S.E.2d 470 (N.C. 1984), the "prosecuting witness," Cottie Brown, had been involved in a sexual relationship with the defendant for six months. They shared an apartment but often fought, and Brown had often left the apartment to stay with her mother. Brown testified that she often enjoyed sexual relations with Alston but also had sex with him at times solely to accommodate him. He occasionally struck her when she refused to give him money or otherwise follow his wishes. She left him after being struck on May 15 and did not have sex with him again until the alleged rape on June 15. Alston encountered her in public in front of the school she attended and used both verbal and physical force in demanding that she tell him where she was now living. At one point he "threatened to 'fix' her face so that her mother could see he was not playing." Id. at 472. They then walked together in an apparently casual way in front of other people, and she told him the relationship was over. He reasserted his right to have sex with her. They then walked to a friend's house where they had gone on previous occasions to have sex. Brown did not ask any passersby for help; she later testified that she assumed they would not help. When in the friend's house, Alston and the friend left her alone for a short while, but she made no effort to escape. The friend then left. Alston proposed that they have sex. Brown said she did not want to, but Alston then began fondling her. She nevertheless complied when he told her to undress and submit to intercourse. Shortly afterward, Brown made a complaint to the police. Two days later Alston came to her apartment, and a similar encounter occurred, ending in intercourse that Brown said she did not fight off because she found that she enjoyed it.

In reviewing Alston's rape conviction, the court noted that

> consent to intercourse freely given can be withdrawn at any time prior to penetration. If the particular act of intercourse for which the defendant was charged was both by force and against the victim's will, the offense is rape without regard to the victim's consent given to the defendant for prior acts of intercourse. [Id. at 475.]

Nevertheless, the court found that in the context of a "continuing sexual relationship" like this one, "determining the victim's state of mind at the time of the alleged rape is obviously more difficult." It held that the state had to prove that Brown had manifested her lack of consent by unequivocal communication of her withdrawal of earlier consent. The court found that the state did indeed establish such evidence in this case but that it had failed to establish the other element — Alston's use or threat of force. In the court's view, Alston may have used or threatened force early in the encounter at the school, but the state had failed to show that this force "related to his desire to have sexual intercourse on that date and was sufficient to overcome the will of the victim." Id. at 476. Indeed, according to the court, Brown had stated that whatever fear she felt on June 15 was based on an earlier experience with Alston and not on specific threats at that moment.

> Although Brown's general fear of the defendant may have been justified on prior occasions, absent evidence that the defendant used force or threats to overcome the will of the victim *to resist the sexual intercourse alleged to have been rape,* such general fear was not sufficient to show that the defendant used the force required to support a conviction of rape. [Id. at 476 (emphasis in original).]

Did the court here find that Brown had explicitly withdrawn her earlier consent to intercourse? If so, was she not raped? Did the court implicitly hold that Brown had indeed consented on June 15? In the court's view, what role does force play independently of the element of lack of consent? What is the difference between a "general fear" and a "specific fear"?

Could *Alston* be reconsidered as a case about sex in an abusive *relationship?* Should the rule be that in such a relationship sex is presumptively rape? As Professor Michelle Anderson notes,[27] often overlooked in *Alston* is that the court also overturned the kidnapping conviction for lack of evidence that when Alston forced her into the house he then intended to rape, saying that his actions were "entirely consistent with the well established pattern of the couple's sexual relationship. During that relationship she frequently remained passive while the defendant at times engaged in some violence at the time of sexual intercourse." 312 S.E.2d at 448. Professor Anderson argues that the court failed to appreciate that the battering cycle in the relationship made rape a tool of dominance, and wrongly concluded not only that there was earlier consent but that consent carried over to the present encounter.

For a parallel case where the court seems to concede that the defendant did not consent, but where it nevertheless found insufficient evidence of force, see Commonwealth v. Berkowitz, 609 A.2d 1338 (Pa. Super. Ct. 1992), discussed in the section on the mens rea of rape, p. 954, *infra*.

7. *Force and consent.* Are force and nonconsent separate elements? Must the prosecution produce other evidence of nonconsent beyond the fact that defendant used or threatened force? If so, does this amount to a requirement of resistance?

One would think that once the prosecution has met the statutory criterion of proving "force," it has effectively mooted any issue of consent. Consider People v. Jansson, 116 Mich. App. 674, 323 N.W.2d 508 (1982), where the defendant was convicted of "criminal sexual conduct in the third degree," and sentenced to 10 to 15 years in prison. The facts were these:

> Carolyn Lamoreaux, the complainant, testified that on January 7, 1979, she was introduced to the defendant by a mutual friend at a Dunkin' Donuts restaurant. The complainant was asked by the defendant if she was looking for a job and she answered she was. The defendant suggested that she fill out an application that night for a full-time secretarial position at his place of employment. The two left the restaurant and drove to the Stedman Agency. The defendant explained the responsibilities of the job while showing the complainant around the building. The two then entered Frank Stedman's office and the defendant and the complainant sat down. During the ensuing conversation, the defendant told the complainant that he was interested in "someone to fuck." The complainant indicated to the defendant that she would not "do things like that." Defendant walked over and turned off the light. The complainant stood up and was grabbed by the defendant. The defendant pulled the complainant to the floor and removed her clothing. He then removed his own clothing and had sexual intercourse with the complainant.
>
> . . . John Stedman testified that he was at the Stedman Agency office on the night of January 7, 1979. He stated that the defendant told the complainant "show Mr. Stedman what you have to offer." The complainant then lifted up her blouse and exposed her breasts. [Id. at 511.]

---

27. From Chastity Requirement to Sexuality License: Sexual Consent and a New Rape Shield Law, 70 G.W. L. Rev. 51, 123-24. (2002).

On appeal, the defendant did not contest the jury's finding that he had used force but asserted that

> because there was no indication in the record that the complainant advised or communicated to the defendant that she did not wish to engage in sexual intercourse, the defendant did not know that the sexual relations were nonconsensual and, therefore, could not have intended to engage in those relations by force or coercion. Without some manifestation of the complainant's unwillingness to engage in sexual relations, defense counsel argues that defendant could not have known of her nonconsent and, therefore, could not have intended to engage in sexual relations against the complainant's will but may rather have assumed that signs of physical resistance by the complainant were what defense counsel terms "the final token manifestations of modesty."
>
> [The] offense required proof beyond a reasonable doubt that sexual penetration was accomplished by force or coercion. MCL 750.520d(1)(b); MSA 28.788(4)(1)(b). Force or coercion includes, but is not limited to, situations where the actor overcomes the victim through the actual application of physical force or physical violence or where the actor coerces the victim to submit by threatening to use force or violence on the victim and the victim believes that the actor has the present ability to execute these threats. . . .
>
> Although consent therefore precludes conviction of criminal sexual conduct in the third degree by force or coercion, the prosecution is not required to prove nonconsent as an independent element of the offense. If the prosecution offers evidence to establish that an act of sexual penetration was accomplished by force or coercion, that evidence necessarily tends to establish that the act was nonconsensual. . . .
>
> If it is established that the actor *overcame the victim,* it necessarily follows that the victim's participation in the act was nonconsensual. Likewise if the actor *coerces the victim* to submit by threats of present or future harm, it necessarily follows that the victim engaged in the act nonconsensually. In short, to prove force or coercion as those terms are defined in the statute is to establish that the victim did not consent.
>
> Defense counsel however would require that there be proved a specific intent to overcome the will of the victim and, as a necessary precondition, knowledge on the part of the actor that the victim was not engaging in the act consensually. In short, defense counsel would have us require some manifestation of nonconsent by the victim. In our judgment, this is simply a suggestion that we require proof that the victim resisted the actor or at least expressed an intent to resist. The express language of the statute precludes any such requirement. [Id. at 513 (emphasis in original).]

Nevertheless, as Professor LaFave points out, many states continue, explicitly or implicitly, to treat "force" or "forcible compulsion," on the one hand, and "nonconsent" on the other hand, as cumulative, not alternative requirements,[28] so that even in cases where the prosecution has established force or forcible compulsion, "consent" remains an affirmative defense. See State v. Jacques, 536 A.2d 535, 537 (R.I. 18-988) (rejecting state's argument that statute cannot logically require force in addition to nonconsensual intercourse). By what reading of the terms "force" and "consent" could they coexist in one sexual encounter? Does the cumulative reading of these terms just indicate that the statutory terms "force" or "forcible compulsion" must require proof of extra-violent force? Does it import a resistance requirement as a way of establishing nonconsent, even in

28. See Wayne R. LaFave, Handbook of Criminal Law 857-58 (4th ed. 2003).

states that would seem to have eliminated an independent requirement of resistance, like California?

E.   NONCONSENT

Some jurisdictions go still a step further, eliminating force as well as resistance as independent requirements and focusing on the fact of nonconsent as the crucial element of the crime. Consider how the next case takes that step.

STATE v. SMITH

Supreme Court of Connecticut

210 Conn. 132, 554 A.2d 713 (1989)

SHEA, J. After a jury trial the defendant was convicted of sexual assault in the first degree in violation of General Statutes §53a-70. . . .

. . . Upon the evidence presented the jury could reasonably have found the following facts. On March 18, 1987, the victim, T, a twenty-six-year-old woman, and her girlfriend, A, a visitor from Idaho, went to a bar in West Haven. T was introduced by a friend to the defendant, who bought her a drink. The defendant invited her and A, together with a male acquaintance A had met at the bar, to dinner at a restaurant across the street. After dinner, the defendant having paid for T's share, the four left the restaurant. The defendant proposed that they all go to his apartment in West Haven. Because A's acquaintance had a motorcycle, the defendant gave them directions to the apartment so that they could ride there, while he and T walked. After a twenty minute walk, the defendant and T arrived at the apartment at about 10 P.M. A and her acquaintance were not there and never arrived at the apartment. When T and the defendant had entered the apartment they sat on the couch in the living room to watch television. After a while the defendant put his arm around T and told her he wanted a kiss. She gave him a kiss. She testified that, "He wouldn't back off. He wouldn't let go of me. So I said, look, I am not kidding. I really don't want to do anything. I don't know you and whatnot." The defendant still held on to T. She testified that he was "still right in my face wanting to kiss me. You know, saying so, saying that you don't think I paid for dinner for nothing, do you."

T testified that she was scared: "At first I didn't know what to do. I did spit in his face and he didn't even take it seriously. Then I tried kicking him off, which was to no avail. He was way too big for me." T described the defendant as "at least six foot two" and "at least two hundred pounds." She testified: "He told me he could make it hard on me or I could make it easy on myself, which I finally decided was probably my best bet." T understood that the defendant was determined to "have sex" with her and that either he would hurt her or she "was going to go along with it." At the point where T ceased resistance, she was "down on the couch" and the defendant was "on top of" her. T testified that she had informed the defendant that she had to pick up her daughter, had insulted him, and had told him that he was "a big man to have to force a woman." She testified, however, that after she decided to "give in," she tried to convince the defendant that she was not going to fight and "was going to go along with him and enjoy it."

The defendant removed T's clothing as she remained on the couch and led her into the bedroom. When she declined his request for oral sex, he did not insist upon it, but proceeded to engage in vaginal intercourse with her. After completion of the act, the defendant said that he knew the victim felt that she had been raped, but that she could not prove it and had really enjoyed herself. After they both had dressed, the defendant requested T's telephone number, but she gave him a number she concocted as a pretense. He also offered her some sherbet, which she accepted and ate while she waited for a cab that the defendant had called. T, however, placed her pink cigarette lighter underneath the couch, so that she would be able to prove she had been in the apartment. When the cab arrived, she left the apartment. She told the cab driver to take her to the police station because she had been raped. At the station she gave her account of the event to the police. The defendant was arrested. The police found T's lighter under the couch in his living room, where T had informed them it was located. . . .

[The court first rejected the defendant's argument that the Connecticut statute contains a mens rea component or a reasonable mistake-of-fact defense.]

Our first degree sexual assault statute, §53a-70, applies to a person who "compels another person to engage in sexual intercourse by the use of force . . . or by the threat of use of force which . . . reasonably causes such person to fear physical injury. . . ." Although the consent of the complainant is not expressly made a defense to such a crime, it is abundantly clear that the draftsmen of our penal code endorsed the principle that "non-commercial sexual activity in private, whether heterosexual or homosexual, between consenting, competent adults . . . is no business of the criminal law." Commission to Revise the Criminal Statutes, Penal Code Comments, (1969) p. 38. A finding that a complainant had consented would implicitly negate a claim that the actor had compelled the complainant by force or threat to engage in sexual intercourse. Consent is not made an affirmative defense under our sex offense statutes, so, as in the case of the defense of alibi, the burden is upon the state to prove lack of consent beyond a reasonable doubt whenever the issue is raised.

. . . While the word "consent" is commonly regarded as referring to the state of mind of the complainant in a sexual assault case, it cannot be viewed as a wholly subjective concept. Although the actual state of mind of the actor in a criminal case may in many instances be the issue upon which culpability depends, a defendant is not chargeable with knowledge of the internal workings of the minds of others except to the extent that he should reasonably have gained such knowledge from his observations of their conduct. The law of contract has come to recognize that a true "meeting of the minds" is no longer essential to the formation of a contract and that rights and obligations may arise from acts of the parties, usually their words, upon which a reasonable person would rely. E. Farnsworth, Contracts §3.6. Similarly, whether a complainant has consented to intercourse depends upon her manifestations of such consent as reasonably construed. If the conduct of the complainant under all the circumstances should reasonably be viewed as indicating consent to the act of intercourse, a defendant should not be found guilty because of some undisclosed mental reservation on the part of the complainant. Reasonable conduct ought not to be deemed criminal.

It is likely that juries in considering the defense of consent in sexual assault cases, though visualizing the issue in terms of actual consent by the complainant, have reached their verdicts on the basis of inferences that a reasonable person would draw from the conduct of the complainant and the defendant under the surrounding circumstances. It is doubtful that jurors would ever convict a defendant who had in their view acted in reasonable reliance upon words or conduct of the complainant indicating consent, even though there had been some concealed reluctance on her part. If a defendant were concerned about such a possibility, however, he would be entitled, once the issue is raised, to request a jury instruction that the state must prove beyond a reasonable doubt that the conduct of the complainant would not have justified a reasonable belief that she had consented.

Thus we adhere to the view expressed in our earlier decisions that no specific intent, but only a general intent to perform the physical acts constituting the crime, is necessary for the crime of first degree sexual assault. We reject the position of the British courts, as well as that adopted in Alaska, that the state must prove either an actual awareness on the part of the defendant that the complainant had not consented or a reckless disregard of her nonconsenting status. We agree, however, with the California courts that a defendant is entitled to a jury instruction that a defendant may not be convicted of this crime if the words or conduct of the complainant under all the circumstances would justify a reasonable belief that she had consented. We arrive at that result, however, not on the basis of our penal code provision relating to a mistake of fact, §53a-6(a), which is applicable only to specific intent crimes, but on the ground that whether a complainant should be found to have consented depends upon how her behavior would have been viewed by a reasonable person under the surrounding circumstances.

. . . Since we have rejected the subjective standard for determining the issue of consent, however, the question for us is whether the evidence is sufficient to prove that a reasonable person would not have believed that T's conduct under all the circumstances indicated her consent.

From our review of the evidence detailed previously, it is clear that the jury could properly have found beyond a reasonable doubt that T's words and actions could not reasonably be viewed to indicate her consent to intercourse with the defendant. According to her uncontradicted testimony, she expressly declined his advances, explaining that she did not know him and wanted to pick up her child. She spat in his face and "tried kicking him off." She "gave in" only after the defendant declared that "he could make it hard" for her if she continued to resist. This statement she could reasonably have regarded as a threat of physical injury. General Statutes §53a-70. Only by entertaining the fantasy that "no" meant "yes," and that a display of distaste meant affection, could the defendant have believed that T's behavior toward him indicated consent. Such a distorted view of her conduct would not have been reasonable. The evidence was more than sufficient to support the verdict.

Notes and Questions

1. How sound is the court's reasoning that nonconsent is the key requirement of the sexual assault statute?

2. How does *Smith* differ from *Barnes*? Would Smith have been convicted under the *Barnes* standard? How about under the *Dorsey* standard?

3. *Mens rea.* The court purports to reject any emphasis on the defendant's mens rea, and to focus instead on the fact of nonconsent. Yet it acknowledges that the defendant cannot be expected to know of the complainant's "undisclosed mental reservation" and suggests that "act" element of nonconsent might have to be inferred by the overt "manifestations" of the complainant's conduct, as they would appear to a reasonable observer. Does the court end up effectively making the question one of the defendant's mental state? If so, what mental state does it require? Does this case confirm the conceptual difficulty of distinguishing act and mental state questions in rape law? We will revisit this question below in examining decisions and commentary explicitly insisting on reference to the defendant's culpable mental state.

4. *Verbal resistance.* Does "no" always in fact mean "no"? A study of Texas undergraduates found that 39.3 percent, including most of those with sexual experience, had sometimes pretended that they did not want sex when in fact they wanted it. On the other hand, most women in the Texas study (60.7 percent) reported that they had never engaged in token resistance and over three-fourths of the women who had engaged in token resistance reported doing so five or fewer times.[29]

Professor Susan Estrich writes:[30]

Many feminists would argue that so long as women are powerless relative to men, viewing a "yes" as a sign of true consent is misguided. For myself, I am quite certain that many women who say yes to men they know, whether on dates or on the job, would say no if they could. I have no doubt that women's silence sometimes is the product not of passion and desire but of pressure and fear. Yet if yes may often mean no, at least from a woman's perspective, it does not seem so much to ask men, and the law, to respect the courage of the woman who does say no and to take her at her word.

But what if the woman says "no" and then later exhibits willingness to have sex? Should there be a per se rule that after an explicit "no" sex is a crime? For an argument to that effect, see Lynne Henderson, Getting to Know: Honoring Women in Law and in Fact, 2 Tex. J. Women & Law 41, 68 (1993) (arguing that any explicit "no" creates a presumption of recklessness). What are the consequences of Professor Henderson's position? Would its premise change as more time passes since the expression of "no"? Does it depend on whether an alleged change of mind comes from verbal persuasion or instead persistence in attempting intercourse?

5. Recall the "earnest resistance requirement" in People v. Dorsey, *supra,* p. 906. New York State ultimately changed its law to include the following language in New York Pen. L. §130.05 (McKinney 1998):

[I]t is an element of every offense defined in [the sections on rape and sexual assault] that the sexual act was committed without the consent of the victim.
   . . . Lack of consent results from
   (a) Forcible compulsion
   (b) Incapacity to consent. . . .

29. Charlene L. Muehlenhard & Lisa C. Hollabagh, Do Women Sometimes Say No When They Mean Yes? The Prevalence and Correlates of Women's Token Resistance to Sex, 54 J. Personality & Soc. Psychology 872 (1988).
   30. Estrich, Real Rape 102 (1987).

Finally, in 2001, the legislature added the offense of rape in the third degree, for which it defined lack of consent as "circumstances under which . . . the victim clearly expressed that he or she did not consent to engage in such act, and a reasonable person in the actor's situation would have understood such person's words and acts as an expression of lack of consent." N.Y. Pen.L. §130.05(d).

6. *The "consent defense."* Courts and commentators may occasionally refer to consent as "a defense" to a rape charge, but such a statement is usually misleading. That is, where the relevant statute clearly makes nonconsent an *element of the crime* of rape, the prosecution would bear the burden of proof beyond a reasonable doubt that sex occurred without the victim's consent.

7. *"Sexual expropriation" as an alternative crime.* Professor Donald Dripps has proposed replacing the independent crime of rape "with a variety of new statutory offenses that would . . . more justly define criminal liability for culpable conduct aimed at causing other individuals to engage in sexual acts."[31] His premise is that "consent" is so amorphous a concept that nonconsent should no longer be an element of rape. Instead, the focus of the criminal law should be the behavior of the defendant in committing a "theft" of the victim's "property" right in sex and bodily integrity. Dripps assumes that there is a greater social interest in freedom from violence than there is in protecting sexual autonomy, and therefore a nonviolent violation of a person's sexual autonomy should not be punished as severely as a physical assault. At the same time, he believes that focusing on the action of the defendant properly respects the complainant's "property" right in bodily integrity. Professor Dripps would create two new statutes to replace rape laws: "Sexually Motivated Assault," a felony, and "Sexual Expropriation," a serious misdemeanor or minor felony.[32]

First, sexually motivated assault would apply in cases in which the accused purposely or knowingly puts the victim in fear of violence for the purpose of causing sexual submission. Second, sexual expropriation would apply when the defendant completes a sexual act over the verbal protests of the victim without purposely or knowingly putting her in fear of physical injury.

Professor Dripps then asserts that the criminal law should ignore other admittedly questionable sexual "transactions," as where, because of a "complex relationship," a woman offers sex not for her own pleasure, but rather for such consideration as fidelity, economic security, or friendship. He concedes that these "transactions" may be nonmutual and unpleasurable, but he treats the means of procuring sex in them as "legitimate." Though these latter transactions may reflect the maldistribution of bargaining power between men and women, he points out that neither the criminal law nor even the civil law of contracts attempts to cure all the maldistribution that somehow arises in our society.[33]

In a reply to Professor Dripps, Professor Robin West argues that Professor Dripps's division of the offense of rape into violent and nonviolent parts wrongly assumes that rape is only violent in the first case, where some collateral threat of violence is the means of procuring intercourse. Rather, she argues, in any case of illegitimately procured sex the act of intercourse itself is necessarily a violent

31. Donald A. Dripps, Beyond Rape: An Essay on the Difference Between the Presence of Force and the Absence of Consent, 92 Colum. L. Rev. 1780 (1992).

32. Id. at 1799-81.

33. Id. at 1789-92, 1801-03. Professor Dripps explains in a follow-up piece that by "legitimate" he meant only that these transactions are lawful, not that they are morally admirable. Donald Dripps, More on Distinguishing Sex, Sexual Expropriation, and Sexual Assault: A Reply to Professor West, 93 Colum. L. Rev. 1460, 1464-65 (1993).

physical act and the notion of a "larcenous taking" of sex becomes an inapt analogy. Professor West challenges Professor Dripps's notion that the "legitimate" transactions in sex that he concedes are not mutually pleasurable fit his image of unhappy but fair exchange. In many of these relationships, Professor West insists, beneath the appearance of fair exchange is the woman's deep fear that an ominous threat of violence or harsh economic deprivation — or even loss of protection from other men's violence — always remains to coerce the woman's apparently voluntary offer of sex.[34]

F. LACK OF AFFIRMATIVE EXPRESSION OF CONSENT

The last step on this continuum is a definition of the actus reus of rape as sexual penetration absent some kind of affirmative expression of consent. Consider this case:

IN THE INTEREST OF M.T.S.
New Jersey Supreme Court
129 N.J. 422, 609 A.2d 1266 (1992)

HANDLER, J. Under New Jersey law a person who commits an act of sexual penetration using physical force or coercion is guilty of second-degree sexual assault. The sexual assault statute does not define the words "physical force." The question posed by this appeal is whether the element of "physical force" is met simply by an act of non-consensual penetration involving no more force than necessary to accomplish that result.

That issue is presented in the context of what is often referred to as "acquaintance rape." The record in the case discloses that the juvenile, a seventeen-year-old boy, engaged in consensual kissing and heavy petting with a fifteen-year-old girl and thereafter engaged in actual sexual penetration of the girl to which she had not consented. There was no evidence or suggestion that the juvenile used any unusual or extra force or threats to accomplish the act of penetration. The trial court determined that the juvenile was delinquent for committing a sexual assault. The Appellate Division reversed the disposition of delinquency, concluding that non-consensual penetration does not constitute sexual assault unless it is accompanied by some level of force more than that necessary to accomplish the penetration.

I

. . . On Monday, May 21, 1990, fifteen-year-old C.G. was living with her mother, her three siblings, and several other people, including M.T.S. and his girlfriend. A total of ten people resided in the three-bedroom town home at the time of the incident. M.T.S., then age seventeen, was temporarily residing at the

34. Robin West, Legitimating the Illegitimate: A Comment on *Beyond Rape*, 93 Colum. L. Rev. 1442, 1448 (1993).

home with the permission of the C.G.'s mother; he slept downstairs on a couch. C.G. had her own room on the second floor. At approximately 11:30 P.M. on May 21, C.G. went upstairs to sleep after having watched television with her mother, M.T.S., and his girlfriend. When C.G. went to bed, she was wearing underpants, a bra, shorts, and a shirt.

At trial, C.G. and M.T.S. offered very different accounts concerning the nature of their relationship and the events that occurred after C.G. had gone upstairs. The trial court did not credit fully either teenager's testimony.

C.G. stated that earlier in the day, M.T.S. had told her three or four times that he "was going to make a surprise visit up in [her] bedroom." She said that she had not taken M.T.S. seriously and considered his comments a joke because he frequently teased her. She testified that M.T.S. had attempted to kiss her on numerous other occasions and at least once had attempted to put his hands inside of her pants, but that she had rejected all of his previous advances. C.G. testified that on May 22, at approximately 1:30 A.M., she awoke to use the bathroom. As she was getting out of bed, she said, she saw M.T.S., fully clothed, standing in her doorway. According to C.G., M.T.S. then said that "he was going to tease [her] a little bit." C.G. testified that she "didn't think anything of it"; she walked past him, used the bathroom, and then returned to bed, falling into a "heavy" sleep within fifteen minutes.

The next event C.G. claimed to recall of that morning was waking up with M.T.S. on top of her, her underpants and shorts removed. She said "his penis was into [her] vagina." As soon as C.G. realized what had happened, she said, she immediately slapped M.T.S. once in the face, then "told him to get off [her], and get out." She did not scream or cry out. She testified that M.T.S. complied in less than one minute after being struck; according to C.G., "he jumped right off of [her]." She said she did not know how long M.T.S. had been inside of her before she awoke. C.G. said that after M.T.S. left the room, she "fell asleep crying" because "[she] couldn't believe that he did what he did to [her]." She explained that she did not immediately tell her mother or anyone else in the house of the events of that morning because she was "scared and in shock." According to C.G., M.T.S. engaged in intercourse with her "without [her] wanting it or telling him to come up [to her bedroom]." By her own account, C.G. was not otherwise harmed by M.T.S. At about 7:00 A.M., C.G. went downstairs and told her mother about her encounter with M.T.S. earlier in the morning and said that they would have to "get [him] out of the house." While M.T.S. was out on an errand, C.G.'s mother gathered his clothes and put them outside in his car; when he returned, he was told that "[he] better not even get near the house." C.G. and her mother then filed a complaint with the police.

According to M.T.S., he and C.G. had been good friends for a long time, and their relationship "kept leading on to more and more." He had been living at C.G.'s home for about five days before the incident occurred; he testified that during the three days preceding the incident they had been "kissing and necking" and had discussed having sexual intercourse. The first time M.T.S. kissed C.G., he said, she "didn't want him to, but she did after that." He said C.G. repeatedly had encouraged him to "make a surprise visit up in her room." M.T.S. testified that at exactly 1:15 A.M. on May 22, he entered C.G.'s bedroom as she was walking to the bathroom. He said C.G. soon returned from the bathroom, and the two began "kissing and all," eventually moving to the bed. Once they were in bed, he said, they undressed each other and continued to kiss and touch for about five minutes. M.T.S. and C.G. proceeded to engage in sexual intercourse. According to M.T.S., who was on top of C.G., he "stuck it in" and "did it [thrust] three times, and then the fourth time [he] stuck it in, that's when [she] pulled [him] off of her." M.T.S. said that as C.G. pushed him off, she said "stop, get off," and he "hopped off right away."

According to M.T.S., after about one minute, he asked C.G. what was wrong; she replied with a back-hand to his face. He recalled asking C.G. what was wrong a second time, and her replying, "how can you take advantage of me or something like that." M.T.S. said that he proceeded to get dressed and told C.G. to calm down, but that she then told him to get away from her and began to cry. Before leaving the room, he told C.G., "I'm leaving. . . . I'm going with my real girlfriend, don't talk to me. . . . I don't want nothing to do with you or anything, stay out of my life . . . don't tell anybody about this . . . it would just screw everything up." He then walked downstairs and went to sleep.

On May 23, 1990, M.T.S. was charged with conduct that if engaged in by an adult would constitute second-degree sexual assault of the victim, contrary to N.J.S.A. 2C:14-2c(1). . . . After reviewing the testimony, the court concluded that the victim had consented to a session of kissing and heavy petting with M.T.S. The trial court did not find that C.G. had been sleeping at the time of penetration, but nevertheless found that she had not consented to the actual sexual act. Accordingly, the court concluded that the State had proven second-degree sexual assault beyond a reasonable doubt. On appeal, following the imposition of suspended sentences on the sexual assault and the other remaining charges, the Appellate Division determined that the absence of force beyond that involved in the act of sexual penetration precluded a finding of second-degree sexual assault. It therefore reversed the juvenile's adjudication of delinquency for that offense.

II

The New Jersey Code of Criminal Justice, N.J.S.A. 2C:14-2c(1), defines "sexual assault" as the commission "of sexual penetration" "with another person" with the use of "physical force or coercion."[35] An unconstrained reading of the statutory language indicates that both the act of "sexual penetration" and the use of "physical force or coercion" are separate and distinct elements of the offense. . . . The trial court held that "physical force" had been established by the sexual penetration of the victim without her consent. The Appellate Division believed that the statute requires some amount of force more than that necessary to accomplish penetration.

The parties offer two alternative understandings of the concept of "physical force" as it is used in the statute. The State would read "physical force" to entail any amount of sexual touching brought about involuntarily. A showing of sexual penetration coupled with a lack of consent would satisfy the elements of the statute. The Public Defender urges an interpretation of "physical force" to mean force "used to overcome lack of consent." That definition equates force

---

35. The sexual assault statute, N.J.S.A.: 2C:14-2c(1), reads as follows:

c. An actor is guilty of sexual assault if he commits an act of sexual penetration with another person under any one of the following circumstances:

(1) The actor uses physical force or coercion, but the victim does not sustain severe personal injury; . . .

Sexual assault is a crime of the second degree.

with violence and leads to the conclusion that sexual assault requires the application of some amount of force in addition to the act of penetration. Current judicial practice suggests an understanding of "physical force" to mean "any degree of physical power or strength used against the victim, even though it entails no injury and leaves no mark." Model Jury Charges, Criminal 3 (revised Mar. 27, 1989). Resort to common experience or understanding does not yield a conclusive meaning. The dictionary provides several definitions of "force," among which are the following: (1) "power, violence, compulsion, or constraint exerted upon or against a person or thing," (2) "a general term for exercise of strength or power, esp. physical, to overcome resistance," or (3) "strength or power of any degree that is exercised without justification or contrary to law upon a person or thing." Webster's Third New International Dictionary 887 (1961). Thus, as evidenced by the disagreements among the lower courts and the parties, and the variety of possible usages, the statutory words "physical force" do not evoke a single meaning that is obvious and plain. . . . Under traditional rape law, in order to prove that a rape had occurred, the state had to show both that force had been used and that the penetration had been against the woman's will. Force was identified and determined not as an independent factor but in relation to the response of the victim, which in turn implicated the victim's own state of mind. "Thus, the perpetrator's use of force became criminal only if the victim's state of mind met the statutory requirement. The perpetrator could use all the force imaginable and no crime would be committed if the state could not prove additionally that the victim did not consent." National Institute of Law Enforcement and Criminal Justice, Forcible Rape — An Analysis of Legal Issues 5 (March 1978) (Forcible Rape). Although the terms "non-consent" and "against her will" were often treated as equivalent, under the traditional definition of rape, both formulations squarely placed on the victim the burden of proof and of action. Effectively, a woman who was above the age of consent had actively and affirmatively to withdraw that consent for the intercourse to be against her will. . . . The presence or absence of consent often turned on credibility. To demonstrate that the victim had not consented to the intercourse, and also that sufficient force had been used to accomplish the rape, the state had to prove that the victim had resisted. According to the oft-quoted Lord Hale, to be deemed a credible witness, a woman had to be of good fame, disclose the injury immediately, suffer signs of injury, and cry out for help. 1 Matthew Hale, History of the Pleas of the Crown 633 (1st ed. 1847). . . . Evidence of resistance was viewed as a solution to the credibility problem; it was the "outward manifestation of nonconsent, [a] device for determining whether a woman actually gave consent." Note, The Resistance Standard in Rape Legislation, 18 Stan. L. Rev. 680, 689 (1966). . . .

At least by the 1960s courts in New Jersey followed a standard for establishing resistance that was somewhat less drastic than the traditional rule. Thus, in 1965 the Appellate Division stated: "[W]e have rejected the former test that a woman must resist 'to the uttermost.' We only require that she resist as much as she possibly can under the circumstances." State v. Terry, 89 N.J. Super. 445, 449, 215 A.2d 374. . . .

Resistance was necessary not only to prove non-consent but also to demonstrate that the force used by the defendant had been sufficient to overcome the victim's will. The amount of force used by the defendant was assessed in relation to the resistance of the victim. In New Jersey the amount of force necessary to establish rape was characterized as "the degree of force sufficient to overcome any resistance that had been put up by the female." State v. Terry, *supra,* 89 N.J. Super., at 451, 215 A.2d 374 (quoting jury charge by trial court). Resistance, often demonstrated by torn clothing and blood, was a sign that the defendant had used significant force to accomplish the sexual intercourse. Thus, if the defendant forced himself on a woman, it was her responsibility to fight back, because force was measured in relation to the resistance she put forward. Only if she resisted, causing him to use more force than was necessary to achieve penetration, would his conduct be criminalized. . . .

Critics of rape law agreed that the focus of the crime should be shifted from the victim's behavior to the defendant's conduct, and particularly to its forceful and assaultive, rather than sexual, character. Reformers also shared the goals of facilitating rape prosecutions and of sparing victims much of the degradation involved in bringing and trying a charge of rape. There were, however, differences over the best way to redefine the crime. Some reformers advocated a standard that defined rape as unconsented-to sexual intercourse; others urged the elimination of any reference to consent from the definition of rape. Nonetheless, all proponents of reform shared a central premise: that the burden of showing non-consent should not fall on the victim of the crime. In dealing with the problem of consent the reform goal was not so much to purge the entire concept of consent from the law as to eliminate the burden that had been placed on victims to prove they had not consented.

Similarly, with regard to force, rape law reform sought to give independent significance to the forceful or assaultive conduct of the defendant and to avoid a definition of force that depended on the reaction of the victim. Traditional interpretations of force were strongly criticized for failing to acknowledge that force may be understood simply as the invasion of "bodily integrity." Susan Estrich, Rape, 95 Yale L.J. 1087, 1105 (1986). In urging that the "resistance" requirement be abandoned, reformers sought to break the connection between force and resistance.

III

. . . [T]he New Jersey Code of Criminal Justice does not refer to force in relation to "overcoming the will" of the victim, or to the "physical overpowering" of the victim, or the "submission" of the victim. It does not require the demonstrated non-consent of the victim. As we have noted, in reforming the rape laws, the Legislature placed primary emphasis on the assaultive nature of the crime, altering its constituent elements so that they focus exclusively on the forceful or assaultive conduct of the defendant. The Legislature's concept of sexual assault and the role of force was significantly colored by its understanding of the law of assault and battery. As a general matter, criminal battery is defined as "the unlawful application of force to the person of another." 2 Wayne LaFave & Austin Scott, Criminal Law, §7.15 at 301 (1986). The application of force is criminal when it results in either (a) a physical injury or (b) an offensive touching. Id. at 301-02. Any "unauthorized touching of another [is] a battery." Perna v. Pirozzi, 92 N.J. 446, 462, 457 A.2d 431 (1983).

Thus, by eliminating all references to the victim's state of mind and conduct, and by broadening the definition of penetration to cover not only sexual intercourse between a man and a woman but a range of acts that invade another's body or compel intimate contact, the Legislature emphasized the affinity between sexual assault and other forms of assault and battery. . . .

The understanding of sexual assault as a criminal battery, albeit one with especially serious consequences, follows necessarily from the Legislature's decision to eliminate nonconsent and resistance from the substantive definition of the offense. Under the new law, the victim no longer is required to resist and therefore need not have said or done anything in order for the sexual penetration to be unlawful. The alleged victim is not put on trial, and his or her responsive or defensive behavior is rendered immaterial. We are thus satisfied that an interpretation of the statutory crime of sexual assault to require physical force in addition to that entailed in an act of involuntary or unwanted sexual penetration would be fundamentally inconsistent with the legislative purpose to eliminate any consideration of whether the victim resisted or expressed non-consent. . . .

Because the statute eschews any reference to the victim's will or resistance, the standard defining the role of force in sexual penetration must prevent the possibility that the establishment of the crime will turn on the alleged victim's state of mind or responsive behavior. We conclude, therefore, that any act of sexual penetration engaged in by the defendant without the affirmative and freely-given permission of the victim to the specific act of penetration constitutes the offense of sexual assault. Therefore, physical force in excess of that inherent in the act of sexual penetration is not required for such penetration to be unlawful. The definition of "physical force" is satisfied under N.J.S.A. 2C:14-2c(1) if the defendant applies any amount of force against another person in the absence of what a reasonable person would believe to be affirmative and freely-given permission to the act of sexual penetration. Under the reformed statute, permission to engage in sexual penetration must be affirmative and it must be given freely, but that permission may be inferred either from acts or statements reasonably viewed in light of the surrounding circumstances. Persons need not, of course, expressly announce their consent to engage in intercourse for there to be affirmative permission. Permission to engage in an act of sexual penetration can be and indeed often is indicated through physical actions rather than words. Permission is demonstrated when the evidence, in whatever form, is sufficient to demonstrate that a reasonable person would have believed that the alleged victim had affirmatively and freely given authorization to the act.

. . . Although it is possible to imagine a set of rules in which persons must demonstrate affirmatively that sexual contact is unwanted or not permitted, such a regime would be inconsistent with modern principles of personal autonomy. . . .

Today the law of sexual assault is indispensable to the system of legal rules that assures each of us the right to decide who may touch our bodies, when, and under what circumstances. The decision to engage in sexual relations with another person is one of the most private and intimate decisions a person can make. Each person has the right not only to decide whether to engage in sexual contact with another, but also to control the circumstances and character of that contact. No one, neither a spouse, nor a friend, nor an acquaintance, nor a stranger, has the right or the privilege to force sexual contact. . . . The insight into rape as an assaultive crime is consistent with our evolving understanding of the wrong inherent in forced sexual intimacy.

IV

In a case such as this one, in which the State does not allege violence or force extrinsic to the act of penetration, the factfinder must decide whether the defendant's act of penetration was undertaken in circumstances that led the defendant reasonably to believe that the alleged victim had freely given affirmative permission to the specific act of sexual penetration. Such permission can be indicated either through words or through actions that, when viewed in the light of all the surrounding circumstances, would demonstrate to a reasonable person affirmative and freely-given authorization for the specific act of sexual penetration. . . .

. . . In this case, . . . [t]he trial court concluded that the victim had not expressed consent to the act of intercourse, either through her words or actions. We conclude that the record provides reasonable support for the trial court's disposition.

Accordingly, we reverse the judgment of the Appellate Division and reinstate the disposition of juvenile delinquency for the commission of second-degree sexual assault.

Notes and Questions

1. *M.T.S.* seems to hold that the state must prove only the minimal physical effort necessary to engage in intercourse and the absence of an affirmative expression of consent. What does it mean for the woman to affirmatively give permission? Does it mean that the criminal law requires a *Miranda*-type procedure for all sexual relations?[36] If it means nothing so explicit, what guidelines does it offer for determining implicit or tacit affirmative expressions of consent? Would those guidelines end up differing from the criteria in *Smith*? In *Barnes*? How would the rule in *M.T.S.* have affected the decision in State v. Alston, *supra*, pp. 921-22? Would it have better addressed the special context of an abusive relationship? Did it overreach in applying the New Jersey statute by simply eliminating the requirement of force? Moreover, what protection does this ruling offer a woman who appears to acquiesce because she is subject to some other psychological force of which the man is aware and over which he has some control — as by threatening to cut off his relationship with her for another? Would this meet the court's test of permission to have sex "freely given"?[37]

2. Does the holding in *M.T.S.* end up moving the focus of rape law back to the conduct of the victim, not that of the defendant — contrary to the aspiration of most recent rape law reform — indeed contrary to statements made in the *M.T.S.* decision itself? Or does it avoid this problem because the focus is on the objective conduct of the victim, not on her thoughts?

3. Consider the following statutory definition of "consent" from Wisconsin: "words or overt actions by a person who is competent to give informed consent indicating a freely given agreement to have sexual intercourse or sexual contact." Wis. Stat. Ann. §940.225(4) (Supp. 1999). Is this consistent with *M.T.S.*? Is it sufficient guidance for courts?

---

36. It would be tempting but misleading to link *M.T.S.* to the controversial code of sexual conduct adopted by Antioch College in 1993, which applied to even minimal physical contact and which required that permission be verbally explicit, not just "affirmative."

37. See Schulhofer, Unwanted Sex, *supra*, at 96.

4. The *M.T.S.* court, like the *Smith* court, tries to focus on the defendant's actus reus, not on his culpable mental state or the victim's state of mind. Does it succeed?

5. Professor Schulhofer has proposed a rule similar to the holding in *M.T.S.*

> An actor is guilty of sexual abuse, a felony of the third degree, if he commits an act of sexual penetration with another person, when he knows that he does not have the consent of the other person.
> Consent, for purposes of this section, means that at the time of sexual penetration there are actual words or conduct indicating affirmative, freely given permission to the act of sexual penetration.[38]

Does this statute define affirmative consent with sufficient precision? Absent a more precise definition, may jurors rely on social mores about how consent is manifested? Are those mores clear and uncontroversial? On the other hand, could a definition of affirmative consent be made more precise without imposing a restrictive legalistic regime on intimate relationships?

G.   INCAPACITY TO CONSENT

Even in jurisdictions that retain requirements of force and resistance as independent requirements or as necessary indicia of nonconsent, a defendant will be guilty of some form of rape or sexual assault where he has sex with a victim who is categorically incapable of offering resistance or of expressing consent, because of a disability, because she is unconscious at the time of the act, or because of youth.

STATE v. MOORMAN
Supreme Court of North Carolina
358 N.E.2d 502 (1987)

Exum, Chief Justice.

. . . Defendant was convicted of second-degree rape and sentenced to 12 years in prison. The intermediate court of appeals reversed, and the state appealed.

On the evening of 31 August 1984 the victim was out with friends. She returned to her dorm room at approximately 1:00 A.M. She entered the room, closed the door, turned on the radio and fell asleep fully clothed. The victim dreamed she was engaging in sexual intercourse. She awoke to find defendant on top of her having vaginal intercourse with her. She tried to sit up, but defendant pushed her back down. Afraid her attacker might injure her, the victim offered no further resistance. Thereafter defendant engaged in anal intercourse with the victim.

---

38. Model Criminal Statute for Sexual Offenses, 202, in id. at 283.

The victim went to the door and turned on the light. Defendant told her not to call the police. He said, "I'm Lynn's (the victim's roommate) friend, I thought you were Lynn and I wouldn't have done this if I had known it was you." The victim told several friends about the incident, but did not report the incident to the North Carolina State Public Safety Department or make a statement until two days later.

Defendant testified in his own behalf as follows:

He knocked on the victim's door. Hearing music, he believed his friend, Lynn, to be present and entered the room. Defendant observed a girl lying on the bed with her back facing him. Defendant called out the name Lynn but received no response. He then kissed the girl on the neck. The girl turned over and invited him to engage in oral sex. Defendant assisted the girl in removing her underpants. They engaged in oral sex, anal and vaginal intercourse. Following a brief rest, they engaged in sexual intercourse again. The girl then ran to the bathroom. When she returned, defendant noticed for the first time that his sexual partner was not Lynn. The victim told the defendant not to worry because it could have happened to anybody. Defendant then left.

The Court of Appeals arrested judgment as to the charge of second-degree rape. It first noted that N.C.G.S. sec. 14-27.3 provides for two theories of second-degree rape: one theory is that the vaginal intercourse was committed "by force and against the will" of the victim, id., (a)(1); the other theory is that such intercourse was committed against one who is "mentally defective," mentally incapacitated, or physically helpless, and the person performing the act should reasonably know. Id., (a)(2). It then noted that N.C.G.S. 14-27.1(3) defines "physically helpless" to mean "(i) a victim who is unconscious; or (ii) a victim who is physically unable to resist an act of vaginal intercourse or a sexual act or communicate unwillingness to submit to an act of vaginal intercourse or a sexual act." The Court of Appeals concluded that a sleeping person is a "physically helpless" person under N.C.G.S. 14-27.2(a)(2). It held than an indictment for the rape of one who is asleep must proceed on the theory that the victim was "physically helpless" pursuant to N.C.G.S. 14-27.3(a)(2) and not on the theory that the rape was "by force and against the will" of the victim as provided in subsection (1). The result in the Court of Appeals was that there is a fatal variance between the indictment and the proof presented at trial, and judgment was arrested.

We conclude that while the state might have elected to proceed under G.S. sec. 14-27.23(a)(2), it was not required to do so and that the evidence in this case supports a conviction of rape on a theory of force and lack of consent. There was, therefore, no fatal variance between the indictment and the proof.

At common law rape occurred when there was sexual intercourse by force and without the victim's consent. Rape also occurred when there was sexual intercourse with a victim who was asleep or otherwise incapable of providing resistance or consent.

In Brown v. State, 174 Ga. App. 913, 331 S.E.2d 891 (1985), defendant had sexual relations with the victim as she lay comatose in her hospital bed. The court said that "[s]exual intercourse with a woman whose will is temporarily lost from intoxication, or unconsciousness arising from use of drugs or other cause, or sleep, is rape." 174 Ga. App. at 913, 331 S.E.2d at 892. An Oklahoma court held that an information which charged the accused with an act of sexual intercourse with a female while she was asleep and at the time unconscious of the nature of the act was sufficient to charge the accused with second degree rape and to give the court jurisdiction to pronounce judgment and sentence. In re Childers, 310 P.2d 776 (Okla. Crim. App. 1957). The court said: "It is easily understood, and universally recognized, that a person who is unconscious by reason of intoxication, drugs, or sleep, is incapable of exercising any judgment in any matter whatsoever." Id. at 778. . . .

As can be seen from the foregoing cases the common law implied in law the elements of force and lack of consent so as to make the crime of rape complete upon the mere showing of sexual intercourse with a person who is asleep, unconscious, or otherwise incapacitated and therefore could not resist or give consent. . . .

Notes and Questions

1. *Mental incapacity.* Model Penal Code §213.1(2) defines a lesser form of rape it calls "gross sexual imposition" that consists of imposing sexual intercourse on a victim by means of fraud or coercion, or with knowledge that the victim "suffers from a mental disease or defect which renders her incapable of appraising the nature of her conduct." Moroever, many states now equate this conduct with the highest level of forcible rape. What level of proof do such provisions require? In White v. Commonwealth, 23 Va. App. 593, 478 S.E.2d 713 (1996), the prosecution chiefly relied on a school psychologist's test, done two years before the incident, reporting that the complainant was at the upper end of the educable range for retarded persons. The court reversed the conviction, holding that the criterion of the complainant's incapacity at the time of the sexual encounter could not be inferred from general or earlier tests. Instead, the prosecution had to prove beyond a reasonable doubt that: (1) the victim was mentally incapacitated at the time of the offense; (2) that her condition prevented the victim from understanding the nature and consequences of the sexual act; and (3) that at the time of the offense the defendant knew or should have known of the victim's condition. What sort of evidence would achieve this proof?

2. *Drunkenness.* What if the woman's capacity to decide on consent or ability to express nonconsent is impaired by alcohol? Recall that the Model Penal Code in §213 defines rape as including intercourse where the accused

> (b) . . . has substantially impaired [the female's] power to appraise or control her conduct by administering or employing without her knowledge drugs, intoxicants or the means for the purpose of preventing resistance; or
>
> (c) the female is unconscious.

Does that mean it is not rape under the MPC where the man knows that the woman is drunk (but not unconscious) and knows that her capacity for consent is impaired, but where he did not cause her to get drunk?

A few states do define rape to include cases where the woman was conscious and involuntarily drunk, but where someone other than the accused was responsible for getting her drunk. E.g., N.Y. Penal Law §130.00(6) (1998). On the other hand, if the woman becomes drunk through voluntary drinking, it may not be rape unless the state can meet the regular statutory test of force or nonconsent. Why should the voluntariness of intoxication matter? Does consent to become intoxicated imply consent to sexual intercourse? One commentator has shown that in a series of recent well-publicized rape cases where the woman arguably was voluntary in her drinking, the defense argued, sometimes successfully, that the woman was drinking as a way of expressing sexual desire or releasing inhibitions, so that, ironically, drunkenness helps prove consent.[39] And Professor Patricia J. Falk, in a comprehensive review of laws on this subject,[40] argues that current statutes offer too little protection to victims who have voluntarily ingested alcohol because these laws rely on tests of whether the victim actively resisted, rather than whether she consented; Professor Falk also argues for aggravated punishment or separate liability for the crime of administering drugs to a victim as a a prelude to sexual assault.

3. *Minority.* The development of the offense of statutory rape is summarized in the following comments by Professor Michelle Oberman:[41]

> Statutory rape . . . was codified in English law in 1275. Essentially, statutory rape criminalizes acts which would not otherwise be classified as rape. Initially, the age of consent was twelve; in 1576, the age was lowered to ten. . . . Early American lawmakers set the age of consent at ten, but over the course of the nineteenth century, the states gradually raised the age, some to as high as eighteen or twenty-one. Some states provided increased penalties for adult men who had sex with pre-pubescent girls, and lesser penalties when the male was younger than the female.
>
> Statutory rape laws were gender-specific, criminalizing sexual relations with young females, but not with young males. . . . American courts in the 19th century originally adopted statutory rape as a strict liability offense, in accordance with English law. It did not matter whether the victim looked older than the age of consent, that she consented, or even that she initiated sexual contact. If she was underage, the law was violated. However, since a statutory rape offense could as easily have been charged as a fornication offense, the age limits in statutory rape laws were viewed as determinative of the level of punishment rather than of liability for the sexual encounter. Therefore, the notion of age as a "sentence enhancer" is integral to the common law construction of statutory rape.
>
> At common law, men accused of statutory rape often asserted two claims in an effort to exculpate themselves: that the accused was reasonably mistaken as to the victim's age, that the victim was "promiscuous," or both. The first of these claims was unsuccessful, for it was not until 1964 that an American court permitted a mistake of fact defense in a statutory rape case. . . . [But the] "promiscuity defense" exculpated the accused if he could demonstrate credible evidence that the minor had behaved promiscuously in the past. . . .
>
> Presently, [the great majority of] jurisdictions have made the crime of statutory rape entirely gender-neutral (i.e. applicable to a person of either gender who has sex with a minor of either gender). Others elected to abolish the crime altogether, by decriminalizing sex among teenagers. Among the states that have adopted gender-neutral statutory rape laws, most impose liability only if an age gap of two to five years exists and the "victim" is under the statutory age of consent.

39. See Karen Kramer, Rule by Myth: The Social and Legal Dynamics Governing Alcohol-Related Acquaintance Rapes, 47 Stan. L. Rev. 115 (1994).

Moreover, recall from Chapter 3, pp. 236-39, *supra,* that the drunkenness of the *defendant* may exculpate when the prosecution is brought under a "specific intent" statute. See People v. Guillett, 342 Mich. 1, 69 N.W.2d 140 (1955) (voluntary intoxication may negate intent in crime of assault with intent to rape).

40. Rape by Drugs: A Statutory Overview and Proposals for Reform, 44 Ariz. L. Rev. 131 (2002).

41. Michelle Oberman, Turning Girls into Women: Re-evaluating Modern Statutory Rape Law, 85 J. Crim. L. & Criminology 15, 24-26, 32-33, 37 (1994).

Despite the widespread reforms in rape law, one vestige of the common law statutory rape offense which the reformers did not eradicate was the common law defense of promiscuity. . . . Not all states chose to classify any victim who was no longer a virgin as promiscuous. Yet, many jurisdictions did, and some even codified this presumption. For example, the 1975 version of Florida's sexual battery statute, which criminalized sexual conduct with a person under the age of eighteen, permitted a defense of consent, so long as the victim was not under the age of twelve. However, Section 794.05 obviated consent as a defense if the child was "under eighteen, unmarried, and previously was chaste."

Statutory rape laws, although infrequently invoked, maintain a unique and useful role within the structure of modern criminal sexual misconduct laws. For instance, a statutory rape violation is an easily documented offense. If the victim is underage, and the perpetrator is a certain number of years older than her, he is guilty. This additional conviction can add several years to a convicted rapist's sentence. Additionally, statutory rape laws permit prosecutors to seek convictions in cases in which there is insufficient evidence to sustain a heightened criminal sexual assault charge (e.g., felony rape) because prosecutors lack proof that intercourse was nonconsensual. In these situations, prosecutors can use modern statutory rape laws to seek convictions which simply would not be obtainable under rape law generally.

While, as Oberman notes, most states have adopted gender-neutral statutory rape laws, they are not constitutionally required to, according to the Supreme Court's decision in Michael M. v. Sonoma County Superior Court, 450 U.S. 464 (1981). Oberman points out that prosecutors rarely charge statutory rape unless the facts very clearly indicate nonconsent. Oberman proceeds to argue that prosecutors thereby drastically overestimate the capacity of adolescent girls to protect themselves from sexual predation, and that this aspect of the date-rape problem has been overlooked by reformers.

The highly calibrated New York statutory scheme illustrates the contemporary approach to statutory rape. New York defines sex with a child under eleven as first-degree rape or sodomy, New York Penal L. §§130.35, 130.50 (1998); sex with a child of less than fourteen as second-degree rape or sodomy, if the defendant is eighteen or over, §§130.30, 130.45; and sex with an adolescent under the age of seventeen as third-degree rape or sodomy, where the defendant is twenty-one or over, §§130.25, 130.40. New York defines sexual contact with a child under eleven as sexual abuse in the first degree, §130.65; sexual contact with a child under fourteen as the misdemeanor of sexual abuse in the second degree, §130.60; and sexual contact with an adolescent under seventeen, by a defendant at least five years older than the victim, as the misdemeanor of sexual abuse in the third degree, §130.55. Where the defendant is less than five years older than a victim under the age of seventeen, sexual contact is sexual abuse in the third degree unless the defendant proves that the victim manifested affirmative consent. Id.

In a reappraisal of the social role of statutory rape laws,[42] Professor Oberman notes that they were originally motivated by highly patriarchal views of young females and fathers' economic concern in ensuring that they could offer a valuable commodity — chastity — in the marriage market. Modern feminists expressed concerns about these laws, but a strong social consensus on the need to prevent teenage pregnancies sparked a revival of statutory rape prosecutions

---

42. Girls in the Master's House: Of Protection, Patriarchy and the Potential for Using the Master's Tools To Reconfigure Statutory Rape Law, 50 DePaul L. Rev. 799 (2002).

late in the twentieth century. In particular, state and federal welfare laws encouraged or required states to pursue these prosecutions in cases where pregnancy resulted,[43] and prosecutors increasingly used them as a back-up to forcible rape charges in nonstranger cases where uncertainty over consent made conviction of the greater charge unlikely.[44] Though feminists resisted this movement out of concern that these laws reinforce patriarchal gender stereotypes and interfere with the sexual autonomy of young females, Professor Oberman urges that feminists can "reclaim" these laws by rediscovering their power to protect young females from abuse in a manner consistent with their healthy social development.[45]

H.   RAPE BY EXTORTION

COMMONWEALTH v. MLINARICH
Supreme Court of Pennsylvania
518 Pa. 247, 542 A.2d 1335 (1988)

NIX, CHIEF JUSTICE.

In the instant appeal we have agreed to consider the Commonwealth's contention that the threats made by an adult guardian to a fourteen-year-old girl to cause her to be recommitted to a juvenile detention facility supplies the "forcible compulsion" element of the crime of rape. For the reasons that follow, we are constrained to conclude that they do not and that the appellee's convictions of rape and attempted rape may not be permitted to stand.

Appellee, Joseph Mlinarich, . . . was . . . arrested and charged with rape as well as multiple counts of attempted rape, involuntary deviate sexual intercourse, corruption of a minor, indecent exposure, and endangering the welfare of a minor. After a jury trial in the Court of Common Pleas of Cambria County appellee was convicted of all charges. . . . Appellee took a direct appeal to the Superior Court, which . . . reversed the rape and attempted rape convictions. . . . The prosecution's appeal [from these reversals] having been allowed, the matter has been ably briefed and argued and is now ripe for resolution. . . .

[Section 3121 of the Crimes Code defines rape as follows: "A person . . . engages in sexual intercourse with another person not his spouse: (1) by forcible compulsion [or] (2) by threat of forcible compulsion that would prevent resistance by a person of reasonable resolution."] For the reasons that follow, we conclude that the term "forcible compulsion" includes both physical force as well as psychological duress. We are constrained to reject the contention that "forcible compulsion" was intended by the General Assembly, in this context, to be extended to embrace appeals to the intellect or the morals of the victim.

. . . It is clear that the legislature did consider the impact that should be given the minority of . . . victims of sexual assaults and specifically provided for it [in its statutory rape provision]. Thus the arguments raised by the Commonwealth based upon the age of the victim in this appeal can only be considered as

---

43. Id. at 810-13.
44. Id. at 815-23.
45. Id. at 824-25.

provided for under the statutory provisions in question. . . . It is also helpful in bringing into focus the issues raised herein to recognize that . . . subsection (2) of section 3121 qualifies the "threat" as being one that "would prevent resistance by a person of reasonable resolution." . . . An "objective" test has been established to determine whether the pressure generated upon the victim by the threat would be such as to overcome the resolve and prevent further resistance of a person of reasonable resolution. Thus any uniqueness in the emotional makeup of the victim is irrelevant in determining whether the threat possessed the requisite force to satisfy this element of the offense. . . .

. . . There has never been a question that the gravamen of the crimes of rape and the later statutory offense of involuntary deviate sexual intercourse was their non-volitional quality. . . . We are . . . satisfied that the adjective "forceful" was employed to establish that the assault must be upon the will. . . . The critical distinction is where the compulsion overwhelms the will of the victim in contrast to a situation where the victim can make a deliberate choice to avoid the encounter even though the alternative may be an undesirable one. Indeed, the victim in this instance apparently found the prospect of being returned to the detention home a repugnant one. Notwithstanding, she was left with a choice and therefore the submission was a result of a deliberate choice and was not an involuntary act. This is not in any way to deny the despicable nature of appellee's conduct or even to suggest that it was not criminal. We are merely constrained to recognize that it does not meet the test of "forcible compulsion" set forth in subsections (1) and (2) of [section] 3121. . . .

In reaching its conclusion that the charges of rape and attempted rape were not established, the majority of the Superior Court erroneously inferred that the term "forcible compulsion" required physical violence. As we have indicated, the term "forcible compulsion" was employed to convey that the result produced must be non-voluntary rather than to describe the character of force itself. Certainly, psychological coercion can be applied with such intensity that it may overpower the will to resist as effectively as physical force. . . . The purpose of the term was to distinguish between assault upon the will and the forcing of the victim to make a choice regardless how repugnant. Certainly difficult choices have a coercive effect but the result is the product of the reason, albeit unpleasant and reluctantly made. The fact cannot be escaped that the victim has made the choice and the act is not involuntary. Accordingly, for the reasons set forth herein, the order of the Superior Court is affirmed.

LARSEN, Justice, dissenting.

Threatening to have her placed in physical confinement unless she complied with his demands, Joseph Mlinarich, at sixty-three years of age, engaged in sustained, systematic sexual abuse of a fourteen-year-old child with low mental abilities, despite her continual crying, her pain and her pleading with him to stop. . . . The jury called these acts rape and attempted rape. The Opinion in Support of Affirmance says the jury was wrong because a person of reasonable resolution would have withstood Mlinarich's threats and advances, and would hold that this fourteen-year-old child voluntarily consented to have sexual intercourse with the sixty-three-year-old Mlinarich of her own free will and volition.

To the affirming members of this Court, the victim "was left with a choice and therefore the submission was as a result of a deliberate choice and was not an involuntary act." The Opinion in Support of Affirmance acknowledges that hers was a "difficult" choice, but states that the sexual intercourse was "the product of the reason, albeit unpleasant and reluctantly made. The fact cannot be escaped that the victim has made the choice and the act is not involuntary." Has civilization fallen so far, have our values become so distorted and misplaced, as to leave a fourteen-year-old child without protection when she is forced to make such an awful "choice"? . . .

One wonders what is the "prescribed level of intensity designed to have an effect upon the will of the victim," . . . that will satisfy the criteria of those who would affirm the Superior Court. . . . If a policeman, or someone posing as a policeman, pulls a female motorist to the side of the road at night and threatens to throw her in jail until morning unless she has intercourse with him, and she complies, would such compulsion satisfy the majority's "prescribed level of intensity"? If a male judge calls a female litigant into his chambers, and tells her he will find her in contempt of court and have her thrown in jail unless she has intercourse with him, and she complies, would such compulsion reach the majority's "prescribed level of intensity"? . . .

In a recent novel by William Styron, "Sophie's Choice," the principal character was forced by a Nazi gestapo officer to make a horrifying choice. She was ordered to either choose one of her two children to remain with her while the other was sent to . . . die, or to watch both of them be sent [to die]. By no conceivable stretch of the imagination could it be said that "Sophie's Choice" was a voluntary, consensual choice, although, in the reasoning and language of the majority, she was "left with choices, albeit difficult and unpleasant ones," and her choice was a "deliberate" exercise of her "free will" and the "product of reason."

Notes and Questions

1. The coercive insistence on sex backed by some material or economic threat is rarely punished in the United States. Similar to *Mlinarich* is State v. Thompson, 792 P.2d 1103 (Mont. 1990), in which a high school principal threatened to deny a 17-year-old female permission to graduate unless she had sex with him. The court upheld dismissal of a charge of sexual intercourse "without consent," then defined under 45-5-501 MCA as occurring where "the victim is compelled to submit by force or by threat of imminent death, bodily injury, or kidnaping." The court acknowledged that the female had submitted under "intimidation, fear and apprehension" but found insufficient evidence of force.

2. *Punishment as extortion.* Some courts have imposed criminal liability under extortion rather than rape laws. In State v. Felton, 339 So. 2d 797 (La. 1976), defendant was a police officer. On several occasions, he found couples in a park area and threatened them with arrest if they did not perform sexual intercourse in his presence, and then threatened the woman with arrest if she did not have sex with him. Under La. R.S. §14:66 (2004), extortion is "the communication of threats to obtain anything of value or any acquittance, advantage, or immunity of any description," and "threats" can include the threat "to do any unlawful injury or any other harm." The court upheld the conviction on the ground that the "acquittance" gained was sexual gratification.

Does *Felton* demonstrate that a general extortion law can fill the gap left by cases like *Mlinarich* and *Thompson*? New York Penal Law defines the misdemeanor of "Coercion" as "compel[ling] or induc[ing] a person to engage in conduct which the latter has legal right to abstain from engaging in" by threat-ening to cause someone to be charged with a crime, to expose a secret, to pro-vide or withhold information relative to the victim's legal claim or defense, or to harm someone through an official act in one's capacity as a public servant. §135.60 (1998). Does this sort of statute correctly describe or adequately punish the wrong committed in *Felton, Mlinarich,* and *Thompson?*

3. *Punishment as sexual assault or rape.* Tenn. Code §§39-13-503(a), 39-11-106(a)(3)(2003), provides that a person can be convicted for either rape or sex-ual battery if: "Force or coercion is used" and "coercion" is defined as "any threat, however communicated, to wrongfully accuse any person of an offense; . . . [e]xpose any person to contempt, hatred or ridicule; . . . [or] harm the credit or business repute of any person." Similarly, MPC §213.1(2) defines Gross Sex-ual Imposition as including intercourse whenever a man compels a victim "to submit by any threat that would prevent resistance by a woman of ordinary res-olution." To which of the above cases would these statutory formulae apply? The drafters tried to offer a standard for resolving sexual extortion cases:

> . . . The threat must be such that submission by the female results from coer-cion rather than bargain. . . . Thus, if a wealthy man were to threaten to withdraw financial support from his unemployed girlfriend, it is at least arguable under the circumstances that he is making a threat "that would prevent resistance by a woman of ordinary resolution." The reason why this case is excluded from liability . . . is not the gravity of the harm threatened — it may be quite substantial — but its essential character as part of a process of a bargain. He is not guilty of compul-sion overwhelming the will of his victim but only of offering her an unattractive choice to avoid some unwanted alternative [comment at 314].

In Lovely v. Cunningham, 796 F.2d. 1 (1st Cir. 1986), a liquor store man-ager befriended a young drifter and over a four-month period, spent $1,000 on him, hired him as an employee to do little work, paid $60 to the local police in restitution for a theft committed by the young man, paid his room rent, and in-vited him to live in his home. Lovely allegedly coerced the victim into sexual re-lations, threatening him with the loss of various of the benefits he had conferred on him, including a threat to sue him for the restitution money and thereby cause him to end up in jail. Lovely was convicted in the New Hampshire courts of aggravated sexual assault, which, under New Hampshire Rev. Stat. Ann. §632-A:2 (1996 & Supp. 2003), occurs when the defendant "coerces the victim to sub-mit by threatening to retaliate against the victim . . . and the victim believes that the actor has the ability to execute these threats in the future." Section 632-A:1 says: "Retaliation" means threats of future physical or mental punishment, kid-napping, false imprisonment, extortion or public humiliation or disgrace. Fi-nally, the state extortion law, §637:5, makes it theft by extortion for a person to "threaten to cause [official] action or [d]o any other act which would not in it-self substantially benefit him but which would harm substantially any other per-son. . . ."

On a habeas corpus appeal in federal court, Lovely noted the confusing se-quence of "threats" described in this statutory scheme and argued that to pun-ish him constituted such a novel and unforeseeable reading of the statutes as to violate his due process right to fair notice. Specifically, Lovely argued that the New Hampshire courts unforeseeably construed "extortion" to include coercion through threats of economic reprisal without the objective of acquiring a victim's property. Lovely also argued that the scheme was unconstitutionally vague, since it might even punish a person who exerts pressure on a lover for continued favors.

Rejecting both these claims, the Court of Appeals agreed that had Lovely merely threatened to end the victim's privilege of free housing, his actions would be no more than "the withholding of an expensive present." Id. at 6. It held, however, that Lovely's threats to make trouble for the victim with the police and to deprive him of his job could support an extortion charge, by analogy to a rape where the rapist coerces sex from the victim by threatening to cause her to lose her job.

I. RAPE BY FRAUD

If force and unconsciousness are primarily significant as indicia of nonconsent, the question arises, what other kinds of circumstances that can interfere with free consent? Model Penal Code §213.1(2) includes some forms of knowing deception among the circumstances that can give rise to liability for gross sexual imposition: "A male who has sexual intercourse with a female . . . commits a felony . . . if . . . (c) he knows that she is unaware that a sexual act is being committed upon her or that she submits because she mistakenly supposes that he is her husband." Consider this case:

BORO v. PEOPLE
California Court of Appeal
163 Cal. App. 3d 1224, 210 Cal. Rptr. 122 (1985)

. . . Ms. R., the rape victim, was employed at the Holiday Inn in South San Francisco when, on March 30, 1984 at about 8:45 A.M., she received a telephone call from a person who identified himself as "Dr. Stevens" and said that he worked at Peninsula Hospital.

"Dr. Stevens" told Ms. R. that he had results of her blood test and that she had contracted a dangerous, highly infectious and perhaps fatal disease; that she could be sued as a result; that the disease came from using public toilets; and that she would have to tell him the identity of all her friends who would then have to be contacted in the interest of controlling the spread of the disease.

"Dr. Stevens" further explained that there were only two ways to treat the disease. The first was a painful surgical procedure — graphically described — costing $9,000, and requiring her uninsured hospitalization for six weeks. A second alternative, "Dr. Stevens" explained, was to have sexual intercourse with an anonymous donor who had been injected with a serum which would cure the disease. The latter, nonsurgical procedure would only cost $4,500. When the victim replied that she lacked sufficient funds the "doctor" suggested that $1,000 would suffice as a down payment. The victim thereupon agreed to the nonsurgical alternative and consented to intercourse with the mysterious donor, believing "it was the only choice I had."

After discussing her intentions with her work supervisor, the victim proceeded to the Hyatt Hotel in Burlingame as instructed, and contacted

"Dr. Stevens" by telephone. The latter became furious when he learned that Ms. R. had informed her employer of the plan, and threatened to terminate his treatment, finally instructing her to inform her employer she had decided not to go through with the treatment. Ms. R. did so, then went to her bank, withdrew $1,000 and, as instructed, checked into another hotel and called "Dr. Stevens" to give him her room number.

About a half hour later the defendant "donor" arrived at her room. When Ms. R. had undressed, the "donor," petitioner, after urging her to relax, had sexual intercourse with her. . . .

Petitioner was apprehended when the police arrived at the hotel room, having been called by Ms. R.'s supervisor. . . .

Upon the basis of the evidence just recounted, petitioner was charged with . . . Count II: section 261, subdivision (4)-rape, "[w]here a person is at the time unconscious of the nature of the act, and this is known to the accused."

The People's position is stated concisely: "We contend, quite simply, that at the time of the intercourse Ms. R., the victim, was 'unconscious of the nature of the act' because of [petitioner's] misrepresentation she believed it was in the nature of a medical treatment and not a simple, ordinary act of sexual intercourse." Petitioner, on the other hand, stresses that the victim was plainly aware of the *nature* of the act in which she voluntarily engaged, so that her motivation in doing so . . . is irrelevant.

Our research discloses sparse California authority on the subject. A victim need not be totally and physically unconscious in order that section 261, subdivision (4), apply. In People v. Minkowski (1962) 204 Cal. App. 2d 832, the defendant was a physician who "treated" several victims for menstrual cramps. Each victim testified that she was treated in a position with her back to the doctor, bent over a table, with feet apart, in a dressing gown. And in each case the "treatment" consisted of the defendant first inserting a metal instrument, then substituting an instrument which "felt different"— the victims not realizing that the second instrument was in fact the doctor's penis. The precise issue before us was never tendered in People v. Minkowski because the petitioner there *conceded* the sufficiency of evidence to support the element of [un]consciousness.

The decision is useful to the analysis, however, because it exactly illustrates certain traditional rules in the area of our inquiry. Thus, as a leading authority has written, "if deception causes a misunderstanding as to the fact itself (fraud in the *factum*) there is no legally-recognized consent because what happened is not that for which consent was given, whereas consent induced by fraud is as effective as any other consent, so far as direct and immediate legal consequences are concerned, if the deception relates not to the thing done but merely to some collateral matter (fraud in the inducement)." (Perkins and Boyce, Criminal Law (3d ed. 1982) ch. 9 §3, p.1079.)

The victims in *Minkowski* consented, not to sexual intercourse, but to an act of an altogether different nature, penetration by medical instrument. The consent was to a pathological, and not a carnal, act, and the mistake was, therefore, in the *factum* and not merely in the inducement.

Another relatively common situation in the literature on this subject — discussed in detail by Perkins (*supra,* at p. 1080) is the fraudulent obtaining of intercourse by impersonating a spouse. As Professor Perkins observes, the courts are not in accord as to whether the crime of rape is thereby committed. "[T]he disagreement is not in regard to the underlying principle but only to its application. Some courts have taken the position that such a misdeed is fraud in the inducement on the theory that the woman consents to exactly what is done (sexual intercourse) and hence there is no rape; other courts, . . . hold such a misdeed to be rape on the theory that it involves fraud in the *factum,* since the woman's consent is to the innocent act of marital intercourse while what is actually perpetrated on her is an act of adultery. Her innocence seems never to have been questioned in such a case and the reason she is not guilty of adultery is because she did not consent to adulterous intercourse. . . .

In California, of course, we have by statute[46] adopted the majority view that such fraud is in the *factum,* not the inducement, and have thus held it to vitiate consent. It is otherwise, however, with respect to the conceptually much murkier statutory offense with which we here deal. . . .

The language itself could not be plainer. It defines rape to be "an act of sexual intercourse" with a nonspouse, accomplished where the victim is "at the time unconscious of the nature of the act. . . ." (§261, subd. (4).) Nor, as we have just seen, can we entertain the slightest doubt that the legislature well understood how to a draft a statute to encompass fraud in the *factum* (§261, subd. 5) and how to specify certain fraud in the inducement as vitiating consent.[47]

. . . [Ms. R.] precisely understood the "nature of her act," but, motivated by a fear of disease, and death, succumbed to petitioner's fraudulent blandishments.

To so conclude is not to vitiate the heartless cruelty of petitioner's scheme, but to say that it comprised crimes of a different order than a violation of section 261, subdivision (4).

Let a peremptory writ of prohibition issue restraining respondent from taking further action upon Count II.[48]

Notes and Questions

1. What result would be reached in *Boro* under the general nonconsent standard of State v. Smith, or the affirmative consent standard of In the Interest of M.T.S.?

2. *Fraud in factum.* The distinction between fraud in the factum and fraud in the inducement derives from commercial law, where the former is far more likely to establish a cause of action than the latter. And a true case of obtaining sex by fraud in the factum would seem to be an obvious case of rape. In McNair v. State, 825 P.2d 571 (Nev. 1992), a gynecologist would arrange for his patients to position themselves for an examination and then engage in anal sexual contact with them. After one patient reported this to the police, others came

46. Section 261, subdivision (5), reads as follows: "Where a person submits under the belief that the person committing the act is the victim's spouse, and this belief is induced by any artifice, pretense, or concealment practiced by the accused, with intent to induce the belief."

47. [Before its repeal], section 268 provided that: Every person who, under promise of marriage, seduces and has sexual intercourse with an unmarried female of previous chaste character, is punishable by imprisonment. . . .

48. [Boro, who engaged in the same conduct with several other women, became infamously known in the California press as "Dr. Feelgood" and proved unrepentant, repeating this scheme with another woman. But in the interim the California legislature had enacted a law explicitly criminalizing this kind of conduct (see Cal. Pen. Code 266(c)), and in 1987 Boro was prosecuted under the new statute. See Patricia J. Falk, Rape by Fraud and Rape by Coercion, 64 Brooklyn L. Rev. 1, 57 (1998). — Eds.]

forward to report the same kind of occurrence. The state sexual assault statute, NRS §200.366(1) (2001) provides:

> A person who subjects another person to sexual penetration or who forces . . . against the victim's will or under conditions in which the perpetrator knows or should know that the victim is mentally or physically incapable of resisting or understanding the nature of his conduct, is guilty of sexual assault.

The court first held that overt force is not necessary as an element and that a victim "is not required to resist more than her age, strength, and the surrounding facts and circumstances would reasonably dictate as manifesting the opposition. . . . Submission is not the equivalent of consent." Instead, it viewed lack of protest to be "simply one among the totality of circumstances to be considered by the trier of fact." The court held that McNair had committed sexual assault "by fraud and deception without the victim's consent." An expert witness described the assault as "the confidence style assault" whereby "[v]ictims experience feelings of betrayal and confusion," an emotional condition that also served to explain any otherwise implausible delay in the victim's report.

3. *Fraud in the inducement.* Is the case for criminal liability in an inducement case like *Boro* that much weaker? Some courts have imposed rape liability in arguably similar situations. Robert Dutton was the pastor of Bethany Christian Missionary Alliance Church. J.A.J. and her husband approached him about joining his church and about getting J.A.J. counseling. In the counseling session, J.A.J. told Dutton that she suffered from low self-esteem, suicidal thoughts, and an eating disorder, among other things. Dutton first discussed scripture with her but then insisted on discussing sexual matters, saying sex was a gift from God and that he was "working" with her on her sexuality. She paid him for these sessions until she joined the church. In one session, purporting to console her for the death of her daughter, Dutton embraced and kissed her. Despite her insistence and his promise that the relationship would remain platonic, at a later session Dutton engaged in intimate sexual contact with her.

A month later, they had intercourse in a motel, with Dutton telling her that this was healthy for her because he, unlike her husband, loved her unselfishly. J.A.J. then wrote him a letter stating she was giving control of her life to him. Shortly thereafter, Dutton told her that sex between a counselor and a counselee was a felony in Minnesota. They had sexual intercourse several more times. Under Minn. Stat. §609.344-45 (2003), the state had to prove that the defendant was purporting to perform psychotherapy, and the complainant was his patient, and that she was emotionally dependent on him, in the sense that she was unable to withhold consent to sex, and that he represented to her that sex was part of the treatment. Dutton was convicted, and on appeal the statute was held applicable to clergy who offered psychotherapy. State v. Dutton, 450 N.W.2d 189 (Minn. Ct. App. 1990). The statute was subsequently amended to make this coverage explicit. Minn. Stat. §609.344(1) (1999).

Is *Dutton* distinguishable from *Boro* on the ground that a recipient of psychotherapy is more vulnerable to manipulation than a recipient of medical therapy? On the other hand, is it clear that Dutton actually deceived J.A.J.? Did he deceive her about any material facts? About his intentions?

In People v. Evans, 85 Misc. 2d 1088, 379 N.Y.S.2d 912 (Sup. Ct. N.Y. Cty. 1975), the defendant, falsely posing as an experimental psychologist, approached

Beth Peterson, a young college student, at LaGuardia Airport and told her he was interested in interviewing her for an academic study. He offered to drive her to her destination, Grand Central Station; she agreed and joined him in a waiting car, along with other people he described as professional colleagues. Evans first drove, however, to a downtown singles bar where, he said, he wanted to record sociological observations of her interactions with male patrons. After several hours at the bar, he proposed that they stop at his apartment so he could pick up his own car. Arriving at the building, he induced her to come upstairs to his apartment (which turned out to be someone else's, which he entered without permission). The apartment was full of toys belonging to the occupants' children, and Peterson questioned why the toys were there; Evans told her the toys were used in primal therapy to enable his patients to restore contact with their childhood selves. Evans explained to Peterson that his research concerned the missing link between the girl and adult woman stage and inquired of her sexual history. After she hesitantly gave answers, he tried to unclothe her, and when she resisted he criticized her for failing to reach her innermost consciousness and for foolishly placing herself at the mercy of a stranger. After a short while, he had sex with her. She then left the apartment and called the police.

The court, after noting that Peterson exhibited neither injuries nor torn clothing, stated:

> The prevailing view in this country is that there can be no rape which is achieved by fraud, or trick, or stratagem. Provided there is actual consent, the nature of the act being understood, it is not rape, absent a statute, no matter how despicable the fraud, even if a doctor persuades her that sexual intercourse is necessary for her treatment and return to good health.
>
> . . . In seduction, unlike rape, the consent of the woman, implied or explicit, has been procured, by artifice, deception, flattery, fraud or promise. . . .
>
> . . . [T]here are no presently existing penal sanctions against seduction.
>
> It is clear from the evidence in this case that Beth Peterson was intimidated; that she was confused; that she had been drowned in a torrent of words and perhaps was terrified. [Id. at 918-19.]

But the court found no evidence of force and resistance.

> It is not criminal conduct for a male to make promises that will not be kept, to indulge in exaggeration and hyperbole, or to assure any trusting female that, as in the ancient fairy tale, the ugly frog is really the handsome prince. [Id. at 922.]

In United States v. Condolon, 600 F.2d 7 (4th Cir. 1979), the operator of a bogus talent agency advertised that he could obtain acting and modeling jobs for women who had sex with him. Disappointed clients complained to the police, and Condolon was ultimately convicted of federal wire fraud. Should he then also have been convicted of rape? Did Condolon make the kind of representation to which the criminal law should seek to hold him?

4. *Statutory solutions.* Many states have enacted legislation to address the varieties of "professional sexual fraud" in specific contexts, some statutes redefining force or nonconsent in medical or other professional situations, and others categorically criminalizing any sexual relations between specified medical professionals and patients, or between psychotherapists and their patients, or clerics and parishioners. These prohibitions reflect growing concern that in such medical or therapeutic relationships, clients or patients cede too much

authority to the professional to fully exercise free will, and also may suffer a kind of aggravated sexual harassment — i.e., the fear that the professional will withhold treatment except in a *quid pro quo* exchange for a sexual relationship.[49] For a detailed review of these laws, see Patricia Falk, Rape by Fraud and Rape by Coercion, 64 Brooklyn L. Rev. 1, 92-108 (1998). Only Tennessee and Alabama have a general criminal prohibition against obtaining sex by fraud. See Tenn. Code §39-13-503(4) (2003) ("The sexual penetration is accomplished by fraud"). Many jurisdictions, however, will prosecute cases that could be called fraud in the inducement in special circumstances, as where the perpetrator lies about or withholds information about a venereal disease. But generally, commentators suggest, states avoid punishing fraud in the inducement because, as compared to the more instrumental motives of commercial transactions, in sex cases it is too difficult to establish that the fraud was the cause of the apparent consent to sexual activity.

5. *Impersonation.* The *Boro* court notes the doctrine that fraudulent impersonation of the victim's husband may constitute rape. But is it limited to husbands? In People v. Hough, 159 Misc. 2d 997, 607 N.Y.S.2d 884 (1994), the court found itself without precedent in a case where a woman had sex with a man named Lamont Hough, thinking he was her boyfriend, Lamont's twin brother, Lenny. The court noted that at least two states had statutes expressly addressing the issue in the context of impersonation of a husband, e.g., "Where the female submitted under a belief that the person committing the act is her husband, and this belief is induced by any artifice, pretense or concealment practiced by the accused with intent to induce such belief." Ariz. Rev. Stat. §13-611; see Model Penal Code §213.1 (2). But it reversed a conviction for the crime of "sexual misconduct," because the statute required, and the proof did not establish, "forcible compulsion" or "incapacity to consent." The court hinted, however, that the state could still proceed under another less punitive statute covering "sexual abuse," which punished sexual acts in "any circumstances . . . in which the victim does not expressly or impliedly acquiesce in the actor's conduct."

J. MENS REA

COMMONWEALTH v. FISCHER
Superior Court of Pennsylvania
721 A.2d 1111 (Pa. Super. 1998)

BECK, J. This case prompts our consideration of the law with respect to forcible compulsion and consent in sexual assault cases. After a careful review of the record and an in-depth analysis of the issue at hand, we affirm.

Appellant, an eighteen-year-old college freshman, was charged with involuntary deviate sexual intercourse (IDSI), aggravated indecent assault and related offenses in connection with an incident that occurred in a Lafayette College campus dormitory. The victim was another freshman student appellant met at school.

49. Schulhofer, Unwanted Sex, *supra*, at 206-26.

At trial, both the victim and appellant testified that a couple of hours prior to the incident at issue, the two went to appellant's dorm room and engaged in intimate contact. The victim testified that the couple's conduct was limited to kissing and fondling. Appellant, on the other hand, testified that during this initial encounter, he and the victim engaged in "rough sex" which culminated in the victim performing fellatio on him. According to appellant, the victim acted aggressively at this first rendezvous by holding appellant's arms above his head, biting his chest, stating "You know you want me," and initiating oral sex.

After the encounter, the students separated and went to the dining hall with their respective friends. They met up again later and once more found themselves in appellant's dorm room. While their accounts of what occurred at the first meeting contained significant differences, their versions of events at the second meeting were grossly divergent. The victim testified that appellant locked the door, pushed her onto the bed, straddled her, held her wrists above her head and forced his penis into her mouth. She struggled with appellant throughout the entire encounter and warned him that "someone would look for her" and "someone would find out." She also told him that she was scheduled to be at a mandatory seminar and repeatedly stated that she did not want to engage in sex, but her pleas went unheeded.

. . . Throughout the incident, appellant made various statements to the victim, including "I know you want it" and "Nobody will know where you are." When the victim attempted to leave, appellant blocked her path. Only after striking him in the groin with her knee was the victim able to escape.

Appellant characterized the second meeting in a far different light. He stated that as he led the victim into his room, she told him it would have to be "a quick one." As a result, appellant figured that their sexual liaison would be brief. Thereafter, according to appellant, he began to engage in the same type of behavior the victim had exhibited in their previous encounter. . . . When she [said] "no," appellant answered, "No means yes." After another verbal exchange that included the victim's statement that she had to leave, appellant again insisted that "she wanted it." This time she answered "No, I honestly don't." Upon hearing this, appellant no longer sought to engage in oral sex and removed himself from her body. However, as the two lay side by side on the bed, they continued to kiss and fondle one another.

. . . According to appellant, the victim enjoyed the contact and responded positively to his actions. At some point, however, she stood up and informed appellant that she had to leave. When appellant again attempted to touch her, this time on the thigh, she told him she was "getting pissed." Before appellant could "rearrange himself," so that he could walk the victim to her class, she abruptly left the room. . . .

The Commonwealth offered physical evidence of sperm found on the victim's sweater. Medical personnel testified to treating the victim on the night in question. Many of the victim's friends and classmates described her as nervous, shaken and upset after the incident.

Defense counsel argued throughout the trial and in closing that appellant, relying on his previous encounter with the victim, did not believe his actions were taken without her consent. Presenting appellant as sexually inexperienced, counsel argued that his client believed the victim was a willing participant during their intimate encounters. In light of his limited experience and the victim's initially aggressive behavior, argued counsel, appellant's beliefs were reasonable.

Further, the victim's conduct throughout the second encounter, as testified to by appellant, would not make appellant's actions "forcible" since it appeared that the victim was enjoying the encounter. Finally, as soon as appellant realized that the victim truly did not wish to engage in oral sex a second time, appellant stopped seeking same. As a result, appellant's actions could not be deemed forcible compulsion.

The jury returned a verdict of guilty on virtually all counts. Appellant was sentenced to two to five years in prison. On direct appeal, he retained new counsel who has raised a single issue of ineffectiveness before this court. He argues that trial counsel provided ineffective assistance in failing to request a jury charge on the defense of mistake of fact. Specifically, appellant claims that counsel should have asked the court to instruct the jurors that if they found appellant reasonably, though mistakenly, believed that the victim was consenting to his sexual advances, they could find him not guilty. . . .

The standard of review for ineffectiveness challenges is clear. Appellant must establish: (1) an underlying issue of arguable merit; (2) the absence of a reasonable strategy on the part of counsel in acting or failing to act; and (3) prejudice as a result of counsel's action or inaction. . . .

Our initial inquiry is whether counsel would have been successful had he requested a mistake of fact instruction. . . . Further, the quality of counsel's stewardship is based on the state of the law as it existed at time of trial; counsel is not ineffective if he fails to predict future developments or changes in the law. . . .

The Commonwealth [relies] on an opinion by a panel of this court. Commonwealth v. Williams, 294 Pa. Super. 93, 439 A.2d 765 (Pa. Super. 1982), concerned the rape and assault of a Temple University student. The facts established that the victim accepted a ride from the appellant on a snowy evening in Philadelphia. Instead of taking the young woman to the bus station, appellant drove her to a dark area, threatened to kill her and informed her that he wanted sex. The victim told Williams to "go ahead" because she did not wish to be hurt.

After his conviction and sentence, appellant filed a direct appeal and argued, among other things, that the trial court erred in refusing to instruct the jury "that if the defendant reasonably believed that the prosecutrix had consented to his sexual advances that this would constitute a defense to the rape and involuntary deviate sexual intercourse charge." 439 A.2d at 767. This court rejected Williams's claim and held:

> The charge requested by the defendant is not now and has never been the law of Pennsylvania. When one individual uses force or the threat of force to have sexual relations with a person not his spouse and without the person's consent he has committed the crime of rape. *If the element of the defendant's belief as to the victim's state of mind is to be established as a defense to the crime of rape then it should be done by our legislature which has the power to define crimes and offenses. We refuse to create such a defense.*

Id. (emphasis supplied.) The Commonwealth insists that under *Williams,* appellant was not entitled to the instruction he now claims trial counsel should have requested.

In response, appellant makes two arguments. First, he argues that the "stranger rape" facts of *Williams* were far different from those of this case, making the case inapplicable. Second, he maintains that the law with respect to rape and sexual assault has changed significantly over the last decade, along with our understanding of the crime and its permutations, making a mistake of fact instruction in a date rape case a necessity for a fair trial.

In support of his argument, appellant draws our attention to many sources, including the evolution of sexual assault case law in this Commonwealth, recent amendments to our sexual offenses statutes, commentary accompanying the Pennsylvania Standard Jury Instructions, law review articles and treatment of the issue in other jurisdictions. Because we find appellant's arguments thoughtful and compelling, we will address them here.

The issues of consent and forcible compulsion raised in sexual assault prosecutions have always been complex. Unless the incident is witnessed by a third party, or is accompanied by conspicuous injury, a rape case is often reduced to a credibility battle between the complainant and the defendant. Our laws have sought continually to protect victims of sexual assault, and in the process, have undergone significant change. Although the rape and IDSI laws have always required the element of "forcible compulsion," that term was not initially defined. The definition of that term and its relation to the concept of consent have been the frequent topic of discussion among lawmakers, courts and scholars.[50]

Not long after *Williams* was decided, our Supreme Court published Commonwealth v. Rhodes, 510 Pa. 537, 510 A.2d 1217 (1986). In that case, a twenty-year-old man was accused of raping an eight-year-old child. The evidence established that the appellant took the victim, whom he knew, to an abandoned building and sexually assaulted her. The child complied with all of the appellant's instructions. . . . A panel of this court . . . held that while the crime of statutory rape clearly was established given the victim's age, there was no evidence of the forcible compulsion necessary for the rape conviction. Our Supreme Court disagreed . . . and stated that "the degree of force required to constitute rape . . . is relative and depends upon the facts and particular circumstances of the case." Defining forcible compulsion as including "not only physical force or violence but also moral, psychological or intellectual force," the court held that forcible compulsion was established. . . .

The *Rhodes* court's inclusion of types of forcible compulsion other than physical was a significant change in the law. Of course, defining those new types was not an easy task. In Commonwealth v. Mlinarich, 518 Pa. 247, 542 A.2d 1335 (1988) . . . appellant was charged with raping a fourteen-year-old girl . . . who had been released to his wife's custody . . . [after she] had spent a period of time in a juvenile detention center. . . . [T]he appellant instructed the girl to disrobe, . . . threatening to send her back to the detention home if she did not comply. The victim acquiesced and, on several occasions thereafter, the appellant engaged in vaginal and oral intercourse with her. After conviction [on several charges] the appellant came before this court[, which] . . . ruled . . . that the rape and attempted rape charges must be reversed for lack of proof of forcible compulsion. Upon review, the Supreme Court was evenly divided and so the reversal by this court was sustained. The Supreme Court's opinion in support of affirmance . . . stated that . . . "certainly difficult choices have a coercive affect but the result is the product of the reason, albeit unpleasant and reluctantly made. The fact cannot

50. It is clear from a reading of the relevant statutes and accompanying case law that the rape and IDSI statutes rely on the same definitions. Therefore, despite the fact that this is an IDSI case, our discussion of rape laws and cases involving rape convictions is relevant to and probative of the issue before us.

be escaped that the victim has made the choice and the act is not involuntary." In his opinion in support of reversal, Justice Larsen . . . implored the legislature to correct what he characterized as a "misreading of its intention."

A correction by the legislature did not occur immediately after *Mlinarich* or even shortly thereafter. . . . [I]t was not until the Supreme Court's decision in Commonwealth v. Berkowitz, 537 Pa. 143, 641 A.2d 1161 (1994), that the legislature amended the law with respect to sexual assaults. *Berkowitz,* like the case before us, involved an incident between two young college students in a dormitory room. The complainant testified that she entered the appellant's room hoping to find his roommate. She stayed in the room at the appellant's request. At some point, the appellant moved toward the complainant, touched her breasts and attempted to put his penis in her mouth. He then removed her pants and undergarments and penetrated her vagina with his penis. Throughout the encounter, the complainant repeatedly told the appellant "no," but she made no attempt to leave even though she could have done so as the appellant was not restraining her in any manner.

Our Supreme Court considered the facts set out above and concluded that the element of forcible compulsion was not established. While recognizing that the complainant said "no" throughout the incident, the court stated that the legislature intended the term forcible compulsion to mean "something more than a lack of consent." 537 Pa. at 150, 641 A.2d at 1165. Berkowitz's rape conviction was reversed.

Less than one year after the *Berkowitz* decision, the legislature amended the sexual assault law by adding a definition for forcible compulsion. . . .

> "Forcible Compulsion." Compulsion by use of physical, intellectual, moral, emotional or psychological force, either express or implied. The term includes, but is not limited to, compulsion resulting in another person's death, whether the death occurred before, during or after sexual intercourse.

18 Pa. C.S.A. §3101.

It is this broader definition, argues appellant in this case, that prompts the necessity for a mistake of fact jury instruction in cases where such a defense is raised. According to appellant:

> The language of the present statute inextricably links the issues of consent with mens rea. To ask a jury to consider whether the defendant used "intellectual or moral" force, while denying the instruction as to how to consider the defendant's mental state at the time of alleged encounter, is patently unfair to the accused.

Appellant's argument is bolstered by the fact that the concept of "mistake of fact" has long been a fixture in the criminal law. The concept is codified in Pennsylvania and provides:

> Ignorance or mistake as to a matter of fact, for which there is reasonable explanation or excuse, is a defense if:
>
> > the ignorance or mistake negatives the intent, knowledge, belief, recklessness, or negligence required to establish a material element of the offense; or the law provides that the state of mind established by such ignorance or mistake constitutes a defense.

18 Pa. C.S.A. §304.

The notion that one charged with sexual assault may defend by claiming a reasonable belief of consent has been recognized in other jurisdictions. The New Jersey Supreme Court has stated:

> If there is evidence to suggest that the defendant reasonably believed that . . . permission had been given, the State must demonstrate either that the defendant did not actually believe that affirmative permission had been freely-given or that such belief was unreasonable under all of the circumstances.

In the Interest of M.T.S., 129 N.J. 422, 609 A.2d 1266, 1279 (1992).

Courts in other jurisdictions have likewise held that jury instructions regarding the defendant's reasonable belief as to consent are proper. See State v. Smith, 210 Conn. 132, 554 A.2d 713 (Conn. 1989) ("We agree with the California courts that a defendant is entitled to a jury instruction that a defendant may not be convicted of this crime if the words or conduct of the complainant under all the circumstances would justify a reasonable belief that she had consented."). See also People v. Mayberry, 15 Cal. 3d 143, 542 P.2d 1337, 125 Cal. Rptr. 745 (Cal. 1975).

Although the logic of these other cases is persuasive, we are unable to adopt the principles enunciated in them because of the binding precedent with which we are faced, namely, *Williams*. In an effort to avoid application of *Williams*, appellant directs our attention to the Subcommittee Notes of the Pennsylvania Criminal Suggested Standard Jury Instructions. The possible conflict between *Williams* and §304 (Mistake of Fact) was not lost on the Subcommittee.

> Quaere whether Williams is wholly consistent with Crimes Code §§302(c) and 304(1). In the Subcommittee's opinion, the courts should recognize as a defense a defendant's non-recklessly held, mistaken belief regarding consent. The jury ought to be told in what circumstances a mistaken belief may preclude a defendant's forceful conduct from being forcible compulsion or threat of forcible compulsion.

Subcommittee Note, Pa. Suggested Standard Crim. Jury Instructions at 15.3121A.

Appellant's insistence that *Williams* should be disregarded in light of the legislature's broader and more complex definition of forcible compulsion is echoed by the Subcommittee:

> In the opinion of the Subcommittee there may be cases, especially now that [the state supreme court] has extended the definition of force to psychological, moral and intellectual force, where a defendant might non-recklessly or even reasonably, but wrongly, believe that his words and conduct do not constitute force or the threat of force and that a non-resisting female is consenting. An example might be "date rape" resulting from mutual misunderstanding. The boy does not intend or suspect the intimidating potential of his vigorous wooing. The girl, misjudging the boy's character, believes he will become violent if thwarted; she feigns willingness, even some pleasure. In our opinion the defendant in such a case ought not to be convicted of rape.

It is clear that the Subcommittee gave extensive thought to the ever-changing law of sexual assault and our understanding of sexual behavior in modern times. We agree with the Subcommittee that the rule in *Williams* is inappropriate in the type of date rape case described above. Changing codes of sexual conduct, particularly those exhibited on college campuses, may require that we give greater weight to what is occurring beneath the overt actions of young men and women. Recognition of those changes, in the form of specified jury instructions, strikes us an appropriate course of action.

. . . Despite appellant's excellent presentation of the issues, there remain two distinct problems precluding relief in this case. First is appellant's reliance on the evolution of our sexual assault laws to avoid the application of *Williams*. As is obvious from our discussion above, the changes in the statute are significant and have served to extend culpability in rape and IDSI cases to a variety of new circumstances, including incidents involving psychological, moral and intellectual force.

. . . This case, however, is not one of the "new" varieties of sexual assault contemplated by the amended statute. It does not involve the failure to resist due to a tender age, . . . or the threat of punishment for failure to comply, as in *Mlinarich*. Nor is it a situation where the complainant admits she offered no resistance and the evidence shows that nothing prevented her escape, as in *Berkowitz*. This is a case of a young woman alleging physical force in a sexual assault and a young man claiming that he reasonably believed he had consent. In such circumstances, *Williams* controls.

We are keenly aware of the differences between *Williams* and this case. Most notable is the fact that Williams and his victim never met before the incident in question. Here, appellant and the victim not only knew one another, but had engaged in intimate contact just hours before the incident in question. It is clear however, that the *Williams* court's basis for denying the jury instruction was its conclusion that the law did not require it and, further, that the judiciary had no authority to grant it. Even if we were to disagree with those conclusions, we are powerless to alter them.

. . . Even if we decide that we are persuaded by appellant's arguments chronicling the history of sexual assault law and the Jury Instructions Subcommittee's views, we face a second barrier. Because this appeal raises ineffective assistance of counsel, we are required to find that appellant's trial lawyer made a mistake. That mistake is the failure to ask the trial court for an instruction that the *Williams* case held is unwarranted. In other words, we would have to find that counsel's failure to argue for a change in the law constituted ineffectiveness. This, of course, is not possible. We simply cannot announce a new rule of law and then find counsel ineffective for failing to predict same.

Assuming that we have the authority to declare that the instruction is one to which appellant should be entitled, we cannot hold that counsel erred in failing to demand it. The relief appellant seeks represents a significant departure from the current state of the law. Despite its compelling nature, it cannot be the basis for an ineffective assistance of counsel claim.

Judgment of sentence affirmed.

Notes and Questions

1. Does Pennsylvania rape law now require proof of negligence? Only where no physical force is used? Section 302 of the Pennsylvania Criminal Code includes provisions identical to Model Penal Code §§2.02(1), 2.02(3), and

2.02(4). Do these provisions require mens rea with respect to the element of "forcible compulsion"? What level of mens rea?

2. The previous cases have chiefly focused on the *actions* of the defendant (and of the victim). Does it make sense in the context of rape to treat these actions as elements of the actus reus of the crime and then shift the focus, as we have for other crimes, to the required mens rea? What if Barnes, for example, had conceded, in retrospect, that Marsha had not consented to have intercourse, but he nevertheless argued that at the time of the alleged rape he honestly, and perhaps reasonably, had believed that she was consenting? Does a claim of mistake of fact seem plausible in a case like this? If the use of force or the absence of consent is an element of the crime of rape, is the defendant entitled to argue that he lacked the requisite mens rea for that element? (Note that the court cites both State v. Smith and In the Interest of M.T.S.) If so, what level of culpability should be required? Do *Smith* and *M.T.S.* in effect require mens rea with respect to nonconsent? If so, what level of mens rea?

3. In People v. Mayberry, 15 Cal. 3d 143, 542 P.2d 1337, 125 Cal. Rptr. 745 (1975), the victim was walking to a grocery store when Mayberry began harassing her and grabbed hold of her arm. He released her after she "dug her fingernails into his wrist," but after she turned to leave, he kicked her, struck her with a bottle, and shouted obscenities at her. He then followed her into the store, and then she accompanied him outside; it was unclear from the evidence whether any passersby were available to help her. When Mayberry proposed having sex, the woman refused, and he then hit her in the chest, knocked her to the ground, and uttered threats. Hoping to "buy time," she told him she wanted to buy some cigarettes. Feeling "completely beaten" and doubting that the storekeeper would help her, she left the store without asking for help. She went with the defendant to his apartment, where she tried to persuade him to "change his mind." The defendant, "without her consent," then engaged in several sexual acts with her, during which he apparently struck and caused bruises over several parts of her body.

On appeal, the state Supreme Court sustained the jury's finding that the woman had not consented. But in the court's view, the defendant's mens rea argument was another matter altogether.

> The [trial] court refused to give requested instructions that directed the jury to acquit Franklin of the rape and kidnaping if the jury had a reasonable doubt as to whether Franklin reasonably and genuinely believed that Miss B. freely consented to her movement from the grocery store to his apartment and to sexual intercourse with him. Franklin contends that the court thereby erred. The Attorney General argues that the court properly refused to give the instructions because "mistake of fact instruction[s] as to consent should be rejected as against the law and public policy." . . .
>
> Penal Code section 26 recites, generally, that one is incapable of committing a crime who commits an act under a mistake of fact disproving any criminal intent. Penal Code section 20 provides, "In every crime . . . there must exist a union, or joint operation of act and intent, or criminal negligence." The word "intent" in section 20 means "wrongful intent." (See People v. Vogel, 46 Cal. 2d 798, 801, fn. 2, 299 P.2d 850.) "So basic is this requirement [of a union of act and wrongful intent] that it is an invariable element of every crime unless excluded expressly or by necessary implication." (Id., at p. 801, 299 P.2d at p. 853.). . .
>
> . . . If a defendant entertains a reasonable and bona fide belief that a prosecutrix voluntarily consented to accompany him and to engage in sexual

intercourse, it is apparent he does not possess the wrongful intent that is a pre-requisite under Penal Code section 20 to a conviction of either kidnaping (§207) or rape by means of force or threat (§261, subds. 2 & 3). . . .

. . . However, Franklin's testimony . . . could be viewed as indicating that he reasonably and in good faith believed that Miss B. consented to accompany him to the apartment and to the subsequent sexual intercourse. In addition, part of Miss B.'s testimony furnishes support for the requested instructions. It appears from her testimony that her behavior was equivocal. Although she did not want Franklin to think she was consenting, her "act" and admitted failure physically to resist him after the initial encounter or to attempt to escape or obtain help might have misled him as to whether she was consenting. We by no means intimate that such is the *only* reasonable interpretation of her conduct, but we do conclude that there was some evidence "deserving of . . . consideration" which supported his contention that he acted under a mistake of fact as to her consent both to the movement and to intercourse. It follows, accordingly, that the requested instructions, if correctly worded, should have been given. 15 Cal. 3d at 151, 154-57.

On retrial, what evidence could Mayberry offer to persuade the jury that he honestly and reasonably believed the woman was consenting, if the jury must treat as an established fact that the woman did not in fact consent?[51]

4. *The policy debate.* Professor Susan Estrich has proposed eliminating the force element and conditioning rape liability on nonconsent plus negligence. Estrich argues that shifting the legal focus to the defendant's mens rea would benefit rape victims:[52]

> To treat what the defendant intended or knew or even should have known about the victim's consent as irrelevant to his liability sounds like a result favorable to both prosecution and women as victims. But experience makes all too clear that it is not. To refuse to inquire into mens rea leaves two possibilities: turning rape into a strict liability offense where, in the absence of consent, the man is guilty of rape regardless of whether he (or anyone) would have recognized nonconsent in the circumstances; or defining the crime of rape in a fashion that is so limited that it would be virtually impossible for any man to be convicted where he was truly unaware or mistaken as to nonconsent. In fact, it is the latter approach which has characterized all of the older, and many of the newer, American cases. In practice, abandoning mens rea produces the worst of all possible worlds: The trial emerges not as an inquiry into the guilt of the defendant (is he a rapist?) but of the victim (was she really raped? did she consent?). The perspective that governs is therefore not that of the woman, nor even of the particular man, but of a judicial system intent upon protecting against unjust conviction, regardless of the dangers of injustice to the woman in the particular case.

51. A later development in California underscores the difficulty of distinguishing actual manifest consent from the defendant's reasonably mistaken perception of consent. In one case the court ruled that the reasonable-mistake-of-fact instruction should only be given where there is "substantial evidence of equivocal conduct [by the complainant] that would have led a defendant to reasonably and in good faith believe consent existed where it did not." People v. Williams, 4 Cal. 4th 354, 841 P.2d 961, 964-65 (1992). In a critique of this decision, Professor Rosanna Cavallaro argues that it illogically denies the mistake defense to a defendant "those who give the most persuasive and consistent account of events," while [a] defendant who describes an encounter in which the complainant's conduct was admittedly equivocal as to consent essentially concedes that point and is doomed to almost certain conviction." A Big Mistake: Eroding the Defense of Mistake of Fact About Consent in Rape, 86 J. Crim. L. & Criminology 815, 838-39 (1996). Does the *Williams* rule unfairly prevent a defendant from pleading in the alternative that the complainant actually consented *and* that, even if she was did not consent, he reasonably inferred that she had?

52. Rape, 95 Yale L.J. 1087, 1099-1101 (1986).

The requirement that sexual intercourse be accompanied by force or threat of force to constitute rape provides a man with some protection against mistakes as to consent. A man who uses a gun or knife against his victim is not likely to be in serious doubt as to her lack of consent, and the more narrowly force is defined, the more implausible the claim that he was unaware of nonconsent.

But the law's protection of men is not limited to a requirement of force. Rather than inquire whether the man believed (reasonably or unreasonably) that his victim was consenting, the courts have demanded that the victim demonstrate her nonconsent by engaging in resistance that will leave no doubt as to nonconsent. The definition of nonconsent as resistance — in the older cases, as utmost resistance, while in some more recent ones, as "reasonable" physical resistance — functions as a substitute for mens rea to ensure that the man has notice of the woman's nonconsent.

The choice between focusing on the man's intent or focusing on the woman's is not simply a doctrinal flip of the coin.

First, the inquiry into the victim's nonconsent puts the woman, not the man, on trial. Her intent, not his, is disputed; and because her state of mind is key, her sexual history may be considered relevant (even though utterly unknown to the man). Considering consent from *his* perspective, by contrast, substantially undermines the relevance of the woman's sexual history where it was unknown to the man.

Second, . . . the resistance requirement is not only ill-conceived as a definition of nonconsent, but is an overbroad substitute for mens rea in any event. The application of the resistance requirement has not been limited to cases in which there was uncertainty as to what the man thought, knew or intended; it has been fully applied in cases where there can be no question that the man knew that intercourse was without consent. Indeed, most of the cases that have dismissed claims that mens rea ought to be required have been cases where both force and resistance were present, and where there was no danger of any unfairness.

Finally, by ignoring mens rea, American courts and legislators have imposed limits on the fair expansion of our understanding of rape. As long as the law holds that mens rea is not required, and that no instructions on intent need be given, pressure will exist to retain some form of resistance requirement and to insist on force as conventionally defined in order to protect men against conviction for "sex." Using resistance as a substitute for mens rea unnecessarily and unfairly immunizes those men whose victims are afraid enough, or intimidated enough, or, frankly, smart enough, not to take the risk of resisting physically. In doing so, the resistance test may declare the blameworthy man innocent and the raped woman guilty.

Professor Lynne Henderson disagrees:[53]

Estrich's analysis has two flaws. First, her assertion that American courts ignore the issue of mens rea to consent is wrong. Second, she is mistaken in thinking that shifting attention to the man's mental state about consent and reducing the mens rea requirement to negligence will relieve the victim of the burden of physical resistance and of having to "prove" she was raped. Estrich contends that absent a mens rea requirement for consent, the question becomes "was this woman raped?" rather than "is this man a rapist?" In fact, focusing on whether or not the man believed he had no consent is no solution at all. First, it returns us to the dangers of the focus on consent of the nineteenth century. Second, the methods of proving mens rea will continue to focus attention on the woman and her credibility. . . .

. . . Absent a confession or admission by the defendant, the prosecutor must introduce evidence of the circumstances surrounding the event to prove mens rea.

53. Review Essay: What Makes Rape a Crime? 3 Berkeley Women's L.J. 193, 211-14 (1988).

Consequently, although the woman's subjective state may not be an issue, her behavior is certainly relevant to establishing whether the defendant "honestly and reasonably" believed that she consented. Thus, resistance once more becomes an issue. . . . Because the defendant in a criminal prosecution has the sixth amendment right to confront his accuser, inquiries focusing on the defendant's mens rea as to consent are [also] likely to reopen the door to more extensive explorations of a victim's sexual past.

Professor David Bryden[54] expresses skepticism whether the focus on the defendant's mens rea or mistake will make a difference in jurisdictions that retain the force-resistance rule, because juries are unlikely to believe that a defendant who used force on a resisting victim honestly believed she consented. Bryden[55] suggests that litigation over mistake will be rare in any event, because in addition to ambiguous cases of consent being screened out before trial, few rape defendants will find it in their interest to argue mistake: "[A] defendant who claims that the victim consented may still get the benefit of jurors' speculation that he made an understandable mistake and should not be punished. Unless he is unusually honest, or the facts are unusually clear, he has no reason to concede that she did not consent, and therefore no reason to assert a mistake defense." Where mistake is litigated now, defendants rarely testify, with the following consequences:[56]

Generally, mistake is a defense to crime when the factual mistake makes the requisite criminal intent impossible. To satisfy the first doctrinal element of the reasonable belief defense, then, a defendant must claim that he did not have the requisite mens rea for the crime of rape because he genuinely and honestly believed the victim was consenting. If he believed, even mistakenly, that the victim was consenting, then he merely intended to have consensual sexual intercourse and had no criminal intent at all.

In practice, this "subjective" aspect of the defense (i.e., did the defendant honestly believe the victim consented) is virtually ignored. Because defendants are entitled to raise the reasonable belief defense without testifying, juries evaluate the defendant's reasonable belief defense without hearing him testify that he in fact believed the victim consented. Moreover, when the defendant does not so testify, a jury may be instructed on the reasonable belief defense if the victim's testimony about *her own* behavior suggests the possibility of reasonable mistake. Thus, the courts focus on the victim's behavior, not the defendant's subjective belief that the victim consented.

The subjective prong of the defense is further discounted because, in practice, the courts have improperly collapsed the two elements. That is, instead of determining whether a *particular* defendant *honestly* believed his victim consented and then whether that belief was reasonable, courts ask whether *any* defendant could have *reasonably* believed the victim consented.

Is it necessarily improper for factfinders to focus on what the defendant could have reasonably believed under the circumstances, rather than requiring the defendant to testify as to his actual beliefs? Isn't this focus almost required by the prosecution's burden to prove mens rea beyond a reasonable doubt?

54. Redefining Rape, at 166-69.
55. Id. at 199-200.
56. Dana Berliner, Note, Rethinking the Reasonable Belief Defense to Rape, 100 Yale L.J. 2687, 2694-95 (1991).

K. EVIDENTIARY REFORMS

Though rules of evidence and procedure fall outside the scope of a book on substantive criminal law, a brief review of changes in evidentiary and procedural rules peculiar to rape cases helps illuminate the evolution of the substantive doctrines of rape.

1. *The "cautionary instruction."* In 1680 Sir Matthew Hale enunciated a famous admonition about rape cases that has influenced the criminal law in the centuries since:

> It is true, rape is a most detestable crime, and therefore ought to severely and impartially be punished with death, but it must be remembered that it is an accusation easily to be made and hard to be proved and harder to be defended by the party accused, thou never so innocent.[57]

This admonition, probably unique to rape cases, was incorporated, often literally, in jury instructions for most of the three centuries since uttered. In recent years, however, most jurisdictions have dropped this practice entirely.

2. *Corroboration and prompt complaint rules.* At common law, a prosecutor trying to win a rape case often confronted serious obstacles in the "corroboration" rule and the "prompt complaint" rule. Both these rules resulted in rape prosecutions being barred or dismissed as a matter of law, no matter how strong the state's case and no matter how plausible the explanation for the lack of corroboration or the delay in the report. Consider this early statement from Davis v. State, 120 Ga. 433, 48 S.E. 180 (1904):

> . . . The law is well established . . . that a man shall not be convicted of rape on the testimony of the woman alone, unless there are some concurrent circumstances which tend to corroborate her evidence. The offense of rape seems to be an exceptional one in this regard. The accused should not be convicted upon the woman's testimony alone, however positive it may be, unless she made some outcry or told of the injury promptly, or her clothing was torn or disarranged, or her persons showed signs of violence, or there were other circumstances which tend to corroborate her story. This rule appears to us to be a sound one. Without it, every man is in danger of being prosecuted and convicted on the testimony of a base woman in whose testimony there is no truth. Of course every woman, when she makes up her mind to prosecute for the offense, will testify that the sexual act was accomplished by force and without her consent. The man is powerless. . . . Our people, be it said to their credit, reverence innocence and virtue in the female sex. When a charge of this sort is made, the people, and the jurors likewise, are apt to let their indignation get the better of their judgment and convict upon evidence which does not authorize it. [120 Ga. at 435.]

In *Davis,* the complainant was a sickly woman who arguably was so enfeebled that she could not resist at all and hence evidenced no signs of violence; further, she did not mention the attack to neighbors whom she encountered soon after because she wanted to first tell her husband, whom she could not immediately find.

---

57. The History of Pleas of the Crown I, LVIII *635 (1680).

Half a century later in State v. Anderson, 137 N.W.2d 781 (Minn. 1965), a father was convicted of committing incest on his 17-year-old daughter. She testified that he had regularly had intercourse with her over the previous five years, during which she made no report to anyone. Reversing the conviction, the court cited the 70-year-old authority of State v. Connelly, 57 Minn. 482, 485, 59 N.W. 479, 481 (1894):

> It is so natural as to be almost inevitable that a female upon whom the crime has been committed will make immediate complaint, if she have a mother or other confidential friend to whom she can make it. The rule is founded upon the laws of human nature.

But the *Anderson* court cited contemporary authority as well, including the eminent Wigmore treatise, 7 Wigmore, Evidence (3 ed.) §2062 ("The unchaste (let us call it) mentality finds incidental but direct expression in the narration of imaginary sex-incidents of which the narrator is the heroine or the victim."); Professor Glanville Williams, Corroboration — Sexual Cases 1962 Criminal L. Rev. 662 ("sexual cases are particularly subject to the danger of deliberately false charges, resulting from sexual neurosis, phantasy, jealousy, spite, or simply a girl's refusal to admit that she consented to an act of which she is now ashamed"); and even the famed psychiatrist Karl Menninger:

> "[F]antasies of rape are exceedingly common in women, indeed one may almost say that they are probably universal.... Of course, the normal woman who has such a fantasy does not confuse it with reality, but it is so easy for some neurotic individuals to translate their fantasies into actual beliefs and memory falsifications that I think a safeguard should certainly be placed upon this type of criminal charge."
> [Cited in 7 Wigmore, Evidence (3 ed.) §2062.]

Professor Morrison Torrey ascribes the notion that a high proportion of rape complaints are unfounded to a variety of "rape myths," including the notion that women make complaints out of fantasy or vengeance or as blackmail.[58] She notes that when police departments characterize complaints as "unfounded," the cases might be dropped because of mundane problems of procedure of evidence-gathering of the sort that typically thwart prosecutions for other crimes. In fact, she asserts, most well-founded rape claims are never reported to the police at all.[59]

In recent years, corroboration and prompt complaint rules have virtually disappeared, and lack of corroboration or prompt complaint are evidentiary factors for the jurors to weigh as they see fit. Consider Pennsylvania Criminal Code §§3105-06 (2002):

§3105. Prompt Complaint

Prompt reporting to public authority is not required in a prosecution under this chapter. Provided, however, that nothing in this section shall be construed to prohibit a defendant from introducing evidence of the complainant's failure to

---

58. When Will We Be Believed? Rape Myths and the Idea of Fair Trial in Rape Prosecutions, 24 U.C. Davis L. Rev. 1013, 1025 (1991).
59. Id. at 1029-31.

promptly report the crime if such evidence would be admissible pursuant to the rules of evidence.

§3106. Testimony of Complainants

The credibility of a complainant of an offense under this chapter shall be determined by the same standard as is the credibility of a complainant of any other crime. The testimony of a complainant need not be corroborated in prosecutions under this chapter. No instructions shall be given cautioning the jury to view the complainant's testimony in any other way than that in which all complainants' testimony is viewed.

3. *The complainant's sexual history.* Well into the twentieth century, rape defendants were permitted to cross-examine complainants about, or put on independence evidence of, the complainant's history of sexual conduct. An early statement of this point of evidence law puts the reason all too bluntly. In People v. Abbott, 19 Wend. 192 (N.Y. 1838), the defendant, a clergyman, appealed his rape conviction on the ground that the trial court wrongly forbade him to question the complainant about her previous sexual conduct with other men.

> The question to the prosecutrix herself, whether she had not had previous criminal connection with other men, was, I think, proper. . . . Any fact tending to the inference that there was not the utmost resistance, is always received. . . . [A]re we to be told that previous prostitution shall not make one among those circumstances which raise a doubt of assent? That the triers should be advised to make no distinction between the virgin and a tenant of the stew? Between one who would prefer death to pollution, and another who, incited by lust and lucre, daily offers her person to the indiscriminate embraces of the other sex? . . . [W]ill you not more readily infer assent in the practiced Messalina, in loose attire, than in the reserved and virtuous Lucretia? . . . No court can overrule the law of human nature, which declares that one who has already started on the road of prostitution, would be less reluctant to pursue her way, than another who remains at her home of innocence. . . . [Id. at 192-93.]

A similar statement can be found over a century later in Packineau v. United States, 202 F.2d 681 (8th Cir. 1953), where a man accused of raping a young woman during an evening of socializing and drinking sought to introduce evidence that she had once cohabited with another man for a week:

> . . . It might be that there are cases were a woman has been set upon and forcibly ravished by strangers coming out of ambush or the like and any inquiry as to her chastity or lack of it is irrelevant.
>
> But in this case the prosecutrix . . . was a "very refined girl, who attended school at the Indian Agency and then went to high school and was attending Haskell, the Indian School at Lawrence, Kansas, where she was preparing herself for nurse's training." Her appearance and the evidence concerning her antecedents tended to enhance the credibility of her testimony, and to offset the unfavorable inferences that might otherwise have been drawn from the part of her night's adventures that were admittedly of her own volition. . . .
>
> That her story of having been raped would be more readily believed by a person who was ignorant of any former unchaste conduct on her part than it would be by a person cognizant of the unchaste conduct defendants offered to prove against her seems too clear for argument. [Id. at 685.]

Can you follow the court's logic? Inquiry into the complainant's sexual history surely does increase the chance of acquittal, but should it? Does it indicate consent on the relevant occasion? Does it indicate dishonesty? Or may it merely decrease the jury's sympathy for the victim?

4. *Rape-shield laws.* In recent years, virtually all states have passed so-called rape-shield laws to address the concerns that evidence of the complainant's sexual history operates to (a) promote the notion that only "chaste" woman deserve the protection of rape laws, and (b) reinforce jurors' perception that past consent to sex necessarily implies consent on the occasion generalizes to the encounter being prosecuted. Legislatures were motivated by arguments and studies showing that juries tended overwhelmingly to favor the defendant in any case where they heard evidence of the complainant's past consensual sexual conduct.[60]

Federal Rule of Evidence 412 is fairly typical:

Rule 412. Sex Offense Cases; Relevance of Victim's Past Sexual Behavior or Predisposition

(a) Evidence generally inadmissible. Evidence of past sexual behavior or predisposition of an alleged victim of sexual misconduct is not admissible in any civil or criminal proceeding except as provided in subdivisions (b) and (c).

(b) Exceptions. Evidence of the past sexual behavior or predisposition of an alleged victim of sexual misconduct may be admitted only if it is otherwise admissible under these rules and is —

(1) evidence of specific instances of sexual behavior with someone other than the person accused of the sexual misconduct, when offered to prove that the other person was the source of semen, other physical evidence, or injury;

(2) evidence of specific instances of sexual behavior with the person accused of the sexual misconduct, when offered to prove consent by the alleged victim;

(3) evidence of specific instances of sexual behavior, when offered in a criminal case in circumstances where exclusion of the evidence would violate the constitutional rights of the defendant. . . .

(c) Procedure to determine admissibility. Evidence must not be offered under this rule unless the proponent obtains leave of court by a motion filed under seal, specifically describing the evidence and stating the purposes for which it will be offered. The motion must be served on the alleged victim and the parties and must be filed at least 15 days before trial unless the court directs an earlier filing or, for good cause shown, permits a later filing.

After giving the parties and the alleged victim an opportunity to be heard in chambers, the court must determine whether, under what conditions, and in what manner and form the evidence may be admitted. The motion and the record of any hearing in chambers must, unless otherwise ordered, remain under seal.

---

60. Anderson, From Chastity Requirement to Sexual License, *supra*, at 104-05, Bryden & Lengnick, *supra*, at 1257-70. On the other hand, some argue that these studies are no longer relevant because they predated constitutional and legislative changes in jury selection that have greatly increased female representation on criminal juries. E.g., Christina Carmody Tilley, A Feminist Criticism of the Rape Shield Laws, 51 Drake L. Rev. 45, 66-73 (2002).

Perhaps the most notable exception to the ban on the complainant's sexual history is that for evidence of past sexual conduct with the defendant himself. Why does the law distinguish this evidence from that of past consensual sex with persons other than the defendant? Is it categorically more logical to infer present consent to sex from the complainant's previous consensual sex with the defendant than it is in regard to sex with "third parties"?[61]

The most comprehensive study of these laws is Michelle J. Anderson, From Chastity Requirement to Sexuality License: Sexual Consent and a New Rape Shield Law, 70 G.W. L. Rev. 51 (2002). Anderson shows how these laws take on a number of forms; the majority, like the Federal Rule, legislate specific exceptions to the presumptive ban on evidence of the complainant's sexual history; others grant judges discretion to create exceptions; or permit sexual history evidence only when it goes to the complaining witness's credibility if she testifies, not to the issue of consent, or require exceptions where necessary to protect the defendant's constitutional right to present exculpatory evidence (see *infra*). Id. at 81-86.

As for the exceptions to the rape shield, a few states, by either statute or judicial decision, go beyond the federal rule by adding an exception for evidence of past sexual conduct with third parties where it establishes an arguably relevant "pattern" of sexual activity with third parties. E.g., Fla. Stat. Ann. 704.022(2) ("a pattern of conduct or behavior on the part of the victim which is so similar to the conduct or behavior in the case that it is relevant to the issue of consent.") Thus, while the rape-shield law generally presumes that past sexual relations with others are situation-bound and cannot support generalizations, some patterns of past sexual activity are said to establish a "modus operandi." State v. Shofner, 302 N.E.2d 830, 832 (N.C. App. 1983). Thus in United States v. Kelly, 33 M.J. 878 (A.M.C.R. 1991), the court admitted evidence, otherwise banned by the rape-shield law, that the complainant had over the previous two years frequently engaged in sexually aggressive conduct while intoxicated. Professor Anderson criticizes this and other "pattern" holdings as prejudicially inferring a general pattern of promiscuous consensual sex from behavior that, in light of modern sexual mores and trends in social activity, support no such inference.[62]

Moreover, whether mentioned in a rape shield law or not, a defendant's Sixth Amendment rights to present exculpatory evidence (the Sixth Amendment's Compulsory Process clause) or to cross-examine or rebut his accusers (the Confrontation Clause) must, where they apply, trump any state-created, constitutional shield law. But drawing the line between the shield laws' legitimate boundaries on relevancy and these vague constitutional commands is not easy. In State v. Colbath, the defendant charged with raping a woman after meeting her in a bar sought to present evidence that the complainant had earlier that day engaged in aggressively suggestive behavior toward several men in the bar. The court ruled that the defendant's Sixth Amendment rights trumped the shield law in cases where such "public displays of general interest in sexual activity can be taken to indicate a contemporaneous receptiveness to sexual

---

61. In this regard, note that though these shield laws are often viewed as the equivalent of certain evidentiary privileges (clergy-parishioner, therapist-patient, husband-wife, attorney-client) that are expressly designed to exclude otherwise perfectly relevant evidence to protect the privacy of certain relationships, shield laws are in fact rules defining what evidence is relevant in the first place.

62. 70 G.W. L. Rev. at 101-05, 140-41.

advances that cannot be inferred from evidence of private behavior with chosen sex partners." 540 A.2d 212 (N.H. 1988).[63]

Professor Anderson concludes that the various exceptions to the shield laws have been construed so broadly as to significantly nullify the shield laws' stated goals. She therefore proposes a new kind of "sexuality license" for women in the form of a virtually categorical shield law. Under this law, no particular past act of consensual sex, or communications about sex with any third party or with the defendant would never lose its "unique, nontransferable" character.[64]

5. *Assessing the success of rape law reform.* How successful have the substantive, procedural, and evidentiary reforms in rape law been in improving rape law enforcement? One major study of rape prosecutions in Michigan before and after major statutory reforms finds only weak evidence of great change in terms of conviction and incarceration of rape defendants generally. Nevertheless, it finds some modest evidence of an increased number of cases of "simple" rape (defined as cases between nonstrangers and not involving great extrinsic physical injury) being reported and bound over for trial.[65] In addition, a report on a survey questionnaire of college students reports that attitudes about women's sexual autonomy changed between 1992 and 1997 in the direction of recognizing claims of rape in nonstranger cases and suggests that changes in laws may be one cause.[66]

L. MARITAL RAPE

PEOPLE v. LIBERTA
New York Court of Appeals
64 N.Y.2d 152, 485 N.Y.S.2d 207 (1984)

WACHTLER, J.

The defendant, while living apart from his wife pursuant to a Family Court order, forcibly raped . . . her in the presence of their 2½ year old son. Under the New York Penal Law a married man ordinarily cannot be prosecuted for raping . . . his wife. The defendant, however, though married at the time of the incident, is treated as an unmarried man under the Penal Law because of the Family Court order. On this appeal, he contends that because of the exemption

---

63. One remarkable exception to the rape-shield law arose in State v. Jacques, 558 A.2d 706 (Me. 1989), where the defendant was prosecuted for molesting two children, aged five and ten. Uncontested evidence showed that these children had previously been sexually molested by persons other than the defendant. The defendant sought to introduce this evidence, but the trial court refused, citing the state rape shield law, which tracked the federal rule. The appellate court reversed, stating, "A defendant . . . must be permitted to rebut the inference a jury might otherwise draw that the victim was so naive sexually that she could not have fabricated the charge." It added that "recognizing the jury's natural assumption that children are innocent of sexual matters," Jacques legitimately sought "to rebut the inference that he was responsible for their unusual sexual knowledge." Id. at 708.

64. 70 G.W. L. Rev. at 1401-2. The key exception in her proposed rule would be for "[e]vidence of negotiations between the complainant and the defendant to convey consent in a specific way or to engage in a specific sexual act at issue." Id. at 147.

65. Cassia C. Spohn & Julie Horney, The Impact of Rape Law Reform on the Processing of Simple and Aggravated Rape Cases, 86 J. Crim. L. & Criminology 861 (1996).

66. George C. Thomas III & David Edelman, Consent to Have Sex: Empirical Evidence About "No", 61 U. Pitt. L. Rev. 579 (2000).

for married men, the statutes for rape in the first degree (Penal Law §130.35) . . . violate the equal protection clause of the federal constitution (U.S. Const., Amend. 14). . . .

Defendant Mario Liberta and Denise Liberta were married in 1978. Shortly after the birth of their son, in October of that year, Mario began to beat Denise. In early 1980 Denise brought a proceeding in the Family Court in Erie County seeking protection from the defendant. On April 30, 1980, a temporary order of protection was issued to her by the Family Court. Under this order, the defendant was to move out and remain away from the family home, and stay away from Denise. The order provided that the defendant could visit with his son once each weekend.

On the weekend of March 21st, 1981, Mario, who was then living in a motel, did not visit his son. On Tuesday, March 24, 1981, he called Denise to ask if he could visit his son on that day. Denise would not allow the defendant to come to her house, but she did agree to allow him to pick up their son and her and take them both back to his motel after being assured that a friend of his would be with them at all times. The defendant and his friend picked up Denise and their son and the four of them drove to defendant's motel.

When they arrived at the motel the friend left. As soon as only Mario, Denise, and their son were alone in the motel room, Mario attacked Denise, threatened to kill her, and forced her . . . to engage in sexual intercourse with him. The son was in the room during the entire episode, and the defendant forced Denise to tell their son to watch what the defendant was doing to her.

The defendant allowed Denise and their son to leave shortly after the incident. Denise, after going to her parents' home, went to a hospital to be treated for scratches on her neck and bruises on her head and back, all inflicted by her husband. She also went to the police station, and on the next day she swore out a felony complaint against the defendant. On July 15, 1981, the defendant was indicted for rape in the first degree and sodomy in the first degree. [The defendant was convicted of rape in the first degree and the conviction was affirmed by the Appellate Division.] . . .

Section 130.35 of the Penal Law provides in relevant part that "A male is guilty of rape in the first degree when he engages in sexual intercourse with a female . . . by forcible compulsion." "Female," for purposes of the rape statute, is defined as "any female person not married to the actor" (Penal Law §130.00, subd. 4). . . . Thus, due to the "not married" language in the definitions of "female" . . . there is a "marital exemption" for . . . forcible rape. . . . The marital exemption itself, however, has certain exceptions. For purposes of the rape . . . [statute], a husband and wife are considered to be "not married" if at the time of the sexual assault they "are living apart . . . pursuant to a valid and effective (i) order issued by a court of competent jurisdiction which by its terms or in its effect requires such living apart, or (ii) decree or judgment of separation, or (iii) written agreement of separation. . . ." (Penal Law §130.00, subd. 4.). . .

Defendant asserts on this appeal that . . . he cannot be convicted of . . . rape in the first degree . . . because [the statute is] unconstitutional. Specifically, he contends that [the statute] violate[s] equal protection because [it] burden[s] some, but not all males (all but those within the "marital exemption"). . . . The lower courts rejected the defendant's constitutional arguments, finding that [the] statute [did not] violate the equal protection clause in the Fourteenth Amendment. Although we affirm the conviction of the defendant, we do not agree with the constitutional analysis of the lower courts and instead conclude that the marital . . . [exemption] must be read out of the statutes prohibiting forcible rape. . . .

As noted above, under the Penal Law a married man ordinarily cannot be convicted of forcibly raping . . . his wife. . . . Although a marital exemption was not explicit in earlier rape statutes, an 1852 treatise stated that a man could not be guilty of raping his wife (O.L. Barbour, Treatise on the Criminal Law of the State of New York, 69). The assumption, even before the marital exemption was codified, that a man could not be guilty of raping his wife, is traceable to a statement made by the seventeenth century English jurist Lord Hale, who wrote: "[T]he husband cannot be guilty of a rape committed by himself upon his lawful wife, for by their mutual matrimonial consent and contract the wife hath given up herself in this kind unto her husband, which she cannot retract" (1 M. Hale, The History of the Pleas of the Crown, 629). Although Hale cited no authority for his statement it was relied on by state legislatures which enacted rape statutes with a marital exemption and by courts which established a common law exemption for husbands.

The first American case to recognize the marital exemption was decided in 1857 by the Supreme Judicial Court of Massachusetts, which stated in dictum that it would always be a defense to rape to show marriage to the victim (Commonwealth v. Fogerty, 74 Mass. 489). Decisions to the same effect by other courts followed, usually with no rationale or authority cited other than Hale's implied consent view. In New York, a 1922 decision noted the marital exemption in the Penal Law and stated that it existed "on account of the matrimonial consent which [the wife] has given, and which she cannot retract" (People v. Meli, 193 N.Y.S. 365, 366 [Sup. Ct.]).

Presently, over forty states still retain some form of marital exemption for rape. While the marital exemption is subject to an equal protection challenge, because it classifies unmarried men differently than married men, the equal protection clause does not prohibit a state from making classifications, provided the statute does not arbitrarily burden a particular group of individuals. Where a statute draws a distinction based upon marital status, the classification must be reasonable and must be based upon "some ground of difference that rationally explains the different treatment" . . . (Eisenstadt v. Baird, 405 U.S. 437, 447).

We find that there is no rational basis for distinguishing between marital rape and non-marital rape. The various rationales which have been asserted in defense of the exemption are either based upon archaic notions about the consent and property rights incident to marriage or are simply unable to withstand even the slightest scrutiny. We therefore declare the marital exemption for rape in the New York statute to be unconstitutional.

Lord Hale's notion of an irrevocable implied consent by a married woman to sexual intercourse has been cited most frequently in support of the marital exemption. Any argument based on a supposed consent, however, is untenable. Rape is not simply a sexual act to which one party does not consent. Rather, it is a degrading, violent act which violates the bodily integrity of the victim and frequently causes severe, long-lasting physical and psychic harm. To ever imply consent to such an act is irrational and absurd. Other than in the context of rape statutes, marriage has never been viewed as giving a husband the right to coerced intercourse on demand. Certainly, then, a marriage license should not be viewed as a license for a husband to forcibly rape his wife with impunity. A married woman has the same right to control her own body as does an unmarried woman. If a husband feels "aggrieved" by his wife's refusal to engage in sexual intercourse, he should seek relief in the courts governing domestic relations, not in "violent or forceful self-help."

The other traditional justifications for the marital exemption were the common law doctrines that a woman was the property of her husband and that the legal existence of the woman was "incorporated and consolidated into that of the husband" (1 Blackstone, Commentaries on the Laws of England, 430 [1966 ed.]). Both these doctrines, of course, have long been rejected in this state. . . .

Because the traditional justifications for the marital exemption no longer have any validity, other arguments have been advanced in its defense. The first of these recent rationales, which is stressed by the People in this case, is that the marital exemption protects against governmental intrusion into marital privacy and promotes reconciliation of the spouses, and thus that elimination of the exemption would be disruptive to marriages. While protecting marital privacy and encouraging reconciliation are legitimate state interests, there is no rational relation between allowing a husband to forcibly rape his wife and these interests. The marital exemption simply does not further marital privacy because this right of privacy protects consensual acts, not violent sexual assaults. Just as a husband cannot invoke a right of marital privacy to escape liability for beating his wife, he cannot justifiably rape his wife under the guise of a right to privacy.

Similarly, it is not tenable to argue that elimination of the marital exemption would disrupt marriages because it would discourage reconciliation. Clearly, it is the violent act of rape and not the subsequent attempt of the wife to seek protection through the criminal justice system which "disrupts" a marriage. Moreover, if the marriage has already reached the point where intercourse is accomplished by violent assault it is doubtful that there is anything left to reconcile. This, of course, is particularly true if the wife is willing to bring criminal charges against her husband which could result in a lengthy jail sentence.

Another rationale sometimes advanced in support of the marital exemption is that marital rape would be a difficult crime to prove. A related argument is that allowing such prosecutions could lead to fabricated complaints by "vindictive" wives. The difficulty of proof argument is based on the problem of showing lack of consent. Proving lack of consent, however, is often the most difficult part of any rape prosecution, particularly where the rapist and the victim had a prior relationship.

Similarly, the possibility that married women will fabricate complaints would seem to be no greater than the possibility of unmarried women doing so. The criminal justice system, with all of its built-in safeguards, is presumed to be capable of handling any false complaints. Indeed, if the possibility of fabricated complaints were a basis for not criminalizing behavior which would otherwise be sanctioned, virtually all crimes other than homicides would go unpunished.

The final argument in defense of the marital exemption is that marital rape is not as serious an offense as other rape and is thus adequately dealt with by the possibility of prosecution under criminal statutes, such as assault statutes, which provide for less severe punishment. The fact that rape statutes exist, however, is a recognition that the harm caused by a forcible rape is different, and more severe, than the harm caused by an ordinary assault. . . . Moreover, there is no evidence to support the argument that marital rape has less severe consequences than other rape. On the contrary, numerous studies have shown that marital rape is frequently quite violent and generally has *more* severe, traumatic effects on the victim than other rape.

Among the recent decisions in this country addressing the marital exemption, only one court has concluded that there is a rational basis for it (see People v. Brown, 632 P.2d 1025 [Colo.]). We agree with the other courts which have analyzed the exemption, which have been unable to find any present justification for it. . . . [T]he marital exemption . . . lacks a rational basis, and therefore violates the equal protection clauses of both the federal and state constitutions (U.S. Const., 14th Amend. §1; N.Y Const., Art I, §11).

[Because the unconstitutionality of the marital exemption left the general rape law intact, the court affirmed the conviction.]

Notes and Questions

1. Is the distinction between marital and nonmarital rape wholly archaic? Can one argue that the psychological shock and loss of faith that accompany marital rape make it at least as harmful as, if not more harmful than, nonmarital rape? On the other hand, should the same standards be imposed for nonconsent in the context of an ongoing marital relationship? Should marital rape be conditioned on sexual intercourse plus the absence of an affirmative manifestation of consent? On sexual intercourse with a person the defendant knows to be asleep or intoxicated or psychologically or mentally impaired? But if you think a marital relationship should alter the law's interpretation of these situations, what about an ongoing sexual relationship outside of marriage?

2. Professor Robin West argues that the marital rape exemption is unconstitutional under several theories of equal protection: It effectively, if not literally, discriminates against women as a group; it implicates the state in reinforcing subordination for women; and it denies married women "equal protection" in the "pure" sense of the term — i.e., it denies them equal access to the organs of state law enforcement to protect them from criminal violence. See Equality Theory, Marital Rape, and the Promise of the Fourteenth Amendment, 42 Fla. L. Rev. 45, 70-71 (1990).

APPENDIX A

A NOTE ON THE MODEL PENAL CODE

C. MCCLAIN AND DAN KAHAN, CRIMINAL LAW REFORM: HISTORICAL DEVELOPMENT IN THE UNITED STATES
1 Encyclopedia of Crime and Justice 422-425 (2002)

The Model Penal Code. The American Law Institute, an organization of lawyers, judges, and legal scholars, was founded in 1923 for the purpose of clarifying and improving the law. One of the major causes that had led to its establishment was dissatisfaction with the state of the criminal law, and thus it is no surprise that criminal law reform occupied a high place on its agenda from the outset. However, it proved difficult to translate this concern into action. The institute was quick to decide that the method of restatement which seemed the appropriate way to proceed in other fields of law was inappropriate for the law of crime. As Herbert Wechsler, a leading theorist of penal jurisprudence, later explained, "The need . . . was less for a description and reaffirmation of existing law than for a guide to long delayed reform." . . . A proposal for a model penal code was advanced in 1931, but the project was large in scope, and the funding to carry it out was not forthcoming during the Depression years.

In 1950 the infusion of a large grant from the Rockefeller Foundation stirred the model penal code project to life again. An advisory committee, made up of distinguished scholars in the field of criminal law, was assembled by the American Law Institute. Wechsler was appointed chief reporter of the enterprise, and Louis Schwartz, another eminent authority in the field, was named co-reporter.

Early in the project's life, Wechsler made it clear that he and his colleagues were confronting a task of immense magnitude. In Wechsler's view, American society had entered the twentieth century without having ever rationally articulated "the law on which men placed their ultimate reliance for protection against all the deepest injuries that human conduct can inflict on individuals and institutions." . . . Instead, the penal law of the various states was a hopelessly disorganized and internally inconsistent mass of common and statute law — with the statutes often more important in their gloss than in their text — less the product of informed, deliberate choice than of accident, chance, and unreflecting imitation. As Wechsler put it, American penal law was a "combination of the old and the new that only history explains." . . .

From beginning to end, Wechsler was the code project's guiding spirit, and he deserves most of the credit for leading the enterprise to successful completion. But the drafting of the Model Penal Code was no solo performance by Wechsler. It was very much a collaborative effort, drawing on the talent of virtually the whole of the academic criminal law establishment, of a goodly number of judges, and of a handful of practitioners. It was also an effort that proceeded carefully and deliberately. The writing of the Code took ten years, from 1952 to 1962, during which time thirteen tentative drafts were circulated for general discussion and comment after debate in the project's advisory committee and on the floor of the American Law Institute.

In 1962 the institute's Proposed Official Draft of the Model Penal Code was promulgated, the greatest attempt since Livingston's time to put the house of penal jurisprudence into some kind of rational order. In truth, the Proposed Official Draft was in many respects a very Livingstonian document. This was seen particularly in its commitment to the principle that the sole purpose of the criminal law was the control of harmful conduct, and in its adherence to the notion that clarity of concept and expression were essential to that purpose's fulfillment. The draft was wholly lacking, however, in that ideological smugness and imperiousness which at times had tarnished the work of Livingston and of his mentor, Bentham. As befitted a product of the mid-twentieth-century American mind, the draft was suffused with a spirit of pragmatism, albeit a pragmatism tempered by principle.

The Code was divided into four parts: general provisions, definitions of specific crimes, treatment and correction, and organization of correction. Each contained significant innovations with respect to existing law. In keeping with the principle that the criminal law's only purpose was to deter blameworthy, harmful conduct, and the converse principle that faultless conduct should be shielded from punishment, new standards of criminal liability were established in the Code's general provisions. In the area of inchoate crimes, for example, the law of attempt was rewritten to sweep away all questions as to factual impossibility and to focus attention on the actor's perception of the circumstances surrounding the commission of his act (§5.01). In conspiracy, on the other hand, the traditional common-law rule that made every member of the conspiracy liable for any reasonably foreseeable crime committed by any other member of the conspiracy was rejected. Instead, an accomplice's liability was limited to those crimes of the principal that the accomplice intended to assist or encourage (§5.03). Thus too, in the interest of protecting faultless conduct, the use of defensive force was declared justifiable in cases of apparent, as opposed to actual, necessity (§3.04). Reasonable mistake of fact was affirmed as a defense in crimes such as bigamy (§230.1). In addition, a limited defense of *ignorantia legis* was made available to defendants who harbored good faith beliefs regarding the innocence of their conduct as a result of reliance on official opinion or as a result of the unavailability to them of the enactment they were accused of violating (§§2.02, 2.04).

The most striking provisions in the Code's general part were those that sought to articulate a new definition of the mental element in crime. The common law used a bewildering variety of terms to designate the mental blameworthiness (mens rea) that had to be present if a person were to be convicted of a criminal offense. For this profusion of terms the Code drafters substituted four modes of acting with respect to the material elements of offenses — purposely, knowingly, recklessly, and negligently — one of which would have to be present for criminal liability to attach (§2.02). The Code achieved a creative compromise in the area of strict liability, allowing for the possibility of such offenses by classifying them as violations punishable only by fines.

In addition to attempting to order and rationalize the general, underlying principles of criminal liability, the Model Penal Code wrought numerous innovations in the definitions of specific offenses. Perhaps the most single achievement in this regard was its substitution of a unified law of theft for the potpourri of common-law offenses that went under the names of larceny, larceny by trick, false pretenses, and embezzlement. It sought, too, to bring greater rationality and fairness to the sentencing of those convicted of crimes. It proposed a scheme of determinate sentencing, under which felonies were classified into three punishment categories and all misdemeanors into two. Upper and lower limits of sentences were set out for each category, with the determination of the exact length left to the discretion of the judge (§§6.06, 6.08). Extended terms were authorized for persistent offenders and professional criminals (§§7.03, 7.04).

The American Law Institute neither expected nor intended that its Model Penal Code would be adopted in toto anywhere, or that it would lead to the establishment of a uniform national penal law. Diversity of political history and of population makeup in the various states made that kind of expectation quite unrealistic. Rather, the institute hoped that the Code would spark a fresh and systematic reevaluation of the penal law in many jurisdictions and that its provisions would be liberally drawn on. The institute was not to be disappointed in this hope. By 1980, in large part owing to the Model Penal Code's example, some thirty states had adopted revised criminal codes, and another nine had code revisions either under way or completed and awaiting enactment. It is no exaggeration to say, as did Sanford Kadish, that within three decades of the time when Code drafts began to be circulated, the Model Penal Code had "permeated and transformed" American substantive law.

A final salutary impact of the Model Penal Code must be mentioned, namely, the impetus that it gave to the effort to codify — for the first time in the true sense of the word — the federal penal law. In 1962, when the Code's Proposed Official Draft was promulgated, the federal criminal law was in a sorrier condition than that of most of the states. It had grown up in an unsystematic, piecemeal fashion since the beginnings of the republic, and the several efforts that had been previously undertaken to place it on a more rational basis had not come to very much. In 1866 Congress, alarmed at the uncontrolled manner in which the corpus of federal criminal law seemed to have been growing since 1800, had impaneled a commission to introduce some order into the confusion. The work of this commission led to the passage of a body of revised statutes, which at least had the virtue of arranging federal penal provisions into some sort of coherent order (U.S. Congress). In 1897 and later in 1909, revisions and rearrangements of federal penal statutes were again undertaken (Appropriations Act of June 4, 1897, ch. 2, 30 Stat. 11; Act of March 4, 1909, ch. 321, 35 Stat. 1088 (codified in scattered sections of 18 U.S.C.)). Finally, in 1948, after eight years of work by another commission, Congress enacted Title 18 of the United States Code, which purported to be the first codification of the federal criminal law. If it was a codification, it was one in the Fieldian rather than the Benthamite-Livingstonian sense — and even that may be a charitable overstatement.

In 1966 Congress established the National Commission on Reform of Federal Criminal Laws to examine the state of the federal penal law and to propose a reformulation. The action was in part taken to appease an anxious public which was insisting that Congress do something about dramatically escalating crime rates, but it was motivated as well by an authentic desire to reform and improve the law. Congress left no doubt that it wished to see a thorough rethinking of the federal law of crimes, and its mandate was heeded. In due course the commission produced a thorough revision of the federal substantive law of crimes, and several bills were promptly introduced for the enactment of some version of it into law.

APPENDIX B

THE MODEL PENAL CODE

PART I.   GENERAL PROVISIONS

Article 1.   Preliminary

Section 1.01.   Title and Effective Date [Omitted]

Section 1.02.   Purposes; Principles of Construction

(1) The general purposes of the provisions of governing the definition of offenses are:

(a) to forbid and prevent conduct that unjustifiably and inexcusably inflicts or threatens substantial harm to individual or public interests;

(b) to subject to public control persons whose conduct indicates that they are disposed to commit crimes;

(c) to safeguard conduct that is without fault from condemnation as criminal;

(d) to give fair warning of the nature of the conduct declared to constitute an offense;

(e) to differentiate on reasonable grounds between serious and minor offenses.

(2) The general purposes of the provisions governing the sentencing and treatment of offenders are:

(a) to prevent the commission of offenses;

(b) to promote the correction and rehabilitation of offenders;

(c) to safeguard offenders against excessive, disproportionate or arbitrary punishment;

(d) to give fair warning of the nature of the sentences that may be imposed on conviction of an offense;

(e) to differentiate among offenders with a view to a just individualization in their treatment;

(f) to define, coordinate and harmonize the powers, duties and functions of the courts and of administrative officers and agencies responsible for dealing with offenders;

(g) to advance the use of generally accepted scientific methods and knowledge in the sentencing and treatment of offenders;

(h) to integrate responsibility for the administration of the correctional system in a State Department of Correction [or other single department or agency].

(3) The provisions of the Code shall be construed according to the fair import of their terms but when the language is susceptible of differing constructions it shall be

interpreted to further the general purposes stated in this Section and the special purposes of the particular provision involved. The discretionary powers conferred by the Code shall be exercised in accordance with the criteria stated in the Code and, insofar as such criteria are not decisive, to further the general purposes stated in this Section.

Section 1.03.   Territorial Applicability [Omitted]

Section 1.04.   Classes of Crimes; Violations

(1) An offense defined by this Code or by any other statute of this State, for which a sentence of [death or of] imprisonment is authorized, constitutes a crime. Crimes are classified as felonies, misdemeanors or petty misdemeanors.

(2) A crime is a felony if it is so designated in this Code or if persons convicted thereof may be sentenced [to death or] to imprisonment for a term that, apart from an extended term, is in excess of one year.

(3) A crime is a misdemeanor if it is so designated in this Code or in a statute other than this Code enacted subsequent thereto.

(4) A crime is a petty misdemeanor if it is so designated in this Code or in a statute other than this Code enacted subsequent thereto or if it is defined by a statute other than this Code that now provides that persons convicted thereof may be sentenced to imprisonment for a term of which the maximum is less than one year.

(5) An offense defined by this Code or by any other statute of this State constitutes a violation if it is so designated in this Code or in the law defining the offense or if no other sentence than a fine, or fine and forfeiture or other civil penalty is authorized upon conviction or if it is defined by a statute other than this Code that now provides that the offense shall not constitute a crime. A violation does not constitute a crime and conviction of a violation shall not give rise to any disability or legal disadvantage based on conviction of a criminal offense.

(6) Any offense declared by law to constitute a crime, without specification of the grade thereof or of the sentence authorized upon conviction, is a misdemeanor.

(7) An offense defined by any statute of this State other than this Code shall be classified as provided in this Section and the sentence that may be imposed upon conviction thereof shall hereafter be governed by this Code.

Section 1.05.   All Offenses Defined by Statute;
Application of General Provisions of the Code

(1) No conduct constitutes an offense unless it is a crime or violation under this Code or another statute of this State.

(2) The provisions of Part I of the Code are applicable to offenses defined by other statutes, unless the Code otherwise provides.

(3) This Section does not affect the power of a court to punish for contempt or to employ any sanction authorized by law for the enforcement of an order or a civil judgment or decree.

Section 1.06.   Time Limitations [Omitted]

Section 1.07.   Method of Prosecution When Conduct Constitutes More Than One Offense

(1) *Prosecution for Multiple Offenses; Limitation on Convictions.* When the same conduct of a defendant may establish the commission of more than one offense, the defendant may be prosecuted for each such offense. He may not, however, be convicted of more than one offense if:

(a) one offense is included in the other, as defined in Subsection (4) of this Section; or

(b) one offense consists only of a conspiracy or other form of preparation to commit the other; or

(c) inconsistent findings of fact are required to establish the commission of the offenses; or

(d) the offenses differ only in that one is defined to prohibit a designated kind of conduct generally and the other to prohibit a specific instance of such conduct; or

(e) the offense is defined as a continuing course of conduct and the defendant's course of conduct was uninterrupted, unless the law provides that specific periods of such conduct constitute separate offenses.

(2) *Limitation on Separate Trials for Multiple Offenses.* Except as provided in Subsection (3) of this Section, a defendant shall not be subject to separate trials for multiple offenses based on the same conduct or arising from the same criminal episode, if such offenses are known to the appropriate prosecuting officer at the time of the commencement of the first trial and are within the jurisdiction of a single court.

(3) *Authority of Court to Order Separate Trials.* When a defendant is charged with two or more offenses based on the same conduct or arising from the same criminal episode, the Court, on application of the prosecuting attorney or of the defendant, may order any such charge to be tried separately, if it is satisfied that justice so requires.

(4) *Conviction of Included Offense Permitted.* A defendant may be convicted of an offense included in an offense charged in the indictment [or the information]. An offense is so included when:

(a) it is established by proof of the same or less than all the facts required to establish the commission of the offense charged; or

(b) it consists of an attempt or solicitation to commit the offense charged or to commit an offense otherwise included therein; or

(c) it differs from the offense charged only in the respect that a less serious injury or risk of injury to the same person, property or public interest or a lesser kind of culpability suffices to establish its commission.

(5) *Submission of Included Offense to Jury.* The Court shall not be obligated to charge the jury with respect to an included offense unless there is a rational basis for a verdict acquitting the defendant of the offense charged and convicting him of the included offense.

Section 1.08.   When Prosecution Barred by Former Prosecution for the Same Offense [Omitted]

Section 1.09.   When Prosecution Barred by Former Prosecution for Different Offense [Omitted]

Section 1.10.   Former Prosecution in Another Jurisdiction: When a Bar [Omitted]

Section 1.11.   Former Prosecution Before Court Lacking Jurisdiction or When Fraudulently Procured by the Defendant [Omitted]

Section 1.12.   Proof Beyond a Reasonable Doubt; Affirmative Defenses; Burden of Proving Fact When Not an Element of an Offense; Presumptions

(1) No person may be convicted of an offense unless each element of such offense is proved beyond a reasonable doubt. In the absence of such proof, the innocence of the defendant is assumed.

(2) Subsection (1) of this Section does not:

(a) require the disproof of an affirmative defense unless and until there is evidence supporting such defense; or

(b) apply to any defense which the Code or another statute plainly requires the defendant to prove by a preponderance of evidence.

(3) A ground of defense is affirmative, within the meaning of Subsection (2)(a) of this Section, when:

(a) it arises under a section of the Code that so provides; or

(b) it relates to an offense defined by a statute other than the Code and such statute so provides; or

(c) it involves a matter of excuse or justification peculiarly within the knowledge of the defendant on which he can fairly be required to adduce supporting evidence.

(4) When the application of the Code depends upon the finding of a fact which is not an element of an offense, unless the Code otherwise provides:

(a) the burden of proving the fact is on the prosecution or defendant, depending on whose interest or contention will be furthered if the finding should be made; and

(b) the fact must be proved to the satisfaction of the Court or jury, as the case may be.

(5) When the Code establishes a presumption with respect to any fact that is an element of an offense, it has the following consequences:

(a) when there is evidence of the facts that give rise to the presumption, the issue of the existence of the presumed fact must be submitted to the jury, unless the Court is satisfied that the evidence as a whole clearly negatives the presumed fact; and

(b) when the issue of the existence of the presumed fact is submitted to the jury, the Court shall charge that while the presumed fact must, on all the evidence, be proved beyond a reasonable doubt, the law declares that the jury may regard the facts giving rise to the presumption as sufficient evidence of the presumed fact.

(6) A presumption not established by the Code or inconsistent with it has the consequences otherwise accorded it by law.

Section 1.13. *General Definitions*

In this Code, unless a different meaning plainly is required:

(1) "statute" includes the Constitution and a local law or ordinance of a political subdivision of the State;

(2) "act" or "action" means a bodily movement whether voluntary or involuntary;

(3) "voluntary" has the meaning specified in Section 2.01;

(4) "omission" means a failure to act;

(5) "conduct" means an action or omission and its accompanying state of mind, or, where relevant, a series of acts and omissions;

(6) "actor" includes, where relevant, a person guilty of an omission;

(7) "acted" includes, where relevant, "omitted to act";

(8) "person," "he" and "actor" include any natural person and, where relevant, a corporation or an unincorporated association;

(9) "element of an offense" means (i) such conduct or (ii) such attendant circumstances or (iii) such a result of conduct as

(a) is included in the description of the forbidden conduct in the definition of the offense; or

(b) establishes the required kind of culpability; or

(c) negatives an excuse or justification for such conduct; or

(d) negatives a defense under the statute of limitations; or

(e) establishes jurisdiction or venue;

(10) "material element of an offense" means an element that does not relate exclusively to the statute of limitations, jurisdiction, venue or to any other matter similarly unconnected with (i) the harm or evil, incident to conduct, sought to be prevented by the law defining the offense, or (ii) the existence of a justification or excuse for such conduct;

(11) "purposely" has the meaning specified in Section 2.02 and equivalent terms such as "with purpose," "designed" or "with design" have the same meaning;

(12) "intentionally" or "with intent" means purposely;

(13) "knowingly" has the meaning specified in Section 2.02 and equivalent terms such as "knowing" or "with knowledge" have the same meaning;

(14) "recklessly" has the meaning specified in Section 2.02 and equivalent terms such as "recklessness" or "with recklessness" have the same meaning;

(15) "negligently" has the meaning specified in Section 2.02 and equivalent terms such as "negligence" or "with negligence" have the same meaning;

(16) "reasonably believes" or "reasonable belief" designates a belief which the actor is not reckless or negligent in holding.

Article 2. General Principles of Liability

Section 2.01. *Requirement of Voluntary Act; Omission as Basis of Liability; Possession as an Act*

(1) A person is not guilty of an offense unless his liability is based on conduct which includes a voluntary act or the omission to perform an act of which he is physically capable.

(2) The following are not voluntary acts within the meaning of this Section:

(a) a reflex or convulsion;

(b) a bodily movement during unconsciousness or sleep;

(c) conduct during hypnosis or resulting from hypnotic suggestion;

(d) a bodily movement that otherwise is not a product of the effort or determination of the actor, either conscious or habitual.

(3) Liability for the commission of an offense may not be based on an omission unaccompanied by action unless:

(a) the omission is expressly made sufficient by the law defining the offense; or

(b) a duty to perform the omitted act is otherwise imposed by law.

(4) Possession is an act, within the meaning of this Section, if the possessor knowingly procured or received the thing possessed or was aware of his control thereof for a sufficient period to have been able to terminate his possession.

Section 2.02. *General Requirements of Culpability*

(1) *Minimum Requirements of Culpability.* Except as provided in Section 2.05, a person is not guilty of an offense unless he acted purposely, knowingly, recklessly or negligently, as the law may require, with respect to each material element of the offense.

(2) *Kinds of Culpability Defined.*

(a) *Purposely.* A person acts purposely with respect to a material element of an offense when:

(i) if the element involves the nature of his conduct or a result thereof, it is his conscious object to engage in conduct of that nature or to cause such a result; and

(ii) if the element involves the attendant circumstances, he is aware of the existence of such circumstances or he believes or hopes that they exist.

(b) *Knowingly.* A person acts knowingly with respect to a material element of an offense when:

(i) if the element involves the nature of his conduct or the attendant circumstances, he is aware that his conduct is of that nature or that such circumstances exist; and

(ii) if the element involves a result of his conduct, he is aware that it is practically certain that his conduct will cause such a result.

(c) *Recklessly.* A person acts recklessly with respect to a material element of an offense when he consciously disregards a substantial and unjustifiable risk that the material element exists or will result from his conduct. The risk must be of such a nature and degree that, considering the nature and purpose of the actor's conduct and the circumstances known to him, its disregard involves a gross deviation from the standard of conduct that a law-abiding person would observe in the actor's situation.

(d) *Negligently.* A person acts negligently with respect to a material element of an offense when he should be aware of a substantial and unjustifiable risk that the material element exists or will result from his conduct. The risk must be of such a nature and degree that the actor's failure to perceive it, considering the nature and purpose of his conduct and the circumstances known to him, involves a gross deviation from the standard of care that a reasonable person would observe in the actor's situation.

(3) *Culpability Required Unless Otherwise Provided.* When the culpability sufficient to establish a material element of an offense is not prescribed by law, such element is established if a person acts purposely, knowingly or recklessly with respect thereto.

(4) *Prescribed Culpability Requirement Applies to All Material Elements.* When the law defining an offense prescribes the kind of culpability that is sufficient for the commission of an offense, without distinguishing among the material elements thereof, such provision shall apply to all the material elements of the offense, unless a contrary purpose plainly appears.

(5) *Substitutes for Negligence, Recklessness and Knowledge.* When the law provides that negligence suffices to establish an element of an offense, such element also is established if a person acts purposely, knowingly or recklessly. When recklessness suffices to establish an element, such element also is established if a person acts purposely or knowingly. When acting knowingly suffices to establish an element, such element also is established if a person acts purposely.

(6) *Requirement of Purpose Satisfied if Purpose Is Conditional.* When a particular purpose is an element of an offense, the element is established although such purpose is conditional, unless the condition negatives the harm or evil sought to be prevented by the law defining the offense.

(7) *Requirement of Knowledge Satisfied by Knowledge of High Probability.* When knowledge of the existence of a particular fact is an element of an offense, such knowledge is established if a person is aware of a high probability of its existence, unless he actually believes that it does not exist.

(8) *Requirement of Wilfulness Satisfied by Acting Knowingly.* A requirement that an offense be committed wilfully is satisfied if a person acts knowingly with respect to the material elements of the offense, unless a purpose to impose further requirements appears.

(9) *Culpability as to Illegality of Conduct.* Neither knowledge nor recklessness or negligence as to whether conduct constitutes an offense or as to the existence, meaning or application of the law determining the elements of an offense is an element of such offense, unless the definition of the offense or the Code so provides.

(10) *Culpability as Determinant of Grade of Offense.* When the grade or degree of an offense depends on whether the offense is committed purposely, knowing, recklessly or negligently, its grade or degree shall be the lowest for which the determinative kind of culpability is established with respect to any material element of the offense.

Section 2.03.   *Causal Relationship Between Conduct and Result; Divergence Between Result Designed or Contemplated and Actual Result or Between Probable and Actual Result*

(1) Conduct is the cause of a result when:

(a) it is an antecedent but for which the result in question would not have occurred; and

(b) the relationship between the conduct and result satisfies any additional causal requirements imposed by the Code or by the law defining the offense.

(2) When purposely or knowingly causing a particular result is an element of an offense, the element is not established if the actual result is not within the purpose or the contemplation of the actor unless:

(a) the actual result differs from that designed or contemplated, as the case may be, only in the respect that a different person or different property is injured or affected or that the injury or harm designed or contemplated would have been more serious or more extensive than that caused; or

(b) the actual result involves the same kind of injury or harm as that designed or contemplated and is not too remote or accidental in its occurrence to have a [just] bearing on the actor's liability or on the gravity of his offense.

(3) When recklessly or negligently causing a particular result is an element of an offense, the element is not established if the actual result is not within the risk of which the actor is aware or, in the case of negligence, of which he should be aware unless:

(a) the actual result differs from the probable result only in the respect that a different person or differing property is injured or affected or that the probable injury or harm would have been more serious or more extensive than that caused; or

(b) the actual result involves the same kind of injury or harm as the probable result and is not too remote or accidental in its occurrence to have a [just] bearing on the actor's liability or on the gravity of his offense.

(4) When causing a particular result is a material element of an offense for which absolute liability is imposed by law, the element is not established unless the actual result is a probable consequence of the actor's conduct.

Section 2.04.   *Ignorance or Mistake*

(1) Ignorance or mistake as to a matter of fact or law is a defense if:

(a) the ignorance or mistake negatives the purpose, knowledge, belief, recklessness or negligence required to establish a material element of the offense; or

(b) the law provides that the state of mind established by such ignorance or mistake constitutes a defense.

(2) Although ignorance or mistake would otherwise afford a defense to the offense charged, the defense is not available if the defendant would be guilty of another offense had the situation been as he supposed. In such case, however, the ignorance or mistake of the defendant shall reduce the grade and degree of the offense of which he may be convicted to those of the offense of which he would be guilty had the situation been as he supposed.

(3) A belief that conduct does not legally constitute an offense is a defense to a prosecution for that offense based upon such conduct when:

(a) the statute or other enactment defining the offense is not known to the actor and has not been published or otherwise reasonably made available prior to the conduct alleged; or

(b) he acts in reasonable reliance upon an official statement of the law, afterward determined to be invalid or erroneous, contained in (i) a statute or other enactment; (ii) a judicial decision, opinion or judgment; (iii) an administrative order or grant of permission; or (iv) an official interpretation of the public officer or body charged by law with responsibility for the interpretation, administration or enforcement of the law defining the offense.

(4) The defendant must prove a defense arising under Subsection (3) of this Section by a preponderance of evidence.

Section 2.05.   *When Culpability Requirements Are Inapplicable to Violations and to Offenses Defined by Other Statutes; Effect of Absolute Liability in Reducing Grade of Offense to Violation*

(1) The requirements of culpability prescribed by Sections 2.01 and 2.02 do not apply to:

(a) offenses which constitute violations, unless the requirement involved is included in the definition of the offense or the Court determines that its application is consistent with effective enforcement of the law defining the offense; or

   (b) offenses defined by statutes other than the Code, insofar as a legislative purpose to impose absolute liability for such offenses or with respect to any material element thereof plainly appears.

   (2) Notwithstanding any other provision of existing law and unless a subsequent statute otherwise provides:

   (a) when absolute liability is imposed with respect to any material element of an offense defined by a statute other than the Code and a conviction is based upon such liability, the offense constitutes a violation; and

   (b) although absolute liability is imposed by law with respect to one or more of the material elements of an offense defined by a statute other than the Code, the culpable commission of the offense may be charged and proved, in which event negligence with respect to such elements constitutes sufficient culpability and the classification of the offense and the sentence that may be imposed therefor upon conviction are determined by Section 1.04 and Article 6 of the Code.

Section 2.06.   Liability for Conduct of Another; Complicity

   (1) A person is guilty of an offense if it is committed by his own conduct or by the conduct of another person for which he is legally accountable, or both.

   (2) A person is legally accountable for the conduct of another person when:

   (a) acting with the kind of culpability that is sufficient for the commission of the offense, he causes an innocent or irresponsible person to engage in such conduct; or

   (b) he is made accountable for the conduct of such other person by the Code or by the law defining the offense; or

   (c) he is an accomplice of such other person in the commission of the offense.

   (3) A person is an accomplice of another person in the commission of an offense if:

   (a) with the purpose of promoting or facilitating the commission of the offense, he

      (i)   solicits such other person to commit it; or

      (ii) aids or agrees or attempts to aid such other person in planning or committing it; or

      (iii) having a legal duty to prevent the commission of the offense, fails to make proper effect so to do; or

   (b) his conduct is expressly declared by law to establish his complicity.

   (4) When causing a particular result is an element of an offense, an accomplice in the conduct causing such result is an accomplice in the commission of that offense, if he acts with the kind of culpability, if any, with respect to that result that is sufficient for the commission of the offense.

   (5) A person who is legally incapable of committing a particular offense himself may be guilty thereof if it is committed by the conduct of another person for which he is legally accountable, unless such liability is inconsistent with the purpose of the provision establishing his incapacity.

   (6) Unless otherwise provided by the Code or by the law defining the offense, a person is not an accomplice in an offense committed by another person if:

   (a) he is a victim of that offense; or

   (b) the offense is so defined that his conduct is inevitably incident to its commission; or

   (c) he terminates his complicity prior to the commission of the offense and

      (i)   wholly deprives it of effectiveness in the commission of the offense; or

      (ii) gives timely warning to the law enforcement authorities or otherwise makes proper effort to prevent the commission of the offense.

   (7) An accomplice may be convicted on proof of the commission of the offense and of his complicity therein, though the person claimed to have committed the offense has not been prosecuted or convicted or has been convicted of a different offense or degree of offense or has an immunity to prosecution or conviction or has been acquitted.

Section 2.07.   Liability of Corporations, Unincorporated Associations and Person Acting, or Under a Duty to Act, in Their Behalf

(1) A corporation may be convicted of the commission of an offense if:

(a)   the offense is a violation or the offense is defined by a statute other than the Code in which a legislative purpose to impose liability on corporations plainly appears and the conduct is performed by an agent of the corporation acting in behalf of the corporation within the scope of his office or employment, except that if the law defining the offense designates the agents for whose conduct the corporation is accountable or the circumstances under which it is accountable, such provisions shall apply; or

(b)   the offense consists of an omission to discharge a specific duty of affirmative performance imposed on corporations by law; or

(c)   the commission of the offense was authorized, requested, commanded, performed or recklessly tolerated by the board of directors or by a high managerial agent acting in behalf of the corporation within the scope of his office or employment.

(2) When absolute liability is imposed for the commission of an offense, a legislative purpose to impose liability on a corporation shall be assumed, unless the contrary plainly appears.

(3) An unincorporated association may be convicted of the commission of an offense if:

(a)   the offense is defined by a statute other than the Code which expressly provides for the liability of such an association and the conduct is performed by an agent of the association acting in behalf of the association within the scope of his office or employment, except that if the law defining the offense designates the agents for whose conduct the association is accountable or the circumstances under which it is accountable, such provisions shall apply; or

(b)   the offense consists of an omission to discharge a specific duty of affirmative performance imposed on associations by law.

(4) As used in this Section:

(a)   "corporation" does not include an entity organized as or by a governmental agency for the execution of a governmental program;

(b)   "agent" means any director, officer, servant, employee or other person authorized to act in behalf of the corporation or association and, in the case of an unincorporated association, a member of such association;

(c)   "high managerial agent" means an officer of a corporation or an unincorporated association, or, in the case of a partnership, a partner, or any other agent of a corporation or association having duties of such responsibilities that his conduct may fairly be assumed to represent the policy of the corporation or association.

(5) In any prosecution of a corporation or an unincorporated association for the commission of an offense included within the terms of Subsection (1)(a) or Subsection (3)(a) of this Section, other than an offense for which absolute liability has been imposed, it shall be a defense if the defendant proves by a preponderance of evidence that the high managerial agent having supervisory responsibility over the subject matter of the offense employed due diligence to prevent its commission. This paragraph shall not apply if it is plainly inconsistent with the legislative purpose in defining the particular offense.

(6)(a) A person is legally accountable for any conduct he performs or causes to be performed in the name of the corporation or an unincorporated association or in its behalf to the same extent as if it were performed in his own name or behalf.

(b)   Whenever a duty to act is imposed by law upon a corporation or an unincorporated association, any agent of the corporation or association having primary responsibility for the discharge of the duty is legally accountable for a reckless omission to perform the required act to the same extent as if the duty were imposed by law directly upon himself.

(c)   When a person is convicted of an offense by reason of his legal accountability for the conduct of a corporation or an unincorporated association, he is subject to the sentence authorized by law when a natural person is convicted of an offense of the grade and the degree involved.

Section 2.08.   Intoxication

(1) Except as provided in Subsection (4) of this Section, intoxication of the actor is not a defense unless it negatives an element of the offense.

(2) When recklessness establishes an element of the offense, if the actor, due to self-induced intoxication, is unaware of a risk of which he would have been aware had he been sober, such unawareness is immaterial.

(3) Intoxication does not, in itself, constitute mental disease within the meaning of Section 4.01.

(4) Intoxication that (a) is not self-induced or (b) is pathological is an affirmative defense if by reason of such intoxication the actor at the time of his conduct lacks substantial capacity either to appreciate its criminality [wrongfulness] or to conform his conduct to the requirements of law.

(5) *Definitions.* In this Section unless a different meaning plainly is required:

(a) "intoxication" means a disturbance of mental or physical capacities resulting from the introduction of substances into the body;

(b) "self-induced intoxication" means intoxication caused by substances which the actor knowingly introduces into his body, the tendency of which to cause intoxication he knows or ought to know, unless he introduces them pursuant to medical advice or under such circumstances as would afford a defense to a charge of crime;

(c) "pathological intoxication" means intoxication grossly excessive in degree, given the amount of the intoxicant, to which the actor does not know he is susceptible.

Section 2.09.   Duress

(1) It is an affirmative defense that the actor engaged in the conduct charged to constitute an offense because he was coerced to do so by the use of, or a threat to use, unlawful force against his person or the person of another, that a person of reasonable firmness in his situation would have been unable to resist.

(2) The defense provided by this Section is unavailable if the actor recklessly placed himself in a situation in which it was probable that he would be subjected to duress. The defense is also unavailable if he was negligent in placing himself in such a situation, whenever negligence suffices to establish culpability for the offense charged.

(3) It is not a defense that a woman acted on the command of her husband, unless she acted under such coercion as would establish a defense under this Section. [The presumption that a woman acting in the presence of her husband is coerced is abolished.]

(4) When the conduct of the actor would otherwise be justifiable under Section 3.02, this Section does not preclude such defense.

Section 2.10.   Military Orders

It is an affirmative defense that the actor, in engaging in the conduct charged to constitute an offense, does no more than execute an order of his superior in the armed services which he does not know to be unlawful.

Section 2.11.   Consent

(1) *In General.* The consent of the victim to conduct charged to constitute an offense or to the result thereof is a defense if such consent negatives an element of the offense or precludes the infliction of the harm or evil sought to be prevented by the law defining the offense.

(2) *Consent to Bodily Harm.* When conduct is charged to constitute an offense because it causes or threatens bodily harm, consent to such conduct or to the infliction of such harm is a defense if:

(a) the bodily injury consented to or threatened by the conduct consented to is not serious; or

(b) the conduct and the injury are reasonably foreseeable hazards of joint participation in a lawful athletic contest or competitive sport or other concerted activity not forbidden by law; or

(c) the consent establishes a justification for the conduct under Article 3 of the Code.

(3) *Ineffective Consent.* Unless otherwise provided by the Code or by the law defining the offense, assent does not constitute consent if:

(a) it is given by a person who is legally incompetent to authorize the conduct charged to constitute the offense; or

(b) it is given by a person who by reason of youth, mental disease or defect or intoxication is manifestly unable or known by the actor to be unable to make a reasonable judgment as to the nature or harmfulness of the conduct charged to constitute the offense; or

(c) it is given by a person whose improvident consent is sought to be prevented by the law defining the offense; or

(d) it is induced by force, duress or deception of a kind sought to be prevented by the law defining the offense.

Section 2.12.   De Minimis Infractions

The Court shall dismiss a prosecution if, having regard to the nature of the conduct charged to constitute an offense and the nature of the attendant circumstances, it finds that the defendant's conduct:

(1) was within a customary license of tolerance, neither expressly negatived by the person whose interest was infringed nor inconsistent with the purpose of the law defining the offense; or

(2) did not actually cause or threaten the harm or evil sought to be prevented by the law defining the offense or did so only to an extent too trivial to warrant the condemnation of conviction; or

(3) presents such other extenuations that it cannot reasonably be regarded as envisaged by the legislature in forbidding the offense.

The Court shall not discuss a prosecution under Subsection (3) of this Section without filing a written statement of its reasons.

Section 2.13.   Entrapment

(1) A public law enforcement official or a person acting in cooperation with such an official perpetrates an entrapment if for the purpose of obtaining evidence of the commission of an offense, he induces or encourages another person to engage in conduct constituting such offense by either:

(a) making knowingly false representations designed to induce the belief that such conduct is not prohibited; or

(b) employing methods of persuasion or inducement that create a substantial risk that such an offense will be committed by persons other than those who are ready to commit it.

(2) Except as provided in Subsection (3) of this Section, a person prosecuted for an offense shall be acquitted if he proves by a preponderance of evidence that his conduct occurred in response to an entrapment. The issue of entrapment shall be tried by the Court in the absence of the jury.

(3) The defense afforded by this Section is unavailable when causing or threatening bodily injury is an element of the offense charged and the prosecution is based on conduct causing or threatening such injury to a person other than the person perpetrating the entrapment.

Article 3.   General Principles of Justification

Section 3.01.   *Justification an Affirmative Defense; Civil Remedies Unaffected*

(1) In any prosecution based on conduct that is justifiable under this Article, justification is an affirmative defense.

(2) The fact that conduct is justifiable under this Article does not abolish or impair any remedy for such conduct that is available in any civil action.

Section 3.02.   *Justification Generally: Choice of Evils*

(1) Conduct that the actor believes to be necessary to avoid a harm or evil to himself or to another is justifiable, provided that:

(a) the harm or evil sought to be avoided by such conduct is greater than that sought to be prevented by the law defining the offense charged; and

(b) neither the Code nor other law defining the offense provides exceptions or defenses dealing with the specific situation involved; and

(c) a legislative purpose to exclude the justification claimed does not otherwise plainly appear.

(2) When the actor was reckless or negligent in bringing about the situation requiring a choice of harms or evils or in appraising the necessity for his conduct, the justification afforded by this Section is unavailable in a prosecution for any offense for which recklessness or negligence, as the case may be, suffices to establish culpability.

Section 3.03.   *Execution of Public Duty*

(1) Except as provided in Subsection (2) of this Section, conduct is justifiable when it is required or authorized by:

(a) the law defining the duties or functions of a public officer or the assistance to be rendered to such officer in the performance of his duties; or

(b) the law governing the execution of legal process; or

(c) the judgment or order of a competent court or tribunal; or

(d) the law governing the armed services or the lawful conduct of war; or

(e) any other provision of law imposing a public duty.

(2) The other sections of this Article apply to:

(a) the use of force upon or toward the person of another for any of the purposes dealt with in such sections; and

(b) the use of deadly force for any purpose, unless the use of such force is otherwise expressly authorized by law or occurs in the lawful conduct of war.

(3) The justification afforded by Subsection (1) of this Section applies:

(a) when the actor believes his conduct to be required or authorized by the judgment or direction of a competent court or tribunal or in the lawful execution of legal process, notwithstanding lack of jurisdiction of the court or defect in the legal process; and

(b) when the actor believes his conduct to be required or authorized to assist a public officer in the performance of his duties, notwithstanding that the officer exceeded his legal authority.

Section 3.04. Use of Force in Self-Protection

(1) *Use of Force Justifiable for Protection of the Person.* Subject to the provisions of this Section and of Section 3.09, the use of force upon or toward another person is justifiable when the actor believes that such force is immediately necessary for the purpose of protecting himself against the use of unlawful force by such other person on the present occasion.

(2) *Limitations on Justifying Necessity for Use of Force.*

(a) The use of force is not justifiable under this Section:

(i) to resist an arrest that the actor knows is being made by a peace officer, although the arrest is unlawful; or

(ii) to resist force used by the occupier or possessor of property or by another person on his behalf, where the actor knows that the person using the force is doing so under a claim of right to protect the property, except that this limitation shall not apply if:

(1) the actor is a public officer acting in the performance of his duties or a person lawfully assisting him therein or a person making or assisting in a lawful arrest; or

(2) the actor has been unlawfully dispossessed of the property and is making a re-entry or recaption justified by Section 3.06; or

(3) the actor believes that such force is necessary to protect himself against death or serious bodily harm.

(b) The use of deadly force is not justifiable under this Section unless the actor believes that such force is necessary to protect himself against death, serious bodily harm, kidnapping or sexual intercourse compelled by force or threat; nor is it justifiable if:

(i) the actor, with the purpose of causing death or serious bodily injury, provoked the use of force against himself in the same encounter; or

(ii) the actor knows that he can avoid the necessity of using such force with complete safety by retreating or by surrendering possession of a thing to a person asserting a claim of right thereto or by complying with a demand that he abstain from any action that he has no duty to take, except that:

(1) the actor is not obliged to retreat from his dwelling or place of work, unless he was the initial aggressor or is assailed in his place of work by another person whose place of work the actor knows it to be; and

(2) a public officer justified in using force in the performance of his duties or a person justified in using force in his assistance or a person justified in using force in making an arrest or preventing an escape is not obliged to desist from efforts to perform such duty, effect such arrest or prevent such escape because of resistance or threatened resistance by or on behalf of the person against whom such action is directed.

(c) Except as required by paragraphs (a) and (b) of this Subsection, a person employing protective force may estimate the necessity thereof under the circumstances as he believes them to be when the force is used, without retreating, surrendering possession, doing any other act which he has no legal duty to do or abstaining from any lawful action.

(3) *Use of Confinement as Protective Force.* The justification afforded by this Section extends to the use of confinement as protective force only if the actor takes all reasonable measures to terminate the confinement as soon as he knows that he safely can, unless the person confined has been arrested on a charge of crime.

Section 3.05. Use of Force for the Protection of Other Persons

(1) Subject to the provisions of this Section and of Section 3.09, the use of force upon or toward the person of another is justifiable to protect a third person when:

(a) the actor would be justified under Section 3.04 in using such force to protect himself against the injury he believes to be threatened to the person whom he seeks to protect; and

(b) under the circumstances as the actor believes them to be, the person whom he seeks to protect would be justified in using such protective force; and

(c) the actor believes that his intervention is necessary for the protection of such other person.

(2) Notwithstanding Subsection (1) of this Section:

(a) when the actor would be obliged under Section 3.04 to retreat, to surrender the possession of a thing or to comply with a demand before using force in self-protection, he is not obliged to do so before using force for the protection of another person, unless he knows that he can thereby secure the complete safety of such other person; and

(b) when the person whom the actor seeks to protect would be obliged under Section 3.04 to retreat, to surrender the possession of a thing or to comply with a demand if he knew that he could obtain complete safety by so doing, the actor is obliged to try to cause him to do so before using force in his protection if the actor knows that he can obtain complete safety in that way; and

(c) neither the actor not the person whom he seeks to protect is obliged to retreat when in the other's dwelling or place of work to any greater extent than in his own.

Section 3.06. *Use of Force for the Protection of Property*

(1) *Use of Force Justifiable for Protection of Property.* Subject to the provisions of this Section and of Section 3.09, the use of force upon or toward the person of another is justifiable when the actor believes that such force is immediately necessary:

(a) to prevent or terminate an unlawful entry or other trespass upon land or a trespass against or the unlawful carrying away of tangible, movable property, provided that such land or movable property is, or is believed by the actor to be, in his possession or in the possession of another person for whose protection he acts; or

(b) to effect an entry or re-entry upon land or to retake tangible movable property, provided that the actor believes that he or the person by whose authority he acts or a person from whom he or such other person derives title was unlawfully dispossessed of such land or movable property and is entitled to possession, and provided, further, that:

(i) the force is used immediately or on fresh pursuit after such dispossession; or

(ii) the actor believes that the person against whom he uses force has no claim of right to the possession of the property and, in the case of land, the circumstances, as the actor believes them to be, are of such urgency that it would be an exceptional hardship to postpone the entry or re-entry until a court order is obtained.

(2) *Meaning of Possession.* For the purpose of Subsection (1) of this Section:

(a) a person who has parted with the custody of property to another who refuses to restore it to him is no longer in possession, unless the property is movable and was and still is located on land in his possession;

(b) a person who has been dispossessed of land does not regain possession thereof merely by setting foot thereon;

(c) a person who has a license to use or occupy real property is deemed to be in possession thereof except against the licensor acting under claim of right.

(3) *Limitations on Justifiable Use of Force.*

(a) *Request to Desist.* The use of force is justifiable under this Section only if the actor first requests the person against whom such force is used to desist from his interference with the property, unless the actor believes that:

(i) such request would be useless; or

(ii) it would be dangerous to himself or another person to make the request; or

(iii) substantial harm will be done to the physical condition of the property which is sought to be protected before the request can effectively be made.

(b) *Exclusion of Trespasser.* The use of force to prevent or terminate a trespass is not justifiable under this Section if the actor knows that the exclusion of the trespasser will expose him to substantial danger of serious bodily harm.

(c) *Resistance of Lawful Re-entry or Recaption.* The use of force to prevent an entry or re-entry upon land or the recaption of movable property is not justifiable under this Section, although the actor believes that such re-entry or recaption is unlawful, if:

(i)   the re-entry or recaption is made by or on behalf of a person who was actually dispossessed of the property; and

(ii)   it is otherwise justifiable under paragraph (1)(b) of this Section.

(d) *Use of Deadly Force.* The use of deadly force is not justifiable under this Section unless the actor believes that:

(i)   the person against whom the force is used is attempting to dispossess him of his dwelling otherwise than under a claim of right to its possession; or

(ii)   the person against whom the force is used is attempting to commit or consummate arson, burglary, robbery or other felonious theft or property destruction and either:

(1)   has employed or threatened deadly force against or in the presence of the actor; or

(2)   the use of force other than deadly force to prevent the commission or the consummation of the crime would expose the actor or another in his presence to substantial danger of serious bodily harm.

(4) *Use of Confinement as Protective Force.* The justification afforded by this Section extends to the use of confinement as protective force only if the actor takes all reasonable measures to terminate the confinement as soon as he knows that he can do so with safety to the property, unless the person confined has been arrested on a charge of crime.

(5) *Use of Device to Protect Property.* The justification afforded by this Section extends to the use of a device for the purpose of protecting property only if:

(a)   the device is not designed to cause or known to create a substantial risk of causing death or serious bodily injury; and

(b)   the use of the particular device to protect the property from entry or trespass is reasonable under the circumstances, as the actor believes them to be; and

(c)   the device is one customarily used for such a purpose or reasonable care is taken to make known to probable intruders the fact that it is used.

(6) *Use of Force to Pass Wrongful Obstructor.* The use of force to pass a person whom the actor believes to be purposely or knowingly and unjustifiably obstructing the actor from going to a place to which he may lawfully go is justifiable, provided that:

(a)   the actor believes that the person against whom he uses force has no claim of right to obstruct the actor; and

(b)   the actor is not being obstructed from entry or movement on land which he knows to be in the possession or custody of the person obstructing him, or in the possession or custody of another person by whose authority the obstructor acts, unless the circumstances, as the actor believes them to be, are of such urgency that it would not be reasonable to postpone the entry or movement on such land until a court order is obtained; and

(c)   the force used is not greater than would be justifiable if the person obstructing the actor were using force against him to prevent his passage.

Section 3.07.   *Use of Force in Law Enforcement*

(1) *Use of Force Justifiable to Effect an Arrest.* Subject to the provisions of this Section and of Section 3.09, the use of force upon or toward the person of another is justifiable when the actor is making or assisting in making an arrest and the actor believes that such force is immediately necessary to effect a lawful arrest.

(2) *Limitations on the Use of Force.*

(a) The use of force is not justifiable under this Section unless:

(i)   the actor makes known the purpose of the arrest or believes that it is otherwise known by or cannot reasonably be make known to the person to be arrested; and

(ii) when the arrest is made under a warrant, the warrant is valid or believed by the actor to be valid.

(b) The use of deadly force is not justifiable under this Section unless:

(i)   the arrest is for a felony; and

(ii) the person effecting the arrest is authorized to act as a peace officer or is assisting a person whom he believes to be authorized to act as a peace officer; and

(iii) the actor believes that the force employed creates no substantial risk of injury to innocent persons; and

(iv) the actor believes that:

(1) the crime for which the arrest is made involved conduct including the use or threatened use of deadly force; or

(2) there is a substantial risk that the person to be arrested will cause death or serious bodily harm if his apprehension is delayed.

(3) *Use of Force of Prevent Escape from Custody.* The use of force to prevent the escape of an arrested person from custody is justifiable when the force could justifiably have been employed to effect the arrest under which the person is in custody, except that a guard or other person authorized to act as a peace officer is justified in using any force, including deadly force, that he believes to be immediately necessary to prevent the escape of a person from a jail, prison, or other institution for the detention of persons charged with or convicted of a crime.

(4) *Use of Force by Private Person Assisting an Unlawful Arrest.*

(a) A private person who is summoned by a peace officer to assist in effecting an unlawful arrest, is justified in using any force that he would be justified in using if the arrest were lawful, provided that he does not believe the arrest is unlawful.

(b) A private person who assists another private person in effecting an unlawful arrest, or who, not being summoned, assists a peace officer in effecting an unlawful arrest, is justified in using any force that he would be justified in using if the arrest were lawful, provided that (i) he believes the arrest is lawful and (ii) the arrest would be lawful if the facts were as he believes them to be.

(5) *Use of Force of Prevent Suicide or the Commission of a Crime.*

(a) The use of force upon or toward the person of another is justifiable when the actor believes that such force is immediately necessary to prevent such other person from committing suicide, inflicting serious bodily injury upon himself, committing or consummating the commission of a crime involving or threatening bodily injury, damage to or loss of property or a breach of the peace, except that:

(i)   any limitations imposed by the other provisions of this Article on the justifiable use of force in self-protection, for the protection of others, the protection of property, the effectuation of an arrest or the prevention of an escape from custody shall apply notwithstanding the criminality of the conduct against which such force is used; and

(ii) the use of deadly force is not in any event justifiable under this Subsection unless:

(1) the actor believes that there is a substantial risk that the person whom he seeks to prevent from committing a crime will cause death or serious bodily harm to another unless the commission or the consummation of the crime is prevented and that the use of such force presents no substantial risk of injury to innocent persons; or

(2) the actor believes that the use of such force is necessary to suppress a riot or mutiny after the rioters or mutineers have been ordered to disperse and

warned, in any particular manner that the law may require, that such force will be used if they do not obey.

(b) The justification afforded by this Subsection extends to the use of confinement as preventive force only if the actor takes all reasonable measures to terminate the confinement as soon as he knows that he safely can, unless the person confined has been arrested on a charge of crime.

Section 3.08. *Use of Force by Persons with Special Responsibility for Care, Discipline or Safety of Others*

The use of force upon or toward the person of another is justifiable if:

(1) The actor is the parent or guardian or other person similarly responsible for the general care and supervision of a minor or a person acting at the request of such parent, guardian or other responsible person and:

(a) the force is used for the purpose of safeguarding or promoting the welfare of the minor, including the prevention or punishment of his misconduct; and

(b) the force used is not designed to cause or known to create a substantial risk of causing death, serious bodily injury, disfigurement, extreme pain or mental distress or gross degradation; or

(2) the actor is a teacher or a person otherwise entrusted with the care or supervision for a special purpose of a minor and:

(a) the actor believes that the force used is necessary to further such special purpose, including the maintenance of reasonable discipline in a school, class or other group, and that the use of such force is consistent with the welfare of the minor; and

(b) the degree of force, if it had been used by the parent or guardian of the minor, would not be unjustifiable under Subsection (1)(b) of this Section; or

(3) the actor is the guardian or other person similarly responsible for the general care and supervision of an incompetent person; and:

(a) the force is used for the purpose of safeguarding or promoting the welfare of the incompetent person, including the prevention of his misconduct, or, when such incompetent person is in a hospital or other institution for his care and custody, for the maintenance of reasonable discipline in such institution; and

(b) the force used is not designed to cause or known to create a substantial risk of causing death, serious bodily harm, disfigurement, extreme or unnecessary pain, mental distress, or humiliation; or

(4) the actor is a doctor or other therapist or a person assisting him at his direction, and:

(a) the force is used for the purpose of administering a recognized form of treatment which the actor believes to be adapted to promoting the physical or mental health of the patient; and

(b) the treatment is administered with the consent of the patient or, if the patient is a minor or an incompetent person, with the consent of his parent or guardian or other person legally competent to consent in his behalf, or the treatment is administered in an emergency when the actor believes that no one competent to consent can be consulted and that a reasonable person, wishing to safeguard the welfare of the patient, would consent; or

(5) the actor is a warden or other authorized official of a correctional institution, and:

(a) he believes that the force used is necessary for the purpose of enforcing the lawful rules or procedures of the institution, unless his belief in the lawfulness of the rule or procedure sought to be enforced is erroneous and his error is due to ignorance or mistake as to the provisions of the Code, any other provision of the criminal law or the law governing the administration of the institution; and

(b) the nature or degree of force used is not forbidden by Article 303 or 304 of the Code; and

(c) if deadly force is used, its use is otherwise justifiable under this Article; or

(6) the actor is a person responsible for the safety of a vessel or an aircraft or a person acting at his direction, and

(a) he believes that the force used is necessary to prevent interference with the operation of the vessel or aircraft or obstruction of the execution of a lawful order, unless his belief in the lawfulness of the order is erroneous and his error is due to ignorance or mistake as to the law defining his authority; and

(b) if deadly force is used, its use is otherwise justifiable under this Article; or

(7) the actor is a person who is authorized or required by law to maintain order or decorum in a vehicle, train or other carrier or in a place where others are assembled, and:

(a) he believes that the force used is necessary for such purpose; and

(b) the force is not designed to cause or known to create a substantial risk of causing death, bodily harm, or extreme mental distress.

Section 3.09.   Mistake of Law as to Unlawfulness of Force or Legality of Arrest; Reckless or Negligent Use of Otherwise Justifiable Force; Reckless or Negligent Injury or Risk of Injury to Innocent Persons

(1) The justification afforded by Sections 3.04 to 3.07, inclusive, is unavailable when:

(a) the actor's belief in the unlawfulness of the force or conduct against which he employs protective force or his belief in the lawfulness of an arrest which he endeavors to effect by force is erroneous; and

(b) his error is due to ignorance or mistake as to the provisions of the Code, any other provision of the criminal law or the law governing the legality of an arrest or search.

(2) When the actor believes that the use of force upon or toward the person of another is necessary for any of the purposes for which such belief would establish a justification under Sections 3.03 to 3.08 but the actor is reckless or negligent in having such belief or in acquiring or failing to acquire any knowledge of belief which is material to the justifiability of his use of force, the justification afforded by those Sections is unavailable in a prosecution for an offense for which reckless or negligence, as the case may be, suffices to establish culpability.

(3) When the actor is justified under Sections 3.03 to 3.08 in using force upon or toward the person of another but he reckless or negligently injures or creates a risk of injury to innocent persons, the justification afforded by those Sections is unavailable in a prosecution for such reckless or negligence towards innocent persons.

Section 3.10.   Justification in Property Crimes

Conduct involving the appropriation, seizure or destruction of, damage to, intrusion on or interference with property is justifiable under circumstances that would establish a defense of privilege in a civil action based thereon unless:

(1) the Code or the law defining the offense deals with the specific situation involved; or

(2) a legislative purpose to exclude the justification claimed otherwise plainly appears.

Section 3.11.   Definitions

In this Article unless a different meaning plainly is required:

(1) "unlawful force" means force, including confinement, which is employed without the consent of the person against whom it is directed and the employment of which constitutes an offense or actionable tort or would constitute such offense or tort except for a defense (such as the absence of intent, negligence, or mental capacity; duress;

youth; or diplomatic status) not amounting to a privilege to use the force. Assent constitutes consent, without the meaning of this Section, whether or not it otherwise is legally effective, except assent to the infliction of death or serious bodily harm.

(2) "deadly force" means force which the actor uses with the purpose of causing or which he knows to create a substantial risk of causing death or serious bodily injury. Purposely firing a firearm in the direction of another person or at a vehicle in which another person is believed to be constitutes deadly force. A threat to cause death or serious bodily injury, by the production of a weapon or otherwise, so long as the actor's purpose is limited to creating an apprehension that he will use deadly force if necessary, does not constitute deadly force;

(3) "dwelling" means any building or structure, though movable or temporary, or a portion thereof, that is for the time being the actor's home or place of lodging.

Article 4.   Responsibility

Section 4.01.   *Mental Disease or Defect Excluding Responsibility*

(1) A person is not responsible for criminal conduct if at the time of such conduct as a result of mental disease or defect he lacks substantial capacity either to appreciate the criminality [wrongfulness] of his conduct or to conform his conduct to the requirements of law.

(2) As used in this Article, the terms "mental disease or defect" do not include an abnormality manifested only by repeated criminal or otherwise antisocial conduct.

Section 4.02.   *Evidence of Mental Disease or Defect Admissible When Relevant to Element of the Offense; [Mental Disease or Defect Impairing Capacity as Ground for Mitigation of Punishment in Capital Cases]*

(1) Evidence that the defendant suffered from a mental disease or defect is admissible whenever it is relevant to prove that the defendant did or did not have a state of mind which is an element of the offense.

[(2) Whenever the jury or the Court is authorized to determine or to recommend whether or not the defendant shall be sentenced to death or imprisonment upon conviction, evidence that the capacity of the defendant to appreciate the criminality [wrongfulness] of his conduct or to conform his conduct to the requirements of law was impaired as a result of mental disease or defect is admissible in favor of sentence of imprisonment.]

Section 4.03.   *Mental Disease or Defect Excluding Responsibility Is Affirmative Defense; Requirement of Notice; Form of Verdict and Judgment When Finding of Irresponsibility Is Made*

(1) Mental disease or defect excluding responsibility is an affirmative defense.

(2) Evidence of mental disease or defect excluding responsibility is not admissible unless the defendant, at the time of entering his plea of not guilty or within ten days thereafter or at such later time as the Court may for good cause permit, files a written notice of his purpose to rely on such defense.

(3) When the defendant is acquitted on the ground of mental disease or defect excluding responsibility, the verdict and the judgment shall so state.

Section 4.04.   *Mental Disease or Defect Excluding Fitness to Proceed*

No person who as a result of mental disease or defect lacks capacity to understand the proceedings against him or to assist in his own defense shall be tried, convicted or sentenced for the commission of an offense so long as such incapacity endures.

Section 4.05.   Psychiatric Examination of Defendant with Respect to Mental Disease or Defect

(1) Whenever the defendant has filed a notice of intention to rely on the defense of mental disease or defect excluding responsibility, or there is reason to doubt his fitness to proceed, or reason to believe that mental disease or defect of the defendant will otherwise become an issue in the cause, the Court shall appoint at least one qualified psychiatrist or shall request the Superintendent of the _____ Hospital to designate at least one qualified psychiatrist, which designation may be or include himself, to examine and report upon the mental condition of the defendant. The Court may order the defendant to be committed to a hospital or other suitable facility for the purpose of the examination for a period of not exceeding sixty days or such longer period as the Court determines to be necessary for the purpose and may direct that a qualified psychiatrist retained by the defendant be permitted to witness and participate in the examination.

(2) In such examination any method may be employed which is accepted by the medical profession for the examination of those alleged to be suffering from mental disease or defect.

(3) The report of the examination shall include the following: (a) a description of the nature of the examination; (b) a diagnosis of the mental condition of the defendant; (c) if the defendant suffers from a mental disease or defect, an opinion as to his capacity to understand the proceedings against him and to assist in his own defense; (d) when a notice of intention to rely on the defense of irresponsibility has been filed, an opinion as to the extent, if any, to which the capacity of the defendant to appreciate the criminality [wrongfulness] of his conduct or to conform his conduct to the requirements of law was impaired at the time of the criminal conduct charged; and (e) when directed by the Court, an opinion as to the capacity of the defendant to have a particular state of mind which is an element of the offense charged.

If the examination cannot be conducted by reason of the unwillingness of the defendant to participate therein, the report shall so state and shall include, if possible, an opinion as to whether such unwillingness of the defendant was the result of mental disease or defect.

The report of the examination shall be filed [in triplicate] with the clerk of the Court, who shall cause copies to be delivered to the district attorney and to counsel for the defendant.

Section 4.06.   Determination of Fitness to Proceed; Effect of Finding of Unfitness; Proceedings if Fitness Is Regained[; Post-Commitment Hearing]

(1) When the defendant's fitness to proceed is drawn in question, the issue shall be determined by the Court. If neither the prosecuting attorney nor counsel for the defendant contests the finding of the report filed pursuant to Section 4.05, the Court may make the determination on the basis of such report. If the finding is contested, the Court shall hold a hearing on the issue. If the report is received in evidence upon such hearing, the party who contests the finding thereof shall have the right to summon and to cross-examine the psychiatrists who joined in the report and to offer evidence upon the issue.

(2) If the Court determines that the defendant lacks fitness to proceed, the proceeding against him shall be suspended, except as provided in Subsection (3) [Subsections (3) and (4)] of this Section, and the Court shall commit him to the custody of the Commissioner of Mental Hygiene [Public Health or Correction] to be placed in an appropriate institution of the Department of Mental Hygiene [Public Health or Correction] for so long as such unfitness shall endure. When the Court, on its own motion or upon the application of the Commissioner of Mental Hygiene [Public Health or Correction] or the prosecuting attorney, determines, after a hearing if a hearing is requested, that the defendant has regained fitness to proceed, the proceeding shall be resumed. If, however,

the Court is of the view that so much time has elapsed since the commitment of the defendant that it would be unjust to resume the criminal proceeding, the Court may dismiss the charge and may order the defendant to be discharged or, subject to the law governing the civil commitment of persons suffering from mental disease or defect, order the defendant to be committed to an appropriate institution of the Department of Mental Hygiene [Public Health].

(3) The fact that the defendant is unfit to proceed does not preclude any legal objection to the prosecution that is susceptible of fair determination prior to trial and without the personal participation of the defendant.

[Alternative: (3) At any time within ninety days after commitment as provided in Subsection (2) of this Section, or at any later time with permission of the Court granted for good cause, the defendant or his counsel or the Commissioner of Mental Hygiene [Public Health or Correction] may apply for a special post-commitment hearing. If the application is made by or on behalf of a defendant not represented by counsel, he shall be afforded a reasonable opportunity to obtain counsel, and if he lacks funds to do so, counsel shall be assigned by the Court. The application shall be granted only if counsel for the defendant satisfies the Court by affidavit or otherwise that as an attorney he has reasonable grounds for a good faith belief that his client has, on the facts and the law, a defense to the charge other than mental disease or defect excluding responsibility.]

[(4) If the motion for a special post-commitment hearing is granted, the hearing shall be by the Court without a jury. No evidence shall be offered at the hearing by either party on the issue of mental disease or defect as a defense to, or in mitigation of, the crime charged. After hearing, the Court may in an appropriate case quash the indictment or other charge, or find it to be defective or insufficient, or determine that it is not proved beyond a reasonable doubt by the evidence, or otherwise terminate the proceedings on the evidence or the law. In any such case, unless all defects in the proceedings are promptly cured, the Court shall terminate the commitment ordered under Subsection (2) of this Section and order the defendant to be discharged or, subject to the law governing the civil commitment of persons suffering from mental disease or defect, order the defendant to be committed to an appropriate institution of the Department of Mental Hygiene [Public Health].]

Section 4.07.   *Determination of Irresponsibility on Basis of Reports;*
Access to Defendant by Psychiatrist of His Own Choice; Form of
Expert Testimony When Issue of Responsibility Is Tried

(1) If the report filed pursuant to Section 4.05 finds that the defendant at the time of the criminal conduct charged suffered from a mental disease or defect which substantially impaired his capacity to appreciate the criminality [wrongfulness] of his conduct or to conform his conduct to the requirements of law, and the Court, after a hearing if a hearing is requested by the prosecuting attorney or the defendant, is satisfied that such impairment was sufficient to exclude responsibility, the Court on motion of the defendant shall enter judgment of acquittal on the ground of mental disease or defect excluding responsibility.

(2) When, notwithstanding the report filed pursuant to Section 4.05, the defendant wishes to be examined by a qualified psychiatrist or other expert of his own choice, such examiner shall be permitted to have reasonable access to the defendant for the purpose of such examination.

(3) Upon the trial, the psychiatrists who reported pursuant to Section 4.05 may be called as witnesses by the prosecution, the defendant or the Court. If the issue is being tried before a jury, the jury may be informed that the psychiatrists were designated by the Court or by the Superintendent of the _____ Hospital at the request of the Court, as the case may be. If called by the Court, the witness shall be subject to cross-examination by the prosecution and by the defendant. Both the prosecution and the defendant may summon any other qualified psychiatrist or other expert to testify, but no

one who has not examined the defendant shall be competent to testify to an expert opinion with respect to the mental condition or responsibility of the defendant, as distinguished from the validity of the procedure followed by, or the general scientific propositions stated by, another witness.

(4) When a psychiatrist or other expert who has examined the defendant testifies concerning his mental condition, he shall be permitted to make a statement as to the nature of his examination, his diagnosis of the mental condition of the defendant at the time of the commission of the offense charged and his opinion as to the extent, if any, to which the capacity of the defendant to appreciate the criminality [wrongfulness] of his conduct or to conform his conduct to the requirements of law or to have a particular state of mind that is an element of the offense charged was impaired as a result of mental disease or defect at that time. He shall be permitted to make any explanation reasonably serving to clarify his diagnosis and opinion and may be cross-examined as to any matter bearing on his competency or credibility or the validity of his diagnosis or opinion.

Section 4.08.   Legal Effect of Acquittal on the Ground of Mental Disease or Defect Excluding Responsibility; Commitment; Release or Discharge

(1) When a defendant is acquitted on the ground of mental disease or defect excluding responsibility, the Court shall order him to be committed to the custody of the Commissioner of Mental Hygiene [Public Health] to be placed in an appropriate institution for custody, care and treatment.

(2) If the Commissioner of Mental Hygiene [Public Health] is of the view that a person committed to his custody, pursuant to paragraph (1) of this Section, may be discharged or released on condition without danger to himself or to others, he shall make application for the discharge or release of such person in a report to the Court by which such person was committed and shall transmit a copy of such application and report to the prosecuting attorney of the county [parish] from which the defendant was committed. The Court shall thereupon appoint at least two qualified psychiatrists to examine such person and to report within sixty days, or such longer period as the Court determines to be necessary for the purpose, their opinion as to his mental condition. To facilitate such examination and the proceedings thereon, the Court may cause such person to be confined in any institution located near the place where the Court sits, which may hereafter be designated by the Commissioner of Mental Hygiene [Public Health] as suitable for the temporary detention of irresponsible persons.

(3) If the Court is satisfied by the report filed pursuant to paragraph (2) of this Section and such testimony of the reporting psychiatrists as the Court deems necessary that the committed person may be discharged or released on condition without danger to himself or others, the Court shall order his discharge or his release on such conditions as the Court determines to be necessary. If the Court is not so satisfied, it shall promptly order a hearing to determine whether such person may safely be discharged or released. Any such hearing shall be deemed a civil proceeding and the burden shall be upon the committed person to prove that he may safely be discharged or released. According to the determination of the Court upon the hearing, the committed person shall thereupon be discharged or released on such conditions as the Court determines to be necessary, or shall be recommitted to the custody of the Commissioner of Mental Hygiene [Public Health], subject to discharge or release only in accordance with the procedure prescribed above for a first hearing.

(4) If, within [five] years after the conditional release of a committed person, the Court shall determine, after hearing evidence, that the conditions of release have not been fulfilled and that for the safety of such person or for the safety of others his conditional release should be revoked, the Court shall forthwith order him to be recommitted to the Commissioner of Mental Hygiene [Public Health], subject to discharge or release only in accordance with the procedure prescribed above for a first hearing.

(5) A committed person may make application for his discharge or release to the Court by which he was committed, and the procedure to be followed upon such application shall be the same as that prescribed above in the case of an application by the Commissioner of Mental Hygiene [Public Health]. However, no such application by a committed person need be considered until he has been confined for a period of not less than [six months] from the date of the order of commitment, and if the determination of the Court be adverse to the application, such person shall not be permitted to file a further application until [one year] has elapsed from the date of any preceding hearing on an application for his release or discharge.

Section 4.09.   *Statements for Purposes of Examination or Treatment Inadmissible Except on Issue of Mental Condition*

A statement made by a person subjected to psychiatric examination or treatment pursuant to Sections 4.05, 4.06 or 4.08 for the purposes of such examination or treatment shall not be admissible in evidence against him in any criminal proceeding on any issue other than that of his mental condition but it shall be admissible upon that issue, whether or not it would otherwise be deemed a privileged communication[, unless such statement constitutes an admission of guilt of the crime charged].

Section 4.10.   *Immaturity Excluding Criminal Conviction; Transfer of Proceedings to Juvenile Court*

(1) A person shall not be tried for or convicted of an offense if:

(a) at the time of the conduct charged to constitute the offense he was less than sixteen years of age[, in which case the Juvenile Court shall have exclusive jurisdiction]; or

(b) at the time of the conduct charged to constitute the offense he was sixteen or seventeen years of age, unless:

(i)   the Juvenile Court has no jurisdiction over him, or,

(ii) the Juvenile Court has entered an order waiving jurisdiction and consenting to the institution of criminal proceedings against him.

(2) No court shall have jurisdiction to try or convict a person of an offense if criminal proceedings against him are barred by Subsection (1) of this Section. When it appears that a person charged with the commission of an offense may be of such an age that criminal proceedings may be barred under Subsection (1) of this Section, the Court shall hold a hearing thereon, and the burden shall be on the prosecution to establish to the satisfaction of the Court that the criminal proceeding is not barred upon such grounds. If the Court determines that the proceeding is barred, custody of the person charged shall be surrendered to the Juvenile Court, and the case, including all papers and processes relating thereto, shall be transferred.

Article 5.   Inchoate Crimes

Section 5.01.   *Criminal Attempt*

(1) *Definition of Attempt.* A person is guilty of an attempt to commit a crime if, acting with the kind of culpability otherwise required for commission of the crime, he:

(a) purposely engages in conduct that would constitute the crime if the attendant circumstances were as he believes them to be; or

(b) when causing a particular result is an element of the crime, does or omits to do anything with the purpose of causing or with the belief that it will cause such result without further conduct on his part; or

(c) purposely does or omits to do anything which, under the circumstances as he believes them to be, is an act or omission constituting a substantial step in a course of conduct planned to culminate in his commission of the crime.

(2) *Conduct Which May Be Held Substantial Step Under Subsection (1)(c).* Conduct shall not be held to constitute a substantial step under Subsection (1)(c) of this Section unless it is strongly corroborative of the actor's criminal purpose. Without negativing the sufficiency of other conduct, the following, if strongly corroborative of the actor's criminal purpose, shall not be held insufficient as a matter of law:

   (a) lying in wait, searching for or following the contemplated victim of the crime;

   (b) enticing or seeking to entice the contemplated victim of the crime to go to the place contemplated for its commission;

   (c) reconnoitering the place contemplated for the commission of the crime;

   (d) unlawful entry of a structure, vehicle or enclosure in which it is contemplated that the crime will be committed;

   (e) possession of materials to be employed in the commission of the crime, that are specially designed for such unlawful use or which can serve no lawful purpose of the actor under the circumstances;

   (f) possession, collection or fabrication of materials to be employed in the commission of the crime, at or near the place contemplated for its commission, where such possession, collection or fabrication serves no lawful purpose of the actor under the circumstances;

   (g) soliciting an innocent agent to engage in conduct constituting an element of the crime.

(3) *Conduct Designed to Aid Another in Commission of a Crime.* A person who engages in conduct designed to aid another to commit a crime that would establish his complicity under Section 2.06 if the crime were committed by such other person, is guilty of an attempt to commit the crime, although the crime is not committed or attempted by such other person.

(4) *Renunciation of Criminal Purpose.* When the actor's conduct would otherwise constitute an attempt under Subsection (1)(b) or (1)(c) of this Section, it is an affirmative defense that he abandoned his effort to commit the crime or otherwise prevented its commission, under circumstances manifesting a complete and voluntary renunciation of his criminal purpose. The establishment of such defense does not, however, affect the liability of an accomplice who did not join in such abandonment or prevention.

Within the meaning of this Article, renunciation of criminal purpose is not voluntary if it is motivated, in whole or in part, by circumstances, not present or apparent at the inception of the actor's course of conduct, that increase the probability of detection or apprehension or which make more difficult the accomplishment of the criminal purpose. Renunciation is not complete if it is motivated by a decision to postpone the criminal conduct until a more advantageous time or to transfer the criminal effort to another but similar objective or victim.

Section 5.02.   Criminal Solicitation

(1) *Definition of Solicitation.* A person is guilty of solicitation to commit a crime if with the purpose of promoting or facilitating its commission he commands, encourages or requests another person to engage in specific conduct that would constitute such crime or an attempt to commit such crime or which would establish his complicity in its commission or attempted commission.

(2) *Uncommunicated Solicitation.* It is immaterial under Subsection (1) of this Section that the actor fails to communicate with the person he solicits to commit a crime if his conduct was designed to effect such communication.

(3) *Renunciation of Criminal Purpose.* It is an affirmative defense that the actor, after soliciting another person to commit a crime, persuaded him not to do so or otherwise prevented the commission of the crime, under circumstances manifesting a complete and voluntary renunciation of his criminal purpose.

Section 5.03.   Criminal Conspiracy

(1) *Definition of Conspiracy.* A person is guilty of conspiracy with another person or persons to commit a crime if with the purpose of promoting or facilitating its commission he:

(a)   agrees with such other person or persons that they or one or more of them will engage in conduct that constitutes such crime or an attempt or solicitation to commit such crime; or

(b)   agrees to aid such other person or persons in the planning or commission of such crime or of an attempt or solicitation to commit such crime.

(2) *Scope of Conspiratorial Relationship.* If a person guilty of conspiracy, as defined by Subsection (1) of this Section, knows that a person with whom he conspires to commit a crime has conspired with another person or persons to commit the same crime, he is guilty of conspiring with such other person or persons, whether or not he knows their identity, to commit such crime.

(3) *Conspiracy With Multiple Criminal Objectives.* If a person conspires to commit a number of crimes, he is guilty of only one conspiracy so long as such multiple crimes are the object of the same agreement or continuous conspiratorial relationship.

(4) *Joinder and Venue in Conspiracy Prosecutions.*

(a)   Subject to the provisions of paragraph (b) of this Subsection, two or more persons charged with criminal conspiracy may be prosecuted jointly if:

(i)   they are charged with conspiring with one another; or

(ii)   the conspiracies alleged, whether they have the same or different parties, are so related that they constitute different aspects of a scheme of organized criminal conduct.

(b)   In any joint prosecution under paragraph (a) of this Subsection:

(i)   no defendant shall be charged with a conspiracy in any county [parish or district] other than one in which he entered into such conspiracy or in which an overt act pursuant to such conspiracy was done by him or by a person with whom he conspired; and

(ii)   neither the liability of any defendant nor the admissibility against him of evidence of acts or declarations of another shall be enlarged by such joinder; and

(iii)   the Court shall order a severance or take a special verdict as to any defendant who so requests, if it deems it necessary or appropriate to promote the fair determination of his guilty or innocence, and shall take any other proper measures to protect the fairness of the trial.

(5) *Overt Act.* No person may be convicted of conspiracy to commit a crime, other than a felony of the first or second degree, unless an overt act in pursuance of such conspiracy is alleged and proved to have been done by him or by a person with whom he conspired:

(6) *Renunciation of Criminal Purpose.* It is an affirmative defense that the actor, after conspiring to commit a crime, thwarted the success of the conspiracy, under circumstances manifesting a complete and voluntary renunciation of his criminal purpose.

(7) *Duration of Conspiracy.* For purposes of Section 1.06(4):

(a)   conspiracy is a continuing course of conduct that terminates when the crime or crimes that are its object are committed or the agreement that they be committed is abandoned by the defendant and by those with whom he conspired; and

(b)   such abandonment is presumed if neither the defendant nor anyone with whom he conspired does any overt act in pursuance of the conspiracy during the applicable period of limitation; and

(c)   if an individual abandons the agreement, the conspiracy is terminated as to him only if and when he advises those with whom he conspired of his abandonment or he informs the law enforcement authorities of the existence of the conspiracy and of his participation therein.

Section 5.04.   Incapacity, Irresponsibility or Immunity of Party to Solicitation or Conspiracy

(1) Except as provided in Subsection (2) of this Section, it is immaterial to the liability of a person who solicits or conspires with another to commit a crime that:

(a) he or the person whom he solicits or with whom he conspires does not occupy a particular position or have a particular characteristic that is an element of such crime, if he believes that one of them does; or

(b) the person whom he solicits or with whom he conspires is irresponsible or has an immunity to prosecution or conviction for the commission of the crime.

(2) It is a defense to a charge of solicitation or conspiracy to commit a crime that if the criminal object were achieved, the actor would not be guilty of a crime under the law defining the offense or as an accomplice under Section 2.06(5) or 2.06(6) (a) or (b).

Section 5.05.   Grading of Criminal Attempt, Solicitation and Conspiracy; Mitigation in Cases of Lesser Danger; Multiple Convictions Barred

(1) *Grading.* Except as otherwise provided in this Section, attempt, solicitation and conspiracy are crimes of the same grade and degree as the most serious offense that is attempted or solicited or is an object of the conspiracy. An attempt, solicitation or conspiracy to commit a [capital crime or a] felony of the first degree is a felony of the second degree.

(2) *Mitigation.* If the particular conduct charged to constitute a criminal attempt, solicitation or conspiracy is so inherently unlikely to result or culminate in the commission of a crime that neither such conduct nor the actor presents a public danger warranting the grading of such offense under this Section, the Court shall exercise its power under Section 6.12 to enter judgment and impose sentence for a crime of lower grade or degree or, in extreme cases, may dismiss the prosecution.

(3) *Multiple Convictions.* A person may not be convicted of more than one offense defined by this Article for conduct designed to commit or to culminate in the commission of the same crime.

Section 5.06.   Possessing Instruments of Crime; Weapons

(1) *Criminal Instruments Generally.* A person commits a misdemeanor if he possesses any instrument of crime with purpose to employ it criminally. "Instrument of crime" means:

(a) anything specially made or specially adapted for criminal use; or

(b) anything commonly used for criminal purposes and possessed by the actor under circumstances that do not negative unlawful purpose.

(2) *Presumption of Criminal Purpose from Possession of Weapon.* If a person possesses a firearm or other weapon on or about his person, in a vehicle occupied by him, or otherwise readily available for use, it is presumed that he had the purpose to employ it criminally, unless:

(a) the weapon is possessed in the actor's home or place of business;

(b) the actor is licensed or otherwise authorized by law to possess such weapon; or

(c) the weapon is of a type commonly used in lawful sport.

"Weapon" means anything readily capable of lethal use and possessed under circumstances not manifestly appropriate for lawful uses it may have; the term includes a firearm that is not loaded or lacks a clip or other component to render it immediately operable, and components that can readily be assembled into a weapon.

(3) *Presumptions as to Possession of Criminal Instruments in Automobiles.* If a weapon or other instrument of crime is found in an automobile, it is presumed to be in the possession of the occupant if there is but one. If there is more than one occupant, it shall be presumed to be in the possession of all, except under the following circumstances:

(a) it is found upon the person of one of the occupants;

(b) the automobile is not a stolen one and the weapon or instrument is found out of view in a glove compartment, car trunk, or other enclosed customary depository, in which case it is presumed to be in the possession of the occupant or occupants who own or have authority to operate the automobile;

(c) in the case of a taxicab, a weapon or instrument found in the passenger's portion of the vehicle shall be presumed to be in the possession of all the passengers, if there are any, and, if not, in the possession of the driver.

Section 5.07.   *Prohibited Offensive Weapons*

A person commits a misdemeanor if, except as authorized by law, he makes, repairs, sells, or otherwise deals in, uses or possesses any offensive weapon. "Offensive weapon" means any bomb, machine gun, sawed-off shotgun, firearm specially made or specially adapted for concealment or silent discharge, any blackjack, sandbag, metal knuckles, dagger, or other implement for the infliction of serious bodily injury that serves no common lawful purpose. It is a defense under this Section for the defendant to prove by a preponderance of evidence that he possessed or dealt with the weapon solely as a curio or in a dramatic performance, or that he possessed it briefly in consequence of having found it or taken it from an aggressor, or under circumstances similarly negativing any purpose or likelihood that the weapon would be used unlawfully. The presumptions provided in Section 5.06(3) are applicable to prosecutions under this Section.

Article 6.   Authorized Disposition of Offenders

Section 6.01.   *Degrees of Felonies*

(1) Felonies defined by this Code are classified, for the purpose of sentence, into three degrees, as follows:

(a) felonies of the first degree;

(b) felonies of the second degree;

(c) felonies of the third degree.

A felony is of the first or second degree when it is so designated by the Code. A crime declared to be a felony, without specification of degree, is of the third degree.

(2) Notwithstanding any other provision of law, a felony defined by any statute of this State other than this Code shall constitute, for the purpose of sentence, a felony of the third degree.

Section 6.02.   *Sentence in Accordance with Code;*
Authorized Dispositions [Omitted]

Section 6.03.   *Fines*

A person who has been convicted of an offense may be sentenced to pay a fine not exceeding:

(1) $10,000, when the conviction is of a felony of the first or second degree;

(2) $5,000, when the conviction is of a felony of the third degree;

(3) $1,000, when the conviction is of a misdemeanor;

(4) $500, when the conviction is of a petty misdemeanor or a violation;

(5) any higher amount equal to double the pecuniary gain derived from the offense by the offender;

(6) any higher amount specifically authorized by statute.

Section 6.04.   *Penalties Against Corporations and Unincorporated Associations; Forfeiture of Corporate Charter or Revocation of Certificate Authorizing Foreign Corporation to Do Business in the State*

(1) The Court may suspend the sentence of a corporation or an unincorporated association that has been convicted of an offense or may sentence it to pay a fine authorized by Section 6.03.

(2) (a) The [prosecuting attorney] is authorized to institute civil proceedings in the appropriate court of general jurisdiction to forfeit the charter of a corporation organized under the laws of this State or to revoke the certificate authorizing a foreign corporation to conduct business in this State. The Court may order the charter forfeited or the certificate revoked upon finding (i) that the board of directors or a high managerial agent acting in behalf of the corporation has, in conducting the corporation's affairs, purposely engaged in a persistent course of criminal conduct and (ii) that for the prevention of future criminal conduct of the same character, the public interest requires the charter of the corporation to be forfeited and the corporation to be dissolved or the certificate to be revoked.

(b) When a corporation is convicted of a crime or a high managerial agent of a corporation, as defined in Section 2.07, is convicted of a crime committed in the conduct of the affairs of the corporation, the Court, in sentencing the corporation or the agent, may direct the [prosecuting attorney] to institute proceedings authorized by paragraph (a) of this Subsection.

(c) The proceedings authorized by paragraph (a) of this Subsection shall be conducted in accordance with the procedures authorized by law for the involuntary dissolution of a corporation or the revocation of the certificate authorizing a foreign corporation to conduct business in this State. Such proceedings shall be deemed additional to any other proceedings authorized by law for the purpose of forfeiting the charter of a corporation or revoking the certificate of a foreign corporation.

Section 6.05.   *Young Adult Offenders*

(1) *Specialized Correctional Treatment.* A young adult offender is a person convicted of a crime who, at the time of sentencing, is sixteen but less than twenty-two years of age. A young adult offender who is sentenced to a term of imprisonment that may exceed thirty days [alternatives: (1) ninety days; (2) one year] shall be committed to the custody of the Division of Young Adult Correction of the Department of Correction, and shall receive, as far as practicable, such special and individualized correctional and rehabilitative treatment as may be appropriate to his needs.

(2) *Special Term.* A young adult offender convicted of a felony may, in lieu of any other sentence of imprisonment authorized by this Article, be sentenced to a special term of imprisonment without a minimum and with a maximum of four years, regardless of the degree of the felony involved, if the Court is of the opinion that such special term is adequate for his correction and rehabilitation and will not jeopardize the protection of the public.

(3) *Removal of Disabilities; Vacation of Conviction.*

(a) In sentencing a young adult offender to the special term provided by this Section or to any sentence other than one of imprisonment, the Court may order that so long as he is not convicted of another felony, the judgment shall not constitute a conviction for the purposes of any disqualification or disability imposed by law upon conviction of a crime.

(b) When any young adult offender is unconditionally discharged from probation or parole before the expiration of the maximum term thereof, the Court may enter an order vacating the judgment of conviction.

[(4) *Commitment for Observation.* If, after pre-sentence investigation, the Court desires additional information concerning a young adult offender before imposing sentence, it may order that he be committed, for a period not exceeding ninety days, to the custody of the Division of Young Adult Correction of the Department of Correction for observation and study at an appropriate reception or classification center. Such Division of the Department of Correction and the [Young Adult Division of the] Board of Parole shall advise the Court of their findings and recommendations on or before the expiration of such ninety-day period.]

Section 6.06.   *Sentence of Imprisonment for Felony; Ordinary Terms*

A person who has been convicted of a felony may be sentenced to imprisonment, as follows:

(1) in the case of a felony of the first degree, for a term the minimum of which shall be fixed by the Court at not less than one year nor more than ten years, and the maximum of which shall be life imprisonment;

(2) in the case of a felony of the second degree, for a term the minimum of which shall be fixed by the Court at not less than one year nor more than three years, and the maximum of which shall be ten years;

(3) in the case of a felony of the third degree, for a term the minimum of which shall be fixed by the Court at not less than one year nor more than two years, and the maximum of which shall be five years.

Alternate Section 6.06.   *Sentence of Imprisonment for Felony;*
Ordinary Terms

A person who has been convicted of a felony may be sentenced to imprisonment, as follows:

(1) in the case of a felony of the first degree, for a term the minimum of which shall be fixed by the Court at not less than one year nor more than ten years, and the maximum at not more than twenty years or at life imprisonment;

(2) in the case of a felony of the second degree, for a term the minimum of which shall be fixed by the Court at not less than one year nor more than three years, and the maximum at not more than ten years;

(3) in the case of a felony of the third degree, for a term the minimum of which shall be fixed by the Court at not less than one year nor more than two years, and the maximum at not more than five years.

No sentence shall be imposed under this Section of which the minimum is longer than one half the maximum, or, when the maximum is life imprisonment, longer than ten years.

Section 6.07.   *Sentence of Imprisonment for Felony: Extended Terms*

In the cases designated in Section 7.03, a person who has been convicted of a felony may be sentenced to an extended term of imprisonment, as follows:

(1) in the case of a felony of the first degree, for a term the minimum of which shall be fixed by the Court at not less than five years nor more than ten years, and the maximum of which shall be life imprisonment;

(2) in the case of a felony of the second degree, for a term the minimum of which

shall be fixed by the Court at not less than one year nor more than five years, and the maximum of which shall be fixed by the Court at not less than ten years nor more than twenty years;

(3) in the case of a felony of the third degree for a term the minimum of which shall be fixed by the Court at not less than one year nor more than three years, and the maximum of which shall be fixed by the Court at not less than five nor more than ten years.

Section 6.08.   Sentence of Imprisonment for Misdemeanors and Petty Misdemeanors; Ordinary Terms

A person who has been convicted of a misdemeanor or a petty misdemeanor may be sentenced to imprisonment for a definite term which shall be fixed by the Court and shall not exceed one year in the case of a misdemeanor or thirty days in the case of a petty misdemeanor.

Section 6.09.   Sentence of Imprisonment for Misdemeanors and Petty Misdemeanors; Extended Terms

(1) In the cases designated in Section 7.04 a person who has been convicted of a misdemeanor or a petty misdemeanor may be sentenced to an extended term of imprisonment as follows:

(a) in the case of a misdemeanor, for a term the minimum of which shall be fixed by the Court at not more than one year and the maximum of which shall be three years;

(b) in the case of a petty misdemeanor, for a term the minimum of which shall be fixed by the Court at not more than six months and the maximum of which shall be two years.

(2) No such sentence for an extended term shall be imposed unless:

(a) the Director of Correction has certified that there is an institution in the Department of Correction, or in a county, city [or other appropriate political subdivision of the State] that is appropriate for the detention and correctional treatment of such misdemeanants or petty misdemeanants, and that such institution is available to receive such commitments; and

(b) the [Board of Parole] [Parole Administrator] has certified that the Board of Parole is able to visit such institution and to assume responsibility for the release of such prisoners on parole and for their parole supervision. . . .

PART II.   DEFINITION OF SPECIFIC CRIMES

Offenses Involving Danger to the Person

Article 210.   Criminal Homicide

Section 210.0.   Definitions

In Articles 210-213, unless a different meaning plainly is required:

(1) "human being" means a person who has been born and is alive;

(2) "bodily injury" means physical pain, illness or any impairment of physical ondition;

(3) "serious bodily injury" means bodily injury which creates a substantial risk of death or which causes serious, permanent disfigurement, or protracted loss or impairment of the function of any bodily member or organ;

(4) "deadly weapon" means any firearm or other weapon, device, instrument, material or substance, whether animate or inanimate, which in the manner it is used or is intended to be used is known to be capable of producing death or serious bodily injury.

Section 210.1.   Criminal Homicide

(1) A person is guilty of criminal homicide if he purposely, knowingly, recklessly or negligently causes the death of another human being.

(2) Criminal homicide is murder, manslaughter or negligent homicide.

Section 210.2.   Murder

(1) Except as provided in Section 210.3(1)(b), criminal homicide constitutes murder when:

(a) it is committed purposely or knowingly; or

(b) it is committed recklessly under circumstances manifesting extreme indifference to the value of human life. Such recklessness and indifference are presumed if the actor is engaged or is an accomplice in the commission of, or an attempt to commit, or flight after committing or attempting to commit robbery, rape or deviate sexual intercourse by force or threat of force, arson, burglary, kidnapping or felonious escape. *, or inher dang of 1st deg*

must in all cases be presumed

(2) Murder is a felony of the first degree [but a person convicted of murder may be sentenced to death, as provided in Section 210.6].

Section 210.3.   Manslaughter

(1) Criminal homicide constitutes manslaughter when:

(a) it is committed recklessly; or

(b) a homicide which would otherwise be murder is committed under the influence of extreme mental or emotional disturbance for which there is reasonable explanation or excuse. The reasonableness of such explanation or excuse shall be determined from the viewpoint of a person in the actor's situation under the circumstances as he believes them to be.

(2) Manslaughter is a felony of the second degree.

Section 210.4.   Negligent Homicide

(1) Criminal homicide constitutes negligent homicide when it is committed negligently.

(2) Negligent homicide is a felony of the third degree.

Section 210.5.   Causing or Aiding Suicide

(1) *Causing Suicide as Criminal Homicide.* A person may be convicted of criminal homicide for causing another to commit suicide only if he purposely causes such suicide by force, duress or deception.

(2) *Aiding or Soliciting Suicide as an Independent Offense.* A person who purposely aids or solicits another to commit suicide is guilty of a felony of the second degree if his conduct causes such suicide or an attempted suicide, and otherwise of a misdemeanor.

Section 210.6.   Sentence of Death for Murder; Further Proceedings to Determine Sentence[1]

(1) *Death Sentence Excluded.* When a defendant is found guilty of murder, the Court shall impose sentence for a felony of the first degree if it is satisfied that:

(a) none of the aggravating circumstances enumerated in Subsection (3) of this Section was established by the evidence at the trial or will be established if further proceedings are initiated under Subsection (2) of this Section; or

1. . . . [T]he Institute took no position on the desirability of the death penalty. . . .

(b) substantial mitigating circumstances, established by the evidence at the trial, call for leniency; or

(c) the defendant, with the consent of the prosecuting attorney and the approval of the Court, pleaded guilty to murder as a felony of the first degree; or

(d) the defendant was under 18 years of age at the time of the commission of the crime; or

(e) the defendant's physical or mental condition calls for leniency; or

(f) although the evidence suffices to sustain the verdict, it does not foreclose all doubt respecting the defendant's guilt.

(2) *Determination by Court or by Court and Jury.* Unless the Court imposes sentence under Subsection (1) of this Section, it shall conduct a separate proceeding to determine whether the defendant should be sentenced for a felony of the first degree or sentenced to death. The proceeding shall be conducted before the Court alone if the defendant was convicted by a Court sitting without a jury or upon his plea of guilty or if the prosecuting attorney and the defendant waive a jury with respect to sentence. In other cases it shall be conducted before the Court sitting with the jury which determined the defendant's guilt or, if the Court for good cause shown discharges that jury, with a new jury empanelled for the purpose.

In the proceeding, evidence may be presented as to any matter that the Court deems relevant to sentence, including but not limited to the nature and circumstances of the crime, the defendant's character, background, history, mental and physical condition and any of the aggravating or mitigating circumstances enumerated in Subsections (3) and (4) of this Section. Any such evidence, not legally privileged, which the Court deems to have probative force, may be received, regardless of its admissibility under the exclusionary rules of evidence, provided that the defendant's counsel is accorded a fair opportunity to rebut such evidence. The prosecuting attorney and the defendant or his counsel shall be permitted to present argument for or against sentence of death.

The determination whether sentence of death shall be imposed shall be in the discretion of the Court, except that when the proceeding is conducted before the Court sitting with a jury, the Court shall not impose sentence of death unless it submits to the jury the issue whether the defendant should be sentenced to death or to imprisonment and the jury returns a verdict that the sentence should be death. If the jury is unable to reach a unanimous verdict, the Court shall dismiss the jury and impose sentence for a felony of the first degree.

The Court, in exercising its discretion as to sentence, and the jury, in determining upon its verdict, shall take into account the aggravating and mitigating circumstances enumerated in Subsections (3) and (4) and any other facts that it deems relevant, but it shall not impose or recommend sentence of death unless it finds one of the aggravating circumstances enumerated in Subsection (3) and further finds that there are no mitigating circumstances sufficiently substantial to call for leniency. When the issue is submitted to the jury, the Court shall so instruct and also shall inform the jury of the nature of the sentence of imprisonment that may be imposed, including its implication with respect to possible release upon parole, if the jury verdict is against sentence of death.

Alternative formulation of Subsection (2):

(2) *Determination by Court.* Unless the Court imposes sentence under Subsection (1) of this Section, it shall conduct a separate proceeding to determine whether the defendant should be sentenced for a felony of the first degree or sentenced to death. In the proceeding, the Court, in accordance with Section 7.07, shall consider the report of the presentence investigation and, if a psychiatric examination has been ordered, the report of such examination. In addition, evidence may be presented as to any matter that the Court deems relevant to sentence, including but not limited to the nature and circumstances of the crime, the defendant's character, background, history, mental and physical condition and any of the aggravating or mitigating circumstances enumerated in Subsections (3) and (4) of this Section. Any such evidence, not legally privileged, which the Court deems to have probative force, may be received, regardless of its admissibility

under the exclusionary rules of evidence, provided that the defendant's counsel is accorded a fair opportunity to rebut such evidence. The prosecuting attorney and the defendant or his counsel shall be permitted to present argument for or against sentence of death.

The determination whether sentence of death shall be imposed shall be in the discretion of the Court. In exercising such discretion, the Court shall take into account the aggravating and mitigating circumstances enumerated in Subsections (3) and (4) and any other facts that it deems relevant but shall not impose sentence of death unless it finds one of the aggravating circumstances enumerated in Subsection (3) and further finds that there are no mitigating circumstances sufficiently substantial to call for leniency.

(3) *Aggravating Circumstances.*

(a) The murder was committed by a convict under sentence of imprisonment.

(b) The defendant was previously convicted of another murder or of a felony involving the use or threat of violence to the person.

(c) At the time the murder was committed the defendant also committed another murder.

(d) The defendant knowingly created a great risk of death to many persons.

(e) The murder was committed while the defendant was engaged or was an accomplice in the commission of, or an attempt to commit, ~~or flight after committing or attempting to commit~~ robbery, rape or deviate sexual intercourse by force or threat of force, arson, burglary or kidnapping, *fel escape, or inher dang of 1st deg*

(f) The murder was committed for the purpose of avoiding or preventing a lawful arrest or effecting an escape from lawful custody.

(g) The murder was committed for pecuniary gain.

(h) The murder was especially heinous, atrocious or cruel, manifesting exceptional depravity.

(4) *Mitigating Circumstances.*

(a) The defendant has no significant history of prior criminal activity.

(b) The murder was committed while the defendant was under the influence of extreme mental or emotional disturbance.

(c) The victim was a participant in the defendant's homicidal conduct or consented to the homicidal act.

(d) The murder was committed under circumstances which the defendant believed to provide a moral justification or extenuation for his conduct.

(e) The defendant was an accomplice in a murder committed by another person and his participation in the homicidal act was relatively minor.

(f) The defendant acted under duress or under the domination of another person.

(g) At the time of the murder, the capacity of the defendant to appreciate the criminality [wrongfulness] of his conduct or to conform his conduct to the requirements of law was impaired as a result of mental disease or defect or intoxication.

(h) The youth of the defendant at the time of the crime.

Article 211. Assault; Reckless Endangering; Threats

Section 211.0. Definitions

In this Article, the definitions given in Section 210.0 apply unless a different meaning plainly is required.

Section 211.1. Assault

(1) *Simple Assault.* A person is guilty of assault if he:

(a) attempts to cause or purposely, knowingly or recklessly causes bodily injury to another; or

(b) negligently causes bodily injury to another with a deadly weapon; or

(c) attempts by physical menace to put another in fear of imminent serious bodily injury.

Simple assault is a misdemeanor unless committed in a fight or scuffle entered into by mutual consent, in which case it is a petty misdemeanor.

(2) *Aggravated Assault.* A person is guilty of aggravated assault if he:

(a) attempts to cause serious bodily injury to another, or causes such injury purposely, knowingly or recklessly under circumstances manifesting extreme indifference to the value of human life; or

(b) attempts to cause or purposely or knowingly causes bodily injury to another with a deadly weapon.

Aggravated assault under paragraph (a) is a felony of the second degree; aggravated assault under paragraph (b) is a felony of the third degree.

Section 211.2.   *Recklessly Endangering Another Person*

A person commits a misdemeanor if he recklessly engages in conduct which places or may place another person in danger of death or serious bodily injury. Recklessness and danger shall be presumed where a person knowingly points a firearm at or in the direction of another, whether or not the actor believed the firearm to be loaded.

Section 211.3.   *Terroristic Threats*

A person is guilty of a felony of the third degree if he threatens to commit any crime of violence with purpose to terrorize another or to cause evacuation of a building, place of assembly, or facility of public transportation, or otherwise to cause serious public inconvenience, or in reckless disregard of the risk of causing such terror or inconvenience.

Article 212.   Kidnapping and Related Offenses; Coercion

Section 212.0.   *Definitions*

In this Article, the definitions given in section 210.0 apply unless a different meaning plainly is required.

Section 212.1.   *Kidnapping*

A person is guilty of kidnapping if he unlawfully removes another from his place of residence or business, or a substantial distance from the vicinity where he is found, or if he unlawfully confines another for a substantial period in a place of isolation, with any of the following purposes:

(a) to hold for random or reward, or as a shield or hostage; or

(b) to facilitate commission of any felony or flight thereafter; or

(c) to inflict bodily injury on or to terrorize the victim or another; or

(d) to interfere with the performance of any governmental or political function.

Kidnapping is a felony of the first degree unless the actor voluntarily releases the victim alive and in a safe place prior to trial, in which case it is a felony of the second degree. A removal or confinement is unlawful within the meaning of this Section if it is accomplished by force, threat or deception, or, in the case of a person who is under the age of 14 or incompetent, if it is accomplished without the consent of a parent, guardian or other person responsible for general supervision of his welfare.

Section 212.2.   *Felonious Restraint*

A person commits a felony of the third degree if he knowingly:

(a) restrains another unlawfully in circumstances exposing him to risk of serious bodily injury; or

(b) holds another in a condition of involuntary servitude.

Section 212.3.   False Imprisonment

A person commits a misdemeanor if he knowingly restrains another unlawfully so as to interfere substantially with his liberty.

Section 212.4.   Interference with Custody

(1) *Custody of Children.* A person commits an offense if he knowingly or recklessly takes or entices any child under the age of 18 from the custody of its parent, guardian or other lawful custodian, when he has no privilege to do so. It is an affirmative defense that:

(a) the actor believed that his action was necessary to preserve the child from danger to its welfare; or

(b) the child, being at the time not less than 14 years old, was taken away at its own instigation without enticement and without purpose to commit a criminal offense with or against the child.

Proof that the child was below the critical age gives rise to a presumption that the actor knew the child's age or acted in reckless disregard thereof. The offense is a misdemeanor unless the actor, not being a parent or person in equivalent relation to the child, acted with knowledge that his conduct would cause serious alarm for the child's safety, or in reckless disregard of a likelihood of causing such alarm, in which case the offense is a felony of the third degree.

(2) *Custody of Committed Persons.* A person is guilty of a misdemeanor if he knowingly or recklessly takes or entices any committed person away from lawful custody when he is not privileged to do so. "Committed person" means, in addition to anyone committed under judicial warrant, any orphan, neglected or delinquent child, mentally defective or insane person, or other dependent or incompetent person entrusted to another's custody by or through a recognized social agency or otherwise by authority of law.

Section 212.5.   Criminal Coercion

(1) *Offense Defined.* A person is guilty of criminal coercion if, with purpose unlawfully to restrict another's freedom of action to his detriment, he threatens to:

(a) commit any criminal offense; or

(b) accuse anyone of a criminal offense; or

(c) expose any secret tending to subject any person to hatred, contempt or ridicule, or to impair his credit or business repute; or

(d) take or withhold action as an official, or cause an official to take or withhold action.

It is an affirmative defense to prosecution based on paragraphs (b), (c) or (d) that the actor believed the accusation or secret to be true or the proposed official action justified and that his purpose was limited to compelling the other to behave in a way reasonably related to the circumstances which were the subject of the accusation, exposure or proposed official action, as by desisting from further misbehavior, making good a wrong done, refraining from taking any action or responsibility for which the actor believes the other disqualified.

(2) *Grading.* Criminal coercion is a misdemeanor unless the threat is to commit a felony or the actor's purpose is felonious, in which cases the offense is a felony of the third degree.

Article 213.   Sexual Offenses

Section 213.0.   Definitions

In this Article, unless a different meaning plainly is required:

(1) the definitions given in Section 210.0 apply;

(2) "Sexual intercourse" includes intercourse per os or per anum, with some penetration however slight; emission is not required;

(3) "Deviate sexual intercourse" means sexual intercourse per os or per anum between human beings who are not husband and wife, and any form of sexual intercourse with an animal.

Section 213.1.   Rape and Related Offenses

(1) *Rape.* A male who has sexual intercourse with a female not his wife is guilty of rape if:

(a) he compels her to submit by force or by threat of imminent death, serious bodily injury, extreme pain or kidnapping, to be inflicted on anyone; or

(b) he has substantially impaired her power to appraise or control her conduct by administering or employing without her knowledge drugs, intoxicants or other means for the purpose of preventing resistance; or

(c) the female is unconscious; or

(d) the female is less than 10 years old.

Rape is a felony of the second degree unless (i) in the course thereof the actor inflicts serious bodily injury upon anyone, or (ii) the victim was not a voluntary social companion of the actor upon the occasion of the crime and had not previously permitted him sexual liberties, in which cases the offense is a felony of the first degree.

(2) *Gross Sexual Imposition.* A male who has sexual intercourse with a female not his wife commits a felony of the third degree if:

(a) he compels her to submit by any threat that would prevent resistance by a woman of ordinary resolution; or

(b) he knows that she suffers from a mental disease or defect which renders her incapable of appraising the nature of her conduct; or

(c) he knows that she is unaware that a sexual act is being committed upon her or that she submits because she mistakenly supposes that he is her husband.

Section 213.2.   Deviate Sexual Intercourse by Force or Imposition

(1) *By Force or Its Equivalent.* A person who engages in deviate sexual intercourse with another person, or who causes another to engage in deviate sexual intercourse, commits a felony of the second degree if:

(a) he compels the other person to participate by force or by threat of imminent death, serious bodily injury, extreme pain or kidnapping, to be inflicted on anyone; or

(b) he has substantially impaired the other person's power to appraise or control his conduct, by administering or employing without the knowledge of the other person drugs, intoxicants or other means for the purpose of preventing resistance; or

(c) the other person is unconscious; or

(d) the other person is less than 10 years old.

(2) *By Other Imposition.* A person who engages in deviate sexual intercourse with another person, or who causes another to engage in deviate sexual intercourse, commits a felony of the third degree if:

(a) he compels the other person to participate by any threat that would prevent resistance by a person of ordinary resolution; or

(b) he knows that the other person suffers from a mental disease or defect which renders him incapable of appraising the nature of his conduct; or

(c) he knows that the other person submits because he is unaware that a sexual act is being committed upon him.

Section 213.3.   *Corruption of Minors and Seduction*

(1) *Offense Defined.* A male who has sexual intercourse with a female not his wife, or any person who engages in deviate sexual intercourse or causes another to engage in deviate sexual intercourse, is guilty of an offense if:

(a) the other person is less than [16] years old and the actor is at least [four] years older than the other person; or

(b) the other person is less than 21 years old and the actor is his guardian or otherwise responsible for general supervision of his welfare; or

(c) the other person is in custody of law or detained in a hospital or other institution and the actor has supervisory or disciplinary authority over him; or

(d) the other person is a female who is induced to participate by a promise of marriage which the actor does not mean to perform.

(2) *Grading.* An offense under paragraph (a) of Subsection (1) is a felony of the third degree. Otherwise an offense under this section is a misdemeanor.

Section 213.4.   *Sexual Assault*

A person who has sexual contact with another not his spouse, or causes such other to have sexual conduct with him, is guilty of sexual assault, a misdemeanor, if:

(1) he knows that the contact is offensive to the other person; or

(2) he knows that the other person suffers from a mental disease or defect which renders him or her incapable of appraising the nature of his or her conduct; or

(3) he knows that the other person is unaware that a sexual act is being committed; or

(4) the other person is less than 10 years old; or

(5) he has substantially impaired the other person's power to appraise or control his or her conduct, by administering or employing without the other's knowledge drugs, intoxicants or other means for the purpose of preventing resistance; or

(6) the other person is less than [16] years old and the actor is at least [four] years older than the other person; or

(7) the other person is less than 21 years old and the actor is his guardian or otherwise responsible for general supervision of his welfare; or

(8) the other person is in custody of law or detained in a hospital or other institution and the actor has supervisory or disciplinary authority over him.

Sexual contact is any touching of the sexual or other intimate parts of the person for the purpose of arousing or gratifying sexual desire.

Section 213.5.   *Indecent Exposure*

A person commits a misdemeanor if, for the purpose of arousing or gratifying sexual desire of himself or of any person other than his spouse, he exposes his genitals under circumstances in which he knows his conduct is likely to cause affront or alarm.

Section 213.6.   *Provisions Generally Applicable to Article 213*

(1) *Mistake as to Age.* Whenever in this Article the criminality of conduct depends on a child's being below the age of 10, it is no defense that the actor did not know the child's age, or reasonably believed the child to be older than 10. When criminality depends on the child's being below a critical age other than 10, it is a defense for the actor to prove by a preponderance of the evidence that he reasonably believed the child to be above the critical age.

(2) *Spouse Relationships.* Whenever in this Article the definition of an offense excludes conduct with a spouse, the exclusion shall be deemed to extend to persons living as man and wife, regardless of the legal status of their relationship. The exclusion shall be inoperative as respects spouses living apart under a decree of judicial separation. Where the definition of an offense excludes conduct with a spouse or conduct by a woman, this shall not preclude conviction of a spouse or woman as accomplice in a sexual act which he or she causes another person, not within the exclusion, to perform.

(3) *Sexually Promiscuous Complainants.* It is a defense to prosecution under Section 213.3, and paragraphs (6), (7) and (8) of Section 213.4 for the actor to prove by a preponderance of the evidence that the alleged victim had, prior to the time of the offense charged, engaged promiscuously in sexual relations with others.

(4) *Prompt Complaint.* No prosecution may be instituted or maintained under this Article unless the alleged offense was brought to the notice of public authority within [3] months of its occurrence or, where the alleged victim was less than [16] years old or otherwise incompetent to make complaint, within [3] months after a parent, guardian or other competent person specially interested in the victim learns of the offense.

(5) *Testimony of Complainants.* No person shall be convicted of any felony under this Article upon the uncorroborated testimony of the alleged victim. Corroboration may be circumstantial. In any prosecution before a jury for an offense under this Article, the jury shall be instructed to evaluate the testimony of a victim or complaining witness with special care in view of the emotional involvement of the witness and the difficulty of determining the truth with respect to alleged sexual activities carried out in private.

Offenses Against Property

Article 220.   Arson, Criminal Mischief, and Other Property Destruction

Section 220.1.   Arson and Related Offenses

(1) *Arson.* A person is guilty of arson, a felony of the second degree, if he starts a fire or causes an explosion with the purpose of:

(a) destroying a building or occupied structure of another; or

(b) destroying or damaging any property, whether his own or another's, to collect insurance for such loss. It shall be an affirmative defense to prosecution under this paragraph that the actor's conduct did not recklessly endanger any building or occupied structure of another or place any other person in danger of death or bodily injury.

(2) *Reckless Burning or Exploding.* A person commits a felony of the third degree if he purposely starts a fire or causes an explosion, whether on his own property or another's, and thereby recklessly:

(a) places another person in danger of death or bodily injury; or

(b) places a building or occupied structure of another in danger of damage or destruction.

(3) *Failure to Control or Report Dangerous Fire.* A person who knows that a fire is endangering life or a substantial amount of property of another and fails to take reasonable measures to put out or control the fire, when he can do so without substantial risk to himself, or to give a prompt fire alarm, commits a misdemeanor if:

(a) he knows that he is under an official, contractual, or other legal duty to prevent or combat the fire; or

(b) the fire was started, albeit lawfully, by him or with his assent, or on property in his custody or control.

(4) *Definitions.* "Occupied structure" means any structure, vehicle or place adapted for overnight accommodation of persons, or for carrying on business therein, whether

or not a person is actually present. Property is that of another, for the purposes of this section, if anyone other than the actor has a possessory or proprietary interest therein. If a building or structure is divided into separately occupied units, any unit not occupied by the actor is an occupied structure of another.

Section 220.2.   Causing or Risking Catastrophe

(1) *Causing Catastrophe*. A person who causes a catastrophe by explosion, fire, flood, avalanche, collapse of building, release of poison gas, radioactive material or other harmful or destructive force or substance, or by any other means of causing potentially widespread injury or damage, commits a felony of the second degree if he does so purposely or knowingly, or a felony of the third degree if he does so recklessly.

(2) *Risking Catastrophe*. A person is guilty of a misdemeanor if he recklessly creates a risk of catastrophe in the employment of fire, explosives or other dangerous means listed in Subsection (1).

(3) *Failure to Prevent Catastrophe*. A person who knowingly or recklessly fails to take reasonable measures to prevent or mitigate a catastrophe commits a misdemeanor if:

(a) he knows that he is under an official, contractual or other legal duty to take such measures; or

(b) he did or assented to the act causing or threatening the catastrophe.

Section 220.3.   Criminal Mischief

(1) *Offense Defined*. A person is guilty of criminal mischief if he:

(a) damages tangible property of another purposely, recklessly, or by negligence in the employment of fire, explosives, or other dangerous means listed in Section 220.2(1); or

(b) purposely or recklessly tampers with tangible property of another so as to endanger person or property; or

(c) purposely or recklessly causes another to suffer pecuniary loss by deception or threat.

(2) *Grading*. Criminal mischief is a felony of the third degree if the actor purposely causes pecuniary loss in excess of $5,000 or a substantial interruption or impairment of public communication, transportation, supply of water, gas or power, or other public service. It is a misdemeanor if the actor purposely causes pecuniary loss in excess of $100, or a petty misdemeanor if he purposely or, recklessly causes pecuniary loss in excess of $25. Otherwise criminal mischief is a violation.

Article 221.   Burglary and Other Criminal Intrusion

Section 221.0.   Definitions

In this Article, unless a different meaning plainly is required:

(1) "occupied structure" means any structure, vehicle or place adapted for overnight accommodation of persons, or for carrying on business therein, whether or not a person is actually present.

(2) "night" means the period between thirty minutes past sunset and thirty minutes before sunrise.

Section 221.1.   Burglary

(1) *Burglary Defined*. A person is guilty of burglary if he enters a building or occupied structure, or separately secured or occupied portion thereof, with purpose to commit a crime therein, unless the premises are at the time open to the public or the actor

is licensed or privileged to enter. It is an affirmative defense to prosecution for burglary that the building or structure was abandoned.

(2) *Grading.* Burglary is a felony of the second degree if it is perpetrated in the dwelling of another at night, or if, in the course of committing the offense, the actor:

(a) purposely, knowingly or recklessly inflicts or attempts to inflict bodily injury on anyone; or

(b) is armed with explosives or a deadly weapon.

Otherwise, burglary is a felony of the third degree. An act shall be deemed "in the course of committing" an offense if it occurs in an attempt to commit the offense or in flight after the attempt or commission.

(3) *Multiple Convictions.* A person may not be convicted for burglary and for the offense which it was his purpose to commit after the burglarious entry or for an attempt to commit that offense, unless the additional offense constitutes a felony of the first or second degree.

Section 221.2. Criminal Trespass

(1) *Buildings and Occupied Structures.* A person commits an offense if, knowing that he is not licensed or privileged to do so, he enters or surreptitiously remains in any building or occupied structure, or separately secured or occupied portion thereof. An offense under this Subsection is a misdemeanor if it is committed in a dwelling at night. Otherwise it is a petty misdemeanor.

(2) *Defiant Trespasser.* A person commits an offense if, knowing that he is not licensed or privileged to do so, he enters or remains in any place as to which notice against trespass is given by:

(a) actual communication to the actor; or

(b) posting in a manner prescribed by law or reasonably likely to come to the attention of intruders; or

(c) fencing or other enclosure manifestly designed to exclude intruders.

An offense under this Subsection constitutes a petty misdemeanor if the offender defies an order to leave personally communicated to him by the owner of the premises or other authorized person. Otherwise it is a violation.

(3) *Defenses.* It is an affirmative defense to prosecution under this Section that:

(a) a building or occupied structure involved in an offense under Subsection (1) was abandoned; or

(b) the premises were at the time open to members of the public and the actor complied with all lawful conditions imposed on access to or remaining in the premises; or

(c) the actor reasonably believed that the owner of the premises, or other person empowered to license access thereto, would have licensed him to enter or remain.

Article 222. Robbery

Section 222.1. Robbery

(1) *Robbery Defined.* A person is guilty of robbery if, in the course of committing a theft, he:

(a) inflicts serious bodily injury upon another; or

(b) threatens another with or purposely puts him in fear of immediate serious bodily injury; or

(c) commits or threatens immediately to commit any felony of the first or second degree.

An act shall be deemed "in the course of committing a theft" if it occurs in an attempt to commit theft or in flight after the attempt or commission.

(2) *Grading.* Robbery is a felony of the second degree, except that it is a felony of

the first degree if in the course of committing the theft the actor attempts to kill anyone, or purposely inflicts or attempts to inflict serious bodily injury.

Article 223.   Theft and Related Offenses

Section 223.0.   Definitions

In this Article, unless a different meaning plainly is required:

(1) "deprive" means: (a) to withhold property of another permanently or for so extended a period as to appropriate a major portion of its economic value, or with intent to restore only upon payment of reward or other compensation; or (b) to dispose of the property so as to make it unlikely that the owner will recover it.

(2) "financial institution" means a bank, insurance company, credit union, building and loan association, investment trust or other organization held out to the public as a place of deposit of funds or medium of savings or collective investment.

(3) "government" means the United States, any State, county, municipality, or other political unit, or any department, agency or subdivision of any of the foregoing, or any corporation or other association carrying out the functions of government.

(4) "movable property" means property the location of which can be changed, including things growing on, affixed to, or found in land, and documents although the rights represented thereby have no physical location. "Immovable property" is all other property.

(5) "obtain" means: (a) in relation to property, to bring about a transfer or purported transfer of a legal interest in the property, whether to the obtainer or another; or (b) in relation to labor or service, to secure performance thereof.

(6) "property" means anything of value, including real estate, tangible and intangible personal property, contract rights, choses-in-action and other interests in or claims to wealth, admission or transportation tickets, captured or domestic animals, food and drink, electric or other power.

(7) "property of another" includes property in which any person other than the actor has an interest which the actor is not privileged to infringe, regardless of the fact that the actor also has an interest in the property and regardless of the fact that the other person might be precluded from civil recovery because the property was used in an unlawful transaction or was subject to forfeiture as contraband. Property in possession of the actor shall not be deemed property of another who has only a security interest therein, even if legal title is in the creditor pursuant to a conditional sales contract or other security agreement.

Section 223.1.   Consolidation of Theft Offenses; Grading;
Provisions Applicable to Theft Generally

(1) *Consolidation of Theft Offenses.* Conduct denominated theft in this Article constitutes a single offense. An accusation of theft may be supported by evidence that it was committed in any manner that would be theft under this Article, notwithstanding the specification of a different manner in the indictment or information, subject only to the power of the Court to ensure fair trial by granting a continuance or other appropriate relief where the conduct of the defense would be prejudiced by lack of fair notice or by surprise.

(2) *Grading of Theft Offenses.*

   (a) Theft constitutes a felony of the third degree if the amount involved exceeds $500, or if the property stolen is a firearm, automobile, airplane, motorcycle, motorboat or other motor-propelled vehicle, or in the case of theft by receiving stolen property, if the receiver is in the business of buying or selling stolen property.

   (b) Theft not within the preceding paragraph constitutes a misdemeanor, except that if the property was not taken from the person or by threat, or in breach of a fiduciary obligation, and the actor proves by a preponderance of the evidence that the amount involved was less than $50, the offense constitutes a petty misdemeanor.

(c) The amount involved in a theft shall be deemed to be the highest value, by any reasonable standard, of the property or services which the actor stole or attempted to steal. Amounts involved in thefts committed pursuant to one scheme or course of conduct, whether from the same person or several persons, may be aggregated in determining the grade of the offense.

(3) *Claim of Right.* It is an affirmative defense to prosecution for theft that the actor:

(a) was unaware that the property or service was that of another; or

(b) acted under an honest claim of right to the property or service involved or that he had a right to acquire or dispose of it as he did; or

(c) took property exposed for sale, intending to purchase and pay for it promptly, or reasonably believing that the owner, if present, would have consented.

(4) *Theft from Spouse.* It is no defense that theft was from the actor's spouse, except that misappropriation of household and personal effects, or other property normally accessible to both spouses, is theft only if it occurs after the parties have ceased living together.

Section 223.2.   Theft by Unlawful Taking or Disposition

(1) *Movable Property.* A person is guilty of theft if he unlawfully takes, or exercises unlawful control over, movable property of another with purpose to deprive him thereof.

(2) *Immovable Property.* A person is guilty of theft if he unlawfully transfers immovable property of another or any interest therein with purpose to benefit himself or another not entitled thereto.

Section 223.3.   Theft by Deception

A person is guilty of theft if he purposely obtains property of another by deception. A person deceives if he purposely:

(1) creates or reinforces a false impression, including false impressions as to law, value, intention or other state of mind; but deception as to a person's intention to perform a promise shall not be inferred from the fact alone that he did not subsequently perform the promise; or

(2) prevents another from acquiring information which would affect his judgment of a transaction; or

(3) fails to correct a false impression which the deceiver previously created or reinforced, or which the deceiver knows to be influencing another to whom he stands in a fiduciary or confidential relationship; or

(4) fails to disclose a known lien, adverse claim or other legal impediment to the enjoyment of property which he transfers or encumbers in consideration for the property obtained, whether such impediment is or is not valid, or is or is not a matter of official record.

The term "deceive" does not, however, include falsity as to matters having no pecuniary significance, or puffing by statements unlikely to deceive ordinary persons in the group addressed.

Section 223.4.   Theft by Extortion

A person is guilty of theft if he obtains property of another by threatening to:

(1) inflict bodily injury on anyone or commit any other criminal offense; or

(2) accuse anyone of a criminal offense; or

(3) expose any secret tending to subject any person to hatred, contempt or ridicule, or to impair his credit or business repute; or

(4) take or withhold action as an official, or cause an official to take or withhold action; or

(5) bring about or continue to strike, boycott or other collective unofficial action, if the property is not demanded or received for the benefit of the group in whose interest the actor purports to act; or

(6) testify or provide information or withhold testimony or information with respect to another's legal claim or defense; or

(7) inflict any other harm which would not benefit the actor.

It is an affirmative defense to prosecution based on paragraphs (2), (3) or (4) that the property obtained by threat of accusation, exposure, lawsuit or other invocation of official action was honestly claimed as restitution or indemnification for harm done in the circumstances to which such accusation, exposure, lawsuit or other official action relates, or as compensation for property or lawful services.

Section 223.5.   *Theft of Property Lost, Mislaid, or Delivered by Mistake*

A person who comes into control of property of another that he knows to have been lost, mislaid, or delivered under a mistake as to the nature or amount of the property or the identity of the recipient is guilty of theft if, with purpose to deprive the owner thereof, he fails to take reasonable measures to restore the property to a person entitled to have it.

Section 223.6.   *Receiving Stolen Property*

(1) *Receiving.* A person is guilty of theft if he purposely receives, retains, or disposes of movable property of another knowing that it has been stolen, or believing that it has probably been stolen, unless the property is received, retained, or disposed with purpose to restore it to the owner. "Receiving" means acquiring possession, control or title, or lending on the security of the property.

(2) *Presumption of Knowledge.* The requisite knowledge or belief is presumed in the case of a dealer who:

(a) is found in possession or control of property stolen from two or more persons on separate occasions; or

(b) has received stolen property in another transaction within the year preceding the transaction charged; or

(c) being a dealer in property of the sort received, acquires it for a consideration which he knows is far below its reasonable value.

"Dealer" means a person in the business of buying or selling goods including a pawnbroker.

Section 223.7.   *Theft of Services*

(1) A person is guilty of theft if he purposely obtains services which he knows are available only for compensation, by deception or threat, or by false token or other means to avoid payment for the service. "Services" includes labor, professional service, transportation, telephone or other public service, accommodation in hotels, restaurants or elsewhere, admission to exhibitions, use of vehicles or other movable property. Where compensation for service is ordinarily paid immediately upon the rendering for such service, as is the case of hotels and restaurants, refusal to pay or absconding without payment or offer to pay gives rise to a presumption that the service was obtained by deception as to intention to pay.

(2) A person commits theft if, having control over the disposition of services of others, to which he is not entitled, he knowingly diverts such services to his own benefit or to the benefit of another not entitled thereto.

Section 223.8.   Theft by Failure to Make Required
Disposition of Funds Received

A person who purposely obtains property upon agreement, or subject to a known legal obligation, to make specified payment or other disposition, whether from such property or its proceeds or from his own property to be reserved in equivalent amount, is guilty of theft if he deals with the property obtained as his own and fails to make the required payment or disposition. The foregoing applies notwithstanding that it may be impossible to identify particular property as belonging to the victim at the time of the actor's failure to make the required payment or disposition. An officer or employee of the government or of a financial institution is presumed: (i) to know any legal obligation relevant to his criminal liability under this Section, and (ii) to have dealt with the property as his own if he fails to pay or account upon lawful demand, or if an audit reveals a shortage or falsification of accounts.

Section 223.9.   Unauthorized Use of Automobiles and Other Vehicles

A person commits a misdemeanor if he operates another's automobile, airplane, motorcycle, motorboat, or other motor-propelled vehicle without consent of the owner. It is an affirmative defense to prosecution under this Section that the actor reasonably believed that the owner would have consented to the operation had he known of it.

Article 224.   Forgery and Fraudulent Practices

Section 224.0.   Definitions

In this Article, the definitions given in Section 223.0 apply unless a different meaning plainly is required.

Section 224.1.   Forgery

(1) *Definition.* A person is guilty of forgery if, with purpose to defraud or injure anyone, or with knowledge that he is facilitating a fraud or injury to be perpetrated by anyone, the actor:

(a) alters any writing of another without his authority; or

(b) makes, completes, executes, authenticates, issues or transfers any writing so that it purports to be the act of another who did not authorize that act, or to have been executed at a time or place or in a numbered sequence other than was in fact the case, or to be a copy of an original when no such original existed; or

(c) utters any writing which he knows to be forged in a manner specified in paragraphs (a) or (b).

"Writing" includes printing or any other method of recording information, money, coins, tokens, stamps, seals, credit cards, badges, trade-marks, and other symbols of value, right, privilege, or identification.

(2) *Grading.* Forgery is a felony of the second degree if the writing is or purports to be part of an issue of money, securities, postage or revenue stamps, or other instruments issued by the government, or part of an issue of stock, bonds or other instruments representing interests in or claims against any property or enterprise. Forgery is a felony of the third degree if the writing is or purports to be a will, deed, contract, release, commercial instrument, or other document evidencing, creating, transferring, altering, terminating, or otherwise affecting legal relations. Otherwise forgery is a misdemeanor.

Section 224.2.   Simulating Objects of Antiquity, Rarity, etc.

A person commits a misdemeanor if, with purpose to defraud anyone or with knowledge that he is facilitating a fraud to be perpetrated by anyone, he makes, alters or utters any object so that it appears to have value because of antiquity, rarity, source, or authorship which it does not possess.

Section 224.3.   *Fraudulent Destruction, Removal or Concealment of Recordable Instruments*

A person commits a felony of the third degree if, with purpose to deceive or injure anyone, he destroys, removes or conceals any will, deed, mortgage, security instrument or other writing for which the law provides public recording.

Section 224.4.   *Tampering with Records*

A person commits a misdemeanor if, knowing that he has no privilege to do so, he falsifies, destroys, removes or conceals any writing or record, with purpose to deceive or injure anyone or to conceal any wrongdoing.

Section 224.5.   *Bad Checks*

A person who issues or passes a check or similar sight order for the payment of money, knowing that it will not be honored by the drawee, commits a misdemeanor. For the purposes of this Section as well as in any prosecution for theft committed by means of a bad check, an issuer is presumed to know that the check or order (other than a post-dated check or order) would not be paid, if:

(1) the issuer had no account with the drawee at the time the check or order was issued; or

(2) payment was refused by the drawee for lack of funds, upon presentation within 30 days after issue, and the issuer failed to make good within 10 days after receiving notice of that refusal.

Section 224.6.   *Credit Cards*

A person commits an offense if he uses a credit card for the purpose of obtaining property or services with knowledge that:

(1) the card is stolen or forged; or

(2) the card has been revoked or cancelled; or

(3) for any other reason his use of the card is unauthorized by the issuer.

It is an affirmative defense to prosecution under paragraph (3) if the actor proves by a preponderance of the evidence that he had the purpose and ability to meet all obligations to the issuer arising out of his use of the card. "Credit card" means a writing, or other evidence of an undertaking to pay for property or services delivered or rendered to or upon the order of a designated person or bearer. An offense under this Section is a felony of the third degree if the value of the property or services secured or sought to be secured by means of the credit card exceeds $500; otherwise it is a misdemeanor.

Section 224.7.   *Deceptive Business Practices*

A person commits a misdemeanor if in the course of business he:

(1) uses or possesses for use a false weight or measure, or any other device for falsely determining or recording any quality or quantity; or

(2) sells, offers or exposes for sale, or delivers less than the represented quantity of any commodity or service; or

(3) takes or attempts to take more than the represented quantity of any commodity or service when as buyer he furnishes the weight or measure, or

(4) sells, offers or exposes for sale adulterated or mislabeled commodities. "Adulterated" means varying from the standard of composition or quality prescribed by or

pursuant to any statute providing criminal penalties for such variance, or set by established commercial usage. "Mislabeled" means varying from the standard of truth or disclosure in labeling prescribed by or pursuant to any statute providing criminal penalties for such variance, or set by established commercial usage; or

(5) makes a false or misleading statement in any advertisement addressed to the public or to a substantial segment thereof for the purpose of promoting the purchase or sale of property or services; or

(6) makes a false or misleading written statement for the purpose of obtaining property or credit; or

(7) makes a false or misleading written statement for the purpose of promoting the sale of securities, or omits information required by law to be disclosed in written documents relating to securities.

It is an affirmative defense to prosecution under this Section if the defendant proves by a preponderance of the evidence that his conduct was not knowingly or recklessly deceptive.

Section 224.8.   *Commercial Bribery and Breach of Duty to Act Disinterestedly*

(1) A person commits a misdemeanor if he solicits, accepts or agrees to accept any benefit as consideration for knowingly violating or agreeing to violate a duty of fidelity to which he is subject as:

(a) partner, agent or employee of another;

(b) trustee, guardian, or other fiduciary;

(c) lawyer, physician, accountant, appraiser, or other professional adviser or informant;

(d) officer, director, manager or other participant in the direction of the affairs of an incorporated or unincorporated association; or

(e) arbitrator or other purportedly disinterested adjudicator or referee.

(2) A person who holds himself out to the public as being engaged in the business of making disinterested selection, appraisal, or criticism of commodities or services commits a misdemeanor if he solicits, accepts or agrees to accept any benefit to influence his selection, appraisal or criticism.

(3) A person commits a misdemeanor if he confers, or offers or agrees to confer, any benefit the acceptance of which would be criminal under this Section.

Section 224.9.   *Rigging Publicly Exhibited Contest*

(1) A person commits a misdemeanor if, with purpose to prevent a publicly exhibited contest from being conducted in accordance with the rules and usages purporting to govern it, he:

(a) confers or offers or agrees to confer any benefit upon, or threatens any injury to a participant, official or other person associated with the contest or exhibition; or

(b) tampers with any person, animal or thing.

(2) *Soliciting or Accepting Benefit for Rigging.* A person commits a misdemeanor if he knowingly solicits, accepts or agrees to accept any benefit the giving of which would be criminal under Subsection (1).

(3) *Participation in Rigged Contest.* A person commits a misdemeanor if he knowingly engages in, sponsors, produces, judges, or otherwise participates in a publicly exhibited contest knowing that the contest is not being conducted in compliance with the rules and usages purporting to govern it, by reason of conduct which would be criminal under this Section.

Section 224.10. *Defrauding Secured Creditors*

A person commits a misdemeanor if he destroys, removes, conceals, encumbers, transfers or otherwise deals with property subject to a security interest with purpose to hinder enforcement of that interest.

Section 224.11. *Fraud in Insolvency*

A person commits a misdemeanor if, knowing that proceedings have been or are about to be instituted for the appointment of a receiver or other person entitled to administer property for the benefit of creditors, or that any other composition or liquidation for the benefit of creditors has been or is about to be made, he:

(a) destroys, removes, conceals, encumbers, transfers, or otherwise deals with any property with purpose to defeat or obstruct the claim of any creditor, or otherwise to obstruct the operation of any law relating to administration of property for the benefit of creditors; or

(b) knowingly falsifies any writing or record relating to the property; or

(c) knowingly misrepresents or refuses to disclose to a receiver or other person entitled to administer property for the benefit of creditors, the existence, amount or location of the property, or any other information which the actor could be legally required to furnish in relation to such administration.

Section 224.12. *Receiving Deposits in a Failing Financial Institution*

An officer, manager or other person directing or participating in the direction of a financial institution commits a misdemeanor if he receives or permits the receipt of a deposit, premium payment or other investment in the institution knowing that:

(1) due to financial difficulties the institution is about to suspend operations or go into receivership or reorganization; and

(2) the person making the deposit or other payment is unaware of the precarious situation of the institution.

Section 224.13. *Misapplication of Entrusted Property and Property of Government or Financial Institution*

A person commits an offense if he applies or disposes of property that has been entrusted to him as a fiduciary, or property of the government or of a financial institution, in a manner which he knows is unlawful and involves substantial risk of loss or detriment to the owner of the property or to a person for whose benefit the property was entrusted. The offense is a misdemeanor if the amount involved exceeds $50; otherwise it is a petty misdemeanor. "Fiduciary" includes trustee, guardian, executor, administrator, receiver and any person carrying on fiduciary functions on behalf of a corporation or other organization which is a fiduciary.

Section 224.14. *Securing Execution of Documents by Deception*

A person commits a misdemeanor if by deception he causes another to execute any instrument affecting, purporting to affect, or likely to affect the pecuniary interest of any person.

Offenses Against the Family

Article 230.   Offenses Against the Family

Section 230.1.   Bigamy and Polygamy

(1) *Bigamy.* A married person is guilty of bigamy, a misdemeanor, if he contracts or purports to contract another marriage, unless at the time of the subsequent marriage:

(a) the actor believes that the prior spouse is dead; or

(b) the actor and the prior spouse have been living apart for five consecutive years throughout which the prior spouse was not known by the actor to be alive; or

(c) a Court has entered a judgment purporting to terminate or annul any prior disqualifying marriage, and the actor does not know that judgment to be invalid; or

(d) the actor reasonably believes that he is legally eligible to remarry.

(2) *Polygamy.* A person is guilty of polygamy, a felony of the third degree, if he marries or cohabits with more than one spouse at a time in purported exercise of the right of plural marriage. The offense is a continuing one until all cohabitation and claim of marriage with more than one spouse terminates. This section does not apply to parties to a polygamous marriage, lawful in the country of which they are residents or nationals, while they are in transit through or temporarily visiting this State.

(3) *Other Party to Bigamous or Polygamous Marriage.* A person is guilty of bigamy or polygamy, as the case may be, if he contracts or purports to contract marriage with another knowing that the other is thereby committing bigamy or polygamy.

Section 230.2.   Incest

A person is guilty of incest, a felony of the third degree, if he knowingly marries or cohabits or has sexual intercourse with an ancestor or descendant, a brother or sister of the whole or half blood [or an uncle, aunt, nephew or niece of the whole blood]. "Cohabit" means to live together under the representation or appearance of being married. The relationships referred to herein include blood relationships without regard to legitimacy, and relationship of parent and child by adoption.

Section 230.3.   Abortion [Omitted]

Section 230.4.   Endangering Welfare of Children

A parent, guardian, or other person supervising the welfare of a child under 18 commits a misdemeanor if he knowingly endangers the child's welfare by violating a duty of care, protection or support.

Section 230.5.   Persistent Non-Support

A person commits a misdemeanor if he persistently fails to provide support which he can provide and which he knows he is legally obliged to provide to a spouse, child or other dependent.

Offenses Against Public Administration

Article 240.   Bribery and Corrupt Influence [Omitted]

Article 241.   Perjury and Other Falsification in Official Matters [Omitted]

Article 242.   Obstructing Governmental Operations; Escapes [Omitted]

Article 243.   Abuse of Office [Omitted]

Offenses Against Public Order and Decency

Article 250.   Riot, Disorderly Conduct, and Related Offenses

Section 250.1.   Riot; Failure to Disperse

(1) *Riot.* A person is guilty of riot, a felony of the third degree, if he participates with [two] or more others in a course of disorderly conduct:

(a) with purpose to commit or facilitate the commission of a felony or misdemeanor;

(b) with purpose to prevent or coerce official action; or

(c) when the actor or any other participant to the knowledge of the actor uses or plans to use a firearm or other deadly weapon.

(2) *Failure of Disorderly Persons to Disperse Upon Official Order.* Where [three] or more persons are participating in a course of disorderly conduct likely to cause substantial harm or serious inconvenience, annoyance or alarm, a peace officer or other public servant engaged in executing or enforcing the law may order the participants and others in the immediate vicinity to disperse. A person who refuses or knowingly fails to obey such an order commits a misdemeanor.

Section 250.2.   Disorderly Conduct

(1) *Offense Defined.* A person is guilty of disorderly conduct if, with purpose to cause public inconvenience, annoyance or alarm, or recklessly creating a risk thereof, he:

(a) engages in fighting or threatening, or in violent or tumultuous behavior; or

(b) makes unreasonable noise or offensively coarse utterance, gesture or display, or addresses abusive language to any person present; or

(c) creates a hazardous or physically offensive condition by any act which serves no legitimate purpose of the actor.

"Public" means affecting or likely to affect persons in a place to which the public or a substantial group has access; among the places included are highways, transport facilities, schools, prisons, apartment houses, places of business or amusement, or any neighborhood.

(2) *Grading.* An offense under this section is a petty misdemeanor if the actor's purpose is to cause substantial harm or serious inconvenience, or if he persists in disorderly conduct after reasonable warning or request to desist. Otherwise disorderly conduct is a violation.

Section 250.3.   False Public Alarms

A person is guilty of a misdemeanor if he initiates or circulates a report or warning of an impending bombing or other crime or catastrophe, knowing that the report or warning is false or baseless and that it is likely to cause evacuation of a building, place of assembly, or facility of public transport, or to cause public inconvenience or alarm.

Section 250.4.   Harassment

A person commits a petty misdemeanor if, with purpose to harass another, he:

(1) makes a telephone call without purpose of legitimate communication; or

(2) insults, taunts or challenges another in a manner likely to provoke violent or disorderly response; or

(3) makes repeated communications anonymously or at extremely inconvenient hours, or in offensively coarse language; or

(4) subjects another to an offensive touching; or

(5) engages in any other course of alarming conduct serving no legitimate purpose of the actor.

Section 250.5.   Public Drunkenness; Drug Incapacitation

A person is guilty of an offense if he appears in any public place manifestly under the influence of alcohol, narcotics or other drug, not therapeutically administered, to the degree that he may endanger himself or other persons or property, or annoy persons in his vicinity. An offense under this Section constitutes a petty misdemeanor if the actor has been convicted hereunder twice before within a period of one year. Otherwise the offense constitutes a violation.

Section 250.6.   Loitering or Prowling

A person commits a violation if he loiters or prowls in a place, at a time, or in a manner not usual for lawabiding individuals under circumstances that warrant alarm for the safety of persons or property in the vicinity. Among the circumstances which may be considered in determining whether such alarm is warranted is the fact that the actor takes flight upon appearance of a peace officer, refuses to identify himself, or manifestly endeavors to conceal himself or any object. Unless flight by the actor or other circumstance makes it impracticable, a peace officer shall prior to any arrest for an offense under this section afford the actor an opportunity to dispel any alarm which would otherwise be warranted, by requesting him to identify himself and explain his presence and conduct. No person shall be convicted of an offense under this Section if the peace officer did not comply with the preceding sentence, or if it appears at trial that the explanation given by the actor was true and, if believed by the peace officer at the time, would have dispelled the alarm.

Section 250.7.   Obstructing Highways and Other Public Passages

(1) A person, who, having no legal privilege to do so, purposely or recklessly obstructs any highway or other public passage, whether alone or with others, commits a violation, or, in case he persists after warning by a law officer, a petty misdemeanor. "Obstructs" means renders impassable without unreasonable inconvenience or hazard. No person shall be deemed guilty of recklessly obstructing in violation of this Subsection solely because of a gathering of persons to hear him speak or otherwise communicate, or solely because of being a member of such a gathering.

(2) A person in a gathering commits a violation if he refuses to obey a reasonable official request or order to move:

(a) to prevent obstruction of a highway or other public passage; or

(b) to maintain public safety by dispersing those gathered in dangerous proximity to a fire or other hazard.

An order to move, addressed to a person whose speech or other lawful behavior attracts an obstructing audience, shall not be deemed reasonable if the obstruction can be readily remedied by police control of the size or location of the gathering.

Section 250.8. Disrupting Meetings and Processions

A person commits a misdemeanor if, with purpose to prevent or disrupt a lawful meeting, procession or gathering, he does any act tending to obstruct or interfere with it physically, or makes any utterance, gesture or display designed to outrage the sensibilities of the group.

Section 250.9. Desecration of Venerated Objects [Omitted]

Section 250.10. Abuse of Corpse [Omitted]

Section 250.11. Cruelty to Animals [Omitted]

Section 250.12. Violation of Privacy [Omitted]

Article 251. Public Indecency

Section 251.1. Open Lewdness

A person commits a petty misdemeanor if he does any lewd act which he knows is likely to be observed by others who would be affronted or alarmed.

Section 251.2. Prostitution and Related Offenses

(1) *Prostitution.* A person is guilty of prostitution, a petty misdemeanor, if he or she:
(a) is an inmate of a house of prostitution or otherwise engages in sexual activity as a business; or
(b) loiters in or within view of any public place for the purpose of being hired to engage in sexual activity.

"Sexual activity" includes homosexual and other deviate sexual relations. A "house of prostitution" is any place where prostitution or promotion of prostitution is regularly carried on by one person under the control, management or supervision of another. An "inmate" is a person who engages in prostitution in or through the agency of a house of prostitution. "Public place" means any place to which the public or any substantial group thereof has access.

(2) *Promoting Prostitution.* A person who knowingly promotes prostitution of another commits a misdemeanor or felony as provided in Subsection (3). The following acts shall, without limitation of the foregoing, constitute promoting prostitution:
(a) owning, controlling, managing, supervising or otherwise keeping, alone or in association with others, a house of prostitution or a prostitution business; or
(b) procuring an inmate for a house of prostitution or a place in a house of prostitution for one who would be an inmate; or
(c) encouraging, inducing, or otherwise purposely causing another to become or remain a prostitute; or
(d) soliciting a person to patronize a prostitute; or
(e) procuring a prostitute for a patron; or
(f) transporting a person into or within this state with purpose to promote that person's engaging in prostitution, or procuring or paying for transportation with that purpose; or
(g) leasing or otherwise permitting a place controlled by the actor, alone or in association with others, to be regularly used for prostitution or the promotion of prostitution, or failure to make reasonable effort to abate such use by ejecting the tenant, notifying law enforcement authorities, or other legally available means; or
(h) soliciting, receiving, or agreeing to receive any benefit for doing or agreeing to do anything forbidden by this Subsection.

(3) *Grading of Offenses Under Subsection (2).* An offense under Subsection (2) constitutes a felony of the third degree if:

(a) the offense falls within paragraph (a), (b) or (c) of Subsection (2); or

(b) the actor compels another to engage in or promote prostitution; or

(c) the actor promotes prostitution of a child under 16, whether or not he is aware of the child's age; or

(d) the actor promotes prostitution of his wife, child, ward or any person for whose care, protection or support he is responsible.

Otherwise the offense is a misdemeanor.

(4) *Presumption from Living off Prostitutes.* A person, other than the prostitute or the prostitute's minor child or other legal dependent incapable of self-support, who is supported in whole or substantial part by the proceeds of prostitution is presumed to be knowingly promoting prostitution in violation of Subsection (2).

(5) *Patronizing Prostitutes.* A person commits a violation if he hires a prostitute to engage in sexual activity with him, or he enters or remains in a house of prostitution for the purpose of engaging in sexual activity.

(6) *Evidence.* On the issue whether a place is a house of prostitution the following shall be admissible evidence: its general repute; the repute of the persons who reside in or frequent the place; the frequency, timing and duration of visits by non-residents. Testimony of a person against his spouse shall be admissible to prove offenses under this Section.

Section 251.3.   *Loitering to Solicit Deviate Sexual Relations*

A person is guilty of a petty misdemeanor if he loiters in or near any public place for the purpose of soliciting or being solicited to engage in deviate sexual relations.

Section 251.4.   *Obscenity [Omitted]*

PART III.   TREATMENT AND CORRECTION [Omitted]

PART IV.   ORGANIZATION OF CORRECTION [Omitted]

TABLE OF CASES

TABLE OF MODEL PENAL
CODE SECTIONS

INDEX